Handbook

OF THE

Linguistic Atlas

OF THE

Middle and South Atlantic States

Handbook
OF THE
Linguistic Atlas
OF THE
Middle and South Atlantic States

Edited by

William A. Kretzschmar, Jr. Editor
Virginia G. McDavid Associate Editor
Theodore K. Lerud Assistant Editor
Ellen Johnson Assistant Editor

The University of Chicago Press
Chicago and London

The University of Chicago Press, Chicago 60637
The University of Chicago Press, Ltd., London
© 1994 by William A. Kretzschmar, Jr.
All rights reserved. Published 1993
Printed in the United States of America
02 01 00 99 98 97 96 95 94 93   1 2 3 4 5

ISBN: 0–226–45282–4   (cloth)
        0–226–45283–2   (paper)

Editorial work on the LAMSAS project
has been made possible by funding from
the Research Tools Program of the
National Endowment for the Humanities.

Library of Congress Cataloging-in-Publication Data

Handbook of the linguistic atlas of the Middle and South Atlantic
    states / edited by William A. Kretzschmar, Jr. ... [et al.].
        p. cm.
    Includes bibliographical references.
    1. Middle Atlantic States—Languages—Maps.   2. Southern
States—Languages—Maps.   3. Middle Atlantic States—Social life
and customs. 4. Southern States—Social life and customs.
I. Kretzschmar, William A., Jr.
G1246.E3H3   1993 <G&M>
427'.974'0223–dc20   93–15245
                                                                                    CIP
                                                                                    MAP

♾ The paper used in this publication meets the
minimum requirements of the American National Standard
for Information Sciences—Permanence of Paper for
Printed Library Materials, ANSI Z39.48–1984.

We offer this volume in memory of

Hans Kurath and **Guy Lowman**

for their roles in the creation of LAMSAS,

and especially in memory of

Raven I. McDavid, Jr.

for his dedication over many years
to LAMSAS,
to the art and science of dialectology,
and to the empirical study of American culture.

Contents

10. Community Sketches and Informant Biographies   165

Figures

Preface

The purpose of this handbook is to help users of the research materials of the Linguistic Atlas of the Middle and South Atlantic States (LAMSAS) to judge the materials accurately and appropriately. To that end, we have included information about the history of the project and the aims of its designers, about communities and informants and how information was collected from them, and about several editorial stages in processing of the information gathered. We have also included at the end a few comments about interpretation. We have not attempted to describe the distribution of linguistic features in the LAMSAS survey area, nor have we attempted to demonstrate the existence of one or more dialects in the region, except for a commentary on these tasks by Raven McDavid in Chapter 8. In the tradition of American Linguistic Atlas work, we are interested to provide the fullest and most accurate record of survey data before the order of interpretation is imposed upon it. This handbook is an adjunct to the presentation of that full and accurate record.

Two special circumstances affect the shape of this handbook: the long history of the project and publications related to it, and current plans for publication of LAMSAS data. While Chapter 1 will discuss the history and nature of LAMSAS in some detail, it is important to emphasize here that LAMSAS has become a historical project. Nobody should claim any longer that LAMSAS describes contemporary American English. That claim might still be made by the editors of the *Dictionary of American Regional English* (*DARE*; Cassidy et al. 1985–) and the *Linguistic Atlas of the Gulf States* (*LAGS*; Pederson et al. 1986–92) because their interviews were conducted in the 1960s and 1970s; LAMSAS interviews were mainly carried out before World War II and were all but complete soon thereafter, before the population migrations and social changes that sharply altered American culture after the war. Editing of LAMSAS data continued during the period between the interviews and the present date. We must describe the procedures of earlier editors as well as our own computer-assisted work, so that users may judge in their proper context both LAMSAS and the many publications derived from it. Those publications, of course, include Kurath's *Word Geography* (1949), Atwood's *Survey of Verb Forms* (1953), and Kurath and McDavid's *Pronunciation of English in the Atlantic States* (1961), which together still constitute the foundations for scholarly opinion on American regional dialects. Only a portion of LAMSAS data was available to be analyzed for these works, however, and their authors manipulated the available data only in particular ways. There is much that users of the data can know about earlier editorial procedures to interpret these founding analyses more appropriately, and there is still much more to learn from the LAMSAS data per se.

The general outline for comprehensive publication of LAMSAS is clear. For other Atlas projects, like the *Linguistic Atlas of New England* (*LANE*; Kurath et al. 1939–43), and the *Linguistic Atlas of the Upper Midwest* (*LAUM*; Allen 1973–76), publication of handbook materials accompanied complete publication of the data. The *Handbook of the Linguistic Atlas of New England* appeared in the same year as the first volume of *LANE* in 1939, and *LAUM* included handbook information in the first volume of the atlas itself, alongside summaries of the data. The *LAGS* publication series appeared subsequent to microform publication of the complete, edited *Basic Materials* (Pederson et al. 1981) and the *Concordance* (Pederson et al. 1986). We do not have the advantage for LAMSAS of having completely assembled and edited the data before preparation of a handbook. There is a complete microfilm set, the *Basic Materials* (McDavid et al. 1982–86), that consists of unedited field records. Publication of the *Linguistic Atlas of the Middle and South Atlantic States* in fascicles, as edited lists, was begun but will not be continued (McDavid and O'Cain 1980). We anticipate that comprehensive publication of LAMSAS data will occur in two ways, in microform and as computer files, as the editorial procedures now under way come to completion. This handbook, then, should serve as an aid for either of these means of publication, as well as a guide for the original paper records now archived at the University of Georgia and for the many analytical publications based on LAMSAS data. It will provide descriptions and illustrations of all of the ways in which LAMSAS data have been recorded and stored, and so will act as a bridge between the different media and means of presentation. We are prevented from making direct reference to these publications, however, because this volume has been prepared as the first part of the comprehensive program, after development of suitable methods for computer processing but before the data have all been entered on disk.

During the life of the project there have been many sources of support for the work. Brown University, the University of Michigan, the University of Chicago, the University of South Carolina, and now, most hospitably of all, the University of Georgia have provided editorial sites, with varying degrees of ancillary support for the faculty editors. The National Endowment for the Humanities has provided the lion's share of extramural editorial funding, beginning with a grant to the project at the University of South Carolina in the late 1970s, continuing with several grants at the University of Chicago in the 1980s and a grant to Lerud at Elmhurst College in 1985, up to our current editorial funding at the University of Georgia. The Hans Kurath Fund of the American Dialect Society has provided important funding to LAMSAS since 1986. Elmhurst College has provided support for work on community and informant sketches and settlement history materials, and the Elmhurst College Department of Geography and Environmental Planning has made a significant contribution to map production. We are grateful to all of our sponsors over the years, and especially to the University of Georgia, the American Dialect Society, and to NEH for their present sponsorship as LAMSAS is brought before the public.

There have also been a great number of workers in the LAMSAS vineyard over the years, and it is not now possible to name them all. Hans Kurath, Guy Lowman, and Raven I. McDavid, Jr., have been principal agents in the creation of LAMSAS, as Chapter 1 will show. Many others in addition to the present editors have had lesser but important roles; we here recognize the contributions of those participants and local advocates whose names we can recover from the files:

Advisory Board (current and former):

Guy Bailey	David Maurer
Ronald Butters	Allan Metcalf
Lurline Coltharp	Michael Miller
Lawrence Davis	William Moulton
John H. Fisher	Lee Pederson
Eric Hamp	Herbert Penzl
Archibald Hill	Thomas Pyles
Robert Hogan	Randolph Quirk
A. M. Kinloch	A. Hood Roberts
James B. McMillan	Edgar Schneider

Additional field workers:

Bernard Bloch	Grace Reuter
Raymond O'Cain	Barbara Rutledge
Lee Pederson	Gerald Udell

South Carolina:

Linda Barnes	Sara Sanders
George Dorrill	Milledge Siegler
David Fischer	Kenneth Toombs
Nell Huffman	William Workman
Raymond O'Cain	

Chicago:

Jeffrey Atwood	Paul Kroeber
Kenneth Brehob	Carol Levine
Laurie Burgess	Nicole Lombardi
Robert Chametzky	Judith Maxwell
A. L. Davis	Patrick Merman
Nancy Dray	Steven Meyer
James Francis	Melanie Miller
Michael Grove	Thad Puig
Gail Hankins	Martha Ratliff
Patricia Hefner	Paul Ries
Suzanne Isaacson	James Williams
Lisa Jacobson	

Georgia:

John Algeo	John Kirk
Judy Blankenship	Heidi Kniskern
Karen Bresnahan	Rafal Konopka
Nancy Condon	Deanna Light
Nellie Felder	Timothy Marsh
Barbara Ferré	Debbie Vaughn
Coburn Freer	

We would also like to recognize the support offered to LAMSAS by the officers and members of the American Dialect Society, whose good will and good offices have been essential to the continuance of LAMSAS work through six decades.

Draft chapters for this handbook were prepared in the early 1980s by Raven I. McDavid, Jr., and he also conducted extensive research and made copious notes for community sketches (Lerud was initiated by Raven into the mysteries of his notecards, and managed to convert the notes to text with assistance of an NEH stipend), both with support from the National Endowment for the Humanities. He conceived of these chapters as continuations of or parallels to the similar chapters in the New England *Handbook*; it is no accident that LAMSAS and *LANE* share methods, and it should not be unexpected that those methods would be described in the same ways, sometimes in the same language. We have profited greatly by Raven's labors, and (not counting community sketches) the sections describing the worksheets, phonetics, and field-worker practices are largely his work. His chapter on dialect areas has been included complete. We have, however, had to rework and augment much material in order to incorporate the new design of LAMSAS for computer processing. We will be pleased if readers can still find evidence of Raven's strong influence.

WAK
VGMcD
TKL
EJ

Works Cited

[This list of references is in no way intended to serve as a bibliography of linguistic geography; it is merely a list of works cited for Chapters 1 through 9. Bibliography of state and local histories is included in the separate state sections of Chapter 10. An excellent bibliography of linguistic geography has been published recently in Volume 1 of Pederson et al. 1986–92; for particular studies of dialectal features and aspects of language variation, one may consult the annual MLA bibliography, annual indices for the journal *American Speech*, McMillan and Montgomery 1989, or Viereck, Schneider and Görlach 1984. *Eds.*]

Allen, Harold B. 1977. Regional Dialects, 1945–1974. *American Speech* 52:163–261.

— 1973–76. *Linguistic Atlas of the Upper Midwest*. 3 vols. Minneapolis: University of Minnesota Press.

Atwood, E. Bagby. 1953. *A Survey of Verb Forms in the Eastern United States*. Ann Arbor: University of Michigan Press.

Avis, Walter. 1961. The "New England short *o*": a Recessive Phoneme. *Language* 37:544–58.

Cassidy, Frederic G., and Joan Hall, eds. 1985-. *Dictionary of American Regional English*. Cambridge: Belknap Press.

Davis, Lawrence M. 1986. Sampling and Statistical Inferences in Dialectology. *Journal of English Linguistics* 19:42–48.

Gilliéron, Jules, and Edmond Edmont. 1902–1910. *Atlas linguistique de France*. Paris: Champion.

Jaberg, Karl, and Jacob Jud. 1928–1940. *Sprach- und Sachatlas Italiens und der Südschweiz*. Zofingen: Ringier.

Kaminkow, Marion J. 1975. *United States Local Histories in the Library of Congress: A Bibliography*. 4 vols. Baltimore: Magna Carta.

Kretzschmar, William A., Jr. 1988. Computers and the American Linguistic Atlas. In A. Thomas, ed., *Methods in Dialectology* (Clevedon, ENG: Multilingual Matters), 200–24.

— 1989. Phonetic Display and Output. In Kretzschmar, Schneider, and Johnson 1989, 47–53.

Kretzschmar, William A., Jr., and Edgar W. Schneider. In preparation. *Postmodern Dialectology: Computers, Statistics, and the Linguistic Atlas of the Middle and South Atlantic States (LAMSAS)*.

Kretzschmar, William A., Jr., Edgar W. Schneider, and Ellen Johnson, eds. 1989. *Computer Methods in Dialectology. Journal of English Linguistics* 22.1.

Kurath, Hans. 1949. *A Word Geography of the Eastern United States*. Ann Arbor: University of Michigan Press.

— 1972. *Studies in Area Linguistics*. Bloomington: University of Indiana Press.

Kurath, Hans, and Raven I. McDavid, Jr. 1961. *The Pronunciation of English in the Atlantic States*. Ann Arbor: University of Michigan Press.

Kurath, Hans, et al. 1939. *Handbook of the Linguistic Geography of New England*. Providence: Brown University, for ACLS.

— 1939–43. *Linguistic Atlas of New England*. 3 vols. in 6 pts. Providence: Brown University for ACLS.

Linn, Michael. 1983. Informant Selection in Dialectology. *American Speech* 58:225–43.

McDavid, Raven I., Jr. 1957. Tape Recording in Dialect Geography: A Cautionary Note. *Journal of the Canadian Linguistic Association* 3:3–8.

— 1970. Changing Patterns of Southern Dialects. In Arthur Bronstein, et al., eds., *Essays in Honor of C. M. Wise* (Hannibal, MO: Standard, Speech Association of America), 206–28. Repr. in W. Kretzschmar, et al., eds, *Dialects in Culture: Essays in General Dialectology by Raven I. McDavid, Jr.* (Tuscaloosa: University of Alabama Press), 295–308.

— 1971. Planning the Grid. *American Speech* 46:9–26.

—— 1984. Linguistic Geography. In Thomas Clark, ed., *Needed Research in American English (1983)*. Publication of the American Dialect Society 71:4–31.

—— 1985. Review of Edward Ives, *The Tape-Recorded Interview*. Journal of English Linguistics 18:54–63.

McDavid, Raven I., Jr., and Raymond O'Cain. 1980. *Linguistic Atlas of the Middle and South Atlantic States*. Fasc. 1-2. Chicago: University of Chicago Press.

McDavid, Raven I., Jr., et al. 1976–78. *Linguistic Atlas of the North-Central States: Basic Materials*. Chicago Microfilm MSS on Cultural Anthropology, gen. ed. Norman McQuown. Series 38.200–08. Chicago: Joseph Regenstein Library, University of Chicago.

—— 1982–86. *Basic Materials: Linguistic Atlas of the Middle and South Atlantic States and Affiliated Projects*. Chicago Microfilm MSS on Cultural Anthropology, gen. ed. Norman McQuown. Series 68.360–64, 69.365–69, 71.375–80. Chicago: Joseph Regenstein Library, University of Chicago.

McMillan, James, and Michael Montgomery. 1989. *Annotated Bibliography of Southern American English*. Tuscaloosa: University of Alabama Press.

O'Cain, Raymond. 1979. *Linguistic Atlas of New England. American Speech* 54:243–78.

Orton, Harold, et al. 1962–71. *Survey of English Dialects: Basic Materials*. Leeds: Arnold.

Paullin, Charles, and John Wright. 1932. *Atlas of the Historical Geography of the United States*. Washington and New York: Carnegie Institution and the American Geographical Society.

Pederson, Lee, et al. 1981. *Linguistic Atlas of the Gulf States: The Basic Materials*. Ann Arbor: University Microfilms International.

—— 1986. *Linguistic Atlas of the Gulf States: A Concordance of Basic Materials*. Ann Arbor: University Microfilms International.

—— 1986–92. *Linguistic Atlas of the Gulf States*. 7 vols. Athens: University of Georgia Press. [1, *Handbook*; 2, *General Index*; 3, *Technical Index*; 4, *Regional Matrix*; 5, *Regional Pattern*; 6, *Social Matrix*; 7, *Social Pattern*.]

US Department of the Interior, Geological Survey. 1970. *The National Atlas of the United States of America*. Washington: USGPO.

Viereck, Wolfgang, Edgar Schneider, and Manfred Görlach, eds. 1984. *A Bibliography of Writings on Varieties of English, 1963–1983*. Amsterdam: John Benjamins.

Wenker, Georg. 1892–1902. *Sprachatlas der Deutschen Reichs*. Marburg.

Wetmore, Thomas H. 1959. *The Low-Central and Low-Back Vowels in the English of the Eastern United States*. Publication of the American Dialect Society, 32.

Wrede, Ferdinand. 1926–56. *Deutscher Sprachatlas*. Marburg: Elwert.

Wright, Joseph. 1898–1905. *The English Dialect Dictionary*. London: Frowde.

Zelinsky, Wilbur. 1973. *The Cultural Geography of the United States*. Englewood Cliffs, NJ: Prentice-Hall.

Acronyms for American Linguistic Atlas Projects

[The following list is derived from McDavid 1984. Additional field work following Kurath's methodology has been executed in a number of other areas (such as Missouri, or the Canadian Maritime Provinces) but without project-level organization. Citations to publications listed above are supplied for works cited in this volume. *Eds.*]

LAMSAS Linguistic Atlas of the Middle and South Atlantic States. McDavid and O'Cain 1980, McDavid et al. 1982–86.

LANE *Linguistic Atlas of New England.* Kurath et al. 1939–43, 1939.

LAUM *Linguistic Atlas of the Upper Midwest.* Allen 1973–76.

LAGS *Linguistic Atlas of the Gulf States.* Pederson et al. 1981, 1986, 1986–92.

LANCS Linguistic Atlas of the North-Central States. McDavid et al. 1976–78.

LAPC Linguistic Atlas of the Pacific Coast (California and Nevada).

LAPN Linguistic Atlas of the Pacific Northwest.

LAO Linguistic Atlas of Oklahoma.

LARMR Linguistic Atlas of the Rocky Mountain Region.

Chapter 1: History and Nature of the Project

The history of LAMSAS cannot be understood without some understanding of the history of the entire project for a Linguistic Atlas of the United States and Canada. The idea for a Linguistic Atlas of the United States and Canada was broached almost simultaneously in 1928 at the annual meetings of various professional groups, by such scholars as Charles C. Fries, Edward Sapir, and Edgar H. Sturtevant. A preliminary meeting in January of 1929 led to a more extensive discussion in August of that year, under the sponsorship of the American Council of Learned Societies. At this later conference it was resolved to begin a survey toward a Linguistic Atlas of the United States and Canada (LAUSC), on the general model of European linguistic atlases as exemplified by Gilliéron's *Atlas linguistique de France* (1902–10); the ACLS accepted the idea in principle, but advised a pilot project in a limited area—New England—where local support could be obtained and where a great deal was already known about the social and demographic history of the region. Hans Kurath was named Director of the project; project headquarters were established first at Yale and then at Brown; field workers were recruited, and two scholars involved in the linguistic atlas of Italy and Southern Switzerland (Jaberg and Jud 1928–40)—Jakob Jud, one of the two directors, and Paul Scheuermeier, principal field investigator—were enlisted to train these field workers in interviewing techniques and phonetic transcription. Field work was completed, on the scale planned by Kurath, by 1933. Editing had begun while field work was still under way; the *Linguistic Atlas of New England (LANE)* was published in three elegant folio volumes, bound as six parts, in 1939–43, with an accompanying handbook (Kurath et al. 1939). The only detail lacking in the execution of Kurath's plan was the analysis and publication of the collateral evidence provided by phonograph recordings made in the later 1930s (for further details of the origins of the American Atlas effort, see O'Cain 1979).

In contrast with the rapid completion of *LANE*, work on the Middle and South Atlantic States has gone very slowly, for a number of reasons. The great Depression struck the United States as the LAUSC project was being organized; universities and foundations found their resources drastically curtailed, and in much of the Atlantic Seaboard such resources did not exist on the scale they did in New England. Funds were barely enough to keep one investigator in the field till 1941; with the involvement of the United States in World War II field work became impossible, and the federal student support that had provided a number of competent editorial assistants came to an end. Linguists who might have worked on the Atlas project were taken into the wartime Intensive Language Program, later into research on exotic languages or into the language teaching program of the Foreign Service Institute and special programs in the teaching of English as a second language. In later years the rise of transformational grammar and sociolinguistics did not encourage strong support for research based on an older model. Even linguists chiefly concerned with American linguistic geography found themselves involved in other tasks. Kurath himself became editor-in-chief of the *Middle English Dictionary* at Ann Arbor, and from the end of World War II was unable to direct editorial operations. The project became a group of autonomous regional surveys, sharing the same general methodology but locally supported and directed. The history of these separate projects has been summarized in Allen 1977 and McDavid 1984.

All of the autonomous Atlas projects share the same essential methodology, detailed discussion of which is the subject of the other chapters of this handbook: communities selected to form a representative grid of the region; informants selected to be representative of the communities; interviewers specially trained to record responses in fine phonetic notation; a questionnaire with questions about everyday speech, administered in as informal a situation as could be obtained. These methods have yielded a massive corpus of answers to questions. They are not methods by which one can arrive at a complete description of the structure of American English, or even a complete description of variation within the language. Instead, these answers to questions may be taken as a sample of American speech at the time of the interviews, and the answers represent and should be used to diagnose the speech of Americans of that time only to the extent that the questions and informants reflect that speech and those people. The LAMSAS files do provide much of the sociocultural information about informants that contemporary field methods would elicit, and so it is possible to analyze the data as the speech of individuals rather than merely as speech representative of communities. The corpus has great historical value if it is called to testify only about what it surveyed and can support, not about all Americans and all of American English at the time of the field work.

Field work. Originally Kurath planned three surveys for the Atlantic Seaboard, with the South Atlantic States and then the Middle Atlantic States to follow New England. The Depression precluded any large group of field workers like the one which had been organized for New England. Kurath was able to get Guy L. Lowman, Jr., who had made the largest contribution to the work in New England, to conduct a preliminary investigation (October 1933–December 1934) from Delaware through Georgia, with a longer, modified questionnaire. The questionnaire was then trimmed to one slightly longer than the one used for New England, and a network of South Atlantic communities was drawn up. Following New England precedent, Kurath secured local support for the work in Virginia and North Carolina, but since there was none available in South Carolina and Georgia he suspended work in the South, while Lowman spent the academic year 1937–38 on a wide-meshed survey of Southern England. On returning from England, Lowman completed the field work in Delaware and Maryland but did not return to South Carolina and Georgia.

Work in the Middle Atlantic States, originally intended to be a separate atlas, was begun in the summer of 1939. By August of 1941 Lowman had completed work in Pennsylvania, West Virginia, New Jersey, the eastern strip of counties in Ohio, New York City, and the Hudson and Mohawk Valleys; he was at work in the Finger Lakes of Upstate New York when he died in an automobile accident.

During the 1937 Linguistic Institute at Ann Arbor, Bloch had used Raven I. McDavid, Jr., of Greenville, South Carolina, as a demonstration informant, and—finding him both interested in regional culture and a good beginning student in linguistics—had encouraged him to develop his

talents and to undertake a more intensive study in South Carolina than Atlas plans had called for. After further study, including training with Bloch and Kurath at the Institutes of 1940 and 1941, McDavid was invited by Kurath to use a small grant to cover as much of South Carolina as possible; he had begun his study when Lowman died. It was planned for him to return to the field full-time in 1942, but American entrance into World War II and his own participation in the Army Intensive Language Program postponed this till the fall of 1945. Work in South Carolina and Georgia and northeast Florida was essentially completed according to Kurath's plans by the spring of 1948, and in Upstate New York and Ontario the following year.

When McDavid became editor-in-chief in 1964, an inventory of the LAMSAS archives suggested to him the need for supplementing the records previously made in Ontario, Upstate New York, South Carolina, Georgia, and Florida. For this task he enlisted Lee Pederson (beginning the Atlas of the Gulf States), Gerald Udell of Missouri, and Raymond O'Cain (completing a dissertation on the speech of Charleston). All of these investigators—and the colleagues and students of Pederson who assisted him—conducted their interviews with the tape recorder and transcribed them later; consequently, to avoid the problems of calibrating a number of transcription practices (which had faced the editors in New England), McDavid retranscribed all of these records. The corpus of records was completed by incorporating four *LANE* records from eastern Long Island (all by Lowman), and 39 from the North-Central Atlas (LANCS; three records from Ontario, 16 from Ohio, and 20 from Kentucky, of which 29 were by McDavid). Of these 1,216 records all but 11 represented the transcriptions of Lowman and McDavid. In 1989 it was decided, in conjunction with computerization of the project, that interviews from Ontario, Ohio, and Kentucky would be omitted from LAMSAS and would be treated instead as part of the North-Central Atlas; at the same time a number of informants with partial interviews were elevated from auxiliary status to primary status (see Chapter 2). These changes result in the total of 1,162 field records from primary informants now included in LAMSAS, all of which contain phonetic transcriptions by either Lowman or McDavid.

Editing and Publication. While editing of *LANE* was being completed, Kurath and his staff began the preparation of list manuscripts (see Chapter 6) of the evidence from the South Atlantic States, in which were included six communities from southern New Jersey and seven from the eastern panhandle of West Virginia. Some two hundred of these manuscripts, incorporating evidence only as far south as North Carolina, had been completed when the student aid program was suspended. No list manuscripts were prepared from the Middle Atlantic States while the archives were in Ann Arbor (1946–64). In the interim Kurath 1949, Atwood 1953, and Kurath-McDavid 1961 appeared, based on the editing so far completed.

When the archives were transferred to Chicago, McDavid adopted as top priority the completion of the list manuscripts, which at this time represented about 8% of the body of material. By the time they were transferred to South Carolina (1974–76) another 80% of the list-manuscript materials were in first draft; some 10% were ready for composition. During the period of editorial activity at South Carolina, about 4% more of the list manuscripts were drafted, and a considerable number made ready for the compositor.

The list-manuscript stage of editorial work proceeded rapidly after Raven McDavid assumed control of the project, but final editing and publication were delayed. In 1974 the University of South Carolina provided generous working space, editorial assistance, and a promising associate editor in O'Cain, but he resigned for personal reasons in 1980. Until the summer of 1983 editorial operations were limited to taking stock and to preparing the field records for microfilming as a measure of security; also during this period the relationship between LAMSAS and the American Dialect Society was formalized so that the Society, which had received reports on Atlas projects and served as the forum for scholarly exchange on Atlas methods and results, now held title to all research materials and assumed a role in the appointment of editorial personnel. It was not until 1986 that Kretzschmar managed to reestablish a secure, suitably appointed editorial site at the University of Georgia.

The format for publication was a more daunting problem. Kurath originally intended that the Middle and South Atlantic States would appear as two separate atlases, each with the data presented cartographically, like the data for *LANE*. A base map and overlays for 180 South Atlantic States list manuscripts were prepared according to *LANE* specifications in the 1940s, but Kurath did not publish the volume. Practical considerations led to the abandonment of the cartographic format: 1) the bulk and the expense of preparing large volumes to be printed lithographically from hand-lettered overlays; 2) the uneven distribution of data from map to map (items with many variants, like *cornbread*, had inadequate space, while the forms of verbs or geographical names left considerable blank space); 3) the difficulty of checking single phonetic features on the maps. Presenting the data in lists would be simpler and more economical, especially if these lists could be reproduced in photo-offset from typed copy. It was also decided to consolidate the data into a single Atlas. Kurath's explorations of the evidence had shown that the Mason-Dixon Line rarely constituted a dialect boundary, and that in most of the South Atlantic States the principal boundaries were those between the coastal plain and the Piedmont, or between the Piedmont and the mountains.

To present the data in tabular form, however, required technology that was not available at the end of World War II. Ultimately the development of the IBM Selectric typewriter, with interchangeable elements, offered a practical solution: A. L. Davis and McDavid designed such an element, produced by Camwil, Inc., of Honolulu, and that provided a suitable way of preparing copy. Final editing proceeded at South Carolina with the help of NEH funding (1976–1980), and the first two fascicles of LAMSAS, containing an introduction and lists of geographical names, were published by University of Chicago Press in 1980 (McDavid and O'Cain 1980).

An NEH site visit in 1980 had recommended computer assistance for fascicles, microfilming the records for safety, completion of the LAMSAS Handbook, and compilation of word indices. After the unexpected resignation of O'Cain the same year, McDavid assembled a new staff at the University of Chicago (including three of the present editors) to work to meet the site-visit recommendations. Work on two more fascicles was completed by 1982, but publication was postponed until computer-assisted production could be resumed. Microfilming of the records began in 1982 and was completed in 1986, with some NEH and corporate funding. Kretzschmar began investigating computer assistance for fascicle production in 1982.

McDavid died in October 1984, and Kretzschmar accepted direction of the project as had been arranged in a contingency plan. Work had just begun on an NEH grant to compile word indices by entering LAMSAS responses in standard spelling into a computer database. The goals of the grant were not accomplished because the software consultant could not provide working customizations of dBase III; all salvageable data, however, have been incorporated into current LAMSAS computer files. In 1985–86 Lerud received NEH funding to complete from McDavid's notes the community sketches and informant biographies for LAMSAS, the largest hurdle preventing publication of the LAMSAS Handbook, and he finished them in good time. Kretzschmar moved with all McDavid's materials to the University of Georgia in the fall of 1986.

Once at Georgia, Kretzschmar arranged for an archive of the original LAMSAS field records, along with those of LANCS and other projects which had employed Atlas methods. He then developed the means to display and print Atlas phonetics with PC-compatible computers (Kretzschmar 1989), designed the database structure for LAMSAS following the lead of *LAGS* (Kretzschmar 1988), and programmed the customizations of commercial software required for data entry and proofreading (see Chapter 7). These methods were tested and improved with assistance of a 1989 grant from the National Science Foundation. In 1990 NEH again provided major funding for final editing and creation of database files, and that work is now well under way. Final arrangements for publication are incomplete, but they will continue in the spirit of the modifications envisioned by Kurath: computer databases, after all, consist essentially of tables.

Chapter 2: Selection of Communities and Informants

Original Plans and Practices

The general guidelines for selection of communities for LAMSAS are the same as those for *LANE* as described in the *Handbook of the Linguistic Geography of New England* (Kurath et al. 1939:39):

> In selecting the communities, consideration was given to the original settlements, as well as to later shifts in population resulting from the development of commercial centers along the seaboard and the growth of industrial centers during the 19th century. Some attention was paid also to evenness of distribution, so that there might be no serious gaps. . . . Care was taken to include not only representative flourishing towns and cities, and stable towns, but also towns that have been going down hill for a century or more . . . . We feel rather confident that the Atlas has not overlooked any provincial center of importance and that rural as well as urban types of communities are well represented. It is readily granted, of course, that some highly individual towns deserving special study have been omitted—for the very reason that they are not representative of a larger district.

A tentative selection of *LANE* communities based on the historical research of Marcus Hansen was made before the inception of field work; Kurath later allowed some latitude to field workers in the final selection of localities for interviews (39). Raven McDavid has commented on the actual application of these principles:

> . . . Kurath adopted a policy of weighted selection of his communities . . . . There were two basic principles: rural communities would be represented more heavily than urban ones; and older areas of settlement would be represented more heavily than more recent ones. This means that in the Atlantic seaboard areas the network is finer meshed along the coast than inland . . . . (1971:16)

The *LANE* procedure—communities selected on the basis of history and culture, rather than randomized selection practices—remained Kurath's preferred method throughout his career (cf. Kurath 1972:10–11).

The basic community unit for LAMSAS is the county. In New England the basic unit was the township, and the change for LAMSAS corresponds to a difference in the organization of local governance (McDavid 1971:17). Occasionally a county is treated as two communities, reflecting differences in settlement patterns; in several instances two adjacent counties have been treated as a single community, with a single community number. As the planning documents indicate, the counties chosen were intended to be representative of their areas and states, according to settlement, ethnicity, and population. Figure 2.1 illustrates the area investigated. Figure 2.2 shows the counties of the LAMSAS region; the division of Figure 2.2 into three parts is a convenience for clear display of the counties, not a logical division employed in the survey plan or suggested for later analysis.

No overall grid of communities was planned before the inception of interviews in either the Middle Atlantic or the South Atlantic sections of the survey area. Instead, a preliminary survey of the South Atlantic area was carried out by Guy Lowman in 1933–34, and Kurath subsequently prepared overall estimates of the number of interviews required. Separate states were then completed in the South Atlantic section, and later in the Middle Atlantic section, as local funding could be obtained.

Kurath's 1935 overall plan for the South Atlantic area, a model of concision in its three pages, remains in the Atlas files. His two guiding principles were that "the entire area settled at the time of the Revolution" in the South Atlantic region would be covered, and that two informants would be

Figure 2.1: Area Investigated for LAMSAS

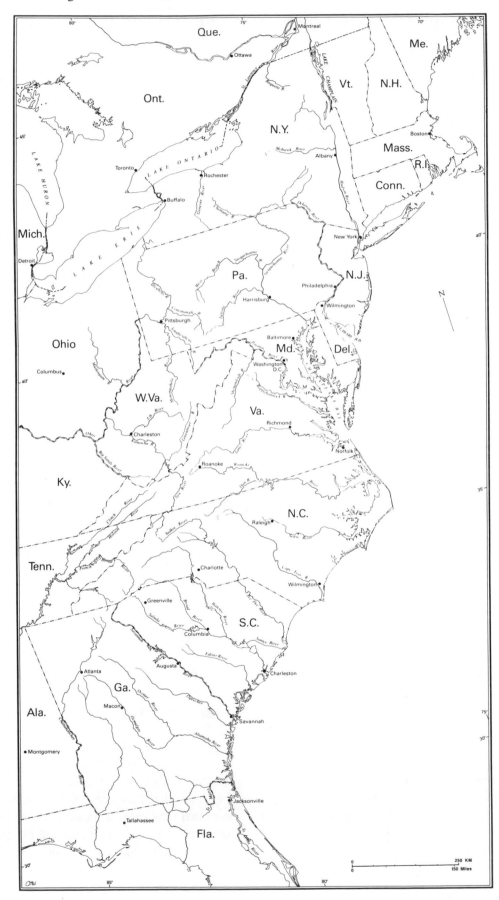

Figure 2.2a: Counties of the LAMSAS Region,
Northern Zone

Figure 2.2b: Counties of the LAMSAS Region,
Central Zone

Figure 2.2c: Counties of the LAMSAS Region, Southern Zone

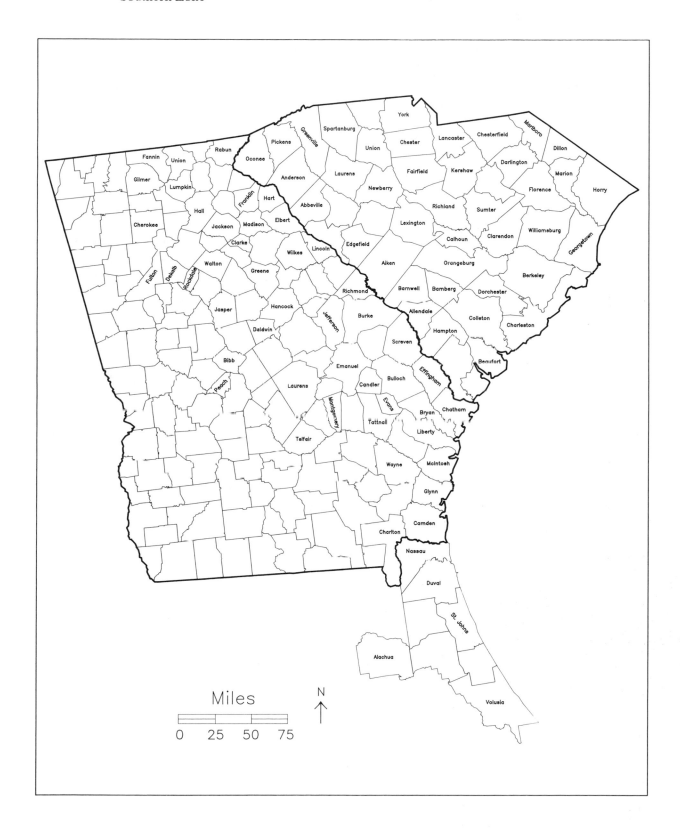

interviewed in each of about 250 communities. His discussion of the plan, previously unpublished, may be included here *in extenso*:

> In my attempt to arrive at a proper distribution of informants as between the several states, I first assigned *one* informant to every 20,000 inhabitants and then adjusted the figures for concentration of population in the cities. Since we shall have no more than 3 or 4 informants in such cities as Baltimore and Richmond, and no more than 2 in cities of 40,000, the quota of informants has been reduced in states that have a large urban population, namely Delaware (40%), Maryland (50%), Virginia (20%). The 50 informants thus eliminated were then distributed over the entire territory. These figures will have to be revised somewhat from the point of view of the history of settlement and the social organization of the several sections. In highly diversified areas (as inferred from historical data) the representation should be greater than in more uniform ones.
>
> Since the Tidewater, the Piedmont, and the Mountains differ more widely from each other in this respect than the several states concerned, the quotas assigned to the several states will probably not be altered substantially.
>
> In selecting communities within each state, the relative uniformity or diversity of the sections must be taken into consideration together with other factors revealed in the historical survey.

The number of communities eventually included in LAMSAS for each South Atlantic state is close to the number planned by Kurath (see Figure 2.3).

Figure 2.3: South Atlantic Communities by State

	Planned	Final
Delaware	4	6
Maryland	23	27
Virginia	57	75
North Carolina	83	75
South Carolina	46	44
Georgia	26	44
Florida	—	5

More communities than planned came to be used in Virginia and Georgia (16 of the extra Georgia communities were added by McDavid in the 1960s and 1970s, long after he had completed other interviewing there in 1948); five communities were also added in northern Florida. While no general Middle Atlantic plan now survives in the LAMSAS files, there is no reason to think that similar principles were not applied for that region.

Two of the state-by-state historical surveys, Virginia and North Carolina (executed by Guy Lowman), remain in the LAMSAS files. They are composed of brief, telescopic paragraphs about each county (community sketches in this handbook are considerably more extensive) which indicate early settlement history and notable events. The Virginia survey is accompanied by a 54-item bibliography.

Kurath's plan for selection of North Carolina communities also exists, with a copy of his transmittal letter to Lowman (May 6, 1936, sent to Lowman in the field, to "General Delivery, Suffolk, Virginia"). The plan contains maps of North Carolina by county which indicate dates of original settlement, concentrations of ethnic populations (Highland Scots, Germans, Scotch-Irish), and 18th-century population figures. There are also lists of counties in which interviews are to be conducted, and of counties in which a cultivated informant is to be interviewed in addition to Type I and II informants (see below for Type definitions). Kurath notes that "the number of communities is somewhat smaller than originally proposed, but I think it corresponds closely to the number investigated in Virginia when the area of the states and their present population are taken into consideration." It is clear that practical considerations entered into actual execution of survey planning. As Kurath wrote in his cover letter,

> The plans as sent are of course to be regarded as tentative. You will wish to make substitutions here and there; and upon closer investigation of the historical facts, you may want to include a few additional communities or drop others. I believe that the number of communities should not be changed much either way.

In the 1935 South Atlantic plan North Carolina was to have included 83 communities; the 1936 North Carolina plan proposes 64 communities; LAMSAS now includes 75 North Carolina communities.

Similarly, the expansion in the number of Virginia communities from those planned was carried out in the field by Lowman.

Figure 2.4 shows the localities selected for LAMSAS; the division of Figure 2.4, like Figure 2.2, into three parts is a convenience for clear display of the localities, not a logical division employed in the survey plan or suggested for later analysis. Little information now remains in the LAMSAS files concerning specific decisions about the selection of particular localities as sites for interviews. Guy Lowman and later Raven McDavid had considerable latitude as field workers in selection of individual localities for interviewing, just as they were involved in planning the state grids. Localities vary from isolated rural districts to neighborhoods in major cities. Some closely related localities are not separately sited in Figure 2.4 (e.g. Brooklyn Heights and East Brooklyn are not specified separately from Brooklyn), and the location of the local post office was used whenever it has not been possible to recover an exact location for the locality name listed in the field record. Localities have been included for some but not all auxiliary informants.

The field workers sought informants through a variety of local contacts, chiefly through people whose activities required them to know their communities intimately: local officials, agricultural agents, newspapermen, local historians, occasionally clergymen. In approaching such local contacts, field workers emphasized cultural identification with the community, intelligence, and cooperativeness, and normally minimized matters of speech except for its freedom from physical defects; they rarely used the word *dialect*, which may often be misunderstood. The closer such persons were identified with the community, the more reliable (in the view of the field workers) were their judgments about potential informants and the more cooperative the informants were likely to be. Field workers used the names of their local contacts when they approached informants, in order to let them know that they had some association in the community.

All informants were expected to be natives of the community and rooted in the local culture. Along the Atlantic Seaboard long local pedigrees were common. Three principal types of speakers were sought:

1) Folk speakers, local usage subject to a minimum of education and other outside influence, in every community. Type I.

2) Common speakers, local usage subject to a moderate amount of education (generally high school), private reading, and other external contacts, in every community. Type II.

3) Cultivated speakers, representing wide reading and elevated local cultural traditions, generally but not always with higher education, in about a fifth of the communities. Type III.

Folk speakers usually represented the oldest stratum of local usage, common speakers the middle generation, though there were exceptions. From information given by local contacts the field worker could tentatively assign an informant to a particular cultural group. If two or more local contacts provided the same kind of information, the assignment was likely to be fairly sure. The classification, however, could be changed on the strength of the interview, which might run from four to twenty-four hours. More than once a retired farmer with a sixth-grade education turned out to be a community leader, widely read and traveled. For this reason, field workers were asked to provide as much information as they could gather on the lives and activities of the informants and on their speech characteristics. This information is recorded in the informant sketches of Chapter 10, and is encoded in the table of informants. It is clearly the case that Type classifications depended entirely on the judgment of the field workers, who used the informant's level of education as the prime determinant of the informant's cultural position; they should not be understood as a rigorous delineation of informants' social class.

African-Americans were not included in the general grid of communities and informants. No African-American informants were interviewed in the Middle Atlantic States; there is no mention of African-Americans in Kurath's South Atlantic plan (though there are entries alluding to Lorenzo Turner's interviews of Gullah speakers in South Carolina and Georgia, which in the end were not included on the LAMSAS informant roster). The North Carolina plan proposes that African-Americans be interviewed in addition to the usual two informants per community. Kurath's cover letter for the plan suggests "that four negroes be interviewed, perhaps two in the eastern part of the state and two in the central part." Kurath also maintained separate listings of African-American informants in his editorial materials. These 41 informants are now integrated by community into the

Figure 2.4a: Localities of the LAMSAS Sample,
               Northern Zone

Legend
Key

1   Bronx
2   Nutley
3   Orange
4   Newark
5   Jersey City
6   Union Center
7   Elizabeth
8   Staten Island
9   Brooklyn
10 Flushing
11 Hancocks Bridge
12 Port Norris

Figure 2.4b: Localities of the LAMSAS Sample, Central Zone

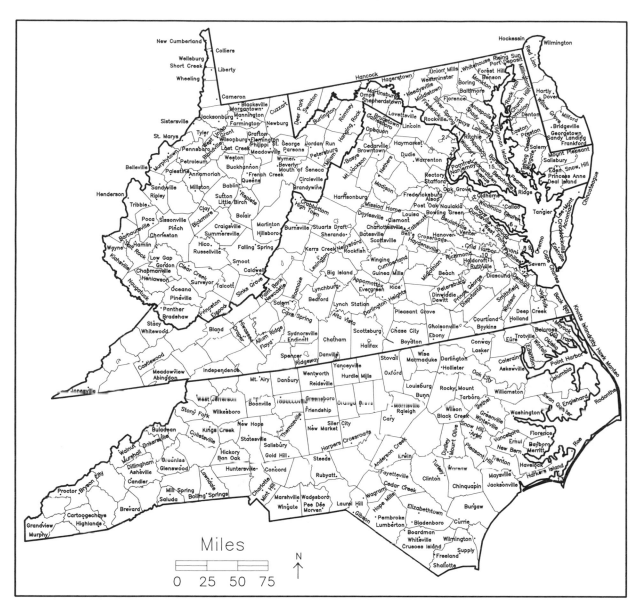

Legend
Key

1 Washington D.C.
2 Herndon
3 Alexandria
4 Woodbridge
5 Horners
6 Mollusk
7 Weems
8 Port Haywood
9 Mathews
10 Providence Forge
11 Messick
12 Grafton
13 Straits
14 King and Queen
15 Prince Frederick

Figure 2.4c: Localities of the LAMSAS Sample,
                 Southern Zone

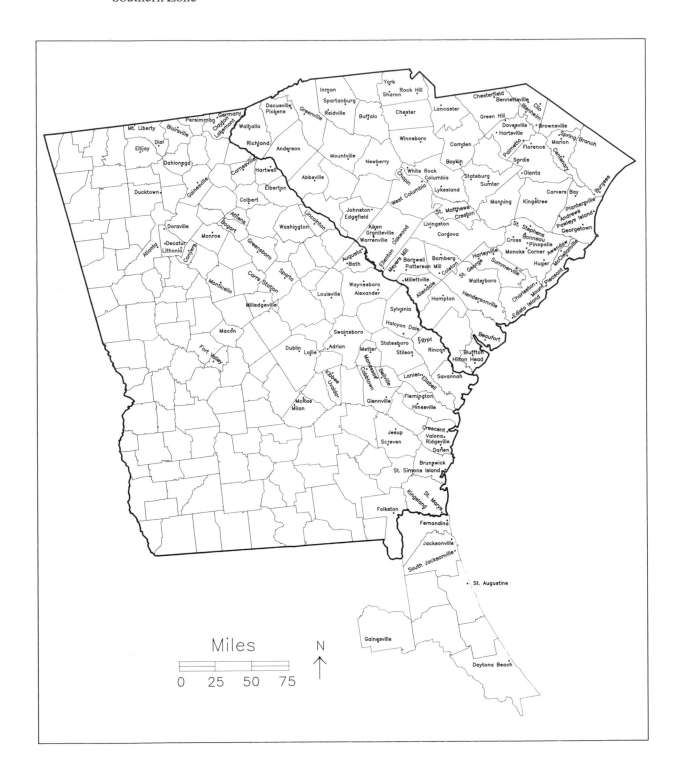

serial listing of LAMSAS informants, and have been included in LAMSAS editorial materials on the same terms as other informants since Raven McDavid assumed direction of the project.

Informants who completed at least a large part of the questionnaire are designated as primary informants and are numbered serially according to the LAMSAS numbering systems. Responses to questions by some other speakers, called auxiliary informants, are also included within LAMSAS. Auxiliary informants include family members or acquaintances of primary informants who happened to contribute a few responses during an interview, or speakers who were selected for interviewing but did not complete very much of an interview. Responses of auxiliary informants are recorded under the number of their family member or acquaintance, or of the primary informant who replaced them for the locality, but the responses are specially marked so that they will not be confused with those of the primary informant. Any biographical information which might be available for auxiliary informants is recorded in Chapter 10, under the number of the associated primary informant but marked with an asterisk (e.g. NC12A*) or as a specially-marked segment of the primary informant's biographical sketch. Auxiliary informants are not included in the master informant table.

Reconsideration of Communities and Informants for Computer Processing

When the computerization of LAMSAS became a real possibility in the late 1980s, it also became necessary to think again about the status of the project's communities and informants. Strict regularity and consistency of community and informant classifications are required for computer processing of the files, and over the decades of field work and editing a number of problems in this regard had arisen. The penultimate LAMSAS roster of communities and informants has been published in the first fascicle of McDavid et al. 1980 and in the front matter, state by state, for the microfilmed LAMSAS field records (McDavid et al. 1982–86). In this stage of the project there were 1,216 primary informants and 518 communities.

The first step in the reconsideration was to remove informants from Ontario, Kentucky, and Ohio from the LAMSAS roster. Only border communities in these areas had been surveyed, and a number of different field workers had executed the interviews, often with work sheets other than those used for the majority of LAMSAS. Moreover, most of these informants' responses had never been added to the LAMSAS list manuscripts, which were to be the primary witness for data entry. No data would be lost permanently by the deletion, since all of Ohio and Kentucky and a large portion of Ontario were included within the LANCS survey and former LAMSAS informants could easily be treated in LANCS. The total number of LAMSAS informants was reduced from 1,216 to 1,136, the number of communities from 518 to 483, by the following cuts: Ontario, 10 communities, 16 informants; Ohio, 18 communities, 44 informants; and Kentucky, 7 communities, 20 informants.

Another category of questionable records was the 58 interviews conducted between 1964 and 1974, 15 years after the completion of all other LAMSAS interviews in 1949. Nineteen new communities were thus introduced, 16 in Georgia and one each in New York, South Carolina, and Florida. Twenty-four of these informants were also included in the *LAGS* project. A number of different field workers executed the interviews, though all were transcribed from tape recordings by Raven McDavid. All of these interviews, however, were retained for the following reasons: all were transcribed by McDavid and they would thus not introduce new problems in interpretation of phonetics; there was no other project under which the 34 records not included in *LAGS* could be treated; and the 15-year hiatus would probably not be considered a destructively long interruption for the long-term historical value of LAMSAS. Computer processing also makes it easy for individual users of the database who do consider the hiatus significant to exclude the late records from their analyses.

A different kind of problem was presented by the classification of auxiliary informants: it was discovered that some auxiliary informants had actually completed large parts of the questionnaire. Conversely, some primary informants had completed relatively small portions of the work sheets. Reclassification of these informants was carried out in accordance with the portion of the work sheets that each informant had finished and the biographical information available for each one.

The 10 auxiliary informants who had completed 50 pages or more of the work sheets were reclassified as primary informants. Another 51 auxiliary informants had completed between a quarter and a half of the questionnaire. Those whose interviews were terminated because of a speech defect or some other problem that caused the field worker to consider them unsuitable as a primary informant were not considered eligible for reclassification.

Figure 2.5: Auxiliary Informants Reclassified as Primary Informants

Number	Former	Original
NY28C	← NY28B*	← 473b*
NY38C	← NY38A*	← 497*
PA14C	← PA14a*	← 95*
PA35C	← PA35B*	← 158*
PA37C	← PA37A*	← 161*
DE2C	← DE2A*	← 15*
MD13G	← MD13A*	← 54*
VA3C	← VA3A*	← 105*
VA20C	← VA20B*	← 150*
VA31C	← VA31A*	← 171*
VA51C	← VA51B*	← 220*
VA61C	← VA61A*	← 245*
NC15C	← NC15A*	← 335*
NC45B	← NC45*	← 409*
SC2C	← SC2A*	← 204.1*
SC6D	← SC6B*	← 208.2*
SC18D	← SC18C*	← 219.3*
SC19E	← SC19C*	← 220.2*
SC29D	← SC29A*	← 230.2*
SC29E	← SC29B*	← 230.1*
SC35D	← SC35B*	← 236.2*
SC35E	← SC35C*	← 236.3*
SC38E	← SC38D*	← 239.4*
SC42M	← SC42N*	← N243*
GA30D	← GA30A*	← 272.1*
GA30E	← GA30B*	← 272.2*

Biographies for the eligible auxiliary informants were then checked for information on age, sex, educational level, and occupation, the four characteristics that were predicted to be of most interest to the eventual users of LAMSAS. If auxiliary informants had completed at least 30 pages of the work sheets and there was information on them for three

of the four characteristics, they were reclassified as primary informants. This process yielded 16 more primary informants. No existing primary informants were reclassified as auxiliary informants because, even if they had completed as little as a quarter of the questionnaire, complete biographical information was available for them. All 26 reclassifications constituted net additions to the LAMSAS informant roster, to make a final total of 1,162.

The main serial numbering system for LAMSAS informants was created after the reclassifications. New informant numbers under the previous numbering system were, however, assigned to all reclassified informants to preserve links with previous LAMSAS publications (see Figure 2.5). For example, community SC 2 had informants SC 2A, SC 2A*, and SC 2B; SC 2A* was reclassified as a primary informant and assigned the number SC 2C, so that SC 2 now contains informants SC 2A, SC 2B, and SC 2C. The letter codes for individual informants were originally assigned according to the Type classification, with A the least sophisticated, B more sophisticated than A, and so on. The new numbers for reclassified informants violate that practice, but they do not require renumbering of any existing primary informants.

The LAMSAS Sample

When Hans Kurath and his field workers planned and executed the network of communities and informants, their major assumption was that careful selection of communities and informants improved the quality of the survey. While this assumption was normal and expected for surveys when LAMSAS began, random selection is now the ideal; probability theory and statistical modeling assume randomness (see Linn 1983 and Davis 1986 for some practical limitations on random sampling). Simply to note that survey research standards have changed, as some may be tempted to do, is a poor reason to refuse to consider evidence collected in earlier times—especially when it cannot be replaced with comparable evidence collected according to modern methods. Instead, it is possible to specify the relationship between the LAMSAS data as collected and a modern sample, and thus to assess any distortion or error which should be anticipated when modern statistical methods are applied to the data.

Several of the survey principles outlined earlier in this chapter have important ramifications for

LAMSAS data viewed as a sample. First and foremost, Kurath and his field workers conceived of their work as a study of elements of language with regard both to area and to population, and so LAMSAS is both an areal sample (or set of samples) and a population sample (or set of samples). It will be necessary to assess the areal qualities of the sample, its evenness of distribution and density of coverage, as well as the relation of the data to the population. The interrelation of area and population is part of the survey design. Evenness in areal sampling cannot correspond to even sampling of the population: population density is different between areas, as between city and countryside. Kurath tried to accommodate these variations by treating urban and rural populations differently in his South Atlantic plan. He began with even sampling by state and population; his redistribution of informants away from states with greater urban populations is a concession to even areal sampling.

Not every member of the American population at the time of the interviews was eligible to be included; Kurath and field workers knew in advance what kind of speakers they wanted to interview. Their first concern was that informants be natives of their region, which excludes the foreign-born and those who had changed their area of residence. A second principle was that adult speakers, particularly the old and middle-aged, were preferable to children as informants. A third principle excluded African-Americans and other non-whites; while Kurath was somewhat more progressive than his time in his allowance of some place in the survey for African-Americans, LAMSAS was typical of its era in the exclusion of non-whites from the general grid. It is necessary, then, to say that LAMSAS is not a sample of the general population of its region at the time of the interviews, but instead a sample of a target population: white, adult natives of their communities. It is generally true that this target population at the time of LAMSAS interviews held the economic power and social sway; it is less certain to what degree the target population also dominated or fairly represented American English in the region at the time of the survey.

LAMSAS data as a sample, then, represent the speech of the target population, not the general population, and targeting a specific population to sample remains an acceptable practice in modern survey design. There were also goals for selection of informants within the target population. Kurath specified that two informants should be interviewed

in each community, one folk speaker and one common speaker, and that in a portion of the communities a cultivated speaker should be interviewed. This practice is known as stratified, or quota, sampling, and it too is still common in modern survey design. What separates LAMSAS methods from those of modern survey research is how individual informants were selected. Today some effort at randomization is expected in order to give every eligible member of a population an equal chance to be selected for the survey. Randomized selection from telephone or street directories is common, but in practice neither of these methods is entirely satisfactory because not everybody has a telephone or a listed address. The question that must be answered about informant selection for LAMSAS, then, is whether every eligible member of the population had an equal chance of being included in the survey, given the planned stratification. Recommendation of informants by local contacts does not seem to introduce an ascertainable bias; however, it also does not offer the same freedom from possible bias (in practical terms) as randomized selection from lists. It would be well to assume that sampling practices represent a larger potential source of error in LAMSAS than they do in modern surveys; the accepted way to accommodate such a difference would be to require a stricter confidence level in statistical testing (e.g. to require $p < .01$, rather than the most commonly used level of $p < .05$). Kretzschmar and Schneider (in preparation) offers more detailed consideration of the application of statistical principles to LAMSAS.

The qualities of the LAMSAS sample as it was finally constituted can be measured against standard population and area figures. In the following set of figures Georgia and Florida are omitted from the comparison because only parts of them were surveyed; the foreign-born and non-white components are also omitted because they are not part of the target population. Figure 2.6 shows a breakdown of the population of the states covered in LAMSAS with figures drawn from the 1940 US Census, the census which best describes the population at the time LAMSAS was planned and executed. The total population of each state is shown in comparison with the native white population; one row for each state shows a division by locality type (urban, rural non-farm, and rural farm) excluding children age 14 or under, followed by a row which includes children. Native white children make up 21% of the population across the board; non-whites and the foreign-born, adults and children, make up about another 23%. The LAMSAS target population thus includes no more than 56% of the population of the region on average, ranging from a high of 62% in West Virginia and Delaware to a low of 39% in South Carolina (where there was a high non-white population). Of the approximately 40 million people living in the states included in Figure 2.6, only some 22 million belonged to the target population, and actually fewer than that number when the effect of population mobility is considered. Sixty-four percent of the population lived in urban areas, which according to the criterion of the 1940 Census includes towns of 2,500 or more. While there are consistently more women than men in urban areas, the opposite was true of rural areas so that, overall, the target population in the LAMSAS region in 1940 was composed almost equally of men and women.

Figure 2.7 shows the LAMSAS sample arrayed in categories similar to those in Figure 2.6; the rural non-farming and rural farming categories have been collapsed because there is too little information in the informant biographies to make a reliable distinction between them. Of the total of 1,162 LAMSAS informants, Figure 2.7 includes only 1,013 because Georgia, Florida, and African-American informants are removed for purposes of comparison, and missing information prevented appropriate categorization of one New York male informant. It is clear that the sample does not represent categories of the target population in the same proportions as in the census. Men are overrepresented overall, though women are somewhat overrepresented in the urban subcategory. This suggests that the field workers may have been biased in seeking more women in urban areas to compensate for selection of men in rural farming localities. Guy Lowman, for instance, selected only women, usually from urban areas, to serve as Type III informants in Virginia and North Carolina. The proportion of urban to rural residents is also skewed: the sample proportion of urban to rural residents is the reverse of that in the census. Comparison of the Georgia and Florida figures at the bottom indicates that those state samples followed the same trends as the other state samples.

Figure 2.8 shows the scale of the sample, the number of people in the target population who were represented by each informant (by individual category, by category overall, and by state overall). The figures show that the scale of coverage was widely different from individual category to individual category, from 1:256,986 for Pennsylvania rural women to 1:3,319 for men from South Carolina urban communities. Two categories were not covered at all: rural Delaware women and North Carolina urban men. Coverage was generally denser in the South Atlantic states than in the Middle Atlantic states where the population is concentrated in urban areas. For density by category, the restatement of the sample scale for the native white population with an urban vs. rural distinction (Figure 2.9) shows the effects of Kurath's redistribution of urban and rural informants. Rural coverage is denser than urban coverage as planned by Kurath, so that about 1:10,000 rural members of the target population were interviewed, but only 1:65,000 urban members. Urban density of coverage is most limited in those states with the highest concentrations of the their population in urban areas, the Middle Atlantic states and Maryland.

Figure 2.10 illustrates the areal scale of the sample. Overall, one informant was interviewed for each 250 sq. miles of the quarter-million sq. miles of the states in the table. States with small land areas, such as New Jersey, Delaware, and Maryland, have denser areal coverage than the larger states. Comparison of the areal scale column with the population scale figures reproduced next to it indicates some of the balancing that Kurath attempted. North Carolina has dense coverage by population but the least dense coverage by area. Areal coverage in New York is about average but its sample density by population is relatively small.

Figure 2.11 compares an index of the mean educational level of each state from census figures with the same index from the sample. The index was computed by assigning values to different levels of education as assigned in the LAMSAS Table of Informants (Chapter 3), from 0 for no schooling up to 6 for four years of college; the values were then multiplied by the number of tokens at each level in each category, and the totals were summed and divided by the cumulative number of tokens. Index averages were then computed for the rows (by state) and columns (by category) but were not weighted by population. While the great majority of LAMSAS informants have been classified by education, only about 70% of each state's population was so categorized in the census. The indices and index averages show consistently that urban residents tend to be better educated than rural residents, and that in rural areas women tend to be slightly better educated than men. The sample indices correspond closely to the census indices, but tend to be slightly higher. Urban women in the sample were the only category as much as one-half level different from the same category in the population.

These measures indicate that the LAMSAS sample is quite faithful to its target population in large terms. Kurath's attempt to balance urban and rural population density against even areal sampling is reflected in modulations in survey scale, and it created a large difference between urban and rural sampling density. Separate analysis of rural and urban informants is well justified by their difference in sampling scales. Stratified sampling by type classification has resulted in a good reflection of mean educational levels from the population to the sample. The greatest sampling bias seems to have occurred by sex. Evident variations between separate states and categories within the sample suggest caution in analysis of sub-samples, particularly when cells from individual categories contain only a few informants or if some cells contain no informants, but such variation seems more the result of known parameters of survey design than bias in the execution of the plan.

A somewhat different measure of the adequacy of the LAMSAS sample can be calculated once it is determined that the LAMSAS informant roster can be considered a reasonable sample (in large terms) of a target population. A typical question to be asked of LAMSAS data might be "What is the proportion of the LAMSAS target population who are likely to use a particular linguistic feature (as opposed to not using the feature), given the results of the LAMSAS sample?" This question is parallel to those asked in political opinion polling and marketing surveys; it also forms the basis of other forms of statistical testing on LAMSAS because it constitutes the "expected" frequency against which actual frequencies of use of linguistic features by different groups of speakers can be compared. Given the generally accepted confidence level for opinion polling (95%) and the number of white LAMSAS informants (1121), and assuming no prior knowledge of the proportion who use the linguistic feature ($\pi = .5$), we may calculate the standard error of the prediction made by the LAMSAS sample about its target population: approximately ±3%. This means that any prediction made by the LAMSAS sample about the percentage of members of its target population who use a particular linguistic feature (as opposed to not using it) has a 95% likelihood of being within 3% of the predicted percentage. This is exactly the standard error accepted in general use by most contemporary pollsters.

The 41 African-American informants in LAMSAS cannot be said to constitute a sample of the non-white population in the same way that the other LAMSAS informants make up a well-planned sample of the native white population. The same selection guidelines do not seem to have been consistently applied to the African-American population. The 41 informants come from just five states: Maryland, Virginia, North Carolina, South Carolina, and Georgia. More African-American informants than elsewhere were interviewed in Georgia (12) and South Carolina (12), states with high non-white populations, but the interviewing scale is still approximately 1:50,000 population in South Carolina, one-tenth the density for the white population. Still, the responses of these informants represent an important source of data about African-American English at the time of the survey. If statistical testing is conducted on the overall LAMSAS informant roster, these informants do help to compensate for the smaller proportions of the target population in the South Atlantic States.

Figure 2.6: Target Populations of States, 1940 Census

NW = Native White   Rural NF = Rural Non-Farming   Rural F = Rural Farming

	Total Population	NW Urban Male	NW Urban Female	NW Rural NF Male	NW Rural NF Female	NW Rural F Male	NW Rural F Female	NW Total	Share of Total
New York	13479142								
Adults		2830429	3064437	519035	517235	263124	212441	7406701	0.55
Incl. Children		3892881	4092284	703254	691922	350734	294941	10026016	0.74
New Jersey	4160165								
Adults		944785	1002946	200347	198350	42916	35620	2424964	0.58
Incl. Children		1274816	1322485	269045	264183	56572	48176	3235277	0.78
Pennsylvania	9900180								
Adults		1947687	2009051	770457	749432	329593	278513	6084733	0.61
Incl. Children		2632883	2777214	1108028	1077050	458651	399903	8453729	0.85
West Virginia	1901974								
Adults		174804	192650	240243	231264	182192	160854	1182007	0.62
Incl. Children		232596	249601	373777	361447	275345	249554	1742320	0.92
Delaware	266505								
Adults		40915	44212	25988	25798	14722	12702	164337	0.62
Incl. Children		53385	56320	34459	33906	19943	17682	215695	0.81
Maryland	1821244								
Adults		312191	329285	154967	149943	75256	65840	1087482	0.60
Incl. Children		405872	420356	210873	204030	103298	92337	1436766	0.79
D. of Columbia	663091								
Adults		171805	192900	0	0	0	0	364705	0.55
Incl. Children		209828	230484	0	0	0	0	440312	0.66
Virginia	2677773								
Adults		260003	279656	208085	197629	253095	236177	1434645	0.54
Incl. Children		335088	353110	299443	286159	370607	348189	1992596	0.74
North Carolina	3571623								
Adults		235392	266044	245377	254545	386431	366106	1753895	0.49
Incl. Children		319102	349331	364581	370255	592842	562478	2558589	0.72
South Carolina	1899804								
Adults		102904	117652	123904	126200	142211	134262	747133	0.39
Incl. Children		139259	152813	182464	183627	216041	205189	1079393	0.57
Total	40341501								
Adults		7020915	7498833	2488403	2450396	1689540	1502515	22650602	0.56
Incl. Children		9495710	10003998	3545924	3472579	2444033	2218449	31180693	0.77

By Community Type:	Urban	Share	Rural NF	Share	Rural F	Share
Adults	14519748	0.641	4938799	0.218	3192055	0.141
Incl. Children	19499708	0.625	7018503	0.225	4662482	0.150

By Sex:	Male	Share	Female	Share
Adults	11198858	0.494	11451744	0.506
Incl. Children	15485667	0.497	15695026	0.503

Figure 2.7: Informants of the LAMSAS Sample by State

(NB: Totals exclude 41 African-American informants, and one New York white male informant not classified by locality type; tables including these informants may be found in Chapter 3.)

	Urban Male	Urban Female	Rural Male	Rural Female	Total
New York	34	34	93	20	181
New Jersey	4	8	32	3	47
Pennsylvania	17	13	124	4	158
West Virginia	4	1	93	13	111
Delaware	2	1	11	0	14
Maryland	6	5	40	8	59
Dist. of Columbia	1	1	0	0	2
Virginia	2	14	70	61	147
North Carolina	0	22	71	57	150
South Carolina	31	22	72	19	144
Subtotals	101	121	606	185	1013

	Urban	Proportion	Rural	Proportion
Subtotal by Locality	222	0.219	791	0.781

	Male	Proportion	Female	Proportion
Subtotal by Sex	707	0.698	306	0.302

Partial States	Urban Male	Urban Female	Rural Male	Rural Female	Total
Georgia	18	20	44	16	98
Florida	2	1	5	1	9
Subtotals	20	21	49	17	107

	Urban Male	Urban Female	Rural Male	Rural Female	Total
Overall Totals	121	142	655	202	1120

	Urban	Proportion	Rural	Proportion
Overall by Locality	263	0.235	857	0.765

	Male	Proportion	Female	Proportion
Overall by Sex	776	0.693	344	0.307

Figure 2.8: LAMSAS Sample Scale by State, Native White Population (1:)

	Urban Male	Urban Female	Rural Male	Rural Female	Total
New York	83248	90131	8410	36484	40921
New Jersey	236196	125368	7602	77990	51595
Pennsylvania	114570	154542	8871	256986	38511
West Virginia	43701	192650	4542	30163	10649
Delaware	20458	44212	3701		11738
Maryland	52032	65857	5756	26973	18432
Dist. of Columbia	171805	192900			182353
Virginia	130002	19975	6588	7112	9759
North Carolina		12093	8899	10889	11693
South Carolina	3319	5348	3696	13709	5188
Overall	69514	61974	6894	21367	22360

Figure 2.9: LAMSAS Sample Scale by State, Native White Population (1:), Urban vs. Rural Division

	Urban	Rural
New York	86689	13379
New Jersey	162311	13379
Pennsylvania	131891	16625
West Virginia	73491	7684
Delaware	28376	7201
Maryland	58316	9292
Dist. of Columbia	182353	
Virginia	33729	6832
North Carolina	22793	9785
South Carolina	4161	5787
Overall	65404	10279

Figure 2.10: LAMSAS Sample Areal Scale, Native White Population

	Number of Informants	Area in Square Miles	Areal Scale (1:sq. mile)	Population Scale
New York	182	47834	263	40921
New Jersey	47	7532	160	51595
Pennsylvania	158	45026	285	38511
West Virginia	111	24084	217	10649
Delaware	14	1983	142	11738
Maryland	59	9881	167	18432
Dist. of Columbia	2	61	31	182353
Virginia	147	39838	271	9759
North Carolina	150	49067	327	11693
South Carolina	144	30280	210	5188
Overall	1014	255586	252	22360

Figure 2.11: 1940 Census Data vs. LAMSAS Sample, Native White Population:
Index of Mean Educational Level

The index is based on the scale of educational levels presented in Chapter 3: 0, none/illiterate; 1, some grade school; 2, grade school; 3, some high school; 4, high school; 5, some college; 6, college graduate.

	Urban Male	Urban Female	Rural Male	Rural Female	Index Average
New York census	3.033	2.950	2.713	2.897	2.949
New York sample	3.235	3.469	2.900	3.789	3.166
New Jersey census	2.966	2.877	2.729	2.799	2.888
New Jersey sample	4.250	4.000	3.031	2.333	3.255
Pennsylvania census	2.879	2.836	2.464	2.570	2.741
Pennsylvania sample	4.438	3.000	2.967	2.500	3.109
West Virginia census	2.946	2.961	2.125	2.242	2.432
West Virginia sample	2.500	5.000	2.376	3.364	2.505
Delaware census	3.029	3.003	2.628	2.763	2.858
Delaware sample	3.500	4.000	2.600		2.846
Maryland census	2.757	2.702	2.615	2.737	2.706
Maryland sample	4.000	3.400	2.270	3.000	2.630
Dist. of Columbia census	3.637	3.544			3.587
Dist. of Columbia sample	1.000	6.000			3.500
Virginia census	3.036	3.145	2.246	2.528	2.659
Virginia sample	2.000	4.538	1.761	2.564	2.350
North Carolina census	3.091	3.194	2.214	2.433	2.566
North Carolina sample		3.905	1.730	2.315	2.290
South Carolina census	3.281	3.434	2.364	2.584	2.743
South Carolina sample	3.767	4.000	2.657	2.750	3.133
Census index average	3.065	3.065	2.455	2.617	
Sample index average	3.188	4.131	2.477	2.827	

Overall Index averages (not weighted by population):

Average of index by category (average of urban and rural averages):
    Census   2.801
    Sample   3.156

Average of index by state (average of index average column):
    Census   2.813
    Sample   2.878

Chapter 3: Tables of Informants and Communities

Table of Informants

The Table of Informants contains coding to identify each informant (5 columns), information about the circumstances of each interview (3 columns), field workers' judgments about informants (3 columns), and sociocultural characteristics for each informant (6 columns).

The three categories of field workers' judgments represent the sociocultural classifications planned originally by Kurath. Information about six more characteristics—age, sex, race, education, occupation, and rurality—was recovered from informant biographies. The number of possible categories is limited to those for which evidence was available in the biographical sketches of informants (Chapter 10).

A. Serial Number. This column contains a unique real number, from 1 to 1162, to identify each informant. These numbers were assigned according to the order of informants in the previous LAMSAS numbering system (C. below), as adjusted for reclassified auxiliary informants. Thus, serial numbers proceed by state beginning with New York in the north and ending with Florida in the south; within each state serial numbers follow the ordering of the old community numbers, which do not have any precise relation to location within the state.

B. Community Number. This column contains an integer which uniquely identifies each of the 483 communities represented by at least one informant. The numbers are organized by state (i.e. numbers in the 100s refer to New York State, in the 200s to New Jersey, and so on), and by the old community numbers within each state (e.g. 101 is the same as NY1, 102 as NY2, and so on). The *serial number* and *community number* identifiers were assigned in order to facilitate computer processing of data, since the older numbering systems had proven difficult to manage under the normal sorting routines employed by computers.

Serial Number	Community Number	State
1–182	101–164	New York
183–229	201–221	New Jersey
230–387	301–367	Pennsylvania
388–498	401–454	West Virginia
499–512	501–506	Delaware
513–574	551–577	Maryland
575–576	599	Dist. of Columbia
577–730	601–675	Virginia
731–887	701–775	North Carolina
888–1043	801–844	South Carolina
1044–1153	901–944	Georgia
1154–1162	951–955	Florida

C. Informant ID Number. This column identifies informants as marked in many previous LAMSAS publications, including McDavid and O'Cain 1980 and McDavid et al. 1982–86. Each code is composed of a two-letter state abbreviation, a community number, and finally a letter for each informant if more than one had been interviewed in the community. For instance, NY 1 identifies an informant from community 1 in New York State, and there is no following letter code because only one informant was interviewed in that community; NY2A, NY2B, and NY2C identify the three informants from community 2 in New York State. The order of the A, B, and other informants in any community was established in order of the *type* classification (I. below), with A the least sophisticated informant, B more sophisticated, and so on. This ordering is no longer strictly valid because of the reclassification and renumbering of some auxiliary informants (see Chapter 2). Separate from these letter codes are the N and M letter codes used to identify the first and second African-American informants from a community. Exclamation points identify cultivated informants (see K. below).

D. Original Informant Number. This column records the original informant identifiers assigned by Kurath and the field workers. They were superseded by *informant id* codes because they did not uniquely identify informants, and because somewhat different ordering systems had been used in different states. These identifiers are presented here because they are often of use for work with documents and publications prepared very early in the history of LAMSAS. Numbers with an asterisk designate some of the informants formerly classified as auxiliary informants (see Chapter 2).

E. Auxiliary Informants. This column indicates by Y or N whether or not responses from any auxiliary informants appear alongside those of the primary informant.

F. Field Worker. This column indicates which field worker conducted the interview. The breakdown below summarizes how many interviews each field worker conducted. McDavid transcribed interviews from tape for all other field workers except Lowman and Bloch.

Code	Name	Number
L	Guy Lowman	826
M	Raven McDavid	278
P	Lee Pederson	19
S	Student	19
Rr	Grace Reuter	7
U	Gerald Udell	5
Rt	Barbara Rutledge	4
O	Raymond O'Cain	3
B	Bernard Bloch	1

G. Work Sheets. This column records which questionnaire was used to conduct the interview (see Chapter 4). The following summary indicates how many interviews were conducted with each questionnaire.

Code	Work Sheets	Number
S	South Atlantic	565
M	Middle Atlantic	465
P	Preliminary South Atlantic	70
C	Combined	57
E	New England	5

H. Year of Interview. This column indicates the year in which each interview took place. The following list records the number of interviews that took place each year.

Year	Number	Year	Number
1933	9	1948	40
1934	65	1949	58
1935	77	1964	1
1936	125	1965	12
1937	80	1966	1
1939	179	1967	3
1940	169	1968	13
1941	135	1970	6
1945	1	1971	5
1946	70	1972	15
1947	96	1974	2

I. Type. This column indicates the *type* classification assigned by the field worker, a subjective measure which was associated by Kurath and his field workers with formal education, private reading, and participation in social activites.

Type I: Folk speakers, local usage subject to a minimum of education and other outside influence.

Type II: Common speakers, local usage subject to a moderate amount of education (generally high school), private reading, and other external contacts.

Type III: Cultivated speakers, representing wide reading and elevated local cultural traditions, generally but not always with higher education (see K. below).

This classification was an important constituent in the planning of the survey and selection of particular informants (see Chapter 2). A count of informants belonging to each *type* is presented below; three informants (formerly auxiliary informants) cannot be classified by *type*.

Type I	582
Type II	439
Type III	138

J. Generation. This column shows another judgment by the field worker. Kurath and the field workers considered that formal education and self-education through reading and association with others were more significant for the character of informants' speech than mere age, and thus this generational A/B distinction was regarded as a sub-classification of *type* (I.). Two former auxiliary informants have no indication of *generation*.

    A. Aged and/or regarded by the field worker as old-fashioned. 696 informants.

    B. Middle-aged or younger and/or regarded by the field worker as more modern. 463 informants.

K. Cultivation. Field workers' judgments of cultivation were supposed to identify those whose speech reflected superior education and elevated social standing in their communities. In all 150 informants were judged to be cultivated. The judgment was not identical with *type* classication: fourteen informants of Type II were thought to be cultivated, and two Type III informants were not so considered. Three former auxiliary informants are not classified by *cultivation*.

L. Sex. This column encodes a binary, purely biological classification, 802 male informants, 360 female informants. Culturally based measures of gender are not available in informant sketches.

M. Age when Interviewed. The number of informants at any particular age is summarized below.

Age	Number	Age	Number	Age	Number
16	1	50	23	73	33
18	1	51	21	74	31
19	1	52	24	75	49
24	2	53	18	76	33
26	1	54	21	77	38
30	1	55	24	78	25
33	1	56	10	79	26
34	2	57	16	80	47
35	3	58	19	81	18
36	9	59	13	82	26
37	8	60	18	83	20
38	8	61	16	84	19
39	12	62	20	85	25
40	13	63	14	86	12
41	12	64	10	87	17
42	16	65	20	88	5
43	16	66	22	89	7
44	19	67	24	90	4
45	22	68	28	91	2
46	13	69	17	92	3
47	16	70	55	94	3
48	21	71	24	95	2
49	21	72	33	100	2

Information is missing regarding the age of six informants.

N. Education. This column encodes seven levels of education attained by informants. The number at each level is summarized below.

Code	Description	Number
0	None/Illiterate.	90
1	Some grade school: 1–4 years.	177
2	Grade school: 5–8 years.	217
3	Some high school: 9–11 years.	249
4	High school: 12 years.	212
5	Some college (also trade schools)	95
6	College graduate.	65

These categories were not defined at the time of the interviews but were created post-hoc from information about years of schooling found in the informant biographies; the assignments are thus subject to doubt. Most of the informants would have finished school before 1915 and before free, public, compulsory education was widespread. School systems were far from standardized, and statements such as "graduated from Jones Academy" are impossible to classify exactly. Grade levels may have been nonexistent in some schools and students may have attended irregularly owing to agricultural or other responsibilities: someone who was "educated through age 18" may conceivably not even have finished grammar school. In the absence of further information, those who attended past the age of 13 (or for 5–8 years) are considered elementary school graduates, and those who attended past the age of 17 (or for 12 years) are considered high-school graduates. Some informants were not formally educated but learned at home. Those who did not go to school but somehow learned to read and write (including ex-slaves denied a formal education) were assigned to level 1. Some informants who were taught at home had parents who were themselves schoolteachers and were assigned to level 2 or 3. Some cultivated women who had governesses as children and later tutors in various subjects were assigned to level 4. Fifty-six informants could not be classified because of missing information.

O. Occupation. Informants were assigned an occupational code according to the classifications given by the U.S. Census for 1940. One census category, Retired, was omitted from LAMSAS classifications and the code for the informant's previous occupation was substituted. Student was not listed as an occupation in the census.

Code	Description	Number
P	Professional and Technical	47
F	Farmers	568
M	Managers, Officials, Proprietors	96
R	Clerical and Sales	29
C	Craftsmen and Foremen	30
O	Operatives	19
H	Private Household Workers	13
S	Service Workers	17
W	Farm Laborers	13
K	Keeping House	278
L	Non-Farm Laborers	27
U	Seeking Work	1
G	Student	2

Many of the informants were listed in the biographies as having more than one occupation. In these cases, and in the absence of clues for which occupation they considered their primary work, only the code for the first job listed was entered. For example, informants described as a farmer and newspaper editor and as a farmer and sawmill worker are both entered as "Farmer". It is usually impossible to determine whether the job listed first was arbitrary or was the occupation with which informants most closely identified themselves. Female informants were more often identified by their marital status than their occupation. The designation *housewife*, sometimes *housekeeper*, seems to collapse the two, meaning both that the informant was a homemaker and that she was married. *Widow* and *single homemaker*, given as comparable occupations, provide evidence for this interpretation. The marital status of male informants is rarely noted. There was insufficient information to identify the occupation of 22 informants.

P. Race. This column encodes a binary distinction between Caucasian and African-American informants. It should be noted that racial designation in LAMSAS is social, not genetic, since people of mixed ancestry may well have been described as "Negro" by field workers. The 41 African-American informants on the LAMSAS roster are now integrated in the serial listings by community, though they remain segregated at the end of the informant listings for each community; they were originally thought of as additions to the overall survey plan (Chapter 2).

Q. Locality Type. Informants have been grouped according to the criteria of the 1940 US Census for relative population of their localities:

U	Urban	277
R	Rural	884

The Urban designation refers to localities with populations greater than 2500. Census categories for Rural Farming and Rural Non-Farming communities have been collapsed into a single Rural category; there is too little evidence in the LAMSAS informant biographies to make reliable farming/non-farming distinctions. LAMSAS communities are typically counties; judgments of *locality type* were based on specific residence within the LAMSAS community. Missing information prevented classification of one informant.

A.	B.	C.	D.	E.	F.	G.	H.	I.	J.	K.	L.	M.	N.	O.	P.	Q.
1	101	NY1	50	N	L	E	33	I	B	N	M	53	3	F	W	R
2	102	NY2A	51.1	N	L	E	33	I	A	N	M	63	0	F	W	R
3	102	NY2B	51.2	N	L	E	33	I	A	N	M	85	3	F	W	R
4	102	NY2C	51.3	Y	L	E	33	II	A	N	F	80	2	K	W	U
5	103	NY3A	401	N	L	M	41	I	A	N	M	71	4	F	W	R
6	103	NY3B	403	N	L	M	41	I	A	N	M	70	3	F	W	R
7	103	NY3C	402	N	L	M	41	I	B	N	M	50	4	F	W	R
8	103	NY3D	404	N	L	M	41	I	B	N	M	48	3	F	W	R
9	104	NY4A	405	N	L	M	41	I	A	N	M	69	2	F	W	R
10	104	NY4B	407	N	L	M	41	I	A	N	M	79	2	O	W	U
11	104	NY4C	408	N	L	M	41	I	B	N	M	51	3	F	W	R
12	105	NY5A	409	N	L	M	41	I	B	N	F	70	4	K	W	U
13	105	NY5B	410	N	L	M	41	I	B	N	M	62	4	R	W	U
14	105	NY5C	411	N	L	M	41	II	B	N	F	51	3	K	W	U
15	105	NY5D	412	N	L	M	41	II	B	N	M	64	2	R	W	U
16	105	NY5E	413	N	L	M	41	II	A	N	F	82	2	K	W	U
17	105	NY5F	414	N	L	M	41	II	B	N	M	53	2	M	W	U
18	105	NY5G	415	N	L	M	41	II	B	N	M	50	4	M	W	U
19	105	NY5H!	416	N	L	M	41	III	A	Y	M	68	6	P	W	U
20	105	NY5I!	417	N	L	M	41	III	B	Y	M	54	6	M	W	U
21	106	NY6A	418	N	L	M	41	I	A	N	F	76	2	K	W	U
22	106	NY6B	419	N	L	M	41	II	B	N	F	48	4	K	W	U
23	107	NY7A	420	N	L	M	41	I	B	N	M	45	2	L	W	U
24	107	NY7B	421	N	L	M	41	I	B	N	M	39	2	O	W	U
25	107	NY7C	422	N	L	M	41	I	B	N	F	43	2	K	W	U
26	107	NY7D	423	N	L	M	41	II	A	N	F	79	2	K	W	U
27	107	NY7E	424	N	L	M	41	II	B	N	M	63	3	R	W	U
28	107	NY7F	425	N	L	M	41	II	B	N	F	67	3	R	W	U
29	107	NY7G	426	N	L	M	41	II	B	N	F	55	3	K	W	U
30	107	NY7H	427	N	L	M	41	II	B	N	M	38	3	R	W	U
31	107	NY7I	428	N	L	M	41	II	A	N	M	85	2	R	W	U
32	107	NY7J!	429	N	L	M	41	III	B	Y	F	59	4	K	W	U
33	107	NY7K!	430	N	L	M	41	III	B	Y	M	60	6	P	W	U
34	107	NY7L!	431	N	L	M	41	III	A	Y	F	76	3	P	W	U
35	107	NY7M!	432	N	L	M	41	III	B	Y	F	62	4	K	W	U
36	108	NY8	432b	N	L	M	41	I	A	N	F	83	2	K	W	U
37	109	NY9A	432c	N	L	M	41	I	A	N	F	75	2	K	W	U
38	109	NY9B	433	N	L	M	41	I	A	N	M	77	4	F	W	R
39	109	NY9C	434	N	L	M	41	II	B	N	F	55	4	K	W	R
40	110	NY10A	435	N	L	M	41	I	B	N	M	59		F	W	R
41	110	NY10B!	436	N	L	M	41	III	A	Y	F	63	4	K	W	U
42	111	NY11	438	N	L	M	41	II	B	N	F	42	5	K	W	R
43	112	NY12A	439	Y	L	M	41	I	A	N	F	67	2	K	W	R
44	112	NY12B	440	N	L	M	41	II	B	N	F	55	6	K	W	R
45	112	NY12C!	441	N	L	M	41	III	A	Y	F	65	3	M	W	U
46	113	NY13A	443	N	L	M	41	I	A	N	M	81	3	F	W	R
47	113	NY13B!	444	N	L	M	41	III	A	Y	F	68	4	K	W	R

A. Serial **B.** Community **C.** Informant ID **D.** Old ID **E.** Auxiliaries **F.** Field Worker **G.** Work Sheets **H.** Year
I. Type **J.** Generation **K.** Cultivation **L.** Sex **M.** Age **N.** Education **O.** Occupation **P.** Race **Q.** Locality

A.	B.	C.	D.	E.	F.	G.	H.	I.	J.	K.	L.	M.	N.	O.	P.	Q.
48	114	NY14A	445	Y	L	M	41	I	A	N	M	78	4	F	W	R
49	114	NY14B	446	N	L	M	41	II	B	N	M	46	4	F	W	R
50	115	NY15A	447	N	L	M	41	I	A	N	M	84	2	F	W	R
51	115	NY15B	448	N	L	M	41	II	B	N	M	49	3	F	W	R
52	116	NY16A	449	N	L	M	41	I	A	N	M	66	3	F	W	R
53	116	NY16B	450	N	L	M	41	II	A	N	M	61	4	F	W	R
54	117	NY17A	451	Y	L	M	41	I	A	N	M	77	1	F	W	R
55	117	NY17B	452	N	L	M	41	II	B	N	M	45	4	F	W	R
56	118	NY18A	453	N	L	M	41	I	A	N	M	82	3	F	W	R
57	118	NY18B	454	N	L	M	41	II	B	N	M	49	2	O	W	R
58	118	NY18C!	455	N	L	M	41	III	A	Y	M	84	4	M	W	U
59	119	NY19	456	N	L	M	41	I	B	N	M	52	3	F	W	R
60	120	NY20A	457	N	L	M	41	I	A	N	M	77	1	F	W	R
61	120	NY20B	458	N	L	M	41	II	B	N	M	35	5	F	W	R
62	121	NY21	459	N	L	M	41	I	A	N	M	73	3	F	W	R
63	122	NY22	460	N	L	M	41	II	B	N	M	51	3	F	W	R
64	123	NY23A	461	N	M	M	48	I	A	N	M	84	2	M	W	U
65	123	NY23B	462a	Y	M	M	48	I	A	N	M	74	3	F	W	R
66	123	NY23C	462b	N	M	M	48	II	A	N	M	75	4	M	W	R
67	124	NY24A	463	N	L	M	41	I	A	N	M	74	3	F	W	R
68	124	NY24B!	464	N	L	M	41	II	B	Y	F	61	3	K	W	U
69	125	NY25A	465	N	M	M	48	I	A	N	M	75	2	F	W	R
70	125	NY25B	466	Y	M	M	48	II	A	N	M	68	2	S	W	R
71	126	NY26A	467	Y	M	M	48	I	A	N	M	82	0	C	W	R
72	126	NY26B	468	N	M	M	48	II	A	N	F	77	2	K	W	R
73	126	NY26C	469	N	M	M	48	II	B	N	M	54	4	M	W	R
74	127	NY27A	470	Y	M	M	48	I	A	N	M	74	1	L	W	U
75	127	NY27B	471	N	M	M	48	II	Λ	N	F	82	3	K	W	U
76	127	NY27C	472	N	M	M	48	II	A	N	M	72	2	F	W	R
77	128	NY28A	473a	N	M	M	48	I	B	N	F	54	2	K	W	U
78	128	NY28B	473b	N	M	M	48	II	A	N	F	87	5	K	W	R
79	128	NY28C	473b*	N	M	M	48	II	A	N	F	85		K	W	R
80	129	NY29A	474a	N	M	M	48	I	A	N	M	84	2	F	W	R
81	129	NY29B	474b	Y	M	M	48	I	B	N	M	67	2	O	W	U
82	129	NY29C	474c	N	M	M	48	II	A	N	M	70	4	M	W	U
83	130	NY30A	475a	N	M	M	48	I	A	N	M	82	2	F	W	R
84	130	NY30B	475b	N	M	M	48	I	A	N	M	87	2	C	W	R
85	130	NY30C	475c	N	M	M	48	I	A	N	M	85	2	F	W	R
86	130	NY30D	475d	N	M	M	48	I	A	N	M	77	2	F	W	R
87	130	NY30E	475e	Y	M	M	48	II	A	N	F	75	4	K	W	R
88	131	NY31A	478a	N	M	M	49	II	A	N	M	94	4	M	W	U
89	131	NY31B	478b	N	M	M	49	II	A	N	M	76	2	F	W	R
90	132	NY32A	479a	Y	M	M	49	I	A	N	M	77	2	F	W	R
91	132	NY32B	479b	N	M	M	49	I	A	N	M	71	2	F	W	R
92	133	NY33A	480	N	M	M	48	I	B	N	M	52	2	S	W	R
93	133	NY33B	481	N	M	M	48	II	B	N	M	50	3	P	W	R
94	133	NY33C	482	N	M	M	48	II	B	N	M	57	4	M	W	R
95	134	NY34A	483	N	M	M	49	I	A	N	M	85	5	F	W	R
96	134	NY34B	484	N	M	M	49	I	A	N	F	65	2	K	W	U
97	134	NY34C	485	N	M	M	49	II	A	N	M	81	5	P	W	R

A.	B.	C.	D.	E.	F.	G.	H.	I.	J.	K.	L.	M.	N.	O.	P.	Q.
98	134	NY34D!	486	N	M	M	49	III	A	Y	M	81	3	M	W	U
99	135	NY35A	487	N	L	M	41	I	A	N	M	78	2	F	W	R
100	135	NY35B	488	N	L	M	41	II	B	N	F	45	3	K	W	R
101	135	NY35C!	489	N	L	M	41	III	B	Y	M	62	4	M	W	U
102	136	NY36A	491	N	L	M	41	I	A	N	M	78	3	F	W	R
103	136	NY36B	492	N	L	M	41	II	B	N	M	52	3	F	W	R
104	137	NY37A	493	N	L	M	41	I	A	N	F	80	3	K	W	R
105	137	NY37B	494	N	L	M	41	II	B	N	M	42	3	L	W	R
106	137	NY37C!	495	N	L	M	41	III	B	Y	F	52	4	K	W	U
107	138	NY38A	497	N	L	M	41	I	A	N	M	81	4	F	W	R
108	138	NY38B	498	N	L	M	41	II	B	N	M	54	4	F	W	R
109	138	NY38C	497*	N	L	M	41				F				W	U
110	139	NY39A	499	N	L	M	41	I	A	N	M	79	4	F	W	R
111	139	NY39B	500	N	L	M	41	II	B	N	M	43	3	F	W	R
112	140	NY40A	501	N	L	M	41	I	A	N	M	79	3	F	W	R
113	140	NY40B	502	N	L	M	41	II	B	N	M	51	3	M	W	U
114	141	NY41	504	N	L	M	41	II	B	N	M	47	3	F	W	R
115	142	NY42A	505	N	L	M	41	I	A	N	M	63	3	F	W	R
116	142	NY42B	506	N	L	M	41	II	B	N	M	45	3	F	W	R
117	143	NY43A	507	N	L	M	41	I	A	N	M	80		F	W	R
118	143	NY43B	507b	N	L	M	41	II	B	N	M	41	3	F	W	R
119	143	NY43C!	508	N	L	M	41	II	B	Y	F	47	4	K	W	U
120	144	NY44A	511	N	L	M	41	II	A	N	M	78	3	F	W	R
121	144	NY44B	512	N	L	M	41	II	B	N	M	38	3	F	W	R
122	145	NY45A	513a	N	M	M	49	I	A	N	M	72	1	H	W	U
123	145	NY45B	513b	N	M	M	49	I	A	N	M	75	2	M	W	U
124	145	NY45C	513c	N	M	M	49	I	A	N	M	70	2	F	W	U
125	145	NY45D!	513d	N	M	M	49	III	A	Y	F	72	6	K	W	U
126	146	NY46A	515a	N	M	M	49	I	A	N	M	82	2	C	W	R
127	146	NY46B	515b	N	P	C	65	I	A	N	M	72	2	F	W	R
128	146	NY46C	515c	N	P	C	65	II	A	N	F	73	2	K	W	U
129	147	NY47A	517	Y	M	M	49	I	A	N	M	57	2	F	W	R
130	147	NY47B	518	N	L	M	41	II	B	N	M	40	5	F	W	R
131	148	NY48A	519a	Y	M	M	49	I	A	N	M	78	2	S	W	R
132	148	NY48B	519b	N	M	M	49	I	A	N	M	76	2	F	W	R
133	148	NY48C	519c	Y	M	M	49	II	A	N	M	63	4	F	W	R
134	148	NY48D	519d	Y	M	M	49	II	B	N	F	60	2	K	W	R
135	149	NY49A	520	N	M	M	49	I	A	N	M	87	2	F	W	R
136	149	NY49B	521	N	L	M	41	I	B	N	M	44			W	
137	149	NY49C	522a	Y	U	C	68	II	A	N	M	80	2	C	W	U
138	149	NY49D	522b	N	U	C	68	II	B	N	F	50		R	W	U
139	150	NY50A	523	N	M	M	49	II	A	N	F	92	4	O	W	R
140	150	NY50B	524	N	M	M	49	II	A	N	M	75	4	M	W	R
141	151	NY51A	525a	N	M	M	49	I	A	N	M	80	2	F	W	R
142	151	NY51B	525b	Y	M	M	49	II	A	N	M	87	4	F	W	R
143	151	NY51C	525c	N	M	M	49	II	A	N	M	75	2	F	W	R
144	151	NY51D	525d	Y	M	M	49	II	A	N	F	70	3	K	W	R

A. Serial **B.** Community **C.** Informant ID **D.** Old ID **E.** Auxiliaries **F.** Field Worker **G.** Work Sheets **H.** Year
I. Type **J.** Generation **K.** Cultivation **L.** Sex **M.** Age **N.** Education **O.** Occupation **P.** Race **Q.** Locality

A.	B.	C.	D.	E.	F.	G.	H.	I.	J.	K.	L.	M.	N.	O.	P.	Q.
145	151	NY51E!	525e	N	M	M	49	III	A	Y	M	89	3	M	W	U
146	152	NY52A	527	Y	M	M	49	I	B	N	F	49	3	K	W	R
147	152	NY52B	528	N	M	M	49	II	A	N	F	77	5	K	W	U
148	152	NY52C	528b	N	U	C	68	II	B	N	F	47	4	M	W	U
149	153	NY53A	529	Y	M	M	49	I	A	N	M	85	2	F	W	R
150	153	NY53B!	530	N	M	M	49	III	A	Y	F	80	5	M	W	U
151	154	NY54A	531	Y	U	C	68	I	A	N	M	74	2	F	W	R
152	154	NY54B	532	N	U	C	68	II	B	N	M	50	4	S	W	U
153	155	NY55A	533	N	M	M	49	I	A	N	M	84	4	F	W	R
154	155	NY55B	534	N	M	M	49	II	A	N	F	85	4	K	W	R
155	156	NY56A	535	N	M	M	49	I	A	N	M	77	2	S	W	R
156	156	NY56B	536	N	M	M	49	II	A	N	M	84	4	C	W	R
157	157	NY57A	537a	N	M	M	49	I	A	N	M	73	4	F	W	R
158	157	NY57B	537b	Y	M	M	49	II	A	N	F	79	5	K	W	R
159	157	NY57C!	537c	N	M	M	49	III	A	Y	F	83	6	P	W	R
160	158	NY58A	539a	N	M	M	49	I	A	N	M	72	3	C	W	U
161	158	NY58B	539b	N	M	M	49	II	A	N	M	81			W	R
162	158	NY58C	539c	N	M	M	49	II	B	N	M	63	5	M	W	U
163	158	NY58D!	539d	Y	M	M	49	III	B	Y	F	60	3	K	W	R
164	158	NY58E!	539e	N	M	M	49	III	B	Y	F	65	6	M	W	U
165	158	NY58F!	539f	N	M	M	49	III	B	Y	F	62	5	K	W	U
166	159	NY59A	543	Y	M	M	49	II	A	N	M	71	3	F	W	R
167	159	NY59B	544	N	L	M	41	II	B	N	M	44	5	F	W	R
168	160	NY60A	545	N	M	M	49	I	A	N	M	87	1	F	W	R
169	160	NY60B!	546	N	M	M	49	III	A	Y	M	74	6	M	W	U
170	161	NY61A	547	N	M	M	49	I	A	N	M	82	2	F	W	R
171	161	NY61B	548	N	M	M	49	II	A	N	M	77	4	C	W	R
172	162	NY62A	551a	N	M	M	49	I	A	N	M	89	3	F	W	R
173	162	NY62B	551b	Y	M	M	49	I	A	N	M	85	2	F	W	R
174	162	NY62C	551c	N	M	M	49	II	A	N	M	85	2	M	W	U
175	162	NY62D!	551d	Y	M	M	49	III	A	Y	F	73	4	K	W	R
176	163	NY63A	556a	Y	M	M	49	I	A	N	M	70	3	F	W	R
177	163	NY63B	556b	Y	M	M	49	II	A	N	M	83	4	M	W	R
178	163	NY63C	556c	N	L	M	41	II	B	N	M	47	4	F	W	R
179	163	NY63D!	556d	N	M	M	49	III	A	Y	M	72	6	P	W	U
180	164	NY64A	557a	N	M	M	49	I	A	N	M	81	3	M	W	U
181	164	NY64B	557b	N	M	M	49	II	A	N	F	80	5	M	W	U
182	164	NY64C!	557c	N	M	M	49	III	B	Y	F	65	6	P	W	U
183	201	NJ1A	1	N	L	S	39	I	A	N	M	70	0	L	W	R
184	201	NJ1B	2	N	L	S	39	II	B	N	M	52	3	F	W	R
185	202	NJ2A	3	Y	L	S	39	I	A	N	M	80	3	F	W	R
186	202	NJ2B	4	N	L	S	39	I	B	N	M	42	3	F	W	R
187	203	NJ3A	5	N	L	S	39	I	A	N	M	86	3	F	W	R
188	203	NJ3B	6	N	L	S	39	II	B	N	M	55	4	F	W	R
189	204	NJ4A	7	N	L	S	39	I	A	N	M	70	3	F	W	R
190	204	NJ4B	8	N	L	S	39	I	B	N	M	53	3	F	W	R
191	205	NJ5A	9	N	L	S	39	I	A	N	M	75	2	F	W	R
192	205	NJ5B	10	N	L	S	39	I	B	N	M	58	2	M	W	R
193	206	NJ6A	11	N	L	M	41	I	A	N	M	75	4	F	W	R
194	206	NJ6B	12	N	L	S	39	I	B	N	M	47	2	F	W	R

A.	B.	C.	D.	E.	F.	G.	H.	I.	J.	K.	L.	M.	N.	O.	P.	Q.
195	207	NJ7A	17	N	L	S	39	I	A	N	M	72	3	L	W	R
196	207	NJ7B!	18	N	L	M	41	III	B	Y	F	49	5	K	W	U
197	208	NJ8A	19	N	L	M	41	I	A	N	M	77	0	F	W	R
198	208	NJ8B	20	N	L	M	41	II	B	N	M	57	4	R	W	R
199	209	NJ9A	21	N	L	M	41	I	A	N	F	76	3	K	W	R
200	209	NJ9B	22	N	L	M	41	II	B	N	M	56	4	F	W	R
201	210	NJ10A	24b	N	L	M	41	I	A	N	M	78	3	L	W	U
202	210	NJ10B	23	N	L	M	41	I	A	N	M	68	3	F	W	R
203	210	NJ10C	24	N	L	M	41	II	B	N	M	49	5	F	W	R
204	210	NJ10D!	24c	N	L	M	41	III	B	Y	M	59	6	M	W	U
205	211	NJ11A	25	N	L	M	41	I	A	N	M	82	3	F	W	R
206	211	NJ11B	26a	N	L	M	41	II	B	N	F	57	4	K	W	U
207	211	NJ11C	26b	N	L	M	41	II	B	N	M	41	5	F	W	R
208	212	NJ12A	27	N	L	M	41	I	A	N	M	80	3	F	W	R
209	212	NJ12B	28	N	L	M	41	II	B	N	M	49	3	F	W	R
210	213	NJ13A	29	N	L	M	41	I	A	N	F	80	0	K	W	R
211	213	NJ13B	30	N	L	M	41	I	B	N	M	47	3	F	W	R
212	214	NJ14A	31	N	L	M	41	I	A	N	M	78	4	F	W	R
213	214	NJ14B	32	N	L	M	41	II	B	N	F	44	4	K	W	R
214	215	NJ15A	33	N	L	M	41	I	A	N	M	70	4	F	W	R
215	215	NJ15B	34	N	L	M	41	I	B	N	M	46	4	F	W	R
216	216	NJ16A	35	N	L	M	41	I	A	N	M	75	1	F	W	R
217	216	NJ16B	36	N	L	M	41	II	B	N	M	45	3	F	W	R
218	217	NJ17A	37	N	L	M	41	I	A	N	M	82	3	F	W	R
219	217	NJ17B	38	N	L	M	41	II	A	N	M	66	3	M	W	U
220	218	NJ18A	41	N	L	M	41	II	A	N	F	68	4	K	W	U
221	218	NJ18B	42	N	L	M	41	II	B	N	F	58	3	K	W	U
222	218	NJ18C!	43	N	L	M	41	III	B	Y	F	57	4	P	W	U
223	218	NJ18D!	44	N	L	M	41	III	B	Y	F	54	6	P	W	U
224	219	NJ19A	45	N	L	M	41	I	A	N	F	75	2	K	W	U
225	219	NJ19B!	46	N	L	M	41	II	A	Y	F	65	4	P	W	U
226	220	NJ20A	47	N	L	M	41	II	A	N	M	80	5	P	W	U
227	220	NJ20B	47b	N	L	M	41	II	B	N	M	61	4	F	W	R
228	221	NJ21A	48	N	L	M	41	I	A	N	M	71	3	F	W	R
229	221	NJ21B	49	N	L	M	41	II	B	N	M	55	3	F	W	R
230	301	PA1A	51	N	L	M	39	I	A	N	M	68	2	O	W	U
231	301	PA1B	52	N	L	M	39	I	B	N	M	43	4	C	W	U
232	301	PA1C	53	N	L	M	39	II	A	N	F	68	3	K	W	U
233	301	PA1D	54	N	L	M	39	II	A	N	M	66	2	R	W	U
234	301	PA1E!	55	N	L	M	39	III	A	Y	M	68	6	P	W	U
235	301	PA1F!	56	N	L	M	39	III	B	Y	M	62	6	M	W	U
236	301	PA1G!	57	N	L	M	39	III	A	Y	M	70	6	M	W	U
237	301	PA1H!	58	N	L	M	39	III	B	Y	F	59	4	K	W	U
238	302	PA2A	59	N	L	M	39	I	A	N	M	70	3	F	W	R
239	302	PA2B	60	N	L	M	39	II	B	N	M	57	5	F	W	R
240	303	PA3A	61	N	L	M	39	I	A	N	F	91	2	K	W	U
241	303	PA3B	62	N	L	M	40	I	A	N	F	67	3	F	W	R

A. Serial **B.** Community **C.** Informant ID **D.** Old ID **E.** Auxiliaries **F.** Field Worker **G.** Work Sheets **H.** Year **I.** Type **J.** Generation **K.** Cultivation **L.** Sex **M.** Age **N.** Education **O.** Occupation **P.** Race **Q.** Locality

A.	B.	C.	D.	E.	F.	G.	H.	I.	J.	K.	L.	M.	N.	O.	P.	Q.
242	303	PA3C	62b	N	L	M	40	II	B	N	M	58	2	F	W	R
243	304	PA4A	63	N	L	M	39	I	A	N	M	80	2	F	W	R
244	304	PA4B!	64	N	L	M	39	III	B	Y	M	48	6	P	W	U
245	305	PA5A	65	Y	L	M	39	I	A	N	M	79	3	L	W	R
246	305	PA5B	65b	N	L	M	40	I	A	N	M	82	3	F	W	R
247	305	PA5C	66	N	L	M	39	I	B	N	M	57	2	W	W	R
248	305	PA5D	67	N	L	M	39	I	A	N	M	67	0	F	W	R
249	305	PA5E!	68	N	L	M	39	III	B	Y	M	49	5	F	W	R
250	306	PA6A	69	N	L	M	39	I	A	N	M	75	3	F	W	R
251	306	PA6B	71	N	L	M	39	I	A	N	M	67	3	S	W	U
252	306	PA6C	71b	N	L	M	40	I	B	N	M	49	2	F	W	R
253	306	PA6D!	72	N	L	M	39	III	A	Y	M	69	6	P	W	U
254	307	PA7A	73	N	L	M	39	I	A	N	M	80	3	F	W	R
255	307	PA7B	74	N	L	M	39	I	B	N	M	53	3	F	W	R
256	307	PA7C	75	N	L	M	39	II	A	N	M	65	4	F	W	R
257	307	PA7D!	76	N	L	M	39	III	B	Y	M	39	6	M	W	U
258	308	PA8A	77	N	L	M	39	I	A	N	M	65	3	L	W	R
259	308	PA8B	78	N	L	M	39	II	B	N	M	46	3	F	W	R
260	308	PA8C	79	N	L	M	40	II	A	N	M	66	5	F	W	R
261	308	PA8D!	80	N	L	M	39	III	A	Y	F	62	3	K	W	U
262	309	PA9A	83	N	L	M	39	I	A	N	M	78	3	F	W	R
263	309	PA9B	83b	N	L	M	40	I	B	N	M	57	3	F	W	R
264	309	PA9C!	84	N	L	M	39	III	A	Y	F	68	4	R	W	U
265	310	PA10	87	N	L	M	39	I	A	N	M	66	3	F	W	R
266	311	PA11A	89	N	L	M	39	I	A	N	M	73	3	F	W	R
267	311	PA11B	90	Y	L	M	40	II	B	N	M	37	3	F	W	R
268	312	PA12A	91	N	L	M	39	I	A	N	M	67	4	C	W	R
269	312	PA12B	92	Y	L	M	39	II	B	N	F	47	3	K	W	U
270	313	PA13A	93	N	L	M	39	I	A	N	M	74	2	F	W	R
271	313	PA13B	94	N	L	M	39	II	B	N	M	47	4	F	W	R
272	314	PA14A	95	N	L	M	40	I	A	N	M	76	3	F	W	R
273	314	PA14B	96	N	L	M	39	II	B	N	M	36	2	R	W	U
274	314	PA14C	95*	N	L	M	40	I	A	N	M	80	3	F	W	R
275	315	PA15A	99	N	L	M	39	I	A	N	M	69	2	F	W	R
276	315	PA15B	99b	N	L	M	39	II	B	N	M	44	4	F	W	R
277	315	PA15C!	100	N	L	M	39	III	B	Y	M	62	6	P	W	U
278	316	PA16A	101	N	L	M	39	I	A	N	M	69	3	F	W	R
279	316	PA16B	102	N	L	M	39	II	B	N	M	39	4	R	W	U
280	316	PA16C	103	N	L	M	39	II	B	N	M	50		C	W	U
281	317	PA17A	105	N	L	M	39	I	A	N	M	72	2	F	W	R
282	317	PA17B	106	N	L	M	39	II	A	N	M	74	4	M	W	U
283	318	PA18A	107	N	L	M	39	I	A	N	F	69	3	K	W	R
284	318	PA18B!	108	N	L	M	39	III	B	Y	M	60	6	P	W	U
285	319	PA19A	113	N	L	M	39	I	A	N	F	70	1	K	W	R
286	319	PA19B	114	N	L	M	39	II	B	N	M	49	3	C	W	R
287	320	PA20A	115	N	L	M	39	I	A	N	M	75	3	F	W	R
288	320	PA20B	116	N	L	M	39	II	B	N	M	44	3	F	W	R
289	321	PA21A	117	N	L	M	39	I	A	N	M	72	2	F	W	R
290	321	PA21B	118	N	L	M	39	II	B	N	M	56		F	W	R
291	322	PA22A	119	N	L	M	39	I	A	N	M	85	2	F	W	R

A.	B.	C.	D.	E.	F.	G.	H.	I.	J.	K.	L.	M.	N.	O.	P.	Q.
292	322	PA22B	120	N	L	M	39	II	B	N	M	48	3	F	W	R
293	323	PA23A	121	N	L	M	39	I	A	N	M	87	4	F	W	R
294	323	PA23B	122	N	L	M	39	II	B	N	M	51	3	F	W	R
295	324	PA24A	123	N	L	M	39	I	A	N	M	74	3	F	W	R
296	324	PA24B	124	N	L	M	39	II	B	N	M	42	4	F	W	R
297	325	PA25A	125	N	L	M	39	I	A	N	M	80	4	F	W	R
298	325	PA25B	126	N	L	M	39	II	B	N	M	52	3	F	W	R
299	326	PA26A	127	N	L	M	39	I	A	N	M	83	4	F	W	R
300	326	PA26B	128	N	L	M	39	II	B	N	M	51	4	F	W	R
301	327	PA27A	131	Y	L	M	39	I	A	N	M	70	4	F	W	R
302	327	PA27B	132	N	L	M	39	I	B	N	M	50	3	F	W	R
303	328	PA28A	135	N	L	M	39	II	A	N	M	72	4	F	W	R
304	328	PA28B!	136	N	L	M	39	III	B	Y	F	50	5		W	U
305	329	PA29A	139	Y	L	M	39	I	A	N	M	60	2	F	W	R
306	329	PA29B	140	N	L	M	39	II	B	N	M	42	3	F	W	R
307	330	PA30A	143	N	L	M	39	I	A	N	M	73	2	F	W	R
308	330	PA30B	144	N	L	M	39	II	B	N	M	48	3	F	W	R
309	331	PA31A	145	N	L	M	40	I	A	N	M	75	1	L	W	R
310	331	PA31B	146	N	L	M	40	I	B	N	M	54	2	C	W	U
311	332	PA32A	147	N	L	M	39	I	A	N	M	80	2	F	W	R
312	332	PA32B	148	N	L	M	39	I	B	N	M	40	4	F	W	R
313	333	PA33A	151	N	L	M	40	I	A	N	M	77	2	F	W	R
314	333	PA33B	152	N	L	M	39	II	B	N	M	46	2	F	W	R
315	334	PA34A	155	N	L	M	39	I	A	N	M	79	4	F	W	R
316	334	PA34B	156	N	L	M	39	II	B	N	M	37	3	F	W	R
317	300	PA34C!	155b	Y	L	M	39	III	A	Y	F	75	4	K	W	U
318	335	PA35A	157	N	L	M	39	I	A	N	M	67	2	W	W	R
319	335	PA35B	158	N	L	M	39	II	B	N	M	46	3	F	W	R
320	335	PA35C	158*	N	L	M	39	II		N	M		4	F	W	R
321	336	PA36A	159	N	L	M	39	I	A	N	M	73	1	S	W	R
322	336	PA36B	160	N	L	M	39	II	B	N	M	50	4	F	W	R
323	337	PA37A	161	N	L	M	40	I	A	N	M	76	2	F	W	R
324	337	PA37B	162	N	L	M	40	II	B	N	M	40	4	F	W	R
325	337	PA37C	161*	N	L	M	40	I	A	N	M	78	0	W	W	R
326	338	PA38A	163	N	L	M	39	I	A	N	M	70	2	F	W	R
327	338	PA38B	164	N	L	M	39	II	B	N	M	42	3	F	W	R
328	339	PA39A	165	N	L	M	40	I	A	N	M	85	4	F	W	R
329	339	PA39B	166	N	L	M	39	II	B	N	M	41	4	F	W	R
330	340	PA40A	167	N	L	M	40	I	A	N	M	77	3	F	W	R
331	340	PA40B	168	N	L	M	39	II	B	N	M	36	3	F	W	R
332	341	PA41A	171	N	L	M	40	I	A	N	M	70	1	W	W	R
333	341	PA41B	172	N	L	M	39	II	B	N	M	58	4	F	W	R
334	342	PA42A	175	N	L	M	40	I	A	N	M	59	3	F	W	R
335	342	PA42B	176	N	L	M	40	I	B	N	M	51	2	F	W	R
336	343	PA43A	177	N	L	M	39	I	A	N	M	79	1	F	W	R
337	343	PA43B	178	N	L	M	39	II	B	N	M	51	4	F	W	R
338	344	PA44A	179	N	L	M	39	I	A	N	M	75	3	F	W	R

A. Serial **B.** Community **C.** Informant ID **D.** Old ID **E.** Auxiliaries **F.** Field Worker **G.** Work Sheets **H.** Year **I.** Type **J.** Generation **K.** Cultivation **L.** Sex **M.** Age **N.** Education **O.** Occupation **P.** Race **Q.** Locality

A.	B.	C.	D.	E.	F.	G.	H.	I.	J.	K.	L.	M.	N.	O.	P.	Q.
339	344	PA44B	180	N	L	M	39	II	B	N	M	51	3	F	W	R
340	345	PA45A	181	N	L	M	40	I	A	N	M	81	4	F	W	R
341	345	PA45B	182	N	L	M	40	II	B	N	M	43	3	F	W	R
342	346	PA46A	185	N	L	M	40	I	A	N	M	61	1	L	W	R
343	346	PA46B	186	N	L	M	40	II	B	N	M	45	3	F	W	R
344	347	PA47A	189	N	L	M	40	I	A	N	M	90	1	F	W	R
345	347	PA47B	190	N	L	M	40	II	B	N	M	49	4	F	W	R
346	348	PA48A	191	N	L	M	40	I	A	N	M	89	3	F	W	R
347	348	PA48B	192	N	L	M	40	I	A	N	M	70	2	F	W	R
348	348	PA48C	193	N	L	M	40	II	B	N	M	44	5	F	W	R
349	349	PA49A	194	N	L	M	40	I	B	N	M	72	3	F	W	R
350	349	PA49B	195	N	L	M	40	II	B	N	M	44	3	F	W	R
351	350	PA50A	196	N	L	M	40	I	A	N	M	80	2	C	W	R
352	350	PA50B	197	N	L	M	40	I	A	N	F	70	3	K	W	U
353	350	PA50C!	198	N	L	M	40	II	B	Y	M	47	4	F	W	R
354	351	PA51A	199	N	L	M	40	I	A	N	F	74	2	O	W	U
355	351	PA51B	200	N	L	M	40	II	B	N	F	50	2	K	W	U
356	352	PA52A	201	N	L	M	40	I	A	N	M	76	2	C	W	R
357	352	PA52B!	202	N	L	M	40	III	B	Y	M	48	5	F	W	R
358	353	PA53A	203	N	L	M	40	I	A	N	M	78	3	F	W	R
359	353	PA53B	204	N	L	M	40	II	B	N	M	43	4	F	W	R
360	354	PA54A	205	Y	L	M	40	I	A	N	F	83	1	K	W	U
361	354	PA54B	206	N	L	M	40	II	B	N	M	53	3	F	W	R
362	355	PA55A	207	N	L	M	40	I	A	N	M	85	3	F	W	R
363	355	PA55B	208	N	L	M	40	II	B	N	M	40	5	F	W	R
364	356	PA56A	211	Y	L	M	40	II	A	N	M	87	5	M	W	R
365	356	PA56B	212	N	L	M	40	II	B	N	M	44	3	F	W	R
366	357	PA57A	213	N	L	M	40	I	A	N	M	75	4	F	W	R
367	357	PA57B	214	N	L	M	40	II	B	N	M	53	3	F	W	R
368	358	PA58A	215	N	L	M	40	I	A	N	M	84	4	F	W	R
369	358	PA58B	216	N	L	M	40	II	B	N	M	42	2	F	W	R
370	359	PA59A	219	N	L	M	40	I	A	N	M	87	1	F	W	R
371	359	PA59B	220	N	L	M	40	II	B	N	F	41	3	K	W	U
372	360	PA60A	221	N	L	M	40	I	A	N	M	77	5	F	W	R
373	360	PA60B	222	N	L	M	40	I	B	N	M	40	3	F	W	R
374	361	PA61A	223	N	L	M	40	I	A	N	M	84	3	F	W	R
375	361	PA61B	224	N	L	M	40	II	B	N	M	40	3	F	W	R
376	362	PA62A	229	N	L	M	40	I	A	N	M	87	3	F	W	R
377	362	PA62B	230	N	L	M	40	I	B	N	M	40	1	F	W	R
378	363	PA63A	231	N	L	M	40	I	A	N	M	74	2	F	W	R
379	363	PA63B	232	N	L	M	40	II	B	N	M	36	3	F	W	R
380	364	PA64A	233	N	L	M	40	I	A	N	M	77	3	L	W	R
381	364	PA64B	234	N	L	M	40	II	B	N	F	43	3	K	W	R
382	365	PA65A	237	N	L	M	40	I	A	N	M	74	3	F	W	R
383	365	PA65B	238	N	L	M	40	II	A	N	M	51	3	F	W	R
384	366	PA66A	239	N	L	M	40	I	A	N	M	81	2	F	W	R
385	366	PA66B	240	N	L	M	40	II	B	N	M	50	3	F	W	R
386	367	PA67A	243	N	L	M	40	I	A	N	M	76	3	F	W	R
387	367	PA67B	244	N	L	M	40	II	B	N	M	37	3	F	W	R
388	401	WV1!	88	N	L	S	39	III	A	Y	F	71	5	K	W	R

A.	B.	C.	D.	E.	F.	G.	H.	I.	J.	K.	L.	M.	N.	O.	P.	Q.
389	402	WV2	89	N	L	S	39	II	B	N	M	54	3	F	W	R
390	403	WV3	91	N	L	S	39	I	A	N	M	78	0	F	W	R
391	404	WV4A	92	N	L	S	39	I	A	N	M	80	0	F	W	R
392	404	WV4B	93	N	L	P	34	I	A	N	M	76	4	F	W	R
393	405	WV5	94	N	L	S	39	I	B	N	M	38	2	F	W	R
394	406	WV6A	95	N	L	S	39	I	A	N	M	87	0	F	W	R
395	406	WV6B	96	N	L	S	39	II	B	N	M	45	4	F	W	R
396	407	WV7A	97	N	L	S	39	I	A	N	M	72	0	F	W	R
397	407	WV7B	98	N	L	S	39	II	B	N	M	55	4	F	W	R
398	408	WV8A	97b	N	L	M	40	I	A	N	M	89	1	F	W	R
399	408	WV8B	98b	N	L	M	40	II	B	N	M	56	4	F	W	R
400	409	WV9A	301	N	L	M	40	I	A	N	M	85	0	F	W	R
401	409	WV9B	302	N	L	M	40	II	B	N	M	52	3	F	W	R
402	410	WV10A	303	N	L	M	40	I	A	N	M	72	0	F	W	R
403	410	WV10B	303b	N	L	M	40	I	A	N	M	76	1	L	W	U
404	410	WV10C	304	N	L	M	40	II	B	N	M	51	3	F	W	R
405	411	WV11A	305	N	L	M	40	I	A	N	M	69	1	F	W	R
406	411	WV11B!	306	N	L	M	40	II	B	Y	M	59	5	F	W	R
407	412	WV12A	307	N	L	M	40	I	A	N	F	80	4	K	W	R
408	412	WV12B	308	N	L	M	40	II	B	N	M	42	3	F	W	R
409	413	WV13A	309	N	L	M	40	I	A	N	M	71	3	F	W	R
410	413	WV13B	310	N	L	M	40	II	B	N	M	36	2	F	W	R
411	414	WV14A	311	N	L	M	40	I	A	N	M	72	3	F	W	R
412	414	WV14B	312	N	L	M	40	II	B	N	M	42	4	F	W	R
413	415	WV15A	313	N	L	M	40	I	A	N	F	79		K	W	R
414	415	WV15B	314	N	L	M	40	II	B	N	M	58	5	F	W	R
415	416	WV16A	315	N	L	M	40	I	A	N	M	66	0	F	W	R
416	416	WV16B	316	N	L	M	40	II	B	N	M	56	4	F	W	R
417	417	WV17A	317	N	L	M	40	I	A	N	M	80	1	F	W	R
418	417	WV17B	317b	N	L	M	40	II	B	N	M	53	3	F	W	R
419	417	WV17C	318	N	L	M	40	II	A	N	M	73	4	F	W	R
420	418	WV18A	319	N	L	M	40	I	A	N	F	75	2	K	W	R
421	418	WV18B	320	N	L	M	40	II	B	N	M	47	2	F	W	R
422	419	WV19A	321	N	L	M	40	I	A	N	M	70	0	F	W	R
423	419	WV19B	322	N	L	M	40	II	B	N	M	40	4	F	W	R
424	420	WV20A	323	N	L	M	40	I	A	N	M	70	3	F	W	R
425	420	WV20B	324	N	L	M	40	II	B	N	F	46	4	K	W	R
426	421	WV21A	325	N	L	M	40	I	A	N	M	80	0	F	W	R
427	421	WV21B	326	N	L	M	40	II	B	N	M	49	2	F	W	R
428	422	WV22A	327	N	L	M	40	I	A	N	M	85	3	F	W	R
429	422	WV22B	328	N	L	M	40	II	B	N	M	34	4	F	W	R
430	423	WV23A	331	N	L	M	40	I	A	N	M	82	2	F	W	R
431	423	WV23B	332	N	L	M	40	II	B	N	M	51	4	F	W	R
432	424	WV24A	335	N	L	M	40	I	A	N	M	74	4	F	W	R
433	424	WV24B	336	N	L	M	40	II	B	N	M	39	4	F	W	R
434	425	WV25A	337	N	L	M	40	I	A	N	M	72	3	F	W	R
435	425	WV25B	338	N	L	M	40	II	B	N	M	39	2	F	W	R

A. Serial **B.** Community **C.** Informant ID **D.** Old ID **E.** Auxiliaries **F.** Field Worker **G.** Work Sheets **H.** Year **I.** Type **J.** Generation **K.** Cultivation **L.** Sex **M.** Age **N.** Education **O.** Occupation **P.** Race **Q.** Locality

A.	B.	C.	D.	E.	F.	G.	H.	I.	J.	K.	L.	M.	N.	O.	P.	Q.
436	426	WV26A	339	N	L	M	40	I	A	N	F	82	3	K	W	R
437	426	WV26B	340	N	L	M	40	II	B	N	M	43	3	F	W	R
438	427	WV27A	341	N	L	M	40	I	A	N	M	75	3	F	W	R
439	427	WV27B	342	N	L	M	40	II	B	N	M	52	3	F	W	R
440	428	WV28A	343	N	L	M	40	I	A	N	F	74	4	K	W	R
441	428	WV28B	344	N	L	M	40	II	B	N	M	43	5	F	W	R
442	429	WV29A	345	N	L	M	40	I	A	N	M	87	1	F	W	R
443	429	WV29B	346	N	L	M	40	II	B	N	F	34		K	W	R
444	430	WV30A	347	N	L	M	40	I	A	N	M	68	0	F	W	R
445	430	WV30B	348	N	L	M	40	I	B	N	M	49	3	F	W	R
446	431	WV31A	349	N	L	M	40	I	A	N	M	63	1	F	W	R
447	431	WV31B	350	N	L	M	40	I	B	N	M	49	1	F	W	R
448	432	WV32A	353	N	L	M	40	I	A	N	F	69	0	K	W	R
449	432	WV32B	354	N	L	M	40	I	B	N	M	45	2	L	W	R
450	433	WV33A	355	N	L	M	40	I	A	N	M	67	1	F	W	R
451	433	WV33B	356	N	L	M	40	II	B	N	M	55	4	F	W	R
452	434	WV34A	359	N	L	M	40	I	A	N	F	67	4	K	W	R
453	434	WV34B	360	N	L	M	40	I	B	N	M	46	2	F	W	R
454	435	WV35A	361	N	L	M	40	I	A	N	M	68	3	F	W	R
455	435	WV35B	362	N	L	M	40	II	B	N	M	49	4	F	W	R
456	436	WV36A	363	N	L	M	40	I	A	N	M	65	2	F	W	R
457	436	WV36B	364	N	L	M	40	II	B	N	M	63	4	F	W	R
458	437	WV37A	365	N	L	M	40	I	A	N	M	79	0	F	W	R
459	437	WV37B!	366	N	L	M	40	III	A	Y	F	69	5	K	W	R
460	438	WV38A	367	N	L	M	40	I	A	N	M	72	1	O	W	R
461	438	WV38B	368	N	L	M	40	I	B	N	M	37	2	O	W	R
462	439	WV39A	369	N	L	M	40	I	B	N	M	58	2	M	W	U
463	439	WV39B	370	N	L	M	40	II	B	N	M	54	3	M	W	U
464	439	WV39C!	371	N	L	M	40	III	B	Y	F	45	5	P	W	U
465	440	WV40A	373	N	L	M	40	I	A	N	M	74	1	F	W	R
466	440	WV40B	374	N	L	M	40	II	B	N	M	45	2	F	W	R
467	441	WV41A	375	N	L	M	40	I	A	N	M	75	1	F	W	R
468	441	WV41B	376	N	L	M	40	I	B	N	M	49	2	F	W	R
469	442	WV42A	377	N	L	M	40	I	A	N	F	72	3	K	W	R
470	442	WV42B	378	N	L	M	40	II	B	N	M	54	4	F	W	R
471	443	WV43A	381	N	L	M	40	I	A	N	M	74	1	F	W	R
472	443	WV43B	382	N	L	M	40	II	B	N	M	35	3	F	W	R
473	444	WV44A	383	N	L	M	40	I	A	N	M	71	4	F	W	R
474	444	WV44B	384	N	L	M	40	I	B	N	M	52	3	F	W	R
475	445	WV45A	385	N	L	M	40	II	A	N	M	72	4	F	W	R
476	445	WV45B	386	N	L	M	40	II	B	N	M	42	2	F	W	R
477	446	WV46A	387	N	L	M	40	I	A	N	M	73	3	F	W	R
478	446	WV46B	388	N	L	M	40	II	B	N	M	48	3	F	W	R
479	447	WV47A	389	N	L	M	40	II	A	N	M	68	4	F	W	R
480	447	WV47B	390	N	L	M	40	II	B	N	M	36	3	F	W	R
481	448	WV48A	391	N	L	M	40	I	A	N	M	75	4	F	W	R
482	448	WV48B	391b	N	L	M	40	I	B	N	M	50	1	F	W	R
483	448	WV48C	392	N	L	M	40	I	B	N	M	45	2		W	R
484	448	WV48D	392b	N	L	M	40	II	B	N	M	42	2	C	W	R
485	449	WV49A	393	N	L	M	40	I	A	N	M	65	0	W	W	R

A.	B.	C.	D.	E.	F.	G.	H.	I.	J.	K.	L.	M.	N.	O.	P.	Q.
486	449	WV49B	394	N	L	M	40	I	B	N	M	36	2	F	W	R
487	450	WV50A	395	N	L	M	40	I	A	N	M	88	1	F	W	R
488	450	WV50B	396	N	L	M	40	II	B	N	M	51	3	F	W	R
489	451	WV51A	261	N	L	M	40	I	A	N	M	66	2	M	W	R
490	451	WV51B	262	N	L	M	40	II	B	N	M	47	3	F	W	R
491	452	WV52A	258	N	L	M	40	I	A	N	M	68	1	F	W	R
492	452	WV52B	259	N	L	M	40	II	B	N	F	36	3	K	W	R
493	452	WV52C!	260	N	L	M	40	III	A	Y	M	70	4	M	W	U
494	453	WV53A	257	N	L	M	40	I	A	N	M	79	4	F	W	R
495	453	WV53B	257b	N	L	M	40	I	A	N	M	61	2	W	W	R
496	453	WV53C!	257c	N	L	M	40	II	B	Y	M	43	2	F	W	R
497	454	WV54A	255	N	L	M	40	I	A	N	M	70	2	F	W	R
498	454	WV54B	256	N	L	M	40	I	B	N	M	41	2	F	W	R
499	501	DE1A	11	N	L	S	39	II	A	N	M	70	3	M	W	U
500	501	DE1B	12	N	L	S	39	II	B	N	M	63	4	M	W	U
501	501	DE1C!	13	N	L	S	39	III	A	Y	F	62	4	K	W	U
502	502	DE2A	15	Y	L	P	34	II	A	N	M	73	2	M	W	R
503	502	DE2B	16	N	L	S	39	II	B	N	M	37	4	F	W	R
504	502	DE2C	15*	N	L	P	34	I	A	N	M	60		F	W	R
505	503	DE3A	18	N	L	S	39	I	A	N	M	75	3	F	W	R
506	503	DE3B	19	N	L	S	39	II	B	N	M	38	2	F	W	R
507	503	DE3C!	17	N	L	S	39	III	A	Y	M	66	5	F	W	R
508	504	DE4	20	N	L	S	39	I	A	N	M	82	1	F	W	R
509	505	DE5A	21	N	L	P	34	I	A	N	M	77	4	F	W	R
510	505	DE5B	22	N	L	S	39	II	B	N	M	38	3	F	W	R
511	506	DE6A	23	N	L	S	39	I	A	N	M	70	0	F	W	R
512	506	DE6B	24	N	L	S	39	II	B	N	M	53	2	F	W	R
513	551	MD1A	27	N	L	S	39	I	A	N	F	95	3	K	W	R
514	551	MD1B	28	N	L	S	39	II	B	N	M	58	6	F	W	R
515	552	MD2A	31a	N	L	S	39	I	A	N	M	82	1	F	W	R
516	552	MD2B	32	N	L	S	39	I	B	N	M	48	2	F	W	R
517	553	MD3A	33	N	L	S	39	I	A	N	M	73	2	L	W	R
518	553	MD3B	34	N	L	S	39	II	B	N	M	43	4	F	W	R
519	554	MD4A	35b	N	L	S	39	I	A	N	F	85	3	K	W	R
520	554	MD4B	35	N	L	S	39	II	A	N	M	80	4	F	W	R
521	554	MD4C	36	N	L	P	34	II	B	N	M	53	3	F	W	R
522	555	MD5A	37	N	L	S	39	I	A	N	M	69	1	O	W	R
523	555	MD5B	38	N	L	S	39	II	B	N	M	48	4	F	W	R
524	556	MD6A	39	Y	L	S	39	I	A	N	F	79	2	K	W	R
525	556	MD6B	40	N	L	S	39	II	B	N	M	58	4	F	W	R
526	557	MD7A	41	N	L	S	39	I	A	N	M	73	1	F	W	R
527	557	MD7B	41b	N	L	S	39	I	B	N	M	44	3	F	W	R
528	557	MD7C!	42	N	L	S	39	III	B	Y	M	55	6	C	W	U
529	558	MD8A	43	N	L	S	39	I	A	N	M	70	0	F	W	R
530	558	MD8B	44	N	L	S	39	II	B	N	M	51	3	F	W	R
531	559	MD9N	N46	N	L	P	34	I	A	N	F	70	1	H	B	R
532	559	MD9A	45	N	L	S	39	II	A	N	F	68	3	K	W	R

A. Serial **B.** Community **C.** Informant ID **D.** Old ID **E.** Auxiliaries **F.** Field Worker **G.** Work Sheets **H.** Year
I. Type **J.** Generation **K.** Cultivation **L.** Sex **M.** Age **N.** Education **O.** Occupation **P.** Race **Q.** Locality

A.	B.	C.	D.	E.	F.	G.	H.	I.	J.	K.	L.	M.	N.	O.	P.	Q.
533	559	MD9B	46	N	L	S	39	II	B	N	M	42	2	F	W	R
534	560	MD10A	49	N	L	S	39	I	A	N	M	82	3	F	W	R
535	560	MD10B	50	N	L	S	39	II	B	N	M	41	3	F	W	R
536	561	MD11	51	N	L	S	39	I	A	N	M	77	1	F	W	R
537	562	MD12A	52	N	L	S	39	I	A	N	F	87	2	K	W	R
538	562	MD12B	53	N	L	S	39	I	B	N	M	52	1	F	W	R
539	563	MD13A	54	N	L	S	39	I	A	N	F	70	4	H	W	U
540	563	MD13B	55	N	L	S	39	I	B	N	M	45		C	W	U
541	563	MD13C	56	N	L	S	39	II	B	N	M	55	5	R	W	U
542	563	MD13D!	57	N	L	S	39	III	A	Y	F	70	4	K	W	U
543	563	MD13E!	58	N	L	P	34	III	A	Y	F	76	4	K	W	U
544	563	MD13F!	59	N	L	S	39	III	B	Y	F	50	4	K	W	U
545	563	MD13G	54*	N	L	S	39	I	A	N	F		1	K	W	U
546	564	MD14	61	Y	L	S	39	II	B	N	M	52	2	F	W	R
547	565	MD15A	62	N	L	S	39	I	A	N	M	71	2	W	W	R
548	565	MD15B	63	N	L	S	39	II	B	N	M	42		F	W	R
549	566	MD16	64	N	L	P	34	I	A	N	F	60		F	W	R
550	567	MD17A	65	N	L	S	39	II	A	N	M	77	2	M	W	U
551	567	MD17B	66	N	L	S	39	II	B	N	M	39	3	F	W	R
552	568	MD18A	67	N	L	S	39	I	A	N	M	65	0	F	W	R
553	568	MD18B	68	N	L	S	39	II	B	N	M	49	4	F	W	R
554	569	MD19A	69	N	L	S	39	I	A	N	M	78	1	F	W	R
555	569	MD19B	70	N	L	S	39	I	B	N	M	38	4	F	W	R
556	570	MD20A	71	N	L	P	34	I	A	N	M	68	1	L	W	R
557	570	MD20B	72	N	L	S	39	II	B	N	M	46		F	W	R
558	570	MD20C!	73	N	L	S	39	III	B	Y	M	33	5	R	W	U
559	571	MD21A	75	N	L	S	39	I	A	N	M	85	1	F	W	R
560	571	MD21B	76	N	L	S	39	I	B	N	M	48		F	W	R
561	572	MD22N	N77	N	L	S	39	I	A	N	M	92	0	F	B	R
562	572	MD22M	N78	N	L	S	39	I	A	N	M	83	0	W	B	R
563	572	MD22A	77	N	L	P	34	I	A	N	M	76	0	F	W	R
564	572	MD22B	78	N	L	S	39	II	B	N	M	54	3	F	W	R
565	572	MD22C!	79	N	L	S	39	III	A	Y	F	65	5	K	W	R
566	573	MD23A	80b	N	L	S	39	I	A	N	M	79	3	F	W	R
567	573	MD23B	80a	N	L	S	39	I	A	N	M	70	0	F	W	R
568	573	MD23C	81	N	L	S	39	II	B	N	M	39	4	F	W	R
569	574	MD24	82	N	L	S	39	I	A	N	M	82	1	F	W	R
570	575	MD25	84	N	L	S	39	II	B	N	M	48	3	F	W	R
571	576	MD26A	83	N	L	S	39	I	A	N	F	70	3	K	W	R
572	576	MD26B	83A	N	L	S	39	II	A	N	M	80	2	M	W	U
573	577	MD27A	85	N	L	S	39	I	A	N	M	76	1	F	W	R
574	577	MD27B	86	N	L	S	39	II	B	N	M	39	3	F	W	R
575	599	DC1A	99	N	L	P	34	I	A	N	M	87	1	C	W	U
576	599	DC1B!	100	N	L	S	39	II	B	Y	F	50	6	P	W	U
577	601	VA1!	101	N	L	S	35	III	B	Y	F	50	5	K	W	U
578	602	VA2A	103	N	L	S	35	I	A	N	M	84	1	F	W	R
579	602	VA2B	104	Y	L	S	35	I	A	N	M	77	1	L	W	R
580	603	VA3A	105	N	L	S	35	I	A	N	M	73	0	F	W	R
581	603	VA3B	106	N	L	S	35	II	B	N	F	50	5	K	W	R
582	603	VA3C	105*	N	L	S	35	I	A	N	M	75	1	F	W	R

A.	B.	C.	D.	E.	F.	G.	H.	I.	J.	K.	L.	M.	N.	O.	P.	Q.
583	604	VA4N	N109	N	L	S	35	I	A	N	F	89		H	B	R
584	605	VA5A	107	N	L	S	35	I	A	N	M	64	1	F	W	R
585	605	VA5B	108	N	L	S	35	II	B	N	F	55	3	K	W	R
586	606	VA6A	113	N	L	S	35	I	A	N	M	81	1	F	W	R
587	606	VA6B	114	N	L	S	35	II	B	N	F	53	2	K	W	R
588	607	VA7A	121	N	L	S	35	I	A	N	M	71	0	F	W	R
589	607	VA7B	122	N	L	S	35	II	B	N	F	54		K	W	R
590	608	VA8A	123	N	L	P	34	I	A	N	M	83	1	F	W	R
591	608	VA8B	124	N	L	S	35	II	A	N	M	71	1	F	W	R
592	608	VA8C!	125	N	L	S	35	III	A	Y	F	62	4	K	W	U
593	609	VA9A	117	N	L	S	35	I	A	N	M	73	1	F	W	R
594	609	VA9B!	118	N	L	S	35	III	A	Y	F	71	4	K	W	R
595	610	VA10A	127	N	L	S	36	I	A	N	M	77	0	F	W	R
596	610	VA10B	128	N	L	S	35	II	B	N	F	60	3	K	W	R
597	611	VA11A	129	N	L	S	36	I	A	N	F	83	0	K	W	R
598	611	VA11B	130	N	L	S	36	II	B	N	F	52	4	K	W	R
599	612	VA12N	N131	N	L	S	36	I	A	N	F	80	0	K	B	R
600	612	VA12A	131	N	L	S	35	I	A	N	M	73	1	F	W	R
601	612	VA12B!	132	N	L	S	35	II	B	Y	M	51	4	F	W	R
602	613	VA13A	133	N	L	S	35	I	A	N	F	74	0	K	W	R
603	613	VA13B	134	N	L	S	35	II	B	N	F	57	2	K	W	R
604	614	VA14A	135	N	L	P	34	I	A	N	F	88	3	K	W	R
605	614	VA14B	136	N	L	S	35	I	B	N	F	57	3	K	W	R
606	614	VA14C	137	N	L	S	35	II	B	N	F	46	3	K	W	R
607	615	VA15N	N139	Y	L	S	36	I	A	N	F	94	0	K	B	R
608	615	VA15A	139	N	L	S	35	I	A	N	M	73	0	F	W	R
609	615	VA15B	140	N	L	S	35	II	B	N	F	45	4	K	W	R
610	616	VA16A	141	N	L	S	35	II	A	N	M	70	4	F	W	R
611	616	VA16B	142	N	L	S	35	II	B	N	M	44	5	S	W	R
612	617	VA17A	143	N	L	S	36	I	A	N	M	64	0	F	W	R
613	617	VA17B	144	N	L	S	36	II	B	N	M	46	3	F	W	R
614	618	VA18	145	N	L	S	36	I	A	N	M	81	3	F	W	R
615	619	VA19A	146	N	L	S	36	I	A	N	M	67	1	L	W	R
616	619	VA19B	147	N	L	S	36	II	A	N	F	61	3	K	W	R
617	619	VA19C!	148	N	L	S	36	III	B	Y	F	55	4	K	W	R
618	620	VA20A	149	N	L	S	36	I	A	N	M	79		F	W	R
619	620	VA20B	150	N	L	S	36	II	A	N	F	63	4	K	W	R
620	620	VA20C	150*	N	L	S	36		B		F	47		K	W	R
621	621	VA21N	N153	N	L	S	36	I	A	N	F	75	0	K	B	R
622	621	VA21A	153	N	L	S	36	I	A	N	F	80	0	K	W	R
623	621	VA21B	154	N	L	S	36	II	B	N	M	56	3	M	W	R
624	622	VA22	155	N	L	S	36	I	A	N	F	86	0	K	W	R
625	623	VA23A	156	N	L	S	36	I	A	N	F	90	0	K	W	R
626	623	VA23B	157	N	L	P	34	I	A	N	F	73	1	K	W	R
627	624	VA24	159	N	L	S	36	II	A	N	F	64	4	K	W	R
628	625	VA25	160	Y	L	S	36	I	A	N	M	76	1	L	W	R
629	626	VA26A	161A	N	L	P	34	I	A	N	M	82	1	C	W	R

A. Serial **B.** Community **C.** Informant ID **D.** Old ID **E.** Auxiliaries **F.** Field Worker **G.** Work Sheets **H.** Year **I.** Type **J.** Generation **K.** Cultivation **L.** Sex **M.** Age **N.** Education **O.** Occupation **P.** Race **Q.** Locality

A.	B.	C.	D.	E.	F.	G.	H.	I.	J.	K.	L.	M.	N.	O.	P.	Q.
630	626	VA26B	161	N	L	S	36	I	A	N	F	78	1	K	W	R
631	626	VA26C	162	N	L	S	36	II	B	N	F	47	4	K	W	R
632	627	VA27	163	Y	L	S	36	I	A	N	F	88	0	K	W	U
633	628	VA28A	164	N	L	S	36	I	A	N	M	84		F	W	R
634	628	VA28B	165	N	L	S	36	II	B	N	F	60	4	K	W	R
635	629	VA29	166	N	L	S	36	I	A	N	M	75	1	F	W	R
636	630	VA30A	167	N	L	S	36	I	A	N	M	79	1	C	W	U
637	630	VA30B!	167a	N	L	S	36	III	B	Y	F	50		K	W	U
638	630	VA30C!	168	N	L	P	34	III	A	Y	F	85	5	K	W	U
639	630	VA30D!	169	N	L	S	36	III	A	Y	F	83	5	K	W	U
640	630	VA30E!	170	N	L	S	36	III	B	Y	F	50	4	K	W	U
641	631	VA31A	171	Y	L	S	36	I	A	N	M	70	1	F	W	R
642	631	VA31B	172	N	L	S	36	II	B	N	M	55	3	R	W	R
643	631	VA31C	171*	N	L	S	36	I	A	N	F	70		K	W	R
644	632	VA32!	175	N	L	S	36	III	A	Y	F	70	4	K	W	U
645	633	VA33A	173	N	L	S	36	I	A	N	F	73	1	K	W	R
646	633	VA33B	174	N	L	S	36	II	B	N	F	47	3	K	W	R
647	634	VA34A	177	Y	L	P	34	I	A	N	F	66	3	K	W	R
648	634	VA34B	178	N	L	S	36	II	B	N	F	45	3	K	W	R
649	635	VA35A	179	N	L	S	36	I	A	N	M	75	0	F	W	R
650	635	VA35B	180	N	L	S	36	II	B	N	F	44	3	K	W	R
651	636	VA36A	181	N	L	S	36	I	A	N	M	75	1	F	W	R
652	636	VA36B	182	N	L	S	36	II	B	N	F	55	3	K	W	R
653	637	VA37	183	N	L	S	36	I	A	N	M	76	1	F	W	R
654	638	VA38	185	N	L	P	34	II	B	N	M	43	5	R	W	R
655	639	VA39!	186	N	L	S	36	III	B	Y	F	47	5	P	W	U
656	640	VA40A	187	N	L	S	36	I	A	N	F	81	1	K	W	R
657	640	VA40B	188	N	L	S	36	II	B	N	M	18	5	G	W	R
658	641	VA41A	191	N	L	S	36	I	A	N	M	80	1	F	W	R
659	641	VA41B	192	N	L	S	36	II	B	N	M	54	2	F	W	R
660	642	VA42A	193	Y	L	S	35	I	A	N	M	75	0	F	W	R
661	642	VA42B	194	N	L	S	35	II	B	N	F	61	4	K	W	R
662	643	VA43N	N195	N	L	S	36	I	A	N	M	86	0	F	B	R
663	643	VA43A	195	N	L	S	36	I	A	N	M	68	1	F	W	R
664	643	VA43B	196	N	L	S	36	II	A	N	M	64	4	F	W	R
665	644	VA44A	199	N	L	S	35	I	A	N	F	74		K	W	R
666	644	VA44B	200	N	L	S	35	II	A	N	M	63	3	M	W	R
667	645	VA45A	201	N	L	P	34	I	A	N	F	67	2	K	W	R
668	645	VA45B	202	N	L	S	35	II	B	N	M	54	3	F	W	R
669	646	VA46N	N207	N	L	P	34	I	A	N	M	70		F	B	R
670	646	VA46A	207	Y	L	P	34	I	A	N	F	72	1	K	W	R
671	646	VA46B!	208	N	L	S	35	III	B	Y	F	55	6	K	W	U
672	647	VA47	211	N	L	S	35	I	A	N	M	80	1	F	W	R
673	648	VA48A	213	Y	L	S	35	I	A	N	F	66	0	W	W	R
674	648	VA48B	214	N	L	S	35	II	A	N	F	62	2	K	W	R
675	649	VA49A	215	N	L	S	35	I	A	N	M	62	1	F	W	R
676	649	VA49B	216	N	L	S	35	II	B	N	F	48	4	K	W	R
677	650	VA50A	217	N	L	S	36	I	A	N	M	76	2	F	W	R
678	650	VA50B	218	N	L	S	36	II	B	N	F	58	4		W	R
679	651	VA51A	219	N	L	S	36	I	A	N	M	82	0	F	W	R

A.	B.	C.	D.	E.	F.	G.	H.	I.	J.	K.	L.	M.	N.	O.	P.	Q.
680	651	VA51B	220	N	L	S	36	II	A	N	F	62	4	K	W	R
681	651	VA51C	220*	N	L	S	36		B	N	F	55		K	W	R
682	652	VA52A	224	N	L	S	35	II	A	N	M	71	4	F	W	R
683	652	VA52B	225	N	L	S	35	II	B	N	F	50	5	K	W	R
684	652	VA52C!	226	N	L	S	35	III	B	Y	F	55	4	K	W	R
685	653	VA53A	227	N	L	S	35	I	A	N	M	82	0	F	W	R
686	653	VA53B	228	N	L	S	35	II	B	N	M	56	3	F	W	R
687	654	VA54A	229	N	L	P	34	I	A	N	M	62	3	F	W	R
688	654	VA54B	230	N	L	S	35	II	B	N	M	44	4	F	W	R
689	655	VA55A	233	Y	L	P	34	I	A	N	M	72	4	F	W	R
690	655	VA55B	234	N	L	S	35	II	B	N	F	62	4	K	W	U
691	656	VA56A	237	N	L	S	35	I	A	N	M	71	1	F	W	R
692	656	VA56B	238	N	L	S	35	II	B	N	F	54	4	K	W	R
693	657	VA57A	239	N	L	S	35	I	A	N	F	79	0	K	W	R
694	657	VA57B	240	N	L	S	35	II	A	N	F	64	4	K	W	R
695	658	VA58	241	Y	L	S	35	I	A	N	M	73	0	F	W	R
696	659	VA59N	N241	N	L	P	33	I	A	N	M	80	0	F	B	R
697	659	VA59A	242	N	L	S	35	II	B	N	F	46	3	K	W	R
698	659	VA59B!	243	N	L	S	35	III	B	Y	F	54	5	K	W	U
699	660	VA60	244	Y	L	S	35	I	A	N	M	80	1	F	W	R
700	661	VA61A	245	N	L	P	33	I	B	N	M	53	1	O	W	R
701	661	VA61B!	246	N	L	S	35	II	B	Y	M	54	3	M	W	U
702	661	VA61C	245*	N	L	P	33	I	A	N	M	76	3	F	W	R
703	662	VA62A	247	Y	L	S	35	I	A	N	F	77	1	K	W	R
704	662	VA62B	248	N	L	S	35	II	B	N	M	55	3	F	W	R
705	663	VA63A	251	N	L	S	35	I	A	N	M	80	0	F	W	R
706	663	VA63B	252	N	L	S	35	I	A	N	F	73	4	K	W	R
707	664	VA64A	255	N	L	S	35	I	A	N	F	83	1	K	W	R
708	664	VA64B	256	N	L	S	35	II	B	N	F	59		K	W	R
709	665	VA65A	257	N	L	P	33	I	A	N	F	70	1	K	W	R
710	665	VA65B	258	N	L	P	33	II	B	N	M	56	2	F	W	R
711	665	VA65C!	259	N	L	S	35	III	B	Y	F	35	6	K	W	U
712	666	VA66A	261	N	L	S	35	I	A	N	F	70	1	K	W	R
713	666	VA66B	262	N	L	S	35	II	A	N	M	52	1	F	W	R
714	667	VA67A	267	N	L	S	35	I	A	N	M	83	1	F	W	R
715	667	VA67B	268	N	L	S	35	II	B	N	F	50	3		W	R
716	668	VA68A	269	N	L	S	35	I	A	N	F	79	0	K	W	R
717	668	VA68B	270	N	L	S	35	II	B	N	M	52	4	F	W	R
718	669	VA69A	273	N	L	S	35	I	A	N	M	76	0	F	W	R
719	669	VA69B	274	N	L	S	35	II	B	N	M	52		M	W	R
720	670	VA70A	275	N	L	P	34	I	A	N	F	61	4	K	W	R
721	670	VA70B	276	N	L	S	35	II	B	N	F	48	4	K	W	R
722	671	VA71A	285	N	L	S	35	I	A	N	M	75	1	F	W	R
723	671	VA71B	286	N	L	S	35	II	B	N	F	51	3	K	W	R
724	672	VA72A	287	N	L	S	35	I	A	N	M	82	2	F	W	R
725	672	VA72B	288	N	L	S	35	II	B	N	M	45	5	F	W	R
726	673	VA73	291	N	L	S	35	I	A	N	M	63	0	F	W	R

A. Serial B. Community C. Informant ID D. Old ID E. Auxiliaries F. Field Worker G. Work Sheets H. Year
I. Type J. Generation K. Cultivation L. Sex M. Age N. Education O. Occupation P. Race Q. Locality

A.	B.	C.	D.	E.	F.	G.	H.	I.	J.	K.	L.	M.	N.	O.	P.	Q.
727	674	VA74A	293	N	L	S	35	I	A	N	M	77	1	F	W	R
728	674	VA74B!	294	N	L	S	36	III	B	Y	F	56	6	K	W	U
729	675	VA75A	297	N	L	S	36	I	A	N	M	74	1	F	W	R
730	675	VA75B	298	N	L	S	36	II	B	N	M	52	4	F	W	R
731	701	NC1	303	N	L	S	36	I	A	N	F	66	0		W	R
732	702	NC2A	301	Y	L	P	34	I	A	N	M	65	3	F	W	R
733	702	NC2B	304	N	L	S	36	II	B	N	M	41	3	F	W	R
734	703	NC3A	305	N	L	S	36	I	A	N	M	79	0	F	W	R
735	703	NC3B	306	N	L	S	36	II	B	N	F	37	4	K	W	R
736	704	NC4A	307	Y	L	S	36	I	A	N	M	83	1	F	W	R
737	704	NC4B	308	N	L	S	36	II	B	N	F	38	4	F	W	R
738	705	NC5A	309	N	L	S	36	I	A	N	F	74	1	K	W	U
739	705	NC5B	310	N	L	S	36	II	B	N	F	44	5	K	W	R
740	706	NC6!	311	N	L	S	36	III	B	Y	F	57	5		W	U
741	707	NC7A	315	Y	L	P	34	I	A	N	F	74	1		W	R
742	707	NC7B	316	N	L	S	36	II	B	N	F	43	2	K	W	R
743	708	NC8N	N317	N	L	S	37	I	A	N	M	80	1	F	B	R
744	708	NC8A	317	N	L	S	36	I	A	N	F	70	0	W	W	R
745	708	NC8B	318	Y	L	S	36	I	B	N	F	41	2	K	W	R
746	709	NC9A	319	N	L	S	36	I	A	N	M	71	1	F	W	R
747	709	NC9B	320	N	L	S	36	II	B	N	F	60	2	K	W	R
748	710	NC10A	321	N	L	P	34	I	A	N	M	76		L	W	R
749	710	NC10B	323	N	L	S	36	I	A	N	F	70		H	W	R
750	710	NC10C	322	N	L	S	36	II	B	N	F	41	4	K	W	R
751	711	NC11A	325	N	L	S	36	I	A	N	M	82	1	F	W	R
752	711	NC11B	326	N	L	S	36	II	B	N	F	39	3	K	W	R
753	712	NC12A	327	Y	L	S	36	I	A	N	M	77	0	F	W	R
754	712	NC12B	328	N	L	S	36	II	B	N	F	46	5	K	W	U
755	713	NC13A	329	N	L	S	36	I	A	N	M	75	1	F	W	R
756	713	NC13B	330	Y	L	S	36	II	B	N	F	40	4		W	R
757	714	NC14N	N331	N	L	S	37	I	A	N	M	77	1	F	B	R
758	714	NC14A	331	N	L	S	36	I	A	N	M	70	2	F	W	R
759	714	NC14B	332	N	L	P	34	II	A	N	F	75	5		W	R
760	714	NC14C!	333	N	L	S	36	III	A	Y	F	67	5	K	W	U
761	715	NC15A	335	N	L	S	36	I	A	N	M	74	0	F	W	R
762	715	NC15B	336	N	L	S	36	I	B	N	F	53	3	K	W	R
763	715	NC15C	335*	N	L	S	36	I	A	N	M	84	0	F	W	R
764	716	NC16A	339	Y	L	S	36	I	A	N	F	74	1	K	W	R
765	716	NC16B	340	N	L	S	36	I	B	N	M	44	1	F	W	R
766	717	NC17A	337	N	L	S	36	I	A	N	M	66	1	F	W	R
767	717	NC17B	338	N	L	S	36	II	B	N	M	48	3	F	W	R
768	718	NC18A	341	N	L	S	37	I	A	N	M	71	0	F	W	R
769	718	NC18B	342	N	L	S	37	II	A	N	F	61	4		W	R
770	719	NC19A	343	N	L	S	36	I	A	N	M	69	2	F	W	R
771	719	NC19B	344	N	L	S	36	II	B	N	M	51	5	F	W	R
772	720	NC20A	345	N	L	P	34	I	A	N	M	69	1	L	W	R
773	720	NC20B	346a	N	L	S	36	I	A	N	M	72	1	L	W	R
774	720	NC20C	346b	N	L	S	36	II	B	N	F	42	4	K	W	R
775	721	NC21A	347	N	L	S	37	I	A	N	F	71	1	K	W	R
776	721	NC21B	348	N	L	S	36	II	B	N	M	45	5	F	W	R

A.	B.	C.	D.	E.	F.	G.	H.	I.	J.	K.	L.	M.	N.	O.	P.	Q.
777	722	NC22A	349	N	L	P	34	I	A	N	M	68		F	W	R
778	722	NC22B	349b	N	L	S	37	II	B	N	F	43	4	K	W	R
779	723	NC23A	351a	N	L	S	37	I	A	N	M	75		F	W	R
780	723	NC23B	351b	Y	L	S	37	II	B	N	F	46	3	K	W	R
781	723	NC23C!	351c	N	L	S	37	III	B	Y	F	48	5	M	W	U
782	723	NC23D!	351d	N	L	S	37	III	B	Y	F	55			W	U
783	724	NC24N	N352	N	L	S	37	I	A	N	M	89		F	B	R
784	724	NC24A	352a	N	L	S	37	I	A	N	F	70	1	K	W	R
785	724	NC24B	352b	N	L	S	37	II	B	N	M	45	4	F	W	R
786	725	NC25N	N353	N	L	P	34	I	B	N	F	60	4	F	B	R
787	725	NC25A	353	N	L	S	37	I	A	N	M	73		F	W	R
788	725	NC25B	354	N	L	P	34	II	A	N	M	68	3	F	W	R
789	726	NC26A	355a	N	L	S	37	I	A	N	F	70	1	K	W	R
790	726	NC26B	355b	N	L	S	37	II	B	N	F	57		K	W	R
791	726	NC26C!	356	N	L	S	37	III	B	Y	F	37	4	K	W	U
792	727	NC27A	357	N	L	S	37	I	A	N	M	70		F	W	R
793	727	NC27B	358	N	L	S	37	II	B	N	F	47	4	K	W	R
794	728	NC28A	361	N	L	S	37	I	A	N	M	73	1	F	W	R
795	728	NC28B	361b	N	L	S	37	I	A	N	M	67	1	F	W	R
796	728	NC28C	362	N	L	S	37	II	B	N	F	40	3	K	W	U
797	729	NC29A	363	Y	L	P	34	I	A	N	M	78	1	F	W	R
798	729	NC29B	364	N	L	S	37	II	B	N	F	43	4	K	W	R
799	730	NC30A	365	N	L	S	36	I	A	N	M	89		F	W	R
800	730	NC30B	366	N	L	S	36	II	A	N	F	65	3		W	R
801	731	NC31A	367	N	L	S	36	I	A	N	M	68		F	W	R
802	731	NC31B	368	N	L	S	36	II	B	N	F	59	3		W	R
803	732	NC32A	369	N	L	P	34	I	A	N	M	73	0	F	W	R
804	732	NC32B!	370	N	L	S	36	III	B	Y	F	59	5	K	W	R
805	733	NC33A	373	N	L	S	36	I	A	N	F	68	1		W	R
806	733	NC33B	374	N	L	S	36	II	B	N	F	40	2	K	W	R
807	734	NC34A	375	N	L	S	36	I	A	N	F	70	0	W	W	R
808	734	NC34B	376	N	L	S	36	II	B	N	F	61	3	K	W	U
809	735	NC35A	377	N	L	P	34	II	A	N	F	80	3	K	W	R
810	735	NC35B	378	N	L	S	37	II	B	N	F	44	1	K	W	U
811	735	NC36N	N381	N	L	S	37	I	A	N	M	77	1	F	B	R
812	736	NC36A	381	N	L	S	37	I	A	N	M	76	1	F	W	R
813	736	NC36B	382	N	L	S	37	I	B	N	M	43	3	F	W	R
814	737	NC37A	383	N	L	S	36	I	A	N	F	65	0	K	W	R
815	737	NC37B	384	N	L	S	36	II	B	N	M	52	5	F	W	R
816	738	NC38N	N385	N	L	S	37	I	A	N	M	81	0	F	B	R
817	738	NC38A	385	N	L	S	37	I	A	N	M	70	0	F	W	R
818	738	NC38B	386	N	L	S	36	II	B	N	F	58	3	K	W	R
819	739	NC39A	389	N	L	S	36	I	A	N	M	77	0	F	W	R
820	739	NC39B!	390	N	L	S	36	III	B	Y	F	45	5	K	W	R
821	740	NC40A	391	N	L	P	34	I	A	N	F	68	1	P	W	R
822	740	NC40B	392	N	L	S	37	II	B	N	M	58	2	F	W	R
823	741	NC41!	393	N	L	S	37	III	B	Y	F	54	5	R	W	U

A. Serial B. Community C. Informant ID D. Old ID E. Auxiliaries F. Field Worker G. Work Sheets H. Year
I. Type J. Generation K. Cultivation L. Sex M. Age N. Education O. Occupation P. Race Q. Locality

A.	B.	C.	D.	E.	F.	G.	H.	I.	J.	K.	L.	M.	N.	O.	P.	Q.
824	742	NC42A	403	N	L	S	37	I	A	N	M	84	1	F	W	R
825	742	NC42B	404	Y	L	S	37	II	B	N	F	44	4	K	W	R
826	743	NC43A	397	N	L	S	37	I	A	N	F	80	0	H	W	R
827	743	NC43B	398	N	L	S	37	II	B	N	M	41	2	F	W	R
828	744	NC44	410	Y	L	S	37	II	B	N	M	49	5	F	W	R
829	745	NC45A	409	N	L	S	37	I	A	N	F	80	0	W	W	R
830	745	NC45B	409*	N	L	S	37	I	A	N	M	75	0		W	R
831	746	NC46A	411	N	L	S	37	I	A	N	M	83	1	F	W	R
832	746	NC46B	412	N	L	S	37	II	B	N	M	44	5	F	W	R
833	746	NC46C!	412b	N	L	S	37	III	B	Y	F	48	6	M	W	U
834	747	NC47	413	N	L	P	34	I	A	N	F	76	1	K	W	R
835	748	NC48	418	N	L	S	37	II	A	N	M	52	4	F	W	R
836	749	NC49	421	N	L	S	37	I	A	N	F	79	1	K	W	R
837	750	NC50A	422	N	L	S	37	II	B	N	M	45	4	F	W	R
838	750	NC50B!	423	N	L	S	37	III	B	Y	F	38	5	R	W	U
839	751	NC51A	427	N	L	S	37	I	A	N	F	76	1	K	W	R
840	751	NC51B	428	N	L	S	37	II	B	N	M	49	5	F	W	R
841	752	NC52N	N429	N	L	S	37	I	A	N	F	90	0	K	B	U
842	752	NC52A	429	N	L	S	37	I	A	N	F	77	1	W	W	R
843	752	NC52B	430	N	L	S	37	II	B	N	M	48	3	F	W	R
844	753	NC53A	431	N	L	S	37	I	A	N	M	82		F	W	R
845	753	NC53B	432	N	L	S	37	II	B	N	F	42	4	K	W	U
846	754	NC54A	433	N	L	P	34	I	A	N	M	79	4	F	W	R
847	754	NC54B	434	N	L	S	37	II	B	N	F	41	4	K	W	U
848	755	NC55	435	N	L	S	37	I	A	N	M	86	0	F	W	R
849	756	NC56A	436	N	L	S	37	II	B	N	F	60	3	K	W	R
850	756	NC56B!	437	N	L	S	37	III	B	Y	F	45	5	K	W	U
851	757	NC57A	438a	N	L	S	37	I	A	N	M	81	1	M	W	R
852	757	NC57B	438b	N	L	S	37	II	B	N	M	36	3	F	W	R
853	758	NC58A	439	N	L	S	36	I	A	N	M	72	1	F	W	R
854	758	NC58B	440	N	L	S	36	I	B	N	F	39	2		W	U
855	759	NC59	441	Y	L	P	34	I	A	N	F	86	1	K	W	R
856	760	NC60	442	N	L	S	37	II	B	N	M	41	3	F	W	R
857	761	NC61A	443	N	L	S	37	I	A	N	M	74	0	F	W	R
858	761	NC61B	444	N	L	S	37	II	B	N	F	40	4	K	W	U
859	762	NC62A	447	N	L	S	36	I	A	N	M	76	1		W	R
860	762	NC62B	448	N	L	S	36	II	B	N	F	52	3	K	W	R
861	763	NC63A	449	N	L	S	36	I	A	N	F	74	1	K	W	R
862	763	NC63B	450	N	L	S	36	II	B	N	F	52	4	M	W	R
863	764	NC64A	453	N	L	S	37	I	A	N	M	86	0	F	W	R
864	764	NC64B	454	N	L	S	37	II	B	N	M	39	2	F	W	R
865	765	NC65A	461	N	L	S	37	I	A	N	F	66	2	K	W	R
866	765	NC65B	462	N	L	P	34	II	A	N	F	64	1	H	W	U
867	766	NC66A	465	N	L	S	37	I	A	N	M	75	0	F	W	R
868	766	NC66B	466	N	L	S	37	II	B	N	F	53	3	K	W	R
869	767	NC67A	469	N	L	S	36	I	A	N	M	84	0	F	W	R
870	767	NC67B	470	N	L	P	34	II	A	N	M	81	1	F	W	R
871	768	NC68A	473	N	L	S	37	I	A	N	F	67	1	K	W	R
872	768	NC68B	474	N	L	S	37	II	B	N	F	42	3	K	W	U
873	769	NC69A	477	N	L	S	37	I	A	N	M	77	0	F	W	R

A.	B.	C.	D.	E.	F.	G.	H.	I.	J.	K.	L.	M.	N.	O.	P.	Q.
874	769	NC69B	478	N	L	P	34	II	A	N	F	57	1	H	W	R
875	770	NC70A	479	N	L	S	36	I	A	N	F	71	0	K	W	R
876	770	NC70B	480	N	L	S	36	II	B	N	M	16	4	G	W	R
877	771	NC71A	481	N	L	S	37	I	A	N	M	78	1	F	W	R
878	771	NC71B	482	N	L	S	36	II	B	N	M	54	5	F	W	R
879	771	NC71C!	483	N	L	S	36	III	B	Y	F	49	6	K	W	U
880	772	NC72A	487	N	L	S	37	I	A	N	M	74	0	F	W	R
881	772	NC72B	488	N	L	S	36	II	B	N	F	45	5	K	W	U
882	773	NC73A	491	N	L	S	36	I	A	N	F	86			W	R
883	773	NC73B	492	N	L	P	34	II	A	N	M	77	1	F	W	R
884	774	NC74A	493	N	L	S	36	I	A	N	M	76	0	F	W	R
885	774	NC74B	494	N	L	S	37	II	B	N	F	57	3	K	W	R
886	775	NC75A	495	N	L	S	36	I	A	N	M	83	0	F	W	R
887	775	NC75B	496	N	L	S	36	II	B	N	F	52	3	K	W	R
888	801	SC1A	203.1	N	L	S	37	I	A	N	F	81	1	K	W	R
889	801	SC1B	203.2	N	L	S	37	II	B	N	F	56	5	K	W	R
890	802	SC2A	204.1	Y	L	S	37	I	A	N	F	70	0	K	W	R
891	802	SC2B	204.2	N	L	S	37	II	B	N	F	48	4	K	W	U
892	802	SC2C	204.1*	N	L	S	37	I	A	N	F	70		K	W	R
893	803	SC3A	205.1	N	L	P	34	I	A	N	M	72	1	F	W	R
894	803	SC3B	205.2	N	M	S	47	I	A	N	M	80	2	F	W	R
895	803	SC3C!	205.3	Y	M	S	47	III	A	Y	F	67	5	K	W	U
896	804	SC4A	206.1	N	M	S	46	I	B	N	M	55	1	L	W	R
897	804	SC4B	206.2	N	M	S	46	II	A	N	F	81	4	K	W	U
898	804	SC4C	206.3	N	M	S	46	II	B	N	M	55	3	M	W	R
899	805	SC5A	207.1	Y	M	S	48	I	A	N	M	79	1	F	W	R
900	805	SC5B	207.2	N	M	S	46	II	A	N	M	80	2	C	W	U
901	805	SC5C	207.2A	N	M	S	46	II	B	N	M	61	2	M	W	U
902	805	SC5D!	207.3	Y	M	S	46	III	A	Y	F	71	4	M	W	U
903	806	SC6N	N208	N	M	S	46	I	A	N	M	77	1	C	B	U
904	806	SC6A	208.1	N	L	P	34	I	A	N	M	60	1	F	W	R
905	806	SC6B	208.2	N	M	S	48	I	A	N	F	79	1	K	W	R
906	806	SC6C!	208.3	Y	M	S	48	III	A	Y	F	68	5	K	W	R
907	806	SC6D	208.2*	N	M	S	48	I	B	N	M	49	1	U	W	U
908	807	SC7N	N209	N	M	S	46	I	A	N	M	83	1	S	B	U
909	807	SC7A	209.1	N	M	S	46	II	A	N	M	75	2	M	W	U
910	807	SC7B	209.2	Y	M	S	46	II	A	N	M	85	1	M	W	U
911	807	SC7C!	209.3	N	M	S	46	III	A	Y	M	78	6	P	W	U
912	807	SC7D!	209.4	Y	M	S	46	III	B	Y	F	50	6	K	W	U
913	808	SC8A	210.1	N	M	S	47	I	A	N	F	74	1	K	W	R
914	808	SC8B	210.2	N	M	S	47	I	A	N	M	58	1	F	W	R
915	808	SC8C	210.3	N	M	S	47	II	A	N	M	67	1	F	W	R
916	809	SC9A	211.1	N	M	S	47	I	A	N	M	75	1	F	W	R
917	809	SC9B	211.2	N	M	S	47	I	A	N	M	65	1	M	W	R
918	809	SC9C!	211.3	N	M	S	47	III	B	Y	M	50	6	P	W	R
919	809	SC9D!	211.4	N	M	S	47	III	A	Y	M	73	6		W	R
920	810	SC10A	212.1	N	M	S	46	I	B	N	F	53	2	K	W	U

A. Serial **B.** Community **C.** Informant ID **D.** Old ID **E.** Auxiliaries **F.** Field Worker **G.** Work Sheets **H.** Year
I. Type **J.** Generation **K.** Cultivation **L.** Sex **M.** Age **N.** Education **O.** Occupation **P.** Race **Q.** Locality

A.	B.	C.	D.	E.	F.	G.	H.	I.	J.	K.	L.	M.	N.	O.	P.	Q.
921	810	SC10B!	212.2	N	M	S	48	III	A	Y	M	85	6	P	W	U
922	810	SC10C!	212.3	N	M	S	48	III	A	Y	F	64	4	K	W	U
923	811	SC11N	N213	N	L	P	34	I	B	N	M	58	2	C	B	U
924	811	SC11M!	2N213	N	M	S	46	III	B	Y	M	44	5	R	B	U
925	811	SC11A	213.1	Y	M	S	46	II	A	N	M	86	2	M	W	U
926	811	SC11B	213.11	N	P	C	65	II	B	N	M	57	2	M	W	U
927	811	SC11C	213.2	N	M	S	46	II	B	N	F	58	2	K	W	U
928	811	SC11D	213.3	N	M	S	46	II	A	N	M	83	2	M	W	U
929	811	SC11E	213.4	N	M	S	46	II	A	N	M	76	4	M	W	U
930	811	SC11F	213.5	N	M	S	46	II	B	N	F	48	4	K	W	U
931	811	SC11G!	213.7	N	M	S	46	III	B	Y	M	24	6	P	W	U
932	811	SC11H!	213.8	N	M	S	46	III	B	Y	M	52	6	M	W	U
933	811	SC11I!	213.9	Y	L	P	34	III	B	Y	F	51	4	K	W	U
934	811	SC11J!	213.10	N	M	S	46	III	B	Y	F	69	4	P	W	U
935	812	SC12A	214.1	N	M	S	47	I	A	N	M	80	2	F	W	R
936	812	SC12B	214.2	N	L	P	34	II	A	N	F	70	3	K	W	R
937	813	SC13	213.6	N	M	S	48	II	B	N	M	52	5	F	W	R
938	814	SC14A	215.1	N	L	P	34	I	A	N	M	84	2	F	W	R
939	814	SC14B	215.2	N	M	S	47	II	B	N	M	51	5	R	W	U
940	815	SC15A	216.1	N	M	S	47	I	A	N	M	83	1	F	W	R
941	815	SC15B	216.2	N	M	S	47	II	A	N	M	68	3	M	W	U
942	815	SC15C	216.3	N	M	S	47	II	A	N	M	85	2	M	W	U
943	816	SC16N	N217	N	M	S	46	I	A	N	M	68	1	F	B	R
944	816	SC16	217.1	N	O	C	67	I	B	N	M	69	2	F	W	R
945	817	SC17A	218.1	N	M	S	46	I	A	N	F	76	2	K	W	R
946	817	SC17B	218.2	N	M	S	46	I	A	N	M	68	2	S	W	R
947	817	SC17C	218.3	N	M	S	46	II	A	N	F	88	4	M	W	R
948	817	SC17D	218.4	N	M	S	46	II	A	N	M	78	6	M	W	R
949	818	SC18N	N219	N	M	S	46	I	A	N	M	75	1	M	B	U
950	818	SC18A	219.1	N	M	S	46	I	B	N	M	68	2	C	W	U
951	818	SC18B	219.2	N	M	S	46	II	B	N	M	62	4	M	W	U
952	818	SC18C!	219.3	N	M	S	46	III	B	Y	F	61	6	K	W	U
953	818	SC18D!	219.3*	N	M	S	46	III	A	Y	F	85	4	K	W	U
954	819	SC19N	N220	N	L	P	34	I	B	N	M	53		F	B	R
955	819	SC19A	220.1	N	M	S	46	II	B	N	F	51	5	F	W	R
956	819	SC19B	220.4	N	P	C	65	II	B	N	M	70	3	M	W	R
957	819	SC19C	220.2	N	M	S	46	II	B	N	F	68	4	K	W	R
958	819	SC19D!	220.3	N	M	S	48	III	B	Y	M	67	4	F	W	R
959	819	SC19E!	220.2*	N	M	S	46	III	A	Y	F	73		K	W	R
960	820	SC20A	221.1	N	M	S	48	I	A	N	M	80	1	F	W	R
961	820	SC20B	221.2	N	M	S	48	II	A	N	M	76	2	F	W	R
962	820	SC20C	221.3	Y	M	S	48	II	A	N	M	72	5	F	W	R
963	820	SC20D!	221.4	N	M	S	48	II	B	Y	M	53	5	F	W	R
964	821	SC21A	222.1	N	L	S	37	I	A	N	F	70	1	F	W	R
965	821	SC21B	222.2	N	L	S	37	II	A	N	F	66	4	K	W	R
966	822	SC22N	N223	N	L	P	34	I	A	N	F	65		H	B	U
967	822	SC22A	223.1	N	M	S	47	II	B	N	M	62	4	M	W	R
968	822	SC22B	223.2	N	L	P	34	II	A	N	F	65	3	K	W	U
969	822	SC22C!	223.3	N	M	S	47	III	A	Y	M	74	6	F	W	R
970	823	SC23A	224.1	N	M	S	47	I	A	N	M	81	1	M	W	R

A.	B.	C.	D.	E.	F.	G.	H.	I.	J.	K.	L.	M.	N.	O.	P.	Q.
971	823	SC23B	224.2	N	M	S	47	I	A	N	M	72	2	F	W	R
972	823	SC23C	224.3	N	M	S	47	II	A	N	M	66	2	F	W	R
973	823	SC23D	224.4	N	M	S	47	II	B	N	M	66		F	W	R
974	823	SC23E!	224.5	N	M	S	47	III	A	Y	M	75		F	W	R
975	824	SC24N	N225	Y	M	S	46	I	A	N	M	82	1	O	B	R
976	824	SC24A	225.1	N	P	C	65	I	A	N	M	67	2	F	W	R
977	824	SC24B	225.11	N	M	S	46	I	A	N	M	84	1	F	W	R
978	824	SC24C	225.2	N	M	S	46	II	A	N	M	65	2	M	W	R
979	824	SC24D!	225.3	N	M	S	46	III	A	Y	M	86	6	P	W	U
980	825	SC25A	226.1	N	L	P	34	I	A	N	F	78	1	K	W	R
981	825	SC25B	226.2	N	M	S	47	II	A	N	M	77	4	F	W	R
982	825	SC25C!	226.3	N	M	S	47	III	B	Y	F	30	6	P	W	U
983	826	SC26A	227.1	N	M	S	47	II	A	N	M	72	2	F	W	R
984	826	SC26B!	227.2	N	M	S	47	III	B	Y	M	55	6	F	W	R
985	827	SC27A	228.1	N	P	C	65	I	B	N	M	71	3	F	W	R
986	827	SC27B	228.2	N	M	S	47	II	A	N	M	75	2	F	W	R
987	828	SC28A	229.1	N	M	S	47	I	A	N	F	78	2	K	W	R
988	828	SC28B	217.2	N	M	S	47	II	B	N	M	39	4	M	W	R
989	828	SC28C	229.2	N	M	S	47	II	B	N	M	44	4	F	W	R
990	828	SC28D	229.3	N	M	S	47	II	B	N	F	19		R	W	R
991	829	SC29A	230.2	N	M	S	47	I	A	N	M	78	3	F	W	R
992	829	SC29B	230.1	N	M	S	47	II	A	N	M	87	2	R	W	U
993	829	SC29C	230.3	N	M	S	47	II	A	N	M	82	3	F	W	R
994	829	SC29D	230.2*	N	M	S	47	I	A	N	M	77	2	F	W	R
995	829	SC29E	230.1*	N	M	S	47	I	A	N	M			F	W	R
996	830	SC30A	231.1	N	L	P	34	I	A	N	M	63	1	F	W	R
997	830	SC30B	231.2	N	M	S	46	II	A	N	M	79	1	M	W	R
998	830	SC30C!	231.3	Y	M	S	46	III	A	Y	F	73	5	K	W	R
999	831	SC31A	232.1	N	M	S	47	I	A	N	M	64	1	M	W	R
1000	831	SC31B	232.2	N	M	S	47	II	A	N	M	86	2	F	W	R
1001	832	SC32A	233.1	Y	M	S	47	II	A	N	M	80	5	F	W	R
1002	832	SC32B	233.2	N	M	S	47	II	A	N	M	86	4	F	W	R
1003	832	SC32C	233.3	N	M	S	47	II	B	N	M	55	5	F	W	R
1004	832	SC32D	233.4	N	M	S	47	III	A	N	M	78	5	P	W	U
1005	833	SC33A	234.1	N	L	P	34	I	A	N	M	75	0	F	W	R
1006	833	SC33B	234.2	N	M	S	47	II	A	N	M	75	2	R	W	U
1007	834	SC34A	235.1	N	M	S	47	I	A	N	M	75	1	F	W	R
1008	834	SC34B	235.2	N	M	S	47	II	A	N	M	73	2	M	W	R
1009	834	SC34C	235.3	N	M	S	47	II	A	N	F	80	4	K	W	U
1010	835	SC35A	236.1	Y	M	S	47	I	B	N	F	59	1	K	W	U
1011	835	SC35B	236.2	N	M	S	47	I	B	N	M	37	2	O	W	U
1012	835	SC35C	236.3	N	O	C	67	II	A	N	M	76	2	F	W	R
1013	835	SC35D	236.2*	N	M	S	47	II	B	N	M			M	W	U
1014	835	SC35E!	236.3*	N	O	C	67	III	A	Y	M	84	6	P	W	R
1015	836	SC36A	237.1	Y	M	S	46	I	A	N	M	73	2	F	W	R
1016	836	SC36B	237.2	Y	M	S	46	I	A	N	F	76	2	K	W	U
1017	836	SC36C	237.3	Y	M	S	46	II	A	N	M	73	5	F	W	R

A. Serial **B.** Community **C.** Informant ID **D.** Old ID **E.** Auxiliaries **F.** Field Worker **G.** Work Sheets **H.** Year **I.** Type **J.** Generation **K.** Cultivation **L.** Sex **M.** Age **N.** Education **O.** Occupation **P.** Race **Q.** Locality

A.	B.	C.	D.	E.	F.	G.	H.	I.	J.	K.	L.	M.	N.	O.	P.	Q.
1018	836	SC36D!	237.4	N	M	S	46	III	A	Y	M	80	6	P	W	U
1019	837	SC37	238	N	P	C	65	I	B	N	M	66		C	W	R
1020	838	SC38N	N239	N	M	S	46	II	A	N	M	73	3	S	B	R
1021	838	SC38A	239.1	N	M	S	46	I	A	N	M	94	0	S	W	R
1022	838	SC38B	239.2	N	M	S	46	II	B	N	M	66	2	M	W	U
1023	838	SC38C!	239.3	N	M	S	46	III	A	Y	M	75	6	P	W	U
1024	838	SC38D!	239.4	N	M	S	46	III	B	Y	F	59	6	P	W	U
1025	838	SC38E!	239.4*	N	M	S	46	III		Y	M		6	P	W	U
1026	839	SC39A	240.1	N	M	S	46	I	A	N	M	62	1	M	W	R
1027	839	SC39B!	240.2	N	M	S	46	III	A	Y	M	84	6	F	W	R
1028	840	SC40A	241.1	Y	M	S	41	I	A	N	M	63	1	F	W	R
1029	840	SC40B	241.2	N	M	S	41	II	A	N	F	78	5	H	W	U
1030	841	SC41A	242.1	N	L	P	34	I	A	N	F	79	2	K	W	U
1031	841	SC41B	242.2	N	M	S	41	II	B	N	M	58	2	F	W	R
1032	842	SC42N	N243	N	M	S	41	I	B	N	F	54	2	H	B	U
1033	842	SC42M	N243*	N	M	S	41	I	A	N	F	100	0	H	B	U
1034	842	SC42A	243.1	N	M	S	41	I	A	N	M	70	1	F	W	R
1035	842	SC42B!	243.2	N	M	S	46	II	B	Y	F	67	6	K	W	U
1036	842	SC42C!	243.3	N	M	S	41	III	A	Y	M	58	6	M	W	U
1037	842	SC42D!	243.4	N	B	E	37	III	B	Y	M	26	6	P	W	U
1038	842	SC42E!	243.5	N	M	S	64	III	B	Y	M	52	6	M	W	U
1039	843	SC43A	244.1	N	M	S	41	I	A	N	M	100		F	W	R
1040	843	SC43B	244.2	Y	M	S	41	I	A	N	M	66	2	F	W	R
1041	843	SC43C	244.3	Y	M	S	41	III	A	N	M	69	6	P	W	R
1042	844	SC44A	245.1	N	M	S	41	I	A	N	M	70	1	F	W	R
1043	844	SC44B	245.2	Y	M	S	41	II	A	N	M	85	3	F	W	R
1044	901	GA1N	N246	N	S	C	72	I	B	N	F	40	3	S	B	U
1045	901	GA1A	246.1	Y	M	S	46	I	B	N	M	72	3	O	W	U
1046	901	GA1B	246.11	N	Rr	C	72	I	A	N	F	77	3	P	W	U
1047	901	GA1C	246.2	N	M	S	46	II	A	N	F	90	4	K	W	U
1048	901	GA1D	246.3	N	M	S	46	II	A	N	M	76	4	R	W	U
1049	901	GA1E	246.4	N	M	S	46	II	B	N	F	36	5	M	W	U
1050	901	GA1F!	246.5	N	L	P	34	III	A	Y	F	78	4	K	W	U
1051	901	GA1G!	246.6	N	M	S	46	III	A	Y	M	76	5	M	W	U
1052	901	GA1H!	246.7	Y	M	S	45	III	B	Y	F	60	5	K	W	U
1053	902	GA2N	N247	Y	M	S	46	I	A	N	M	67	1	F	B	R
1054	902	GA2A	247.1	N	M	S	46	I	A	N	M	78	3	F	W	R
1055	902	GA2B	247.2	N	M	S	46	II	B	N	M	43	5	F	W	R
1056	903	GA3A	248.1	N	L	P	34	I	A	N	M	80	2	F	W	R
1057	903	GA3B	248.2	N	M	S	48	I	A	N	F	83	1	K	W	R
1058	904	GA4N	N249	N	L	P	34	I	B	N	M	53	0	F	B	R
1059	904	GA4A	249.1	N	M	S	47	II	A	N	M	77	1	C	W	R
1060	904	GA4B	249.2	N	M	S	47	II	A	N	M	72	2	L	W	R
1061	904	GA4C!	249.3	N	M	S	47	III	B	Y	F	58	4	K	W	R
1062	905	GA5A	250.1	N	M	S	47	II	B	N	M	57	5	O	W	R
1063	905	GA5B	250.2	N	M	S	47	II	B	N	M	60	4	M	W	R
1064	905	GA5C	250.3	N	M	S	47	II	B	N	M	66		S	W	U
1065	905	GA5D!	250.4	N	M	S	47	II	A	Y	M	80	5	M	W	U
1066	905	GA5E!	250.5	N	M	S	47	II	B	Y	M	61	2	R	W	U
1067	906	GA6A	251.1	N	M	S	47	I	A	N	M	79	1	O	W	R

A.	B.	C.	D.	E.	F.	G.	H.	I.	J.	K.	L.	M.	N.	O.	P.	Q.
1068	906	GA6B!	251.2	N	M	S	47	III	A	Y	M	78	2	M	W	R
1069	907	GA7	256	N	M	S	47	I	A	N	M	87	1	L	W	R
1070	908	GA8A	257.1	N	M	S	47	I	A	N	F	86	2	K	W	R
1071	908	GA8B	257.2	N	M	S	47	II	B	N	F	50	5	P	W	U
1072	909	GA9A	257A.1	N	Rr	C	72	I	B	N	F	74	2	K	W	R
1073	909	GA9B	257A.2	N	Rr	C	72	I	B	N	M	60	3	F	W	R
1074	910	GA10A	258.1	N	L	P	34	I	A	N	M	67	2	F	W	R
1075	910	GA10B	258.2	N	M	S	48	II	A	N	M	84	2	F	W	R
1076	911	GA11N	N258A	N	S	C	72	I	B	N	F	60	2	K	B	R
1077	912	GA12A	259.1	Y	M	S	46	II	B	N	M	54	3	R	W	R
1078	912	GA12B!	259.2	N	Rr	C	68	III	B	Y	M	61	6	P	W	U
1079	913	GA13A	260.1	N	L	P	34	I	A	N	M	69	1	F	W	R
1080	913	GA13B!	260.2	N	M	S	47	III	A	Y	M	83	6	P	W	R
1081	914	GA14A	261.1	N	M	S	46	I	A	N	M	76	1	F	W	R
1082	914	GA14B	261.3	N	M	S	46	I	A	N	M	70	2	C	W	U
1083	914	GA14C	261.2	N	M	S	46	II	A	N	F	88	1	F	W	R
1084	915	GA15A	262.1	N	L	P	34	I	A	N	M	83	1	F	W	R
1085	915	GA15B	262.2	N	M	S	48	I	A	N	M	92	1	F	W	R
1086	916	GA16A	263.2	Y	M	S	47	I	A	N	F	61		K	W	R
1087	916	GA16B	263.1	N	M	S	47	II	A	N	F	85	2	K	W	R
1088	916	GA16C	263.21	N	S	C	70	II	B	N	F	72	5	K	W	U
1089	916	GA16D!	263.3	N	M	S	47	III	B	Y	F	54	6	K	W	U
1090	917	GA17N	N264	N	P	C	65	I	B	N	F	48	3	R	B	R
1091	917	GA17	264	N	P	C	65	II	B	N	M	71	5	M	W	R
1092	918	GA18A	264A.1	Y	Rt	C	72	I	A	N	M	82	1	F	W	R
1093	918	GA18B	264A.2	N	Rt	C	72	I	A	N	F	70	2	K	W	U
1094	919	GA19A	265.1	Y	M	S	47	I	A	N	M	71	2	M	W	R
1095	919	GA19B	265.2	N	M	S	47	I	A	N	M	72	2	F	W	R
1096	920	GA20A	266.1	N	M	S	47	I	A	N	M	77	1	F	W	R
1097	920	GA20B	266.2	N	M	S	47	I	A	N	M	75	2	F	W	R
1098	921	GA21A	267.1	N	Rr	C	71	I	A	N	F	71	3	K	W	R
1099	921	GA21B	267.2	N	M	S	47	I	A	N	F	74	2	O	W	U
1100	922	GA22A	268A.1	N	P	C	65	I	B	N	M	60	2	S	W	U
1101	922	GA22B	268A.2	N	M	S	47	II	A	N	M	75	4	F	W	R
1102	923	GA23A	268.1	N	M	S	47	I	A	N	M	55	2	L	W	U
1103	923	GA23B	268.11	N	S	C	72	II	A	N	F	80	3	K	W	U
1104	923	GA23C	268.2	N	S	C	72	II	B	N	F	58	4	K	W	U
1105	923	GA23D!	268.3	N	M	S	47	III	A	Y	F	62	6	K	W	U
1106	923	GA23E!	268.4	N	P	C	68	III	B	Y	F	67	5	K	W	U
1107	923	GA23F!	268.5	N	S	C	72	III	B	Y	F	24	6	P	W	U
1108	924	GA24N	N269	N	S	C	70	I	A	N	M	68	0	L	B	U
1109	924	GA24A	269.1	N	L	P	34	I	A	N	M	64	0	F	W	R
1110	924	GA24B	269.2	Y	M	S	47	I	A	N	M	66	0	F	W	R
1111	925	GA25N	N269A	N	S	C	72	I	A	N	F	71	1	K	B	R
1112	926	GA26	270A	N	Rr	C	71	I	B	N	M	49	2	M	W	R
1113	927	GA27!	270	N	P	C	65	III	B	Y	M	48		M	W	U
1114	928	GA28	271A	N	P	C	65	II	A	N	M	80	3	R	W	U

A. Serial **B.** Community **C.** Informant ID **D.** Old ID **E.** Auxiliaries **F.** Field Worker **G.** Work Sheets **H.** Year **I.** Type **J.** Generation **K.** Cultivation **L.** Sex **M.** Age **N.** Education **O.** Occupation **P.** Race **Q.** Locality

A.	B.	C.	D.	E.	F.	G.	H.	I.	J.	K.	L.	M.	N.	O.	P.	Q.
1115	929	GA29A	271.1	N	M	S	47	I	A	N	M	87	1	F	W	R
1116	929	GA29B	271.2	Y	M	S	47	II	A	N	F	67	5	K	W	R
1117	930	GA30A	272.1	N	M	S	46	I	B	N	M	71	2	C	W	R
1118	930	GA30B	272.2	N	M	S	46	II	A	N	M	77	4	C	W	U
1119	930	GA30C!	272.3	N	Rr	C	68	III	A	Y	M	77	5	P	W	U
1120	930	GA30D	272.1*	N	M	S	46	I	A	N	M	77	2	F	W	R
1121	930	GA30E	272.2*	N	M	S	46	II	A		F	87	4	K	W	U
1122	931	GA31	272A	N	S	C	71	I	A	N	F	73	0	K	W	R
1123	932	GA32	272B	N	P	C	68	I	B	N	F	61	3	K	W	R
1124	933	GA33A	272C1	N	S	C	72	I	A	N	F	75	2	K	W	R
1125	933	GA33B	272C2	N	S	C	72	I	B	N	F	62	2	O	W	R
1126	934	GA34N	N273	N	M	S	47	I	A	N	M	75	2	S	B	U
1127	934	GA34A	273.1	N	L	P	34	II	A	N	F	65	2	K	W	R
1128	934	GA34B	273.2	N	M	S	47	II	B	N	M	62	2	F	W	R
1129	935	GA35N	N273A	N	S	C	71	I	A	N	F	80	1	F	B	R
1130	936	GA36N	N274A	N	Rt	C	72	I	A	N	M	69	1	L	B	R
1131	937	GA37N	2N274	N	S	C	71	I	A	N	F	82	2	H	B	U
1132	937	GA37M!	NC274	N	P	C	68	III	B	Y	M	55	6	P	B	U
1133	937	GA37A	274.1	N	M	S	47	I	A	N	M	95	2	F	W	R
1134	937	GA37B	274.2	N	M	S	47	II	A	N	M	75	3	M	W	R
1135	937	GA37C	274.21	N	S	C	70	II	B	N	F	45	3	K	W	U
1136	937	GA37D!	274.7	N	P	C	68	III	B	Y	M	59	6	P	W	U
1137	937	GA37E!	274.8	N	S	C	70	III	B	Y	F	53	6	P	W	U
1138	937	GA37F!	274.3	N	M	S	47	III	A	Y	F	84	6	K	W	U
1139	937	GA37G!	274.4	N	M	S	47	III	B	Y	M	51	6	P	W	U
1140	937	GA37H!	274.5	Y	M	S	47	III	A	Y	M	73	4	P	W	U
1141	937	GA37I!	274.6	N	P	C	68	III	B	Y	F	59	5	K	W	U
1142	938	GA38	275	N	P	C	66	I	A	N	M	79		M	W	U
1143	939	GA39	275A	N	P	C	68	II	A	N	M	66	4	M	W	R
1144	940	GA40	276A	N	S	C	70	I	A	N	F	72	3	K	W	R
1145	941	GA41	276B	N	S	C	74	I	A	N	M	81	2	S	W	R
1146	942	GA42A	276.1	N	M	S	47	I	A	N	F	74	1	K	W	R
1147	942	GA42B	276.2	N	M	S	47	II	A	N	M	73	3	F	W	R
1148	943	GA43	277	N	L	P	34	I	A	N	M	85	1	F	W	R
1149	944	GA44A	278.1	N	M	S	47	I	A	N	M	91	1	F	W	R
1150	944	GA44B	278.2	N	M	S	47	I	A	N	M	80	2	F	W	R
1151	944	GA44C	278.3	N	M	S	47	I	A	N	M	72	4	F	W	R
1152	944	GA44D	278.4	N	M	S	47	II	A	N	M	70	5	M	W	R
1153	944	GA44E	278.5	N	S	C	72	II	A	N	M	72	3	C	W	R
1154	951	FL1	252	N	M	S	47	I	A	N	F	70	1	M	W	U
1155	952	FL2A	253.1	N	M	S	47	I	A	N	F	69	2	K	W	R
1156	952	FL2B	253.2	N	S	C	70	II	B	N	M	58	6	R	W	U
1157	952	FL2C!	253.3	N	M	S	47	III	A	Y	M	85	6	M	W	U
1158	953	FL3A	254.1	N	M	S	47	I	A	N	M	65	2	F	W	R
1159	953	FL3B!	254.2	N	M	S	47	II	A	Y	M	77	6	F	W	R
1160	954	FL4	254A	N	Rt	C	74	I	B	N	M	56	2	F	W	R
1161	955	FL5A	255.1	N	M	S	47	I	A	N	M	74	2	F	W	R
1162	955	FL5B	255.2	N	M	S	47	II	A	N	M	75	2	O	W	R

Figure 3.1: LAMSAS Base Map

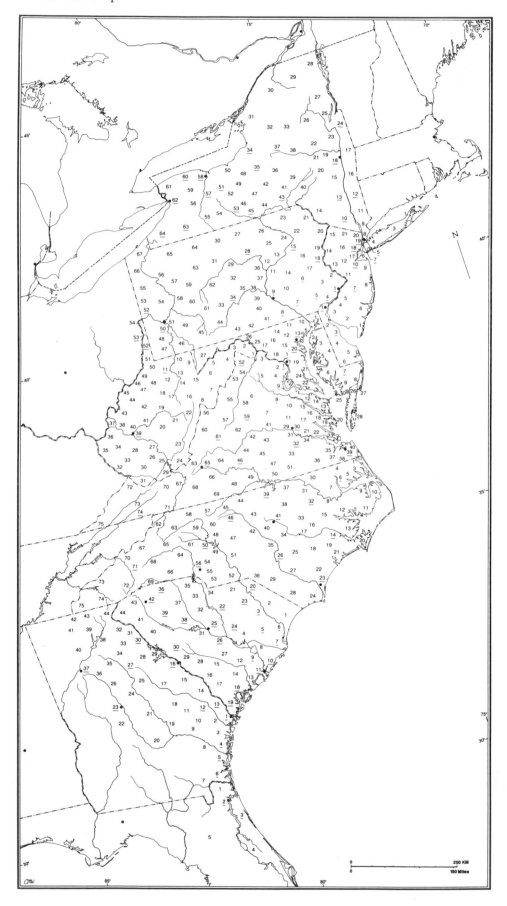

Table of Communities

The Table of Communities contains only three columns per entry: one for county names, one for the old community number (= the part of the Informant ID from the Table of Informants that contains the state abbreviation), and one for the new community number (= Community Number in the Table of Informants). Communities are most often counties; wherever one county was broken into more than one community, more than one community number is assigned to it. Italicized entries among the county names represent major cities; the names of the cities are in many cases not identical with the names of the counties in which they are located, and city boundaries may not constitute a separate and complete LAMSAS community. Specific localities where interviews took place within communities are identified in this handbook only in the informant biographies. Figure 3.1, the LAMSAS base map, illustrates the locations of the 483 LAMSAS communities according to the old state-by-state numbering system.

Abbeville	SC 40	840
Accomack	VA 25/26/27	625/626/627
Adams	PA 41	341
Aiken	SC 29	829
Alachua	FL 5	955
Albany	NY 18	118
Albemarle	VA 59	659
Alexandria	VA 1	601
Allegany	NY 55	155
Allegheny	PA 50/51	350/351
Allendale	SC 16	816
Anderson	SC 41	841
Annapolis	MD 20	570
Anne Arundel	MD 20	570
Anson	NC 52	752
Appomattox	VA 44	644
Arlington	VA 1	601
Armstrong	PA 58	358
Ashe	NC 62	762
Asheville	NC 71	771
Atlanta	GA 37	937
Atlantic	NJ 6	206
Augusta	GA 16	916
Augusta	VA 57	657
Baldwin	GA 24	924
Baltimore	MD 11/12/13	561/562/563
Bamberg	SC 15	815
Barbour	WV 14	414
Barnwell	SC 28	828
Bath	VA 60	660
Beaufort	NC 12	712
Beaufort	SC 18/19	818/819
Beaver	PA 52	352
Bedford	PA 44	344
Bedford	VA 64	664
Bergen	NJ 20	220
Berkeley	SC 8/9	808/809
Berkeley	WV 2	402
Berks	PA 6	306
Bertie	NC 7	707
Bibb	GA 23	923
Bladen	NC 27	727
Blair	PA 33	333
Bland	VA 70	670
Boone	WV 28	428
Bradford	PA 26	326
Braxton	WV 19	419
Bronx	NY 8	108
Brooke	WV 53	453
Brooklyn	NY 5	105
Broome	NY 43	143
Brunswick	NC 24	724
Brunswick	VA 51	651
Bryan	GA 2	902
Buchanan	VA 72	672
Buckingham	VA 42	642
Bucks	PA 2	302
Buffalo	NY 62	162
Bulloch	GA 12	912
Buncombe	NC 71	771
Burke	GA 15	915
Burlington	NJ 7	207
Butler	PA 54	354
Cabarrus	NC 54	754
Cabell	WV 36	436
Caldwell	NC 65	765
Calhoun	SC 26	826
Calhoun	WV 42	442
Calvert	MD 21	571
Cambria	PA 61	361
Camden	GA 6	906
Camden	NJ 5	205
Camden	NC 3	703
Cameron	PA 31	331
Campbell	VA 46	646
Candler	GA 11	911
Cape May	NJ 1	101
Carbon	PA 16	316
Caroline	MD 4	554

County	State	Number	County	State	Number
Caroline	VA 10	610	Davidson	NC 48	748
Carroll	MD 14	564	Dekalb	GA 37	937
Carteret	NC 20	720	Delaware	NY 40	140
Caswell	NC 44	744	Delaware	PA 4	304
Catawba	NC 64	764	Dinwiddie	VA 32/22	632/633
Cattaraugus	NY 63	163	District of Columbia	DC 1	599
Cayuga	NY 48	148	Doddridge	WV 48	448
Cecil	MD 1	551	Dorchester	MD 6	556
Centre	PA 32	332	Dorchester	SC 12	812
Charles	MD 23/24	573/574	*Dover*	DE 3	503
Charles City	VA 21	621	Duplin	NC 18	718
Charleston	SC 10/11/13	810/811/813	Dutchess	NY 12	112
Charleston	WV 39	439	Duval	FL 2	952
Charlotte	NC 56	756	Edgecombe	NC 32	732
Charlton	GA 7	907	Edgefield	SC 30	830
Chautauqua	NY 64	164	Effingham	GA 13	913
Chatham	GA 1	901	Elbert	GA 30	930
Chatham	NC 42	742	Elk	PA 63	363
Chemung	NY 45	145	Emanuel	GA 18	918
Chenango	NY 41	141	Erie	NY 62	162
Cherokee	GA 40	940	Erie	PA 67	367
Cherokee	NC 75	775	Essex	NJ 18	218
Chester	PA 5	305	Essex	NY 27	127
Chester	SC 33	833	Essex	VA 15	615
Chesterfield	SC 21	821	Evans	GA 10	910
Chesterfield	VA 31	631	Fairfax	VA 2	602
Chowan	NC 6	706	Fairfield	SC 32	832
Clarendon	SC 4	804	Fannin	GA 42	942
Clarion	PA 57	357	Fauquier	VA 5	605
Clarke	GA 34	934	Fayette	PA 46	346
Clay	WV 41	441	Fayette	WV 27	427
Clearfield	PA 62	362	Florence	SC 3	803
Cleveland	NC 66	766	Floyd	VA 68	668
Clinton	NY 28	128	Forsyth	NC 60	760
Clinton	PA 29	329	Franklin	GA 32	932
Colleton	SC 14	814	Franklin	NY 29	129
Columbia	NY 16	116	Franklin	NC 38	738
Columbia	PA 13	313	Franklin	PA 42	342
Columbia	SC 25	825	Franklin	VA 66	666
Columbus	NC 28	728	Frederick	MD 16/17	566/567
Cortland	NY 42	142	Frederick	VA 52	652
Craig	VA 63	663	Fulton	GA 37	937
Craven	NC 14	714	Fulton	NY 22	122
Crawford	PA 66	366	Fulton	PA 43	343
Cumberland	NJ 2	202	Garrett	MD 27	577
Cumberland	NC 26	726	Gates	NC 4	704
Cumberland	PA 40	340	Genesee	NY 59	159
Cumberland	VA 43	643	Georgetown	SC 6/7	806/807
Currituck	NC 1/2	701/702	Gilmer	GA 41	941
Dare	NC 10	710	Gloucester	NJ 4	204
Darlington	SC 23	823	Gloucester	VA 19	619
Dauphin	PA 9	309	Glynn	GA 5	905

Goochland	VA 41	641	Kanawha	WV 39/40	439/440
Grant	WV 6	406	Kent	DE 3/4	503/504
Granville	NC 39	739	Kent	MD 2	552
Grayson	VA 71	671	Kershaw	SC 22	822
Greenbrier	WV 23	423	King and Queen	VA 16	616
Greene	GA 27	927	King William	VA 17	617
Greene	NY 15	115	Kings	NY 5	105
Greene	NC 16	716	Lackawanna	PA 22	322
Greene	PA 47	347	Lancaster	PA 7	307
Greene	VA 58	658	Lancaster	SC 34	834
Greenville	SC 42	842	Lancaster	VA 13	613
Guilford	NC 46	746	Laurens	GA 21	921
Halifax	NC 31	731	Laurens	SC 39	839
Halifax	VA 49	649	Lawrence	PA 53	353
Hall	GA 38	938	Lebanon	PA 10	310
Hamilton	NY 26	126	Lee	VA 75	675
Hampshire	WV 4	404	Lehigh	PA 17	317
Hampton	SC 17	817	Lewis	NY 32	132
Hancock	GA 25	925	Lewis	WV 18	418
Hancock	WV 54	454	Lexington	SC 31	831
Hanover	VA 11	611	Liberty	GA 3	903
Harford	MD 10	560	Lincoln	GA 29	929
Harnett	NC 35	735	Lincoln	WV 34	434
Harrisburg	PA 9	309	Livingston	NY 57	157
Harrison	WV 12	412	Logan	WV 33	433
Hart	GA 31	931	Loudoun	VA 3	603
Henrico	VA 29/30	629/630	Louisa	VA 7	607
Henry	VA 69	669	Lumpkin	GA 39	939
Herkimer	NY 33/38	133/138	Lunenburg	VA 47	647
Highland	VA 56	656	Luzerne	PA 15	315
Horry	SC 1	801	Lycoming	PA 28	328
Houston	GA 22	922	*Macon*	GA 23	923
Howard	MD 15	565	Macon	NC 74	774
Hudson	NJ 19	219	Madison	GA 33	933
Hunterdon	NJ 13	213	Madison	NY 36	136
Huntingdon	PA 34	334	Madison	NC 70	770
Hyde	NC 11	711	Madison	VA 6	606
Indiana	PA 60	360	*Manhattan*	NY 7	107
Iredell	NC 61	761	Marion	SC 2	802
Isle of Wight	VA 35	635	Marion	WV 11	411
Jackson	WV 43	443	Marlboro	SC 20	820
Jacksonville	FL 2	952	Marshall	WV 51	451
James City	VA 22	622	Martin	NC 8	708
Jasper	GA 26	926	Mason	WV 37	437
Jefferson	GA 17	917	Mathews	VA 20	620
Jefferson	NY 31	131	McDowell	NC 68	768
Jefferson	PA 59	359	McDowell	WV 31	431
Jefferson	WV 1	401	McIntosh	GA 4	904
Jersey City	NJ 19	219	McKean	PA 64	364
Johnston	NC 34	734	Mecklenburg	NC 55/56	755/756
Jones	NC 19	719	Mecklenburg	VA 50	650
Juniata	PA 38	338	Mercer	NJ 11	211

Mercer	PA 55	355	Pamlico	NC 13	713
Mercer	WV 29	429	Pasquotank	NC 5	705
Middlesex	NJ 10	210	Passaic	NJ 21	221
Middlesex	VA 18	618	Peach	GA 22	922
Mifflin	PA 35	335	Pender	NC 22	722
Mineral	WV 5	405	Pendleton	WV 7/8	407/408
Mingo	WV 32	432	Perquimans	NC 5	705
Mitchell	NC 67	767	Perry	PA 39	339
Monmouth	NJ 9	209	Philadelphia	PA 1	301
Monongalia	WV 10	410	Pickens	SC 43	843
Monroe	NY 58	158	Pike	PA 20	320
Monroe	PA 19	319	Pitt	NC 15	715
Monroe	WV 24	424	*Pittsburgh*	PA 51	351
Montgomery	GA 19	919	Pittsylvania	VA 48	648
Montgomery	MD 18	568	Pleasants	WV 46	446
Montgomery	NY 21	121	Pocahontas	WV 22	422
Montgomery	NC 51	751	Polk	NC 69	769
Montgomery	PA 3	303	Potter	PA 30	330
Montour	PA 12	312	Preston	WV 9	409
Morgan	WV 3	403	Prince Edward	VA 45	645
Morris	NJ 16	216	Prince George	VA 34	634
Nansemond	VA 37	637	Prince Georges	MD 19	569
Nassau	FL 1	951	Prince William	VA 4	604
Nassau	NY 4	104	Princess Anne	VA 40	640
Nelson	VA 62	662	Pulaski	VA 67	667
Newark	NJ 18	218	Putnam	NY 11	111
Newberry	SC 38	838	Putnam	WV 38	438
New Castle	DE 1/2	501/502	Queen Annes	MD 3	553
New Hanover	NC 23	723	Queens	NY 5	105
New York	NY 7	107	Rabun	GA 44	944
New York City	NY 5/6/7/8	105/106/107/108	*Raleigh*	NC 41	741
Niagara	NY 61	161	Raleigh	WV 26	426
Nicholas	WV 20	420	Randolph	NC 47	747
Norfolk	VA 38/39	638/639	Randolph	WV 16	416
Northampton	NC 30	730	Rensselaer	NY 17	117
Northampton	PA 18	318	Richland	SC 25	825
Northampton	VA 28	628	Richmond	GA 16	916
Northumberland	PA 11	311	Richmond	NY 6	106
Northumberland	VA 14	614	*Richmond*	VA 30	630
Ocean	NJ 8	208	Ritchie	WV 47	447
Oconee	SC 44	844	Roanoke	VA 65	665
Ohio	WV 52	452	Robeson	NC 29	729
Oneida	NY 37	137	*Rochester*	NY 58	158
Onondaga	NY 35	135	Rockbridge	VA 61	661
Onslow	NC 21	721	Rockdale	GA 36	936
Ontario	NY 51	151	Rockingham	NC 45	745
Orange	NY 10	110	Rockingham	VA 55	655
Orange	NC 43	743	Rowan	NC 49/50	749/750
Orangeburg	SC 27	827	Russell	VA 73	673
Orleans	NY 60	160	Salem	NJ 3	203
Oswego	NY 34	134	Sampson	NC 25	725
Otsego	NY 39	139	Saratoga	NY 23	123

Savannah	GA 1	901	Union	NC 53	753
Schenectady	NY 19	119	Union	PA 36	336
Schoharie	NY 20	120	Union	SC 37	837
Schuyler	NY 46	146	Upshur	WV 17	417
Schuylkill	PA 14	314	Venango	PA 56	356
Scotland	NC 36	736	Volusia	FL 4	954
Screven	GA 14	914	Wake	NC 40/41	740/741
Seneca	NY 49	149	Walton	GA 35	935
Shenandoah	VA 53	653	Warren	NJ 14	214
Snyder	PA 37	337	Warren	NY 25	125
Somerset	MD 9	559	Warren	NC 37	737
Somerset	NJ 12	212	Warren	PA 65	365
Somerset	PA 45	345	Warren	VA 54	654
Southampton	VA 36	636	Warwick	VA 24	624
Spartanburg	SC 36	836	*Washington*	DC 1	599
Spotsylvania	VA 8	608	Washington	MD 25/26	575/576
Stafford	VA 9	609	Washington	NY 24	124
Steuben	NY 53/54	153/154	Washington	PA 48	348
St. Augustine	FL 3	953	Washington	VA 74	674
St. Johns	FL 3	953	Wayne	GA 8	908
St. Lawrence	NY 30	130	Wayne	NY 50	150
St. Marys	MD 22	572	Wayne	NC 17	717
Stokes	NC 57	757	Wayne	PA 21	321
Suffolk	NY 1/2/3	101/102/103	Wayne	WV 35	435
Sullivan	NY 14	114	Webster	WV 21	421
Sullivan	PA 25	325	Westchester	NY 9	109
Summers	WV 25	425	Westmoreland	PA 49	349
Sumter	SC 24	824	Westmoreland	VA 12	612
Surry	NC 58	758	Wetzel	WV 50	450
Susquehanna	PA 23	323	Wicomico	MD 7	557
Sussex	DE 5/6	505/506	Wilkes	GA 28	928
Sussex	NJ 15	215	Wilkes	NC 63	763
Swain	NC 73	773	Williamsburg	SC 5	805
Talbot	MD 5	555	*Wilmington*	DE 1	501
Tattnall	GA 9	909	*Wilmington*	NC 23	723
Taylor	WV 13	413	Wilson	NC 33	733
Telfair	GA 20	920	Wirt	WV 44	444
Tioga	NY 44	144	Wood	WV 45	445
Tioga	PA 27	327	Worcester	MD 8	558
Tompkins	NY 47	147	Wyoming	NY 56	156
Transylvania	NC 72	772	Wyoming	PA 24	324
Trenton	NJ 11	211	Wyoming	WV 30	430
Tucker	WV 15	415	Yadkin	NC 59	759
Tyler	WV 49	449	Yates	NY 52	152
Tyrrell	NC 9	709	York	PA 8	308
Ulster	NY 13	113	York	SC 35	835
Union	GA 43	943	York	VA 23	623
Union	NJ 17	217			

Chapter 4: Work Sheets and Collection of Information

The first work sheets for systematic field investigation of North American English were developed by Kurath in 1929–31. After six weeks' use in the field they were modified and slightly abridged; it is this version that is published in the *Handbook of the Linguistic Geography of New England* (Kurath et al. 1939).

For Lowman's preliminary investigation of the South Atlantic States (1933–35) Kurath drafted a much longer set of work sheets (marked P in the tables below, Preliminary South Atlantic), adding to the New England version several kinds of items: a) those like *vase* and *played truant* which had been dropped from the final New England version but which promised to be productive; b) items that previous investigations of Southern speech had found regionally or socially significant, e.g. *house* and *houses* for positional allophones of /au/, names for the peanut and the dragonfly, designations for poor whites and unskilled part-time preachers. Kurath deleted items unproductive in the South and reduced the proportion of grammatical items. This final Southern version (marked S, South Atlantic) was used by Lowman from southern New Jersey through North Carolina, and later by McDavid in South Carolina, Georgia, and northeastern Florida.

For the Middle Atlantic States, Kurath deleted some of the items of peculiarly Southern significance (including several grammatical items associated with the speech of African-Americans), restored such New England items as the *stone boat* and *sled*, and added some items associated with regional culture, such as *hay barrack* in the Hudson Valley. This version (marked M, Middle Atlantic) was used for New York, New Jersey 6a and 7–21, Pennsylvania, and West Virginia 8–45.

A slightly modified version which preserved features of both the Middle Atlantic and South Atlantic work sheets was used by Pedersen and his students in interviews in the 1960s and 1970s (marked C, Combined).

Field workers occasionally modified the work sheets. Thus Lowman added *frowning* and *now* as pronunciation items in the South Atlantic States, affirmative *anymore* ("mules are scarce *anymore*")

as a syntactic item in the Middle Atlantic. McDavid added *bed sink* 'bed-alcove off the kitchen' in Upstate New York. Furthermore, though the primary response was clearly indicated and always sought, field workers often probed for related items, as Lowman for varieties of squash, McDavid for types of cornbread.

Hans Kurath's Directions for Field Work

[The following instructions from Kurath to his field workers were first used in the New England survey (see Kurath et al. 1943:48–50) and remained appropriate for LAMSAS. They are here reproduced from a stencil copy initialled by Kurath. *Eds.*]

1. Beware of preconceived notions. Do not be misled by what you know, but trust your ear and eye. Rejoice in discovering new facts, and in having your "expectations" disappointed. Alertness and keenness of perception are the important factors in this work.

2. The investigator must take care to secure natural, unguarded responses. Slow and emphatic utterance differs from normal speech, especially insofar as normally weak syllables are concerned. For this reason the interview should be carried on as far as possible in the form of a conversation. If the desired expression is first uttered in isolation, the subject should be led or directed to utter it in context, under normal stress and at the usual speed. A question such as "How would you say it if you were talking to your wife or a neighbor?" often sets the subject right.

3. If the isolation and the "bound" form differ, the context of the latter should be written down either in phonetic notation or in the conventional spelling whenever it deviates from that given in the work sheets. Phonetic notation should be used if the pronunciation of the desired expression seems to be influenced by the surrounding sounds.

4. Never urge your subject to speak plainly. If the first response is not caught on the wing and you must ask for a repetition of the utterance, make

sure whether the response is natural, or emphatic and over-careful. The natural response should be secured either by a direct request (i.e. by asking "How would you say it if you were talking to your wife, neighbor, etc.?") or by leading up to it from a new angle. In certain cases it will be better to drop the matter temporarily and to take it up at a later meeting.

5. Do not suggest a response by asking "Do you say so-and-so?" until all other methods are exhausted. If the response is secured by direct suggestion, prefix *sug.* to it. The approach should be indirect, i.e. thru the idea.

Do not press too hard for an answer. If the subject lacks the information ask someone else in the house or in the community. *All responses secured from auxiliary subjects* must be starred, and the subject should be identified in the right-hand column.

6. Do not explain to your subjects in the course of your interview in what respects his pronunciation differs from yours or someone else's, since it may lead to conscious avoidance of normal speech. Defer all explanations until the entire interview has been completed. A courteous promise to this effect should satisfy the subject and serve to hold his interest.

7. The careful selection of authorities for the various generations and the diverse social and racial elements is of supreme importance.

The middle-aged generation (40-60) must be represented in all communities. If either the older or the younger generation differs markedly from the middle-aged generation, for whatever reason, it must be represented in our survey. The pronunciation of "old-timers" is of the greatest interest. Your "authorities" will often tell you how their parents used to speak, or what new expressions their children use. All such information must be put down in the right-hand column. It is very valuable.

A representative of the oldest families must be secured in all communities, preferably a middle-aged or an aged person.

In all communities a representative of the lower classes must be studied; in rural communities a simple but intelligent farmer, in urban communities a working man or a storekeeper.

8. Persons who have traveled a good deal or have attended college outside of their section of the country must be avoided.

Persons who speak two dialects (say, an urban and a rustic dialect) may furnish important leads, but they are not desirable authorities unless they command both equally well and are in the habit of setting one off against the other. They are also apt to be opinionated. The ideal authority is one who cannot help talking the way he does.

Concerning the Handling of the Blank Books

[The "blank books" were bound notebooks containing blank, lined pages, with a vertical line dividing the right from the left sides of each page, in which the field worker was to enter biographical information and the responses and comments of the informant. Each book held twice as many pages as required for the interview: field workers used carbon paper to make an instant second copy as they wrote. The pages were perforated at the binding, and the original and carbon-copy pages were torn out and separately filed at the editorial office. *Eds.*]

I.

1. The name of the village, town, county, and state as well as the full name of the subject should be entered both in conventional spelling and in phonetic notation.

2. Education: Formal schooling and extent of reading (newspapers, periodicals, fiction, scientific and technical literature).

3. Social contacts: Working companions, business contacts, intimate friends; membership in church, club and other organizations; travel.

4. Family history: Birth place of father and mother, cultural and social standing, ancestry. If the family history has been published or is accessible in manuscript, give bibliographical information.

5. General character of the community: Number of inhabitants: racial elements with an estimate of their size; industrial, residential or rural; historical or antiquarian society, library schools.

6. Character sketch: Alertness and intelligence, extent and accuracy of information, attitude toward the investigator and his task, naturalness or guardedness in utterance, interest in 'improving' the language.

II.

1. All records must be made in duplicate. Use only first-class thin carbon paper, which will be sent to you from headquarters, so that the carbon copy will be absolutely clear and easy to read.

2. The left-hand column is for the phonetic record, the right-hand column for comments and definitions.

3. Number the pages while you record. This procedure has the advantage of giving you a control, but it will require that you write down chance observations on points that come further on in the questionnaire in a separate notebook. Optional.

4. In order to speed up the interview and to avoid irritation on the part of the subject, it will be well for you to go over the parts of the work sheets that are to be handled in a particular session with great care before confronting the subject. After the first interview you will be sufficiently familiar with the personality of your subject and his range of information and interests to be able to formulate your questions beforehand with the purpose of securing the desired responses in the quickest and surest way. Many of your subjects will be busy men and women and will have little patience with "floundering." Moreover, our time and our manpower is limited and we must strive to make the best of it. After each interview the record should be checked over as soon as possible so that errors may be detected and points singled out for further inquiry and definition. If the record seems unsatisfactory, the subject's usage should be verified during the following interview. *However, the original record must not be changed*; corrections and explanations should be offered in the right-hand column.

5. It is of the greatest importance to record the subject's attitude (hesitation, doubt, amusement, etc.) as well as illuminating comments offered by him. The observer's reaction is of equal importance; uncertainty of perception, doubt concerning the genuineness of the response, certainty in the perception of surprising responses, etc. The signs that should be used are listed on a separate sheet.

6. A journal is indispensable. A looseleaf booklet which can be conveniently carried in the coat pocket will best serve the purpose. One section of it should be used for interviewing, observations on the characteristics of the speech and the personality of these subjects [*sic*]. Entries concerning the personal history, the family history, and the nature of the community should be made day by day and a summary of the most important facts should be given in the blank books when the transcript has been completed.

Another section should be reserved for recording engagements; to prevent loss of time and to avoid confusion, it is important to date up subjects in advance.

A third section should contain a separate leaf for each tentatively selected community on which you may enter the names and addresses of informants, possible subjects, and information concerning the community or prospective subjects.

This pocket notebook should be your inseparable companion. — Hans Kurath, c. 1935.

Work Sheet Tables

Four tables are presented here as finding aids for the material in the work sheets. All questions from each version of the work sheets are included in the tables here, though not all of them will be entered as separate computer files (see Chapter 7). Since only seventy informants responded to questions that were limited to the Preliminary South Atlantic States work sheets, these responses have been combined with the files to which they are most closely related. In some cases, these have been labelled as inappropriate responses (i.e. responses that do not match the questionnaire cue), for instance *rented a room* in the file for 'living room'. In other cases, the target of the question was similar enough to allow the responses to the preliminary work sheets to be merged with the other responses, e.g. *chunk* in the file for 'backlog'.

Work Sheets by Topic suggests the general flow of the questionnaire by topic.

Work Sheets by Headword is a detailed alphabetical listing of words used to identify question types in the work sheets. This list is not the same as an index of the responses elicited, which cannot be prepared until all LAMSAS data is entered on computer. The headwords do, however, suggest some of the likely contents of LAMSAS data files, since they either represent the expected response to the question (for pronunciation questions) or a common lexical or grammatical feature which categorizes expected responses. Each headword compound or phrase has been exploded so that the table makes reference to every separate word among the headwords from the final copy of the worksheets (the articles *a*, *an*, and *the* are not listed separately unless the target of a question). For instance, for the headword phrase *to his stomach* (080.4), there are three entries in the list that explode the phrase—"to his stomach", "his stomach [to ..]", and "stomach [to his ..]"—but there are no entries corresponding to the variant phrases actually elicited from informants (e.g. *in his stomach, at his stomach*). The next column is a brief indication of the context in which the question was meant to have been posed (field workers did not use fixed, prearranged questions). There follows a suggestion of whether the responses for the question are likely to contain primarily pronunciation (p), grammatical (g), or lexical (l) variation. Finally there are two number codes, the first representing the page and line of the work sheet (e.g. 014.7 = page 14, line 7); numbers without a decimal point and line number generally indicate questions restricted to the preliminary South Atlantic States version of the work sheets. The second code gives the number of the list manuscript in which the responses to the question were intended to be included.

Work Sheets by Work Sheet Number reproduces the page and line of the work sheet (e.g. 001.2 = page 1, line 2), a designation of the version of the work sheets in which the question was asked if elicitation was limited to a particular version, and finally the headword from the final copy of the worksheets. For questions with limited elicitation, the letters P, S, and M refer to the Preliminary South Atlantic, the South Atlantic, and the Middle Atlantic work sheets, respectively. The letter X indicates questions systematically asked only by Raven McDavid (i.e. in interviews in Upstate New York, South Carolina, Georgia, and Florida).

Work Sheets by List Manuscript Number indicates the number of the list manuscript and the page and line designation from the work sheets, followed by the headword for the list manuscript (see Chapter 6). The advantage of this table is that list manuscripts were planned according to general topics, such as *Geography* or *Sport and Play*, and thus the table offers a breakdown of questions by topic which is not restricted by work sheet sequence. This table includes all lists as originally planned, though not all have been or will be completed. The plan sometimes called for separate lists for different response types elicited by the same question (e.g. *bog* and *swamp* for 029.5). The organizing principle behind

the database, one table per question, requires that such lists be combined in the computer files (see Chapter 7).

Work Sheets by Topic

1.1–1A.6	numerals
1A.7–5.2	expressions of time
5.3–7.5	the weather
7.6–12.1	the dwelling
12.2–13.8	*verb forms*
14.1–20.6	vehicles, utensils, implements
20.7–24.5	vehicles, implements
24.6–25.7	*verb forms*
26.1–29.2	clothing and bedding
29.3–32.1	topography, roads
32.2–32.7	*prepositions*
33.1–39.4	domestic animals, calls to animals
39.5–41.1	*adverbs*
41.2–42.1	farm crops
42.2–44.2	*pronouns*
49.3–51.8	food, cooking, mealtime
52.1–53.3	*pronouns*
54.1–57.3	fruits, vegetables
57.4–58.7	*verb phrases*
59.1–61.3	animals
61.4–62.8	trees, berries
63.1–66.7	the family
67.1–69.8	persons, names, nicknames
70.1–71.2	*adverbs, conjunctions*
71.3–73.1	the human body
73.2–75.7	personal characteristics, emotions
76.1–80.5	illness and death
81.1–85.8	social life and institutions
86.1–87.8	names of states, cities, countries
88.1–88.5	*noun forms, conjunctions*
89.1–90.3	religion, superstition
90.4–94.1	*adverbs, exclamations, salutations*
94.2–102.8	various activities
103.1–104.10	miscellaneous expressions

Work Sheets by Headword

***	call to calves	l	037.6	257.0
***	call to chickens	l	038.5	264.0
***	call to cows from pasture	l	037.5	255.0
***	call to cows to stand still	l	037.5	256.0
***	call to hogs	l	038.3	263.0
***	call to horses from pasture	l	037.8	259.0
***	calls to oxen, etc. in plowing	l	037.7	258.0
***	call to sheep	l	038.4	262.0
***	grunt of affirmation	p	103.7	628.0
***	grunt of negation	p	103.8	629.0
***	/i/ for he, she, it, they	g	042	
***	/m/ for him, her, it, them	g	042	
***	miscellaneous containers	l	019.2	180.0
***	miscellaneous boats	l	024.5	215.0
***	other bread from wheat flour	l	044.4	335.1
***	other bread from corn meal	l	044.7	340.0
***	pet names for children	l	064	
a-raring	he's .. to get you	g	075	
across	I ran .. him (met by chance)	l	032.6	477.0
across [clear ..]	it goes .. the bed	l	028.9	397.0
across [swam ..]	he ..	g	095.6	615.0
actress		l	069.1	498.0
address	will you .. this letter	p	100.7	705.0
address	noun	p	100	705.1
afire [a house ..]	he ran like ..	l	097	
afraid		l	074.3	520.0
after him	named ..	l	032.7	456.0
after next [Sunday ..]		l	003.7	094.0
after writing	I'm .. a letter (= 'have written')	g	089	706.2
after [look ..]	she has to .. the baby	l	065	457.3
afternoon	before supper	l	002.4	101.0
again [come back ..]		l	093.1	481.0
ago [year ..]	a ..	p	005.2	109.0
ague	define	l	077	
ain't done nothing [I ..]	multiple negation	g	040.5	771.0
ain't I?		g	025.4	721.0
ain't you?	you are going, ..? (tag)	g	012.6	721.1
Alabama		p	086.6	015.0
all at once		p	001a.5	085.0
all excited	he was .. (with expectation)	l	075	
all gone	the oranges are ..	p	055.2	596.0
almost	it's .. midnight	l	070.1	763.0
always		p	103.4	758.0
am I going to	.. get some	g	024.7	722.0
am [as I ..]	he's as tall ..	g	042.6	643.0
American		p	069.2	505.0
an apple [give me ..]	indef. article before vowel	p	051.7	324.0
an old man	indef. article before vowel	p	051	
and by [by ..]	she'll be all right ..	p	076.2	760.0
and cigarettes [cigars ..]		p	057.3	375.0

and him not there	I wouldn't go to his house ..	g	088	
and him [me ..]		g	042.4	648.0
and his overcoat on his arm	he went out ..	g	088	
and hungry [good ..]	I'm ..	l	090	
and I [you ..]	.. are going	g	042.2	646.0
and ironing [washing ..]	laundry	l	010.5	415.0
and laughing [singing ..]	they were .. (a- prefix)	g	057.4	476.0
and order [law ..]		p	085.7	590.0
and pepper [salt ..]		p	051.7	344.0
and still [but yet ..]	.. I won't go	l	105	
andirons		l	008.3	382.0
angry	sudden outburst? habitual?	l	075.2	519.0
another chance [give me ..]		p	099.2	604.0
answer [an ..]	I expect ..	p	100.6	605.0
any [I don't care for ..]	to decline food	l	049.7	374.0
anymore	we buy our bread .. (affirmative)	l	104.6	758.2
anywhere		g	040.2	757.0
appendicitis		p	080.1	552.0
apple [give me an ..]	indef. article before vowel	p	051.7	324.0
April	other months	p	001a.7	089.0
apron		p	026.3	424.0
are they going to	.. get some	g	024.7	722.0
are thrashed [oats ..]		g	042.1	160.0
are you? [How ..]	greetings to friend, (intonation)	l	092.7	478.0
are [there ..]	.. lots of them	g	025.2	724.0
are [those cabbages ..]	.. big	g	055a.1	303.0
Arkansas		p	086.8	020.0
arm [and his overcoat on his ..]	he went out ..	g	088	
armful of wood		l	019.8	159.0
as good [twice ..]		p	001a.6	086.0
as he is	as tall ..	g	043.1	644.0
as I am	he's as tall ..	g	042.6	643.0
as I want to	I don't know ..	g	088.2	787.0
as not [like ..]	he'll have trouble ..	g	041.1	769.0
ashes [white ..]		p	008.8	385.0
Asheville		p	087.3	024.0
Asia		p	087	033.1
ask	I'll .. him	p	104.1	704.0
ask for it? [How much do you ..]	in store	l	094	597.1
asked	I .. him	p	104.2	704.0
at a loss	he had to sell it ..	l	094.5	598.0
at home	he isn't ..	g	032.2	461.0
at once [all ..]		p	001a.5	085.0
at the bell [listen ..]		l	105	
at [up ..]	I was .. the Browns'	l	082.6	775.0
ate	we .. at six o'clock	p	048.4	683.0
Atlanta		p	087	030.1
attic		l	009.7	402.0
Aunt Sarah		p	068.1	445.0
aunt [your ..]		p	067.8	444.0
automobile	can you drive an ..	l	023.6	218.0
awfully	it's .. cold	l	090	

awkward	in appearance	l	073.3	512.0
awkward fellow	that ..	l	073	
axle		p	021	
baby carriage		l	064.4	611.0
back again [come ..]		l	093.1	481.0
backlog		l	008.5	383.0
backward		p	040	
backwoodsman	a .. (neutral, jocular, derogatory)	l	069.8	500.0
bacon	sliced	l	046.6	357.0
bad with [got in ..]	he .. me	l	101	622.3
badly	he's feeling ..	g	039	
bag [paper ..]		l	019.6	182.0
baker's bread	homemade bread and ..	l	045.1	338.0
ballad	ever for hymn?	l	089.8	473.0
Baltimore		p	087.1	022.0
bank barn	in ground	l	014	
Baptist		p	089.1	569.0
barbed wire fence		p	016.3	144.0
barn	incl. compounds	p	014.2	128.0
barn [bank ..]	in ground	l	014	
barnyard		l	015.5	140.0
barrel	container for meal/flour	p	019.1	178.0
barrow		p	035.4	241.0
basket	clothes ..	p	020.1	417.0
bastard	normal, euphemistic, jocular terms	l	065.7	454.0
bath towel		l	018.5	173.0
bawl	of calf being weaned	l	036.2	229.0
be glad [we shall ..]	.. to see you	g	081	
be you going	(finite be)	g	026	723.0
be [I shall ..]	.. disappointed if you don't	g	081	
be [used to ..]	she .. afraid	g	074.4	749.0
beans [lima ..]		l	055a.3	309.0
beans [shell ..]	to ..	l	055a.2	311.0
beans [string ..]		l	055a.4	310.0
beard		p	071.5	531.0
beatinest	he is the .. fellow	l	066	
beautiful		p	089.7	506.0
because	I like it .. it tastes good	l	088.5	784.0
bed [in ..]	he's still ..	l	076	
bed [laid in ..]	he .. all morning	g	097.1	691.0
bedspread		l	028.7	393.0
beef [dried ..]		l	046	
been thinking [I've ..]		g	013.6	726.0
before last [Sunday ..]		l	003.6	095.0
began	he .. to talk	g	102.2	670.0
behind the door	the broom is ..	l	010.4	777.0
beholden	I'm not .. to anybody	l	057.5	671.0
bell [listen at the ..]		l	105	
belly bumper	coast lying down; hit water flat	l	095.4	610.0
belongs to	he .. be careful (= should)	g	058.1	746.1
best man		l	082.3	468.0
better [some ..]	he is ..	l	076	

big to-do	social affair	l	082	
biscuits	a pan of ..	g	044.5	336.0
bit [e'er a ..]	not see any more trouble, ..	l	040	
bitten	by a dog	g	033.3	672.0
blew		g	006.3	673.0
blocks	I live three .. from here	g	085	
blood pudding		l	047.1	360.2
boar	normal, farmers' term, polite	l	035.3	240.0
boat [stone ..]	for removing stones from field	l	021.8	201.0
boil	discharging sore	l	077.5	554.0
boiled eggs		p	046.1	347.0
bolster	large pillow	l	028.9	395.0
borrow		p	095.1	601.0
Boston		p	087	030.1
both of us		g	042.3	647.0
boyfriend	her ..	l	081.3	458.0
boys [those ..]	it was ..	g	052.1	660.0
bracelet		p	028.3	428.0
branch	small, fresh water	l	030.5	047.0
bread [baker's ..]	homemade bread and ..	l	045.1	338.0
bread [wheat ..]	in loaves	l	044.3	335.0
bridesmaid		l	082.4	469.0
bring [go ..]	.. me a knife	g	098.3	185.0
bristles	stiff hair on hog's back	p	035.6	242.0
broken	the glass is ..	g	048.8	674.0
broom		p	010.4	186.0
brought		g	027.4	675.0
brush		p	022.2	187.0
buck fever		l	077	
bucket		l	017.2	161.0
bucket [dinner ..]		l	017	161.0
bug [lightning ..]		l	060a.3	282.0
bulge	the pockets ..	p	027.7	422.0
bulk [in ..]	we bought our groceries ..	p	051.5	594.0
bull	normal, farmers' term, polite	l	033.4	225.0
bullfrog		l	060.2	272.0
bumper [belly ..]	coast lying down; hit water flat	l	095.4	610.0
buried me [I ..]	.. a son	g	078	568.1
burlap sack	cloth	l	019.7	183.0
burned off	it's .. (of fog)	l	006	123.1
burr	walnut ..	l	054.7	331.0
burst	past	g	018.7	676.0
bushels	forty ..	g	041.8	156.0
but yet and still	.. I won't go	l	105	
butcher		p	046.8	592.0
by and by	she'll be all right ..	p	076.2	760.0
by the time I get there	church will be over ..	l	089.9	762.0
cabbages are [those ..]	.. big	g	055a.1	303.0
calf		p	033.7	227.0
California		p	086	020.2
calm [keep ..]		p	075.4	522.0
calve	Daisy is going to ..	l	033.8	228.0

came	he .. over to see me	g	102.4	677.0
can	I .. do it; unstressed	p	057.6	742.0
can [I sure ..]		p	091.3	625.0
can [than I ..]	he can do it better ..	g	043.2	645.0
can't [I ..]	stressed	p	057.7	741.0
Canada		p	087	033.3
canal	drainage, transport	p	030.2	048.0
Captain	.. Smith	p	068	
car [street ..]		l	085	
care for any [I don't ..]	to decline food	l	049.7	374.0
care [he doesn't ..]		g	013.1	733.0
careless		p	074.6	514.0
Carolina [North ..]		p	086.4	012.0
Carolina [South ..]		p	086.4	012.0
carriage [baby ..]		l	064.4	611.0
carried	I .. a bag of meal	l	098.1	198.0
cartridge		p	022.4	192.0
castrate		l	036.1	247.0
catch	.. the ball	p	098.5	620.0
catty-cornered	at intersection	l	085.1	587.0
cattywampus	furniture at an angle	l	085.2	587.1
caught	who .. it	g	098.6	678.0
caught a cold	he ..	g	076.3	543.0
cemetery		l	078.8	567.0
certainly	strong affirmation	l	091.1	626.0
chair		p	008.9	377.0
chance [give me another ..]		p	099.2	604.0
Charleston		p	087.2	025.0
chat	they used to .. for hours	l	100	603.2
cheese is [most ..]	.. round	p	047	
cheese [cottage ..]		l	047.4	353.0
cherry tree		p	062.1	289.0
chest		p	072.4	532.0
chew		p	050.2	370.0
Chicago		p	087.5	026.0
chicken coop		l	036.8	138.0
children		l	064.3	439.0
children [head of ..]	two ..	g	055a.6	302.0
chimney		p	008.1	386.0
china		p	017.1	167.0
chipmunk		l	059.8	267.0
chittlings	intestines	p	037.3	246.0
chore time		l	037.4	253.0
Christmas [Merry ..]		l	093.2	482.0
chronically ill	he is ..	l	075	
chum	same sex	l	066	
chunk	split wood for a stove	l	008	
cigars and cigarettes		p	057.3	375.0
Cincinnati		p	087.4	028.0
circuit rider		l	067	
Civil War		l	085.6	591.0
clabber	curdled milk	l	047.3	352.0

clam [hard ..]		l	060	
clapboards		l	011.2	409.0
class		p	083	
clean up		l	010	186.1
clear across	it goes .. the bed	l	028.9	397.0
cleared	we .. the land	g	041.4	150.0
clearing up		l	005.4	112.0
cliff		p	031.2	043.0
climbed	he .. a tree	g	096.3	679.0
clingstone	.. peach	l	054.3	320.0
closet	built in	l	009.5	389.0
cloth [file ..]	damp cloth for wiping floor	l	010.8	186.2
clothes [here's your ..]		g	025.1	413.0
clouding up		l	005.5	113.0
clouds		p	005.6	113.3
coal hod		l	023.1	181.0
coast	the boys .. down the hill	l	095.3	609.0
coat		p	027.1	419.0
cobbler	deep fruit pie	l	047.6	345.0
coffee [make some ..]	I'll ..	l	048.6	366.0
coffin		l	079.1	566.0
cog wheel		p	022	
cold [caught a ..]	he ..	g	076.3	543.0
college		p	083.7	578.0
Colonel	.. Brown	p	068.4	491.0
come back again		l	093.1	481.0
come cooler weather	we'll go hunting ..	g	058	
common	complimentary sense?	l	073	
cooler weather [come ..]	we'll go hunting ..	g	058	
coop [chicken ..]		l	036.8	138.0
Cooper [Mrs. ..]	slow, fast	p	067.5	488.0
core	apple ..	l	054.5	325.0
cork	for bottle	l	020.4	175.0
corn crib		l	014.3	133.0
corn [sweet ..]	grown to be eaten on cob	l	056.2	312.0
cornbread	large cakes	l	044.6	339.0
costs	it .. too much	p	094.6	597.0
cottage cheese		l	047.4	353.0
cough	he has a ..	p	076.5	544.0
could [might ..]	I .. do it	g	058.7	745.0
county seat		l	085.4	588.0
couples	two ..	g	083	
courting her	he is .. (normal, jocular terms)	l	081.1	462.0
cow		p	033.5	226.0
cow stable	separate, in barn	l	015.1	135.0
cowpen	for milking cows in field	l	015.2	136.0
creek	tidal stream	l	030.3	045.0
creek	small, fresh water	l	030.5	045.0
creeps	the baby .. on the floor	l	096.2	618.0
crib [corn ..]		l	014.3	133.0
crop	a big ..	p	041.3	153.0
crop [second ..]	of hay	l	041.5	152.0

crouch	.. down	l	096.4	617.0
crowd [the whole ..]	jocular, disparaging	l	082.8	475.0
cup	tin ..	l	016	
curse [don't ..]	don't .. like that	p	092	
cut it half in two		l	105	
dad	normal, familiar	l	063.5	431.0
dairy	store milk/butter; commercial?	p	015.4	134.0
damn it!	strong oath	l	092.1	637.0
dance	a ..	l	083.1	471.0
Daniel	.. Webster	p	067	
dare go [you don't ..]		g	058.2	743.0
darn it!	mild oath	l	092.1	638.0
dauber [dirt ..]		p	060a.6	285.0
daughter		p	064.7	437.0
day [fine ..]	a ..	l	005.3	111.0
day [gloomy ..]		l	005	113.2
day [good ..]	meeting, parting	p	002.5	103.0
dead [done ..]	he is ..	g	057.9	737.0
deaf		p	077.3	546.0
Detroit		p	087	030.1
devil	neutral, jocular terms	l	090.1	574.0
dew	we had a ..	p	007.4	126.0
did	he .. it last night	g	102	734.1
didn't used to	she .. do that	g	074.5	750.0
died	neutral, veiled, crude terms	l	078.5	561.1
died from [he ..]		l	078.7	561.0
digest	it's hard to ..	p	050	
dinner bucket		l	017	161.0
diphtheria		p	079.7	551.0
directly	she'll be all right ..	l	076	760.1
dirt dauber		p	060a.6	285.0
dish towel	for drying	l	018.4	172.0
dishcloth	for washing	l	018.3	171.0
dishes [wash the ..]		p	018.1	169.0
dived	he .. in	g	095.7	616.0
do it [I ..]		g	012.7	730.0
do it [I won't ..]		g	058.5	751.0
do she smell it	Lord help me ..	g	088	
do you ask for it? [How much ..]	in store	l	094	597.1
do you do? [How ..]	to stranger (intonation)	l	092.8	479.0
do you?	you don't think so, ..?	g	013.2	729.0
do [does he ..]	what ..	g	012.8	731.0
does he do	what ..	g	012.8	731.0
does it [he ..]		g	012.7	730.0
does [he ..]	stressed	g	012.9	732.0
doesn't care [he ..]		g	013.1	733.0
dog		p	033.1	248.0
don't care for any [I ..]	to decline food	l	049.7	374.0
don't curse	don't .. like that	p	092	
don't dare go [you ..]		g	058.2	743.0
Don't I know it!		l	013.3	735.0
don't know [I ..]	.. as I want to	p	088.2	786.0

don't pay him no mind	don't pay him .. (=attention)	g	105	
don't remember	I .. that	l	100.4	712.1
don't worry		p	079.5	542.0
Don't you touch it!		l	098.2	734.0
done dead	he is ..	g	057.9	737.0
done nothing [I ain't ..]	multiple negation	g	040.5	771.0
done worked [I ..]		g	057.8	736.0
door [behind the ..]	the broom is ..	l	010.4	777.0
door [shut the ..]		l	011.1	405.0
doubletree		l	021.3	206.0
doughnut		l	045.2	337.0
down in	he lives .. Columbia	l	082.7	774.0
down [going ..]	the wind is ..	l	007.3	115.0
down [kneeled ..]	she ..	g	096.5	710.0
down [knock you ..]	I'll (=introduce)	l	105	
down [lie ..!]	to a dog	l	033	
down [lie ..]	I have to ..	g	096.6	540.0
down [like to fell ..]	I .. (= 'almost')	l	070.2	684.0
down [sat ..]	he ..	g	049.4	697.0
down [sit ..!]	invitation to dinner	l	049.3	697.0
down [turned him ..]	she ..	l	082.1	466.0
dragged		g	021.5	707.0
dragonfly		l	060a.4	283.0
draining	they are .. the marshes	p	030.1	038.0
drank	I .. it	g	049.1	680.0
dreamed	I .. all night	g	097.2	708.0
dress up	she likes to ..	l	028.1	414.0
dresser		l	009.2	391.0
drew	he .. it out	g	104.4	681.0
dried beef		l	046	
driven		g	011.4	682.0
drizzle		l	006.7	122.0
drizzling		l	006	122.1
drought		l	007.1	124.0
drove		g	011.3	682.0
drowned	he was ..	g	096.1	563.0
drowsy		l	076	540.1
drunk	how much have you ..	g	049.2	680.0
due	the bill is ..	p	094.7	600.0
dues	pay your ..	p	094.8	600.0
e'er a bit	not see any more trouble, ..	l	040	
ear [right ..]		p	071.4	527.0
earthworm	large size	l	060.5	279.0
eaten	we've already ..	g	048.5	683.0
education		l	083.6	577.0
eggs [boiled ..]		p	046.1	347.0
eight		p	001.4	067.0
eighty [up in ..]	he's ..	l	005	108.2
either you or I	.. will have to do it	g	071	
either [nor me ..]	resp. to "I won't do it"	g	071.2	649.0
eleven		p	001.6	070.0
eleven [quarter of ..]		l	004.5	106.0

elm		p	061	
England [New ..]		p	086.1	004.0
evening	after supper	l	002.6	101.0
ewe		p	035.1	237.0
excited [all ..]	he was .. (with expectation)	l	075	
face [minister's ..]		l	047	360.6
far off	you were not .. (= 'nearly right')	g	070	
far [how ..]	.. is it?	p	070.4	056.0
farthest [the ..]	two miles is .. I can go	g	043.3	057.0
father		p	063.4	430.0
faucet	sink, barrel, garden	l	018.6	174.0
February		p	001a.7	088.0
feet	nine .. high	g	007.7	055.0
fell down [like to ..]	I .. (= 'almost')	l	070.2	684.0
fellow [awkward ..]	that ..	l	073	
fellows [these ..]		g	052	
felly		l	021.1	202.0
fence [barbed wire ..]		p	016.3	144.0
fence [picket ..]		l	016.2	143.0
fence [rail ..]		l	016.4	145.0
fertile		p	029	039.2
fever		l	077	
fever [buck ..]		l	077	
fiancee [his ..]		l	082	
field	potato ..	l	016.1	148.0
fifth		p	001a.4	083.0
file cloth	damp cloth for wiping floor	l	010.8	186.2
file the floor	wipe with a damp cloth	l	010.9	186.3
find us	can we .. a trail back	g	044	
fine day	a ..	l	005.3	111.0
first		p	001a.3	081.0
fists		p	072.2	535.0
fitted	it .. me exactly	g	027.5	709.0
five		p	001.3	064.0
fix	I'll have to .. the table	l	098	621.2
flesh [proud ..]		l	078.2	557.0
floor [file the ..]	wipe with a damp cloth	l	010.9	186.3
Florida		p	086.5	014.0
flowers [pick ..]		l	101.5	298.0
fog		p	006.8	123.0
fog grass	dry grass in spring	l	041	
foggy		p	006.9	123.0
food		l	048.1	334.0
fool	only of men? of women?	l	073.4	513.0
for any [I don't care ..]	to decline food	l	049.7	374.0
for goodness sake!	surprise	l	092.3	639.0
for it? [How much do you ask ..]	in store	l	094	597.1
for it? [What will you take ..]	private deal	l	094	597.2
for you [wait ..]		l	099.1	782.0
forehead		p	071.3	526.0
fortnight		l	003.8	096.0
forty		p	001a.1	077.0

forward		p	040.3	754.0
fought	they .. all the time	g	104.3	685.0
four		p	001.2	063.0
fourteen		p	001.7	073.0
France		p	087.7	032.0
freestone	.. peach	l	054.4	321.0
from the south	the wind is ..	l	006.4	118.0
from [he died ..]		l	078.7	561.0
frost	we had a ..	l	007.4	125.0
frown		p	082.9	685.1
frowning		p	082.9	685.1
froze over		g	007.5	686.0
frying pan		l	017.5	164.0
funeral		l	079.2	564.0
funnel		l	019.3	176.0
furniture		p	009.3	390.0
furrows		p	041.2	151.0
garbage pail		l	017.4	166.0
garden	vegetable ..	p	050.5	149.0
gave	that's the one you .. me	g	102.1	687.0
gelding		l	034	231.1
General	.. Lee (title, not primary address)	p	068.3	490.0
gentleman	there's a .. at the door	p	067	
genuine		p	051.4	365.0
Georgia		p	086.5	013.0
get rid of him	I'll have to ..	l	099.4	603.0
get there [by the time I ..]	church will be over ..	l	089.9	762.0
get up!	to start horses	l	038.1	260.0
ghosts		l	090.2	575.0
giblets		l	037	
girl		p	064.8	438.0
girlfriend [his ..]		l	081.4	459.0
give me an apple	indef. article before vowel	p	051.7	324.0
give me another chance		p	099.2	604.0
glad [mighty ..]	I'm .. to see you	l	090.6	480.0
glad [we shall be ..]	.. to see you	g	081	
glass of water		p	048.7	367.0
gloomy day		l	005	113.2
go bring	.. me a knife	g	098.3	185.0
go [if you ..]	.. I won't stay	g	088	
go [you don't dare ..]		g	058.2	743.0
goad	for oxen	l	019.5	213.0
goal	games, children's games	l	098.4	621.0
God	reverential	p	089.3	570.0
God [My ..!]	profane	l	089.4	571.1
going down	the wind is ..	l	007.3	115.0
going on ten	he's ..	l	005	108.1
going to [am I ..]	.. get some	g	024.7	722.0
going to [are they ..]	.. get some	g	024.7	722.0
going [be you ..]	(finite be)	g	026	723.0
going [I'm ..]		g	024.6	719.0
going [we're ..]		g	024.6	719.0

gone [all ..]	the oranges are ..	p	055.2	596.0
good and hungry	I'm ..	l	090	
good day	meeting, parting	p	002.5	103.0
good morning	till what time	p	002.3	103.0
good night		p	003.1	102.0
good [twice as ..]		p	001a.6	086.0
good-bye!	when parting for a long time	l	093	
good-natured		l	073.2	515.0
goodness sake! [for ..]	surprise	l	092.3	639.0
got in bad with	he .. me	l	101	622.3
got me	I .. a new suit	g	027	
got sick	she ..	l	076.1	539.0
government	the federal ..	p	085.5	589.0
granary	store other than corn	l	014	133.1
grandfather	formal, normal, familiar	l	064.1	442.0
grandmother	formal, normal, familiar	l	064.2	443.0
grass [fog ..]	dry grass in spring	l	041	
grasshopper		l	061.1	280.0
grease	.. the wagon	p	023.7	222.0
greasy		p	023.8	222.0
great	it's a .. idea	p	104	635.1
greens	edible tops of root vegetables	l	055a.5	308.0
grew		g	065.6	688.0
grindstone		l	023.5	191.0
grits	coarsely ground corn	l	050.6	342.2
grocery store	small or large	l	094	
grove [maple ..]		l	061.6	292.0
grown		g	065.6	688.0
guardian		p	066.4	452.0
Gullah	dialect, people	l	069	
gully	channel cut by stream in field	l	030.4	041.0
gums		p	071.8	530.0
gutters		l	011.6	408.0
had it to rain harder [we've ..]		g	105	
had me	I .. a new suit	g	027	
half in two [cut it ..]		l	105	
half past seven		l	004.4	105.0
half shoes		l	028	
hammer	other tools	p	020.6	184.0
hanged	the murderer was ..	g	085.8	689.0
Happy New Year		l	093.3	483.0
hard clam		l	060	
harder [we've had it to rain ..]		g	105	
harness	.. the horses	l	038.6	208.0
harrow	kinds	l	021.7	200.0
haslet	edible insides of pig or calf	l	037.2	245.0
hasn't [he ..]	weakly stressed	g	012.4	728.1
hasn't [he ..]	stressed	g	012.5	728.0
hauling	he was ... wood in his wagon	l	021.4	214.0
haunches	define	l	072.7	538.0
haunted house		p	090.3	576.0
have helped [might ..]	you ..	g	058.6	744.0

have my [I ..]	.. troubles	g	012.2	650.0
have our [we ..]	.. troubles	g	012.2	650.0
have your [you ..]	.. troubles	g	012.2	650.0
Haven [New ..]		p	087	030.1
haven't [I ..]	weakly stressed	g	012.4	728.1
haven't [I ..]	stressed	g	012.5	728.0
haycock	in field at haying time	l	014.6	132.0
haystack	stored in field	l	014.5	131.0
hazy		l	005	113.4
he died from		l	078.7	561.0
he do [does ..]	what ..	g	012.8	731.0
he does	stressed	g	012.9	732.0
he does it		g	012.7	730.0
he doesn't care		g	013.1	733.0
he hasn't	weakly stressed	g	012.4	728.1
he hasn't	stressed	g	012.5	728.0
he is [as ..]	as tall ..	g	043.1	644.0
head of children	two ..	g	055a.6	302.0
headcheese	recipes	l	047.1	360.0
heads of lettuce	two ..	g	055a.6	301.0
hear a lot of people to say that [we ..]		g	105	
heard [I've ..]		l	012.3	727.0
hearth		p	008.2	381.0
heavy rain	short duration	l	006.1	119.0
help yourself		l	049.5	372.0
helped myself	I ..	g	049.6	373.0
helped [might have ..]	you ..	g	058.6	744.0
hen [setting ..]		l	036.7	251.0
hen [wet ..]	he was mad as a ..	l	075	
her [courting ..]	he is .. (normal, jocular terms)	l	081.1	462.0
her [it's ..]		g	042.5	641.0
her [no kin to ..]		l	066.6	449.0
here [Look ..!]	exclamation; serious, jesting	p	070.5	634.0
here's your clothes		g	025.1	413.0
hers	it's ..	g	043.4	653.0
highway		l	031.5	049.0
hill		l	031	042.1
him down [turned ..]	she ..	l	082.1	466.0
him no mind [don't pay ..]	don't pay him .. (=attention)	g	105	
him not there [and ..]	I wouldn't go to his house ..	g	088	
him out of it [sweet talk ..]	she'll ..	l	105	
him up [wake ..]	transitive	l	076.6	540.3
him [after ..]	named ..	l	032.7	456.0
him [get rid of ..]	I'll have to ..	l	099.4	603.0
him [it's ..]		g	042.5	641.0
him [lighted ..]	he .. a pipe	g	044	
him [me and ..]		g	042.4	648.0
him [sic ..]!	call to dog to attack	l	033.1	254.0
himself	he'd better do it ..	g	044.2	658.0
his	it's ..	g	043.4	652.0
his arm [and his overcoat on ..]	he went out ..	g	088	
his fiancee		l	082	

his girlfriend		l	081.4	459.0
his overcoat on his arm [and ..]	he went out ..	g	088	
his stomach [to ..]	sick ..	l	080.4	547.0
hoarse		p	076.4	545.0
hod [coal ..]		l	023.1	181.0
hog pen		l	015.3	137.0
hogs		p	035.5	239.0
hoist		p	104.5	197.0
hollow	topography	l	030	034.2
home [at ..]	he isn't ..	g	032.2	461.0
home [take you ..]	may I .. (riding, walking)	l	097.5	460.0
hominy	whole grain of corn	l	050.6	342.1
hoofs		p	034.7	234.0
hookey [played ..]		l	083.5	581.0
hoops		p	020.3	179.0
hoot owl		l	059.2	271.0
hornets		l	060a.5	287.0
horse		p	034.2	231.0
horse [near ..]	on left	l	039.4	207.0
horseshoes		p	034.6	235.0
horseshoes	game	l	034.8	235.0
hospital		p	084.5	560.0
hotel		p	084.3	584.0
house		p	014.1	127.0
house afire [a ..]	he ran like ..	l	097	
house [haunted ..]		p	090.3	576.0
house [in the ..]	she's ..	l	032	461.1
How are you?	greetings to friend, (intonation)	l	092.7	478.0
How do you do?	to stranger (intonation)	l	092.8	479.0
how far	.. is it?	p	070.4	056.0
how is it that	.. you're here?	l	081	
How much do you ask for it?	in store	l	094	597.1
how often	.. do you go	p	071.1	759.0
humor	in a blister	l	077	
humor	he's in a good ..	p	099.3	516.0
hundred		p	001a.2	079.0
hung	he .. himself	g	085	689.0
hungry [good and ..]	I'm ..	l	090	
hurrah!		p	093	
husband [my ..]	I must ask ..	l	063.1	435.0
husks	around ear of corn	l	056.1	315.0
I ain't done nothing	multiple negation	g	040.5	771.0
I am [as ..]	he's as tall ..	g	042.6	643.0
I buried me	.. a son	g	078	568.1
I can [than ..]	he can do it better ..	g	043.2	645.0
I can't	stressed	p	057.7	741.0
I do it		g	012.7	730.0
I don't care for any	to decline food	l	049.7	374.0
I don't know	.. as I want to	p	088.2	786.0
I done worked		g	057.8	736.0
I get there [by the time ..]	church will be over ..	l	089.9	762.0
I going to [am ..]	.. get some	g	024.7	722.0

I have my	.. troubles	g	012.2	650.0
I haven't	weakly stressed	g	012.4	728.1
I haven't	stressed	g	012.5	728.0
I just knew it!		l	101.7	690.0
I know it [Don't ..!]		l	013.3	735.0
I shall be	.. disappointed if you don't	g	081	
I sure can		p	091.3	625.0
I think	.. I'll have time	l	094.1	630.0
I think so		l	103.9	631.0
I want off		g	085.3	748.0
I want to [as ..]	I don't know ..	g	088.2	787.0
I was talking		g	013.5	725.0
I were you [if ..]	.. I wouldn't wait	g	026	
I won't do it		g	058.5	751.0
I [ain't ..?]		g	025.4	721.0
I [either you or ..]	.. will have to do it	g	071	
I [neither you nor ..]	.. can do anything about it	g	071	
I [says ..]		g	014	
I [you and ..]	.. are going	g	042.2	646.0
I'd rather	.. not	p	090.5	767.0
I'm going		g	024.6	719.0
I'm not		g	025.3	720.0
I'm not sure		g	013.4	627.0
I've been thinking		g	013.6	726.0
I've heard		l	012.3	727.0
idea [the ..!]		l	092.6	635.0
if I were you	.. I wouldn't wait	g	026	
if you go	.. I won't stay	g	088	
if you're a mind to	you can ..	g	101.3	753.0
ill [chronically ..]	he is ..	l	075	
Illinois		p	086	030.1
in bad with [got ..]	he .. me	l	101	622.3
in bed	he's still ..	l	076	
in bed [laid ..]	he .. all morning	g	097.1	691.0
in bulk	we bought our groceries ..	p	051.5	594.0
in eighty [up ..]	he's ..	l	005	108.2
in it	there's too much ..	g	104	774.1
in the house	she's ..	l	032	461.1
in two [cut it half ..]		l	105	
in [down ..]	he lives .. Columbia	l	082.7	774.0
in [pitch ..]	you better .. and help	l	097	
Indiana		p	086	030.1
inflamed wound		l	078	
instead of	.. helping me	p	088.4	783.0
intend to	we .. go	l	101.2	752.0
into	we burn coal .. the stove	l	008	388.1
iodine		p	078.3	558.0
Ireland		p	087.7	031.0
Irishman		l	069	
ironing [washing and ..]	laundry	l	010.5	415.0
is it that [how ..]	.. you're here?	l	081	
is it? [What time ..]		l	004.2	104.0

is poor [who ..]	a man ..	g	053.1	666.0
is [as he ..]	as tall ..	g	043.1	644.0
is [most cheese ..]	.. round	p	047	
is [mumps ..]	the .. dangerous	g	079.7	
it half in two [cut ..]		l	105	
it on [put ..]		p	102.7	756.0
it that [how is ..]	.. you're here?	l	081	
it to rain harder [we've had ..]		g	105	
it wasn't me		g	025.6	642.0
it wonders me		l	104.9	640.1
it [damn ..!]	strong oath	l	092.1	637.0
it [darn ..!]	mild oath	l	092.1	638.0
it [do she smell ..]	Lord help me ..	g	088	
it [Don't I know ..!]		l	013.3	735.0
it [Don't you touch ..!]		l	098.2	734.0
it [he does ..]		g	012.7	730.0
it [How much do you ask for ..?]	in store	l	094	597.1
it [I do ..]		g	012.7	730.0
it [I just knew ..!]		l	101.7	690.0
it [I won't do ..]		g	058.5	751.0
it [in ..]	there's too much ..	g	104	774.1
it [smell of ..]	just ..	g	051.1	713.0
it [swallow ..]	he couldn't ..	p	057.2	371.0
it [sweet talk him out of ..]	she'll ..	l	105	
it [What time is ..?]		l	004.2	104.0
it [What will you take for ..?]	private deal	l	094	597.2
it's her		g	042.5	641.0
it's him		g	042.5	641.0
it's me		g	042.5	640.0
it's them		g	042.5	641.0
Italian	noun	p	069	
ivy [poison ..]		l	062.3	297.0
jacket [yellow ..]		l	060a.7	286.0
January		p	001a.7	087.0
jaundice		l	079.8	553.0
jelly		p	051.6	362.0
Jersey [New ..]		p	086.2	007.0
Jew		l	069	
John [Master ..]		l	069.5	489.0
John [Uncle ..]		p	068.2	446.0
joined	they .. the church	p	089.2	573.0
joint		p	072.3	536.0
Judge	.. Marshall	p	068.5	492.0
junk		l	010.2	404.0
junk room		l	010.3	403.0
just a minute		p	070.3	110.0
just knew it! [I ..]		l	101.7	690.0
justice of the peace	other county officials	l	069	
keep calm		p	075.4	522.0
keep [to ..]	I'd like .. it	g	080	
keg		p	020.2	177.0
Kentucky		p	086.7	017.0

kerosene		l	024.2	221.0
kettle		l	017.6	162.0
kin to her [no ..]		l	066.6	449.0
kind of a pencil [what ..]	.. is that	l	104.7	664.2
kissing	normal, jocular terms	l	081.5	464.0
kitchen		l	009.8	399.0
kneeled down	she ..	g	096.5	710.0
knew it! [I just ..]		l	101.7	690.0
knitted	they .. sweaters	g	027	
knock you down	I'll (=introduce)	l	105	
know it [Don't I ..!]		l	013.3	735.0
know [I don't ..]	.. as I want to	p	088.2	786.0
laid in bed	he .. all morning	g	097.1	691.0
lamb [pet ..]		l	035	
lane	from public road to house	l	031.7	051.0
last [Sunday before ..]		l	003.6	095.0
laughing [singing and ..]	they were .. (a- prefix)	g	057.4	476.0
launch	.. the boat	p	024.4	216.0
laurel [mountain ..]		l	062.6	293.0
law and order		p	085.7	590.0
lets out	school .. at four	l	083.3	579.0
lettuce [heads of ..]	two ..	g	055a.6	301.0
lever		l	022	
library		p	084.1	582.0
lie down	I have to ..	g	096.6	540.0
lie down!	to a dog	l	033	
lighted him	he .. a pipe	g	044	
lightning bug		l	060a.3	282.0
lightwood		l	008.6	384.0
like	it seems .. he won't	l	088.6	711.1
like as not	he'll have trouble ..	g	041.1	769.0
like to fell down	I .. (= 'almost')	l	070.2	684.0
like [looks ..]	the boy .. his father	l	065.3	455.0
like [made out ..]	he .. he knew it all	l	100.1	711.0
lima beans		l	055a.3	309.0
lines	for driving	l	039.1	209.0
listen at the bell		l	105	
little way [a ..]		l	039.5	058.0
little [a ..]	.. different	l	091	
little [some ..]	I've got .. oil (=some)	l	105	
lively	old people? young?	l	074.1	510.0
liverwurst		l	047.1	360.1
living room		l	007.6	376.0
loam	poor soil	l	029.7	039.0
locusts		p	061	280.0
loft	places for hay in barn	l	014.4	129.0
long sweetening		l	051	
long way [a ..]		l	040.1	059.0
look after	she has to .. the baby	l	065	457.3
Look here!	exclamation; serious, jesting	p	070.5	634.0
looks like	the boy .. his father	l	065.3	455.0
loss [at a ..]	he had to sell it ..	l	094.5	598.0

lot of people to say that [we hear a ..]		g	105	
lot [a ..]	.. of them	l	091	
Louis [St. ..]		p	087.5	027.0
Louisiana		p	086.6	016.0
Louisville		p	087.4	029.0
lovinger	she is a .. child	g	066.1	441.0
low	of cow during feeding time	l	036.3	230.0
lowland	flat low-lying, along stream	l	029.3	034.0
made out like	he .. he knew it all	l	100.1	711.0
magnolia		l	062.8	295.0
make some coffee	I'll ..	l	048.6	366.0
makes	What .. him do it?	g	013.7	739.0
mama	normal, familiar	l	063.6	433.0
mammy [Negro ..]		l	069	
man [an old ..]	indef. article before vowel	p	051	
man [best ..]		l	082.3	468.0
mantel		l	008.4	380.0
maple grove		l	061.6	292.0
maple [sugar ..]		l	061.5	291.0
mare		l	034	231.1
married		p	082.2	467.0
marsh	along the sea	p	029.6	037.0
Martha		p	067.2	485.0
Mary		p	067.1	484.0
Maryland		p	086.3	010.0
Mass		p	089	
Massachusetts		p	086.1	005.0
Master John		l	069.5	489.0
Matthew		p	067.4	487.0
me an apple [give ..]	indef. article before vowel	p	051.7	324.0
me and him		g	042.4	648.0
me another chance [give ..]		p	099.2	604.0
me either [nor ..]	resp. to "I won't do it"	g	071.2	649.0
me off [spelled ..]	relieved from duty	l	004	110.2
me [got ..]	I .. a new suit	g	027	
me [had ..]	I .. a new suit	g	027	
me [I buried ..]	.. a son	g	078	568.1
me [it wasn't ..]		g	025.6	642.0
me [it wonders ..]		l	104.9	640.1
me [it's ..]		g	042.5	640.0
me [next to ..]	he was sitting right ..	l	032	777.2
meadow	low-lying grassland	p	029.4	035.0
medicine show		l	069	
Merry Christmas		l	093.2	482.0
merry-go-round		l	022.5	613.3
Michigan		p	086	030.1
midwife		l	065.2	497.0
might could	I .. do it	g	058.7	745.0
might have helped	you ..	g	058.6	744.0
mighty glad	I'm .. to see you	l	090.6	480.0
miles	ten ..	g	088.1	054.0
milk [strain the ..]		p	047.5	351.0

mind to [if you're a ..]	you can ..	g	101.3	753.0
mind [don't pay him no ..]	don't pay him .. (=attention)	g	105	
minister's face		l	047	360.6
minnows		l	061.2	277.0
minute [just a ..]		p	070.3	110.0
Miss	.. Mary (familiar term of address)	l	067	
Miss	.. Brown (formal term of address)	p	067	
miss you	we're going to ..	p	100	
Missouri		p	086.8	019.0
molasses		p	051.2	363.0
mole	animal	l	059	
mongrel		l	033.2	249.0
morning [good ..]	till what time	p	002.3	103.0
most cheese is	.. round	p	047	
moth		l	060a.1	281.0
moths		p	060a.2	281.0
mountain		p	031.1	042.0
mountain laurel		l	062.6	293.0
mourning	in ..	p	079.3	565.0
mouth		p	071.6	528.0
mouth organ		l	020.5	474.0
Mrs. Cooper	slow, fast	p	067.5	488.0
much do you ask for it? [How ..]	in store	l	094	597.1
muck	rich soil	l	029.7	039.1
mumps is	the .. dangerous	g	079	
mush		l	050.3	342.0
mushroom		p	056.8	332.0
music		p	089.6	472.0
muskmelon		l	056.7	318.0
My God!	profane	l	089.4	571.1
my husband	I must ask ..	l	063.1	435.0
my wife	I must ask ..	l	063.2	436.0
my [I have ..]	.. troubles	g	012.2	650.0
myself [helped ..]	I ..	g	049.6	373.0
ne'er a one	I couldn't find ..	g	040.4	770.0
near horse	on left	l	039.4	207.0
necklace		l	028.4	429.0
Negro	neutral	l	069.3	502.0
Negro mammy		l	069	
neither you nor I	.. can do anything about it	g	071	
Nelly		p	067.3	486.0
nephew		p	066.2	447.0
New England		p	086.1	004.0
New Haven		p	087	030.1
New Jersey		p	086.2	007.0
New Orleans		p	087.6	030.0
new suit		p	027.6	418.0
New Year [Happy ..]		l	093.3	483.0
New York		p	086.2	006.0
next to me	he was sitting right ..	l	032	777.2
next [Sunday after ..]		l	003.7	094.0
nigger	derogatory	l	069.4	503.0

night [good ..]		p	003.1	102.0
nine		p	001.5	068.0
no kin to her		l	066.6	449.0
no mind [don't pay him ..]	don't pay him .. (=attention)	g	105	
nohow	he didn't hurt me ..	g	040.6	772.0
none	he didn't give me ..	g	040.7	773.0
nor I [neither you ..]	.. can do anything about it	g	071	
nor me either	resp. to "I won't do it"	g	071.2	649.0
North Carolina		p	086.4	012.0
northeast		p	006.6	116.0
northwest		p	006.6	116.0
not sure [I'm ..]		g	013.4	627.0
not there [and him ..]	I wouldn't go to his house ..	g	088	
not [I'm ..]		g	025.3	720.0
not [like as ..]	he'll have trouble ..	g	041.1	769.0
nothing		p	103.1	669.0
nothing [I ain't done ..]	multiple negation	g	040.5	771.0
now		p	082.1	758.1
nurse		p	084.6	496.0
oats are thrashed		g	042.1	160.0
of a pencil [what kind ..]	.. is that	l	104.7	664.2
of children [head ..]	two ..	g	055a.6	302.0
of eleven [quarter ..]		l	004.5	106.0
of him [get rid ..]	I'll have to ..	l	099.4	603.0
of it [smell ..]	just ..	g	051.1	713.0
of it [sweet talk him out ..]	she'll ..	l	105	
of lettuce [heads ..]	two ..	g	055a.6	301.0
of oxen [yoke ..]	two ..	g	033.6	224.0
of people to say that [we hear a lot ..]		g	105	
of the peace [justice ..]	other county officials	l	069	
of us [both ..]		g	042.3	647.0
of water [glass ..]		p	048.7	367.0
of wood [armful ..]		l	019.8	159.0
of yeast	a cake ..	p	045.6	343.0
of [instead ..]	.. helping me	p	088.4	783.0
of [out ..]	he fell .. the bed	g	034.5	778.0
off	he fell .. the horse	g	034.4	779.0
off [burned ..]	it's .. (of fog)	l	006	123.1
off [far ..]	you were not .. (= 'nearly right')	g	070	
off [I want ..]		g	085.3	748.0
off [spelled me ..]	relieved from duty	l	004	110.2
office [post ..]		p	084.2	586.0
often [how ..]	.. do you go	p	071.1	759.0
Ohio		p	086.2	009.0
oil		p	024.1	220.0
old man [an ..]	indef. article before vowel	p	051	
old [three years ..]	he is ..	p	005.1	108.0
oldest	he's the ..	l	064.6	440.0
on	.. the table	l	102	
on his arm [and his overcoat ..]	he went out ..	g	088	
on purpose	he did it ..	l	103.6	768.0
on ten [going ..]	he's ..	l	005	108.1

on [put it ..]		p	102.7	756.0
on [tell ..]	you won't .. me, will you	l	101	
once [all at ..]		p	001a.5	085.0
one		p	001.1	060.0
one [ne'er a ..]	I couldn't find ..	g	040.4	770.0
onions		p	055.7	306.0
or I [either you ..]	.. will have to do it	g	071	
oranges		p	055.1	326.0
orchard [the ..]		p	053.2	290.0
order [law and ..]		p	085.7	590.0
organ [mouth ..]		l	020.5	474.0
Orleans [New ..]		p	087.6	030.0
orphan	only in institution?	l	066.3	451.0
ought to	you .. go	p	058.3	746.0
ought to take	you .. it easy	g	080	
oughtn't to	you .. go	g	058.4	747.0
our [we have ..]	.. troubles	g	012.2	650.0
ours	it's ..	g	043.4	654.0
out like [made ..]	he .. he knew it all	l	100.1	711.0
out of	he fell .. the bed	g	034.5	778.0
out of it [sweet talk him ..]	she'll ..	l	105	
out [lets ..]	school .. at four	l	083.3	579.0
out [worn ..]		g	075.7	525.0
over there	it's ..	l	052.2	755.0
over [froze ..]		g	007.5	686.0
over [warmed ..]		l	050.1	368.0
overalls		l	027	
overcoat on his arm [and his ..]	he went out ..	g	088	
owl [hoot ..]		l	059.2	271.0
owl [screech ..]		l	059.1	270.0
owns [who ..]	he's the man .. the orchard	g	053.2	665.0
oxen [yoke of ..]	two ..	g	033.6	224.0
oysters		p	060.1	278.0
pail		l	017.3	161.0
pail [garbage ..]		l	017.4	166.0
palings	in fence	l	016	
pallet	bed on floor	l	029.2	398.0
palm	of hand	p	072.1	534.0
pan [frying ..]		l	017.5	164.0
Panama		p	087	033.2
pancakes	wheat flour	l	045.4	341.0
pantry		l	010.1	400.0
pants		l	027.3	421.0
paper bag		l	019.6	182.0
parents		p	063.7	434.0
past seven [half ..]		l	004.4	105.0
pasture	for grazing stock	p	015.6	141.0
pay him no mind [don't ..]	don't pay him .. (=attention)	g	105	
peace [justice of the ..]	other county officials	l	069	
peaked	from ill-health	l	072.8	508.0
peanuts		l	054.6	329.0
peekaboo		l	105	

peepers	small frogs	l	060.3	273.0
pen [hog ..]		l	015.3	137.0
pencil [what kind of a ..]	.. is that	l	104.7	664.2
Pennsylvania		p	086.2	008.0
people thinks	.. he did it	g	013.8	738.0
people to say that [we hear a lot of ..]		g	105	
pepper [salt and ..]		p	051.7	344.0
pet lamb		l	035	
Philadelphia		p	087.1	021.0
pick flowers		l	101.5	298.0
picket fence		l	016.2	143.0
pillow		p	028.8	395.0
pit	peach ..	l	054.2	322.0
pitch in	you better .. and help	l	097	
played hookey		l	083.5	581.0
pleaded	he .. guilty	g	023	
plow	kinds	l	021.6	199.0
poached	.. eggs	p	046.2	348.0
pocosin	swamp with no outlet	l	029	036.0
poison ivy		l	062.3	297.0
poisonous		p	062	297.1
poor whites	Whites' and Negroes' terms	l	069.6	501.0
poor [who is ..]	a man ..	g	053.1	666.0
pop [soda ..]	bottled carbonated drinks	l	049	
porch	front, back	l	010.7	410.0
porgy	fish	l	059	
pork [salt ..]		l	046.3	355.0
pork [smoked ..]		l	046.4	356.0
post office		p	084.2	586.0
posts		p	016.5	146.0
potato [sweet ..]		l	055.6	300.2
potatoes		l	055.5	300.0
poultry	feed the ..	l	036.6	250.0
pounds	two ..	g	045.5	595.0
preacher	esp. untrained, part-time	l	067.6	504.0
pregnant	normal, jocular terms	l	065.1	453.0
prettier		g	026.2	507.0
pretty well	in resp. to 'how are you?'	l	079.4	541.0
privy	outdoor	l	012.1	412.0
proud flesh		l	078.2	557.0
psalm		p	089	
public square		l	085	
pudding [blood ..]		l	047.1	360.2
pull		p	097.6	195.0
pumpkin		p	056.5	316.0
purpose [on ..]	he did it ..	l	103.6	768.0
purse		l	028.2	427.0
pus		l	077.6	555.0
push		p	097.7	196.0
put it on		p	102.7	756.0
quarter of eleven		l	004.5	106.0
queer	define	l	074.7	518.0

quilt	washable	l	029.1	394.0
quinine		p	078.4	559.0
quite	.. (+ adjective)	l	074.1	511.0
radishes		p	055.3	304.0
rag [wash ..]		l	018	173.1
rail fence		l	016.4	145.0
rain harder [we've had it to ..]		g	105	
rain [heavy ..]	short duration	l	006.1	119.0
ram	normal, farmers' term, polite	l	034.9	236.0
ran	he .. away	g	102.3	694.0
rancid		l	047.2	354.0
rang		g	011	
raspberries		l	062.5	328.0
rather	it's .. cold	l	090.4	766.0
rather [I'd ..]	.. not	p	090.5	767.0
ravine		l	030	041.1
real	those are .. dogs (intensive)	p	091.8	764.0
really	he .. dreaded the place	l	091.7	765.0
reared	she has .. three children	l	065	
recognize	I didn't .. you	l	100	
reins	for riding	l	039.2	209.0
relatives	her .. (near and extended family)	l	066.5	448.0
remember	I .. that	l	100.3	712.0
remember [don't ..]	I .. that	l	100.4	712.1
rented a room		g	010	412.3
Reverend Simpson		l	067	
rheumatism	.. is painful	l	079.6	550.0
rhododendron		l	062.7	293.0
rice		p	050.6	342.3
rid of him [get ..]	I'll have to ..	l	099.4	603.0
ridden		g	034.3	692.0
rider [circuit ..]		l	067	
right ear		p	071.4	527.0
right smart	he owns a .. of land	l	091	
rind	bacon ..	l	046.5	358.0
rinses	she .. the dishes	p	018.2	170.0
rising	the wind is ..	l	007.2	114.0
river	large, fresh water	p	030.5	045.0
road [side ..]		l	031.6	050.0
rolliches		l	047.1	360.4
rolls [sweet ..]	kinds	l	045	
roof		p	011.5	406.0
room [junk ..]		l	010.3	403.0
room [living ..]		l	007.6	376.0
room [rented a ..]		g	010	412.3
roots		p	061.4	305.0
rose	the sun ..	g	003.3	693.0
Russia		p	087.8	033.0
sack [burlap ..]	cloth	l	019.7	183.0
sake [for goodness ..!]	surprise	l	092.3	639.0
salad	fruit ..	p	050	
salt and pepper		p	051.7	344.0

salt pork		l	046.3	355.0
sample	.. of cloth	l	026.1	425.0
Sarah [Aunt ..]		p	068.1	445.0
sat down	he ..	g	049.4	697.0
Saturday	other days	p	002.2	093.0
sauce	sweet, for pudding	l	048.2	346.0
sausage		p	046.7	359.0
saw	he .. me go in	g	102.5	695.0
sawhorse	A-frame; X-frame	l	022.1	193.0
say that [we hear a lot of people to ..]		g	105	
say [they ..]	he did it	g	013.9	740.0
says I		g	014	
scallions		l	055.8	307.0
scarce	money is .. these days	p	095.2	599.0
scarcely	I could .. see him	p	095	599.1
schoolteacher	female	l	067.7	493.0
scrapple		l	047.1	360.3
screech owl		l	059.1	270.0
seat [county ..]		l	085.4	588.0
second		p	001a.3	082.0
second crop	of hay	l	041.5	152.0
secretary		p	068.7	495.0
seesaw		l	022.5	613.1
seesawing	they are ..	l	022.6	613.0
serenade	after wedding	l	082.5	470.0
sermon		l	089.5	572.0
setting hen		l	036.7	251.0
seven		p	001.4	066.0
seven [half past ..]		l	004.4	105.0
seventy		p	001a.2	078.0
shades [window ..]		l	009.4	379.0
shafts	buggy	l	020.8	204.0
shall be glad [we ..]	.. to see you	g	081	
shall be [I ..]	.. disappointed if you don't	g	081	
she smell it [do ..]	Lord help me ..	g	088	
sheaf	of wheat, oats	l	041.6	154.0
shell beans	to ..	l	055a.2	311.0
shins		l	072.6	537.0
shock	of wheat, corn (how many sheaves)	l	041.7	154.0
shoes [half ..]		l	028	
shopping	I'll have to do some ..	l	094.2	593.0
shoulders		p	072.5	533.0
show [medicine ..]		l	069	
shrank	the collar ..	g	027.8	696.0
shucks	impatience or disgust	l	092.5	636.0
shut the door		l	011.1	405.0
sic him!	call to dog to attack	l	033.1	254.0
sick [got ..]	she ..	l	076.1	539.0
side road		l	031.6	050.0
sidewalk		l	031.8	053.0
sifter	flour	l	018	178.5
silk	corn .. (on the ear)	l	056.4	314.0

since		p	103.5	761.0
singing and laughing	they were .. (a- prefix)	g	057.4	476.0
singletree		l	021.2	205.0
sir [yes ..]	also ma'am; how common?	l	091.5	624.0
sit down!	invitation to dinner	l	049.3	697.0
sitting	he was .. at the table	l	049	
six		p	001.3	065.0
sixth		p	001a.4	084.0
skillful	he is quite .. at plowing	l	073	
skin		l	072	
skunk		l	059.4	268.0
sled	play, work	l	022.7	608.0
smart [right ..]	he owns a .. of land	l	091	
smell it [do she ..]	Lord help me ..	g	088	
smell of it	just ..	g	051.1	713.0
smoked pork		l	046.4	356.0
snack	between meals	l	048.3	369.0
snappy	it's rather ..	l	007	
so [I think ..]		l	103.9	631.0
soda pop	bottled carbonated drinks	l	049	
sofa		l	009.1	378.0
some better	he is ..	l	076	
some coffee [make ..]	I'll ..	l	048.6	366.0
some little	I've got .. oil (=some)	l	105	
somersault		l	095.5	614.0
something		p	103.2	668.0
soot		p	008.7	388.0
South Carolina		p	086.4	012.0
south [from the ..]	the wind is ..	l	006.4	118.0
southeast wind		l	006.5	117.0
southwest wind		l	006.5	117.0
spelled me off	relieved from duty	l	004	110.2
spiderweb	in house and outdoors	l	061.3	288.0
spoiled	the meat is ..	p	046.9	361.0
spoon	other utensils	p	017.8	165.0
Springfield		p	087	030.1
square [public ..]		l	085	
squash		p	056.6	317.0
Squire	.. John	l	069	
squirrel	kinds	l	059.6	266.0
St. Louis		p	087.5	027.0
stable	for horses	l	015	
stable [cow ..]	separate or in barn	l	015.1	135.0
stairs		l	010.6	401.0
stallion	normal, farmers' term, polite	l	034.1	232.0
start	school will .. in September	l	083.4	580.0
station		l	084.7	585.0
stem	of a strawberry	l	062	
still [but yet and ..]	.. I won't go	l	105	
stirrups		p	039.3	211.0
stock	feed the ..	l	036.5	223.0
stole	who .. my pencils?	l	100.2	602.0

stomach [to his ..]	sick ..	l	080.4	547.0
stomp	.. with your foot	p	097.4	619.0
stone	threw a .. at the dog	l	032.1	040.0
stone	cherry ..	l	054.1	323.0
stone boat	for removing stones from field	l	021.8	201.0
stone wall		l	016.6	147.0
store [grocery ..]	small or large	l	094	
stout		l	072	
stovepipe		l	023.2	387.0
strain the milk		p	047.5	351.0
stranger		l	066.7	499.0
strawberries		p	062.4	327.0
street car		l	085	
string beans		l	055a.4	310.0
strong	.. person	p	073.1	509.0
strop		p	022.3	188.0
stub	of one's toe	l	070	684.1
student		l	068.6	494.0
such	it's .. a good one	p	103.3	662.0
sugar maple		l	061.5	291.0
suit [new ..]		p	027.6	418.0
sumac		p	062.2	296.0
Sunday after next		l	003.7	094.0
Sunday before last		l	003.6	095.0
sunrise		l	003.2	099.0
sunset		l	003.4	100.0
sure can [I ..]		p	091.3	625.0
sure [I'm not ..]		g	013.4	627.0
suspenders		l	028.5	423.0
swallow it	he couldn't ..	p	057.2	371.0
swam across	he ..	g	095.6	615.0
swamp	inland	l	029.5	036.0
sweated	he ..	g	077.4	714.0
sweet corn	grown to be eaten on cob	l	056.2	312.0
sweet potato		l	055.6	300.2
sweet rolls	kinds	l	045	
sweet talk him out of it	she'll ..	l	105	
sweetening [long ..]		l	051	
swelled up	it ..	g	077.7	698.0
swing	board suspended by rope	l	022	
switch	for punishing children	l	019	
swollen	it's still ..	g	077.8	698.0
sycamore		l	061.7	294.0
syrup	maple ..	p	051.3	364.0
tag	the children play ..	l	098	
take for it? [What will you ..]	private deal	l	094	597.2
take you home	may I .. (riding, walking)	l	097.5	460.0
take [ought to ..]	you .. it easy	g	080	
taken	have you .. your medicine	g	077.1	699.0
talk him out of it [sweet ..]	she'll ..	l	105	
talking [I was ..]		g	013.5	725.0
talking [you were ..]		g	013.5	725.0

tassel		p	056.3	313.0
tattletale	children's names for such	l	101.4	622.0
taught you	who .. that	l	101.1	701.0
teeth		p	071.7	529.0
tell on	you won't .. me, will you	l	101	
tell [to ..]	he came over .. me	g	080.5	606.0
ten		p	001.5	069.0
ten [going on ..]	he's ..	l	005	108.1
Tennessee		p	086.7	018.0
terrapin	on land	l	060.7	276.0
Texas		p	086	020.1
than I can	he can do it better ..	g	043.2	645.0
that tree	at a distance	g	052	
that [how is it ..]	.. you're here?	l	081	
that [we hear a lot of people to say ..]		g	105	
the idea!		l	092.6	635.0
theater		l	084.4	583.0
theirs	it's ..	g	043.4	657.0
them [it's ..]		g	042.5	641.0
them's	.. the fellows I mean	g	052	
themselves	they've got to look out for ..	g	044.1	659.0
there are	.. lots of them	g	025.2	724.0
there [and him not ..]	I wouldn't go to his house ..	g	088	
there [by the time I get ..]	church will be over ..	l	089.9	762.0
there [over ..]	it's ..	l	052.2	755.0
these fellows		g	052	
they going to [are ..]	.. get some	g	024.7	722.0
they say	he did it	g	013.9	740.0
think so [I ..]		l	103.9	631.0
think [I ..]	.. I'll have time	l	094.1	630.0
thinking [I've been ..]		g	013.6	726.0
thinks [people ..]	.. he did it	g	013.8	738.0
thirteen		p	001.7	072.0
thirty		p	001a.1	076.0
this way	do it ..	p	052.3	661.0
this year		p	004.6	107.0
those boys	it was ..	g	052.1	660.0
those cabbages are	.. big	g	055a.1	303.0
those were	.. the good old days	g	025	
thousand		p	001a.2	080.0
thrashed [oats are ..]		g	042.1	160.0
three		p	001.2	062.0
three years old	he is ..	p	005.1	108.0
threw	he .. a stone at the dog	g	032.1	702.0
thunderstorm		l	006.2	120.0
Thursday	other days	p	002.2	092.0
time I get there [by the ..]	church will be over ..	l	089.9	762.0
time is it? [What ..]		l	004.2	104.0
time [chore ..]		l	037.4	253.0
time [wasting ..]	he is ..	l	099	603.1
tire		l	021.1	202.0
tired	normal and strong terms	l	075.5	523.0

to be [used ..]	she .. afraid	g	074.4	749.0
to fell down [like ..]	I .. (= 'almost')	l	070.2	684.0
to her [no kin ..]		l	066.6	449.0
to his stomach	sick ..	l	080.4	547.0
to keep	I'd like .. it	g	080	
to me [next ..]	he was sitting right ..	l	032	777.2
to rain harder [we've had it ..]		g	105	
to say that [we hear a lot of people ..]		g	105	
to take [ought ..]	you .. it easy	g	080	
to tell	he came over .. me	g	080.5	606.0
to [am I going ..]	.. get some	g	024.7	722.0
to [are they going ..]	.. get some	g	024.7	722.0
to [as I want ..]	I don't know ..	g	088.2	787.0
to [belongs ..]	he .. be careful (= should)	g	058.1	746.1
to [didn't used ..]	she .. do that	g	074.5	750.0
to [if you're a mind ..]	you can ..	g	101.3	753.0
to [intend ..]	we .. go	l	101.2	752.0
to [ought ..]	you .. go	p	058.3	746.0
to [oughtn't ..]	you .. go	g	058.4	747.0
to-do [big ..]	social affair	l	082	
toad		l	060.4	274.0
toadstool		l	057.1	333.0
tomatoes		p	055.4	319.0
tomorrow		p	004.1	098.0
tongue	wagon	l	020.7	203.0
took	I .. it	g	077.2	699.0
tooth		p	071.7	529.0
torn up	the road was all ..	g	102.6	700.0
touch it! [Don't you ..]		l	098.2	734.0
touchy	easily offended	l	075.1	517.0
tourist		l	069	
toward		p	032.5	776.0
towel [bath ..]		l	018.5	173.0
towel [dish ..]	for drying	l	018.4	172.0
toys		l	101.6	607.0
tree [cherry ..]		p	062.1	289.0
tree [that ..]	at a distance	g	052	
trough		p	035.8	244.0
troughs		p	035.8	244.0
tube	inner ..	p	024.3	219.0
tuberculosis		l	080	
Tuesday		p	002.1	090.0
turn	of corn, grist to mill	l	019.8	157.0
turned him down	she ..	l	082.1	466.0
turnpike		l	031	049.0
turtle	in water	l	060.6	275.0
tusks		p	035.7	243.0
twelve		p	001.6	071.0
twenty		p	001.8	074.0
twenty-seven		p	001.8	075.0
twice as good		p	001a.6	086.0
two		p	001.1	061.0

two [cut it half in ..]		l	105	
umbrella	an old ..	p	028.6	426.0
Uncle John		p	068	446.0
Uncle William		p		
underwear		l	026	
uneasy	un- prefix	p	074.2	521.0
unless	I won't go .. he does	l	088.3	785.0
unwrapped	I .. it	p	094.4	715.0
up at	I was .. the Browns'	l	082.6	775.0
up in eighty	he's ..	l	005	108.2
up [clean ..]		l	010	186.1
up [clearing ..]		l	005.4	112.0
up [clouding ..]		l	005.5	113.0
up [dress ..]	she likes to ..	l	028.1	414.0
up [get ..!]	to start horses	l	038.1	260.0
up [swelled ..]	it ..	g	077.7	698.0
up [torn ..]	the road was all ..	g	102.6	700.0
up [wake ..]	intransitive	l	076.7	540.2
up [wake him ..]	transitive	l	076.6	540.3
up [woke ..]	intransitive	g	097.3	703.0
up [wrapped ..]		p	094.3	716.0
us [both of ..]		g	042.3	647.0
us [find ..]	can we .. a trail back	g	044	
used to be	she .. afraid	g	074.4	749.0
used to [didn't ..]	she .. do that	g	074.5	750.0
valley	on roof	l	011.7	407.0
varmints	define, kinds	l	059.5	265.0
vase		l	017.7	168.0
vegetables	home grown	p	050.4	299.0
vest		l	027.2	420.0
vinky		l	047.1	360.5
Virginia		p	086.3	011.0
vomit	neutral and crude terms	l	080.2	548.0
wait for you		l	099.1	782.0
wake him up	transitive	l	076.6	540.3
wake up	intransitive	l	076.7	540.2
wall [stone ..]		l	016.6	147.0
walnut		p	054.7	330.0
want off [I ..]		g	085.3	748.0
want to [as I ..]	I don't know ..	g	088.2	787.0
War [Civil ..]		l	085.6	591.0
wardrobe	movable	l	009.6	392.0
warmed over		l	050.1	368.0
was talking [I ..]		g	013.5	725.0
was [we ..]	.. going to do it anyway	g	025.5	725.1
wash rag		l	018	173.1
wash the dishes		p	018.1	169.0
washing and ironing	laundry	l	010.5	415.0
Washington		p	087.1	023.0
wasn't me [it ..]		g	025.6	642.0
wasp		p	060a.6	284.0
wasting time	he is ..	l	099	603.1

watch	a gold ..	p	004.3	189.0
water [glass of ..]		p	048.7	367.0
waterfall		l	031.4	044.0
way [a little ..]		l	039.5	058.0
way [a long ..]		l	040.1	059.0
way [this ..]	do it ..	p	052.3	661.0
we have our	.. troubles	g	012.2	650.0
we hear a lot of people to say that		g	105	
we shall be glad	.. to see you	g	081	
we was	.. going to do it anyway	g	025.5	725.1
we're going		g	024.6	719.0
we've had it to rain harder		g	105	
weather [come cooler ..]	we'll go hunting ..	g	058	
Wednesday		p	002.1	091.0
well . . .	hesitation	l	091.6	632.0
well [pretty ..]	in resp. to 'how are you?'	l	079.4	541.0
went	he .. down to the store	g	104	
were talking [you ..]		g	013.5	725.0
were you [if I ..]	.. I wouldn't wait	g	026	
were [those ..]	.. the good old days	g	025	
wet hen	he was mad as a ..	l	075	
wharf		l	031.3	217.0
what kind of a pencil	.. is that	l	104.7	664.2
What time is it?		l	004.2	104.0
What will you take for it?	private deal	l	094	597.2
what-all	.. did he say?	g	043.8	664.0
what?	upon not understanding a remark	l	052.4	633.0
wheat bread	in loaves	l	044.3	335.0
wheel	.. the baby	l	064.5	612.0
wheel [cog ..]		p	022	
wheelbarrow		p	023.3	194.0
whenever	I'll do it .. I can	g	104.9	759.1
whetstone		l	023.4	190.0
while	quite a ..	l	004	110.1
whilst	.. I was talking	g	088	
whinny	of horse	l	036.4	233.0
whip		p	019.4	212.0
whipping	he got a ..	l	065.4	457.0
white ashes		p	008.8	385.0
whites [poor ..]	Whites' and Negroes' terms	l	069.6	501.0
who is poor	a man ..	g	053.1	666.0
who owns	he's the man .. the orchard	g	053.2	665.0
who-all	.. was there?	g	043.7	663.0
whoa!	to stop horses	p	038.2	261.0
whole	the .. thing	p	103	
whole crowd [the ..]	jocular, disparaging	l	082.8	475.0
whose	there's a boy .. father is rich	g	053.3	667.0
why!	exclamation (stressed)	l	092	
why, yes!		l	091	
widow		l	063.3	450.0
wife [my ..]	I must ask ..	l	063.2	436.0
will you take for it? [What ..]	private deal	l	094	597.2

wind [southeast ..]		l	006.5	117.0
wind [southwest ..]		l	006.5	117.0
window shades		l	009.4	379.0
winklehawk	three-cornered tear	l	027.9	421.1
wire fence [barbed ..]		p	016.3	144.0
wish	I .. you could come tonight	g	058	
wishbone		l	037.1	252.0
with	.. milk (before voiced sound)	p	032.4	780.0
with [got in bad ..]	he .. me	l	101	622.3
without	.. milk	p	032.3	781.0
woke up	intransitive	g	097.3	703.0
won't do it [I ..]		g	058.5	751.0
wonders me [it ..]		l	104.9	640.1
wood [armful of ..]		l	019.8	159.0
woodpecker		l	059.3	269.0
woodshed	wood, tools	l	011.8	411.0
wool		p	035.2	238.0
work	I/we/they .. all day	g	013	
worked [I done ..]		g	057.8	736.0
worn out		g	075.7	525.0
worry [don't ..]		p	079.5	542.0
wound	noun	p	078.1	556.0
wound [inflamed ..]		l	078	
wrapped up		p	094.3	716.0
writing [after ..]	I'm .. a letter (= 'have written')	g	089	706.2
written	I have .. him	g	100.5	706.0
year ago	a ..	p	005.2	109.0
Year [Happy New ..]		l	093.3	483.0
year [this ..]		p	004.6	107.0
years old [three ..]	he is ..	p	005.1	108.0
yeast [of ..]	a cake ..	p	045.6	343.0
yellow	the yolk is ..	p	045.8	350.0
yellow jacket		l	060a.7	286.0
yes	habitual affirmation	l	091.4	623.0
yes sir	also ma'am; how common?	l	091.5	624.0
yes [why, ..!]		l	091	
yesterday		p	003.5	097.0
yet and still [but ..]	.. I won't go	l	105	
yoke of oxen	two ..	g	033.6	224.0
yolk		p	045.7	349.0
York [New ..]		p	086.2	006.0
you and I	.. are going	g	042.2	646.0
you ask for it? [How much do ..]	in store	l	094	597.1
you do? [How do ..]	to stranger (intonation)	l	092.8	479.0
you don't dare go		g	058.2	743.0
you down [knock ..]	I'll (=introduce)	l	105	
you go [if ..]	.. I won't stay	g	088	
you going [be ..]	(finite be)	g	026	723.0
you have your	.. troubles	g	012.2	650.0
you home [take ..]	may I .. (riding, walking)	l	097.5	460.0
you nor I [neither ..]	.. can do anything about it	g	071	
you or I [either ..]	.. will have to do it	g	071	

you take for it? [What will ..]	private deal	l	094	597.2
you touch it! [Don't ..]		l	098.2	734.0
you were talking		g	013.5	725.0
you [do ..?]	you don't think so, ..?	g	013.2	729.0
you [ain't ..?]	you are going, ..? (tag)	g	012.6	721.1
you [How are ..?]	greetings to friend, (intonation)	l	092.7	478.0
you [if I were ..]	.. I wouldn't wait	g	026	
you [miss ..]	we're going to ..	p	100	
you [taught ..]	who .. that	l	101.1	701.0
you [wait for ..]		l	099.1	782.0
you're a mind to [if ..]	you can ..	g	101.3	753.0
you-all	when are .. coming again?	g	043.5	651.0
you-all's	it's ..	g	043.4	656.0
your aunt		p	067.8	444.0
your clothes [here's ..]		g	025.1	413.0
your [you have ..]	.. troubles	g	012.2	650.0
yours	it's ..	g	043.4	655.0
yourself [help ..]		l	049.5	372.0

Work Sheets by Work Sheet Number

001.1		one	002.1			Tuesday
001.1		two	002.1			Wednesday
001.2		four	002.2			Saturday
001.2		three	002.2			Thursday
001.3		five	002.3			good morning
001.3		six	002.4			afternoon
001.4		eight	002.5			good day
001.4		seven	002.6			evening
001.5		nine	003.1	X		good night
001.5		ten	003.2			sunrise
001.6		eleven	003.3			rose
001.6		twelve	003.4			sunset
001.7		fourteen	003.5			yesterday
001.7		thirteen	003.6			Sunday before last
001.8		twenty	003.7			Sunday after next
001.8		twenty-seven	003.8	X		fortnight
001a.1		forty	004		P	spelled me off
001a.1		thirty	004		P	while
001a.2		hundred	004.1			tomorrow
001a.2		seventy	004.2			What time is it?
001a.2	M	thousand	004.3			watch
001a.3		first	004.4			half past seven
001a.3		second	004.5			quarter of eleven
001a.4		fifth	004.6			this year
001a.4		sixth	005		P	gloomy day
001a.5		all at once	005		P	going on ten
001a.6		twice as good	005		P	hazy
001a.7		April	005		P	up in eighty
001a.7		February	005.1			three years old
001a.7		January	005.2			year ago

005.3		fine day
005.4		clearing up
005.5		clouding up
005.6	X	clouds
006	P	burned off
006	P	drizzling
006.1		heavy rain
006.2		thunderstorm
006.3		blew
006.4		from the south
006.5		southeast wind
006.5		southwest wind
006.6		northeast
006.6		northwest
006.7		drizzle
006.8		fog
006.9		foggy
007	P	snappy
007.1		drought
007.2		rising
007.3		going down
007.4	X	dew
007.4		frost
007.5		froze over
007.6		living room
007.7		feet
008	P	chunk
008	P	into
008.1		chimney
008.2		hearth
008.3		andirons
008.4		mantel
008.5		backlog
008.6		lightwood
008.7		soot
008.8		white ashes
008.9		chair
009.1		sofa
009.2		dresser
009.3		furniture
009.4		window shades
009.5		closet
009.6		wardrobe
009.7		attic
009.8		kitchen
010	P	clean up
010	P	rented a room
010.1		pantry
010.2		junk
010.3	S,M	junk room
010.4		behind the door
010.4		broom
010.5		washing and ironing
010.6		stairs
010.7		porch
010.8	X	file cloth
010.9	X	file the floor
011	P	rang
011.1		shut the door
011.2		clapboards
011.3		drove
011.4		driven
011.5		roof
011.6		gutters
011.7		valley
011.8	MP	woodshed
012.1		privy
012.2		I have my
012.2		we have our
012.2		you have your
012.3		I've heard
012.4		he hasn't
012.4		I haven't
012.5		he hasn't
012.5		I haven't
012.6	X	ain't you?
012.7		he does it
012.7		I do it
012.8		does he do
012.9		he does
013	P	work
013.1		he doesn't care
013.2	S	do you?
013.3	S	Don't I know it!
013.4		I'm not sure
013.5		I was talking
013.5		you were talking
013.6		I've been thinking
013.7	S	makes
013.8		people thinks
013.9		they say
014	P	bank barn
014	P	granary
014	P	says I
014.1		house
014.2		barn
014.3		corn crib
014.4		loft
014.5		haystack
014.6		haycock
015	P	stable
015.1		cow stable
015.2	S	cowpen
015.3		hog pen

015.4		dairy	021.4		hauling
015.5		barnyard	021.5		dragged
015.6		pasture	021.6		plow
016	P	cup	021.7		harrow
016	P	palings	021.8	MP	stone boat
016.1		field	022	P	cog wheel
016.2		picket fence	022	P	lever
016.3		barbed wire fence	022	P	swing
016.4		rail fence	022.1		sawhorse
016.5		posts	022.2		brush
016.6		stone wall	022.3		strop
017	P	dinner bucket	022.4		cartridge
017.1		china	022.5	X	merry-go-round
017.2		bucket	022.5		seesaw
017.3		pail	022.6		seesawing
017.4		garbage pail	022.7	MP	sled
017.5		frying pan	023	P	pleaded
017.6		kettle	023.1		coal hod
017.7		vase	023.2		stovepipe
017.8		spoon	023.3		wheelbarrow
018	P	sifter	023.4		whetstone
018	P	wash rag	023.5		grindstone
018.1		wash the dishes	023.6		automobile
018.2		rinses	023.7		grease
018.3		dishcloth	023.8		greasy
018.4		dish towel	024.1		oil
018.5		bath towel	024.2		kerosene
018.6		faucet	024.3		tube
018.7		burst	024.4		launch
019	P	switch	024.5		miscellaneous boats
019.1		barrel	024.6		I'm going
019.2		miscellaneous containers	024.6		we're going
019.3		funnel	024.7		am I going to
019.4		whip	024.7		are they going to
019.5		goad	025	P	those were
019.6		paper bag	025.1		here's your clothes
019.7		burlap sack	025.2		there are
019.8		armful of wood	025.3		I'm not
019.8		turn	025.4		ain't I?
020.1		basket	025.5		we was
020.2		keg	025.6		it wasn't me
020.3		hoops	026	P	be you going
020.4		cork	026	P	if I were you
020.5		mouth organ	026	P	underwear
020.6		hammer	026.1		sample
020.7		tongue	026.2		prettier
020.8		shafts	026.3		apron
021	P	axle	027	P	got me
021.1		felly	027	P	had me
021.1		tire	027	P	knitted
021.2		singletree	027	P	overalls
021.3		doubletree	027.1		coat

027.2		vest
027.3		pants
027.4		brought
027.5		fitted
027.6		new suit
027.7		bulge
027.8		shrank
027.9	X	winklehawk
028	P	half shoes
028.1		dress up
028.2		purse
028.3		bracelet
028.4		necklace
028.5		suspenders
028.6		umbrella
028.7		bedspread
028.8		pillow
028.9		bolster
028.9	X	clear across
029	P	fertile
029	P	pocosin
029.1		quilt
029.2	S	pallet
029.3		lowland
029.4		meadow
029.5		swamp
029.6		marsh
029.7	M	loam
029.7	M	muck
030	P	hollow
030	P	ravine
030.1		draining
030.2		canal
030.3		creek
030.4		gully
030.5		branch
030.5		creek
030.5		river
031	P	hill
031	P	turnpike
031.1		mountain
031.2		cliff
031.3		wharf
031.4		waterfall
031.5		highway
031.6		side road
031.7		lane
031.8	M	sidewalk
032	P	in the house
032	P	next to me
032.1		stone
032.1		threw

032.2		at home
032.3		without
032.4		with
032.5		toward
032.6		across
032.7		after him
033	P	lie down!
033.1		dog
033.1		sic him!
033.2		mongrel
033.3		bitten
033.4		bull
033.5		cow
033.6		yoke of oxen
033.7		calf
033.8		calve
034	P	gelding
034	P	mare
034.1		stallion
034.2		horse
034.3		ridden
034.4		off
034.5		out of
034.6		horseshoes
034.7		hoofs
034.8		horseshoes
034.9		ram
035	P	pet lamb
035.1		ewe
035.2		wool
035.3		boar
035.4		barrow
035.5		hogs
035.6		bristles
035.7		tusks
035.8		trough
035.8		troughs
036.1		castrate
036.2		bawl
036.3		low
036.4		whinny
036.5		stock
036.6		poultry
036.7		setting hen
036.8		chicken coop
037	P	giblets
037.1		wishbone
037.2		haslet
037.3		chittlings
037.4		chore time
037.5		call to cows from pasture
037.5		call to cows to stand still

037.6		call to calves
037.7		calls to oxen, etc. in plowing
037.8		call to horses from pasture
038.1		get up!
038.2		whoa!
038.3		call to hogs
038.4		call to sheep
038.5		call to chickens
038.6		harness
039	P	badly
039.1		lines
039.2		reins
039.3		stirrups
039.4		near horse
039.5		a little way
040	P	backward
040	P	e'er a bit
040.1		a long way
040.2		anywhere
040.3		forward
040.4		ne'er a one
040.5		I ain't done nothing
040.6		nohow
040.7		none
041	P	fog grass
041.1		like as not
041.2		furrows
041.3		crop
041.4		cleared
041.5		second crop
041.6		sheaf
041.7		shock
041.8		bushels
042	P	/i/ for he, she, it, they
042	P	/m/ for him, her, it, them
042.1		oats are thrashed
042.2		you and I
042.3		both of us
042.4		me and him
042.5		it's her
042.5		it's him
042.5		it's me
042.5		it's them
042.6		as I am
043.1	S	as he is
043.2		than I can
043.3		the farthest
043.4		hers
043.4		his
043.4		ours
043.4		theirs
043.4		you-all's

043.4		yours
043.5		you-all
043.7		who-all
043.8		what-all
044	P	find us
044	P	lighted him
044.1		themselves
044.2		himself
044.3		wheat bread
044.4		other bread from wheat flour
044.5		biscuits
044.6		cornbread
044.7		other bread from corn meal
045	P	sweet rolls
045.1		baker's bread
045.2		doughnut
045.4		pancakes
045.5		pounds
045.6		of yeast
045.7		yolk
045.8		yellow
046	P	dried beef
046.1		boiled eggs
046.2		poached
046.3		salt pork
046.4		smoked pork
046.5		rind
046.6		bacon
046.7		sausage
046.8		butcher
046.9		spoiled
047	P	minister's face
047	P	most cheese is
047.1		blood pudding
047.1		headcheese
047.1		liverwurst
047.1	M	rolliches
047.1		scrapple
047.1	M	vinky
047.2		rancid
047.3		clabber
047.4		cottage cheese
047.5		strain the milk
047.6		cobbler
048.1		food
048.2		sauce
048.3		snack
048.4		ate
048.5		eaten
048.6		make some coffee
048.7		glass of water
048.8		broken

049	P	sitting
049	P	soda pop
049.1		drank
049.2		drunk
049.3		sit down!
049.4		sat down
049.5		help yourself
049.6		helped myself
049.7		I don't care for any
050	P	digest
050	P	salad
050.1		warmed over
050.2		chew
050.3		mush
050.4		vegetables
050.5		garden
050.6	X	grits
050.6	X	hominy
050.6	X	rice
051	P	an old man
051	P	long sweetening
051.1		smell of it
051.2		molasses
051.3		syrup
051.4		genuine
051.5		in bulk
051.6		jelly
051.7		give me an apple
051.7		salt and pepper
052	P	that tree
052	P	them's
052	P	these fellows
052.1		those boys
052.2		over there
052.3		this way
052.4		what?
053.1		who is poor
053.2		the orchard
053.2		who owns
053.3		whose
054.1		stone
054.2		pit
054.3		clingstone
054.4		freestone
054.5		core
054.6		peanuts
054.7		burr
054.7		walnut
055.1		oranges
055.2		all gone
055.3		radishes
055.4		tomatoes

055.5		potatoes
055.6		sweet potato
055.7		onions
055.8		scallions
055a.1		those cabbages are
055a.2		shell beans
055a.3		lima beans
055a.4		string beans
055a.5		greens
055a.6	S	head of children
055a.6		heads of lettuce
056.1		husks
056.2		sweet corn
056.3		tassel
056.4		silk
056.5		pumpkin
056.6		squash
056.7		muskmelon
056.8		mushroom
057.1		toadstool
057.2		swallow it
057.3		cigars and cigarettes
057.4		singing and laughing
057.5		beholden
057.6		can
057.7		I can't
057.8		I done worked
057.9	S	done dead
058	P	come cooler weather
058	P	wish
058.1		belongs to
058.2		you don't dare go
058.3		ought to
058.4		oughtn't to
058.5		I won't do it
058.6		might have helped
058.7	S	might could
059	P	mole
059	P	porgy
059.1		screech owl
059.2		hoot owl
059.3		woodpecker
059.4		skunk
059.5		varmints
059.6		squirrel
059.8		chipmunk
060	P	hard clam
060.1		oysters
060.2		bullfrog
060.3		peepers
060.4		toad
060.5		earthworm

060.6		turtle		065.6		grown
060.7		terrapin		065.7		bastard
060a.1		moth		066	P	beatinest
060a.2		moths		066	P	chum
060a.3		lightning bug		066.1	S	lovinger
060a.4		dragonfly		066.2		nephew
060a.5		hornets		066.3		orphan
060a.6	S	dirt dauber		066.4		guardian
060a.6		wasp		066.5		relatives
060a.7		yellow jacket		066.6	S	no kin to her
061	P	elm		066.7		stranger
061	P	locusts		067	P	circuit rider
061.1		grasshopper		067	P	Daniel
061.2		minnows		067	P	gentleman
061.3		spiderweb		067	P	Miss
061.4		roots		067	P	Miss
061.5		sugar maple		067	P	Reverend Simpson
061.6		maple grove		067.1		Mary
061.7	MP	sycamore		067.2		Martha
062	P	poisonous		067.3		Nelly
062	P	stem		067.4		Matthew
062.1		cherry tree		067.5		Mrs. Cooper
062.2		sumac		067.6		preacher
062.3		poison ivy		067.7		schoolteacher
062.4		strawberries		067.8		your aunt
062.5		raspberries		068	P	Captain
062.6		mountain laurel		068	P	Uncle William
062.7		rhododendron		068.1		Aunt Sarah
062.8		magnolia		068.2		Uncle John
063.1		my husband		068.3		General
063.2		my wife		068.4		Colonel
063.3		widow		068.5		Judge
063.4		father		068.6		student
063.5		dad		068.7		secretary
063.6		mama		069	P	Gullah
063.7		parents		069	P	Irishman
064	P	pet names for children		069	P	Italian
064.1		grandfather		069	P	Jew
064.2		grandmother		069	P	justice of the peace
064.3		children		069	P	medicine show
064.4		baby carriage		069	P	Negro mammy
064.5		wheel		069	P	Squire
064.6		oldest		069	P	tourist
064.7		daughter		069.1		actress
064.8		girl		069.2		American
065	P	look after		069.3		Negro
065	P	reared		069.4		nigger
065.1		pregnant		069.5	S	Master John
065.2		midwife		069.6	S	poor whites
065.3		looks like		069.8		backwoodsman
065.4		whipping		070	P	far off
065.6		grew		070	M	stub

070.1		almost	076	P	in bed
070.2		like to fell down	076	P	some better
070.3		just a minute	076.1		got sick
070.4		how far	076.2	S	by and by
070.5		Look here!	076.3		caught a cold
071	P	either you or I	076.4		hoarse
071	P	neither you nor I	076.5		cough
071.1		how often	076.6	X	wake him up
071.2		nor me either	076.7	X	wake up
071.3		forehead	077	P	ague
071.4		right ear	077	P	buck fever
071.5		beard	077	P	fever
071.6		mouth	077	P	humor
071.7		teeth	077.1		taken
071.7		tooth	077.2		took
071.8		gums	077.3		deaf
072	P	skin	077.4		sweated
072	P	stout	077.5		boil
072.1		palm	077.6		pus
072.2		fists	077.7		swelled up
072.3		joint	077.8		swollen
072.4		chest	078	P	I buried me
072.5		shoulders	078	P	inflamed wound
072.6		shins	078.1		wound
072.7		haunches	078.2		proud flesh
072.8		peaked	078.3		iodine
073	P	awkward fellow	078.4		quinine
073	P	common	078.5		died
073	P	skillful	078.7		he died from
073.1		strong	078.8		cemetery
073.2		good-natured	079	P	mumps is
073.3		awkward	079.1		coffin
073.4		fool	079.2		funeral
074.1		lively	079.3		mourning
074.1		quite	079.4		pretty well
074.2		uneasy	079.5		don't worry
074.3		afraid	079.6		rheumatism
074.4		used to be	079.7		diphtheria
074.5		didn't used to	079.8		jaundice
074.6		careless	080	P	ought to take
074.7		queer	080	P	to keep
075	P	a-raring	080	P	tuberculosis
075	P	all excited	080.1		appendicitis
075	P	chronically ill	080.2		vomit
075	P	wet hen	080.4		to his stomach
075.1		touchy	080.5		to tell
075.2		angry	081	P	how is it that
075.4		keep calm	081	P	I shall be
075.5		tired	081	P	we shall be glad
075.7		worn out	081.1		courting her
076	P	directly	081.3		boyfriend
076	X	drowsy	081.4		his girlfriend

081.5		kissing		086.3		Maryland
082	P	big to-do		086.3		Virginia
082	P	his fiancee		086.4		North Carolina
082.1	S	now		086.4		South Carolina
082.1		turned him down		086.5		Florida
082.2		married		086.5		Georgia
082.3		best man		086.6		Alabama
082.4		bridesmaid		086.6		Louisiana
082.5		serenade		086.7		Kentucky
082.6		up at		086.7		Tennessee
082.7		down in		086.8		Arkansas
082.8		the whole crowd		086.8		Missouri
082.9	S	frown		087	P	Asia
082.9	S	frowning		087	P	Atlanta
083	P	class		087	P	Boston
083	P	couples		087	P	Canada
083.1		dance		087	P	Detroit
083.3		lets out		087	P	New Haven
083.4		start		087	P	Panama
083.5		played hookey		087	P	Springfield
083.6		education		087.1		Baltimore
083.7		college		087.1	M	Philadelphia
084.1		library		087.1		Washington
084.2		post office		087.2		Charleston
084.3		hotel		087.3	S	Asheville
084.4		theater		087.4		Cincinnati
084.5		hospital		087.4		Louisville
084.6		nurse		087.5		Chicago
084.7	MP	station		087.5		St. Louis
085	P	blocks		087.6		New Orleans
085	P	hung		087.7		France
085	P	public square		087.7		Ireland
085	P	street car		087.8		Russia
085.1		catty-cornered		088	P	and him not there
085.2		cattywampus		088	P	and his overcoat on his arm
085.3		I want off		088	P	do she smell it
085.4		county seat		088	P	if you go
085.5		government		088	P	whilst
085.6		Civil War		088.1		miles
085.7		law and order		088.2		as I want to
085.8		hanged		088.2		I don't know
086	P	California		088.3		unless
086	P	Illinois		088.4		instead of
086	P	Indiana		088.5		because
086	P	Michigan		088.6		like
086	P	Texas		089	P	after writing
086.1		Massachusetts		089	P	Mass
086.1		New England		089	P	psalm
086.2	M	New Jersey		089.1		Baptist
086.2		New York		089.2		joined
086.2	MP	Ohio		089.3		God
086.2	M	Pennsylvania		089.4		My God!

089.5		sermon
089.6		music
089.7		beautiful
089.8	S	ballad
089.9		by the timc I get there
090	P	awfully
090	P	good and hungry
090.1		devil
090.2		ghosts
090.3		haunted house
090.4		rather
090.5		I'd rather
090.6		mighty glad
091	P	a little
091	P	a lot
091	P	right smart
091	P	why, yes!
091.1		certainly
091.3		I sure can
091.4		yes
091.5		yes sir
091.6		well ..
091.7	S	really
091.8		real
092	P	don't curse
092	P	why!
092.1		damn it!
092.1		darn it!
092.3		for goodness sake!
092.5		shucks
092.6		the idea!
092.7		How are you?
092.8		How do you do?
093	P	good-bye!
093	P	hurrah!
093.1		come back again
093.2		Merry Christmas
093.3		Happy New Year
094	P	grocery store
094	P	How much do you ask for it?
094	P	What will you take for it?
094.1		I think
094.2		shopping
094.3		wrapped up
094.4		unwrapped
094.5		at a loss
094.6		costs
094.7		due
094.8		dues
095	P	scarcely
095.1		borrow
095.2		scarce

095.3		coast
095.4		belly bumper
095.5		somersault
095.6		swam across
095.7		dived
096.1		drowned
096.2		creeps
096.3		climbed
096.4		crouch
096.5		kneeled down
096.6		lie down
097	P	a house afire
097	P	pitch in
097.1		laid in bed
097.2		dreamed
097.3		woke up
097.4		stomp
097.5		take you home
097.6		pull
097.7		push
098	P	fix
098	P	tag
098.1		carried
098.2		Don't you touch it!
098.3		go bring
098.4		goal
098.5		catch
098.6		caught
099	P	wasting time
099.1		wait for you
099.2		give me another chance
099.3		humor
099.4		get rid of him
100	P	address (n.)
100	P	chat
100	P	miss you
100	P	recognize
100.1		made out like
100.2		stole
100.3		remember
100.4		don't remember
100.5		written
100.6		an answer
100.7		address (v.)
101	P	got in bad with
101	P	tell on
101.1		taught you
101.2		intend to
101.3		if you're a mind to
101.4		tattletale
101.5		pick flowers
101.6		toys

101.7		I just knew it!
102	P	did
102	P	on
102.1		gave
102.2		began
102.3		ran
102.4		came
102.5		saw
102.6		torn up
102.7		put it on
103	P	whole
103.1		nothing
103.2		something
103.3		such
103.4		always
103.5		since
103.6		on purpose
103.7		grunt of affirmation
103.8		grunt of negation
103.9		I think so
104	P	great
104	P	in

104	P	in it
104	P	went
104.1		ask
104.2		asked
104.3		fought
104.4		drew
104.5		hoist
104.6	M	anymore
104.7	M	what kind of a pencil
104.9	X	it wonders me
104.9	M	whenever
105	P	but yet and still
105	P	cut it half in two
105	P	don't pay him no mind
105	P	knock you down
105	P	listen at the bell
105	P	peekaboo
105	P	some little
105	P	sweet talk him out of it
105	P	we hear a lot of people to say that
105	P	we've had it to rain harder

Work Sheets by List Manuscript Number

Geography

004.0	086.1	New England
005.0	086.1	Massachusetts
006.0	086.2	New York
007.0	086.2	New Jersey
008.0	086.2	Pennsylvania
009.0	086.2	Ohio
010.0	086.3	Maryland
011.0	086.3	Virginia
012.0	086.4	North Carolina
012.0	086.4	South Carolina
013.0	086.5	Georgia
014.0	086.5	Florida
015.0	086.6	Alabama
016.0	086.6	Louisiana
017.0	086.7	Kentucky
018.0	086.7	Tennessee
019.0	086.8	Missouri
020.0	086.8	Arkansas
020.1	086	Texas
020.2	086	California
021.0	087.1	Philadelphia
022.0	087.1	Baltimore
023.0	087.1	Washington
024.0	087.3	Asheville

025.0	087.2	Charleston
026.0	087.5	Chicago
027.0	087.5	St. Louis
028.0	087.4	Cincinnati
029.0	087.4	Louisville
030.0	087.6	New Orleans
030.1	087	Atlanta
030.1	087	Boston
030.1	087	Detroit
030.1	086	Illinois
030.1	086	Indiana
030.1	086	Michigan
030.1	087	New Haven
030.1	087	Springfield
031.0	087.7	Ireland
032.0	087.7	France
033.0	087.8	Russia
033.1	087	Asia
033.2	087	Panama
033.3	087	Canada

Topography

034.0	029.3	lowland
034.1	031	valley
034.2	030	hollow

035.0	029.4	meadow
035.1	029.4	swale
036.0	029	pocosin
036.0	029.5	swamp
036.1	029.5	names of swamps
036.2	029.5	bog
036.3	029.5	hammock
037.0	029.6	marsh
038.0	030.1	draining
038.1	030.1	ditch it
039.0	029.7	loam
039.1	029.7	muck
039.2	029	fertile
040.0	032.1	stone
040.1	032.1	brick
041.0	030.4	gully
041.1	030	ravine
042.0	031.1	mountain
042.1	031	hill
042.2	031.1	notch
042.3	031.1	names of mountains, hills, gaps
043.0	031.2	cliff
043.1	031.2	bluff
044.0	031.4	waterfall
045.0	030.3	creek
045.0	030.5	creek
045.0	030.5	river
045.1	030.5	names of rivers
046.0	030.6	names of streams
046.1	030.3	inlet
046.2	030.5	pond
047.0	030.5	branch
047.1	030.5	slough
048.0	030.2	canal
049.0	031.5	highway
049.0	031	turnpike
050.0	031.6	side road
051.0	031.7	lane
051.1	031.7	gap
053.0	031.8	sidewalk
054.0	088.1	miles
054.1	088.1	rods
055.0	007.7	feet
056.0	070.4	how far
057.0	043.3	the farthest
058.0	039.5	a little way
059.0	040.1	a long way

Numerals

060.0	001.1	one
061.0	001.1	two

062.0	001.2	three
063.0	001.2	four
064.0	001.3	five
065.0	001.3	six
066.0	001.4	seven
067.0	001.4	eight
068.0	001.5	nine
069.0	001.5	ten
070.0	001.6	eleven
071.0	001.6	twelve
072.0	001.7	thirteen
073.0	001.7	fourteen
074.0	001.8	twenty
075.0	001.8	twenty-seven
076.0	001a.1	thirty
077.0	001a.1	forty
078.0	001a.2	seventy
079.0	001a.2	hundred
080.0	001a.2	thousand
081.0	001a.3	first
082.0	001a.3	second
083.0	001a.4	fifth
084.0	001a.4	sixth
085.0	001a.5	all at once
086.0	001a.6	twice as good

Time

087.0	001a.7	January
088.0	001a.7	February
089.0	001a.7	April
090.0	002.1	Tuesday
091.0	002.1	Wednesday
092.0	002.2	Thursday
093.0	002.2	Saturday
094.0	003.7	Sunday after next
095.0	003.6	Sunday before last
096.0	003.8	fortnight
097.0	003.5	yesterday
098.0	004.1	tomorrow
099.0	003.2	sunrise
100.0	003.4	sunset
101.0	002.4	afternoon
101.0	002.6	evening
102.0	003.1	good night
103.0	002.5	good day
103.0	002.3	good morning
104.0	004.2	What time is it?
105.0	004.4	half past seven
106.0	004.5	quarter of eleven
107.0	004.6	this year
108.0	005.1	three years old

108.1	005	going on ten
108.2	005	up in eighty
109.0	005.2	year ago
110.0	070.3	just a minute
110.1	004	while
110.2	004	spelled me off

Weather

111.0	005.3	fine day
112.0	005.4	clearing up
113.0	005.5	clouding up
113.1	005.5	falling weather
113.2	005	gloomy day
113.3	005.6	clouds
113.4	005	hazy
114.0	007.2	rising
115.0	007.3	going down
116.0	006.6	northeast
116.0	006.6	northwest
117.0	006.5	southeast wind
117.0	006.5	southwest wind
118.0	006.4	from the south
119.0	006.1	heavy rain
120.0	006.2	thunderstorm
121.0	006.7	shower
122.0	006.7	drizzle
122.1	006	drizzling
123.0	006.8	fog
123.0	006.9	foggy
123.1	006	burned off
124.0	007.1	drought
125.0	007.4	frost
126.0	007.4	dew

The Farm

127.0	014.1	house
128.0	014.2	barn
129.0	014.4	loft
130.0	014.7	hay mow
131.0	014.5	haystack
132.0	014.6	haycock
133.0	014.3	corn crib
133.1	014	granary
134.0	015.4	dairy
135.0	015.1	cow stable
136.0	015.2	cowpen
137.0	015.3	hog pen
138.0	036.8	chicken coop
139.1	015	miscellaneous farm buildings
140.0	015.5	barnyard

141.0	015.6	pasture
143.0	016.2	picket fence
144.0	016.3	barbed wire fence
145.0	016.4	rail fence
146.0	016.5	posts
147.0	016.6	stone wall

Agriculture

148.0	016.1	field
149.0	050.5	garden
150.0	041.4	cleared
151.0	041.2	furrows
152.0	041.5	second crop
153.0	041.3	crop
154.0	041.6	sheaf
154.0	041.7	shock
156.0	041.8	bushels
157.0	019.8	turn
159.0	019.8	armful of wood
160.0	042.1	oats are thrashed

Containers and Utensils

161.0	017.2	bucket
161.0	017	dinner bucket
161.0	017.3	pail
162.0	017.6	kettle
164.0	017.5	frying pan
165.0	017.8	spoon
166.0	017.4	garbage pail
167.0	017.1	china
167.1	017.1	china egg
168.0	017.7	vase
169.0	018.1	wash the dishes
170.0	018.2	rinses
171.0	018.3	dishcloth
172.0	018.4	dish towel
173.0	018.5	bath towel
173.1	018	wash rag
174.0	018.6	faucet
175.0	020.4	cork
176.0	019.3	funnel
177.0	020.2	keg
178.0	019.1	barrel
178.5	018	sifter
179.0	020.3	hoops
180.0	019.2	miscellaneous containers
181.0	023.1	coal hod
182.0	019.6	paper bag
183.0	019.7	burlap sack
184.0	020.6	hammer

185.0	098.3	go bring
186.0	010.4	broom
186.1	010	clean up
186.2	010.8	file cloth
186.3	010.9	file the floor
187.0	022.2	brush
188.0	022.3	strop
189.0	004.3	watch
190.0	023.4	whetstone
191.0	023.5	grindstone
192.0	022.4	cartridge
193.0	022.1	sawhorse

Vehicles

194.0	023.3	wheelbarrow
195.0	097.6	pull
196.0	097.7	push
197.0	104.5	hoist
198.0	098.1	carried
199.0	021.6	plow
200.0	021.7	harrow
201.0	021.8	stone boat
202.0	021.1	felly
202.0	021.1	tire
203.0	020.7	tongue
204.0	020.8	shafts
205.0	021.2	singletree
206.0	021.3	doubletree
207.0	039.4	near horse
208.0	038.6	harness
209.0	039.1	lines
209.0	039.2	reins
211.0	039.3	stirrups
212.0	019.4	whip
213.0	019.5	goad
214.0	021.4	hauling
215.0	024.5	miscellaneous boats
216.0	024.4	launch
217.0	031.3	wharf
218.0	023.6	automobile
219.0	024.3	tube
220.0	024.1	oil
221.0	024.2	kerosene
222.0	023.7	grease
222.0	023.8	greasy

Domestic Animals

223.0	036.5	stock
224.0	033.6	yoke of oxen
225.0	033.4	bull

226.0	033.5	cow
227.0	033.7	calf
228.0	033.8	calve
229.0	036.2	bawl
230.0	036.3	low
231.0	034.2	horse
231.1	034	gelding
231.1	034	mare
232.0	034.1	stallion
233.0	036.4	whinny
234.0	034.7	hoofs
235.0	034.6	horseshoes
235.0	034.8	horseshoes
236.0	034.9	ram
237.0	035.1	ewe
238.0	035.2	wool
239.0	035.5	hogs
240.0	035.3	boar
241.0	035.4	barrow
242.0	035.6	bristles
243.0	035.7	tusks
244.0	035.8	trough
244.0	035.8	troughs
245.0	037.2	haslet
246.0	037.3	chittlings
247.0	036.1	castrate
248.0	033.1	dog
249.0	033.2	mongrel
250.0	036.6	poultry
251.0	036.7	setting hen
252.0	037.1	wishbone
253.0	037.4	chore time

Calls to Animals

254.0	033.1	sic him!
255.0	037.5	calls to cows
256.0	037.5	calls to cows to stand still
257.0	037.6	calls to calves
258.0	037.7	calls to oxen, horses (plowing)
259.0	037.8	calls to horses
260.0	038.1	get up!
261.0	038.2	whoa!
262.0	038.4	calls to sheep
263.0	038.3	calls to pigs
264.0	038.5	calls to chickens

Wild Animals

265.0	059.5	varmints
266.0	059.6	squirrel
267.0	059.8	chipmunk

268.0	059.4	skunk
269.0	059.3	woodpecker
270.0	059.1	screech owl
271.0	059.2	hoot owl
271.1	059.2	miscellaneous owls
272.0	060.2	bullfrog
273.0	060.3	peepers
274.0	060.4	toad
275.0	060.6	turtle
275.2	060.6	cooter
276.0	060.7	terrapin
276.1	060.7	gopher
277.0	061.2	minnows
278.0	060.1	oysters
279.0	060.5	earthworm
279.2	060.5	other worms (than earthworm)
280.0	061.1	grasshopper
280.0	061	locusts
281.0	060a.1	moth
281.0	060a.2	moths
282.0	060a.3	lightning bug
283.0	060a.4	dragonfly
284.0	060a.6	wasp
285.0	060a.6	dirt dauber
286.0	060a.7	yellow jacket
287.0	060a.5	hornets
288.0	061.3	spiderweb

Trees and Shrubs

289.0	062.1	cherry tree
290.0	053.2	the orchard
291.0	061.5	sugar maple
292.0	061.6	maple grove
293.0	062.6	mountain laurel
293.0	062.7	rhododendron
294.0	061.7	sycamore
295.0	062.8	magnolia
296.0	062.2	sumac
297.0	062.3	poison ivy
297.1	062	poisonous
298.0	101.5	pick flowers

Vegetables

299.0	050.4	vegetables
300.0	055.5	potatoes
300.2	055.6	sweet potato
301.0	055a.6	heads of lettuce
302.0	055a.6	head of children
303.0	055a.1	those cabbages are
304.0	055.3	radishes

305.0	061.4	roots
306.0	055.7	onions
307.0	055.8	scallions
308.0	055a.5	greens
309.0	055a.3	lima beans
310.0	055a.4	string beans
311.0	055a.2	shell beans
312.0	056.2	sweet corn
313.0	056.3	tassel
314.0	056.4	silk
315.0	056.1	husks
316.0	056.5	pumpkin
317.0	056.6	squash
318.0	056.7	muskmelon
318.1	056.7	cantaloupe
318.2	056.7	honeydew
319.0	055.4	tomatoes
320.0	054.3	clingstone
321.0	054.4	freestone
322.0	054.2	pit
323.0	054.1	stone
324.0	051.7	give me an apple
325.0	054.5	core
326.0	055.1	oranges
327.0	062.4	strawberries
328.0	062.5	raspberries
328.1	062.5	dewberries
329.0	054.6	peanuts
330.0	054.7	walnut
331.0	054.7	burr
332.0	056.8	mushroom
333.0	057.1	toadstool

Food and Cooking

334.0	048.1	food
335.0	044.3	wheat bread
335.1	044.4	other bread from wheat flour
336.0	044.5	biscuits
337.0	045.2	doughnut
338.0	045.1	baker's bread
339.0	044.6	cornbread
340.0	044.7	other bread from corn meal
341.0	045.4	pancakes
342.0	050.3	mush
342.1	050.6	hominy
342.2	050.6	grits
342.3	050.6	rice
343.0	045.6	of yeast
343.1	045.6	emptings
344.0	051.7	salt and pepper
345.0	047.6	cobbler

346.0	048.2	sauce
347.0	046.1	boiled eggs
348.0	046.2	poached
349.0	045.7	yolk
350.0	045.8	yellow
351.0	047.5	strain the milk
352.0	047.3	clabber
353.0	047.4	cottage cheese
354.0	047.2	rancid
355.0	046.3	salt pork
356.0	046.4	smoked pork
357.0	046.6	bacon
358.0	046.5	rind
359.0	046.7	sausage
360.0	047.1	headcheese
360.1	047.1	liverwurst
360.2	047.1	blood pudding
360.3	047.1	scrapple
360.4	047.1	rolliches
360.5	047.1	vinky
360.6	047	minister's face
361.0	046.9	spoiled
362.0	051.6	jelly
363.0	051.2	molasses
364.0	051.3	syrup
365.0	051.4	genuine
366.0	048.6	make some coffee
367.0	048.7	glass of water
368.0	050.1	warmed over
369.0	048.3	snack
370.0	050.2	chew
371.0	057.2	swallow it
372.0	049.5	help yourself
373.0	049.6	helped myself
374.0	049.7	I don't care for any
375.0	057.3	cigars and cigarettes

Dwellings

376.0	007.6	living room
376.1	009.9	bedroom
377.0	008.9	chair
378.0	009.1	sofa
379.0	009.4	window shades
380.0	008.4	mantel
381.0	008.2	hearth
382.0	008.3	andirons
383.0	008.5	backlog
384.0	008.6	lightwood
385.0	008.8	white ashes
386.0	008.1	chimney
387.0	023.2	stovepipe

388.0	008.7	soot
388.1	008.6	into
389.0	009.5	closet
390.0	009.3	furniture
391.0	009.2	dresser
392.0	009.6	wardrobe
393.0	028.7	bedspread
394.0	029.1	quilt
395.0	028.9	bolster
395.0	028.8	pillow
397.0	028.9	clear across
398.0	029.2	pallet
399.0	009.8	kitchen
400.0	010.1	pantry
401.0	010.6	stairs
402.0	009.7	attic
403.0	010.3	junk room
404.0	010.2	junk
405.0	011.1	shut the door
406.0	011.5	roof
407.0	011.7	valley
408.0	011.6	gutters
409.0	011.2	clapboards
410.0	010.7	porch
411.0	011.8	woodshed
412.0	012.1	privy
412.3	010	rented a room

Clothing

413.0	025.1	here's your clothes
414.0	028.1	dress up
415.0	010.5	washing and ironing
416.0	010.5	laundry
417.0	020.1	basket
418.0	027.6	new suit
419.0	027.1	coat
420.0	027.2	vest
421.0	027.3	pants
421.1	027.9	winklehawk
422.0	027.7	bulge
423.0	028.5	suspenders
424.0	026.3	apron
425.0	026.1	sample
426.0	028.6	umbrella
427.0	028.2	purse
428.0	028.3	bracelet
429.0	028.4	necklace

Family

430.0	063.4	father

431.0	063.5	dad
432.0	063.6	mother
433.0	063.6	mama
434.0	063.7	parents
435.0	063.1	my husband
436.0	063.2	my wife
437.0	064.7	daughter
438.0	064.8	girl
439.0	064.3	children
440.0	064.6	oldest
441.0	066.1	lovinger
442.0	064.1	grandfather
443.0	064.2	grandmother
444.0	067.8	your aunt
445.0	068.1	Aunt Sarah
446.0	068.2	Uncle John
447.0	066.2	nephew
448.0	066.5	relatives
449.0	066.6	no kin to her
450.0	063.3	widow
451.0	066.3	orphan
452.0	066.4	guardian
453.0	065.1	pregnant
454.0	065.7	bastard
455.0	065.3	looks like
456.0	032.7	after him
457.0	065.4	whipping
457.3	065	look after

Social Relations

458.0	081.3	boyfriend
459.0	081.4	his girlfriend
460.0	097.5	take you home
461.0	032.2	at home
461.1	032	in the house
462.0	081.1	courting her
463.0	081.1	going with her
464.0	081.5	kissing
465.0	082.1	gave him the mitten
466.0	082.1	turned him down
467.0	082.2	married
468.0	082.3	best man
469.0	082.4	bridesmaid
470.0	082.5	serenade
471.0	083.1	dance
472.0	089.6	music
473.0	089.8	ballad
474.0	020.5	mouth organ
475.0	082.8	the whole crowd
476.0	057.4	singing and laughing
477.0	032.6	across

Greetings and Salutations

478.0	092.7	How are you?
479.0	092.8	How do you do?
480.0	090.6	mighty glad
481.0	093.1	come back again
482.0	093.2	Merry Christmas
483.0	093.3	Happy New Year

Names, Titles, Occupations

484.0	067.1	Mary
485.0	067.2	Martha
486.0	067.3	Nelly
487.0	067.4	Matthew
488.0	067.5	Mrs. Cooper
489.0	069.5	Master John
490.0	068.3	General
491.0	068.4	Colonel
492.0	068.5	Judge
493.0	067.7	schoolteacher
494.0	068.6	student
495.0	068.7	secretary
496.0	084.6	nurse
497.0	065.2	midwife
498.0	069.1	actress
499.0	066.7	stranger
500.0	069.8	backwoodsman
501.0	069.6	poor whites
501.1	069.6	poor white trash
502.0	069.3	Negro
503.0	069.4	nigger
504.0	067.6	preacher
505.0	069.2	American

Personal Characteristics

506.0	089.7	beautiful
507.0	026.2	prettier
508.0	072.8	peaked
509.0	073.1	strong
510.0	074.1	lively
511.0	074.1	quite
512.0	073.3	awkward
513.0	073.4	fool
514.0	074.6	careless
515.0	073.2	good-natured
516.0	099.3	humor
517.0	075.1	touchy
518.0	074.7	queer
519.0	075.2	angry
520.0	074.3	afraid

521.0	074.2	uneasy
522.0	075.4	keep calm
523.0	075.5	tired
524.0	075.5	give out
525.0	075.7	worn out

Body Parts

526.0	071.3	forehead
527.0	071.4	right ear
528.0	071.6	mouth
529.0	071.7	teeth
529.0	071.7	tooth
530.0	071.8	gums
531.0	071.5	beard
532.0	072.4	chest
533.0	072.5	shoulders
534.0	072.1	palm
535.0	072.2	fists
536.0	072.3	joint
537.0	072.6	shins
538.0	072.7	haunches

Illness and Death

539.0	076.1	got sick
540.0	096.6	lie down
540.1	076	drowsy
540.2	076.7	wake up
540.3	076.6	wake him up
541.0	079.4	pretty well
542.0	079.5	don't worry
543.0	076.3	caught a cold
544.0	076.5	cough
545.0	076.4	hoarse
546.0	077.3	deaf
547.0	080.4	to his stomach
548.0	080.2	vomit
549.0	080.3	throw up
550.0	079.6	rheumatism
551.0	079.7	diphtheria
552.0	080.1	appendicitis
553.0	079.8	jaundice
554.0	077.5	boil
555.0	077.6	pus
556.0	078.1	wound
557.0	078.2	proud flesh
558.0	078.3	iodine
559.0	078.4	quinine
560.0	084.5	hospital
561.0	078.7	he died from
561.1	078.5	died

562.0	078.5	passed away
562.1	078.6	kicked the bucket
563.0	096.1	drowned
564.0	079.2	funeral
565.0	079.3	mourning
566.0	079.1	coffin
567.0	078.8	cemetery
568.0	078.8	graveyard
568.1	078	I buried me

Religion

569.0	089.1	Baptist
570.0	089.3	God
571.1	089.4	My God!
572.0	089.5	sermon
573.0	089.2	joined
574.0	090.1	devil
574.1	090.1	boogeyman
575.0	090.2	ghosts
576.0	090.3	haunted house

Public Institutions

577.0	083.6	education
578.0	083.7	college
579.0	083.3	lets out
580.0	083.4	start
581.0	083.5	played hookey
582.0	084.1	library
583.0	084.4	theater
584.0	084.3	hotel
585.0	084.7	station
586.0	084.2	post office
587.0	085.1	catty-cornered
587.1	085.2	cattywampus
588.0	085.4	county seat
589.0	085.5	government
590.0	085.7	law and order
591.0	085.6	Civil War

Business

592.0	046.8	butcher
593.0	094.2	shopping
594.0	051.5	in bulk
595.0	045.5	pounds
596.0	055.2	all gone
597.0	094.6	costs
597.1	094	How much do you ask for it?
597.2	094	What will you take for it?
598.0	094.5	at a loss

599.0	095.2	scarce
599.1	095	scarcely
600.0	094.7	due
600.0	094.8	dues
601.0	095.1	borrow
602.0	100.2	stole
603.0	099.4	get rid of him
603.1	099	wasting time
603.2	100	chat
604.0	099.2	give me another chance
605.0	100.6	an answer
606.0	080.5	to tell

Sport and Play

607.0	101.6	toys
608.0	022.7	sled
609.0	095.3	coast
610.0	095.4	belly bumper
611.0	064.4	baby carriage
612.0	064.5	wheel
613.0	022.6	seesawing
613.1	022.5	seesaw
613.2	022.5	joggling board
613.3	022.5	merry-go-round
614.0	095.5	somersault
615.0	095.6	swam across
616.0	095.7	dived
617.0	096.4	crouch
618.0	096.2	creeps
619.0	097.4	stomp
620.0	098.5	catch
621.0	098.4	goal
621.2	098	fix
622.0	101.4	tattletale
622.3	101	got in bad with

Affirmations and Interjections

623.0	091.4	yes
624.0	091.5	yes sir
625.0	091.3	I sure can
626.0	091.1	certainly
627.0	013.4	I'm not sure
628.0	103.7	grunt of affirmation
629.0	103.8	grunt of negation
630.0	094.1	I think
631.0	103.9	I think so
632.0	091.6	well . . .
633.0	052.4	what?
634.0	070.5	Look here!
635.0	092.6	the idea!

635.1	104	great
636.0	092.5	shucks
637.0	092.1	damn it!
638.0	092.1	darn it!
639.0	092.3	for goodness sake!

Pronouns

640.0	042.5	it's me
640.1	104.9	it wonders me
641.0	042.5	it's her
641.0	042.5	it's him
641.0	042.5	it's them
642.0	025.6	it wasn't me
643.0	042.6	as I am
644.0	043.1	as he is
645.0	043.2	than I can
646.0	042.2	you and I
647.0	042.3	both of us
648.0	042.4	me and him
649.0	071.2	nor me either
650.0	012.2	I have my
650.0	012.2	we have our
650.0	012.2	you have your
651.0	043.5	you-all
652.0	043.4	his
653.0	043.4	hers
654.0	043.4	ours
655.0	043.4	yours
656.0	043.4	you-all's
657.0	043.4	theirs
658.0	044.2	himself
659.0	044.1	themselves
660.0	052.1	those boys
661.0	052.3	this way
662.0	103.3	such
663.0	043.7	who-all
664.0	043.8	what-all
664.2	104.7	what kind of a pencil
665.0	053.2	who owns
666.0	053.1	who is poor
667.0	053.3	whose
668.0	103.2	something
669.0	103.1	nothing

Verbs: Principal Parts

670.0	102.2	began
671.0	057.5	beholden
672.0	033.3	bitten
673.0	006.3	blew
674.0	048.8	broken

675.0	027.4	brought
676.0	018.7	burst
677.0	102.4	came
678.0	098.6	caught
679.0	096.3	climbed
680.0	049.1	drank
680.0	049.2	drunk
681.0	104.4	drew
682.0	011.4	driven
682.0	011.3	drove
683.0	048.4	ate
683.0	048.5	eaten
684.0	070.2	like to fell down
684.1	070	stub
685.0	104.3	fought
685.1	082.9	frown
685.1	082.9	frowning
686.0	007.5	froze over
687.0	102.1	gave
688.0	065.6	grew
688.0	065.6	grown
689.0	085.8	hanged
689.0	085	hung
690.0	101.7	I just knew it!
691.0	097.1	laid in bed
692.0	034.3	ridden
693.0	003.3	rose
694.0	102.3	ran
695.0	102.5	saw
696.0	027.8	shrank
697.0	049.4	sat down
697.0	049.3	sit down!
698.0	077.7	swelled up
698.0	077.8	swollen
699.0	077.1	taken
699.0	077.2	took
700.0	102.6	torn up
701.0	101.1	taught you
702.0	032.1	threw
703.0	097.3	woke up
704.0	104.1	ask
704.0	104.2	asked
705.0	100.7	address
705.1	100	address
706.0	100.5	written
706.2	089	after writing
707.0	021.5	dragged
708.0	097.2	dreamed
709.0	027.5	fitted
710.0	096.5	kneeled down
711.0	100.1	made out like
711.1	088.6	like

712.0	100.3	remember
712.1	100.4	don't remember
713.0	051.1	smell of it
714.0	077.4	sweated
715.0	094.4	unwrapped
716.0	094.3	wrapped up

Verbs: Be, Have, Do

719.0	024.6	I'm going
719.0	024.6	we're going
720.0	025.3	I'm not
721.0	025.4	ain't I?
721.1	012.6	ain't you?
722.0	024.7	am I going to
722.0	024.7	are they going to
723.0	026	be you going
724.0	025.2	there are
725.0	013.5	I was talking
725.0	013.5	you were talking
725.1	025.5	we was
726.0	013.6	I've been thinking
727.0	012.3	I've heard
728.0	012.5	he hasn't
728.0	012.5	I haven't
728.1	012.4	he hasn't
728.1	012.4	I haven't
729.0	013.2	do you?
730.0	012.7	he does it
730.0	012.7	I do it
731.0	012.8	does he do
732.0	012.9	he does
733.0	013.1	he doesn't care
734.0	098.2	Don't you touch it!
734.1	102	did
735.0	013.3	Don't I know it!
736.0	057.8	I done worked
737.0	057.9	done dead

Verbs: Agreement

738.0	013.8	people thinks
739.0	013.7	makes
740.0	013.9	they say

Verbs: Modals

741.0	057.7	I can't
742.0	057.6	can
743.0	058.2	you don't dare go
744.0	058.6	might have helped
745.0	058.7	might could

746.0   058.3   ought to
746.1   058.1   belongs to
747.0   058.4   oughtn't to
748.0   085.3   I want off
749.0   074.4   used to be
750.0   074.5   didn't used to
751.0   058.5   I won't do it
752.0   101.2   intend to
753.0   101.3   if you're a mind to

Adverbs

754.0   040.3   forward
755.0   052.2   over there
756.0   102.7   put it on
757.0   040.2   anywhere
758.0   103.4   always
758.1   082.1   now
758.2   104.6   anymore
759.0   071.1   how often
759.1   104.9   whenever
760.0   076.2   by and by
760.1   076   directly
761.0   103.5   since
762.0   089.9   by the time I get there
763.0   070.1   almost
764.0   091.8   real
765.0   091.7   really
766.0   090.4   rather

767.0   090.5   I'd rather
768.0   103.6   on purpose
769.0   041.1   like as not
770.0   040.4   ne'er a one
771.0   040.5   I ain't done nothing
772.0   040.6   nohow
773.0   040.7   none

Prepositions

774.0   082.7   down in
774.1   104   in it
775.0   082.6   up at
776.0   032.5   toward
777.0   010.4   behind the door
777.2   032   next to me
778.0   034.5   out of
779.0   034.4   off
780.0   032.4   with
781.0   032.3   without
782.0   099.1   wait for you
783.0   088.4   instead of

Conjunctions

784.0   088.5   because
785.0   088.3   unless
786.0   088.2   I don't know
787.0   088.2   as I want to

Chapter 5: Phonetics and Field Worker Practices

The general guidelines for phonetic transcription for LAMSAS are the same as those for *LANE* (Kurath et al. 1943:122–123):

1. In transcribing the responses of their informants, the field workers and scribes of the Linguistic Atlas used a finely graded alphabet based on that of the International Phonetic Association (IPA).

The use of this alphabet is founded on the assumption that every configuration of the vocal organs produces a characteristic sound, and that every sound is determined by a characteristic configuration of the organs. (It is granted that similar acoustic effects may be produced in different ways: for example, that the effect of lip rounding may be produced not only by actual protrusion of the lips but also by retraction of the tongue.) However, although the field workers took pains to ascertain as well as they could the positions and movements of the vocal organs of their informants, they were obliged to rely largely on auditory impressions. Movements at the back of the oral cavity, in the pharynx and in the larynx cannot be observed without instruments; and even the observation of tongue movements ordinarily visible to the eye with the speaker's cooperation had often to be neglected for fear of embarrassing or offending the informant. The securing of natural responses is far more important than minute phonetic observation.

2. The symbols for the phonetic alphabet, therefore, are to be understood as representing primarily *sounds as heard*. The field workers, in transcribing a sound, usually thought also in terms of articulation, and tried, so far as they were able, to refer their acoustic impression to the configuration of the vocal organs which produced it. But in the last analysis it is the sound itself which governed the field workers' choice of symbols.

3. The field workers' phonetic notations . . . are not phonemic, but on the contrary intentionally phonic, that is *impressionistic*. The phonemic pattern of an informant's speech can be determined only after long and careful study, and only on the basis of a large body of material first recorded impressionistically—certainly not under the conditions of field work, which require that the interviews proceed as rapidly as possible, and that the informant's first utterance be transcribed as accurately as his last.

The pronunciation of two sections, of two generations or of two individuals often differs strikingly; but in most cases the differences are without phonemic value. Thus the difference between [faɪv] and [fɐɪv], between [kau kəu kɐʊ], between [bəd bɤ·d bɜɪd], etc. is nonphonemic, but of the greatest importance to linguistic geography and dialectology, and to historical grammar as well. Moreover, unsuspected phonemic differences can be found only if there is full and accurate phonic evidence. Accordingly, the field workers were instructed to record what they heard as accurately and minutely as they could, without attempting to normalize their transcriptions or to interpret their auditory impressions in terms of a phonemic system. If two utterances of the same word by the same informant struck their ears as different—no matter how small the difference might be—they were to write them differently. As a result, the field workers' records may well include some observations of minute phonetic detail too trivial to be of much use to the linguist. But on the other hand this procedure has several advantages: small differences which may turn out to possess phonemic importance are not overlooked; positional and accentual variants of phonemes, required for the proper description of a dialect, are duly observed; and such non-phonemic differences in pronunciation as are characteristic of regional and social dialects automatically come to light. Moreover, the field worker is relieved of the time-consuming and hazardous task of deciding on the spot how much of his auditory impression is phonemically relevant.

These principles remained in effect throughout interviewing for LAMSAS, and received their fullest analysis in Kurath and McDavid 1961. In 57 late interviews the tape-recorder was employed by others in the field and Raven McDavid transcribed from the tape, but McDavid saw no great advantage for transcription from tape; as he discussed the matter most fully in McDavid 1985 (cf. McDavid 1957), he preferred that field workers should make an initial transcription even while taping the interview, and argued that the tape recorder may be a disadvantage if it causes well-trained field workers to relax their vigilance, or if it encourages use of inadequately trained field workers because an expert editor is available to do the transcription at the editorial office. The New England *Handbook* discussed differences in phonetic transcription between nine field workers. In this chapter we need treat only Lowman (826 records) and McDavid (278 records, 57 transcriptions of taped interviews). The one remaining record was prepared by Bloch, whose practices are discussed in detail in the New England *Handbook*. Discussion of individual vowels and consonants in large part recapitulates the material in the New England *Handbook* (125–40) but is keyed specially to Lowman's and McDavid's habits. Additional material on field worker practices is appended after treatment of separate sounds.

Figure 5.1 reproduces the vowel chart from *LANE* (123), Figure 5.2 the consonant chart (133). These charts have the advantage of employing handwritten symbols which correspond to the handwritten symbols of the field records and list manuscripts, subject to minor variations in field worker practices. McDavid and O'Cain 1980 employed the vowels, consonants, and diacritical marks as reproduced in Figures 5.3, 5.4, and 5.5 (2–3). These symbols were produced with a special typing element for the IBM Selectric-II typewriter, and incorporate several minor changes from *LANE* phonetics in consonants and diacritics. The text of this handbook and all other LAMSAS materials prepared with computer assistance utilize the computer phonetics described in Chapter 7. Phonetic typography for the computer is based on the symbol set from McDavid and O'Cain 1980, but offers additional resources.

Vowels and Diphthongs

LAMSAS vowel symbols are presented in Figure 5.1 which has been reproduced from the New England *Handbook* (with discussion, 123–25; see also Kurath and McDavid 1961) and in Figure 5.3. The "central values" of the symbols [i ɪ e ɛ æ a ɔ ʌ o ʊ u] may be approximately defined as the vowels of *beat, bit, bait, bet, bat, psalm, bought, but, boat, put, boot,* respectively, in the "Inland Northern" (New England *Handbook*, 124: "west of the Hudson River, north of the Ohio River") pronunciation adopted as a standard of reference for *LANE*. Symbols shown in parentheses in the diagram denote rounded vowels, thirteen of which are paired with corresponding unrounded vowels: [i y], [ɪ ʏ], [e ø], [ɛ œ], [ɨ ʉ], [ɯ ʉ], [ɜ ɞ], [ɯ u], [ɤ ʊ], [ɑ ɒ]; three rounded vowels are not paired in this way: [o ɵ ɔ]. Four symbols have different values from those in the IPA alphabet: [a] is low-central, not low-back; [ʌ] is advanced lower mid-back, not the unrounded counterpart of [ɔ] and not the corresponding sound of standard British; [ɵ] is advanced higher mid-back weakly rounded, not midway between [ø] and [o]; [ɤ] is unrounded [ʊ], not unrounded [o]. Two vowel symbols used in LAMSAS are not included in the IPA alphabet: [ɚ ɑ].

Individual Vowels

[ɛ] denotes the vowel of *bet/mess* in "Inland Northern" speech. It is slightly lower than the corresponding sound in standard British English (written [e] by Daniel Jones in "broad" transcription), though still considerably higher than the sound transcribed [ɛ] in French *père, bête*. [ɵ], the rounded counterpart of [ɛ], is rare. Lowman wrote IPA [œ] for [ɵ]; the symbols have been regularly edited.

Figure 5.1: *LANE* Vowel Chart (Kurath et al. 1943)

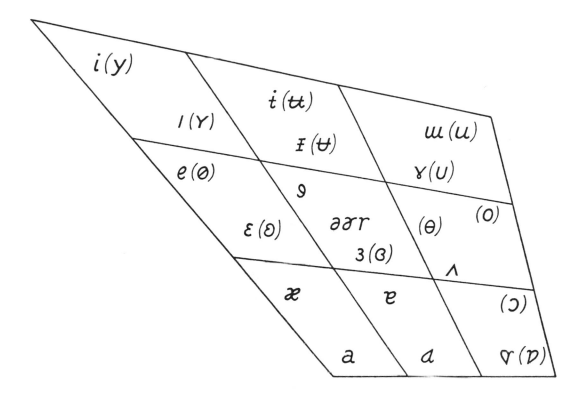

Figure 5.2: *LANE* Consonant Chart (Kurath et al. 1943)

		BILABIAL	LABIODENTAL	DENTAL	ALVEOLAR	PALATALIZED ALVEOLAR	RETROFLEX	ALVEOLO-PALATAL	PALATO-ALVEOLAR	PALATAL	RETRACTED PALATAL	ADVANCED VELAR	VELAR	GLOTTAL
STOPS	55	p b		ṭ ḓ	t d	ṭ ḓ	ṭ ḓ			c ɟ	č ɟ̌	k̂ ĝ	k g	ʔ
NASALS	56	m	ɱ	ṇ	n	ɳ	ɳ			ɲ	ɲ̌	ŋ̂	ŋ	
LATERALS	57			ḷ	ⱡ	ɭ	l			ʎ				
FLAPS	58			ɾ̣	ɾ / ɹ		ɽ							
FRICATIVES	59	φ β	f v	s̱ ẕ / θ ð	s z / ɹ / r / R	s̱ ẕ / ɟ	ṣ ẓ / ɟ̣ / ṛ	ʃ ʒ	ʂ ʐ	ʃʒ / l̠ʒ	č̣ ɟ̣̌	x̂ ɣ̂	x ɣ	h ɦ / ɦ̣
FRICTIONLESS CONTINUANTS 60		(ɥ) (w)	F ʋ		ɾ		ʈ			ʝ ɥ	ʝ̌ ɥ̌	w̄	w	

Figure 5.3: LAMSAS Vowel Chart (McDavid and O'Cain 1980)

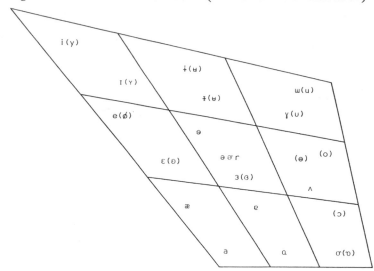

Figure 5.4: LAMSAS Consonant Chart (McDavid and O'Cain 1980)

	BILABIAL	LABIODENTAL	DENTAL	ALVEOLAR	PALATALIZED ALVEOLAR	RETROFLEX	ALVEOLO-PALATAL	PALATO-ALVEOLAR	PALATAL	RETRACTED PALATAL	ADVANCED VELAR	VELAR	GLOTTAL
STOPS	p b		ṯ ḏ	t d	ṯ̦ ḏ̦	ṭ ḍ			c ɟ	c̀ ɟ̀	k̀ g̀	k g	ʔ
NASALS	m	ɱ	ṉ	n	ṋ	ṇ			ɲ	ɲ̀	ŋ̀	ŋ	
LATERALS			ḻ	l ɫ	ḻ̦	!			ʎ				
FLAPS			ɾ̻	ɾ ɹ	ɾ̦	ɽ							
FRICATIVES	ɸ β	f v	s̠ z̠ θ ð ṯ ṟ̬	s z ɹ r ʀ	ș z̦ ṯ̦ ɾ̦	ṣ ẓ ṛ ṛ̣	ʃ ʒ ʃ̣ ʒ̣	ɕ̀ ʑ̀	ɕ ʝ	ɕ̀ ʝ̀	x̀ ɣ̀	x ɣ	h ɦ ɧ
FRICTIONLESS CONTINUANTS	(ɥ) (w)	F ʋ	ɹ ʀ		ɻ				ɟ ɥ	ɟ̀ ɥ̀	ẁ	w	

Figure 5.5: LAMSAS Diacritics (McDavid and O'Cain 1980)

‹	ə‹ k̀	fronting	˜	ə̃ ʔ̃	nasalization	,	ə̦	pharyngealization	'	ʿp pʿ	aspiration
›	ə› c̀	backing	˳	ə̞ ɾ	rounding	–	ɱ	velarization	·	oˑ	long
ˆ	ə̂	raising	˕	ʊ̝	spreading	ˍ	ṯ	dentalization	:	o:	overlong
ˇ	ə̌	lowering	˳	ə̥ ḏ̥	unvoicing	ˍ	ṯ	lenis	˘	ə̆	short
.	ə̣	r-color	˯	ṱ	voicing	̑	b̑	implosive	ʔt ᵘᵗ		coarticulation
.	ṭ	retroflexion	'	ə̓ ʼt	glottalization	̯	ɾ̯	linkage			

Lowman also wrote [ɵ] for [ɵ], the rounded counterpart of [ɜ]; this is systematically emended to [ɵ].

[ɨ ʉ] denote high-central vowels, respectively unrounded and rounded, usually tense. [ɨ] occurs rarely; [ʉ] is common, especially in words like *music, beautiful, new*; in the Midland and parts of the South it also appears in such words as *do, fool*.

[ɪ̵ ʊ̵] denote lower high-central vowels, respectively unrounded and rounded, usually lax. [ɪ̵] occurs very frequently in weak-stressed syllables of words like *habit, because, merry* and as the second element of the diphthongs in *bait, bite, boy*, sometimes also as a stressed vowel in words like *bristles, river*. A lowered [ɪ̵] approaches [ə] in its acoustic effect.

In his early records McDavid often wrote [ɪ] for the weak-stressed vowel of *habit* and for the second element of diphthongs. An [ɪ] in such positions in McDavid's early records is usually to be interpreted as equivalent of [ɪ̵].

[ɜ ɞ ɵ] are used chiefly to write the stressed vowel of *bird* when pronounced without retroflection. [ɜ] is somewhat higher, perhaps also somewhat farther front, than the corresponding sound in standard British English (written [əː] by Jones in "broad" transcription. A retracted [ɜ] approaches [ʌ] in its acoustic effect. [ɞ] denotes a fully rounded variety of [ɜ]. [ɵ] is rare; it denotes a mid-central vowel considerable higher and slightly more advanced than [ɜ], usually very tense. The relation of [ɵ] to [ɜ] is roughly the same as the relation of [e] to [ɛ].

McDavid sometimes writes [ɜ] as in *yellow* where there is no "historical *r*" in the background. The phonemic assignment of this vowel is sometimes debatable (see Kurath and McDavid 1961:169–70).

[ɵ] often occurs as the first member of the diphthong in *boat*—especially in records by Lowman from east Pennsylvania, west Pennsylvania, and east North Carolina.

[ə] denotes the common "obscure" mid-central vowel heard in weak-stressed syllables in words like *about, confess, sofa*. In stressed syllables [ə] is chiefly used to write the first element of diphthongs of the type [əɪ əʊ] (common in eastern Virginia and in Canada), rarely also a monophthong higher and more advanced than [ʌ] in words like *cut*.

[ɒ] denotes a rounded low-back vowel, [ɑ] its unrounded counterpart. [ɑ] was introduced into the Atlas alphabet for the Southern field work, to eliminate some of the diversity in practice among the New England field workers.

In his Preliminary Southern records, Lowman used ɒ̣ to indicate an unrounded low-back vowel [ɑ]; ɒ̤ to indicate a lightly rounded vowel [ɑ]. These have been emended by the editors to [ɑ] and [ɒ̈] respectively.

[a ɑ ɑ ɒ] denote low vowels; [æ e ɔ] denote higher-low vowels, that is vowels higher than those in the series [a–ɒ] but lower than mid position.

After McDavid's first records there is little difference between his records and Lowman's in the low-back range. Of such differences, McDavid is somewhat more inclined than Lowman to indicate diphthongization (up-gliding or centering). In communities investigated by both of them, McDavid (like Bloch in New England) often writes [ɔˑ] where Lowman writes [ɒˑ] (Wetmore 1959).

[ɐ] is used chiefly for the first element of diphthongs in words like *bite, boat*; McDavid (less often Lowman) sometimes uses it for a low variety of /ʌ/ or for a raised variety of [a].

[ʌ] denotes the vowel of *cut* as pronounced in the North-Central United States. The corresponding standard British English sound (written [ʌ] by Daniel Jones) is considerably lower and somewhat farther advanced than the American sound. A vowel somewhat higher than this North-Central [ʌ] is often heard in the South Midland, which McDavid often writes as [ɤˑ ɤˢ].

[ɵ] is used chiefly for an extreme variety of the so-called "New England short *o*" as in the rural Northern pronunciation of words like *whole, home, coat* (see Avis 1961). It also appears for weak-stressed *o* in words like *swallow*.

[ɤ] denotes a somewhat advanced lower high-back unrounded vowel, the unrounded counterpart of [ʊ]. It appears occasionally as a variant of [ʊ] in words like *good*, sometimes as a variant of [ɜ] in words like *bird*, sometimes as a glide before velar consonants as in *log* [lɔᵞg]. In McDavid's records it is used for the relatively high South Midland vowel in *cut*, usually written [ɤˢ ɤˑ].

[ɚ] denotes a strongly retroflex mid-central vowel as in the most common American pronunciation of words like *bird*. Both Lowman and McDavid use [ɚ] for a strongly retroflex vowel in all positions; thus they would write [bɚd bɜɚd fɑðɚ faðɚ fiɚ kaɚt]. In accordance with use of the retroflection diacritic, [ɚ ɹ] denote varieties of [ɚ ɹ] in which the *r*-color is still stronger.

Lowman, who discriminated most carefully among the different varieties of this sound, defines his use of the symbols in question as follows (May 1935):

> I use [ə] for a vocalic sound. The tip and blade are greatly retracted; the rest of the tongue is laterally contracted and very high, so that the sides of the tongue touch the roof of the mouth in the palatal, velar and uvular sections. When this raising or curling back is more extreme or more noticeable I use [ɚ]; in this case the back part of the tongue is usually lower than for [ə]. Where the sound suggests a consonant I use [r], or [ɹ] for the more extreme type, chiefly in sequences like [ɜr ɚɹ]. I use [ɜ] for a weakly r-colored [ə], usually without retraction of the tongue tip. [ɜ ɝ] differ from [ə ɚ] chiefly in length.

In some areas where very strong r-coloring occurs, Lowman writes the syllabic of *bird* as [ᵊr ᵊɹ]. These have been changed by the editors to [ɚr ɚɹ].

In *bird* McDavid distinguishes between [ɜɚ ɝɚ] and [ɚ ɚ]; in the former, constriction increases during the syllabic; in the latter it is strong from the beginning.

Shift Signs and Diacritics Used with Vowels

In order to avoid the necessity of using special symbols for the innumerable shades of sound intermediate between any two of the vowels, the phonetic alphabet of the Linguistic Atlas provides shift signs in the form of small arrowheads, which are placed after a vowel symbol to indicate varieties heard as articulated in a higher, a lower, a more advanced, or a more retracted position than the vowel denoted by the unmodified letter. These shift signs must be interpreted on the basis of the vowel diagram.

For stressed vowels and for the first members of diphthongs, Lowman writes the shift signs before the vowel; in editing these have been placed after the vowel.

An arrowhead pointing *to the left* indicates, after a front-vowel symbol, a vowel articulated exceptionally far forward; after a central vowel symbol, a fronted vowel (one approaching front position); after a back-vowel symbol, a centered vowel (one approaching central position). Thus [aᶜ] is an extremely advanced variety of [a]; [ɑᶜ] a vowel

between [a] and [a] but nearer to [a]; [ɑᶜ] is a vowel between [ɑ] and [a] but nearer to [ɑ].

An arrowhead pointing *to the right* indicates after a front-vowel symbol, a centered vowel (one approaching central position); after a central-vowel symbol, a backed vowel (one approaching back position); after a back-vowel symbol, a vowel articulated exceptionally far back. Thus [aᐟ] is a vowel between [a] and [a] but nearer to [a]; [aᐟ] is a vowel between [a] and [ɑ] but nearer to [a]; [ɑᐟ] is an extremely retracted variety of [ɑ].

An arrowhead pointing *up* indicates a vowel articulated in a higher and usually also in a somewhat more advanced position: compare the sloping sides of the vowel diagram. Thus [æˏ] is a vowel between [æ] and [ɛ] but nearer to [æ]; [aˏ] is a vowel between [a] and [ɐ] but nearer to [a]; [oˏ] is a vowel between [o] and [u] but nearer to [o] (not a vowel between [o] and [ʊ] since [ʊ] is not in the direct line of fully back vowels).

An arrowhead pointing *down* indicates a vowel articulated in a lower and usually also in a somewhat more retracted position: compare the sloping sides of the vowel diagram. Thus [ɛˎ] is a vowel between [ɛ] and [æ] but nearer to [ɛ]; [ɔˎ] is a vowel between [ɔ] and [ɒ] but nearer to [ɔ]; [iˎ] is a vowel between [i] and [e] but nearer to [i] (not a vowel between [i] and [ɪ], since [ɪ] is not in the direct line of fully front vowels).

The varieties of unrounded high vowels, from front to back, can thus be represented by the series [iᶜ i iᐟ ɨᶜ ɨ ɨᐟ ɯᶜ ɯ ɯᐟ]. The varieties of rounded back vowels, from high to low, can be represented by the series [uˏ u uˎ oˏ o oˎ ɔˏ ɔ ɔˎ ɒˏ ɒ ɒˎ].

Double shift signs (one pointing to the left or right, the other up or down) are used to indicate shades of sound for which single shift signs are inadequate. These combinations must be interpreted according to the statements above. Thus [iˎᶜ] is a vowel between [i] and [ɨ] and [ɪ] but nearest to [i]; [oˎᶜ] is a vowel between [o] and [ɵ] and [ɔ] but nearest to [o]; [əˎᶜ] is a vowel between [ə] and [ɛ] (or [e]) and [ɨ] but nearest to [ə]; [aˎᶜ] is a vowel between [a] and [ɐ] but nearer to [a].

Lowman occasionally used double shift signs in the same direction, indicating an extreme modification; these have been changed editorially to single shift signs.

The diacritic for labialization [˯] (equivalent to the IPA diacritic) may be written under symbols for unrounded vowels to indicate weak rounding, as [ɯ], and under symbols for rounded vowels to indicate over-rounding, as [y̰].

The diacritic for lip spreading [˳] is written under symbols for rounded vowels to indicate slight unrounding, and under symbols for unrounded vowels to indicate over-spreading. It is thus possible to represent six degrees of lip-rounding, as [ɯ̣ ɯ ɯ̣ y̰ u y̰]. See below for a separate use of [˳] with consonants.

Lowman's and McDavid's last records use the IPA [˳] to indicate rounding; this has been emended to [˳].

Lowman normally indicates unrounding by the IPA symbol [( ] as [g(o(u]; this has been emended to [˳], as in [go̰u].

The diacritic for nasalization [˜] may be written over any vowel symbol to indicate nasal resonance, produced by pronouncing the vowel with the velum relaxed so as to allow part of the air current to escape through the nose. The modification so marked may vary from a very faint nasal tinge to a very strong nasality.

When the speech of a given informant is colored throughout by a "nasal twang" that affects all or most of his oral sounds (except stops), the nasality is usually not indicated for every sound but is mentioned once and for all in the general statement characterizing the informant's speech. Lowman sometimes did not mark nasalization on off-glides of a nasalized vowel followed by a nasal consonant [pĩˤn].

The diacritic for retroflection [ˎ] may be written under any vowel symbol to indicate the acoustic effect of *r*-color, whether this is produced by actual raising and inversion of the tongue tip or by retraction and lateral contraction of the body of the tongue. Thus [a̡ o̡ ə̡ ɜ̡] denote retroflex or *r*-colored [a o ə ɜ] respectively; [ɚ] denotes a variety of [ə] in which the retroflection inherent in this vowel is especially strong or noticeable.

The diacritic for retroflection may also be written under consonants.

The diacritic for breath or devocalization [˳] may be written under any vowel symbol to indicate voicelessness. Voiceless vowels are not uncommon in unstressed syllables between voiceless consonants.

Length Marks

The method used to mark vowel length (quantity) is that of the IPA, with such deviations in practice as will appear from the following statement. The rules here formulated apply to vowels in both strongly and weakly stressed syllables, and to both elements of a diphthong.

Vowels heard as neither distinctly long nor distinctly short are not specially marked. Half-long vowels are usually treated in the same way, though the remark "half-long" is sometimes entered in the commentary when the field worker considers this degree of length for any reason worth noticing.

Vowels which strike the field worker as distinctly long are marked with a single raised dot [·] as [a·]. In practice the field workers occasionally write the single dot to mark half-long vowels appearing in contexts where short vowels are more usual, as in *bid* [bɪ·d] with half-long [ɪ].

Vowels which strike the field worker as overlong—that is, as appreciably longer than ordinary long vowels—are marked with a colon, as [a:]. Overlong vowels are rare. Still longer vowels, when they occur, may be marked with a double colon as [a::]; they are rarely recorded except in calls to animals.

Vowels which strike the field worker as appreciably shorter than ordinary short vowels are marked with a breve [˘] as [ä]. In practice, the field workers occasionally write the breve to mark vowels of ordinary shortness appearing in contexts where long or half-long vowels are more usual, as in *home* [hŏm].

Very short vowels heard as mere glides without forming the peak of a syllable are written with superior letters, as in *frost* [froᵊst], *five* [faᶦv], *beans* [bᵊi·nz bi·ᶦnz] and the like.

Lowman often writes superior letters for vowels which are short but clearly syllabic, as in *because* [bᵊkɔz]. These have been replaced with on-line letters marked with a breve, as in *because* [bŏkɔz]; any syllabic vowel, no matter how short, is written on the line.

Some very short superior vowels are marked with a breve or (occasionally with Lowman in NC) by a second degree of superior symbols. These have been changed to unmodified superior vowels, on the principle that any sound indicated by a superior letter is intrinsically very short and obscure.

The diacritic [ˎ] is used *beneath* a vowel symbol to indicate pharyngealization [a̡]. The diacritic ['] is used *above* a vowel symbol to indicate glottalization. Both of these diacritics are rarely used.

Diphthongs

A diphthong, definable as a vocalic sound characterized by a continuous movement of the tongue or lips resulting in a continuous audible glide, is written with two symbols (occasionally with three, when the middle part of the glide is for some reason prominent). A falling diphthong, one with decreasing stress, is written with the first symbol on the line, the second either on the line or superior, according to the length of the glide. A rising diphthong, one with increasing stress, is written with the first symbol superior, the second on the line. Both symbols in a diphthong may be modified by any of the diacritics used with vowels and may be followed by shift signs.

Of the two symbols used in writing a diphthong, the first regularly denotes the acoustic impression of the glide at its beginning, interpreted as the position from which the tongue (or lip) movement starts. The second symbol may denote either (A) the position to which the articulatory organ actually moves before the beginning of the next sound, or (B) the position toward which the glide tends but which the articulating organ does not actually reach before the beginning of the next sound. The exact point at which a diphthongal glide ends is often difficult to determine by ear, though sometimes the end of the glide leaves a clear auditory impression. The following transcriptions of a diphthong of the [aɨ] type illustrate the two methods used by the field workers: (A) [aɨ ae aɛ aɛ͵ aɪ] the glide begins at [a] and appears to end respectively at [ɨ e ɛ ɛ͵ ɪ]; (B) [aɪ aɨ aj] the glide begins at [a] and moves toward some variety of high-front vowel, or generally in an upward and forward direction. Note that [aɨ aɪ] may represent either method of transcription. In short, the transcription of the second symbol of the diphthong in method B claims only a direction for the glide, while a transcription according to method A makes a stronger claim for the actual position of the articulating organ at the termination of the glide.

Both Lowman and McDavid have used both methods, but ultimately settled on method A. Lowman had generally reached this point by the time he began his work in the South Atlantic States. McDavid used both methods in his South Atlantic records. For a time in late 1947 he was fairly consistent in [ij ʉw]. His later records (NY) are of method A.

The length of each element in a falling diphthong is noted in the usual manner. If the first element is long (that is, if the glide which characterizes the diphthong is drawled or is preceded by a momentary hold with no perceptible change in quality) it is marked with a single dot; if it is very short (that is, if the glide appears to move away from its starting position very abruptly) it is marked with a breve. The second element is treated similarly, with the added provision that if it is so faint as to be no more than a scarcely audible vanishing glide, it may be written with a superior letter. If the whole diphthong is long, each element may be marked with the sign of length; if the whole element is short, each element may be marked with a breve. The following series illustrates various distributions of length (though by no means all possible combinations) in a diphthong of the [aɨ] type: [aːˑ aˑɨ aɨ aˑɨ̆ aɨ̆ ăɨ ăɨ̆ aᶦ ăᶦ].

Lowman sometimes writes [ă·ɨ̆], etc., to indicate that the first element is longer than the second but that the whole diphthong is short. Such transcriptions have been simplified by the omission of the breve on the first element.

When two contiguous vowel symbols are not intended to represent a diphthong, they are separated by a hyphen, thus *drawing* [drɔ-ɪŋ] *real* [ri-əl] when pronounced in two syllables (cf. *boil* [bɔɪl bɔ-ɪl], *fear* [fɪɚ fi-ɚ]). But the hyphen is not used (A) between a stressed diphthong and a following weak-stressed vowel, as in *rowen* [raʊɪn raʊən]; (B) between a weak-stressed vowel and a following stressed vowel or diphthong, if the stress mark is written as in *piazza* [piˈæzə] *create* [kriˈet]; (C) between identical vowel symbols, as in *tidying* [taɪdɪŋ taɨdɨŋ]; or (D) elsewhere if no misunderstanding can arise. In computer files and printouts, the vertical bar | replaces the hyphen for this purpose (see Chapter 7).

Consonants

LAMSAS consonant symbols are presented in Figure 5.2, reproduced from the New England *Handbook* (with discussion, 132–33; see also Kurath and McDavid 1961), and in Figure 5.4. The following deviations from the alphabet of the IPA should be noted:

1) The symbols [ḷ] and [ɫ] have been added.
2) The diacritics appearing in [ṣ ċ ġ] are not recognized in this use by the IPA.

3) The symbols [r ɹ] have slightly different values than those usually assigned to them by the IPA.

4) The symbol [ʀ] has a totally different value from that assigned to it by the IPA.

5) Several LAMSAS symbols are shaped somewhat differently from the New England chart and from IPA but without differences of value: [č ž] are palato-alveolar fricatives, [ɤ] is a velar fricative, [ɓ ɗ ƙ] are implosives. [č ž] are represented in McDavid and O'Cain 1980 with a single vertical stroke above the base symbol.

6) All LAMSAS retroflex consonants are indicated by adding the dot for retroflexion (not a curl) below the symbols for alveolar consonants: [ḷ ḍ ṇ ḻ ḽ ɾ̣ ṣ ẓ ɟ̣ ṛ].

The terms at the head of the columns in the table indicate the point of articulation:

bilabial: the lower lip against the upper lip.

labiodental: the lower lip against the upper front teeth.

dental: the tip or blade of the tongue against the edge or back of the upper front teeth.

alveolar: the tip or blade of the tongue or both, against the upper gums or the teeth-ridge, rarely just back of the teeth-ridge.

palatalized alveolar: the same, with the front of the tongue raised toward or touching the anterior or mid point of the hard palate.

retroflex: the tip (rarely the blade) of the tongue against a point back of the teeth-ridge or against the anterior part of the hard palate.

alveolo-palatal: the blade and front of the tongue against the teeth-ridge and the anterior part of the hard palate, the opening being smallest at the teeth ridge.

palato-alveolar: the front of the tongue against the teeth-ridge and the hard palate, the opening being smallest at the hard palate.

palatal: the front of the tongue against the anterior or mid part of the hard palate.

retracted palatal: the front of the tongue against back part of the hard palate, or still farther back.

advanced velar: the back of the tongue against the anterior part of the soft palate, or still farther forward.

velar: the back of the tongue against the mid (rarely the back) of the soft palate.

glottal: formed by closure or (slight) contraction of the glottis, the configuration of the oral cavity being of only secondary importance.

Terms for manner of articulation are defined below.

When two symbols appear side by side in a single compartment of the table, the first denotes a voiceless, the second a voiced consonant. It is usually to be assumed that the voiceless sound is stronger (fortis) than its voiced counterpart (and in the case of stops also slightly shorter). When only one symbol appears without another beside it in the same compartment, it denotes a voiced consonant, except that [ʔ] and [h̩] in the last column are voiceless.

When two or more symbols appear one below another in a single compartment of the table, they denote sounds of the same class articulated at the same point but differing in some other respect. Consult the description of the individual sounds.

Diacritics Used with Consonant Symbols

Voiceless consonants for which no separate symbols are provided are written by adding a small circle below the symbol for the corresponding voiced sounds as [r̥ l̥ ŋ̊]. When symbols for voiceless and voiced consonants occur side by side, the same diacritic may be added to the latter to indicate a voiceless sound somewhat more weakly articulated than the usual voiceless variety: thus [z̥ d̥ d̥ʒ̊] are respectively weaker (lenis instead of fortis) than [s t tʃ].

Lenis voiceless consonants, which are stronger than those marked by adding the voiceless diacritic to the symbol for a voiced consonant (*halbfortis* in German dialectology), are indicated by adding the diacritic [_] below the symbol for a voiceless consonant, as [t̲ ʃ̲ p̲]. Other devices such as [͜] appear in some list manuscripts and field records. This usage of the underscore diacritic is not the same as as use of the underscore with vowels to indicate unrounding.

The diacritic for voicing [ˬ] may be written below symbols for voiceless consonants to indicate a voiced sound somewhat more strongly articulated and sometimes also shorter than the usual voiced variety: thus [s̬ t̬ tʃ̬] are respectively stronger and sometimes shorter (fortis instead of lenis) than [z d dʒ].

The diacritic for retroflection [.] is used with consonant symbols in two ways: it is written below symbols for alveolar consonants, thus [ṭ ḍ ṇ ḷ ḽ ɾ̣ ṣ ʐ ɻ ɾ]. It is also written below other consonant symbols to indicate the acoustic effect of *r*-color, usually produced by raising and inversion of the tongue tip during the articulation of the consonant; thus [w̡] is [w] with simultaneous tongue tip action, [ʃ̡] is [ʃ] with raised tongue-tip, etc.

The diacritic for labialization [˷] may be written below any consonant symbol to indicate the acoustic effect of lip rounding. When written below a symbol for a bilabial consonant, the diacritic indicates protrusion of the lips, often resulting in a characteristic labial off-glide; when written below other consonant symbols, it indicates labialization (lip-rounding simultaneous with the articulation of the tongue).

The diacritic for nasalization [˜] may be written above any symbol denoting an oral continuant (laterals, fricatives, and frictionless consonants) to indicate nasal resonance.

Velarized consonants, that is consonants modified by raising the back of the tongue toward the soft palate (except for [ɫ ɟ ʀ ʁ] are indicated by a line through the letter [ɼ ʍ] These last are rare.

Syllabic consonants, that is consonants which form the peak of a syllable, are marked with the diacritic [ˌ], but this diacritic is used only when needed for an unambiguous reading of the form. Thus in *table* [teɪbl] the diacritic is not written under the [l], since the phonetic context shows that this must be syllabic; but in *leveling* [lɛvl̩ŋ] the diacritic is written, since in such a form the [l] may or may not be syllabic.

Consonants which strike the field worker as distinctly long or as "double" are written with doubled symbols as in *land, picture, bulge* [læennd], [pɪkktʃə], [bʌlldʒ] or in phrases like *what time, some men, this year* [hwʌt taɪm], [sʌmmɛn], [ðɪʃ ʃɪə]. When the long consonant is the peak of a syllable, it is marked with the usual sign of length, as in *wool* [w·l̩], *sh!* (a call to animals) [ʃː], *unh-huhnh* (grunt of affirmation) [ˌm̩ːˈm̩m̩ː].

McDavid always writes doubled consonants; Lowman often writes the dot, thus [læennd] vs. [læn·d]. This inconsistency has been eliminated by the editors.

Consonants which strike the field workers as distinctly short, though distinctly audible, may be marked with a breve, as in *April, glass* [eɪp̆ɪl], [ğlæs]. Faintly articulated consonants, not only short but also indistinct, may be written with superior letters, as in [eɪpʳɪl], [pɪᵏtʃə], [læsᵗ].

Lowman often marks the flap with a breve, as *three* [θɾ̆i̥·]. The breve has sometimes been eliminated in list manuscripts—editors have thought that a flap is by definition instantaneous—and this slight inconsistency in list manuscripts and computer files may thus create a distinction without a difference.

The diacritic [ˈ] before a consonant is used to indicate weak glottalization, as [kæᵊˈp], [ræˈt], [beɾˈkn̩].

The diacritic [ˌ] beneath the symbol for a alveolar consonant, is used to indicate dentalization, as *width* [wɪt̪θ].

Individual Consonants by Classes

Stops: sounds formed by a complete stopping and abrupt release of the air current at some point in the larynx or mouth, the nasal passage being shut off by the velum.

[p ṭ t ṱ t̠ c ċ ḱ k] denote strong (fortis) voiceless stops, as a rule slightly aspirated when initial in a word or in a stressed syllable, otherwise unaspirated. In final position they may be written superior to indicate weak unexploded stops.

[b ḍ d d̠ ḏ ʈ ɟ ġ g] denote weak (lenis) voiced stops. When initial in a word or, especially, final in a phrase, these sounds are often partly or wholly voiceless (and may be written as ᵇb̥i· æd̥ᵈ]).

[pʻ ṭʻ tʻ ṱʻ t̠ʻ cʻ ċʻ ḱʻ kʻ] denote voiceless stops with exceptionally strong or noticeable aspiration, or slightly aspirated stops in contexts where the unaspirated variety is more common.

[pʰ ṭʰ tʰ ṱʰ t̠ʰ cʰ ċʰ ḱʰ kʰ] denote voiceless stops with very striking aspiration.

A still stronger degree of aspiration may be indicated by [ph ṭh th ṱh t̠h ch ċh ḱh kh].

Lowman commonly writes [pʰ ṭʰ tʰ ṱʰ t̠ʰ cʰ ċʰ ḱʰ kʰ] to indicate a degree of aspiration which McDavid writes as [pʻ ṭʻ tʻ ṱʻ t̠ʻ cʻ ċʻ ḱʻ kʻ].

[pᶲ pᶠ tˢ ḱˢ kˣ] and the like denote affricated voiceless stops, in which the oral occlusion is broken gradually, with a resulting fricative off-glide. When this off-glide is still slower, stronger, or more noticeable, the sounds may be written [pɸ pf ts ḱs kx]. When the affrication is noticeably stronger than the stop, the stop may be written with a superior symbol, as [ᵖɸ ᵖf ᵗs ᵏs ᵏx].

[bᵝ vᵛ dᶻ gʳ] and the like denote affricated voiced stops; they parallel the voiceless stops of the preceding paragraph in transcription alternatives.

[ˈp ˈṭ ˈt ˈṱ ˈt̠ ˈc ˈċ ˈḱ ˈk] denote glottalized

stops, with a simultaneous glottal closure. This is usually released before the release of the oral closure, less commonly after it or at the same time.

['p 't 't 't 't 'c 'c 'k 'k] denote preaspirated stops, in which the occlusion is preceded by a short but audible puff of breath.

[p̬ t̬ t̬ t̬ t̬ c̬ c̬ k̬ k̬] denote strong (fortis) voiced stops, usually somewhat shorter as well as more energetically articulated than [b ḍ d d̬ ḍ t̬ j ġ g].

[b̥ d̥ d̥ d̥ j̊ g̊ g] denote weak (lenis) unaspirated voiceless stops, usually somewhat longer as well as less energetically articulated than [p t̬ t t̬ t̬ c c̀ k̬ k]. They may also be written to indicate unaspirated stops in initial position.

[p̱ ṯ ṯ ṯ ṯ c̱ c̱ ḵ ḵ] indicate "half-fortis" stops, between [p t̬ t t̬ t̬ c c̀ k̬ k] and [b̥ d̥ d̥ d̥ j̊ g̊ g]. They are rarely recorded, chiefly by Lowman in New York and Pennsylvania.

[t̬ d̬] denote palatalized alveolar stops, articulated like [t d] with the tip and blade of the tongue touching the teeth or ridge but modified by raising the front of the tongue toward the hard palate (sometimes by actual contact) so as to produce a characteristic palatal coloring.

[c ɟ] denote true palatal stops, articulated with the tip of the tongue lowered and the front of the tongue touching the anterior or mid part of the hard palate.

[k̇ ġ] denote velar stops articulated in a somewhat more advanced position than [k g]. In practice the field workers use [k̇ ġ] chiefly for advanced velar stops in contexts where the less advanced variety is more common, as in *car, garden, girl*. Velar stops contiguous to high-front vowels, as in *keep, geese, weak*, are normally more advanced than velar stops contiguous to central or back vowels, but are usually written simply as [k g].

[tʃ dʒ] denote the consonants in *church, judge*. These are regularly so written, though the stop element is probably often more palatalized and somewhat farther retracted than ordinary [t d]. When the palatalization is especially distinct, the sounds may be written as [tʃ̬ dʒ̬] or [t̬ʃ̬ d̬ʒ̬].

[ʔ] denotes a strong (but unaspirated) glottal stop. It may occur initially before a vowel in hesitating or emphatic utterance, as in *all* [ʔɔl], or less commonly in final position after a vowel when the utterance is abruptly broken off, as in *whoa* [woʊʔ], or else in medial or final position as a substitute for some other stop, usually [t] or [b], as in *little, sit,*

actress [lɪʔl], [sɪʔ], [æʔtrɪs].

Implosive stops [ɓ ɗ ɠ], accompanied by glottal *release* are rarely indicated, almost always in Lowman's records.

Nasals: Sounds differing from stops in that the velum is lowered to let the air current escape through the nose. The symbols in the consonant table are self-explanatory. Voiceless nasals are indicated by adding the diacritic [̥], as [m̥ n̥ ŋ̥].

A flapped [n], articulated by a quick up-and-down movement of the tongue tip with momentary contact between this and the teeth-ridge, is sometimes heard as a substitute for the combination [nt] in words like *center, into*. It is usually written as a nasalized flap [ɾ̃], less often as [nɾ].

Laterals: sounds formed by contact of the tip (and blade) of the tongue, or of the front of the tongue with some part of the roof of the mouth, in such a way that the air current is free to pass along one side or both sides of the tongue, usually without friction.

[l] denotes the normal weakly velarized *l* of American English, articulated with the tip of the tongue touching the teeth-ridge in the median line.

[l̩] denotes a distinctly "clear" *l*, that is an alveolar [l] with the front of the tongue evenly rounded and the back relatively flat or sloping, so as to produce the timbre of a front vowel.

[ɫ] denotes a distinctly "dark" (velarized) *l*, that is an alveolar [l] with the front of the tongue slightly depressed and the back raised toward the soft palate, so as to produce the timbre of a back vowel.

Lowman occasionally and still less frequently McDavid indicate a very "dark" *l* by a double slanting line. These have been emended to [ɫ] with the notation "[ɫ] very dark" in the commentary.

Since [ɫ] is the usual post-vocalic allophone, McDavid frequently wrote it in his early records in the South Carolina Low Country, where Lowman's and McDavid's later records have [l]. These have been changed to [l].

[l̡] denotes a distinctly palatalized *l*, that is an alveolar [l] with the front of the tongue either raised toward or actually touching the anterior part of the hard palate, so as to produce a strong palatal timbre sometimes accompanied by an off-glide written as [j] or [ʲ].

[ɭ] denotes a retroflex *l*, homorganic with [t d]. It may be neutral, slightly "dark", or slightly "clear", according to the phonetic context. [ɭ] is used only by

McDavid and denotes a retroflex *l* with distinct velar timbre: a "dark" retroflex *l*.

[ʎ] denotes a true palatal *l*, homorganic with [c j]. The symbol is rarely used.

Superior lateral symbols, especially [ˡ] and [ɬ], denote sounds resembling true laterals but formed without actual contact between the tip of the tongue and the roof of the mouth, heard frequently in words like *will* and *milk*. When these sounds are heard as completely vocalized (when they are acoustically identical with vowels or vocalic glides) they are written with vowel symbols, as in [wɪᵘ], [mɪɯk] and the like.

Flaps or *taps*: sounds formed by a single quick up-and-down movement of the tongue tip, usually but not always with momentary contact between this and some point on the roof of the mouth.

[ɾ] denotes an alveolar flapped *r*. It may represent a variant of the /r/ phoneme, as in *three* and *very* [θri· vɛɾɪ] or of the /t/ phoneme, as in *water* and *butter* [wɒɾə], [bʌɾə bʌɾə]. [ɾ̃] is one possibility for writing flapped *n*.

[ɺ] denotes a flapped *l* (which may be neutral, slightly "clear", or slightly "dark"), formed like [ɾ] but with lateral constriction of the tongue at the moment of contact. This sound seems to be limited to the position after initial consonants, as in *blue*, *slow* [bɺu·], [sɺou].

[ɽ] denotes a retroflex flapped *r*, formed like [ɾ] but homorganic with [ṭ ḍ]. It is usually a variant of the /r/ phoneme, less commonly of the /t/ phoneme.

Fricatives: sounds formed by constricting the oral or glottal passage so that the passing air current sets up audible friction at the point of narrowing.

[ɸ f s̺ θ s s̪ ʂ ʃ ʆ č ç ċ x̣ x h] denote strong (fortis) voiceless fricatives. Weaker (lenis) varieties may be written by adding [˕], the "half-fortis" diacritic, to these symbols, oftener by adding the diacritic for breath to the symbols for the corresponding voiced sounds.

[ß v z̺ ð z ɹ ʁ z̪ ɻ ẓ ɭ ʑ ɿ ʒ ʓ ž j ĵ ɣ̇ ɣ ɦ] denote weak (lenis) voiced fricatives. When initial in a word or final in a phrase, these sounds are often partly or wholly devoiced (equivalent to [ß̥ v̥ z̺̥ ð̥ z̥ ɹ̥ ʁ̥ z̪̥ ɻ̥ ẓ̥ ɭ̥ ʑ̥ ɿ̥ ʒ̥ ʓ̥ ž̥ j̥ ĵ̥ ɣ̣̇ ɣ̥]). This fact is indicated by the field workers only when the devocalization is complete or especially noticeable.

[ɸ ß f v] denote bilabial and labiodental fricatives respectively.

[s̪ z̪ θ ð] denote dental (rarely interdental) fricatives, distinguished from each other by different kinds of tongue contact and opening. [s̪ z̪] like [s

z] are (in Jespersen's terminology) rill spirants, articulated so as to leave a narrow channel along the median line of the tongue; [θ ð] are slit spirants, articulated so as to leave a wide flat passage over a large part of the tongue.

[s z ɹ ʁ] denote alveolar fricatives, distinguished from each other by different kinds of tongue contact and opening. [s z] are rill spirants articulated by the blade of the tongue. [ɹ] is a strongly fricative slit spirant articulated by the tip of the tongue, often heard after alveolar stops or fricatives in words like *try*, *dry* or in the [sɹ-] pronunciation of *shrank* [sɹæŋk]. [ʁ] is a fricative and strongly velarized slit spirant, rare except in Lowman records and uncommon even there (it may appear in coarticulation).

[s̗ z̗ ɻ̗] denote palatalized alveolar fricatives, homorganic with [t̗ d̗], distinguished from each other in the same way as [s z ɹ].

[ʂ ʐ ɻ] denote retroflex or retracted alveolar fricatives, homorganic with [ṭ ḍ], distinguished from each other in the same way as [s z ɹ].

[ʃ ʒ ʆ ʓ] denote alveolar-palatal fricatives, as heard in *ship* and *leisure* and as part of the affricates in *church* and *judge*. [ʆ ʓ] are distinguished from [ʒ] by a palatal timbre, usually produced by advancing the front of the tongue nearer to the hard palate.

[č ž] denote palato-alveolar or advanced palatal fricatives, roughly intermediate in acoustic effect between [ʃ ʒ] and [ç j], sometimes heard in phrases like *this year*, *these years* [ðɪč (j)iə], [ðiž (j)iəz].

[ç j] denote palatal fricatives, as heard in German *ich*, *ja*. [j] is also used for a frictionless continuant symbol.

[x ɣ] denote velar fricatives, homorganic with [k g]. An advanced velar fricative, [ɣ̇], modified by raising of the tongue tip, is sometimes used to denote a peculiar kind of *r*-sound heard after initial [g] in words like *green* and *grow*.

[ċ j̇ x̣ ɣ̇] denote respectively retracted palatal and advanced velar fricatives, representing nuances intermediate between [ç j] and [x ɣ].

[h ɦ] denote the ordinary *h* sounds of English, articulated with the tongue and lip position of the following sound. Thus [ha] is equivalent to [ɑ̥a], [hi] to [i̥i], [hw] to [w̥w], etc. "Voiced *h*" [ɦ] is murmured rather than fully voiced; [h̗] denotes a distinctly palatalized [h], i.e. one with front-vowel timbre, that is used in a context where central or back-vowel timbre is more common; it is sometimes replaced by [ḣ].

Frictionless continuants: sounds formed by narrowing or modifying the shape of the oral passage, but not sufficient to create audible friction.

[ɥ w] are entered in the first compartment of this row within parentheses, to indicate that the protrusion of the lips which characterizes these sounds is only a part of their articulation. The difference between [ɥ] and [w] is exactly analogous to the difference between the vowels [y] and [u].

[ꜰ   v] denote sounds resembling [f v] but with less friction and usually shorter.

[r] denotes the common alveolar or slightly post-alveolar frictionless *r*-sound of American English, as in the most usual pronunciation of *red, run, gray, arrow, far away*.

If a word ending in [r] is recorded in a context in which it is immediately followed by a word beginning with a vowel (as *father* in the context *father and mother*), but if this following word does not appear as part of the entry, a notation is made in the commentary to indicate the environment.

[ʀ] denotes a velarized frictionless *r*. [ɹ] denotes a sound of the same kind but articulated farther back.

[j ɥ] denote frictionless palatal continuants, distinguished from each other by the position of the lips: for [j] the lips are unrounded (neutral), for [ɥ] they are rounded and sometimes protruded. The voiceless counterparts of these sounds are written [j̥ ɥ̥]. Observe that [j] is used also (though rarely) for the voiced counterpart of [ç], and for this reason [j] is entered in the consonant table twice.

[w] denotes a frictionless velar continuant articulated with rounded lips. The initial consonant of *white, wheel* and the like is variously written. Transcriptions range from [w̥] (completely voiceless), through [hw] (voiceless at the beginning), [ʰw] (voiced except for a scarcely audible voiceless beginning) and [ʱw] (fully voiced except for a half-voiced or murmured beginning), to [w] (voiced throughout).

Coarticulation is indicated in two ways: by a ligature joining the two consonants [maunʔtn], or less commonly by writing the symbols above each other; the latter transcriptions have been edited into strings with ligatures, as [vɛvr̩ɪ] or [vɛvr̩ɪ].

Accentuation

Stress. Word and sentence stress, the relative prominence of syllables in polysyllabic words and in groups of two or more words, is marked in accordance with the practice of the IPA. A primary stress (the chief stress in the word or word group) is indicated by a superior vertical stroke [ˈ] immediately preceding the stressed syllable; a secondary stress is indicated by an inferior vertical stroke [ˌ] preceding the syllable.

McDavid sometimes tried to indicate four degrees of stress, with a degree intermediary between [ˈ] and [ˌ] marked in various ways, usually with [ˋ]. These markings have been emended to secondary stresses in single words, to primary stresses in phrases.

The extent to which stress is indicated is a matter of judgment, by field workers, editors, or both, and thus stress is not represented comprehensively at any stage from field transcription through final corrected data files. If there is a consistent stress pattern, as in *Georgia*, it is often described in a narrative accompanying the list manuscript or data file and is marked in the responses themselves only for exceptions. If there is great variety (*Louisiana, automobile, how are you?*), the position of the stresses is indicated in the entries wherever the information is available.

The observation of stress (or rather of the relative prominence of syllables, produced jointly by stress, pitch, and length) is beset with serious difficulties during the conditions of field work. The tendency of informants to offer some words with an overcareful or overemphatic pronunciation, as well as their hesitation or uncertainty in pronouncing others, often produces unnatural distributions of stress in the recorded forms. The difference between primary and secondary stresses is likely to be obscured or to disappear: compounds normally pronounced with the main stress on either the first or the second member may be given even stress, (as ˈstone ˈwall instead of ˈstone wall or stone ˈwall), and the usual stress pattern may even be reversed when contrasting two similar expressions (as hay ˈstack and hay ˈmow instead of the normal ˈhay stack and ˈhay mow). Moreover, the degree and the distribution of the stress often depend largely upon the context in which the expression happened to be uttered, but since the full context was only rarely recorded, the clue to many exceptional stress phenomena has been lost.

When a word or compound is described as having even stress, it is to be understood that according to circumstances either the first or the second stress may be the stronger, or that the two may be equal in force. The determining influences are usually of three kinds: sentence rhythm (cf. *he is ˈfourˈteen*; *he is ˈfourˌteen ˈyears*; *he is ˈjust fourˈteen*; *a ˈstone ˈwall*; *the ˈold ˌstone ˈwall*; *the ˈstone ˌwall fell*, etc.); contrast or distinction (cf. *ˈthirteen, ˈfourteen, ˈfifteen* in counting; *back ˈporch* and *back ˈstoop, ˈback porch* and *ˈfront porch*, etc.); or emphasis (cf. *for the ˈlast ˈfourˈteen ˈyears*, etc.)

Intonation

The intonation (rise and fall of pitch) was recorded only for certain special phrases, such as greetings and calls to domestic animals, in which the pitch pattern is more or less fixed by habit and may be regarded as an integral part of the expression. In recording these phrases, the field workers used a system of straight lines, curves, and dots on a staff of three levels, written under the phonetic transcription or in the right-hand column of the field book (see the New England *Handbook*, pp. 141–42). Intonation has not been included in final LAMSAS computer files.

Word Division

When an entry is a phrase containing two or more words, the words are separated by spaces for the sake of convenience in reading. This rule is observed even when the phonetic divisions between syllables do not coincide with the word division. The rule governing the separation of words is observed also when the final consonant of one word and the initial consonant of the following word are partially assimilated, thus *this year* [ðɪs̜ jɪə], [ðɪʃ jiə], [ðɪˢ ʃiə], and even when these two sounds are completely assimilated, provided the following consonant is long or "double": thus [ðɪʃ ʃiə]. When the resulting consonant is short, however, so that a single consonant belongs equally to both words, the words are not separated: thus [ðɪʃiə]. It is sometimes difficult to decide where the boundary between two words should be drawn. In such cases the words are usually not divided: thus *used to* [justə].

In writing a phrase of two words, the field workers sometimes indicate that the stress on the second word sets in before or together with the final consonant of the first word, so that the consonant belongs phonetically to the following syllable: thus *far off* [faˈrɔf], *New England* [nuˈwiŋglənd], *post office* [ˈpousˌdɔfɨs].

Field Workers

Guy S. Lowman, Jr., was the principal field worker for LAMSAS, even more than for LANE. He did all of the interviewing from October 1933 until his death in a car accident in July 1941. Lowman was trained first by Miles Hanley at Wisconsin and then by Daniel Jones for a doctorate at University College, London. He was a meticulous observer of fine phonetic distinctions, notably in vowels and in the qualities of /r/, with little normalizing in terms of his own phonemic system, little overtranscription, accurate indication of quantity and stress, and good definition of the currency of words and pronunciations by social and age groups. He observed fewer lexical variants than some other investigators, paid less attention to word meanings, and recorded relatively few forms from free conversation. Working very fast, he suggested rather frequently. He generally got along well with his informants.

Raven I. McDavid, Jr., was first attracted to the Atlas project when he served as a demonstration informant for Bernard Bloch at the Linguistic Institute of 1937 (this interview is included in the LAMSAS roster as number 1037, SC 42D). Afterward, in addition to private study, he received intensive training from Bloch and Kurath at the Institutes of 1940 and 1941, and later attended the Institutes of 1946-49 and 1954-58.

In general, he had good rapport with his informants. In his interviews McDavid emphasized history, folklore, and local traditions, encouraging alternate responses, synonyms and variant pronunciations. When he could not get a natural response, he would often leave the item blank; on the other hand, he recorded a very large number of conversational responses, especially for grammatical forms. Definitions are generally clear and full.

In comparison with the practices of the New England field workers, McDavid's transcriptions can be described as minute; he prided himself on freedom from systematization (in terms of both his own system and that of the informants), avoidance of overtranscription, and consistent marking of quantity and stress.

Records by the following investigators were taped and later transcribed by McDavid. For this reason only their interviewing practices are noted.

Lee Pederson, now Director of the Linguistic Atlas for the Gulf States (*LAGS*), studied under McDavid at Chicago, with additional training from

Norman McQuown. At the time of his first interviews in LAMSAS territory he had completed nearly forty interviews for his dissertation on the speech of Chicago. More at home in urban than in rural environments when he began investigating Southern speech, he adapted extremely well and showed initiative and ingenuity in locating suitable informants and persuading them to talk. He often included items from the New England work sheets, though he probed less than McDavid for synonyms. He tended to suggest more than McDavid. His rapport with informants was generally excellent, and his tapes provide many conversational forms.

Grace Rueter and Barbara Rutledge, students of Pederson and natives of Georgia, both participated actively in the Survey of Rural Georgia and the *LAGS* project. Somewhat more at home in rural Southern culture than Pederson, and learning from his experience, they followed his general interviewing techniques.

Other students of Pederson, who usually did single interviews as class projects, varied greatly, though their practices generally followed those of Pederson. Their records are less useful than those of Pederson, Rueter, and Rutledge, because of their inexperience, but they help to fill in some of the gaps in the coverage of the secondary settlements of Georgia.

Gerald Udell, a student of McDavid at Chicago (and before that at Western Reserve), had considerable field experience before his work for LAMSAS, in gathering evidence for his 1966 dissertation on the speech of Akron. He had studied with McQuown, and with Kurath and others at a Linguistic Institute at Michigan. Udell's interviews were deliberately paced, and followed the work sheet order rather closely. He did relatively little probing for variants, and allowed little time for free conversation from which spontaneous forms might be picked up. He enjoyed good rapport with his informants.

Raymond K. O'Cain, a doctoral student of McDavid at Chicago, contributed two field records to LAMSAS (for which he was Associate Editor 1973–80): the very full SC 35C and the fragmentary SC 16. He had excellent rapport with his informants, encouraged free conversation, and was leisurely in his interviewing, so his records have many spontaneous forms. He enjoyed probing for synonyms and alternate responses, and was excellent in his definitions of variants.

Variant Practices of Lowman and McDavid

1) Lowman indicated two degrees of aspiration for initial voiceless stops [p p^h]. McDavid indicated three [p p' p^h].

2) Lowman wrote half-fortis voiceless unaspirated stops as [p̬ t̬ ḳ s̬]. McDavid wrote them as [p t̬ ḳ s̬]. In editing, these have been changed to [p̬ t̬ ḳ s̬].

3) Lowman wrote glottalized stops before syllabic [-m -n -ŋ -ɫ] as [-ʔpm -ʔtn -ʔkŋ -ʔtɫ]. In his field records McDavid wrote them as [-pʔm -tʔn -kʔŋ -tʔɫ]. In his transcriptions of tapes he followed Lowman's practice. In editing they are marked as [-'pm -'tn -'kŋ -'tɫ].

4) Lowman wrote [-'t-] consistently in intervocalic position, as if indicating pre-aspiration. For aspirated intervocalic stops, McDavid wrote [-t'-], following Lowman's practice only when preaspiration was clear. Such transcriptions are left unchanged in editing.

5) Lowman wrote [ʎ] for both palatalized [ʎ] and clear [l]. McDavid distinguished the two. In editing, Lowman's [ʎ] is changed to [l], except in contexts where palatalization is almost certain, as in *million*.

6) McDavid wrote flap [ɹ] and retroflex [ɽ ɻ] more often than Lowman. In editing the two last are changed to [l ɻ].

7) McDavid occasionally wrote [-t⁷], etc., to indicate unreleased stops; in editing these are changed to Lowman's [-'t].

8) McDavid followed the Atlas vowel alphabet strictly and wrote [ɵ ɵ] where Lowman wrote [œ ɵ] respectively. In editing, Lowman's symbols are changed to those of the Atlas alphabet.

9) McDavid occasionally wrote [ʀ] to indicate a frictionless velar open consonant.

10) Lowman put shift signs for vowel shading before stressed vowels and before the first members of diphthongs [ᶜʊ ᴣaɨ]. McDavid followed Atlas conventions and wrote shift signs after all vowels. In editing, Atlas conventions are followed.

11) Lowman indicated rounding by a double curve [ɽ ǫ]. McDavid followed the Atlas convention of writing rounding as [ɽ ǫ] in most of his LAMSAS field records. In editing, Atlas conventions are followed.

12) For spreading (unrounding) of vowel sounds McDavid followed the Atlas convention of underlining [ʋ]; Lowman used the open parenthesis [(ʋ]. In editing, Atlas conventions are followed.

Chapter 6: Field Records, List Manuscripts, and Initial Editing

The first editorial steps actually took place in the field. Since most interviews were not completed in a single sitting, field workers were supposed to look over the results of each day's labors to see what responses had been elicited that required correction or elucidation and what questions still needed to be asked. They were also supposed to transfer conversational responses gathered on the fly from the extra pages at the back of the field book (or from any other place that had served the moment) to the appropriate page and line of the field book. Any comments or corrections the field worker wished to enter in the field book were supposed to go in the right margin; the original transcription was not to be altered by any later reconsideration of what the field worker had first heard.

The field books in which the field workers recorded their transcriptions have not remained intact. They were designed to be taken apart into separate pages, one original page and one carbon copy for every page of the work sheets (see Chapter 4). The separate pages have at different times in LAMSAS history been filed by informant and by page and state (e.g. all of the page 86s from one state's interviews together in a folder). The original field records are now filed by page and state in the University of Georgia Library Special Collections archive. Some pages have been lost over the years—an inventory of missing pages accompanies the records in the archive—but the original transcriptions on the field records remain unretouched. Any later marking on the pages, such as renumbering with new informant ID numbers, has been kept clearly separate from the transcriptions, and there is little of it. The major exceptions are the records from Georgia and South Carolina. The original Georgia field records disappeared from storage at the University of Chicago, and "original" pages were then reconstituted from the carbons. The cluttered appearance of some South Carolina field book pages, the result of McDavid's elicitation of many synonyms and alternate pronunciations, required that these records be recopied in more orderly fashion before being submitted to the camera for microfilming.

McDavid et al. 1982–86 is a comprehensive set of microfilms of the original field records, plus some other comparable sets of records such as Lowman's Southern England interviews, Turner's Gullah interviews, and Alexander's Canadian Maritime interviews. The field records were photographed state by state. The microfilms were to serve as a guarantee of safety for the records; the installment for each state was provided with front matter sufficient to explain the contents, but no editorial corrections were attempted.

The original field records and microfilms should be used with caution. Figure 6.1 illustrates a sample field book page by Lowman, Figure 6.2 a page by McDavid. Both pages require some paleographical skill to interpret—the field workers were after all transcribing on the fly. Moreover, the transcriptions in the field records have not been edited to reconcile variant transcription practices, such as Lowman's placement of shift signs before vowels when McDavid placed them after (see Chapter 5).

The major editorial task before the mid-1980s was the creation of list manuscripts. Each list manuscript contains a serial listing, in a prescribed order by informant within each state, of the responses provided for each elicitation cue, normally one list manuscript for each line of each page of the work sheets. Kurath started to compile list manuscripts for the South Atlantic States data while the New England Atlas was still being published and Lowman was in the field; responses from additional states were added as the states were completed. In the ten years following his acceptance of the editor's chair in 1964, Raven McDavid completed approximately 80% of the entries, some for existing partial lists and some for lists that had not yet been started. Further work on the lists occurred during editorial operations at the University of South Carolina. Virginia McDavid has recently been finishing incomplete list manuscripts before they are used for data entry. List manuscripts in the LAMSAS files, therefore, are frequently products of work at different times by different hands.

The chief reason for making list manuscripts was access to the material. Kurath had compiled list

Figure 6.1: Sample Field Book Page (Guy Lowman)
Informant 99 (NY35A), page 19

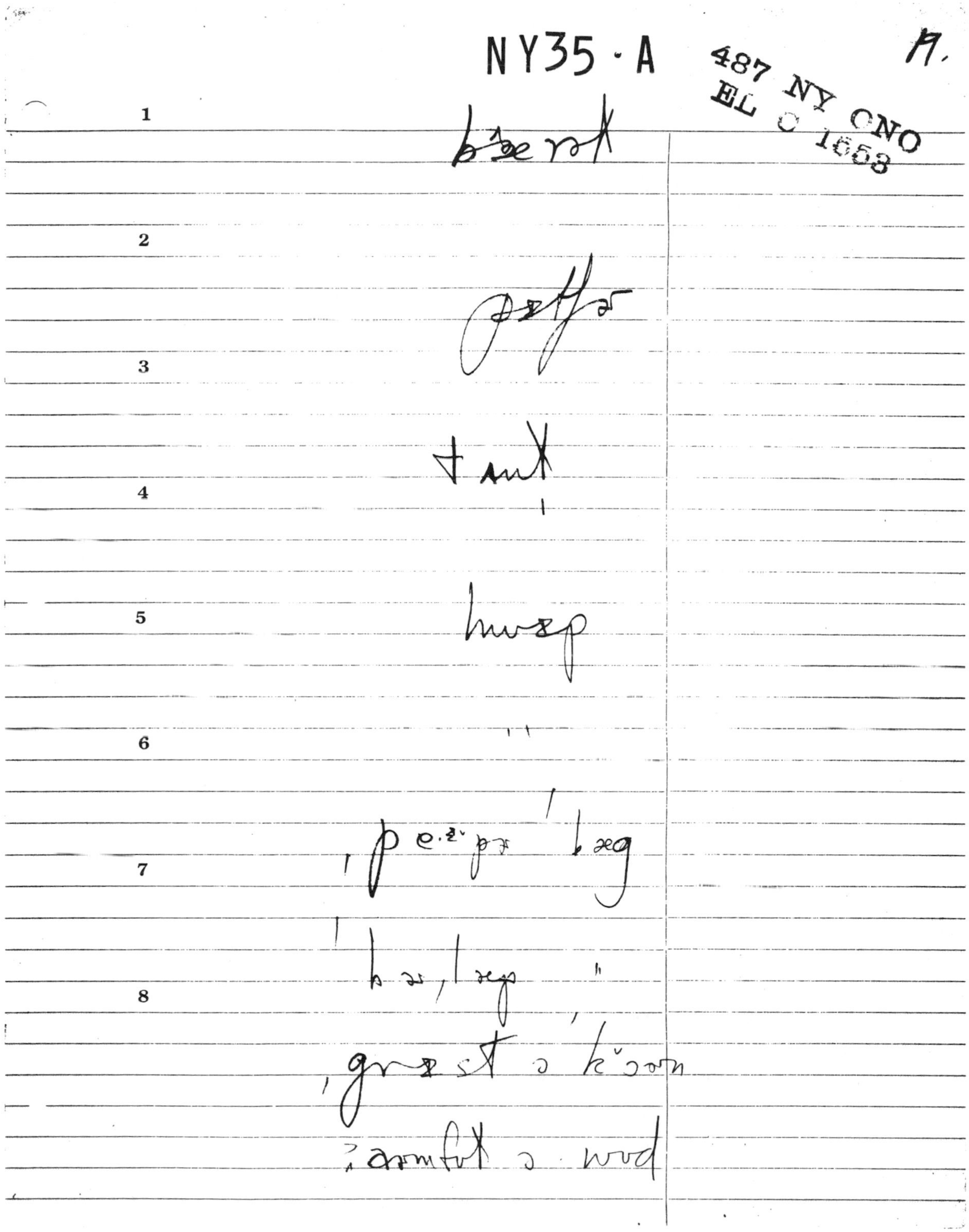

Figure 6.2: Sample Field Book Page (Raven McDavid)
Informant 88 (NY31A), page 19

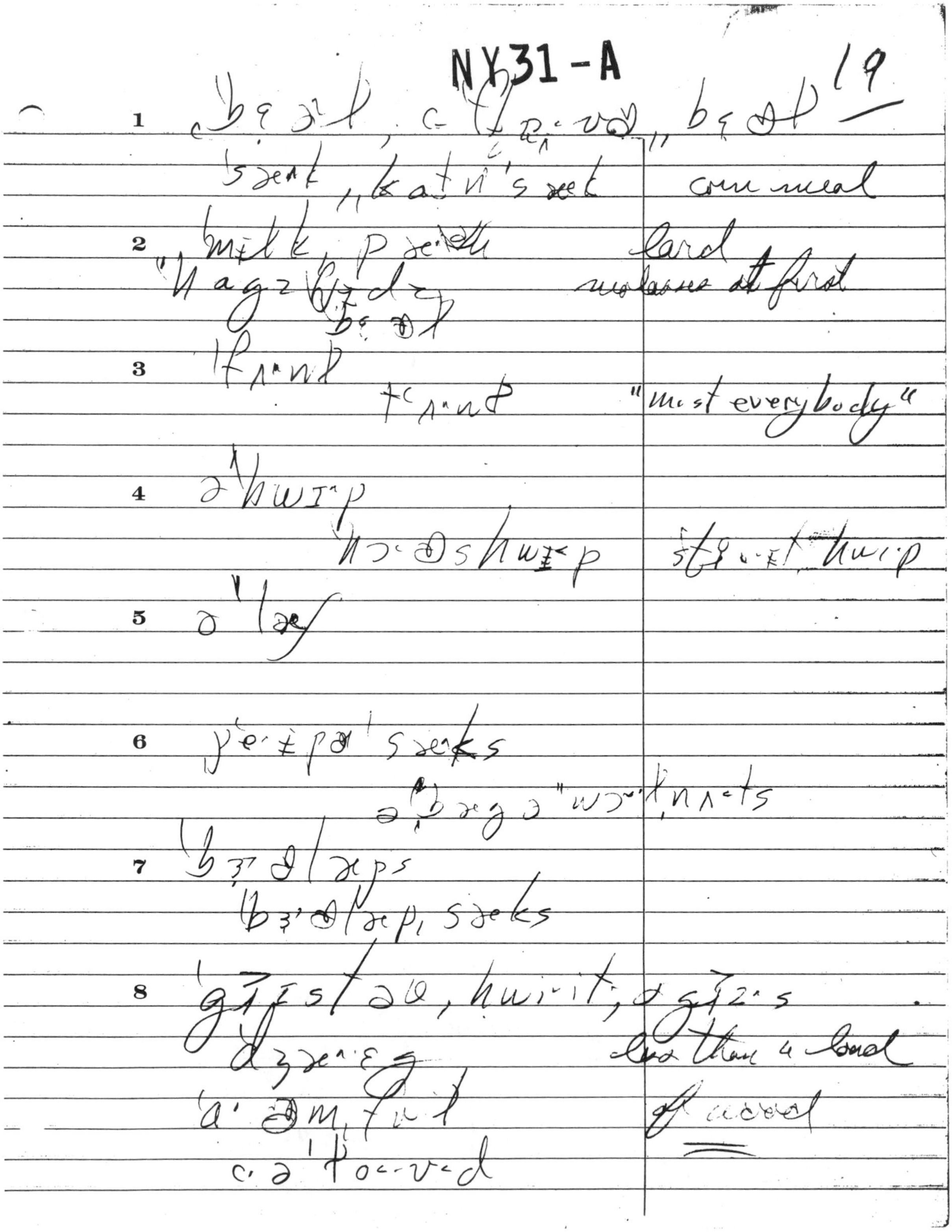

Figure 6.3: Sample List Manuscript Page (list number 212)

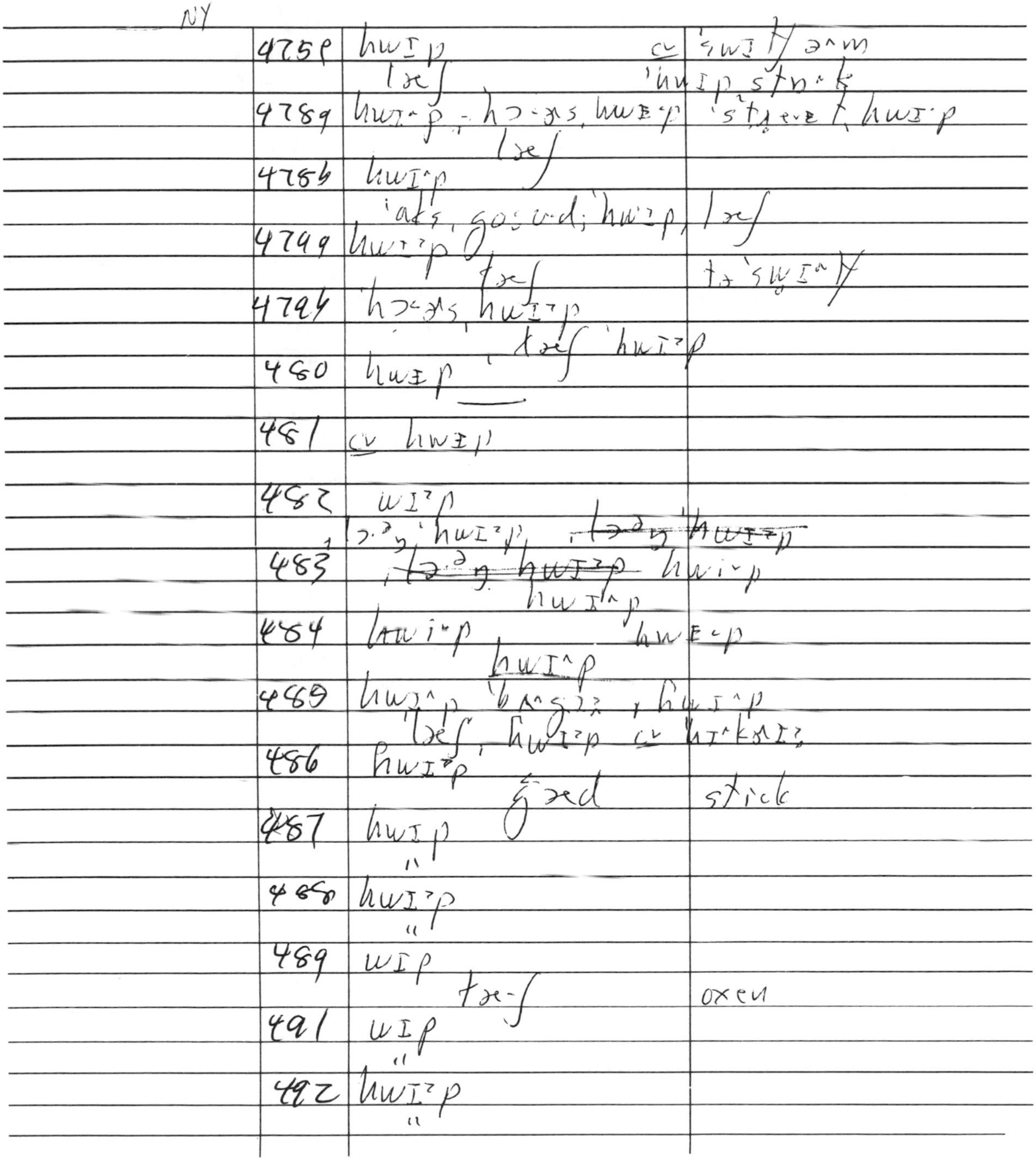

manuscripts of the New England responses; they allowed an opportunity to reconcile transcription practices while making legible entries in a regular order from which draftsmen could prepare the *LANE* maps. Kurath later realized that his analyses of New England speech (for Kurath 1949 and elsewhere) were conducted mainly from the lists, which allowed for easy creation of symbol maps, not from the published maps where it was more difficult to organize and interpret the data. Eventually Kurath decided to use the list format for publication (see Chapter 1). A sample list manuscript page is reproduced as Figure 6.3.

In addition to their organization of responses, the list manuscripts were themselves organized according to a general plan. As printed in the new indices for the second edition of the New England *Handbook* and illustrated for LAMSAS in Chapter 4, Kurath and later McDavid conceived of list manuscripts as presenting responses according to conceptual or grammatical categories such as *Domestic Animals* or *Pronouns*. While the pages of the work sheets were roughly arranged into similar categories, the plan for list manuscripts superseded the plan of the work sheets so that information gathered from disparate work-sheet pages was gathered into lists in the same category; indeed, in some cases information gathered in response to different cues from different pages and lines of the work sheets was entered into the same list. For example, list 723 was planned for responses illustrating finite *be*, and the responses were to be drawn from questions on pages 4, 24, 25, 42, 43, 46, and 92 of the work sheets. The case is extreme but not unique.

Conversely, data gathered in response to the cue from a single page and line of the work sheets could be presented in different lists. A common example is page 86, line 5: two state names, *Georgia* and *Florida*, were supposed to be elicited for this page and line (a not uncommon practice for numerals and geographical names), and the *Georgia* responses were to be put on list 13, *Florida* responses on list 14. Another way in which the responses from a single page/line cue could be separated is by content. In the New England *Atlas* some planned maps were separated into an A map and B map to allow sufficient room for complex sets of responses. For LAMSAS, Raven McDavid planned to make numerous subsidiary lists which would separate the responses by lexical type or other criterion. For example, for work sheet page 29 line 3, intended to elicit terms for 'flat low-lying land along a stream',

there was to be a main list for *lowland* (list 34) and subsidiary lists for *valley* (34a) and for *hollow, cove* (34b).

In practice, for those few subsidiary lists actually executed and for the main lists related to them, it happened that words of similar pronunciation from different page/line cues were grouped in the same lists: *ravine* was elicited from page 29 line 3 but also from page 30 line 4, the cue for 'a channel cut by a stream in a road or field', and responses from both sources were entered on list 41a; *gully* was also elicited in response to these questions, and was entered on list 41. The problem with such separation is that, while it might be valuable to group lexemes together to study their pronunciation, there was no list manuscript in which all of an informant's responses to a single cue would be located, and it was possible that some of the responses that fell between the lists might not be recorded. Since a great many of the planned subsidiary lists were not prepared, it is sometimes difficult to know how complete the main lists might be without checking against the field records. These problems are aggravated by the gradual preparation of numerous lists by many hands over many years, because decisions made about list creation by one editor might not always be effectively transmitted to later editors. The problems of the list manuscripts are not carried over into the computer files, which are organized by page and line of the work sheets and reassemble all responses to a single cue (see Chapter 7).

Two major benefits of list preparation were editorial reconciliation of transcriptions and regularization of codes for the status of responses. The code list (in large part recapitulated from the New England *Handbook*, pp. 143–46) and the editors' list of reconciliation practices are presented below. A separate code list for the computer files is described in Chapter 7.

Labels and Other Symbols

Besides the linguistic forms transcribed by the field workers in the phonetic alphabet presented above, the entries in LAMSAS list manuscripts sometimes contain various labels to indicate (A) the manner in which the response was secured, (B) the informant's attitude toward the response, (C) the status of the form offered according to the informant's comments, and (D) doubt on the field worker's part as to the accuracy of the transcription.

A separate labeling system is employed for LAM-SAS computer files (see Chapter 7).

(A) Labels indicating the manner in which the response was secured are abbreviations (small letters followed by a period) immediately preceding the form. They are used to mark all responses not secured as straightforward answers to the usual form of the question. Each of these abbreviations most often applies only to the one form to which it is prefixed in field records; abbreviations in list manuscripts apply to all the forms following the symbol.

cv marks a form recorded from the informant's conversation, not in answer to a question. Such forms are especially valuable as samples of spontaneous natural usage. In McDavid's records, most of the strictly grammatical items, such as the forms of auxiliary verbs, the case forms of pronouns and double negation, were secured in this way.

cr marks a form offered by the informant as a spontaneous correction of some other form, usually the one immediately preceding it in the entry. Such forms are often self-conscious attempts at elegance or correctness, but sometimes a conscientious informant may correct his affected first response to a more natural form.

r marks a form repeated at the field worker's request, usually because the field worker did not hear the first utterance clearly or was not sure that it was transcribed correctly. The notation of the first utterance is sometimes included in the field record preceding the repeated form, sometimes omitted. Since immediate repetition increases the formality of the interview and the likelihood of unnatural responses, McDavid avoided this after his early interviews; instead he would come back to the item later. Responses secured in this fashion are not marked with *r*.

f marks a form secured by insisting on an answer when the informant is reluctant to give one. Such forms are to be accepted with reservations, since an informant may sometimes be forced by the field worker's persistence into offering a response which does not represent his normal usage. This symbol is replaced in list manuscripts by *s*.

s marks a form suggested (that is, actually pronounced) by the field worker and repeated by the informant. A suggested response is not recorded by the field worker unless he has reason to suppose that it represents the informant's natural usage, but since this question cannot always be decided satisfactorily under the conditions of field work, forms marked as suggested—especially grammatical items—are in general to be regarded as less trustworthy than responses secured in other ways. A suggested form is not entered by the field worker unless the informant actually pronounced it and signified that it was natural.

Lowman was especially inclined to suggest forms in which he was particularly interested if his informants failed to offer them spontaneously, and in his later records systematically suggested a number of terms which he had found it difficult to secure by indirect questioning. McDavid preferred indirect questioning and observation of free conversation.

(B) Labels indicating the informant's attitude toward the response (usually toward the word or phrase offered, sometimes toward the subject-matter to which this refers) are marks of punctuation immediately preceding the form. Each of these marks applies only to the single form to which it is prefixed.

: a colon marks a hesitating response, regardless of the cause of the hesitation. This may be uncertainty on the informant's part, his inability to recall the term, or his disinclination to utter it (for words which he regards as indelicate).

! an exclamation point marks a form at which the informant evinces amusement, whether this is caused by the phonetic character of the term, by its meaning or connotation, or by the broader subject matter to which it refers.

? a query marks a form concerning which the informant expresses doubt, whether this refers to its meaning, to its pronunciation or to its naturalness.

(C) Labels indicating the status of the form offered according to the comments or explicit statements of the informant are arbitrary superior symbols immediately preceding the form.

⌐ marks a form not used by the informant, but offered as an expression used by others. Very often this label is amplified by a statement in the commentary indicating whether the informant has heard the form in question from natives of the community or from strangers, from educated or uneducated persons, and the like.

→ marks a form characterized by the informant as recently introduced, new, used only by the younger generation or the like, especially if the informant states that it has come into currency since the informant's own speech habits became fixed. In LAMSAS computer files all forms cited as being new or modern are specially marked; no distinction is made between between new forms not used by the informant and new forms that the informant believes to be natural.

* (or **) marks a form offered not by the informant from whom the entry is usually recorded (the main informant) but by an auxiliary informant, generally a native of the same community and often a member of the main informant's immediate family. The auxiliary informant is usually identified either in the commentary or in the informant biographies. Forms offered by an auxiliary informant are entered only if they provide information—a word or a feature of pronunciation—not given by the principal informant. If they are exactly alike in all respects, phonetically, status, etc., they are omitted.

† marks a form characterized by the informant as old, heard from older people, obsolete, no longer used or the like, whether it is one which he himself used formerly or one which he only has heard from older people. A statement in the commentary may indicate the status of old terms more precisely. In LAMSAS computer files all forms cited as being old or obsolete are specially marked; no distinction is made between between old forms not used by the informant and old forms that the informant believes to be natural.

Lowman systematically asked for or suggested older variants of the expressions used by his informants; McDavid tried to elicit older forms from his informants, but rarely suggested. As a result there are probably more terms marked with the † sign in Lowman's records than in McDavid's.

In most of Lowman's records and the later records by McDavid the symbols are replaced by marginalia which have been converted into the symbols as follows:

> *h.* "heard" becomes ⊥.
> *o.* "old". Described in the commentary.
> *o.f.* "old-fashioned". Described in the commentary.
> *o.h., h.o.* "old-heard", "heard old" becomes †.
> *o.n., o. nat.* "old natural". Described in the commentary.
> *as a ch., o. as a ch., n. as a ch., o.n. as a ch.,* etc. "as a child", "old, as a child", "natural as a child". Described in the commentary.

(D) The label indicating the field worker's doubt as to the accuracy of the transcription is a query in parentheses (?) immediately following the form. When the field worker's uncertainty refers to only one feature in the transcription (for example, to the quality of a particular vowel in the word), the reference of the label is more fully explained in the commentary.

The label indicating certainty as to the accuracy of a transcription is a check in parentheses (√) immediately following the form (less often by a *sic* in the commentary).

In actual field work, doubt as to the accuracy of a transcription was indicated by a wavy underline under the doubtful symbol or symbols; certainty (especially for transcriptions which might seem to the editors to involve a slip in notation) was marked by a double underline.

Forms marked by the field worker as doubtful are included in the entries only if no other form (or no other form of the same type) was recorded from the same informant.

Substitution Symbols

Under this head are grouped a number of signs used to avoid the repetition of identical words or parts of words in a single entry or to represent forms not given in phonetic transcription. Substitution symbols are not used in LAMSAS computer files.

The swing dash (~) is used to replace a word or group of words (or each of two or more noncontiguous words) repeated without change in a single entry: thus

[hæf pæst sɛvən, ha·f pa·st ~] to repeat the word [sɛvən],

[hæf pæst sɛvən, ha·f ~ sɛbm] (to repeat the word [pæst]),

[hæf pæst sɛvən, ~ sɛbm] (to repeat the words [hæft pæst]),

[hæf pæst sɛvən, ~ æftə ~] (to repeat the words [hæf] and [sɛvən]).

~ is also used to replace one member of a compound written as two words repeated without change in a single entry: thus [hwijlbærou, ~ barə] (to repeat the first member [hwijl]), [hwijlbærou, ~ barə, wijl~] (to repeat the first member [hwijl] and then the second member of the immediately preceding entry [barə]).

The hyphen (–) is used to replace a sequence of sounds (usually a syllable or a group of syllables) repeated without change in two or more forms of the same word in a single entry: thus [jɛstədeɪ, jɪstə–] (to repeat the syllable [deɪ]), [jɛstədi, jɪs–] (to repeat the syllables tədi]), [jɛstədɪ, –deɪ] (to repeat the syllables [jɛstə]).

The equal sign (=) is used after a semicolon to indicate that all the forms preceding the semicolon are to be repeated after it. Thus, in the list which shows the preterite and past participle of the verb *drive*, separated by a semicolon [drouv;   =] (preterite *drove*, participle also *drove*), [drouv, driv; =] (preterite either *drove* or *driv*, participle the same), [drouv;   =, drivən] (preterite *drove*, participle either *drove* or *driven*).

When no response was secured for a given item, either because the question was not asked or for some other reason, the line for the informant's responses is marked with a dash (–).

Other symbols are occasionally used—a triangle (Δ), numerals either standing alone or suffixed as exponents to linguistic forms, etc.—and are explained in the headnote for the list manuscript in which they appear.

Reconciliation of Phonetic Practices in List Manuscripts

The following directions were compiled and approved by Raven McDavid for editors at the University of South Carolina (1976–80), and represent a composite list of practices by all those who had worked earlier on list manuscripts. The South Carolina editors completed and corrected a number of list manuscripts in order to compose camera-ready pages with a Selectric typewriter for McDavid and O'Cain 1980. Directions which apply only to that publication have been deleted. A few of the practices described here have been modified for LAMSAS computer files (see Chapter 7).

General

I. Vowels

1. Superior symbols of vowels presumably carrying a syllable should be replaced by an on-line symbol with the breve (˘). [ræbᵊt] = [ræbăt], also [ᵊl ᵊn ᵊr] = [ăl ăn ăr]. BUT [ᵊə] (unchanged), since [ə] is considered a vowel and the superior vowel would be an on-glide.

2. An off-glide between a nasalized vowel and a nasal consonant should also be written as nasalized. [ãᵊn] = [ãə̃n].

3. [œ] = [ə]. Be sure the latter is distinguished from [ɵ].

4. Breves on superior symbols should be eliminated. [aə̆] = [aᵊ]. Superior characters are by definition very short and obscure.

II. Consonants

1. Glottalized stops, marked in the field records with a superior comma ['t], should be so marked in the manuscript.

2. Consonant symbols followed by length marks in the field records are to be written as double symbols [p·] = [pp] EXCEPT where the long consonant is syllabic, as in grunts of affirmation and negation, and other interjections: [ˌʔmˈm̩n:].

3. On line ligatures are to be retained. [ßw] ≠ [ßw]. A ligature is assumed (not to be written) if a segment is written above the line [ᵝw] = [ᵝw].

4. Syllabic marks are to be eliminated EXCEPT if essential to a proper reading of the syllabification: [laɪtnɪn] but [laɪtn̩ɪn]

5. Special symbols for retroflex consonants [ṭ ḍ ṇ ḷ ṛ] should be replaced by the symbols for alveolar consonants plus the accompanying diacritic for retroflextion [t ḍ ṇ ṛ].

6. The palatalized lateral [lʲ] should be replaced by the 'clear l' [l] unless the context makes a palatalized [lʲ] probable, as *glass, stallion*. This occurs oftenest in Lowman and Bloch.

III. Suprasegmentals

1. The elements of a compound word should be separated unless the second number is normally unstressed.

2. If a stress pattern predominates, it should be stated in the headnote. Thereafter, only exceptions should be entered. (This is particularly important since GSL marks stress much less frequently than RIM) For a complicated item like *Louisiana*, all stress marks should be retained.

IV. Doubtful Observations

1. Forms with a wavy underline [æ̰ɨ] should be eliminated EXCEPT

   a. When no other form is recorded.

   b. If a different type of pronunciation, construction, etc., is represented.

2. When doubtful forms are retained, substitute a question mark in parentheses (?) *after* the doubtful form and put a specific statement in the commentary as to what was doubtful. *field record* [fɜtɨl]; *list MS.* [fɜtɨl] (?); commentary [ɜ]. The commentary should employ the most economical manner of specifying the doubtful portion.

3. The double underline, if really significant, should be replaced by *sic* in the commentary, otherwise eliminate it. [ɜ̲]; commentary [ɜ] *sic*.

V. Labelling

1. : ? (hesitating, doubtful) to be replaced by (?).

2. Heard forms

   a. Forms characterized by informants as 'rare' were labeled ⊥ 'heard' by Kurath and Bloch. Continue this practice.

   b. In the marginal notes of the FW's:

   h. is to be replaced by ⊥

   h.o./o.h. are to be replaced by †

   c. → should be used only with 'recent' forms, but retained wherever it appears in the records by RIM. Otherwise, modern forms are better summarized in the commentary.

3. Suggested forms

   a. *s.f.* (suggested, forced) should be replaced by *s*.

   b. *s.h.* to be replaced by *s.*⊥

   c. *s.o.h./s.h.o.* to be replaced by †.

4. Auxiliary responses ("starred forms"). Starred forms should be freely eliminated EXCEPT when:

   a. No other form is recorded.

   b. The starred form differs (even if by as little as a shift sign) from that of the primary informant. *cf.* IV.2.

VI. Commentaries

1. Semicolons or commas separate parts of a single commentary entry (for one informant) in the community, except that a period must be used if part of the entry is a full sentence.

2. Cross references in the commentaries should be by key word. E.g. in some appropriate place there will be a cross-reference to places where weak preterites of strong verbs can be found. For *drawed (up)* there will be a note to see *shrank*.

3. Labels in the commentaries

   If the commentary refers to a labeled entry (one preceded by ?, !, →, ⊥, †, *, etc.) the label itself is sufficient to identify a form if the label appears with only *one* form.

4. Starred forms should be identified in the commentary *only* if two conditions are met:

   a. They differ markedly (cf. IV. 2) from the response of the primary informant.

   b. The auxiliary informant who offered them is not previously mentioned in the *vita*.

5. Where informants are bilingual the foreign language responses should normally be entered in the commentary, especially if identified as such. If the only response is in the foreign language, it should be entered in the main list.

Lowman

A. Vowels

1. Normally Lowman wrote shift signs before stressed vowels and before the first elements of diphthongs (but after weak stressed vowels—especially final—and after the second members of diphthongs). The shift signs should be written so that they always *follow* the symbol they modify. [ᐠi] = [iᐠ]

2. Lowman frequently wrote [ii uu uᵘ] etc., where the first and second elements are alike (also, rarely, [ᐠiiᐠ]). Writing cursively, Lowman apparently entered the shift signs only after transcribing the whole utterance, and sometimes did not put them in. Thus, look

elsewhere in the record(s) for cues to interpret [ii] and the like:

    a. On the same page.

    b. Elsewhere in the same record.

    c. In the records of adjacent communities.

    d. If cues are lacking, put a lowering shift sign on the first element.

3. Change [ə] to [ɘ] always. (*cf.* General I.3).

4. [ij ej uw ow aj *a*w] etc., to be retained.

5. [eɨ̆ ăʊ] to be changed to [e·ɨ a·ʊ], etc.

6. Diacritics for rounding/unrounding

    [ɜ] = [ɜ̜], etc.

    [(o] = [ǫ], etc. (L *never* uses _ except as indicated below)

    NB: in the early Lowman records, [v] only

    [v] = [ɑ]

    [v̰] = [ɒ]

7. To determine if post-vocalic schwa is on or above the line, follow 2a-c above.

B. Consonants

1. [k̜ g̜] = [k̇ ġ]

2. Glottalization of stops should be diacritically marked *before* the symbol (*cf.* General II.1)

    [p'] = ['p]

McDavid

A. Vowels

1. See Lowman A.6 (rounding): sometimes found in later records.

2. See Lowman A.7.

B. Consonants

1. [kj gj] = [k̇j ġj].

    [kʲ gʲ] *stet.*

In later SAS records transcribed from tapes

    [k̜ g̜] = [k̇ʲ ġʲ]

2. [ʀ], whether as an on-line symbol or as a modifier (= velarized [r], should be replaced by [ʁ]).

3. In all SAS records made before 1964: intervocalic [-ɚ-], whether on-line or superior, should be replaced by [-r-].

4. Final [-ɫ] = [-l] in all SC-GA Low-Country records before August 1947:

    SC 205.2,3; 206.1-3; N208; 209 (all); 210-211; 212.1; 213.1, 213.2-5, 2N213, 213.7,8,10; 214.2; 215.1; 216.1-3; N217; 219 (all); 220.1,2; 223.1-3; 225 (all); possibly 229; 233 (all); GA 246.1-4, 6-7; possible 247.

5. McDavid frequently wrote [ɫ̩ l̩ ṇ m̩], especially after intervocalic /-r-/ [-r- -ɚ-], in environments where Lowman wrote [ᵊn ə̃n en]. These transcriptions have been left unchanged since many of them reflect McDavid's practice of recording wherever possible from free conversation.

Bloch (One record: SC 243.4, SC42D)

A. [ə] to be replaced by [ɚ] (note [ɘ] = [ɘ]).

B. [l̩] to be replaced by [l̩] unless the context makes a palatalized [l̩] probable, as *glass*, *stallion*.

Chapter 7: LAMSAS Computerization

An NEH site visit to the University of South Carolina editorial site in 1980 suggested that ways be found to bring computer assistance to production of the camera-ready list manuscripts then being published (McDavid and O'Cain 1980). The most difficult problem at the time was Atlas phonetics, which could be neither displayed nor printed out with the systems, large or small, that were then available. Technical advances in the middle 1980s made it possible to develop good computer facilities for editing phonetic transcriptions, and the full range of Atlas phonetics was available both for on-screen editing and in hard copy from the laser printer by the late 1980s (Kretzschmar 1989).

LAMSAS Computer Phonetics

LAMSAS computer phonetics take advantage of the 256 codes available to display characters in text mode on IBM PC compatible computers. A subset of these codes, known as the ASCII set, conventionally represents the symbols of the Roman alphabet, Arabic numerals, a few additional symbols, and a selection of "control codes" used to control computer operations. The ASCII set takes up a large part of the first 128 codes, but some of the first 128 codes and the majority of the remaining 128 codes are available to represent other symbols. Different brands of computers and software packages make use of these additional codes for special purposes; on IBM PC compatible computers the most common symbol sets are composed of line-graphics symbols and some common combinations of characters plus diacritical marks, such as ä. The software in use for the LAMSAS system remaps all available codes to represent phonetic symbols not included in the normal ASCII set, diacritical marks, and a selection of other useful symbols, as illustrated in Figure 7.1. Sixteen codes, those that correspond to important computer control codes and codes reserved by the software packages in use for LAMSAS, are not mapped with characters for display.

There are no composite characters, i.e. combinations of base symbol with diacritical mark in a single character space, mapped to the display codes because there are far too many possible combinations to be mapped within a single run of 256 codes. While it would be possible to map composite characters if it were assumed that there would be many possible runs of 256 codes in multiple fonts, such a practice would require font coding to be inserted in databases and texts along with the phonetics codes; font coding differs between different software packages and, in the absence of a standard markup language (SGML) or set of text encoding conventions (TEI) as were being developed in the late 1980s, it was decided that the greatest number of potential users of LAMSAS files would be able (in theory) to find ways to display these mappings of phonetics independent of particular software packages with just the single 256-code set. Later developments in IBM compatible display technology, VGA and SVGA display systems, have borne out this judgment.

In practice, with the software in use for LAMSAS, phonetics are displayed on the computer monitor in strings. For instance, ɨ appears on the screen as ɪ – in a sequence of two units; in a complex hypothetical example, ą̈ would appear on the screen as a sequence of no fewer than seven units, ə ˛ ˘ ˉ ˄ ˒ . The order in which the symbols are entered is conventional, an amplification of the ordering used for handwritten list manuscripts: first the base symbol, then on-line overstrike diacritics, then subscript diacritics, then superscript diacritics, and finally on-line diacritics representing height, frontness, and length. If more than one diacritic of the same type is called for, e.g. ˘ ˉ, the diacritics are entered in ascending order of the numeric codes to which each is mapped.

In order to achieve a composite appearance in hard copy that corresponds to hand-written versions of phonetic transcriptions, the files containing strings of phonetic symbols and diacritics are processed by a kerning program before being sent to the printer. The kerning program compares each set of codes (usually pairs, but some larger sets are specified) in the text file against a list of over 10,000 sets which require adjustment; when the program identifies a set that needs adjustment before printing, it inserts new codes as necessary to locate symbols and diacritics correctly with respect to each other when the file is sent to the printer. For instance, in a 12 point Roman font for the laser printer, the ɪ – string is converted to ɪ\i-11d\|27d ¯ \|-27d . The added codes move the overscore diacritic down and to the left so that it forms the bar on the small-cap ɪ, then restores normal print positioning for the next symbol to be printed. The LAMSAS list of sets requiring adjustment is updated frequently as new combinations of symbols and diacritics requiring adjustment are discovered during data entry and proofreading. There is a specific list of kerning adjustments for each of the fourteen bit-mapped Times Roman fonts in use to print LAMSAS data on a laser printer.

All customized elements of the LAMSAS computer phonetics system, including screen fonts, printer fonts, and kerning lists—but not including commercial software with which they are used—are available from the LAMSAS editorial office for the cost of reproduction and shipping.

Figure 7.1: LAMSAS Computer Character Mapping

Subscript Diacritics: (141 = ̦) (142 = ̣) (143 = ̥)
(144 = ̬) (145 = ̠) (146 = ̯) (147 = ̮) (148 = ̱)
(149 = ̱) (150 = ̩) (151 = ̮) (152 = ̞) (153 = ̝)
(154 = ̟) (155 = ̭) (156 = ̜) (157 = ̹) (158 = ̨)
(159 = ‿) (172 = ̡)

Superscript Diacritics: (134 = ˝) (135 = ')
(136 = ̔) (137 = ̃) (138 = ˚) (139 = ̂) (140 = ⁀)
(167 = ') (187 = ˙) (219 = ˇ) (220 = ˋ) (221 = ˘)
(223 = ¯) (224 = ¨) (234 = ´) (254 = ˜)

Stress Markings and Online Diacritics: (094 = ^)
(195 = ˊ) (205 = ˋ) (229 = ˈ) (233 = ‿) (245 = ˌ)
(132 = ˕) (133 = ˔) (160 = ̡) (171 = ˰)
(186 = ·) (188 = ‹) (189 = ˬ) (190 = ›)
(191 = –) (251 = ~)

Vowels (apart from standard keyboard): (161 = ʏ)
(163 = ɵ) (164 = ɘ) (165 = ɐ) (166 = ɤ)
(168 = ɷ) (169 = ɯ) (170 = œ) (176 = ə)
(177 = ɪ) (178 = ɛ) (179 = ɜ) (180 = ɚ)
(181 = ɑ) (182 = ɒ) (183 = ɔ) (184 = ʌ)
(185 = ʊ) (192 = ɞ) (201 = ɩ) (222 = ɶ)
(225 = æ)

Consonants (apart from standard keyboard):
(194 = ʙ) (197 = ɪ̵) (198 = ꜰ) (199 = ɓ)
(200 = ʜ) (202 = ᴊ) (203 = ɦ) (204 = ʟ)
(206 = ɲ) (208 = ᴘ) (209 = ɟ) (210 = ʀ)
(211 = ɼ) (213 = ɹ) (214 = ʁ) (215 = ɣ)
(216 = ɿ) (217 = ʎ) (226 = β) (227 = ɾ)
(228 = ð) (230 = ɸ) (231 = ʔ) (232 = ɥ)
(235 = ɰ) (236 = ɬ) (237 = ɱ) (238 = ŋ)
(240 = ɖ) (241 = ɾ) (242 = ɹ) (243 = ʃ)
(246 = ʋ) (247 = ʍ) (248 = ʈ) (249 = θ)
(250 = ʒ)

Other Special Symbols and Characters: (001 = ×)
(002 = ÷) (003 = ≠) (004 = ±) (005 = ←)
(006 = μ) (016 = √) (017 = †) (018 = χ)
(019 = →) (020 = ⁊) (021 = §) (022 = σ)
(023 = α) (024 = ↑) (025 = ↓) (028 = ©)
(029 = Σ) (030 = Δ) (031 = £) (127 = ffi)
(128 = fi) (129 = ffl) (130 = fl) (131 = ff)
(162 = ") (175 = ȷ) (193 = Æ) (196 = Đ)
(207 = Ø) (212 = Ᵽ) (218 = Ʒ) (239 = ø)
(244 = þ) (252 = π) (255 =)

Standard Keyboard: (032 =) (033 = !)
(034 = ") (035 = #) (036 = $) (037 = %)
(038 = &) (039 = ') (040 = ( ) (041 =))
(042 = *) (043 = +) (044 = ,) (045 = -)
(046 = .) (047 = /) (048 = 0) (049 = 1)
(050 = 2) (051 = 3) (052 = 4) (053 = 5)
(054 = 6) (055 = 7) (056 = 8) (057 = 9)
(058 = :) (059 = ;) (060 = <) (061 = =)
(062 = >) (063 = ?) (064 = @) (065 = A)
(066 = B) (067 = C) (068 = D) (069 = E)
(070 = F) (071 = G) (072 = H) (073 = I)
(074 = J) (075 = K) (076 = L) (077 = M)
(078 = N) (079 = O) (080 = P) (081 = Q)
(082 = R) (083 = S) (084 = T) (085 = U)
(086 = V) (087 = W) (088 = X) (089 = Y)
(090 = Z) (091 = [ ) (092 = \ ) (093 =])
(095 = _) (096 = ') (097 = a) (098 = b)
(099 = c) (100 = d) (101 = e) (102 = f)
(103 = g) (104 = h) (105 = i) (106 = j)
(107 = k) (108 = l) (109 = m) (110 = n)
(111 = o) (112 = p) (113 = q) (114 = r)
(115 = s) (116 = t) (117 = u) (118 = v)
(119 = w) (120 = x) (121 = y) (122 = z)
(123 = {) (124 = |) (125 = })

Unassigned: 000, 007, 008, 009, 010, 011, 012, 013, 014, 015, 026, 027, 126, 173, 174, 253

Database and File Structure

The scale of the data collected for LAMSAS makes it impractical for most purposes to store all of it in a single file; simple retrievals of information would then take a long time because of the sheer quantity of information that would need to be searched, even at computer speeds. A hierarchical file and database system has therefore been created in order to manage LAMSAS data effectively.

The primary level of organization of the data is by single responses. Every separate response is entered in both standard orthography and in phonetic transcription; it is associated with a simple grammatical tag, and with coding to specify who said it (serial number, informant id number, and old informant number, as in the Table of Informants in Chapter 3), and with the circumstances under which it was uttered, including page and line numbers for the work sheet cue, commentary by the informant and field worker, and comment codes corresponding to the signs used in list manuscripts. One other code is entered for each response: a doubt flag is included so that each response can be marked as being, for any of many possible reasons, less reliable than normal responses. Each response is entered in full; no repetition or substitution codes are employed as in the list manuscripts, because each response is designed to be separately retrievable and such codes would prevent that. If no response was recorded from an informant two different entries are possible: if there is evidence that the informant was not asked the question (as is available for many incomplete field records), "NA" is entered to indicate "Not Asked"; if there is no such evidence, "NR" is recorded to indicate "No Response". If more than one response was given by an informant, each of the responses is separately encoded with a repetition of the informant's identification coding.

Responses with their associated coding and information are then grouped into tables according to the elicitation cue on a particular page and line of the work sheets. The structure of a table may best be imagined as that of a text table, with one row for every response and with columns corresponding to each way of storing the response (standard spelling or phonetics) and to each associated code or comment. Tables created with LAMSAS database software are readily convertible to standard ASCII files, which may then be imported by many different kinds of software packages. Most tables contain all of the information collected for a single page/line unit of the work sheets; whenever two separate cues were listed on the same page and line of the work sheets, such as *North Carolina* and *South Carolina* on page 86, line 4, two tables are created, one for each separate cue. If a response to a cue is clearly inappropriate, such as the response *manure* to the question about 'an enclosure for cattle next to a barn', it is still recorded but is coded as an inappropriate response. All information recorded in phonetics for a particular page and line is retained, as either an appropriate or an inappropriate response. Information not recorded in phonetics is relegated to the commentary. This level of organization explicitly abandons the plan for list manuscripts in favor of the work sheets. List manuscripts imposed implicit interpretations on the data according to the selection of responses incorporated in each list; organization by work sheet page and line restores the connection between an elicitation cue and its response, whether the connection is explicit through questioning or implicit through the association of a conversational response to the cue by a field worker. Figure 7.2 shows sample proof printouts that illustrate the tabular character of LAMSAS computer files. They also illustrate the process of association of data with page and line numbers instead of planned list manuscripts: the sample responses come from different LAMSAS computer files, P19#4 *whip* and L19#5 *goad*, but the responses were entered on the same list manuscript (Figure 6.3). One may also note that the two comments illustrated, "switch them" in Figure 7.2 and "to switch" in Figure 7.3, happened to have been transcribed in phonetics in the field, and they are encoded for the computer as inappropriate responses in the rows following the responses for which they are included as comments.

The name of each table indicates unambiguously the page and question number. A letter code is prefixed to indicate the nature of the responses as showing mainly grammatical (G), lexical (L), or phonetic (P) variation. Thus table G4#4 contains data for line 4 from page 4, of grammatical type; L29#3 contains data from page 29, line 3, of lexical type; P1#2A contains data from page 1, line 2, of phonetic type. The "A" suffix found in the last example indicates that the table contains responses to the first elicitation cue for this page and line (*three*); table P1#2B contains responses to the other elicitation cue for page 1, line 2 (*four*). Table names are typically carried over into ASCII files made from

Figure 7.2a: Sample Proof Printout (P19#4 *whip*)   *Figure 7.2b*: Sample Proof Printout (P19#5 *goad*)

Figure 7.2a

ID	No.	Word	Transcription	Codes	Note
NY30E	475e	whip	hwɪp	N|N|	
NY30E	475e	switch them	ˈswɪtʃ əˌm	E|Y| INA/CNV	"switch them"
NY31A	478a	horsewhip	ˈhɔˤəsˌhwɪˤp	N|N|	
NY31A	478a	straight whip	ˈstɹ̥e·ɹt ˌhwɪ·p	O|N|	
NY31A	478a	whip	hwʌp	N|N|	
NY31B	478b	whip	hwʌp	N|N|	
NY32A	479a	whip	hwɪˤp	N|N|	
NY32B	479b	horsewhip	ˈhɔˤəsˌhwɪˤp	N|N|	
NY33A	480	whip	hwɪp	N|N|	
NY33B	481	whip	hwɪp	N|N| CNV	
NY33C	482	whip	wɪˤp	N|N|	
NY34A	483	whip	hwiˑp	N|N|	
NY34B	484	whip	hwɪˤp	N|N|	
NY34C	485	buggy whip	ˈbʌgɪˤ ˌfɪwɪˤp	O|N|	
NY34C	485	whip	hwɪˤp	N|N|	
NY34D!	486!	whip	fɪwɪˤp	N|N|	
NY35A	487	whip	hwɪp	N|N|	

Figure 7.2b

ID	No.	Word	Transcription	Codes	Note
NY30E	475e	lash	læʃ	N|N|	
NY30E	475e	whipstock	ˈhwɪpˌstɒˑk	N|Y| INA	
NY31A	478a	lash	læʃ	|N|	
NY31B	478b	oxgoad	ˈɑksˌgɔsʊd	N|N|	
NY31B	478b	whiplash	ˈhwɪpˌlæʃ	N|N|	
NY32A	479a	lash	læʃ	N|N|	
NY32A	479a	to switch	tə ˈswɪtʃ̥	V|Y| INA	"to switch"
NY32B	479b	lashwhip	ˌlæʃˈhwɪˤp	N|N|	
NY33A	480	NR		|N|	
NY33B	481	NR		|N|	
NY33C	482	long whip	ˈlɔˑŋ ˌhwɪˤp	O|N|	
NY34A	483	whip	hwʌp	N|N|	
NY34B	484	NR		|N|	
NY34C	485	hickory	ˈhɪˌkəɹɪ	N|N| CNV	stick
NY34C	485	lashwhip	ˈlæʃˌfɪwɪˤp	N|N|	
NY34D!	486!	goad	gæd	N|N|	
NY35A	487	whip	hwɪp	N|N|	

them, with the addition of the file extension .asc, such as G4#4.ASC, P1#2A.ASC.

All of the tables from a particular page of the work sheets are grouped together into databases, a total of 104 databases for all LAMSAS data. This level of organization will not be apparent to users of separate ASCII files made from individual tables, but it is a convenience for data management in editorial operations.

In addition to the tables and databases that store LAMSAS responses, there is a single database which records informant information. One of its tables includes the information presented in Chapter 3 as the Table of Informants. Two other tables record pages that are missing from the field records. The missing pages tables distinguish those pages that are missing because they were never asked from those pages that have somehow been lost in the history of the project.

Detailed examples of the manipulation of data from the several tables and databases for purposes of interpretation will be published in Kretzschmar and Schneider [in preparation].

Data Entry and Proofreading

The greatest problem in the creation of tables and files for the LAMSAS corpus has been time: the amount of time it takes to enter all of the data with their associated information, the amount of time it takes to proofread and correct them, and the question of how to reduce both of these amounts. Automation of procedures saves both time and human error but, as a review of typical procedures will reveal, even the most efficient procedures are time-consuming for work of this complexity.

The first step for preparation of any new table is to assess the state of the data. List manuscripts normally provide a more efficient record from which to enter data, both because they are serial listings of responses and because editorial reconciliation of phonetics has already been conducted. It is important, however, to consider how many list manuscripts might have been made from responses from a single page and line of the work sheets: sometimes subsidiary lists were made, sometimes one list manuscript was made of responses from more than one page and line or from more than one cue on one page and line. It is also important to note the amount of duplication among responses, i.e. whether the same word occurs consistently in

pronunciation files or whether one or a few lexical variants dominate the responses for a lexical file. Even in pronunciation files it is helpful to note whether there are common segments.

The next step is to duplicate materials and data as far as possible. Since some information starts out the same in every table, such as the series of three informant numbering codes and negative marking for the doubt flag, and the table structure itself is always the same, the new, empty table is copied from an exemplar and then renamed as appropriate. Common elements discovered in assessment of the list manuscript can then be added globally, and can be edited as necessary when going through the file response by response.

In most cases the grammatical code can be pre-entered according to the system shown in Figure 7.3.

Figure 7.3: LAMSAS Grammatical Codes

N = noun	J = conjunction
V = verb	P = preposition
M = pronoun	X = verb auxiliary
C = copula	D = determiner (article)
A = adjective	R = relative pronoun
B = adverb	T = existential 'there', 'it', etc.

S = complete clause
E = word group with verb
Q = word group with preposition
O = word group with noun
K = word group with adjective or adverb

Only one letter is used to characterize each response, according to the following guidelines:

Verb plus PP or NP should be E.
S is used only if a subject, predicate, and, where appropriate, object, can be identified.
Preposition plus NP should be Q.
Choose S if possible, then E, then Q, O, and K.

Grammatical codes are not intended to be prescriptive or overly precise; they are meant only as aids to future analyses.

The final step in data entry is to proceed through the table as it was created and globally changed, to add or edit responses as necessary. Each row of the table is brought to the screen in the order established by informant serial numbers, and the information that was pre-entered is displayed in the screen

Figure 7.4: LAMSAS Data Entry Screen

```
┌──────────────────────────────────────────────────────────────┐
║ Serial ID: 246        Informant ID: PA5B      Old Number: 65b ║
║                                                                ║
║ St Orthog: twenty-seven                       Gram Flag: N     ║
║                                               Comment Code:    ║
║ Phonetics: twɛˀnt̬ɪ–ˏ$sɛvm̩                                     ║
║                                                                ║
║    Doubtflg:  N   Comtext:                                     ║
║ -------------------------------------------------------------- ║
║                                                                ║
║ Serial ID: 247        Informant ID: PA5C      Old Number: 66  ║
║                                                                ║
║ St Orthog: twenty-seven                       Gram Flag: N     ║
║                                               Comment Code:    ║
║ Phonetics: twɛn{ɾ}ɪ–ˏ$sɛ{ə}vəˇn                                ║
║                                                                ║
║    Doubtflg:  N   Comtext:                                     ║
└──────────────────────────────────────────────────────────────┘
```

Figure 7.5: LAMSAS Phonetic Macro System

Key	1	2	3	4	5	6	7	8	9	0
Alt	ɪ$_{177}$	ɛ$_{178}$	ɜ$_{179}$	ɚ$_{180}$	a_{181}	ʋ$_{182}$	ɔ$_{183}$	ʌ$_{184}$	ʊ$_{185}$	ˈ$_{229s}$
Ctrl	ɨ	{ɛ}	̈$_{221}$	{ɚ}	ʋ$_{165}$	ɑ$_{222}$	{ɔ}	ə̃	ʉ	ˌ$_{245s}$

Key	Q	W	E	R	T	Y	U	I	O	
Alt	ɾ$_{241}$	˷151	ə$_{176}$	ɻ̯	ṭ	θ$_{249}$	ɪ$_{197}$	ɪ̈	˳143	
Ctrl	ɹ$_{242}$	{w}	{ə}	{ɻ̯}	t̡	ɤ$_{166}$	ʉ	{ɪ̈}	θ	

Key	A	S	D	F	G	H	J	K	L	;
Alt	æ$_{225}$	ʃ$_{243}$	ð$_{228}$	– 148	ʔ$_{231}$	ɦ$_{203}$	˧ 160	k̓	ł$_{236}$	˙186
Ctrl	æ̃	z̦	{d}	ɨ	ɾ$_{227}$	{h}	{j}	ʞ$_{235}$	ļ	· 142

Key	Z	X	C	V	B	N	M	,		
Alt	ʒ$_{250}$	˷159lg	c̓	ʋ$_{246}$	ß$_{226}$	ŋ$_{238}$	ɱ$_{237}$	˴141		
Ctrl	{z}	͡140lg	˜254	ˬ144	ß	ɲ$_{206}$	ɰ$_{169}$	ˌ150		

Key	↑	↓	←	→	(cursor keys)					
Alt	ˆ171	ˇ189	ˋ188	ˊ190						
Ctrl	ᷓ	᷆	᷄	᷈						

format illustrated in Figure 7.4. Any additional responses for a particular informant are entered by duplicating an existing row and editing the information in it as necessary, a function supported by LAMSAS database software; duplicating rows saves time and also error, even in this editing step. Another technique, use of a macro program, also saves time and error. While it is possible to enter the display codes for phonetic symbols by holding down the ALT and SHIFT keys and entering the numeric code with the keyboard, that method requires the keyboarder to look up the numeric code and then make several keystrokes. With a macro program, these sets of keystrokes (whether for one symbol or for an entire phonetic string) can be mapped mnemonically to key combinations, such as the ALT key plus the "l" key to yield ł, or the CTRL key plus the "l" key to yield ļ. The LAMSAS macro system (Figure 7.5) also allows the keyboarder to create macros that correspond to entire strings for common lexical or pronunciation variants discovered during assessment of the list manuscript. Substituting the single keystrokes of macros for multiple keystrokes of phonetic and other strings has, we estimate, reduced data entry time by half.

Several new practices have been introduced to facilitate data entry and as improvements on previous list manuscript practices.

All entries. The database program requires that a maximum number of characters be specified for each kind of entry, such as the standard spelling response or phonetic transcription. Entries for the commentary very occasionally exceed the number of characters permitted: field workers in rare cases transcribed in phonetics an extended passage from an informant, which was included as commentary although not directly relevant to any response or cue. When this occurs, the discourse is broken into convenient units; a new row is created for each unit and marked as an inappropriate response. If some appropriate response ever does exceed the maximum number of characters permitted, it will be broken into appropriate units and put in more than one row, with notice of the editorial change in the commentary for the response.

Standard spelling entries for responses. These were not attempted in list manuscripts. In the computer files such spellings are standardized, not "eye dialect" spellings. The first authority for permissible spellings is the *LAGS General Index* (Pederson et al. 1986-92, vol. 2). After that, spellings found in the following dictionaries are considered permissible:

Oxford English Dictionary, *Random House Dictionary of the English Language* (*Second Edition, Unabridged*), *Webster's Third New International Dictionary*, *Dictionary of American Regional English* (Cassidy and Hall 1985-), *English Dialect Dictionary* (Wright 1898-1905).

Status of missing responses. If there is evidence that the informant was not asked the question, such as a notation in the informant's biographical sketch that the field record was incomplete, "NA" is entered to indicate "Not Asked"; if there is no such evidence, "NR" is recorded to indicate "No Response". For informants who formerly were auxiliary informants, "NR" is entered for the standard spelling response in the absence of an actual response or of other information about the incompleteness of the record.

Phonetic transcriptions. Two conventions are followed in the computer files that do not appear in hard copy. A dollar sign ($) is used instead of a space to separate words in the entries; it is converted to an extra-wide space in hard copy. Superscript symbols in transcriptions are enclosed in curly braces ({ }) in the computer files to avoid having to enter font coding; the braces are replaced with the requisite font coding before printing, so that superscripts appear above the line in hard copy.

The | symbol (vertical bar, or pipe) is used instead of the hyphen to separate vowels that are adjacent but do not form a diphthong.

When the stop consonants [p, b, t, d, k, g] are marked with a breve (˘) to indicate shortness in list manuscripts, they are changed in computer files to enclosure in curly braces ({ }) to mark weak realization (converted to superscription in printouts).

Entries including the ~ or – signs in list manuscripts (repetition signs) are expanded so as to include the full string indicated by the sign.

Comment Codes. The list of comment codes, somewhat adjusted and augmented from those used for the list manuscripts, is presented in Figure 7.6. The effect of each code on the doubt flag is also indicated: any single dubious code results in the doubt flag, a column in the table used for quick identification of such responses, being reset from "N" to "Y". See Chapter 6 for an explanation of field record and list manuscript symbols. The last two codes were not used in list manuscripts. INA is usually applied to material recorded in phonetics in the right margin of list manuscripts as commentary, but is also applied, infrequently, to transcribed material in the response area of the list manuscript

Figure 7.6: LAMSAS Comment Codes

New Code	Former Symbols	Description	Doubt Flag
CNV	cv, c., +	conversational	N
SUG	s., f.	suggested, forced	Y
COR	cr.	corrected	Y
REP	r.	repeated	Y
HES	:	hesitation	Y
DBT	?	doubt	Y
AMS	!	amusement	Y
HRD	⌐, h.	heard	Y
OLD	†, o.f.	old-fashioned, obsolete	Y
NEW	→	recently introduced	Y
AUX	*, a.	from auxiliary inf.	Y
AUX2	**	from second aux. inf.	Y
FDT	(?)	FW doubt	Y
SIC	(√)	FW certain	N
INA		inappropriate to cue	Y
DDT		data entry doubtful	Y

or field record (frequently as the informant's commentary on a response). Foreign language responses are also marked INA. DDT is reserved for the few cases in which entries from the field record or list manuscript are completely illegible or otherwise opaque to the editors.

Certain comment codes may be inferred from the commentary and have been added to codes derived from list manuscript signs. Any item that is reported as used by someone (supposedly) other than the informant ("father said", "uneducated", etc.) are marked HRD. (N) in the commentary is replaced by "Used by Negroes" in the commentary, with HRD entered as a comment code. If the comment is "old-fashioned" or "o.f." or "old" the remark is not entered in the narrative commentary and OLD entered as a comment code. OLD may also be added if the comment implies that the form is now obsolete, as in "as a boy", "grandfather said", etc. "Modern" or "new" are deleted from the commentary and NEW is entered as code. Other comments implying that the item is of recent usage may justify entering NEW as well, but are still included in the narrative commentary.

In addition to improvements, some changes in LAMSAS practices over the years cause data-entry problems, particularly informant numbering:

1. Informants previously considered auxiliary informants but now as primary informants are not listed separately in list manuscripts, but instead are represented as starred responses amongst responses from a primary informant (see Chapter 2). For example, NY28C is not listed in the list manuscript, and starred responses for NY28B should be listed for NY28C, not for NY28B. Also, the doubt flag and comment for AUX which should be present if there is a starred response under NY28B should be deleted.

2. The same problem occurs with some informants who were changed from auxiliary to primary informants at the time of the last renumbering.

$$MD26B \leftarrow \quad 83A\ (83^* - MD26A^*)$$
$$VA26A \leftarrow \quad 161A\ (161^* - VA26B^*)$$
$$VA30B \leftarrow \quad 167A\ (167^* - VA30A^*)$$
$$SC5C \leftarrow \quad 207.2A\ (207.2^* - SC5B^*)$$

Sometimes they have been added to the list manuscript, sometimes not.

3. African-American informants from Maryland, Virginia, and North Carolina are sometimes listed together on a separate page found in the front of many list manuscripts.

4. Order changes were made when the old numbers were changed to the informant id numbers. If the list manuscript was originally completed using the old numbering system the order is not the same as that in the computer file. It is sometimes necessary to compare the numbering systems to resolve sequence problems.

After all data have been entered, a hard copy is printed from the computer file and the copy is read in tandem against the list manuscript—and the field records if necessary to resolve problems. For entries from McDavid's field records (parts of New York, South Carolina, Georgia, and Florida), the number of responses in the field records is routinely counted and compared to the number in the list manuscripts, to ensure that all variant responses are recorded. Aural tandem proofreading takes about twice as long as initial entry of the data.

When proofreading is complete and corrections have been made, the computer file is subjected to an automated error-checking program. This program looks for anomalous conditions in the file, such as blank rows and entries, and compares the entries in the file against the missing pages table. The program generates a list of exceptional cases, such as blank rows or responses present when the missing pages table indicated no response should be present, and automatically changes lacking responses to "NA" (question not asked) or "NR" (question probably asked but no response elicited) depending on the data in the missing pages table. An editor then reviews all anomalous conditions, making changes as required and performing a final check for errors in non-phonetic columns which may have been overlooked during tandem proofreading. Finally, a text file is prepared to accompany the data file, in which an editor reproduces any headnote or comments by Kurath or McDavid, prepares a tally of the separate standard-spelling responses, describes any important editorial problems encountered during data entry, and notes related files that may be of interest. The text file is cross-referenced to Kurath 1949 or Kurath and McDavid 1961 if the item was included there.

Chapter 8: Dialects of the LAMSAS Region

by Raven I. McDavid, Jr.

[This prospectus was written by Raven McDavid in 1984 and is presented here without substantial alteration. It does not reflect developments in LAMSAS or in dialectology more generally since 1984, but we trust that it is valuable in itself as an expression of the best ideas of classic dialectology and as the mature judgment of its author. Important book-length analyses of Atlantic States dialects made in large part from LAMSAS evidence are Kurath 1949, Atwood 1953, and Kurath and McDavid 1961. *Eds.*]

A linguistic atlas is a historical document: evidence on the usage of a speech community at a particular time. It is not necessarily to be taken as a report of the condition of the language at the time when the evidence is published, which may be considerably later. Rarely does field work lead to immediate publication, as with the *Linguistic Atlas of New England*: field work 1931–33, publication 1939–43. More typical is the history of the dialect survey of Germany: Wenker sent out his first questionnaires in 1876; although he published his conclusions in the *Sprachatlas der Deutschen Reichs* (1892–1902), they were not accessible to scholars (there being only two copies, one in Marburg and the other in Berlin) until 1926, when the first section of Wrede's *Deutscher Sprachatlas* appeared; the final published section appeared in 1956.

Since 1933, when Guy Lowman began LAMSAS field work, many forces have redistributed the population of the Atlantic Seaboard and altered its dialectal patterns: World War II and the subsequent Cold War, punctuated by military involvement in Korea and Vietnam; economic readjustment under the New Deal and later social legislation; easier access to education (especially higher education) for a larger proportion of the population; growth of new industrial centers, especially in the South, the Southwest, and the Pacific States; megalopolitan aggregation, with declining central cities and spawning of one-class suburbs; accelerated migration from the countryside and small towns, with a sharp decline in rural population; attrition of family farming, and growing industrialized agriculture (often known as *agribusiness*). Consolidated schools and increasing employment of women in industry and business have altered the patterns of family living.

Along with these developments have come dramatic alterations of American ethnic patterns. Even during the major period of field work the African-American population of the South—especially the rural South—was declining sharply, and African Americans were becoming concentrated in the inner cities of metropolitan areas, particularly in the Northeast and the Middle West. A familiar example is Washington, DC, which in 1930 was only 25% African American but in 1960 was nearly 60% (the proportion has since increased). On the other hand, Beaufort County, South Carolina, 90% African American in 1910 was barely 40% African American in 1960, and the proportion is now much less; Hilton Head, in 1930 a community of African-American yeomanry with 4% white population, has become an expensive playground for the affluent white. Figure 8.1 charts these changes in African-American population distribution. In none of the LAMSAS communities investigated in the 1930s had the immigration of Hispanic Americans (Cubans, Mexicans, Puerto Ricans, etc.) created striking ethnic groups: in northeastern Florida there were only minor traces of the centuries of Spanish dominion. Today every city has its Hispanic neighborhoods.

None of these changes began with the 1930s. From the beginning the American population has been one of diverse origins, English-speaking and other; it has undergone geographic and social mobility, and it has been responsive to the intertwining influences of industrialization, urbanization, and general access to education. It is just that these forces have operated with greater intensity (and publicity) during the past half-century.

It would be foolish to assert that the linguistic patterns of the Atlantic Seaboard, or indeed of any community on the Atlantic Seaboard, are now the

Figure 8.1: Change in African-American Population
(Source: US Census Data)

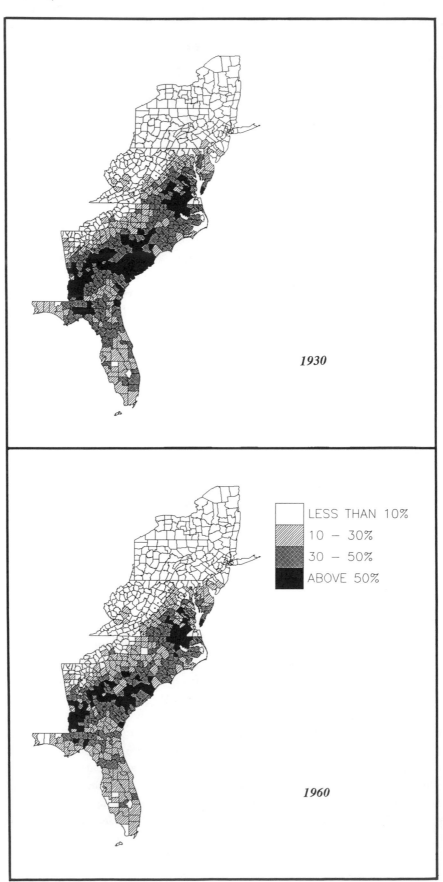

same as they were when the field work was done. Indeed, the rationale of the Linguistic Atlas project, as designed by Kurath, was a recognition of the dynamic dialect situation in English-speaking North America. No American linguistic survey at any time could rationally follow the traditional European models and confine itself to uneducated rural speech. The Atlas project recognized social differences and the potentiality for linguistic change by investigating three social levels: folk, common, and cultivated speech. This is not a complete picture of American social classes—no two communities have exactly the same patterns—but it indicates the relative status of linguistic forms at that time and suggests the direction of linguistic change. If the subsequent operation of demographic and cultural forces has produced a different picture from that which one might have predicted from the evidence of 1939–49, the earlier evidence is even more valuable, like the evidence from past censuses.

Innovations and Survivals. Innovations arise largely through the forces of industrialization, urbanization, and mass education. They normally establish themselves in the center of a *focal area* and spread outward. Focal areas generally have well-defined centers—like Philadelphia, Pittsburgh, and Charleston—and a well-defined shape; the *isoglosses* (imaginary lines indicating the limits of individual linguistic features) delimiting these areas are generally close together; they thrust outward along major arteries of communication; in border communities, when usage is divided, forms characteristic of the area are found among the younger and better educated. Among the more distinctive focal areas of the LAMSAS region are the Hudson Valley, the Delaware Valley, the Upper Ohio Valley, the Virginia Piedmont, and the South Carolina-Georgia Low Country.

Survivals of older usage are characteristically found in *relic areas*, which tend to preserve forms lost in other parts of the speech community. A relic area characteristically lacks a well-defined center; the isoglosses defining it are irregularly spaced and shrink inward along major arteries of communication; in marginal communities of divided usage characteristic forms are found among the older and less-educated speakers. In the LAMSAS region some of the more distinctive relic areas are the Delmava Peninsula and Chesapeake Bay, the North Carolina coast, and the Carolina-Georgia mountains.

Both focal areas and relic areas are generally old areas of settlement: the former developed centers and grew around them; the latter did not. *Transition areas*, the third type, are often more recent areas of settlement, where cultural patterns are fluctuating in response to pressures from other regions; they have few distinctive forms of their own; they are highly receptive to forms from neighboring areas, and the isoglosses delimiting such areas may overlap and intersect in patterns of bewildering complexity (the alternative term *graded areas* reflects such patterns of isoglosses). Transition areas may be of considerable extent: in the LAMSAS region the two most important are the Inland Northern from northwestern New England to northeastern Ohio and beyond, and the South Midland from the Shenandoah Valley through the Carolina and Georgia Piedmont to the southwest. Inland Northern speech forms are interlarded with those from eastern New England, the Hudson Valley, the North Midland, and Canada; the South Midland with those from the Virginia Piedmont and the South Carolina-Georgia Low Country.

One must recognize, however, that the picture can change. The Inland Northern and the South Midland were the chief eastern areas from which the Mississippi Valley and the West were settled. As population grew, so grew new centers of industry, commerce, and culture, attracting natives of other regions; with the drop in farm population, rural Inland Northerners and South Midlanders have swarmed into the cities. From Rochester to Minneapolis the Inland North is studded with economic and cultural centers; in the southeast a corresponding expansion has taken place along the main line of the Southern Railway, which skirts the Blue Ridge from Charlottesville to Atlanta.

Whatever their status—focal, relic, or transition—dialect areas may be grouped according to their patterns of settlement. LAMSAS includes three regional belts: Northern, Midland, and Southern. For LAMSAS the North comprises western New England, New York City, and the Hudson Valley, and their over spill into Western New York, the northern tier of Pennsylvania, and the Western Reserve of northern Ohio. The Midland comprises Pennsylvania—except for the northern strip of Yankee settlement—and its derivatives west and southwest. Within the Midland area there is a division between North Midland and South Midland regions, the former leaning toward the North, the latter toward the South. The North Midland includes three strong cultural foci—the Delaware Valley (originally Quakers), the Susquehanna Valley (largely German), and the Upper Ohio Valley (Ulster Scots), plus the transition area of northern West Virginia. The South Midland, largely a transition area as we have seen, includes the Shenandoah Valley, southern West Virginia and southwestern Virginia, the Carolina-Georgia Piedmont, and the Carolina-Georgia mountains—the last until recently a striking relic area. Before 1860 all of this region belonged to the slave-holding states, dominated by the Southern planter and mercantile elite of the coastal plain. Members of that elite moved inland, taking their speech ways with them—as their opposite numbers from eastern New England took theirs to the Inland North. There is some reason for grouping South Midland and Southern into a macro-Southern. On the other hand, there have been deep-seated differences between the regions since the earliest settlement. The South was plantation, mercantile, and Anglican, with early settlement largely from Southern England, and many Africans; the South Midland was yeoman farming (later industrial), Presbyterian, and evangelical, with early settlement dominated by Ulster Scots and Germans, and a small number of Africans. Although the inland areas held a majority of the white population by 1776, they did not have proportionate economic and political weight. The long neglect of the Trans-Allegheny region created a resentment which made it easy for Unionists to detach West Virginia from the parent state. Forces less dramatic but no less real have persisted in the Carolinas and Georgia into the twentieth Century; in Virginia proper the differences between the Piedmont and the Shenandoah are apparent when one crosses the Blue Ridge—resulting in one of the sharpest dialect boundaries in the English-speaking world.

The dialectal South of LAMSAS has two principal focal areas, the Virginia Piedmont with its cultural center now at Richmond with Fredericksburg and Petersburg as satellites, and the South Carolina-Georgia Low Country from Georgetown to St. Augustine, with Charleston as its center. Economically, Charleston has been outstripped by both Savannah and Jacksonville, but it retains some cultural preeminence, enhanced by its importance as a military base. Relic areas are Chesapeake Bay, the Albermarle Sound-Neuse Valley area of northwestern North Carolina, and the Cape Fear-Peedee valleys on the border between the Carolinas. A blend of influences from eastern Virginia and Charleston created the new plantation country of middle Georgia, which with its speech spread into the plantation areas of the Lower South.

Closer analysis reveals many smaller areas, more or less distinctive, including linguistic and cultural backwaters even within the focal areas, such as the Jersey Pinelands southeast of Philadelphia. But the areas here mentioned reflect striking parallels of lexical, grammatical, and phonological patterns, found by detailed (but not exhaustive) examination of the field data (see McDavid 1970).

Non-English Elements. As the sketch of settlement history (Chapter 9) indicates, the ethnic composition of the older population of the LAMSAS area was far more complex than that of New England. In the 1650s the Jesuit martyr Father Jogues reported that there were fifteen languages and dialects in New Amsterdam, a village of no more than 2000 inhabitants; by 1700 Philadelphia and Charleston were comparably polyglot. In the countryside, from the Mohawk Valley to the Savannah Valley there were German settlements of various origins. There were Holland Dutch in the Hudson and Delaware valleys, and Swedes and Finns on both sides of the Delaware before the Penn proprietary was established. Highland Scots came to the Cape Fear Valley after the Jacobite rebellion was crushed at Culloden in 1745. Welsh—Quakers and Baptists—settled in Pennsylvania and South Carolina. There were a few colonial French Huguenots as planters and upland yeomanry in South Carolina and as merchants in the cities, and scattered groups of the displaced Acadians, and from adjacent Quebec the northern counties of New York have drawn immigrants and some of their linguistic forms (notable *shivaree*). In the LAMSAS region the only traces of older Hispanic influence are around St. Augustine, less from the early Spanish dominion than from the later Turnbull settlement of Minorcans; on the other hand, displaced Sephardic Jews, ultimately of Spanish and Portuguese origin, were important in New York and South Carolina. Other European colonial groups, such as the Polish glass makers in Virginia, have been almost forgotten.

Of the dozens of aboriginal languages spoken in the LAMSAS region, only the Iroquoian survive—Six Nations in New York, Cherokee in western North Carolina—though Catawba, of Siouan stock, lingered in South Carolina till the time of field work. A variety of African languages were spoken by the involuntary immigrants of the colonial period and early nineteenth century. Speakers of these tongues were most numerous in the Low Country of South Carolina, where slavery was recognized from the beginning of the colony, and where Gullah, a unique North American English-based Creole, developed before the Revolution and still survives. In Virginia, though the first Africans arrived in 1619, large-scale importation was coeval with that in South Carolina: previous to 1670 life expectations in Virginia were so low that landowners found it more practicable to engage whites on seven-year indentures than to invest capital in the purchase of Africans. There is far less evidence of a plantation Creole in Virginia than in South Carolina. Unlike the situation in the Caribbean, where the African population was maintained only by constant importations (it actually declined in the first decades after emancipation), in North America it grew largely by natural increase. Tiny Barbados alone received more than 60% as many Africans as the English and French colonies on the mainland. There was also a large African population in the New York City area, dating from the period of Dutch dominion in northern Brazil.

The linguistic influence of these other tongues on North American English has interested students from the colonial period. Sometimes a loan is identified with a dialect region, as the Algonquian *skunk* in the North (and expanding at the expense of the transferred English *polecat*); German *smearcase* in the North Midland, against an assortment of regional and local terms elsewhere (all losing ground to the commercial term *cottage cheese*); or the African *cooter* 'turtle', with the South Carolina and Georgia Low Country. Sometimes these loans are highly localized, like *awendaw* 'soft corn bread' (of unknown aboriginal origin) in the Charleston area, or the probable German *liverel* 'liver sausage' near Charlotte. All reflect the complex interrelationships of linguistic groups in a newly settled country.

Social Differences. The social classes of seventeenth-century England, and their speech, were imperfectly reflected in North America. The peasantry did not migrate; the nobility and gentry did not settle, though some of them served as colonial administrators. Lord Fairfax, associated with George Washington, was a notable exception.

Two efforts were made to establish an indigenous landed aristocracy. To encourage the settlement of New Netherlands, the Dutch West India Company created a number of patroonships—large landholdings, with tenants paying quitrents—but only that of

Rensselaerswyck, in the Albany area, endured. After the British conquest of 1664, Rensselaerswyck was converted into one of the large manors created by the British, chiefly in the Hudson Valley, which lasted till the abolition of quitrents in the 1830s. The Lords Proprietors of Carolina sought to install a landed feudal system, with generous Low-Country baronial grants, but in these colonies as elsewhere the local elite was open to the ambitious and energetic. By the Revolution the first families of the colonies had sorted themselves out, in Quaker Pennsylvania as well as in Anglican Virginia and South Carolina, and to some degree—particularly in the South—it is still true that family status may be independent of wealth and even education. For this reason the assignment of informants to social classes is an approximation, though an approximation based on previous study of the community, the judgments of the intermediaries, and the interpersonal relationships of investigator and informant during an interview of considerable length. A summary of the character and status of each informant is found in Chapter 10 of this handbook, and in the apparatus accompanying the microfilmed field records (McDavid et al. 1982–86).

Differences between classes of informants are most obvious in grammar, less in pronunciation and vocabulary. They are most distinctive in the oldest settlements, especially in the South Atlantic States, where cultivated and common speech may be sharply differentiated. They are less distinctive in such inland areas as Upstate New York, western Pennsylvania, and West Virginia; in such communities the sharpest distinction may be between the folk speech and the common, or the classes may shade imperceptibly into each other. For this reason, further investigations are desirable, in all types of communities, to indicate the direction of change since the LAMSAS interviews.

Urban Speech. Although the influence of cultural centers has always been recognized, the first European surveys were restricted to village speech. Cities were first included in the Atlas of Italy and Southern Switzerland (Jaberg and Jud 1928–40), but the urban informants were unsophisticated, like those in the villages. The *Survey of English Dialects* (Orton et al. 1962–71) had two interviews in Metropolitan London and one each in Leeds, Sheffield, and York, but again of the folk type. A major innovation in the American surveys has been the interviewing of urban informants of all three major cultural types, recognizing that the cities of English-speaking North America were centers of commerce, industry, and culture before the Revolution, and that new centers have arisen with the spread of settlement. Almost every urban area of any antiquity has been investigated, and a considerable number of younger ones.

Interviewing in urban areas has been complicated by the nature of the urban population. The cultivated speakers of long-established families are generally easy to find, since that group has persisted. Urban common speech is also easily investigated. But the tradition of geographical and social mobility makes urban folk speakers more difficult to identify and locate. As the native urban working class has moved up and out, it has been replaced by immigrants from outside (Irish, Germans, Poles, Italians), and then from other parts of America (African Americans, French Canadians, Hispanics, Southern poor whites), to whom the traditional speech patterns of their new urban environment were alien.

Finally, the most recent movement to urban areas has come in a period of metropolitan growth, with suburban and exurban sprawl; most of the older cities like New York and Philadelphia have lost population while the suburbs around them have burgeoned, and industry and population have moved out into the countryside. The only American cities to show steady growth in this century have been those that have suburbanized themselves, like Atlanta and Charlotte and Houston and Los Angeles. The growth and simultaneous decentralization of corporations have made businessmen and technologists, the new elite, as mobile as military and naval personnel. Since LAMSAS field work was largely completed before these recent changes, one may be sure that newer investigations of urban speech will disclose different patterns from those revealed by the Atlas evidence—and for that reason it is important to use this evidence as a base line.

The Speech of African Americans. Wherever African Americans have lived, their speech has never been more monolithic than that of the whites around them. They have participated in various activities, and even under slavery had their own class distinctions, from house servants through yard servants and skilled craftsmen to the humblest field hands. At the time of the LAMSAS field work, more African Americans still lived in the rural South; now a majority of them live in the urban north and west, generally in spreading black belts, with fewer informal interracial contacts than customary in the South.

In the South the principal situations in which African Americans lived till World War II were three: 1) coastal plantations, 2) upland farms, 3) cities and towns.

1) Although the coastal plantation system—resembling in many ways the village society of feudalism—had been shattered by the Confederate War and subsequent reconstruction, vestiges remained for nearly a century. Many African Americans were employed in labor-intensive cultivation of export crops (e.g. cotton and tobacco) under (ideally) a paternalistic management, with white overseers to help administer production. Although most African Americans were unskilled laborers, some were highly skilled craftsmen. Community life was stable, with little mobility and few contacts outside the neighborhood. The archetype was the rice plantation of the lower Santee in South Carolina.

2) Although some of the large upland farms were called plantations, they were normally smaller, and their economy was less complex than one found near the coast. African Americans were most frequently share-tenants (as were many whites—indeed, share-cropping was originally designed for the landless whites), with annual contracts, little supervision, a good deal of mobility from one farm to another, more contacts with whites than found on the plantations, and less identification with the immediate community.

3) In smaller towns, urban African Americans were most commonly domestic servants and service employees, generally unskilled. In the larger cities there were some professionals, chiefly teachers and clergymen, and some individual entrepreneurs, notably undertakers. A number of cities, furthermore, had their African-American elites, going back to pre-Emancipation days. Domestic servants working for the upper-class families were clients as well as employees, and had prestige in the African-American community from this connection.

In all Southern communities economic and cultural opportunities for the African Americans were less than those for the local whites, but whites enjoyed far fewer advantages than those of other regions, so that in practice there were many lower-class members of the white caste less well off than middle-class African Americans (though the comparison was rarely mentioned). If education and transportation and many services were segregated in the South, there was always a great deal of informal contact between the races. Where there was segregated housing—and it did not always exist—

there were no massive black belts like those in New York and Chicago, but rather small African-American enclaves scattered throughout the community. As a rule, Southern African Americans and whites were familiar with each other's speech ways. For practical purposes, the only variety of African-American speech alien to Southern whites was the Gullah of the South Carolina-Georgia coast, a dialect also bewildering to most inland African Americans. The recent heavy migration of uneducated Southern African Americans to the central cities of Northern metropolitan areas has produced a new kind of segregation, where there is less opportunity for traditional local speech ways to be observed and emulated. The parallels between the Northern black belts and the earlier plantations in the West Indies and coastal America where indigenous creoles developed suggests that the similarities between various urban African-American dialects today can be explained best as the result of a neo-creolization. Paradoxically, as African Americans have gained equality before the law, they have had fewer casual contacts with whites. This was noted in parts of the South by the 1880s, and is certainly true of Northern cities today.

Afterword. Relationships between varieties of American English can be determined only by examining the full range of data, phonological and morphological and syntactical and lexical. The Linguistic Atlases represent only a sample; as field work proceeded, investigators observed that many interesting forms had not been marked for systematic study. Such forms constitute part of the task for the next generation of students.

Chapter 9: Settlement History

The settlement history of the Middle and South Atlantic States is far more complicated than that of New England.

The area stretches from the St. Lawrence Valley to the neighborhood of Daytona Beach, Florida, from the eastern tip of Long Island to the Ohio border. It is four and a half times the size of New England, with nearly five times the population. New York or Pennsylvania alone has far more people than all of New England.

There is a wide range of climatic conditions; thus an item like 'a shelter for cattle' can evoke a wide range of referents—from the large multipurpose barn in Upstate New York, to a few sheets of galvanized iron on a crude frame in parts of the coastal South. Parenthetically, for a long time Florida had the highest rate of cattle deaths from exposure of all the states, Minnesota the lowest.

The history of settlement varies. In New England, most of the coastal communities were settled by 1675, and the whole region was pretty well staked out by the time of the Revolution. For the LAMSAS area the first settlements (not counting the first Spanish outpost at St. Augustine in 1565) vary from Jamestown in 1607 to Savannah in 1733, a spread of over 126 years. Much of New York, Pennsylvania, and Georgia was not opened up till after 1800, and the Central Adirondacks not till the end of the nineteenth century.

There was far greater ethnic diversity among the settlers in the Middle and South Atlantic States than in New England. In New England even the ubiquitous Ulster Scots contributed a minimal leavening of the colonial Yankee stock; the Southern Irish did not reach New England till the 1830s, and foreign language groups became important only in the twentieth century. But the earliest settlements in New York, New Jersey, Pennsylvania, and Delaware were made by Dutch, Swedes, and Finns. German and German-Swiss settlements were scattered from the Mohawk Valley to the Altamaha; the Ulster Scots covered the same expanse of territory, generally in greater density. There were Highlanders in North Carolina and Georgia, Huguenots in almost every colony, especially in the towns, Sephardic Jews, notably in New York, Philadelphia, and Charleston, and Africans in varying proportions, to say nothing of the Welsh in Pennsylvania and South Carolina and the Barbadians who dominated colonial Charleston. Nor was the situation of any ethnic group the same in every colony.

Each colony had its own agricultural system and special products. Maryland, Virginia, and the Albemarle Sound area had tobacco; South Carolina, a little later, had rice and indigo. All colonies exported furs, hides, and timber; the Carolinas and Georgia also exported naval stores.

The extent of urbanization varied. Philadelphia, New York, and Charleston were comparable to British provincial cities by the beginning of the eighteenth century; Virginia had no city until Norfolk, which developed after 1750 in time to be destroyed in the Revolution; Baltimore began to develop about 1790. The population of the three major cities was extremely diverse, and it is debatable which one was the most diverse. For example, as late as 1820 there were more Jews in Charleston than in New York.

Finally, the systems of local government were quite varied. The New England system of townships was extended to New York, New Jersey, and Pennsylvania—the last two with the borough as something incorporated, smaller than a city but larger than a village. Further south there were militia districts or legislative districts; in Delaware, and occasionally in other colonies, they were called hundreds, an Old English term meaning an area supplying a hundred armed men. To add to the complication, in South Carolina, for a while, a district meant something larger than a county—often with counties as sub-divisions. In the South the parish was also a unit of civil as well as ecclesiastical government. Townships were imposed on Virginia and the Carolinas by the occupation governments of the 1860s, but Virginia soon returned to the old system of districts. After 1868 the South Carolina Low Country converted the older parishes into townships, keeping the old names, but many of the inhabitants still refer to them as parishes. Virginia

Figure 9.1: Topography of the LAMSAS Region

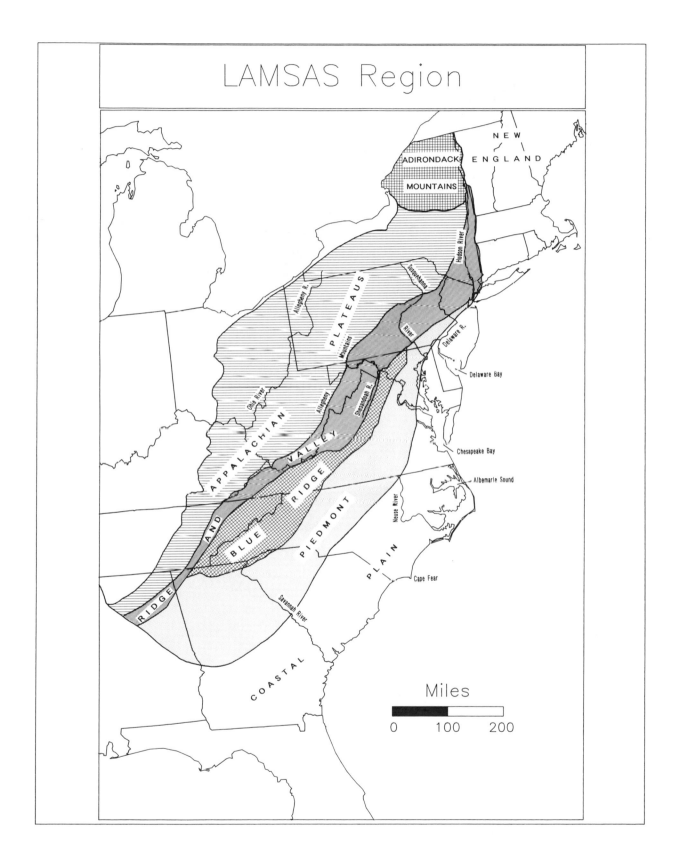

Figure 9.2a: Population Density, 1790–1850
(Source: Paullin and Wright 1932:76B, 76E, 77A)

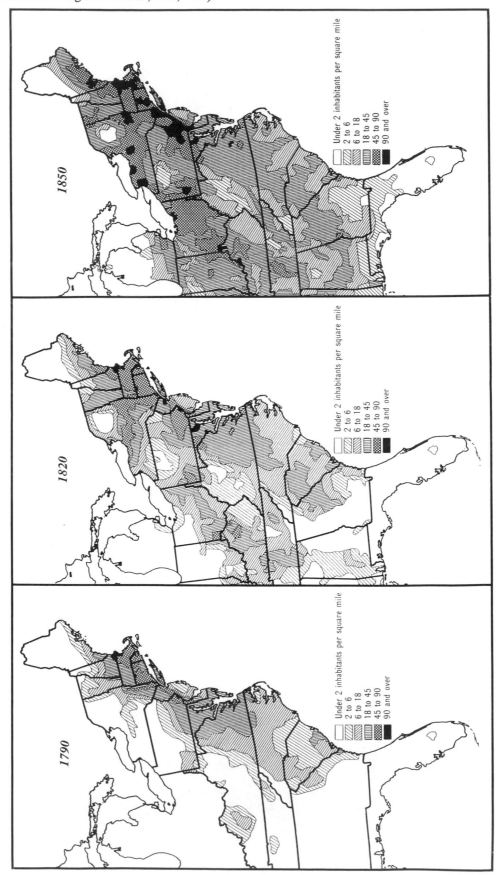

Figure 9.2b: Population Density, 1880–1930
(Source: Paullin and Wright 1932:78A, 79B, 79D)

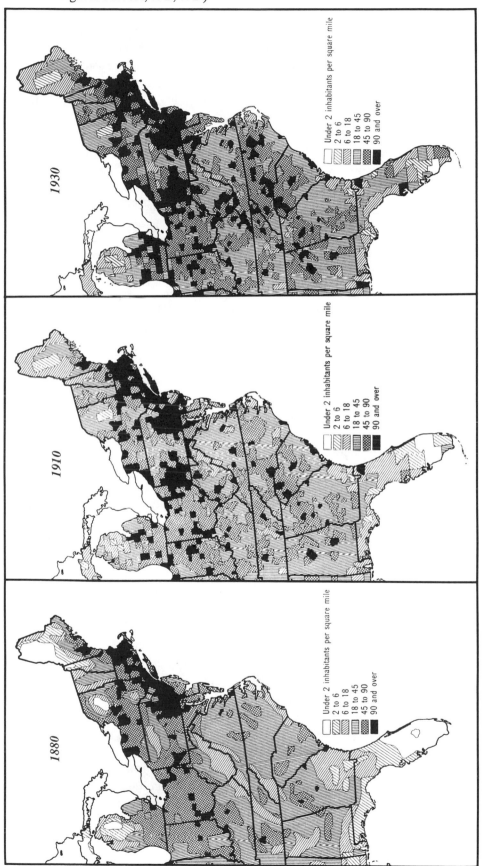

also has a system of independent cities, within counties and sometimes housing the county building, but not under county government. Recently some counties, or their rural parts, have converted themselves into cities, so that the City of Chesapeake, once rural Norfolk County, issues licenses for hunting deer and bear within the city limits. These differences in local government, and the frequent splitting of counties and townships, make it very hard to get comparable figures from census to census, particularly below the county level.

Land Areas. The LAMSAS area includes five major geographic regions as represented in Figure 9.1. Moving inland from the coast, these may be defined as follows: 1) The Atlantic Coastal Plain, extending inland from the Continental Shelf stretching from Long Island in the north down along the coast to Georgia and Florida; 2) the Piedmont area, which begins the ascent into the Appalachian Highlands, embracing the middle portions of Virginia and North Carolina and most of the western half of South Carolina and the northern half of Georgia; 3) the Blue Ridge of North Carolina and Virginia; 4) the rolling ridge and valley formations of the Shenandoah Valley; and 5) the Appalachian Plateaus, extending south from the Adirondacks through western Pennsylvania and eastern Ohio and Kentucky.

Patterns of Settlement. The settlement of the Middle and South Atlantic States spans the period from the establishment of St. Augustine as a Spanish outpost in 1565 to the massive westward and northward migrations following the Civil War. The six parts of Figure 9.2 will give a general idea of the movement of settlers in the region in terms of population densities between 1790 and 1930.

Three broad cultural belts are represented in the LAMSAS region: 1) the Northern, comprising New York City and the Hudson Valley and their overspill into Western NY, the northern tier of Pennsylvania, and the Western Reserve of Northern Ohio; 2) the Midland, comprising Pennsylvania and its derivatives west (North Midland) and southwest (South Midland), with its core in the Philadelphia area in southeastern Pennsylvania, settled by 1750 by largely German, Scotch-Irish, and English; and 3) the South, with two principal hearth areas, one in the Chesapeake Bay area with its center at Williamsburg-Newport in eastern Virginia (where English settlers were firmly established by 1690), and extending southward to the northeastern corner of North Carolina and northward along the coast

nearly to Baltimore; and the other in the Savannah-Charleston nexus of the South Carolina-Georgia Low Country, a thriving English settlement area by 1730. Figure 9.3 presents a general view of the cultural areas of the LAMSAS region with reference to the traditional areal terms of American dialect geography (compare Pederson et al. 1986–92, vol. 1, Figure 23, and Zelinsky 1973:118–19).

Figure 9.4 illustrates the growth of transportation linkages to accommodate the general directions of settlement. Settlers from the New York City and Hudson Valley hearth area moved west into western NY, the northern tier of Pennsylvania, and finally into the Western Reserve of northern Ohio. Stemming from the Philadelphia cradle area, several cultural foci and two major patterns may be distinguished. A North Midland pattern saw settlement along the Delaware Valley (originally mainly Quakers), the Susquehanna Valley (largely German) and the Upper Ohio River Valley (largely Ulster Scots), with some groups continuing south along the Ohio River. A second group, South Midlanders, proceeded south along the Shenandoah Valley through southern West Virginia and southwestern Virginia into the Carolina-Georgia Appalachian Highlands. Thus, a pattern of German and Scotch-Irish settlement, comprising mainly yeoman farmers, proceeded along these lines, in contrast to the largely English plantation culture which moved Upcountry from the Coastal Plain. In the South, settlers proceeded south from the Williamsburg-Newport area along the Piedmont into North Carolina, South Carolina, and Georgia. Movements along this route apparently included not only English settlers, but Germans and Scotch-Irish from the Baltimore area and even from as far north as Philadelphia. Finally, settlers from the Charleston area generally proceeded inland into the Deep South, though a smaller stream moved up through the mountains toward Kentucky; Savannah settlers proceeded inland as well as south toward northeastern Florida.

In general, after 1660 the English government was somewhat averse to emigration from England proper, though migration from Scotland and Ireland was encouraged. After 1689, there was a falling off in migration from Britain until 1768: the greatest English migration occurred in 1770–75. The years after 1728 saw increased Irish migration, with German migration being second to Irish in 1720–60. Early on, more than half the colonists south of New England were servants (many indentured);   as

Figure 9.3: Cultural Areas of the LAMSAS Region
(Source: Zelinsky 1973:118–19; Pederson et al.
1986–92:I, Figure 23.)

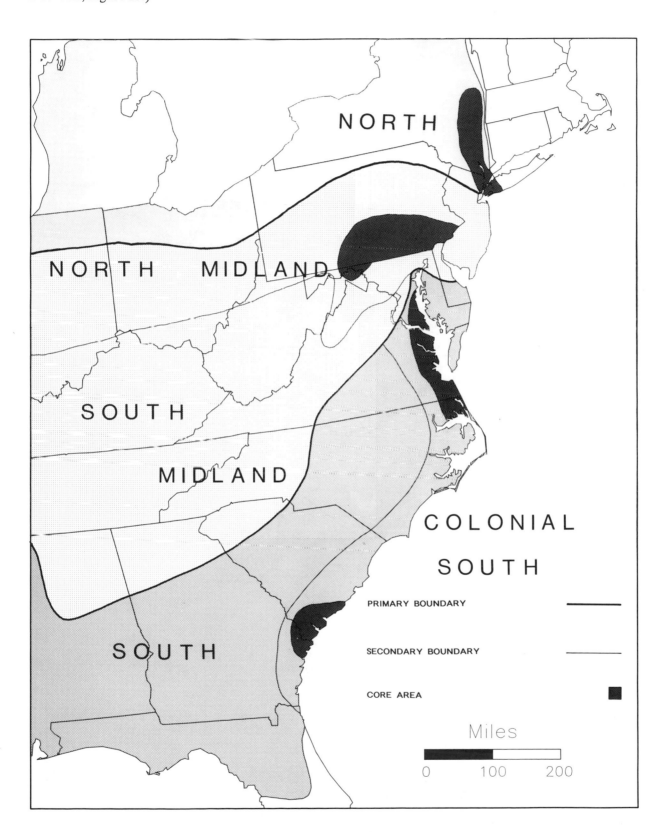

Figure 9.4a: Growth of Transportation Routes, 1675–1800
(Source: US Department of the Interior Geological Survey 1970:135)

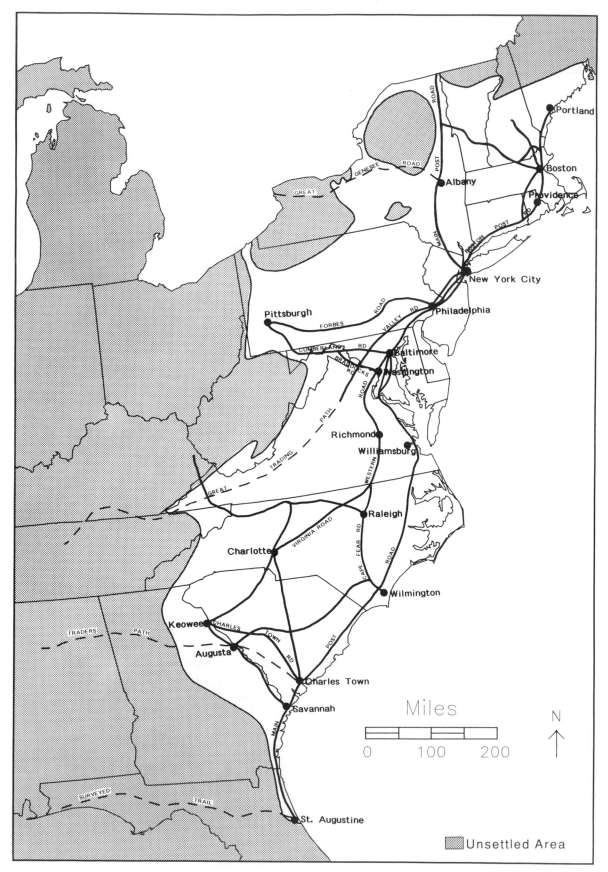

Figure 9.4b: Growth of Transportation Routes, 1850–1890
(Source: US Department of the Interior Geological Survey 1970:137)

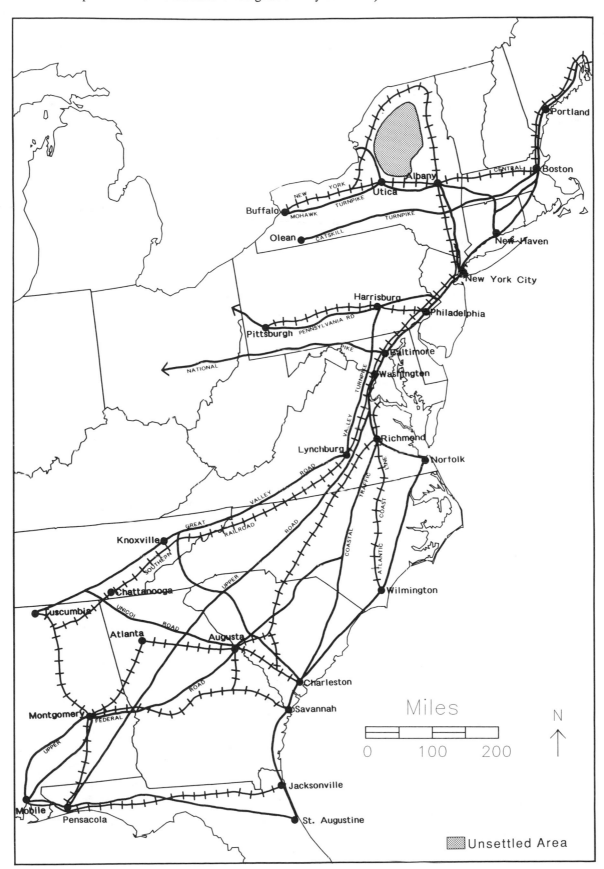

the principal labor supply, they were not superseded by Africans until the eighteenth century. On the verge of the Revolution, the total population of the colonies was approximately 3 million; of these, approximately 40% were Scottish, Welsh, Germans, Irish, Dutch, French, and other immigrant groups, and approximately 23% were Africans, almost all slaves. All the South Atlantic States lost population by migration between 1820 and 1831: whites migrated west toward California, while southern African Americans migrated north. Immigrants from three key groups came in large numbers in the nineteenth century: Germans, 5,200,000; Irish, 4,000,000; British, 3,300,000. Before 1860, large numbers of Scandinavians had also arrived, as well as some French, and immigrants included large numbers of Roman Catholics and Jews as well as members of Protestant sects. Immigrants who arrived from southern and eastern Europe in the late-nineteenth century were more urbanized than the then-current population, and contributed to the general cultural movement from farm to city.

The New York City / Hudson Valley Area. The Italian navigator Verrazano was probably in the New York City / Manhattan area as early as 1524. The Harbor was discovered by Hudson in 1609; a trading post was established by 1614. Dutch and Protestant Walloon settlers arrived by 1623. Peter Stuyvesant served as the last Dutch governor of New Netherland in 1646–64, but English settlement of the area had already begun by 1646. The population of Manhattan was about 1,400 at the time of the English takeover in 1669. By 1700, the Dutch portion of the population was down to about 60%, as English and French came to dominate the merchant class. Greenwich Village was originally a settlement of Scottish weavers; there was also some Jewish immigration in the seventeenth century. Germans followed in the eighteenth century.

Concord, Massachusetts, became the first inland settlement in 1635; shortly after, from 1640 on, Long Island was settled, with many New Englanders migrating there. By 1662 the Long Island English settlements had united with either the New Haven colony or the Connecticut colony. Newark and Elizabeth, NJ, were settled by 1666 from Connecticut. By about 1670 much of Long Island was inhabited: there were several Dutch towns in the west, with the remainder of the settlements English. By 1696, settlers from Dorchester arrived in west Jersey and Westchester County, New York, as well

as other counties east of the Hudson (some also continued to South Carolina). From 1709, numbers of Germans from the Palatinate migrated into the Hudson Valley, and from there eventually to Pennsylvania. Between 1781 and 1800, groups of settlers moved from New England to north and west New York State and to the northern strip of Pennsylvania and the upper Susquehanna Valley. Some settlers continued on to Marietta, Ohio, and the Western Reserve; dairying in the Western Reserve followed the New England and New York State pattern.

Pennsylvania and the Philadelphia Hearth Area. The hearth area (i.e. core or origin of a cultural region) of Philadelphia constitutes an important starting point for the eventual settlement of the West. From there, settlers followed essentially two routes, one tending toward the Susquehanna and Upper Ohio Valleys, and the transition area of northern West Virginia, and the other moving southwesterly along the edge of the Virginia Blue Ridge, through the Great Valley of Tennessee toward the Carolina/Georgia Piedmont and mountains. The Great Valley Road linked Pennsylvania and the Shenandoah Valley with the eastern Tennessee backcountry; it extended from Lancaster to Knoxville. Both Pennsylvanians and Virginians used this route, followed by large numbers of German and Scotch-Irish immigrants. Early advances into Middle Tennessee formed a major staging ground for the eventual development of the West. Most of the Shenandoah Valley was settled by 1750.

Large numbers of Quakers arrived in the Delaware Valley in the middle of the seventeenth century, having been persecuted in Britain by both the Commonwealth and the Restoration. By the late seventeenth century, a number of Finnish settlers were given inland farms to persuade them to move out of the Delaware Valley.

The Middle Colonies were characterized by amalgamation of ethnic stocks; the insular Pennsylvania German community stands out as an exception. By 1750 100,000 Germans were in the colonies, most in Pennsylvania. In 1847–54 alone, 800,000 Germans arrived, with the largest number settling in Pennsylvania. Some Czechs, Hungarians, and Jews also arrived, and were for the most part assimilated rapidly.

As many as two-thirds of Pennsylvania immigrants in the eighteenth century came in under indentures; one reason that slavery was discouraged there was competition with free labor. In 1820–1920, 4.5 million Irish arrived in the U.S., with large numbers in New York and Pennsylvania.

The South. In general, the Chesapeake Bay/Wilmington-Newport, Delaware, hearth area contributed settlers who moved through the Carolinas into the upper Piedmont of Georgia and East Alabama. This settlement route was reinforced from the South, perhaps most notably by settlers of both English and German descent from the Wilmington-New Bern area of North Carolina. Groups of Virginia settlers also moved westward and followed the Great Valley Road into east Tennessee.

Approximately 6,000 settlers lived on Chesapeake Bay in 1640; tobacco was the chief crop early, with indentured servants providing the bulk of the seventeenth-century labor supply. Up to 1666, 30% to 40% of Virginia landholders had come in under indenture. Possibly as many as 50,000 felons were among the settlers in Maryland and Virginia from 1719 to 1722; Scottish "border ruffians" were also liable for transportation there. Settlers from New England arrived in Guilford County, North Carolina, about 1700; by 1709, approximately 600 Palatine Germans had migrated to New Bern in North Carolina and they began to move inland from there. Both Virginians and North Carolinians moved westward to the Nashville Basin area; both tobacco and cotton farmers were attracted by the soil and convenient waterways.

Colonial Chesapeake society, the society of the Tidewater and Piedmont of Virginia, Maryland, and northeastern North Carolina, can be characterized as prevailingly English, and as the closest thing in the Middle and South Atlantic States to European aristocracy, despite its largely middle-class origins. Some Scots, Huguenots, Germans, and Scotch-Irish were also among the early settlers. Eventually, the expansion of slavery functioned to forestall continued European immigration. By the mid-eighteenth century, in Maryland (and the other colonies) slaves had come to outnumber the white working class, and approximately 45% of the population of the Chesapeake area was of African descent. Economically, the area had its apogee around 1765, when it was characterized by a stable agrarian society with a natural political liberalism.

The 1730s in Virginia saw the movement of numbers of Pennsylvania Germans into western Virginia and the general westward movement of numbers of Virginians into the Back Country. In 1738–76 there was road building in this area, with villages appearing along the Great Philadelphia Wagon Road, the Fall Line, and near road junctions. Virginia and Maryland extended local government to the Upper Piedmont and Shenandoah Valley. Yet the mountains of Virginia created an insuperable obstacle to total unity.

The Blue Ridge of Virginia comprised a melting pot for German, Ulster Scot, and east Virginia poor whites, though Germans predominated in many of the small towns of the Valley of Virginia and western North Carolina. Many came from Pennsylvania, but others also came directly from Germany. The Germans generally were not interested in slavery.

The Appalachians were settled chiefly from central and western Pennsylvania and from the North Carolina and South Carolina Piedmont; the settlement routes followed streams, with the earliest settlements appearing in valleys. The settlement of the Appalachians occurred chiefly from 1800 to 1850, with population increasing as a result of coal mining from 1850 to 1900.

The South Carolina Low Country, from Charleston to Savannah, was another major hearth area. The settlement route moved up to Augusta, then along the Fall Line from Augusta to Columbus, and finally through Alabama and Mississippi to Natchez. As early as 1696, settlers arrived in South Carolina from Dorchester in New England. British colonies were established in this area from the 1730s on. Though the area looked to the older Charleston settlement for direction and cultural leadership, its thoroughfare was the Savannah River that provided the means for settlement of the Upcountry. The Savannah settlement soon attracted not only English, but German settlers, most notably a group of German refugees known as Salzburgers.

Colonial Carolina society was smaller and more compact than Chesapeake society, with its focus on "Charles Town". It was a plantation culture of large estates, especially rice and indigo. Charleston was the only large mercantile town south of Philadelphia, and in the middle-eighteenth century it dominated Savannah, St. Augustine, and other growing Gulf-area towns to the west. The cities of Charleston and Savannah were 50% African American, with the rural Low Country of the region up to 95% African American. Though the white residents of the area were largely Anglophile in manners, the population tended to be more variegated than that of Chesapeake society. Charleston was characterized by a lively culture of private societies, but put little emphasis on education or local government.

By 1735 Augusta was established, providing a staging ground for occupation of the Piedmont. Soon both Georgia and South Carolina reflected the plantation culture. By 1775, the Upcountry had a larger population (especially a larger white population) than the Tidewater area, but it still lacked the wealth, prestige, and political power of the Tidewater. The domestic history of the South is for many years the history of a contest between its eastern and western sections; with the cotton culture dominant, the Piedmont was eventually assimilated to the plantation areas, forcing the migration of small farmers to the Ohio Valley and Gulf states. Little white immigration to the South occurred after 1790.

Settlement of the Back Country—past Savannah, the Shenandoah Valley, and the Upper Piedmont—proceeded rapidly, with approximately 250,000 settlers moving to these areas between 1730 and 1770. In South Carolina, frontier townships were established in the Back Country especially in 1760–70; the economy there by 1770 consisted mainly of small subsistence farms, with the settlers primarily of Scotch-Irish and German extraction. German Lutherans arrived from Pennsylvania and Charleston, as well as from Salzburg, and were prominent in the early settlement of South Carolina, with a group arriving 1788–94, and a North Carolina synod of Lutherans had been established by 1803. The minimal agriculture of the Back Country area at first involved the growing of grain rather than cotton or tobacco, and herding and hunting also played a major economic role in frontier society. However, as mentioned above, most of the South Carolina Back Country eventually succumbed to the economy of the plantation as the soil conditions in the coastal areas worsened.

The Georgia Piedmont developed rapidly, with the population of Georgia doubling between 1790 and 1800. Most development occurred in the eastern Piedmont, but settlers moved west as tracts of land extending to the Ocmulgee River were acquired. The upper Piedmont and the Georgia highlands remained unsettled until 1835, when the Cherokees were forced out.

Meanwhile, South Carolina planters took the best land through the Savannah Basin and along the coast and rivers of lower Georgia. The Charleston hearth area also influenced the development of northern Florida, which had been under Spanish influence since the initial establishment of St. Augustine in 1565. After a brief interlude of English ascendancy between 1763 and 1768, this area, never heavily populated, remained under Catalan influence until the arrival of the planters.

The South never had the closely knit settlements of New England towns, owing to differences in climate, to the availability of navigable streams, and to the fact of less hostility from the Indians. Though the South is identified with the agrarian plantation culture, it is significant that, in the South of the 1850s, of a total of approximately 6 million Southerners, fewer than 350,000 were slave owners, with fewer than 10,000 owning enough land to be described as "planters". Nonetheless, it is true that by 1860 there was only one city, New Orleans, of over 50,000 in the Deep South, while the border states had four such cities: Baltimore (212,418), St. Louis (160,773), Louisville (68,033), and Washington DC (61,122).

Bibliographical Note. Local bibliographies and community histories are included in Chapter 10. Local histories differ greatly in quantity and quality. To one [i.e. Raven McDavid] reared in other disciplines, it is sometimes surprising that they are so numerous or so generally bad. Recent histories are not necessarily better than their predecessors; what they may gain in explicit social theory, they often lose in explicit information about the origins of the early settlers and what they did. Even as research for the LAMSAS settlement and community histories got underway, Marion Kaminkow's four-volume bibliography of local histories in the Library of Congress appeared (1975), later expanded by supplements. We must be more selective with sources than Marcus Hansen and Julia Bloch were in preparation of materials for the New England *Handbook*. Still, the patterns of population and economic growth emerge, sometimes reinforcing old (or new) legends, sometimes refuting them. For instance, the overseas slave trade played a relatively small part in the growth of the black population after 1800; the growth was attributable simply to natural increase. And a combination of Union bayonets and moral revulsion could not have snatched the transmontane counties from the Old Dominion to create West Virginia, had the way not been paved by a long history of neglect by the magnates of the Tidewater and the Piedmont.

Chapter 10: Community Sketches and Informant Biographies

The proper interpretation of the LAMSAS records requires some knowledge of the history and character of the communities investigated, and of the life and personality of the informants interviewed. The information is presented here in a series of individual case histories. For each community and for each informant there is a brief account of the essential facts, together with bibliographical references to facilitate a more intensive study of local history.

Community Sketches

The communities investigated for LAMSAS are numbered serially for each state or province (the District of Columbia, originally part of the plan for Virginia, is here treated as a single community). The historical sketches and the informant biographies are presented in the following order:

State	Number of Communities
New York	64
New Jersey	21
Pennsylvania	67
West Virginia	54
Delaware	6
Maryland	27
District of Columbia	1
Virginia	75
North Carolina	75
South Carolina	44
Georgia	44
Florida	5

The basic community unit for LAMSAS is the county; occasionally a county is treated as two communities, reflecting differences in settlement patterns. Within each county the political subdivision where each informant was interviewed is given—township, district, borough, hundred, parish—according to the local situation (in the South Carolina Low Country, official townships are still popularly known as parishes, as they were in the colonial period); specific locality is given, with the name of the post office at the time the interview was conducted (many small post offices have since been abandoned). The locality may vary from an isolated rural area to a major city.

In several instances two adjacent counties have been treated as a single community, with a single community number. In such communities the sequence of the historical sketches and the vitae follows the order of the informants, with the least sophisticated first. In a number of instances a single county has been treated as more than one community.

Each historical sketch presents, in principle, the following information:

1) The name of the county, then the locality, the post office, and the township (or analogous civil division). In larger communities the neighborhood is sometimes specified, especially when it was originally an independent community, such as Flushing in the Borough of Queens, New York.

2) The date when the county was established (if possible, the date of minor civil divisions), the date of settlement, and, for urban places, the date of incorporation. Some of these dates are only approximate, since historians sometimes disagree on when permanent settlement began.

3) Provenience of the settlers, with information on the areas from which they came.

4) Notes on the early history of the community. These are based on notes compiled by members of the LAMSAS staff and local associates, sometimes from county or local histories, sometimes from the state histories listed at the end of each state.

5) A description of the present character of the community, with notes on principal industries or agricultural products, the make-up of the population and the like. This description is based on notes made by field workers from first-hand observation, from reports of local consultants and informants, and from published sources.

6) Population of the county figures for 1790, 1820, 1850, 1880, 1910, 1930, and 1960, sometimes also population estimates of still earlier dates. For counties organized after 1790 (the great majority) figures begin with the first census after organization.

For localities within a county, similar figures are given where the locality is large enough to be listed in the census tables. In some cases, the African-American population is given separately as an aid to appraising the changing demography. In most rural counties the percentage of African Americans has decreased since 1930; in the urban communities it has generally increased. The 1930 census was chosen to provide data comparable to that incorporated in *LANE*; that for 1960 to indicate the situation at the time intensive editing was resumed.

7) Bibliographical notes on published histories of the county and the particular locality, including such items as vital records, genealogies, personal reminiscences, or local fiction or poetry. No attempt has been made to offer an exhaustive bibliography. Further information may be found in the sources listed under *Bibliographies*, *General Histories*, and *Special Studies* at the end of each state; for counties or localities with no published history, such works may be the principal source of historical information. For intensive studies, the various bibliographies of local history and the publications of local historical societies are especially valuable.

On some counties and localities a good deal of historical material has been published, though some may be accessible only locally and early publications may be out of print. The amount of such information varies greatly from state to state; the presidential suggestion of 1876 that each county celebrate the national centennial by preparing a history was followed unevenly, since at the time much of the South was still under military occupation and in many Southern communities local records had been destroyed during the conflict of 1861–65. Recent county histories are very uneven; few of them provide the kinds of information about townships and localities that one finds in the histories produced in New York, New Jersey, and Pennsylvania in 1876–1900. Above-average age, size, and historical consciousness of a community do not necessarily yield local histories of high quality; more important is the activity of local historians: neither New York nor Charleston has its history as well interpreted as Rochester. Although a number of county histories (as well as state ones) have been produced in response to the Bicentennial of 1976, they generally are not as useful as those a century earlier, where such exist.

The local bibliographies and community histories are subject to certain problems. Sometimes the notations of the field worker have given us false scents: *Rowanta* District, Dinwiddie County, Virginia, was recorded from one local informant as *Low Warranty*, suggesting an ideal place for a retired politician to set up a used-car lot. Other places were simply not found in the census records, or were mislaid in the change in the designation of the minor civil divisions—from parish to district to township—or were simply gobbled up in new developments, like the rustic towns of Kings County, New York, hardly discernible in Brooklyn, or like Ellenton, South Carolina, taken over for the Savannah River plant of the Atomic Energy Commission, or like others that have been exploited for mines, factories, reservoirs, and military bases.

Informant Biographies

Each historical sketch is followed immediately by the vitae of the informants interviewed in that community. Among white informants, the most old-fashioned (generally also the oldest) is listed first, while the most modern or sophisticated (often also the youngest) is entered last, according to the alphabetical code assigned in each informant id number. The order depends partly on the actual age of the informants, partly on the amount of formal education they have received, partly on their social status in the community, partly on their general personality: their receptiveness to new ideas, their interest in the present and so on. Every community is different in its value system.

For African-American informants, the letter N is used in the informant identification number, rather than the A, B . . . M sequence used for whites. Only in New York City were there enough people interviewed to reach M in the alphabet; this M informant is white. Elsewhere, an M designates the second African-American informant interviewed in a community. It should be noted that no African Americans were interviewed at all north of Maryland. Biographies of the African-American speakers are first within a community, reflecting both their status (usually) as "folk" type speakers and as a supplement to the sampling plan (see Chapter 2). Better-educated African Americans (some are in the "cultivated" category) and former auxiliary informants who were recently reclassified as primary informants violate the general sequence of informants by Type (cf. the Table of Informants and the discussion of informant selection in Chapters 2 and 3).

Biographies for the most highly educated informants, or those from the highest social class, conclude with the term "Cultivated". For informants judged as cultivated, the informant id number is followed by an exclamation point. These speakers, whose phonemic systems were analyzed for Kurath and McDavid 1961, illustrate the regional differences that exist within standard speech in the US.

Each vita presents information on the following points, so far as it is available in the field record (if the informant lives in a locality that is different from the immediately preceding location for which there is a historical sketch, this is noted first—often only the voting district or post office is different).

1) The informant's sex and occupation.

2) The informant's age, sometimes only approximate.

3) The informant's birthplace. Note that county (and state, abbreviated with the two-letter postal code) names are added to locality names in the vitae only when the locality referred to is outside the informant's own county (or state). Distances in miles are often cited for convenience in referring to such communities. Such distances are measured (approximately) from the informant's residence.

4) The informant's residence in other parts of the same state, in other states, or abroad. If there is no specific mention of residence elsewhere, it may be assumed that the informant has been a life-long resident of the home community. Travel experience may also be noted in this section. The speakers are not necessarily assigned to the community of their birth. The community given for them at the beginning of the biography, or in the immediately preceding local history sketch, may reflect where they are currently living, where they were born, or where they spent most of their lives. Even though speakers were specifically sought who were natives of their communities, the relatively large number of LAMSAS informants who had traveled or lived elsewhere attests to the high rate of mobility characteristic of US culture.

5) The birthplace of the parents and ancestors. (F. = father; M. = mother; PGF = paternal grandfather; MGF = maternal grandfather; PGM = paternal grandfather; PGF's F = paternal grandfather's father; PGF's PGF, etc.). Ordinarily the record is taken back through the male line, then each succeeding female line. Sometimes detailed genealogies are abridged in the interest of convenience.

6) The informant's education: grammar school, high school (academy), and college (seminary, normal school, university); and the extent of the informant's reading and of other experiences or activities which may have affected the informant's socio-cultural level. In rural communities the grammar school attended by older informants was often a one-room "district school" or "old-field school", with terms of only two or three months.

7) Social contacts, especially with particular classes of the local population; church affiliation, membership in clubs and fraternal organizations, and the like; participation in community activities. The extent of this information varies greatly from record to record.

8) The informant's character and personality as described by the field worker: temperament, habits, interests, and the like. This section also often gives a brief assessment of the interview. Difficulties in communication or scheduling are noted, as well as whether others were present. The general circumstances of the interview and degree of rapport established with the field worker are discussed. This part of the sketch often contains information of linguistic interest, particularly notes on nonstandard usage, taboo reactions, and other language-related attitudes. Comments on the use of "folk" forms, particularly, are sometimes included here as evidence of the degree of informality for the interview.

Sometimes information on auxiliary informants is given at the end of a sketch rather than in this section. Especially if a separate interview was conducted with the auxiliary informant, as opposed to the auxiliary informant merely being present, as a friend or relative, at the interview with the primary informant, the biography of the auxiliary informant is given a separate paragraph. The informant identification number for an auxiliary informant will be the same as the number of the associated primary informant, followed by an asterisk.

9) The informant's speech: familiarity with other dialects, attitude toward "correctness", individual characteristics (especially such as do not appear from the individual transcriptions in the field records: tempo, intonation, firmness of articulation, nasality, etc.). Sometimes the field worker added a note on local peculiarities not illustrated in the speech of the informant.

The informant's family name was always recorded by the field worker, both in conventional spelling and in phonetic transcription, but usually with the explicit understanding that it would not be published. A number of informants, despite their willingness to help, would have refused to be interviewed if the field workers had not promised that they would remain anonymous. On the other hand, many informants referred to published genealogies of their families. Confidentiality prevents publication of information that would personally identify informants.

List of Abbreviations

acc.	according
AfAm	African-American
Am.	American
Assn.	Association
assoc.	associated
asst.	assistant
b.	born
Balt.	Baltimore
bro.	brother
c.	circa
cent.	century
Co.	. . . County
co.	county
cos.	counties
comm.	community
cons.	consonant(s)
DAR	Daughters of the American Revolution
dept.	department
diph.	diphthong(al)
dist.	district
E.	east, eastern
Ed., ed.	education
est.	established
F	female
F.	father
Feds	Federal troops (Civil War)
Ft.	Fort
ft.	feet
FW	field worker
govt.	government
GP	grandparents
HS	High School
h.s.	high school
I.	Island
inc.	incorporated
incl.	including
inf.	informant
infs.	informants
info.	information
LANE	Linguistic Atlas of New England
M.	mother
mfg.	manufacturing
MGF	maternal grandfather
MGM	maternal grandmother
mi.	mile(s)
mo.	month
mod.	moderate(ly)
monoph.	monophthong(al)
Mt.	Mount
mtn.	mountain
N.	north, northern
natl.	national
NE	northeast
New Eng.	New England
NYC	New York City
occ.	occasional(ly)
org.	organized
orig.	original(ly)
PGF	paternal grandfather
PGM	paternal grandmother
Phila.	Philadelphia
Pitts.	Pittsburgh
P.O.	post office
pop.	population
prob.	probably
pronun.	pronunciation
pt.	point
R.	River
Rev.	Revolutionary War
RR	railroad
S.	south, southern
Shen.	Shenandoah
Soc.	Society
TB	tuberculosis
U.	University
UDC	United Daughters of the Confederacy
uninc.	unincorporated
unstr.	unstressed
us.	usual(ly)
V.A.	Veterans Administration
vocab.	vocabulary
VP	Vice-President
W.	west, western
WCTU	Women's Christian Temperance Union
wks.	weeks
Wm.	William
WS	work sheets
WWI	World War I
WWII	World War II
yr.	year

New York

1, 2, 3. Suffolk County (Long Island)

Settled by the Dutch and the English. Many New Englanders migrated to the island in the 1640s. By c. 1670 it was all inhabited: several Dutch towns in the W., the remainder of the settlements English. The English towns were at first independent, governing themselves by majority vote in town meetings. By 1662 the Long I. English settlements had united with either the New Haven Colony or the CT Colony. After New Haven and CT Colonies were united, Long I. became part of NY. Pop. 1790: 16,440, 1820: 24,272, 1850: 36,922, 1880: 53,888, 1910: 96,138, 1930: 161,055, 1960: 666,784.

Bailey, Paul 1949. *Long Island, a History of Two Great Counties, Nassau and Suffolk.* 3 vols. NY: Lewis Historical Pub. Co.

Bayles, Richard M. 1874. *Historical and Descriptive Sketches of Suffolk County. . . .* Port Jefferson: The Author.

Bigelow, Stephanie S. 1968. *Bellport and Brookhaven. . . .* Bellport: Bellport-Brookhaven Historical Society.

Bruce, James E., and Richard P. Harwood, comps. 1977. *Long Island as America.* Port Washington, NY: Kennilait Press.

Cooper, J. L., et al. 1882. *. . . History of Suffolk County. . . .* NY: W. W. Munsell.

Fernow, B., comp. 1883. *Documents Relating to the History of the Early Colonial Settlements Principally on Long Island. . . .* Albany: Weed, Parsons.

Flint, Martha Bockeé. 1896. *Long Island before the Revolution: A Colonial Study.* NY. Repr. 1967 (Port Washington: I. J. Friedman).

Fuller, Myron L. 1914. *The Geology of Long Island.* Washington: Government Print. Office.

Furman, Gabriel. 1875. *Antiquities of Long Island. . . .* Ed. by Frank Moore. NY: J. W. Bouton.

Gabriel, Ralph Henry. 1921. *The Evolution of Long Island; A Story of Land and Sea.* New Haven: Yale University Press.

Godfrey, Kenneth. 1976. *Historic Orient Village.* Orient, NY: Oysterponds Historical Society.

Gould, Zell Morris, and Henrietta M. Klaber. 1953. *Colonial Huntington, 1653–1800.* Huntington: Huntington Press.

Halsey, William Donaldson. 1935. *Sketches from Local History.* Bridgehampton: Harry Lee Pub. Co.

Hazelton, Henry Isham. 1925. *The Boroughs of Brooklyn and Queens, Counties of Nassau and Suffolk, Long Island, 1609–1924.* NY: Lewis Historical Pub. Co.

Hedges, Henry P. 1897. *A History of the Town of East Hampton, New York. . . .* Sag-Harbor: J. H. Hunt.

Howell, Nathaniel Robinson. 1952. *Know Suffolk, the Sunrise County. . . .* Islip: Buys Bros.

McDermott, Charles J. 1966. *Suffolk County.* NY: J. H. Heineman.

Overton, Jacqueline, and Bernice Marshall. 1961. *Long Island's Story, with a Sequel. . . .* 2nd ed. Port Washington: I. J. Friedman.

Platt, Henry C. 1876. *Old Times in Huntington.* Huntington, NY: Long Islander Print.

Rattray, Jeannette Edwards. 1953. *East Hampton History. . . .* Garden City: Country Life Press.

Rattray, Jeannette Edwards. 1955. *Ship Ashore! A Record of Maritime Disasters off Montauk and Eastern Long Island 1640–1955.* NY: Coward-McCann.

Sammis, Romanah. 1937. *Huntington-Babylon Town History.* Huntington: Huntington Historical Society.

Senlock, Richard B., and Pauline W. Sealy. 1940. *Long Island Bibliography.* Ann Arbor, MI: Edwards Bros.

Thompson, Benjamin Franklin. 1843. *History of Long Island. . . .* 2nd ed. NY: Gould, Banks.

Wevgold, Marilyn E. 1974. *The American Mediterranean: An Environmental, Economic, and Social History of Long Island Sound.* Port Washington, NY: Kenrilaut Press.

Wilson, Rufus Rockwell. 1902. *Historic Long Island.* NY: Berkelcy Press.

Wood, Silas. 1828. *A Sketch of the First Settlement of the Several Towns on Long Island. . . .* 3rd ed. Brooklyn: A. Spooner.

1885. *History of Suffolk County. . . .* Babylon: Budget Steam Print.

Orient, Southold Twp.

Southold settled 1640 under the direction of New Haven by a congregation from Hingham, Norfolk, England. By 1662, Southold had joined New Haven. Southold eventually determined to belong to the new Colony of CT, and submitted in 1676 to NY's jurisdiction only under protest. Rural town in NE part of island; excellent farms, fishing. Many wealthy old families here from early times. Pop. 1790: 3,222, 1820: 2,968, 1850: 4,723, 1880: 7,267, 1910: 10,577, 1930: 11,669.

NY 1: M, farmer, justice of the peace, 53. — Old local families. — Ed.: until 16. — Congregational; not much social life. — Intelligent, cooperative, quick witted. — Rapid tempo. Rather short vowels. Less retroflexion than some older speakers here have. — LANE WS.

Easthampton

Settled 1649 from Lynn, MA. Several of the pioneers of Milford, CT, moved on to Easthampton and Southampton. Many Kentish early. Newcomers to town voted on after careful investigation. Along with Southampton and Southold, drew up plans of govt. and maintained close relations with CT. In 1658, Easthampton joined the CT Colony; like Southold, it finally accepted NY's jurisdiction with reluctance. Located on the SE shore of the island. Always a rural community, now filled with large estates. East Hampton village inc. 1920. Pop. 1790: 1,497, 1820: 1,646, 1850: 2,122, 1880: 2,515, 1910: 4,722, 1930: 6,569.

NY 2A: M, farmer, fisherman, 63. Has always lived in backwoods area just N. of village of East Hampton. — Old local stock. — Probably illiterate (only 4 mos. of school). — No social contacts. Leads semi-Indian life. — Thinks quickly but not clearly. Content of his speech sometimes illogical and confused. — Rapid tempo. Fairly precise articulation, without the strong New Eng. stress. — LANE WS; Incomplete.

Sagaponack, Southampton Twp.

Settled 1640 from Lynn, MA. Many early inhabitants from Yorkshire. Union with CT Colony 1644. Whaling off the shore during the 17th and early 18th cent. Later shipbuilding brought prosperity. Located on southern shore W. of Easthampton. Many large estates. Sag Harbor village began with a temporary population of fishermen and became a well established settlement c. 1730. Center of shipbuilding. Sagaponack a rural community. Pop. 1790: 3,402, 1820: 4,229, 1850: 6,501, 1880: 6,352, 1910: 11,069, 1930: 15,341.

NY 2B: M, farmer, carpenter, 85. — Old local families. — Ed.: till 16. — Presbyterian. — Intelligent; rather ponderous. Gave trustworthy information. — Deliberate tempo. Some nasalization. — LANE WS; Incomplete.

NY 2C: Bridgehampton, Southampton Twp. — F, housewife, 80. B. and brought up in a rural section SW of the village of East Hampton, but has lived since her marriage in the village of Bridgehampton (c. 5 mi. W.), twp. of Southampton. — Old local stock. — Ed.: grammar school (daughter a librarian). — Many social contacts. — Frail health and failing memory. Not a very satisfactory inf. — Speech typical of the region. — LANE WS; Incomplete.

NY 2C*: M, carpenter, "old". — Old Bridgehampton stock. — Very rustic, nasal speech. — LANE WS; Incomplete.

Brookhaven Village, Brookhaven P.O. and Twp.

1st settled 1655 from Boston; Twp. inc. 1666. Large colonial estates. Village to WW II; since SUNY Stony Brook, atomic labs. Twp. pop. 1790: 3,224, 1820: 5,218, 1850: 8,595, 1880: 11,544, 1910: 16,737, 1930: 28,291, 1970: 245,260.

NY 3A: M, farmer, retired local coal dealer, 71. B. same house. — F. b. Brookhaven Village, PGF b. Easthampton, PGM b. Moriches (E. in same Twp.); M., MGF both b. South Haven (2 mi. E. in Twp.), MGF's F. b. Hempstead (Nassau Co.), MGM b. Twp. — Ed.: public school till 20 (graduated). — Presbyterian (F. Episcopalian).

Huntington

1646 deed; 1655 settlement; all associations with eastern towns. Settled early from New Haven, CT and MA. Twp. inc. 1666. Babylon formed from Huntington 1872. Congregational and Presbyterian by 1658; Methodists and Roman Catholics by early 19th cent. Orig. commercial port; now largely pleasure. Pop. 1790: 3,260, 1820: 4,935, 1850: 7,481, 1880: 8,098, 1910: 12,004, 1930: 25,582, 1970: 200,172.

NY 3B: M, farmer, 70. B. Melville (same twp.); here last 18 yrs. — F., PGF, PGM, M., MGF, MGM all b. Melville. — Ed.: till 16. — Presbyterian.

Coram, Brookhaven Twp.

Coram oldest interior settlement (pre-Rev.); farming. Seat of Twp. govt. since Rev. or before. Baptist church 1747; public town meetings by 1800.

NY 3C: M, farmer, 50. B. same house. — F. b. same house, PGF, PGF's F. b. Mt. Sinai (6 mi. N. in Twp.), PGM b. Port Jefferson (in Twp.); M., MGF b. Middle Island (6 mi. E. in Twp.), MGM b. Coram (prob. all from earliest settlers). — Ed.: locally till 18. — Presbyterian.

Fort Salonga, Northport P.O., Huntington Twp.

Ft. Salonga a British fort during Rev.; captured and destroyed in 1781 by raid from CT. Now agricultural. Northport once a thriving seaport and shipbuilding town.

NY 3D: M, farmer, 48. B. same house. — F. b. same farm, PGF, PGM, M., MGF, MGF's F., MGM all born same twp. — Ed.: till 17. — Presbyterian.

4. Nassau County

Formed 1898 from Queens. Busiest along S. shore. Large estates, country clubs, middle class developments; commuter pop. Market gardening for NYC; fishing: clams, oysters. Recreational areas (incl. racetracks); aircraft industries; artists' colonies. NY businessmen came to dominate communities. Methodists and Episcopalians. Colleges include Adelphi and Hofstra. Industry developed in WWII. Jewish pop. increased significantly. Pop. 1890: 128,059, 1900: 152,999, 1910: 284,041, 1930: 1,079,129, 1960: 1,809,578.

Clarke, Mary Louise. 1952. *East Meadow: Its History: Our Heritage, 1658–1952*. East Meadow.

Cox, John, Jr., ed. 1916–31. *Oyster Bay Town Records 1653–1763*. NY: T. A. Wright.

Darlington, O. G. 1949. *Glimpses of Nassau County History*. Mineola: Nassau County Trust Co.

Federal Writers' Project of the WPA. 1939. *New York Learns*. NY: M. Barrows and Co.

Irvin, Frances. 1926. *Historic Oyster Bay*. East Norwich.

Marshall, Bernice S. 1937. *Colonial Hempstead*. Lynbrook: The Review-Star Press.

Moore, Charles Benjamin. 1879. *Early History of Hempstead. . . .* NY: Trow's.

Onderdonk, Henry, Jr. 1878. *The Annals of Hempstead 1643–1832. . . .* Hempstead: L. Van de Water.

Smits, Edward J. 1974. *Nassau: Suburban USA; The First 75 Years of Nassau County, New York, 1899–1974*. Syosset, NY: Doubleday.

1937–. *Nassau County Historical Journal*. Uniondale: Nassau County Historical and Genealogical Society.

Old Brookville, Glen Head P.O., Oyster Bay Twp.

New Eng. outpost 1640. Dutch settlement at Oyster Bay soon after 1650. Boundary of Dutch and English claims; as a result, village has 2 main streets a block apart. 1732 Dutch Reformed Church. Large estates in 19th cent. Democratic stronghold before WWI. Growth peaked 1953–56; pop. quadrupled from WWII to 1960s.

NY4A: M, retired farmer, 69. B. same house. — F. b. same house, PGF b. Westchester Co., came to Old Brookville at 2, PGF's F., PGM, PGM's F. b. Westchester Co.; M. b. Manhasset, Nassau Co., MGF, MGF's F., MGM, MGM's F. b. Jericho, Nassau Co. — Ed.: public school; 6 yrs. at Friends Academy, Locust Grove. — Society of Friends.

Hempstead Twp., Freeport P.O.

Settled 1643; settlers from Stamford, CT and originally from Hampstead, England; also from MA. Frontier post where English and Dutch grants met; accepted Dutch rule until 1664. At least 15% from Yorkshire (1647); many of first group scattered during troubles of 1650s. Strong loyalist settlement. Quaker stronghold in colonial days. Freeport largest of S. side villages; sport fishing; near Jones Beach. Oystering. Rapid growth since 1875. Small industries after WWI. Intensively developed in 1960s.

NY 4B: M, retired boatman, 79. B. same neighborhood. — F., PGF b. Freeport, PGF's F. b. Hempstead, PGM b. Baldwin; M. b. Baldwin, MGF, MGF's F., MGF's M. b. Oceanside (Nassau Co.), MGM, MGM's F. b. Baldwin. — Ed.: locally until 10–12. — Methodist parentage.

East Meadow, Hempstead P.O. and Twp.

Farming community till 20th cent.; Barnum farm largest. Development after WWII. See previous community description for Twp.

NY 4C: M, farmer, 51. B. same house. — F., PGF, PGM b. Elmont in Co.; M., MGF, MGF's F. b. East Meadow, MGM b. Hempstead. — Ed.: until 14, some local night school afterwards. — Methodist.

New York City

Fur trade in area by 1610. Fort Amsterdam, lower end of Manhattan, by 1626. Peter Stuyvesant 1646–64; English conquest 1664. Public schools under Dutch, abolished by English. Pop. began with a Dutch/English nucleus. Irish influx 1833–67, soon outnumbered old stock. Lower East Side an Irish area; Irish into civil service c. 1837. 1867–1900 Germans became largest nationality group in NYC; 1900–25 Jews and Italians became 1st and 2nd groups. AfAm and Puerto Rican influx begun by 1930.

Condit, Carl W. 1980. *The Port of New York: A History of the Rail and Terminal System from the Beginnings to Pennsylvania Station.* Chicago: University of Chicago Press.

East, Robert A., and Jacob Judd. 1975. *The Loyalist Americans: A Focus on Greater New York.* Tarrytown, NY: Sleepy Hollow Restorations.

Federal Writers Project. 1938. *New York Panorama: A Comprehensive View of the Metropolis. . . .* NY: Random House.

Federal Writers Project. 1939. New York City Guide. *American Guide Series.* NY: Random House.

Glazer, Nathan, and Daniel P. Moynihan. 1963. *Beyond the Melting Pot.* Cambridge, MA: MIT.

Klein, Alexander. 1955. *The Empire City. . . .* NY: Rinehart.

Kouwenhoven, John Atlee. 1953. *The Columbia Historical Portrait of New York. . . .* Garden City: Doubleday.

Kouwenhoven, John Atlee. 1964. *The New York Guidebook.* NY: Dell Pub. Co.

Lamb, Martha J. 1877–96. *History of the City of New York: Its Origin, Rise, and Progress.* 3 vols. NY: A. S. Barnes.

Leonard, John William. 1910. *History of the City of New York, 1609–1909. . . .* 2 vols. NY: The Journal of Commerce and Commercial Bulletin.

Mandelbaum, Seymour J. 1965. *Boss Tweed's New York.* NY: J. Wiley.

Nevins, Allan. 1948. *The Greater City: New York 1898–1948.* NY: Columbia University Press.

Pomerantz, Sidney I. 1938. *New York: An American City 1783–1803; A Study of Urban Life.* NY: Columbia University Press.

Richardson, James F. 1970. *The New York Police: Colonial Times to 1901.* NY: Oxford University Press.

Rodgers, Cleveland. 1948. *New York: The World's Capital City. . . .* NY: Harper.

Rusannaike, Ira. 1972. *Population History of New York City.* Syracuse: University Press.

Still, Bayrd. 1956. *Mirror for Gotham: New York as Seen by Contemporaries from Dutch Days to the Present.* NY: University Press.

Stokes, Isaac Newton Phelps. 1939. *New York Past and Present. . . .* NY: Plantin Press.

Wilson, James Grant. 1892–93. *The Memorial History of the City of New York. . . .* 4 vols. NY: New York History Co.

Writers' Program. 1941. *A Maritime History of New York.* Garden City, NJ: Doubleday, Doran and Co.

5. Brooklyn, Kings Co., and Queens Co.

1st settlement in Brooklyn area c. 1626; 1st land grant 1636. Town organized c. 1646: 1st town of New Netherland to be politically organized. Inc. as village 1801; charter 1816; inc. as city 1834. In early 19th cent., a "suburban", quiet community, in contrast with NYC. Bushwick settled by 1638; Swedes and Norwegians by 1650; French by 1660; became part of Williamsburg c. 1817. Williamsburg (called "Dutchtown") annexed 1855; Brooklyn then 3rd largest city in US. Public-supported ed. under Dutch, not under English; to 1830, little schooling for poor. "American Lyceum" founded in NYC in 1831; Brooklyn Lyceum (founded 1833) led to Brooklyn Institute of Arts and Sciences. In 1865, c. 1/3 of pop. foreign-born; Irish, German, English. Also more Scandanavians than in NYC proper. By 1865, NY state legislature controlled Brooklyn's police, etc. Prospect Park 1874. Brooklyn Bridge authorized 1869; constr. started 1870; opened 1883. 1st rapid transit 1885. Series of annexations in 1880s and 90s; city and county became coterminus in 1890s. Consolidation with NY argued from 1833 on; passed in 1898. Navy yard here at one time; shipping, knitwear. Manufacturers Assn. of NY organized here 1894; Chamber of Commerce 1913. Except for Gravesend, Dutch official language of Kings Co. under British; endured till end of 18th cent. Kings was not only smallest but least populous Long Island co. till end of 18th cent. Queens Co. settled first (Flushing) 1643; charter 1645. Early settlers English, Quakers, Huguenots. Developed by rapid transit: 1st link to Manhattan, Queensboro Bridge in 1909. Long I. RR 1910. Both NYC airports in Queens. In 1924, Brooklyn/Queens had largest Jewish pop. of any NY community. Brooklyn 2nd leading center in chemicals by 1880; several major corps. there today. Pop. Kings 1790:

4,495, 1820: 11,187, 1850: 138,882, 1880: 599,495, 1910: 1,634,351, 1930: 2,560,401, 1960: 2,627,319. Queens 1698: 3,568, 1731: 7,995, 1756: 10,786, 1790: 16,014, 1820: 21,519, 1850: 36,833, 1880: 90,574, 1910: 284,041, 1930: 1,079,129, 1960: 1,809,578.

Armbruster, Eugene, L. 1918. *The Bruijkleen Colonie (Borough of Brooklyn) 1638–1918*. NY.

Bailey, J. T. 1840. *An Historical Sketch of the City of Brooklyn*. . . . Brooklyn: The Author.

Bergen, Teunis G. 1881. *Register, in Alphabetical Order, of the Early Settlers of Kings County*. New York: S. W. Green's Son.

Dubois, Anson. 1884. A History of the Town of Flatlands. In Henry M. Stiles, ed. . . .*History of the County of Kings and the City of Brooklyn, New York, from 1683 to 1884* (Brooklyn: W. W. Munsell and Co.), vol. 1, 64–79.

Furman, Gabriel. 1824. *Notes, Geographical and Historical, Relating to the Town of Brooklyn*. . . . Brooklyn: A. Spooner.

Hazelton, Henry Isham. 1925. *The Boroughs of Brooklyn and Queens, Counties of Nassau and Suffolk, Long Island 1609–1924*. 5 vols. NY: Lewis Historical Pub. Co.

Onderdonk, Henry. 1865. *Queens County in Olden Times*. Jamaica: C. Welling.

Ostrander, Stephen M. 1894. *A History of the City of Brooklyn and Kings County*. Ed. by Alexander Black, 2 vols. Brooklyn: Pub. by Subscription.

Stiles, Henry Reed. 1884. *The Civil, Political, Professional, and Ecclesiastical History. . . of the County of Kings and the City of Brooklyn, New York, from 1683 to 1884*. NY: W. W. Munsell and Co.

Syrett, Harold C. 1944. *The City of Brooklyn; 1865–1898*. NY: Columbia University Press.

Vanderbilt, Gertrude Lefferts. 1881. *The Social History of Flatbush and Manners and Customs of the Dutch Settlers in Kings County*. NY: D. Appleton.

Waller, Henry D. 1899. *History of the Town of Flushing, Long Island*. Flushing: J. H. Ridenour.

Weld, Ralph Foster. 1938. *Brooklyn Village, 1816–1834*. NY: Columbia University Press.

Weld, Ralph Foster. 1950. *Brooklyn is America*. NY: Columbia University Press.

1882. *History of Queens County*. . . . NY: W. W. Munsell.

Flatlands, Brooklyn P.O., Kings Co.

Settled as early as 1624; 1st purchase 1637; charter 1667. Marshland; squatters. Boundary disputes with Flatbush. Taken into Brooklyn 1894. Pop. 1790: 423, 1820: 512, 1850: 1,155, 1880: 3,127.

NY 5A: F, housewife, 70. B. same house. F., PGF, PGF's F., PGF's PGF b. same house, PGF's M. b. NYC, PGM, PGM's F. b. Manhattan, PGM's M. b. Flatbush; M. b. New Utrecht, MGF, MGF's F., MGF's M. b. Blelyn, MGM b. Newtown, Queens. — Ed.: Erasmus Hall Academy, Brooklyn. — Dutch Reformed Church.

NY 5B: Brooklyn, Kings Co. — M, restaurant cashier, 62. B. downtown Brooklyn; moved to Manhattan 1933. — F., PGF, PGF's F., PGM, M. all b. Lower Manhattan, MGF, MGM b.

England. — Ed.: till 18, Boys' H.S. Commercial Course. — Methodist Episcopal.

Ozone Park, Queens Co.

Maritime and industrial center (shipping declining since WWII).

NY 5C: F, housewife, 51. B. Brooklyn; to Ozone Park, Queens age 39. — F. b. Brooklyn, PGF, PGF's F. b. downtown Manhattan (English or N. Irish descent), PGM, M, MGF b. downtown Manhattan, MGF's F. b. England, Yorkshire, MGF's M., MGM b. downtown Manhattan. — Ed.: until 18, 3 yrs. h.s. — Methodist.

NY 5D: Brooklyn, Kings Co. — M, letter-carrier, probation bureau in magistrates' courts, 64. B. here; lived in Larchmont, Westchester Co. 1928–38. — F. b. NYC, PGF b. Chaplin Hill, CT, PGF's F. b. Hampton, CT, PGM b. CT; M. b. NYC, MGF b. Albany, MGM b. PA (Quaker). — Ed.: public schools in Brooklyn till 14. — NY Oratorio Society, Gilbert and Sullivan, Spanish War vet, instructing officer in WWI.

Flatbush, Brooklyn P.O., Kings Co.

Midway between E. River and Jamaica Bay. Founded 1634. 1st church on Long I., Dutch, 1655. Orig. heavily timbered. Boundary disputes with Flatlands and with Newtown (Queens). English made official school language in 1776. Erasmus Hall 1786. Farming till late 19th cent. Relatively isolated till rapid transit and automobile. Taken into Brooklyn 1894. Pop. 1790: 941, 1820: 1,027, 1850: 3,177, 1880: 7,634.

NY 5E: East Brooklyn, East New York, Flatbush. — F, widow, 82. B. East Brooklyn; moved to East New York when 21; when 47 to Flatbush; when 68 to Rockville Center, Nassau Co. (record made there). — F., PGF both b. Lower Manhattan, PGF's F. b. MA, PGM b. MA (Huguenot descent); M. b. Brooklyn, MGF b. Newburgh-on-Hudson (lived in NH), MGF's F. b. Dracut, MA, MGM b. Peekskill (Westchester Co.), MGM's M. of Holland Dutch descent, daughter of a Methodist minister. — Ed.: public school till 14. — Methodist.

NY 5F: Brooklyn, Queens Co. — M, secretary-treasurer of the Hat Institute, 53. B. Brooklyn; lives now at Huntington, Long I. (20 yrs.). — F., PGF b. Brooklyn (PGF of old Amityville, Long I., stock), PGM b. Brooklyn; M. b. Lower Manhattan. Entire family of "English" stock (prob. old Long I. Yankee). — Ed.: Brooklyn till 14. — Methodist.

NY 5G: M, coal and oil business (old family business), 50. B. downtown Brooklyn. — F., PGF b. Lower Brooklyn, PGF's F. b. 1797 Brooklyn Village (Dutch descent), PGM, PGM's F. b. Brooklyn Village (latter of English descent); M., MGF b. downtown Brooklyn (MGF Scottish descent), MGM b. N. Ireland. — Ed.: h.s. in Brooklyn. — Methodist.

Brooklyn Heights, Kings Co.

Old, distinctive, residential; fashionable till very recently.

NY 5H!: M, civil engineer, 68. B. Brooklyn Heights; moved to Morningside Heights age 30 when married (record made there); traveled widely, but did not stay in one place. — F. b. S. Manhattan, PGF, PGM b. prob. near Jamaica, Long I.; M., MGF b. Brooklyn, MGF's F. b. England. — Ed.: private school, Brooklyn; Columbia U. School of Mines. — F. Dutch Reformed; M. Congregational, later Episcopalian. — Cultivated.

Flushing, Queens Co.

Village orig. settled in 1643 from Netherlands and MA; focus of Quaker fight for toleration. Summer colony for Manhattan in 19th cent.

NY 5I!: M, manufacturing, banking, 54. B. here. Winters in FL, summers in Maine. — F. b. Flushing Village, PGF, PGF's F. b. on Willets Point (now Fort Totten) near Bayside, Queens, PGM b. here or Long I.; M. b. Flushing (Quaker), MGM b. NYC. — Ed.: Hill School at Pottstown, PA; 4 yrs. at Yale U. — Congregational (Episcopalian father). — Cultivated.

6. Richmond County (Staten Island)

Richmond Co. est. 1683. Territorial rights sold to W. India Co. in 1637; patroonship 1640–41; patent 1642. 1st permanent settlement 1661; possibly an early Walloon settlement. English grants after 1664. Prob. 1st industries in New Netherland a distillery and a buckskin tannery. Waldensians as early as 1658; Huguenots and other French by 1678. In 1668, separated from NJ, became part of NY (NJ boundary est. 1833). Dutch spoken extensively in 18th cent. Chief British base in Rev. 1st ferry 1755; municipal ferry system 1890. 1st factory a cleaning and dyeing works c. 1826. Chiefly farming and fishing till 1830. RR planned 1851, opened 1860. Socially prominent families from NYC and South. Highest percent of native-born residents; many old families of French, English, and Dutch descent. Lawn tennis 1st played in US here. Shad fisheries through 19th cent. Shipbuilding; oyster beds (overworked); bird sanctuary. Verrazano Bridge 1964 (ferries to Brooklyn abandoned after this). Soap. oil storage and refining, printing, lumber mill; some iron deposits; breweries from 1851. Pop. 1790: 3,835, 1820: 6,135, 1850: 15,061, 1880: 38,991, 1910: 85,969, 1930: 158,346, 1960: 221,911.

Bayles, Richard M., ed. 1887. *History of Richmond County (Staten Island) New York, from Its Discovery to the Present Time.* NY: L. E. Preston.

Clute, John J. 1877. *Annals of Staten Island. . . .* NY: C. Vogt.

Leng, Charles W. 1930. *Staten Island and Its People, a History, 1609–1929.* 4 vols. NY: Lewis Historical Pub. Co.

Morris, Ira K. 1898–1900. *Morris's Memorial History of Staten Island. . . .* 2 vols. NY: Memorial Pub. Co.

Smith, Dorothy Valentine. 1968. *This Was Staten Island.* Staten Island: Staten Island Historical Society.

Smith, Dorothy Valentine. 1970. *Staten Island: Gateway to New York.* Philadelphia: Chilton Book Co.

Steinmeyer, Henry George. 1950. *Staten Island 1524–1898.* Staten Island: Staten Island Historical Society.

NY 6A: Huguenot, Annadale P.O., Staten Island. — F, widow, 76. B. Huguenot. — F. b. locally, PGF b. Staten I., PGM b. this part of Staten I.; M., MGF, MGM all b. Princes Bay, S.

end of Staten I. — Ed.: till 14. — Huguenot Dutch Reformed. — Somewhat senile; very glad to talk. — Fair articulation.

Tottenville

S. tip of Staten Island. Waldensian church c. 1660. Grant in 1674; Methodists early. Chartered 1894. Ferry to Amboy from 17th cent. Picturesque village into 20th cent.

NY 6B: F, housewife, 48. B. here. — F., PGF, PGF's F. all b. Staten I. (French Huguenot descent), PGF's M. b. Staten I., PGM, PGM's F. b. Staten I. (English descent); M. b. Staten I., MGF b. near Toms River, NJ, MGM b. Staten I. — Ed.: public schools till 17, 2 yrs. St. Louis Academy here. — Methodist.

7. New York City (Manhattan)

Verrazano possibly in area as early as 1524. Harbor discovered by Hudson 1609; trading 1614. Settlement by 1623: Protestant Walloons. 1st slaves owned by Company, brought to Manhattan 1626 to work on public projects. Private slaveholding by 1646. Stuyvesant 1647; English settlers as early as 1646. Dutch inc. as city, 1655 (church services conducted in Dutch in NYC till 1890s). Pop. of Manhattan about 1400 at time of English takeover in 1669. Greenwich Village orig. a settlement of Scottish weavers; also some Jewish immigration in 17th cent. 1st municipal charter in US 1686. Dutch down to about 60% of pop. by 1700; English and French came to dominate merchant class; Chamber of Commerce 1768. Germans in 18th cent. Irish before Am. Rev. Kings College (Columbia) founded 1754, also 1st public library. Rise of port started by colonial wars; heyday of privateering 1754–60. Slums of Lower East Side date from before 1800. C. 1810, rise in trade made NYC larger than Phila.; dominated cotton trade by 1830. Merchant class stable, even in 1837 depression; involved with both European trade (43%) and trade with South (19%). Had passed Charleston in trade by 1820; 3 1/2 times as much by 1850. First RR to NYC 1851; Grand Central Station 1871. Central Park est. 1856–76. Large Jewish migration began 1881 with death of Alexander II; Jewish and Italian patronage grew with La Guardia. Harlem est. as village 1658; farming till 1830, then suburb. AfAm influx into Harlem began 1903; essentially complete by 1930; high unemployment in Depression (never recouped). Port Authority 1921. Pop. 1790: 33,131, 1820: 123,706, 1850: 515,547, 1880: 1,206,299, 1910: 2,331,542, 1930: 1,867,312, 1960: 1,698,281.

Abbott, Wilbur C. 1929. *New York in the American Revolution.* NY: C. Scribner's Sons.

Archdeacon, Thomas, J. 1976. *New York City, 1664–1710: Conquest and Change.* Ithaca: Cornell University Press.

Armstrong, William. 1848. *The Aristocracy of New York.* NY: New York Pub. Co.

Bales, William Alan. 1967. *Tiger in the Streets.* NY: Dodd, Mead.

Barck, Oscar Theodore, Jr. 1931. *New York City during the War for Independence.* Columbia Univ. Press.

Barrett, Walter. 1885. *The Old Merchants of New York City.* 4 vols. NY: Thomas R. Knox and Co.

Barrett, Walter. 1885. *The Old Merchants of New York City.* 4 vols. NY: Thomas R. Knox and Co.

Beach, Moses Y. 1846. *Wealth and Biography of the Wealthy Citizens of New York City.* 10th ed. NY: The Sun Office.

Benson, Lee. 1966. *The Concept of Jacksonian Democracy: New York as a Test Case.* NY: Princeton U. Press.

Brace, Charles Loring. 1880. *The Dangerous Classes of New York.* 3rd ed. NY: Wynkoop and Hallenbeck.

Colton, Julia M. 1901. *Annals of Old Manhattan.* NY: Brentano.

Coon, Horace. 1947. *Columbia: Colossus on the Hudson.* NY: E. P. Dutton and Co.

Danforth, B. J. 1974. *The Influence of Socioeconomic Factors upon Political Behavior: A Quantitative Look at New York City Merchants 1828–1844.* New York U. dissertation.

Duffus, Robert L. 1930. *Mastering a Metropolis.* NY: Harper and Bros.

Edwards, George W. 1917. *New York as an Eighteenth Century Municipality 1731–1776.* NY: Columbia University Press.

Ellis, Edward Robb. 1966. *The Epic of New York City.* NY: Coward-McCann.

Foner, Philip S. 1941. *Business and Slavery: The New York Merchants and the Irrepressible Conflict.* Chapel Hill: University of North Carolina Press.

Footner, Hulbert. 1937. *New York: City of Cities.* Philadelphia: J. S. Lippincott Co.

Harrington, Virginia. 1935. *The New York Merchant on the Eve of the Revolution.* NY: Columbia University Press.

Harris, Charles T. 1928. *Memories of Manhattan in the Sixties and Seventies.* NY: Derrydale Press.

Headley, Joel Tyler. 1873. *The Great Riots of New York: 1712 to 1873. . . .* NY: E. B. Trent.

Hone, Philip. 1936. *The Diary of Philip Hone, 1828–1851,* ed. by Allan Nevins. NY: Dodd, Mead.

Howe, Irving. 1976. *World of Our Fathers.* NY: Simon and Schuster.

Innes, J. H. 1902. *New Amsterdam and Its People.* NY: C. Scribner's Sons.

Johnson, James W. 1930. *Black Manhattan.* NY: Knopf.

Judd, Jacob, and Irwin Polishedi, eds. 1973. *Aspects of Early New York History and Politics.* Tarrytown: Sleepy Hollow Restorations.

Kessler, Henry H., and Eugene Reubin. 1959. *Peter Stuyvesant and His New York.* NY: Random House.

Lanier, Henry W. 1923. *A Century of Banking? in New York: 1822–1922.* NY: George H. Doran Co.

Longstreet, Stephen. 1975. *City on Two Rivers.* NY: Hawthorn Books.

Lydon, James G. 1970. *Pirates, Privateers, and Profit.* Upper Saddle River, NJ: Gregg Press.

Lyman, Susan Elizabeth. 1964. *The Story of New York. . . .* NY: Crown Pub.

Mandelbaum, Seymour J. 1965. *Boss Tweed's New York.* NY: J. Wiley.

McKay, Richard C. 1934. *South Street: A Maritime History of New York.* NY: G. P. Putnam's Sons.

Miller, Douglas T. 1967. *Jacksonian Aristocracy: Class and Democracy in New York.* NY: Oxford University Press.

Mohl, Raymond A. 1971. *Poverty in New York: 1783–1824.* NY: Oxford University Press.

Monaghan, Frank, and Marvin Lowenthal. 1943. *This Was New York: The Nation's Capital in 1789.* Garden City: Doubleday, Doran and Co.

Morris, Lloyd. 1951. *Incredible New York.* NY: Random House.

Mott, Hopper Striker. 1908. *The New York of Yesterday; A Descriptive Narrative of Old Bloomingdale.* NY: Putnam's.

Myers, Gustavus. 1971. *A History of Tammany Hall.* NY: B. Franklin.

Orafsky, Gilbert S. 1966. *Harlem: The Making of a Ghetto; Negro New York 1890–1930.* NY: Harper and Row.

Peterson, Arthur E. 1917. *New York as an Eighteenth Century Municipality (prior to 1831).* NY: Columbia University Press.

Pierce, Carl H. 1903. *New Harlem.* NY: New Harlem Pub. Co.

Pool, David de Sola, and Tamar de Sola Pool. 1955. *An Old Faith in the New World: Portrait of Shearith Israel, 1654–1954.* NY: Columbia University Press.

Pool, David de Sola. 1953. *Portraits Etched in Stone: Early Jewish Settlers 1682–1831.* NY: Columbia University Press.

Pratt, E. E. 1911. *Industrial Causes of Congestion of Population in New York City.* NY: Columbia University Press.

Riker, James. 1904. *History of Harlem.* NY: New Harlem Pub. Co.

Riker, James. 1904. *Revised History of Harlem.* NY: New Harlem Pub. Co.

Rodgers, Cleveland. 1948. *New York: The World's Capital City. . . .* NY: Harper.

Russell, William F., and Edward C. Elliott, eds. 1937. *The Rise of a University.* 2 vols. NY: Columbia University Press.

Still, Bayrd. 1956. *Mirror for Gotham. . . .* NY: University Press.

Stokes, Isaac Newton Phelps. 1915. *The Iconography of Manhattan Island 1498–1909.* 6 vols. NY. Repr. 1967 (NY: Arno Press).

Van Rensselaer, Mariana Griswold. 1909. *History of the City of New York in the Seventeenth Century.* NY: Macmillan.

Wertanbaker, Thomas J. 1948. *Father Knickerbocker Rebels.* NY: C. Scribner's Sons.

NY 7A: M, stevedore on Staten Island, 45. B. here. — F., PGF both b. here, PGF's F. b. in Ireland, PGM b. here (Irish parentage); M., MGF both b. here, MGF's F. b. Germany (Lutheran), MGM prob. b. Germany (Lutheran). — Ed.: parochial schools till 10 or 11, public schools till 12. — Roman Catholic.

NY 7B: M, chauffeur, 39. B. here. — F. b. here, PGF, PGM both b. Ireland; M. b. here, MGF b. Scotland, MGM b. Ireland. — Ed.: parochial school. — Roman Catholic.

NY 7C: F, housewife, 43. B. here. — F., PGM both b. here; M. b. here, MGF b. Fishkill (Dutchess Co.), MGM b. here (old Long I. stock). — Ed.: public school till 14. — Roman Catholic. — Probably untrustworthy. — Coarse voice.

NY 7D: F, widow, 79. B. here; spent 3 yrs. in Hackensack, NJ, when 31. — F., PGF, PGF's M., PGM all b. here (PGM of

Holland Dutch descent); M., MGM both b. here (Holland Dutch descent). — Ed.: public school till 13. — Baptist.

NY 7E: M, salesman in hatter's shop, 63. B. here. Age 39–47 in Springfield, MA; 47–54 in Hartford, CT; then back here. — F. b. on East Side, PGF b. perhaps in NYC (English descent); PGM, M., MGM all b. NYC. — Ed.: public school till 15. — Methodist, now believer in Divine Science.

NY 7F: F, homemaker until 43, then saleslady, bookkeeper, clerk, 67. B. on West Side; last seven summers in Catskills (Shandaken, Ulster Co.). — F. b. here, PGF b. London, England, PGM b. here (Holland Dutch descent); M. b. on West Side, MGF, MGM both b. London, England. — Ed.: till 16. — Methodist (grandparents were Church of England).

NY 7G: F, housewife, school board member, 55. B. here, when 20 moved to Brooklyn. — F. b. here, PGF b. Londonderry, Ireland (Catholic), PGF's F., PGF's M. both b. N. Ireland (PGF's M. daughter of a Presbyterian minister), PGM b. Londonderry, Ireland (Catholic); M. b. here, MGF, MGM both b. Co. Derry, Ireland (both Catholic). — Ed.: public school till 14, evening school off and on. — Roman Catholic.

NY 7H: M, receiving clerk, Museum of City of NY, 38. B. here. 1 yr. in CA; last 5 yrs. in the Bronx. Lived in Bergen Co., NJ, for 10 yrs. and commuted to work. — F., PGF both b. here, PGF's F. b. Alsace-Lorraine, PGF's M. b. Ireland, PGM b. PA; M. b. Greenwich Village, MGF b. US, MGM b. Ireland. — Ed.: 1 yr. h.s. in NYC. — Roman Catholic.

NY 7I: M, retired bookkeeper for large concerns, 85. B. Lower East Side of Manhattan; has lived in White Plains since age 60 (record made there, in Westchester Co.). — F., PGF, PGF's F. all b. Lower Manhattan (first ancestor in this line to NYC in 1635 from England), PGM b. Scotland and came as a child; M., MGF both b. Lower Manhattan (MGF Congregational minister). — Ed.: public school till 14. — Episcopalian.

NY 7J!: F, 59. B. here. — F. b. Rochester, NH (on summer vacation from NYC), PGF b. Rochester, NH (lived in NYC), PGM b. Rochester, NH; M., MGF, MGF's F., MGM, MGM's F. all b. NYC (MGM's F. of old colonial stock). — Ed.: Brown School (very fashionable). — Episcopalian. — Cooperative; upper social level. Her mother trained her strictly in social behavior, never to talk of money or servants, always to enjoy calling and entertaining. — Aggressive, vigorous speech. The regular (but occasionally wavering) use of the broad /a/ inf. feels to be derived from her parents. — Cultivated.

NY 7K!: M, lawyer, 60. B. here. When 43, went to S. Orange, NJ for 8 or 9 yrs. — F. b. Greenwich Village, PGF b. Easton, PA, PGM b. here; M. b. here, MGF b. Charleston, SC, MGM b. here. [Distinguished name, related to US Supreme Court Justice — RIM.] — Ed.: private schools in NYC; Columbia U. and Law School. — Sephardic. — Cultivated.

NY 7L!: F, writer (prose and verse), 76. B. here; in Paris 3 yrs. during WWI. — F. b. Highwood, NJ (name of his country place), PGF b. Albany, NY, PGF's F. Pres. of Columbia College, PGF's PGF b. Devonshire, England, with Clive in India, then in Antigua, West Indies, then to NY, PGF's PGM b. in Scotland (daughter of a Rev. general of Morris Co., NJ), PGF's M. b. Hudson Valley, PGM b. Highwood, NJ, PGM's M. b. here; M., MGF, MGF's F. all b. in Albany (M. educated in NYC), MGF's M., MGM b. Elizabeth, NJ. — Ed.: German drawing master, French governess at home; St. Agnes, Bishop Doane's School in Albany 2 yrs., 14–16. — Episcopalian. — Cultivated.

NY 7M!: F, housewife, 62. B. Hastings-on-Hudson (Westchester Co.) in summer at country home. — F. b. at country home in Astoria now a part of Long Island City in Queensboro, but lived in downtown Manhattan, PGF b. here, PGF's F. b. here or near here (of English Quaker stock from Long I., near Oyster Bay), PGF's M. b. near Flushing, Queens Co., PGM b. NY or RI, PGM's F. Governor of RI, b. RI, PGM's M. b. perhaps near Pelham Manor in old Westchester; M., MGF both b. here, MGF's F. b. Orange Co., NY, MGF's M. b. Stamford, CT, MGM b. here, MGM's F. of German descent (Leipzig), MGM's M. b. Ireland (Protestant). — Ed.: governess at home, Brearley School 6 yrs. (12–18). — Episcopalian. — Cultivated.

8. Bronx

Probably settled by Dutch before 1640; in 1641 Jonas Bronk (Scandinavian), first known settler, arrived. New England dissenters, 1643. Some Irish, 1840; Bronx part of Westchester Co. Pop. largely German in 1850. Never a definite political territory in its growth; taken piecemeal from Westchester with Bronx River as its axis. Geological extension of Manhattan. Inc. as Borough of the Bronx 1898; separate co. 1914. Pop. more than doubled between 1898 and 1910; mainly Italians, Jews, AfAms, Puerto Ricans. 1/2 Jewish by 1930. Church of England from 1702. Rapid transit to Manhattan from 1886. Montefiore Hospital from 1913. Roman Catholic religion not tolerated until 1784: 1st Bronx parish 1843. 54 Jewish congregations in 1927. Several colleges, including NYU and Fordham. 16% devoted to park purposes (more than in all the other 4 boroughs). Industries include RR yards, clothing, metalworking, food products, pianos and other musical instruments. Pop. 1900: 200,507, 1910: 430,980, 1930: 1,265,258, 1960: 1,424,815.

Comfort, Randall, ed. 1906. *History of Bronx Borough.* NY: North Side News Press.

Cook, Harry T. 1913. *The Borough of the Bronx, 1639–1913.* . . . NY: The Author.

Hufeland, Otto. 1929. *A Check List of Books, Maps, Pictures and Other Printed Matter Related to the Counties of Westchester and Bronx.* White Plains: Westchester Historical Society.

Jenkins, Stephen. 1912. *The Story of the Bronx.* . . . NY: G. P. Putnam's Sons.

McNamara, John. 1978. *History in Asphalt: The Origin of Bronx Street and Place Names, Borough of the Bronx.* Harrison: Harbor Hill Books.

Tieck, William A. 1968. *Riverdale, Kingsbridge, Spuyten Duyvil, New York City: A Historical Epitome of the Northwest Bronx.* Old Tappan, NJ: F. H. Revell Co.

Wells, James L., et al., eds. 1927. *The Bronx and Its People: A History, 1609–1927*. 3 vols. NY: Lewis Historical Pub. Co.

NY 8: West Farms (record made in Westchester). — F, single homemaker, 83. B. West Farms, moved to Westchester aged 71. — F. b. Bronxdale, in Bronx, PGF, PGM b. Lancashire, England; M. b. West Farms, Bronx, MGF b. prob. in England, MGM b. Long I. — Ed.: West Farms public school (no h.s.). — (Dutch) Reformed.

9. Westchester County

English settlers from CT 1650–1664. Late 17th cent., Huguenot settlement, New Rochelle. Co. formed 1863; included what is now Bronx. 21 twps. Boundary with CT long in dispute. Pop. 1790: 23,941, 1820: 32,638, 1850: 58,263, 1880: 108,988, 1910: 283,055, 1930: 520,947, 1960: 808,891.

Albion, Robert Greenhalgh. 1939. *The Rise of New York Port*. NY: C. Scribner's Sons.

Baird, Charles W. 1882. *History of Bedford Church*. NY: Dodd, Mead.

Barrett, Robertson T. 1955. *The Town of Bedford: A Commemorative History 1680–1955*. Bedford: Town of Bedford.

Bolton, Robert, Jr. 1848. *A History of the County of Westchester. . . .* 2 vols. NY: A. S. Gould.

Bonner, William T. 1924. *New York, the World Metropolis 1623–1924*. NY: R. L. Polk and Co.

Burnham, Alan. 1963. *New York Landmarks*. Middletown, CT: Wesleyan University Press.

Caro, Robert A. 1974. *The Power Broker: Robert Moses and the Rule of New York*. NY: Vintage.

Conklin, Margaret Swancott. 1939. *Historical Tarrytown and North Tarrytown. . . .* Tarrytown: Tarrytown Historical Society.

Crandell, Richard F. 1954. *This is Westchester: A Study of Suburban Living*. NY: Sterling Pub. Co.

Dawson, Henry B. 1886. *Westchester County, New York during the American Revolution*. NY: Morrisania.

French, Alvah P., ed.-in-chief. 1925. *History of Westchester County*. 4 vols. NY: Lewis Historical Pub. Co.

Griffin, Ernest Freeland, ed. 1946. *Westchester County and Its People. . . .* 3 vols. NY: Lewis Historical Pub. Co.

Hansen, Harry. 1950. *North of Manhattan: Persons and Places of Old Westchester*. NY: Hastings House.

Hinitt, Dorothy Humphreys, comp. 1974. *The Burning of Bedford, July 1779, as Reported in Contemporary Documents and Eyewitness Accounts*. Bedford: Bedford Historical Society.

Hufeland, Otto. 1926. *Westchester County during the American Revolution*. White Plains: Westchester Historical Society.

Hufeland, Otto. 1929. *A Check List of Books, Maps, Pictures and Other Printed Matter Related to the Counties of Westchester and Bronx*. White Plains: Westchester Historical Society.

Jay, John. 1862. *Correspondence between John Jay, Esquire, and the Vestry of St. Matthew's Church, On the Slavery Question*. Bedford.

Scharf, J. Thomas. 1886. *History of Westchester County. . . .* 2 vols. Philadelphia: L. E. Preston.

Shonnard, Frederic, and W. W. Spooner. 1900. *History of Westchester County. . .to 1900*. NY: New York History Co.

Westchester County Emergency Work Bureau. 1939. *Historical Development of Westchester County: A Chronology*. 2 vols. White Plains: Westchester County.

1880. *A "Centennial Souvenir" Brief History of Tarrytown. . . .* Tarrytown: G. L. Wiley.

1966–72. *Town of Bedford Historical Records*. Bedford: Bedford Historical Society.

Tarrytown, Greenburgh Twp.

Philipse ("richest man in the colonies") purchase, c. 1672–93. Dutch settlement. About 1,000 inhabitants in 1842. C. 1930 said to be primarily a service center for large and small estates. Now suburban. Problem of etymology: Irving's folk etymology "too long at the tavern" or Dutch *tarwe* 'wheat'.

NY 9A: F, widow, 75. B. Ossining (West Co.), came here when 1 1/2 yrs. old. — F. b. Drewville (Putnam Co.), came to Ossining as a boy, PGF b. Putnam Co. (French descent), PGM b. Putnam Co.; M. b. Ossining, MGF b. Ireland (Protestant), MGM b. near Saratoga (partly of Holland Dutch descent). — Ed.: till 18 (grammar school). — Methodist. — Quick, alert. — Moderate tempo. Good articulation.

Middle Patent, Bedford P.O., North Castle Twp.

1640 Indian grant to New Haven. 1701–2 "middle patent" grant between CT and Bedford. Name applied to NE corner of Twp. (See next description for Bedford.)

NY 9B: M, farmer, 77. B. NYC and came here as infant. — F. b. Greenburgh (West. Co.), PGF, PGF's F., PGM all b. Cross River, Lewisboro (West. Co.); M. b. Riversville, near Greenwich, CT, MGF b. Greenwich, CT, MGM b. Mt. Pleasant (now under the waters of the Kensico Reservoir, in West. Co.). — Ed.: till 18. — Methodist.

Cross River, Bedford P.O. and Twp.

1640 purchase for New Haven; 1655 confirmed to Stamford; late 17th cent. confirmed to NY. 1681 dissenters arrived from Massachusetts Bay via CT. Small village in 1742: 45 dwellings. Cross family early settlers; from Fairfield, CT, to small settlement on the Cross River.

NY 9C: F. homemaker, 55. B. here. — F., PGF, PGF's F. all b. here, PGF's M. b. Greenwich, CT, PGM, PGM's F., PGM's M. b. here; M. b. Bedford Village, MGF b. Orange Co., NY near Thompson Ridge, MGM, MGM's F., MGM's M. b. here (MGM's and PGF's lines were cousins, descended from the first settlers of Bedford, from Stamford, CT). — Ed.: locally, then h.s. Mt. Kisco, Blair Hall in Blairstown, NJ. — Presbyterian.

10. Orange County

1666 purchase from Indians; some Dutch, Huguenots. Land grants 1690–1720. C. 1709 Palatine settlement; later English, Scotch, Irish. Intensive farming; iron mines in the 18th cent. 1800 turnpikes. Industries include milk and milk transport, foundry, cut glass. Pop. 1790: 18,492, 1820: 41,213, 1850: 57,145, 1880: 88,220, 1910: 116,001, 1930: 130,383, 1970: 221,657.

Akers, Dwight. 1937. *Outposts of History in Orange County.* Washingtonville: Blooming Grove Chapter, D. A. R.

Clark, Robert Bruce. 1895. *The First Presbyterian Church, Goshen, 1720–1895.* NY: A. D. F. Randolph.

Coleman, R. 1909. *A Few Biographical Sketches of Goshen People and Reminiscences. . . .* Newburgh: Woolsey Print.

Coleman, R. 1909. *Some Traditions of Goshen and Its People.* Newburgh: Woolsey Print.

Eager, Samuel W. 1846–47. *An Outline History of Orange County. . . .* Newburgh: S. T. Callahan.

Fugliomeni, M. P. 1976. *The Flickering Flame: Treachery and Loyalty in the Mid-Hudson during the American Revolution.* Washingtonville: Spear Printing.

Headley, Russel, ed. 1908. *The History of Orange County.* Middleton: Van Deusen and Elms.

Moffat, Almet S., comp. 1928. *Orange County: A Narrative History. . . .* Washingtonville.

Roberts, Mildred F. 1970. *The Origin of Orange County, from 1683 to 1847.* Orange, CA.

Ruttenber, E. M. 1875. *History of the County of Orange. . . .* Newburgh: E. M. Ruttenber.

Ruttenber, E. M., and L. H. Clark, comps. 1881. *History of Orange County. . . .* Philadelphia: Everts and Peck.

Seese, Mildred P. 1945. *A Tower of the Lord in the Land of Goshen — A History Written in Commemoration of the 225th Anniversary of the First Presbyterian Church.* Goshen: Windy Hill Book Mill.

Seese, Mildred Parker. 1941. *Old Orange Houses. . . .* Middletown: Whitlock Press.

Sharts, Elizabeth. 1960. *Land o' Goshen: Then and Now.* Ed. by Mildred Parker Sesse. Goshen: The Bookmill.

Stickney, Charles E. 1867. *A History of the Minisink Region. . .in Orange County.* Middletown: C. Finch and I. F. Guiwits.

Zimm, Louise H., et al. 1946. *Southeastern New York: A History of the Counties of Ulster, Dutchess, Orange, Rockland, and Putnam.* 3 vols. NY: Lewis Historical Pub. Co.

1884–1919. *Publications of the Historical Society of Newburgh and the Highlands.* Newburgh.

1895. *Portrait and Biographical Record of Orange County. . . .* NY: Chapman Pub. Co.

1964. *Goshen, the Spirit of '64: The Story of Goshen on Its 250th Anniversary.* Goshen.

Mt. Salem, Unionville P.O., Greenville Twp.

Formed 1854 from Minisink Twp. Pop. decline 1900–1920.

NY 10A: M, farmer, 59. B. neighborhood. — F. b. same twp., PGF b. adjacent farm, PGF's F. of Scotch-Irish descent, PGF's M. b. neighborhood, PGF's MGF b. Putnam Co., NY, PGM, PGM's F., PGM's M. b. Sussex Co., NJ (3 mi. away); M. b. 5 mi. NE in Wawayanda Twp., MGF b. Minisink Twp., MGF's F. b. Long Island, MGF's M. b. Minisink, MGF's MGF b. Long I., MGM b. near Goshen in Co. (Scotch-Irish descent).

Goshen

Co. seat. First settled 1703; patent to John Bridges and Company. English and Scotch settlers early. Twp. organized 1788. Goshen Village inc. 1843. Very fertile soil, dairying, foundry. National center of light-harness racing. Pop. 1790:

2,448, 1820: 3,441, 1850: 3,149, 1880: 4,387, 1910: 3,081, 1930: 2,891, 1960: 3,906.

NY 10B!: F, housewife, 63. B. Goshen. — F., PGF b. Goshen, PGF's F. b. Westtown, Orange Co. (Scotch Presbyterian descent), PGM b. Kingston, Ulster Co.; M., MGF, MGM b. Orange Co., MGM's F. of French-Huguenot descent. — Ed.: h.s. here. — Episcopalian. — Clear articulation. [ɔ·n] as in NJ. — Cultivated.

11. Putnam County

1697 all in Philipse Patent. In 1720 individual settlements; largely English from CT and Long I. Settlers from CT and Cape Cod c. 1740. First church Congregationalist c. 1742; other denominations by the end of the century. Co. taken from Dutchess Co. 1812. Industries: cattle raising (beef, then dairy), mining to 1900. Pop. 1820: 11,268, 1850: 14,138, 1880: 15,181, 1910: 14,665, 1930: 13,744, 1960: 31,722.

Blake, William J. 1849. *The History of Putnam County. . . .* NY: Baker and Scribner.

Pelletreau, William S. 1886. *History of Putnam County, New York.* Philadelphia: W. W. Preston.

Zimm, Louise Hasbrouck, et al., eds. 1946. *Southeastern New York, a History of the Counties of Ulster, Dutchess, Orange, Rockland and Putnam.* 3 vols. NY: Lewis Historical Pub. Co.

Putnam Valley (record made in Shrub Oak, Mohegan Lake P.O., Yorktown Twp. [Westchester Co.]).

Mohegan Lake a trading center for vacationers. Has a prep school. Pop. 1930: 100.

NY 11: F, housewife, 42. B. Putnam Valley, moved to Shrub Oak when 22 yrs. old. — F. b. Mahopack Falls (Putnam Co.), PGF b. Putnam Co., PGM b. Lake Mahopack (Putnam Co.); M. b. IL and returned as infant to Co., at Peekshill Hollow, MGF, MGF's F. b. Mohegan Lake (Westchester Co.), MGF's M., MGM, MGM's F., MGM's M. b. Putnam Valley. — Ed.: Putnam Valley, h.s. in Peekshill, business college in Poughkeepsie. — Methodist.

12. Dutchess County

11 authentic crown patents. First resident 1627; slow to develop village life. Co. formed 1683. In 1714, 416 free residents, 29 slaves; almost all Dutch. "Anti-rent" war 1766; quitrent riots in 1850s. AfAm pop. consistently under 5% 1714–1950. In 18th cent., 2nd most populous co. in NY; predominantly Dutch. Early textile center; excellent specialized agriculture continues today. Borden condensed milk located here. Pop. 1790: 45,266, 1820: 46,615, 1850: 58,995, 1880: 79,184, 1910: 87,661, 1930: 105,452, 1960: 176,008.

Booth, Henry. 1878. *Relics in Poughkeepsie, New York.* Washington, DC.

Coon, Edwin C. 1967. *Old First: A History of the Reformed Church of Poughkeepsie, New York.* NY: William-Frederick Press.

Federal Writers Project. 1937. Dutchess County. *American Guide Series.* Philadelphia: William Penn Association of Philadelphia.

Filkin, Francis. 1911. *Account Book of a Country Store Keeper in the Eighteenth Century at Poughkeepsie.* Poughkeepsie: Vasser Bros. Institute.

Griffin, Clyde. 1969. Workers Divided: The Effect of Class and Ethnic Differences in Poughkeepsie, New York, 1850–1880. In Stephen Thernstrom and Richard Sennett, eds., *Nineteenth-Century Cities* (New Haven: Yale University Press), 49–97.

Hasbrouck, Frank, ed. 1909. *The History of Dutchess County.* Poughkeepsie: S. A. Matthieu.

King, Charles Donald. 1959. *History of Education in Dutchess County.* NY.

Lossing, Benson J. 1867. *Vassar College and Its Founder.* NY: C. A. Alvord, Printer.

MacCracken, Henry Noble. 1956. *Old Dutchess Forever! The Story of an American County.* NY: Hastings House.

MacCracken, Henry Noble. 1958. *Blithe Dutchess: The Flowering of an American County from 1812.* NY: Hastings House.

Platt, Edmund. 1905. *The Eagle's History of Poughkeepsie from the Earliest Settlements 1683 to 1905.* Poughkeepsie: Platt and Platt.

Reynolds, Helen Wilkinson, ed. 1911–1919. *The Records of Christ Church. . . .* Poughkeepsie: F. B. Howard.

Reynolds, Helen Wilkinson. 1924. *Poughkeepsie: The Origin and Meaning of the Word.* Poughkeepsie: Dutchess County Historical Society.

Smith, Philip H. 1877. *General History of Dutchess County. . . .* Pawling: The Author.

Van Gieson, Acmon P. 1893. *Anniversary Discourse and History of the First Reformed Church of Poughkeepsie.* Poughkeepsie: The Consistory.

Zimm, Louise Hasbrouck, et al., eds. 1946. *Southeastern New York, a History of the Counties of Ulster, Dutchess, Orange, Rockland and Putnam.* 3 vols. NY: Lewis Historical Pub. Co.

1789–. *The Poughkeepsie Journal.* Poughkeepsie.

1914–1951. *Dutchess County Historical Society Year Book.* Poughkeepsie.

1924–58. *Dutchess County Historical Society Collections.* 8 vols. NY: William-Frederick Press.

Pecksville, Peck Slip, Holmes P.O., East Fishkill Twp.

Fishkill Twp. at least from 1717. Largely rural; farming people: Dutch, some French, English late. E. Fishkill Twp. set off 1850.

NY 12A: F, widow, antique dealer, 67. B. locally (Beekman Twp.). — F. b. near Quaker Hill (S. end) near edge of Sherman Twp., CT, PGF lived in Patterson, Putnam Co.; M. b. locally (Pawling Twp.), MGM b. Luddingstonville, just over line in Putnam Co. — Ed.: till 14 (not "steady"). — Baptist (Methodist parentage).

NY 12A*: M, farmer, elderly.

North Clove, LaGrangeville P.O., Union Vale Twp.

Twp. formed 1827. Old iron mines; now almost wholly agricultural. Clove in S. part of Twp.

NY 12B: F, housewife, 55. B. here. — F. b. here, PGF, PGF's F. b. neighborhood (PGF's F. of Palatine German descent),

PGF's M. b. Dover in Co., PGM, PGM's F. b. Washington in Co.; M., MGF, MGF's F. and M., MGM, MGM's F. and M. all b. LaGrange (MGF's F. son of a Hessian soldier). — Ed.: district school here; then boarding school W. NY; Starkie Seminary 4 yrs. — Christian Church.

Poughkeepsie

Township 1788; village 1799; city 1854. 1683 first settlement (purchase from Indians); predominantly Dutch at outset. Settlers in 18th cent. included Walloons, French, English, Palatines, Irish, and Scots. State capital during Revolution. Developed in part as a whaling post. Vassar College founded 1861; coed in 1969. City grew till panic of 1873; German and Irish immigration 1850–1880; Irish tended to advance more slowly than Germans. Furniture and coffin making, once imp., disappeared. Industries include shipping and distribution of lumber, machinery, clothing; Smith Bros. cough drops till after WWII. Pop. 1790: 2,529, 1820: 5,726, 1850: 13,944, 1880: 20,207, 1910: 27,936, 1930: 40,288, 1960: 38,330.

NY 12C!: F, county historian of Dutchess Co., trustee of Dutchess Co. Historical Society and Free Library (formerly librarian at Hyde Park), 65. B. here. — F., PGF b. here, PGF's F. b. in RI, PGF's M. b. here, PGM b. here, PGM's F. b. Brooklyn, PGM's M. b. Dutchess Co.; M. b. LaGrange in Co., MGF, MGF's F. b. Union Vale in Co., MGF's M. b. Co., MGM, MGM's F., MGM's PGF all b. Beekman in Co. — Ed.: till 14 in public school. Due to curvature of the spine, education continued only at home. — Episcopalian (born Dutch Reformed). — Cultivated.

13. Ulster County

3rd oldest settlement, after NYC and Albany. Chartered 1661. 1652 settled by Thomas Chambers, Englishman; other early settlers primarily Dutch, with some Flemish and English. 1660s Indian raid: 24 killed, 48 prisoners. 1676 Huguenot settlement at New Paltz. Palatines settled 1708–10. Some Quakers wouldn't sign "Articles of Association". Scots, Swiss, Norse, Swedes, Poles immigrated more recently. Industries: millstones, glass (1800–50), tanneries (to 1880), cement, quarries; poultry, dairying, rich agriculture including fruit. Pop. 1790: 29,397, 1820: 30,934, 1850: 59,384, 1880: 85,838, 1910: 91,769, 1930: 80,155, 1960: 118,804.

Beers, F. W. 1875. *County Atlas of Ulster, New York.* NY: Walker and Jewett.

Brink, Benjamin Myer. 1902. *The Early History of Saugerties 1660–1825.* Kingston: R. W. Anderson.

Child, Hamilton, comp. 1871. *Gazetteer and Business Directory of Ulster County, for 1871–2.* Syracuse: Hamilton Child.

Clearwater, Alphonso T., ed. 1907. *The History of Ulster County.* Kingston: W. J. Van Deusen.

Fried, Marc B. 1975. *The Early History of Kingston and Ulster County, New York.* Kingston: Marbletown.

Heidgerd, Ruth P. 1977. *Ulster County in the Revolution.* New Paltz: Ulster County Bicentennial Commission.

Sylvester, Nathaniel Bartlett. 1880. *History of Ulster County. . . .* Philadelphia: Everts and Peck.

Van Buren, Augustus H. 1923. *A History of Ulster County under the Dominion of the Dutch.* Kingston.

Zimm, Louise Hasbrouck, et al., eds. 1946. *Southeastern New York, a History of the Counties of Ulster, Dutchess, Orange, Rockland and Putnam.* 3 vols. NY: Lewis Historical Pub. Co.

――― 1896. *Commemorative Biographical Record of Ulster County, New York.* Chicago: J. H. Beers.

Mt. Marion, Saugerties P.O. and Twp.

1667 included in Kingston Charter. Town chartered 1811. Sawmill there before 1663. Early settlers mostly Dutch, with some English and a few Huguenots. Palatines arrived 1710. 18th century Dutch from Kingston. Irish immigrants in 19th cent. Varied industries, including textiles, tanning, quarries, paper, leather, canvas; once exported blue stone for sidewalks, etc. Saugerties terminus and port of call for river steamers. Pop. decline after 1875.

NY 13A: M, farmer, 81. B. locally. — F. b. town of Ulster, PGF, PGM b. Co.; M. b. town of Ulster, MGF b. Co. (inf. feels totally of old Holland Dutch descent). — Ed.: till 18 (off and on). — Dutch Reformed. — Quick, volatile type. — Uses [r] in postvocalic position instead of [ə]. Retroflexion weak in stressed syllables (indicating perhaps that it is a new characteristic in the region, or that retroflexion was difficult for the Dutch to acquire). Inf.'s mother could speak some Dutch.

The Mountain Road, Hurley P.O. and Twp.

Old Hurley settled as "Nieuw Dorp" from Kingston 1661. Town est. 1708. Temporary state capital 1777. Declining pop. 1900–1920; not heavily settled.

NY 13B!: F, unmarried homemaker, 68. B. here; between ages 40–60 spent 3 mos. each winter in NYC (Brooklyn). — F. b. here, PGF, PGF's F., PGF's PGF all b. Greenkill, town of Rosendale (PGF's PGF a member of Continental Congress), PGF's M. b. here, PGM lived in Hurley; M., MGF b. Stone Ridge, Marbletown Twp. — Ed.: country school, Kingston HS. — Dutch Reformed. — Descendant of old famous families; lived in lovely old brick house. — Genuine, unaffected speech of the old Kingston type. — Cultivated.

14. Sullivan County

Formed 1809 from Ulster Co. Few settlers c. 1790. 1826–28, Delaware and Hudson Canal (to Kingston) to take PA coal to NYC. 1830s Erie RR. Industries: tanneries (early 19th cent.), dairying, charcoal, potash. Resort area, esp. for NYC Jews: "borscht belt". Pop. 1810: 6,108, 1820: 8,900, 1850: 25,088, 1880: 32,491, 1910: 33,808, 1930: 35,272, 1960: 45,272.

Child, Hamilton, comp. 1872. *Gazetteer and Business Directory of Sullivan County for 1872–3.* Syracuse: Hamilton Child.

Curley, E. 1930. *Old Monticello.* Monticello: The Republican Watchman.

Heidt, William. 1956. *Francis Knapp's 103 years of Brief History of the Development of Sullivan County.* NY: New-York Historical Society.

Quinlan, James Eldridge. 1873. *History of Sullivan County.* . . . Liberty: G. M. Beebe and W. T. Morgans.

South Hill, Grahamsville P.O., Neversink Twp.

Twp. organized 1798. 1743 first settlers (Germans and English); driven off in Rev. Grahamsville named for "Graham's disaster" (ambush 1778). Some New England settlers from CT; some from England. Location of a Quaker meeting house. Pop. 1800: 858, 1820: 1380, 1850: 2281.

NY 14A: M, farmer, 78. B. here. — F., PGF both b. adjoining farm (Holland Dutch descent), PGM Scotch-Irish descent; M. b. Esopus (Ulster Co.) and came to Claryville in Co. age 3, MGF, MGM b. Ulster Co. — Ed.: till 18. — Dutch Reformed. — Quick, intelligent; yet gruff, suspicious, uninterested (his wife, NY 14A*, finished the last few pages of the record).

NY 14A*: F, wife of NY 14A.

Monticello, Thompson Twp.

Co. seat since 1809; inc. 1820. 1749 first settlement; abandoned during French and Indian War. 1795 first permanent settlement: William Thompson from CT via NYC. Most early settlers English (many from CT), some Dutch. Monticello founded c. 1802 by Samuel F. Jones. Turnpike 1804. Country remained wild a long time. Now a resort center. Pop. 1810: 1,300, 1820: 1,897, 1850: 3,198, 1880: 941, 1910: 1,941, 1930: 3,450, 1960: 5,222.

NY 14B: M, farmer, 46. B. here. — F., PGF b. Twp., PGF's F., PGM, PGM's F. b. Orange Co. (PGF, PGM descendants of a Southold, Long I., family); M., MGF both b. Sackett Lake in Twp., MGM, MGM's F. both b. CT. — Ed.: public schools and h.s. in Monticello. — Methodist. — Quick, understanding person. — Good articulation. (Note: it was difficult for FW to hear and is not correctly recorded, but inf. actually distinguishes an [ɔɚ] (*hoarse*) and an [ɔ˞] (*horse*) type of sound throughout.)

15. Greene County

Formed from Ulster and Albany in 1800. English and Dutch settlement from the 1690s. Peaceful history. 1703 King's Highway; 1801 Susquehanna Turnpike. In Catskills; industries include farming, cement. Pop. 1800: 12,584, 1820: 22,996, 1850: 33,126, 1880: 32,695, 1910: 30,214, 1930: 25,808, 1960: 31,372.

Atkinson, Oriana (Torrey). 1970. *Not Only Ours: A Story of Greene County New York.* Durham:

Beecher, Raymond. 1977. *Out to Greenville and Beyond: Historical Sketches of Greene County.* Cornwallville: Hope Farm Press.

Brace, H., et al. 1884. *History of Greene County.* . . . NY: J. B. Beers.

Chadwick, George Halcott. 1932. *The "Old Times" Corner.* Catskill: Greene County Historical Society.

Gallt, Frank A. 1915. *Dear Old Greene County.* Catskill.

Vedder, J. Van Vechten. 1927. *History of Greene County.* Vol. 1. Catskill: Greene County Recorder.

Goshen Street, Jewett P.O. and Twp.

Twp. first settled c. 1784. First settlers English (via Martha's Vineyard and CT) and Dutch. Organized 1850. Mountainous, general farming, light industry.

NY 15A: M, farmer, 84. B. locally (Ashland). — F. b. Ashland, PGF b. CT; M. b. Lexington (Greene Co.) near Shandakin (Ulster Co.). — Ed.: till 10 or 12. — Presbyterian. — Quick, alert, intelligent; secluded. — Very interesting low tongue position of [oˇ·ᵁˇ] sound.

NY 15B: Jewett. — M, farmer and insurance business, 49. B. here. — F. b. here, PGF b. Greene Co. (of CT descent); M., MGF b. Hunter (Greene Co.). — Ed.: till 17. — Presbyterian. — Quick, intelligent. — Moderate articulation.

16. Columbia County

Formed 1786 from Albany Co. 1640 farmers here; 1684–85 Livingston Manor, Livingston patent. Many Dutch settlers; Scotch and English in N. Palatines came in 1710; many remained (Germantown). In 1784 Nantucket whalers came to Hudson. Heavy political influence (e.g., Van Buren group). Industry: iron, paper, textiles, cement. Pop. 1790: 27,732, 1820: 38,330, 1850: 43,073, 1880: 47,928, 1910: 43,658, 1930: 41,617, 1960: 47,322.

Bradbury, Anna R. 1908. *A History of the City of Hudson. . . .* Hudson: Record Printing and Pub. Co.

Ellis, Franklin. 1878. *History of Columbia County.* Philadelphia: Everts and Ensign.

Hunt, Thomas. 1928. *A Historical Sketch of the Town of Clermont.* Hudson: Hudson Press.

Maynard, Mary S. 1979. *A Guide to Local History and Genealogical Resources in Columbia County.* Brookville.

Williams, M. 1900. *Columbia County at the End of the Century. . . .* 2 vols. Hudson: Hudson Gazette.

1894. *Biographical Review. . . of Columbia County.* Boston: Biographical Review Pub. Co.

Clermont, Germantown P.O., Clermont Twp.

Lower Livingston Manor. Clermont organized 1788; Dutch spoken into 19th cent. Only 3 Dutch families until 1709. Palatines immigrated in 1710 (Germantown); also English and Scottish in 18th cent. Village uninc. to 1928; existed as a hamlet in 1790. First chartered public school in NY state in Clermont (1791). Good farming; purely agricultural twp. to 1900.

NY 16A: M, farmer and fruitgrower, 66. B. here. — F. b. locally, PGF b. Amenia in Dutchess Co., PGF's F, PGF's M. b. RI, PGM b. Berne (Albany Co.); M., MGF, MGM, MGM's F. all b. Germantown. — Ed.: till 15. — Episcopalian.

Blue Shores, Hudson P.O., Livingston Twp.

Hudson settled 1783 by 30 Quaker fisherman and families from Martha's Vineyard. 1785 received 3rd city charter in NY. Whaling port; West India trade. Blue Shores a stop on the old Albany Post Road from well before 1836. Twp. org. 1788; Germans, Dutch. In S. part of Co.

NY 16B: M, farmer and fruitgrower, 61. B. here. — F. b. Red Hook in Dutchess Co. and came here as a baby, PGF b. Red Hook, PGM b. Livingston; M., MGF, MGM b. Livingston (all of Holland Dutch descent). — Ed.: till 19. — Lutheran.

17. Rensselaer County

Formed from Albany in 1791. 1624 Walloon settlement attempted; 1630 first settlement. Ft. Crail built by 1642. Center of anti-rent riots. Confluence of Hudson and Mohawk. Rensselaer patroonship: undisturbed to 1839. Troy in Co. is a shirtmaking and collar making center. Pop. 1800: 30,442, 1820: 40,153, 1850: 73,363, 1880: 115,328, 1910: 122,276, 1930: 119,781, 1960: 142,585.

Anderson, George Baker. 1897. *Landmarks of Rensselaer County.* Syracuse: D. Mason.

Craib, Stephanie Hicks, and Roderick Hull Craib. 1948. *Our Yesterdays, a History of Rensselaer County.* Troy.

Federal Writers Project. 1941. *A Souvenir of the Founding of Rensselaer County, 1791.* Troy: Whitehurst Printing Co.

Hayner, Rutherford. 1925. *Troy and Rensselaer County.* 3 vols. NY: Lewis Historical Pub. Co.

Sylvester, Nathaniel Bartlett. 1880. *History of Rensselaer County.* Philadelphia: Everts and Peck.

Weise, Arthur James. 1880. *History of the Seventeen Towns of Rensselaer County.* Troy: S. M. Francis and Tucker.

Petersburg

1754 Indian raid: many killed and captured. Formed 1791 from Stephentown, part of old Rensselaerswyck Manor. First settlements c. 1750: Dutch, with some settlers from RI and elsewhere in New Eng. Shirt factories from 1870. Farming and resort area.

NY 17A: M, retired farmer, 77. B. locally (Grafton); left Grafton at age 60 for Berlin in Co.; in Petersburg 1 yr. only. — F. b. Petersburg (on mtn.), PGF b. Moon Holler in Petersburg Twp., PGF's F. Rev. soldier, PGM b. Moon Holler; M., MGF b. Grafton, MGF's F. b. on the ocean, on way from Ireland, MGM, MGM's F., MGM's M. b. Grafton. — Ed.: Petersburg till 14 (very little: completed 3rd grade). — Christian.

NY 17A*: M, farmer.

South Schodack, Schodack Twp.

Formed 1795 from Rensselaerswyck; SW corner of Co. First settlers Dutch, prob. before 1660. Mohican Indians once here. Small settlement.

NY 17B: M, farmer, administrative asst. in Co. Soil Conservation, 45. B. locally. — F., PGF, PGF's F. all b. S. Schodack, PGF's PGF of Holland Dutch descent, PGF's M. b. Schodack, PGM, PGM's F. b. S. Schodack, PGM's M. b. Schodack (of French Canadian descent); M., MGF, MGM all b. Nassau in Co., MGM's F. b. Nassau (English descent). — Ed.: country school here and Albany HS. — Dutch Reformed.

18. Albany County

1st settlers 1636; strongest feudal area in America. Predominantly Dutch through colonial period. Co. created 1683; very large: 50 counties have been taken from it! West India Company supported settlement to 1629; then patroons. Palatines thrust frontier westward for protection of Albany. Battlefront during the Rev. Expansion after 1783, esp. from New Eng. In 1841 "Western RR" (from Boston) opened up NY state to New Eng. Pop. 1790: 75,921, 1820: 38,116, 1850:

93,279, 1880: 154,890, 1910: 173,666, 1930: 211,953, 1960: 272,926.

Banks, A. Bleecker. 1888. *Albany Bi-centennial*. Albany: Banks and Bros.

Barnes, William. 1851. *The Settlement and Early History of Albany....* Albany: Gould, Banks and Gould.

Beers, S. N., et al. 1866. *New Topographical Atlas of the Counties of Albany and Schenectady, New York*. Philadelphia: Stone and Stewart.

Brinkman, W. 1945. *Historical Data of Town of Guilderland*. NY: Guilderland

Clough, Wilson Ober. 1977. *Dutch Uncles and New England Cousins*. New Orleans: Polyanthos.

Federal Writers Project. 1938. Albany — Past and Present. *American Guide Series*. Albany.

Fernow, Berthold. 1886. *Albany and Its Place in the History of the U. S....* Albany: C. Van Benthuysen.

Gregg, Arthur B. 1936. *Old Hellebergh*. Altamont: The Altamont Enterprise.

Gregg, Arthur B. 1965. *Below the Hellebergh: The Story of Altamont, New York*. Altamont: Altamont Enterprise Print.

Hislop, Codman. 1936. *Albany: Dutch, English, and American*. Albany: Argus Press.

Howell and Tenney. 1886. *Bi-Centennial History of Albany...1609 to 1886*. NY: W. W. Munsell.

Kimball, Francis P. 1942. *The Capital Region of New York*. 3 vols. NY: Lewis Historical Pub. Co.

Munsell, Joel. 1850–59. *The Annals of Albany*. 10 vols. Albany: J. Munsell.

Munsell, Joel. 1865–71. *Collections on the History of Albany....* 4 vols. Albany: J. Munsell.

Nissenson, S. G. 1937. *The Patroon's Domain*. NY: Columbia University Press.

Parker, Amasa J., ed. 1897. *Landmarks of Albany County*. Syracuse: D. Mason.

Reynolds, Cuyler. 1906. *Albany Chronicles....* Albany: J. B. Lyon Co.

Tenney, Jonathan. 1883. *New England in Albany*. Boston: Crocker and Co.

1924–. *Dutch Settlers Society of Albany Year Book*. Albany.

1924. *Albany's Tercentenary: America's Oldest City*. Albany: J. B. Lyon Co.

Filkins Mill, East Berne P.O., Berne Twp.

Formed from Rensselaersville 1795. Swiss settlement 1750. 1786 New Englanders from CT, VT, NH, Long I. (mixed farming, dairying). Berne Twp. settled during Rev.; Scottish under Van Rensselaer patroonship. Seat of anti-rent convention 1846.

NY 18A: M, farmer, 82. B. neighborhood (Berne Twp.). — F. b. here, PGF b. Stonington, CT, PGM b. near Windham in Greene Co. (Dutch descent); M. b. here, MGF b. Windham Co., CT (near Putnam), MGM b. Berne. — Ed.: till 16. — Mother is Christian, wife is Methodist.

Altamont, Guilderland Twp.

Twp. formed 1803. Settled by Dutch before 1750. Slave auctions as late as 1814. Altamont inc. as a village in 1890; mainly Dutch, some French and English surnames. Largest

and most prosperous village in Twp. (formerly Knauersville). Industries: glassmaking (1785–1815), hay market, shipping point, farming, summer resort.

NY 18B: M, formerly farmer, now truck driver, 49. B. locally (Dunnsville). — F., PGF b. Twp., PGF's F. b. Co. (of old German stock, name said to be Polish); PGF's M. b. Co., PGM, PGM's M. b. Guilderland; M., MGF, MGF's F., MGF's PGF, MGF's M. b. Guilderland, MGM, MGM's M. b. Bethlehem Twp. (Albany Co.). — Ed.: grade school. — Lutheran.

Albany

First settlement in NY: Ft. Nassau in 1614. Ft. Orange 1617; families by 1624. 1630 Rensselaerswyck: only patroonship to survive colonial times. In 1685 village relinquished as part of manor; city charter 1686. Important fur trade center; key to frontier defense. Personality determined by role as state capital (since 1797). "Albany Congress" in 1784 to secure united colonial action. Diverse ethnic groups in colonial times: Walloons (first); also Norwegians, Danes, Germans, Scots, Irish. In 1797 first Roman Catholic church in upstate NY here. 1807 machine shops and stove-making; flour milling till c. 1830. Middle 19th cent. new immigrants: Irish, Germans, Italians. Called the "oldest city in the U.S". Noted for the expensive quality of its funerals. Pop. 1790: 3,498, 1820: 12,630, 1850: 50,763, 1880: 90,758, 1910: 253, 1930: 127,412, 1960: 129,726.

NY 18C!: M, steel and iron manufacturer, bank director, former head of Chamber of Commerce, 84. B. here. — F. b. Esperance in Co., PGF b. N. Ireland, came as infant, PGM b. N. Ireland; M., MGF b. Albany, MGF's F. of English descent intermarried with Dutch, MGM b. near Albany (of Dutch descent). — Ed.: Albany Free Academy. — Presbyterian. — Blind for 25 yrs. but remained active in business. — Cultivated.

19. Schenectady County

Formed 1809 from Albany. Settled 1658 by Alexander Glen; family house of 1713 still stands. Mostly Dutch settlers early; also a Scots family. Massacre in 1690; rebuilt with aid of Indians. Fur trade by 1727, after Albany monopoly broken. Pop. 1810: 10,201, 1820: 13,081, 1850: 20,054, 1880: 23,538, 1910: 88,235, 1930: 125,021, 1960: 152,896.

Beers, S. N., et al. 1866. *New Topographical Atlas of the Counties of Albany and Schenectady, New York*. Philadelphia: Stone and Stewart.

Greene, Nelson, ed. 1925. *History of the Mohawk Valley, Gateway to the West, 1614–1925. ...* 4 vols. Chicago: Clarke.

Howell and Munsell. 1886. *History of the County of Schenectady from 1662 to 1886*. NY: W. W. Munsell.

MacMurray, J. W., ed. 1883. *History of the Schenectady Patent....* Albany: J. Munsell's Sons.

Yates, Austin A. 1902. *Schenectady County, New York: Its History to the Close of the Nineteenth Century*. NY: New York History Co.

Duanesburg

Largest twp. in Co. 1740 1st purchase (Anthony Duane); in 1765 first settled by PA Germans and erected as twp. by patent. 1793 Christ Church built, "oldest unaltered Episcopal

Church in NY". In 1810 2nd most imp. twp. in Co.; importance has waned with urbanization.

NY 19: M, farmer, justice of the peace, 52. B. here. — F., PGF b. here, PGM b. Princeton in Co. (both grandparents of Scottish descent); M., MGF b. Duanesburg, MGF's F. b. Duanesburg (of Yankee stock), MGM, MGM's F., MGM's M. b. nearby. — Ed.: till 16. — Episcopalian. — Complacent, rather set in ways. — Quick tempo, short vowels. Weak articulation.

20. Schoharie County

Formed 1795 from Albany and Otsego Cos. First settled toward end of 17th cent.; Dutch settlers. 1712–13 Palatine settlers. Wheat growing; furnished army supplies 1758. Revolutionary War battleground. Heavy New Eng. influx after Rev. Hilly; rich soil. Pop. 1800: 9,808, 1820: 23,154, 1850: 33,548, 1880: 32,910, 1910: 23,855, 1930: 19,667, 1960: 22,616.

Brown, John M. 1823. *Brief Sketch of the First Settlement of the County of Schoharie, by the Germans.* . . . Schoharie: L. Cuthbert.

Noyes, Marion F., ed. 1964. *A History of Schoharie County.* Richmondville: Richmondville Phoenix.

Roscoe, William E. 1882. *History of Schoharie County.* . . . Syracuse: D. Mason.

Sias, Solomon. 1904. *A Summary of Schoharie County.* . . . Middleburgh: P. W. Danforth.

Simms, Jeptha R. 1845. *History of Schoharie County.* . . . Albany: Munsell and Tanner.

Simms, Jeptha R. 1882–83. *The Frontiersmen of New York.* . . 2 vols. Albany: G. C. Riggs.

Vrooman, John J. 1958. *The Promised Land: The Story of the Palatine Emigration from Their Rhineland Homes to the Hudson and Schoharie Valleys.* Johnstown: Baronet Litho Co.

1937–. *Schoharie County Historical Review.* Schoharie County Historical Society.

Pine Grove, Middleburg P.O., Broome Twp.

Middleburg founded in 1712 by Palatine Germans; oldest settlement in Schoharie Valley. Middle Fort defended in Rev. against Tories and Indians (1780). Twp. founded 1797; Dutch and English settlers.

NY 20A: M, farmer, 77. B. locally. — F. b. Twp., PGF b. Columbia Co., near Taghkanic, PGM b. Twp. (both Holland Dutch); M., MGF b. Albany/Schoharie Co. line, near Livingstonville, MGM b. England, step-MGM b. Co. — Ed.: off and on when "a mind to". — Methodist. — Cooperative, secluded.

Sharon Springs, Sharon Twp.

Settled 1784 from CT. Twp. taken from Schoharie Twp. 1797. Many Tories in area during American Rev. First hotel 1825; also a spa in the early 19th cent. (still operating).

NY 20B: M, farmer, 35. B. here. — F., PGF b. here, PGF's F. b. Twp., PGF's PGF b. Wilbraham, MA, PGF's PGM b. Twp., PGF's MGF b. Germany, PGF's MGM b. Canajoharie, PGM of Fly Creek, Otsego Co.; M. b. Sloansville in Co., MGF, MGF's F. b. Twp., MGM, MGM's F. b. Montgomery Co., Root Twp., MGM's M. of Scottish descent or birth. — Ed.:

here; 1 yr. at Rutgers, age 17. — Dutch Reformed. — Mild, cooperative.

21. Montgomery County

Highland settlement c. 1770; Loyalists uprooted in Rev. Taken from Albany Co. in 1772 as Tryon Co.; name changed 1784. Settled by some Dutch, many Palatines; then Yankees. Urban; various industries: carpets, textiles, brooms, and brushes, flour sacks and other containers, linseed oil, Beechnut. Pop. 1790: 28,839, 1820: 37,569, 1850: 31,992, 1880: 38,315, 1910: 57,567, 1930: 60,070, 1960: 57,240.

Beers, F. W., ed. 1878. *History of Montgomery and Fulton Counties.* . . . NY: F. W. Beers.

Buckley, W. A. 1892. *A Descriptive Geography of Montgomery County.* . . . Amsterdam, NY: Daily Democrat Print.

Campbell, William W. 1831. *Annals of Tryon County.* NY: J. and J. Harper.

Frothingham, Washington, ed. 1892. *History of Montgomery County.* Syracuse: D. Mason.

Salt Springville, Fort Plain P.O., Minden Twp.

Twp. formed 1798. Area settled by Germans from Schoharie c. 1720–50; post Rev. settlements from VT. Ft. Plain a military post 1776–83; later a canal port. Twp. developed with Erie Canal; diversified industry (mostly knit goods c. 1920).

NY 21: M, farmer, 73. B. here. — F. b. here, PGF b. here (German Palatine descent), PGM b. Co.; M., MGF, MGM all b. here (all Palatine Mohawk "Dutch"). — Ed.: till 16. — Universalist. — Slightly impatient, loud voice, still alert. — Fair articulation, moderate tempo.

22. Fulton County

Formed from Montgomery Co. 1838. Johnstown (Sir Wm. Johnson) laid out 1761; grew with canal and RR. 1st settled by Scots and Irish; Dutch and Palatines in S. part of Co. Leather goods center. Pop. 1840: 18,049, 1850: 20,171, 1880: 30,985, 1910: 44,534, 1930: 46,560, 1960: 51,304.

Beers, F. W., ed. 1878. *History of Montgomery and Fulton Counties.* . . . NY: F. W. Beers.

Cook, Alice B., comp. 1940. *Historical Sketch of Fulton County.* Johnstown: Board of Supervisors of Fulton County.

Frothingham, Washington. 1892. *History of Fulton County.* Syracuse: D. Mason and Co.

South Mayfield, Gloversville P.O., Mayfield Twp.

Gloversville had glovemaking from 1760; Perthshire glovers brought over by Sir William Johnson. Settlers Scottish, some from PA, New Englanders, some Dutch. Twp. formed 1793; industries: lime, timber, gloves.

NY 22: M, farmer, 51. B. here. — F., PGF b. Twp., PGF's F., PGF's PGF both b. Braunschweig, Germany, PGM b. Twp., PGM's F. a Dutchman, PGM's M. a Vermonter; M., MGF b. Saratoga Co., MGM b. MI, MGM's F. b. Mohawk Valley. —

Ed.: till 15. — Methodist. — Conservative, hearty. — Vigorous articulation.

23. Saratoga County

Formed from Albany 1791. 1713–44 "Old Saratoga" (Schuylers); wiped out by French and Indians in 1745. Saratoga patent 1684; reduced and renegotiated 1768. 1st temperance organization here. Appalachian foothills. Industries include resorts, racing; worsted, wool, knit goods. Pop. 1800: 24,483, 1820: 36,052, 1850: 45,646, 1880: 55,156, 1910: 61,917, 1930: 63,314, 1960: 89,096.

Allen, C.C., comp. 1912. *Schuylerville, New York, the "Historical Village"*. Schuylerville: Historical Week Committee.

Anderson, George Baker, comp. 1899. *Our County and Its People*. . . . Boston: Boston History Co.

Brandow, John Henry. 1919. *The Story of Old Saratoga*. . . . 2nd ed. Albany: Brandow Print.

Shorey, Mabel Pitkin. 1959. *The Early History of Corinth*. Corinth.

Sylvester, Nathaniel Bartlett. 1878. . . . .*History of Saratoga County*. Philadelphia: Everts and Ensign.

Vanderwerker, J. B. 1938. *Early Days in Eastern Saratoga County*. Schuylerville.

Vanderwerker, J. B. 1938. *Early Days in the Vicinity of Northumberland and Bacon Hill*. Schuylerville.

Corinth, Corinth Twp.

Formed 1818 from Hadley. 1st settlements on Hudson, N. of Twp., before Rev. New Englanders among first settlers. Water power led to misc. industries, including paper mills. Pop. 1820: 1,490, 1850: 1,501, 1880: 1,737, 1910: 3,102, 1930: 2,613, 1960: 3,193.

NY 23A: M, ran a store, worked in paper mill, 84. B. here, lived 2 yrs. Troy. — F., PGF (perhaps), PGM, M. b. Corinth. — Ed.: common school. — Methodist; Good Templars. — Fine old gentleman; somewhat crippled with rheumatism, mind a little shaky. Although initially suspicious, later very cooperative. Many items may be unreliable: responses suggested by FW or daughter received unusually vigorous assent. — A number of old-fashioned pronunciations: [ˈfæsɪt], [təˈmætə]. Stresses usually strong, strong pharyngealization, nasality. Voice medium in pitch, but often cracked to a falsetto, esp. under stress.

Bacon Hill, Schuylerville, Northumberland Twp.

Twp. formed 1798 from Saratoga. On Hudson. 1st settlement 1765 near Bacon Hill. Bacon Hill (formerly Fiddletown and Pope's Corners) named for Ebenezer Bacon (from CT), tavern keeper here in 1794. Schuylerville originally settled in 1689 as Saratoga; destroyed by Indians in 1745; inc. 1831 and named after Gen. Philip Schuyler (Schuyler's flax mill 1767). Has abandoned cotton mills, small industries. Pop. Schuylerville 1880: 1,617, 1910: 1,614, 1930: 1,411, 1960: 1,361.

NY 23B: M, farmer, formerly 25 yrs. in paper box factory, 74. B. Brownville, same twp. Lived 1 yr. in Hackensack; 6 mos. NYC. — F. b. Brownville, PGF's F. b. Scotland, PGF's M. of local family, PGM from Bullston in Co.; M., MGF b. Bennington, MGF's F. a Dutchman captured from Burgoyne, MGM from Bennington, English descent. — Ed.: local twp. schools, 1 yr. h.s. in Schuylerville. — Methodist; Mason. — Plainspoken, unaffected; knows farming and rural life intimately. — Free, rapid speech, not always distinct. Little variation in pitch; stresses moderate. Stressed vowels moderately long (about twice as long as most). Moderate nasality. Final consonants often weakly articulated. Not very familiar with other dialects, but recognizes some words as "southern". A few aux. responses from wife, also of community, slightly better ed. with some notions of "correctness". Also very cooperative.

NY 23C: Schuylerville, Saratoga Twp. — M, banker and accountant, 75. B. locally (Victory Mills). Lived 2 yrs. Boston, 8 yrs. N. Andover, MA. — F. local, Dutch descent, PGF b. Pittstown, PGF's M. b. West Sand Lake, PGM b. Nynich Kill, near Troy; M. local, Dutch descent, MGF b. West Sand Lake. Family history available from Dutch Settlers' Society of Albany. — Ed.: h.s. graduate. — Dutch Reformed (by background, but not formal member); village and Twp. historian, 2 terms justice of the peace, member town board. — Very cooperative; talked very freely. Steeped in local history. — Weak articulation of final consonants (esp. lenis ones). Stressed vowels moderately long. Nasality. Tempo moderate to fast. Some notions of propriety: almost never used *ain't* of double neg., but regularly used *it don't*. Fairly high-pitched voice. Slurred utterance.

24. Washington County

Formerly Charlotte Co., renamed 1784. Orig. part of Albany Co. First settlement at Ft. Edward; first settlers chiefly from New Eng., some Scotch-Irish, etc. Textiles, paper mills. Pop. 1790: 14,033, 1820: 38,831, 1850: 44,750, 1880: 47,871, 1910: 47,778, 1930: 46,482, 1960: 48,476.

Bascom, Robert O. 1903. *The Fort Edward Book*. . . . Ft. Edward: J. D. Keating.

Brayton, Isabella, comp. 1929. *The Story of Hartford*. . . . Glens Falls: Bullard Press.

Brislin, Anne E. 1962. *Narratives of Old Fort Edward*. Fort Edward: Bd. of Ed., Fort Edward Public Schools.

Corey, Allen. 1850. *Gazetteer of the County of Washington*. . . . Schuylerville.

Gibson, James. 1937. *History of Washington County, New York*. Fort Edward: Honeywood Press.

Hill, William H., comp. 1932. *History of Washington County*. Fort Edward: Honeywood Press.

Johnson, Crisfield. 1878. *History of Washington County*. Philadelphia: Everts and Ensign.

Lamb, Wallace E. 1940. *The Lake Champlain and Lake George Valleys*. 3 vols. NY: American Historical Co.

Miller, Samuel D. 1896. *History of Hartford*. Fort Edward: Keating.

Stone, William L. 1901. *Washington County: Its History to the Close of the Nineteenth Century*. NY: New York History Co.

Van de Water, Frederic F. 1946. *Lake Champlain and Lake George*. Indianapolis: Bobbs-Merrill Co. Repr. 1969 (Port Washington: I. J. Friedman).

1866. *New Topographical Atlas of Washington County, New York*. Philadelphia: Stone and Stewart.

North Hartford, Hartford P.O. and Twp.

Twp. formed from Westfield Twp. 1793. Grants in 1764; prob. no settlement till a decade later. 1st settled from CT. "Provincial patent" to officers of NY infantry. Grew up as trading center. Baptist meeting house in 1789. Early distilleries. Industry declined 1850–1900; shift to dairying, potatoes. Twp. pop. c. 1842: 2,158.

NY 24A: M, farmer, 74. B. locally (West Hartford). — F. b. W. Hartford, PGF b. Cambridge in Co., PGF's F. and M. b. Stonington, Westerly area (RI, now CT), PGM b. W. Hartford, PGM's F. b. Stonington, PGM's M. b. perhaps W. Hartford.; M. b. Hartford, MGF b. MA, MGM b. prob. Hartford. — Ed.: till 20 (winters when could). — Baptist. — Somewhat quavering voice; some prolongation.

Fort Edward, Fort Edward Twp.

1st settlers 1762: Nathaniel Gage; Scots, English, (possibly a few Germans) from CT. Twp. taken from Argyle Twp. 1818. Champlain Canal 1822: Ft. Edward to Lake Champlain. Village inc. 1849. Paper manufacturing, various industries. Pop. 1820: 1,631, 1850: 2,328, 1880: 4,680, 1910: 5,740, 1930: 3,850, 1960: 3,737.

NY 24B!: F, unmarried homemaker, 61. B. here. — F. b. Argyle in Co., PGF b. N. Ireland, PGM b. Argyle; M., MGF b. Ft. Edward, MGF's F. and M. both b. England, MGM b. Co., MGM's F. a Quaker. — Ed.: public schools, institute here 3 yrs. — Episcopalian. — Cultivated.

25. Warren County

Formed 1813 from Washington Co. Queensburg Patent 1762; settlement 1763. Border country in colonial/Indian wars. Settlement slow; difficult access; settled from VT and downstate. Farming largely subsistence. Misc. industry, including lumbering, cement, lime, graphite, garnets, tourism; Glens Falls an insurance center. Pop. 1820: 9,453, 1850: 17,199, 1880: 25,178, 1910: 32,223, 1930: 34,174, 1960: 44,002.

Brown, William Howard, ed. 1963. *History of Warren County*. Board of Supervisors of Warren Co.
Federal Writers Project. 1942. *Warren County: A History and Guide*. Glens Falls: Warren Co. Board of Supervisors.
Mason, Howard C. 1963. *Backward Glances*. 3 vols. Glens Falls: Mimeoprint Services.
O'Brien, Kathryn E. 1978. *The Great and Gracious on Millionaires' Row*. Sylvan Beach: North County Books.
Smith, H. P., ed. 1885. *History of Warren County*. Syracuse: D. Mason.

Weverton, Johnsburg Twp.

Weverton a backwoods settlement; pop. 225 c. 1930. Johnsburg in NW corner of Co. Largest twp. in Co.; formed from Thurman Twp. in 1805. John Thurman arrived 1790, soon after Rev.; 1st settlers include English, Scots, Irish, New Englanders. Older industries lumbering, tanning, whiskey, garnet. Resort country.

NY 25A: M, retired farmer, also worked as logger, rafter, team-driver, garnet miner, 75. B. Johnsburg. — F., PGF b.

Johnsburg, PGF's F. and M. both b. Wales, PGM b. Washington Co., of Welsh descent; M. b. Sweetsburg (Broome Co., Quebec). — Ed.: 8th grade, Johnsburg. — Methodist; Mason (past grand master), Odd Fellows, Maccabees. — Amateur genealogist, folk historian; a wealth of anecdotes and proverbs. Knows area well. Cooperative, friendly, unpretentious, independent. Simply but deeply religious. — Much nasality; moderately strong stresses. Pitch med. to low, rising on stress. Some simplification of consonant clusters. Stressed vowels moderately long. [ɛʊ] diph. common.

Warrensburg Twp.

Formed 1813 from Thurman. First settlers in area c. 1786. Lumbering 1810–20. Industries: textiles (wool), gloves, shirts, wood pulp and paper, tourism, water power. Warrensburg Village "queen village of the Adirondacks". Early farms generally small. Twp. Pop. 1842: 1,469.

NY 25B: M, caretaker (formerly school janitor, shirt cutter, paper mill worker, mail carrier), 68. B. neighborhood, lived 67 yrs. Stony Creek (same Co.). — F. b. neighborhood, PGM b. Co. — Ed.: about 8th grade, Stony Creek. — Methodist; Odd Fellows. — Cooperative and intelligent, understood purpose of interview. Some notions of "correctness" despite use of folk grammatical forms. Aux. forms offered by wife (more likely to offer "correct" forms). — Clear and natural articulation; tempo and stresses moderate. Some nasality, though less than normal for area. Fairly careful articualtion of final consonants; stressed vowels moderately long.

26. Hamilton County

First settler Wells c. 1790; others from Long I. Some Indians; Fr. Canadians more recently. 1st town 1805. Co. est. provisionally 1816; permanently 1836 from Montgomery Co. Isolated; small permanent population. Industries include farming, lumbering, mining (now played out), tanning (1870–1900), maple sugar. Pop. 1820: 1,251, 1850: 2,188, 1880: 3,923, 1910: 4,373, 1930: 3,929, 1960: 4,267.

Aber, Ted, and Stella King. 1965. *The History of Hamilton County*. Lake Pleasant: Great Wilderness Books.
Aber, Ted, and Stella King. 1961. *Tales from an Adirondack County*. Prospect: Prospect Books.
Donaldson, Alfred Lee. 1921. *A History of the Adirondacks*. 2 vols. NY: Century Co. Repr. 1963 (Port Washington: I. J. Friedman).
Hochschild, Harold K. 1952. *Township 34: A History. . . of an Adirondack Township in Hamilton Co. . . . . NY.*

Lake Pleasant, Lake Pleasant Twp.

1st settler 1795 from Columbia Co.; others from Mohawk Valley, RI, CT. Twp. formed 1812. Summer people: hotels first, then summer homes; summer camps for children.

NY 26A: M, carpenter, farmer, lumberman, handyman, 82. B. 2 mi. away at Fish Mt. House, lived 2–3 yrs. NYC aged 20–22. — F. b. Scotland; M. b. Piseco (adjacent twp.), MGF b. NY, MGM b. Lake Pleasant. — Ed.: no formal schooling. — Methodist. — Suspicious and uncooperative initially; deaf and somewhat slow-witted. No linguistic taboos; unconstrained use of folk forms. Aux. forms offered by daughter. — Slow to respond. Strong stresses; slow tempo. Utterances slurred and muffled. Nasality present.

Speculator, Lake Pleasant Twp.

See above for Twp. Speculator inc. 1925. A summer and winter resort; training camp for fighters. Pop. 1930: 261.

NY 26B: F, widowed homemaker, 77. B. Wells, W. Hill (nearby), spent some winters in Hudson and NYC. — F. b. Wells, of German stock, PGF spoke no English until 11 yrs. old, PGM b. US, prob. near Palatine Bridge; M., MGF, MGM b. Schoharie Co. (MGF of Holland Dutch descent). — Ed.: Wells common school. — Methodist; Ladies Aid. — Very cooperative and intelligent. Many folk-grammatical forms; willingly volunteered old-fashioned forms. Well-to-do and sure of status in community. — Moderate tempo, occasionally somewhat fast. Fairly strong stresses; low pitch, seldom spoke loudly. Some nasality.

NY 26C: M, hotel keeper, 54. B. Broadalbin, Fulton Co. Moved here age 5. In US Marines WWI. — No family history obtained. — Ed.: h.s. — Cooperative within limits of knowledge. Enjoyed interview, likes people, fairly talkative. Not too sure of recollections of old times. — Fairly fast speech; little nasality. [ɔ] and [o] fall together before [r].

27. Essex County

Formed 1799 from Clinton Co. 2nd largest in state; mountainous, 5 ranges. Ticonderoga "most important military position in N. NY". 1st colonization by French — faded away. Also settled from N. England. Little pop. variation since 1880. Industries: tourism and summer homes, iron, lumber, graphite mines (till 1921). Pop. 1800: 8,514, 1810: 9,472, 1820: 12,811, 1850: 31,148, 1880: 35,515, 1910: 33,458, 1930: 33,959, 1960: 35,300.

Bascom, Frederick G., ed. 1946. *Letters of a Ticonderoga Farmer.* Ithaca: Cornell University Press.

Cook, Flavius J. 1858. *Home Sketches of Essex County.* Keeseville: W. Lansing.

Cook, Joseph. 1909. *An Historical Address. . . the First Centennial Anniversary of the Settlement of Ticonderoga.* Ticonderoga: Ticonderoga Historical Society.

Gilchrist, Helen Ives. 1924. *Fort Ticonderoga in History.* Fort Ticonderoga: Fort Ticonderoga Museum.

Johnson, Ellen (Adkins). 1956. *Streetroad: Its History and Its People.* Ithaca: Linguistica.

Smith, H. P., ed. 1885. *History of Essex County. . . .* Syracuse: D. Mason.

Stoddard, Seneca Ray. 1873. *Ticonderoga Past and Present.* Albany: Weed, Parsons and Co.

Watson, Winslow C. 1869. *The Military and Civil History of the County of Essex.* Albany: J. Munsell.

Ticonderoga

Fort originally erected here by French in 1750 ("Ft. Carillon"). 1st grants 1764; abandoned in Rev. Post-Rev. settlers from CT, MA, VT (possibly also some Germans). Stock raising, boat building. Industries: timber 1780–1840, iron (deposits worked off and on), agriculture, pulp and paper, pencils (local graphite); tourists since c. 1830. Twp. formed from Crown Point Twp. 1804; village inc. 1889. Museum of

NY State Historical Assn. Pop. 1820: 1,493, 1850: 2,669, 1880: 3,304, 1910: 4,940 (town), 1930: 3,680, 1960: 5,617 (town).

NY 27A: M, log-cutter, RR worker, worked as fireman in pulp mill, farmed when younger, 74. B. Crown Point; 35 yrs. here. — F. b. Crown Point, PGF buried Crown Point, was in battle of Plattsburg; M., prob MGM b. Crown Point. — Ed.: Crown Point till about 3rd grade. — Methodist; Odd Fellow. — Enjoyed talking about old times, emphasizing boyhood poverty and hardships. No attempt to conceal folk-grammatical forms. Some taboo reactions (see 33#4, 65#7). Folk forms not reliable when asked, but appeared in free speech. — Stresses fairly strong, tempo med. to slow. Much nasality. — Aux. forms from wife, about same age, b. neighborhood, quicker and slightly better read. Fewer folk-grammatical forms.

NY 27B: Hague Road, Ticonderoga P.O. and Twp. — F, widow, keeps rooming house, 10 yrs. nursing, 82. B. Ticonderoga; spent 2 winters in CA, lived 1 yr. Hague after married. — F. b. Franklin, VT, came to NY when young, PGF "from West"; M. b. Hague, MGF, MGM both from Hague section ("New Hague"). — Ed.: Ticonderoga, through "Academy". — Methodist, church societies. — Quick, nervous little woman; hard-working. Hesitant about her knowledge, though generally satisfactory. Activities generally confined to household, family, intimate friends. Some suggestion necessary, but confirmation and rejection prompt. — Stresses fairly strong. Husky quality to voice, moderately low register rising sharply on stresses.

NY 27C: North Ticonderoga, Ticonderoga. — M, farmer, 72. B. same farm (family there 105 yrs.). — F., PGF, PGF's F., PGF's M. all b. locally, PGM from Schroon, W. part of Co.; M., MGF both b. on next road, MGM b. locally (RI stock: coopers). — Ed.: Ticonderoga grade school. — Congregationalist; Honorary Mohawk Grange (master 10 yrs.); director community building, Dairyman's League, Masons. — Very cooperative and intelligent, quick mind. Old family in area; interested in old times, esp. American Indian culture. Grammatical forms mixed: inf. says he sometimes talks like his grandfather (no education) and sometimes like his grandmother (a schoolteacher). — Fairly fast speech; slightly slurred articulation. Little intonation range. Moderately strong stresses.

28. Clinton County

Formed 1788 from Washington Co. 1st permanent settlement 1783. Some settlers from VT. Industries: water power, iron ore, timber.

Averill, H. K., Jr. 1885. *A New Geography and History of Clinton County, New York.* 2nd ed., rev. and enlarged. Plattsburgh: Telegram Printing House.

Hurd, Duane Hamilton. 1880. *History of Clinton and Franklin Counties.* Philadelphia: J. W. Lewis.

Palmer, Peter Sailly. 1877. *History of Plattsburgh. . .to Jan. 1, 1876.* Plattsburgh.

Porter, M. 1944. *Old Plattsburgh.* Plattsburgh.

Porter, Marjorie Lansing. 1964. *Plattsburgh, 1785 — 1815 — 1902.* G. Little Press.

1898. *Old Chazy: Reminiscences of Old Chazy Given by Descendants of the Early Settlers.* Plattsburgh: Clinton County Farmer.

Plattsburg

Twp. organized 1785. Founded late 1700s by Platt Brothers from Poughkeepsie; 1st settlement c. 1783. Near naval battles of 1776 and 1814. Pop. half French-Canadian; also settlers from Long I., NH, and VT. US Military Reservation; 1916 volunteer training camp. Industries: water power, wood pulp, paper products. 2nd largest city on Lake Champlain. Pop. (City) 1790: 458, 1820: 3,519, 1850: 5,618, 1880: 8,283, 1910: 11,138, 1930: 13,349, 1960: 20,172.

NY 28A: F, housewife, 54. B. locally (Schuyler Falls Twp.). Since married has lived some in Bridgeport, CT; Springfield, MA; and Niagara Falls; back to vicinity when 28. — F. b. Schuyler Falls Twp., PGF, PGM b. Canada (prob. Quebec); M. b. Schuyler Falls Twp., MGF b. perhaps in VT, MGM b. Schuyler Falls. — Ed.: Saranac Twp till 8th grade (approx.). — Methodist. — Very cooperative and friendly. Likes to talk about old times; devoted to memory of mother who was a ballad singer; knows many more old forms than she uses. — Definite drawl. Nasality. Strong stresses; stressed vowels usually long. A few affectations ([aɪ̌ðə], [təˈmatəz]) prob. from her yr. or so in MA.

Chazy

Formed from Champlain Twp. 1804. 1st settler Jean Fromboise (only Frenchman to stay); started apple growing in N. country. Settlers from VT, MA, CT. Farming; famous for black marble. Pop. 1930: 500.

NY 28B: F, widowed homemaker, former school teacher, 87. B. Chazy Landing. A few winters in Providence, a few in FL; 1 yr. in Plattsburg while husband in business. — F., PGF b. Alburg, VT, PGM from Isle la Motte, VT, PGM's F. b. in Scotland and came to settle in Alburg, VT; M., MGF b. Chazy, MGF's F. and M. from CT, MGM b. Chazy. — Dignified, self-assured, hard-working. Mind still good. Knows both village and rural life; intimately associated with history of community. Excellent rapport with FW. Very few forced responses. Both folk and standard forms; some taboos (on "bastard" item and profanities). — Tempo moderate; stressed vowels generally about 50% longer than unstressed; stresses moderately strong. Nasality moderate. Little simplification of clusters. False teeth. No drawl; voice barely shows "cracking" of old age.

Champlain

Organized 1788. Settled late 1790s by French Canadians. Bookbinding machines, peonies.

NY 28C: F, widowed homemaker, 85. B. Mooers Twp. (next twp. W.); spent a while in Rouses Pt. (5 mi. E.). — Information on family history, ed., social contacts not obtained. — A good middle group inf.; impossible to complete interview due to real or imagined business. — Moderate tempo. Nasality. Velar fricative usual.

29. Franklin County

Formed 1808 from Clinton Co. First white settlement late 18th cent.; settlers from VT and Clinton Co., also Essex Co. Severe winters; called "Siberia of New York". Said to be the "least valuable Co. in the state". Pop. growth slow since 1860. Dairying, potatoes, hay, vegetables, oats, livestock. 1890 illegal Chinese immigration. Pop. 1810: 2,717, 1820: 4,439, 1850: 25,102, 1880: 32,390, 1910: 45,717, 1930: 45,694, 1960: 44,742.

Hough, Franklin B. 1853. *A History of St. Lawrence and Franklin Counties.* . . . Albany: Little and Co.

Hurd, Duane Hamilton. 1880. *History of Clinton and Franklin Counties.* Philadelphia: J. W. Lewis.

Ives, H. L. 1915. *Reminiscences of the Adirondacks.* Potsdam: E. Fay.

Landon, Harry F. 1932. *The North Country.* . . . 3 vols. Indianapolis: Historical Pub. Co.

Seaver, Frederick J. 1918. *Historical Sketches of Franklin County.* . . . Albany: J. B. Lyon Co.

1952. *Sesqui-Centennial of Malone, 1802–1952.* Malone.

Brainardsville, Belmont Twp.

Twp. formed from Chateaugay in 1833. Relatively recent settlement (1820s). Rocky and wild. Brainardsville in NE of Co.; settled c. 1840. Mainly wilderness crossroads — denuded by lumbering.

NY 29A: M, farmer, 84. B. west of Watertown; part of childhood in Bangor, Moira (St. Lawrence Co.), rest of life in Malone (Franklin Co.). — F. b. Ireland (a Methodist minister, hence travels); M. b. St. Lawrence Co., MGF's F. was ship captain, MGM b. St. Lawrence Co. — Ed.: till 5th grade, took bookkeeping, in Bangor, Malone, Chateaugay. — Methodist, Grange; Farm Bureau. — Talkative; becoming somewhat senile; tired toward end of interview. Old-fashioned, somewhat eccentric: doesn't believe in education and tries to discourage young people from it. Close-fisted but hospitable and charitable. No religious, racial prejudices. — Moderate tempo; strong stresses. Slurred utterance. Strong nasality. Some weak final consonants.

Malone

Formed from Chateaugay 1805 as Harison; became Malone in 1812. Settlers from New Eng., esp. VT; French Canadians recently. Much barren land; early developed "service industries": sawmill, distillery, etc. RR in 1851. Other industries: textiles, hydroelectric power, shirts, brooms, metals, milk and cheese. Pop. 60% French-Canadian (bilingual). Pop. (Town) 1820: 1,130, 1850: 4,550, 1880: 7,909, 1910: 10,154, 1930: 8,657, 1960: 11,997.

NY 29B: M, hostler (in roundhouse) for 48 yrs. with NYC RR, 67. B. here. — F., PGF, PGM all b. Ormstown, Quebec, Canada (between Malone and Montreal); M., MGF, MGM b. Malone. — Ed.: till 5th grade in Malone. — Catholic, Holy Name Society; Brotherhood of Locomotive Enginemen. — Slow, patient, hospitable, hard-working. Prompted a good deal by son (inf. bedridden 20 yrs. with arthritis), whose independent responses are starred. Mostly town-bred, except for acquaintance with RR. — Tempo moderate to fast; moderate stresses. Traces of French, both in vocab. and pronun. (family is bilingual, inf.'s wife speaks better French than English), esp. in occasional [ʈ] for [θ]. Much nasality. Weak final consonants.

NY 29C: M, 23 yrs. wholesale grocer, now local magistrate, 70. B. 6 mi. E. of Chateaugay; moved to Chateaugay when 15–16; c. 20 yrs. old worked in P.O. in Plattsburg, 1 season with Ringling Bros. as minstrel, 1 yr. with Armour in Boston and Portland; 2 yrs. in Colorado; 23 yrs. as grocer in Malone. — F. b. Cherubusco, E. of Chateaugay, PGF b. VT, first settler in community, PGM b. VT; M., perhaps MGF b. Malone. — Ed.: Chateaugay HS. — Elks; attends, but not member of Congregational Church. — Cooperative, genial, hospitable. Fair-minded, practical (good Yankee type). Many fine anecdotes. Good mind. — Tempo moderate. Slight drawl. Some nasality. Fairly deep voice. Wide intonation range. Utterances generally clear.

30. St. Lawrence County

Formed 1802 from Clinton Co. Industry along St. Lawrence (growth with Seaway project). 1626 Jesuits at La Galette (near Ogdensburg); fort in area by 1749; capture by English 1760. 10 twps. surveyed by 1787; Macomb purchase (1787–78). Settlers from VT, Albany. RRs 1850, 1857. Largest Co. in NY. General farming, dairying inland; mining (esp. iron). Large landholdings by NYC elite. Pop. 1810: 7,885, 1820: 16,037, 1850: 68,617, 1880: 85,997, 1910: 89,005, 1930: 90,960, 1960: 111,239.

> Blankman, E. 1898. *Geography of St. Lawrence County.* Canton: Plaindealer Presses
> Curtis, Gates, comp. 1894. *Our County and Its People.* Syracuse: D. Mason.
> Durant, Samuel W. 1878. *History of St. Lawrence County. . . . Philadelphia: L. H. Everts.
> Hough, Franklin B. 1853. *A History of St. Lawrence and Franklin Counties. . . .* Albany: Little and Co.
> Sanford, Carlton E. 1903. *Early History of the Town of Hopkinton. . . .* Boston: Bartlett Press.
> Webster, Clarence J. 1945. *St. Lawrence County: Past and Present.* Watertown.
> 1946–1959. *North Country Life.* Ogdensburg: G. G. Cole.

East Hill, South Colton, Colton Twp.

Formed from Parishville 1843 (previously Hopkinton). First settlement 1824; 19th cent. industries: starch factory, lumber, water power. Still sparsely settled in 1893; lumbering, dairying (cheese and butter). South Colton 5 mi. "above" Colton; 1st sawmill there 1837.

NY 30A: M, farmer, some lumbering, 82. B. Macomb, moved age 9 to Long Bow, edge of Parishville Twp. — F. b. Genesee Co.; M. b. Macomb. — Ed.: local schools, 5th reader. — Baptist, Grange. — Convivial, vigorous for his age. Enjoyed interviews; excellent rapport with FW. No pretentions. — Tempo moderate; very strong nasality. Deep voice, slurring. Not much intonation range; voice tends to crack under excitement.

Fort Jackson, Hopkinton Twp.

Twp. formed 1805; named for Roswell Hopkins, 1st settler c. 1802. British raid 1814. Settlers largely from VT, also MA, CT. Still much wilderness in 1893. Industries: tanneries,

sawmills, gristmills, distillery, carding mill. Ft. Jackson formed 1824 around sawmill, woolen mill briefly.

NY 30B: M, mason, tax collector, 87. B. here; lived 1 yr. Providence. — F. b. Highgate, VT, lived IL, PGF, PGM b. Vergennes, VT, moved to Highgate; M. b. Lawrence Twp, MGF, MGM b. Essex Co. — Ed.: in village, district school (no h.s.). — Universalist (F. and M. Baptist); once belonged to Odd Fellows. — Vigorous, both physically and mentally; independent. Does occasional chores for neighbors, works when he pleases. Congenial, kind-hearted. Well-rooted locally, knows community. — Many old-fashioned pronunciations (e.g., [grɪnstən]). Voice in low register. Nasality; moderate tempo; fairly strong stresses. "Irish intonation"; same speech-tunes FW has noted among Irish of Charleston's Beaver Island.

NY 30C: Hopkinton. — M, retired farmer, has been carpenter, 85. B. here. — F. b. Canada, across Vergennes, VT, line, PGF b. Canada; M. b. Bangor, NY, MGF, MGM prob. Canadian. — Ed.: common schools. — Methodist. — Cooperative, but tended to tire. Well rooted in community. — Moderate tempo, moderately strong stresses. Nasality. Somewhat rasping voice with weakening of final stops and some slurring. Vowels seldom prolonged.

NY 30D: Ft. Jackson, Hopkinton Twp. — M, creamery in VT 9 yrs., farmed 45–46 yrs., 77. B. locally. — F. from W. Berkshire, VT, near Canadian line; M. b. S. Franklin Co. — Ed.: local schools, 8th grade. — Methodist; Odd Fellows, Grange, Maccabees. — Good, old-fashioned type. Good sense of humor, quick mind, but tended to tire. Locally rooted; unpretentious, easy-going. Didn't fully understand interview purpose, but cooperative within those limits. — Tempo moderate, strong nasality, slight drawl. Some weakening of final consonants. Stressed vowels moderately long.

NY 30E: Hopkinton. — F, housewife, 75. B. Twp. Lived 2 yrs. CT, 1 yr. Malone, 2 winters in FL. — Sister of inf. NY 30C. — Ed.: district school, village; h.s. in Winthrop. — Congregationalist; formerly Eastern Star member. — Excellent interview: pleasant and successful. Proceeded rapidly, with much humor and teasing between inf. and husband. Aware of past tradition, strong local roots. Fewer folk forms than brother. — Both show mod. strong stress, nasality. Husband has some "Yankee drawl", more folk forms, much [ɛʊ] in all environments.

31. Jefferson County

Formed from Oneida 1805. Rapid settlement after Rev. Extinction of Indian claims 1784; 1st surveys 1789; Macomb purchase 1791. First settlement 1797–78. RRs 1850s–1870s. 1st still 1804; 1st brewery 1807. Potash first industry: gone by 1860. Other industries: dairying (cheese), paper and pulp, water power, agriculture, grazing. Pop. 1810: 15,140, 1820: 32,952, 1850: 68,153, 1880: 66,103, 1910: 80,382, 1930: 83,574, 1960: 87,835.

> Child, Hamilton, comp. 1866. *Gazetteer and Business Directory, of Jefferson County, for 1866–7.* Watertown: Hamilton Child.

Clarke, T. W. 1941. *Emigres in the Wilderness*. NY: Macmillan.

Coughlin, J., comp. 1905. *Jefferson County Centennial 1905*. Watertown: Hungerford-Holbrook.

Durant, Samuel W., and Henry B. Pierce. 1878. . . .*History of Jefferson County*. Philadelphia: L. H. Everts.

Emerson, Edgar C. 1898. *Our County and Its People*. Boston: Boston History Co.

Gould, Ernest C., comp. 1955. *Jefferson County Sesquicentennial Program and Historical Almanac: 1805–1855*. Carthage: Carthage Republican Tribune Press.

Haddock, John A., comp. 1895. *The Growth of a Century. . . Jefferson County, from 1793 to 1894*. Albany: Weed-Parsons.

Horton, William H., ed. 1890. . . .*Geographical Gazetteer of Jefferson County: 1684–1890*. Syracuse: Hamilton Child.

Hough, Franklin B. 1854. *A History of Jefferson County*. . . . Albany: J. Munsell.

Landon, Harry F. 1932. *The North Country*. . . . 3 vols. Indianapolis: Historical Publishing Co.

Oakes, R. A., comp. 1905. *Genealogical and Family History of the county of Jefferson*. . . . 2 vols. NY: Lewis Pub. Co.

Stone Mills, Watertown P.O., Orleans Twp.

Twp. formed 1821 from Brownville. German settlers 1828–30. Lime kilns at one time. Stone Mills settled 1806–7, in part by French emigres. In SW corner of Twp.; rolling terrain. Watertown settled 1800 by New Englanders; paper mills started 1809; some other light industry.

NY 31A: M, retired storekeeper, former telegrapher, 94. B. locally, pretty good deal of traveling in US, a month in Europe. — F. b. Orange Co., NY, left at age 6 (a mechanic), PGF Scottish; M. b. Mohawk Valley, Herkimer Co. (schoolteacher), MGF (German), MGM both b. Herkimer Co. — Ed.: Adams Collegiate Institute (Adams, Jefferson Co.); some reading; has studied Esperanto. — Methodist; Foresters one winter; has been postmaster. — Excellent inf., few signs of aging (hearing good). Collector of anecdotes; cooperated gladly when told interview would help preserve local lore. Reliable; uses folk and standard forms interchangeably (occ. notes he used certain forms as a child). Talked freely. — Articulation clear; strong stresses (and opinions).

Theresa

Formed in 1841 from Alexandria Twp.; area settled by New Englanders in 1817. Village inc. 1871. Early settlers from CT, VT, W. MA, Herkimer Co., Quebec, Germany, England; a number of Mormon settlers in the 1830s. Light industries: gristmill, sawmill, carding mill, foundry, water power. Good farming; cheese and butter.

NY 31B: M, retired farmer, newspaper correspondent (Twp. historian), ran cooperative store, 76. B. West Theresa, lived a little in Philadelphia when with publishing house. — F., PGF b. here, PGF's F. b. near Cooperstown, PGM b. here (1st white child in Twp.), PGM's F. and M. from Deerfield, MA; M. b. here, MGF b. near Plymouth, VT, came here age 2 (built 1st church in Watertown, 1st bridge over Black River), MGM b. near Sackets Harbor in Co. — Ed.: local district school. — Methodist; Mason, Rotary, Grange a long while, 9 yrs. patron

of Eastern Star. — Hospitable, talked freely. Strong local roots; little experience outside area. Many folk forms in speech, but *ain't* only interrogative; no double neg. — Talked a bit out of right-hand corner of mouth, but no discernible effect on articulation. Fast speech, staccato.

32. Lewis County

Part of Macomb Purchase (1791); formed from Oneida 1805. 1st settlers 1794 from MA and CT; also some Mennonites and Amish. 1st road 1798; state roads 1803. Black River Canal 1855. Industries: hay, dairying, cheese, Christmas trees, maple sugar and syrup. Pop. 1810: 6,433, 1820: 9,227, 1850: 24,564, 1880: 31,416, 1910: 24,849, 1930: 23,747, 1960: 23,249.

Beers, D. G. 1875. *Atlas of Lewis County, New York*. Philadelphia: Pomeroy, Whitman and Co.

Bender, Arletha Zehr. 1964. *A History of the Mennonites in Lewis County*.

Bowen, G. Byron, ed. 1970. *History of Lewis County, 1880–1965*. Lowville: Board of Legislators of Lewis Co.

Drew, Hazel C. 1961. *Tales from Little Lewis*. Lyons Falls: History.

Hough, Franklin B. 1883. *History of Lewis County*. . . . Syracuse: D. Mason.

Hough, Franklin Benjamin. 1872. *Lewis County*. Albany: Munsell.

Highmarket, Constableville P.O., Highmarket Twp.

Highest point in Co., much wilderness remains even in 1949. Irish influx c. 1842; in 1855 1/4 twp. natives of Ireland, also a few French and Germans. Constableville a small post village.

NY 32A: M, farmer, worked in veneer mill a couple of yrs. (in PA), freight house c. 6 mos. (Erie, PA), state forest ranger, 77. B. 12 mi. NE in Lyons Falls, came here as baby; with only the above exceptions, has lived in immediate neighborhood ever since. — F. Irish; M. Irish (Co. Mayo), came with her parents through Philadelphia before settling in Co. by 1860. — Ed.: local schools till c. 8th grade. — Catholic, Knights of Columbus, Holy Name Society; Grange, has been Twp. supervisor. — Soft-spoken, yet subdued sense of humor. Interview conducted under adverse circumstances (snowstorm); pp. 32-104, 1-7 done in one sitting as inf. unavailable for 3rd sitting even if roads cleared. — Usually a drawl, but some words (e.g., *January, February*) noticeably clipped. Lacks the usual nasality of upstate NY. — A few aux. forms from a neighbor, a farmer, native to the area, age 40.

New Bremen, Lowville P.O., New Bremen Twp.

Twp. formed 1848; over half of pop. Europeans at this time. By 1947, a cheese factory, tanneries gone, goldmining unsuccessful; in 1966 red granite for cement blocks. Lowville a "characteristic North Country village". Home of Dr. Franklin B. Hough, "father of American forestry". Pop. Twp. 1848: 1345, 1880: 2414, 1960: 1963.

NY 32B: M, farmer, 71. B. 4 mi. S. — F. b. Twp., PGF, PGM from Alsace-Lorraine; M. b. Twp., MGF, MGM from Germany (Bavaria). — Ed.: common school, New Bremen. — Baptist, Grange, Elks, Twp. Supervisor. — Quick mind, good talker (fairly profane). Busy, but interested in local history and folklore. Unassuming, excellent rapport with FW. — Deep, resonant voice; comparatively little nasality.

33. Herkimer County

Formed 1791. Cheese district from 1795. Palatines at first; New Englanders after Rev. North a wilderness: now Adirondack Park. Pop. 1800: 14,479, 1820: 31,017, 1850: 38,244, 1880: 42,669, 1910: 56,356, 1930: 64,006, 1960: 66,370.

Beers, F. W., ed. 1879. . . .*History of Herkimer County.* . . . NY: F. W. Beers.

Benton, Nathaniel S. 1856. *A History of Herkimer County.* . . . Albany: J. Munsell.

Child, Hamilton. 1869. *Gazetteer and Business Directory of Herkimer County, New York, for 1869–70.* Syracuse: H. Child.

Grady, Joseph F. 1933. *The Adirondacks: Fulton Chain — Big Moose Region: The Story of a Wilderness.* Little Falls: Press of the Journal and Courier Co.

Hardin, George A., ed. 1893. *History of Herkimer County.* . . . Syracuse: D. Mason.

Thistlethwaite, W. 1915. *The Romance of Old Forge.* Utica: Utica Daily Express.

1904. *Souvenir of Ilion.* Ilion: Citizen Print.

1952. *Ilion, 1852–1952.* Ilion.

1954. *Herkimer County Commemorative Brochure.* Herkimer: Dept. of Archives and History.

Old Forge, Webb Twp.

Old Forge a foundry in early 19th cent. Revived with RR; summer visitors, sportsmen. Twp. formed 1918; resort area. Early settlement faded; permanent occupation came with NYC resort development.

NY 33A: M, policeman 14 yrs., bush pilot, guide, 52. B. here. — F. b. Canada. — Ed.: local schools. — Quick mind; talked freely and naturally. Knows local community intimately. Busy year-round. — Husky voice. Low nasality. Not much range in pitch. Moderate to fast tempo; little slurring.

NY 33B: M, skilled woodsman, construction worker, 50 "even". B. here. Lived 2 yrs. in NYC. — F. b. Port Leyden, PGF from France; M. b. Moose River, MGF, MGM b. Canada. — Ed.: 3 yrs. h.s. here. — Catholic, formerly Knights of Columbus. — Quick, good sense of humor. No inhibitions: many anecdotes. Talkative, well-liked, very proud of family. — Fast talk; stresses moderately strong. Little nasality or slurring. Final stops usually clear.

Big Moose, Webb Twp.

Big Moose bought 1793 by John Brown of Providence, RI; surveyed, laid out in twps. Abandoned 1819–92, until coming of RR. Camp, resort hotel.

NY 33C: M, resort owner, 57. B. here. Went to school in Utica. — F. b. Lewis Co.; M. b. Altmar, N. of Syracuse, MGF, MGM b. Sperryville in Lewis Co. — Ed.: h.s. — Presbyterian; Mason, Chm. Chamber of Commerce Planning Committee, Hotel Assn., Fire Dept. — Intelligent, cooperative, hospitable. Well-rooted in community: one of leading citizens. No

pretentions. — Fair proportion of folk verb forms; no *ain't*s or double negatives observed. Fairly fast speech, pleasant voice, nasality less than usual in comm. Not much slurring; final consonants generally clear.

34. Oswego County

Formed 1818 from Oneida. French outpost 1684. Large-scale trading post 1726. English fort 1727; captured and destroyed by French 1756; refortified by English 1758. British base in Revolution (off and on): not surrendered to US till 1796. 1789 beginning of permanent settlement; settlers from CT, also some French and Dutch. First twp. 1792. Canal branch from Syracuse 1829. Newspaper from 1850. Strawberries, onions. Pop. 1820: 12,374, 1850: 62,198, 1880: 77,911, 1910: 71,664, 1930: 69,645, 1960: 86,118.

Churchill, John C., et al., eds. 1895. *Landmarks of Oswego County.* Syracuse: D. Mason.

Clark, George T. 1896. *Oswego: An Historical Address.* . . . Oswego.

Faust, Ralph Milligan. 1934. *The Story of Oswego: With Notes about the Several Towns in the County.* Oswego: R. M. Faust.

Johnson, Crisfield. 1877. . . .*History of Oswego County.* Philadelphia: L. H. Everts.

Snyder, Charles M. 1968. *Oswego, From Buckskin to Bustles.* Port Washington: I. J. Friedman.

Snyder, Charles McCool. 1962. *Oswego County, New York, in the Civil War.* Oswego: Oswego County Historical Society.

Tyler, R. H. 1880. *Oswego County Fifty Years Ago.* Address. . . . August 21, 1879. Fulton: Morrill Bros.

Welch, Edgar Luderne. 1902. *Historical Souvenir of Pulaski and Vicinity.*

Fruit Valley, Oswego P.O. and Twp.

Oswego Twp. formed from Hannibal 1818. Fortified after 1722; old Ft. Ontario goes back to 1755. Settled in late 1790s. First propeller ship, Vandalia, built in 1841. Flour milling in 19th cent. Misc. light manufacturing; harbor; canal to Syracuse. Fruit Valley settled 1797.

NY 34A: M, retired farmer, 85. B. here. Lived 6 yrs. in city of Oswego. — F. b. here, PGF came from East as a child (MA or CT), PGM came as child from CT; M., MGF b. Twp. — Ed.: h.s., Oswego Normal 2 yrs. — Baptist; Grange, Historical Society. — FW was ill, thus limited number of cv. forms obtained. Inf. cooperative, hospitable, unassuming; a good plain Yankee type. Thoroughly versed in rural culture of comm. — Voice mid-register; mod. tempo; mod. strong stresses; no nasality.

Oswego

First settlers, village laid out 1797. Shipbuilding in early 19th cent. Misc. industries: Kingsford Starch (plant moved 1923), Kingsford foundry, shipping of salt, milling, paper, woolens. Consolidated school movement; Oswego Normal 1861. Pop. (city) 1820: 992, 1850: 2,445, 1880: 21,116, 1910: 23,368, 1930: 22,652, 1960: 22,155.

NY 34B: F, widow, seamstress, 65. B. here; lived a few yrs. in Auburn as a child. — F. b. Ireland, came to US as child; M. b.

Kingston, Ont. — Ed.: local schools. — Roman Catholic. — Slow of speech and reaction. Suspicious, broke off interview. Little knowledge of things outside the household. Speech a bit guarded.

Pulaski, Richland Twp.

Twp. formed 1807 from Williamstown (before organization of Co.). 1st settlers from Canada in 1801. Pulaski expanded 1804–16; settlers from New Eng. and Mohawk Valley. Alternate Co. seat. Waterpower, grist and sawmills. Pop. Pulaski 1880: 1,501, 1910: 1,788, 1930: 2,046, 1960: 2,256.

NY 34C: M, lawyer, 81. B. here; lived a few yrs. NYC. — F. b. N. NY, PGF b. Co., PGM daughter of a Tory; M. local, MGF b. Herkimer Co., MGM's family orig. from Lyme, NH. Inf.'s paternal lineage from England to Watertown, MA 1635 on record. — Ed.: public schools, Syracuse U. (didn't finish). Read law privately. — Methodist; Mason, formerly Sons of Veterans. — Oldest native citizen of village. Had been ill; a little slow. Interview not completely satisfactory: wife tried to answer all the questions, wouldn't withdraw. Many responses should probably be labelled SUG. Some good political anecdotes. — Pleasant voice, moderate tempo. Uses both folk and standard grammatical forms. Relatively little nasality.

NY 34D!: Oswego. — M, fur merchant, 81. B. here. Has travelled widely. — F. b. Wolcott Co., near Waterbury, came to Oswego as a child; M. b. Yorkshire, England, stonecutter family, came to Oswego as a child. — Ed.: local schools, 1st yr. h.s. Read a lot. — Never joined anything, "not even my church" (Congregationalist); Historical Society. — Cooperative, self-educated, cultivated. Hard-working. Very quick mind. Knew his limits: didn't pretend to know about rural life (city-bred). — A little finicky on notions of correctness (typical for self-educated). Very few folk forms. Pleasant voice, mod. tempo, fairly wide pitch range. — Cultivated.

35. Onondaga County

Co. formed from Herkimer Co. 1794; 1st settler c. 1786 from VT; others chiefly from New Eng. and NY to develop salt works. Land of military tract allotted 1791. First Germans c. 1808. Developed by Erie Canal. Industries and products: flour, iron and steel, salt products, chemicals, pottery, chinaware, wheat, tobacco, hay. Dairying in rural areas. Pop. 1800: 7,406, 1820: 41,467, 1850: 85,890, 1880: 117,893, 1910: 200,298, 1930: 291,606, 1960: 423,028.

Baker, Anne Kathleen. 1941. *A History of Old Syracuse, 1654–1899*. Fayetteville: Manlius.

Bannan, Theresa. 1911. *Pioneer Irish of Onondaga (about 1776–1847)*. NY: G. P. Putnam's Sons.

Beauchamp, William M. 1908. *Past and Present of Syracuse and Onondaga County*. . . . 2 vols. NY: Clarke.

Beauchamp, William M., ed. 1913. *Revolutionary Soldiers Resident or Dying in Onondaga County.* . . . Syracuse: McDonnell Co.

Bruce, Dwight H., ed. 1891. *Memorial History of Syracuse*. . . . Syracuse: H. P. Smith.

Bruce, Dwight H., ed. 1896. *Onondaga's Centennial*. 2 vols. Boston: Boston History Co.

Chase, Franklin H. 1924. *Syracuse and Its Environs, a History*. 3 vols. NY: Lewis Historical Pub. Co.

Chase, Franklin Henry. 1920. *Where to Find It: Bibliography of Syracuse History*. Syracuse: Onondaga Historical Association.

Cheney, Timothy C. 1914. *Reminiscences of Syracuse*. Comp by Parish B. Johnson. Syracuse: Onondaga Historical Association.

Child, Hamilton. 1868. *Gazetteer and Business Directory of Onondaga County, New York, for 1868–9*. Syracuse: Hamilton Child.

Clark, Joshua V. H. 1849. *Onondaga, or Reminiscences of Earlier and Later Times.* . . . 2 vols. Syracuse: Stoddar and Babcock.

Clayton, W. Woodford. 1878. *History of Onondaga County.* . . . Syracuse: D. Mason.

Durston, H. 1935–38. *History of Manlius*. Manlius.

Faigle, Eric Henry. 1936. *Syracuse, A Study in Urban Geography*. University of Michigan dissertation.

Hand, M. C. 1889. *Syracuse: From a Forest to a City*. Syracuse: Masters and Stone.

Hasbrouck, Mary Josephine, ed. 1942. *Early Onondaga in Letters to Young Students, by "An Old Lady"*. Syracuse: Bardeen's.

Mulford, Henry DuBois. 1894. *Onondaga County Centennial, Historical Address*. Syracuse: Onondaga Historical Association.

Munson, Lillian Steele. 1969. *Syracuse: The City that Salt Built*. NY: Pageant Press.

Northrup, A. 1896. *The Formative Period: Some Intellectual and Moral Influences in the History of Onondaga County*. Syracuse.

Powell, E. Alexander. 1938. *Gone are the Days*. Boston: Little, Brown.

Smith, Carroll E. 1904. *Pioneer Times in the Onondaga Country*. Syracuse: C. W. Bardeen.

Strong, Gurney S. 1894. *Early Landmarks of Syracuse*. Syracuse: Times Pub. Co.

Teall, Sarah Sumner. 1915. *Onondaga's Part in the Civil War*. Syracuse: Onondaga Historical Association.

Van Schaack, Henty C. 1873. *A History of Manlius Village.* . . . Fayetteville: The Recorder.

1875. *Re-Union of the Sons and Daughters of the Old Town of Pompey. . .Also, a History of the Town. . . Biographical Sketches of Its Early Inhabitants*. Pompey: The Re-Union Meeting.

Kakatt, Elbridge P.O. and Twp.

Twp. organized 1829; 1st settlers 1790s predominantly from New Eng. Indian mounds.

NY 35A: M, farmer, former assessor, 78. B. here. — F. b. Twp., PGF b. Orange Co.; M. b. Co., MGF b. Province of New Brunswick in Canada (Scots name), MGM b. Dutchess Co. (Palatine name). — Ed.: till 12. — Presbyterian.

Oran, Manlius P.O., Pompey Twp.

Twp. organized 1794, "original twp."; 1st settlement 1791. One of first settlements in Military Tract. Early settlers principally from New Eng. (CT). Apple orchards. Oran in E. part of Twp., near Madison Co. line. Settled 1793 from

Stockbridge, MA; "was more thriving in past than now". Manlius the location of Manlius Military Academy (1869).

NY 35B: F, housewife, 45. B. near DeRuyter, Fabius Twp., came here when married at age 16. — F., M. both b. Fabius Twp. — Ed.: till 16. — Methodist. — Extremely quick and alert. — Rapid tempo; short vowels. Good articulation.

Syracuse

In 1654, mission of Father LeMoyne: discovered Lake Onondaga, site for settlements. 1786 1st settler, Ephraim Webster from VT; agent among Indians. Other settlers 1780s–90s; state control of salt works in 1797. Strong Irish community by 1812. Inc. as village 1825; Co. seat 1828. 1st US plank road built 1837. RR 1839. Chartered as a city 1847; Salina merged with Syracuse. Syracuse University est. 1867. Many German musical groups. 1st inland source of salt production. Diversification of industry since Civil War: barge canal, clay products, china, silverware, foundries, salt and salt products (87 industries — mostly light); L.C. Smith: guns and typewriters; Franklin Auto. State fairgrounds here.

NY 35C!: M, president of gear co., 62. B. here, presumably. — F. pioneer in salt mining industry in central NY; M. "a descendant of one of city's oldest families" (obituary). Both parents "natives of Syracuse and educated in local and/or select schools" (local historical assoc.). Wife equally well-placed. — Ed.: local schools; graduated from Phillips-Andover Academy, Andover, MA. — St. Paul Episcopal Church; Sons of the American Revolution, Century Club, Cazenovia Club, Trustee of Syracuse Museum of Fine Arts. — Cultivated.

36. Madison County

Formed 1806 from Chenango Co. Diversified terrain. Colgate U. here from 1819. In 1875, hops, dairying, stock raising, grain, hay, wool. Still general farming, dairying; also lakes, resorts. Pop. 1810: 25,144, 1820: 32,208, 1850: 43,072, 1880: 44,112, 1910: 39,289, 1930: 39,790, 1960: 54,635.

Atwell, Christine O. 1928. *Cazenovia, Past and Present: A Descriptive and Historical Record.* . . . Orlando: Florida Press.

Hammond, L. M. 1872. *History of Madison County.* Syracuse: Truair, Smith.

Lehman, K., ed. 1943. *Madison County Today.* Oneida Castle.

Monroe, J. H. 1911. *Cazenovia: Looking Backward Through 118 Years.*

Smith, James H. 1880. *History of Chenango and Madison Counties.* . . . Syracuse: D. Mason.

Smith, James H. 1981. *History of Madison and Chemung Counties, New York.* Syracuse: University Press.

Smith, John E., ed. 1899. *Our County and Its People.* Boston: Boston History Co.

Wood, Silas. 1894. *Biographical Review: Leading Citizens of Madison County.* Boston: Biographical Review Pub. Co.

1858. *Benefaction of William Evans, Esq., to the Town of Smithfield.* Syracuse.

Fenner Corners, Cazenovia P.O., Fenner Twp.

Twp. formed from Cazenovia and Smithfield 1823; highest point in Co. First settlement 1793: early settlers from CT, RI, VT, MA, Albany and Oneida Cos., Scotland. 1st industries: gristmill, carding mill. Cazenovia settled from 1793; Cazenovia College 1824 (Methodist). 1860–62 Gerrit Smith Miller began American football here. "Orderly village with shaded streets and classical and Colonial homes". Fenner Corners near center of Twp.; has faded as a village.

NY 36A: M, farmer, 78. B. Twp.; last 5 yrs. here in Canastota. — F. b. Twp., PGF b. NYS ("Dutch" descent), PGM b. Twp. (Yankee descent); M. b. Sullivan Twp., MGF, MGM b. CT. — Ed.: till 16. — Baptist. — Keen interest. — Toothless articulation.

Peterboro, Smithfield Twp.

Twp. formed from Cazenovia 1807. 1794 leased from Oneidas by Peter Smith, Indian trader and shrewd investor. 1st settler 1795; early settlers from CT, RI, some from Hudson Valley. Peterboro 1st village. Glass factory 1808–30; center of anti-slavery agitation. Twp. and village both declining in 19th cent. Pop. Peterboro 1930: 330.

NY 36B: M, farmer, 52. B. Twp. — F. b. Twp., PGF b. Co., PGM b. near Meadville, PA; M., MGM b. Stockbridge Twp. — Ed.: till 16. — Methodist. — Intelligent, cooperative local type. Conservative; limited amenities. — Unhurried tempo. Definite type of articulation.

37. Oneida County

Formed 1798 from Herkimer Co. Several forts during the time of the French and Indian War. Some pre-Rev. settlements; many abandoned during the Revolution. Post-Rev. settlement chiefly from New Eng. (esp. CT); in 1784, some settlers from lower Mohawk Valley and Hudson Valley (Germans and Yankees). Originally a lumbering Co.; also limestone, glassmaking in 19th cent. Hamilton College est. 1788; orig. Indian school. Lake Ontario and Susquehanna watershed; dairying and general agriculture. Sterling and plate; copper and brass; diversified industry. Pop. 1800: 22,047, 1820: 50,997, 1850: 99,566, 1880: 115,475, 1910: 154,157, 1930: 198,763, 1960: 264,401.

Bagg, M. M. 1877. *Pioneers of Utica. . . to the year 1825.* . . . Utica: Curtiss and Childs.

Bagg, M., ed. 1892. *Memorial History of Utica.* 2 vols. Syracuse: Mason.

Beers, D. G. 1874. *Atlas of Oneida County, New York.* Philadelphia: D. G. Beers and Co.

Brown, Dorothy W. 1953. *Oneida County.* Utica: Oneida Historical Society.

Canfield, W. W., and J. E. Clark. 1909. *Things Worth Knowing about Oneida County.* Utica: T. J. Griffiths.

Clarke, Thomas Wood. 1952. *Utica, for a Century and a Half.* Utica: Widtman Press.

Cookinham, Henry J. 1912. *History of Oneida County, from 1700 to the Present Time.* 2 vols. Chicago: Clarke Pub. Co.

Devereaux, L., ed. 1939. *Utica and Its Savings Bank, 1839–1939.* NY.

Durant, S. W. 1878. *Oneida Biography*. Philadelphia: Everts.

Durant, Samuel W. 1878. . . .*History of Oneida County*. Philadelphia: Everts and Fariss.

Galpin, William Freeman. 1941. *Central New York. . . Oneida, Madison, Onondaga, Cayuga, Tompkins, Cortland, Chenango Counties. . . .* 4 vols. NY: Lewis Historical Pub. Co.

Jones, Pomroy. 1851. *Annals and Recollections of Oneida County. . . .* Rome, NY: The Author.

Miller, Blandina Dudley. 1895. *A Sketch of Old Utica*. Utica: L. C. Childs.

Mowris, J. A. 1866. *117th Regiment (4th Oneida) 1862 to June 1865*. Hartford: Case.

New Century Club. 1900. *Outline History of Utica and Vicinity*. Utica: L. C. Childs.

O'Callaghan, E. B., comp. 1849. Papers Relating to the Oneida Country and Mohawk Valley. In E. B. O'Callaghan, *The Documentary History of the State of New York* (Albany) vol. 1, 507–34.

Old Home Week Corp. 1914. *Old Home Week Souvenir, Utica, New York, Aug. 3–10, 1914*. Utica: T. J. Griffiths.

Tracey, William. 1838. *Notices of Men and Events Connected with the Early History of Oneida County*. Utica: R. Northway, Jr.

Utica, New York, First Bank and Trust Co. 1926. *The Tale of the Treasure Chest, Being Somewhat the Story of Old Fort Schuyler and Its People*. Utica: Moser and Cotins.

Wager, Daniel E. 1896. *Our Country and Its People*. Boston: Boston History Co.

1881–1905. *Year Book. . . of the Oneida Historical Society*. 10 vols. Utica: Roberts.

1882. *Semi-centennial of the City of Utica. . . .* Utica: Oneida Historical Society.

1932. *Old Home Day and Centennial Celebration, Marcy, New York*. Rome: Franklin Press.

1932. *Town of Marcy Centennial*. Rome: Franklin Press.

Lee Center, Lee Twp.

Twp. formed from Western in 1811. 1st settlement in area 1790; early settlers from MA, RI, CT, VT, Ireland. An active little village at the end of the 19th cent.: tanning, furniture and cabinet making. Pop. 1820: 2186, 1850: 3025.

NY 37A: F, widowed homemaker, 80. B. Western Twp. (Oneida Co.); here last 50 yrs. — F. b. Western, PGF b. near Troy, NY (descendant of signer of Declaration of Indep.), PGM b. near Troy, NY; M., MGF, MGM all b. Western. — Ed.: till 16. — Society of Friends. — Quaint; loves to dance and make merry; forbids mention of age. Has tried to write stories but can't spell. Little senility. — Sharply raised voice.

Maynard, Marcy P.O. and Twp.

Twp. formed from Deerfield 1832. 1st settlement 1793 from VT (Irish, Welsh). Maynard a small settlement; not in Co. histories. Pop. Twp. 1840: 1799, 1880: 1857.

NY 37B: M, market gardener (former carpenter), 42. B. neighborhood; spent 6 yrs. in Utica, moved back here age 32. — F. b. Twp., PGM b. Wales; M. b. Deerfield Twp., MGF b. CT (Scotch-Irish descent). — Ed.: here first, then 1 yr. h.s. in

Utica. — Methodist. — Quick, alert. Calm temperament. — Good tempo. Clear articulation.

Utica

Old Fort Schuyler here, 1758–60, French and Indian War. Palatine immigrants 1773; c. 1790 settlers from CT, MA, RI, Long Island, England, Scotland. 1798 1st village charter; org. as city 1832. A major center of industry by 1812. Early 19th cent. some Welsh, Irish, German (Lutheran parishes) immigrants; also some Italians to work in knitting mills. Industries: glass (till 1836), farm implements, pottery, millstones, lumber products, cigars and tobacco, soap and candles, textiles and knit goods, flour, coffins, hydroelectric power, beer, furnaces, metal products, firearms, machinery; also dairy country.

NY 37C!: F, separated homemaker, 52. — F. b. Paris (Oneida Co.), just outside of Utica; M., MGF b. Utica, MGF's F. b. Berne (Albany Co.), MGM b. Mexico in Oneida Co., MGM's F. b. Springfield (Otsego Co.), MGM's M. b. Mexico (Oneida Co.). — Ed.: 1 yr. public school, then private school here, then at St. Mary's Episcopal School in Garden City, Long I. 2 yrs. — Episcopalian. — Cultivated.

38. Herkimer County

Formed 1791 from Montgomery Co. Palatine settlers from Schoharie Valley 1722. Large patents, Dutch and English; New Englanders from Rev. times. US cheesemaking begun here by New Englanders c. 1800. Originally grain producing; later dairying. 1742 Canal to Lake Oneida; roads 1790–1809; plank roads 1847–55.

Beers, F. W., ed. 1879. *History of Herkimer County. . . .* NY: F. W. Beers.

Benton, Nathaniel S. 1856. *A History of Herkimer County. . . .* Albany: J. Munsell.

Child, Hamilton. 1869. *Gazetteer and Business Directory of Herkimer County, New York, for 1869–70*. Syracuse: H. Child.

Grady, Joseph F. 1933. *The Adirondacks: Fulton Chain — Big Moose Region: The Story of a Wilderness*. Little Falls: Press of the Journal and Courier Co.

Hardin, George A., ed. 1893. *History of Herkimer County. . . .* Syracuse: D. Mason.

Thistlethwaite, W. 1915. *The Romance of Old Forge*. Utica: Utica Daily Express.

1904. *Souvenir of Ilion*. Ilion: Citizen Print.

1952. *Ilion, 1852–1952*. Ilion.

1954. *Herkimer County Commemorative Brochure*. Herkimer: Dept. of Archives and History.

Columbia Center, Ilion P.O., Columbia Twp.

Twp. formed 1812 from Warren. In S. part of Co., one of earliest Palatine settlements. Yankee influx in 1790s. Columbia Center near center of Twp: crossroads village (1892). Ilion location of Remington gun shops; later diversified. Few recent immigrants (village ordinance prohibited sale of land to foreigners).

NY 38A: M, farmer, painting and decorating, 81. B. here. — F. b. here (Mohawk "Dutch" = German Palatine), PGF b. Schuyler (Herkimer Co.), PGM b. Twp. (Irish Protestant descent); M., MGF, MGM, MGM's F. all b. Twp. (MGM's F. of Mohawk "Dutch" = German Palatine descent). — Ed.: till 20. — Dutch Reformed. — Alone, unoccupied. Fairly quick mind. — Rather weak articulation.

NY 38B: Ilion Gorge, Ilion P.O., Litchfield Twp. — M, farmer (former Twp. supervisor), 54. B. here, but lived ages 1–21 near Chittenango, Madison Co. — F. b. Danube Twp in Co., PGF b. Ireland, PGM b. Fords Bush in Montgomery Co.; M. b. Litchfield Twp., MGF b. Montgomeryshire, Wales, MGM b. Wales. — Ed.: h.s. in Chittenango. — Presbyterian. — Self-depreciative sense of humor (Welsh temperament?). — Weak articulation. Rising pitch inflection.

Paines Hollow, Mohawk P.O., German Flats Twp.

Twp. organized 1788 (first in Co.); originally settled by Palatines; 9000 acres patented by German Lutherans, 1725. Raided in French and Indian War and Rev. Rebuilt by Germans and Yankees. Paines Hollow settled 1797. Industries in area include cheese, paper mills, desks, knitting mills. Pop. Twp. 1850: 3855.

NY 38C: F, married.

39. Otsego County

Formed in 1791 from Montgomery Co. Settlement as early as 1739; first land grants 1768. Earliest settlers Scots and Dutch. Source of Susquehanna. Reportedly 1st for raising Cheviot sheep. Hops in 1890s. General farming, cattle, dairying; misc. industries. Pop. 1800: 21,636, 1820: 44,856, 1850: 48,638, 1880: 51,397, 1910: 47,216, 1930: 46,710, 1960: 51,942.

Bacon, Edwin F. 1902. *Otsego County: Geographical and Historical, from the Earliest Settlement to the Present.* . . . Oneonta: The Oneonta Herald.

Beardsley, Levi. 1852. *Reminiscences. . . Early Settlement of Otsego County.* NY: C. Vinten.

Butterfield, Lyman H. 1954. Cooper's Inheritance: The Otsego Country and Its Founders. *New York History* 35:374–411.

Butterfield, Roy L. 1959. *In Old Otsego: A New York County Views Its Past.* Cooperstown:History.

Child, Hamilton, comp. 1872. *Gazetteer and Business Directory of Otsego County, for 1872-3.* Syracuse: Hamilton Child.

Cooper, James Fenimore. 1921. *Legends and Traditions of a Northern County.* NY: G. P. Putnam's Sons.

Cooper, W. 1810. *A Guide in the Wilderness, or the History of the First Settlements in the Western Counties of New York, with Useful Instructions to Future Settlers.* Dublin, Ireland. Repr. 1949 (Cooperstown: Freeman's Journal Co.).

Hurd, Duane Hamilton. 1878. . . .*History of Otsego County.* Philadelphia: Everts and Fariss.

Jones, Louis C. 1965. *Growing Up in the Cooper Country.* . . . Syracuse: University Press.

Peck, J. 1796. *The Political Wars of Otsego: Or the Downfall of Jacobinism and Despotism.* . . . Cooperstown: E. Phinney.

1893. *Biographical Review. . . of Otsego County.* Boston: Biographical Review Pub. Co.

Elliot Hill, Worcester P.O., Decatur Twp.

Twp. formed from Worcester 1808; in SE part of Co. 1st settlements 1790 from CT and the Hudson Valley. Pop. 1842: 1071.

NY 39A: M, farmer, 79. B. here. — F. b. here, PGF, PGF's F. both b. Oswego, NY (perhaps Yankee descent), PGM b. Oswego, NY (Indian-"Dutch" descent); M. b. neighborhood, MGF b. Seward (Schoharie Co.; German-"Dutch" descent), MGM b. Milford in Co. — Ed.: till 20. — Methodist.

Schuyler Lake, Exeter Twp.

Twp. formed from Richfield in 1799. English settlers early. Schuyler Lake here. Residential; resort and vacation trade. Pop. 1842: 1,423.

NY 39B: M, farmer, 43. B. Otsego Twp. — F., PGF b. Otsego Twp., PGM b. Co.; M., MGF b. Otsego Twp., MGM b. Co. — Ed.: till 17. — Baptist. — Cooperative; rather conservative. — Moderate tempo.

40. Delaware County

Formed from Ulster and Otsego Counties 1797. 1st settlers 1762–63 from Ulster Co. Most settlements abandoned during the Rev.; most settlers from New England, some from Long Island. Scottish immigration slightly later. Much of Co. under a quit-rent rule till 1844. Lumbering (till woods depleted): rafted to Philadelphia and Baltimore. A watershed: Hudson Valley and Delaware R. Other industries: tanning, sugar, small grains, corn, potatoes (largely for local consumption), dairying. Pop. 1800: 10,228, 1820: 26,587, 1850: 39,834, 1880: 42,721, 1910: 45,575, 1930: 41,163, 1960: 43,540.

Beers, F. W. 1869. *Atlas of Delaware County.* NY: Beers, Ellis and Soule.

Delaware County Bicentennial Book Committee. 1976. *The Spirit of Delaware County: A Look Back from 1976.* Delhi: The Committee.

Devine, J. 1933. *Three Centuries in Delaware County.* NY: Swiss Alps of Delaware Co.

Gould, Jay. 1856. *History of Delaware County.* . . . Roxbury: Keeny and Gould.

Monroe, John D. 1949. *Chapters in the History of Delaware County.* Margaretville: Delaware County Historical Association.

Munsell, W., ed. 1880. *History of Delaware County.* NY: W. W. Munsell.

Murray, David, ed. 1898. *Delaware County History of the Century 1797-1897.* Delhi: W. Clark.

North, Arthur W. 1924. *The Founders and the Founding of Walton.* . . . Walton: Walton Reporter Co.

Wood, Leslie C. 1950. *Holt! T'Other Way!.* Middletown: the author.

1895. *Biographical Review. . . of Delaware County.* Boston: Biographical Review Pub. Co.

Lee Hollow, Bovina Center P.O., Bovina Twp.

Formed 1820 from 3 twps.; 2nd smallest (in area and pop.) in Co. First settler in 1791 (English descent); settler in 1794 from Long Island. Also Scottish settlers later. Pop. decline 1820–80. Excellent dairying.

NY 40A: M, farmer, 79. B. in Bovina Center. — F. b. Bovina Center, PGF b. Co., PGM b. Hamden in Co.; M., MGF b. Roxbury in Co., MGM of Holland Dutch descent. — Ed.: till 15. — Methodist (father Presbyterian). — Alert; still hard at work. — Articulation still pretty good.

Walton

Twp. est. 1797; named for Walton patent (1770). 1st permanent settlement 1784. Walton Village on branch of Delaware; inc. 1851. Industries include gristmills, tanning, potash, wool and flax, distilling, butter, milk (for NYC), brick, machine shop.

NY 40B: M, grocer, 51. B. Andes in Co. — F. b. Andes, PGF b. Dundee, Scotland, PGM b. Scotland; M. b. Andes, MGF b. Co. (of old Palatine stock here), MGM b. Andes (Scottish parentage). — Ed.: 3 yrs. h.s. in Andes. — Methodist Episcopal. — Quick, intelligent; good citizen with good local background. — Rapid tempo; short vowels. Fairly good articulation.

41. Chenango County

Formed 1798 from Herkimer and Tioga Cos.; N. part became Madison Co. in 1806. First settlers from New Eng., esp. CT. "Broken and hilly"; agriculture "respectable", livestock. Watershed; mill sites. Other industries: dairying, some hops and wheat, hay, oats, corn, maple syrup. Pop. 1800: 15,666, 1820: 31,215, 1850: 40,311, 1880: 39,891, 1910: 35,575, 1930: 34,665, 1960: 43,243.

Barber, Gertrude A., comp. 1950. *Index to Wills of Chenango County, New York*. NY.
Clark, Hiram C. 1850. *History of Chenango County*. . . . Norwich: Thompson and Pratt.
Smith, James H. 1880. *History of Chenango and Madison Counties*. . . . Syracuse: D. Mason.
1898. *Book of Biographies: This Book Contains Biographical Sketches of the Leading Citizens of Chenango County*. Buffalo: Biographical Pub. Co.

Plymouth

Formed 1806 from Norwich; 1st settlements c. 1794: several French families, most of whom removed to OH, also some English, New Eng. settlers. Plymouth Village in center of Twp. Pop. 1842: 1,625.

NY 41: M, farmer, 47. B. Twp., spent 3 yrs. in Norwich. — F., PGF b. Twp.; M. b. Twp. — Ed.: till 17. — Baptist. — Quick, intelligent. Genuine speech. — Good tempo. Excellent articulation.

42. Cortland County

Formed 1808 from Onondaga Co. Long, snowy winters. Part of "Military Tract" (Revolutionary bonus). 1st settlement 1791, from New Haven; early settlers mainly from New Eng. First road c. 1800; RR charter 1826. Hilly; river transport important early. Little manufacturing before 1850; maple syrup made here. State Teachers College. Pop. 1810: 8,868,

1820: 16,507, 1850: 25,140, 1880: 25,825, 1910: 29,249, 1930: 31,709, 1960: 41,113.

Al-Khayat, H. 1959. *A Geographic Analysis of the Growth of Cortland*. Syracuse: University Press.
Blodgett, Bertha E. 1932. *Stories of Cortland County*. Cortland: Cortland County Historical Society.
Blodgett, Bertha Eveleth. 1932. *Stories of Cortland County for Boys and Girls*.
Cornish, Cornelia Baker. 1935. *The Geography and History of Cortland County*. . . . Ann Arbor: Edwards Bros.
Goodwin, H. C. 1859. *Pioneer History: Or, Cortland County and the Border Wars of New York*. . . . NY: A. B. Burdick.
Kurtz, D. Morris. 1883. *Past and Present: A Historical and Descriptive Sketch of Cortland*. . . . Binghamton: Republican Book and Job Print.
Reusswig, Harriett M. 1934. *Cortland 1792–1854*. Syracuse University Master's thesis.
Smith, H. P., ed. 1885. *History of Cortland County*. . . . Syracuse: D. Mason.
Welch, Edgar L., comp. 1899. *"Grip's" Historical Souvenir of Cortland*. Cortland: Standard Press.
1898. *Book of Biographies. . . Biographical Sketches of Leading Citizens of Cortland County*. . . . Buffalo: Biographical Pub. Co.
1957–. *Cortland County Chronicles*. Cortland: Cortland County Historical Society.
1958. *Cortland County Sesquicentennial Celebration* [1808–1958]. Cortland.

South Hill, Cranes Mills, Truxton P.O. and Twp.

Twp. formed 1808; highest part of Co. Early settlers from CT, NH, RI, VT, NJ, MA; Westchester, Dutchess, Saratoga Cos.; Baptists and Presbyterians. 2nd largest twp. in Co. Furniture made here as late as 1920s. Pop. 1842: 3,658.

NY 42A: M, farmer, 63. B. Taylor Twp. in Co. — F. b. Twp., PGF b. Saratoga Co., PGM b. Cuyler Twp.; M. b. Cincinnatus Twp., MGF b. near Lake Champlain in VT. — Ed.: till 19 (off and on). — Methodist.

East Homer, Cortland P.O., Homer Twp.

Twp. organized 1794. Watershed of Susquehanna and Lake Ontario. 1st settlement 1791; early settlers from CT, MA, NJ; Congregationalists. For a long while Homer Village the most important in Co. Later settlers from VT, RI, Hudson and Mohawk Valleys, and Orange, Washington, and Albany Cos. Village green reminiscent of New Eng.; brick houses. Dairying, cheese, farm implements, flannel shirts, fishing tackle, canned beans. Cortland has 30 industries and State Teachers College. Many Italians brought from NYC for bean packing.

NY 42B: M, farmer, 45. B. Truxton. — F. b. Truxton Twp., PGF b. CT; M. b. Truxton Twp., MGF, MGM b. England. — Ed.: till 17. — Methodist.

43. Broome County

Formed 1806 from Tioga Co. 1st permanent settlements in 1725; settlers from New Eng. and Wyoming Valley. First sawmill 1788; first gristmill 1790. Developed early as a center of trade; on Susquehanna and Chenango Rivers. Turnpike 1806.

Chenango Canal; Erie RR. Maple sugar, shoe factories, agriculture; industry around Binghamton. Pop. 1810: 8,130, 1820: 14,343, 1850: 30,660, 1880: 49,483, 1910: 78,809, 1930: 147,022, 1960: 212,661.

Burr, George. 1876. *Historical Address Relating to the County of Broome.* . . . Binghamton: Carl, Stoppard Print.

Child, Hamilton, comp. 1872. *Gazetteer and Business Directory of Broome and Tioga Counties, New York, for 1872–73.* Syracuse: H. Child.

Lawyer, William S., ed. 1900. *Binghamton, Its Settlement, Growth and Development.* . . *1800–1900.* Boston: Century Memorial Pub. Co.

Lewis, Frank P. 1924. *La Fayette and Lisle.* Seattle.

Merrill, A. 1953-54. *Southern Tier.* 2 vols. NY: American Book-Stratford Press.

Seward, William Foote, ed.-in-chief. 1924. *Binghamton and Broome County: A History.* 3 vols. NY: Lewis Historical Pub. Co.

Smith, H. P., ed. 1885. *History of Broome County.* Syracuse: D. Mason.

Walker, Olive Brooks. 1962. *Lisle: State, Town, Village.* Whitney Point: Pennysaver Co.

Whitney's Point Reporter. 1898. *Whitney's Point, Old and New, 1791–1898.* Whitney's Point: The Reporter.

Wilkinson, J. B. 1840. *The Annals of Binghamton, and of the Country Connected with It, from the Earliest Settlement.* Binghamton: Cooke and Davis.

1867. *History of Broome County: From 1806 to 1867.* Syracuse: G. V. Luce.

1894. *Biographical Review.* . . *Sketches of the Leading Citizens of Broome County.* . . . Boston: Biographical Review Pub. Co.

1934. *Commemorating the Centennial of the Incorporation of Binghamton.* . . *1834–1934.* Johnson City: Johnson City Pub. Co.

Whitney Point, Nanticoke Twp.

Twp. formed 1831 from Lisle. 1st settled 1793; early settlers from CT, PA, MA, RI, Orange Co. In W. part of Co. Upland; few narrow ravines. Purely agricultural; had lumber and flour mills. Declining pop. since 1870. Whitney Point named 1824; formerly Patterson's Point. Inc. 1871. Trading center for wealthy farm community; light industry.

NY 43A: M, farmer, 80. B. here. — F. b. Triangle Twp., PGF b. Schoharie Co. near Petersburg, PGF's F. b. Rensselaer Co., PGF's PGF of Hopkinton, RI, PGM b. Gilboa (Schoharie Co.); M. b. Greene (Chenango Co.), MGF b. England, MGM b. Fenton (Chenango Co.). — Methodist.

Center Lisle, Lisle P.O. and Twp.

Twp. formed 1801 from Union; 1st settlement 1791–92 from MA. NE of Binghamton. Center Lisle a small trading center; inc. 1866. Pop. decline since 1870.

NY 43B: M, farmer, town supervisor, 41. B. neighborhood. — F. b. Twp., PGF b. Lapier (Cortland Co.), PGM b. Twp.,

PGM's F. from PA; M., MGF, MGM MGM's F. all b. Twp. — Ed.: till 15. — Congregational.

Binghamton

1785 site ceded to whites, sold 1786 to Wm. Bingham, Philadelphia merchant. 1st settlers 1787; called Chenango then. Inc. as a village 1834; as a city 1867. RR junction since middle 19th cent. 26 different "ethnic types" in 1940 (strong Czech and Slovak communities). Industries: water power, washing machines, electronics, glass, work clothes, textiles, shoes, cigars (largest industry in 1855), flour, furniture and woodworking, tanning, IBM. SUNY here. Pop. 1880: 17,317, 1910: 48,443, 1930: 76,662, 1960: 75,941.

NY 43C!: F, housewife, 47. B. here. — Parents died when inf. young; reared by maternal grandparents. F. b. S. of Binghamton, PGF b. Owego (Tioga Co.; French Huguenot descent), PGM b. Portland, ME; M., MGF b. here, MGF's F. b. Susquehanna Co., PA, MGF's M. b. Barker in Co., MGM b. Union in Co. and came to Binghamton as a child, MGM's F., MGM's PGM b. Union, MGM's M. b. here, MGM's MGF b. in NY (Holland Dutch descent), MGM's MGM b. NY. — Ed.: h.s. in Binghamton. — Episcopalian. — Apologetic, loquacious, cooperative. Urban type. Antiquarian interests. Otherwise essentially middle-class in manner and outlook. — Moderate tempo. — Cultivated.

44. Tioga County

Formed from Montgomery Co. in 1791. First settlers c. 1785 from Wyoming Valley (PA), New Eng., and "Boston Ten" Twps. C. 1788 Owego was geographical center of Iroquois domain. Turnpike from 1797; RR to Ithaca from 1834. Lehigh U. est 1864. Light industry early; dairying, orchards. Pop. 1800: 6,889, 1820: 16,971, 1850: 24,880, 1880: 32,673, 1910: 25,624, 1930: 25,480, 1960: 45,272.

Beers, F. W. 1869. *Atlas of Tioga County, New York.* NY: Beers, Ellis and Soule.

Child, Hamilton, comp. 1872. *Gazetteer and Business Directory of Broome and Tioga Counties, New York, for 1872–73.* Syracuse: H. Child.

Gay, William B., ed. 1887. *Historical Gazetteer of Tioga County, 1785–1888.* Syracuse: W. B. Gay and Co.

Kingman, L. W., ed. 1897. *Our County and Its People.* 2 vols. Elmira: W. A. Fergusson.

Merrill, A. 1953-54. *Southern Tier.* 2 vols. NY: American Book-Stratford Press.

Pierce, Henry B. 1879. *History of Tioga, Chemung, Tompkins, and Schuyler Counties, New York.* Philadelphia: Everts and Ensign.

Sexton, John L., Jr. 1885. *An Outline History of Tioga and Bradford Counties in Pennsylvania, Chemung, Steuben, Tioga, Tompkins, and Schuyler in New York.* Elmira: Gazette Co.

Willis, Nathaniel P. 1839. *À l'Abri, or The Tent Pitch'd.* NY: S. Colman.

Red Brush, Owego, Lounsberry P.O., Nichols Twp.

Twp. formed 1824. 1st settlement c. 1787; early settlers from NJ, Westchester Co., Monroe Co. (PA), CT. More improved land than any other twp. in Co. Chiefly dairying.

NY 44A: M, farmer, 78. B. here. — F. b. Twp., PGF from Saratoga Co., PGM b. Lounsberry, PGM's F. English descent; M. b. neighborhood, MGF b. Lounsberry, MGF's F. a Rev. soldier from Down East, MGM b. neighborhood (Scottish parentage). — Ed.: till 21 (off and on). — Methodist.

Halsey Valley, Barton Twp.

Twp. formed 1824; first settlement 1791 from Wyoming Valley, PA via Nichols Twp. Other early settlers from New Eng., Scotland, S. England, and other NY cos. Dairying, light industry, railroads.

NY 44B: M, farmer, 38. B. Hagodorn Hill (Spencer Twp.); here since age 19. — F., PGF b. Spencer Twp., PGF's F. b. Orange Co. (War of 1812 veteran), PGM b. Chemung Co. just across line; M. b. Spencer Twp., MGF b. Barton Twp., MGF's PGF of Holland Dutch descent, MGM b. Barton Twp. — Ed.: till 16. — Methodist (half-hearted).

45. Chemung County

Formed from W. Tioga 1830; first settlement 1786, early settlers from PA, Ireland, NY. Formerly center of Iroquois civilization. Chemung and rest of S. tier bypassed by main stream of migration westward. Farming and livestock, dairying. Chemung Canal (later N. Branch Canal) in 1832. Uplands better grass than grain, valleys fine crops. 60% of farms given up since WWII; in 1970 only 1% of pop. "rural farm". Pop. 1840: 20,732, 1850: 28,821, 1880: 43,065, 1910: 54,662, 1930: 74,680, 1960: 98,706.

Byrne, Thomas E., ed. 1976. *Chemung County 1890–1975.* Elmira: Chemung Co. Historical Soc.

Chemung County Historical Society Writers' Group. 1961. *Chemung County. . . Its History.* Elmira: Chemung County Historical Society.

Cheney, T. Apoleon. 1868. *Historical Sketch of the Chemung Valley. . . .* Watkins.

Child, Hamilton, comp. 1868. *Gazetteer and Business Directory of Chemung and Schuyler Counties, New York, for 1868–9.* Syracuse: Hamilton Child.

Galatian, A. B., comp. 1868. *History of Elmira, Horseheads, and the Chemung Valley. . . .* Elmira: A. B. Galatian.

Merrill, A. 1953-54. *Southern Tier.* 2 vols. NY: American Book-Stratford Press.

Ottman, W. 1900. *A History of the City of Elmira.* Cornell University dissertation.

Pierce, Henry B. 1879. *History of Tioga, Chemung, Tompkins, and Schuyler Counties, New York.* Philadelphia: Everts and Ensign.

Sexton, John L., Jr. 1885. *An Outline History of Tioga and Bradford Counties in Pennsylvania, Chemung, Steuben, Tioga, Tompkins, and Schuyler in New York.* Elmira: Gazette Co.

Taylor, Eva. 1937. *A Short History of Elmira.* Elmira: Steele Memorial Library.

Towner, Ausburn. 1892. *Our County and Its People: A History of the Valley and County of Chemung. . . .* Syracuse: D. Mason.

Towner, Ausburn. 1907. *A Brief History of Chemung County. . . .* NY: A. S. Barnes.

Zimmerman, Eugene. 1927. *The Foolish History of Horseheads, New York.* Horseheads: E. Zimmerman.

1902. *A Biographical Record of Chemung County, New York.* NY: S. J. Clarke Pub. Co.

Dun Hill, Elmira P.O., Big Flats Twp.

Twp. formed from Elmira 1822; first settler 1787. Navigable feeder of Chemung Canal. Big Flats village has Erie RR: tobacco mfg. and trading center in late 19th cent. Suburbanized since WWII.

NY 45A: M, estate caretaker, former butcher, farmed 10 yrs., once drove ice wagon, 72. B. Mt. Zoar Hill, moved to Elmira age 9, there till 30 yrs. old, then to Southport till age 52. — F., PGF, PGM all b. Schuyler Co.; M. b. Ballton (E. of here). — Ed.: till 4th grade (Mt. Zoar). — No church affiliation ("never joined none"). — Mercurial, suspicious. Great story teller; full of local lore and gossip. No travel; not bookish; no idea of purpose of interviews. Got angry at end when being questioned about numbers and calendar terms and wouldn't continue. — Tempo moderate. Very strong stresses. Much slurring. Some simplification of final clusters.

Tompkins Corners, Horseheads P.O., Catlin Twp.

Twp. settled from Catherine in 1823, much still unsettled in 1842. Horseheads named because Sullivan's men killed horses for food, left heads. Bricks and optical goods made here. Tompkins Corners first deeds 1791; settlement after War of 1812 from NJ, Canada, CT. Small hamlet on S. line of Twp.; farm trading center, small industries. Latest settled part of Co. Pop. Twp. 1825: 1105, 1850: 1474, 1875: 1426.

NY 45B: M, storekeeper, 75. B. locally; spent a few years in Big Flats. — F. from Tioga Co., PA, PGF from near Philadelphia, PGF's F. killed in War of 1812, PGM from Tioga Co., PA; M. b. Co., MGF, MGM both local. — Ed.: local schools. — Methodist. — Suspicious; difficult for FW to get vita. Serious-minded. Tired, wouldn't complete interview. Good folk type, using folk grammar almost exclusively, talking freely, many cv. forms. — Voice in medium register. Utterance somewhat slurred. Some nasality.

NY 45C: Big Flats. — M, retired farmer, 71. B. Tompkins Corners (left and sold farm about 2 yrs. ago). — Ed.: district schools. — Strong personality, sure of what he knows. No nostalgia for "the good old days". Sense of humor; fluently profane. Inf. had a stroke and was unable to continue (no family history taken). — Strong stresses, nasality, medium pitch.

Elmira

Formed from Chemung 1792 (named Newtown then). Seneca Indian village destroyed in 1779. First settler 1788; early settlers from PA; others from New Eng., Ireland, Scotland, CT, MA. Inc. as village; named in 1828. Episcopal congregation here by 1833. Erie RR 1844; Chemung Canal 1854. Elmira College founded 1855. Underground railway. Industries: precision tools, steel, office equipment and business machines, fire engines, chemicals, gears, glass bottles. Pianos and organs c. 1900, chocolates to 1932, munitions in WWII. Summer home and grave of Mark Twain here. Pop. 1840: 4,791, 1850: 8,166, 1880: 20,541, 1910: 37,176, 1930: 47,397, 1960: 46,517.

NY 45D!: F, single homemaker, did newspaper work locally, taught 3 yrs. Long I., Binghamton, 72. B. here; traveled abroad. — F. b. Independence (Allegany Co.), prominent: banker, judge, assemblyman, PGF, PGM b. Independence; M. b. Leonardsville, near Utica, MGF's M. from near Schenectady, MGM from Newport. — Ed.: Elmira public schools, Elmira College. — Congregationalist, University Club, College Club, local literary society. — Excellent inf.: quick, assured, straightforward answers. Friendly. — Speech fairly rapid. Slurred, much sandhi. Voice medium register. Stresses fairly strong; fairly wide intonation range. — Cultivated.

46. Schuyler County

Formed 1854; much settlement from PA. Cultivated by Iroquois; undulating, hilly. Chemung Canal; branch of Lehigh Valley RR here. Finger Lakes. Pop. 1860: 18,840, 1880: 18,842, 1910: 14,004, 1930: 12,909, 1960: 15,044.

Bell, Barbara. 1962. *Little Tales from Little Schuyler*. Watkins Glen: History.

Child, Hamilton, comp. 1868. *Gazetteer and Business Directory of Chemung and Schuyler Counties, New York, for 1868-9*. Syracuse: Hamilton Child.

Pierce, Henry B. 1879. *History of Tioga, Chemung, Tompkins, and Schuyler Counties, New York*. Philadelphia: Everts and Ensign.

Sexton, John L., Jr. 1885. *An Outline History of Tioga and Bradford Counties in Pennsylvania, Chemung, Steuben, Tioga, Tompkins, and Schuyler in New York*. Elmira: Gazette Co.

Upson, R. 1938. *The Early Development of the Four Finger Lake Counties: Being the Settlement and Agricultural History of Schuyler, Seneca, Tompkins, and Yates Counties 1790-1870*. Cornell University Master's thesis.

1903. *A Biographical Record of Schuyler County. . . .* NY: Clarke Pub. Co.

1954. *Schuyler County, New York: The First Hundred Years*. Watkins Glen.

Monterey, Barkers Mill, Painted Post P.O., Orange Twp.

Twp. formed c. 1840 from division of Jersey. Germans from NJ settled here c. 1806; Brigham Young's family also early settlers. Painted Post formerly an Indian center wiped out by Sullivan-Clinton 1779. Ingersoll Rand Corp. here: machine shops, foundry, branch plant. Monterey thriving in 1875; cheese factory.

NY 46A: M, carpenter, formerly barber, undertaker's helper, sawmill operator, 82. B. here. — F. b. Townsend (now in Co.), PGM Holland Dutch; M. b. near Monterey, MGF from Scottish Highlands, MGM b. Monterey (Holland Dutch). — Ed.: common school. — Presbyterian; Maccabees, has been town clerk. — Very cooperative. Talks freely. Knows locality intimately: flora, fauna, and folkways. Many anecdotes; enjoyed interview. — Dialect unaffected by outside world and almost unaffected by reading (absence of *ain't* only possible effect of schoolma'ams). Tempo moderate to slow; pitch medium without much range. Nasality.

Reading Center, Watkins Glen, Reading Twp.

Twp. formed 1809 from Frederickstown, Steuben Co. Settled c. 1797 from PA, CT, NY. Reading a small village

"hamlet". Hay, fruit, grapes. See 46C community for Watkins Glen. Pop. 1842: 1,535.

NY 46B: M, farmer, 72. B. border of Schuyler and Steuben Cos. Worked 2 yrs. in PA when young. — PGF, PGM from Switzerland; M.'s family "genuine Yanks". No further info. — Ed.: 6th grade (expelled). — Rustic; excellent example of old-time uncultivated speech. Difficult interview (inf. deaf?). — Slight interference caused by loss of teeth. Distinct nasal twang.

Townsend, Watkins Glen, Dix Twp.

Twp. formed 1835; early settlers 1797-98 from Cumberland Co., PA, E. NY, CT. Townsend near W. line of Twp. Post office by 1826; trading center for farmers. Watkins Glen named after land purchaser who bought a good deal of Tompkins Co. Farm shipping, industrial and tourist center; Glen Spring health resort (mineral spring). Auto racing.

NY 46C: F, housewife, 73. B. Co. Lived 2 yrs. Richmond as a child, a few yrs. each in Watertown, Mecklenburg, Philadelphia. — M.'s family were French and Dutch. Many generations in Co. — Ed.: 8th grade. — Presbyterian; Grange, Ladies Auxiliary of the Red Men. — Old native Yankee stock. Charming and good-natured. — Distinct nasalization of vowels; drawl.

47. Tompkins County

Formed from Cayuga and Seneca Cos. in 1817; part to Schuyler in 1854. First settlers 1789 from MA, NY, CT to site of Ithaca. Cornell founded 1868. Industries: cement, salt. Pop. 1820: 20,681, 1850: 38,746, 1880: 34,445, 1910: 33,647, 1930: 41,490, 1960: 66,164.

Becker, Carl L. 1943. *Cornell University: Founders and the Founding*. Ithaca: Cornell University Press.

Goodrich, George E., ed. 1898. *The Centennial History of the Town of Dryden: 1797-1897*. Dryden: J. G. Ford.

Heidt, William, Jr. 1965. *Forests to Farm in Caroline*. Ithaca: Dewitt Historical Soc. of Tompkins Co.

Kensler, Gladys M., and Bruce L. Melvin. 1930. *A Partial Sociological Study of Dryden, New York*. Ithaca: Cornell University Agricultural Experiment Station.

Lee, Hardy Campbell. 1947. *A History of Railroads in Tompkins County*. Ithaca: DeWitt Historical Society of Tompkins County.

Norris, W. Glenn. 1944. *Old Indian Trails in Tompkins County*. Ithaca: De Witt Historical Society of Tompkins County.

Norris, W. Glenn. 1951. *The Origin of Place Names in Tompkins County*. Ithaca: DeWitt Historical Society of Tompkins County.

Norris, W. Glenn. 1961. *Early Explorers and Travelers in Tompkins County*. Ithaca: De Witt Historical Society of Tompkins County.

Pierce, Henry B. 1879. *History of Tioga, Chemung, Tompkins, and Schuyler Counties, New York*. Philadelphia: Everts and Ensign.

Rumsey, H. 1857. *History of Dryden from 1797-1857 by the Old Man in the Clouds: Transcribed by B. Clark, Town of Dryden Historian*.

Selkreg, John H. 1894. *Landmarks of Tompkins County....* Syracuse: D. Mason.

Sexton, John L., Jr. 1885. *An Outline History of Tioga and Bradford Counties in Pennsylvania, Chemung, Steuben, Tioga, Tompkins, and Schuyler in New York.* Elmira: Gazette Co.

Upson, R. 1938. *The Early Development of the Four Finger Lake Counties: Being the Settlement and Agricultural History of Schuyler, Seneca, Tompkins, and Yates Counties 1790–1870.* Cornell University Master's thesis.

Vidich, Arthur J., and Joseph Bensman. 1958. *Small Town in Mass Society.* Princeton: University Press.

Walrath, F. 1927. *A History of the Agriculture of Tompkins County.* Cornell University dissertation.

Windy Knob, Cooper Street, Newfield P.O. and Twp.

Newfield 7 mi. S. of Ithaca. Organized 1811; first settled 1800. Hilly and broken terrain.

NY 47A: M, farmer, 57. B. locally. Lived 7 yrs. between Cayute and Sullivanville (Schuyler and Chemung Cos.). — F. b. near Bath, Steuben Co., moved to area as child, PGF from PA, PGM b. near Trumbull's Corners, PGM's F. and M. from Orange and Dutchess Cos.; M. b. Enfield Twp. in Co., MGF b. NY, MGF's F. b. Scotland, MGM a sister of PGM. — Ed.: 8th grade. — Grange. — Excellent inf. Tremendous number of folk forms not encountered elsewhere. Some reading, but no effect on grammar. Plenty of stories, many off-color. Cooperative, generous with time, independent. Good sense of humor. Quick answers; his comments show him a reliable judge of items. Several malapropisms. — Pitch mod. high; nasality. Some final consonants unreleased or unclearly articulated. Vowels generally fairly short though relative length differences exist.

Caroline Center

Formed 1811; 11 mi. SE of Ithaca. First settled 1795; some Southerners (MD and VA) here 1805: kept slaves until NY abolition in 1827. Upland, dairying.

NY 47A*: M, farmer. — German descent. — Old-fashioned.

Dryden

Formed from Ulysses 1803; "a neat village 11 mi. NE of Ithaca". 1st settler 1795; early settlers from VT, NJ, RI, MA, CT, NH, N. Ireland, Hudson Valley. Twp. #23 in Military Tract. Pop. increase to 1835, decrease 1835–95. Depreciation of farmland 1870–95. 1850 first use of coal. Lumbering, grain raising; later dairying.

NY 47B: M, farmer, 40. B. same house. — F. b. here, PGF b. locally, PGF's F. b. NJ, Holland Dutch descent, PGM b. neighborhood, PGM's F. and M. b. Twp.; M. b. here, MGF b. Twp., MGF's F. and M. b. Windsor, CT, MGM b. Twp., MGM's F. b. Twp. — Ed.: country school here, h.s. Ithaca, 1 yr. Cornell. — Presbyterian. — Quick, appreciative, diffident. — Average speech. Somewhat weak articualtion. Short vowels and diphthongs.

48. Cayuga County

Formed 1799 from Onondaga Co.; part of "Onondaga military tract". Varied terrain, climate: more severe climate in S.

Erie Canal 1825; 1st RR 1838. Products include hay, grain, apples, dairying, livestock, stone and clay. Pop. 1800: 15,871, 1820: 38,897, 1850: 55,458, 1880: 65,081, 1910: 67,106, 1930: 64,751, 1960: 73,942.

Allen, Henry M. 1958. *A Story of Cayuga County.* Auburn, NY: Jacobs Press.

Barnes, William. 1875. *Seventh Annual Address, Delivered before the Pioneers' Association.* Albany: Weed, Parsons and Co.

Hopkins, Lazelle R. 1933. *Facts Regarding Weedsport, New York.* Livingston: privately printed.

Merriman, C., et al. 1963. *Brutus, Macedonia, Weeds Basin, Weeds Port....* Weedsport: Weedsport Central School.

Snow, B., ed. 1908. *History of Cayuga County.* Auburn.

Snow, D. 1940. *Early Cayuga Days: Folklore and Local History of a New York County.* State Teacher's College, Albany, Master's thesis.

Storke, Elliot G. 1879. *History of Cayuga County....* Syracuse: D. Mason.

Wheeler, Cyrenus, Jr. 1882. *The Inventors and Inventions of Cayuga County.* Auburn: The Author.

Cato

Became separate twp. 1802 (orig. part of Aurelius). On E. border of Co. 1st settlement c. 1800 from upper Hudson Valley, also from VT and NH.

NY 48A: M, school janitor, worked in store, 78. B. Meridian, same Twp. — F. and M. b. Germany, came over when married. — Ed.: country schools. — Disciples (Union Church); Maccabees. — Good-natured. A bit slow, but patient and cooperative. A second party participated in first interview (pp. 7–50); many of these responses might be labeled SUG. Possibly a few aux. forms have been recorded but not marked. — Moderately slow speech. Fairly strong stresses. Some nasality.

Meridian, Weedsport P.O., Cato Twp.

Meridian near N. line of Twp. 1st settlement 1804, principally from New Eng. Trading center; small manufacturing. Lumber and feed mills at Weedsport.

NY 48B: M, retired farmer, 76. B. here. — F. b. locally, PGF b. NJ, PGF's F. b. Holland, PGM from "down east"; M., MGF b. Twp. — Ed.: district school. — Presbyterian; Grange leader, school board. — Potentially good inf., but poor rapport with FW. Talked freely at first, but later became tired and suspicious. Not much sense of humor. — Fairly deliberate speech; nasality; strong stresses.

Benton's Corners, Ira P.O. and Twp.

Twp. formed from Cato 1821; NE corner of Co. 1st settlements 1800 from upper Hudson Valley (chiefly Yankee); some Germans, some from PA. Benton's Corners a crossroads; Benton family in area early 1800s.

NY 48C: M, farmer, 63. B. here. — F., PGF b. here, PGF's F. from Greenville, NY, PGF's M. from CT, PGM from Sodus; M. from Lysander, NY, MGF, MGF's F. from Pompey, MGM's family orig. Dutch. Full family tree. 7 generations lived same land; 5 born same house. — Ed.: seminary. — Methodist; Mason, Grange, Farm Bureau. — Very good interview, ideal conditions. Free talker. Strong local roots, proud of tradition. Unaffected. Some aux. responses from wife. — No taboos. Fairly fast speech; strong stresses; some nasality.

Victory, Cato P.O., Victory Twp.

Twp. formed from Cato 1821. First settlement 1800; earliest settlers from Montgomery Co., Ireland, Rensselaer Co. (Dutch), Herkimer. Victory village small; first settled 1806.

NY 48D: F, housewife, 60. B. here. — F., PGF b. here, PGF's F. from Hudson Valley, PGF's M. b. Washington, NY (Mayflower descendant), PGM related to inf. NY 48C, PGM's F. from Benton's Corners; M. from Victory, MGF lived here, MGM prob. local. Most of ancestors came from Dutchess Co. Kin to FDR. — Ed.: common school. — Methodist; Eastern Star, American Legion Auxiliary, Grange, Red Cross. — Very cooperative and hospitable; quick mind. Ideal interview, which inf. seemed to enjoy. Utterly reliable. A few aux. forms from husband, a local farmer. — Much nasality. Vowels overlong (not marked). Strong stresses. Very open diphthong in *make*, etc., transcribed here as [æ˄ɪ]. Speech of Victory is noticed as "different" by natives of Cato (5 mi. E.).

49. Seneca County

Formed 1810 from Cayuga Co. First settled in 1780s from PA, MA, Ulster Co. Many settlers of German background. Turnpikes in 1800; 1st RR c. 1836. Lowest percent of Yankee nativity in NY. Industries: pumps, fire engines, metal products, pipe fittings, livestock, diversified farming, fruit. Pop. 1810: 16,609, 1820: 23,619, 1850: 25,441, 1880: 29,278, 1910: 26,972, 1930: 24,983, 1960: 31,984.

Becker, John E. 1949. *A History of the Village of Waterloo. . . .* Waterloo: Waterloo Library and Historical Society.

Hawley, Charles. 1884. *Early Chapters of Seneca History: Jesuit Missions in Sonnontouan, 1656–1684.* Auburn: Knapp, Peck and Thomson.

Nichols, Beach. 1874. *Atlas of Seneca County, New York.* Philadelphia: Pomeroy, Whitman and Co.

Patterson, Maurice L. 1976. *Between the Lakes: The History of South Seneca County.* Interlaken: I.T. Pub. Corp.

Upson, R. 1938. *The Early Development of the Four Finger Lake Counties: Being the Settlement and Agricultural History of Schuyler, Seneca, Tompkins, and Yates Counties 1790–1870.* Cornell University Master's thesis.

Welch, Edgar Luderne. 1903. *"Grip's" Historical Souvenir of Waterloo.* Syracuse.

Welch, Edgar Luderne. 1904. *"Grip's" Historical Souvenir of Seneca Falls.* Syracuse.

Willers, Diedrich, ed. 1894. *Centennial Celebration of the Official Organization of the Town of Romulus. . . .* Geneva: Courier Job Dept.

Willers, Diedrich. 1894. *Historical Address, June 13, 1894.* Geneva: Courier Job Dept.

Willers, Diedrich. 1900. *Centennial Historical Sketch of the Town of Fayette. . . .* Geneva, NY: Press of W. F. Humphrey.

1876. *History of Seneca County. . . 1786–1876.* Philadelphia: Everts, Ensign, and Everts.

1895. *Portrait and Biographical Record of Seneca and Schuyler Counties. . . .* NY: Chapman Pub. Co.

1904. *Centennial Anniversary of Seneca County. . . .* Seneca Falls: Seneca Falls Historical Society.

1948. *Centennial Volume of Papers of the Seneca Falls Historical Society.* Seneca Falls: The Society.

Romulus

Organized as twp. 1799; first settlers c. 1789 from Hudson Valley, PA. Agricultural area; earliest settlements on W. shore, Seneca Lake. No inc. village here as of 1894.

NY 49A: M, retired, former farmer, butcher, wholesaler, 87. B. Varick (next twp.). — F. from PA; M., MGF, MGM b. Fayette (Varick). — Ed.: Varick district schools. — Good inf., but a bit restless. Likes people. Much talk about his experiences as a butcher. — Sing-song intonation. Voice cracks under stress. Some weak final consonants.

Fayette

Home of Joseph Smith at time he discovered Book of Mormon. 1st settler 1789 from PA; other early settlers from CT, NJ, Hudson Valley, Mohawk Valley, Long I., NYC. Many PA Germans (at one time had German lang. schools); some Scotch-Irish. 1st Mormon Church 1830. Pop. Twp. 1842: 3,902.

NY 49B: M, 44. No further vita.

Waterloo

Twp. formed from Junius 1829. Early settlement 1780s from Ulster Co. and "east"; some Irish. Waterloo village Seneca outlet of Seneca-Cayuga Canal. On site of older Indian settlement. Pop. Twp. 1850: 3,795, 1880: 4,399, 1910: 4,429, 1930: 2,921, 1960: 6,891.

NY 49C: M, machinist, 80. B. here; some travel. — F. and M. b. Germany, came to NY when young. — Ed.: till 6th grade. — Episcopalian; Mason, German Lodge, Republican Club. Has been alderman, 3 terms mayor, justice of the peace 15 yrs. — Interview was repeated after 4 yrs. (defective tape). Inf. had since undergone major surgery and suffered great personal loss; was somewhat depressed. Some aux. forms from son, machinist, 48, h.s. grad active in comm. organizations.

Seneca Falls

First settlers shortly after Rev. Diversified industries early. Village founded 1815; incorporated 1831. Village flourishing: water power (Seneca outlet), flour mills, other manufacturing. Cradle of women's rights movement. Pop. Twp. 1930: 6,449.

NY 49D: F, telephone operator, clerk, 40. B. here. — F. b. nearby (Montezuma), PGF, PGM b. England; M. b. here, MGF b. Ireland, MGM b. Interlaken, NY. — Voice clear, somewhat precise, not affected.

50. Wayne County

Formed 1823 from Ontario and Seneca Cos. Includes "Montezuma Marshes", now a wildlife preserve. First settlers c. 1787 from RI, Long I., and NJ, later from Middle States and MD. 1st road west 1796; RR pass service 1853. Contains Palmyra Twp., where Joseph Smith, founder of Mormons, "began his public career". Products: onions, celery, black raspberries, apples. Pop. 1830: 33,643, 1850: 44,953, 1880: 51,700, 1910: 50,179, 1930: 49,995, 1960: 67,989.

Beers, D. G. 1874. *Atlas of Wayne County, New York*. Philadelphia: D. G. Beers and Co.

Clark, Lewis H. 1883. *Military History of Wayne County*. Sodus: L. H. Clark, Hulett and Gaylord.

Cowles, George W., ed. 1895. *Landmarks of Wayne County*. Syracuse: D. Mason.

Green, Walter Henry. 1945. *History, Reminiscences, Anecdotes, and Legends of Great Sodus Bay, Sodus Point, Sloop Landing, Sodus Village, Pultneyville, Maxwell, and the Environing Regions. . . .* Sodus.

Jacobs, Stephen W. 1974. *Wayne County: The Aesthetic Heritage of a Rural Area, A Catalog for the Environment*. Lyons: Wayne County Historical Society.

McIntosh, W. 1877. *History of Wayne County. . . .* Philadelphia: Everts, Ensign and Everts.

Sodus

First settlement 1794; early settlers from MD, CT, Philadelphia, E. NY, NH, ME, MA. Sodus Point raided during War of 1812. Silk raising attempted in 1830s: failed because mulberry trees couldn't stand winters. Branch of PA RR here; excellent harbor. Orchards, cheese factory, trading center, light industries; limestone, some iron. Pop. 1830: 3,528, 1850: 4,598, 1880: 5,285, 1910: not listed, 1930: 1,623 (?), 1960: 6,587.

NY 50A: F, retired dressmaker, 92. B. Twp. Lived 12 yrs. Auburn. — F. b. Coumans, Greene Co., came to Sodus as child, PGF, PGM b. Coumans; M. b. Co. (Richardsons Corners), MGF b. Dutchess Co., MGM b. Bullston Springs. — Ed.: "Old Academy", Sodus. — Episcopalian; Red Man Auxiliary. — Active, talked freely. Enjoyed interviews; many anecdotes about family, life in community. — As often in upstate NY, post-vocalic /r/ frequently unconstricted.

NY 50B: M, businessman, county treasurer, once farmer, 75. B. Marion Village, Marion Twp. Lived 6 yrs. in Lyons (same co.). — F., PGF b. Palmyra, PGF's F. moved to area from Long I., PGM b. Palmyra; M. b. Oneida Co., came to Wayne Co. as child. — Ed.: Marion Collegiate Institute. — Methodist, Chamber of Commerce, Masons, Grange. — Cooperative, but with limited time. A few notions of correctness. Many cv. forms.

51. Ontario County

Formed from Montgomery Co. 1789. Orig. included all the land of which the preemptive rights had been ceded to MA. Many cos. eventually formed from it. S. part hilly and broken; N. beautiful rolling country. Early settlers mainly from New Eng.; also from VA, MD, PA, NY, England, Scotland, Ireland, some from Canada. Products include grains, stock, fruit, apples, grapes, wine.

Adams, John Quincy. 1929. *Historic Geneva*. Geneva: Geneva Historical Society.

Brigham, A. 1862. *Brigham's Geneva, Seneca Falls, and Waterloo Directory. . . 1862–63, with a History of the Towns*. Geneva, NY: Steam Power Press of the Geneva Gazette.

Brumberg, G. David 1977. *Geneva, New York: A Community Study, 1786–1860*. Miami (Ohio) University dissertation.

Child, Hamilton, comp. 1867. *Gazetteer and Business Directory of Ontario County, for 1867–8*. Syracuse: Hamilton Child.

Conover, G. 1880. *Early History of Geneva (formerly called Kanadesaga)*. Geneva, NY: Courier Steam Presses.

Conover, George S. 1879. *Echoes of Seneca Lake: or, Reminiscences of a Centennarian*. Waterloo: Waterloo Library and Historical Society.

Conover, George S. 1880. *Early History of Geneva. . . .* Geneva, NY: Courier Steam Presses.

Conover, George S., ed., and Lewis Cass Aldrich, comp. 1893. *History of Ontario County. . . .* Syracuse: D. Mason.

Hedrick, Ulysses P. 1942. Early Geneva. *New York History* 23:149–158.

McIntosh, W. 1876. *History of Ontario County. . . .* Philadelphia: Everts, Ensign, and Everts.

Milliken, Charles F. 1911. *A History of Ontario County and Its People*. 2 vols. NY: Lewis Historical Pub. Co.

Monroe, J. 1912. *A Century and a Quarter of History, Geneva from 1787 to 1912*. Geneva: W. F. Humphrey.

Nichols, Beach. 1874. *Atlas of Ontario County, New York*. Philadelphia.

Pottle, E. 1954. *Naples 1789–1889: Address of July 4, 1889*.

Smith, Warren Hunting. 1931. *An Elegant but Salubrious Village, A Portrait of Geneva. . . .* Geneva: W. F. Humphrey.

Taylor, Frank H. 1902. *Geneva on Seneca Lake*. Geneva: Chamber of Commerce.

West Richmond, Livonia, Richmond Twp.

Twp. formed 1789; W. Richmond a small village. 1st settlement in area 1790. Many small villages in area, none inc. Nurseries, area always agricultural. Twp. dry from 1861 but originally famous for its distilleries.

NY 51A: M, farmer, 80. B. here. — F. b. here, PGF came as child from Paulette, VT, PGF's F. b. Paulette, built house here, PGM b. neighborhood (Allen's Hill), PGM's F. moved to Allen's Hill age 41 (1801), PGM's M. b. VT; M. b. nearby (Hemlock), MGF, MGM b. Rehoboth, MA, moved to Co. after marriage. — Ed.: common schools. — "Believe in all churches, don't belong to any"; Grange, Odd Fellows, Farm Bureau, NY Archaeological Society. — Close and prolonged contact between inf. and FW (snow-bound for 2 days) resulted in a wealth of purely cv. forms. Very successful farmer; lives well, but not extravagantly. Hospitable, kindly. Interested in Indian relics, other curios; plays old-time music with friends. Inherited many books, but doesn't read much (no discernible effect on speech). — Slurred utterances. Voice in medium register. Nasality. Strong stresses, increasing when excited.

Geneva

1st major settlement in W. NY. Village existed from 1788, surveyed 1789, charter 1806, city 1898 (old Seneca capital). Cultural center from beginning; prominent families. Large Episcopal group. Center of land speculation; wealth mostly derived from agriculture. Geneva College (later Hobart) founded 1825. "One of most beautifully situated places in the state". Principal street parallel with lake shore; mansions, terraced gardens. Retirement village. Industries and products: textiles, nurseries, canneries, cereal mills, optical goods, enamelware. Pop. City 1880: 7,412, 1910: 12,446, 1930: 16,053, 1960: 17,286.

NY 51B: M, farmer, 87. B. nearby. Lived 7 yrs. in Gorham Twp. (10 mi. W.). — F. b. PA, lived Baltimore, came to Geneva at 21, PGF b. Scotland, drowned on ocean voyage, PGM b. Scotland; M. b. Geneva Twp., MGF, MGM b. near Albany. — Ed.: district school, Geneva Union School, 4 yr. course at Chautauqua, state diploma, Albany. — Presbyterian; Grange. — Good, cooperative inf. Some gaps in knowledge, refused to guess on items where not certain. Fairly talkative. A few aux. forms from wife, also native, about same age and experience.

Naples

Center for grape growing and wine making. 1852 grape culture; 1856 wine: Germans from Rhine, later Swiss and French. 1st settled c. 1790. Also trade center, natural gas, wool. Pop. 1820: 1,038, 1850: 2,376, 1880: 2,699, 1910: 2,349, 1930: 1,070, 1960: 1,955.

NY 51C: M, farmer, 75. B. adjacent twp. Lived here last 10 yrs. — F. from S. VT, came to Italy Twp. (adjacent) in 1860s; MGF from Fulton Co., "New York Dutch", MGM from NW CT. — Ed.: till about 8th grade. — Methodist; Grange, Farm Bureau. — Good inf., vigorous, alert mind. Hard-working; interview curtailed somewhat. Some reading; probably more "modern" than younger inf. in comm. Sure of own usage. Good many folk forms (esp. double neg.). — Fast speech. Less /-r/ constriction than FW expected.

NY 51D: F, housewife, antique dealer, 70+. B. outside Naples. — No family history obtained, but FW later learned that family was one of earliest in the region (Rev. land grant). — Ed.: about h.s., all local. — Baptist, sings in choir; belongs to just about everything. — Talkative, though a bit suspicious. Nervous, quick reactions. A number of aux. forms from husband, present for part of interview; he contributed all profane forms, whether starred or not.

NY 51E!: Geneva. — M, businessman, 89. B. Auburn Co. (15 mi. E.), moved to Geneva age 4. Lived 1 yr. FL. — F. b. Auburn, PGF b. CT, a silversmith, lived in Cooperstown and Batavia before moving to Auburn; M. b. Auburn, MGF b. Middlebury, VT, MGF's F. b. NH. — Ed.: till 15, expelled from h.s. — Christian Science; Geneva Historical Society, Trustee Hobart College. — Good Yankee type in several respects: self-educated, reads, hard-working, alert to opportunities. Although successful and proud of it, tolerant of ideas and opinions with which he may not agree (supported rights of liberal professors against pressures from rest of community). Completely at ease, spoke freely. No pretensions. — Cultivated.

52. Yates County

Formed in 1823 from Ontario Co.; part of Massachusetts tract. Exploration by Society of Friends, 1786; first settlement 1788. Early settlers from New England and PA. Varied terrain. Vineyards, black raspberries. Pop. 1830: 19,009, 1850:

20,590, 1880: 21,087, 1910: 18,642, 1930: 16,848, 1960: 18,614.

Ackerman, H. S. 1947. *New York and New Jersey Cemeteries*. Ridgewood.

Aldrich, Lewis Cass, ed. 1892. *History of Yates County*. Syracuse: D. Mason.

Bootes, Thelma Burton, comp. 1955. *Inscriptions from Three Abandoned Cemeteries in Yates County*. [From S. C. Cleveland, *History of Yates County*.] Middlesex.

Cleveland, Stafford C. 1873. *History and Directory of Yates County*. Penn Yan: S. C. Cleveland.

Cleveland, Stafford Canning. 1873. *History and Directory of Yates County*. . . . Penn Yan.

Hammersley, Sydney Ernest. 1957. *The History of Waterford*. Waterford.

Lamb, Wallace Emerson. 1955–56. *Sectional Historical Atlas of New York State*. Phoenix, NY: F. E. Richards.

McNall, Neil Adams. 1957. *An Agricultural History of the Genesee Valley, 1790–1860*. Philadelphia: University of Pennsylvania Press.

Melone, Harry R. 1932. *History of Central New York Embracing Cayuga, Seneca, Wayne, Ontario, Tompkins, Cortland, Schuyler, Yates, Chemung, Steuben, and Tioga counties*. . . . Indianapolis: Historical Pub. Co.

Stork, W., ed. 1898. *Student's Handbook of Yates County*. Penn Yan.

Upson, R. 1938. *The Early Development of the Four Finger Lake Counties: Being the Settlement and Agricultural History of Schuyler, Seneca, Tompkins, and Yates Counties 1790–1870*. Cornell University Master's thesis.

Wolcott, Walter. 1895. *The Military History of Yates County*. . . . Penn Yan: Express Book and Job Print.

West Italy, Naples P.O., Italy Twp.

Twp. formed from Naples (Ontario Co.) 1815. Extreme W. of Co. Rugged terrain; highest elevation in Co. Yankee, English settlers. Methodists est. first church. Pop. 1627 in 1850; declined since.

NY 52A: F, housewife, occasional newspaperwoman, 49. B. here. — F. b. England; M. b. here, MGF, MGM b. England. — Ed.: some h.s. (local). — Methodist; Grange. — Quick, alert mind. Cooperative, talked freely. — Folk forms normal. No trace of bookishness. Fairly fast speech. Nasality very strong. Less /-r/ constriction than FW expected. — A few aux. forms from husband; same comm. and similar background.

Penn Yan, Milo P.O., Benton Twp.

Penn Yan agricultural area. Settled by New Englanders (Yankees) and PA immigrants; hence the name "Penn Yan". Village inc. 1833. Light industries, winemaking and distilling, tourism. Twp. of Benton formed 1810 from Jerusalem; settlers from NJ, MA, CT, and Hudson Valley. Milo fronts on both Keuka and Seneca Lakes; first settlers "Universal Friends". Milo Twp. formed from Benton 1825. Water power; distilleries, then paper mills. Pop. Penn Yan 1880: 165, 1910: 4,597, 1930: 5,329, 1960: 5,770.

NY 52B: F, housewife, 77. B. Jerusalem Twp. (edge of Benton and Potter Twp.). — F., PGF b. Potter Twp., PGF b. Elmira; M., MGF, MGM old Yates County families. — Ed.: h.s., some seminary. — Methodist; Grange, Aux. of Sons of Union Veterans. — Good mind, memory. Cooperative, seemed to enjoy interview. Strong local roots. — Talked moderately fast, strong stresses.

NY 52C: Milo, Penn Yan, Milo Twp. — F, campgrounds manager, 47. B. locally (Barrington). Short vacations to Detroit, Canada, and Washington, DC. — F. b. Co. (Yatesville); M., MGF, MGM all from Montrose, PA. — Ed.: h.s. grad. — Methodist; Grange, 4-H Club leader, Home Bureau. — Assured woman; above-average intelligence. — Many glottal stops, prob. undertranscribed as /t/ or /k/.

53 & 54. Steuben County

Formed from Ontario in 1796; almost all originally in Massachusetts cession. 1st settlement in area c. 1786; early settlers from VT, CT, E. NY, PA (Yankee and PA settlements). Early a base for Indians. Several other cos. formed from Steuben in the 19th cent. First vines 1836; winemaking an important business in the latter half of the 19th cent. and the 20th cent. Intricate hill country; watershed between Lake Ontario and Susquehanna. Some natural gas and petroleum; sulphur. Good agriculture in Genesee Valley: truck gardening, nurseries, fruit (esp. apples). Corning Glass located here. Pop. 1800: 1,788, 1820: 21,989, 1850: 63,771, 1880: 77,586, 1910: 83,362, 1930: 82,671, 1960: 97,691.

Clayton, W. W. 1879. *History of Steuben County.* . . . Philadelphia: Lewis, Peck.

Cowan, Helen I. 1941. *Charles Williamson, Genesee Promoter*. Rochester.

Cowan, Helen I. 1942. Charles Williamson and the Southern Entrance to the Genesee Country. *New York History* 23:260–74.

Denniston, Goldsmith. 1862. *Survey of the County of Steuben.*

Folts, James D., Jr. 1976. *Bibliography of Steuben County, New York*. Corning: Southern Tier Library System.

Hakes, Harlo, et al., eds. 1896. *Landmarks of Steuben County*. Syracuse: D. Mason.

Hull, Nora, ed. 1893. *The Official Records of the Centennial Celebration, Bath. . . June 4–7, 1893*. Bath: Press of the Courier Co.

McMaster, Guy H. 1853. *History of the Settlement of Steuben County*. Bath: R. S. Underhill.

Mulford, W. 1909. *Settlement of Steuben County, New York*. Corning.

Near, Irvin W. 1890. *The Early History of Hornellsville.* . . . Hornellsville: Evening Tribune Printing House.

Near, Irvin W. 1911. *A History of Steuben County.* . . . 2 vols. Chicago: Lewis Pub. Co.

Roberts, Millard F. 1891. *Historical Gazetteer of Steuben County.* . . . Syracuse: M. F. Roberts.

Rogers, S. 1893. *Centennial Celebration of Settlement of the Town of Bath*. Bath.

Smith, L. 1948. *Half a Century of Village Development: The Social and Economic Development of Bath, Geneva, Canandaigua, New York, 1786–1836.* Cornell University Master's thesis.

Stuart, William M. 1935. *Who's Who in Steuben. . . Steuben's Place in History*. Dansville: F. A. Owen.

Thrall, W. B. 1942. *Pioneer History and Atlas of Steuben County.* . . . Perry.

Unionville, Bath P.O. and Twp.

Co. seat; inc. as a village 1836. Bath laid out 1793 by Chas. Williamson; planned to be a "great city". Overpromotion; tried to induce settlement by rich Virginians and Marylanders. Williamson built lavishly, by 1796 Bath had a printing office, a newspaper, and a theater. Some settlement from VA and MD in 1803. Also Scots, and settlers from PA, CT, England, Ireland, RI, the Hudson Valley, ME, VT, MA (first settlers mostly Scots and Germans). For years before Erie Canal, most active and important place in W. NY. Frontier industries: sawmill, gristmill, flour mill, distilleries. 3 turnpikes here before 1812. Also rich farming area: wine and champagne country. Unionville a rural settlement to the SE, in hills. Pop. Bath 1800: 452, 1820: 2,578, 1850: 6,185, 1880: 7,396, 1910: 8,554, 1930: 4,015, 1960: 11,978.

NY 53A: M, farmer, 80. B. same house. — F. b. along Seneca Lake, PGF b. Ireland, PGM's family from Greene Co., NY; M. b. here, MGF from PA, MGM from Greene Co. — Ed.: till 9th grade. — Presbyterian (not member); Grange, Masons, Maccabees. — Good inf.: cooperative, patient, good sense of humor. Many anecdotes, esp. on weather lore. Still active. No taboos or inhibitions. Inf. somewhat deaf. — Voice not strong; medium to high pitch. Not fast, but somewhat clipped. Nasality. Many final consonants weak or lost; /-r/ not always constricted (less than usual for upstate NY). — A few aux. forms from son, a folk type himself.

NY 53B!: Bath. — F, helped run secretarial school, was public stenographer, is amateur local historian, 80. B. here; lived 6 mos. in NYC, 1 yr. in Hammondsport. — F. b. Bath, PGF b. Unadilla (Delaware Co.), came here age 16, PGM b. Bath (sister of MGM's F.); M. b. Syracuse, MGF lived Syracuse, later Springfield, IL, MGM b. Bath, MGM's F. was atty. gen. of NY State, congressman. — Ed.: private schools (Bath, Haverling, Buffalo); summer school Cornell. — Christian Science. — Good inf. Strong local roots. Knows little about farm life, but good honest responses. Good mind, sense of humor. Curious about interview implications; unnecessarily concerned with failure to give "right" answer. A representative of the "genteel tradition" of cultivated families in old Bath. — High pitch when stressed. Postvocalic /-r/ is often noticeably unconstricted. Naturally says /bin/ for *been* in both direct and cv. responses. Some "broad a". — Cultivated.

Canisteo

Residential center for Hornell workers; shopping center for farmers. Kanisteo Kastle, refuge of misc. runaways and outlaws (1690–1760s); settled 1788 by survivors of Wyoming Massacre in PA. First settlement on flats; later settlers from CT, NJ, MA, Hudson Valley, Mohawk Valley, Finger Lakes, Otsego Co. Village organized 1796; inc. 1873. Shoe factory 1868; wood products.

NY 54A: M, dairy farmer, worked Railway Express Co. 20 yrs., 74. B. here. Lived elsewhere in Co. (Adrian, Corning, Hornell), 4 yrs. Niagara Falls. — F., PGF, PGM; M., MGF, MGM all b. Adrian (5 mi. E.). — Ed.: till 8th grade. — Methodist (loosely attached). — Alternated between reacting quickly to questions and missing the point entirely. Inf. lacked characteristic "twang" of community, perhaps because he had a cigar in his mouth during most of the interview. Much prompting by wife, born PA, but moved to NY as infant.

Hornell

Formed from Canisteo 1820; named after George Hornell, its first settler, whose father was a native of Sweden. Had saw and gristmills. First settled 1790; settlers largely from Wyoming Valley, PA. Erie RR shops (branch to Buffalo 1852); wood products, tanneries, textiles, gloves, machinery, wire, carriages and wagons.

NY 54B: M, fireman, 42. B. Greenwood (18 mi. S.). Lived in Canisteo. 2 yrs. Korea; Marines in WWII. — F. b. Canada, died young; M., MGF, MGM (and their parents) all b. Co. (Rexville). — Ed.: h.s. — Roman Catholic; American Legion.

55. Allegany County

Formed 1806 from Genesee; 1st settlement 1798, Elm Valley near Wellsville. Part of MA tract; 2 W. tiers in Holland Land Co. purchase. Canal 1836 (now defunct); Erie RR. In 1855, 20% of pop. from E. NY; others from PA and NJ. Products and industries: maple sugar, lumbering (1900; also woodworking and tanning), caskets, dairying (cheese factories), machine shops, oil well equipment, RR shops, water power. 80% of NY oil reserves in this co.; oil fields declining but still producing. Pop. 1810: 1,942, 1820: 9,330, 1850: 37,808, 1880: 41,810, 1910: 41,412, 1930: 38,025, 1960: 43,978.

Beers, F. W., ed. 1879. *History of Allegany County.* NY: F. W. Beers.

Child, Hamilton. 1875. *Gazetteer and Business Directory of Allegany County, for 1875.* Syracuse: Hamilton Child.

Doty, Lockwood R., ed. 1925. *History of the Genesee Country. . . .* 4 vols. Chicago: Clarke Pub. Co.

Flanagan, Margaret. 1939. *History and Folklore of Allegany County.* New York State College for Teachers thesis.

Gilbert, Helen Josephine White, ed. 1910. *Rushford and Rushford People.* Rushford: H. J. W. Gilbert.

Minard, J. 1911. *Civic History and Illustrated Progress of Cuba, 1822–1910.* Cuba.

Minard, J. S. 1905. *Recollections of the Log School House Period, and Sketches of Life and Customs in Pioneer Days.* Cuba: Free Press Print.

Minard, John S. 1896. *Allegany County and Its People.* Alfred: W. A. Ferguson.

1950. *Cuba: Incorporated as a Village for a Century, 1850–1950.* Cuba: Cuba Centennial Committee.

Rushford

Twp. cut off from Caneadea 1816; first settled 1809. Early settlers from MA, CT, VT, Mohawk Valley. First town meeting 1816; "union graded free school" from 1867. Thriving village in 1848. Methodist church. Industries: woolen mill, gristmill, cheese factory (center for pineapple cheese), flax raising, tannery, some oil and gas. General farming and dairying. Pop. Twp. 1910: 1260.

NY 55A: M, farmer, former school teacher, 84. B. 9–10 mi. E. Lived outside Rushford village, moved to Farmersville (6 yrs.),

returned to village 1937. — F. b. Houghton, PGF b. VT, moved to S. IL, PGM b. near Houghton; M. b. here, MGF b. VT, MGM's family from Herkimer Co. — Ed.: school in village, old academy. — Methodist; Odd Fellows, Grange. — Good inf., hospitable, spoke freely. Scornful of linguistic taboos. Hard-working, serious farmer. Well-rooted in community. A good hard-headed Yankee. — Little in speech to show effect of classroom: *ain't,* double negs., folk preterites all common. Moderate tempo; medium pitch. Much nasality. Stressed vowels moderately long. No perceptible drawl.

NY 55B: Hardys Corner, Cuba P.O., Rushford Twp. — F, widow, 85. B. nearby. Spent several winters in NJ. — F. b. Rushford, PGF perhaps from PA; M. b. Rushford, MGF, MGM b. VT. — Ed.: rural schools, Rushfield Academy. — Baptist. — Excellent inf. An example of good old-fashioned Yankee middle class, uncontaminated by modern influences. Small, prim, and erect, with flashes of dry Yankee humor. — A number of folk forms. Moderate tempo; voice med. to high. Post-vocalic consonants somewhat relaxed.

56. Wyoming County

Formed from S. part of Genesee Co. 1841; orig. part of Holland Land Co. Surveyed 1798; twps. delineated by 1799. First permanent settlers in Co. 1802; early settlers from MA, CT, VT, E. NY (by 1855 perhaps 75% of Yankee stock). Irish settlers 1830s. 1st roads from Batavia in 1802; no turnpikes in Co. 1837–54 Genesee Canal; abandoned 1878. First RR 1843. Industries generally small, diversified: salt works, textiles, packaging. Also stock, wool, dairying, grain and fruit, maple sugar. Tendency for rural pop. to decline. Pop. 1850: 31,981, 1880: 30,907, 1910: 31,880, 1930: 28,764, 1960: 34,793.

Beers, F. W., ed. 1880. *History of Wyoming County.* NY: F. W. Beers.

Beers, S. N., et al. 1866. *New Topographical Atlas of Genesee and Wyoming Counties, New York.* Philadelphia: Stone and Stewart.

Child, Hamilton. 1870. *Gazetteer and Business Directory of Wyoming County, New York, for 1870–71.* Syracuse: H. Child.

Douglass, H., comp. 1935. *Famous Sons and Daughters of Wyoming County.* Warsaw: Wyoming County Newspapers.

Douglass, Harry S. 1957. *"Progress with a Past": Arcade, New York, 1807–1957.* Arcade: Arcade Sesquicentennial and Historical Society.

Hodge, Darwin Grant. 1912. *Arcade, New York.* Arcade: D. G. Hodge.

Horton, J. T., et al. 1947. *History of Northwestern New York.* 3 vols. NY: Lewis Historical Pub. Co.

Tomlinson, G. 1894. *From Youth to Seventy and What I Saw by the Way.* LeRoy: LeRoy Times Co.

1895. *Biographical Review. . . of Livingston and Wyoming Counties.* Boston: Biographical Review Pub. Co.

1947–. *Historical Wyoming.* Arcade.

Arcade

Small post village in China Twp. Village known as Arcade from Reynolds Arcade building in Rochester. First settled 1809, most early settlers from VT. Incorporated 1871. Much abolition activity here in 19th cent. Borden powdered milk here. Other products and industries: wood products (bowling pins, barrels, shoe lasts), automobile tools, dairying, cheese, apples, potatoes, hay.

NY 56A: M, plant guard, 77. B. here. — F. b. Eagle, next twp., PGF lived here a while, moved to MI, PGM local; M. b. Machias, MGF, MGM b. VT, moved to Machias. — Ed.: 7th grade. — Volunteer fireman, Good Templars Lodge. — Never traveled over 50 mi. from home. Physically vigorous. Sociable, sense of humor. Knows all details of local life, and makes no effort to cover up. Independent thinker: strong Townsendite. Did not understand purpose of interview. — Voice not too loud (part of interview in semi-whisper in deference to landlord's family). Much nasality; fairly wide intonation range. Basic pitch fairly low.

NY 56B: M, painter and decorator, 84. B. here. — F. b. Hartford, NY; M. b. Wayne Co. — Ed.: local schools, Arcade Academy, Union Schools. — Congregational Church. — Cooperative; great talker. Not too much sense of humor. Disclaimed much knowledge of farm life, but generally had accurate knowledge. Impeccable local roots; likes to talk about old times. — Fairly fast speech. Nasality. Articulation not clear: generally had cigar in mouth. Moderately strong stresses.

57. Livingston County

Formed from Ontario and Genesee Cos., 1821. Part of MA tract. First settled c. 1790 from CT and PA; also many Scots early. 1st antislavery convention here. Pioneers in agricultural experiment: e.g., sheep, beef cattle. Pop. 1830: 27,729, 1850: 40,875, 1880: 39,562, 1910: 38,037, 1930: 37,560, 1960: 44,053.

> Ashton, John. 1951. *Open-Country Holdings in Northern Livingston County, New York.* Cornell University Master's thesis.
> Beers, F. W., ed. 1872. *Atlas of Livingston County, New York.* NY: F. W. Beers.
> Doty, Lockwood R. 1876. *A History of Livingston County. . . .* Geneseo: E. E. Doty.
> Smith, James H. 1881. *History of Livingston County. . . .* Syracuse: D. Mason and Co.
> 1895. *Biographical Review. . . of Livingston and Wyoming Counties.* Boston: Biographical Review Pub. Co.

Livonia

Twp. formed from Pittstown 1808. 1st settler c. 1794 from CT (many early settlers from CT). N. half undulating; S. half hilly; good wheat soil.

NY 57A: M, farmer and coal dealer, 73. B. here. — F. b. Devonshire, came to US at 2; M. b. Co., lived near Livonia Center, MGF, MGM b. in general area, settled in E. Bloomfield. — Ed.: h.s. here; Cook Academy, Montour Falls. — Congregational Comm. Church (was Baptist); Mason, active fireman, Grange once, Royal Arch. — Strenuous interview. Although initially suspicious, inf. insisted on finishing in one session. Free talker, once underway; many cv. forms. Seemed to know local details well; not bookish. — Fairly fast speech.

Nasality. Wide intonation range. Slurring; consonant articulation not clear.

NY 57B: F, housewife, 79. B. here. Lived 8 yrs. Geneseo. — F. b. Bergen (Genesee Co.), PGF prob. b. Bergen, family orig. from Scotland; M., MGF b. Livonia. — Ed.: Livonia public schools, 1 yr. Geneseo Normal. — Methodist, Women's Christian Temperance Union, local social, card, and literary club. — Very good inf. Quick mind; knows community in detail. — Some aux. forms from husband, local with similar background. — Interview interrupted. Incomplete.

NY 57C!: Beecher Road, Lima P.O., Livonia Twp. — F, ex-teacher, 83. B. here. Taught 2 yrs. in NC, 5 yrs. in KY; 1 winter in AZ, some travel. — F. b. here, PGF came from Litchfield, CT, PGM from VT. — Ed.: Syracuse Univ., Columbia, Lima-Genessee Wesleyan Seminary (now Junior College). — Presbyterian, Missionary Society; Women's Christian Temperance Union. — Cooperative, although didn't altogether understand purpose of interview. Interview conducted in one session. Well-read, respected, knows community well. Some taboo reactions. — Pleasant voice, fairly fast speech. Aware of differences in usage, but unaffected. Relatively little nasality. — Cultivated.

58. Monroe County

Formed from Ontario and Genesee Cos., 1821; earliest settlements in what is now SE of Co. (Pittsford). First settlers (c. 1789) from MA, VT, PA; settlement speeded up after War of 1812. Ridge parallel with Lake Ontario; productive soil. Some Quakers; religious and other movements: Mormons, spiritualist, temperance, women's suffrage, abolitionism, anti-Masonic. Productive farms and prosperous industry (mostly light): grains, fruit, nurseries (50 in Co. by 1855), dairying, livestock, wool. In 1920, although small and only 1/8 of pop. rural, leading agricultural co. in NY. Pop. 1830: 49,855, 1850: 87,650, 1880: 144,903, 1910: 283,212, 1930: 423,881, 1960: 586,387.

> Beers, F. W. 1872. *Atlas of Monroe County, New York.* Philadelphia: F. W. Beers and Co.
> Bragdon, George C., ed. 1902. *Notable Men of Rochester and Vicinity, XIX and XX Centuries.* Rochester: Dwight J. Stoddard.
> Brownyard, Mary Jane. 1964. *The Diary of Mary Jane Brownyard.* Silver Springs, Md.
> Butler, William Mill. 1884. *The Semi-Centennial Souvenir. . . with a Chronological History of Rochester.* Rochester: Post-Express Printing Co.
> Child, Hamilton, comp. 1869. *Gazetteer and Business Directory of Monroe County, for 1869–70.* Syracuse: Hamilton Child.
> Cumpston, Dorothy. 1952. *The Building of Brighton, a Town with an Interesting Past and a Promising Future.* Brighton.
> Devoy, John, comp. 1895. *Rochester and the Post Express: A History of the City of Rochester.* Rochester: Post Express Printing Co.
> Elwood, G. 1894. *Some Earlier Public Amusements of Rochester.* Rochester.
> Federal Writers Project. 1937. *Rochester and Monroe County. American Guide Series.* Rochester: Scrantom's.

Fitch, Charles E. 1911. Rochester, Past and Present. In J. N. Larned, *A History of Buffalo* (NY: Progress of the Empire State Co.).

Folts, James D., Jr. 1978. *The Genesee Region, 1790 to the Present: A Guide to Its History*. Rochester: Genesee Valley History Project.

Foreman, E., ed. 1931–34. *Centennial History of Rochester*. 4 vols. Rochester: Rochester Historical Society.

Hanford, Franklin. 1911. *On the Origin of the Names of Places in Monroe County*. Scottsville: I. Van Hooser.

Hosmer, Howard C. 1971. *Monroe County, 1821–1971.* . . . Rochester: Rochester Museum and Science Center.

Kelsey, J. 1854. *Lives and Reminiscences of Pioneers of Rochester and Western New York*. Rochester.

Lee, Florence. 1958. *The Founding of Monroe County*. Rochester: County of Monroe.

Lee, Florence. 1970. *Pleasant Valley: An Early History of Monroe County and Region.* . . . NY: Carlton Press.

McIntosh, W. H., ed. 1877. *History of Monroe County.* . . . Philadelphia: Everts, Ensign and Everts.

McKelvey, Blake. 1945. *Rochester, the Water-Power City.* . . . Cambridge, MA: Harvard University Press.

McKelvey, Blake. 1949. *Rochester, the Flower City, 1855– 1890*. Cambridge, MA: Harvard University Press.

McKelvey, Blake. 1956. *Rochester: The Quest for Quality.* . . . Cambridge, MA: Harvard University Press.

McKelvey, Blake. 1961. *Rochester: An Emerging Metropolis, 1925–1961*. Rochester: Christopher Press.

McKelvey, Blake. 1973. *Rochester on the Genesee: The Growth of a City*. Syracuse: Syracuse University Press.

Merrill, A. 1946. *Rochester Sketchbook*. Rochester: L. Heindl.

O'Reilly, Henry, ed. 1838. *Settlement in the West: Sketches of Rochester, with Incidental Notices of Western New York.* . . . Rochester: W. Alling.

Osgood, H. 1892. *The Struggle for Monroe County*. Rochester.

Osgood, Howard L. 1894. *Rochester: Its Founders and Founding*. Rochester.

Osgood, Katharine Rochester Montgomery. 1937. *Backward Glances at Old Rochester*. Buffalo: Foster and Stewart Pub. Corp.

Parker, Jenny Marsh. 1884. *Rochester: A Story Historical*. Rochester: Scranton, Wetmore.

Peck, William F. 1884. *Semi-Centennial History of the City of Rochester.* . . . Syracuse: D. Mason.

Peck, William F. 1908. *History of Rochester and Monroe County.* . . . 2 vols. NY: Pioneer Pub. Co.

Peck, William, et al. 1895. *Landmarks of Monroe County.* . . . Boston: Boston History Co.

Pugsley, F. 1939. *Pittsford Sesquicentennial, 1789–1939*. Pittsford.

Rosenberg, Stuart E. 1954. *The Jewish Community in Rochester, 1843–1925*. NY: Columbia University Press.

Strong, Augustus Hopkins. 1916. *Reminiscences of Early Rochester.* . . . Rochester: Rochester Historical Society.

Williams, Helen Reynolds, ed. 1964. *Sesquicentennial History of the Town of Brighton. . . 1814–1964*. Brighton: Sesquicentennial Committee.

1860. *Early History of Rochester*. Rochester: G. W. Fisher.

1922–48. *Rochester Historical Society Publications*. Rochester: The Society.

Brighton, Rochester P.O., Brighton Twp.

Twp. first settled 1789; older than Rochester, though now swallowed up in it (actually 3 mi. E.). Formed from Smallwood and Penfield 1814. Many Dutch; early Dutch Reformed Church. Early settlers from MA, Hudson Valley, VT, CT, N. Ireland, RI. Little industry, mainly residential (suburban sprawl in past 30 yrs.), commuters. Some farming: nursery stock, market gardens. Gypsum beds (now mined out). Station on Erie Canal. Pop. 1830: 3,128, 1850: 3,117, 1880: 3,736, 1910: 3,998, 1930: 9,065, 1960: 27,849.

NY 58A: M, blacksmith, mechanic, carriage and truck body building, auto repair, 72. B. locally. — F. b. Rochester, moved to Brighton 1866, PGF, PGM b. Isle of Man, married before emigrating; M. b. Rochester, MGF, MGM b. Nottinghamshire, married before emigrating. — Ed.: local schools, Rochester Business Institute (no h.s.). — Presbyterian; Brighton Historical Society, volunteer fireman and treasurer of Old Brighton Vol. Fire Dept., asst. superintendent of cemetery. — Serious, slow to react, somewhat deaf. Difficulty in handling transition from one block of material to the next. Cooperative, although didn't altogether understand purpose of interview. Strong local roots and intimate knowledge of area. — Slurred, indistinct speech (accentuated by chewing tobacco). Nasality, strong stresses.

Pittsford, Pittsford Twp.

Formed from Smallwood 1814; first settlement 1789 from Washington Co., NY; other early settlers from Pittsford, VT (1792), RI, CT, England, MA (first permanent settlements in E. Monroe Co.). Residential suburb of Rochester (6 mi. SE). Little manufacturing before 1860. Smuggling to Canada during War of 1812. Rolling, highly productive farmland; cheesemaking. Pop. Village 1830: 1,831, 1850: 2,061, 1880: 2,236, 1910: 1,205, 1930: 1,460, 1960: 1,749.

NY 58B: M. B. Murder Kill Hundred, DE, came to Pittsford when 3 yrs. old; spent 1 1/2–2 yrs. out West (OK), 7 yrs. in Brooklyn, 1 yr. in Rochester. — F. b. Windsor area, CT; MGF, MGM from Windsor area. — Good Yankee type; well-to-do, likes to tinker, proud of firearms collection. Knows area intimately. Talkative, no inhibitions, great story teller. — Fast speech. Speech not perceptibly affected by stay in West. Strong nasality. /-r/ occasionally without constriction. Unreleased final stops.

Rochester

First settler "Indian" Allen in 1789; left 1792. First allotments 1812; inc. as village 1817; as city 1834. Co. seat from 1821. Erie Canal built through town 1823; flour mills, operation of canal transportation. 1837 1st RR, to Batavia. 1840 nursery industry est. ("Flower City"). 1847 station on the underground RR. Center for religious movements, women's suffrage movement. In 1855 44% foreign-born, chiefly Germans. By 1930, substantial numbers of Italians, Germans, Canadians, English, Poles, Irish, and Russians, but no distinct "foreign quarter". Literary and cultural center: museum, Historical Society, art gallery. U. of Rochester originally Baptist; est. 1850, coed 1893; heavily endowed. Lake port, once milling center. Varied industries, including Eastman, Bausch and Lomb, Xerox, sewing machines, shoes, men's clothing, electrical equipment, machine tools, RR signals, dental equipment, glass-lined tanks. Pop. 1830: 8,207, 1850: 36,403, 1880: 89,366, 1910: 218,149, 1930: 328,132, 1960: 318,611.

NY 58C: M, nursery business, 63. B. Cortland, moved to Rochester as boy. — F., PGF from Rochester, PGF's F. came to Rochester 1810; M. from Cortland, MGF and MGM b. Ireland, married before emigrating. — Ed.: Cortland Normal. — No organizations. — Intelligent, fairly good inf., although tired. — Nasality. Slight prolongation of stressed vowels, although not drawl.

Bushnell Basin, Pittsford P.O., Perinton Twp.

Twp. formed from Boyle 1812. Bushnell Basin 11 mi. SE of Rochester. 1st settlement 1793; settlers from CT via NH. Other early settlers from MA, Hudson Valley, Mohawk Valley. For a while, terminal of Erie Canal. Sandy loam, general farming, fruit orchards from 1810. In 1860s was a small trading center.

NY 58D!: F, housewife, 60. B. Rochester; always lived in Monroe Co., no travel until late in life. — F. b. Rochester, PGF b. Haddam, CT, came to Bergen, Genesee Co., PGF's F., PGF's PGF, PGF's M. from Haddam, PGM b. Poole, Dorset, England; M. b. Orleans Co. (next co. W.), MGF, MGF's F. b. Pleasant Valley, NY (came out 1820), MGF's M. b. NYC, MGM b. Ridgeway, MGM's F. b. NY State, MGM's M. came into Auburn, "military tract". — Ed.: private school, "Columbia", till 16. Played basketball. — Presbyterian; Historical Society, Landmark Society, YWCA, Garden Club. — Cultivated, assured of place in society, interested in history of comm. Seemed to enjoy interview; talked freely. — No hesitation about using folk grammatical forms if situation calls for them. Small amount of nasality. Fairly rapid speech. /r-/ velarized, fricative, rounded; other infs. in area have same characteristic. The comparative lack of constriction of /-r/ seems characteristic of cultivated Rochester infs. — Cultivated. — A number of aux. forms from brother (lawyer, 62, always lived in Co.). These mostly complemented inf.'s responses; where they differ, brother's responses are starred. Chief diffs. are that brother has more constriction of /-r/ and less frequent use of [ɝ ɝ] type diphthongs in *word*, etc.

NY 58E: Rochester. — F, single, "rentier", 65. B. here. Several visits to England. — F. b. Springfield, MA, area, came here from Worcester as a young man, F's family always in W. MA; MGF's F. from VA, MGF's M. b. VA, MGM b. here, MGM's M. b. Roswell. Genealogy available, but inf. not very interested. — Ed.: private school, boarding school in Northampton, MA, Smith College. — Episcopalian; Genesee Valley Club, Chatterbox Club, Corner Club, Cosmopolitan Club (NYC), AAUW City Club. — Many young contacts; much more active in mind and body than most her age. Excellent inf. Strong-willed; socially assured. Hospitable and cooperative. Knows town better than country, but had much info. on rural life (worked on farm as a girl). — Voice relatively clear. Wide intonation range. Tempo rather rapid. Little nasality. Stresses fairly strong. /-r/ wavers; nearly all Rochester infs. (esp. cultivated) had less constriction than FW anticipated. — Cultivated.

NY 58F!: Rochester. — F, housewife, 62. B. here. 2–3 yrs. school in Baltimore, summers Nantucket. — F., PGF b. Rochester, PGF's F. from CT, PGM b. CT; M. b. Albany, came to Rochester for school, MGF, MGF's F. b. Albany. — Ed.: private schools here; St. Timothy's, Baltimore. — Episcopalian; Roundabout Club, Wednesday Club, Landmark Soc., Hospital Board, nursing education. — Good inf.; quick mind. An assurance that comes from her social position (one of the most cultivated infs. FW has ever interviewed). Natural; charming conversationalist. — Moderate tempo. Wide intonation range; well-modulated voice. Less /-r/ constriction than expected. — Cultivated.

59. Genesee County

Formed from Ontario Co. 1802; several cos. since taken from it. Early settlers from CT, Phila., NJ, VT, Hudson Valley. 1/2 Holland Purchase lands sold by 1821. Birthplace of Anti-Masonic Party; birthplace of Anti-Slavery Party. Politically dominated to 1860 by New Englanders (generally Episcopalians); indigenous New Yorkers underrepresented. Wheat first major crop, but less important after RRs and opening of prairie states. Highly fertile; orchards from 1820. Slow industrialization.

Beers, F. W., ed. 1890. *Gazetteer and Biographical Record of Genesee County, 1788–1890*. Syracuse: J. W. Vose.

Beers, S. N., et al. 1866. *New Topographical Atlas of Genesee and Wyoming Counties, New York*. Philadelphia: Stone and Stewart.

Cooley, La Verne C. 1952. *Tombstone Inscriptions from the Abandoned Cemeteries and Farm Burials of Genesee County*. Batavia.

Cowan, Helen I. 1942. Charles Williamson and the Southern Entrance to the Genesee Country. *New York History* 23:260–74.

Fairchild, Herman L. 1928. *Geologic Story of the Genesee Valley and Western New York*. Rochester: the author.

Hungerford, Edward. 1946. *The Genesee Country*. . . . NY: Gallery Press.

Katlowski, Kathleen Smith. 1973. *The Social Composition of Political Leadership: Genesee County, New York, 1821–1866*. University of Rochester dissertation.

Kennedy, John. 1895. *The Genesee Country*. Batavia: Calkins and Lent.

North, S., ed. 1899. *Our County and Its People*. Boston.

Schmidt, Carl Frederick. 1960. *The Le Roy Settlement*. Scottsville:

Williamson, Charles. 1804. *A Description of the Genesee Country*. NY: R. Munro.

1952. *The Sesquicentennial of Genesee County, 1802–1952*. Batavia.

1962. *A History of the Town of Bethany*. Bethany: Sesquicentennial Committee.

Bergen P.O., Le Roy Twp.

Twp. formed from 1812; village of Le Roy founded 1812. First settler 1793. Saltworks. Birthplace of stringless bean; hometown of Jello. Industries developed from local water power. "Thriving village. . . more than its share of fine old post-Colonial houses". Bergen a small village 16 mi. NE of Batavia. Pop. Le Roy Twp. 1820: 2,611, 1850: 3,473, 1880: 4,469, 1910: 5,442, 1930: 4,474, 1960: 6,779.

NY 59A: M, farmer, 4 yrs. travelling salesman, 71. B. locally (6 mi. NW). — F. b. England, came over age 21; M. b. Ely, near London, England. — Ed.: Le Roy; about 2 yrs. h.s. — Methodist; Farm Bureau, Grange, Masons. — Strong local roots; detailed knowledge of community. No linguistic taboos. — Fast speech, with much assimilation. Nasality. Vowels shorter than found elsewhere in NY. — Wife, born Bergen of local family, similar age and education, amplified or corrected many of inf.'s responses. Disagreements indicated by FW; similarities in overall speech characteristics were far more numerous.

Bethany Center, East Bethany P.O., Bethany Twp.

Twp. formed from Batavia 1812. Bethany Center 8 mi. SE of Batavia. Early settlers from CT. Mainly agricultural area.

NY 59B: M, farmer, 44. B. Twp. — F. b. Pavilion Twp., PGF, PGM b. Co.; M. b. edge of Wyoming Co., MGF b. Wyoming Co., MGM b. near Cayuga Lake. — Ed.: till 18. 3 yrs. h.s. in Batavia, 1 yr. business college in Buffalo. — Presbyterian.

60. Orleans County

Formed 1824 from Genesee Co.; 1st settlers 1803 (chiefly New Englanders). Apple growing from 1805. 1st quarry 1837: quarrying (sandstone) second to agriculture. Level or slightly undulating; gradual inclination to lake except in extreme S. Larger percentage of land in farms than in any other Co. Products and industries: limestone, iron, grain and fruits, beans. Pop. 1830: 17,732, 1850: 28,501, 1880: 30,128, 1910: 32,000, 1930: 28,795, 1960: 34,156.

Child, Hamilton, comp. 1869. *Gazetteer and Business Directory of Orleans County, New York, for 1869.* Syracuse: H. Child.

Signor, Isaac S., ed. 1894. *Landmarks of Orleans County....* Syracuse: D. Mason.

Thomas, Arad. 1853. *Sketches of the Village of Albion....* Albion: Willsea and Beach.

Thomas, Arad. 1871. *Pioneer History of Orleans County.* Albion: H. A. Bruner.

1879. *Historical Album of Orleans County.* NY: Sanford and Co.

Lyndonville, Yates Twp.

Twp. formed from Ridgeway in 1822. 1st settler in Lyndonville 1809, but few settlers until after War of 1812. 1st settler of German descent from Jefferson Co.; other early settlers from PA, E. NY, ME, MA, VT, NH. Small village: churches and shops.

NY 60A: M, retired farmer, 87. B. Somerset Twp. (next W.). Has lived elsewhere in Co., 3 yrs. IA. — F., prob. PGF b. Niagara Co.; M. b. Twp., MGF b. here, MGM from Stillwater, Saratoga Co. — Ed.: Yates Acad. 2 yrs. (local). — Presbyterian; Odd Fellows, Maccabees, Grange. — Good inf.; talked freely. No pretensions; very little reading. Strong local roots. Likes people; good rapport with FW. Tended to tire at end of long sessions; place names rather hard to get at. — Tempo moderate to slow. Stresses fairly strong. Voice somewhat harsh. Fair amount of nasality. Some weakening of final consonants.

Albion

Twp. formed from Barre Twp. 1875. Village originally Newport (grew up around Erie Canal work); inc. 1828. Co. seat. First settlement 1811 from further E. in NY; other early settlers from RI, PA, MA, NH, CT, VT, Hudson Valley, Mohawk Valley, England. Small industries; packing (canned tomatoes and peas), stone quarries. Timber trade early, but ceased when supply depleted; cattle and sheep raised for market. Pop. 1850: 2,251, 1880: 5,147, 1910: 5,016, 1930: 4,578, 1960: 6,416.

NY 60B!: M, retired govt. worker, 74. B. Eagle Harbor. Moved Albion 2 yrs. ago. — F. b. Knollesville (S. of Albany), PGF, PGM b. CT; MGF, MGM b. Genesee Co. — Ed.: district school, private school, military school; N. Falls, Trinity. — Grandparents were Universalists but inf. confirmed Episcopalian; Grange, has served in legislature, active in local dramatics. — Strong local roots, and proud of them. Likes to talk. Hoping to please FW, he offered folk forms from his boyhood, rather than from his present speech; this difficulty partly offset by the wealth of cv. forms which emerged in the interview. Good example of the cultivated type who'll use the folk idiom whenever it seems a good idea. — Rapid speech; nervous (chain-smoker). Stresses fairly strong; articulation generally fairly clear. Some nasality. — Cultivated.

61. Niagara County

Formed 1808 from Genesee Co. French post in 1726; first European settler 1727. Niagara on Corovelli's map (Paris) as early as 1688. Important in Indian trade. Involved in Holland Purchase 1792–93. RR from 1830. Center of electrochemical and electrometallurgical industries. Flour; paper and pulp. Fruit growing: apples, Bartlett pears, grapes, peaches (1st in apples in US). Pop. 1810: 8,971, 1820: 22,990, 1850: 42,276, 1880: 54,173, 1910: 92,036, 1930: 149,329, 1960: 242,269.

Aiken, John, et al. 1961. *Outpost of Empires: A Short History of Niagara County.* Phoenix, NY: F. E. Richards.

Dow, Charles Mason. 1921. *Anthology and Bibliography of Niagara Falls.* Albany: J. B. Lyon Co.

Newell, Ray A. 1950. *History of Newfane.* Lockport: Niagara County Historical Society.

Pechuman, L.L. 1959. *Niagara County and Its Towns (A Series of Maps).* Lockport: Historical Atlas.

Pool, William, ed. 1897. *Landmarks of Niagara County.* Syracuse: D. Mason.

Porter, Peter A. 1913. *Old Niagara County's Share in the Battle of Lake Erie.* Niagara Falls: Niagara Frontier Historical Society.

Wiley, Samuel T., and W. Scott Garner, eds. 1892. *Biographical and Portrait Cyclopedia of Niagara County.* Philadelphia: Gresham Pub. Co.

Williams, Edward T. 1921. *Niagara County... a Concise Record of Her Progress and People, 1821–1921.* 2 vols. Chicago: J. H. Beers.

1878. *History of Niagara County.* New York: Sanford and Co.

1902. *Souvenir History of Niagara County.* Lockport: The Lockport Journal.

Olcott, Newfane Twp.

Twp. formed 1824; includes Niagara Falls, NY. 1st settlement in area at Olcott in 1807–8; early settlers from Canada, NJ, PA, NY, later Germany, E. NY, CT, England. One of earliest gristmills here. Chiefly a summer resort; good harbor, lighthouse. Predominantly rural, agricultural.

NY 61A: M, farmer, 82. B. Twp.; lived a while in Wilson Twp., 2 mi. W. — F. from Rutland, VT, came here as child, worked on a canal boat, PGF raised in Rutland, PGM prob. b. VT; M., MGF, prob. MGM b. Wilson. — Ed.: local schools, till 8th grade. — Methodist (not a member, but attends); paid into farm organization. — Strong local roots; well respected in comm. A good Yankee type. Prosperous farmer and good businessman; hardworking. A bit taciturn, but cooperative. Some travel, but seems not to have influenced speech. — Moderate to slow tempo. Fairly clear utterance. Medium pitch. Nasality. Slight drawl. Stressed vowels moderately long; final consonants fairly distinct.

NY 61B: M, "chemical engineer" (refrigeration), former pro baseball player, 77. B. Lockport in Co., came to Olcott when married. — F. b. Milton, PA, lived in NYC before coming to Lockport, PGF b. Holland; M. b. Ireland. — Ed.: quit h.s. (Lockport) just before graduation. — Presbyterian; Eagles, "Ancient Order of Heptosophs" (now defunct). — Very fine interview. Inf. extremely cooperative, natural; excellent rapport with FW. Plenty of anecdotes. Has done all sorts of work, but movements now limited. A little bit of Puritan conscience (occasionally hesitated over a "swear word" if attention directed). Good sense of humor. — Tempo somewhat fast; stresses variable, sometimes very strong. Clear utterance. No drawl. Voice mid-low pitch, pleasant. "Irish" quality in voice. Much nasality. Unreleased final consonants normal. Stressed vowels mod. long. No contrast of [ɔ] and [o] before [r].

62. Erie County

Formed from Niagara Co. 1821. Contains city of Buffalo and industrial and residential suburbs; small villages, agriculture in S. and E. of Co. All within Holland Company purchase, except strip on Niagara R. 1679 LaSalle built ship for westward expedition; ship lost on return. French fort on Niagara R. from 1687; captured by British 1759. Buffalo-Batavia road 1803. Majority of settlers Yankees; also some PA Germans and some Mohawk Germans. Rent riots in 1830s. 1st RR 1833. Many German immigrants in 19th cent. after Erie Canal opened. Portland cement; electric power. Pop. 1830: 35,719, 1850: 100,993, 1880: 219,884, 1910: 528,985, 1930: 762,408, 1960: 1,064,688.

Anderson, Doris. 1946. *An Informal History of Eden.* Eden.

Ball, Sheldon. 1825. *Buffalo in 1825: Containing Historical and Statistical Sketches.* Buffalo: S. Ball.

Baxter, Henry H., and Erik Heyl. 1965. *Maps: Buffalo Harbor 1804–1864.* Buffalo: Lower Lakes Marine Chapter, Buffalo and Erie Co. Hist. Soc.

Becker, Sophie C. 1904. *Sketches of Early Buffalo and the Niagara Region.* Buffalo.

Bingham, R. 1931. *The Cradle of the Queen City: History of Buffalo to the Incorporation of the City.* Buffalo: Buffalo Historical Society.

Devoy, J. 1896. *History of the City of Buffalo and Niagara Falls.* Buffalo: The Times.

Dunn, Walter S., Jr., ed. 1972. *History of Erie County 1870–1970.* Buffalo: Buffalo and Erie County Historical Society.

Glovack, J. 1952. *Survey of Clarence and Its Educational System.* Buffalo: University of Buffalo.

Hawes, Lucy Williams. 1886. *Buffalo Fifty Years Ago.* Buffalo: Courier Co.

Hill, Henry Wayland, ed.-in-chief. 1923. *Municipality of Buffalo, New York: A History, 1720–1923.* 4 vols. New York: Lewis Historical Pub. Co.

Horton, J. T., et al. 1947. *History of Northwestern New York.* 3 vols. NY: Lewis Historical Pub. Co.

Johnson, Crisfield. 1876. *Centennial History of Erie County.* Buffalo: Matthews and Warren.

Ketchum, William. 1864–65. *An Authentic and Comprehensive History of Buffalo. . . .* 2 vols. Buffalo: Rockwell, Baker, and Hill.

Larned, J. N. 1911. *A History of Buffalo. . . with Sketches of the City of Rochester. . . and the City of Utica. . . .* 2 vols. New York: Progress of the Empire State Co.

Severance, F., ed. 1912. *Picture Book of Earlier Buffalo (Views of the City from 1820 to 1870).* Buffalo: Buffalo Historical Society.

Smith, H. Perry. 1884. *History of the City of Buffalo and Erie County. . . .* 2 vols. Syracuse: D. Mason.

Snow, Julia F. 1908. *Early Recollections of Buffalo.* Buffalo: Matthew-Northrup Works.

Sweeney, Daniel J., comp. 1920. *History of Buffalo and Erie County, 1914–19.* Buffalo: City of Buffalo.

Welch, Samuel M. 1891. *Home History: Recollections of Buffalo during the Decade from 1830 to 1840, or, Fifty Years Since.* Buffalo: Peter Paul and Bro.

White, Truman C., ed. 1898. *Our County and Its People.* 2 vols. Boston: Boston History Co.

1828. *A Directory for the Village of Buffalo. . . to Which is Added a Sketch of the History of the Village, from 1801 to 1828.* Buffalo: L. P. Crary.

1866. *New Topographical Atlas of Erie County, New York.* Philadelphia: Stone and Stewart.

1879–. *Buffalo Historical Society Publications.* Buffalo.

1902. *Men of Buffalo. . . .* Chicago: A. N. Marquis.

1906. *Memorial and Family History of Erie County, New York.* 2 vols. NY: Genealogical Pub. Co.

1908. *A History of the City of Buffalo. . . .* Buffalo: The Buffalo Evening News.

Clarence

Organized 1808; c. 18 mi. NE of Buffalo. C. 1799, 1st permanent settlement in Co. here. Many Germans after 1830, 1848; W. part settled mainly by Germans (wealthy).

NY 62A: M, farmer, 89. B. locally (near Newstead Twp.). — F. b. Scotland, came here when young; M. b. England, died young. — Ed.: local school till age 15–16. — Presbyterian, Maccabees, Dairymen's League. — Difficult interview: inf. very deaf. Inf. entirely untraveled and shows no outside influence in grammar. Solid folk type; best on farm realia, weak on abstract terms. No interest in anything but farming. — Voice in moderate range. Stresses and aspiration medium to very strong. Slow speech. Intonation range limited, except as function of stress. Stressed syllables have sharply falling intonation.

Eden

Organized 1812. 16 mi. S. of Buffalo. Settled 1808 by New Englanders; many Germans and Swiss. Trading center; canning, market gardening.

NY 62B: M, farmer, former constable, has organized phone system, 82. B. here; spent 3 winters in Savannah and 4 in FL. — F. b. here, PGF b. New Hartford, CT, PGM b. near Cleveland, OH; M. b. here, MGF b. locally (N. Boston), MGM b. here (one of first families to settle here). — Ed.: till 8th grade. — Raised Presbyterian; formerly Grange, Maccabees. — Somewhat tired; a bit skeptical. Simple, hardworking; definitely old stock. Well-known in comm. Wife contributed aux. forms, is of same age and general background. She has some notions of "correctness", but these do not interfere. — Some influence of other dialects from winter stays. Crack in voice; medium range. Tempo medium to slow. Nasality. "Short o". Centered beginning of /ai au/. Utterance somewhat slurred. Final cons. often weak.

Delaware Park, Buffalo P.O. and Twp.

First permanent settler 1784. Buffalo originally laid out in 1801 by Holland Land Co. Military post 1812; burnt by British 1813. Inc. as village 1816 (reincorporated 1822); Co. seat 1823; inc. as city 1832. Important harbor from 1821. 1830s Irish and German immigrants; in 1855 over 40% of pop. German; several German newspapers for a time. Timber port for Upper Great Lakes; cattle: market and packing; steel industry important. RR center by 1850s. By 1855 largest grain port in the world. Industry developed: flour mills, textiles, leather, iron, machine shops. Many Poles by mid 19th cent. (now 2nd largest Polish comm. in US); many Italians by 1890. C. 1890 immigrant labor hostility directed against S. and E. Europeans. 1920 chemical industry increased, greater diversification (result of availability of electric power). Other industries: engineering, drugs, dyes, aviation, cement. SUNY Buffalo here; also Grosvenor Library. Pop. 1830: 8,668, 1850: 42,261, 1880: 155,134, 1910: 423,715, 1930: 573,076, 1960: 532,759.

NY 62C: M, president of sign co., 85. B. here. 6 mos. in NYC as sign painter. 16 short trips to all states. Once abroad to Belgium with Rotary. — F. b. Alsace-Lorraine, came here age 15; M. b. Germersheim on the Rhine. — Ed.: till about 8th grade. — Lutheran; Octogenarians Club, Buffalo Historical Club, Buffalo Club, Rotary, United Taxpayers Club. — Cooperative, hospitable; likes people, talked freely. Knows everyone of prominence in Buffalo. Not much experience with rural life, but steeped in city lore. — No pretense at knowing other dialects. Understands German but doesn't speak it. Fast speech. Intonation range moderately wide. Much nasality. Aspiration fairly strong. Initial and final voiced consonants often unvoiced. Unstressed vowels short.

Orchard Park

Formed 1818; originally in twp. of East Hamburg. First settlers in area from VT; some Quakers early. Canal enlarged first 1836–62, again 1895–1903. New Barge Canal 1917.

Prosperous; residential; estates of wealthy Buffalonians. Barrel factory. Pop. 1930: 1,144, 1960: 3,278.

NY 62D!: F, housewife, antique dealer, 73. B. here. Lived 3 yrs. Denver, 19 yrs. Buffalo. — F. b. Twp., PGF b. Utica, came here about 1820, PGM from VT; M., MGF b. here. — Ed.: local and Buffalo schools. — Quaker, local literary club. — Joint interview with husband, with either or both answering; impossible to separate responses, and unnecessary since backgrounds were very much the same. Strong local roots; active in community. Quick minds. Many anecdotes. — Aux. forms from husband, newspaperman, former justice of the peace, b. here but lived 4 yrs. in Washington, DC, as child, 11 yrs. Buffalo. — Fast speech, not overstressed, pleasant to listen to. Clear utterance. Little nasality. Wide intonation range. — Cultivated.

63. Cattaraugus County

Formed 1803 from Genesee Co. 1st settlers 1798: missionaries from Society of Friends. Many early settlers from CT. Orig. Holland Land Company. 1804 Olean Port head of steamboat navigation. Genesee Valley Canal built 1856; abandoned 1878. Erie RR 1851; others after. State park; Indian reservation. Varied terrain, some hills. Products and industries: lumbering, tanning, oil (end of 19th cent.), dairying, maple syrup, apples, grapes. Pop. 1820: 4,090, 1850: 38,950, 1880: 55,806, 1910: 65,919, 1930: 72,398, 1960: 80,187.

Adams, William, ed. 1893. *Historical Gazetteer and Biographical Memorial of Cattaraugus County.* Syracuse: Lyman, Horton.

Beers, D. G. 1869. *Atlas of Cattaraugus county, New York.* NY: D. G. Beers.

Donovan, Michael C. 1959. *Historical Review of Cattaraugus County.* Olean.

Ellis, Franklin. 1879. *History of Cattaraugus County.* Philadelphia: L. H. Everts.

Hall, Lizzie Gregg. 1940. *West of the Cayuga.* NY: Pegasus Pub. Co.

Manley, John, comp. 1857. *Cattaraugus County. . . .* Little Valley: J. Manley.

1958. *Cattaraugus County Sesquicentennial, 1808–1958.* Ellicottville: Sesquicentennial Corp.

Willoughby, Great Valley P.O. and Twp.

Twp. formed from Olean in 1818; first settlers 1812. Early settlers from NH, VT, Hudson Valley, CT, Germany, Ireland, RI, Scotland. Uneven and hilly; good crops. Originally a lumbering town. Cheese factories, dairying. Pop. 1820: 171, 1850: 1638, 1880: 1859.

NY 63A: M, farmer, 70. B. here. Lived 6 mos. Albany, a few winters in the South, has visited ID. — F. b. here, PGF, PGM b. MA; M. b. here, MGF b. "up north", MGM perhaps b. Holland. — Ed.: local schools, 2 yrs. Academy in Franklinville. — Evangelistic United Brethren. — Utterly natural, no inhibitions. Wife, local background, contributed aux. forms; equally uninhibited. No concern for grammar. Good mind and memory. Affable, independent, hard working, frugal. No obvious effect on speech from winters in South. — Talks rather rapidly. Slurring noticeable (sandhi). Nasality strong.

Fairly strong stresses. Stops sharply exploded, though no excess aspiration.

Randolph

Twp. formed from Conewango 1826. First settlement 1820: village had depot, schools, churches, etc. Academy in 19th cent. Early settlers from VT, Genesee Valley, CT, England, MA, NH, NJ, Ireland (many from Monroe Co.). Diversified industry: paints, furniture, tannery, machinery, cheese.

NY 63B: M, banker, formerly farmer, hardware business, 83. B. here. — F. b. Mt. Holly, VT, came here at 25, PGF b. Attleboro, MA, PGM from VT; M. b. adjacent twp. (to NE), MGF, MGM b. New Berlin, NY (Otsego Co.). — Ed.: h.s., local. — Congregationalist background; Masons (50 yrs.). — Yankee trader type. Family came in with lumbering (lived same house 100 yrs.). Somewhat taciturn, but later opened up when son appeared (a few aux. forms). Knows little of other dialects. — Speech somewhat clipped. Nasality. Strong stresses. Vowels all relatively short.

Elkdale, Salamanca P.O., Little Valley Twp.

Twp. formed from Perry 1818. Co. seat. 1st settlements c. 1807; early settlers from CT, MA, Mohawk Valley, Scotland, England, VT, Hudson Valley, Genesee Valley, NH, France, Germany. Hilly and elevated upland; gas, trace of oil. Elkdale trading center for Twp. Cutlery, washing machines, wood products, dairying. (See below for Salamanca.)

NY 63C: M, farmer, 47. B. here. — F. b. Twp., PGF b. Norwich, MA, PGM b. Co., PGM's F. and M. b. MA; M. b. Ellicottville, 8 mi. N., MGF b. MA, near Norwich (Welsh descent), MGM b. Schoharie Co. (Dutch). — Ed.: till 18. — Congregational.

Salamanca

Formed 1854 from Little Valley (orig. Bucktooth: name changed 1862). Settled from CT, Genesee Valley, E. NY, N. PA, MA, N. Ireland, VT, Canada, Germany. Indian reservation since 1797. Inc. as a village 1878; as a city 1913; now largest city in Co. RR division pt. and junction. Natural gas important in development. Misc. industries: stonecutting, tanneries, furniture; market town, becoming winter and summer resort. Pop. 1930: 9,654.

NY 63D!: M, lawyer, 72. B. Randolph, always lived in Co. — F. b. Co. (Napoli), PGF, PGF's F. and M. b. Port Judith, RI, PGM b. Napoli; M., prob. MGF b. Napoli, MGF's F. b. Berkshires, MA, MGM's family from CT. — Ed.: Hamilton; read law in F.'s office. — Congregationalist; NY State Historical Assn., Mason, Director of Salamanca Trust. — Good example of cultivated speech: perhaps the most cultivated inf. FW interviewed in NY. Sure of position. Sticks to standard language, but abhors schoolmarmese (one or two *ain'ts*, very few folk preterites). Steeped in local culture. Very well read. Very hospitable. Recognizes both social and regional dialect differences; recognizes his own multidialectalism. — Very pleasant voice. Wide intonation range. Tempo slow. Stresses fairly strong. No overall nasality (although present before nasal). Some weakening of final cons. Stressed vowels fairly long. — Cultivated.

64. Chautauqua County

Formed from Genesee Co. in 1808. Part of Holland Purchase. 1st settler 1796 from VT; early settlers also from PA, MA, E. NY, N. Ireland; settled along lake. Former French military post. Chautauqua Inst. here from 1874. Many religious, utopian, and reform movements. Many nationalities immigrated in 19th cent.: English, Swedes, Irish, Germans, Danes, Italians, Greeks, Poles, Jews, Dutch; also Albanians in 1913. Erie RR completed 1851; rapid pop. growth followed. Grape growing begun 1824, became commercial in 1874: table grapes and grape juice, wine (mainly along Lake Erie). Greatest grape-producing co. in US in 1920. Also other fruits, vegetables, and dairying. Other products: woodworking and wood products, woolens, machine shops, steel office furniture, voting machines, ironworks. Decline in number of farms since 1900. Pop. 1820: 12,568, 1850: 50,493, 1880: 65,342, 1910: 105,126, 1930: 126,457, 1960: 145,377.

Anderson, Arthur Wellington. 1932. *The Conquest of Chautauqua: Jamestown and Vicinity in the Pioneer and Later Periods*. Jamestown: Journal Press.

Anderson, Arthur Wellington. 1936. *The Story of a Pioneer Family*. Jamestown: Jamestown Historical Society.

Beers, Frederick W. 1881. *Illustrated Historical Atlas of the County of Chautauqua, New York*. NY.

Child, Hamilton, comp. 1873. *Gazetteer and Business Directory of Chautauqua County, New York for 1873–74*. Syracuse: H. Child.

Dilley, Butler F., ed. 1891. *Biographical and Portrait Cyclopedia of Chautauqua County*. Philadelphia: J. M. Gresham.

Doty, W. J., et al. 1940. *Historical Annals of Southwestern New York*. 3 vols. NY: Lewis Historical Pub. Co.

Downs, John P., et al. 1921. *History of Chautauqua County. . . .* 3 vols. NY: American Historical Society Inc.

Edson, Obed. 1894. *History of Chautauqua County*. Boston: W. A. Fergusson.

Hill, F. F., et al. 1943. *Erin: The Economic Characteristics of a Rural Town in Southern New York*. Ithaca: New York State College of Agriculture, Dept. of Agricultural Economics.

McMahon, Helen Grace. 1958. *Chautauqua County, A History*. Buffalo: H. Stewart.

Merrill, A. 1953-54. *Southern Tier*. 2 vols. NY: American Book-Stratford Press.

Taylor, H. C. 1873. *Historical Sketches of the Town of Portland. . . .* Fredonia: W. McKinstry.

Warren, Emory F. 1846. *Sketches of the History of Chautauqua County*. Jamestown: J. W. Fletcher.

Woodward, J. 1902. *Address at the Centennial Celebration of the First Settlement of Chautauqua County, June 24, 1902, at Westfield*. Jamestown.

Young, A. 1875. *History of Chautauqua County*. Buffalo.

1867. *New Topographical Atlas of Chautauqua County, New York*. Philadelphia: William Stewart.

1904. *The Centennial History of Chautauqua County*. Jamestown: Chatauqua History Co.

Westfield

Formed 1829 from Portland and Ripley. Village inc. 1833. First settler 1802 from Northumberland Co., PA; others from CT, PA, Mohawk Valley, NH, Genesee Valley, VT, MA, St.

Lawrence Valley, N. Ireland, Hudson Valley, Finger Lakes. Rolling land of great fertility along lake. Natural gas, farming, grape growing, dairying, small industries. Important as a "crossroads". Welch's grape juice. Pop. 1930: 3,466.

NY 64A: M, village clerk, laundry business, 81. B. Chautauqua; also lived Portland. — F. b. Portland, PGF b. NYC, PGM "Holland Dutch and Irish"; M. b. E. of Chautauqua. — Ed.: 2 yrs. h.s. — Family is Presbyterian, but not inf.; Masons. — Very cooperative. Good sense of humor. A bit deaf but uses hearing aid. Has noticed diffs. between area speech and speech of PA ("was louder"). — Fairly loud, vigorous speech. Strong stresses. Nasality. Some drawl; stressed vowels fairly long.

NY 64B: F, florist and former schoolteacher, 80. B. W. Portland (next town). Came to Westfield age 21, in 1890. — F. b. Kent, England, came to Co. as child, PGF, PGM b. Kent Co., England; M. b. Portland, MGF b. Potter's Hollow, Albany Co., MGM b. Schoharie Co., came to Portland as infant. — Ed.: West Portland and Westfield "teachers' class". — Presbyterian, church Women's Society; Grange, Eastern Star. — Very cooperative. Enjoyed interview. No pretensions. — Slow speech. Nasality. High pitch; rising intonation towards end of sentence, esp. on stressed syllable. Unreleased and weakly articulated final stops.

NY 64C!: F, librarian in public schools, has taught, 65. B. Co. (Canawaugo); moved here at 6. Lived 9 yrs. MS, 2 yrs. AZ. — F., PGF, PGM b. Co. (Charlotte Center); M. b. Co., near Fredonia, MGF b. Arkwright, near Fredonia, MGM b. VT. — Ed.: local schools; A.B. U. of Michigan; M.A. Columbia U.; B.S. in Library Science Geneseo State. — Presbyterian; DAR, AAUW, Librarian Societies, former Eastern Star. — Enjoyed interview. Sure of position in comm. — Good knowledge of local vocabulary. Rather deliberate speech. Medium range of intonation. Small amount of nasality. — Cultivated.

Bibliographies

Cole, G. Glyndon, ed. 1968. *Historical Materials Relating to Northern New York*. Plattsburgh: North Country Reference and Research Resources Council.

Flagg, Charles A., and Judson T. Jennings. 1901. *Bibliography of New York Colonial History*. Albany: University of the State of New York.

Marshall, Shelby, and Martha D. Noble, comps. 1980. *Handbook to Historic Resources of the Upper Hudson Valley*. Albany: Fort Orange Press.

Nestler, Harold. 1968. *A Bibliography of New York State Communities, Counties, Towns, and Villages*. Port Washington: T.J. Friedman.

General Histories

Barber, John Warner, and Henry Howe. 1851. *Historical Collections of the State of New York. . . .* NY: Clerk, Austin, and Co.

Bliven, Bruce, Jr. 1981. *New York: A Bicentennial History*. NY: Norton.

Brodhead, John R. 1853–71. *History of the State of New York*. 2 vols. NY: Harper.

Donaldson, Alfred L. 1921. *A History of the Adirondacks*. 2 vols. NY: Century Co.

Dunn, J. T. 1951. Checklist of Current New York State History Magazines (rev.). *New York History* 32:236–42.

Ellis, David M., James A. Frost, Harold C. Syrett, and Harry J.Carman. 1967. *A History of New York State*. Ithaca: Cornell University Press.

Flick, Alexander C. 1933–37. *History of the State of New York*. NY: Columbia Univ. Press.

Greene, Nelson, ed. 1931. *History of the Valley of the Hudson*. 5 vols. Chicago: Clarke Pub. Co.

Horton, John Theodore, Edward T. Williams, and Harry S. Douglas. 1947. *History of Northwestern New York: Erie, Niagara, Wyoming, and Orleans*. 3 vols. NY: Lewis Historical Pub. Co.

Kammen, Michael. 1975. Colonial New York: A History. In Milton M. Klein and Jacob E. Cook, eds., *A History of the American Colonies* (NY: Scribners).

Smith, William, Jr. 1972. *The History of the Province of New York*. 2 vols., ed. by Michael Kammer. Cambridge, MA: Harvard University Press.

Stevens, John Austin. 1884. The English in New York. In Justin Winsor, ed., *Narrative and Critical History of America* (Boston: Houghton, Mifflin), vol. 3, 385–420.

Sullivan, James, ed. 1927. *History of New York State 1523–1927*. 5 vols. NY: Lewis Historical Pub. Co.

Writers Program of the WPA. 1940. *New York: A Guide to the Empire State*. NY: Oxford University Press.

1917–1945. *New-York Historical Society Quarterly Bulletin*. NY: New-York Historical Society.

1919–. *New York History*. Albany: New York State Historical Association.

1945–1974. *New York Folklore Quarterly*. Ithaca: New York Folklore Society.

Special Studies

Adams, Samuel H. 1953. *The Erie Canal*. NY: Random House.

Archdeacon, Thomas J. 1976. *New York City, 1664–1700: Conquest and Change*. Ithaca: Cornell University Press.

Bachman, Van Cleaf. 1969. *Peltriesor Plantations: The Economic Policies of the Dutch West India Company in New Netherland 1629–1639*. Baltimore: Johns Hopkins Press.

Balen, Willem Julius van. 1943. *Holland aan de Hudson*. Amsterdam: Amsterdamsche Boek en Courantmaatschappij.

Banemi, Patricia. 1971. *A Fractious People: Politics and Society in Colonial New York*. NY: Columbia University Press.

Beauchamp, W. M. 1893. *Indian Names in New York*. Fayetteville: H. C. Beauchamp.

Becker, Carl L. 1909. *History of Political Parties in the Province of New York, 1760–1776*. Madison, WI.

Benson, Lee. 1955. *Merchants, Farmers, and Railroads: Railroad Regulation and New York Politics, 1850–1887*. Cambridge, MA: Harvard University Press.

Brewster, William. 1954. *The Pennsylvania and New York Frontier. . . .* Philadelphia: G. S. MacManus Co.

Bridenbaugh, Carl. 1981. *Early Americans*. NY: Oxford University Press.

Bruyer, Eric. 1955. A Chapter in the Growth of the New York State Dairy Industry 1850–1900. *New York History* 36:736–45.

Chazanof, William. 1970. *Joseph Elliott and the Holland Land Company: The Opening of Western New York*. Syracuse: Syracuse University Press.

Cheyney, Edward P. 1887. *Anti-Rent Agitation in the State of New York*. NY: G. E. Stechert.

Christensen, Gardell Dano. 1969. *Colonial New York*. Camden, N.J.: Nelson.

Christman, Henry. 1945. *Tin Horns and Calico: A Decisive Episode in the Emergence of Democracy*. NY: Holt.

Clinton, George. 1918. Evolution of the New York Canal System. *Publication of the Buffalo Historical Society* 22:273-95.

Condon, Thomas J. 1968. *New York Beginnings: The Commercial Origins of New Netherland*. NY:New York University Press.

Cross, Whitney R. 1950. *The Burned-Over District*. Ithaca: Cornell University Press.

Ellis, D. M. 1951. The Yankee Invasion of New York 1783–1850. *New York History* 32:1-17.

Ellis, D. M. 1954. New York and Middle Atlantic Regionalism. *New York History* 35:3-13.

Ellis, David M. 1946. *Landlords and Farmers in the Hudson-Mohawk Region, 1790-1880*. NY: Octagon Books.

Eltiner, Irving. 1880. Dutch Village Communities on the Hudson River. *Johns Hopkins Urban Studies in History and Political Science* 4:1-69.

Evans, Paul D. 1924. *The Holland Land Company*. Buffalo: Buffalo Historical Society.

Evjen, John Olaf 1916. *Scandinavian Emigrants in New York 1630-1674. . . .* Minneapolis: K. C. Holber.

Fernow, Berthold. 1884. New Netherland, or the Dutch in North America. In Justin Winsor, ed., *Narrative and Critical History of America* (Boston: Houghton, Mifflin), 4:395-442.

Fernow, Berthold. 1887. The Middle Colonies. In Justin Winsor, ed., *Narrative and Critical History of America* (Boston: Houghton, Mifflin), 5:189-231.

Fiske, John. 1899. *The Dutch and Quaker Colonies in America*. NY: Houghton, Mifflin.

Flick, Alexander C. 1901. *Loyalism in New York during the American Revolution*. NY. Repr. 1969 (NY: Arno Press).

Flick, Alexander C., and Peter Nelson. 1967. *The American Revolution in New York. . . .* Port Washington: Friedman.

Fox, Dixon R. 1919. *The Decline of Aristocracy in the Politics of New York*. NY: Columbia University Press.

Fox, Dixon Ryan. 1979. *Yankees and Yorkers*. Reprint. Westerport, CT: Greenwood Press.

French, J. H. 1860. *Gazetteer of the State of New York*. Syracuse: R. P. Smith.

Harlow, Alvin F. 1947. *The Road of the Century: The Story of the New York Central*. NY: Creative Age Press.

Hedrick, Ulysses Prentiss. 1933. *History of Agriculture in the State of New York*. Albany: New York State Agriculture Society.

Hicks, Frederick C. 1929. *High Finance in the Sixties: Chapters from the Early History of the Erie Railway*. New Haven. Repr. 1966 (Port Washington: Kennikat Press).

Higgins, Ruth Loving. 1931. *Expansion in New York with Especial Reference to the Eighteenth Century*. Columbus, OH. Repr. 1976 (Philadelphia: Porcupine Press).

Hill, Henry W. 1908. An Historical Review of Waterways and Canal Construction in New York State. *Publication of the Buffalo Historical Society* 12.

Hoglund, A. William. 1953. Abandoned Farms and the "New Agriculture" in New York State at the Beginning of the Twentieth Century. *New York History* 34:185-203.

Howell, George R. 1897. *The Date of the Settlement of the Colony of New York*. Albany: New York Society of the Order of the Founders and Patriots of America.

Judd, Jacob, and Irwin H. Polishook, eds. 1874. *Aspects of Early New York Society and Politics*. Tarrytown.

Kemp, William W. 1913. *Support of Schools in Colonial New York by the S.P.G.F.P.*. NY: Teachers College, Columbia University.

Kenney, Alice P. 1975. *Stubborn for Liberty: The Dutch in New York*. Syracuse: University Press.

Kim, Sung Bok. 1978. *Landlord and Tenant in Colonial New York*. Chapel Hill: UNC Press.

Kimball, Francis P. 1937. *New York: The Canal State*. Albany: Argus Press.

Kobrin, David. 1971. *The Black Minority in Early New York*. Albany: Office of State History.

Launitz-Schürer, Leopold S. 1980. *Loyal Whigs and Revolutionaries: The Making of the Revolution in New York, 1765-1776*. NY: New York University Press.

Leder, Lawrence H. 1961. *The Politics of Colonial New York*. Chapel Hill: UNC Press.

Mather, J. H., and L. P. Brockett. 1848. *A Geographical History of the State of New York*. Utica: H. H. Hawley and Co.

McKee, Samuel, Jr. 1935. *Labor in Colonial New York 1664-1776*. NY. Repr. 1965 (Port Washington: Friedman).

McManus, Edgar J. 1966. *A History of Negro Slavery in New York*. Syracuse: Syracuse University Press.

McNall, Neil V. 1952. *An Agricultural History of the Genesee Valley 1790-1860*. Philadelphia: University of Pennsylvania Press.

Miller, Douglas T. 1967. *Jacksonian Aristocracy: Class and Democracy in New York 1830-1860*. NY: Oxford University Press.

Munger, William P. 1941. *Historical Atlas of New York*. Phoenix, NY: F. E. Richards.

O'Callaghan, E. B. 1882. *Catalogue of the Library of the Late E. B. O'Callaghan. . . Historian of New York*, comp. by E. W. Nash. NY.

Rosenberry, Lois (Kimball) Mathews. 1910. The Erie Canal and the Settlement of the West. *Publication of the Buffalo Historical Society* 14: 187-203.

Ruttenber, Edward M. 1906. *Footprints of the Red Man: Indian Geographical Names in the Valley of Hudson's River, in the Valley of the Mohawk, and on the Delaware*. Newburgh: New York State Historical Association.

Schnore, Leo F., ed. 1975. *The New Urban History: Quantitative Explorations of American Historians*. Princeton: University Press.

Severance, Frank H., ed. 1909. *Canal Enlargement in New York State*. Buffalo: Buffalo Historical Society.

Spencer, C. W. 1917. Land Systems of Colonial New York. *Proceedings of the New-York Historical Association* 401.

Tarr, Ralph S. 1910. Location of the Towns and Cities of Central New York. *American Geography Society Bulletin* 42:738-64.

Thompson, Harold W. 1939. *Body, Boots, and Britches*. Philadelphia. Repr. 1962 (NY: Dove Pub.).

Thompson, John H. 1966. *Geography of New York State*. Syracuse: University Press.

Turner, Orasmus. 1850. *Pioneer History of the Holland Purchase of Western New York*. Buffalo. Index comp. 1946 by Laverne C. Cooley (Baldwin: Buffalo, Jewett, Thomas).

Turner, Orasmus. 1851. *History of the Pioneer Settlement of the Phelps and Gorham Purchase. . . .* Rochester. 2nd ed. 1852 (Rochester: Alling).

Warren, Sam Bass, Jr. 1972. *The Urban Wilderness*. NY: Harper and Row.

Werner, E. A. 1884. *Civil List and Constitutional History of the Colony and State of New York*. Albany.

Whitford, N. E. 1906. *History of the Canal System of the State of New York*. Albany: Brandon Print. Co.

Whitford, Noble E. 1921. *History of the Barge Canal of New York State*. Albany: J. B. Lylow Co., Printers.

Wilson, George. 1890. *Portrait Gallery of the Chamber of Commerce of the State of New York*. NY: Press of the Chamber of Commerce.

Young, Alfred F. 1967. *The Democratic Republicans in New York*. Chapel Hill: UNC Press.

New Jersey

1. Cape May County

Co. created 1685. Cape christened by Cornelius Jacobsen Mey in 1623. 1st land purchase by Dutch in 1630; land purchase by Swedes in 1641. Settlers from New Haven c. 1640. 1st evidence of English settlement 1685; earliest settlers from Long Island and New England. Seasonal whaling at first. Early landowners English; some Scots and Irish, Quakers. Baptists from 1712; Presbyterians from 1714. Oldest seaside resort 1801; island resorts (developed as a resort area after Civil War and with development of RR). Long isolated from rest of state by the Great Cedar Swamp. Present boundaries est. 1891. Pop. 1790: 2,571, 1820: 4,265, 1850: 6,433, 1880: 9,765, 1910: 19,745, 1930: 29,486, 1960: 48,555.

Beesley, Maurice. 1857. *Sketch of the Early History of Cape May County, to Accompany the Geological Report of the State of New Jersey for Said County....* Trenton: Office of the True American.

Beesley, Maurice. 1857. *Sketch of the Early History of the County of Cape May....* Trenton: Office of the True American.

Howe, Paul S. 1921. *Mayflower Pilgrim Descendants in Cape May County....* Cape May: A. R. Hand.

Richards, Horace Gardiner. 1954. *A Book of Maps of Cape May 1610–1876.* Cape May: Cape May Geographic Society.

Stevens, Lewis T. 1897. *The History of Cape May County, from the Aboriginal Times to the Present Day....* Cape May City: L. T. Stevens.

1900. *Biographical, Genealogical, and Descriptive History of the First Congressional District of New Jersey....* NY: Lewis Pub. Co.

1931–. *The Cape May County Magazine of History and Genealogy.* Cape May: County Historical and Genealogical Society.

Goshen, Middle Twp.

In 1710, Goshen 1st settlement in mid Cape May Co. Shipbuilding here 1859–98; center for farmers and fishermen. Still a small village in 1973.

NJ 1A: M, worked on state highways, oyster dredger, 70. B. Dowdy's Tavern near Milmay, Atlantic Co., came here when 10. — F. b. Dowdy's Tavern, PGM b. near Mullica Hill, Gloucester Co.; M. b. Mullica Hill, MGM b. near Swedesboro, MGM's M. part Indian. — Illiterate. — Methodist. — Primitive mentality, grudging responses. — Easy-going articulation.

Beesleys Point, Marmora P.O., Upper Twp.

Beesleys Pt. settled 1690 by an Irish Tory. Small village: neck of land between salt marshes. Quaker settlement, whaling early. Upper Twp. pop. 1840: 1217; level, well-timbered.

NJ 1B: M, farmer, 52. B. Marmora, 1 1/2 mi. S. — F. b. Seaville in Co., PGF b. Seaville, PGM b. Palermo in Co.; M., MGF b. Palermo, MGM b. Beesley's Pt. (of Scottish descent). — Ed.: 1 yr. h.s. in Ocean City. — Methodist (Baptist parents). — Genial, quick, intelligent. Enjoyed interview.

2. Cumberland County

Formed in 1748 from Salem Co. Present boundaries (with minor exceptions) since 1822. First settlers Dutch and Swedes; some settlers from New Eng. as early as 1641. Gouldtown (Benjamin Gould d. 1777), mulatto settlement, early. 1st congregation, Baptists, 1685; also Presbyterians, Quakers in 17th century. Some settlers direct from England in early 19th cent. Co. most southern in NJ; sandy loam and sand; fruits and vegetables. Industries for the most part dependent on forest. Pop. 1790: 8,248, 1820: 12,668, 1850: 17,189, 1880: 37,687, 1910: 55,153, 1930: 69,895, 1960: 106,850.

Craig H. Stanley, comp. 1938. *Cumberland County Genealogical Data; Records Pertaining to Persons Residing in Cumberland County Prior to 1800.* Merchantville: H. S. Craig.

Cushing, Thomas. 1883. *History of the Counties of Gloucester, Salem, and Cumberland, with Biographical Sketches of Their Prominent Citizens.* Philadelphia: Everts and Peck.

Elmer, Lucius Q. C. 1869. *History of the Early Settlement and Progress of Cumberland County, New Jersey; and of the Currency of This and the Adjoining Colonies.* Bridgeton: G. F. Nixon.

Mints, Margaret Louise. 1968. *The Great Wilderness.* Millville: Wheaton Historical Association.

Nichols, Isaac T. 1907. *Historic Days in Cumberland County 1855–1865....* Bridgeton.

Pierce, Arthur D. 1960. *Smuggler's Woods: Jaunts and Journeys in Colonial and Revolutionary New Jersey.* New Brunswick: Rutgers University Press.

Souder, H., ed.-in-chief. 1923. *Who's Who in New Jersey.* Cumberland County ed. NY: National Biographical News Service.

1896. *Biographical Review; this Volume Contains Biographical Sketches of Leading Citizens of Cumberland County.* Boston: Biographical Review Pub. Co.

Robinstown, Port Norris P.O., Commercial Twp.

Twp. formed 1874 from Donne. Port Norris center first for timber, later oystering (29 shippers by 1955).

NJ 2A: M, farmer, 80. B. here. — F. b. Berrytown, 2 mi. S., PGF prob. b. near Egg Harbor, Atlantic Co., PGM b. Newport in Co.; M. b. 1 mi. W. in Dragson, MGF, MGM b. Cape May Co., MGM's M. b. Co. — Ed.: till 17 on and off. — Baptist. — Old-fashioned, obliging.

Dorchester

Founded shortly after 1800 by Swedes. Town laid out 1814. Earliest settlement before 1698 for oystering. Swedes, English in early 18th cent. Ferry 1815; shipyards continuously.

NJ 2A*: M, waterman, farmer, 82. B. Jericho in W. part of Co. — Parents b. near Jericho. — Ed.: limited. — Aging. — Responses prob. not typical of community since much time spent at sea.

Mauricetown, Commercial Twp.

Twp. descr. above. Early settlers in Mauricetown Dutch (1623), Swedes (1631). Village from 1789; town laid out, renamed 1814. Seafaring village; oyster shipping in 19th cent. Prosperous in sailing days; now quiet.

NJ 2B: M, farmer, 42. B. here. — F., PGF b. here, PGM b. Burlington Co.; M., MGF b. Port Norris, Cumberland Co. — Ed.: here till 15. — Methodist. — Quick, bright, but none too sympathetic toward questioning. — Very rapid tempo; short vowels.

3. Salem County

Est. 1681. Swedes and Finns arrived 1638; first settled in 1641 from New Haven; Soc. of Friends settled in 1675. First landowners English, Dutch, Swedes. Important shipping center in colonial times; glass works. Co. seat Salem, a colonial town on industrial outskirts; still relatively isolated. Friends, Baptists from 1670s, 1680s. Church of England from 1736. Fox hunting. Stop on underground RR. Many AfAms among recent immigrants. Soil depletion has encouraged migration westward. Pop. 1726: 3,977, 1790: 10,437, 1820: 14,022, 1850: 19,467, 1880: 24,579, 1910: 26,999, 1930: 36,834, 1960: 58,711.

Chandler, Catherine V. S. 1969. *Supplement to John Davis. . .Early Salem County. Salem County Historical Society Publications*, v. 4.

Craig, H. 1926. *Genealogical Data: The Salem Tenth in West New Jersey.* Merchantville: The Author.

Craig, Stanley, comp. 1934. *Salem County Genealogical Data: Records Pertaining to Persons Residing in Salem County Prior to 1800.* Merchantville: H. S. Craig.

Cushing, Thomas. 1883. *History of the Counties of Gloucester, Salem, and Cumberland, with Biographical Sketches of Their Prominent Citizens.* Philadelphia: Everts and Peck.

Sharpe, Edward S. 1908. *The Descendants of the Pioneers.* Salem.

Shourds, Thomas. 1876. *History and Genealogy of Fenwick's Colony.* Bridgeton: G. F. Nixon.

Sickler, Joseph S. 1937. *The History of Salem County; Being the Story of John Fenwick's Colony, the Oldest English-Speaking Settlement on the Delaware River.* Salem: Sunbeam Pub. Co.

Stewart, Frank H. 1929. *Foraging for Valley Forge by General Anthony Wayne in Salem and Gloucester Counties. . .* Woodbury: Gloucester County Historical Society.

Stewart, Frank H. 1932. *Salem County in the Revolution.* Camden: Sinnickson Chew.

Van Meter, Anna H. 1892. *Relics of Ye Olden Days in Salem County.* Salem: R. Gwynne.

1876. *Combination Atlas Map of Salem and Gloucester Counties, New Jersey.* Philadelphia: Everts and Stewart.

1964. *Fenwick's Colony; Salem County Pictorial 1675–1964.* Salem: Salem Tercentenary Committee.

Harmony, Salem P.O., Quinton Twp.

Twp. est. 1873. Fenwick colony at Salem from 1664. Glass factory; tomato growing from 1820; Dupont plants on Delaware since 1891.

NJ 3A: M, farmer, 86. B. 1/2 mi. W. — F., PGF b. here; M. b. Lower Creek in Co., MGM b. here. — Ed.: a little till 20. — Baptist. — Old and feeble, but obliging; somewhat forgetful.

Hancocks Bridge, Lower Alloway Creek Twp.

Twp. est. 1767; inc. 1798. Largest portion purchased from proprietor by those who came to America 1676–83 (English surnames). Friends settled here 1685; meeting house here from at least 1756. Hancock scene of massacre of continental militiamen by Tories in 1778. Small crossroads village; fish hatchery est. 1928.

NJ 3B: M, farmer, 55. B. here. — F. b. Mattington Twp., N. of Salem, PGF b. prob. in DE (descendant of one of first settlers of Boston), PGM b. Cumberland Co.; M. descended from 3 generations of Quakers, all of whom were b. here and can trace their descent back to earliest English settlers. — Ed.: here till 14, h.s. in Salem, then prep school in Bucks Co., PA. — Quaker. — Good middle-class type, not particularly quick.

4. Gloucester County

Co. constituted 1686; inc. 1710. Dutch settlement here as early as 1624; abandoned and occupied by English in 1635; reoccupied by Dutch. Also Swedish settlement 1636; English settlement 1664. Irish (Quakers) 1661. Fox hunting. Stop on Underground RR. Prosperous farming; glass. Pop. 1726: 2,229, 1790: 13,363, 1820: 23,071, 1850: 14,655, 1880: 25,886, 1910: 37,368, 1930: 70,802, 1960: 134,840.

Collins, Nicholas. 1936. *The Journal and Biography of Nicholas Collins, 1746–1831.* Philadelphia: New Jersey Society of Philadelphia.

Cushing, Thomas. 1883. *History of the Counties of Gloucester, Salem, and Cumberland, with Biographical Sketches of Their Prominent Citizens.* Philadelphia: Everts and Peck.

Eastlack, John Cawman. 1952. *Gloucester County in the 1850's: Being the Diary of John C. Eastlack.* Woodbury: Gloucester County Historical Society.

Gibson, George. n. d. *Gloucester County Residents, 1850.* G. and F. Gibson.

Godfrey, Carlos E. 1922. *The True Origin of Old Gloucester County.* Camden: Camden County Historical Society.

McGeorge, Isabella C. 1917. *Ann C. Whitall, the Heroine of Red Bank.* Woodbury: Gloucester County Historical Society.

Mickle, Isaac. 1845. *Reminiscences of Old Gloucester: or, Incidents in the History of the Counties of Gloucester, Atlantic, and Camden. . . .* Philadelphia: T. Ward.

Minotty, Paul, comp. 1968. *The Records of the Moravian Church at Oldman's Creek.* Woodbury: E. G. Van Name.

New Jersey Historical Records Survey Project. 1940. *Revolutionary War Documents*. Prepared by the Gloucester County Historical Project. Newark: New Jersey Historical Records Survey Project.

Simpson, Hazel B., ed. 1965. *Under Four Flags: Old Gloucester County, 1686–1964*. . . . Woodbury: Board of Chosen Freeholders, Gloucester County.

Stewart, Frank H. 1927. *History of the Battle of Red Bank*. Woodbury: Board of Chosen Freeholders of Gloucester County.

Stewart, Frank H. 1929. *Foraging for Valley Forge by General Anthony Wayne in Salem and Gloucester Counties*. Woodbury: Gloucester County Historical Society.

Stewart, Frank H., ed. 1924–37. *Notes on Old Gloucester County*. Woodbury.

Stewart, Frank H., ed. 1939–41. *Gloucester County in the Civil War*. Woodbury: Constitution Co.

Stewart, Frank H., ed. 1942. *Gloucester County under the Proprietors*. Woodbury: Constitution Co.

1876. *Combination Atlas Map of Salem and Gloucester Counties, New Jersey*. Philadelphia: Everts and Stewart.

1930. *The Organization and Minutes of the Gloucester County Court, 1686–7*. Woodbury: Gloucester County Historical Society.

1947–. *Bulletin of the Gloucester County Historical Society*. Woodbury: The Society.

Almonessen, Sewell P.O., Deptford Twp.

Twp. originated in 1695; inc. 1798. Twp. among original municipal districts of NJ. 1st settlers primarily English. Almonessen on E. border of Twp., near Camden Co. line. Gristmill c. 1800; cotton mill later. Resort park in 1874.

NJ 4A: M, farmer, carpenter, 70. B. 1 mi. away. — F. b. here, PGF b. Co., PGM b. Williamstown; M., MGF, MGM b. Co. — Ed.: till 16. — Baptist father; Quaker mother. — Quick, bright, understood purpose of interview. Somewhat sensitive about his speech.

Oak Grove, Swedesboro P.O., Logan Twp.

Twp. est. 1877. Site of first permanent settlers of NJ; Swedes, English, Irish, Germans before Rev. Produce for Phila. market (later NYC). 1st local settlement in Oak Grove c. 1740. Oldest Methodist church (1793) in Co. here. Swedesboro formerly Raccoon, renamed 1762. Farm produce. Swedish center till Rev., settled from DE originally. Moravians arrived in 1741. Swedish church built 1784 became Trinity Episcopal Church 1786. Pop. Twp. 1940: 1630.

NJ 4B: M, farmer, 53. B. here. — F. b. here, PGF b. Co. (of old Swedish stock); M. b. Repaupo, MGM b. Co. — Ed.: here, winters till 18. — Methodist. — Not a satisfactory inf. Considerable speech difficulty. Although generally quick to respond, responses often not to the point. — Slovenly articulation.

5. Camden County

Formed 1848 from Gloucester Co.; city of Camden created 1828. 1st settlement 1678. Campbell's foods here from 1892. Now essentially a suburb. Pop. 1850: 25,422, 1880: 62,942, 1910: 142,029, 1930: 392,035.

Boyer, Charles S. 1922. *The Civil and Political History of Camden County and Camden City*. Camden: Priv. Print.

Cooper, Howard M. 1909. *Historical Sketch of Camden*. Camden: H. B. Ketler.

Dorwart, Jeffery M., and Philip English Mackey. 1976. *Camden County, New Jersey, 1616–1976: A Narrative History*. Camden: Camden County Cultural and Heritage Commission.

Fisher, Lorenzo F. 1858. *A Local History of Camden*. . . . Camden: F. A. Cassedy.

Mickle, Isaac. 1845. *Reminiscences of Old Gloucester: Or, Incidents in the History of the Counties of Gloucester, Atlantic, and Camden*. . . . Philadelphia: T. Ward.

Orr, Hector. 1873. *A Sketch of Camden City*. . . . Camden: Bonsall and Carse.

Prowell, George R. 1886. *The History of Camden County*. Philadelphia: L. J. Richards.

Stackhouse, Asa M. 1905. *The King's Highway and the Pensauken Graveyard*. Moorestown: Settle Press.

Traubel, Horace. 1889. *Camden's Compliment to Walt Whitman, May 31, 1889; Notes, Addresses, Letters, Telegrams*. Philadelphia: D. McKay.

Wescott, Ralph W. 1952. *Walt Whitman in Camden*. Trenton: Walt Whitman Foundation and New Jersey Dept. of Conservation and Economic Development.

1897. *Biographical Review, Containing Life Sketches of Leading Citizens of Burlington and Camden Counties*. Boston: Biographical Review Pub. Co.

Brooklyn, Sicklerville P.O., Winslow Twp.

Twp. formed 1845 from Gloucester Twp. Extreme S. of Co. RR junction. Glassmaking.

NJ 5A: M, farmer, 75. B. here. — F. b. here, PGF b. Co. (of German descent), PGM b. Millville, Cumberland Co.; M., MGF, MGM b. Millville (MGF of German descent). — Ed.: irregularly till 12. — Methodist. — Quick, very obliging, glad to be of service, not aware of real purpose of interview.

Cedar Brook, Winslow Twp.

Winslow above; Cedar Brook a small village.

NJ 5B: M, general merchant, 58. B. Bates' Mill, worked at RR station in Orston (a few miles N. in Co.) when 18–20. — F. b. Bates' Mill in Co., PGF b. Co. (of Welsh descent), PGM b. Kittle Run, Burlington Co.; M., MGF b. Haddonfield in Co. — Ed.: till 14. — Methodist. — Placid, docile, not overly bright. — Slow, drawling tempo.

6. Atlantic County

Formed 1837 from Gloucester Co. Now dominated by Atlantic City resort area. Coast explored 1614; most early colonists from England. RR from Phila. opened in 1854. Shipbuilding, privateering; cranberries. Pop. 1840: 8,726, 1850: 8,951, 1880: 18,704, 1910: 71,894, 1930: 124,823, 1960: 160,880.

Collins, Anna C. 1892. *History of the Methodist Episcopal Church on Port Republic and Smithville Charge*. Camden: Gazette Printing House.

Hall, John F. 1900. *The Daily Union History of Atlantic City and County.* . . . Atlantic City: Daily Union Printing Co.

Heston, Alfred M. 1904. *Absegomi: Annals of Eyren Haven and Atlantic City, 1609–1904.* . . . Camden: A. M. Heston.

Mickle, Isaac. 1845. *Reminiscences of Old Gloucester: Or, Incidents in the History of the Counties of Gloucester, Atlantic, and Camden.* . . . Philadelphia: T. Ward.

Willis, Laura L. T., et al., eds. 1915. *Early History of Atlantic County.* . . . Kutztown, PA: Atlantic County Historical Society.

Port Republic

Founded 1774, after Chestnut Creek destroyed by British. 1st settlement in what is now Atlantic Co. Resort before 1860. Organized as city 1905.

NJ 6A: M, farmer, 75. B. here. — F., PGF b. Co.; M. b. Millville in Co., MGF, MGM b. Co. — Ed.: till 19. — Methodist. — Aging, not sharp mentally.

Steelmanville, Pleasantville P.O., Egg Harbor Twp.

Twp. oldest in Co.; originally contained all of Co. Pianos, knife handles once made here. Small industry; vineyards. Steelmanville named after Swedish settler. Pleasantville existed from 17th cent.; residential suburb of Atlantic City.

NJ 6B: M, farmer, 47. B. Northfield, 5 mi. NE. — F. b. Bakersville (now Northfield), PGF, PGM b. Atlantic Co.; M. b. Northfield, MGF, MGM b. Pleasantville. — Ed.: till 11. — Methodist. — Quick, bright, cooperative; of humble background.

7. Burlington County

Est. 1681; present boundaries 1710. Quakers settled in 1677; earlier 3 Dutch families and some Swedes. 1st Anglican parish in NJ (St. Mary's) here 1702. Burlington 2nd town in W. Jersey; largest Co. in NJ. Small industries: shoemaking in 19th cent., canning. Also iron, textiles, paper (some failed industries). Pop. 1726: 4,129, 1790: 18,095, 1820: 28,822, 1850: 55,402, 1910: 66,563, 1930: 93,541, 1960: 224,499.

Bisbee, Henry H. 1971. *Sign Posts: Place Names in History of Burlington County.* Willingboro: Alexia Press.

Brown, Henry A. 1878. *The Settlement of Burlington.* . . . Burlington.

De Cou, George. 1937. *Historical Sketches of Rancocas and Neighborhood.* Mt. Holly.

Hills, George M. 1876. *History of the Church in Burlington.* Trenton: W. S. Sharp.

Hoppin, James M. 1880. *Memoir of Henry Armitt Brown, Together with Four Historical Orations.* Philadelphia: J. B. Lippincott and Co.

Morris, Margaret H. 1949. *Her Journal, with Biographical Sketch and Notes by John W. Jackson.* Philadelphia: G. S. MacManus Co.

Schermerhorn, William E. 1927. *The History of Burlington.* . . . Burlington: Press of Enterprise Pub. Co.

Stackhouse, Asa M. 1905. *The King's Highway and the Pensauken Graveyard.* Moorestown: Settle Press.

Stokes, Edward C. 1927. *Address. . .at the 250th Anniversary Celebration of the Founding of the City of Burlington.* Burlington: Press of Enterprise Pub. Co.

Woodward, Evan M., and John F. Hageman. 1883. *History of Burlington and Mercer Counties, with Biographical Sketches.* . . . Philadelphia: Everts and Peck.

1777–86. *New Jersey Gazette.* Burlington.

1897. *Biographical Review, Containing Life Sketches of Leading Citizens of Burlington and Camden Counties.* Boston: Biographical Review Pub. Co.

South Park, Chatsworth P.O., Tabernacle Twp.

Twp. est. 1901. Legend of Hessian settlers after Trenton. Former Indian reservation, liquidated in late 19th cent. Sparse pop. Pine barrens; some iron. Chatsworth came into existence when RR built c. 1880. Called "city of the pines".

NJ 7A: M, woodsman, 72. B. 2 1/2 mi. N. — F., PGF b. Co.; M. b. nearby in Co. — Ed.: till 16. — Methodist. — Sometimes slow in responding. — Note rounded [ʌ‿ˑ]; [ɒɚ] in earlier half of record should read [a‿ɚ] (FW's note).

Rancocas, Burlington P.O., Willingboro Twp.

Twp. settled by Quakers; some Germans later. 1st settlements along Rancocas River. Twp. a bedroom suburb of Phila. from 1858. Friends meeting house in Rancocas from 1772. Received name Rancocas 1838. R. Creek flows into Delaware. Residence of Wm. Franklin (son of Ben). Last colonial govt. Burlington settled in 1677 by Quakers from Yorkshire and London; inc. 1784. Capital of W. Jersey till after Rev. Still relatively isolated; shipping disappeared; abortive silkworm culture. Library from 1757, one of oldest in country. Pop. Burlington 1820: 2,758, 1850: 4,536, 1880: 6,090, 1910: 8,336, 1930: 10,844, 1960: 12,687.

NJ 7B!: F, housewife, 49. B. Twp. — F. b. nearby in Co., PGF b. Twp., PGF's F., PGM b. Co.; M. b. Twp., MGF b. Penns Manor, Bucks Co., PA (lived on island between Morrisville, PA, and Trenton, NJ), MGF's M. b. Penns Manor, MGM b. Twp., MGM's M. b. Co. — Ed.: Friends School here till 14, 3 yrs. public h.s. in Phila., 2 yrs. Drexel Institute, Phila. — Society of Friends. — Cultivated.

8. Ocean County

Formed 1850 from Monmouth Co. Many of earliest settlers from Long Island. Privateering and shipbuilding at time of Rev. Formerly eelgrass industry; also saltworks, charcoal, iron, resorts (latter esp. in late 19th cent.); fish, oysters, and cranberries. Admiral Farragut Academy; Lakehurst Naval Air Station. Pop. 1850: 10,032, 1880: 14,455, 1910: 21,318, 1930: 33,069, 1960: 108,241.

Blackman, Leah. 1880. *History of Little Egg Harbor Township.* . . . Camden. Repr. 1963 (Tuckerton: Great John Mathis Foundation).

Salter, Edwin. 1874. *Old Times in Old Monmouth: Historical Reminiscences of Old Monmouth County.* . . . Freehold: Monmouth Democrat. Repr. 1980 (Baltimore: Genealogical Publishing Co.).

Salter, Edwin. 1890. *A History of Monmouth and Ocean Counties, Embracing a Genealogical Record of Earliest Settlers.* . . . Bayonne: E. Gardner.

Zinkin, Vivian. 1976. *A Study of the Place Names of Ocean County, New Jersey 1609–1849*. Town Rivers.

Warren Grove, Little Egg Harbor Twp.

Twp. formed 1740; inc. 1798. Originally in Burlington Co. Settled prior to 1698. Shipbuilding, shellfish; summer people. Also cotton and paper. Warren Grove village on edge of Twp.

NJ 8A: M, farmer, woodsman, 77. B. Browns Mill, Burlington Co. — F., PGF b. same house (PGF of original English stock, perhaps from Canterbury, Kent), PGM b. nearby; M. b. near Tom's River in Co., MGF b. 2 mi. N. of here, MGM b. near Pointville, Burlington Co. — No ed. — Methodist. — Old-fashioned; aging. — Moderate tempo; good moderate articulation.

Barnegat, Union Twp.

Twp. est. 1846. First settled c. 1700. Whaling at one time; seafaring community. Quakers among early settlers; both pacifists and profiteers in American Rev. Barnegat became dominated by Swedes; attracted new Swedish immigrants. Pop. Twp. 1940: 1,045.

NJ 8B: M, bank cashier, 57. B. Tuckerton, Ocean Co., came here when 23. — F., PGF, PGF's F., PGM b. Tuckerton (PGF's F. fought in Rev.); M. b. New Gretna, Burlington Co. (just over line from Ocean Co.), MGF b. Bass River, Burlington Co. (of Tory descent), MGM b. Bass River (just over line from Ocean Co.). — Ed.: local h.s. till 18, then S. Jersey Inst. at Bridgeton (military prep school). — Presbyterian.

9. Monmouth County

Co. est. 1683; one of four original cos. of Jersey. Most N. of seacoast cos.: Jersey Highlands, hills, rivers. 1st settled c. 1645. Attempted settlement of English in 1663 repulsed by Dutch. Purchase from Indians 1663; patent 1665. Immigration by Scottish (1680–85), Dutch (1690-95); some from NY. Many Quakers in the late 18th cent. 1st road ordered 1668; 6 principal roads in Co. by 1764. 1st RR 1852. Industries: iron-working, textiles, clothing, pottery, misc. light industries; resorts from early 19th cent. Pop. 1726: 4,879, 1790: 16,918, 1820: 25,038, 1850: 30,313, 1880: 55,538, 1910: 94,734, 1930: 147,209, 1960: 334,401.

Applegate, John S. 1911. *Early Courts and Lawyers of Monmouth County*. NY: L. Middleditch.

Beekman, George C. 1901. *Early Dutch Settlers of Monmouth County*. Freehold: Moreau Bros.

Ellis, Franklin. 1885. *History of Monmouth County*. Philadelphia: R. T. Peck.

Hornor, William S. 1932. *This Old Monmouth of Ours: History, Tradition, Biography, Genealogy, Anecdotes*. Freehold: Moreau Bros.

Leonard, Thomas H. 1923. *From Indian Trail to Electric Rail. . . .* Atlantic Highlands: The Atlantic Highlands Journal.

Martin, George C. 1914. *The Shark River District. . . .* Asbury Park: Martin and Allardyce.

Salter, Edwin. 1874. *Old Times in Old Monmouth: Historical Reminiscences of Old Monmouth County. . . .* Freehold: Monmouth Democrat. Repr. 1980 (Baltimore: Genealogical Publishing Co.).

Salter, Edwin. 1890. *A History of Monmouth and Ocean Counties, Embracing a Genealogical Record of Earliest Settlers. . . .* Bayonne: E. Gardner.

Van Benthuysen, P. F. 1974. *Monmouth County, New Jersey: A Bibliography of Published Works 1676–1973*. Sea Bright: Ploughshare Press.

1922. *History of Monmouth County 1664–1920*. 3 vols. NY: Lewis Historical Pub. Co.

1935–1948. *Monmouth County Historical Association Bulletin*. Freehold.

Union Hill, Englishtown P.O., Manalapan Twp.

Twp. formed 1848; border twp. on NW of Co. Area settled by Scots c. 1685; oldest house 1702. Englishtown Washington's headquarters at Battle of Monmouth; principal village in Twp.

NJ 9A: F, housewife, 76. B. 1 mi. away. — F. b. Twp., PGF b. Co., PGM, PGM's F., PGM's M. b. Twp; M., MGF, MGM b. Co. (MGF of French descent). — Ed. till 16. — Presbyterian.

Tennent, Englishtown P.O., Manalapan Twp.

Tennent is Scottish country. Church built 1692; second church 1752. Earlier Old Scots meeting house (Presbyterian).

NJ 9B: M, farmer, 56. B. Twp. — F. b. near Allentown in W. end of Co., came here as boy, PGF b. near Allentown, PGM b. near Cranbury (of Holland Dutch descent); M. b. same house, MGF, MGM b. NY. — Ed.: till 18. — Presbyterian. — Quick, alert; intellectual curiosity. — Quick, vigorous speech.

10. Middlesex County

Co. authorized 1675; established 1682. First settlers arrived 1666 from Newbury, MA. Other early settlers from NH/ME border, RI; also some Dutch from Long Island. Scottish Covenanters 1685. RRs in 19th cent. Pop. 1726: 4,009, 1790: 15,956, 1820: 21,470, 1850: 28,635, 1880: 52,286, 1910: 114,426, 1930: 212,208, 1960: 433,856.

Benedict, William H. 1925. *New Brunswick in History*. New Brunswick: W. H. Benedict.

Clayton, W. Woodford. 1882. *History of Union and Middlesex Counties, with Biographical Sketches. . . .* Philadelphia: Everts and Peck.

Demarest, William H. S., comp. 1932. *The Anniversary of New Brunswick, 1680–1730–1930*. New Brunswick: J. Heidingsfeld Co.

Federal Writers Project. 1938. *Monroe Township, 1838–1938*. New Brunswick.

Guest, Moses. 1823. *Poems on Several Occasions, to Which are Annexed Extracts from a Journal*. Cincinnati: Looker and Reynolds.

Jones, William Northey. 1925. *The History of St. Peter's Church*. NY: Patterson Pr.

Schmidt, George Paul. 1964. *Princeton and Rutgers: The Two Colonial Colleges of New Jersey*. Princeton: Van Nostrand.

Steele, Richard H. 1867. *Historical Discourse Delivered at the Celebration of the 150th Anniversary of the First Reformed Dutch Church, New Brunswick*. New Brunswick: The Consistory.

Wall, John P. 1901. *New Brunswick during the War of 1812.* New Brunswick.

Wall, John P., ed. 1921. *History of Middlesex County, 1664–1920.* NY: Lewis Historical Pub. Co.

Whitehead, William A. 1856. *Contributions to the Early History of Perth Amboy....* NY: D. Appleton.

Perth Amboy

Twp. formed 1693; Scottish, well est. by 1702. 1st charter of incorporation 1718; enlarged 1720. State charter and incorporation 1784. Chosen as seat of proprietary govt. in 1665. In addition to Scots, Londoners, Dutch, Irish, a few Huguenots among settlers (Danes more recently); also from Long Island and Staten Island. Capital of E. Jersey 1684. Proportion of Tories highest in NJ. Church of England 1st church here. Oldest inc. city in NJ. Pioneer in adult education. Summer resort 1800–1860; industrialization after 1860. Underground RR, Abolitionists. RRs from 1832. Labor troubles 1912 (Guggenheim refineries). Bridge to Staten Island. Still had volunteer fire dept. in 1950s. Good harbor. Industries include clay products, chemicals, copper and other smelting, dry docks, Vaseline. Pop. 1820: 798, 1850: 1,865, 1880: 4,808, 1910: 32,121, 1930: 43,516, 1960: 38,007.

NJ 10A: M, oysterman, 78. — F., PGF b. Perth Amboy (PGF's F. fought in Rev.); MGM b. Staten Island. — Ed.: till 15. — Methodist. — Rough, hearty voice; very old-fashioned speech; retroflexion appears to be an intrusive new feature.

Prospect Plains, Cranbury P.O., Monroe Twp.

Twp. est. 1838. 1st settled 1685 by Scots; later, some Dutch. Prospect Plains on W. border of Twp., has a RR station. Cranbury created 1872; 1st settled late 17th cent. Had a church at least by 1739. Village grew up around gristmill; coffee and spice mills, distilleries at one time.

NJ 10B: M, farmer, 68. B. S. Brunswick Twp., about 3 mi. away. — F., PGF b. Cranbury Twp. (PGF of Scotch descent); M. b. S. Brunswick Twp., MGM b. Cranbury Twp. — Ed.: till 16. — Presbyterian.

NJ 10C: North of Cranbury, Cranbury P.O. and Twp. — M, farmer and asst. administrator, Middlesex Co. Soil Conservation Assoc., 49. B. Monroe Twp., 2 mi. away. — F. b. Ocean Co., came here when 15, PGF, PGM b. England; M. b. Co., MGF, MGM b. England. — Ed.: till 18, then 8 mos. in business college. — Presbyterian. — Quick, businesslike manner. — Genuine in his responses.

New Brunswick

Inc. 1784. 1st settled by English settlers from Long Island in 1681. Dutch Reformed Church from 1717; Dutch settlers from Albany 1730. Named for George I, "Duke of Brunswick". Shipping point for grain in 1815. Originally rejected "College of NJ" (later Princeton); Queen's College (later Rutgers) founded by Governor Wm. Franklin as counterweight to Princeton. Rutgers (chartered 1766; opened 1771) state run since 1917, several branches. Labor battles 1836. Limit of NYC commuting area. Products and industries: paper, rubber goods (waterproofing), glass (fruit jars), surgical dressings, tools, wallpaper, machine works, water heaters.

Pop. 1850: 10,017, 1880: 17,166, 1910: 23,388, 1930: 34,555, 1960: 40,139.

NJ 10D!: M, treasurer of building company, formerly electrical engineer, 59. B. here. — F., PGF, PGF's F. b. New Brunswick; M., MGF, MGM b. Cranbury, Middlesex Co. (both sides of Holland Dutch descent). — Ed.: local public schools, Rutgers U. (4 yrs. engineering). — Dutch Reformed. — Cultivated.

11. Mercer County

Set off from Hunterdon and Burlington Cos., 1838. Named for Gen. Mercer, who died of wounds after battle of Princeton. Orig. settled by "Yorkshire Quakers"; a few Swedes, later more polyglot. Heavily settled by mid 18th cent. Rolling terrain. Pop. 1840: 21,502, 1850: 27,992, 1880: 58,061, 1910: 125,657, 1930: 187,143, 1960: 266,392.

Collins, Varnum Lansing. 1914. *Princeton.* NY: Oxford University Press.

Ege, Ralph. 1908. *Pioneers of Old Hopewell....* Hopewell: Race and Savidge.

Gedney, Lida C. 1931. *The Town Records of Hopewell.* NY: New Jersey Society of the Colonial Dames of America.

Hageman, John F. 1879. *History of Princeton and Its Institutions....* Philadelphia: J. B. Lippincott.

Haven, Charles C. 1866. *Annals of the City of Trenton, with Random Remarks and Historical Reminiscences.* Trenton: State Gazette Office.

Hewitt, Louise, comp. 1916. *Historic Trenton.* Trenton: Smith Press.

Hinsdale, Horace G. 1888. *An Historical Discourse, Commemorating the Centenary of the Completed Organization of the First Presbyterian Church.* Princeton: The Princeton Press.

Lee, Francis B., ed. 1907. *Genealogical and Personal Memorial of Mercer County.* NY: Lewis Pub. Co.

Podmore, Harry J. 1927. *Trenton, Old and New.* Trenton: Kenneth W. Moore Co.

Raum, John O. 1871. *History of the City of Trenton....* Trenton: W. T. Nicholson.

Schmidt, George Paul. 1964. *Princeton and Rutgers: The Two Colonial Colleges of New Jersey.* Princeton: Van Nostrand.

Ulyat, William C., comp. 1877. *An Account of the Centennial Celebrations at Princeton, New Jersey, June 27, 1876, and Jan.3, 1877.* Princeton: Press Printing Office.

Walker, Edwin R., et al. 1929. *A History of Trenton 1679–1929....* Princeton: Princeton University Press.

Wertenbaker, Thomas Jefferson. 1946. *Princeton 1746–1896.* Princeton: Princeton University Press.

Woodward, Evan M., and John F. Hageman. 1883. *History of Burlington and Mercer Counties, with Biographical Sketches....* Philadelphia: Everts and Peck.

1940. *Historic Princeton. . . .* Princeton: Princeton Municipal Improvement, Inc.

1971–. *Princeton History.* Princeton: Historical Society of Princeton.

Federal City, Flemington P.O. (Hunterdon Co.), Hopewell Twp.

Twp. founded by English Baptists c. 1706. 1704–5 Episcopal church here was first non-Quaker church in province.

1757 1st Baptist school for higher ed. in US here. Local museum. Former Lindbergh estate here. Poor soil, fit only for grazing. Federal City was projected site for national capital. Early settlers from Long Island and Middlesex Co.

NJ 11A: M, farmer, 82. B. Twp. — F., PGF, PGF's F., PGF's PGF (of Long I. ancestry) b. Twp., PGM b. Twp., M., MGF (of Scottish ancestry), MGM (of Holland Dutch descent) all b. Twp. — Ed.: till 15. — Presbyterian.

Trenton

First settled c. 1680 by a Quaker miller. Bought by William Trent (Scottish) of Phila. 1714. Chartered 1745; state capital 1790; inc. as a city 1792. Germans and Dutch from colonial times; later many Italians and Hungarians. Methodists from 1773; 1st Roman Catholic parish in NJ here 1814. Manufacturing center, diverse (shoes in 19th cent.); waterpower led to development of industries, originally flour milling, later more diversified: iron and steel, steel products, tools, RR equipment, lime, pottery, paper and paper products, brass (and other nonferrous metalworking), textiles, rubber, shoes. Pop. 1820: 3,942, 1850: 6,461, 1880: 29,910, 1910: 96,815, 1930: 123,356, 1960: 114,167.

NJ 11B: F, widow, 57. B. near center of Trenton. — F. b. Trenton, PGF, PGF's F. b. Cazenovia, NY, PGF's PGF b. near Cazenovia, NY, of Norwich, CT, stock, PGM b. Baltimore, MD; M., perhaps MGF, MGM b. Trenton, MGM's F. b. France (came over as a servant of the Bonapartes on Lafayette's second visit). — Ed.: till 18. — Presbyterian.

Rosedale, Princeton P.O., Lawrence Twp.

Twp. est. 1816. Area settled 1696 by Quakers; other settlers from S. Jersey and MA. Rosedale largely univ. town: research institute, some light industry. No AfAms until after WWII. Princeton inc. as a borough 1813; has service and technical organizations related to education: ETS, Inst. for Advanced Study here. Princeton University chartered 1746; originally the Presbyterian college. 1795 abortive proposal to unite with Queens (Rutgers).

NJ 11C: M, farmer, 41. B. same house. — F. b. on Hunterdon Co. line near Hopewell Twp. of Mercer Co., PGF, PGM b. Hunterdon Co.; M. b. Hopewell Twp. near Pennington, MGF b. Twp., MGM b. Bucks Co., PA, near Darlington. — Ed.: till 16 plus 2 semesters business college in Trenton. — Baptist. — More old-fashioned than age would indicate; obliging.

12. Somerset County

Co. formed 1688 from Middlesex; present boundaries 1738. Purchases from Indians for widow of Sir George in 1681; sold to E. Jersey Proprietors 1682. Possibly some settlements as early as 1681; early settlers include many Dutch (from Albany, Long Island, etc.), English, Palatinate Germans, some Scots; possibly some Huguenots. Pop. 1726: 2,271, 1790: 12,796, 1820: 16,506, 1850: 19,692, 1880: 27,162, 1910: 38,820, 1930: 65,132, 1960: 153,913.

Honeyman, A. Van Doren, ed. 1873. *Our Home: A Monthly Magazine.* . . . Somerville: Cornell and Honeyman.

Honeyman, A. Van Doren, ed. 1912–19. *Somerset County Historical Society Quarterly.* Somerville: Somerset County Historical Society.

Honeyman, A. Van Doren, ed.-in-chief. 1927. *Northwestern New Jersey: A History of Somerset, Morris, Hunterdon, Warren and Sussex Counties.* 4 vols. NY: Lewis Historical Pub. Co.

Mellick, Andrew D. 1889. *The Story of an Old Farm.* . . . Somerville: The Unionist-Gazette. Repr. 1948 (New Brunswick: Rutgers University Press).

Mellick, Andrew D. 1948. Lesser Crossroads. In Hubert G. Schmidt, ed., *The Story of an Old Farm* (New Brunswick: Rutgers University Press).

Messler, Abraham. 1878. *Centennial History of Somerset County.* Somerville: C. M. Jameson.

Schumacher, Ludwig. 1900. *The Somerset Hills.* . . . NY: New Amsterdam Book Co.

Snell, James P., comp. 1881. *History of Hunterdon and Somerset Counties, with Illustrations and Biographical Sketches.* . . . Philadelphia: Everts and Peck.

Van Horn, James H., comp. 1965. *Historic Somerset.* New Brunswick: Historical Societies of Somerset County

1938. *Somerset County — 250 Years.* Somerville: Somerset Press.

Neshanic Station, Branchburg Twp.

Twp. est. 1845; first settlements in area c. 1685: Scots, Dutch, English. Located centrally on W. border of Co.

NJ 12A: M, farmer, 80. B. Montgomery Twp. — F. b. Hillsboro, PGF of English descent, PGM b. Hillsboro Twp. (of Holland Dutch descent); M., MGF b. Hillsboro Twp. (MGF of Holland Dutch descent), MGM b. Neshanic. — Ed.: till 15. — Dutch Reformed.

New Center, Somerville P.O., Hillsboro Twp.

Twp. est. 1771; inc. 1798. Military depots here. Somerville had part of Continental Army encamped there during Rev. Trading center for farming area since 17th cent. Pop. Twp. 1940: 2,648.

NJ 12B: M, farmer, 49. B. Twp. — F. b. Twp., PGF, PGF's F. (of Holland Dutch descent), PGF's M. (of English descent), PGM all b. Bridgewater Twp.; M., MGF, MGF's F., MGF's M. b. Bridgewater Twp. (both great-grandparents of Holland Dutch descent), MGM b. Somerville. — Ed.: till 17. — Dutch Reformed.

13. Hunterdon County

Formed 1713 from Burlington Co. 1st settlers c. 1676, Quakers W. of Trenton. Settlers of diverse origins: English, Scottish, Scotch-Irish, also Dutch Huguenots; Germans by 1721; recently S. and E. Europeans. Mines, furnaces, forges in colonial times. Indian raids in 1750s. Woodlands not considered important till late 18th cent. In 18th cent., wealthiest and most populous co.; wheat, flour, grazing; called "breadbasket of the colonies". Potatoes later, tomatoes introduced c. 1847; also grains, hay, fruit, eggs, bees. Selective breeding of livestock after 1800. Relatively few industries (always basically rural and agricultural): some steel, limestone, paper, rubber goods. Pop. 1726: 3,377, 1790: 20,153, 1820: 28,513, 1850:

28,990, 1880: 38,570, 1910: 33,569, 1930: 34,728, 1960: 54,107.

Deats, Hiram E. c. 1920. *Tombstone Inscriptions from Hunterdon County Cemeteries*. Flemington.

Honeyman, A. Van Doren, ed. 1873. *Our Home: A Monthly Magazine*. . . . Somerville: Cornell and Honeyman.

Honeyman, A. Van Doren, ed.-in-chief. 1927. *Northwestern New Jersey: A History of Somerset, Morris, Hunterdon, Warren and Sussex Counties*. 4 vols. NY: Lewis Historical Pub. Co.

Messler, Abraham. 1873. *Forty Years at Raritan: Eight Memorial Sermons*. NY: A. Lloyd.

Mott, George S. 1878. *The First Century of Hunterdon County*. Flemington: E. Vosseller. Repr. 1961 (Flemington: Hunterdon County Historical Society).

Mott, George S. 1894. *History of the Presbyterian Church in Flemington. . .with Sketches of Local Matters for Two Hundred Years*. NY: W. B. Ketcham.

Schmidt, Hubert Glasgow. 1945. *Rural Hunterdon, an Agricultural History*. New Brunswick: Rutgers University Press.

Schmidt, Hubert Glasgow. 1959. *Some Hunterdon Place Names: Historical Sketches about Communities and Localities*. . . . Flemington: D. H. Moreau.

Schrabisch, Max. 1917. *Archaeology of Warren and Hunterdon Counties*. Trenton: MacCrellish and Quigley Co.

Snell, James P., comp. 1881. *History of Hunterdon and Somerset Counties, with Illustrations and Biographical Sketches*. . . . Philadelphia: Everts and Peck.

Voorhees, Oscar M. 1929. *The Exterior and Interior Bounds of Hunterdon County*. Flemington: H. E. Deats.

Vosseller, Elias. 1901. *Tucca — Ramma — Hacking*. Flemington: H. E. Deats.

1891–1901. *Hunterdon Historical Series*. Flemington: H. E. Deats.

1891–1905. *The Jerseyman: A Quarterly Magazine of Local History and Genealogy*. . . . Flemington: H. E. Deats.

1898. *Portrait and Biographical Record of Hunterdon and Warren Counties*. . . . NY: Chapman Pub. Co.

Snydertown, Ringoes P.O., East Amwell Twp.

Twp. formed 1846 from Amwell; in SE corner of Co. One of finest agricultural districts in Co. 1st settlement c. 1720; Germans, Presbyterians among early settlers. Snydertown still a small settlement of a few families in 1927. Ringoes orig. site of a tavern owned by John Ringo; 1st settlers here mostly Germans. A small crossroads.

NJ 13A: F, widow, 80. B. Mercer Co., 1/4 mi. from Hunterdon Co. line of West Amwell Twp. — F., PGF, PGM, M., MGM b. near Moore's Station, Hopewell Twp., Mercer Co. — Illiterate. — Methodist. — Not very bright; forgetful. — Unable to fully comprehend purpose.

Copper Hill, Flemington P.O., Raritan Twp.

Twp. formed 1838 from Amwell Twp. Area settled c. 1740 by Dutch, Scots. Largely agricultural. Copper Hill a hamlet; former site of a failed copper mine (small quantities of excellent ore in 1840). Flemington a small courthouse town, notorious for Hauptmann trial.

NJ 13B: M, farmer, 47. B. Kingwood Twp. — F., PGF b. near Mercer Co. line (PGF remotely of German descent), PGM b. Co.; M., MGF b. Kingwood Twp., MGM b. Flemington, MGM's F. (a county sheriff) b. NY, perhaps Sullivan Co. — Ed.: till 16. — Christian Church.

14. Warren County

Formed 1824 from Sussex Co. Dutch settlers as early as 1650 (deserted); 1690 to stay. Also Ulster Scots and Germans among early settlers. Land acquired 1713 from Indians; 1st grants 1725; by 1730, most of good land taken up by proprietors. 1831 Morris Canal. Maximum rural pop. c. 1840; declining since. More RR lines here than any other NJ co. Pop. 1830: 18,627, 1850: 22,358, 1880: 36,589, 1910: 43,187, 1930: 49,319, 1960: 63,220.

Honeyman, A. Van Doren, ed.-in-chief. 1927. *Northwestern New Jersey: A History of Somerset, Morris, Hunterdon, Warren and Sussex Counties*. 4 vols. NY: Lewis Historical Pub. Co.

Schrabisch, Max. 1917. *Archaeology of Warren and Hunterdon Counties*. Trenton: MacCrellish and Quigley Co.

Snell, James P., et al., comp. 1881. *History of Sussex and Warren counties, with Illustrations and Biographical Sketches*. . . . Philadelphia: Everts and Peck.

1898. *Portrait and Biographical Record of Hunterdon and Warren Counties*. . . . NY: Chapman Pub. Co.

Pairson's Corner, Union Brick neighborhood, Blairstown P.O. and Twp.

Twp. formed 1845 from Knowlton. Blairstown small village and shipping point; built up by John Blair, successful merchant. Prep school; no industry of consequence.

NJ 14A: M, farmer, 78. B. Frelinghuysen. — F. b. Twp., PGF, PGF's F. b. Sussex Co., PGF's PGF of English descent, PGM b. Hope Twp., PGM's F. of Dutch Holland descent; M. b. 1 mi. from Sussex Co. line near Tranquility, MGM b. near Johnsonsburg, Warren Co., MGM's F. of Mayflower English descent. — Ed.: till 19. — Methodist.

Vienna, Independence Twp.

Twp. est. 1782; inc. 1798. Vienna "a beautiful country town, whose streets are lined with sugar maples". 1st settlers c. 1770: English, Ulster Scots, Dutch. Onetime foundry (made double corn plows), sawmill, woodworking shop (industrial 1860–1900). Pop. Twp. 1940: 1,046.

NJ 14B: F, homemaker, 44. B. Twp. — F. b. Twp., PGF b. Hope Twp. in Co., PGF's F. b. Frelinghuysen Twp., PGF's PGF descendant of Francis Cooke of the Mayflower, PGF's PGM b. near Johnsonsburg in Sussex Co. (of Holland Dutch descent), PGF's M., PGM b. Co.; M. b. Mansfield Twp., MGF b. near Johnsonsburg in Co., MGF's F. b. Hunterdon Co., MGF's M., MGM, MGM's M. b. Co. — Ed.: h.s. — Methodist.

15. Sussex County

Formed 1753 from Morris Co. Early settlers from Hudson Valley (Ulster Co.) c. 1650; further settlement 1690. Dutch churches from 1715; Ulster Scots from Ireland c. 1735;

Presbyterian church at least by 1744. First group of settlers English and Scottish, second group from Holland and Germany, third group from France, Ireland, Wales, Norway. Indian depredations during Rev. Ironworks during 18th cent. By 1790, second in pop. behind Hunterdon. Pop. 1772: 9,229, 1790: 19,500, 1820: 32,752, 1850: 22,989, 1880: 23,539, 1910: 26,781, 1930: 27,830, 1960: 49,255.

Clement, John. 1877. *Sketches of the First Emigrant Settlers.* Camden: S. Chew.

Honeyman, A. Van Doren, ed.-in-chief. 1927. *Northwestern New Jersey: A History of Somerset, Morris, Hunterdon, Warren and Sussex Counties.* 4 vols. NY: Lewis Historical Pub. Co.

Schaeffer, Casper. 1907. *Memoirs and Reminiscences, Together with Sketches of the Early History.* . . . Hackensack: Priv. Print.

Snell, James P., et al., comp. 1881. *History of Sussex and Warren Counties, with Illustrations and Biographical Sketches.* . . . Philadelphia: Everts and Peck.

Webb, Edward A., comp. 1872. *The Historical Directory of Sussex County, Containing a Brief Summary of Events from Its First Settlement.* . . . Andover.

Newton P.O., Stillwater Twp.

Twp. had a Presbyterian Church from 1771; Lutherans and Calvinists in area early. A log schoolhouse by 1814; Dutch Reformed church by 1823. In W. Co., on Blue Mt. range. Newton settled c. 1750: first settlement by Germans; later some settlers from Netherlands, still later English and Scots. Tory area. Some shoe manufacturing; largest dairy center in NJ.

NJ 15A: 5 mi. NE of Stillwater. — M, farmer, 70. B. Twp. — F., PGF b. Twp., PGF's F., PGF's M. b. Hunterdon Co. (both of Holland Dutch descent), PGM b. Wallpack Twp.; M., MGF b. Wallpack Twp., MGF's F. b. PA, MGM b. Shawnee, Monroe Co., PA (of PA Dutch descent). — Ed.: till 18. — Methodist.

The Plains, Augusta P.O., Frankford Twp.

Twp. formed 1797; inc. 1798. 1st settlers from CT, also Dutch and Germans, some Huguenots. 1st school here 1750. Some importance as commercial center. Augusta a RR junction; small village.

NJ 15B: M, farmer, 46. B. Twp. — F., PGF (German descent) b. Stillwater Twp., PGM b. Co.; M., MGM b. Co. — Ed.: till 19. — Methodist.

16. Morris County

Formed from Hunterdon Co. 1739. NJ Highlands. First settlement 1695 by Dutch. In 1707 S. part settled by Germans from Phila.; some English settlers in 1713. Turnpikes from 1801; Morris Canal 1831–71; RR from 1835. Iron mines from 1714; still productive. 3 river systems: Delaware, Passaic, Raritan. Varied agriculture. Pop. 1748: 4,436, 1790: 16,216, 1820: 21,368, 1850: 30,158, 1880: 50,861, 1910: 74,704, 1930: 110,445, 1960: 261,620.

Crayon, Joseph P. 1902. *Rockaway Records of Morris County Families.* . . . Rockaway: Rockaway Pub. Co.

Doremus, George S. 1926. *The American Revolution and Morris County.* Rockaway: Record Print.

Halsey, Edmund D., et al. 1882. . . .*History of Morris County.* . . . NY: W. W. Munsell.

Historical Records Survey. 1937. *Archives and Historical Sketch, Morris County.* Morristown: Board of Chosen Freeholders, County of Morris.

Honeyman, A. Van Doren, ed.-in-chief. 1927. *Northwestern New Jersey: A History of Somerset, Morris, Hunterdon, Warren and Sussex Counties.* 4 vols. NY: Lewis Historical Pub. Co.

Hoskins, Barbara, et al. 1960. *Washington Valley.* . . . Morristown.

Thayer, Theodore. 1975. *Colonial and Revolutionary Morris County.* Morristown: Morris County Heritage Commission.

Tuttle, Joseph F. 1876. *The Revolutionary Forefathers of Morris County.* . . . Dover: B. H. Vogt.

1899. *Biographical and Genealogical History of Morris County, New Jersey.* NY: Lewis Pub. Co.

1914. *A History of Morris County, New Jersey, Embracing Upwards of Two Centuries, 1710–1913.* NY: Lewis Historical Pub. Co.

Jacksonville Rd., Kinnelon, Towaco P.O., Pequannick Twp.

Twp. est. 1738. Earliest puchases in Co. here; one of 3 original twps. Early settlers from NY, Long Island, and (prob.) Bergen Co. (chiefly Dutch). Farming at first; iron district. Kinnelon (borough) est. 1922. Towaco a suburban center; real estate development. Sand quarries.

NJ 16A: M, farmer, handyman, team driver in Boonton when 40, 75. B. Twp. — F. b. Twp.; M. b. near Oakland and Crystal Lake in Bergen Co., came here when married, MGF b. Bergen Co. — Very little ed. — Dutch Reformed.

Jacksonville Rd., Towaco P.O., Montville Twp.

Twp. formed 1867. Agricultural twp.; rolling land, rough and mountainous to E. Early settlers Dutch; then English settlers (c. 1714). Dutch Reformed area. Orchards; distilleries at one time. Residential. Pop. Twp. 1940: 3,207.

NJ 16B: M, farmer, 45. When 21 to Waterbury, CT, 1 1/2 yrs, then home 2 yrs., then garage in NY 1 yr., then home, then out west 1 1/2 yrs. — F. b. Towaco, PGF, PGM b. Twp.; M., MGM b. Twp., MGM's F. of English descent. — Ed.: till 8th grade, 2 yrs. business school in Paterson. — Methodist.

17. Union County

Formed 1857 from Essex Co. 1664 Nichols grant: 1st settlement at Elizabeth. Early settlers from Long Island; some also from New Haven, Watertown, CT, MA, NY; a few Dutch, some directly from northern England. Heavily timbered uplands. Pop. 1860: 27,780, 1880: 55,571, 1910: 140,197, 1930: 305,209, 1960: 504,255.

Ahern, Simeon J. 1879. *Elizabeth: A Glance at the Past and Future of the City.* Elizabeth.

Clayton, W. Woodford. 1882. *History of Union and Middlesex Counties, with Biographical Sketches.* . . . Philadelphia: Everts and Peck.

Elizabeth, New Jersey, Sesqui-centennial Committee. 1926. *Revolutionary History of Elizabeth*. Elizabeth.

Hatfield, Edwin F. 1868. *History of Elizabeth, Including the Early History of Union County*. NY: Carlton and Lanahan.

Honeyman, A. Van Doren, ed.-in-chief. 1923. *History of Union County, 1664–1923*. 3 vols. NY: Lewis Historical Pub. Co.

Miller, George J. 1942. *The Printing of the Elizabethtown Bill in Chancery*. Perth Amboy: Board of General Proprietors of the Eastern Division of New Jersey.

Murray, Nicholas. 1844. *Notes, Historical and Biographical, concerning Elizabethtown*. . . . Elizabeth-town: E. Sanderson.

Ricord, Frederick W., ed. 1897. *History of Union County*. . . . Newark: East Jersey History Co.

Union Center, Union P.O. and Township

Twp. est. 1808; called "Connecticut Farms", settled from CT as early as 1667. Other early settlers from Southampton, MA; some from England. Presbyterian church from 1730. Truck farming; relatively little industry. Union Center formed from Connecticut Farms; small, attractive trading center. Pop. Twp. 1940: 24,730.

NJ 17A: M, retired farmer, 82. B. nearby. — F. b. here, PGF b. Twp., PGM b. Brooklyn, NY; M., MGF b. Springfield Twp., MGM b. Morris Co. (PGF and MGF descendants of original 17th cent. English settlers). — Ed.: till 17. — Presbyterian.

Elizabeth

Settled 1664 from Long Island; originally purchase from Indians. Town 1665, capital of NJ; charter 1740, 1789; chartered as city 1855. Formerly terminus of highways and RRs; declined as port: factories now inland. Original site of Princeton ("College of NJ") 1746-47. Congregational, Presbyterian churches early; Roman Catholics not tolerated until c. 1830. "Industrial park" 1835. German, Irish immigrants; Slavs and Italians around the time of WWI. Was transfer point for rail passengers before Newark Bay bridged. Diversified industry (overflow from NY): iron and steel fittings, stoves, Singer sewing machines (Singer Co. here from 1873), Bethlehem shipbuilding, automobiles, chemicals, tool and die works, commercial photography, wood products. Pop. 1880: 28,229, 1910: 73,409, 1930: 114,589, 1960: 107,698.

NJ 17B: M, office manager, 66. B. just across street. — F., PGF b. same neighborhood (Union Twp.), PGF's F., PGF's PGF, PGF's PGF's F. b. in what is now Elizabeth on Westfield Ave., PGF's PGF's PGF b. England, came here via New Haven, PGF's PGF's PGM b. Denmark, PGF's PGM b. Twp., PGF's M., PGF's MGF b. Westfield, PGM b. Long Hill, Myersville, Morris Co., PGM's F. b. Myersville; M. b. Elizabeth, MGF b. N. Shields, Northumberland, England, MGM, MGM's F., MGM's PGF b. Lyon's Farms, Union Twp., MGM's M. b. Twp. — Ed.: till 17. — Presbyterian.

18. Essex County

Est. 1675; named 1682; boundaries defined 1710. First settlers from Branford, CT, in 1666. Mineral prospecting in 18th cent.; whaling in 1832. 1st roads 1698; RR from 1832. Profitable quarrying. Movement towards urbanization from beginning. Pop. 1726: 4,230, 1790: 11,785, 1820: 23,071, 1850: 73,950, 1880: 189,929, 1910: 521,886, 1930: 833,513, 1960: 923,545.

Atkinson, Joseph. 1878. *The History of Newark*. . . . Newark: W. B. Guild.

Bigelow, Samuel F. 1890. *Biographical Sketch of Moses Bigelow*. Newark: Newark Common Council.

Brown, Elizabeth S., comp. 1907. *The History of Nutley*. Nutley: Woman's Public School Auxiliary.

Condict, Jemima. 1930. *Jemima Condict, Her Book: Being a Transcript of the Diary of an Essex County Maid During the Revolutionary War*. Newark: Carteret Book Club.

Cunningham, John T. 1966. *Newark*. Newark: New Jersey Historical Society.

Folsom, Joseph F., ed.-in-chief. 1925. *The Municipalities of Essex County, 1666–1924*. NY: Lewis Historical Pub. Co.

Gasser, C. Albert. 1904. *Men of Newark*. . . . Newark: Schultz and Gasser.

Hill, Frank P., and Varnum Lansing Collins. 1902. *Books, Pamphlets, and Newspapers Printed at Newark, New Jersey, 1776–1900*. Newark: Courier-Citizen Co.

Hoyt, James. 1860. *The Mountain Society*. . . . NY: C. M. Saxton, Barker, and Co.

Pierson, David L. 1917. *Narratives of Newark*. . . . Newark: Pierson Pub. Co.

Pierson, David L. 1922. *History of the Oranges to 1921*. . . . NY: Lewis Historical Publishing Co.

Ruzicka, Rudolph. 1917. *Newark: A Series of Engravings*. . . . Newark: Carteret Book Club.

Shaw, William H., comp. 1884. *History of Essex and Hudson Counties*. Philadelphia: Everts and Peck.

Stevens, Thomas W. 1916. *Book of Words: The Pageant of Newark*. Newark: Committee of One Hundred.

Whittemore, Henry. 1896. *The Founders and Builders of the Oranges*. . . . Newark: L. J. Hardham.

Wickes, Stephen. 1892. *History of the Oranges,. . .1666–1806*. Newark: New England Society of Orange.

1796–1909. *The Sentinel of Freedom*. Newark.

1864. *Records of the Town of Newark, 1666–1836*. Newark: New Jersey Historical Society.

1866. *Proceedings Commemorative of the Settlement of Newark*. . . . Newark: New Jersey Historical Society.

1898. *Biographical and Genealogical History of the City of Newark and Essex County*. NY: Lewis Pub. Co.

1913. *A History of the City of Newark, 1666–1913*. . . . NY: Lewis Historical Pub. Co.

Nutley

NE section of original Newark Twp. 1874 Twp. of Franklin; renamed Nutley 1902. Late settlement: developed by Dutch from Bergen Co. in early 18th cent. Few English settlers before 1700. Quarries from 17th cent., many abandoned. Artists' and writers' colony after 1865. Some specialized industrialization in 20th cent., but mainly residential suburb since 1920. Pop. 1910: 6,009, 1930: 20,572, 1960: 29,513.

NJ 18A: F, homemaker, 68. B. New York City, to Ann Arbor, MI, when a few mos. old for 2 yrs., then to Jersey City till 16, then to East Orange, NJ, till 33; here for last 35 yrs. — F. b.

Staten Island, NY, PGF b. Morris Co., NJ, PGM b. Bordentown, NJ; M. b. Washington St., NYC, MGF b. Nyack, Rockland Co., NY, MGM b. Spring Valley, Rockland Co., NY. — Ed.: 1 yr. h.s. Jersey City, 3 yrs. East Orange. — Methodist.

NJ 18B: F, homemaker, 58. B. NYC (E. 115th St., still rural when she was a child), in Nutley for last 25 yrs. — F. b. NYC (around W. 33rd St.), PGF b. Catskill, Greene Co., NY, came as child to NYC, PGM b. Albany; M. b. NYC (East 26th St.), MGF b. Belleville, Essex Co., NJ, MGM b. Nutley (of old Holland Dutch descent). — Ed.: some h.s.; many yrs. of private music and piano instruction. — Methodist (family Presbyterian).

Newark

Founded 1666; anti-proprietary revolt 1672. Burned in Rev. Inc. as a city 1836. First settlement mostly from CT. "More Puritan than much of New England". Growth began c. 1794 with bridges over Passaic and Hackensack. Whaling from at least 1825; shoemaking center early 19th cent. Originally Congregationalist; later became Presbyterian. Irish and Scottish immigrants in 17th cent.; large German pop. in 19th cent.; later Italians and Poles; most recently AfAms. Jewish community from 1840s. 1st RR 1833. Literary group 1865–70. Army port in WWI. 3rd oldest US city; some of worst urban decay in US. Products and industries: airports, brewing (since 1850s), insurance (Prudential), machines, jewelry, toilet products, electrical equipment, chemicals, paints and varnish, foundry work. Pop. 1820: 6,507, 1850: 38,894, 1910: 347,469, 1930: 442,337, 1960: 405,220.

NJ 18C!: F, church social service director, 57. B. Newark. — F. b. Newark, PGF b. Greenock, Scotland, PGM b. NYC (Hester St.), PGM's F. b. Auburn, NY; M. b. Newark, MGF, MGF's F. b. Irvington, Essex Co., MGF's M. b. NYC, MGM, MGM's F., MGM's M. b. Rhinebeck, NY. — Ed.: Newark private schools till 18. — Presbyterian. — Cultivated.

Orange

Twp. est. 1806; inc. as a town 1860; inc. as city 1872. Settled by 1678. Like Newark, reinforced by settlers from CT and Long Island. English, Dutch, French settled by 1680 in what is now S. Orange. Copper mines 1719; first gristmill 1735. Dispute over land titles in 1750s: proprietary claims upheld against those who had only Indian titles. "Mountain society" to 1782; small hamlets. 1st Presbyterian church 1720; heavily Presbyterian in 18th cent. A "watering place": very fashionable 1812–24. Became suburban residential area early. European immigration in 1850s. Products and industries: shoes, felt hats, electrical supplies, drugs, office equipment. Pop. 1820: 2,830, 1850: 4,835, 1880: 13,207, 1910: 29,630, 1930: 35,399, 1960: 35,789.

NJ 18D!: F, music teacher, 54. B. Newark, to East Orange when 4, to Orange when 37. — F., PGF, PGF's F. b. Newark, PGM of PA family; M., MGF, MGM b. Newark. — Ed.: private grammar schools, public h.s. in East Orange, Vassar. — Presbyterian. — Cultivated.

19. Hudson County

Formed 1840 from Bergen Co. (Old Bergen Twp.). Settlement as early as 1643; devastated by Indians in 1645, 1655. In 1658 Quakers arrived; resettlement by Dutch. 1790 bridges over Hackensack and Passaic; turnpike. Ferries to New York City important in growth. Orig. agricultural comm., NY market. Called "most German co. in US": at one time 9 German newspapers, including 2 dailies. Pop. 1840: 9,483, 1850: 21,822, 1880: 187,944, 1910: 537,231, 1930: 690,730, 1960: 610,734.

Connors, Richard J. 1971. *A Cycle of Power.* . . . Metuchen: Scarecrow Press.

Eaton, Harriet P. 1899. *Jersey City and Its Historic Sites.* Jersey City: Woman's Club.

Foster, Mark S. 1968. Frank Hague of Jersey City: The "Boss" as Reformer. *New Jersey History* 86.2:106–117.

Harvey, Cornelius B., ed. 1900. *Genealogical History of Hudson and Bergen Counties.* NY: New Jersey Genealogical Pub. Co.

McKean, Dayton D. 1940. *The Boss: The Hague Machine in Action.* Boston: Houghton Mifflin.

McLean, Alexander. 1895. *History of Jersey City.* . . . Jersey City: Press of the Jersey City Printing Co.

Shaw, Douglas V. 1973. *The Making of an Immigrant City: Ethnic and Cultural Conflict in Jersey City, New Jersey, 1850–1877.* Ann Arbor. Repr. 1976 (NY: Arno Press).

Shaw, William H., comp. 1884. *History of Essex and Hudson Counties.* Philadelphia: Everts and Peck.

Van Winkle, Daniel, ed.-in-chief. 1924. *History of the Municipalities of Hudson County, 1630–1923.* NY: Lewis Historical Pub. Co.

Van Winkle, Daniel. 1902. *Old Bergen: History and Reminiscences.* . . . Jersey City: J. W. Harrison.

Winfield, Charles H. 1872. *History of the Land Titles in Hudson County, 1609–1871.* NY: Wynkoop and Hallenbeck.

Winfield, Charles H. 1874. *History of the County of Hudson.* . . . NY: Kennard and Hay.

Winfield, Charles H. 1891. *A Monograph on the Founding of Jersey City.* NY: Caxton Press.

Jersey City

Inc. 1819. Begun in 1804 by Hamiltonians to counter New York City's shipping primacy; initially failed, scheme revived in 1820. Pavonia settlement here 1633 (failed); palisaded town 1660. Bergen Reformed Church (1662) probably oldest in NJ (spoke Dutch there into 19th cent.). Episcopal church from 1808. Underground RR station. Co. seat of (new) Hudson Co., 1840. Large Irish pop. (Irish dominant after 1877), also many English and Germans. Long open-shop city. Shipping, RR yards. In 19th cent., pop. grew by migration from NYC. St. Peter's College founded 1878. Diversified industry: sugar, tobacco, glass, porcelain, graphite (pencils), Colgate, RR shops, steel. Pop. 1850: 6,856, 1880: 120,722, 1910: 267,779, 1930: 316,715, 1960: 276,101.

NJ 19A: F, widow, 75. B. same house. — F., PGF, PGF's F. b. Old Bergen (now part of Jersey City), paternal grandparents spoke Dutch; M., MGF, MGM b. Old Bergen. — Ed.: public schools till 14 or 15. — Dutch Reformed. — Obliging, slightly diffident in her ability to grasp purpose; ordinary ed., good background. — Very genuine, unaffected speech; good articulation.

NJ 19B: F, retired kindergarten teacher, 65. B. Jersey City near Bergen Square. — F., PGF, PGF's M. b. Freehold, Monmouth Co., NJ (F. brought here as baby), PGF's F. b. Freehold or Shrewsbury, NJ, PGM b. NYC, PGM's F. b. Freehold of long line that originally came from Isle of Jersey, PGM's M. b. Cummington, MA; M. b. Jersey City, MGF, MGF's F. and M., MGM b. Old Bergen (now part of Jersey City), MGM's F. and M. b. Jersey City (both of old Dutch stock). — Ed.: local public schools and Bergen School for Girls. — Dutch Reformed.

20. Bergen County

Bergen first village in NJ. Co. formed 1683. Dutch settlers at least from 1634. Many Dutch, some English arrived in late 17th cent.; other early settlers from NY, Long Island, Hudson Valley. Turnpike 1804; first RR 1832. Early 18th cent., Irish and Scotch-Irish settled in N. part. Dutch predominant language in 1840. Pop. 1726: 2,673, 1790: 12,601, 1820: 18,138, 1850: 14,725, 1880: 36,788, 1910: 138,002, 1930: 364,977, 1960: 780,225.

Clayton, W. Woodford., comp. 1882. *History of Bergen and Passaic Counties.* . . . Philadelphia: Everts and Peck.

Durie, Howard I. 1970. *The Kakiat Patent in Bergen County.* . . . Pearl River, NY: Star Press.

Harvey, Cornelius B., ed. 1900. *Genealogical History of Hudson and Bergen Counties.* NY: New Jersey Genealogical Pub. Co.

Keesey, Ruth M. 1957. *Loyalty and Reprisal: The Loyalists of Bergen County, New Jersey.* Columbia University dissertation.

Leiby, Adrian C. 1962. *The Revolutionary War in the Hackensack Valley: The Jersey Dutch and the Neutral Ground, 1775–1783.* New Brunswick: Rutgers Univ. Press.

Leiby, Adrian Coulter. 1964. *The Huguenot Settlement of Schraalenburgh: The History of Bergenfield, New Jersey.* Bergenfield: Bergenfield Free Public Library.

Taylor, Benjamin C. 1857. *Annals of the Classis of Bergen.* 3rd ed. NY: Board of Publication of the Reformed Dutch Church.

Van Winkle, Daniel. 1902. *Old Bergen: History and Reminiscences.* . . . Jersey City: J. W. Harrison.

Westervelt, Frances A., comp. 1905–22. *Annual Report.* Hackensack: Bergen County Historical Society.

Westervelt, Frances A., ed. 1923. *History of Bergen County, 1630–1923.* 3 vols. NY: Lewis Historical Pub. Co.

1970–. *Bergen County History.* River Edge: Bergen County Historical Society.

Park Ridge

Washington Twp. formed 1840 from Harrington. Park Ridge est. 1894. Site of Campbell wampum factory. Early settlers chiefly of Dutch descent, many directly from Holland. Borough from 1894. Industries and products: carbon paper, inked ribbons, paper boxes, labels, sweaters, clothing. Pop. 1880: 2,853, 1910: 1,301, 1930: 2,229, 1960: 6,389.

NJ 20A: M, newspaper editor and publisher, 80. B. here. — F. b. Park Ridge, PGF b. Twp., PGF's F. descendant of the first school teacher in Nieuw Amsterdam, PGM b. Old Tappan, Bergen Co., NJ; M. b. Park Ridge, MGF, MGF's F. b. Staten Island, NY, MGF's M., MGM, MGM's F. b. Park Ridge (all lines but that of MGF of Holland Dutch descent). — Ed.: till 18, then local academy for a short time. — Dutch Reformed.

Oradell, Palisade Twp.

Twp. formed from Hackensack 1871. Oradell a borough from 1894. Residential community to 1923. Renowned for stockbreeding. Also manufacture of machines for moistening gummed tape. Pop. 1880: 2,302, 1930: 2,360, 1960: 7,487.

NJ 20B: M, farmer, 61. B. here. — F. b. Englewood, Bergen Co., NJ, PGF, PGM b. Germany; M. b. Palisade Twp., MGF b. Bergen Co., perhaps at River Edge (of old Holland Dutch stock), MGM b. Schralberg (now Dumont), Bergen Co. (of old local French Huguenot and Dutch stock). — Ed.: till 18. — Dutch Reformed.

21. Passaic County

Formed 1837 from Bergen Co. Area first settled c. 1679; early settlers Dutch, most from Netherlands, via Hudson Valley; some from New York City area. Industrialized in latter 19th cent., esp. textiles. Some German and Slovak immigration. Pop. 1840: 16,734, 1850: 22,569, 1880: 68,860, 1910: 215,902, 1930: 302,129, 1960: 406,618.

Clayton, W. Woodford, comp. 1882. *History of Bergen and Passaic Counties.* Philadelphia: Everts and Peck.

Ebner, Michael Howard. 1974. *Passaic New Jersey, 1855–1912.* University of Virginia dissertation.

Nelson, William, comp. 1895. *Records of the Township of Paterson, 1831–1851.* Paterson: Evening News Job Print.

Nelson, William. 1877. *Historical Sketch of the County of Passaic, Especially of the First Settlement and Settlers.* Paterson: Chiswell and Wurts.

Nelson, William. 1901. *History of the City of Paterson and the County of Passaic, New Jersey.* Paterson: Press Prtg. and Pub. Co.

Scott, William W. 1922. *History of Passaic and Its Environs.* 3 vols. NY: Lewis Historical Pub. Co.

Whitehead, John. 1901. *The Passaic Valley in Three Centuries.* NY: New Jersey Genealogical Co.

Wayne

Twp. set off from Manchester in 1847. Settled in 17th cent. by Dutch. Powder and other explosives; brick. Pop. 1940: 6,868.

NJ 21A: M, farmer, 71. B. same house. — F., PGF b. Wayne, PGM b. Pompton Plains, Morris Co.; M. b. Pompton Plains (2 mi. from Co. line and 3 mi. from house), MGF b. Pompton Plains. — Ed.: till 15. — Dutch Reformed. — Pretty quick, intelligent, cooperative. — Rather rapid tempo; note [v] for [w].

Lower Preakness, Paterson P.O., Wayne Twp.

Preakness E. side of Wayne Twp., near Paterson. Sponsored by A. Hamilton 1791. Cotton, silk made here. 1828 first "sympathy strike"; silk and dye strikes 1933–34. Relatively small establishments, antiquated; "family shop" still common to WWII.

NJ 21B: M, farmer, 55. B. 1/2 mi. away. — F., PGF b. Paterson, PGM b. N. Paterson, formerly called Guffle Hill; M., MGF b. Preakness (all of old Holland Dutch descent). — Ed.: till 16 (1 yr. h.s.). — Dutch Reformed.

Bibliographies

Bibliography Committee. 1967. *New Jersey and the Negro: A Bibliography, 1715–1966*. Trenton: New Jersey Library Association.

Burr, Nelson R. 1964. *A Narrative and Descriptive Bibliography of New Jersey*. Princeton: Van Nostrand.

Humphrey, Constance H. 1931. Checklist of New Jersey Imprints to the end of the Revolution. In *The Papers of the Bibliographic Society of America* 24:43–149.

McCormick, Richard P. 1965. *New Jersey: A Student's Guide to Localized History*. NY: Teacher's College Press.

Morsch, Lucile M. 1939. *Checklist of New Jersey Imprints, 1784–1800*. Baltimore: Historical Records Survey (US). Repr. 1964 (NY: Kraus Reprint Corp.).

New Jersey Historical Records Survey Project. 1941. *The Historical Records Survey in New Jersey: Description of Its Purpose, Account of Its Accomplishments, Bibliography of Its Publications*. Newark: Historical Records Survey.

Perry, Doris M. 1960. *This is New Jersey: A Bibliography*. 3rd rev. ed. Trenton: Trenton State College.

Stevens, Henry, and William A. Whitehead. 1858. *An Analytical Index to the Colonial Documents of New Jersey, in the State Paper Offices of England*. NY: D. Appleton & Co.

Worton, Stanley N., et al. 1964. *New Jersey: Past and Present*. NY: Hayden Book Co.

General Histories

Barber, John W. 1844. *Historical Collections of the State of New Jersey*. NY: S. Tuttle.

Barber, John W. and Henry Howe. 1868. *Historical Collections of New Jersey, Past and Present*. New Haven. Repr. 1966 (Spartanburg, SC: Reprint Co.).

Bebout, John E., and Ronald J. Grele. 1964. *Where Cities Meet: The Urbanization of New Jersey*. Princeton: Van Nostrand.

Carpenter, William H. 1853. *The History of New Jersey from Its Earliest Settlement to the Present Time*. Philadelphia: Lippincott, Grambo.

Cunningham, John T. 1966. *New Jersey, America's Main Road*. Garden City, NY: Doubleday.

Federal Writers Project. 1939. *New Jersey: A Guide to Its Present and Past*. NY: Viking Press.

Fleming, Thomas J. 1984. *New Jersey: A History*. NY: Norton.

Gordon, Thomas Francis. 1834. *The History of New Jersey. . . .* Trenton: D. Fenton.

Kull, Irving Stoddard, ed. 1930–32. *New Jersey: A History*. 5 vols. NY: American Historical Society.

Lee, Francis Bazley. 1902. *New Jersey As a Colony and As a State*. NY: Publishing Society of New Jersey.

Lundin, C. Leonard. 1940. *Cockpit of the Revolution: The War for Independence in New Jersey*. Princeton: Princeton Univ. Press.

McCormick, Richard P. 1950. *Experiment in Independence: New Jersey in the Critical Period, 1781–1789*. New Brunswick: Rutgers Univ. Press.

McCormick, Richard P. 1964. *New Jersey from Colony to State, 1609–1789*. Princeton: Van Nostrand.

Myers, William S. 1945. *The Story of New Jersey*. 5 vols. NY: Lewis Historical Publishing Co.

Pomfret, John E. 1956. *The Province of West New Jersey, 1609–1702: A History of the Origins of an American Colony*. Princeton: Princeton University Press.

Pomfret, John E. 1973. *Colonial New Jersey: A History*. NY: Scribner.

Pomfret, John Edwin. 1962. *The Province of East New Jersey, 1609–1702: The Rebellious Proprietary*. Princeton: University Press.

Raum, John O. 1877. *The History of New Jersey, from Its Earliest Settlement*. Philadelphia: J. E. Potter.

Roome, William. 1883. *The Early Days and Early Surveys of East New Jersey*. Morristown: Jerseyman Steam Press Print.

Smith, Samuel. 1765. *The History of the Colony of Nova-Caesaria, or New Jersey*. Burlington. Repr. 1978 (Burlington, NJ: James Parker).

Tanner, Edwin Platt. 1908. *The Province of New Jersey, 1664–1738*. NY: Columbia University Press.

1847–. *New Jersey History*. Newark: New Jersey Historical Society.

1880–1928. *Documents Relating to the Colonial, Revolutionary and Post-Revolutionary History of the State of New Jersey*. Vols. 1–33. Newark: New Jersey Historical Society.

Special Studies

Beck, Henry C. 1936. *Forgotten Towns of Southern New Jersey*. NY. Repr. 1983 (New Brunswick: Rutgers Univ. Press).

Beck, Henry C. 1937. *More Forgotten Towns of Southern New Jersey*. NY: E. P. Dutton.

Beck, Henry C. 1956. *The Roads of Home: Lanes and Legends of New Jersey*. New Brunswick. Repr. 1983 (New Brunswick: Rutgers Univ. Press).

Beck, Henry C. 1963. *The Jersey Midlands*. New Brunswick. Repr. 1984 (New Brunswick: Rutgers Univ. Press).

Beck, Henry C. 1964. *Tales and Towns of Northern New Jersey*. New Brunswick. Repr. 1983 (New Brunswick: Rutgers Univ. Press).

Black, Frederick R. 1973. The West Jersey Society 1765–1784. *Pennsylvania Magazine of Historical Biography* 97:379–406.

Brush, John E. 1958. *The Population of New Jersey*. 2nd ed. New Brunswick: Rutgers Univ. Press.

Chambers, Theodore Relinghuysen. 1895. *The Early Germans of New Jersey*. Dover, NJ. Repr. 1969 (Baltimore: Genealogical Pub. Co.).

Cook, G. H., and C. C. Vermeule. 1887. *Atlas of New Jersey*. New Jersey Geological Survey.

Cooley, Henry Scofield. 1896. *A Study of Slavery in New Jersey*. Baltimore: Johns Hopkins Press.

Cowen, David L. 1964. *Medicine and Health in New Jersey: A History*. Princeton: Van Nostrand.

Cranmer, H. Jerome 1964. *New Jersey in the Automobile Age: A History of Transportation*. Princeton: Van Nostrand.

Davis, Philip Curtis. 1978. *The Persistence of Partisan Alignment: Issues, Leaders, and Votes in New Jersey, 1840–60*. Washington University dissertation.

Demarest, William H. S. 1924. *History of Rutgers College 1766–1924*. New Brunswick: Rutgers College.

Federal Writers Project. 1938. *Stories of New Jersey, Its Significant Places, People, and Activities.* NY: M. Barrows and Co.

Federal Writers Project. 1938. *The Swedes and Finns in New Jersey.* Bayonne: Jersey Printing Co.

Foster, John Y. 1868. *New Jersey and the Rebellion: A History of the Service of the Troops and People of New Jersey in Aid of the Union Cause.* Newark: M. R. Dennis.

Gerlach, Larry R. 1976. *Prologue to Independence: New Jersey in the Coming of the American Revolution.* New Brunswick: Rutgers.

Keen, Gregory B. 1884. Note on New Albion. In Justin Winsor, ed. *Narrative and Critical History of America,* vol. 3:457–68.

Kemmerer, Donald L. 1940. *Path to Freedom: The Struggle for Self-Government in Colonial New Jersey, 1703–1776.* Princeton. Repr. 1968 (Cos Cob, CT: J. E. Edwards).

Lane, Wheaton Joshua. 1939. *From Indian Trail to Iron Horse: Travel and Transportation in New Jersey, 1620–1860.* Princeton: Princeton University Press.

Leiby, Adrian C. 1964. *The Early Dutch and Swedish Settlers of New Jersey.* Princeton: Van Nostrand.

McCormick, Richard P. 1953. *The History of Voting in New Jersey.* New Brunswick: Rutgers University Press.

McMahon, William H. 1973. *South Jersey Towns: History and Legend.* New Brunswick: Rutgers University Press.

Mulford, Isaac S. 1851. *A Civil and Political History of New Jersey.* Philadelphia: C. A. Brown.

Murray, David. 1899. *History of Education in New Jersey.* Washington, DC: US Bureau of Education.

Myers, Albert C., ed. 1912. *Narratives of Early Pennsylvania, West New Jersey, and Delaware, 1630–1707.* NY. Barnes and Noble.

Nelson, William. 1902. *The New Jersey Coast in Three Centuries.* NY: Lewis Pub. Co.

Parsons, Floyd W., ed. 1928. *New Jersey: Life, Industries, and Resources of a Great State.* Newark: New Jersey State Chamber of Commerce.

Pierce, Arthur D. 1957. *Iron in the Pines: The Story of New Jersey's Ghost Towns and Bog Iron.* New Brunswick. Repr. 1984 (New Brunswick: Rutgers University Press).

Pierce, John R. 1964. *The Research State: A History of Science in New Jersey.* Princeton: Van Nostrand.

Pomfret, John Edwin. 1964. *The New Jersey Proprietors and Their Lands 1664–1776.* Princeton: D. Van Nostrand.

Sackett, William E. 1895–1914. *Modern Battles of Trenton.* Trenton: J. L. Murphy.

Schmidt, Hubert G. 1954. *Agriculture in New Jersey: A 300-Year History.* New Brunswick: Rutgers University Press. Repr. 1973.

Snyder, John P. 1969. *The Story of New Jersey's Civil Boundaries 1606–1968.* Trenton: Bureau of Geology and Topography.

Snyder, John P. 1973. *The Mapping of New Jersey: The Men and the Art.* New Brunswick: Rutgers University Press.

Steward, William, and Theophilus G. Steward. 1913. *Gouldtown, a Very Remarkable Settlement of Ancient Date. . . .* Philadelphia: J. B. Lippincott.

Stockton, Frank R. 1896. *Stories of New Jersey.* NY. Repr. 1987 (New Brunswick: Rutgers University Press).

Wacker, Peter O. 1968. *The Musconetcong Valley of New Jersey: A Historical Geography.* New Brunswick: Rutgers University Press.

Weiss, Harry B. 1971. *The Personal Estates of Early Farmers and Tradesmen of Colonial New Jersey, 1670–1750.* Trenton: New Jersey Agriculture Society.

Weiss, Harry Bischoff. 1964. *Life in Early New Jersey.* Princeton: D. Van Nostrand.

Werner, Charles J. 1930. *Eric Mullica and His Descendants: A Swedish Pioneer in New Jersey.* New Gretna: C. J. Werner.

Widmer, Kemble. 1964. *The Geology and Geography of New Jersey.* Princeton: Van Nostrand.

Wilson, Edmund P. 1923. New Jersey: The Slave of Two Cities. In Ernest Gruening, ed., *These United States* (NY), 56–66.

Wilson, Harold F. 1964. *The Story of the Jersey Shore.* Princeton: Van Nostrand.

Woodward, Carl R. 1937. *The Development of Agriculture in New Jersey.* New Brunswick: New Jersey Agricultural Experimental Station, Rutgers University.

Woodward, Carl R., and Ingrid N. Waller 1932. *New Jersey's Agricultural Experiment Station 1880–1930.* New Brunswick: New Jersey Agricultural Experiment Station.

Wright, William C., ed. 1972. *New Jersey Since 1860* [New Jersey History Symposium, 1971]. Trenton: New Jersey Historical Commission.

Wright, William C., ed. 1972. *New Jersey Since 1860: New Findings and Interpretations.* Trenton: New Jersey Historical Commission.

Wright, William C., ed. 1973. *New Jersey in the American Revolution* [New Jersey History Symposium, 1972]. Trenton: New Jersey Historical Commission.

1874. *New Jersey Geological Survey Report on a Survey of the Boundary Line between New Jersey and New York.* Trenton.

1879. *Minutes of the Provincial Congress and the Council of Safety of the State of New Jersey* [1775–1776]. Trenton: Naar, Day and Naar.

1913. *A Preliminary Report of the Archeological Survey of the State of New Jersey.* Trenton: American Museum of Natural History.

1949–57. *New Jersey Industrial Directory.* Union City: Hudson Dispatch.

1953–. *New Jersey Genesis.* NY: Carl M. Williams.

Pennsylvania

1. Philadelphia County and City

Site first settled by Swedes, Dutch, Finns. Dutch involved in trade; Swedes farmed (preferred draining marsh to clearing forests). City laid out 1682 by Thomas Holme; city charter 1701. 1st printing press in Middle colonies here 1685; public grammar school by 1689. Quaker dominance until c. 1735. Natural focus for trading area: ag. products to W. Indies, sugar and other prods. to England, manufactured goods to colonies. Shipbuilding (1st US naval yard); early industry. Intellectual center of colonies; 1st financial capital of US. Influence of Ben Franklin strong; 1st circulating library 1731, American Philosophical Society founded 1743, Academy for the Education of Youth (which eventually became the U. of PA) founded 1753. Scotch-Irish and German immigration 1727–42. Road to Pittsburgh by 1758; Lancaster Turnpike by 1790. Center of Revolutionary spirit; colonial capital 1774–89 (exc. time of occupation), also 1790–1800. Later center of anti-slavery sentiment. RRs by 1834; 1st RR center. In 1854 city took in all of Phila. County. Many Jews, Italians, Russians, foreign-born Germans, Irish by 1930. Flat terrain. Fairmount Park largest municipal park in the country. "Neighborhood" idea very important: more than 100 identified in 1976. Germantown (c. 1707) oldest real suburb in Phila. and probably oldest in America (predominantly German until Revolution); Kensington and Frankford industrial sections in NE Phila. Still hereditary upper class, based on business wealth and power; often descendants of past elite. Major seaport. Diversified industry, including leather products, textiles, clothing, hats, sugar refining, transportation equipment, paper products; medical center. Pop. Co. 1790: 54,336, 1820: 135,637, 1850: 408,762, 1880: 847,170, 1910: 1,549,008, 1930: 1,950,961, 1960: 2,002,512. City 1790: 28,522, 1820: 63,802, 1850: 121,376, thereafter same as Co. (city absorbed Co. in 1854).

Balch, Thomas, ed. 1855. *Letters and Papers Relating Chiefly to the Provincial History of Pennsylvania*. Philadelphia: Privately printed. Crissy and Markley Printers. American Culture Series, 226.6.

Baltzell, Edward Digby. 1958. *Philadelphia Gentlemen*. Glencoe, IL: Free Press.

Blumin, Stuart. 1969. Mobility and Change in Ante-Bellum Philadelphia. In Stephen Themstrom and Roland Sennett, eds., *Nineteenth-Century Cities* (New Haven, CT: Yale University Press), 165–208.

Bowen, Daniel. 1839. *A History of Philadelphia. . . .* Philadelphia: D. Bowen.

Bridenbaugh, Carl. 1942. *Rebels and Gentlemen: Philadelphia in the Age of Franklin*. NY: Reynal and Hitchcock.

Brookhouser, Frank. 1957. *Our Philadelphia*. Garden City, NY: Doubleday.

Browning, Charles H. 1912. *Welsh Settlement of Pennsylvania*. Philadelphia: W. J. Campbell.

Buck, Solon J. 1939. *The Planting of Civilization in Western Pennsylvania*. Pittsburgh: University of Pittsburgh Press.

Cheyney, Edward Potts. 1940. *History of the University of Pennsylvania*. Philadelphia: University of Pennsylvania Press.

Cutler, William W., III, and Howard Gillette, Jr., eds. 1980. *The Divided Metropolis: Social and Spatial Dimensions of Philadelphia, 1800–1975*. Westport, CT: Greenwood Press.

Darlington, Mary C. 1920. *History of Colonel Henry Bouquet and the Western Frontiers of Pennsylvania, 1747–1764*. Privately printed.

Davis, Allen F., and Mark H. Huller. 1973. *The Peoples of Philadelphia*. Philadelphia: Temple University Press.

Drinker, Elizabeth Sandwith. 1889. *Extracts from the Journal of Elizabeth Drinker, from 1759 to 1807*. Ed. by Henry D. Biddle. Philadelphia: J. B. Lippincott.

Du Bois, W. E. Burghardt. 1899. *The Philadelphia Negro*. Philadelphia. Repr. 1967 (NY: Schocken Books).

Faris, John T. 1918. *Romance of Old Philadelphia*. Philadelphia and London: J.B. Lippencott Company.

Federal Writers Project. 1937. *Philadelphia, a Guide to the Nation's Birthplace*. Philadelphia: William Penn Association of Philadelphia.

Fisher, Sidney George. 1967. *A Philadelphia Perspective: The Diary of Sidney George Fisher. . . 1834–1871*. Ed. by Nicholas B. Wainwright. Philadelphia: Historical Society of Pennsylvania.

Garran, Anthony N. B. 1963. Proprietary Philadelphia as Artifact. In Oscar Handlin and John Burchard, eds. *The Historian and the City* (Cambridge, MA: Harvard University Press), 177–201.

Hall, Norman F. 1935. Modern Philadelphia. *Bulletin of the Geographical Society of Philadelphia* 33:16–22.

Hershberg, Theodore, ed. 1981. *Philadelphia: Work, Space, Family, and Group Experience in the Nineteenth Century*. NY.

Hershberg, Theodore. 1971. Free Blacks in Antebellum Philadelphia. *Journal of Social History* 5

Hershberg, Theodore. 1973. *The Philadelphia Social History Project*. Stanford University dissertation.

Hocker, Edward W. 1933. *Germantown, 1683–1933*. Philadelphia: The Author.

Jackson, Joseph. 1931–33. *Encyclopedia of Philadelphia. . . .* 4 vols. Harrisburg: National Historical Association.

James, F. Cyril. 1940. The Bank of North America. *Pennsylvania Magazine of History and Biography* 64:56–87.

Jenkins, Charles F. 1902. *The Guide Book to Historic Germantown*. Germantown.

Keyser, Naaman Henry, et al. 1907. *History of Old Germantown*. Germantown: H. F. McCann.

Klimm, Lester E. 1935. The Physical Site of Penn's "Greene Towne". *Bulletin of the Geographical Society of Philadelphia* 33:1–8.

Klimm, Lester E. 1935. The Regional Plan and Some of Its Proposals. *Bulletin of the Geographical Society of Philadelphia* 33:23–27.

Lemon, James T. 1972. *The Best Poor Man's Country: A Geographical Study of Early Southeastern Pennsylvania.* Baltimore: Johns Hopkins University Press.

Lippincott, Horace Mather. 1917. *Early Philadelphia.* Philadelphia: J. B. Lippincott Co.

Livingood, James Weston. 1947. *The Philadelphia-Baltimore Trade Rivalry, 1780–1860.* Harrisburg: Pennsylvania Historical and Museum Commission.

Nash, Gary B. 1973. Slaves and Slaveowners in Colonial Philadelphia. *William and Mary Quarterly* 30:223–256.

Oberholtzer, Ellis Paxson. 1912. *Philadelphia: A History of the City and Its People.* . . . 4 vols. Philadelphia: Clarke.

Pennypacker, Samuel Whitaker. 1899. *The Settlement of Germantown.* . . . Philadelphia: W. J. Campbell.

Peyton, Jesse E. 1895. *Reminiscences of the Past.* Philadelphia: J. B. Lippincott Co.

Peyton, Jesse Enlows. 1895. *Reminiscences of the Past.* Philadelphia: J. B. Lippincott Co.

Pullinger, Herbert. 1926. *Old Germantown.* Philadelphia: David McKay.

Roach, Hanna B. 1968. The Planting of Philadelphia: A Seventeenth-Century Real Estate Development. *Pennsylvania Magazine of History and Biography* 92:3–47, 143–95.

Scharf, John Thomas. 1884. *History of Philadelphia: 1609–1884.* Philadelphia: L. H. Everts.

Shackleton, Robert. 1918. *The Book of Philadelphia.* Philadelphia: Pennsylvania Publishing Co.

Shryock, Richard H. 1940. Philadelphia and the Flowering of New England: An Editorial. *Pennsylvania Magazine of History and Biography* 64:305–13.

Spencer, David. 1908. *Historic Germantown.* Germantown: H.F. McCann.

Starkey, Otis P. 1935. The Situation and the Growth of Philadelphia. *Bulletin of the Geographical Society of Philadelphia* 33:9–15.

Tinkcom, Harry M., and Margaret M. Tinkcom. 1955. *Historic Germantown.* . . . Philadelphia: American Philosophical Society.

Warner, Sam B. 1963. Innovation and the Industrialization of Philadelphia, 1800–1850. In Oscar Handlin and John Burchard, eds., *The Historian and the City* (Cambridge, MA: Harvard University Press), 63–69.

Warner, Sam Bass, Jr. 1967. *If All the World Were Philadelphia: A Framework for Urban History, 1774–1930.* St. Louis: Washington University Institute for Urban and Regional Studies.

Warner, Sam Bass. 1968. *The Private City: Philadelphia in Three Periods of Its Growth.* Philadelphia: University of Pennsylvania Press.

Watson, John Fanning. 1830. *Annals of Philadelphia.* . . . Philadelphia: E. L. Carey.

Westcott, Thompson. 1876. *The Official Guide Book to Philadelphia.* . . . Philadelphia: Porter and Coates.

Weygandt, Cornelius. 1938. *Philadelphia Folks.* NY: D. Appleton-Century Co.

Wolf, Stephanie Grauman. 1976. *Urban Village: Population, Community, and Family Structure in Germantown, Pennsylvania, 1683–1800.* Princeton, NJ: Princeton University Press.

1719–46. *The American Weekly Mercury.* Philadelphia: Andrew Bradford.

1771–77. *Pennsylvania Packet.* Philadelphia: John Dunlap.

1775–81. *The Pennsylvania Evening Post.* Philadelphia: B. Towne.

1781–92. *The Freeman's Journal, or, the North-American Intelligencer.* Philadelphia: Francis Bailey.

1782–96. *The Independent Gazetteer.* Philadelphia: Eleazer Oswald.

1784–92. *Pennsylvania Mercury.* Philadelphia: Daniel Humphreys.

1788–90. *The Federal Gazette, and Philadelphia Evening Post.* Philadelphia: Andrew Brown.

1790–94. *General Advertiser.* Philadelphia: B. F. Bache.

1791–93. *National Gazette.* Philadelphia: Childs and Swaine.

1795–98. *The Philadelphia Minerva.* Philadelphia: Woodruff and Turner.

1797–1800. *Porcupine's Gazette.* Philadelphia: William Cobbett.

1798. *Carey's United States' Recorder.* Philadelphia: James Carey.

1799–1800. *The Constitutional Diary and Philadelphia Evening Advertiser.* Philadelphia: James Carey.

1807–73. *The Tickler.* Philadelphia: George Helmbold.

1812–25. *Grotjan's Philadelphia Public Sale Report.* Philadelphia: Peter A. Grotjan.

1953. *Historic Philadelphia.* Philadelphia: American Philosophical Society.

PA 1A: Kensington. — M, weaver, 68. B. here. — F. b. here, PGF b. Germany, PGM probably b. here; M. b. here, MGF b. Ireland (Protestant), MGM b. Ireland (Protestant) came here at age of 3. — Ed.: till 11. — Presbyterian. — Poor neighborhood; fairly quick at answering but dull; apparently saw no point to the interview. — Claimed he had asthma but FW suspects his articulation is slightly defective; very front [aˀ·] peculiar (perhaps German or Scottish).

PA 1B: M, elevator inspector, 43. B. here. — F. b. here, PGF b. perhaps in Germany, PGM b. Leipsig, DE (of old DE stock); M. b. here, MGF, MGF's F. b. here (of Scottish descent), MGF's M. b. here; MGM, MGM's F., MGM's M. b. here. — Ed.: till 18, Phila. Trade School. — Baptist. — Quick; FW asked questions rapidly; mother listened; may not have understood purpose of interview. — Mother says [æ·ʊ̆] where he usually says [aᶜ·ʊ̆] or [aᶺ·ʊ̆].

PA 1C: Frankford. — F, housewife, 68. B. here. — F. b. Phila., PGF (of German descent), PGM b. Germantown, Phila. (of French Huguenot and German descent); M. b. here, MGM b. England, came here as a child. — Ed.: here till 15 or 16. — Methodist. — Has stayed young with her children (one daughter is a teacher), quite modern, quick, rather sparkling personality; occasionally forgetful; confused by what she was told before interview, embarrassed at beginning of interview.

PA 1D: West Philadelphia. — M, receptionist; formerly in shipping dept., then travelled collecting accounts, then business executive, all with same advertising company, 66. B. S. Phila. — F. b. S. Phila. (Methodist), PGF b. S. Phila., PGF's F. b. here (of "German" descent), PGF's M. b. here, PGM b. here; M. b. S. Phila., MGF, MGM b. Ireland (both Catholic). — Ed.: till 14. — Presbyterian. — Pleasant, hearty person who understood immediately and enjoyed the interview thoroughly; because of travel and contacts, very modern, although with limited formal education. — Phonetic pattern essentially stable.

PA 1E!: M, civil engineer, treasurer of insurance co., 68. B. here. 1895–1925 in Utica, NY, but returned here often to visit his family. — F., PGF, PGF's F., PGF's PGF b. here, PGF's PGF's F. b. Kennett Square, Chester Co., PGF's PGF's PGF b. Wales, came 1682, PGF's M. b. England, came 1793, PGM, PGM's F. b. here (of English stock), PGM's M. b. here; M, MGF b. here, MGF's F. b. NJ, MGF's M. b. near Bridgeport, CT, MGM b. here, MGM's F. Scottish Presbyterian. — Ed.: Episcopal Academy here, U. of PA. — Episcopal. — A conscientious and exact mind; reliable; lives in an old house in the old part of town (no one else does). — Articulation defect (not an ideal subject); the [aɪ], [ɛʌɪ], [ɔː] and loss of [r] before certain consonants in certain words typical of old-fashioned cultivated Phila. usage. — Cultivated.

PA 1F!: Germantown. — M, manager, later an engineer, 62. B. here. — F., PGF b. Fox Chase, Montgomery Co. (just outside N. Phila.), PGF's F., PGF's PGF b. Phila. (of German descent), PGF's PGM b. Phila. (of Welsh descent), PGF's M. b. Phila., PGM b. Penllyn, Montgomery Co., PGM's F. b. Mont. Co. of Welsh descent); M. b. Phila., MGF b. Burlington, NJ, MGM, MGM's F., MGM's PGF b. Phila. (of English descent, from Banbury, W. Ox.). All of quaker stock. — Ed.: Friends School, Germantown, Haverford College. — Society of Friends. — A cultivated, very human and cooperative informant. — His wife, born in NY but living in Phila. since infancy, has a very cultivated, highly cosmopolitan type of speech [bɜəd] *bird*, [fɑˈˑm], [kɑˈˑnt]. As the result of her speech, he uses a compromise vowel in [kæʔˑnt kaʔˑnt], etc., but his [ɚ] is always present, except in words where Philadelphians normally omit it. — Cultivated.

PA 1G!: M, merchant, corporation executive, 70. B. Ferry Bank, Westchester (location of country summer home). — F. b. here, PGF b. Green Hill Farms (edge of Phila.), PGF's F. b. Reading during the British siege of Phila., returned the next year (1778), PGF's PGF, PGF's PGF's F. b. here, PGF's PGF's PGF b. London, came in 1682, PGF's PGF's PGM b. probably Burlington, NJ, PGF's PGF's M. b. here, PGF's PGM b. here, PGF's PGM's F. b. Germany in Hildesheim, of Austrian descent, PGF's M. b. here, PGF's MGF b. Elkton, MD, PGF's MGM b. Lower Merion, Montgomery Co.; PGM b. Baltimore, MD, PGM's F. b. West River, Anne Arundel Co., MD, PGM's M. b. Baltimore, MD; M. b. here, MGF b. Hull, Yorkshire, England, came here as a boy, MGF's F. b. Lincolnshire, MGF's M. b. East Riding, Yorkshire; MGM, MGM's F. b. Bucks Co., MGM's PGF b. Hunterdon Co., NJ; MGM's M. b. Bucks Co. (of Holland Dutch, Long Island, NY stock via NJ). — Ed.: Wm. Penn Charter School (here), Haverford College. — Episcopalian; Am. Philosophical Society; VP Agricultural Society. — Quick, business-like type; volunteered to answer the questions because inf. recommended to FW had a speech difficulty; at least pretended to be cooperative. FW had to ask the questions very rapidly because informant's time was limited. — Cultivated.

PA 1H!: Germantown. — F, housewife (government and social service experience), 59. B. here. — F. b. here, PGF b. Salem, MA (of old Salem stock), PGM, PGM's F., PGM's PGF b. here (of English stock), PGM's PGM b. Germantown (of German descent), PGM's M., PGM's MGF b. here (of English descent), PGM's MGM b. here (of English descent); M., MGF, MGF's F. b. here, MGF's PGF b. Ireland, MGF's M., MGF's MGF b. here (of Welsh descent), MGF's MGM b. here, MGM, MGM's F. born here (of English descent); MGM's M. b. here (descended from Welshman who came to PA with William Penn). — Ed.: Friends School, Germantown. — Society of Friends. — Gracious, cultivated person, who understood purpose of interview; cooperative; poised; deliberate. Well-to-do, excellent family background. — Utterance clear and precise; tempo moderate. Vowels tend to be short, but the [aˈɪ] diphthong tends to be prolonged. The [l] is not as dark as [ɫ] in S. Jersey (where it tends to be very strongly velarized). — Cultivated.

2. Bucks County

Organized 1682; surveyed 1685 (first division into twps.). 1st settlement Swedes c. 1670; also Finns early. English predominated among early settlers; Scotch-Irish in 1720, 1740; Dutch 1725–35 and Germans (in upper twps.) 1740–68. Many Quakers among early settlers: 7 Quaker congregations by 1750. Also Dutch Reformed, Mennonites, Baptists, Presbyterians, Lutherans in first half of 18th cent.; Methodists shortly thereafter. Turnpike from 1803; Delaware Canal 1827–32; first RR 1832. Early industries: lumbering, shipbuilding, ironmaking. Also agriculture, limestone. Pop. 1790: 25,401, 1820: 37,842, 1850: 56,091, 1880: 68,656, 1910: 76,530, 1930: 96,727, 1960: 308,567.

Battle, J. H., ed. 1887. *History of Bucks County*. Philadelphia: A. Warner.

Brown, George W. 1882. *Historical Sketches*. Philadelphia: J.P. Murphy.

Buck, William J. 1855. *History of Buck's County*. Willow Grove.

Buck, William Joseph. 1887. *Local Sketches and Legends. . . *. Philadelphia: The Author.

Bye, Arthur Edwin. 1970. *Bucks County Tales, 1685–1931*. Correll Press.

Cheelemay, Barry N. 1978. *Surburbanization and Community: Growth and Planning in Postwar Bucks County*. University of Pennsylvania dissertation.

Davis, W. W. H. 1876. *The History of Bucks County. . . .* Doylestown: Democrat Book and Job Office Print.

Fisher, Allen S. 1935. *Lutheranism in Bucks County, 1734–1934*. Tinicum.

Hampton, Vernon Boyce. 1940. *In the Footsteps of Joseph Hampton*. Doylestown: Bucks Co. Historical Society.

Hotchkin, Samuel F. 1892. *The York Road, Old and New. . . *. Philadelphia: Binder and Kelly.

Hotchkin, Samuel F. 1893. *The Bristol Pike*. Philadelphia: J.W. Jacobs.

MacReynolds, George. 1955. *Place Names in Bucks County. . . .* 2nd ed. Doylestown: Bucks County Historical Society.

McNealy, Terry A. 1970. *A History of Bucks County*. Fallsington.

Parry, Oliver Randolph. 1915. *"Coryell's Ferry" in the Revolution (now New Hope)*. The Fanwood Press.

Reeder, Eastburn, comp. 1971 [1900]. *Early Settlers of Solebury Township*. Doylestown: Bucks County Historical Society.

Roberts, Clarence V. 1925. *Early Friends Families of Upper Bucks.* . . . Philadelphia: The Author.

Smith, Charles W. 1855. History of the Township of Wrightstown. Appendix to William J. Buck, *History of Buck's County*. Philadelphia: W. J. Buck.

Underhill, Sarah Gilpin. 1934. *The Indians of Bucks County, Pennsylvania, 250 Years Ago*. Philadelphia: Friends' Historical Association.

Watson, John. 1804. *An Account of the First Settlement of the Townships of Buckingham and Solebury*. Philadelphia: Pennsylvania Historical Society.

1908–. *A Collection of Papers Read before the Bucks County Historical Society*. Easton: Bucks County Historical Society.

Lurgan, New Hope, Upper Makefield Twp.

Makefield Twp. from 1692; Upper Makefield set off 1737. Area settled as early as 1683; early settlers English Friends. Lurgan a hamlet named after town in Armagh. Seat of old-time schoolhouse "Lurgan College". New Hope site of mills built in 1790s; site of old canal; artists' colony since 1900.

PA 2A: M, farmer, 70. B. Pineville (4 mi. W.). — F. b. Penns Park, Wrightstown Twp. (8 mi. W.), PGF prob. b. near Pineville (of Holland Dutch descent), PGM, PGM's F. b. here; M., MGF b. Pineville, MGM of Quaker stock. — Ed.: here till 15. — Presbyterian. — Very controlled emotionally, plain and straightforward; quick and logical.

Aquetong, New Hope, Solebury Twp.

Twp. set off by 1702. Settled as early as 1687; English and Scotch-Irish among early settlers. Copper mine. Aquetong a crossroads hamlet from the 18th cent.

PA 2B: M, farmer, 57. B. here. — F. b. New Hope, PGF b. Co.; M., MGF, MGM b. Co. — Ed.: Solebury, then 2 yrs. Friends Central Preparatory School in Phila., 1 yr. business school in Trenton. — Society of Friends (as all 4 grandparents). — Rather quick and alert, but at end somewhat suspicious. — Clear speech.

3. Montgomery County

Cut off from Philadephia Co. in 1784. First settlement 1682: north end Germans, SE Welsh and Swedes, W. Welsh (Anglicans). By 18th cent., more than half German. Last Indian claims extinguished 1692. Numerous Friends Houses before Rev. Mennonite settlement by 1702; outgrowth of Germantown. Lutherans most numerous denomination, chiefly 1710–70; 1st Lutheran Church in America congregation 1709. Undulating terrain; limestone and marble, iron ore, some copper, paper, textiles. Pop. 1790: 22,929, 1820: 35,793, 1850: 58,291, 1880: 96,494, 1910: 169,590, 1930: 285,804, 1960: 516,682.

Bean, Theodore W., ed. 1884. *History of Montgomery County*. Philadelphia: Everts and Peck.

Buck, William J. 1859. *History of Montgomery County.* . . . Norristown: E. L. Acker.

Develin, Dora Harvey. 1922. *Historic Lower Merion and Blockley: Also the Erection or Establishment of Montgomery County*. Bala.

Hopkins, G. M., et al. 1871. *Atlas of the County of Montgomery*. Philadelphia.

Hunsicker, Clifton S. 1923. *Montgomery County: A History*. NY: Lewis Historical Pub. Co.

Jenkins, Howard M. 1897. *Historical Collections Relating to Gwynedd.* . . . 2nd ed. Philadelphia: The Author.

Lippincott, Horace Mather. 1948. *A Narrative of Chestnut Hill, with Some Account of Springfield, Whitemarsh and Cheltenham Townships in Montgomery County*. Jenkintown: Old York Road Pub. Co.

1895–. *Historical Sketches*. Norristown: Historical Society of Montgomery County.

1915. *Industrial Conditions in Montgomery County*. Washington: US Bureau of Foreign and Domestic Commerce.

1936–. *Bulletin*. Norristown: Historical Society of Montgomery County.

1951. *The Montgomery County Story*. Norristown: Commissioners of Montgomery County.

Trooper

Norristown (inf.'s birthplace, nearby) settled 1688; laid out 1785; incorporated as borough 1812. Co. seat from 1784. English and Germans. Most populous independent borough in US. Diverse manufacturing nearby; marble, granite, limestone, iron. Pop. Norristown 1820: 827, 1850: 6,024, 1880: 13,063, 1910: 27,875, 1930: 35,853, 1960: 38,925.

PA 3A: F, widow, 91. B. Norristown in Co., moved to Trooper when infant, lived there till 14. Came then to Roxborough, Phila., present residence. — F., PGF, PGM, M., MGF b. Co. (all of PA German ancestry). — Ed.: at Trooper (father a teacher in a country school). — Baptist. — Rather old-fashioned; plain, substantial background. Not aware of purpose of interview; questions often seemed senseless to her, answered quickly from sense of duty.

Spring House, Lower Gwynedd Twp.

Gwynedd Twp. divided c. 1890. Gwynedd an original twp., antedates Co. Part of "Welsh tract" bought in 1683. Welsh Friends Meeting House from 1700. Twp. from c. 1700: Welsh migration 1691; almost exclusively Welsh till 1730, then Germans. Spring House settled from 1698; agricultural and prosperous. 1st tavern 1763; 1st hotel 1832.

PA 3B: M, farmer, 67. B. Upper Dublin Twp., 3 mi. S. — F. b. Upper Dublin Twp., PGF b. near Marcus Hook, Delaware Co., came here as a young man, PGF's F. b. Scotland, PGM b. S. Phila. (of German parentage); M. b. near Southampton in Bucks Co., MGF b. in England and settled in NJ, MGM b. in Germany. — Ed.: till 17. — Church of the Brethren. — Old-fashioned farmer, one of the few left in an area rapidly being converted into estates of wealthy Philadelphians; quick, unable to sleep well. — Slightly indistinct utterance.

PA 3C: M, farmer, 58. B. here. — F. b. Phila., came here at age 5, PGF b. Co., PGF's F. b. Upper Fairmount Park in

Phila., PGF's PGF b. Lower Dublin Twp., now in Phila., PGF's PGF's F. b. Dublin Twp., PGF's PGF's PGF b. Norton, Cheshire, England (1666), PGF's PGF's PGM b. Cheshire, England, PGF's PGF's M. b. Staffordshire, England, PGF's PGM b. Oxford Twp., now in Phila., PGF's PGM's F. b. Berkshire, England, PGF's M. b. Co., PGM, PGM's F., PGM's M. b. Mt. Holly, NJ (of English descent on father's side, 4 generations in Mt. Holly); M., MGF, MGF's F. b. Co., MGF's PGF descendant of one of the first Germans of Germantown, Phila. Co., MGF's M. b. Whitpain Twp. in Co., MGM b. Quakertown, Bucks Co., MGM's M. b. Abington in Co. — Ed.: till 14. — Society of Friends. — Living in old country place very close to edge of Phila. where mostly country estates of wealthy Phila. people are now; practically the only farmer of old native stock in this English-speaking section. Quiet, honest, trustworthy responses; quick and cooperative, often deliberative, not to be hurried. — High [ɔ:] as compared to Chester and Delaware Co. (The entire northern part of Montgomery Co. is PA German-speaking.)

4. Delaware County

Co. formed 1789. 1st settlement by Dutch c. 1635; Swedes settled as early as 1643. English from 1664; Friends settled 1672. Many settlers from Chester, England, in 1682. 1st mill in PA 1643–44. Swedish Lutherans and Friends early (no German Lutherans until 1878); also Episcopalians, Baptists, Presbyterians, and Roman Catholics in early 18th cent. Haverford College (1833), Swarthmore College (1864), Villanova (1842). Water power led to industry in the late 18th cent., esp. textiles and paper; also carpets, steel works, oil refining, machine tools, chemicals, Scott paper, electrical equipment. Pop. 1790: 9,472, 1820: 14,810, 1850: 24,679, 1880: 56,101, 1910: 117,906, 1930: 280,264, 1960: 553,154.

Armstrong, Edward, ed. 1860. Record of Upland Court. . . 1676. . . 1681. *Memoirs of the Historical Society of Pennsylvania* 7:9–203.

Ashmead, Henry Graham. 1883. *Historical Sketch of Chester, on Delaware*. Chester: Republican Steam Print.

Ashmead, Henry Graham. 1884. *History of Delaware County*. Philadelphia: L. H. Everts.

Barker, James N. 1827. *Sketches of the Primitive Settlements on the River Delaware*. Philadelphia: Carey, Lee and Carey.

Cope, Gilbert, et al., eds. 1904. *Historic Homes and Institutions. . . of Chester and Delaware Counties*. 2 vols. NY: Lewis Pub. Co.

Jordan, John W., ed. 1914. *A History of Delaware County, and Its People*. NY: Lewis Historical Pub. Co.

Lemon, James T., and Gary P. Nash. 1968. The Distribution of Wealth in Seventeenth-Century America: A Century of Changes in Chester County, Pennsylvania, 1693–1802. *Journal of Social History* 2:1–24.

Martin, John Hill. 1877. *Chester (and Its Vicinity,) Delaware County*. Philadelphia: W. H. Pile.

Palmer, Charles, ed. 1932. *A History of Delaware County*. Harrisburg: National Historical Association.

Smith, George. 1862. *History of Delaware County. . . .* Philadelphia: H. B. Ashmead.

1941. *Inventory of the Delaware County Archives*. Media: Historical Records Survey.

Pennington Heights, Bethel Twp.
   Twp. org. 1694. Small pop., no RRs.

PA 4A: M, farmer, 80. B. here. — F. b. here, PGF b. perhaps in Chester Co. (of Dutch descent), PGM b. here; M. b. Brandywine Hundred, DE, came here when 3 yrs. old, MGF b. perhaps in Ireland, came to Dupont's, Brandywine Hundred, DE, MGM b. Brandywine Hundred, DE. — Ed.: till 14 (off and on). — Baptist and Methodist. — Quick, nervous, talkative; very simple, rural.

Chester
   1st settled 1645 (farming); 1st streets laid out 1680. Name changed 1682 (many English settlers from Chester). 1847 lost Co. seat to Media. Brickmaking by 1680s. Industrial development after 1850: shipyards and other heavy industry. Pop. 1790: 673, 1820: 657, 1850: 1,667, 1880: 14,997, 1910: 38,537, 1930: 59,164, 1960: 63,658.

PA 4B!: M, engineer, surveyor, 48. B. here. — F. b. Chester, PGF b. Co., PGF's F. b. prob. in Co. (of English descent), PGF's M. b. old Chester Twp. (of Scotch-Irish descent, Quaker), PGM b. Nether Providence Twp. in Co., PGM's F. b. Germany, PGM's M. b. Marple Twp. in Co.; M. b. Chester, MGF b. Monmouth Co., NJ, MGF's F. b. Leicestershire, England, MGF's M. b. in Cornwall, MGM b. Nether Providence Twp., MGM's F. b. in France in a port where his father's ship docked (Irish), MGM's M. b. perhaps in Ireland. — Ed.: here through h.s.; Drexel Institute in Phila., 6 yrs., night school, commuter. — Methodist. — Quick, intelligent, cooperative, but inclined to be disquisitional; wanted to reflect, report on community, rather than to react naively and spontaneously; would like to buy a copy of LAMSAS for the Delaware Co. Historical Society at Chester, but not that of any other region (anti-New England). — Cultivated.

5. Chester County

Oldest of PA cos. (one of the original 3); organized by Swedes as Upland, 1682. Dutch settlers from 1634, Swedes and English later; also Germans, Welsh, some Acadians (1756). 1st Scotch-Irish settlements in PA beginning 1710. Quakers from 1700; also Baptists (1711), Presbyterians (1710), Lutherans (1770), Episcopal (1729), Methodists (1774), Roman Catholics (1730–57), Mennonites (1725). General farming: livestock, dairying, apples, peaches, poultry, mushrooms. Products and industries: textiles, quarrying, brick, canning, cigar-making, iron and steel, paper. Pop. 1790: 27,039, 1820: 44,451, 1850: 66,438, 1880: 83,481, 1910: 109,213, 1930: 126,629, 1960: 210,608.

Bull, D. E. 1973. *The Process of Settlement in Eighteenth-Century Chester County, Pennsylvania*. University of Pennsylvania dissertation.

Carlson, Robert Eugene, ed. 1981. *Chester County (Pennsylvania) Bibliography*. Kennett Square: KNA Press.

Fluck, Jonathan L. 1892. *A History of the Reformed Churches in Chester County*. Norristown: Herald Printing and Binding Rooms.

Futhey, John Smith. 1881. *History of Chester County. . . .* Philadelphia: L. H. Everts.

Heathcote, Charles W., ed. 1932. *A History of Chester County*. Harrisburg: National Historical Association.

Heathcote, Charles William. 1926. *History of Chester County*. West Chester: H. K. Temple.

Highley, George Norman, comp. 1964. *History of Malvern, Chester County*. Downington: Chester Valley Press.

Philips, George Morris. 1919. *An Account of 21 Citizens of West Chester, Pennsylvania, Now Living, Who are More Than Ninety Years Old*. West Chester: H.F. Temple.

Smedley, Lucy I. 1971. *Index to Families and Persons in History of Chester County*. Danboro: R.T. and M.C. Williams.

Smedley, Robert Clemens. 1883. *History of the Underground Railroad in Chester and the Neighboring Counties of Pennsylvania*. Lancaster: Office of the Journal.

Wiley, Samuel T. 1893. *Biographical and Portrait Cyclopedia of Chester County, Comprising an Historical Sketch. . . .* Philadelphia: Gresham Pub. Co.

1898–. *Bulletins*. West Chester: Chester County Historical Society.

1936–. *Chester County Collections*. West Chester: Anderson and Darlington.

Uwchlan, Uwchlan Twp.

Settled c. 1712 by Welsh Friends. German Reformed in 19th cent.

PA 5A: M, laborer, 79. B. Charlestown Twp., last 55 yrs. here. — F. b. Co., prob. in Charlestown Twp., PGF b. Co. (of Scotch descent); M. b. near Phoenixville in Co., MGF b. Chester Co. ("English", but of "Dutch" descent). — Ed.: till 15. — Lutheran; violinist (fiddler). — Occasionally slow at associations.

PA 5A*: Birchrunville. — F, 79. B. here. — F., M. b. here or in vicinity. — Deaf.

Marshallton, West Chester P.O., West Bradford Twp.

Twp. formed 1731 after division of Bradford. English settlers. Marshallton a crossroads hamlet. West Chester Co. seat.

PA 5B: M, farmer and miller, 82. B. Pocopson Twp. (1 1/2 mi. S.). — F., PGF, PGF's F. b. Twp. (Scotch-Irish descent), PGM b. East Bradford Twp.; M. b. near Goshenville in Co., MGF b. Co. (all of M.'s people Quaker). — Ed.: till 17. — Society of Friends. — Calm, quiet, living in a tiny village; respectable, ordinary background. Deliberate, intelligent; perfect rapport with FW. Because of antiquarian interests, felt it a duty to answer; pride in local culture tempered by a natural humility (referred to FW by a Quaker minister). — His [ɒ˞·] instead of [ɔ:] seems to show Wilmington cultural affinities for the region (spent 8 or 9 mos. in Wilmington when 21).

PA 5C: Eagle, Uwchlan Twp. — M, farm laborer, 57. B. here. — F. b. W. Whiteland, Chester Co., PGF b. prob. in Co. (French descent); M. b. Co., MGF, MGM of Dutch descent. — Ed.: here till 12 or 13. — Lutheran. — Quick, intelligent. — His high [ʌ˞·] is noteworthy. Of German descent, but not German-speaking.

West Fallow Field Twp.

Twp. split 1743. Settled by English. W. border of Co. Paper mills in 19th cent.

PA 5D: Cochranville P.O. — M, farmer, 67. B. near here. — F., PGF b. Nickel Mines, Lancaster Co. (of Scotch-Irish descent); M., MGF b. near Colmar, Chester Co. (Scotch-Irish descent). — Ed.: none. — Methodist. — Unable to read (rare in this area); mind good, clear, quick. — Fairly slow tempo.

Elkdale, New London Twp.

Twp. formed 1714 out of London Company territory. London Co. bought 65,000 acres from Penn, 17,000 in Chester Co. Shareholders remained in London.

PA 5E!: 1/2 mi. NE of Elkdale. — M, farmer, 49. B. here. — F. b. here, PGF b. near here, PGM b. near Oxford; M., MGF b. Twp., MGF's F. b. near there, MGM b. other side of Oxford (all of Scotch-Irish descent). — Ed.: h.s. here, Oxford Private School 1 yr., PA State College 1 yr. — Presbyterian. — Rather quick, cooperative, but poor subject. — Indistinct utterance, some speech defects. — Cultivated.

6. Berks County

Formed 1752. Settlers 1701–15 Swedes, Friends, Huguenots, Palatines; 1720 more Palatines; Dutch (most of early settlers Germans). Also some Welsh, Ulster Scots. 1st highway 1727; 1st canal 1828; 1st RR 1833. Roads radiating from Reading 1756–76. Dominated by Lutheran and Reformed to 1910. 1st Lutheran cong. (Swedes) 1703; others (Friends, Baptists, Amish) followed. German language strong. From wheat to general farming (more intensive in recent years); truck farming, dairying, pork, orchards. Misc. industries: iron and steel, copper. Pop. 1790: 30,179, 1820: 46,275, 1850: 77,129, 1880: 122,597, 1910: 183,222, 1930: 231,717, 1960: 275,414.

Albright, Raymond F. 1948. *Two Centuries of Reading, Pennsylvania, 1748–1948*. Reading: Historical Society of Berks County.

Balthaser, Francis W. 1925. *The Story of Berks County*. Reading: Reading Eagle Press.

Brunner, David B. 1881. *The Indians of Berks County*. Reading: Spirit of Berks Book and Job Printing Office.

Burkhardt, Franklin A. 1937 *Romance and History along the Easton-Reading King's Highway*. Allentown.

Croll, Philip C. 1895. *Ancient and Historic Landmarks in the Lebanon Valley*. Philadelphia: Lutheran Publication Society.

Croll, Philip Columbus. 1923. *Annals of Womelsdorf, Pennsylvania, and Community, 1723–1923*. Reading: Reading Eagle.

Fox, Cyrus T., ed.-in-chief. 1925. *Reading and Berks County: A History*. 3 vols. NY: Lewis Historical Pub. Co.

Fryer, Benjamin Alderfer. 1939. *Congressional History of Berks District, 1789–1939*. Reading: Historical Society of Berks County.

Montgomery, Morton L. 1886. *History of Berks County*. Philadelphia: Everts, Peck and Richards.

Montgomery, Morton L. 1898. *History of Reading. . . .* Reading: Times Book Print.

Montgomery, Morton L., comp. 1909. *Historical and Biographical Annals of Berks County. . . .* Chicago: J. H. Beers.

Montgomery, Morton Luther. 1894. *History of Berks County in the Revolution, from 1774 to 1783*. Reading: C. F. Haage, Printer.

Nolan, James Bennett. 1927. *Early Narratives of Berks County*. Reading: Historical Society of Berks County.

Nolan, James Bennett. 1929. *The Foundation of the Town of Reading.* . . . Reading: School District.

Nolan, James Bennett. 1931. *George Washington and the Town of Reading in Pennsylvania*. Reading: under the auspices of the Chamber of Commerce of Reading, Pa.

Nolen, John. 1910. *Replanning Reading*. Boston: G.H. Ellis Co.

Rupp, Israel Daniel. 1844. *History of the Counties of Berks and Lebanon*. Lancaster: G. Hills.

Stahle, William. 1841. *The Description of the Borough of Reading*. Reading: The Author.

1941. *Inventory of the Berks County Archives*. Reading: Historical Records Survey.

PA 6A: Bethel Twp. — M, farmer, 75. B. here. — F., PGF, PGM b. here; M., MGF b. here. — Ed.: till 17 (learned English first at school). — Reformed Church. — Slightly senile, genial; has great difficulty with English.

Reading

Laid out 1748 by Penn's agents. Original settlers chiefly German, some Friends, some English (friends and relatives of Penn). Named for Penn's birthplace: Reading, Berks, England. Co. seat 1752; inc. as borough 1783; inc. as city 1847. Canals from 1820s; Reading RR from 1833. Very important up to Rev. period. Hessian POWs held here during Revolution. Telegraph co. from 1847; oldest in US. Early center of hat making (earliest local industry). Heavy industry from 2nd half of 19th cent.: iron and steel, steel products, high grade alloys, one of first centers of auto making, textiles. Albright College from 1928 (consolidation of several Evangelical schools). Choral society, symphony orchestra. Pop. 1790: 2,225, 1820: 4,332, 1850: 15,743, 1880: 43,278, 1910: 96,071, 1930: 111,171, 1960: 98,177.

PA 6B: M, barber, 67. B. here (when a young man, lived in country a few yrs. and learned to speak PA German). — F. b. here, PGF b. prob. in Reading (a tailor); M. b. Reading, MGF b. prob. in Reading (drove canalboat). — Ed.: here till 16. — Methodist. — Very willing to help, though first interview was slow due to inf.'s inability to understand the project. — [r] after vowels does not appear except with extreme effort; usually only a brief uvular gulp.

Hamburg, Tilden Twp.

Area first settled 1732, mostly by Germans. Frontier in French and Indian War. Agriculture, some brickmaking. Hamburg created as a borough in 1837. Knitting mills, diversified industry. 2nd most important town in Co.; grew with turnpike, canal, RR. Pop. Hamburg 1790: 329, 1850: 1,035, 1880: 2,010, 1910: 2,301, 1930: 3,637, 1960: 3,747.

PA 6C: M, farmer, 44. B. here. — F., PGF b. Twp., PGM b. Co.; M., MGF b. Tilden Twp. — Ed.: till 13. — Lutheran. — Quick, alert, rather interested in project, but not altogether reassured; hardworking. Not familiar with some English words, heard very little English at home before he went to school, uses English only to read the paper and converse with strangers. — FW's transcription of medial [ṭ] is probably an error for [t] or [d̦].

PA 6D!: Reading. — M, architect, 69. B. here. — F. b. here, PGF b. Lancaster, PGF's F. b. Montgomery Co., PGF's PGF b. Einbach, Hanover (educated at Gottingen), PGF's PGM b. PA, PGM b. Co., PGM's F. prob. b. PA; M. b. Co., came to Reading as a girl, MGF, MGM b. Co. — Ed.: till 17, then Boston Tech for 4 yrs.; 1 yr. in Europe. — Lutheran. — A cultivated person of the older school; pleasant, agreeable, cooperative; prob. felt questions and project were slightly foolish and inconsequential. — Slight traces in rhythm, intonation, and medial unvoicing of stops of German origin, but unnoticeable to the ordinary person. — Cultivated.

7. Lancaster County

Formed 1729. 1st permanent settlers Mennonites c. 1709; came to escape persecution in Switzerland. Huguenots followed. Scotch-Irish c. 1715; also some Quakers, Welsh. Legacy of religious liberty, including pacifism; numerous religious groups est. in first half of 18th cent., including (in addition to Mennonites) "Solitary Brethren", Reformed, Lutheran, Moravians, Amish (chiefly in E. part of Co.), Reformed Mennonites, "River Brethren". At one time said to be 22 to 30 sects of Germans in Co. Turnpike to Phila. from 1792; canal on Susquehanna from 1797; RR from 1826. Mennonites first farmers, prosperous general farming. A few Acadians settled 1758. Intensive farming. Electric power from Susquehanna starting in 1920s. Cigar tobacco; copper mining, paper making in 18th cent. A center of rifle making. Other products and industries: limestone, iron making, shoemaking, hats, stockyards, watches (Hamilton), chocolates. Pop. 1790: 36,147, 1820: 67,975, 1850: 98,944, 1880: 139,447, 1910: 167,029, 1930: 196,882, 1960: 278,359.

Bausman, Lottie M. 1915. The Garden of Pennsylvania. *Lancaster County Historical Society Historical Papers and Addresses* 19:311–314.

Bausman, Lottie M. 1917. *A Bibliography of Lancaster County, 1745–1912*. Philadelphia: Patterson and White Co.

Bridgens, H. F. 1864. *Bridges' Atlas of Lancaster County, Pennsylvania*. Lancaster: D.S. Bare.

Diffenderffer, Frank R. 1876. *The Three Earls: An Historical Sketch*. New Holland: Ranck and Sandoe.

Diffenderffer, Frank R. 1905. *The Early Settlement and Population of Lancaster County and City*. Lancaster: Reprinted from the New Era.

Diffenderffer, Frank R. 1905. *The Ephrata Community 120 Years Ago*. Lancaster: Reprinted from the New Era.

Diffenderffer, Frank R. 1905. *The Story of a Picture*. Lancaster: The New Era.

Doll, Eugene Edgar, and Anneliese M. Fanke. 1944. *The Ephrata Cloisters: An Annotated Bibliography*. Philadelphia: Carl Schurz Foundation.

Ellis, Franklin, and Samuel Evans. 1883. *History of Lancaster County.* . . . Philadelphia: Everts and Peck.

Ernst, James E. 1963. *Ephrata, a History*. Allentown: Pennsylvania German Folklore Society.

Eshleman, H. F. 1919. *Papers Read before the Lancaster Historical Society*. Lancaster.

Eshleman, H. Frank. 1917. *Historic Background and Annals of the Swiss and German Pioneer Settlers of Southeastern Pennsylvania....* Lancaster.

Eshleman, Henry Frank. 1908. *Lancaster County Indians.* Lancaster.

Godcharles, Frederic A. 1920. The Influence of Lancaster County on the Pennsylvania Frontier. In *Lancaster County Historical Society Historical Papers and Addresses* 24:77–82.

Harris, Alexander. 1872. *A Biographical History of Lancaster County....* Lancaster: E. Barr.

Hertz, Daniel Rhine. 1894. *History of Ephrata, Pennsylvania.* Philadelphia: H. Ferkler, Printer.

Klein, Frederic Shriver. 1964. *Old Lancaster, Historic Pennsylvania Community from Its Beginnings to 1865.* Lancaster.

Klein, Harry M. J. 1924. *Lancaster County, a History.* 4 vols. NY: Lewis Historical Pub. Co.

Kollmorgen, Walter M. 1942. *Culture of a Contemporary Rural Community: The Old Order Amish of Lancaster County.* Washington.

Meginness, John F., ed. 1903. *Biographical Annals of Lancaster County....* Chicago: J. H. Beers.

Mombert, Jacob I. 1869. *An Authentic History of Lancaster County.* Lancaster: J. E. Barr.

Riddle, William. 1910. *Cherished Memories of Old Lancaster — Town and Shire.* Lancaster: Intelligencer Printing House.

Rupp, I. Daniel, comp. 1844. *History of Lancaster County.* Lancaster: G. Hills.

Sachse, Julius Friedrich. 1899–1900. *The German Sectarians of Pennsylvania, 1708–1800.* Philadelphia: the author.

Scott, Beulah Mohart. 1864. *Index of Bridgens Atlas of Lancaster County, Pennsylvania.* Lancaster: D. S. Bare.

Sener, Samuel Miller. 1901. *Lancaster Townstead.* Lancaster.

Slaymaker, Samuel R. 1973. *Captive's Mansion.* NY: Harper and Row.

Wood, Jerome A. 1974. The Negro in Early Pennsylvania: The Lancaster Experience, 1730–90. In Elinor Miller and Eugene D. Genovese, eds., *Plantation, Town, and County: Essays on the Local History of American Slave Society* (Urbana, IL: University of Illinois Press).

Wood, Jerome H. 1970. *Conestoga Crossroads: Lancaster County, Pennsylvania, 1730–1790.* Ann Arbor: University Microfilms.

1771–77. *Pennsylvania Packet.* Philadelphia: John Dunlap.

1894. *Portrait and Biographical Record of Lancaster County.* ... Chicago: Chapman Pub. Co.

1896–. *Lancaster County Historical Society Historical Papers and Addresses.* Lancaster: The Society.

1941. *Inventory of the Lancaster County Archives.* Lancaster: Historical Records Survey.

Cherry Hill, Peach Bottom P.O., Fulton Twp.

Twp. formed c. 1848. Earliest settlers from MD. Some Scotch-Irish settlers as early as 1732; many families left and Germans replaced them. Quakers from 1749; Presbyterians 1763; Baptists 1808. 2 AfAm churches in 1883. Rural; slate quarries.

PA 7A: M, farmer, 80. B. Drumore Twp. — F. b. Drumore Twp. in Co., PGF b. Montgomery Co. and came here (Quaker), PGM b. Drumore Twp., PGM's F. of Quaker stock (Cornish name); M. b. Bart Twp. near Christiana in Co., MGF, MGM b. Co. (of Presbyterian and Quaker stock, respectively). — Ed.: Silver Spring (here) till 17. — Presbyterian. — Fairly quick (somewhat higher type than desirable for the old-fashioned informant).

Chestnut Level, Drumore Twp.

Twp. est. 1729. 1st settled c. 1700 by Scotch-Irish. Presbyterian church from 1730. Iron and steel at one time; iron ore, general farming, dairying, tobacco.

PA 7B: M, farmer, 53. B. here. — F., PGF, PGF's F. b. here, PGF's M. b. here, PGM, PGM's F., PGM's M. b. Bart Twp. in Co.; M., MGF b. here, MGF's M. b. here, MGM b. near Delta, York Co. (names indicate Scotch-Irish descent). — Ed.: here till 16, 1 term local academy. — Presbyterian. — Busy, business-like; quick and fairly intelligent. — Deep, full-powered voice, but somewhat muffled articulation without much lip action.

Fairmount, West Earl Twp.

Earl Twp. original in 1729; W. Earl formed 1828. 1st settlers (Swiss) arrived in 1717; then Mennonites, Welsh, Palatines. Lutherans, Reformed. 1730 first book of German poetry printed in America. Sect of 7th Day Baptists (celibates) in nearby Ephrata from 1737; declined after Rev. Agricultural, stock-raising.

PA 7C: M, farmer, 65. B. near Ephrata (1 mi. W.). — F. b. East Earl Twp., PGF, PGM b. Peckway in Co.; M. b. near Akron in Co., MGF b. Co., MGM b. near Farmersville in Co., MGM's F., MGM's M. b. Co. — Ed.: till 18. — Lutheran (father Mennonite and mother Dunkard). — Quick, intelligent, well-to-do farmer; has travelled on vacations.

Lancaster

Town laid out 1730; settled by Palatine Germans as early as 1709. Quakers, Germans, Anglicans settled early. Inc. as borough 1742; city charter 1818. English innkeeper and brewery 1721. Four churches by 1744: Lutheran, Reformed, Episcopal, Roman Catholic. Franklin and Marshall College est. here 1787. Turnpike from Phila. in 1796. State capital 1799–1812; candidate for US capital. Cotton mills (1845), iron and steel, watches. Pop. 1790: 297, 1820: 6,633, 1850: 12,369, 1880: 25,769, 1910: 47,227, 1930: 59,949, 1960: 61,055.

PA 7D!: M, merchant, 39. B. here. — F., PGF, PGF's F. b. here, PGF's PGF b. Hesse-Darmstadt, Germany, PGF's M. b. here, PGM, PGM's F., PGM's M. b. Carlisle, Cumberland Co., PA; M. b. here, MGF b. Elizabethtown, MGF's F. b. here, MGF's M. b. Ireland, MGM b. New Providence, Lancaster Co., MGM's M. b. Ireland. — Ed.: city schools, Franklin and Marshall Academy, Franklin and Marshall College. — Lutheran (mother an Episcopalian). — Most cordial and obliging, but rather slow. — Articulation not too good. — Cultivated.

8. York County

Formed 1749 from Lancaster Co. 1st settlers from MD; Scotch-Irish c. 1722. 1st "authorized" settlements 1729; border troubles with MD to 1757. Largely PA Germans (tended to supplant Scotch-Irish): "industry, economy, honesty, morality". Topographically like German homeland. Band of German settlements across Co. by the time Co. est. Most York Co. Germans immediately from Lancaster Co.; most already well off. Also some English settlers. Turnpike from 1804; Susquehanna Canal 1814; RR from 1828. Products and industries: iron and steel (from 1756), textiles, whiskey, lime, farm implements, paper. Pop. 1790: 37,747, 1820: 38,747, 1850: 57,450, 1880: 87,841, 1910: 136,405, 1930: 167,135, 1960: 238,336.

Carter, William C. 1834. *History of York County.* . . . York. Rev. ed. 1930 (Harrisburg: Aurand Press).

Gibson, John, ed. 1886. *History of York County.* . . . Chicago: F. A. Battey Pub. Co.

Heilman, Vernon D., et al. 1940. *An Index to Gibson's History of York County.* York: Historical Society of York County.

Heisey, John W. 1971. *York County in the American Revolution.* York: Historical Society of York County.

Miller, Lewis. 1966. *Lewis Miller, Sketches and Chronicles.* York: Historical Society of York County.

Prowell, George R. 1906. *A Brief History of York County.* York.

Prowell, George R. 1907. *History of York County.* 2 vols. Chicago: J. H. Beers.

Prowell, George Reeser. 1925. *The Invasion of Pennsylvania by the Confederates under General Robert E. Lee, and Its Effect upon Lancaster and York Counties.* Lancaster: Conestoga Publishing Co.

Rupp, Israel Daniel. 1845. *History of York County.* Lancaster: G. Hills.

Scott, Beulah Mohart. 1876. *Index of Atlas of York County, Pennsylvania.* Philadelphia: Pomeroy, Whitman and Co.

Wentz, Abdel Ross. 1916. *The Beginnings of the German Element in York County.* . . . Lancaster: Pennsylvania-German Society.

Wiley, Samuel T. 1897. *Biographical and Portrait Cyclopedia of the Nineteenth Congressional District of Pennsylvania.* Philadelphia: Dunlap and Clarke.

1939–. *Yearbook.* . . . York: Historical Society of York County.

Slate Hill, Delta P.O., Peach Bottom Twp.

Twp. est. 1815; extreme SE of Co. Slate mines; fertile agricultural regions. Quarries at Slate Hill discovered early; commercial exploitation began c. 1812. Many workers of Welsh descent. Delta org. as a borough 1880. Land purchased 1744 from Penn estate; settled same yr. by Scotch-Irish.

PA 8A: M, laborer and carpenter, 65. B. here. — F. b. near Delta, near Colsontown, York Co., PGF of Welsh descent; M. b. near Colsontown. — Ed.: here off and on till 18. — Methodist. — Somewhat feeble.

PA 8B: Delta, Peach Bottom Twp. — M, farmer, 46. B. here. — F. b. here, PGF, PGM, PGM's F. b. York Co.; M., MGF, MGM b. here. — Ed.: till 16 (2 yrs. h.s.). — Presbyterian. — Rather intelligent; reserved.

Sherman's Valley, Hanover P.O., West Manheim Twp.

Twp. formed 1858. A few titles in Manheim from MD. Palatines and Dunkers from Baden. "Sherman's Church" in Sherman's Valley: St. David's Lutheran and Reformed. Hanover a market town (rich agriculture) with misc. industry.

PA 8C: M, farmer, 66. B. here. — F., PGF b. here (on this same farm), PGF's F. b. in Amsterdam, Holland, PGM, PGM's F. b. Manheim Twp.; M., MGF b. Twp., MGM b. Co. — Ed.: till 21; Normal Academy in Hanover, 1 term. — Lutheran. — Careful, deliberate, honest, cooperative; quick at understanding and glad to be of help.

York

Town laid out 1741; inc. as a borough 1787; as a city 1887. Germans early; some English and Scotch-Irish. 1st PA town W. of Susquehanna. US capital during British occupation of Phila.; seat of Cont. Congress 1777–78. Lutherans from 1733; Episcopalians, Presbyterians, German Reformed, R. Catholic, Moravians, 7th Day Baptists also in 18th cent. Paper mill from 1800; iron works after 1800. 1st US-built locomotive here 1831. Also machinery, iron and steel products, RR cars, paper, farm implements. Pop. 1790: 2,076, 1820: 2,183, 1850: 6,863, 1880: 13,940, 1910: 44,750, 1930: 55,254, 1960: 54,504.

PA 8D!: F, widow, 62. B. here. — F., PGF b. York, PGF's F., PGF's M. b. Chester Co., PGM, PGM's F. and M., PGM's MGF b. York; M. b. York, MGF, MGF's F. b. New Oxford, Adams Co., MGF's M. b. Marsh Run, Adams Run, MGM, MGM's F., MGM's PGF, MGM's PGM b. Dummanway near Cork in Ireland, MGM's M., MGM's MGF, MGM's MGM b. York. — Ed.: Young Ladies Seminary in York, school in Phila. 2 or 3 yrs. until 16. — Episcopalian. — Charming, cultivated, courteous; enjoyed interview thoroughly; expansive, happy woman whose thinking is conservative and conventional. — Cultivated.

9. Dauphin County

Formed 1785 from Lancaster Co. 1st permanent settlers Scotch-Irish in 1718; Germans later. Purchases 1736, 1749. On frontier in French and Indian War. 1st road to Phila. 1736. 3 Presbyterian churches by 1750; also Reformed and Lutheran churches in 18th cent. Iron manufacturing before Rev.; coal mining from c. 1825, limestone. Pop. 1790: 19,004, 1820: 21,653, 1850: 35,754, 1880: 76,148, 1910: 136,152, 1930: 165,231, 1960: 220,255.

Donehoo, George P. 1927. *Harrisburg, the City Beautiful, Romantic and Historic.* Harrisburg: The Telegraph Press.

Egle, William Henry, ed. 1886. *Centenary Memorial of the Erection of the County of Dauphin.* . . . Harrisburg: Telegraph Print. House.

Egle, William Henry. 1883. *History of the Counties of Dauphin and Lebanon.* Philadelphia: Everts and Peck.

Frost, James Arthur. 1951. *Life on the Upper Susquehanna, 1783–1860.* NY: King's Crown Press.

Kelker, Luther Reily. 1907. *History of Dauphin County.* 3 vols. NY: Lewis Pub. Co.

Linn, John Blair, comp. 1877. *Annals of Buffalo Valley: 1755–1855.* Harrisburg: L. S. Hart, Printer.

McFarland, John Horace. 1907. *The Awakening of Harrisburg.* Philadelphia: National Municipal League.

Morgan, George H, comp. 1858. *Annals, Comprising Memoirs, Incidents and Statistics of Harrisburg.* Harrisburg: G. A. Brooks.

Morgan, George H. 1877. *Centennial: The Settlement, Formation and Progress of Dauphin County, from 1785 to 1876.* Harrisburg: Telegraph Steam Book and Job Print.

Posey, Lauretta. 1956. *A Preliminary Checklist of Imprints, Harrisburg, Pennsylvania, 1836–1840, with a Historical Introduction.* Washington: Catholic University of America.

Rupp, Israel Daniel. 1846. *The History and Topography of Dauphin....* Lancaster: G. Hills.

Scott, Beulah Mohart. 1875. *Combination Atlas Map of Dauphin County, Pennsylvania.* Philadelphia: Everts and Stewart.

Yagodinski, Mary Anne. 1958. *A Check List of Harrisburg, Pennsylvania Imprints from 1857 to 1865: With a Historical Introduction.* Catholic University of America thesis.

1896. *Commemorative Biographical Encyclopedia of Dauphin County....* Chambersburg: J. M. Runk.

Manada Hill, Grantville P.O., East Hanover Twp.

Twp. formed 1785. Manada Hill area settled by Scotch-Irish and Germans. Manada Gap important for pre-Rev. travel; suffered in French and Indian War.

PA 9A. M, farmer, 78. B, here. — F, PGF b. here, PGF's F. b. in Belgium, came before 1800, PGM b. here; M. b. here, MGF, MGM b. Lebanon Co. — Ed.: till 17. — Lutheran. — Quick, excitable, easy to lose his temper, but genial and expansive; well-to-do. — Occasionally not at home with English words.

Linglestown, Harrisburg P.O., Lower Paxton Twp.

Twp. remaining when Upper Paxton created in 1767 (Middle Paxton created 1787). Linglestown village plot set off in 1765. Some German settlers; majority Scotch-Irish and English. Productive farming country.

PA 9B: M, farmer, 57. B. here. — F., PGF, PGM b. here; M. b. here, MGF, MGM b. Dauphin Co. — Ed.: till 16. — Lutheran. — Simple; saw no sense to the interview; referred to FW by local justice of the peace who also did not understand the purpose of the interviews. — Grew up speaking PA German at home but changed over to English at school, and now there is little trace of German in his English. Either has slight speech difficulty (laxness of articulation), or his [ł] is just a reaction from German [ł].

Harrisburg

John Harris est. ferry here 1712; 1733 grant to Harris validated by treaty between Indians and Penn heirs. Town laid out 1785. 1st church (German Reformed) 1788; Presbyterian church 1802. Inc. as borough 1791; as city 1860. State capital since 1812. Canal opened 1834; 1st RR 1835. Silk mills. Military base in Civil War. Canal and RR center; industry; RR yards. Pop. 1790: 875, 1820: 2,990, 1850: 7,834, 1880: 30,762, 1910: 64,186, 1930: 80,339, 1960: 79,697.

PA 9C!: F, 68. B. here. — F., PGF b. here, PGF's F. b. Phila., PGF's M. b. Barbados, West Indies, daughter of a German trader, PGM b. Phila.; M., MGF b. here, MGM b. perhaps Dauphin Co. — Ed.: private school. — YWCA asst. secy. — Timid, sensitive, high-strung; incessant talker; good lineage. — Rapid, precise speech. — Cultivated.

10. Lebanon County

Formed 1816 from Dauphin Co. Earliest settlers Palatines from 1711; also Scotch-Irish c. 1720. Purchase from Indians in 1732; 1st surveys 1733: Germans, with some Scotch-Irish (mostly in N.). Also Swiss and Huguenots, Moravians, various German groups. Indian depredations during the French and Indian War. Diverse industries: iron ore, iron and steel products, limestone quarries, chocolates. Productive farming. Pop. 1820: 16,975, 1850: 26,071, 1880: 38,476, 1910: 59,565, 1930: 67,103, 1960: 90,853.

Croll, Philip Columbus. 1909. *Lebanon County Imprints.* Harrisburg: Pennsylvania Federation of Historical Societies.

Egle, William Henry. 1883. *History of the Counties of Dauphin and Lebanon.* Philadelphia: Everts and Peck.

Hark, Joseph Maximillian. 1914. *Moravian Influence in the Settlement and Early Development of Lebanon County.* Lebanon: read before the Lebanon Co. Historical Society.

Heilman, Uriah H. 1909. *Descriptive and Historical Memorials of Heilman Dale.* Philadelphia.

Rupp, I. Daniel. 1844. *History of the Counties of Berks and Lebanon.* Lancaster: G. Hills.

Shenk, Hiram H. 1930. *A History of the Lebanon Valley in Pennsylvania.* Harrisburg: National Historical Society.

1904. *Biographical Annals of Lebanon County.* Chicago: Beers.

Heilmandale, Lebanon P.O., North Annville Twp.

Annville Twp. laid out 1799; N. Annville founded 1845. Annville Academy est. c. 1835. Iron works from 1756. Heilmandale in 1793 had a paper mill, lumber, flaxseed oil; by 1930, all industry gone, "only a few houses near RR". Almost all German; Lutheran and Reformed church from 1733. Level terrain, fertile. Lebanon laid out c. 1750. Strongly German flavor. Center of PA iron ore fields; Bethlehem Steel. Productive farming.

PA 10: M, farmer, 66. B. here. — F., PGF, PGF's F. b. here, PGF's PGF b. Germany, PGM b. S. Annville Twp.; M. b. here, MGF, MGM b. N. Cornwall Twp. — Ed.: till 17. — Lutheran (of Mennonite parentage). — Quick, intelligent, good farmer. — Bilingual.

11. Northumberland County

First explored by French, 1615–16. First survey 1768; Co. est. 1772. Early settlers mainly Scotch-Irish (from Cumberland Valley) and English; later outnumbered by Germans. Indian depredations during American Rev. First highway 1768; turnpike from 1805. First steamboat 1826; RR at least by 1847. Middle belt of PA; "ridge and valley" topography. Coalfields first discovered c. 1780; first used in forge 1810; first shipment 1826. Pop. 1790: 17,161, 1820: 15,424, 1850:

23,272, 1880: 53,123, 1910: 111,420, 1930: 128,504, 1960: 104,138.

Bell, Herbert C. 1891. *History of Northumberland County. . .* . Chicago: Brown, Runk.
Rupp, Israel Daniel. 1847. *History and Topography of Northumberland. . . .* Lancaster: G. Hills.
1899. *Book of Biographies*. Buffalo: Biographical Pub. Co.

Turbotville, Lewis Twp.

Extreme NE part of Co. Turbotville laid out 1820; inc. as borough 1859. 1st settled by Germans and Scotch-Irish. Originally Snydertown. Little industry.

PA 11A: M, farmer, 73. B. Lycoming Co., came here at 7 mos. — F. b. McEwansville in Co., PGF b. near Milton in Co., PGM b. Co. (both of Scotch-Irish descent); M. b. Clinton Twp. in Lycoming Co., MGF, MGM b. Dauphin Co. (both of Scotch-Irish descent). — Ed.: till 18 (4 mos. a yr.). — Lutheran. — Somewhat senile, but pretty quick and willing; one of the few Scotch-Irish in this predominantly "Dutch" region.

Northumberland, Point Twp.

Twp. est. 1786. Northumberland laid out 1775; inc. as a borough 1828. Within forks of Susquehanna. 1st settler c. 1760 from NJ; further settlement in 1770: German (from Lancaster Co.) and Scotch-Irish, English. Practically abandoned in Rev.; resettled 1784–85. Residence of Joseph Priestly 1794–1804. Iron works in 1866. Other light industry; RR yards decreasing in importance; coal dredging in river. Pop. Northumberland 1850: 1,041, 1880: 2,293, 1910: 3,517, 1930: 4,483, 1960: 4,156.

PA 11B: M, farmer, 37. B. on edge of Northumberland borough. — F. b. here, PGF b. near Elysburg-Paxinos in Co. (spoke "Dutch"), PGF's F. b. Shamokin Twp. in Co. in 1810, PGF's PGF lived in Berks Co. and moved to Shamokin Twp. in 1810 (of German descent), PGM b. between Paxinos and Sunbury in Co.; M., MGF b. borough of Northumberland, MGM b. near Mifflinburg, Union Co. (neither GP could speak "Dutch"). — Ed.: till 17 (spent 2 yrs. in h.s. doing the same year's work). — Lutheran. — Quick answers; offhand manner.

PA 11B*: Southern Northumberland Co. — M, farmer, middle-aged. — F., M. b. Co. — Ed.: average. — English-speaking in a predominantly German-speaking neighborhood; no particular interest in project; busy.

12. Montour County

Set off 1850. 1st settled 1768; devastated by Indian raids in Am. Rev.; resettlement 1780. Early settlers from PA: Germans, Scotch-Irish, some Quakers. "Center turnpike" 1808; several RRs in 19th cent. Broken terrain. Limestone, iron ore, iron and steel manufacturing. Pop. 1850: 13,239, 1880: 15,468, 1910: 14,868, 1930: 14,517, 1960: 16,730.

Battle, J. H., ed. 1887. *History of Columbia and Montour Counties. . . .* Chicago: A. Warner.
Brower, D. H. B. 1881. *Danville, Montour County: A Collection of Historical and Biographical Sketches*. Harrisburg: L. S. Hart, Printer.

Foulke, Arthur Toye. 1969. *My Danville Where the Bright Waters Meet*. North Quincy, MA: Christopher Pub. House.

White Hall P.O., Anthony Twp.

Twp. formed 1849 from Perry Twp. Scotch-Irish area. Whitehall on the E. side of Twp. 1st settled c. 1800 from Ireland; Germans later. Center of excellent agricultural district.

PA 12A: M, carpenter and laborer, 67. B. White Hall. — F., PGF b. White Hall (of English descent); M. b. on edge of Columbia Co., near White Hall, MGF, MGM b. Columbia Co. (inf. thinks his mother's people were early settlers here from NJ). — Ed.: till 19. — Baptist. — Drinking problem; homeless, sheltered by neighbors; quick. — Has worked about too much to be considered a very old-fashioned inf.

Danville P.O., Valley Twp.

Twp. formed 1769; settled by Germans and some Scotch-Irish. Danville site of old Delaware village. Surveyed 1769; originally purchased by Philadelphians. Inc. as a borough 1849. Many Germans early. Presbyterians organized (1st org. religious body in Co.) 1778; Methodists 1791. First store 1780. Iron and steel from 1838; pioneers in use of anthracite. Products and industries: iron and steel, alloys, limestone, textiles. State Hospital here. Pop. Danville 1850: 3,302, 1880: 8,346, 1910: 7,517, 1930: 7,185, 1960: 6,889.

PA 12B: F, housewife, 47. B. Mahoning Twp. (E. of Danville), moved to Valley Twp. when 6 or 7. — F., PGF b. Liberty Twp. in Co. (F. could talk a little "Dutch"); M., MGF, MGM b. Co. (MGF could talk a little "Dutch"). — Ed.: till 15 or 16. — Methodist. — Pleasant; did not have much understanding of the project but answered quickly; took husband's place because his parents were not born here; her son looked at the questionnaire and suggested one or two responses to her, e.g., "bagged it" for "played hookey".

13. Columbia County

Formed 1813 from Northumberland Co. Appalachian Mt. belt; broken hills. First settlements 1772: English and Welsh Quakers; largely German later (few Scotch-Irish). Frontier during Rev., several forts. Lutheran and Reformed; many Methodists. Canals from 1826; 1st RR 1854. Iron ore, limestone, anthracite. Pop. 1820: 17,621, 1850: 17,710, 1880: 32,409, 1910: 48,467, 1930: 48,803, 1960: 53,489.

Battle, J. H., ed. 1887. *History of Columbia and Montour Counties. . . .* Chicago: A. Warner.
Freeze, John G. 1883. *A History of Columbia County*. Bloomsburg: Elwell and Bittenbender.

Greenwood Valley, Orangeville P.O., Greenwood Twp.

Twp. org. 1799; one of original twps. N. central part of Co. 1st survey and settlement 1769. Quakers a major part of pop. from 1795 to 1880s. Methodists from 1809; Presbyterians from 1843. Greenwood Valley settled c. 1770; abandoned in Rev. Resettlement 1785–86; mixed settlement. 1st road 1798.

PA 13A: M, farmer, 74. B. here. — F. b. Mt. Pleasant Twp., PGM b. Columbia Co.; M., MGF, MGM b. Greenwood Twp. — Ed.: till 21 (very little). — Church of Christ. — Slight hesitation in speech; otherwise, good old-fashioned inf.

PA 13B: 2 mi. W. of Rohrsburg. — M, farmer, 47. B. here. — F. b. here, PGF (of PA Dutch ancestry), PGM b. Schuylkill Co.; M., MGM b. here. — Ed.: till 19. — Methodist. — At first skeptical, but then rather understanding of the project; quick.

14. Schuylkill County

Co. formed 1811. 1736, 1749 purchased from Six Nations. Germans first settlers by 1747; also Welsh (in coalfields), Irish; Slavs and S. Europeans later. Coal discovered c. 1790; first used successfully 1795; 1st industrial use 1812. Mines developed rapidly: stimulated development of river navigation, canals, RRs. Frontier in French and Indian War. Also lumbering early. 1st main road, "King's Highway", 1770. Many labor troubles beginning with boatmen's strike 1835. Militant antidraft activists in 1863. 800 mi. of RR by 1864: densest in world. Pop. 1820: 11,311, 1850: 60,713, 1880: 129,974, 1910: 207,894, 1930: 235,505, 1960: 173,027.

Elliott, Ella Zerbey. 1916. *Blue Book of Schuylkill County.* Pottsville: Republican.

Henning, David C. 1911. *Tales of the Blue Mountains.* Pottsville: Historical Society of Schuykill County, Pa.

Rupp, Israel Daniel. 1845. *History of Northampton. . . and Schuylkill. . . .* Harrisburg: Hickok and Cantine, Printers.

Schalck, Adolf W., ed. 1907. *History of Schuylkill County. . . . 2 vols.* Harrisburg: State Historical Association.

Wallace, Francis B., comp. 1865. *Memorial of the Patriotism of Schuylkill County, in the American Slaveholder's Rebellion.* Pottsville: B. Bannan.

Yearley, Clifton K. 1961. *Enterprise and Anthracite: Economics and Democracy in Schuylkill County, 1820–1875.* Baltimore: Johns Hopkins University Press.

1881. *History of Schuylkill County.* NY: W. W. Munsell.

1905–10. *Publications of the Historical Society of Schuylkill County.* 2 vols. Pottsville: The Society.

1916. *Schuylkill County.* 2 vols. Chicago: J. H. Beers.

Valley View P.O., Hegins Twp.

Twp. formed 1853. First settler c. 1775; most of earliest settlers German. Some coal; little industry.

PA 14A: M, retired farmer, now a turkey grower, 76. B. Klingerstown. — F. b. Klingerstown, PGF b. Oley, 10 mi. E. of Reading in Berks Co., came here as boy with his father, PGF's F. b. prob. in Berks Co., PGM b. Berwick, Columbia Co.; M., MGF b. near here, on the line in Dauphin Co., MGM b. Dauphin Co. — Ed.: till 16. — Reformed. — Very quick, intelligent, cooperative; has learned English pretty well.

Ashland

Formed from Butler Twp.; surveyed 1847; inc. as a borough 1857. Butler settled mainly by German and Scotch-Irish (mainly German). Iron works in Ashland from 1853; misc. industry (knitting mill, shirt factory), chiefly metal products. Mostly English and Scottish to 1900. Pop. 1930: 7,184.

PA 14B: M, bank clerk, 36. B. here. — F. b. near Mahanoy City in Co., PGF, PGM b. England; M. b. Germantown near Ashland, MGF, MGM b. Wales. — Ed.: till 14. — Methodist. — Rather quick, alert in answering; apparent expansiveness and sense of humor cut short by FW's curt style of questioning; family history oddly meager. — FW writes [r], not [ɚ], after vowels; a short glide without palatal bunching. The [l̩] is no doubt PA German influence.

Pitman (P.O.)

Small village; 1st settlers German. Mining.

PA 14C: M, farmer, 80. B. here. — F., M. b. here. — Ed.: Reads English. — FW was sick during interview; feeling miserable. — First PA German-speaking inf. FW attempted to record; inf. had had a stroke, spoke indistinctly, had only limited knowledge of English. The use of [ɾ] medially between vowels and after [t] and [d] is noteworthy for [r]. Medial [t] and [d] are normally [t̬] or [d̬].

15. Luzerne County

Est. 1786; largest Co. in PA. CT settlement (English stock) began as early as 1755; part of CT settlement (supported by CT govt.) of 1770s. Moravians also among first settlers, but only as missionaries. Frontier; Indian raids in 1750s, 1760s, 1777–80. By 1783, 6,000 Yankees in NE PA. 1st turnpike from 1802; 1st canal from 1828; 1st RR charters 1831. Coal discovered in 1760s; came to dominate Co. Germans came in as Yankees moved west. Presbyterians from 1770; Methodists from 1781; Episcopal, Baptists, Lutherans, and Reformed later. Iron and steel making from 1778. Pop. 1790: 4,904, 1820: 20,027, 1850: 56,072, 1880: 133,065, 1910: 343,186, 1930: 445,109, 1960: 346,972.

Bedford, George R. 1919. *Some Early Recollections. . . .* Wilkes-Barre: Wyoming Historical and geological society. Proceedings and collections. Vol. 16, pp. 1-107.

Bradsby, Henry C., ed. 1893. *History of Luzerne County. . . .* Chicago: S. B. Nelson.

Brower, Edith. 1923. *Little Old Wilkes-Barre As I Knew It. . . .* Wilkes-Barre.

Dougherty, Charles B. *The Story of Bowman's Hill, Wilkes-Barre.* Wilkes-Barre.

Ferrell, R. W., comp. 1911. *Wilkes-Barre, the Diamond City.* Wilkes-Barre: Board of Trade.

Harvey, Oscar Jewell. 1909. *A History of Wilkes-Barré. . . .* Wilkes-Barre: Raeder Press.

Harvey, Oscar Jewell. 1914. *The Beginnings of Luzerne County.* Wilkes-Barre: Wyoming Historical and Geological Society.

Harvey, Oscar Jewell. 1923. *Wilkes-Barre's Earliest Newspapers.* Wilkes-Barre: Wyoming Historical and Geological Society.

Johnson, Frederick C. 1911. *Rev. Jacob Johnson, Pioneer Preacher. . . .* Wilkes-Barre: Wilkes-Barre Record Print.

Joyce, Mary Hinchcliffe. 1928. *Pioneer Days in the Wyoming Valley.* Philadelphia.

Kulp, George B. 1885–90. *Families of the Wyoming Valley.* 3 vols. Wilkes-Barre: E. B. Yordy, Printer.

Pearce, Stewart. 1860. *Annals of Luzerne County.* Philadelphia: J. B. Lippincott Co.

Plumb, Henry Blackman. 1885. *History of Hanover Township. . . and Also a History of Wyoming Valley, in Luzerne County. . . .* Wilkes-Barre: R. Baur, Printer.

1880. *History of Luzerne, Lackawanna and Wyoming Counties.* NY: W. W. Munsell and Co.

1906. *Wilkes-Barre. . . Its History, Its Natural Resources, Its Industries, 1769–1906.* Wilkes-Barre: Committee on Souvenir and Program.

1938. *Inventory of the Luzerne County Archives.* Harrisburg: Historical Records Survey.

Mooretown, Sweet Valley P.O., Ross Twp.

Twp. formed 1842; first settlers 1793 from CT. NW of Co. Hilly farming country; grain, grass, timber. Sweet Valley the preeminent village of Twp. Mooretown named after 1799 settler Wm. Moore (Irish).

PA 15A: M, farmer, 69. B. Lake Twp. (5 mi. NE of here). — F., PGF b. Union Twp. in Co., PGF's F. of CT Yankee stock, PGM b. Co. (of Welsh parentage); M. b. here, MGF b. England (came here as a young man), MGM b. England. — Ed.: till 13. — Methodist. — Occasionally slow in associations.

Muhlenburg, Shickshinny P.O., Union Twp.

Twp. formed 1813. First settled 1773 by Germans and some English. Many early settlers (before 1778) from CT and Delaware Valley; Dutch and Germans later (early 19th cent.). Hilly, little cleared land in 1860. Coal.

PA 15B: M, farmer, 44. B. here. — F., PGF, PGF's F. b. Union Twp., PGF's PGF b. Berks Co. (of Scotch descent), PGF's PGM b. Berks Co. (of English-speaking, PA Dutch descent), PGF's M. b. near Forty Fort in Co., PGF's MGF, PGF's MGM b. CT, PGM b. Reyburn, Union Twp., PGM's F., PGM's M. b. Lehigh Co.; M., MGF, MGF's F. b. Union Twp., MGF's PGF b. Forty Fort in Co., MGF's PGF's F. b. CT (same person as PGF's MGF), MGF's M. b. near Nanticoke in Co., MGM, MGM's F. b. Union Twp., MGM's PGF of CT origin, MGM's M. b. Union Twp., MGM's MGF b. CT (of Scottish descent). — Ed.: till 19. — Quiet-spoken, quick, alert; difficult for FW to hear him because radio was going full blast and children were studying aloud.

Kingston

Twp. one of 11 original (1790). Inc. as a borough 1857; first settlers c. 1769 from CT. Site of Forty Fort, center of Wyoming Massacre of 1778. Now a suburb of Wilkes-Barre (across the Susquehanna). Coal in Twp. Well known for Wyoming Seminary. Pop. Twp. 1820: 1,228, 1850: 2,454, 1880: 5,878, 1910: 6,449, 1930: 21,600, 1960: 20,261.

PA 15C!: M, druggist, 62. B. here. — F., PGF, PGF's F. b. here, PGF's PGF b. CT, PGM b. Knowlton, Sussex Co., NJ (of Scotch-Irish descent); M. b. E. Smithfield, Bradford Co., came here when 6 mos. old, MGF b. MA (of French Huguenot descent), MGM, MGM's F. b. Kingston (of Yankee stock). — Ed.: public schools; Wyoming Seminary, Kingston; Lafayette College 4 yrs. at Easton (B.S. in chemistry). — Presbyterian. — Quick, alert, cooperative, natural; fine old family in reduced circumstances. — Cultivated.

16. Carbon County

Formed 1843 from Lehigh Co. 1st settlement 1746 by Moravian missionaries. Coal discovered 1791. Lehigh Coal and Navigation Co. formed 1818; canal and coal RR from 1827. Mountainous and wild; coal and lumber. Pop. 1850: 15,686, 1880: 31,923, 1910: 52,846, 1930: 63,380, 1960: 52,889.

Brenckman, Fred. 1913. *History of Carbon County.* Harrisburg: J. J. Nungesser.

Laciar, Jacob D. 1867. *Patriotism of Carbon County, and What Her People Contributed during the War for the Preservation of the Union.* Mauch Chunk.

Mathews, Alfred. 1884. *History of the Counties of Lehigh and Carbon. . . .* Philadelphia: Everts and Richards.

Rupp, Israel Daniel. 1845. *History of Northampton, Lehigh, Monroe, Carbon, and Schuylkill Counties. . . .* Harrisburg: Hickok and Cantine, Printers.

White, Josiah. 1909. *Josiah White's History.* Philadelphia: Press of G.H. Bichanan.

1894. *Portrait and Biographical Record of Lehigh, Northampton and Carbon Counties.* Chicago: Chapman Pub. Co.

Little Gap, Palmerton P.O., Lower Towamensing Twp.

Twp. formed 1841; 1st settlers Germans c. 1760. 1798 Lutheran and Reformed churches. Sand, building stone, textiles. Little Gap at gap in Blue Mts. Settlers by 1756 (largely German). Palmerton laid out 1898. Smelting town; New Jersey Zinc Co. Workers predominantly native born, white, Protestant.

PA 16A: M, farmer, 69. B. here. — F., PGF b. Little Gap, PGM b. Kunkletown, just across the line in Monroe Co.; M., MGF, MGM b. Kunkletown. — Ed.: here till 16. — Reformed. — Highly intelligent, quick; said he'd enjoy answering questions for "the German Atlas". — English plain, vigorous, intelligible, but very German; he doesn't understand many words. [ř] for medial [r]; [ɑrɹ] is fairly front, not [ɒrɹ] as in Reading.

Mauch Chunk

Twp. formed 1827. 1st warrant 1774; 1st survey 1798. 1st settlers largely German; also some English and Scots. Town started c. 1815, CT navigation of the Lehigh; inc. 1816. Co. seat 1840. Methodist church from 1826. Developed by Lehigh Coal and Navigation. Center of coal field; dependent on railroading and mining; foundries. Pop. 1850: 3,727, 1880: 4,082, 1910: 3,952, 1930: 3,206, 1960: 3,816.

PA 16B: M, clerk, 39. B. here. — F. b. Wilkes-Barre and came here when 1 1/2 yrs. old, PGF b. Bloomsburg, Columbia Co., PGF's F., PGF's M. of New England ancestry, PGM b. here, PGM's F., PGM's PGM b. Chester Co., PA (Quaker); M. b. Lansford in Co., MGF b. N. Ireland and came here, MGM b. Summit Hill in Co., MGM's F. b. Scotland, MGM's M. b. Scotland and came here via Canada. — Ed.: h.s. — Presbyterian. — Quick, alert, cooperative.

East Mauch Chunk (now Jim Thorpe)

First settled 1824; inc. as a borough 1854. East bank of Lehigh River. Largely residential to WWI. Developed by

Lehigh Coal and Navigation. In 1960 E. Mauch Chunk and part of Mauch Chunk were consolidated and designated as Jim Thorpe borough. Pop. 1880: 1,853, 1910: 3,548, 1930: 3,739, 1960: (Jim Thorpe borough) 5,945.

PA 16C: M, railroad engineer, 50. B. here. — F. b. here (of German descent); M. b. here (of Welsh parentage). Parents spoke only English. — Methodist. — His labials are all articulated as labiodentals owing to the conformation or manner of using lower lip. [b] and [v] are thus difficult to distinguish.

17. Lehigh County

Formed 1812 from Northampton Co. 1st settlements c. 1729, mainly by Palatine Germans; early settlers overflow from Bucks and Montgomery Cos. Reformed from 1725; Mennonites from 1735; Lutherans from 1741. Also Presbyterians in area c. 1728. 1st road 1735; Lehigh Canal 1827; RRs from 1846. Early one of best agricultural cos. in state. Later a center of manufacturing: iron and steel products, tools, cement, trucks, furniture, slate, textiles, shoes, brick, granite, and tile. Pop. 1820: 18,895, 1850: 32,479, 1880: 65,969, 1910: 118,832, 1930: 172,893, 1960: 227,536.

> Hauser, James J. 1902. *A History of Lehigh County*. 2nd ed. Allentown: Jacks, the Printer.
> Martin, John Hill. 1872. *Historical Sketch of Bethlehem. . . with Some Account of the Moravian Church*. Philadelphia. Repr. 1971 (NY: AMS Press).
> Mathews, Alfred. 1884. *History of the Counties of Lehigh and Carbon. . . .* Philadelphia: Everts and Richards.
> Roberts, Charles Rhoads. 1914. *History of Lehigh County. . . .* Allentown: Lehigh Valley Pub. Co.
> Williams, David G. 1950. *The Lower Jordan Valley Pennsylvania German Settlement*. Allentown: H. Ray Haas and Co.
> 1908–. *Proceedings and Papers Read before the Lehigh County Historical Society*. Allentown: The Society.

Kuhnsville/Chapmans, Allentown P.O., Upper Macungie Twp.

Twp. one of original; divided 1832. Area settled c. 1730. Mainly Germans; also French Protestants. Productive farming; limestone, iron ore. Chapmans a small village 7 mi. from Allentown; some growth since 1915 with cement mills nearby. Pop. 1900: c. 60, 1914: 117.

PA 17A: M, farmer, now peddler, 72. B. N. Whitehall (10 mi. NE). — F. b. Northampton, PGF b. Germany, PGM b. N. Whitehall; M., MGF b. Washington Twp. in Co., MGM b. N. Whitehall. — Ed.: till 14. — Reformed. — Genial; somewhat explosive and dogmatic.

Allentown

Laid out by James Allen c. 1762; originally called the Borough of Northampton. Settled as early as 1723. Germans from beginning; market town at first. Reformed and Lutherans in 18th cent.; others later. Iron and cement since 1850; silk, cotton textiles from 1890s. Muhlenberg College (Lutheran) founded 1867. PA German still spoken; still newspaper columns. German musical societies. Products and industries: iron, textiles, boots and shoes, cigars, furniture, bricks. Pop. 1850: 3,779, 1880: 18,063, 1910: 51,913, 1930: 92,563, 1960: 108,347.

PA 17B: M, merchant, bank director, 74. B. here. — F., PGF b. here, PGF's F. b. PA (of German descent), PGM b. Whitehall Twp. in Co.; M. b. Allentown, MGF, MGM b. Lehigh Co. — Ed.: city public schools. — Lutheran. — Not particularly impressed with project, but cooperative. Grew up speaking German and learned English at school and as an errand boy; lived near an Irish section. — Articulation somewhat indistinct.

18. Northampton County

Created 1752. Possibly early Dutch settlement, abandoned after 1664. 1st settlers thereafter Scotch-Irish c. 1728; later (1739) Germans arrived and largely supplanted Scotch-Irish. Bethlehem and Nazareth founded by Moravians. 1761–89 65% German in name; 30% Scotch-Irish; 5% other. Today 45% place names of German origin. By 1940 40% foreign-born of foreign parentage (many S. and E. Europeans). Steel from 1857, silk and rayon from 1887, cement from 1895, limestone, zinc. Unsurpassed in soil fertility. Pop. 1790: 24,220, 1820: 31,765, 1850: 40,235, 1880: 70,312, 1910: 127,667, 1930: 169,304, 1960: 201,412.

> Chidsey, Andrew D. 1940. *A Frontier Village, Pre-Revolutionary Easton*. Easton: Northampton County Historical and Genealogical Society.
> Clyde, John C. 1879. *Genealogies, Necrology, and Reminiscences of the "Irish Settlement". . . .* Frazer: The Author.
> Condit, Uzal W. 1889. *The History of Easton. . . 1739–1885*. Easton: G. W. West.
> Crage, Thomas J. 1959. *A Preliminary Checklist of Easton, Pennsylvania, Imprints, 1800–76, with a Historical Introduction*. Washington: Catholic Univ. of America.
> Ellis, F. 1877. *. . . .History of Northampton County* Philadelphia: P. Fritts.
> Federal Writers Project. 1939. *Northampton County Guide*. Bethlehem: Times Pub. Co.
> Kieffer, Henry Martyn, ed. 1902. *Some of the First Settlers of "the Forks of the Delaware" and Their Descendants*. Easton: H. M. Kieffer.
> Raup, H. F. 1938. The Pennsylvania-Dutch of Northampton County: Settlement Forms and Culture Patterns. *Bulletin of the Geographic Society of Philadelphia* 36:1–15.
> 1926. *The Scotch-Irish of Northampton County. . . .* Easton: Northampton County Historical and Genealogical Society.

Mt. Bethel

Twp. organized 1796; 1st settlement 1730. One of oldest settled parts of Co. Area contains Ulster Scots; Presbyterians c. 1730. Some French, Germans by 1746. Village founded 1835; small trading center.

PA 18A: F, housewife, 69. B. here. — F., PGF b. here (both PGF and PGM of PA German descent); M. b. Northampton Co., MGF b. in Germany, MGM b. NJ, just across the river. — Ed.: here till 16. — Reformed. — Not too intelligent (may have looked at FW's book to get some of her responses).

Pierce, Easton P.O.

Easton laid out 1737–38. Co. seat 1752; inc. 1789; city charter 1837. 1st settler arrived 1739; early settlers Scotch-

Irish and German. Roman Catholics from 1737; Reformed from 1745; Evangelical Lutherans from 1763; Presbyterians 1798. Lehigh Canal from 1824. Lafayette College chartered 1826. By 1940 about 35% AfAms and foreign born, many central and S. Europeans. Almost 200 factories; various products. Pop. 1930: 34,468.

PA 18B!: M, architect, 60. B. here (on RR in PA towns and in NY 1901–8). — F. b. New Haven, CT, came here when 1 mo. old, PGF b. New Haven, came here when 21, PGM b. East Haven, CT, came here to be married; M., MGF b. Easton, MGF's F. b. N. Ireland, MGF's M. b. Bucks Co., MGM b. Easton, MGM's F. b. Phillipsburg, NJ, MGM's M. b. Easton, MGM's MGF b. Warren Co., NJ, MGM's MGM b. Easton, MGM's MGM's F. b. Scotland, MGM's MGM's M. b. Easton, MGM's MGM's MGF and MGM b. Germany. — Ed.: Lafayette College, Easton (engineering). — Presbyterian. — Cultivated, quick, intelligent. — Cultivated.

19. Monroe County

Co. formed 1835. Oldest survey 1727. Dutch from NY 1st settlers; before 1730 (possibly some settlements as early as 1700 on Minisink Flats on Delaware). English and Scotch-Irish 1748. Germans largest group of early settlers. 1st church (Dutch Reformed) 1742; Presbyterians, Lutherans, Methodists, and Baptists by 1800. Generally mountainous, upland swamp. Resort area, textiles. Pop. 1840: 9,879, 1850: 13,270, 1880: 20,175, 1910: 22,941, 1930: 28,286, 1960: 39,567.

> Burrell, Abram A. 1870. *Reminiscences of George La Bar...*
> . Philadelphia: Claxton, Remsen and Haffelfinger.
> Keller, Robert Brown. 1927. *History of Monroe County.*
> Stroudsburg: Monroe Pub. Co.
> Mathews, Alfred. 1886. *History of Wayne, Pike and Monroe Counties.* Philadelphia: R. T. Peck.
> Rupp, Israel Daniel. 1845. *History of Northampton, Lehigh, Monroe, Carbon, and Schuylkill Counties. . . .* Harrisburg: Hickok and Cantine, Printers.

Marshalls Creek, Middle Smithfield Twp.

Smithfield Twp. formed 1746–48; later divided. Area settled permanently c. 1740; possible settlement of Hollanders from NY as early as 1664. English, German, Dutch. Indian depredations 1755–64. Hilly to broken terrain. Marshalls Creek lake ice cut in winter; summer resort. Marshalls Creek pop. 1930: 125.

PA 19A: F, widow, 70. B. here. — F., PGF, PGF's F., PGF's M. b. here, PGM b. here; M. b. here, MGF b. Sussex Co., NJ, MGM b. Co., MGM's F. b. here. — Ed.: 3 winters. — Baptist. — Quick, bright, but very excitable; FW spoke softly and quickly and got immediate reactions. — Very rustic speech.

Cresco P.O., Barrett Twp.

Cresco had 15 hotels c. 1940; anglers' and deer hunters' rendezvous. Pop. 1930: 400.

PA 19B: M, road foreman, 49. B. here. — F., PGF, PGM b. here; M. b. Mountainhome in Co., MGF b. Price Twp. in Co., MGM b. Canadensis in Co. — Ed.: till 16. — Methodist. — Alert, business-like, but not always as quick as might be. Phlegmatic temperament.

20. Pike County

Formed 1814 from Wayne Co. Earliest settlements by Hudson Valley Dutch before 1680; abandoned. 1760 settlement also abandoned. Also English and German settlers. Once timber country; farming in river flats, quarrying. Mtn. resorts; hunting and fishing. Pop. 1820: 2,890, 1850: 5,581, 1880: 9,663, 1910: 8,033, 1930: 7,483, 1960: 9,158.

> Gardiner, Abraham Sylvester, comp. 1888. *Tom Quick: Or, The Era of Frontier Settlement.* Chicago: Knight and Leonard Co., Printers.
> Schrabisch, Max 1930. *Archaeology of the Delaware River Valley between Hancock and Dingman's Ferry in Wayne and Pike Counties.* Harrisburg: Pennsylvania Historical Commission.
> 1900. *Commemorative Biographical Record of Northeastern Pennsylvania. . . Susquehanna, Wayne, Pike and Monroe. . . .* Chicago: J. H. Beers.

Long Meadow/Dingman's Ferry, Milford P.O., Delaware Twp.

Twp. original. Dingman's Ferry first settled 1735; early settlers Dutch from NY, English from NH and NJ. Resort area. Milford Co. seat; large estates, tourist establishments. Pop. Dingman's Ferry 1930: 250.

PA 20A: M, farmer, 75. B. Lehman Twp. (worked as a young man in NY and NJ some). — F. b. Lehman Twp. in Co., PGF b. PA, PGF's F. b. in Scotland and taken prisoner by Gen. Washington, PGM b. here; M., MGF b. Lehman Twp., MGM b. Dingman's Ferry. — Ed.: till 16 (off and on). — Methodist. — Somewhat senile; enjoyed FW's company, but probably thought questions silly.

PA 20B: M, farmer, 44. B. here. — F. b. Middle Smithfield Twp., just over the line in Monroe Co., came here when young, PGF b. Lehman Twp. in Co., PGF's PGF b. Germany, came to Northhampton Co., PA in 1775, PGF's M. b. Monroe Co., PGF's MGF b. Germany, PGM b. Nazareth, Northhampton Co., PGM's F., PGM's M. b. Bucks Co.; M. b. Lehman Twp. in Co., MGF b. Conyngham, Luzerne Co., came here when 14, MGF's F., MGF's PGF, MGF's PGM b. Wantage, Sussex Co., NJ, MGF's M. b. Luzerne Co., MGF's MGF, MGF's MGM b. NJ, MGM b. Lehman Twp., MGM's F. b. Montange, Sussex Co., NJ, MGM's PGF, MGM's PGM b. NY State, MGM's M. b. Co., MGM's MGF, MGM's MGF, MGM's MGM came here from Orange Co., NY in 1774. — Ed.: till 15. — Presbyterian. — Rather intelligent, but indifferent and not always quick; answered from sense of obligation.

21. Wayne County

Formed 1798. Part of CT settlement c. 1770; abandoned after Wyoming massacre. Many Germans also, from CT and NY State. Early industries water power, glass, textiles, paper, machinery, general farming and dairying; edge of coalfields. Developed through Delaware and Hudson Canal Co., 1826–28. Lumbering important till c. 1890. RR from 1827. Little arable land, rocky, forests. Pop. 1800: 2,562, 1820: 4,127, 1850: 21,890, 1880: 33,513, 1910: 29,236, 1930: 28,420, 1960: 28,237.

> Goodrich, Phineas G. 1880. *History of Wayne County.* Honesdale: Haines and Beardsley.

Schrabisch, Max 1930. *Archaeology of the Delaware River Valley between Hancock and Dingman's Ferry in Wayne and Pike Counties.* Harrisburg:Pennsylvania Historical Commission.

Stocker, Rhamanthus Menville. 1906. *History of the First Presbyterian Society of Honesdale.* Honesdale: Herald Press Association.

1900. *Commemorative Biographical Record of Northeastern Pennsylvania. . . Susquehanna, Wayne, Pike and Monroe. . . .* Chicago: J. H. Beers.

1902. *Centennial and Illustrated Wayne County.* 2nd ed. Honesdale: B. F. Haines.

Scott Center, Starucca P.O., Scott Twp.

Twp. formed 1821. NE corner of PA. "Most sparsely pop. twp". Settlement slow; mainly Yankees. Settlers from S. Wayne Co., Delaware Co. (NY), MA, Long Island, CT; various stocks, including French and English. Scott Center sawmill c. 1823–24; some settlers from NJ.

PA 21A: M, farmer, 72. B. here. — F. b. here, PGF, PGM b. CT; M. b. Gibson, Susquehanna Co. and came here, MGF, MGM b. RI. — Ed.: till 13. — Baptist. — Rather quick, bright; rural type. — Distinction between [oᴖ] and [ɔᴖ] and other W. New Eng. features.

Laurella, Honesdale P.O., Berlin Twp.

Twp. formed 1826. 1st settler c. 1801. Benefitted by Delaware and Hudson Canal, turnpikes, and Honesdale branch of Erie RR. Most settlers of English descent; some Germans. Honesdale named for Philip Hone, mayor of NY and pres. of D&H Canal Co. Coal storage, shipping point after 1808. Misc. industry, including shoes, textiles. Pop. Honesdale 1930: 5,490.

PA 21B: M, farmer, 56. B. here. — F. b. here, PGF b. England came here via Phila., PGM (of English descent); M. b. Equinunk in Co., MGM b. S. Canaan in Co. — Sharp; not particularly in sympathy with the project, answered from sense of obligation.

22. Lackawanna County

Formed 1878. Settlers as early as 1771 from CT and NY; Germans 1809–10. Methodists from 1791; other churches in 19th cent. N. limit of anthracite fields; iron and steel (esp. in Scranton). Forge from 1797; canal from 1823. Irish control of city govt. in Scranton c. 1866; city inc. 1866. S. and E. Europeans arrived in latter 19th cent.; Poles from c. 1847. Pop. decline in Scranton since 1920s and collapse of anthracite market. Textiles later. Pop. 1880: 89,269, 1910: 259,570, 1930: 310,397, 1960: 234,531.

McKune, Robert H. 1882. *Memorial of the Erection of Lackawanna County.* Scranton: Walter.

Murphy, Thomas. 1928. *Jubilee History. . . of Lackawanna County.* 2 vols. Indianapolis: Historical Pub. Co.

Weyburn, Samuel Fletcher, comp. 1932. *Following the Connecticut Trail from the Delaware River to the Susquehanna Valley.* Scranton: Anthracite Press.

Weyburn, Samuel Fletcher, ed. 1929. *Memorial of the Fiftieth Anniversary of Lackawanna County.* Scranton: Lackawanna Historical Society.

Weyburn, Samuel Fletcher. 1928. *A Story of Lackawanna County and Lackawanna Historical Society.* Scranton: The Society.

1880. *History of Luzerne, Lackawanna and Wyoming Counties.* NY: W. W. Munsell.

1887–. *Publications of the Lackawanna Historical Society.* Scranton: The Society.

1897. *Portrait and Biographical Record of Wyoming and Lackawanna Counties. . . .* Chicago: Chapman Pub. Co.

Fleetville, Dalton P.O., Benton Twp.

Twp. formed 1838; first settler a Yankee 1810–11. 10 sizeable lakes; once water power, now popular resorts. First store in Fleetville 1838. Dalton a residential suburb of Scranton; dairying, vegetable gardening.

PA 22A: M, farmer, 85. B. here. — F. b. RI and walked here when 17, PGF, PGM b. RI (both Baptists); M. b. Abington Twp. in Co., MGF, MGM b. CT. — Ed.: till 12 (off and on). — Baptist. — Rather quick; at first thought questions nonsense, but was finally persuaded to continue; rather W. New Eng. type.

PA 22B: M, farmer, subassessor, 48. B. here. — F. b. Benton Twp., PGF b. Falls, Wyoming Co., PGF's F. b. RI (of French Huguenot descent), PGM b. here, PGM's F. b. RI; M. b. here, MGF b. Middletown, NY (of German descent), MGM b. here, MGM's F. b. in New Eng., MGM's M. b. NJ. — Ed.: till 16. — Baptist. — Very quick, intelligent; rustic. — Short vowels, New Eng. type, but does not distinguish [ɔɚ].

23. Susquehanna County

Formed 1810 from Luzerne Co. Conflicting settlements 1750s; Indians sold land to both claimants. 1st noticed 1779 during Sullivan campaign; part of CT settlement. Susquehanna River watershed; settled mainly from New England. First road 1762; turnpikes early 19th cent. Large landownings by Philadelphians. Pop. 1820: 9,960, 1850: 28,688, 1880: 40,354, 1910: 37,746, 1930: 33,806, 1960: 33,137.

Blackman, Emily C. 1873. *History of Susquehanna County.* Philadelphia. Repr. 1970 (Baltimore: Regional Pub. Co.).

DuBois, James T., and William J. Pike. 1888. *The Centennial of Susquehanna County.* Washington: Gray and Clarkson, Printers.

Stocker, Rhamanthus M. 1887. *Centennial History of Susquehanna County.* Philadelphia: R. T. Peck.

Taylor, Robert J., and Julian P. Boyd, eds. 1930–71. *The Susquehanna Company Papers.* 11 vols. Wilkes-Barre: Wyoming Historical and Geological Society.

1900. *Commemorative Biographical Record of Northeastern Pennsylvania. . . Susquehanna, Wayne, Pike and Monroe. . . .* Chicago: J. H. Beers.

Harford

Twp. formed 1808 from Nicholson. First settlers c. 1790 from MA; Congregationalists. Settled from VT, CT, Hudson Valley, Ulster. Small industries.

PA 23A: M, farmer, 87. B. Brooklyn (near Dimock). When small child, left and went to Meshappen, then to Bridgewater, then to Harford when 11. — F. b. Brooklyn in Co., PGF b. near Great Bend in Co. (PGF and PGM of English descent — "Yankee"); M., MGF b. Lanesboro in Co. (of Yankee descent). — Ed.: first in Bridgewater, then Harford till 18. — Methodist. — Very old in appearance, but still quick and intelligent; willing. — [oɚ] and [ɔɚ] as in W. New Eng.

Heart Lake, New Milford Twp.

Twp. founded 1807. First survey 1784; first settlers c. 1789: one from Boston, most from CT. 1st road 1791. Some Scots among early settlers; settlers also from NY, VT, Long I., N. NJ, NH, MA. General farming, dairying; lumber, butter, leather. Heart Lake in W. part of Twp.

PA 23B: M, farmer, 51. B. here. — F. b. here, PGF b. Mattewan, NY, PGM b. near Peekskill, NY; M. b. here, MGM b. Wayne Co., PA, at Aldenville. — Ed.: till 16. — Baptist. — Interested in history of settlement; rather quick and intelligent.

24. Wyoming County

Formed 1842 from Luzerne Co. Settlers mainly from New England. Agriculture and manufacturing: leather, lumber, agr. implements, grain; hill pasturage. Pop. 1850: 10,655, 1880: 15,598, 1910: 15,509, 1930: 15,517, 1960: 16,813.

> Barnes, Archy Wright. 1945. *Genealogical Notes on the Ancestry of Some Early Settlers in the Upper Wyoming Valley....*
> Harding, Garrick M. 1901. *Wyoming and Its Incidents.* Wilkes-Barre: Wyoming Valley Chapter, DAR.
> Joyce, Mary Hinchcliffe. 1928. *Pioneer Days in the Wyoming Valley.* Philadelphia.
> Peck, George. 1858. *Wyoming.* NY: Harper and Bros.
> 1880. *History of Luzerne, Lackawanna and Wyoming Counties.* NY: W. W. Munsell.
> 1897. *Portrait and Biographical Record of Wyoming and Lackawanna Counties....* Chicago: Chapman Pub. Co.

Fox Hollow/Jenningsville, Mehoopany P.O., Windham Twp.

Twp. one of oldest in Co.; formed 1787 or earlier. 1st settlers largely from CT. Nearly all river land taken up by 1800; inland settlement later. Jenningsville largely Yankees; sawmill from 1805, tannery later.

PA 24A: M, farmer, 74. B. Mehoopany Twp; came here when 31. — F. b. Middle Smithfield Twp. in Monroe Co., came here when 2 yrs. old, PGF (of English descent), PGM (of "Dutch" descent) b. Monroe Co.; M. b. Mehoopany Twp., MGF b. NH, MGM b. Mehoopany Twp., MGM's F. of English descent. — Ed.: till 21 (off and on). — Baptist. — Quick, bright, but of higher type than is desired for the old-fashioned inf. (daughter is a doctor in Lancaster).

Roger Hollow, Mehoopany Twp.

Twp. formed 1844 from Windham Twp. 1st settler 1775; early settlers mainly Yankees from CT.

PA 24B: M, farmer, 42. B. here. — F., PGF b. here, PGM b. Forkston in Co., PGM's F. b. CT; M. b. here, MGM b. NJ, came here when very young (of Holland Dutch descent). — Ed.: till 18. — Methodist. — Timid man who answered as a

duty, but quickly. — Uses only [ɔɚ] in contrast to the old-fashioned inf.

25. Sullivan County

Formed 1847 from Lycoming Co. Midway between N. and W. branches of Susquehanna. 1st settlement c. 1768 from CT; broken up. Surveyed 1793. English among early settlers. Adventist colony 1864. Isolated; no important stream. Woolen manufacture attempted early. Other products and industries: timber, fishing, resorts, leather making, coal, copper, lead, iron ore, limestone; abortive glass making. Pop. 1850: 3,694, 1880: 8,073, 1910: 11,293, 1930: 7,499, 1960: 6,251.

> Ingham, Thomas J. 1899. *History of Sullivan County.* Chicago: Lewis Pub. Co.
> Streby, George. 1903 *History of Sullivan County.* Dunshore: Sullivan Gazette.

Bethel/Estella, Forksville P.O., Elkland Twp.

Twp. formed 1804. Settled in 1790s from England; some Quakers and a few Mohawk Valley Germans among early settlers. Election dist. est. 1808. Bethel somewhat isolated; founded 1814.

PA 25A: M, farmer, 80. B. 10 mi. W. in Fox Twp., moved here after marriage. — F. b. Fox Twp. in Co., PGF b. NY State, PGF's F. b. Germany, PGM b. NY State; M. b. Fox Twp. in Co. — Ed.: till 18. — Methodist. — Quick, intelligent, interested in archaic things; rather better than average type, but old-fashioned and rustic in an isolated farming and lumbering region.

PA 25B: Elkland Church/Estella. — M, farmer, 52. B. here. — F. b. here, PGF b. Yorkshire, England, came here when 17, PGM b. Fox Twp. in Co. (of Yankee stock); M. b. Forks Twp. in Co., MGF b. Lycoming Co. (partly of French origin), MGM b. here, MGM's F. of English origin. — Ed.: here till 17. — Wesleyan Methodist. — Quick, cooperative. — Uses only [ɔɚ] in contrast to the old-fashioned inf.

26. Bradford County

Formed 1810 from Luzerne; orig. Ontario, name changed 1812. Traders and missionaries (Moravian) in area from 1745; 1st settlement by Palatine Germans in 1770. Further settlement from CT; evacuated during Revolution. Baptists, Presbyterians, Methodists in late 18th cent.; others later. Turnpike from 1807; Canal from 1854; RR 1869. Uneven surface, table lands. Farming: grains, potatoes, hay, livestock. Lumbering once. Coal, flagstones, iron, oil. Pop. 1820: 11,554, 1850: 42,831, 1880: 58,541, 1910: 54,526, 1930: 49,039, 1960: 54,925.

> Bradsby, Henry C. 1891. *History of Bradford County.* Chicago: S. B. Nelson.
> Craft, David. 1878. *History of Bradford County.* Philadelphia: L. H. Everts.
> Heverly, Clement F. 1926. *History and Geography of Bradford County, 1615-1924.* Towanda: Bradford County Historical Society.
> Perkins, Julia Anna. 1906. *Early Times on the Susquehanna.* 2nd ed. Binghamton, NY: Herald Co.

Rupp, Israel Daniel. 1846. *The History and Topography of Dauphin, Cumberland, Franklin, Bedford, Adams, and Perry Counties....* Lancaster: G. Hills.

Warren Center P.O., Warren Twp.

Twp. formed 1813. Extreme NE of Bradford County. Settled 1796–1800, mainly by Yankees from MA, RI, CT, VT. Warren Center had 2 stores and a grist mill c. 1891.

PA 26A: M, farmer, 83. B. here (spent one yr. in Nebraska when 50). — F. b. S. Warren, PGF, PGM b. near CT River in MA; M. b. Jackson Valley on edge of Susquehanna Co., MGF, MGM b. Scotland. — Ed.: till 20. — Methodist. — Bachelor, somewhat hard of hearing. — Very old-fashioned in speech; W. New Eng. speech type.

Camptown, Wyalusing P.O., Herrick Twp.

Twp. formed 1837. E. of center of Co. New Eng. settlers c. 1810. Camptown high table land; 1st settler 1792. Large Irish pop. Wyalusing a residential community. Settled by New Englanders in the 1750s; Moravian mission to Indians till 1772.

PA 26B: M, farmer, 51. B. here. — F., PGF, PGF's F. b. here, PGF's PGF b. CT, PGM b. E. part of Co.; M. b. here, MGF b. Phila. (of Scottish descent), MGM b. Co. — Ed.: here till 18. — Presbyterian (Methodist parentage; mother died when he was 4). — Somewhat deliberate, not to be hurried; makes up his own mind; accurate. — Interesting distinction between "new", "blue" [nuˑ bluᵂ] and "knew", "blew" [nɪˑuˤ blĭŭˤ]; clear-cut speech with short vowels; typical New Eng. intonation with short groups of words as rhythm units.

27. Tioga County

Formed 1804 from Lycoming Co. 2nd largest PA Co. Purchase of NW PA from Iroquois in 1784. State Line Rd. 1786. 1st settlement near Lawrenceville 1787; by 1800, settlers from VA, DE, MD, Phila., Ireland, NY, RI. NE influence predominant; few Germans among first settlers. Coal discovered 1792; 1st RR 1840. Lumbering in 19th cent.; tanneries came and went. Pop. decline 1890–1930. Agriculture (dairying) still leads; also coal, iron ore, clay, salt, forests. Tourism in recent yrs. Pop. 1810: 1,687, 1820: 4,021, 1850: 23,987, 1880: 45,814, 1910: 42,829, 1930: 31,811, 1960: 36,614.

Heaps, John C. 1970. *Headwaters Country: The Story of Tioga County.* State College: Himes Print.

Meginness, J. F. 1897. *History of Tioga County.* Harrisburg: R.C. Brown.

Sexton, John L. 1885. *An Outline History of Tioga and Bradford Counties....* Elmira, NY: Gazette Co.

Cherry Flats/Whitneyville, Mansfield P.O., Covington Twp.

Twp. formed 1815 from Tioga. Settlers chiefly from New Eng. and NY State. Glassworks to 1897, wood products, tanneries. Small mine, mink farm. One of best agricultural twps. 1st settler 1804 in Cherry Flats. Whitneyville in NE Charleston Twp., settled c. 1823. Mansfield has farming, tourists, toy factory, milk condenser; Mansfield State U.

PA 27A: M, farmer, 70. B. here. — F. b. here, PGF b. Clymer, NY, PGM b. NY State; M. b. Charleston Twp. in Co., MGF, MGM b. in Wales. — Ed.: till 18. — Parents Methodist. — Hard-working, miserly, crippled man; his wife thought the questions were nonsense and refused to allow him to complete them; questionnaire completed with 17-year-old son after page 71 (27A*).

PA 27A*: M. 17 (son of 27A). — F's side of the family, as above; M., MGF, MGM b. here, MGM's F., MGM's M, b. NY State. — Answered questions to complete father's interview after page 71; did so surreptitiously, from sense of duty. — Rather old-fashioned in speech himself. Incomplete.

Niles Valley, Wellsboro P.O., Middlebury Twp.

Twp. formed 1832. Settled c. 1799/1800; early settlers from NH, CT, VT, MA. Rugged, mountainous, general farming, tobacco, orchards. Niles Valley near S. boundary of Twp. Trading village; declined since 1900. Wellsboro was a lumbering center; tourists, hunting, Corning Glass, coal mines and gas wells.

PA 27B: M, farmer and birch distiller, 50. B. here. — F. b. near the edge of Potter Co., came here when young, PGF b. near Potter Co. (partly German descent), PGM b. Co.; M., MGF, MGM b. Co. — Ed.: till 16. — Methodist. — Answered from sense of obligation. — Rather W. New Eng. in character and speech.

28. Lycoming County

Formed 1795 from Northumberland Co. Visited by explorers as early as 1615. Settlers began to arrive c. 1737; pioneers chiefly Scotch-Irish; mixed pop. early included English Quakers, Germans, settlers from New Eng., NJ (many Dutch), NY. Rapid settlement after 1784. 1st road completed 1796; canal 1828–89; RR from 1839. Presbyterian church from 1793. "Fair play system": squatters' law in unorganized territory. Contrasting scenery: mountains, narrow and sterile valleys, fertile (limestone) valleys. Products and industries: coal, iron ore, limestone, non-ferrous metals, clays, slate and flagstone, agriculture, lumbering. Pop. 1800: 5,414, 1820: 13,517, 1850: 26,257, 1880: 57,486, 1910: 80,813, 1930: 93,421, 1960: 109,367.

Collins, Emerson, ed. 1906. *Genealogical and Personal History of Lycoming County.* NY: Lewis Pub. Co.

Federal Writers Project. 1939. *A Picture of Lycoming County.* Williamsport: Commissioners of Lycoming County.

Lloyd, T. W. 1929. *Lycoming County.* 2 vols. Indianapolis: Historical Pub. Co.

Meginness, J. F. 1892. *History of Lycoming County.* 2 vols. Chicago: Brown.

Meginness, John F. 1889. *Otzinachson: Or, a History of the West Branch Valley of the Susquehanna.* Rev. ed. Williamsport: Gazette and Bulletin Print. House.

Wolf, George D. 1969. *The Fair Play Settlers of the West Branch Valley, 1769–1784: A Study of Frontier Ethnography.* Harrisburg: Pennsylvania History and Museum Commission.

1876. *History of Lycoming County....* Philadelphia: D. J. Stewart.

Huntersville, Hughesville P.O., Wolf Twp.

Twp. formed 1834. 1st settled c. 1778. Stone products. Huntersville small settlement. Hughesville once a lumbering village; furniture factories.

PA 28A: M, farmer and road caretaker, 72. B. here. — F. b. here, PGF, PGF's F. b. MD; M. b. near Benton, Columbia Co. — Ed.: here till 20. — Lutheran. — Uninterested, unsympathetic, uncooperative; better educated and informed than FW would have liked; FW may have been misinformed about his ancestors.

Williamsport

Town laid out as Co. seat in 1796. 1st tracts 1769; at least one German among early settlers. Organized as borough 1806; as city 1866. Yankee influence still strong. Presbyterians and Methodists by late 18th cent.; others later. One of world's greatest lumbering centers 1850–1900. Iron and steel production begun 1837; also tanneries (till 1890), shoes, flour mills, distilleries. Pop. 1910: 31,860, 1930: 45,729, 1960: 41,967.

PA 28B!: F, 50. B. here. — F. b. Jersey Shore, Lycoming Co., came here when 6 years old, PGF b. 1823 in Hopkinton, MA, went when 3 yrs. old to Speedsville, near Ithaca NY, PGF's F. b. Hopkinton, MA (descendant of man who came to Watertown, MA in 1630), PGF's M. b. Uxbridge, MA, PGM b. Speedsville, NY, PGM's F., PGM's M. of Butter Nut Valleye, NY; M. b. here, MGF, MGF's F. b. 5 miles N. of here, MGF's PGF b. Northampton Co., near Bath, MGF's PGF's F. b. Donegal, N. Ireland, MGF's PGF's M. b. N. Ireland, MGF's PGM b. Northampton Co., near Bath, MGF's PGM's F., MGF's PGM's M. b. Northampton Co., MGF's M. b. here, MGF's MGF b. Northampton Co., MGF's MGF's F. b. N. Ireland, MGF's MGF's PGF b. N. Ireland (same person as MGF's PGF's F.), MGF's MGF's M. b. Bucks Co., MGF's MGM b. near Phila., MGF's MGM's F. of the Navy, MGM b. here, MGM's F. b. NJ (of Welsh descent), MGM's M. b. here, MGM's MGF, MGM's MGM b. N. Ireland. — Ed.: Dickinson Seminary (now the Junior College) here. — Presbyterian. — Cultivated city informant of wealthy department store family; cooperative; quick; nervous. — Speech very local; slight impediment when confused. — Cultivated.

29. Clinton County

County formed 1839 from Centre and Lycoming Cos. 1st settlement 1765; largely Scotch-Irish from Carlisle area. Some English and Dutch, Germans later. Evacuated 1778; resettled 1783. Irish influx with West Branch Canal in 1833. Mountainous and uneven; Susquehanna watershed. Highly productive valleys: coal, iron ore, fire clay, limestone, potter's clay, glass, sand, lumbering. Pop. 1840: 8,323, 1850: 11,207, 1880: 26,278, 1910: 31,545, 1930: 32,619, 1960: 37,619.

Federal Writers Project. 1942. *A Picture of Clinton County*. Harrisburg: Commissioners of Clinton County.

Furey, J. Milton. 1892. *Historical and Biographical Work, or, Past and Present of Clinton County*. . . . Williamsport: Pennsylvania Grit Print. Houses.

Linn, John Blair. 1883. *History of Centre and Clinton Counties*. Philadelphia: L. H. Everts.

Maynard, D. S. 1875. *Historical View of Clinton County*. . . . Lock Haven: Enterprise Print. House.

Meginness, John F. 1889. *Otzinachson: Or, a History of the West Branch Valley of the Susquehanna*. Rev ed. Williamsport: Gazette and Bulletin Print. House.

Rupp, Israel Daniel. 1847. *History and Topography of Northumberland, Huntingdon, Mifflin, Centre, Union, Columbia, Juniata and Clinton Counties*. . . . Lancaster: G. Hills.

Loganton P.O., Green Twp.

Twp. organized 1840. 1st settled c. 1800 by Germans; uplands later by Scotch-Irish. Iron ore; attempt at one time to make iron. Loganton laid out 1840; inc. as borough 1869. Largely German.

PA 29A: M, farmer, over 60. B. 6 mi. E. — F. b. here, PGF b. N. of Loganton on the mtn., PGF's F. b. near Liverpool, Perry Co. (of Swiss descent), PGM b. Booneville in Co.; M. b. Carroll in Co., MGF, MGM b. Schuylkill Co. — Ed.: till 12. — Lutheran. — Quick, alert. — Uses [ɫ] in English, usually uses [l] in German (German dying out here).

Beech Creek

Twp. formed 1850; in S. part of Co. 1st settler 1793; others c. 1800. Fertile bottomland; lumbering first industry. Borough formerly a hardwood forest. Settled c. 1812. Small trading center.

PA 29A*: M, farmer, 83. B. here. — F. b. here, PGF b. Phila., PGF's F. b. in France or Holland, PGF's M. b. Phila., PGM b. here, PGM's F. of Scotch-Irish descent, PGM's M. of English descent; M. (came here as a child), MGF, MGM b. Leicestershire, England. — Christian. — Elderly, impatient, irascible, somewhat hard of hearing; not in very good health; distinguished family. — Remembers hearing his mother's parents' English accent.

Mackeyville, Lamar Twp.

Original twp. (was in Centre Co.). Settled c. 1800 by English; then mostly Germans. C. 1833 attempt at iron-making failed. Productive agriculture; iron ore. Mackeyville a small village formed c. 1830.

PA 29B: M, farmer, 42. B. here. — F., PGF b. Twp., PGF's F., PGM b. Co.; M., MGF, MGM b. Co. — Ed.: till 16. — Lutheran. — Very quick, intelligent, cooperative person who sympathized with the importance of the project and understood its nature. — Full, deep, resonant voice with strong, long [ɝ·]. [a] and [ʋ˄] appear to belong to the same phoneme. [a] appears always before /p t k/.

30. Potter County

Formed 1804 (but still attached to Lycoming). 1784 purchase from Indians. 1st settlement 1808; pioneers mostly from New Eng. and NY. N. part of Co. first settled. Some from SE PA; Germans in 1830s from Alsace; Irish settlement 1840. Lumbering in mid-19th cent. on Allegheny River. 1st RR 1880. Valley table land; agricultural: wheat, corn, fruits, grazing, dairying. Also chemicals, coal and iron, pulp and paper; however, most industry dissolved with end of lumbering. Pop. 1810: 29, 1820: 186, 1850: 6,048, 1880: 13,797, 1910: 29,729, 1930: 17,489, 1960: 16,483.

> Beebe, Victor L. 1934. *History of Potter County.* Coudersport: Potter County Historical Society.
>
> Leeson, Michael A. 1890. *History of the Counties of McKean, Elk, Cameron and Potter.* Chicago: University of Chicago Press.
>
> Lyman, Robert Ray. 1969. *The Life and Times of Major Isaac Lyman, Founder of Potter County, Pennsylvania.* Coudersport: Potter County Historical Society.
>
> 1952. *The Old Bull Colony in Potter County, 1852: One Hundredth Anniversary. . . .* Coudersport.

West Bingham, Genesee P.O., Bingham Twp.

Twp. organized 1830. 1st settlements c. 1820 from NY. Early settlers largely English, some Dutch. Genesee and upper Chemung drainage.

PA 30A: M, farmer, 73. B. here. — F. b. Upper Lisle, Broom Co., NY, and came here age 8, PGF b. Orange Co., VT, PGM b. NY or VT; M. b. here, MGF b. RI near Providence, MGM b. RI. — Ed.: till 16 (3 mos. a year). — Methodist. — Quick, intelligent, genial; proud of his "folkways"; a typical "Yankee". — The [ɚ] is a short, weakly retroflex sound. All vowels and diphthongs tend to be short.

Fox Hill, Ulysses Twp.

Twp. organized 1832; enlarged 1879. 1st settlement c. 1825 from NY. Lumbering, coal.

PA 30B: M, farmer, 48. B. here. — F., PGF b. here, PGF's F. b. NY or New Eng., PGM b. here; M. b. Ompstead in Co., MGF b. here, MGF's F. b. Germany. — Ed.: till 16. — Methodist. — Good natured, loquacious, quick. — Typical New Eng. intonation and small groups of words as unit of rhythm in sentence; short vowels.

31. Cameron County

Formed 1860 from several cos. Frontier in Rev.; Indian/White troubles till late. First settlements 1804–15; English and Germans from PA, NJ, New Eng. (came up Susquehanna). Fertile valleys; cereals and grasses on uplands. Lumbering (to neglect of agriculture), coal, tanneries. Pop. 1870: 4,273, 1880: 5,159, 1910: 7,644, 1930: 5,307, 1960: 7,586.

> Leeson, Michael A. 1890. *History of the Counties of McKean, Elk, Cameron and Potter.* Chicago: University of Chicago Press.
>
> McKnight, William James. 1905. *A Pioneer Outline History of Northwestern Pennsylvania. . . .* Philadelphia: J. B. Lippincott Co.

Rich Valley, Emporium P.O., Shippen Twp.

Rich Valley settled 1811; 3rd settlement in Co. Holland Company lands. First settlers from NJ (Dutch and English). Rugged terrain: 1000–2112 ft. in elevation. Lumber in 19th cent., mtns. denuded by 1890. Explored for oil (no luck); coal. Emporium settled 1810. Co. seat. Grew with lumber boom; radio factory, tannery, sportsmen's supplies.

PA 31A: M, lumberwoods worker, some farming, 75. B. here (2 yrs. in Buffalo, NY, when over 50). — F. b. near Cuba, NY, PGF b. perhaps near Cuba, NY (of Scottish descent), PGM b. NY with a PGM of Mayflower stock; M., perhaps MGF b. here, MGF's F. b. in NJ (probably of English descent), MGM b. Clearfield Co. — Ed.: till 9. — Wesleyan Methodist. — Quick, intelligent.

PA 31B: M, carpenter, former woodsman, 54. B. here. — F. b. here, PGF b. Loch Haven, Clinton Co., PGF's F., PGM of NJ Dutch descent; M. b. here, MGF b. this side of Loch Haven, Clinton Co. — Ed.: till 13. — Methodist. — Very quick, alert. — Note the [ɚ·] symbol throughout instead of the [r] which the FW has been using further W. Inf.'s use of [ɚ] agrees with types E. of him.

32. Centre County

Formed 1800 from several cos. Survey, first settlers in 1766 (S. part); settlers in N. part 1768 and after: Scotch-Irish predominant, some English, German, French. Settlements abandoned 1779; resettlement 1784. 1st road 1771; canals by 1834; 1st RRs 1857. German Reformed as early as 1789. Iron furnaces from 1792. Woolen mills, tannery, RR shops in 19th cent. Penn State in Co. Pop. 1790: 7,562, 1800: 13,609, 1820: 13,796, 1850: 23,355, 1880: 37,922, 1910: 43,424, 1930: 46,294, 1960: 78,580.

> Linn, John Blair. 1883. *History of Centre and Clinton Counties.* Philadelphia: L. H. Everts.
>
> Maynard, D. S., comp. 1877. *Industries and Institutions of Centre County. . . .* Bellefonte: Richie and Maynard.
>
> Rupp, Israel Daniel. 1847. *History and Topography of Northumberland, Huntingdon, Mifflin, Centre, Union, Columbia, Juniata and Clinton Counties.* Lancaster: G. Hills.
>
> 1898. *Commemorative Biographical Record of Central Pennsylvania.* Chicago: J. H. Beers.

Holt's Hollow, Johnson's Run/Milesburg, Bellefonte P.O., Boggs Twp.

Twp. formed 1814; named for Andrew Boggs, first settler of Co. (pre-Revolutionary). Early settlers Scotch-Irish, some English and Germans. Surveys 1760; most land taking in 1790s. Methodists from late 18th cent.; ironworks and tannery in 19th cent. Milesburg laid out 1793 (small village); Indian village nearby has disappeared. Bellefonte center for farmers, hunters, fishermen; limestone. Surveyed 1769; settled shortly after.

PA 32A: M, farmer, 80. B. here. — F. b. near Pleasant Gap in Co., PGF (of English descent), PGM (partly Dutch) b. Co.; M. b. near Yarnell in Co., MGF of Dutch descent, MGM not Dutch. — Ed.: till 14. — Advent Church. — Feeble, uninterested in questions. — Old-fashioned.

PA 32B: Wingate, Boggs Twp. — M, farmer, 40. — F. b. Union Twp. in Co., PGF b. Co., PGM b. Liberty Twp. in Co.; M., MGF b. Beech Creek on edge of Clinton Co., MGM b. on the boat coming to America from Germany. — Ed.: here till 19. — Methodist. — Slow. — Very vigorous voice with long strong [ɚ·].

33. Blair County

Formed 1846 from Huntingdon and Bedford Cos. Traders in area c. 1734; squatters 1746; purchase from Indians 1754. Some Scotch Irish settlers by 1749; Germans by 1755; also some Dutch, English early. First Presbyterians, then Lutherans; also Mennonites early. One of most mountainous cos. in PA. Military frontier during Rev. Transportation center (RR, canal) in 19th cent. Products and industries: farming, dairying, fruit, lumber, iron and metal products, lead, zinc, brick, paper and paper products, chemicals. Pop. 1850: 21,777, 1880: 52,740, 1910: 108,858, 1930: 139,840, 1960: 137,270.

> Africa, J. Simpson. 1883. *History of Huntingdon and Blair Counties*. Philadelphia: L. H. Everts.
> Davis, Tarring S., ed. 1931. *A History of Blair County*. 2 vols. Harrisburg: National Historical Association.
> Ewing, James H., ed. 1880. *History of the City of Altoona and Blair County*. . . . Altoona: H. Slep's Mirror Print. House.
> Sell, Jesse C. 1911. *Twentieth Century History of Altoona and Blair County*. . . . Chicago: Richmond-Arnold Pub. Co.
> Wolf, George A., ed.-in-chief. 1945. *Blair County's First Hundred Years*. . . . Altoona: Mirror Press.
> 1896. *A History of Blair County*. Altoona: C. B. Clark.
> 1938. *A History of Blair County*. Altoona: Altoona Senior High School.

Blue Knob/Portage, Portage P.O., Greenfield Twp.

Twp. formed from Bedford Co. 1846. SW part of Co. 1st settlers mostly German, c. 1770. Iron furnaces in 19th cent., now gone.

PA 33A: M, farmer, 77. B. here. — F. b. here, PGM b. Bedford Co.; M., MGF b. here, MGM (stepGM) b. WV. — Ed.: till 13. Spoke PA "Dutch" as a child, but has not used the language in mature life. — United Brethren. — Quick, intelligent; rather well-off and progressive. — Slight PA "Dutch" accent evident from his vigorous and slightly far forward articulation. Note pronunciation [mæntəl] as indication of non-English antecedents.

Baughman Settlement, Tyrone P.O., Snyder Twp.

Twp. original in Co. (formed 1846). Extreme N. of Co. Area settled before Rev. Iron furnaces from 1805: gone now. Tyrone settled 1850 (previously immigrants from N. Ireland). Formerly a forge; now paper and textile mills.

PA 33B: M, farmer, 46. B. here. — F. b. here, PGF b. Germany, PGM b. nearby in Clearfield Co.; M. b. Van Scoyok in Co., MGF perhaps of Yankee descent, MGM b. just across line in Centre Co. — Ed.: till 13. — Church of the Brethren (wife), Lutheran (parents). — Vigorous, friendly, quick, intelligent, cooperative.

34. Huntingdon County

Formed 1787 from Bedford Co. 1st settlement Scotch-Irish c. 1754 (also some English); Germans later. 1st public road 1772; turnpike 1817; PA RR main line 1850. Central mountainous range; broken terrain. Grew with iron industry. Iron ore, coal, limestone; misc. industry. Pop. 1790: 7,565,

1820: 20,139, 1850: 24,786, 1880: 33,954, 1910: 38,304, 1930: 39,021, 1960: 39,457.

> Africa, J. Simpson. 1883. *History of Huntingdon and Blair Counties*. Philadelphia: L. H. Everts.
> Lytle, Milton Scott. 1876. *History of Huntingdon County*. . . . Lancaster: W. H. Roy.
> Rupp, Israel Daniel. 1847. *History and Topography of Northumberland, Huntingdon, Mifflin, Centre, Union, Columbia, Juniata and Clinton Counties*. Lancaster: G. Hills.

Nossville, Blair's Mills P.O., Tell Twp.

Twp. formed 1810; on SE border of Co. 1st grant 1755. Uneven terrain. Nossville a "flourishing little hamlet" c. 1880.

PA 34A: M, farmer, 79. B. here. — F., PGF b. Dublin Twp. in Co.; M., MGM b. Tell Twp. — Ed.: till 18. — United Brethren. — Quick, alert, intelligent; limited education and experience with the outside world. Limited understanding of the project; suspicious, interview carried out under very informal circumstances. — Pretty good articulation.

Cassville, Cass Twp.

Twp. formed 1843. Mountainous area. 1st settler in area c. 1773; mostly Scotch-Irish, some Germans among early settlers. Cassville laid out 1797; inc. as a borough 1853. Residential, trading; no industry to 1880s.

PA 34B: M, farmer, 37. B. here. — F., PGF, PGF's F. b. here, PGF's PGF b. Washington Co., MD (of German descent), PGF's M. b. near Backlog in Co. (of "Irish" descent), PGM b. Fulton Co. — M., MGF, MGM b. here. — Ed.: till 17. — Methodist. — Very quick, intelligent; natural.

Huntingdon

Laid out 1767 by Wm. Smith, first provost of U. of PA; named for Countess of Huntingdon, benefactor of Univ. 1st settler c. 1760; early settlers Scotch-Irish and English, Germans later. Co. seat 1787; inc. as borough 1796. Busy industrial center: boilers, machines, sewer pipes, radiators, paper tablets. Pop. 1820: 848, 1850: 1,470, 1880: 4,125, 1910: 6,861, 1930: 7,558, 1960: 7,234.

PA 34C!: F, 75. B. here. — F., M. b. here; grandparents all of old stock in vicinity. — Ed.: here, and finishing school in Phila. — Presbyterian. — Wealthy spinster in an old house; interested in local charities; somewhat senile, unable to understand the purpose of the questioning. Perhaps because of ill health, she stopped about p. 76 and a younger woman took her place. — Cultivated.

PA 34C*: F, "younger". (Substitute for PA 34C c. p. 76.) She stopped abruptly on p. 6 when there were only ten more pages to be done, and nothing would induce her to continue.

35. Mifflin County

Formed 1789 from Cumberland and Northumberland Cos. Opened by purchase 1754. 1st settlers 1754, mainly Scotch-Irish. Germans (esp. Amish) later; predominant now. Rugged mountains and fertile valleys. Canal from 1829. No large industries to 1879. Sand deposits, some iron ore. Pop.

1790: 7,562, 1820: 16,618, 1850: 14,980, 1880: 19,577, 1910: 27,785, 1930: 40,335, 1960: 44,348.

Cochran, Joseph. 1879. *History of Mifflin County.* Harrisburg.

Ellis, F., ed. 1886. *History of That Part of the Susquehanna and Juniata Valleys, Embraced in the Counties of Mifflin, Juniata, Perry, Union and Snyder. . . .* Philadelphia: Everts, Peck and Richards.

Stroup, John Martin. 1939. *The Genesis of Mifflin County.* Lewiston. Repr. 1957 (Lewiston: Mifflin County Historical Society).

Stroup, John Martin. 1942. *The Pioneers of Mifflin County.* Lewiston.

Irishtown, Mattawana P.O., Bratton Twp.

Twp. formed 1850 from Oliver, named after earliest settler (c. 1754). 1st settlers Scots and English; later Germans and Irish.

PA 35A: M, farm laborer, 67. B. here. — F. b. near Mt. Union, just over line in Huntingdon Co., PGF b. in France, PGM b. in Hare's Valley above Mapleton in Huntingdon Co. (of "Dutch" descent); M. b. Duncannon, Perry Co., came here when very young, MGF of "Dutch" descent, MGM b. Thompsontown, Juniata Co. (of "Dutch" descent). — Ed.: till 14. — Dunkard. — Slightly senile and hard of hearing; talkative, likes to have someone listen to him; rather limited intelligence and outlook, but quick in reactions when he grasps the point. — Articulation not too good. — New beginning on p. 63 after a lapse of about four mos.

Ferguson Valley, McVeytown P.O., Oliver Twp.

Twp. formed 1835 from Wayne. 1st settlers (c. 1760s) largely English and Scotch-Irish; one Spaniard. Ferguson Valley settled c. 1780. Some ironmaking, sand works. McVeytown inc. as borough 1833. Rolling farm country; somewhat desolate.

PA 35B: M, farmer, 46. B. here. — F., PGF b. here; M., MGF b. near Huntingdon Co. line, MGM b. Co. — Ed.: here till 17. — Dunkard (Brethren). — Quick, cooperative.

PA 35C: M, farmer, age unknown. — Family of Scotch-Irish descent. — Ed.: had taught. — Presbyterian. — Good education for his community; taciturn; slow.

36. Union County

Formed 1813 from Northumberland Co. Scattered settlements by 1754; permanent settlements by 1769. Scotch-Irish and German, latter came to predominate. Presbyterians 1773; Methodists by 1817. Bucknell Univ. in Lewisburg (Co. seat). Mountainous, but not rugged; Susquehanna watershed. Agriculture, light industry. Pop. 1820: 18,619, 1850: 26,083, 1880: 16,905, 1910: 16,249, 1930: 17,468, 1960: 25,646.

Ellis, F., ed. 1886. *History of That Part of the Susquehanna and Juniata Valleys, Embraced in the Counties of Mifflin, Juniata, Perry, Union and Snyder. . . .* Philadelphia: Everts, Peck and Richards.

Lontz, Mary Belle. 1966. *Union County, 1855–1965.* Milton.

Mauser, I. H. 1880. *History of Lewisburg, Containing Also a Chronological History of Union County.* Lewisburg: the author.

Allenwood P.O., Gregg Twp.

Twp. organized 1865. 1st warrants and settlements 1769. Allenwood a village, laid out in 1815 as Uniontown. Early settlers English, Scotch-Irish, German.

PA 36A: M, retired barber (some farming), 73. B. here. — F. b. here, PGF (of Scotch-Irish descent), PGM ("Dutch") b. Co.; M. b. Gregg Twp., MGF (traveling through), MGM b. here (of Scotch-Irish descent). — Ed.: Sunday school. — Methodist. — Uneducated, humble ancestry; pretty quick. — Slight hesitation in speech; not vigorous.

White Deer Valley, Allenwood P.O., Greg Twp.

Settled by 1800. Mixed pop.: German, Irish, Dutch, English. Very fertile.

PA 36B: M, farmer, 50. B. here. — F. b. 2 mi. over line in Lycoming Co., PGF b. here, PGF's F. b. Belfast, Ireland, PGM b. Lycoming Co. (of Scotch-Irish descent); M. b. here, MGF b. here (of York or Lancaster Co. origin), MGM b. here (of Scottish and Welsh origin). — Ed.: here till 18. — Baptist. — Rather tense and nervous. — He appears to distinguish between [a] and [v_{Λ}].

37. Snyder County

Formed from Union Co. 1855. Pre-Rev. settlement (Indian massacre of settler in 1755). 1st settlers Mohawk Valley Germans c. 1745; a few Scotch-Irish, some English 1755, 1769, but predominantly German. Frontier forts in 1750s. Lutheran and Reformed from 1760; most congregations are of German groups. Center of state, mostly in Susquehanna watershed. Some iron (no longer commercially valuable), timber rafting 1840–80, boatbuilding for canal till 1901. Coal dredging, brickmaking, cigar making; other manufacturing sporadic. Pop. 1860: 15,035, 1880: 17,797, 1910: 16,800, 1930: 18,836, 1960: 25,922.

Dunkelberger, George Franklin. 1948. *The Story of Snyder County. . . .* Selinsgrove: Snyder County Historical Society.

Fisher, Charles A. 1938. *The Snyder County Pioneers.* Selinsgrove.

Wagenseller, George Washington, comp. 1919–. *Snyder County Annals. . . .* Middleburgh: The Middleburgh Post.

1914–. *Snyder County Historical Society Bulletin.* Selinsgrove: The Society.

Troxelville, Adams Twp.

Twp. formed 1874 from Beaver Twp. Pop. mainly German descent. Troxelville founded 1856. Predominantly German; Lutheran Church by 1817. Trading center. Pop. Troxelville 1948: c. 100.

PA 37A: M, farmer, 76. B. here; lived in Kansas 18–20 yrs. old. — F., perhaps PGF b. here; M., prob. MGF b. here, MGM b. across the mountain in Union Co. — Ed.: till 14 (not regular). — Reformed. — Quick, alert, elderly man. Retired from farming 15 yrs. ago; plenty of leisure; more well-to-do than many other elderly infs. — Fairly fluent in English; he and his wife would have preferred an inquiry into the German language.

Independence, Port Treverton P.O., Chapman Twp.

Twp. settled c. 1766 by Germans; English later, also some Scotch-Irish before Rev. Lutherans, United Brethren; predominantly German. Independence a small village on Susquehanna; old horse-change on stage route. Nucleus of village a tavern dating from 1784.

PA 37B: M, farmer, 40. B. here. — F., PGF b. here, PGF's F. of German descent, PGM b. Co. (of German descent); M., MGF, MGM b. here. — Ed.: till 19. — United Brethren in Christ. — Quick, alert, provincial; understood purpose of project and was keenly interested. — The open [ʋ·] and [ɚ] are different from PA German further E. where [ɔ:] and [ᴦ] obtain.

Port Ann

Small village, 3 mi. E. of Troxelville.

PA 37C: M, farm laborer, 78. B. here. — Parents b. here (of PA German descent). — Illiterate. — Hard of hearing; hearty; couldn't see any sense to the questions. — Incomplete: left to go hunting at p. 34.

38. Juniata County

Formed 1831 from Mifflin Co. 1st settlements c. 1749 by Scotch-Irish; Germans later. To Rev. most landowners nonresident. Mountainous; Juniata watershed. Small amounts of iron ore. Chiefly farming; small industries: brick, textiles, clothing. Pop. 1840: 11,080, 1850: 13,029, 1880: 18,227, 1910: 15,013, 1930: 14,325, 1960: 15,874.

Jones, U. J. 1856. *History of the Early Settlement of the Juniata Valley.* Philadelphia. Repr. 1940 (Harrisburg: Telegraph Press).

Rupp, Israel Daniel. 1847. *History and Topography of Northumberland, Huntingdon, Mifflin, Centre, Union, Columbia, Juniata and Clinton Counties.* Lancaster: G. Hills.

1897. *Commemorative Biographical Encyclopedia of the Juniata Valley.* Chambersburg: J. M. Runk.

1936. *A History of the Juniata Valley.* 3 vols. Harrisburg: National Historical Association.

Spruce Hill, Port Royal P.O., Spruce Hill Twp.

Twp. formed 1858. 1st settlers Scotch-Irish c. 1762. Center for building arks, to ship goods down Juniata. Spruce Hill a small village; had P.O. in 1880s.

PA 38A: M, farmer, laborer, 70. B. here. — F. b. on edge of Perry Co., came here when 25, PGF b. Perry Co. (of French descent, but name sounds Irish to FW), PGM b. Co.; M. b. Fermanagh Twp. in Co., MGF b. Co. — Ed.: till 14. — Methodist. — Fairly alert; lives on a pension on the mountainside; one of the few uneducated Scotch-Irish surviving in a country that has become largely "Dutch" (both parents could speak "Dutch", esp. his mother). — Poor enunciation.

Lost Creek Valley, Mifflintown P.O., Fermanagh Twp.

Twp. existed as early as 1762 (antedates Mifflin Co.). Landowners by 1763; chiefly Scotch-Irish in beginning. Germans from 1795; a few Holland Dutch. Laid out 1791; Co. seat 1831. Farming country. Lost Creek Valley site of first settlement in Twp.

PA 38B: M, farmer, 42. B. here. — F. b. E. Salem in Co., PGF b. Co. ("Dutch"), PGM b. Snyder Co. ("Dutch"); M. b. here, MGF b. Schuylkill Co. ("Dutch"), MGM "Dutch". — Ed.: here till 15. — Methodist. — Slight trace of German phonetic character although he has never spoken the language: /i/ is very short and high, /s/ is very clear and hissing. [ðɪs jɪə] is his only pronunciation; he cannot make the English assimilation of [ʃ] when /s/ is followed by /j/.

39. Perry County

Formed 1820 from Cumberland Co. 1st settlement 1741 (Germans), removed; Scotch-Irish settlement 1750–55. Germans eventually predominated. Indian depredations 1756; frontier warfare during the French and Indian War, Pontiac War. Presbyterians first; then Lutheran and Reformed. 1st road 1790; canal and RR from 1834. In Susquehanna/Juniata watershed. Still very rural in 1921. General farming, fruit and dairying; limestone, iron ore, small amount of coal. Pop. 1820: 11,284, 1850: 20,088, 1880: 27,522, 1910: 24,136, 1930: 21,744, 1960: 26,582.

Hain, Harry H. 1922. *History of Perry County.* . . . Harrisburg: Hain-Moore Co.

Rupp, Israel Daniel. 1846. *The History and Topography of Dauphin, Cumberland, Franklin, Bedford, Adams, and Perry Counties.* . . . Lancaster: G. Hills.

Wright, Silas. 1873. *History of Perry County.* . . . Lancaster: Wylie and Griest, Printers.

Eshcol/Ickesburg, Millerstown P.O., Saville Twp.

Twp. formed 1817 from Tyrone. 1st settled 1774 by Scotch-Irish; Germans arrived 1790s. Ickesburg laid out c. 1818; originally a village and trading center built around a sawmill and a distillery. Eshcol a hamlet built around a mill and a church: chiefly German, some Scotch-Irish. Millerstown a farming community; busy in canal building period.

PA 39A: M, farmer, 85. B. here (when 22 and 25 visited IL in summer). — F. b. near Bixlers Mills, Madison Twp. in Co., PGF b. near here, PGF's F. b. perhaps Lebanon Co. (of Mennonite Swiss ancestry), PGM b. here; M. b. Tuscarora Twp. in Co., MGF b. Co. (of English descent), MGM b. Co. (of "Irish" descent). — Ed.: till 19 (his brother went to Princeton; his father would have sent him to the Academy, but he didn't like school). — Reformed. — Alert; of better family background than most of FW's elderly infs. — Articulation a little weak at times.

New Bloomfield, Center Twp.

Twp. formed 1830. First settled 1753 from N. Ireland; other Scotch-Irish in 1755. Germans by 1767; also some English. New Bloomfield Co. seat from 1823; inc. as a borough 1831. 1st settled c. 1780. Scotch-Irish and Germans, some Dutch. 1st church Union; Lutheran and Reformed.

Also Presbyterians early. Academy in 19th cent. No industry; local market.

PA 39B: M, farmer, 41. B. here. — F., PGF b. here, PGF's F. b. Berks Co., PGM b. Pine Hill near Delville toward Duncannon; M. b. Co., MGF b. Loysville in Co., MGM b. Co. — Ed.: here till 15, New Bloomfield Academy till 18. — Lutheran. — In general, quick responses; occasionally a little slow at comprehending.

40. Cumberland County

Co. organized 1750; 6th oldest co. in PA. A seed bed of Scotch-Irish settlements in America; early Scotch-Irish settlements 1715; increased after 1734. Germans 1757–60 and after 1770. Almost all Presbyterians to 1750; Episcopalians, Lutherans, Methodists and others shortly thereafter. Dickinson College (1783) here; also a state college. Valley between mountain ridges; Susquehanna watershed. Good farming. Iron ore and iron making, timber, textiles, leather and rubber goods (Goodyear), metal and metal products, food products. Pop. 1790: 18,243, 1820: 23,606, 1850: 34,327, 1880: 45,977, 1910: 54,479, 1930: 68,236, 1960: 124,816.

Ball, Raymond Martin. 1943. *The Townships of Mother Cumberland....* Washington, PA.

Donehoo, George P., ed-in-chief. 1930. *A History of the Cumberland Valley in Pennsylvania.* 2 vols. Harrisburg: Susquehanna History Association.

Rupp, Israel Daniel. 1846. *The History and Topography of Dauphin, Cumberland, Franklin, Bedford, Adams, and Perry Counties....* Lancaster: G. Hills.

Stewart, Harriet Wylie. 1916. *History of the Cumberland Valley, Pennsylvania.* Middle Spring.

Wiley, Samuel T. 1897. *Biographical and Portrait Cyclopedia of the Nineteenth Congressional District.* Philadelphia: C. A. Ruoff.

Wing, Conway P. 1879. *...History of Cumberland County...* Philadelphia: J. D. Scott.

1886. *History of Cumberland and Adams Counties.* Chicago: Warner, Beers.

1951. *History of Cumberland County.* Carlisle: Hamilton Library and the Historical Association of Cumberland County.

1951. *Two Hundred Years in Cumberland County.* Carlisle: Hamilton Library and Historical Association of Cumberland County.

Newburg, Hopewell Twp.
Twp. laid out in 1735 as part of Lancaster Co. Earliest settlements c. 1731; almost all Scotch-Irish before Revolution. Newburg laid out 1819. Declining in pop. by 1930.

PA 40A: M, farmer, 77. B. here. — F. b. here, PGF b. Big Spring near Newville in Co. (of Scotch-Irish descent), PGM b. N. Ireland (or of that descent); M. b. near Doubling Gap on edge of Perry Co., MGF b. Germantown in Perry Co. (of German descent), MGM b. in the mountains near Germantown. — Ed.: till 15. — Zion Lutheran. — Well-educated, better read than most elderly infs.; insecure; ill-health. — Rapid speech.

Mount Hope, Newville P.O., Upper Mifflin Twp.
Twp. formed from Mifflin 1886. Originally settled by Scotch-Irish. First settlers prob. c. 1734–36. Indian massacres in 1750s. Newville a crossroads industrial community.

PA 40B: M, farmer, 36. B. here. — F. b. here, PGF b. here or in Juniata Co., PGM b. Co.; M., MGF, MGM b. Co. — Ed.: till 16. — Evangelical Church. — Reflective and deliberate, not to be hurried or pushed; however, very quick in general. — Moderate articulation.

41. Adams County

Formed 1800 from York Co. 1st settlement 1734, principally Scotch-Irish; Germans shortly thereafter. Not surveyed till 1766–68. Border dispute with MD early. 1st road 1742; 1st RR 1855. Gettysburg (Co. seat) site of battle, college. Diversified terrain; misc. products and industry: farming, stock raising, iron ore, limestone. Pop. 1800: 13,172, 1820: 19,370, 1850: 25,981, 1880: 32,455, 1910: 34,319, 1930: 37,128, 1960: 51,906.

McPherson, Edward. 1889. *The Story of the Creation of Adams County....* Lancaster: Inquirer Print. Co.

Rupp, Israel Daniel. 1846. *The History and Topography of Dauphin, Cumberland, Franklin, Bedford, Adams, and Perry Counties....* Lancaster: G. Hills.

1880. *History and Directory of the Boroughs of... Adams County.* Gettysburg: John T. Reily.

1886. *History of Cumberland and Adams Counties.* Chicago: Warner, Beers.

Hunterstown, Gettysburg P.O., Strahan Twp.
Twp. original; center of Co., just E. of Gettysburg. Hunterstown plotted 1749–50; farmers' market town. Gettysburg laid out 1780s as Marsh Creek; renamed by 1787. Orig. settled by Scotch-Irish; Germans eventually prevailed. Became Co. seat in 1800; inc. as a borough 1806. Gettysburg College (1832) oldest Lutheran college in country. Highway hub. Quiet college town before battle; now battlefield commercialized, many tourists.

PA 41A: M, farm laborer (makes chairs, axe handles at home), 70. B. here. — F., PGF b. here (PGF of "Irish" descent), PGM b. here; M. b. here, MGF, MGM b. Germany. — Ed.: till 10 (very little). — Mother Presbyterian, father Methodist. — Conversational, many tall tales; felt complimented by the questioning.

Fairfield, Hamiltonban Twp.
Twp. original. Copper; iron manufacturing c. 1830. Fairfield surveyed 1801.

PA 41B: M, farmer, school director, director of local bank, 58. B. Highland Twp. (3 mi. E.). — F. b. Freedom Twp., Adams Co., PGF, PGM b. near Westminster, Carrol Co., MD (both of Scottish descent); M. b. Highland Twp. in Co., MGF, MGM b. Franklin Twp. in Co. (both of German descent). — Ed.: till 18. — Reformed. — Quick, alert; easily amused, genial; not particularly impressed with project. — Manner of utterance rather rustic.

42. Franklin County

Formed 1784 from Cumberland Co. 1st settlement 1730, mainly Scotch-Irish; Germans arriving by 1742. Also heavy German influx 1790–1800. Presbyterians by 1734; Lutherans and Reformed by 1742; also Methodists, United Brethren, German Baptists, and Mennonites in 18th cent. 1st turnpike 1809; RR by 1837. Chambersburg Co. seat; John Brown conspiracy organized here c. 1859. Principally agricultural county; also water power, iron ore, foundries, limestone, some copper. Pop. 1790: 15,655, 1820: 31,892, 1850: 39,904, 1880: 49,855, 1910: 59,775, 1930: 65,010, 1960: 88,172.

Donehoo, George P., ed-in-chief. 1930. *A History of the Cumberland Valley in Pennsylvania*. 2 vols. Harrisburg: Susquehanna History Association.
McCauley, I. H. 1878. *Historical Sketch of Franklin County*. 2nd ed., enl. Harrisburg: Patriot Pub. Co.
Rupp, Israel Daniel. 1846. *The History and Topography of Dauphin, Cumberland, Franklin, Bedford, Adams, and Perry Counties*. . . . Lancaster: G. Hills.
Stoner, Jacob H. 1947. *Historical Papers, Franklin County and the Cumberland Valley*. Comp. by Lu Cole Stoner. Chambersburg: Craft Press.
1887. *History of Franklin County*. . . . Chicago: Warner, Beers.
1905. *The Kittochtinny Magazine: A Tentative Record of Local History and Genealogy West of the Susquehanna*. Chambersburg: G.O. Seilhamer.

Oak Grove, Chambersburg P.O., Letterkenny Twp.

Twp. formed 1761–62. 1st settlers c. 1736. Nearly in center of Co. Chambersburg laid out 1764. Scotch-Irish made first settlement c. 1730. Organized as a borough 1803. Burned by Confederates in 1864 in retaliation for Union depredations. Headquarters of John Brown. Wilson College for women founded here c. 1869. Industrial town (paper, machinery) in midst of farming area.

PA 42A: M, farmer, 59. B. Horse Valley (12 mi. NW). — F., PGF b. Horse Valley, PGF's F. of German descent, PGM b. Horse Valley; M., MGF, MGM b. Horse Valley. — Ed.: till 17. — United Brethren. — Old-fashioned.

Criders Church, Chambersburg P.O., Hamilton Twp.

Twp. formed 1752. 1st settlers in area mainly Scotch-Irish. Criders Church (United Brethren) est. 1840.

PA 42B: M, farmer, 51. B. St. Thomas (a few mi. away). — Parents, paternal and maternal GPs all from St. Thomas area (perhaps Irish descent). — Ed.: grade school. — United Brethren.

43. Fulton County

Formed 1850 from Bedford Co. 1st settlements Scotch-Irish between 1730–40; dispossessed c. 1750. Settlement accelerated again after 1758; Scotch-Irish and Scots. Old turnpike 1814–15. Thinly pop. Mountainous and hilly; good farm country. Leather, tanning; iron ore, timber, limestone, some coal. Pop. 1850: 7,567, 1880: 10,149, 1910: 9,703, 1930: 9,231, 1960: 10,597.

Greathead, Elsie S. 1936. *The History of Fulton County*. McConnellsburg: Fulton County News.
Marks, William E. 1941. *Biographical Survey, Fulton County*.
1884. *History of Bedford, Somerset, and Fulton Counties, Pennsylvania*. Chicago: Waterman, Watkins.

Buck Valley, Hancock (MD) P.O., Union Twp.

Twp. formed 1864. Part of Buck Valley; surveyed 1795. Settled from MD, NJ, SE PA, primarily by Scotch-Irish and English; Germans later.

PA 43A: M, farmer, 79. B. here. — F. b. Bethel Twp. in Co., PGF lived near McConnellsburg; M., MGM b. on the mtn. on edge of Bedford Co. — Ed.: 2 or 3 yrs. — Christian. — Occasionally slow at understanding; couldn't see sense in the project.

Pigeon Cove, Warfordsburg P.O., Bethel Twp.

Twp. formed 1773. Settled by English, Scotch-Irish, German; many from MD (of all groups); many from NJ (mainly English and Scotch).

PA 43B: M, farmer, 51. B. here. — F. b. Belfast Twp. in Co., PGF's F. b. in Germany or England; M. b. Bethel Twp., MGF b. Co., MGM b. Ireland and came to America when 14 (Protestant). — Ed.: till 18. — Christian Church. — Quick responses. — Deep, full voice; resonant. [aˑɛ] instead of [aɨ] seems to indicate MD influence, as does distinction of [ɔˑ·] and [ɑ] phonemes which is not found in the northernmost part of the country.

44. Bedford County

Formed 1771 from Cumberland Co. 1st white exploration from VA 1625. Settlers in area as early as 1710 (killed by Indians 1732). Ft. Bedford 1755–59; town laid out 1766. Scotch-Irish settlers from 1750; some Germans by 1760; also some English among early settlers. Allegheny Mtns.; headwaters of Juniata R. Agriculture (once very fertile valley) and industry: coal early, limestone, fireclay, timber in 19th cent., cigars, foundries and furnaces, RR shops, woolen mills, planing mills. Pop. 1790: 13,124, 1820: 20,248, 1850: 23,052, 1880: 34,929, 1910: 38,879, 1930: 37,309, 1960: 42,451.

Blackburn, E. Howard, and William H. Welfley. 1906. *History of Bedford and Somerset Counties*. . . . 3 vols. NY: Lewis Pub. Co.
Rupp, Israel Daniel. 1846. *The History and Topography of Dauphin, Cumberland, Franklin, Bedford, Adams, and Perry Counties*. . . . Lancaster: G. Hills.
1884. *History of Bedford, Somerset, and Fulton Counties, Pennsylvania*. Chicago: Waterman, Watkins.
1971. *The Kernel of Greatness*. Bedford: Bedford County Heritage Commission.

Clearville, Monroe Twp.

Twp. formed c. 1840. Most early settlers from E. PA (Scotch-Irish and German); some from MD. Clearville a "small village, pleasantly situated". Mixed settlers: Welsh, Scotch-Irish, German. Mainly Protestant. Largest twp. in Co.

PA 44A: M, farmer, 75. B. E. Providence Twp., 5 mi. NE. — F. b. Twp., PGF b. Cumberland Valley in Co., PGM b. Twp., PGM's F. b. Clear Ridge in Co., PGM's PGF b. Hesse-Cassel, Germany; M. b. E. Providence Twp., MGF b. Monroe Twp., MGF's F., MGF's M. of "Irish descent", MGM b. Twp. — Ed.: till 16. — Methodist. — Obliging, conversational, quick at responding; occasionally senile and unable to understand.

Clear Ridge, Everett P.O., West Providence Twp.

Twp. formed 1854 (Providence formed c. 1780). Early settlers in the area mainly Scotch-Irish and English from E. PA and MD; also Germans fairly early.

PA 44B: M, farmer, 51. B. here. — F., PGF b. here (of VA stock), PGM b. here, PGM's M. b. Colerain Twp.; M., MGF b. here, MGF's M. of Welsh descent, MGM b. here (step MGM, step MGM's F. b. here). — Ed.: till 17. — Christian. — Not very quick at understanding.

45. Somerset County

Formed 1775 from Bedford Co. 1st settlement c. 1762; English and Welsh. Germans, Quakers, Tories by 1769; also some Scotch-Irish and Holland Dutch. Baptists first; Reformed, Evangelical Lutheran, Brethren followed. Sixth largest co. in PA. Mountainous, undulating terrain; highest elevation in state of PA. Agriculture; lumber (19th cent.), coal, iron ore, natural gas, limestone, maple syrup, clothing. Pop. 1800: 10,188, 1820: 13,974, 1850: 24,416, 1880: 33,110, 1910: 67,717, 1930: 80,764, 1960: 77,450.

Blackburn, E. Howard, and William H. Welfley. 1906. *History of Bedford and Somerset Counties.* . . . 3 vols. NY: Lewis Pub. Co.

Cassady, John C. 1932. *The Somerset County Outline.* Scottdale: Mennonite Pub. House.

Doyle, Frederic Clyde. 1945. *Early Somerset County.* Somerset: Somerset County Historical Society.

1884. *History of Bedford, Somerset, and Fulton Counties, Pennsylvania.* Chicago: Waterman, Watkins.

Humbert, Confluence P.O., Lower Turkeyfoot Twp.

Twp. formed 1848 by division of Turkeyfoot. Turkeyfoot est. as twp. 1773; first settlement c. 1755 by 20 families from NJ, mostly Baptists, prob. English. Also some Scotch-Irish among early settlers; others from VA and MD. Agricultural lime manufactured since 1840. Humbert a small mining and lumbering town which sprang up after Virginia Coal Co. opened mines in 1901. Confluence a borough, shipping point on RR.

PA 45A: M, farmer, 81. B. here. Has lived various places along Laurel Ridge around Confluence, Humbert, etc. Presently living with daughter 1 mi. over the line in Fayette Co. — F. b. Upper Turkeyfoot Twp. near Kingwood in Co., PGF of German descent; M. b. Mechanicsburg in Co., MGF b. near Meyersdale in Co. — Ed.: till 18. — Methodist. — Fairly quick, alert, genial; not completely aware of purpose of the project.

Boone/Shanksville, Friedens P.O., Stony Creek Twp.

Twp. formed c. 1792. 1st permanent settler in 1766 from E. PA. Germans most numerous; also Welsh and Ulster Scots.

Shanksville settled c. 1798; first settler from near Hagerstown, MD. Gristmill and woolen mill, sawmills. Village laid out 1829; inc. as a borough 1912. Everett laid out 1795. Grew slowly till RR (1862); then pop. quadrupled in 20 yrs. Fields, coal mines, iron furnaces, quarries.

PA 45B: M, farmer, 43. B. here. — F., PGF b. here, PGF's F. of German descent, PGM b. here; M., MGF b. Shade Twp. — Ed.: till 15. — Lutheran. — Quick, alert. — Distinct PA German accent: forward articulation, unvoicing.

46. Fayette County

Formed 1783 from Westmoreland Co. Frontier with France in 1750s; peaceably settled after French and Indian War. 1st settlement from VA c. 1752 interrupted by French and Indian War; resumed 1758. Thereafter settled more aggressively from VA. 1st road c. 1759; RR at least from 1844; Monongahela opened to navigation c. 1844. Coal, iron ore and iron making, limestone, fire clay. Pop. 1790: 13,325, 1820: 27,285, 1850: 39,112, 1880: 58,842, 1910: 107,449, 1930: 198,542, 1960: 169,340.

Abraham, Evelyn. 1936. *Over the Mountains.* Uniontown: The Herald-Genius.

Ellis, Franklin, ed. 1882. *History of Fayette County.* . . . Philadelphia: L. H. Everts.

Gresham, John M., ed. 1889. *Biographical and Portrait Cyclopedia of Fayette County.* Chicago: J. M. Gresham.

Jordan, John W., ed. 1912. *Genealogical and Personal History of Fayette and Greene Counties.* 3 vols. NY: Lewis Historical Pub. Co.

Shepherd, Henry Elliott, ed. 1900. *Nelson's Biographical Dictionary and Historical Reference Book of Fayette County.* . . . Uniontown: S. B. Nelson.

Sheppard, Muriel E. 1947. *Cloud by Day: The Story of Coal and Coke and People.* Chapel Hill: University of N.C. Press.

Veech, James. 1910. *The Monongahela of Old.* Pittsburgh.

Greenbriar/Ohiopyle, Dunbar P.O., Stewart Twp.

Twp. formed 1857; E. side of Co. 1st English-speaking settlers arrived 1772. Early settlers from E. PA, NJ. Ohiopyle only village in Twp.; RR there 1871. Salt licks in early 19th cent.

PA 46A: M, laborer (some timber work), 61. B. here. — F., M. b. here (inf. thinks all of old stock in Co.). — Ed.: very little (part of 3 winters). — Baptist. — Quick, uneducated, humble. — [ɔː] and [ɑ] are distinct, although the middle-aged type from Luzerne Twp. uses only one phoneme, [ɑ˞·], for both.

Dawson, Lower Tyrone Twp.

Twp. formed 1877 from Tyrone, which existed before Rev. First settler 1766; early settlers from VA, MD, some from E. PA via MD. Dawson first settled 1786; inc. as a borough in 1872. Almost completely Scotch-Irish. Has some mines.

PA 46B: M, farmer, 45. B. Luzerne Twp. near Brownsville (moved here 4 yrs. ago). — F., PGF b. Luzerne Twp. (of English descent); M. b. Luzerne Twp. — Ed.: till 16. — Presbyterian. — Only average education, but very alert, gifted with intellectual curiosity; appreciated project. — The [ɒ˞· ɑ·]

forms appear to be the same phoneme, with rounding actually almost never present.

47. Greene County

Formed 1796 from S. Washington Co. Ohio Co. territory 1748; some settlements c. 1754, eventually wiped out. Permanent settlement beginning 1766; early settlers from VA. Predominantly Scotch-Irish. In Monongahela Valley. Natural forests, corn, grass, small grains, coal, iron, salt. Pop. 1800: 8,605, 1820: 15,554, 1850: 22,136, 1880: 28,273, 1910: 28,882, 1930: 41,767, 1960: 39,424.

> Bates, Samuel P. 1888. *History of Greene County*. Chicago: Nelson, Rishforth.
>
> Evans, Lewis K. 1941. *Pioneer History of Greene County*. Waynesburg: Waynesburg Republican.
>
> Garretson, Lucretia E. D. 1945. *History of Greene County, Pennsylvania by A. J. Waychoff*. Des Moines.
>
> Hanna, William. 1882. *History of Greene County*.
>
> Meginness, John F. 1857. *Otzinachson: Or, A History of the West Branch Valley of the Susquehanna*. Philadelphia: H. B. Ashmead.

PA 47A: New Freeport. — M, farmer, carpenter, 90. B. Franklin Twp. When 4 or 5 moved to Jackson Twp.; when 6 to New Freeport; and in spring to Hill Twp., 2 mi. away, where he has been nearly all his life. — F. b. below Waynesburg, Franklin Twp., in Co., PGF b. Co. (descendant of Englishman who came to America with Wm. Penn); M. b. below Waynesburg, MGF's M. "Irish", MGM b. below Waynesburg. — Ed.: 6 mos. — Church of God. — Very quick, alert, old-fashioned type.

Waynesburg, Whitely Twp.

Twp. originally a VA settlement. Waynesburg laid out 1796. Agricultural center. Location of Waynesburg College (1849). Pop. 1820: 298, 1850: 852, 1880: 1,208, 1910: 3,545, 1930: 4,915, 1960: 5,188.

PA 47B: M, farmer, 49. B. here. — F., PGF b. here, PGF's F. b. MD, PGM b. Co.; M. b. Franklin Twp. in Co., raised by foster parents (both of Greene Co.). — Ed.: till 18. — Methodist. — Obliging conversationalist; quick, alert; occasional slight difficulties in grasping questions. — Rather old-fashioned, carelessly articulated, gruff-voiced speech.

48. Washington County

Formed from Westmoreland Co. 1773. Monongahela Valley; early settlements close to Monongahela. Traders before 1740; driven out 1754. 1st settlers from VA. Influx of Scotch-Irish in 1773, esp. from E. PA and Ulster. VA had set up counties (and courts) in SW PA by 1776; conflicting VA-PA claims early. Presbyterians dominant early; church by at least 1798. First turnpike 1816; Monongahela navigation 1817. Coal mining, industrial sand (glass) early; limestone, oil and gas, steel industry; also agriculture (cattle, wool). Pop. 1790: 23,901, 1820: 40,038, 1850: 44,939, 1880: 55,418, 1910: 143,680, 1930: 204,802, 1960: 217,271.

> Creigh, Alfred. 1871. *History of Washington County*. . . . 2nd ed., rev. Harrisburg: B. Singerly, Printer.
>
> Crumrine, Boyd, ed. 1882. *History of Washington County*. . . . Philadelphia: L. H. Everts.
>
> Crumrine, Boyd. 1909. *The Bibliography of Washington County, Pennsylvania*. Harrisburg: Pennsylvania Federation of Historical Societies.
>
> Forrest, Earle R. 1926. *History of Washington County*. 3 vols. Chicago: Clarke Pub. Co.
>
> McFarland, Joseph F. 1910. *Twentieth Century History of the City of Washington and Washington County*. . . . Chicago: Richmond-Arnold Pub. Co.
>
> 1893. *Commemorative Biographical Record of Washington County*. . . . Chicago: J. H. Beers.
>
> 1910. *Publications of the Washington County, Pennsylvania, Historical Society*. Washington, PA: The Society.

Burnsville, West Finley Twp.

Twp. formed 1826 (Finley est. 1788). Extreme SW of Co. 1st settled c. 1780 by Scotch-Irish. Farming; sheep and stock raising. Burnsville est. c. 1832. Primarily Presbyterian; pop. c. 200 in 1900.

PA 48A: M, farmer, carpenter, 89. B. E. Finley (5 mi. E.). — F. b. E. Finley, PGF, PGM b. Dublin, Ireland (Protestant, came here just after marriage); M. b. E. Finley, MGF b. PA prob. in Co. (he and MGM of "German" descent). — Ed.: till 17 (4 mos. yearly, off and on). — United Brethren. — Quick, intelligent, somewhat senile. — Articulation not perfect (teeth); he differs from the N.-of-Pittsburgh type (which the middle-aged inf. from this co. approximates) in distinguishing [ɑɾ] and [ɔɾ] and in using an unrounded vowel in *not, knob*.

Buffalo, Hopewell Twp.

Twp. est. 1781; an original twp. One of first settlers arrived in 1779 with a VA land title; Scotch-Irish, English, and Germans among early settlers. Farming; mainly Presbyterians. Buffalo a hamlet of 12 dwellings in 1880, including a post office and a store.

PA 48B: M, farmer, 70. B. Buffalo Twp. — F. b. Buffalo Twp., PGF, PGM b. prob. Washington Co.; M. prob. b. Co., MGF of Scotch-Irish descent. — Ed.: till 15 (8th grade). — United Presbyterian. — Vigorous, hearty; rather humble, but not particularly old-fashioned in character.

Sugar Run, Eighty-Four P.O., Nottingham Twp.

Twp. formed 1781. Hilly area. Largely Presbyterian. Pop. declining. Sugar Run largely rural to 1900.

PA 48C: M, farmer, 44. B. Union Twp. — F., PGF b. here, PGF's F. of Holland Dutch descent, PGM b. OH (of English descent); M. b. Union Twp., MGF b. England, MGM b. Union Twp., MGM's F. b. Ireland (Protestant), MGM's M. of Irish descent. — Ed.: till 18; 6 mos. at California Normal School, California, PA; 2 yrs. business college in Washington, PA. — Presbyterian. — Not very well-off; quick, nervous. — Rather shrill, high-pitched voice; old-fashioned speech.

49. Westmoreland County

Formed 1773 from Bedford Co. First settlers c. 1758: squatters and military allotments. First permanent settlers in late 1760s; early settlers primarily Scotch-Irish. Hannastown 1st Co. seat; burnt 1782. Dispute between PA and VA settlers over boundaries. Presbyterians dominant early: 7 congregations before Rev., and 5 others by 1790. Also Reformed, Evangelical Lutheran, United Brethren, Methodist, Mennonites. Heavily Scotch-Irish, some Quakers and Germans. Turnpike from 1806; canal and RR from 1826. Agricultural co. till 1860, then coal and iron and limestone, eventually steelmaking. Other products: salt, oil, gas, clay, granite, glass, aluminum. Pop. 1790: 16,018, 1820: 30,540, 1850: 51,726, 1880: 78,036, 1910: 231,304, 1930: 294,995, 1960: 352,629.

Albert, George Dallas. 1882. *History of the County of Westmoreland.* . . . Philadelphia: L. H. Everts.

Bomberger, Christian. 1941. *A Short History of Westmoreland County.* . . . Jeannette: Jeannette Pub. Co.

Gresham, John M., ed. 1890. *Biographical and Historical Cyclopedia of Westmoreland County.* Philadelphia: J. M. Gresham.

Wiley, Samuel T. 1890. *Westmoreland County Biography.* Philadelphia: Dunlap and Clarke.

Crisp, Rector P.O., Cook Twp.

Twp. formed 1855. Settled early by English, Scots, Scotch-Irish.

PA 49A: M, farmer, 72. B. here; lived 3 yrs. at Manor Station in Co. — F. b. Twp., PGF b. Co., PGF's F. b. Dublin, Ireland (Protestant), PGM b. Keffer in Co., PGM's F. b. Co.; M. b. here, MGF b. Co. (partly "Dutch" descent), MGM b. here ("Irish" descent). — Ed.: till 15. — United Brethren. — Very quick, alert; said he enjoyed the "interrogation". — Not particularly old-fashioned.

Mansville/Stahlstown, Ligonier P.O., Cook Twp.

Stahlstown on edge of Twp.; named after early German settler. Ligonier laid out 1820. Resort; mining, dairying, farming center.

PA 49B: M, farmer, 44. B. here. — F., PGF b. here, PGF's F. prob. b. here (of Scotch-Irish descent), PGM b. here, PGM's F. prob. b. here (of "German" descent); M., MGF, MGM, MGM's F. b. Ligonier Twp. (of Scotch-Irish and German descent). — Ed.: till 17. — Methodist. — Vigorous, hearty; glad to talk. — Rather old-fashioned speech; prolongation of vowels.

50, 51. Allegheny County

Formed in 1788 from Westmoreland and Washington Cos. At confluence of Allegheny and Monongahela Rivers. NY traders may have reached W. PA as early as 1692; Virginia-Ohio Co. had post here before 1750. Settlements in W. PA by 1755. Disputed territory: VA claim, French 1754, British 1758. 1st town at Pittsburgh by 1769. Originally settled chiefly by Scotch-Irish. Presbyterians dominant in early days; also Moravians, Methodists, Baptists, Evangelical Protestants, and Episcopalians in 18th cent.; Reformed and Lutheran, Roman Catholics shortly thereafter. Pittsburgh Academy est. 1819; became U. of Pitts. 1908. Duquesne U. est. 1878. Natural resources include coal, oil, gas; other products: glass, iron and steel. Pop. 1790: 10,322, 1820: 34,921, 1850: 138,290, 1880: 355,869, 1910: 1,018,463, 1930: 1,374,410, 1960: 1,628,587.

Baldwin, Leland D. 1937. *Pittsburgh: The Story of a City.* Pittsburgh: University of Pittsburgh Press.

Bruce, Thomas. 1894. *Heritage of the Trans-Allegheny Pioneers.* Baltimore: Nichols, Killam and Maffitt.

Church, Samuel Harden. 1908. *A Short History of Pittsburgh.* . . . NY: De Vinne Press.

Craig, Neville B. 1851. *The History of Pittsburgh.* . . . Pittsburgh: J. H. Mellor.

Durant, Samuel W. 1876. *History of Allegheny County.* . . . Philadelphia: L. H. Everts.

Fleming, George Thornton. 1922. *History of Pittsburgh and Environs.* 5 vols. NY: American Historical Society.

Harper, Frank C. 1931. *Pittsburgh of Today.* 4 vols. NY: American Historical Society.

Harper, Frank C. 1957. *Pittsburgh, Forge of the Universe.* . . . NY: Comet Press Books.

Holt, Michael F. 1969. *Forging a Majority: The Republican Party in Pittsburgh, 1848–1860.* New Haven, CT: Yale University Press.

Kelly, George E., ed. 1938. *Allegheny County, a Sesqui-Centennial Review.* Pittsburgh: Allegheny County Sesqui-Centennial Committee.

Killikelly, Sarah H. 1906. *The History of Pittsburgh.* . . . Pittsburgh: B. C. and Gordon Montgomery Co.

Lambing, A. A., and J. E. White. 1888. *Allegheny County: Its Early History and Subsequent Development.* Pittsburgh: Allegheny County Centennial Committee.

Lorant, Stefan. 1964. *Pittsburgh.* Garden City, NY: Doubleday.

Macartney, Clarence E. 1936. *Not Far from Pittsburgh: Places and Personalities in the History of the Land beyond the Alleghenies.* Pittsburgh: Gibson Press.

Reiser, Catherine Elizabeth. 1951. *Pittsburgh's Commercial Development, 1800–1850.* Harrisburg: Pennsylvania Historical and Museum Commission.

Swetnam, George. 1958. *Where Else But Pittsburgh?* Pittsburgh: Davis and Warde.

Thurston, George H. 1888. *Allegheny County's Hundred Years.* Pittsburgh: A. A. Anderson, Printers.

1889. *History of Allegheny County.* Chicago: A. Warner.

Elizabeth

River port up Monongahela. Twp. formed 1788. 1st land patent 1769. Many early settlers from E. PA. Elizabeth borough oldest town on Monongahela; inc. 1834. Boatyard, fertile land, coal from 1815, boatbuilding in 19th cent. Pop. 1790: 1,597, 1820: 2,493, 1850: 3,970, 1880: 3,361, 1910: 2,587, 1930: 2,939, 1960: 2,597.

PA 50A: M, carpenter and farmer, now roadworker, 80. B. here. — F. b. here, PGF of PA "Dutch" descent; M. b. here, MGF b. Twp. — Ed.: till 12. — United Presbyterian. — Not well; hard of hearing, slow and confused in comprehension.

McKeesport, Elizabeth Twp.

Title acquired 1755; town laid out 1795. 1st inhabitants chiefly Scotch-Irish. Inc. as borough 1834; as city 1890. Center of conflict during Whiskey Rebellion. Growth from 1830 with opening of coal mines and various metal-producing shops (plates, alloys). Highly developed industry; large foreign population (1,000 Swedes by 1888). Pop. 1850: 1,392, 1880: 8,212, 1910: 42,694, 1930: 54,632, 1960: 45,489.

PA 50B: F, housewife, over 70. B. here. — F. b. here, PGF prob. b. PA (of Scotch descent), PGM of Scotch descent; M., MGF maybe Irish descent. — Ed.: till 17. — United Presbyterian Church. — Quick, alert, cooperative mind; volunteered to answer because of husband's deafness. — Speech not as conservative as her husband's.

Forward Twp., Elizabeth P.O.

1st settlers from NJ in 1766. No villages, no churches as of 1888. Coal, paper.

PA 50C!: M, farmer, 47. B. here. — F., PGF, PGF's F. b. here, PGF's PGF, PGF's PGM b. County Down, Ireland, PGF's M. b. west PA, near here, PGM b. New Concord, OH, PGM's F. b. Youngstown, Westmoreland Co., PA, PGM's M. b. OH ("Dutch"); M., MGF, MGF's F. b. Elizabeth Twp., MGF's PGF b. Fayette Co., near Laurel Hill (of "Dutch" descent), MGF's M., MGM, MGM's F. b. Elizabeth Twp., MGM's PGF b. Scotland, MGM's PGM lived Westmoreland Co., MGM's M. b. Elizabeth Twp. — Ed.: h.s. in Elizabeth. — Presbyterian. — Rather quick, intelligent; an established local farming family. — Cultivated.

Wilkinsburg

"Typical residential suburb". Settled 1780; predominantly Scotch-Irish at the beginning. Inc. as a borough 1887. Some coal interests here. Pop. 1850: 3,019, 1880: 4,426, 1910: 18,924, 1930: 29,639, 1960: 30,066.

PA 51A: F, sewing at home, 74. B. Allegheny City (now part of the N. side of Pittsburgh). — F. b. Belfast, Ireland, came here as a boy; M. b. Allegheny City (now Pittsburgh), MGF b. Ireland (Protestant). — Ed.: grade school. — United Presbyterian. — Friendly, cooperative, loquacious; quick, alert in reactions.

Green Tree Borough, Pittsburgh

Borough formed 1885 from Union Twp. Exclusively agricultural with suburban propensities. C. 1765 was private manor of the Penns; sold 1786. Trading center with the West from before 1800; shipbuilding. 1834 RR and canal link with Phila.; other canals to OH and Lake Erie. 1836 damming of Monongahela. Pittsburgh surveyed for town 1784; inc. as borough 1794. Germans had first church; Lutherans, Presbyterians, Episcopal in 18th cent. Allegheny and Monongahela join here. Turnpikes, canals, first steamboat to New Orleans by 1811. Steady growth as manufacturing center, esp. for steel. Arms manufacturing 1861–65 (had also prospered during the War of 1812). By 1865, 1/2 steel in US, 1/3 glass manufactured here. AfAms imported as strikebreakers 1875. Large foreign-born pop. from S. and E. of Europe. Shift to sheet and rolled steel in 1930s (autos and canning). U. of Pitts. est. 1787. Products and industries (in addition to steel and glass): coal, coke, clay, electrical equipment, chemicals, pickles, preserves; large banking center. Also developed as a distributing center: 1st for rivers, then RRs.

PA 51B: F, housewife, middle-aged. B. Pittsburgh (Fulton), came here from Pittsburgh 12 years ago. — F. b. Pitts., PGF b. Windsor, CT, PGM b. Pitts.; M. b. Pitts., MGF, MGM b. Ireland (MGF Presbyterian). — Ed.: 7th grade. — Episcopal.

— Somewhat reserved, but very cooperative; respectful toward the educated; guileless in expression and phrasing for the most part. — Good articulation.

52. Beaver County

Formed 1800 from Allegheny and Washington Cos. Ohio Company grant (VA) 1748. Ft. McIntosh on present site of Beaver 1778; 1st land patent (VA) 1779. Earliest settlers included a German and others from Ireland, NW VA, and from near Phila. Presbyterians and Scotch-Irish prevailed among earliest immigrants. Harmony Society here 1825. Canal authorized 1831. Area somewhat isolated till opening of RRs c. 1849; settlement retarded by Indian troubles and conflicting land claims. Products and industries: farming (esp. sheep and grains), coal, iron ore, fire clay, sandstone, petroleum, shipbuilding, water power. Pop. 1800: 5,776, 1820: 15,340, 1850: 26,689, 1880: 39,605, 1910: 78,353, 1930: 149,062, 1960: 206,948.

Bausman, Joseph H. 1904. *History of Beaver County.* . . . 2 vols. NY: Knickerbocker Press.

Bryan, Robert M. 1924. *Historical Events of South Side, Beaver County, Pennsylvania.* Hookstown.

Federal Writers' Project. 1937. *Harmony Society in Pennsylvania.* Philadelphia: William Penn Association.

Jordan, John W., ed. 1914. *Genealogical and Personal History of Beaver County.* 2 vols. NY: Lewis Historical Pub. Co.

1888. *History of Beaver County.* Philadelphia: A. Warner.

1968. *Bibliography of the Harmony Society.* Ambridge: William Penn Association.

Cannelton, Darlington Twp.

Twp. formed 1847 from Little Beaver. Rolling terrain, fertile soil. Presbyterian cong. by 1798. Cannelton named for bed of cannel coal. Roman Catholic church here by 1861. Mining village.

PA 52A: M, coal miner, small farmer, 76. B. here. — F., PGF, PGM b. here; M., MGF b. here (MGF of "Dutch" descent). — Ed.: till 12 or 14 (off and on). — Methodist. — Somewhat senile.

Darlington

Borough settled c. 1795; town laid out 1804. Predominantly Scotch-Irish and Presbyterian. Village barely held its own since RRs. Academy here 19th cent.

PA 52B!: M, farmer, 48. B. here. — F., PGF b. Frankfort Springs in Co., PGF's F. b. Culpeper, VA, PGM b. Butler Co., OH; M., MGF b. here, MGF's F. b. Westmoreland Co., PA, MGM b. here. — Ed.: till 16 Slippery Rock (2 years Normal School). — Presbyterian. — Intelligent, somewhat self-conscious; somewhat better education than many; has traveled some (CA, NY). — Cultivated.

53. Lawrence County

Formed 1849 from Beaver and Mercer Cos. First attempt at settlement 1793; 1st permanent settlement 1794. Settled chiefly by Scotch-Irish; some Germans, some English and Dutch. Welsh immigrants in 1890s to work tinplate shops. Diversified farming; iron and iron mfg. (from 1810), coal, limestone, oil, gas, clay. Pop. 1850: 21,079, 1880: 33,312, 1910: 70,032, 1930: 97,258, 1960: 112,965.

Durant, Samuel W. 1877. *History of Lawrence County.* Philadelphia: L. H. Everts.

Hazen, Aaron L. 1908. *Twentieth Century History of New Castle and Lawrence County.* Chicago: Richmond-Arnold Pub. Co.

Richards, Bart. 1968. *Lawrence County: A Compact History.* New Castle: New Castle Area School District.

Weller Hill/Princeton, New Castle P.O., Slippery Rock Twp.

Twp. one of 13 original twps. in Co. Has had limestone quarries and iron furnaces. Princeton laid out 1841. New Castle an early trading center (capital of Delawares, 1756). Co. seat; laid out 1802, inc. 1867. Industrial and RR center; cement works, metal products, brewery, hotelware potteries; formerly steel and tin mills (closed in 1930s).

PA 53A: M, farmer, 78. B. here. — F. b. here, PGF b. Mercer Co. (perhaps Irish); M. b. Allegheny Co. and came here when young, MGF Scotch descent. — Ed.: till 17. — Presbyterian. — Senile; somewhat slow and deaf. — Old-fashioned.

PA 53B: Weigletown, New Castle P.O., Slippery Rock Twp. — M. farmer, 43. B. here. — F. b. here, PGF b. Shenanggo Twp., PGF's F. of Scotch-Irish descent, PGM b. here (of "Irish" descent); M., MGF b. here, MGF's F. lived here, MGF's M. b. Allegheny Co., PA, MGM, MGM's F., MGM's M. of Butler Co. — Ed.: h.s. at Grove City, Mercer Co. — United Presbyterian. — Quick, alert.

54. Butler County

Formed 1800 from Allegheny Co. Earliest settlers 1790s; mainly Scotch-Irish, some Germans (some from MD), English (from NY). Also settlers from Westmoreland Co., PA, and from New Eng. Various Utopian colonies (mainly German), such as Harmony Society. 1st settlers largely Presbyterian; Lutherans by 1796 and a Roman Catholic church by 1806; others later. Important early oil well in 1859, field exploited till end of 19th cent., now played out. 1st utilization of natural gas 1872. Other industries: clay, limestone, coal, iron ore, salt wells. Pop. 1800: 3,916, 1820: 10,193, 1850: 30,346, 1880: 52,536, 1910: 72,689, 1930: 80,480, 1960: 114,639.

Brown, Robert C., ed. 1895. *History of Butler County.* Chicago: R. C. Brown.

McKee, James A. 1909. *Twentieth Century History of Butler and Butler County.* . . . Chicago: Richmond-Arnold Pub. Co.

Sipe, C. Hale. 1927. *History of Butler County.* 2 vols. Indianapolis: Historical Pub. Co.

1883. *History of Butler County.* Chicago: Waterman, Watkins.

Nixon, Butler P.O., Penn Twp.

One of 13 original twps. in Co. English and Scots arrived in the 1790s. Mainly agricultural. Butler laid out 1803. Diversified industry: plate-glass, refrigerators, RR cars, metal products, machinery and supplies for oil fields, coal, gas, limestone. Labor 90% American born.

PA 54A: F, housewife, 83. B. Adams Twp., came here 55 years ago. — F. b. Adams Twp., PGF, PGM of German descent; M. b. Adams Twp., MGF of Scotch descent, MGM b. Craubery Twp. in Co. (of Scottish descent). — Ed.: 4 mos. yearly for 4 or 5 years (ages 10–14). — Baptist father, Presbyterian mother. — Patient, willing to cooperate in an altruistic spirit, although she may not have understood completely the nature of the project; senile reaction and imperfect perception of questions at times. — Slightly hard of hearing; articulation fairly good.

PA 54A*: Butler. — M, "aged". — Senile; family objected to questioning.

Brownsdale, Butler P.O., Penn Twp.

Brownsdale a small settlement founded 1844. Local village market; once had oil fields.

PA 54B: M, farmer, 53. B. here (spent 3 years S. of Pittsburgh). — F., PGF b. here, PGM b. Lima, OH; M., MGF b. Forward Twp. — Ed.: till 15. — Methodist. — Very quick, alert; somewhat bored. — Articulation not too loud or clear.

55. Mercer County

Formed 1800 from Allegheny Co. 1st settlements 1795 after Wayne's victory at Fallen Timbers. 1st settlers principally Scotch-Irish and Presbyterian from E. PA and Ireland. Also Methodists, Baptists, and Lutherans by 1805; others later. 1st turnpike 1816; canal by 1836, RRs later. Agriculture, coal, iron and steel. Pop. 1800: 3,228, 1820: 11,681, 1850: 33,172, 1880: 56,161, 1910: 77,699, 1930: 99,246, 1960: 127,519.

Durant, Samuel W. 1877. *Eighty Years of Mercer County, 1796–1876.* Philadelphia: Everts.

Stokely, Benjamin. 1850. Remarks and General Observations on Mercer County. *Pennsylvania Historical Society Memoirs* 4.2:65–82.

White, John G., ed. 1909. *A Twentieth Century History of Mercer County.* 2 vols. Chicago: Lewis Pub. Co.

1888. *History of Mercer County.* Chicago: Brown, Runk.

1971–. *Mercer County History.* Mercer: Mercer County Historical Society.

Leesburg, Volant P.O., Springfield Twp.

Twp. formed 1805. S. part of Co. 1st settlement 1796; early settlers German, Scotch-Irish, Irish, English. Leesburg a small hamlet with a market. 1st house there 1828.

PA 55A: M, farmer, 85. B. on the line of Lawrence Co. — F. b. Plain Grove, Lawrence Co., PGF perhaps b. in England, PGM, PGM's F. b. Plain Grove Twp., Law. Co.; M. b. Pine Twp., Mercer Co. — Ed.: till 19 (off and on). — Presbyterian. — Intelligent, somewhat feeble. — Not as old-fashioned as might be expected.

Pleasant Valley, Mercer P.O., Findley Twp.

Twp. formed 1847 from Springfield. S. part of Co. Fertile soil, good grazing. 1st settlers arrived 1799 from SE and SW PA; English, Scotch-Irish, Irish, a few Germans. Mercer settled c. 1800. Once a nationally known horse mart; also a mechandising center till rise of Pittsburgh, Sharon, and Youngstown. Potatoes.

PA 55B: M, farmer, 40. B. here. — F. b. here, PGF b. Co., PGM b. Springfield Twp. in Co.; M., MGF, MGM b. Co. (MGF of Lawrence Co. stock). — Ed.: till 18 (h.s.), 8 week course at State College. — Presbyterian. — Quick, intelligent.

56. Venango County

Formed 1800 from Allegheny and Lycoming Cos. French and English forts here in middle 18th cent. Area open to settlement after Ft. Stannix treaty in 1784. First permanent settlement 1790. Early settlers from SW PA, central PA, MD, Ireland, NJ, NY; many Scotch-Irish, some English, Irish-Catholics, Germans. Settlement slow till after War of 1812. Presbyterians active from 1801; others followed. First oil strike in US here c. 1857, but oil production fell off after 1865. Iron, coal, dairying. Pop. 1800: 1,130, 1820: 4,915, 1850: 18,310, 1880: 43,670, 1910: 56,359, 1930: 63,226, 1960: 65,295.

> Babcock, Charles A. 1919. *Venango County.* . . . 2 vols. Chicago: J. H. Beers.
> Bell, Herbert C., ed. 1890. *History of Venango County.* Chicago: Brown, Runk.
> Eaton, Samuel John Mills. 1876. *Centennial Discourse: A Sketch of the History of Venango County.* Franklin: Venango Spectator Job Office.
> Newton, J. H., ed. 1879. *History of Venango County.* . . . Columbus, OH: J. A. Caldwell.

Hannasville, Cochranton P.O., Canal Twp.

Twp. formed 1835 from Sugar Creek. NW part of Co. 1st settlements c. 1797: Ulster Scots, some English. Primarily agricultural; lumbering in 19th cent. Hannasville only village in Twp. Cochranton an agricultural village with rich pastures; settled as early as 1800.

PA 56A: M, justice of the peace, farmer, teacher, school director, 87. B. Allegheny Twp. in Co. — F. b. here, PGF of Scotch-Irish descent, PGM b. Co.; M. b. here, MGF b. Center Co. ("a PA Dutchman"), MGM b. here (of "Irish" descent). — Ed.: till 21 (2 summers at Edinboro Normal School). — Baptist. — At first highly flattered, toward the end somewhat cantankerous, feeling the questions were silly; was persuaded by a friend to continue. Was aware of and regretted his own senility at times in reacting. — Despite his schoolteaching, his speech is about the most old-fashioned in the community when he is talking naturally.

PA 56A*: M, 87. — Parents b. here. — Senile in reactions; likes to talk.

Nickleville, Emlenton P.O., Richland Twp.

Twp. est. as Richland 1806. 1st settlement in 1796 from Westmoreland Co.; early settlers Scotch-Irish and English, some Germans and French. Nickleville a small village, laid out after 1828.

PA 56B: M, dairy farmer, 44. B. here. — F., PGF, PGM b. here; M., MGF b. Rockland Twp. in Co. (MGF of Dutch descent), MGM b. near Fertigs in Co. — Ed.: till 16. —

Presbyterian. — Quick, alert; perhaps not too appreciative of the importance of the study.

57. Clarion County

Formed 1839 from Armstrong and Venango Cos. Settlement open 1785 after Ft. Stannix purchase. 1st settler arrived 1792 from NY; by 1800 settlers from Westmoreland and Centre Cos. Early settlers Scotch-Irish, English, and German. Presbyterian church est. 1802; Lutheran and Reformed by 1815. 1st state road 1803; 1st turnpike 1822; steamboats on upper Allegheny 1829. Oil strike 1864; 1st oil pipeline 1870; production declined after 1877. Was 3rd largest lumber producer in 1887. Clarion State College. Tableland broken up by watercourses into ridges and rolls; drainage into Allegheny. Iron (now gone), coal, limestone, petroleum, natural gas. Pop. 1850: 23,565, 1880: 40,328, 1910: 36,638, 1930: 34,531, 1960: 37,408.

> Davis, A. J., ed. 1887. *History of Clarion County.* . . . Syracuse, NY. Repr. 1968 (Rimersburg: Record Press).
> 1898. *Commemorative Biographical Record of Central Pennsylvania, Counties of Centre, Clearfield, Jefferson, and Clarion.* Chicago: Beers.

Kissinger Mines, Rimersburg P.O., Madison Twp.

Twp. formed c. 1839. In SW corner of Co. Settled c. 1800 by Scotch-Irish and Germans. Coking plants, coal mines, defunct ironworks. Rimersburg settled in 1829 (by a tavernkeeper); community laid out c. 1837. More Germans than Scots among early settlers. Inc. as a borough 1853. Clarion Collegiate Institute 1858. Coal mining town; agriculture, stock raising.

PA 57A: M, farmer, 75. B. here; spent 1 winter in Allegheny Co. when 26. — F. b. Perry Twp., PGF of Scottish descent, PGM b. Perry Twp.; M. b. Perry Twp., MGF of Scottish descent. — Ed.: till 20. — Presbyterian. — Intelligent, somewhat higher type than usually selected; somewhat slow and feeble.

East Brady P.O., Madison Twp.

East Brady 2nd largest town in Co. Borough on Allegheny R.; rapid yet steady growth. Residence of employees of Bradys Bend Iron Co. 1st settlers c. 1820; 1st residents 1850s; town laid out 1866 (cut off from Madison Twp. then). Beginning of coal mining 1878. 1st church United Presbyterian. Since closing of ironworks, dependent on coal and RR, shipping for oil and gas. Pop. 1880: 1,242, 1910: 1,493, 1930: 1,563, 1960: 1,282.

PA 57B: M, dairy farmer, 53. B. West Monterey. — F. b. Toby Twp., PGF of "Dutch" descent; M. b. Perry Twp., MGF b. Porter Twp., MGM b. Co. — Ed.: till 17. — Methodist. — A very quick, alert mind. — A slight indistinctness of articulation and forward articulation orally, which FW at first mistakenly supposed to be traces of a "Dutch" accent: prob. an individual speech difficulty.

58. Armstrong County

Formed 1800 from Lycoming, Westmoreland, and Allegheny Cos. Armstrong purchase 1771; some settlers from VA. Indian troubles till 1794; no permanent settlement till

1796. Early settlers Scotch-Irish (from Westmoreland Co.) and Germans (from Lehigh and Northampton). Steamboats by 1828; PA canal by 1825; RRs after 1837. Lumbering in 19th cent.; iron mfg. from 1825. Also coal, salt, oil fields, limestone, brickworks, natural gas, distilleries. Pop. 1800: 2,399, 1820: 10,324, 1850: 29,560, 1880: 47,641, 1910: 67,880, 1930: 79,298, 1960: 79,524.

> Smith, R. W. 1883. *History of Armstrong County, Pennsylvania.* Chicago: University of Chicago Press.
> Wiley, Samuel T., ed. 1891. *Biographical and Historical Cyclopedia of Indiana and Armstrong Counties.* Philadelphia: J. M. Gresham.
> 1914. *Armstrong County.* 2 vols. Chicago: J. H. Beers.

Brick Church, Kelly Station P.O., Burrell Twp.

Twp. formed 1855. Originally settled by Germans, Scotch-Irish, Dutch. Salt works (not very profitable). Brick Church a crossroads; orig. an Evangelical Lutheran church.

PA 58A: M, farmer, 84. B. here. — F. b. Parkes Twp., PGF b. S. part of Bedford Co., PA, near Cumberland, MD, PGF's F. b. Germany, PGM b. near Gettysburg, PA; M. b. Parkes Twp., MGF b. perhaps in Germany, MGM b. Parkes Twp. — Ed.: till 18. — Lutheran. — Fairly quick, intelligent, generous; occasionally somewhat slow. — Old-fashioned; articulation not perfect.

Brick Church, Ford City P.O., Boggs Twp.

Formed 1878 from Pine Co. Coal in N.; little industry. 1st glass plant set up in Ford City 1887. Main plant of Pittsburgh Plate Glass here.

PA 58B: M, farmer, road supervisor, 42. B. here. — F., PGF b. here, PGF's F. b. perhaps Germany, PGM b. here; M. b. Kittanning Twp., MGM b. Burrell Twp., MGM's F. b. Kittanning Twp. (partly "Irish" and "Dutch"). — Ed.: till 8th grade. — Presbyterian. — Rather dull in orientation. — Articulation not too good.

59. Jefferson County

Formed 1804 from Lycoming Co. Meades Trail 1787. 1st settled 1796; early settlers from central PA (dispossessed after Rev.) and N. Ireland. Scotch-Irish prevailed; some English (New Eng. and NY), few Germans. Lumbering early; chief industry in late 19th cent., developed by New Englanders. 1st RR 1873–74. Hilly, many streams (were used for logging). Farming and stock raising; coalfields, sandstone, limestone, salt, some iron, natural gas, maple sugaring. Pop. 1810: 161, 1820: 561, 1850: 13,518, 1880: 27,935, 1910: 63,090, 1930: 52,114, 1960: 46,792.

> McKnight, William James. 1917. *Jefferson County, Pennsylvania: Her Pioneers and People.* 2 vols. Chicago: Beers. Repr. 1975 (Evansville, IN).
> Scott, Kate M., ed. 1888. *History of Jefferson County.* . . . Syracuse, NY: D. Mason.
> 1898. *Commemorative Biographical Record of Central Pennsylvania, Counties of Centre, Clearfield, Jefferson, and Clarion.* Chicago: Beers.

Anita, McCalmont Twp.

Twp. formed 1857. 1st settlers in the 1830s from Westmoreland and Centre Cos.: Ulster Scots, Welsh, English, German. 1st school 1840s; 1st church 1870s. High terrain, watershed; lumber beginning 1830. Anita a good-sized town; sawmilling.

PA 59A: M, farmer, 87. B. here. — F. b. S. Mahoning, just one mi. over line in Indiana Co., PA, PGF, PGM b. Dublin, Ireland (Protestant); M. b. near Frostburg, McCalmont Twp., MGF b. W. of Oliveburg in Perry Twp., Jefferson Co. (of Scottish descent), MGM b. near Frostburg, Perry Twp. (of Scotch-Irish descent). — Ed.: very little. — Presbyterian. — In good health, but somewhat senile in his reactions; his very vigorous "PA Dutch" wife enjoyed the sessions and kept him in good spirits. — Articulation not too good.

Mt. Pleasant, Summerville P.O., Beaver Twp.

Twp. formed 1850. 1st settlers in 1816 from CT; Scots and Germans from Dauphin Co. in 1834. Coal, limestone, iron ore. Named for Presbyterian Church (1837) nearby; Baptist church est. in 1840. Agriculture, glass works; formerly coke, auto parts. Pop. Mt. Pleasant 1960: 6,107.

PA 59B: F, housewife, 41. B. here (Rose Twp.). — F., PGF b. Rose Twp., PGF's F. b. Westmoreland Co. (of PA Dutch descent), PGM b. Westmoreland Co. (unable to speak PA Dutch); M. b. Stanton, Rose Twp., MGF b. perhaps Rose Twp., MGM b. Stanton, Rose Twp., MGM's F. b. Westmoreland Co., MGM's M. b. Brookville, Jefferson Co. — Ed.: till 15. — Lutheran. — Highly intelligent, quick, alert; willing to cooperate because she knew the project was under the proper auspices.

60. Indiana County

Formed 1803 from Westmoreland Co. 1st attempted settlement 1764; others arrived 1772. Mainly Scotch-Irish at first; Germans later. First mill W. of Alleghenies est. here 1769. Presbyterian church est. 1790; also some Lutherans early. PA Canal 1831; Indiana Branch RR 1886. Allegheny Mtns.; Susquehanna and Allegheny watersheds; small valleys and hills. Salt works, coal, limestone, lumbering (19th cent.), mineral paint. Pop. 1810: 6,214, 1820: 8,882, 1850: 27,170, 1880: 40,527, 1910: 66,210, 1930: 75,395, 1960: 75,366.

> Caldwell, J. A. 1880. *Indiana County, 1745–1880.* Newark, NJ: Caldwell.
> Stephenson, Clarence D. 1978. *Indiana County 175th Anniversary History.* Indiana: A. G. Halldin Pub. Co.
> Stewart, J. T. 1913. *Indiana County.* 2 vols. Chicago: J. H. Beers.
> Taylor, Alexander Wilson. 1953. *Indiana County.*
> Wiley, Samuel T., ed. 1891. *Biographical and Historical Cyclopedia of Indiana and Armstrong Counties.* Philadelphia: J. M. Gresham.

Crete, Indiana P.O., Center Twp.

Twp. formed 1807. Early settlers mostly Scotch-Irish; area mainly Scotch-Irish with some Germans from NY, elsewhere in PA. Indiana area settled before Rev. Indiana founded 1805. Station on underground RR. Rubber tires, hosiery.

PA 60A: M, farmer, 77. B. near Elder's Ridge, Connemaugh Twp., came here age 4. — F. b. Connemaugh Twp. near Saltsburg, PGF b. Co. Tyrone, Ireland, PGM b. near Saltsburg in Co.; M. b. near Elder's Ridge, MGF b. Connemaugh Twp., MGF's F. lived Nowrytown, Young Twp. (b. in SC), MGF's PGF b. Scotland, MGF's M., MGM b. near Elder's Ridge. — Ed.: till 20 (3 terms at Indiana Normal). — Presbyterian. — Dignified, stubborn, rather good background. — Old-fashioned.

Jacksonville, Blairsville P.O., Black Lick Twp.

Twp. formed 1807. Early settlers mostly Scotch-Irish and English. Jacksonville laid out 1830. Predominantly Scotch-Irish, some Germans; Presbyterians and Methodists. Blairsville laid out 1818; inc. as a borough 1825. 1st settled 1792. Canal port, turnpike. Agriculture; enamelware, coal, stone, clay, glass works, RR repair shops.

PA 60B: M, farmer, 40. B. here. — F., PGF b. here (PGF of Scotch-Irish descent), PGM b. here, PGM's F. of Scotch-Irish descent; M., MGF b. here (MGF of Scotch-Irish descent). — Ed.: till 16. — United Presbyterian. — Quick, intelligent; rather humble background and lifestyle.

61. Cambria County

Formed 1804 from Huntingdon and Somerset Cos. 1st settlement 1790; Germans dominant group in 1791 (mostly from SE PA). Also Scotch-Irish direct from Ulster; some Irish Catholics among early settlers. Turnpike authorized 1810; canal auth. 1825; RR from 1834. Tableland: Susquehanna and Allegheny drainage. Growing (some wheat); coal, iron ore, iron and steel making, formerly lumber. Resort country. Pop. 1810: 2,117, 1820: 3,287, 1850: 17,773, 1880: 46,811, 1910: 166,131, 1930: 203,146, 1960: 203,283.

Caldwell, J. A. 1890. *Atlas of Cambria County.* Philadelphia: Atlas Pub. Co.

Gable, John E. 1926. *History of Cambria County, Pennsylvania.* 2 vols. Topeka: Historical Publishing Co.

Storey, Henry Wilson. 1907. *History of Cambria County, Pennsylvania.* 3 vols. NY: Lewis Historical Pub. Co.

Summerhill/South Fork, Sidman, Lovett P.O., Croyle Twp.

Summerhill Twp. created 1810; Croyle Twp. created 1858 from Summerhill. Mill here 1801. Lovett a town on S. Fork. Pop. South Fork 1910: 4,592, 1960: 2,053.

PA 61A: M, farmer (on RR one yr., coal miner 20 yrs.), 84. B. Summerhill. — F. b. here, PGF, PGF's F. b. Bedford Co. in Woodcock Valley, PGF's PGF b. Ireland (Catholic), PGF's M. b. Bedford Co. ("Dutch"), PGM, PGM's F. b. S. Cambria Co. (latter "Dutch"); M., MGF b. here, MGF's F., MGF's M. b. Bedford Co. ("Dutch"), MGM b. Bedford Co., MGM's F. b. MD (of English descent), MGM's M. b. Bedford Co. (of English descent). — Ed.: till 15 or 16. — Lutheran. — Intelligent; almost the only available elderly person who grew up English-speaking here. — Old-fashioned, somewhat feeble; imperfect articulation.

North Ebensburg, Ebensburg P.O., Cambria Twp.

Twp. formed c. 1798; antedates Co. Ebensburg settled as early as 1791 by Welsh. Congregational church here by 1797.

Village in 1807; inc. as a borough 1825. Co. seat. Onetime resort; agriculture; many residents work in mines. Pop. 1820: 168, 1850: 600, 1880: 1,123, 1910: 1,978, 1930: 3,063, 1960: 4,111.

PA 61B: M, farmer, 40. B. here. — F. b. Nicktown in Co., PGF b. Cardiganshire, Wales, came to Phila. aged 12, PGM b. here, PGM's F. b. N. Wales, PGM's M. b. Wales; M. b. here, MGF b. Cardiganshire, Wales, MGM b. Wales. — Ed.: till 16. — Congregational (a Welsh settlement). — Somewhat reticent, self-conscious, but willing to participate in a new game. — Lacking in clear, vigorous articulation.

62. Clearfield County

Formed 1804 from Huntingdon and Lycoming Cos. Late settlement: Scotch-Irish most numerous, then some Germans. Headwaters on W. branch of Susquehanna, behind main Allegheny ridge. Once heavily forested; now reforestation. Agriculture not emphasized till latter 19th cent., but farming declining now. Lumbering principal industry to 1880; also coal, fire clay, iron ore, limestone, oil, gas, nickel products, knit goods, woolen mills. Pop. 1810: 875, 1820: 2,342, 1850: 12,586, 1880: 43,408, 1910: 93,768, 1930: 86,727, 1960: 81,534.

Aldrich, Lewis Cass, ed. 1887. *History of Clearfield County.* . . . Syracuse, NY: D. Mason.

Wall, Thomas Lincoln. 1925. *Clearfield County.* . . . Clearfield: The Author.

1898. *Commemorative Biographical Record of Central Pennsylvania.* Chicago: J. H. Beers.

Fairview, Morrisdale P.O., Graham Twp.

Twp. formed 1856. Heavy lumbering in the mid 19th cent. Chiefly farming, some coal. Fairview has a United Brethren church and school. Heavily Democratic, except during Greenback period.

PA 62A: M, farmer (some lumbering when younger), 87. B. here; spent 3 mos. in the South when 20; about 10 or 15 yrs. ago went to KY and WV for a few days each yr. — F. b. here, PGF b. Germany, PGM b. here, or in adjoining twp., PGM's F. b. perhaps in Germany; M. b. Bradford Twp. in Co., MGF b. Germany, MGM b. Bradford Twp., MGM's F. of German descent. — Ed.: till 15. — Brethren. — Somewhat senile, but well-preserved; appeared to enjoy answering. — Articulation not too good.

Salem/West Decatur, Blue Ball P.O., Boggs Twp.

Twp. formed 1838. Settled before Co. est. Mainly Germans, Scotch-Irish, English. Hilly, rough; coal, fireclay. Salem in N. part of Twp. Has United Brethren church; also location of the first church (Lutheran and Reformed), c. 1798, W. of Susquehanna and N. of Harrisburg. W. Decatur location of an early stage coach stop. Blue Ball named for a type of clay. Pop. Salem 1930: 35.

PA 62B: M, farmer, 40. B. here. — F. b. here, PGF b. Co. (German), PGM b. Samborne in Co. (German); M. b. Bradford Twp., MGF, MGM b. Spring Valley in Co. (both

German). — Ed.: till 12 (3rd grade). — United Brethren. — Quick, alert. — Slight PA German accent evident in forward articulation and unvoicing.

63. Elk County

Formed in 1843 from 3 other cos. First settler arrived 1798; many early settlers from New England and NY. Scotch-Irish and English. 1st permanent settlement 1803. Presbyterian church by 1801; others followed. Turnpike by 1824. Timber in 19th cent. "Oil stampede" after 1876. Other industries: gas, coal, building stone. Pop. 1850: 3,531, 1880: 12,800, 1910: 35,871, 1930: 33,431, 1960: 37,328.

> 1890. *History of the Counties of McKean, Elk and Forest. . . .* Chicago: J. H. Beers.
> 1956. *Who's Who in Elk County. . . .* St. Marys: Lenze Commercial Studios.

Winslow Hill, Benezett

Formed 1846 from Gibson Twp. Settled by 1813. Susquehanna watershed. Oil, gas, salt, coal, fire clay.

PA 63A: M, farmer, 74. B. here. — F. b. here, PGF b. perhaps in Jefferson Co., PA (of Bostonian ancestry, back to the Mayflower), PGM b. Bristol, CT; M. b. Kersey in Co., MGF, MGM b. Ireland (both Catholic). — Ed.: till 14. — Roman Catholic. — Intelligent, quick; occasionally somewhat senile; did not really understand purpose of study.

Kersey P.O., Fox Twp.

Twp. original, est. 1843. S. central Co.; watershed. Settled 1812; 1st settlers English, some Germans later. Coal, limestone. 1st settler in Kersey 1812–13; set up mill. Laid out 1846. English, Irish, Germans in 1st settlement; many Germans later.

PA 63B: M, farmer, 36. B. here (when 21 at Jamestown, NY, for 6 mos.; then at Ridgeway, Elk Co., 3 yrs.; then Cleveland, OH, 1 yr.; then Jamestown, NY, 1 1/2 yrs.). — F. b. here, PGF b. Nittany Valley, Center Co., PGF's F. of Welsh descent, PGM b. here, PGM's F. of English descent, PGM's M. of PA Dutch descent; M. b. Caldonia, Jay Twp., Elk Co., MGF b. Fox Twp., MGF's F. b. VT, MGF's M. b. English Center, Lycoming Co. — Ed.: till 14 (1st yr. h.s.). — Methodist. — Quick, intellectually curious; able to understand purpose and importance of the study.

64. McKean County

Formed 1804 from Lycoming Co. 1st settlement 1807 by an Englishman; major settlement by 1816: Scotch-Irish from E. PA and Susquehanna Valley and English from New Eng. and NY (no Germans among pioneers). Holland Land Company territory c. 1810. Allegheny River watershed; tableland, cut up by streams. 1st road surveyed 1797; 1st RRs in 1850s. Co. economy developed by oil and gas. Lumbering in 19th cent.; salt works in 1830s; grazing and dairying. Pop. 1810: 142, 1820: 728, 1850: 5,254, 1880: 42,565, 1910: 47,868, 1930: 55,167, 1960: 54,517.

> Lillibridge, C. W. 1945. *McKean County, 1804–1945.* Smethport: McKean County Schools.

> Stone, Rufus Barrett. 1926. *McKean, the Governor's County.* NY: Lewis Historical Pub. Co.
> 1890. *History of the Counties of McKean, Elk and Forest. . . .* Chicago: J. H. Beers.

Jander Run/Shinglehouse, Genesee (Potter Co.), Little Genessee, NY, P.O., Ceres Twp.

Twp. oldest in Co. (original in 1804); NE corner of Co. 1st settlement c. 1797; Quakers from NY among early settlers. Oil and gas developed in 1880s.

PA 64A: M, lumbering, foreman for highway dept., 77. B. here (Bell's Run neighborhood); when 20, spent 1 year in MI woods. — F. b. here, PGF b. MA (partly "Irish"), PGM b. near Belfast, NY, near here in Allegany Co., NY (of "Irish" descent); M. b. Susquehanna Co., PA, came here as a very young child; MGF b. Susquehanna Co. ("Irish" descent), MGM (partly of American Indian descent). — Ed.: till 17. — Baptist. — Better than average background; enjoyed conversation. — Rather old-fashioned Yankee speech; only fairly good articulation.

West Eldred, Eldred

Twp. formed 1878. Oil and gas in 1870s; lumbering (Allegheny Valley). Town inc. 1880. Largely Yankee.

PA 64B: F, housewife, 43. B. here. — F. b. here, PGF b. perhaps NY; M. b. here, MGF b. near Rochester, NY, MGM b. here. — Ed.: till 15. — Methodist. — Quick, intelligent; glad to cooperate in a worthwhile project. — Quick speech with short vowels.

65. Warren County

Formed 1800 from Allegheny and Lycoming Cos. Purchases 1794 by Holland Land Company. Town (later borough) of Warren surveyed 1795. Settlement in 1790s, predominantly Yankee (NY and Eastern States). Early settlers English, Scots, some NY Dutch; Germans later. Steamboats on the Allegheny c. 1830; 1st RR c. 1859. Scandinavian influx (chiefly Swedes) after 1865. Methodist church 1809; Presbyterian church 1822. Lumbering till 1840; oil pumped by 1845. Coal, iron ore, sandstone (for building). Pop. 1800: 233, 1820: 1,976, 1850: 13,671, 1880: 27,981, 1910: 39,573, 1930: 41,453, 1960: 45,582.

> Howden, J. A., and A. Odbert. 1878. *Atlas of Warren County.* Washington:
> Schenck, J. S., ed. 1887. *History of Warren County. . . .* Syracuse, NY: D. Mason.

Yankee Bush/Fairview, Warren P.O., Sugar Grove Twp.

Twp. formed 1821. In N. part of Co. 1st settler came upriver from Pittsburgh in 1797; early settlers from Long Island, Ireland, Scotland, MA, NY, Hudson Valley. Swedes in 1850s; Swedish Lutheran Church 1856. Presbyterians first religious denomination. Little industry; brickmaking. Fairview and Yankee Bush small settlements. Fairview inc. 1868. Retired farmers and Erie commuters. Basket weaving shop, tool factory; hay, berries.

PA 65A: M, farmer, 74. B. here. — F. b. Co., PGF, PGM b. NY (of Yankee descent); M. b. Conawango Twp. in Co., MGF

b. on Lake Erie, NY, MGF's F. ("Irish"), MGM b. NY (of German descent). — Ed.: till 16 (off and on). — Mother Methodist. — Quick, alert, old-fashioned character.

Tidioute Creek Road, Torpedo P.O., Triumph Twp.

Twp. formed 1878. 1st school 1818; Yankees and Scotch-Irish among 1st settlers. Oil in 1860s; pop. decline after oil boom. Tidioute founded by Harmony Society in the early 1800s. Prosperity during the oil boom; now rustic. Pop. Tidioute 1930: 970.

PA 65B: M, farmer, 51. B. here (lived in Tidioute, ages 1 1/2–17). — F. b. Eldred Twp. in Co., PGF b. Co. (of "Irish" descent), PGM (of Scotch-Irish descent); M. b. here, MGF of Scotch-Irish descent, MGF's F. lived in Forest Co., MGM of Irish and "Dutch" descent. — Ed.: Tidioute till 17 (part of h.s.). — Methodist Episcopal. — Rather old-fashioned and not too quick.

66. Crawford County

Formed 1800 from Allegheny Co. 1st settlement in 1788 from Northumberland Co.; others from Scotland via NJ and the Wyoming Valley. 1st settlers have English surnames, but fact of Presbyterian preaching as early as 1799 suggests Scotch-Irish. Also some Germans among early settlers. Also Lutheran and Baptist churches before 1810. Early products: wheat, corn, oats, barley, rye, hay; also grazing. Salt trade 1800–1819; cheese making by 1870. Meadville Theological Seminary est. 1844; later moved to Chicago. Rolling terrain; coal, iron ore, oil. Pop. 1800: 2,346, 1820: 9,397, 1850: 37,849, 1880: 68,607, 1910: 61,565, 1930: 62,980, 1960: 77,956.

Bates, Samuel P. 1899. *Our County and Its People.* Boston: W. A. Fergusson.

Child, Hamilton, comp. 1874. *Gazetteer and Business Directory of Crawford County, for 1874.* Syracuse, NY: H. Child.

Huidekoper, Alfred. 1840. Incidents in the Early History of Crawford County, Pennsylvania. *Memoirs of the Historical Society of Pennsylvania* 4.2 113–163.

1885. *History of Crawford County.* Chicago: Warner, Beers.

Conneaut Lake P.O., East Fallowfield Twp.

Twp. formed 1804 (original twp.), divided 1841. First settlements 1790; Scotch-Irish and German. By 1874, Twp. had cheese factories, a flour mill, and an oil barrel factory. Conneaut Lake largest natural lake in PA; resort village.

PA 66A: M, farmer, 81. B. here. — F. b. here, PGF b. Stony Pt. (4 mi. W.); M., MGF b. Co. (MGF partly "Irish"). — Ed.: till 12. — Methodist. — Intelligent, but somewhat senile. — He appears to have only one phoneme in the [v] territory, whereas the younger inf. from a completely "Yankee" neighborhood in the co. has the distinction between [a] and [vʌ·].

Conneaut Center, Linesville P.O., Conneaut Twp.

Twp. formed 1811. W. border of Co. Settled 1790s from Ireland, W. PA, NJ, SE PA. Level or gently rolling. Methodists c. 1818; Quakers to 1840s. Linesville a "tidy country town, with wide streets and detached houses".

PA 66B: M, farmer, 50. B. here. — F., PGF b. here, PGF's F. came here from NY (German), PGM b. Erie Co., PA; M. b. here, MGF b. NY. — Ed.: till 16. — Congregational. — Quick, alert, cooperative. — Speech seems very typical of the Western NY and Western Reserve of Ohio type, which is in accord with his ancestry. Use of [ɪu ɛʊ]; distinction of [a vʌ·], of [ɔʌɚ oʌɚ]. (Cf. the vastly different type used by the old-fashioned inf. who lives near a neighborhood largely of PA Dutch descent.)

67. Erie County

Formed 1800 from Allegheny Co. Holland Land Company 1793–95. 1st settlers 1795 from Ontario Co., NY; most settlers English from New Eng. and NY, though some Scotch-Irish from PA as well. City of Erie laid out in 18th cent. as port and industrial center. 1st turnpike 1796; Erie extension canal 1844–71; RRs by 1850s. Vineyards on lakeshore; some natural gas, iron; salt wells in past. Pop. 1800: 1,468, 1820: 8,541, 1850: 38,742, 1880: 74,688, 1910: 115,117, 1930: 175,277, 1960: 250,682.

Child, Hamilton, comp. 1873. *Gazetteer and Business Directory of Erie County. . . .* Syracuse, NY: H. Child.

Federal Writers Project. 1938. *Erie: A Guide to the City and County.* Philadelphia: William Penn Association of Philadelphia.

Miller, John. 1909. *A Twentieth Century History of Erie County.* 2 vols. Chicago: Lewis Pub. Co.

Moorhead, I. 1883. Erie County. In William H. Egle, *History of the Commonwealth of Pennsylvania.* Philadelphia: E. M. Gardner.

Reed, J. E. 1925. *History of Erie County, Pennsylvania.* 2 vols. Indianapolis: Historical Pub. Co.

Sanford, Laura G. 1862. *The History of Erie County.* Philadelphia: J. B. Lippincott Co.

Whitman, Benjamin. 1896. *Nelson's Biographical Dictionary and Historical Reference Book of Erie County. . . .* Erie: S. B. Nelson.

1884. *History of Erie County.* Chicago: Warner, Beers.

Arbuckle, Wattsburg P.O., Venango Twp.

Twp. formed 1800. 1st settler 1795; early settlers from NY and Northumberland Co, PA. Presbyterian services early (1801). Wattsburg a small butter producing center.

PA 67A: M, farmer, 76. B. here; when about 40, he traveled here and in adjoining part of NY and OH selling pianos by horse and team. — F., PGF b. here, PGF's F. b. NY (of Mayflower descent), PGM b. on Lake Erie in Harbor Creek Twp., Erie, PA; M. b. here, MGF b. near Troy, NY (of Holland Dutch descent), MGM b. Greene Twp. in Co. — Ed.: till 18 (4 mos. in the winter). — Baptist. — Rather quick, intelligent, but hypersensitive; pious. — Old-fashioned "Yankee" speech.

Wattsburg, Amity Twp.

Twp. formed 1826 from Union. Early settlers 1790s; Irish and English, many Yankees from NH, VT, NY. Distinctly rural; no RRs even in early 20th cent. Dairying. Wattsburg 1st settled 1796 from VT and the Mohawk Valley. Site laid out 1828; inc. as a borough 1833. No major industries; fur depot, woodworking, butter market, grazing.

PA 67B: M, farmer, 37. B. Venango Twp., 1 1/2 mi. N. in Co.; molder and radiator maker 5 yrs. at Corry, in Co. — F. b. Union City in Co., PGF b. Hatch Hollow in Amity Twp., PGF's F. b. NY (of Scotch-Irish descent), PGF's M. b. NY (of German descent); M. b. here, MGF b. NY, MGF's F. of English descent, MGM b. Warren Co., MGM's F. of English descent. — Ed.: till 15. — Methodist. — Highly intelligent; discerning mind; quick, cooperative. — The clear cut precision of "Yankee" articulation; short vowels.

Bibliographies

Bining, Arthur Cecil, ed. 1946. *Writings on Pennsylvania History: A Bibliography*. Harrisburg: Pennsylvania Historical and Museum Commission.

Hoenstine, Floyd G. 1958. *Guide to Genealogical and Historical Research in Pennsylvania*. Hollidaysburg.

Proud, Robert. 1903. *The Proud Papers (Robert Proud, Historian of Pennsylvania)*. Philadelphia: Morris Press.

Read, George Edward, ed. 1902. *Papers of the Governors, 1681–1902*. Harrisburg: Pennsylvania Archives.

Wilkinson, Norman B., et al. 1957. *Bibliography of Pennsylvania History*. 2nd ed. Harrisburg: Pennsylvania History and Museum Commission.

1908. *Calendar of the Papers of Benjamin Franklin in the Library of the University of Pennsylvania*. Philadelphia: University of Pennsylvania Library.

1940. *An Annotated Catalog of the Alexander C. Robinson Collection of Western Pennsylvania*. Sewickley: Public Library.

1949. *Guide to the Manuscript Collections in the Historical Survey of Pennsylvania*. Philadelphia: Historical Records Survey.

1959. *Preliminary Guide to the Research Materials of the Pennsylvania Historical and Museum Commission*. Harrisburg: The Commission.

1970–. *Pennsylvania Historical Bibliography*. Harrisburg: Pennsylvania Historical and Museum Commission.

General Histories

Agnew, Daniel. 1887. *A History of the Region of Pennsylvania, North of the Ohio and West of the Allegheny River. . . .* Philadelphia: Kay and Brother.

Bolles, Albert S. 1899. *Pennsylvania: Province and State. . . 1609 to 1790*. Philadelphia: Burt Franklin.

Bomberger, Christian M. 1934. *Twelfth Colony Plus: The Formative Years of Pennsylvania. . . .* Jeanette: Jeannette Pub. Co.

Brown, Isaac B. 1905. *Early Footprints of Developments and Improvements in Extreme Northwestern Pennsylvania*. Harrisburg: Dept. of Internal Affairs. Extracts from part one of the annual report for 1904, pp. 6-75.

Buck, Solon J., and Elizabeth Hawthorn Buck. 1939. *The Planting of Civilization in Western Pennsylvania*. Pittsburgh: University of Pittsburgh Press.

Carpenter, William H. 1854. *The History of Pennsylvania from Its Earliest Settlement to the Present Time*. Philadelphia: Lippincopp, Grameo and Co.

Cochran, Thomas Childs. 1978. *Pennsylvania: A Bicentennial History*. NY: Norton.

Cornell, William M. 1876. *The History of Pennsylvania from the Earliest Discovery to the Present Time*. Philadelphia: Quaker City Publishing House.

De Armond, Anna Janney. 1969. *Andrew Bradford, Colonial Journalist*. NY: Greenwood Press.

Dingwall, E. 1937. *Pennsylvania, The State without an Army, 1681–1756*. London: C.W. Davis Co. Ltd.

Donehoo, George P. 1926. *Pennsylvania, a History*. 2 vols. NY: Lewis Publishers.

Dunaway, Wayland Fuller. 1935. *A History of Pennsylvania*. NY: Prentice-Hall.

Egle, William Henry. 1876. *An Illustrated History of the Commonwealth of Pennsylvania. . . .* Harrisburg: DeWitt C. Goodrich.

Ellis, Franklin, et al. 1886. *History of That Part of the Susquehanna and Juniata Valleys Embraced in the Counties of Mifflin, Juniata, Perry, Union, and Snyder*. Ed. by F. Ellis and A.N. Hungerford. 2 vols. Philadelphia. Repr. 1975.

Fisher, Sydney G. 1897. *Pennsylvania, Colony and Commonwealth*. Philadelphia: H.T. Coates and Co.

Giddens, Paul Henry. 1947. *Pennsylvania Petroleum, 1750–1872: A Documentary History*. Titusville: Pennsylvania Historical and Museum Commission.

Giddens, Paul Henry. 1948. *Early Days of Oil, a Pictorial History of the Beginnings of the Industry in Pennsylvania*. Princeton: Princeton University Press.

Godcharles, Frederic Antes. 1933. *Pennsylvania: Political, Governmental, Military and Civil*. 4 vols. NY: American Historical Society.

Hazard, Samuel, ed. 1860. *General Index to the. . . Pennsylvania Archives. . . .* Philadelphia: J. Severns and Co.

Jenkins, Howard Malcomb. *Pennsylvania: Colonial and Federal*. Philadelphia: Pennsylvania Historical Publishing Association.

Klein, Philip Shriver, and Ari Arthur Hoogenboom. 1980. *A History of Pennsylvania*. 2nd ed. University Park: Pennsylvania State University Press.

McKnight, William James. 1905. *A Pioneer Outline History of Northwestern Pennsylvania*. Philadelphia: Lippincott.

Pennsylvania Writers' Project. 1942. *Pennsylvania Cavalcade*. Philadelphia: University of Pennsylvania Press.

Pennypacker, Samuel Whitaker. 1883. *Historical and Biographical Sketches*. Philadelphia: R.A. Tripple.

Proud, Robert. 1797–98. *The History of Pennsylvania in North America, from. . . 1681 till after the Year 1742. . . with a Brief Description of the Said Province, 1760–1770*. Philadelphia: Z. Poulson.

Rupp, Israel Daniel. 1848. *Early History of Western Pennsylvania. . . .* Pittsburgh: A. P. Ingram. Republished 1851.

Sharpless, Isaac. 1919. *Political Leaders of Provincial Pennsylvania*. NY: Macmillan.

Sheaver, P. W. 1875. *An Historical Map of Pennsylvania*. Philadelphia: Historical Society of Pennsylvania.

Shenk, Hiram Herr, ed. 1932. *Encyclopedia of Pennsylvania*. Harrisburg: National Historical Association.

Stevens, Sylvester Kirby. 1956. *Pennsylvania: Keystone State*. 2 vols. NY: American Historical Co.

Thomas, Gabriel. 1698. *An Historical and Geographical Account of. . . Pensilvania, and of West New Jersey. . . .* London. Rev. ed. 1938 (Harrisburg: Aurand Press).

Wallace, Paul A. W. 1962. *Pennsylvania: Seed of a Nation*. NY: Harper and Row.

Wood, T. K., ed. 1945–. *Now and Then: A Quarterly Magazine of History and Biography.* Muncy: Mimcu Historical Society.

Writers Program. 1940. *Pennsylvania: A Guide to the Keystone State.* NY: Oxford University Press.

1782. *Journals of the House of Representatives.* [November 1776 through October 1781] Philadelphia: J. Dunlap.

1826–95. *Memoirs.* Philadelphia: Historical Society of Pennsylvania.

1874–1935. *Pennsylvania Archives.* Philadelphia: J. Severns and Co.

1877–. *The Pennsylvania Magazine of History and Biography.* Philadelphia: Historical Society of Pennsylvania.

1883–84. *Historical Register: Notes and Queries, Biographical and Genealogical.* Harrisburg: Lane S. Hart.

1918–. *Western Pennsylvania Historical Magazine.* Pittsburgh: Historical Society of Western Pennsylvania.

1934–. *Pennsylvania History.* Philadelphia: University of Pennsylvania Press.

1944–. *The Pennsylvanian.* Washington: Pennsylvania Historical Junto.

1954. *The Pennsylvania Magazine of History and Biography — Indexes.* Philadelphia: Historical Society of Pennsylvania.

Philadelphia, 1789–1804. Gazette of the United States. Philadelphia: John Fenno.

Special Studies

Anderson, Florence S. 1960. *The Delaware River and Valley.* Philadelphia: Franklin Pub. and Supply Co.

Applegarth, Albert C. 1892. *Quakers in Pennsylvania.* Baltimore: Johns Hopkins University Press.

Ashley, George H., and J. French Robinson. 1912. *Oil and Gas Fields of Pennsylvania.* Harrisburg: Dept. of Internal Affairs, Bureau of Topographic and Geological Survey.

Balch, Thomas. 1914. *The Swedish Beginning of Pennsylvania and Other Events in Pennsylvania History.* Worcester, MA: American Antiquarian Society.

Barton, Thomas. 1764. *The Conduct of the Paxton-Men.* Philadelphia: A. Steuart.

Bining, Arthur C. 1954. *Pennsylvania's Iron and Steel Industry.* Gettysburg: Pennsylvania Historical Association. Pennsylvania History Studies, No. 5.

Bishop, Avard Longley. 1907. *The State Works of Pennsylvania.* New Haven: Tuttle, Morehouse and Taylor Press.

Bodnar, John E., ed. 1973. *The Ethnic Experience in Pennsylvania.* Lewisburg: Bucknell University Press.

Boyd, Julian P. 1935. *The Susquehannah Company: Connecticut's Experiment in Expansion.* New Haven, CT: Tercentenary Commission of the State of Connecticut.

Boyd, Julian P., and Robert J. Taylor, eds. 1930–71. *The Susquehanna Company Papers.* 11 vols. Wilkes-Barre: Wyoming Historical and Geological society.

Bronner, Edwin B. 1962. *William Penn's Holy Experiment: The Founding of Pennsylvania, 1681–1701.* NY: Temple University Publications.

Browning, Charles Henry. 1912. *Welsh Settlement of Pennsylvania.* Philadelphia. Repr. 1967 (Baltimore: Genealogical Pub. Co.).

Chambers, George. 1856. *A Tribute to. . . the Scotch and Irish Early Settlers of Pennsylvania.* Chambersburg: M. Keiffer.

Dale, James W. 1871. *Earliest Settlement by Presbyterians on the Delaware River. . . .* Philadelphia.

Day, Sherman. 1843. *Historical Collections of the State of Pennsylvania: Containing a Copious Selection of. . . Traditions, Biographical Sketches. . . Topographical Descriptions. . . .* Philadelphia: G. W. Gorton.

Diffenderffer, Frank R. 1900. *The German Immigration into Pennsylvania through the Port of Philadelphia. . . .* Lancaster. Repr. 1977 (Baltimore: Genealogical Pub. Co.).

Dunaway, Wayland F. 1928. The English Settlers in Colonial Pennsylvania. *Pennsylvania Magazine of History and Biography* 52:317–41.

Dunaway, Wayland Fuller. 1944. *The Scotch-Irish of Colonial Pennsylvania.* Chapel Hill: University of North Carolina Press.

Dunbar, John Raine, ed. 1957. *The Paxton Papers.* The Hague: M. Nijhoff.

Egle, William Henry, ed. 1893. *Journals and Diaries of the War of the Revolution.* Harrisburg: E. K. Meyers.

Eshleman, Henry Frank. 1917. *Historic Background and Annals of the Swiss and German Pioneer Settlers of Southeastern Pennsylvania. . . .* Lancaster.

Espenshade, Abraham Howry. 1925. *Pennsylvania Place Names.* State College: Pennsylvania State College.

Falckner, Daniel. 1909. *A Contribution to Pennsylvania History.* Lancaster: Pennsylvania-German Society.

Fisher, Sydney George. 1896. *The Making of Pennsylvania.* Philadelphia. Repr. 1969 (Port Washington, NY: I. J. Friedman).

Fisher, Sydney George. 1919. *The Quaker Colonies.* New Haven: Yale University Press.

Folsom, Burton W. 1981. *Urban Capitalists: Entrepreneurs and City Growth in the Lackawanna and Lehigh Valleys, 1800–1920.* Baltimore: Johns Hopkins University Press.

Garland, Robert. *The Scotch-Irish in Western Pennsylvania.* Pittsburgh: Carnegie Library.

Gipson, Lawrence H. 1935. *Crime and Its Punishment in Provincial Pennsylvania.* Bethlehem: Lehigh University Press Studies in Humanities, 15.

Glenn, Thomas A. 1911–13. *Welsh Founders of Pennsylvania.* Oxford: Fox, Jones and Co.

Godcharles, Frederic Antes. 1924. *Daily Stories of Pennsylvania.* Milton.

Gordon, Thomas Francis. 1832. *Gazetteer of the State of Pennsylvania.* Philadelphia. Repr. 1975 (New Orleans: Polyanthos).

Graeff, Arthur Dundore. 1939. *The Relations between the Pennsylvania Germans and the British Authorities (1750–1776).* Norristown: Pennsylvania German Society.

Hall, William M. 1890. *Reminiscences and Sketches, Historical and Biographical.* Harrisburg: Meyers Printing House.

Harpster, John W., ed. 1938. *Pen Pictures of Early Western Pennsylvania.* Pittsburgh: University of Pittsburgh Press.

Hazard, Samuel, ed. 1828–31. *The Register of Pennsylvania: Devoted to the Preservation of Facts and Documents.* Philadelphia: W. F. Geddes.

Herrick, Cheesman Abiah. 1926. *White Servitude in Pennsylvania.* Philadelphia: J. J. McVey.

Hinke, William John. 1934. *Pennsylvania German Pioneers.* 3 vols. Norristown: Pennsylvania German Society.

Holcomb, William P. 1886. Pennsylvania Boroughs. *Johns Hopkins University Studies in History and Political*

Science 4.4:129–80. Baltimore: Johns Hopkins University Press.

Horn, William F. 1945. *The Horn Papers: Early Westward Movement on the Monongahela and Upper Ohio, 1765–1795*. Waynesburg: Published for a committee of the Green County Historical Society by the Herald Press.

Hotchkin, Samuel Fitch. 1897. *Rural Pennsylvania*. Philadelphia: G.W. Jacobs.

Ireland, Owen S. 1973. The Ethnic-Religious Dimension of Pennsylvania Politics, 1778–1779. *William and Mary Quarterly* 30:423–448.

Janney, Samuel M. 1888. *Peace Principles Exemplified in the Early History of Pennsylvania*. Philadelphia: Friends' Book Association.

Johnson, Amandus. 1911. *Swedish Settlements on the Delaware*. . . . 2 vols. Philadelphia. Repr. 1969 (Baltimore: Genealogical Pub. Co.).

Kephart, Horace. 1902. *Pennsylvania's Part in the Winning of the West*. St. Louis: Bureau of Publicity of the Louisiana Purchase Exposition.

Klees, Frederic. 1950. *The Pennsylvania Dutch*. NY: Macmillan.

Klett, Guy S. 1937. *Presbyterians in Colonial Pennsylvania*. Philadelphia: University of Pennsylvania Press.

Knipe, Irvin P. 1917. *The Pennsylvania-German in the Civil War*. Lancaster: Press of the New Era Printing Co.

Kuhns, Levi Oscar. 1901. *The German and Swiss Settlements of Colonial Pennsylvania*. NY. Repr. 1971 (Ann Arbor, MI: Gryphon Books).

Lemon, James T. 1967. Urbanization and the Development of Eighteenth-Century Southeastern Pennsylvania and Adjacent Delaware. *William and Mary Quarterly* 24:501–542.

Lemon, James T. 1972. *The Best Poor Man's Country: A Geographical Study of Early Southeastern Pennsylvania*. Baltimore: Johns Hopkins University Press.

Lyman, Robert R. 1971. *Forbidden Land: Strange Events in the Black Forest*. Coudersport: Potter Enterprise.

Maginness, John Franklin. 1857. *Otzinachson: Or, History of the West Branch Valley of the Susquehanna*. Philadelphia: H.B. Ashmead. Reprinted 1889 (Williamsport: Gazette and Bulletin Printing House).

Marshall, Christopher. 1877. *Extracts from the Diary of Christopher Marshall, 1774–1781*. Albany: J. Munsell.

McClure, Alexander Kelly. 1905. *Old Time Notes of Pennsylvania*. Philadelphia: J. R. Winston.

Miller, Ernest C. 1974. *Pennsylvania's Oil Industry*. 3rd ed., rev. Gettysburg: Pennsylvania Historical Society.

Murphy, Raymond E. 1933. *Mineral Industries of Pennsylvania*. Harrisburg: Greater Pennsylvania Council.

Murphy, Raymond Edward, and Marion Murphy. 1937. *Pennsylvania: A Regional Geography*. Harrisburg: Pennsylvania Book Service.

Nash, Gary B. 1968. *Quakers and Politics: Pennsylvania, 1681–1726*. Princeton, NJ: Princeton University Press.

Pastorius, Francis Daniel. 1898. *Pastorius' Description of Pennsylvania, 1700*. Trans. by Lewis H. Weiss. Boston: Directors of the Old South.

Paxson, Henry D. 1926. *Sketch and Map of a Trip from Philadelphia to Tinicum Island*. Philadelphia: Buchanan.

Raup, Hallock Floyd. 1940. The Susquehanna Corridor: A Neglected Trans-Appalachian Route. *Geographical Review* 30:439–50.

Richards, Henry Melchior Muhlenberg. 1908. *The Pennsylvania-German in the Revolutionary War, 1775–1783*. Lancaster: The Society.

Richardson, Charles Francis. 1916. *Charles Miner, a Pennsylvania Pioneer*. Wilkes-Barre.

Rodney, Richard Seymour. 1930. *Early Relations of Delaware and Pennsylvania*. Wilmington: Historical Society of Delaware.

Rosenberger, Jesse Leonard. 1902. *The Pennsylvania Germans*. Chicago: The American Lumberman. Republished 1923, 1966 (Chicago: University of Chicago Press).

Russ, William A., Jr. 1966. *How Pennsylvania Acquired Its Present Boundaries*. University Park: Pennsylvania Historical Association.

Sapio, Victor A. 1970. *Pennsylvania and the War of 1812*. Lexington: University Press of Kentucky.

Schmidt, Ernst Reinhold 1882. *The Founding of Pennsylvania: The German View of Our Bicentennial*. Philadelphia.

Schotter, Howard Ward. 1927. *The Growth and Development of the Pennsylvania Railroad Company*. Philadelphia: Allen, Lane and Scott.

Sharpless, Isaac. 1898. *A Quaker Experiment in Government*. Philadelphia: Ferris.

Sharpless, Isaac. 1900. *Two Centuries of Pennsylvania History*. Philadelphia: J. B. Lippincott.

Sipes, William B. 1875. *The Pennsylvania Railroad*. . . . Philadelphia: Pennsylvania Railroad Press.

Stevens, Sylvester K., Ralph W. Cordier, and Florence O. Benjamin. 1968. *Exploring Pennsylvania*. 3rd ed. NY: Harcourt, Brace.

Thayer, Theodore. 1953. *Pennsylvania Politics and the Growth of Democracy, 1740–1776*. Harrisburg: Pennsylvania History and Museum Commission.

Tolles, Frederick Barnes. 1948. *Meeting House and Counting House*. Chapel Hill, NC: Institute of Early American History and Culture.

Turner, Edward Raymond. 1911. *The Negro in Pennsylvania*. Washington: American Historical Association.

Tyler, David Budlong. 1958. *The American Clyde: A History of Iron and Steel Ship-Building on the Delaware from 1840 to World War I*. Newark: University of Delaware Press.

Volwiler, Albert Tangeman. 1926. *George Croghan and the Westward Movement, 1741–1782*. Cleveland: Clark.

Watson, John Fanning. 1830. *Memorials of Country Towns and Places in Pennsylvania*. Philadelphia: Pennsylvania Historical Society.

Watts, R. L. 1925. *Rural Pennsylvania*. NY: Macmillan.

Weygandt, Cornelius. 1939. *The Dutch Country*. NY: Appleton-Century Co.

Wickersham, James Pyle. 1969. *A History of Education in Pennsylvania*. NY: Arno Press.

Wildes, Harry Emerson. 1940. *The Delaware*. NY: Farrar and Rinehart.

Wood, Ralph Charles, ed. 1942. *The Pennsylvania Germans*. Princeton, NJ: Princeton University Press.

Wright, John Ernest T., et al. 1938. *With Rifle and Plow: Stories of the Western Pennsylvania Frontier*. Pittsburgh: University of Pittsburgh Press.

Yoder, Clayton P. 1972. *Delaware Canal Journal*. Bethlehem: Canal Press.

1848. *The Bulletin of the Historical Society of Pennsylvania*. Philadelphia: Pennsylvania Historical Society.

1887–94. *The Historical Journal: Devoted Principally to Northwestern Pennsylvania*. Williamsport: Gazette and Bulletin Print. House.

1902–. *Pennsylvania State College Library Bulletin*. University Park, PA.

1909. *Publications of the Pennsylvania History Club*. Philadelphia: Pennsylvania History Club.

1941. *Wilderness Chronicles of Northwestern Pennsylvania*. Harrisburg: Frontier Forts and Trails Survey.

1953–. *Tableland Trails*. Oakland, MD: Maryland Hist. Soc.

West Virginia

1. Jefferson County

Formed in 1801 from Berkeley Co. Pop. 1820: 13,087, 1850: 15,357, 1880: 15,005, 1910: 15,889, 1930: 15,980, 1960: 18,665.

Bushong, Millard Kessler. 1941. *A History of Jefferson County, West Virginia*. Charles Town: Jefferson Pub. Co.

Bushong, Millard Kessler. 1972. *Historic Jefferson County*. Boyce, VA: Carr Pub. Co.

Cartmell, Thomas Kemp. 1963. *Shenandoah Valley Pioneers and Their Descendants*. 2nd ed. Berryville, VA: Chesapeake Book Co.

Crickard, Madeline W., comp. 1969. *1810 Jefferson County, Virginia Census*. Beverly: Crickard.

Dandridge, Danske. 1910. *Historic Shepherdstown*. Charlottesville, VA: Michie Co.

Jefferson County Historical Tour Organization. 1951. *Jefferson County, West Virginia, Historical Tour*. Ranson: Whitney and White.

Kenamund, Alva D. 1963. *Prominent Men of Shepherdstown, during Its First Two Hundred Years*. Shepherdstown: Jefferson Co. Hist. Pub.

Norris, J. E., ed. 1890. *History of the Lower Shenandoah Valley Counties of Frederick, Berkeley, Jefferson, and Clarke*. . . . Chicago: A. Warner.

Phillips, Edward Hamilton. 1949. *The Transfer of Jefferson and Berkeley Counties from Virginia to West Virginia*. University of North Carolina thesis.

Slonaker, A. G. 1967. *A History of Shepherd College, Shepherdstown, West Virginia*. Parsons: McClain Print. Co.

1951. *Historical Booklet. . . 1801–1951*. Charles Town: Jefferson County Sesqui-Centennial, Inc.

Shepherdstown, Shepherdstown Dist.

Settled c. 1730 by Jorst Hite and his followers who came from Germany, having first settled in NY and PA. Scotch-Irish Presbyterians soon followed. 1737–40 Hite helped immigrants from England, Ireland, France, Scotland, and Wales settle. Shepherdstown originally chartered in 1762 as Mecklinberg, laid out by Thomas Shepherd; name changed to Shepherd's Town in 1798, Shepherdstown in 1867. Site of Shepherd College, small four-year state-supported liberal arts college. Largely agricultural area: grain, fruit, and vegetable farms. Pop. 1930: 888, 1940: 945, 1970: 1,328.

WV 1!: F, widow, 71. B. same house, 3 yrs. in NY age 30–33. — F., PGF local, PGF's F. b. Shropshire, England, PGF's M. b. Berkeley Co., of German descent, PGM b. Berkeley Co., of old Holland Dutch stock; M. b. here, MGF b. Vincennes, IN, MGF's F. b. Prussia, came over with General Von Steuben, MGF's M. b. Crown Point, NY, MGF's MGF b. Stornoway, Scotland (a Brit. general), MGM, MGM's MGF local. — Ed.: private school here; 3 yrs. St. Timothy's, Cantonsville, MD. — Episcopalian. — Charming, intelligent, cooperative. Lives in house which has been in family 5 generations. — Speech similar to Baltimore or Montgomery Co., MD. Uses post-vocalic /r/ very rarely, though general population uses it and her children have it. — Cultivated.

2. Berkeley County

Once part of Frederick Co., VA. Became Berkeley in 1772; included all of what is now Jefferson and Morgan Cos. Named for Norborne Berkeley, Baron of Boutetort, Colonial Governor of VA under George III. First Co. officials sworn in May 19, 1772. Once site of principal village of the Tuscarora Indians. Pop. 1790: 19,713, 1820: 11,211, 1850: 11,771, 1880: 17,380, 1910: 21,999, 1930: 28,030, 1960: 33,791.

Aler, F. Vernon. 1888. *Aler's History of Martinsburg and Berkeley County, West Virginia*. . . . Hagerstown, MD: Mail Pub. Co.

Bell, Annie Walker Burns, comp. 1934. *Third Census of the United States (Year 1810) for the County of Berkeley, State of Virginia*. Washington.

Berkeley County Jaycee-ettes. 1961. *Berkeley County and Martinsburg in the Civil War, 1861–1865*. Martinsburg: Berkeley County Junior Chamber of Commerce.

Crickard, Madeline W., comp. 1970. *1810 Census of Berkeley County, Virginia*. Beverly: Crickard.

Doherty, William Thomas. 1972. *Berkeley County, U.S.A.*. Parsons: McClain Print. Co.

Evans, Willis Fryatt. 1928. *History of Berkeley County, West Virginia*. Wheeling.

Gardiner, Mabel Henshaw. 1938. *Chronicles of Old Berkeley*. . . . Durham, NC: Seeman Press.

Grove, Max W. 1968. *The 1820 Census of the United States of America for Berkeley County*. Hedgesville.

Grove, Max W. 1970. *Reconstructed Census, 1774–1810, Berkeley County, Virginia*. Colesville, MD: Eastern West Virginia Press. U. S. Census Office.

Josephus, Jr. [pseud. for Joseph Barry]. 1872. *The Annals of Harpers Ferry*. . . . 2nd ed. Martinsburg: Berkeley Union.

Norris, J. E., ed. 1890. *History of the Lower Shenandoah Valley Counties of Frederick, Berkeley, Jefferson, and Clarke*. . . . Chicago: A. Warner.

Phillips, Edward Hamilton. 1949. *The Transfer of Jefferson and Berkeley Counties from Virginia to West Virginia*. University of North Carolina thesis.

1968–. *The Berkeley Journal*. Martinsburg: Berkeley County Historical Society.

Martinsburg, Hedgesville Dist.

Named for Thomas B. Martin, nephew of Lord Fairfax, proprietor of that area of VA. Laid out in October, 1778; quickly became a prosperous town with substantial homes and a market house. By 1810, Martinsburg was the Co. seat and had become a resort center as well as an agricultural area. August 5, 1863, became a part of WV. By 1920 had textile

mills, limestone quarries, B&O RR workshops, and participated substantially in the Shenandoah Valley pottery industry.
On the nation's second line of defense in WWII. Large Newton D. Baker Hospital (later converted to a V.A. hospital)
cared for numerous military sick. Numerous industries,
including Dupont, General Motors, Lockheed, and Corning
Glass. Has built a large vocational-technical school. High
land prices, many of the buyers are retired officials from DC.
Still large agricultural areas: orchards, corn, sorghum. Pop.
1810: 1,200, 1820: 1,561, 1850: 2,190, 1880: 6,335, 1910:
10,698, 1930: 14,857, 1960: 15,179.

WV 2: Hedgesville, Martinsburg P.O., Hedgesville Dist. — M,
farmer, 54. B. 15 mi. S. near Arden, came here at age 6. — F.
b. Cumberland, MD, came here as infant, PGF b. Morgan Co.,
WV, PGM b. Frederick (German descent); M. b. Martinsburg,
MGF b. between Bunker Hill, WV, and Winchester, VA,
MGM b. Berkeley Co. (German descent). — Ed.: here till 17.
— Methodist. — Typical farmer. Hard of hearing; unsophisti-
cated; cooperative.

3. Morgan County

Formed in 1820 from Hampshire and Berkeley Cos.
Settled c. 1730. Pop. 1820: 2,500, 1850: 3,557, 1880: 5,777,
1910: 7,848, 1930: 8,406, 1960: 8,376.

Newbraugh, Frederick T. 1967. *Warm Springs Echoes:
About Berkeley Springs and Morgan County.* Berkeley
Springs: The Morgan Messenger.

Omps, Berkeley Springs P.O., Rock Gap Dist.

Omps and Rock Gap small rural communities on edge of
Cacapon State Park, resort area frequented by tourists from
DC and Eastern shore. Little changed from 1940s. Mostly
farming area; Omps has (1974) 6 houses, Rock Gap 7. Pop.
Omps: 1960: c. 25.

WV 3: M, farmer 78. B. 5 mi. S. on Timber Ridge. — F.'s and
M.'s families both from Timber Ridge area, of "Dutch"
descent. — Illiterate. — United Brethren. — Hospitable; little
knowledge of outside world. — Lax articulation, homonymy of
war/wore, etc.

4. Hampshire County

Oldest co. in WV. Formed from parts of Frederick and
Augusta Cos., VA, in 1754. Pop. 1755: 570, 1782: 7,982,
1790: 7,346, 1820: 10,889, 1850: 14,036, 1880: 10,336, 1910:
11,694, 1930: 11,836, 1960: 11,795.

Brannon, Selden W. 1976. *Historic Hampshire.* Parsons:
McClain Print. Co.
Federal Writers Project. 1937. *Historic Romney, 1762–
1937.* Romney.
Maxwell, Hu. 1897. *History of Hampshire County, West Vir-
ginia....* Morgantown: A. B. Boughner.
Michael, Glen E. 1976. *Hampshire County, Virginia (Now
West Virginia), 1782–1850: Heads of Families and Index
to the United States Census.* Winchester, VA: The
Author.
Pugh, Maud. 1946–48. *Capon Valley....* 2 vols. Capon
Bridge.

Hanging Rock

Settled c. 1754. Provenience of settlers, same as 4B (Romney); Hanging Rock 4 mi. N. of Romney. Originally site of
Indian Village, probably Delaware Indians; part of area
known in VA as Old Fields. Agricultural: trees had been
cleared away before white settlers came. Ft. William built
nearby in 1754. In 1940, village consisted of one house. 1960
WV Gazeteer listed the population of Hanging Rock as 0.
1974 official highway map showed Hanging Rock as having 8
houses, 3 farms, and one store. Name comes from 300-ft. cliff
which rises from the edge of the South Branch River; gap
existed before the river. — No village today; mainly agricultural area.

WV 4A: Augusta, Hanging Rock P.O., Sherman Dist. — M,
farmer, 80. B. 12 mi. SW, Peters neighborhood. — F. local,
PGF of Frederick Co., MD, family (English descent), PGM
local; M. b. 8 mi. SW, MGF local (English descent), MGM,
step-MGM local. — Illiterate. — Baptist (New School). —
Quick, intelligent, genial; completely unschooled, no knowledge of outside world. — Clear articulation, moderately rapid
tempo.

Romney

Second oldest city in WV. Settled c. 1730 by Dutch, Irish,
Scotch, English. Later settlements by captured Hessians who
elected to remain. Established at site of Ft. Pearsoll, built in
1756 during French-Indian Wars. Named Co. seat in 1762;
Lord Fairfax named it for Romney, one of the Cinque ports of
England. Oct. 9, 1770, Washington reported to have spent the
night in a house (which still stands) on lot #96. Early in 19th
cent., tobacco-growing area. B&O stop of great importance
during Civil War. Stronghold for Stonewall Jackson's forces
during the 2 Battles of Bull Run. — In 1940s, a small town
populated mainly by orchard growers; no Catholics and only 3
AfAms. Character of town relatively unchanged in 70s. Location of WV schools for the Deaf and Blind. Pop. 1880: 371,
1910: 1,112, 1930: 1,441, 1960: 2,703.

WV 4B: M. farmer, carpenter, 76. B. Staunton, VA, returned
here as infant (under 3). — F. b. here, PGF b. Springfield,
WV, or Fistersville, VA (northeast of Staunton), where
ancestors settled; M. b. here, MGF of German descent. —
Ed.: till 18. — Quick-thinking, very natural, thoroughly
enjoyed questions; friendly, democratic, Confederate
sympathies. — Tempo rapid; vowels short. Usage of *room*,
etc., varies in community.

5. Mineral County

One of five cos. in WV to be established after the admis-
sion of the state into the Union in 1863; formed by the division of Hampshire Co. Created in 1866 and covered 330
square miles. Early settlers were Dutch, Irish, Scotch, and
English. In 1880, 5.6% of population was foreign-born
(Ireland and Germany); in 1910 4.9% foreign-born (Italy and
England). AfAms constituted 3.6% of population in 1910;
3.1% in 1940. Pop. 1870: 6,332, 1880: 8,630, 1910: 16,674,
1930: 20,084, 1960: 22,354.

Wood, Leonora W. 1938. *Sesqui-Centennial of Frankfort...
1787–1938.* Frankfort: Mineral County Historical
Society.

Burlington, Welton Dist.

Settled in 1820, 46 yrs. before the forming of Mineral Co. By 1830, when Burlington Presby. Ch. was established, 12 families made up entire population. Coal and lumber industries; some agriculture. According to 1960 census, Burlington was uninc. 1974 official highway map showed Burlington as having a post office, a school, a children's home, and a one-street shopping district. Pop. 1960: c. 200.

WV 5: M, farmer, 38. B. here. — F. PGF b. Hampshire Co. (German descent), PGM b. Hampshire Co.; M. b. near Grant Co. line, MGF, MGM b. Hardy Co. — Ed.: 8 yrs. — Methodist. — Quick, intelligent in naïve responses, limited general understanding and orientation. — Articulation gentle; tempo moderate.

6. Grant County

Formed in 1866 from Hardy Co. Settled c. 1740 by German, Dutch, English, Scotch-Irish settlers. Land patented in 1746 to Benjamin Chambers. Largely agricultural area: orchards, truck gardens, and lumber. The Grant Co. area was first surveyed in 1746, and was included in the inheritance of Thomas, Sixth Lord Fairfax. Earliest co. name was Spottsylvania. In 1734 Orange Co. formed from Spottsylvania; in 1738 the districts of Augusta and Frederick were formed from Orange Co. In 1754 Hampshire Co. was formed from parts of Augusta and Frederick; in 1786 Hardy Co. was formed from Hampshire; and in 1866, Grant, named for U. S. Grant, was formed from Hardy Co. One of five cos. created by the legislature of WV after the state was established. Pop. 1870: 5,567, 1880: 5,542, 1910: 7,828, 1930: 8,441, 1960: 8,304.

> Judy, Elvin Lycurgus. 1951. *History of Grant and Hardy Counties, West Virginia.* Charleston: Charleston Print. Co.

Jordan Run (Maysville), Union Dist.

Pop. 1960: c. 120.

WV 6A: M, farmer, 87. B. 7 1/2 mi. from here, up mountain. — F. b. here, PGF, PGM b. Germany; M. b. 4 mi. down creek, MGF b. Germany, MGM b. here. — Illiterate. — United Brethren. — Vigorous in mind and body despite age and short stature. Cooperative, patient, somewhat puzzled by questions, but pleased that he was the only man of his age in Co. who could give all information sought. — Articulation good; moderate tempo.

Petersburg, Milroy Dist.

Co. seat since late 1890s. First settled in 1745 as part of Hampshire Co.; inc. 1910. Settled by German, Dutch, English, Irish, Scotch-Irish. Early mill site. Some small coal production. Small rural community with fewer than 400-person increase in population from 1940–70; character of community little changed between 1940 and 1975. Pop. 1880: 268, 1920: 834, 1930: 1,410, 1960: 2,089.

WV 6B: M, farmer, 45. B. here. — F. b. South Mill Creek, Grant Co., PGF b. Grant Co., PGM b. Pendleton Co.; M. b. MO but came here as infant, MGF b. Pendleton Co., MGM b. Hardy Co. — Ed.: here till 18. — United Brethren. — Limited abilities, perhaps overshadowed by elderly father, a pioneer

school teacher, with whom he lives. — Articulation average; tempo moderate.

7 & 8. Hardy County and Pendleton County

Hardy County

Formed in 1786 from parts of Hampshire Co. and named after a VA man, Samuel Hardy. Area first settled in 1740 by Dutch, Irish, Scotch, and English. Home of Lost River State Park. Chief agricultural products: lumber, hay, grain, livestock; leading industries: dairying, poultry processing, and cabinet manufacturing. Pop. 1790: 7,336, 1820: 8,700, 1850: 9,543, 1880: 6,794, 1910: 9,163, 1930: 9,816, 1960: 9,308.

> Judy, Elvin Lycurgus. 1951. *History of Grant and Hardy Counties, West Virginia.* Charleston: Charleston Print. Co.
>
> Moore, Alvin Edward. 1963. *History of Hardy County of the Borderland.* Parsons: McClain Print. Co.

Milam, South Fork Dist.

Established in 1786, with 4 residents. Still an uninc. village in 1960, with a population of 30. Located mainly in an agricultural area with emphasis on livestock, dairy, and poultry farming. Had a post office in 1974. Pop. 1789: 4, 1960: 30.

WV 7A: Swedeland, Milam P.O., Bethel Dist. — M, farmer, 72. B. 5 mi. S. of line in Pendleton Co., near Swedeland, has lived 13 yrs. 1 1/2 mi. N. of line in Hardy Co. — F. b. near here, Hardy Co., PGF b. Grant Co. (could speak "Dutch", name could be Dutch or Swedish), PGM b. near Petersburg, Grant Co.; M. b. Brandywine. — Illiterate. — Mother a Mennonite. — Good natured, slowed down a little by age; probably didn't understand purpose of interview too well. — Articulation fairly clear; tempo moderate.

Pendleton County

Formed in 1787 from Augusta, Hardy, and Buckingham Cos., VA. Located on S. Fork of S. Branch of the Potomac. First settlement in 1745; by 1777 settlement consisted of several families. Settlers were Dutch from NY, Germans from PA, and Scotch-Irish and English from VA. Contains parts of Monongahela and George Washington Natl. Forests. Chief products: lumber, livestock, hay, grain, and poultry. Pop. 1790: 2,452, 1820: 4,846, 1850: 5,795, 1880: 8,022, 1910: 9,348, 1930: 9,660, 1960: 8,093.

> Baggs, Elsie Byrd. 1960. *A History of Franklin, the County-Seat of Pendleton County, West Virginia.* Staunton, VA: McClure Print. Co.
>
> Bell, Annie Walker Burns, comp. 1934. *Third Census of the U.S. (Year 1810) for the County of Pendleton, State of Virginia....* Washington.
>
> Calhoun, Harrison Mayberry. 1974. *Twixt North and South.* Ed. by Harlan M. Calhoun. Franklin: McCoy Pub. Co.
>
> Morton, Oren F. 1910. *A History of Pendleton County, West Virginia.* Franklin. Repr. 1974 (Baltimore: Regional Pub. Co.).
>
> Morton, Oren Frederic. 1922. *A Handbook of Highland County and a Supplement to Pendleton and Highland History.* Monterey, VA: Highland Record.

Brandywine, Bethel Dist.

Largely agricultural grazing and pasturing area; forest land, lying between G. Washington Natl. Forest on the E. and Monongahela Natl. Forest on the W. In 1940, village included 3 businesses, 3 churches, 2 schools, approximately 40 dwellings. In 1974, approximately 7 businesses, 60–70 families, 2 churches, post office. Some iron ore production, but no significant amount. Pop. 1960: c. 200.

WV 7B: M, farmer, 55. B. here. — F., PGF, PGF's F. b. here, PGF's PGF b. Germany, PGF's PGM b. Fort Seybert in Co., PGF's M. b. Highland Co., VA (probably English descent); M. b. here, MGF b. Rockingham Co., VA (German descent), MGM, MGM's F. b. Fort Seybert, MGM's PGF b. here, MGM's M., MGM's MGF, MGM's MGF's F. b. Fort Seybert. — Ed.: here till 20. — Church of Christ. — Quiet, well-mannered, living comfortably on father's old farm. Intelligent, interested in project, took several pages of notes on FW's comments on usage elsewhere. — Articulation a little weak, but speech distinct. Somewhat nasal. Calm, deliberate tempo.

Mouth of Seneca, Union Dist.

Located on the N. Fork of the S. Branch of the Potomac. Largely forest land and agricultural grazing land. Even in 1910 largely just a trading point. In 1940, a post office, a church, a school, about 15 dwellings, and one business establishment. In 1974, approximately three business establishments, a church, a school, a post office, and 12 families. Pop. 1960: c. 5.

WV 8A: Carr Schoolhouse, Mouth of Seneca P.O., Union Dist. — M, farmer, 89. B. 7 1/2 mi. away, edge of Grant Co. — F. b. perhaps in VA, came here as a boy (of "Dutch" descent); M. b. edge of Grant and Pendleton Cos., MGF b. probably in VA ("Dutch"). — Almost no education. — Wife Mennonite; parents unconverted. — Well-preserved, but becoming forgetful. Enjoyed company. — Some prolongation.

Circleville, Circleville P.O. and Dist.

Located on the N. Fork of the S. Branch of the Potomac. Small community surrounded by agricultural area, largely grazing and pasture, with some timbering. In 1940, post office, 1 school, 1 business, 12 dwellings. In 1974, post office, 1 church, about 7 occupied dwellings. Pop. 1960: c. 150.

WV 8B: M, farmer and livestock dealer, 56. B. here. — F., PGF, PGF's F. local, PGF's PGF Ulster Scot, settled in 1781, PGF's M. b. Crabbottom, Highland Co., VA (German descent), PGM, PGM's F., PGM's PGF b. Dist. (English stock, came here via Phila. in 1767), PGM's PGM, PGM's M. b. Co.; M., MGF b. Dist., MGF's F., MGF's M. b. Co. (German descent), MGM b. Dist., MGM's F., MGM's M. b. Highland Co., VA. — Ed.: till 21. — Methodist. — Quick, alert, rugged, genuine. — Articulation clear; vowels somewhat prolonged.

9. Preston County

Formed from Monongalia Co. and named after James Patton Preston, a Rev. hero and governor of VA. Covers 653.88 sq. mi. Settled by the Welsh, Scotch, Irish, and Germans. In 1850, 1.2% of the population was AfAm (0.5% free and 0.7% slave). In 1880 3.7% of the population was foreign-born (Ireland and Germany); in 1910 5.2% was foreign-born (Italy and Germany) and 0.6% was AfAm. Important industries:

coal, limestone, iron ore, lumber, and cement. Also an agricultural area with buckwheat, hay, and grains as the main products. Pop. 1820: 3,422, 1850: 11,708, 1880: 19,091, 1910: 28,341, 1930: 29,043, 1960: 27,233.

Ayersman, George P. 1949. *Educational Development of Preston County.* Marshall College thesis.
McRae, Duncan. 1891. *Prospectus of Preston County.* . . . Kingwood: Journal Printing House.
Morton, Oren F. 1914. *A History of Preston County, West Virginia.* 2 vols. Kingwood: Journal Pub. Co.
Wiley, Samuel T. 1882. *History of Preston County, West Virginia.* Kingwood: Journal Printing House.

Newburg, Reno Dist.

One of the area's early churches was served by Rev. Jesse M. Purinton, father of Professor D. B. Purinton who served as president of WV University. The B&O RR runs by this small inc. village. Pop. 1910: 823, 1930: 745, 1940: 696, 1970: 494.

WV 9A: Fellowsville, Newburg P.O., Reno Dist. — M, farmer, 85. B. here. — F. b. Dist., PGF b. near Denver, in Co. (German descent); M. b. Dist., MGF b. England. — Illiterate. — Methodist. — Alert, gentle, genial; somewhat suspicious; rather unaware of purpose of interview, but able to talk just the same. — Some neighbors of old native stock in the area use [ɔʌɚ] for both [oɚ] and [ɔɚ] words in all cases.

Cuzzart, Pleasant Dist.

Very small, uninc. settlement. Major religion in the community is Methodist Episcopal. In 1940, had a post office, two saw mills, one school, a church, and a cemetery. Still uninc. in 1974 and had grown very little. Pop. 1960: c. 65.

WV 9B: M, farmer, 52. B. Grant Dist., 10 mi. W. — F., PGF b. Dist. (English descent), PGM b. Dist., PGM's F. b. Ireland; M., MGF b. Dist. — Ed.: till 16. — Methodist. — Intelligent; suspicious of purpose once in the middle of the interview.

10. Monongalia County

Formed in 1776 from Dist. of West Augusta, VA. Original settlers were predominantly English along with many Scotch-Irish, Scottish, Irish, and Welsh (largest city Morgantown named after Morgan Morgan; he and Evan Evans were two of the original settlers). Evidence of a settlement as early as 1694 on site of present Rivesville. Oldest church is Forks of Cheat Baptist: 1775. Many forts built in 1770s and 1780s because of Indians, Rev., and Dunmore's War. After 30 Years War Germans, French, Huguenots, Walloons, and Calvinists moved into area. Major industries and products are coal, chemicals, glass and glassware, petroleum, livestock, hay, grain, fruit, vegetables, forestry, and dairying. Part of Cooper's Rock State Forest in Co. Pop. 1783: 2,383, 1790: 4,768, 1820: 11,060, 1850: 12,387, 1880: 14,985, 1910: 24,334, 1930: 50,083, 1960: 55,617.

Atkinson, Mary Davis, comp. 1972. *Monongalia County, West Virginia, 1776–1810.* Beltsville, Md.
Callahan, James Morton. 1926. *History of the Making of Morgantown, West Virginia.* Morgantown: West Virginia University.

Crickard, Madeline W., comp. 1974. *1820 Monongalia County, Virginia Census*. Beverly: Crickard.

Crickard, Madeline W., comp. 1976. *1850 Census of Monongalia County, Virginia*. Beverly: Crickard.

Lathrop, J. M., et al. 1886. *An Atlas of Marion and Monongalia Counties, West Virginia*. Philadelphia: D. J. Lake and Co.

Schmoyer, Jerry H. 1970. *The Historical, Cultural and Archeological Resources of Monongalia County, West Virginia*. Morgantown: Schmoyer.

1895. *Biographical and Portrait Cyclopedia of Monongalia, Marion and Taylor Counties, West Virginia*. Philadelphia: Rush, West and Co.

1928. *Sesqui-Centennial of Monongalia County.* . . . Morgantown: Monongalia Historical Society.

1954. *The 175th Anniversary of the Formation of Monongalia County, West Virginia, and Other Relative Historical Data*. Morgantown: Monongalia Historical Society.

Blacksville, Western (formerly Clay) Dist.

Settled in 1766. Site of Baldwin blockhouse 1770–75. Ft. Baldwin built about 1774 on present site of town. Ft. Worley erected in 1780s. Laid out as town in 1829; inc. 1897. In 1940s town had a post office and several scattered dwellings. Until 1960s town was agricultural and rural. Since then large deep mining operations have changed nature of town; Blacksville mine is rated as one of the largest and most modern in state. Pop. 1910: 204, 1930: 269, 1940: 261, 1970: 211.

WV 10A: Foley Run, Blacksville P.O., Clay Dist. — M, farmer, 72. B. same house. — F. b. Hampshire Co., came here when 2 yrs. old, PGF, PGM b. Hampshire Co.; M., MGF b. Dist., MGF's F. of Scotch-Irish descent, MGM b. Greene Co., PA (German descent). — Ed.: none. — Christian. — Quick, alert, genuine; patient, cooperative. Never learned to read or write. — His slightly centralized and short [ăɹ̆] in all positions may be in the Scotch-Irish tradition of W. PA. Only one phoneme in the [ɔɚ] territory.

Morgantown, Eastern (formerly Clinton) Dist.

Founded 1766–68 by Zackquill Morgan on site of settlement established in 1758 by Thomas Decker. In 1770 Ft. Coburn and in 1774 Fts. Burris and Keras built. Ft. Morgan built between 1767 and 1774; Fort Morgantown established 1774 or 1775. In 1790, 4 houses in Morgantown; 1814 Monongalia Academy; 1849 Morgantown Female Collegiate Institute; 1858 Woodburn Seminary. 1860 Borough of Morgantown inc. and boundaries set. 1866–67 WVU established (originally WVU Agricultural College) by acquisition of property of the Academy and the Woodburn Seminary, now c. 19,000 enrolled. Co. seat. Major industries education, mining, glass and glassware, farming. Pop. 1860: 741, 1880: 745, 1910: 9,150, 1930: 16,186, 1960: 22,487.

WV 10B: Dalton, Morgantown P.O., Clinton Dist. — M, sawmilling, farming, timbering, 76. B. 3 mi. E. of Morgantown in Morgan Dist. — F. b. Morgan Dist., PGF b. below Winchester, VA, PGM b. Co.; M. b. Co., MGF b. Elizabeth, Allegheny Co., PA. — Ed.: two yrs., 3 mos. each. — Methodist. — Aged, feeble; willing to talk when able. — Slightly indistinct

articulation. He distinguishes [oɚ ɔɚ] whereas the middle-aged informant does not.

WV 10C: M, dairy farmer, 51. B. same farm. — F. b. Dist., PGF, PGF's F. b. Co., perhaps near Winchester, VA, PGM b. Co., PGM's F. b. near Winchester, VA; M. b. Co., MGF b. Co. (English descent), MGM b. Co. (German descent). — Ed.: till 21 (one semester h.s. here). — Methodist. — Satisfactory, cooperative. — Uses [ɔɚ] for both phonemes, whereas old-fashioned type distinguishes [oɚ ɔɚ].

11. Marion County

Created in 1842 from Monongalia and Harrison Counties. Got its name from Rev. hero Francis Marion ("The Swamp Fox"). Main industries are coal, glass, natural gas, mining, and machinery; livestock, hay, grain, dairying, and poultry are also important. In 1880, pop. made up primarily of whites born in WV, VA, and PA; foreign-born came from Ireland and Germany. In 1910, 80.2% of pop. native-born, 6.8% of mixed parentage, 11% foreign-born (Italy and Austria), and 2% AfAm. Pop. 1850: 10,552, 1880: 17,198, 1910: 42,794, 1930: 66,655, 1960: 63,717.

Dunnington, George A. 1880. *History and Progress of the County of Marion, West Virginia*. Fairmont: G. A. Dunnington.

Hoffman, Joseph E. 1963. *Marion County Centennial Yearbook, 1863–1963*. Fairmont: Marion County Centennial Committee.

Lathrop, J. M., et al. 1886. *An Atlas of Marion and Monongalia Counties, West Virginia*. Philadelphia: D. J. Lake and Co.

Lough, Glenn D. 1969. *Now and Long Ago: A History of the Marion County Area*. Fairmont: Marion Co. Hist. Soc.

Newman, Dora Lee, dir. 1917. *Marion County in the Making*. Fairmont: Fairmont High School.

Pinnell, William George. 1953. *A Survey of the Economic Base of Marion County*. West Virginia University thesis.

1895. *Biographical and Portrait Cyclopedia of Monongalia, Marion and Taylor Counties, West Virginia*. Philadelphia: Rush, West and Co.

Dent's Run, Mannington P.O. and Dist.

3 mi. W. of the inc. city of Mannington. Relatively small settlement: only a few farms and homes. Presbyterian religious background. Dent's Run boasts first religious services held in the dist.; first church in area built soon after 1800. Mannington pop. 1890: 908, 1900: 1,681, 1910: 2,672, 1940: 3,145, 1970: 2,759.

WV 11A: M, farmer, 69. B. here. — F. b. Dist., PGF, PGF's F. b. OH, PGM b. Dent's Run; M. b. Dent's Run, MGF, MGM, MGM's F. b. in Co. (the latter of VA Tuckahoe descent, from E. of the Blue Ridge). — Ed.: practically none. — Methodist. — Marginal existence. Quick, cooperative to the extent of his ability.

Davis Ridge, Farmington P.O., Lincoln Dist.

Located 2 mi. SE of Farmington. No post office; its business is conducted through Farmington. Farmington is a small village on the B&O RR: mostly non-farm dwellings, a few small businesses and 1 church. Farmington pop. 1910: 519, 1930: 819, 1940: 880, 1970: 709.

WV 11B!: M, farmer, 59. B. same house. — F. b. Dist., PGF b. Co., PGF's F. b. VA or DE (1st ancestor from England to DE), PGM b. Dist., PGM's F. English descent; M, MGF b. Monongalia Co. (German descent), MGM b. Monongalia Co. — Ed.: a few terms at Fairmont Teachers College. — Methodist; chairman of the agricultural assoc. of the Monongalia Valley, member of the school board. — Deliberative, reflective, patient, honest in intent. Difficult to interrogate because of his refusal to be led into spontaneous expression. — Articulation not vigorous. — Cultivated.

12. Harrison County

Formed in 1784 from Monongalia Co., settled in 1764, chiefly by Scotch-Irish migrating from MD and VA. In 1780s and 1790s some migration of Rev. veterans who took up unappropriated land in payment for service with Continental Army. In 1852 Irish immigrants arrived to work on developing B&O RR. 1895–1905 ore workers from PA moved into W. Harrison Co. 1900–1920, French and Belgians came to work in the glass factories; Greeks, Russians, Hungarians, Italians, and Spaniards came to the coal mines and steel and zinc plants. AfAms also came to work in the mines, increasing what had been a very small AfAm pop. In 1940 the leading industries in the co. were glass and glassware, coal chemicals, petroleum, natural gas, lumber, chinaware, and pottery: also some agricultural products. Pop. 1790: 2,080, 1820: 10,942, 1850: 11,728, 1880: 20,181, 1910: 48,381, 1930: 78,567, 1960: 77,856.

Boram, Ron, ed. 1976. *Harrison County 76*. Clarksburg: Clarksburg-Harrison Bicentennial Commission.

Crickard, Madeline W., comp. 1969. *1810 Harrison County, Virginia Census*. Beverly: Crickard.

Davis, Dorothy. 1970. *History of Harrison County, West Virginia*. Ed. by Elizabeth Sloan. Clarksburg: American Association of University Women.

Harmer, Harvey W. 1940. *Old Grist Mills of Harrison County*. Charleston: Charleston Print. Co.

Harmer, Harvey Walker. 1956. *Covered Bridges of Harrison County, West Virginia*. Charleston: Education Foundation.

Haymond, Henry. 1910. *History of Harrison County, West Virginia*. Morgantown: Acme Pub. Co.

Lathrop, J. M., et al. 1886. *An Atlas of Harrison County, West Virginia*. Philadelphia: D. J. Lake and Co.

Martin, Tom. 1966. *Early Clarksburg and Harrison County*. Clarksburg: Tom Martin.

1895. *Biographical and Portrait Cyclopedia of Monongalia, Marion and Taylor Counties, West Virginia*. Philadelphia: Rush, West and Co.

Wilsonburg, Wilsonburg P.O., Sardis Dist.

Located just W. of Clarksburg (industrial center). In 1940, Wilsonburg had 2 schools, 1 church, 100 mixed farm and nonfarm dwellings, 1 business, and a trolley line to Clarksburg. On B&O RR. In 1962 coal mine opened in nearby Mars and rural character of Wilsonburg changed. Many residents commute to Clarksburg. Pop. 1900: 350, 1910: 410, 1967: 200.

WV 12A: Isaacs Creek, Wilsonburg P.O., Sardis Dist. — F, widow, 80. B. Dist (adjoining farm). — F. b. Clark Dist. in Co., PGF b. perhaps in VA; M. b. Clark Dist. in Co., MGF b. Co., MGF's F. b. VA, MGF's PGF, MGF's PGM b. Germany, MGF's M., MGM, MGM's M. b. PA, MGM's MGF b. Ireland. — Ed.: till 18. — Baptist. — Slightly hard of hearing. Feeble at times; rather inquisitive at times as to purpose of a question. — Clear enunciation.

Lost Creek, Grant Dist.

Settled 1800 by PA 7th Day Baptists, inc. 1946. First church, 1808; post office, 1826; B&O RR 1879. Farming, mining, suburban commuting to Clarksburg. Pop. 1950: 798.

WV 12B: M, merchant (hardware store), farmer, 42. B. Dist. Spent one summer in OH. — F. b. Dist., PGF b. Co. (Scotch-Irish and Indian descent); PGM, M., MGF b. Lost Creek, MGM b. Westmoreland Co., PA. — Ed.: till 17. — Methodist. — Extremely quick, intelligent; good orientation; suitable selection for this rather progressive co.

13. Taylor County

Formed in 1844 from parts of Harrison, Barbour, and Marion Cos. For early settlement see Harrison and Barbour (12. and 14.). Tygart River flood control dam is located near Grafton, the Co. seat. WV Industrial School for Boys is located at Pruntytown. In 1850 AfAms constituted 4.4% of pop. (1.3% were free); by 1940 only 2.9%. 1880–1930 large population increase result of coal boom and coming of the RRs. In 1910, 5.2% of pop. foreign-born (mainly Italy and Germany). Leading industries and agricultural products include coal, livestock, hay grain, dairying, poultry, some manufacturing (boxes), and in 1940 glass, glassware, and chinaware. Pop. 1850: 5,367, 1880: 11,455, 1910: 16,554, 1930: 12,785, 1960: 15,010.

1895. *Biographical and Portrait Cyclopedia of Monongalia, Marion and Taylor Counties, West Virginia*. Philadelphia: Rush, West and Co.

Belgium, Grafton P.O., Booth's Creek Dist.

On US Route 50. In 1940 Belgium had about 6 farms, 9 nonfarm dwellings, and 1 business. Area surrounded by coal mines (but only 2 coal mines in area in 1974).

WV 13A: M, farmer, 71. B. Dist. — F, PGF b. Dist., PGF's F. b. VA, PGM b. Co.; M., MGM b. Dist. — Ed.: till 16. — Baptist. — Not very old-fashioned. — His [ɔ˞ɚ] and [ɔ˞ɚ] sound rather alike at times; at first FW was not aware that he distinguished two phonemes in this acoustic area. Rather measured tempo; good articulation. Some prolongation of vowels and diphthongs.

Meadland, Flemington P.O., Booth's Creek Dist.

At intersection of Co. roads 3 and 8. In 1940 shown as farming area with one school and one church and graveyard. Much mining to the east. A 12-acre tomato packing plant in nearby Flemington. By 1974, farming units had disappeared to a great extent and non-farm dwellings had increased in number.

WV 13B: M, farmer, 36. B. same farm. — F. b. Harrison Co., came back here age 12, PGF, PGF's F. b. Flemington Dist., Taylor Co., PGF's PGF Irish descent, PGF's M. b. Dist.; M. b. Dist., MGF b. Co., MGM b. Dist. — Ed.: till 8th grade. — Baptist. — Somewhat intelligent. Son of an uneducated, extremely old-fashioned-talking but well-to-do banker. — Articulation not perfect. No [ɔ˞ ɔ˞] distinction.

14. Barbour County

Formed in 1843 from Harrison, Lewis, and Randolph Cos.; settled in mid-18th cent. by Germans, Irish, English, Scottish, Welsh, Dutch, and French who settled originally in NY, NJ, CT, PA, MD, and VA (Virginians made up the greatest number). Earliest settlement in 1754 at mouth of Dunkard's Creek, now Beverly. Home of "Guineas", a group of partly AfAm people who, according to folklore, were among the earliest settlers and originated from an AfAm and an Englishman. Great variation in color among the Guineas with some having blond hair and blue eyes; their dialect is uniquely theirs. Leading industries and products of Co. are coal, lumber, buckwheat, dairying, livestock, fruit, poultry, grain. Pop. 1850: 9,005, 1880: 11,870, 1910: 15,858, 1930: 18,628, 1960: 15,474.

Maxwell, Hu. 1899. *The History of Barbour County. . . .* Morgantown: Acme Pub. Co.

West Virginia Geological Survey. 1918. *Barbour and Upshur Counties and Western Portion of Randolph County.* Wheeling: Wheeling News Lithograph Co.

Meadowville, Belington P.O., Glade Dist.

Belington settled in 1768 and inc. in 1894. Settlement pattern similar to that for Co. Meadowville, originally Glady Creek, was settled in the 1780s and 90s, and in 1904 was still listed as a post village. When Meadowville and Belington were first settled, they were in co. of W. Augusta, VA; also in Monogalia, Harrison, and Randolph Cos. before being in Barbour Co. in 1843. Fort built in 1784 at Meadowville by Henry Phillips, Welshman. Belington is a lumbering center; other products include wheat, corn, potatoes, beef, and dairy items. Community was a terminus for B&O, WV Central, and Roaring Creek RRs. Also many sandstone and limestone products. In 1940 Meadowville area had 5 churches and nearly all dwellings were farms; by 1974 dwellings were mainly non-farm, and only 1 church was left.

WV 14A: Meadowville, Belington P.O., Glade Dist. — M, farmer, 72. B. 2 mi. S. — F. b. Dist., PGF b. Co. ("Irish" descent), PGM, PGM's F. b. Cove Dist.; M., MGF b. near Belington. — Ed.: till 15. — Methodist. — Vigorous; some difficulty understanding questions.

Philippi, West Dist.

Co. seat; first settled c. 1780. Settlers came from England, Scotland, Ireland, Germany, Holland, France, and Wales by way of DE, NH, CT, MA, NJ, NY, and MD, although most settlers came from eastern WV, E. of the Alleghenies. Chartered in 1844; inc. in 1905. Site of the first land battle of the Civil War. Coal mining and farming major industries; RR terminus for shipment of lumber. Small college, Alderson-

Broaddus, est. in 1909, 1970 enrollment c. 1000. Pop. 1880: 400, 1910: 1,038, 1930: 1,737, 1940: 1,955, 1970: 3,002 (includes college students).

WV 14B: Fox Hall, Philippi P.O., Pleasant Dist. — M, farmer, miner, 42. B. Dist. — F. b. Dist., PGF b. near Morgantown, WV, perhaps in PA (Scotch-Irish descent); M. b. Philippi Dist. — Ed.: till 18. — Methodist. — Willing; some difficulty understanding questions. — Imperfect articulation.

15. Tucker County

Formed in 1856 from Randolph Co.; see Randolph Co. (16.) for early settlement. Rugged, mountainous, forested terrain. Contains Blackwater Falls State Park and part of Monongahela Natl. Forest. As in many other WV cos., Tucker's pop. jumped in 1880–1910. In 1880 0.4% of the pop. foreign-born; in 1910 16.1% foreign-born (Italy and Austria). Paper mills developed early; much lumbering in 1940 but decreased by 1970. Pop. 1860: 1,428, 1880: 3,151, 1910: 18,675, 1930: 13,374, 1960: 7,450.

Lord, James H. 1967. *An Economic Profile of Tucker County, West Virginia.* Morgantown: West Virginia Center for Appalachian Studies and Development, West Virginia University.

Maxwell, Hu. 1884. *History of Tucker County, West Virginia, from the Earliest Explorations and Settlements to the Present Time.* Kingwood: Preston Pub. Co.

St. George, St. George Dist., Tucker Co.

Settled 1776; uninc. Had first sawmill W. of the Alleghenies, first paper mill and first academy of higher ed. in Tucker Co. Bypassed by the RR, St. George declined. In 1937 had several dwellings, both farm and non-farm, and 3 churches; in 1974 some dwellings, 1 church. Pop. 1890: 316, 1900: 152, 1910: 245, 1930: 2,012.

WV 15A: F, housewife, 79. B. just over line in Preston Co. and moved here when 1 yr. old. Spent several months in Webster Co. during Civil War as a child. — F. b. Co., PGF b. in (lower end of) old VA near the Shenandoah Valley, PGF's F. b. England and came over in same boat as George Washington's father, acc. to inf.'s anachronistic account, PGM b. near St. George (spoke "Dutch"), PGM's F. b. Co. ("Dutch" descent); M. b. Co., MGF b. Preston Co., MGF's F. b. Germany, MGM, MGM's M. b. Co., MGM's MGF an American Indian. — Vigorous, healthy, honest, and willing to cooperate. Slightly hard of hearing and forgetful at times. — Good clear articulation.

Parsons, Black Fork Dist., Tucker Co.

Co. seat; inc. 1893. In 1940 had several farm dwellings, some non-farm (row houses), saw mills and a coal mine, one school, one church, one business establishment. 1974 map shows mainly non-farm dwellings, no school, sawmill, or mine. Pop. 1910: 1,780, 1930: 2,001, 1940: 2,077, 1970: 1,829.

WV 15B: Horseshoe Run, Parsons P.O., St. George Dist. — M, farmer, 58. B. adjoining house. — F., PGF b. adjoining farm, PGF's F. b. on S. Branch of the Potomac (English descent), PGM b. near Hanover, PA; M. b. Hollow Meadows, Black Fork Dist., MGF, MGM b. near Kerns, Randolph Co.

— Ed.: till 28, St. George Academy, business college in Lexington, KY for 6 mos. — Presbyterian. — Obliging, but rather hesitant. Politely said he enjoyed the interview very much.

16. Randolph County

Formed from Harrison Co. in 1787; parts annexed later. Settled 1753. Settlers mainly from British Isles, primarily hunters, not farmers. In 1879, colony of 100 Swiss; by 1898 only 6 families remained. WV Central and Pittsburgh RRs came in 1889. First newspaper founded 1874. Pop. jump 1880–1910 a result of coal boom. In 1880 6.2% foreign-born (Ireland and Germany); in 1910 1.4% AfAm and 7.9% foreign-born (Italy and Austria). Forest land. Industries and products include lumber, coal, potatoes, hay, grain, livestock, dairying. First steam sawmill in 1878. First religious service held by Presbyterians in 1786. Pop. 1790: 951, 1820: 3,357, 1850: 5,243, 1880: 8,102, 1910: 36,028, 1930: 25,049, 1960: 26,349.

Bosworth, Albert S. 1916. *A History of Randolph County, West Virginia, from Its Earliest Exploration and Settlement to the Present Time. . . .* Elkins.

Cobb, William Henry. 1923. *Indian Trails, Frontier Forts, Revolutionary Soldiers and Pioneers of Randolph County, West Virginia.* Elkins: Chenoweth Society.

Kek, Anna Dale. 1976. *Randolph County Profile — 1976: A Handbook of the County.* Parsons: McClain Print. Co.

Maxwell, Hu. 1898. *The History of Randolph County, West Virginia.* Morgantown: Acme Pub. Co.

West Virginia Geological Survey. 1918. *Barbour and Upshur Counties and Western Portion of Randolph County.* Wheeling: Wheeling News Lithograph Co.

Wymer, Monongahela Natl. Forest P.O., Dry Fork Dist.

Settlement pattern similar to Co. In NE part of Co.; predominantly farming area. Pop. 1960: c. 40.

WV 16A: M, farmer, 66. B. Dist. Spent 3 yrs. in Pocahontas Co. c. 1917–20. — F. b. Dist., PGF b. PA (Scotch-Irish descent), PGM Scotch-Irish descent; M., MGF b. Dist., MGF's F. Scotch-Irish descent, MGM b. perhaps IL. — Ed.: none. — Mother: Dunkard; wife: Mennonite. — Isolated. Genial, obliging, moderately quick, intelligent.

Beverly, Beverly Dist.

Originally chartered in 1790 and formerly known as Edmonton. Settlement pattern similar to Co. Ft. Westfall built 1774; Ft. Wilson, probably one of most importance in Co., built 4 mi. N. of Beverly in 1774. First Co. seat; first Co. court held in 1787. The name *Beverly* first appeared in court records in 1791. An official post office. In 1940, several farm dwellings, 1 church, 4 schools; in 1974 no church, no schools, most farm dwellings have disappeared. Pop. 1910: 438, 1930: 431, 1940: 484, 1970: 441.

WV 16B: M, farmer, 36. B. Dist. — F., PGF b. Dist., PGF's F. prob. b. Dist. (German descent), PGM b. Dist., PGM's F. German descent; M., MGF, MGF's F., MGM b. Dist. (German descent). — Ed.: till 19. — Methodist. — Cooperative, quick responses. — Slightly indistinct articulation.

17. Upshur County

Formed in 1851 from Randolph, Barbour, and Lewis Cos. Area settled by John and Samuel Pringle after they had deserted from the King's army; lived in a hollowed out sycamore tree near Turkey Run. After the French and Indian War the brothers left the woods in search of people to bring back and settle the area. State game farm located in Co. near French Creek. Increase in pop. between 1880 and 1910 caused by RRs, lumbering, and coal. Chief industries and products: lumber, coal, buckwheat, natural gas, potatoes, livestock, dairying, strawberries. Pop. 1860: 7,292, 1880: 10,249, 1910: 16,629, 1930: 17,944, 1960: 18,292.

Cutright, William Bernard. 1907. *The History of Upshur County, West Virginia. . . .* Buckhannon.

Hornbeck, Betty Dutton. 1967. *Upshur Brothers of the Blue and the Gray.* Parsons: McClain Print. Co.

Liggett, Thomas J., comp. 1980. *Census of Upshur County, 1860.* Buckhannon: Upshur County Genealogical Society.

Morgan, French. 1963. *Yesterdays of Buckhannon and Upshur.* Buckhannon: Republican-Delta.

West Virginia Geological Survey. 1918. *Barbour and Upshur Counties and Western Portion of Randolph County.* Wheeling: Wheeling News Lithograph Co.

Queens, Washington Dist.

James Tenney, Sr., first settler in area, settled above Queens in 1817. He built the first grist mill in the area in 1818. Most of early settlers Methodist; area still primarily Methodist. In 1940 3 schools, a sawmill, 2 churches, and several farm dwellings; in 1974 the sawmill and schools are gone and most dwellings are non-farm. Pop. 1960: c. 65.

WV 17A: M, farmer, 80. B. Dist. — F. b. Pendleton Co. and came here as a boy; M. b. Dist. — Ed.: very little. — Mind failing.

French Creek, Meade Dist.

Uninc.; settled in early 19th cent. by New Englanders. Has State game farm and mixture of farm and non-farm dwellings; Holly River State Park nearby. Pop. 1960: c. 165.

WV 17B: M, farmer, 53. B. 4 mi. S. — F. b. Co., PGF b. Co. or in Pendleton Co. where family originated (German descent); M. b. Banks Dist. — Ed.: till 17. — Methodist. — Slow. — Some prolongation.

Buckhannon, Meade Dist.

Co. seat. Inc. in 1852 by VA, in 1933 by WV. Established in 1816. Early became educational center, the home of Buckhannon Academy, later to become the present WV Wesleyan, a small 4-yr. liberal arts school. Buckhannon has annual strawberry festival. Blacklick Run, SW of Buckhannon, had extensive lumbering and mining in 1940; in 1974 no mining activities in area and few sawmills exist. Pop. Buckhannon 1910: 2,225, 1930: 4,374, 1940: 4,450, 1970: 7,353 (includes students at Wesleyan).

WV 17C: Black Lick Run, Abbott, Buckhannon P.O., Meade Dist. — M, farmer, 73. B. Dist. — F. b. Dist., PGF, PGM b. MA; M. b. Co., MGF "Dutch" descent, MGM b. Co., MGM's

F. "Dutch" descent. — Ed.: till 21. — Presbyterian. — Somewhat suspicious, somewhat senile, but generally cooperative. — Slightly hurried, indistinct speech at times.

18. Lewis County

Created in 1816 from Harrison Co.: settlement pattern and early history similar. Early industries hunting and trapping; by 1900 Lewis was one of the foremost stock raising cos. Present industries include glass, glassware, petroleum, natural gas, lumber, livestock, hay, grain, and poultry. Pop. 1820: 4,247, 1850: 10,031, 1880: 13,269, 1910: 18,281, 1930: 21,794, 1960: 19,711.

Cook, Roy Bird. 1924. *Lewis County in the Civil War.* . . . Charleston: Jarrett Print. Co.

Cook, Roy Bird. 1925. *Lewis County in the Spanish-American War.* Charleston: Jarrett Print. Co.

Smith, Edward Conrad. 1920. *A History of Lewis County, West Virginia.* Weston: The Author.

Bablin, Collins Settlement Dist.

Uninc. settlement in southernmost tip of Co., S. of Duffy which was the P.O. in 1940. Now Ireland, N. of Duffy, is the nearest P.O. Settlement began in 1770s; panic of 1837 reduced construction of Staunton and Parkersburg Turnpike and as a result some displaced Irish and German workers settled in area. In 1940 Bablin was a farming village; farming has since declined. Pop. Duffy 1970: c. 25.

WV 18A: F, housewife, 75. B. Dist. — F. PGF, PGM b. Dist.; M., MGF b. Co., MGM b. near Huttonsville, Randolph Co. — Ed.: till 12, off and on. — Methodist. — Somewhat senile; timid. — Indistinct in utterance.

Weston, Courthouse Dist. and Hackers Creek Dist.

Settlement began in 1770s (see Harrison Co., 12.); inc. 1913. Co. seat. Town originally started as Preston, then changed to Flesherville in 1819, and then to Weston later that year. 1837 panic brought some Irish and German settlers. Home of state mental hospital. Small town atmosphere, but surrounding area includes mining as well as farming. Pop. 1890: 2,143, 1910: 2,212, 1930: 8,646, 1940: 8,268.

WV 18B: M, farmer, 47. B. Freemans Creek Dist., in Co. (33 yrs. in present Dist.). — F., PGF b. Hackers Creek Dist. (of French descent from VA), PGM b. Highland Co., VA (German descent); M., MGF, MGM b. Co. — Ed.: till 18 (8th grade). — Methodist. — Quick, sailing interview; less than 3 hrs.

19. Braxton County

Formed in 1836 from parts of Lewis, Kanawha, and Nicholas Cos. Settlers of Scotch-Irish descent came to area about 1790 directly from the British Isles or from eastern VA and western MD. Once important salt works located at Bulltown, site of massacre of friendly Delawares, Captain Bull and his family, by frontiersman. Braxton Game Refuge in Co. 1880–1910 increase in pop. largely due to migration of native-born, some foreign-born (Italy and Hungary). Major industries and agricultural products: lumber, natural gas, livestock, poultry, dairying, hay, and grain. Pop. 1840: 2,575,

1850: 4,212, 1880: 9,787, 1910: 23,023, 1930: 22,579, 1960: 15,152.

Boggs, Forrest Jones. 1953. *Flora of Braxton County, West Virginia.* West Virginia University thesis.

Sutton, John Davison. 1919. *History of Braxton County and Central West Virginia.* Sutton.

Little Birch, Holly Dist.

Uninc.; settled about 1812. Small community about 7 mi. S. of Sutton. Listed as a post village in 1904. Farming and lumbering major industries, but by 1974 dwellings nearly all non-farm and sawmill and coal mine gone. Pop. 1960: c. 100.

WV 19A: Crites Mtn., Little Birch P.O., Holly Dist. — M, farmer, 70+. B. Dist. — F. b. Dist., PGF, PGM b. Co.; M., MGF b. on Nicholas Co. line, about 2 mi. from here, MGM b. Nicholas Co. — Illiterate. — Methodist. — Unsophisticated; strong, nervous laughter. — No teeth.

Sutton, Holly Dist.

Formerly known as Newville, originally settled c. 1795 by an Irishman, Daniel O'Brien, who made his home in a hollow sycamore tree. By 1826 became the Co. seat, called Suttonsville; in 1837 name was changed to Sutton. Inc. 1873. Burned by Confed. troops in Dec., 1861. Many cattle farms because of rich bottomland along Elk River. At one time salt was mined for local consumption, but process was abandoned in 1868. 1910 first sawmill was built; by 1940s area was lumbered out and coal mining became leading industry, esp. during WWII. In 1974 trees were mainly nut trees used for commercial production (e.g., black walnuts). After WWII, coal mining declined and pop. decreased. In 1940s c. 200 petroleum and gas wells were drilled. Good soil has kept area primarily agricultural and rural; limestone produced and consumed locally as agricultural lime. Pop. 1880: c. 800, 1910: 1,121, 1930: 1,205, 1940: 1,083, 1970: 1,018.

WV 19B: Morrison Church, Sutton P.O., Holly Dist. — M, farmer and lumberman, 40. B. Weston, Lewis Co.; came here when less than 1 yr. old. Spent 3 mos. in Akron, OH. — F. b. Co., 20 mi. N., PGF prob. b. in Co.; M., MGF, MGM b. Co. — Ed.: till 18. — Methodist. — Alert.

20. Nicholas County

Formed in 1818 from parts of Kanawha (39.), Greenbrier (23.), and Randolph (16.) Cos.: settlement patterns similar to those of these cos. Early settlers included Scotch-Irish and German, bringing with them the Presbyterian and Mennonite faiths. After 1800 settlement increased rapidly; first substantial dwelling built in 1805 by John Hamilton at Cross Lane. 1850 1.8% of pop. was AfAm (all slave). In 1880 5.6% were foreign-born (Irish and German); in 1910 3.6% were AfAm and 4.9% were foreign-born (Italy, England). Carnifex Ferry Battlefield Park and parts of the Monongahela Natl. Forest are located in Co. Industries and products include lumber, clothespins, mining, buckwheat, livestock, oats, potatoes, poultry, coal. Pop. 1820: 1,853, 1850: 3,963, 1880: 7,223, 1910: 17,699, 1930: 20,686, 1960: 25,414.

Blair, John P. 1974. *The Growth Prospects of Nicholas County*. Morgantown: West Virginia University Regional Research Institute.

Brown, William Griffee. 1954. *History of Nicholas County, West Virginia*. Richmond, VA: Dietz Press.

Critchfield, Mary Roberts. 1949. *Nicholas County in World War II*. West Virginia University thesis.

McMichael, Edward V. 1965. *Archeological Survey of Nicholas County, West Virginia*. West Virginia Geological and Economic Survey.

Craigsville, Cherry Dist. (formerly Beaver)

Primarily a small lumbering community at intersection of State Routes 20 and 41. Decline in number of farm dwellings by 1974. Pop. 1960: 250.

WV 20A: M, farmer (some RR building and grading for lumber companies locally), 70. B. Dist. — F. b. Dist., PGF b. Greenbrier Co., PGF's F. of German descent or birth, PGM b. Greenbrier Co.; M. b. Dist., MGF b. England. — Ed.: till 16, off and on. — Northern Methodist (Southern Methodist parents). — Excitable; cooperative. — Prolonged vowels and diphthongs.

Summersville (Muddlety), Birch Dist. (formerly Hamilton)

Co. seat; est. 1824, inc. 1897. Summersville Reservoir Project located about 4 mi. SW on Gauley River. Muddlety, supposedly named after Indian game mumbletypeg, is in central Nicholas Co., N. of Summersville. Served by B&O RR. In 1940 sparsely settled with a mixture of farm and non-farm dwellings; by 1974 had become less agricultural or rural in nature. Pop. 1910: 204, 1930: 536, 1940: 642, 1970: 2,174.

WV 20B: Muddlety, Summersville P.O., Hamilton Dist. — F, housewife, 46. B. Dist., 3 mi. N. — F. b. Dist., PGF b. Greenbrier Co., PGF's F. b. Craig Co., VA (Scotch-Irish descent), PGM b. Dist., PGM's F., PGM's M. b. VA (both Scotch-Irish descent); M., MGF b. Dist., MGF's F. b. VA (Scotch-Irish descent), MGM b. Dist., MGM's F. of Scotch-Irish descent. — Ed.: till 20. — Methodist. — Cooperative.

21. Webster County

Created in 1860 from Nicholas, Braxton, and Randolph Cos.; for early settlement see these cos., esp. Randolph (16.). First settlers in 1770s; early settlers chiefly from VA, many from Bath Co. Industries and products include lumber, coal, potatoes, buckwheat, oats, honey, livestock, poultry. Pop. 1860: 1,555, 1880: 3,707, 1910: 9,680, 1930: 14,216, 1960: 13,719.

Dodrill, William Christian. 1915. *Moccasin Tracks, and Other Imprints*. Charleston: Lovett Print. Co.

Hamrick, Gordon Thomas. 1968. *Webster County, West Virginia: An Economic Survey*. West Virginia University thesis.

Miller, Sampson Newton. 1969. *Annals of Webster County, West Virginia, before and since Organization, 1860*. Webster Springs: Webster Springs Star.

Thomas, R. L. 1942. *Webster County*. Webster Springs: Webster Springs Star.

Jerryville (Bolair), Fork Lick Dist.

In 1937 Jerryville was a mining town but not shown on state map; now no longer exists since coal mine closed. This is a very sparsely settled area of the Monongahala Forest, served by the Gauley River and the B&O RR. In 1937 Bolair had 1 sawmill, 1 church, 1 school, 1 small business, and 1 coal mine; in 1974 most farm dwellings had disappeared and there were 9 small businesses, 4 churches, and 1 school. Pop. Jerryville 1960: c. 5.

WV 21A: Gauley River, Bolair, Jerryville P.O., Fork Lick Dist. — M, farmer and local beekeeper, 80. B. same house. — F., PGF b. on Birch River on edge of Co., PGF's F., PGM b. Pendleton Co. (PA "Dutch" descent); M., MGF, MGM, MGM's F. all b. nearby on Elk River (latter said to be "Hessians" because they used to be "ill" and fight). — Illiterate. — Southern Methodist. — Isolated. Genial, cooperative, slightly senile.

Replete, Hacker Valley Dist.

Small, rural community in NW Co. Several seasonal dwellings; small decline in number of farms from 1937–74. Pop. 1960: c. 10.

WV 21B: Browns Mtn., Replete P.O., Hacker's Valley Dist. — M, farmer, lumbering on state roads 8 yrs. now, 49. B. adjoining farm. — F. b. on Holly R. in Co., PGF b. VA (PA "Dutch" descent), PGM b. Highland Co., VA, PGM's F. Scotch-Irish descent; M. b. Upshur Co., MGF b. VA (both MGF and MGM claimed to be part Indian). — Ed.: till 14. — Southern Methodist. — Quick, alert, amiable, rural. — Long vowels and diphthongs.

22. Pocahontas County

Est. in 1821 from parts of Bath, Pendleton, and Randolph Cos., VA. First settled in 1744–50 by Scotch-Irish, French Huguenots, and Germans. Second wave of settlers in 1795–1815 from lower valleys of VA. In 1770s and 80s six forts were erected to fend off Indians, to be used by Revolutionary forces, and to be used in Dunmore's War. In 1910 AfAms were 3% of pop. and foreign-born were 5.5% (Italy and Austria). Major industries and products: lumbering, livestock, poultry, maple sugar, honey, and potatoes. Pop. 1830: 2,542, 1850: 3,598, 1880: 5,591, 1910: 14,740, 1930: 14,555, 1960: 10,136.

Price, William T. 1901. *Historical Sketches of Pocahontas County, West Virginia*. Marlinton: Price Bros.

Marlinton, Edray Dist.

Inc. 1900. First settled in 1749 by Jacob Marlin and Steven Sewell. Ft. Greenbrier, c. 1760, site of present Marlinton. In 1793 the first Presby. church, Oak Grove, was organized. First newspaper 1883. Co. seat, situated on Greenbrier River and served by C&O RR. Borders Monongahala Natl. Forest. Pop. 1910: 1,045, 1930: 1,586, 1940: 1,644, 1970: 1,271.

WV 22A: Elk, Marlinton P.O., Edray Dist. — M, farmer, 85. B. Dist. — F. b. Dist., PGF b. Co. (VA Valley Scotch-Irish descent), PGM b. Dist.; M. b. Marlinton, MGF of VA Valley Scotch-Irish descent, MGM b. Co. — Ed.: till 16. — Presbyterian. — Trusting; senile in reactions. — Short vowels and diphthongs (the VA influence).

Hillsboro, Little Levels Dist.

Home of Pearl Buck, now a historical site. Largely forested area with most dwellings farm units. In 1974, area still almost entirely rural, though restoration of Pearl Buck home attracted some tourists. Pop. 1910: 181, 1930: 220, 1940: 224, 1970: 210.

WV 22B: M, farmer and carpenter, 34. B. in Dist., 4 1/2 mi. SE. — F. b. Green Bank Dist. in N. of Co., PGF b. Amherst Co., VA (German descent), PGM b. Amherst Co., VA; M., MGF b. Dist., MGF's F. b. Augusta Co., VA (Scotch-Irish descent), MGM b. Greenbrier Co., MGM's F. b. VA (English descent). — Ed.: in Beard, then h.s. at Renick in Greenbrier Co. — Presbyterian. — Cooperative. — Articulation not altogether vigorous.

23. Greenbrier County

Est. in 1778 from Montgomery and Botetourt Cos., VA. In 1755, Ft. Savannah (now Lewisburg) was erected. Ft. Donally erected in 1767, 10 mi. from Lewisburg. Col. John Stuart, a Scottish Virginian, is known as the "Father of Greenbrier Co.", and the first Co. clerk's office was in his home in Ft. Spring Dist. White Sulphur Springs (mineral waters) a resort since 1778. Early industries also included chair making, milling, and operating a cattle market. 1783 C&O RR opened; 1820, first newspaper. Timbering industry began in 1880s. State fair held at Lewisburg. Contemporary industries and products include coal, lumber, road materials, livestock, hay, grain, poultry, fruit, and dairy products. Pop. 1783: 682, 1790: 6,015, 1820: 7,041, 1850: 10,022, 1880: 15,060, 1910: 24,833, 1930: 35,878, 1960: 34,446.

Cloninger, Judith McClung. 1972. *Greenbriar County, Virginia, Now West Virginia, 1850 Census.* St. Louis: Micro-Records Pub. Co.

Cole, Joseph R. 1917. *History of Greenbrier County.* Lewisburg.

Dayton, Ruth Woods. 1942. *Greenbriar Pioneers and Their Homes.* Charleston: West Virginia Pub. Co.

Smoot, Meadow Bluff Dist.

Uninc. small community in W. central Co., probably settled in late 18th century. Predominantly farming community; in 1937 there was a quarry which was no longer there in 1974. Pop. 1960: c. 250.

WV 23A: M, farmer, clerk, 82. B. Smoot. — F., PGF b. Smoot, PGM b. Co.; M., MGF b. Co. — Ed.: till 15, off and on. — Methodist. — Quick, alert, cooperative; only occasional senility interference (a 3-hr. interview). — Short vowels and diphthongs (the VA influence).

Renick, Falling Spring Dist.

Inc. in 1906 as Falling Spring but has been known as Renick since at least the 1930s. Small predominantly farming town W. of Greenbrier River, C&O RR, and the Monongahela Natl. Forest. Pop. 1910: 270, 1930: 355, 1940: 388, 1970: 265.

WV 23B: M, farmer, 51. B. Frankford Dist. — F., PGF b. Meadow Bluff Dist. in Co., PGF's F., PGM b. Co.; M., MGF b. Dist., MGF's F. "Irish" descent, MGM b. Co. — Ed.: till 20.

— Presbyterian, member of local draft board. — Quick, alert. Not particularly impressed with purpose or value of study. — Articulation OK. Tendency toward short vowels and diphthongs.

24. Monroe County

Est. from Greenbrier Co. in 1799. First explored about 1671; first settled 1749 by Scotch-Irish and some Germans. Prior to Civil War a few families held large land tracts and were slaveholders; practice of freeing slaves common, esp. by will. Other inhabitants were primarily tenant farmers. Co. almost entirely agricultural with no coal or natural gas deposits and minimal industries. Has good open valley forms; always in touch with Virginian culture. Pop. 1800: 4,188, 1820: 5,580, 1850: 10,204, 1880: 11,501, 1910: 13,055, 1930: 11,949, 1960: 11,584.

Lynch, Leona. 1950. *Monroe County, West Virginia, in the Civil War.* West Virginia University thesis.

Morton, Oren F. 1916. *A History of Monroe County, West Virginia.* Staunton, VA: McClure Co.

Dutch Corner, Caldwell P.O. (Greenbrier Co.), Second Creek Dist.

Dutch Corner not identified on 1937 or 1974 map; Caldwell (nearest P.O.) is a small non-farming community on Howard's Creek. Pop. 1960: c. 200.

WV 24A: M, farmer, 74. B. Dist. — F. b. Dist, PGF of German descent; M. b. Dist. — Ed.: till 18. — Methodist. — Quick, alert, cooperative; somewhat higher type that that selected in some places. — Short vowels and diphthongs (the VA influence).

Sinks Grove, Second Creek Dist.

First house built by Alexander Leach about 1839. Located in N. Co. Predominantly farming area; has a post office. Pop. 1960: c. 100.

WV 24B: M, farmer, 39. B. 8 mi. S. in Union Dist. — F., PGF b. Dist., PGF's F. b. Ireland (Protestant), PGM b. Pickaway in Co. (Scotch-Irish descent); M., MGF b. Union Dist., MGM b. Greenbrier Co. near Lewisburg ("Dutch" descent). — Ed.: till 21 (h.s. at Sinks Grove). — Presbyterian. — Quick, alert, cooperative. — Rather good speech.

25. Summers County

Formed in 1871 from parts of Monroe, Mercer, Greenbrier, and Fayette Cos.; see them for settlement. First land grant in this area by Thomas Jefferson in 1781. Co. has Bluestone Lake, Bluestone Lake Park, and Pipestem State Park. Great pop. increase from 1880–1910 due to AfAms and other non-foreign migrants to the coal fields. Very rugged, mountainous, heavily forested area. Leading industries include lumbering, livestock, production of hay and grain, and tourism. Pop. 1880: 9,033, 1910: 18,420, 1930: 20,468, 1960: 15,640.

Miller, James H. 1908. *History of Summers County from the Earliest Settlement to the Present Time.* Hinton.

Bargers Springs, Talcott P.O., Greenbrier River Dist.

Rural community served by Co. route 17 and the Greenbrier River. In 1937 scattered farm and seasonal dwellings and 1 school; in 1974 still farm dwellings and number of non-farm dwellings had increased.

WV 25A: M, farmer and timbercutter, 72. B. Greenbrier Dist. in Co.; spent 6 yrs. in AR age 35–40. — F. b. Dist., PGF b. Co., PGF's F. b. England, PGM b. Monroe Co.; M. b. Co., MGF b. Botetourt Co., VA, MGF's F. b. Scotland, MGF's M. "Dutch" descent, MGM French descent. — Ed.: till 21, off and on. — Baptist. — Cooperative, quick. — Articulation OK. Vowels and diphthongs tend to be short.

Lowell, Talcott P.O., Greenbrier River Dist.

Settled about 1775–80. On Greenbrier River and C&O RR. Rural community; area in general still mostly farming.

WV 25B: M, farmer, 39. B. same house. — F., PGF, PGF's F. b. same house, PGF's PGF b. VA in Botetourt Co. (Welsh descent), PGM, PGM's F. b. Lowell; M., MGF, MGM, step-MGM all b. on edge of Greenbrier Co. near Alderson. — Ed.: till 17 (8th grade). — Presbyterian. — Better-than-average type. — Prolongation of vowels and diphthongs.

26. Raleigh County

Formed in 1850 from part of Fayette Co. Early settlers primarily Irish, Scotch-Irish, English. In 1880 population was primarily native-born with 1,740 from VA, 61 from OH, 43 foreign-born (British Isles). After 1880, immigrants were primarily from Italy, Austria, and Hungary. Industries and products: coal, lumber, potatoes, poultry, strawberries, cattle, ponies (for mines), mining equipment, building blocks, electronic parts. In 1940 pop. was 14.9% AfAm and 2.3% foreign-born. Pop. 1850: 1,765, 1880: 7,367, 1910: 25,633, 1930: 68,072, 1960: 77,826.

Bone, Dewey. 1950. *History of Education in Raleigh County*. Marshall College thesis.

Clear Creek, Clear Fork Dist.

A rural area in N. of Co. Mainly a farming area; 2 sawmills and a school in 1937 had disappeared by 1974. Pop. 1960: c. 400.

WV 26A: Toneys Fork, Clear Creek P.O., Clear Fork Dist. — F, widow, 82. B. neighborhood. — F. b. Maple Fork, Raleigh Co., PGF, PGM b. Giles Co., VA; M. b. Dist. — Ed.: till 20, off and on. — Baptist parents, now Advent Church. — Fairly good local background; somewhat forgetful at times; somewhat slow. — Articulation not perfect. Tendency toward drowsy prolongations, but short diphthongs before voiceless consonants.

Surveyor, Trap Hill Dist.

Earliest settlers were primarily Irish, Scotch-Irish, English, and a few German and French. Small community in W. Co. Between 1937 and 1974 character of village changed from farm to non-farm as pop. increased. Pop. 1960: c. 125.

WV 26B: M, farmer, 43. B. Dist. — F. b. Glen White, Raleigh Co., PGF, PGM b. Floyd Co., VA; M., MGF, MGM b. Clear

Fork, Raleigh Co. — Ed.: till 16. — Methodist (Dunkard father). — Cooperative; rather better than local average type. — Shorter diphthongs before voiceless consonants.

27. Fayette County

Formed in 1831 from parts of Greenbrier, Kanawha, Nicholas, and Logan Cos., VA. Area explored as early as 1651; first white man came in 1671. Much of the public land given as payment for service in the French and Indian and Revolutionary wars. 1888–1903 Fayette was the leading coal producing county in WV; pronounced pop. jump 1880–1910 appears to be due to the coal boom. Few slaves prior to emancipation, but by 1910 AfAms made up 17.9% of county pop. Before 1880 many migrants from England and Wales; in 1910 predominantly from Italy and Austria. Pop. 1840: 3,924, 1850: 3,955, 1880: 11,580, 1910: 51,903, 1930: 72,050, 1960: 61,731.

Darlington, L. N. 1933. *Early Loup Creek, Fayette County, 1798–1865*. Fayetteville: Tribune.

Donnelly, Clarence Shirley. 1953. *History of Oak Hill, West Virginia*. Charleston: priv. print.

Donnelly, Clarence Shirley. 1958. *Historical Notes on Fayette County, West Virginia*. Oak Hill.

Holliday, Robert Melvin. 1956. *Politics in Fayette County*. Montgomery: Montgomery Herald.

Holliday, Robert Melvin. 1960. *A Portrait of Fayette County*. Oak Hill: Fayette Tribune.

Humphreys, Milton Wylie. 1875. *Military Operations, 1861–1863: Fayette County, West Virginia*. Fayetteville: C. A. Goddard.

Peters, J. T. 1926. *History of Fayette County*. . . . Charleston: Jarrett Print. Co.

Sargent, Webster, Crenshaw, and Folley. 1965. *An Economic Base Study of Fayette County, West Virginia*. Montpelier: Central Planning Office.

Russellville, Nuttall Dist.

Small rural community in E. Co. on edge of Greenbrier Co., on the Nicholas, Fayette, and Greenbrier RR and the Meadow River. In 1937 mixture of farm and non-farm dwellings, post office, 1 church, 1 school, 1 small business, 2 sawmills; little change in 1974 except school is gone. Pop. 1960: c. 100.

WV 27A: M, farmer, 75. B. same house. — F., PGF b. Sewell Dist., PGF's F. b. Greenbrier Co., PGM b. Sewell Dist; M. b. Monroe Co. and came to Sewell Dist when 1 yr. old, MGF b. Monroe Co., MGM b. Sewell Dist. — Ed.: till 16. — Southern Methodist. — Cooperative; occasionally slow or forgetful; perhaps somewhat better speaker than some his age. — Articulation OK; shorter diphthongs when followed by voiceless consonants.

Hico, New Haven Dist.

Hico a small community in E. Co. Marked decline in farms and increase in non-farm dwellings between 1937–1974. Pop. 1960: c. 765.

WV 27B: Hawver, Hico P.O., Nuttall Dist. — M, farmer, 52. B. Dist. — F., PGF b. Co., PGF's F. b. England, PGM b. Co., PGM's F. of "German" descent; M. b. Dist., MGF b. Holland and came when 18 yrs. old, MGM b. Canada (of English descent). — Ed.: till 15 (mother was a schoolteacher; died when he was 12). — Presbyterian. — Slightly self-conscious. — Tendency to prolong. Somewhat shorter diphthongs before voiceless consonants.

28. Boone County

Formed in 1847 from parts of Kanawha (40.), Cabell (36.), and Logan (33.); see them for settlement. Pop. increase 1880–1910 due to coal and railroad. Major industries and products: coal, lumber, natural gas, corn, and strawberries. Pop. 1850: 3,237, 1880: 5,824, 1910: 10,331, 1930: 24,586, 1960: 28,764.

Gordon, Crook Dist.

FW visited area 3 mi. E. of Gordon. Small community in central Co.; contained school and coal mines in 1937, but these were gone by 1974. Pop. 1960: c. 300.

WV 28A: F, widow, 74. B. Dist. — F. prob. b. Tazewell Co. and came here age 10; M. b. Whitesville in Co. — Ed.: till 20. — Free Will Baptist. — Busy, though well-off. Old-fashioned speaker, whose speech did not change much even when self-conscious. Needed reassurance to continue. Somewhat unaware of purpose of the interview.

Low Gap, Washington Dist.

In E. Co. School, coal mine, farming in 1937; school and coal mine gone by 1974 and farming almost nonexistent.

WV 28B: M, farmer, 43. B. Dist. — F., PGF, PGM b. Co.; M. b. Co., MGF b. perhaps in Lincoln Co., MGM of Scottish descent. — Ed.: 2 summers of Spring Normal school at Dawville in Boone Co. Business college at Lexington, KY 3 mos. — Missionary Baptist. — Somewhat defensive.

29. Mercer County

Formed in 1837 from parts of Giles and Tazewell Cos., VA. Earliest settlers 1775 came from eastern VA, others came from Ireland, Wales, England, Scotland, and NY. Mostly farmers prior to 1883, but Norfolk and Western RRs brought in large construction gangs in 1883. First coal mine opened 1884. Influx of AfAms, Hungarians, Italians between 1880–1930. Pinnacle Rock State Park and Camp Creek State Park are in Co. Industries and products: coal, lumber, hay, grain, dairying, livestock, poultry, manufacturing. Pop. 1840: 2,233, 1850: 4,222, 1880: 7,467, 1910: 38,371, 1930: 61,393, 1960: 69,206.

Hendrick, Charles B. 1931. *Official Blue Book of Mercer County, West Virginia.* Princeton, WV: Mercer County Blue Book Association.

Johnston, David E. 1906. *A History of the Middle New River Settlements and Contiguous Territory.* Huntington: Standard Print. and Pub. Co.

McCormick, Kyle. 1957. *The Story of Mercer County.* Charleston: Charleston Print. Co.

Straley, Harrison W. 1925. *Memoirs of Old Princeton.* Princeton, WV.

1937. *Centennial Review and Souvenir Program of Mercer County.* Bluefield: Mercer County Centennial Association.

Elgood (Christians Ridge), Plymouth Dist.

Uninc. Christians Ridge is rural area in E. Co.; Elgood is a few mi. to the N. Farming declined, schools and sawmill disappeared between 1937 and 1974. Pop. 1960: c. 25.

WV 29A: Christians Ridge, Elgood P.O., East River Dist. — M, farmer, 87. B. Dist. — F. unknown; M., MGF b. Dist., MGF's F. b. Rockingham Co., VA, MGM b. McDowell Co., WV. — Ed.: 1 mo. (after age 21), never before that. — Christian Baptist. — Old-fashioned. — Articulation OK.

Athens (Bent Mtn.), Princeton P.O., Plymouth Dist.

Incorporated 1906. Bent Mtn. is a farming area in E. central Co. In nearby Athens is Concord College, small 4-yr. state-supported school. Pop. 1910: 575, 1940: 682, 1970: 1,000.

WV 29B: Bent Mtn., Athens, Princeton P.O., Plymouth Dist. — F, housewife, 34. B. Dist. — F. b. Dist., PGF, PGM b. Co.; M. b. Dist., MGF b. NC, MGM b. Co. — Slow. — Prolongation.

30. Wyoming County

Created in 1850 from Logan Co. (33.). Pioneer industries were the raising of corn, potatoes, sweet potatoes, rye, tobacco, flax, turnips, wheat, and oats. Many early settlers operated their own grist mills. Ginseng digging an early source of income. Road construction began 1850; first newspaper 1878. 1889 commercial timbering began; 1919 first natural gas well completed. Coal operations began in 1907 after the VA RR arrived. Increase 1910–30 of foreign-born and AfAms, who came to work in the mines. Industries and products: coal, natural gas, lumber, livestock, poultry, hay and grain. Pop. 1850: 1,645, 1880: 4,322, 1910: 10,392, 1930: 20,926, 1960: 34,836.

Bowman, Mary Keller. 1965. *Reference Book of Wyoming County History.* Parsons: McClain Print. Co.

Cooke, Kennis. 1952. *A History of Education in Wyoming County.* Marshall College thesis.

McGraw, Darrell V. 1949. *Wyoming County in World War II.* West Virginia University thesis.

Pineville (Bear Hole Fork), Center Dist.

Incorporated 1907; Co. seat. Bear Hole Fork is a rural area just E. of Pineville in S. central Co. Non-farm dwellings; school and sawmill have disappeared since 1937. Pop. 1910: 334, 1930: 536, 1940: 769, 1970: 1,175.

WV 30A: Bear Hole Fork, Pineville P.O., Center Dist. — M, farmer, saw logging, 68. B. near mouth of Laurel Fork in Oceana Dist. — F., PGF b. Oceana Dist. in Co., PGF's F. b. NC; M. b. Fayette Co., came at 13 to Oceana Dist., MGF b. Fayette Co. — Ed.: none. — Missionary Baptist. — Timid; unaware of purpose of the interview; trouble understanding questions. — Prolonged vowels, diphthongs.

Oceana, Oceana Dist.

Settled 1797; inc. 1947. Co. seat 1850–1907. In NW Co. By 1974, farming had declined and former coal mine was gone. Pop. 1910: 129, 1960: c. 1,303.

WV 30B: M, farmer, 49. B. Dist. – F., M., MGF, MGF's F. b. Dist., MGF's PGF, MGF's PGM b. Giles Co., VA., MGM b. Co. – Ed.: till 15. – Methodist. – Rather unsophisticated. – High vowels; prolongation.

31. McDowell County

Created in 1858 from Tazewell Co., VA. Big jumps in pop. in 1880, 1910, and 1930 due to coal boom. Co. 30.6% AfAm by 1910, 25% in 1930. 13.1% foreign-born in 1910 (mainly Italy, Hungary). Migrants to Co. after 1930 were mainly non-foreign whites. One of state's largest coal-producing cos.; boom started after opening in 1887 of Flat Top Mtn. Tunnel, which brought RR to McDowell. Industries and products in addition to coal: lumber, livestock, corn, potatoes. Pop. 1860: 1,535, 1880: 3,074, 1910: 47,856, 1930: 90,479, 1960: 71,359.

DAR, Colonel Andrew Donnally Chapter. 1959. *McDowell County History: A Pictorial History of McDowell County, West Virginia Covering both the Old and the New*. Fort Worth, TX: University Supply and Equipment Co.

Panther (Trace Fork), Sandy River Dist.

Trace Fork very sparsely settled area on NW border of Panther State Forest in W. Co. By 1974 mostly non-farm dwellings; very rural. Pop. 1960: c. 250.

WV 31A: Trace Fork, Panther P.O., Sandy River Dist. – M, farmer and timberman, 63. B. Dist. – F. b. Dist., PGF not b. in Co. (killed by Democratic bushwhackers in Civil War), PGM b. Dist., PGM's F. b. Bluefield, Mercer Co., WV; M. b. in a house divided by the VA-WV line next to Buckhannon Co., VA, MGF b. on Buckhannon Co., VA line in WV, MGF's F. b. perhaps in Giles Co., VA (killed by Democratic bushwhackers in the Civil War); MGM b. Buckhannon Co., VA. – Ed.: 4 mos. only at age 14–15. – Baptist and Holiness. – Talkative, genial. Not the most primitive type by any means. Majority of pop. in community had parents born in Buckhannon Co., VA or in KY. – Prolonged vowels, diphthongs.

Bradshaw, Sandy River Dist.

Small town in SW Co.; served by Norfolk and Western RR. 3 coal mines in 1937; these were gone by 1974 though several non-farm dwellings and a post office remained. Pop. 1960: c. 950.

WV 31B: Crane Ridge, Bradshaw P.O., Sandy River Dist. – M, farmer, 49. B. Dist. – F. b. Dist., PGF b. Mingo Co., WV, PGF's M. b. KY, PGM b. Wise Co., VA (partly "Dutch"); M. b. Dist., MGF b. Wise Co., VA, MGM partly "Dutch". – Ed.: till 5th grade (14 yrs. old). – Baptist. – Not very alert. – Prolonged vowels and diphthongs.

32. Mingo County

Created in 1895 from Logan Co. (33.); see Logan for early settlement. Site of infamous Hatfield-McCoy feud. Major pop. gain in 1910–30 due to coal industry; influx esp. of AfAms, Austrians, Italians. Industries and products: corn, livestock, lumber, potatoes, coal. Pop. 1900: 11,359, 1910: 19,431, 1930: 38,319, 1960: 39,742.

Barnes, John. 1970. *A Case Study of the Mingo County Economic Opportunity Commission*. University of Pennsylvania thesis.

Perry, Huey. 1977. *"They'll Cut Off Your Project": A Mingo County Chronicle*. NY: Praeger.

Naugatuck, Hardee Dist.

In W. Co., served by the Tug River and the Norfolk and Western RR. Mainly non-farm dwellings; coal mine nearby in 1937 but gone by 1974. Pop. 1960: c. 350.

WV 32A: F, housewife and washerwoman, 69. B. Dist. – F. b. Dist., PGF b. on Beech Creek in McDowell Co., PGM b. on Elk Creek in Mingo Co.; M., MGF, MGM b. Dist. – No education. – Baptist. – FW met inf. in a country store while looking for someone else; inf. was a volunteer. Repetitive, self-assertive, independent; humble, subdued, hardworking. Loved being center of attention, but quite un-self-conscious in responses. Completely ignorant of the outside world. – Quick, high-pitched, nervous, drawling speech. High front long [ɪ˱˔·ᵊ] and [ɛ˱˔·ᵊ]. *Last*, *past*, *aunt* rhyme with *laced*, *paste*, *ain't*.

WV 32B: M, timberman, 45. B. Dist. – F., PGF b. Dist., PGM b. Warfield Dist., Mingo Co.; M. b. KY and settled here as a child, MGF "a rambler". – Ed.: till 12–13. – Baptist. – Willing; occasionally slow due to high blood pressure.

33. Logan County

Formed in 1824 from parts of Giles, Tazewell, Kanawha, and Cabell Cos., VA. Settled 1790s by migrants from eastern VA and other east coast areas; first settlers were farmers, carpenters, and laborers. First permanent settlement started by William Dingess (of German descent) in 1799. First store opened, near present city of Logan, between 1820–23, dealing in ginseng, furs, pelts, and household goods. 1904 first RR. Then coal production and big pop. jump 1910–1930; included AfAms and foreign-born whites, esp. from Italy and Hungary. Pop. 1830: 3,860, 1850: 3,620, 1880: 7,329, 1910: 14,476, 1930: 58,534, 1960: 31,570.

Albert, Ethel Evans. 1974. *Logan County, Virginia, Marriage Records, 1853–1860, and 1850 Census*. Kingsport, TN: Albert.

Harvey, Helen Barger. 1942. *From Frontier to Mining Town in Logan County (West Virginia)*. University of Kentucky thesis.

Hurst, Mary Bland. 1930. *Social History of Logan County, West Virginia, 1753–1923*. NY. Repr. 1961 (Cleveland, OH: Micro Prints Inc.).

Ragland, H. C. 1949. *Logan County*. Logan: Banner.

Swain, George Thomas. 1927. *History of Logan County, West Virginia. . . .* Logan: G. T. Swain.

Chapmanville (Crawley's Creek), Guyan Dist.

Inc. 1947. Earliest lumber company in Co. built on Crawley's Creek in 1876 by 2 men, Garret and Runyon. Forests were quickly depleted and by 1900 industry had declined dramatically. Area is in NW Co. Farming declined between 1937–74 and the one school disappeared. Pop. 1960: 1,158.

WV 33A: Crawley's Creek, Chapmanville P.O. and Twp. — M, farmer, logging, lumbering, horse/cattle trading, 67. B. Dist. — F. b. Boone Co. and came here as a minor, PGF b. perhaps in VA (part Indian), PGM b. Boone Co. (partly of "Irish" descent); M. b. Dist., MGF b. perhaps in TN (possibly "Irish" descent), MGM b. KY, near Beavers Creek (part Indian). — Ed.: 3 mos. — Baptist. — Old-fashioned, good-hearted. — Prolonged vowels and diphthongs.

Henlawson (Mitchell Heights), Guyan Dist.

Inc. 1949. Mitchell Heights not on state map in 1937. The area is S. of Logan, the Co. seat in NW of Co. Served by Guyandotte River and C&O RR. Near Chief Logan State Park. Farming declined 1937–74. Pop. Henlawson 1960: c. 1,670.

WV 33B: Logan: Mitchell Heights, Henlawson P.O., Logan Dist. — M, farmer, logging, sawmill, 55. B. on Tug River, 40 mi. SW in Mingo Co.; came here when 7 yrs. old. — F. b. Tazewell Co., VA, enlisted in Confed. Army at 16 and settled when 20 on Tug River in present Mingo Co., PGF of "Irish" descent; M. b. on Tug River, MGF of "Dutch" descent, MGM half-Indian. — Ed.: till 20. — Christian. — Quick, intelligent. Initially somewhat suspicious. — High front tongue position for front vowels. Prolonged vowels and diphthongs.

34. Lincoln County

Formed in 1867 from parts of Cabell, Putnam, Kanawha, and Boone Cos. Named for Abraham Lincoln. Leading industries and products: petroleum, natural gas, lumber, tobacco, corn, and potatoes. Pop. 1870: 5,053, 1880: 8,739, 1910: 20,481, 1930: 19,156, 1960: 20,267.

Lambert, F. B. 1925. *Lincoln County.* Hamlin: Carroll High.

Hamlin, West Hamlin P.O., Carroll Dist.

Chartered 1867; incorporated 1908. Settled by Scotch-Irish from VA. English and Irish from other WV cos. and English and German 1870–1900. Originally a terminus for salt and lumber distribution. C. 1900 gas wells opened in area causing influx of Germans and Irish from OH and to some extent from southern VA. In 1940, gas and oil wells as well as some coal mines were in operation. Pop. 1937: 850, 1974: 1024.

WV 34A: F, housewife, 67. B. Union Dist., 10 mi. S. — F., PGF b. Union Dist., PGM b. Raleigh Co.; M., MGF b. Carroll Dist. — Ed.: till 20. — Mormon. — Inf. took the place of her husband, who was deaf. Timid; old-fashioned.

WV 34B: M, farmer, 46. B. Dist. — F. b. Dist., PGF, PGF's F. b. Kanawha Co., PGF's PGF b. France, PGM b. Kanawha Co.; M., MGF, MGM b. Duval Dist., Lincoln Co. (MGM "Dutch" descent). — Ed.: till 14. — Methodist. — Average intelligence; cooperative.

35. Wayne County

Formed 1842 from Cabell Co. Named for General Anthony Wayne of Rev. fame. Cabwaylingo State Forest is located in Co. Much of Co. was given to a number of military men, as far back as French and Indian War, as land grants. Leading industries and products: porcelain, insulation,

natural gas, lumber, cement and concrete; hay and grain, tobacco, livestock, dairying, poultry, fruit, vegetables, sorghum. Pop. 1850: 4,760, 1880: 14,739, 1910: 24,081, 1930: 31,206, 1960: 38,977.

Kiahsville, Stonewall Dist.

Settled in late 1820s by immigrants from Giles Co., VA. Remained a small community. In late 19th century coal mines opened nearby. A post office. In 1937 predominantly farm housing. Town moved in 1969–70 when East Lynn Dam and Reservoir system was built; predominantly non-farm dwellings by 1974. Pop. 1960: c. 10.

WV 35A: Maynard Branch, Kiahsville P.O., Grant Dist. — M, farmer, 68. B. Dist. — F. b. KY, but came here before 7 yrs. old, PGF b. NC, PGM b. perhaps KY; M. b. Dist, MGF, MGM b. Co. (MGF of Protestant Irish descent). — Ed.: till 15. — Baptist. — Alert, conscientious, cooperative. Somewhat apologetic. — Rather good, clear articulation. [ʌ] vowel tends to lengthen but in general not much lengthening of vowels and diphthongs.

Wayne, Union Dist.

Co. seat. Formed in 1842 as Trout's Hill; inc. in 1882 as Wayne. Turn of century brought RRs, gas, oil to Wayne although area still remained agricultural in nature; many farms under lease for oil. Pop. 1910: 384, 1930: 675, 1940: 801, 1970: 1,354.

WV 35B: M, farmer, 49. B. Butler Dist., 4 mi. away. — F. b. Butler Dist, PGF b. VA (partly "Irish"), PGM b. perhaps KY; M. b. Butler Dist., MGF b. Co. (of old VA stock), MGM b. Butler Dist. — Ed.: till 20. — Baptist (Methodist parents). — Moderately good articulation; some prolongation.

36. Cabell County

Formed from Kanawha in 1809. Settled c. 1790. Settlers were particularly Scottish, Irish, English from Giles, Tazewell, and Amherst Cos., VA, English resettling from Kanawha and Greenbrier Cos., and Germans from MD and PA by way of Pittsburgh. Pop. jump between 1880–1940 largely due to Germans having originally settled in OH. Lumbering and furniture-making major industries before the Civil War. Once a shipping point for meat packing firm, but locks and dams of Guyandotte destroyed during Civil War and not restored. Leading industries and products: glass, nickel alloys, railway and mine cars, clothing, steel rails, chemicals, shoes, lumber, natural gas, tobacco, dairying, fruit, poultry, sorghum. Pop. 1810: 2,717, 1820: 4,789, 1850: 6,299, 1880: 13,744, 1910: 46,685, 1930: 90,786, 1960: 108,202.

Smith, Wiatt, ed. 1910. *Program: Guyandotte Centennial, 1810–1910.* Huntington: Guyandotte Centennial and Cabell County Home Coming Association.
Wallace, George Selden. 1935. *Cabell County Annals and Families.* Richmond, VA: Garrett and Massie.

Salt Rock, McComas Dist.

Uninc.; settled about 1801. Meed River Church est. 1807. First court session, 1809, held at home of William Merritt in Salt Rock. Area almost entirely agricultural: far removed from pop. centers of Co. Almost all non-farm dwellings by 1974. Pop. 1960: c. 150.

WV 36A: Merritt Creek, Salt Rock P.O., McComas Dist. — M, farmer, 65. B. Dist. — F. b. Dist., PGF prob. b. Co., PGF's F. b. VA; M., MGF b. Dist., MGF's F. b. VA. — Ed.: till 14. — United Baptist. — Understood that he was being interviewed as an "old-fashioned" type, and enjoyed it. — Articulation slightly unclear.

Tom Creek, Barboursville P.O., McComas Dist.

A rural area settled in 1803 by Henry Peyton from Amherst Co., VA. Predominantly a non-farm area in 1937 and 1974; coal mine had disappeared by 1974.

WV 36B: M, farmer, 63. B. Dist. — F. b. Dist., PGF b. perhaps in England; M. b. Dist. — Ed.: till 19. — Northern Methodist. — Rather progressive for his age; cooperative, intelligent.

37. Mason County

Formed in 1804 from W. portion of Kanawha. Visited in 1669 by LaSalle, in 1749 by Celoron, in 1750 by Gist, and in 1770 by Washington. Co., like Putnam, part of military land grants of 1754. Settlers mainly military patentees, English and Scottish originally settling in eastern VA. Leading industries and products: electric power, coal, lumbering, ship building, plastics, chemicals, furniture, clothing, salt and brine, hay, grain, tobacco, dairy products, poultry, fruit, and vegetables. Pop. 1810: 1,791, 1820: 4,868, 1850: 7,539, 1880: 22,293, 1910: 23,019, 1930: 20,788, 1960: 24,459.

Hamilton, H. Cliff, and Zelda Knapp. 1961. *"Moving Up": A Slogan for Educational Advancement in the Schools of Mason County.* Charleston: West Virginia State Dept. of Education.

Macher, Violette S. 1972. *Mason County Cemetery Inscriptions.* Middleport, OH: Quality Print. Shop.

Tribble, Union Dist.

Uninc. but earlier listed as a post office. Settled in early 19th century. Lumbering important in area. By 1974 no post office and few dwellings.

WV 37A: M, farmer, 79. B. same farm. — F. b. Dist., PGF b. OH (perhaps Yankee descent), PGM b. Co. (perhaps Yankee descent); M. b. 3 mi. over line in Putnam Co., MGF b. PA ("Irish" descent), MGM b. PA ("Dutch" descent). — Ed.: none. — United Brethren. — Senile. Very difficult to find anyone whose parents were born in Co.

Henderson, Clendenin Dist. (formerly Arbuckle)

Inc. 1893. Part of land surveyed by Washington in 1770. Quiet rural area, though farming declined in 1940–70; listed as a post office in 1970. Pop. 1960: 601.

WV 37B!: F, spinster, 69. B. same house; spent one summer in Texas age 40. — F. b. same house, PGF b. Co., PGF's F., PGF's M. b. Augusta Co., VA (both Scotch-Irish descent), PGM b. Co., PGM's F., PGM's M. b. VA (Shenandoah Valley); M. b. near Buffalo, now over line in Putnam Co., MGF b. near Arbuckle P.O., MGF's F. b. Monroe Co., MGF's M. b.

near Arbuckle P.O., MGF's MGF prob. b. VA. — Ed.: till 18 (few mos. at Marshall College). — Southern Methodist. — Somewhat prim and self-conscious, essentially a local cultivated type. Interested in traditions, but unimpressed by the importance of this study. — Cultivated.

38. Putnam County

Formed in 1848 from parts of Kanawha, Mason, and Cabell Cos. Named in honor of General Israel Putnam, New England patriot and soldier. Settled originally by Scotch-Irish, English, and Germans from Albemarle and Berkshire Cos., VA. German immigration 1870–90 from OH. Much of Co. part of military land grants issued for service during the French and Indian War (1754, George Washington surveyed the area). After Civil War and with coming of the RR, coal mining and lumbering extensive; yet agricultural nature of the area has remained. Chemical industry also important since 1890s. Other products: rayon pulp, tobacco, hay, grain, livestock, dairying. Pop. 1850: 5,335, 1880: 11,735, 1910: 18,587, 1930: 16,737, 1960: 23,561.

Rust, Mary Jane Hansford. 1975. *Recollections and Reflections of Mollie Hansford, 1828–1900.* Ed. by William D. Wintz.

Wintz, William D. 1967. *The History of Putnam County.* Charleston: Upper Vandalia Historical Society.

Poca (Lanham, Heizer), Pocatalico Dist.

Poca inc. 1958, Lanham uninc. village. First school in area opened 1827; mill constructed 1844. Center for coal mining, iron ore, and lumber (2 sawmills). After WWII, coal and lumber industry decreased, replaced by large chemical plants. Between 1937 and 1970, farming declined and 3 coal mines in Heizer area were closed. 2 schools in 1937, but these were gone by 1970, though number of non-farm dwellings had increased. Pop. 1960: 607.

WV 38A: Lanham, Poca P.O., Pocatalico Dist. — M, miner and farmer, 72. B. on edge of Kanawha Co. but raised in Putnam Co.; spent several years in Greenbrier Co. — F. b. Union Dist., Putnam Co., PGF b. VA (Protestant Irish descent), PGM b. on Poca River in Kanawah Co.; M. b. Union Dist., Putnam Co. — Ed.: part of 3 terms. — Baptist. — Quick, alert conversationalist; high interest in project. — Good articulation. Remarkable that his [ʋʌ·] is so open (instead of [ɔ·]).

WV 38B: Heizer, Poca P.O., Pocatalico Dist. — M, miner, 37. B. same house. — F. b. Dist, PGF b. Scott Dist. on other side of river, Putnam Co., PGF's F., PGF's M. b. Botetourt Co., VA, PGM, PGM's F., PGM's M. b. Co.; M. b. on edge of Kanawha Co., MGF b. Poca Dist., Kanawha Co., MGF's F. b. VA. — Ed.: till 12. — Advent father, Baptist mother. — Quick, alert, with good sense of humor; cooperative. — Rather clear articulation.

39 & 40. Kanawha County

Formed in 1788 from parts of Greenbrier and Montgomery Cos. (VA). Settlers, primarily of English descent, came from eastern VA. Also Palatinate Germans and Scotch-Irish immigrated from SE PA and the Valley of VA. First explored by Washington in 1772. First coal from Lewisburg to the Kanawha Valley in 1774. First permanent settlement in 1773.

1808 salt making, an important pioneer industry, began. In 1819 the first newspaper was published and the first steamboat ascended the Kanawha River. 1827 and 1832 stagecoach service began to Lewisburg and Lexington, KY, respectively. By 1840, more than 200,000 tons of coal were being consumed annually by the Kanawha salt furnaces. Coal production boomed after the Civil War; natural gas extracted as early as 1841 and oil extraction began in early 20th cent. Effective train service by 1873 and 1865–1915 saw a significant growth in manufacturing. Kanawha State Forest located here. WV State College (once AfAm, now integrated), Morris Harvey College (private small 4-yr. liberal arts college), and the College for Graduate Studies in Co. Leading industries and products: chemicals, brines, coal, glass and glassware, petroleum, natural gas, axes and tools, electrical power, enamelware, lumber, mine machinery and equipment, dairying, poultry, hay and grain, fruit, vegetables, livestock. Pop. 1800: 3,239, 1820: 6,399, 1850: 15,353, 1880: 32,466, 1910: 81,457, 1930: 157,667, 1960: 252,825.

Atkinson, George Wesley. 1876. *History of Kanawha County*. Charleston: The West Virginia Journal.

Cook, Roy Bird. 1930. *Daniel Boone: Little Known History of the Famous Pioneer, Trail-Blazer, Indian Fighter in the Kanawha Valley of West Virginia*. Charleston.

Dayton, Ruth Woods. 1947. *Pioneers and Their Homes on Upper Kanawha*. Charleston: West Virginia Pub. Co.

Ganyard, David Wayne. 1967. *The Degree of Relationship between Bituminous Coal Mining and Chemical Manufacturing in the Kanawha County Region*. Ohio State University dissertation.

Laidley, W. S. 1911. *History of Charleston and Kanawha County, West Virginia. . . .* Chicago: Richmond-Arnold Pub. Co.

McMichael, Edward V. 1969. *Excavation of the Murad Mound, Kanawha County, West Virginia, and an Analysis of Kanawha Valley Mounds*. Morgantown: West Virginia Geological and Economic Survey.

Russell, Michael J. 1972. *The Planning Commission in County Government: The Kanawha County Planning and Zoning Commission*. West Virginia University thesis.

Rust, Mary Jane Hansford. 1975. *Recollections and Reflections of Mollie Hansford, 1828–1900*. Ed. by William D. Wintz. St. Albans: Wintz.

South Charleston, Dist. 4

Est. 1906; inc. 1919. Largely urban area developed as a result of large chemical industries in the area. On S. side of Kanawha River, opposite Charleston. Pop. 1930: 5,904, 1960: 19,180.

WV 39A: M, merchant, former painter, 58. B. Charleston on the S. side near the C&O RR station; only moved to S. Charleston a few months ago. — F. b. Hanover Co., VA and came here as a young man; M. b. Charleston, MGF's F. b. Scotland, MGM b. WV on a farm. — Ed.: Charleston till 15 (6th grade). — Baptist. — Enjoyed being interviewed; rootless, but honest, reliable, good-natured in answering. — Somewhat lazy articulation; tendency to prolongation.

Charleston, Dist. 5

Co. seat and state capital. Chartered in 1794 as Charles Town; changed to Charleston in 1819. In 1788, George Clendenin and a party of rangers, mostly English, arrived on site of present day Charleston to establish a fort, Ft. Lee, as a protectorate against the Indians. Charleston in a narrow valley with high hills on each side, served by Elk and Kanawha Rivers. In 1808 Charleston was described as a long row of cabins along the river with a narrow street in front. By 1940 there were 11 dry goods stores, 6 grocery stores, 2 saw and grist mills, 1 newspaper, and 1 bank. 1823 first steamboat reached Charleston; 1824 packet boat service initiated; 1890 first streetcar service. In 1884 approx. 20% of pop. was AfAm; in 1930 only 11.2%. Present-day Charleston is a thriving metropolis: Morris Harvey College and business schools are there. Also Civic Center, municipal auditorium, symphony orchestra, local theatrical group. Extensive sports: water sports, AA professional baseball team, and National Track and Field Hall of Fame. 2 daily newspapers and 3 TV stations; became a Port of Entry in 1973 and is a transportation center with 4 airlines, 8 commercial barge lines, and 19 motor traveling companies. An industrial park is located within city limits. In 1910, foreign-born had come mainly from Russia and Germany. Pop. 1850: 1,050, 1880: 4,192, 1910: 22,996, 1930: 60,408, 1960: 85,796.

WV 39B: M, laundry owner, 54. B. here. — F. b. 5 mi. N. of Charleston, PGF b. VA (Scotch-Irish descent), PGM b. Co.; M. b. neighborhood, MGF b. Co. ("Dutch" descent), MGM "Welsh" descent. — Ed.: city schools till 14–15. — Baptist. — Genial, expansive, successful manager of a large modern laundry. — Natural; perhaps somewhat influenced by schoolteachers and an OH-born wife.

WV 39C!: F, weaving teacher, 45. B. here. — Extensive family history: F., PGF b. Charleston, PGF's family from VA (traced back 5 generations), Scottish, English, French Huguenot descent, PGM b. Vincennes, IN, PGM's family primarily from VA (traced back 8 generations), same background as PGF's; M., MGF b. Charleston, MGF's family from VA, NY, MD, NC (traced back 8 generations), Scottish, Alsatian descent, MGM b. Marietta, OH, MGM's family from CT, NJ, NY, NH, RI (traced back 5 generations). — Ed.: h.s. here; year Natl. Park Seminary in MD near Wash., DC. — Episcopalian. — Somewhat overcooperative. — Cultivated.

Sissonville, Dist. 4 (formerly Poca)

Uninc.; see Kanawha Co. for early settlement. In 1883 Sissonville had 5 general mercantile stores, a post office, and a Methodist church. In 1937 area overwhelmingly rural. By 1974 all dwellings have become non-farm. Sissonville still a post office with 2 churches and 4 small businesses. Pop. 1960: c. 900.

WV 40A: Grapevine, Sissonville P.O., Poca Dist. — M, farmer, 74. B. Dist. — F. b. Dist., PGF b. Co.; M. b. Dist., MGF b. "away off". — Ed.: very little. — Adventist. — Excitable; did not understand purpose of interview initially, was reassured by schoolteacher son; occasionally forgetful. — Pretty good articulation.

Pinch, Dist. 1 (formerly Elk)

Small community in N. central Kanawha Co.; uninc. Near Elk River and B&O RR. In 1937 dwellings almost all farm, with many oil and gas wells nearby. In 1974 predominantly non-farming; no evidence of mines or wells on official map. Pop. 1960: c. 500.

WV 40B: Upper Pinch, Pinch P.O., Elk Dist. — M, farmer, 45. B. Dist. — F. b. Mink Shoal Dist., PGF b. Blue Creek Dist., PGF's F. b. VA, PGM b. Roane Co.; M. b. Campbells Creek in Co., MGF b. Co. — Ed.: till 14. — Baptist. — Quick, alert.

41. Clay County

Formed in 1858 from parts of Kanawha (39.), Braxton (19.), and Nicholas (20.) Cos.; see these for settlement. Largely agricultural and forested land although some coal, natural gas, and petroleum are found. Earliest industry timbering, rafting logs down Elk River to Charleston. Present industries and products include coal, lumber, natural gas, petroleum, hay, grain, livestock, poultry, camper manufacturing. Pop. 1860: 1,787, 1880: 3,460, 1910: 10,233, 1930: 13,125, 1960: 11,942.

Bickmore, Pleasant Dist.

Uninc.; in S. part of Co. Mixed farm and non-farm dwellings, post office; still one coal mine in 1974. Pop. 1960: c. 130.

WV 41A: M, farmer, 75. B. Henry Dist., 10 mi NE. — F. b. Ash Co., NC and came here young, PGF b. Ash Co., NC; M. b. Floyd Co. or Grayson Co., VA. — Ed.: 2 mos., then 4 mos. — Baptist. — Very genial, hospitable; humble background. — Slow, drawling vowels.

Clay, Henry Dist.

Incorporated 1895; formerly known as Henry, Clay Court House, and Marshall. In early days yellow-root and ginseng were legal tender. In 1937 there were many row houses, probably occupied by miners, and several farm and non-farm dwellings. In 1974, a post office and very few dwellings. Pop. 1920: 342, 1930: 444, 1940: 511, 1970: 486.

WV 41B: Mountain Home, Clay P.O., Henry Dist. — M, farmer, 49. B. Dist. — F. b. Dist.; M. b. Co. — Ed.: till 12–14. — Missionary Baptist. — Timid but cooperative.

42. Calhoun County

Formed in 1856 from Gilmer Co. Settled about 1810 mostly by VA migrants (Scotch-Irish, Scottish, English). First white man 1772. Corn was the chief crop of early settlers; later supplanted by fruit (both crops now small). 1818 the first school was held in a cave; first school building erected 1824. Since Civil War, Calhoun has become one of the leading gas and oil producing cos. in the state. Leading industries and products: petroleum, natural gas, lumber, hay and grain, livestock, poultry, rubber fabricators industry, and Sav-a-Tool, Inc. Pop. 1860: 2,502, 1880: 6,072, 1910: 11,258, 1930: 10,866, 1960: 7,948.

1956. *Calhoun County Centennial: 1856–1956*. Grantsville: Calhoun County Centennial Corp.

Annamoriah, Sheridan Dist.

Uninc. Annamoriah is in NW Co. Post office. Farming has decreased between 1937–74. Pop. 1960: c. 75.

WV 42A: Katys Run, Annamoriah P.O., Sheridan Dist. — F, housewife, 72. B. Lee Dist.; lived in Parkersburg for a few yrs. — F, PGF b. Co., PGF's F. b. Roane Co. ("Irish" descent), PGF's M. of Irish descent, PGM b. Co.; M. b. Co., MGF of "Irish" and "Dutch" descent, MGM b. Co. — Ed.: till 15. — Baptist. — Old-fashioned, isolated type.

Sycamore, Millstone P.O., Sherman Dist.

Unincorporated. Millstone is a village in central Co. In 1937 primarily farm dwellings, several oil and gas wells; 1974 wells remain, but mixed farm and non-farm dwellings. Pop. Millstone 1960: c. 150.

WV 42B: M, farmer, 54. B. Dist. — F. b. Dist. on edge of Ritchie Co., came here age 1 1/2 yrs., PGF b. Ritchie Co., PGF's F. of "Irish" descent, PGM b. Ritchie Co.; M. b. Dist., MGF, MGM b. Barbour Co. — Ed.: till 20. — Methodist. — Quick, intelligent; somewhat above type usually selected.

43. Jackson County

Formed in 1831 from parts of Kanawha (39.), Wood (45.), and Mason (37.) Cos.; settled in 1796 (see above cos.). Pop. jump between 1850–80 due to migration from other parts of the state. Foreign-born 1880 (less than 1%) mainly from British Isles, Germany, and Canada. Kaiser Aluminum and Chemical located in Co. Other leading industries: pulpwood, oil and gas, poultry, livestock, hay and grain, tobacco. Pop. 1840: 489, 1850: 6,544, 1880: 16,312, 1910: 20,956, 1930: 16,124, 1960: 18,541.

Moore, Dean W. 1971. *Washington's Woods: A History of Ravenswood and Jackson County, West Virginia*. Parsons: McClain Print. Co.

Morrison, Okey J. 1898. *The Slaughter of the Pfost-Greene Family of Jackson County, West Virginia*. Cincinnati: Gibson and Sorin Co.

Sandyville, Ravenswood Dist.

Uninc. First settlement about 1808. Listed as post office in 1883. Area reputed to have some of finest farming lands in state. Sandyville is in central Co.; farming there has declined somewhat between 1937–74. Pop. 1960: c. 300.

WV 43A: M, farmer and timberworker, 74. B. Dist. — F. b. Silverton in Co., PGF, PGF's F. b. Crow Summit, 1 mi. from here in Dist., PGM b. Jackson Co. on Ohio River; M. b. on the little Kanawha River in what is now Wirt Co. (formerly Jackson), came here when 9 yrs. old, MGF partly Scotch-Irish, MGM b. near Little Kanawha River toward Gilmer Co. ("Dutch" descent). — Ed.: 2 terms only (4 mos. each). — Baptist. — Quick, alert. Never traveled.

Ripley (Parchment Valley), Ripley Dist.

Settled 1833; inc. 1852. Became Co. seat in 1833. Parchment Valley (listed as post office in 1883) is a rural area SW of Ripley in S. central Co. In 1937 all dwellings were farms and there was 1 school; in 1974 little has changed although there is a decline in the number of dwellings. Pop. 1910: 591, 1930: 669, 1960: 2,756.

WV 43B: Parchment Valley, Ripley Dist. — M, farmer, 35. Spent 3 yrs. in Mahoning Co., OH, when 23–24. — F. b. Co., PGF b. OH, PGM b. Co.; M. b. Millwood in Co., MGF b. OH. — Ed.: till 16. — Baptist. — Somewhat sensitive; occasionally slow; not altogether cooperative and had to be persuaded to participate.

44. Wirt County

Formed 1848 from Wood and Jackson Cos., VA. First explored 1772; settled 1796. Methodist and Baptist first denominations establishing churches. Oil boom began 1860s in Burning Springs. First steamboat had reached Wirt Courthouse in 1842, and because of oil boom the Little Kanawha Navigation Co. was organized in 1860. In spite of French and Irish inhabitants, few or no Catholics in Co. in 1910. Farms in 1910 were small and individually owned. Many Wirt residents migrated to industrial OH in early 20th century. Leading industries and products: lumber, petroleum, hay and grain, livestock, poultry, dairying. Pop. 1850: 3,353, 1880: 7,104, 1910: 9,047, 1930: 6,358, 1960: 4,391.

Reed, Louis. 1967. *Warning in Appalachia: A Study of Wirt County, West Virginia*. Morgantown: West Virginia University Library.

Palestine (Lynn Camp), Elizabeth (formerly Tucker) Dist.

Lynn Camp takes its name from a camp constructed of lynn logs built by hunters in the late 18th cent. In early 19th cent. there was a grist mill on Lynn Camp Creek. Baptist church organized 1880. Lynn Camp Run is a rural area in central Co. In 1937 mixed farm and non-farm dwellings; in 1974 farm dwellings in majority. Pop. 1960: c. 100.

WV 44A: Lynn Camp, Palestine P.O., Tucker Dist. — M, farmer, 71. B. Dist. — F. b. Elizabeth Dist. in Co., PGF, PGM b. perhaps in VA; M. b. Reedy Dist. in Co. — Ed.: till 19. — Baptist. — Somewhat senile.

Reedy Creek, Palestine P.O., Elizabeth Dist.

Settlers came mainly from Harrison Co., VA. First explored 1772. First settler, John Shepherd, built a cabin on Left Hand Reedy in 1806; in 1810 a grist mill and in 1818 a school were erected on Right Hand Reedy. Area very rural, S. of Palestine in central Co. Basically a farming area in 1937 and 1974.

WV 44B: M, farmer, 52. B. Dist. — F. b. Dist., PGF b. Co., PGF's F. perhaps b. Co., PGF's PGF b. France, PGF's M. b. Co., PGM b. Dist; M. b. Tuckers Dist, MGF b. Co. — Ed.: till 15. — Baptist. — Cooperative. — Rather powerful voice.

45. Wood County

Formed in 1798 from Harrison Co., VA. Early settlers in 1770 from Washington, Greene, and Fayette Counties, VA. Significant pop. jumps in 1850–80 and 1880–1910 not due to foreign settlers; in 1910 only 2.2% of pop. foreign-born (German and Irish). Growth in pop. a result of industrial growth in Ohio River Valley. Leading industries and products: nylon,

shovels, tools, plastic, glass and glassware, pharmaceuticals, porcelain, electrical and oil field equipment, steel and metal products, petroleum, dairying, poultry, livestock, fruits, hay and grain. Pop. 1800: 1,217, 1820: 5,860, 1850: 8,450, 1880: 25,006, 1910: 38,001, 1930: 56,521, 1960: 78,331.

Beckwith, Nancy Stout. 1955. *The Story of Washington Bottom, Wood County, West Virginia*. Parkersburg: Banner Print. Co. Sponsored by the West Augusta Historical and Genealogical Society.

Beckwith, Nancy Stout. 1969. *Gleanings from Wood County, West Virginia*. Washington, WV.

Black, Donald F. 1975. *History of Wood County, West Virginia*. Marietta, OH: Richardson Print Corp.

Cunningham, Will. 1957. *Historical and Educational Development of Wood County to 1933*. West Virginia University thesis.

Gibbens, Alvaro F. 1899. *Wood County Formation*. Morgantown: Acme Press.

Gibbons, Alvaro F. 1899. *Wood County Centennial, 1799–1899*. Morgantown: Acme.

Gibbons, Alvaro F. 1899. *Wood County Formation*. Morgantown: Acme Press.

Parrish, W. H. 1897. *Art Work of Wood County*. Chicago: University of Chicago Press.

Shaw, S. C. 1878. *Early Wood County*. Parkersburg: Job Printer.

Shaw, Stephen Chester. 1878. *Sketches of Wood County*. Parkersburg. Repr. 1932 (Clarksburg: W. G. Tetrick).

Crum Hill, Belleville P.O., Harris Dist.

Uninc. Belleville, nearest P.O., located in western Co., adjacent to the OH River and served by the B&O RR. Some decline in farming between 1937 and 1974. Pop. Belleville 1960: c. 50.

WV 45A: M, farmer (formerly carpenter), 72. B. Dist.; ages 38–44 in lumber business on edge of Charleston, WV. — F. b. Dist., PGF b. perhaps in Ireland (Prot.); PGM b. Dist.; M. b. 1 mi. over line in Jackson Co., MGF b. OH ("German" descent), MGM b. Jackson Co., MGM's F. "Irish" descent. — Ed.: till 21. — Methodist. — Occasionally forgetful. — Open [vʌ˙]. [ɪðə].

Murphytown, Parkersburg P.O., Clay Dist.

Uninc. Post office. Mixed farm and non-farm dwellings in 1937 with 3 oil and gas wells and 3 pumping stations nearby. Many dwellings gone and slight decline in farming by 1974. Pop. 1960: c. 200.

WV 45B: Murphytown, Loomis Ridge, Parkersburg P.O., Clay Dist. — M, farmer, 42. B. Dist. — F. b. Dist., PGF, PGF's F., PGF's M., PGM, PGM's F., PGM's M. all b. Beaver Co., PA (PGF's family Welsh descent, PGM's family Scotch descent); M. b. Dist., MGF b. Beaver Co., PA, MGF's F., MGF's M. b. PA ("Irish" and "Dutch" descent respectively), MGM, MGM's F. b. PA ("Dutch" descent), MGM's M. b. Beaver Co., PA. — Ed.: till 14. — Baptist. — Quick, alert, cooperative.

46. Pleasants County

Formed 1851 from Wood, Tyler, Ritchie Cos., VA. First settled in late 18th cent. Early settlers arrived by flatboat on the Ohio River. In 1840s great numbers of cattle, hogs, and sheep were being driven through Co. to the Pittsburgh and Baltimore markets. Oil discovered in 1850 and subsequent rush occurred; most immigrants native-born from other cos. and OH (0.8% foreign-born in 1880 from Ireland and Germany). Timbering also reached its height in the 1880s. In 1880, an influx of Italians to work on RR which was completed in 1884. In 1909, mussel shell gathering for use in pearl button factories and in 1910 a button factory was built. First newspaper 1877 and a school by 1843 at Clay Point. Colin Anderson Center, institution for the mentally retarded, located in Co. Industries and products: petroleum, poultry, hay and grain, livestock, dairying. Divisions of American Cyanimid, Cabot Corp., and an oil refining company located here. Pop. 1860: 2,945, 1880: 6,256, 1910: 8,074, 1930: 6,545, 1960: 7,124.

Pemberton, Robert L. 1929. *A History of Pleasants County, West Virginia*. St. Marys: Oracle Press.

St. Marys, Washington Dist.

Co. seat. Settled 1786; chartered 1815; inc. 1872. During the peak of timbering, coopering was the chief business of St. Marys. Oil refinery opened in 1913 and glassware factory in 1916–17. Post office in area by 1974. Significant decline in farming 1937–74. Pop. 1910: 1,358, 1930: 2,182, 1940: 2,201, 1970: 2,183.

WV 46A: Clay Point, St. Marys P.O., Union Dist. — M, farmer, 73. B. 1 1/2 mi. below toward St. Marys, Union Dist. — F. b. Union Dist., PGF lived here (Irish descent in part), PGM b. Washington Co., OH; M. b. PA, moved to OH as infant, here when about 13, MGF, MGM b. PA (MGF a "PA Dutchman"). — Ed.: till 17. — Christian. — Unsophisticated, old-fashioned; genial, fond of talking, although unable to see the sense of the interview.

Schultz, St. Marys P.O., Jefferson Dist.

Rural Community in SW Co. Dwellings changed from predominantly farm to predominantly non-farm between 1937–74. Pop. 1960: c. 50.

WV 46B: M, farmer, oil field worker, now school bus driver, 40. B. Dist. — F., M. b. Dist. — Ed.: till 15. — Baptist. — Quick, alert. — Somewhat indistinct speech.

47. Ritchie County

Formed in 1843 from parts of Wood, Harrison, and Lewis Cos., VA. First settled 1800. Development of roads in 1830s and 40s brought many settlers from surrounding area. Tobacco industry in late 19th cent. attracted workers to area. Leading industries and products: petroleum, natural gas, clothing, glass and glassware, livestock, hay and grain. Pop. 1850: 3,902, 1880: 13,474, 1910: 17,875, 1930: 15,494, 1960: 10,877.

Horris, T. M. 1975. *A Brief History of Ritchie County*. Comp. by Stephen D. Six. Harrisville: Ritchie Gazette.

Petroleum (Racy), Grant Dist.

Uninc. Racy is a rural area SW of Petroleum in eastern Co. Area in 1937 overwhelmingly farming; yet many oil and gas wells and sawmills nearby. Predominantly non-farming in 1974; one church and 3 oil and gas wells. Pop. 1960: c. 100.

WV 47A: Racy, Petroleum P.O., Grant Dist. — M, farmer, 68. B. Dist. — F. b. Dist., PGF b. near Winchester, VA, PGM b. Dist.; M. b. Dist., MGF, MGM b. Marion Co. or Monongalia Co. (MGF's F. b. Wales). — Ed.: till 19. — Methodist. — Friendly, alert; perhaps somewhat higher type than usually selected. — Rather good articulation.

Pennsboro (Hushers Run), Clay Dist.

Inc. 1885 as a town and 1915 as a city. Hushers Run is a rural area in N. of Co. W. of Pennsboro, nearest P.O. Farming declined 1937–74. Pennsboro itself is location of "Old Stone House" built in 1810 and long a well-known tavern in stage coach days. 1858 first RR reached Pennsboro and in 1866 first church, United Brethren, established. First newspaper in early 1880s. A shirt factory and a marble yard were established in first decade of 20th cent. Pop. 1910: 930, 1930: 1,616, 1940: 1,738, 1970: 1,575.

WV 47B: Hushers Run, Pennsboro P.O., Clay Dist. — M, farmer, 36. B. Union Dist. in Co., 4 mos. in MO when 16. — F. b. Union Dist. in Co., PGF b. Monongalia Co., near PA, PGF's F. b. PA, prob. Green Co. ("Dutch" descent), PGF's M. b. Monongalia Co. ("Dutch" descent) (PGF's MGF froze to death on a buffalo chase), PGM b. Union Dist., PGM's F., PGM's PGM, PGM's M. all born Barbour Co. (PGM's M. of "Dutch" descent); M. b. Union Dist. in Co., MGF, MGF's F. b. Marion Co., MGF's M. b. Monongalia Co., near PA ("Dutch" descent), MGM b. Wood Co. — Ed.: till 16. — Methodist. — Quick, alert. Humble surroundings.

48. Doddridge County

Formed in 1845 from parts of Harrison (12.), Lewis (18.), Ritchie (47.), and Tyler (49.) Cos., VA; see these cos. for settlement. Leading industries and products: petroleum, natural gas, livestock, and poultry. Pop. 1850: 2,750, 1880: 10,552, 1910: 12,672, 1930: 10,488, 1960: 6,970.

Buckeye, Grant Dist.

P.O. Salem in Ten Mile Dist. in Harrison Co. Dist. First settled in 1811 by Jesse Davis. First religious service (Seventh Day Baptist) 1820. 1829 first school; 10 schools by 1880. 1841 first grist mill; 1845 first sawmill. Buckeye Run rural area in E. Co.; farming declined there in 1937–74.

WV 48A: M, farmer, 75. B. Dist. — F. b. Dist., PGF b. VA (partly Tuckahoe), PGM b. Harrison Co.; M. b. Dist., MGM b. Harrison. — Ed.: till 19. — Seventh-Day-Baptist. — Somewhat senile, but on the whole very alert.

Blandville, New Milton Dist.

Uninc. First cabin in New Milton Dist. was erected in 1820 on Meat House Fork, near what is now known as Blandville. First grist mill and first sawmill in Dist. in 1830, first school and first church (Baptist) in 1832. Pop. 1960: c. 50.

WV 48B: M, farmer, 50. B. Dist. — Parents b. Co. — Ed.: till 5th grade. — Slow, dull.

West Union, West Union Dist.

Co. seat. Inc. 1881. Settled beginning of 18th cent. Town was established just across Island Creek from Lewisport when an effort was being made to change the name of that settlement to Union; hence the name West Union. First business est. 1820, followed soon by a post office. 1845 first Co. court and first circuit court convened at the home of Martha Davis. In 1846 first school was built and first religious meeting was held (combined Baptist and Christian). 1858 the entire town burned, but est. of B&O RR led to town's rebuilding. First newspaper was established in 1868. Pop. 1910: 779, 1940: 1,020, 1970: 1,128.

WV 48C: M. B. Dist.; spent few years in Harrison Co. — Parents b. Co. — Ed.: common school. — Self-conscious; abrupt halt on p. 77 because he'd gotten tired of sitting for 2 hrs. and didn't see any sense to it.

Sugar Camp, New Milton Dist.

Blandville nearest P.O. A village in central Co., S. of Blandville. Farming area.

WV 48D: M, rig building (oil and gas), farmer, 42. — B. Dist.; spent one fall and winter in Preston Co. age 16. — F. b. Dist., PGF Scotch-Irish descent; M. b. Grant Dist. in Co., MGF b. Harrison Co. (Irish Prot. descent), MGM b. Harrison Co. — Ed. till 14. — Seventh-Day-Baptist. — Very quick, alert, intelligent. — Good articulation.

49. Tyler County

Formed in 1814 from Ohio Co., VA. Majority of early settlers migrated westward through the Shenandoah Valley and then northward from VA, Loudon Co. Settlers were predominantly Virginians but some Pennsylvanians were included. Co. originally rich in fertile soil for farming and game for hunting. Now largely industrial; fertility of the land is gone and most of the inhabitants are lower-middle-class laborers employed in the various industries of the OH Valley. 1860 first newpaper was published; 1883 Co. fair was organized. In 1884 the world's greatest gas well, "Big Moses", was drilled in Co., producing 100 million cubic feet of gas per day. In 1880 principal crops were corn, wheat, oats, tobacco, grass. Exports included tobacco, grain, stock, lumber, and cooperage. Today leading industries and products are: glass and glassware, chinaware, pottery, petroleum, natural gas, chemicals, dairying, poultry. Pop. 1820: 2,314, 1850: 498, 1880: 11,073, 1910: 16,211, 1930: 12,785, 1960: 10,026.

Pursley, Sistersville P.O., Lincoln Dist.

Sistersville established 1815, inc. 1839. First grist mill 1800 at present site of Sistersville; first school 1810; first religious service 1816. Sistersville originally Co. seat, but seat was moved to more accessible location, Middlebourne. In 1880 Sistersville had a woolen mill, a flour mill, a steam tannery, a weekly newpaper, and a job printing establishment. In 1883 Pursley listed as a post office. Pop. Sistersville 1900: 2,979, 1910: 2,684, 1930: 3,072, 1940: 2,702, 1970: 2,177.

WV 49A: M, farm worker, 65. B. neighborhood; worked on steamboats aged 12–15 between Pittsburgh and New Orleans; one summer in Nebraska at 18. — F. unknown; M. b. on Big Sanko in Co., MGM lived on Little Buffalo, 2 mi. from Sistersville, MGM's F. of English descent. — Ed.: none. — Christian. — Very quick, alert mind; understood purpose of the study; humble surroundings. — Speech very archaic and

not influenced by his boyhood steamboating; clear articulation; lengthened [aˑɛ] is the chief "Southern" characteristic.

Tyler, McElroy Dist.

Uninc. Settled 1818; predominantly farming area until about 1940. Inhabitants largely workers in surrounding industries. Little business in Tyler so people travel to larger town for schools, shopping, work, and recreation. Community therefore remains rural in character. Pop. 1820: c. 37, 1850: 54, 1880: 110, 1910: 86, 1930: 81, 1967: 90.

WV 49B: M, farmer, 36. Parents b. Co. — Ed.: country school. — Quick, highstrung, nervous. Rather suspicious; however, quick and spontaneous at answering. Counting on pp. 1 and 1A and the first question on p. 12 seemed to unnerve him and he stopped firmly at the bottom of p. 13.

50. Wetzel County

Created in 1846 from Tyler Co. (49.); settled in 1780 (see Tyler for provenience of settlers). In 1880 industries and products included farming, stock raising, lumbering, grain. Wool was growing into a major industry. The county had 3 woolen mills, 10 grist mills, 22 saw mills, 4 tanneries, 5 cooper shops, and 1 large oil barrel factory. First grist mill 1790; first newspaper 1870. Pop. 1850: 4,284, 1880: 13,896, 1910: 23,855, 1930: 22,334, 1960: 19,347.

Curtis, Mary G. 1958. *The 1850 Census of Wetzel County, Virginia, Now West Virginia.* Stockton, CA: U.S. Census Office.

McEldowney, John E. 1901. *History of Wetzel County, West Virginia.*

Jacksonburg, Grant Dist.

Settled about 1790; first settlers from Shenandoah Valley, followed by settlers from OH and PA. Original settlers attracted by coal mines now abandoned; miners now work in Marshall Co. (51.) mines. Shortline RR came to Jacksonburg. Town is in S. Co. on Fishing Creek and B&O RR. Sawmills and pumping stations in the area. Area declined somewhat between 1937 and 1974.

WV 50A: M, farmer, carpenter, 88. — F. b. Church Dist. in Co., PGF b. Monongalia Co. on Dunkard Creek, PGF's F. b. England (came with Cornwallis, deserted, and was wounded at Bunker Hill), PGM b. Monongalia Co.; M. b. Jacksonburg, MGF b. near Winchester, VA, MGM b. near Barracksville, Marion Co., MGM's F. of "Irish" descent, MGM's M. killed by Indians in Wetzel Co. — Ed.: 4 or 5 terms of 3 mos. — Baptist. — Quick, intelligent, well-preserved; occasionally somewhat fatigued. — Prob. of a somewhat higher speech type than usually selected.

WV 50B: M, farmer and real estate, 51. B. in vicinity. — F., PGF b. Dist., PGF's F. b. PA perhaps Green Co. (of Scotch-Irish descent), PGM b. near Littleton in Church Dist., Wetzel Co. (Scotch-Irish descent); M. b. on Marion Co. line, MGF, MGM b. Marion Co. — Ed.: till 16. — Presbyterian. — Overweight community patriarch; enjoyed the interview, although he had trouble understanding certain questions.

51. Marshall County

Formed in 1835 from Ohio Co. (52.), VA. First settled 1753 by migrants from E. VA, PA, MD, and Germany. Major industries in 1940 included iron, steel, glassware, coal, clothing, mechanical toys, enamelware, natural gas, hay and grain, dairying, fruit, vegetables, and sheep raising. Since 1940 chemicals have become a major product. Pop. 1840: 6,937, 1850: 10,138, 1880: 18,840, 1910: 32,388, 1930: 39,831, 1960: 38,041.

Boyd, Peter. 1927. *History of the Northern West Virginia Panhandle, Embracing Ohio, Marshall, Brooke, and Hancock Counties.* Topeka, KS: Historical Pub. Co.

Newton, J. H. 1879. *History of the Pan-Handle.* Wheeling: Caldwell.

Powell, Scott. 1925. *History of Marshall County.* Moundsville.

Cameron, Dist. 3 (formerly Liberty)

Inc. 1861. In 1937, a sparsely settled farming area in W. Co. adjacent to the Penn Central RR and the Ohio River. Farming and number of gas and oil wells declined between 1937 and 1974. In 1974 no dwellings in area, but one coal mine and one small business. Pop. 1910: 1,660, 1930: 2,281, 1940: 1,994, 1970: 1,524.

WV 51A: Cameron Ridge, Cameron P.O., Liberty Dist. — M, storekeeper, always a farmer, 66. B. Cameron Dist., about 15 mi. N.; spent one summer in S. MO. — F. b. Cameron Co., PGF b. near Cumberland, MD (Scotch-Irish descent), PGM b. near Cumberland, MD (English descent); M. b. Dist., MGF b. Berlin, Germany, MGM b. Cameron Ridge. — Ed.: till 21 (very little). — Church of God (parents Latter Day Saints). — Cooperative, quick, intelligent. Old-fashioned type.

WV 51B: Big Run, Cameron P.O., Liberty Dist. — M, farmer, 47. B. Dist. — F. b. Dist., PGF perhaps b. Co., PGM b. Co. (both Scotch-Irish descent); M. b. Dist., MGF prob. b. Marshall Co. (Methodist descent), MGM b. Dist. — Ed.: till 16. — Christian. — Cooperative, occasionally a little slow. — He and the middle-aged inf. from Monongalia Co. use one phoneme, [ɔɚ], for words of the *four, for* type, as in most parts of PA except in Green Co., where FW's middle-aged inf. distinguished [oɚ ɔɚ] as in VA usage.

52. Ohio County

Formed in 1776 from the Dist. of West Augusta, VA. Settled 1773 by Scotch-Irish from PA, E. VA, and MD. Early settlers mostly Presbyterians. Has many institutions of higher education: West Liberty State College (est. 1870); West Liberty Academy (1838–1870); Wheeling College, 4-yr. liberal arts Catholic college (1954); WV Northern Community College (1972). 1880–1930 immigrants (Germany, Ireland, Austria) and AfAms attracted by extensive industrial development, esp. steel and metal industries. Major industries and products: metal products, iron, steel, coal, paint, tools, garments, pipe fittings, stogies, chewing tobacco, meat packing, bakery products, dairying, fruits and vegetables, hay and grain, poultry. Pop. 1790: 5,212, 1820: 9,182, 1850: 18,005, 1880: 37,457, 1910: 57,572, 1930: 72,077, 1960: 68,437.

Amos, Nancy Lee. 1952. *Ohio County and the Second World War.* West Virginia University thesis.

Bell, Annie Walker Burns, comp. 1934. *Third Census of the U.S. (Year 1810) for the County of Ohio, State of Virginia. . . .* Washington.

Boyd, Peter. 1927. *History of the Northern West Virginia Panhandle, Embracing Ohio, Marshall, Brooke, and Hancock Counties.* Topeka, KS: Historical Pub. Co.

Cranmer, Gibson Lamb. 1902. *History of Wheeling City and Ohio County. . . .* Chicago: Biographical Pub. Co.

McGhee, Lucy Kate. 1964. *Ohio County, West Virginia, 1810: United States Census of Ohio County, Virginia.* Washington: US Census Office.

Newton, J. H. 1879. *History of the Pan-Handle.* Wheeling: Caldwell.

Wilde, Joseph L. *History of Wheeling during the Past Forty Years.*

Liberty, West Alexander, PA P.O.

Located in NE Co. just S. of Castleman Run Public Fishing area. Decline in farming 1937–74.

WV 52A: Potomac, West Alexander, PA P.O., Liberty Dist. — M, farmer, 68. B. Richland Dist.; when 7–13 lived near West Liberty on a farm in Brooke Co. that adjoined Ohio Co., 1 yr. in PA, then mostly in Liberty Dist. — F. b. Buffalo Dist., Brooke Co. (1/2 mi. from Ohio Co.); M., MGM b. Dist. — Ed.: through 3rd reader. — Methodist. — Very quick, alert. — Fairly short vowels; good articulation.

Waddells Run (probably Southells Run), Short Creek P.O. (Brooke Co.), Richland Dist.

Rural area in NW Co.

WV 52B: F, housewife, 36. B. Buffalo Dist., Brooke Co., on a farm which touched Ohio Co.; when 18 to West Liberty, Ohio Co. (winters there when 6–10); came here when married 13 yrs. ago. — F. b. Co. near West Liberty; M. b. near Potomac in Co., MGF b. Marshall Co. (Scottish descent). — Ed.: till 17. — Christian. — Quick, alert, cooperative.

Wheeling, Triadelphia Dist.

Co. seat. Settled in 1769 by Ebenezer Zane and his followers from OH; inc. 1806. Zane and his group built Ft. Henry at this site, that of the last battle of the Rev. 1818–19 first church (Methodist Episcopal) established. Institution Hall, known as WV State Shrine, is in Wheeling, where WV was founded after the VA cos. W. of the Alleghenies withdrew from VA and joined the Union (1863). Wheeling was state capital until 1870 and again from 1875–80. Many institutions of higher learning: Linsley Military Academy, Mount de Chental Academy, Wheeling College, WV Northern Community College. Has 2 large recreational parks; industrial city with radio and TV stations. Served by major state and interstate highways and the Ohio River. Pop. 1850: 11,435, 1880: 30,737, 1910: 41,641, 1930: 61,659, 1960: 53,400.

WV 52C!: Leatherwood Lane, Woodsdale, Wheeling P.O., Triadelphia Dist. — M, formerly manufacturing (foundry), 70. B. Wheeling. — F. b. Wheeling, PGF b. CT, PGM b. England, near Chelsea; M. b. Wheeling, MGF b. near Pittsburgh, MGM b. York, PA, MGM's F. b. England (Church of England),

MGM's M. b. Baltimore, MD. — Ed.: Leatherwood village school; 3 yrs. at prep school in Providence, RI (ages 16–19). — Episcopalian. — Intellectual interests, incl. this study; cooperative; perhaps somewhat untypical and influenced by his 3 yrs. in Providence, RI. — Cultivated.

53. Brooke County

Formed in 1797 from Ohio Co., VA. Settled by people of German, Irish, Scotch-Irish, and Welsh descent. From 1790–1850, main activities were agriculture, small industries, mining, and transportation via the Ohio River. 1806–50 Wellsburg one of leading ship building centers in the world. Mining was done on a small scale in the early 1800s and was much increased in the 20th cent. In 1812 first bank was established; in 1873 paper manufacturing established. Large pop. jump 1910–30 owing to steel and tar industries. Many immigrants from Great Britain, Italy, elsewhere in Europe, and surrounding area. Major industries and products: metal products and containers, plastic containers, coal, paper bags, tar and chemicals, electric power, glass and glassware, dairying, and fruit. Pop. 1800: 4,706, 1820: 6,631, 1850: 5,054, 1880: 6,013, 1910: 11,098, 1930: 24,663, 1960: 28,940.

> Boyd, Peter. 1927. *History of the Northern West Virginia Panhandle, Embracing Ohio, Marshall, Brooke, and Hancock Counties.* Topeka, KS: Historical Pub. Co.
> Caldwell, Nancy Lee. 1976. *A History of Brooke County.* Ed. by Catherine Manion. Wellsburg: Brooke County Historical Society.
> Jacob, John G. 1882. *Brooke County.* Wellsburg: Herald.
> Newton, J. H. 1879. *History of the Pan-Handle.* Wheeling: Caldwell.
> 1963. *Brooke County, Virginia and West Virginia, Official Centennial Program: Photograph Album, Advertisements of County Businesses and Industries.* Follansbee: Follansbee Review Press.

Wellsburg, Cross Creek Dist.

Co. seat since 1797. Chartered 1791 as Charlestown; chartered as Wellsburg 1887. Inc. Earliest settlements in Co. were centered in Wellsburg-Follansbee area. 1806–50 Wellsburg one of the leading shipbuilding centers of the country. In 1813 country's first glass industry est. at Wellsburg. In E. Co. on Ohio River and Penn Central RR. Pop. 1900: 2,588, 1910: 4,189, 1930: 6,400, 1970: 4,600.

WV 53A: Genteel Ridge, Wellsburg P.O., Buffalo Dist. — M, farmer, 79. B. Dist.; traveled in his old age. — F. b. Hagerstown, MD, and came here young (died when inf. only 2 yrs. old); M. b. Pierces Run, Dist., MGF b. Dist., MGF's F. ancestry partly "Turk", MGM b. Dist. — Ed.: till 20. — Baptist (now Methodist). — Quick, alert; comparatively well-off.

Colliers, Weirton Dist.

Uninc. Developed as a RR and mining town but now most residents work in the steel industry. In 1880 site of world bare-knuckle championship. Lies in NE Co. served by Penn Central RR. Post office. Became gradually more urban 1937–74. Pop. 1960: c. 900.

WV 53B: M, farmhand, 61. B. Dist. — Parents b. Co. — Ed.: ordinary. — Suspicion and lack of interest; overworked.

WV 53C!: Tent Community, Colliers P.O., Cross Creek Dist. — M, farmer, postmaster, 43. B. same house. — F. b. same house, PGF b. Dist., PGF's F. b. Co., PGF's PGF, PGF's PGM b. Winchester, VA, PGM b. Co., PGM's F. b. Sistersville, Tyler Co., PGM's PGF b. Baltimore Co., MD, PGM's M. b. near Baltimore; M. b. Dist., MGF, MGF's F. b. Co., MGF's PGF b. MD, MGM b. Wheeling. — Ed.: till 14. — United Presbyterian. — Quick, alert; occasionally not altogether honest in first reactions, but essentially a reliable, trustworthy inf.; enjoyed interview. — No [ɔɚ] distinction; [a] and [ɒˑ] are distinct; good articulation. — Cultivated.

54. Hancock County

Formed in 1848 from Brooke Co.; settled c. 1770. First churches, both Presbyterian, est. in 1790 and 1794. In 1794 first iron furnace; 1795 first gunpowder factory. Cannonballs used by Commodore Perry at the Battle of Lake Erie were manufactured at the iron foundry of Peter Tarr, on King's Creek. First school opened 1812. Tomlinson Run State Park located here. Co. highly industrial; growth of industry at beginning of 20th cent. attracted many immigrants (Austria, England, Greece, Ireland, Italy) and AfAms to area. Leading industries and products: iron, steel, chinaware, pottery, brick and fire clay, sheet metal, tin products, apples, dairying, livestock. Pop. 1850: 4,050, 1880: 4,882, 1910: 10,465, 1930: 28,511, 1960: 39,615.

> Boyd, Peter. 1927. *History of the Northern West Virginia Panhandle, Embracing Ohio, Marshall, Brooke, and Hancock Counties.* Topeka, KS: Historical Pub. Co.
> Lindsay, Susan. 1949. *Hancock County in World War II.* West Virginia University thesis.
> Newton, J. H. 1879. *History of the Pan-Handle.* Wheeling: Caldwell.
> Welch, Jack. 1963. *History of Hancock County: Virginia and West Virginia.* Wheeling: Wheeling News Printing and Litho. Co.

New Cumberland (Hardin Run and Langfitt Run), Clay Dist.

Laid out in 1839. Inc. in 1872 (formerly known as Cuppy Town and Vernon). Small town in W. Co. on the Ohio River and Penn Central RR. First known building in New Cumberland was Ft. Chapman, erected 1796. Nearby are deposits of gas, oil, clay, and coal. Clay was responsible for the development of the town; first mine 1830. 1832 first brick factory; 1844 first post office. Hardin Run is rural area east of New Cumberland, Langfitt Run rural area in central Co.; farming declined both areas 1937–74. Pop. New Cumberland 1890: 2,305, 1910: 1,807, 1930: 2,300, 1940: 2,098, 1970: 1,909.

WV 54A: Hardin Run, New Cumberland P.O., Clay Dist. — M, farmer, teamster in local oil field, 70. B. Dist. — F., PGF b. Dist., PGF's F. of English descent, PGM b. Co., PGM's F. Scotch-Irish; M. b. Co., MGF b. Washington Co., PA (Scotch-Irish descent). — Ed.: till 15, off and on. — Methodist. — Intelligent old-timer.

WV 54B: Langfitt Run, New Cumberland P.O., Clay Dist. — M, farmer, 41. B. same house. — F. b. adjacent farm, PGF b. S. part of Beaver Co., PA, PGF's F., PGF's M. b. Beaver Co., PA (both English descent), PGM b. Co., PGM's F. of Scotch-Irish descent; M., MGF b. 2 mi. away in Co., MGF's F. b. PA (partly Irish), MGF's M. b. PA, MGM, MGM's F., MGM's M. b. Brooke Co. — Ed.: till 8th grade (15 or 16). — Christian Church (Campbellite). — Quick, intelligent. Fairly old-fashioned.

Bibliographies

Davis, Innis C., et al. 1938. *Bibliography of West Virginia*. Charleston: State Dept. of Archives and History.

Hess, James W. 1974. *Guide to Manuscripts and Archives in the West Virginia Collection*. Morgantown: West Virginia University Library.

Munn, Robert F. 1960. *Index to West Virginiana*. Charleston: Education Foundation.

Shetler, Charles. 1960. *Guide to the Study of West Virginia History*. Morgantown: West Virginia University Library.

1940. *A Preliminary Bibliography Relating to Churches in West Virginia, Virginia, Kentucky, and Southern Ohio*. Charleston: West Virginia Historical Records Survey.

General Histories

Ambler, Charles H. 1938. *A History of West Virginia*. NY: Prentice-Hall.

Ambler, Charles Henry, and Festus P. Summers. 1958. *West Virginia, the Mountain State*. 2nd ed. Englewood Cliffs, NJ: Prentice-Hall.

Ambler, Charles Henry. 1936. *George Washington and the West*. Chapel Hill: University of North Carolina Press.

Ash, Jerry W., and Stratton L. Douthat. 1976. *West Virginia USA*. Baltimore: Waverly Press.

Ball, Arthur. 1954. *Voices from Vale and Hill*. NY: Exposition Press.

Boughter, Isaac F., et al. 1927. *West Virginia History and Government Told by Contemporaries*. 12 vols. Fairmont: Dept. of History and Govt.

Boughter, Isaac Fegley. 1927. *Outlines in the History and the Government of West Virginia*. Ann Arbor, MI: Edwards Bros.

Boyd, Peter. 1927. *History of the Northern West Virginia Panhandle, Embracing Ohio, Marshall, Brooke, and Hancock Counties*. Topeka, KS: Historical Pub. Co.

Callahan, James M. 1923. *History of West Virginia*. Chicago: American Historical Society.

Callahan, James Morton. 1913. *Semi-Centennial History of West Virginia*. Charleston: Semi-Centennial Commission of West Virginia.

Cometti, Elizabeth, and Festus P. Summers. 1966. *The Thirty-Fifth State*. Morgantown: West Virginia University Library.

Conley, Philip, and Bob B. Stutler. 1966. *West Virginia, Yesterday and Today*. Charleston: Education Foundation, Inc.

Curry, Richard Orr. 1964. *A House Divided: Statehood Politics and the Copperhead Movement in West Virginia*. Pittsburgh: University of Pittsburgh Press.

Federal Writers Project. 1941. *West Virginia: A Guide to the Mountain State*. NY: Oxford University Press.

Hale, John P. 1897. *History and Mystery of the Great Kanawha Valley*. 2 vols. Charleston: Butler Printing Co.

Lambert, Oscar D. 1958. *West Virginia, Its People and Its Progress*. 3 vols. Hopkinsville, KY: Library of American Lines.

Lewis, Virgil Anson. 1889. *History of West Virginia*. Philadelphia: Hubbard Bros.

Miller, Thomas Condit, and Hu Maxwell. 1913. *West Virginia and Its People*. NY: Lewis Historical Pub. Co.

Myers, Sylvester. 1915. *History of West Virginia*. 2 vols. Wheeling: Wheeling News Lithograph Co.

Norton, J. H., ed. 1879. *History of the Pan-Handle*. Wheeling: Caldwell.

Rice, Otis K. 1970. *The Allegheny Frontier: West Virginia Beginnings, 1730–1830*. Lexington: University Press of Kentucky.

Rice, Otis K. 1971. *West Virginia: The State and Its People*. Parsons: McClain Printing Co.

Rucker, Maude Applegate, comp. 1930. *West Virginia, Her Land, Her People, Her Traditions, Her Resources*. NY: W. Neale

Shawkey, Morris P. 1928. *West Virginia. . . .* 5 vols. Chicago: University of Chicago Press.

West Virginia DAR. 1962. *Glimpses of West Virginia History*. Beckley: Biggs-Hohnson-Withrow.

Williams, John Alexander. 1976. *West Virginia: A Bicentennial History*. NY: Norton Co.

1939–. *West Virginia History*. Charleston: West Virginia Dept. of Archives and History.

Special Studies

Agricultural Extension Division. 1924–28. *History of West Virginia Communities*. 2 vol. Morgantown: West Virginia University College of Agriculture, Forestry and Home Economics.

Ambler, Charles H. 1902. The Cleavage between Eastern and Western Virginia. *American History Review* 15:762–80.

Ambler, Charles H. 1910. *West Virginia: Stories and Biographies*. NY: Rand, McNally, and Co.

Ambler, Charles Henry. 1910. *Sectionalism in Virginia from 1776 to 1861*. Chicago: University of Chicago Press.

Anderson, Hugh E. 1936. *Facts of West Virginia: Its Institutions and Its People*. Charleston: Woodyard Commercial Printers.

Artley, Malvin Newton. 1955. *The West Virginia Country Fiddler*. Chicago Musical College thesis.

Atkinson, George W., and Alvaro F. Gibbens. 1890. *Prominent Men of West Virginia*. Wheeling: W.L. Callin.

Barb, Jean Milliken. 1949. *Strikes in the Southern West Virginia Coal Field, 1912–1922*. West Virginia University thesis.

Botler, Alexander Robinson. 1860. *My Ride to the Barbecue, or, Revolutionary Reminiscences of the Old Dominion*. NY: S. A. Rollo.

Brooks, Morgan M. 1934. *Pioneer Settlers of the Buckhannon Valley*. West Virginia Wesleyan College thesis.

Byrne, George, ed. 1915. *1915 Hand-Book of West Virginia*. Charleston: West Virginia Panama-Pacific Exposition Commission.

Carpenter, Charles. 1929. Our Place Names. *The West Virginia Review* 6.11:422, 440.

Carpenter, Charles. 1974. *West Virginia, People and Places*. Richwood: J. Comstock.

Clagg, Sam Edward. 1975. *West Virginia Historical Almanac*. Huntington: Clagg.

Clerk of the Senate. 1916–. *West Virginia Blue Book*. Charleston: Jarrett Printing.

Comstock, Jim. 1974. *West Virginia Commonplace Book*. Richwood: Comstock.

Conley, Philip M. 1919. *The West Virginia Encyclopedia.* Charleston: West Virginia Pub. Co.

Crickard, Madeline W. 1971. *1810 Census Lists for Counties in Virginia, Now West Virginia.* Beverly.

Davis, Innes C., comp. 1937. *Some Events and Persons of Importance in the History of West Virginia.* Charleston: West Virginia Dept. of Archives and History.

Dunaway, Wayland F. 1922. *History of the James River and Kanawha Company.* NY: Columbia University Press.

Gannett, Henry. 1904. *A Gazetteer of Virginia and West Virginia.* Washington. Repr. 1975 (Baltimore: Genealogical Pub. Co.).

Hale, John P. 1886. *Trans-Allegheny Pioneers.* Cincinnati. 3rd ed. 1971 (Raleigh, NC: Derreth Print. Co.).

Hall, Granville Davisson. 1902. *The Rending of Virginia.* Chicago: Mayer and Miller.

Hall, Granville Davisson. 1915. *The Two Virginias.* Chicago: Mayer and Miller.

Hamilton, Eleanor Meyer. 1977. *The Flair and the Fire: The Story of the Episcopal Church in West Virginia.* Charleston: Diocese of West Virginia, Protestant Episcopal Church.

Hiden, Martha Woodroof. 1957. *How Justice Grew: Virginia Counties.* . . . Williamsburg, VA: Virginia 350th Anniversary Celebration Corp.

Hiner, Mary. 1933. *The Scotch-Irish and Academics in the Transallegheny Frontier.* West Virginia University thesis.

Historical Activities Committee. 1972. *West Virginia's Counties and Courthouses.* National Society of the Colonial Dames of America.

Hughes, Josiah 1913. *An Epitome of West Virginia History and Civil Government.* Countesville: The Author.

Hughes, Josiah. 1932. *Pioneer West Virginia.* Charleston: The Author.

Ice, John R., comp. 1933. *New Descriptive Atlas of West Virginia.* Clarksburg: Clarksburg Pub. Co.

Johnson, Gerald W. 1970. *West Virginia Politics: A Socio-Cultural Analysis of Political Participation.* University of Tennessee dissertation.

Johnston, David E. 1906. *A History of Middle New River Settlements and Contiguous Territory.* Huntington. Repr. 1969 (Radford: Commonwealth Press).

Kenny, Hamill. 1945. *West Virginia Place Names: Their Origin and Meaning, Including the Nomenclature of the Streams and Mountains.* Piedmont: Place Name Press.

Kenny, Hamill. 1961. Settling *Laurel's* Business. *Names* 9:160–62.

Kiplinger, John L. 1935. *The Influence of the Press in the Making of West Virginia.* West Virginia University thesis.

Krakowski, Paul. 1951. *Pronunciation Guide to West Virginia Place Names.* Morgantown: West Virginia University School of Journalism.

Lambert, Oscar D. 1935. *Pioneer Leaders of Western Virginia.* Parkersburg: Scholl Print. Co.

Lambert, Oscar D. 1941. *Camps and Firesides West of the Alleghenies.* Charleston: West Virginia Pub. Co.

Lane, Winthrop D. 1921. *Civil War in West Virginia.* NY. Repr. 1969 (NY: Arno Press).

Lang, Theodore F. 1895. *Loyal West Virginia from 1861 to 1865.* Baltimore: Deutsch Pub. Co.

Mastroguiseppe, Agostine David. 1969. *George Cookman Sturgiss, the Buckeye West Virginian.* West Virginia University thesis.

Maury, Matthew Fontaine, and William Morris Fontaine. 1876. *Resources of West Virginia.* Wheeling: Register Co.

McGregor, James Clyde. 1922. *The Disruption of Virginia.* NY: Macmillan.

McWhorter, John Camillus. 1927. *The Cabin Home of the West Virginia Pioneer.* Buckhannon: Buckhannon Record.

McWhorter, Lucullus Virgil, et al. 1915. *The Border Settlers of Northwestern Virginia from 1768 to 1795.* . . . Hamilton, OH. Repr. 1975 (Baltimore: Genealogical Pub. Co.).

Miller, Thomas C. 1904. *History of Education in West Virginia.* Charleston: Tribune Print. Co.

Mockler, William E. 1973. *West Virginia Surname: The Pioneer.* Parsons: West Virginia Dialect Society.

Morgan, R. S. 1893. *Columbian History of Education in West Virginia.* Charleston: M. W. Donnelly.

Osborne, Ray K. 1966. *Unto These Hills and Beyond the Sea.* R. K. Osborne.

Permar, Robert, et al., eds. 1928. *West Virginia.* West Virginia Biographical Association.

Perry, Lester. 1971. *Forty Years of Mountain Politics, 1930–1970.* Parsons: McClain Print. Co.

Pessen, Edward. 1973. *Riches, Class, and Power before the Civil War.* Lexington, MA: D. C. Heath.

Rosengarten, William Q., ed. 1967. *West Virginia Incorporated and Unincorporated Communities.* Charleston: West Virginia Dept. of Commerce.

Rucker, Maude Applegate, comp. 1930. *West Virginia, Her Land, Her People, Her Traditions, Her Resources.* NY: W. Neale

Shawkey, Morris P. 1928. *West Virginia: A Book of Geography, History, and Industry.* Boston: Ginn and Co.

Shawkey, Morris Purdy. 1928. *West Virginia, in History, Life, Literature and Industry.* Chicago: Lewis Pub. Co.

Stallings, James L. 1967. *Resources of the Upper South Branch Valley, West Virginia.* West Virginia University thesis.

Strother, David Hunter. 1974. *Porte Crayon Sampler.* Richwood: Jim Comstock Pub.

Tams, W. P. 1963. *The Smokeless Coal Fields of West Virginia: A Brief History.* Morgantown: West Virginia University Library.

West Virginia Centennial Committee on Folklore. 1963. *The West Virginia Centennial Book of One Hundred Songs, 1863–1963.* Morgantown: Patrick W. Gainer.

Whetzel, Virgil L. 1969. *Reservoir Impacts on Economic Activity, Land Use and Land Values in Appalachia.* West Virginia University thesis.

Willey, William P. 1901. *An Inside View of the Formation of the State of West Virginia.* Wheeling: News Pub. Co.

Williams, John Alexander. 1976. *West Virginia and the Captains of Industry.* Morgantown: West Virginia University Library Press.

1938. *West Virginia County Formations and Boundary Changes.* Charleston: Historical Records Survey.

Delaware

1 & 2. New Castle County

"Hundreds" = townships here as far back as 1687. 1703 Welsh Tract c. 10 mi. from Wilmington. Earliest settlers predominantly Dutch (c. 1655) and Swedish (c. 1638; 20–25% Swedish in 1790). Quakers strongest in 18th cent. Best farming country in early 19th cent.: wheat and potatoes; tobacco an important export crop. Has gradually come to dominate the state; Wilmington became Co. seat 1884. Pop. 1790: 19,688, 1820: 27,899, 1850: 42,780, 1880: 77,716, 1910: 123,188, 1930: 161,032, 1960: 307,446.

Booth, Elizabeth. 1884. *Reminiscences by Elizabeth Booth of New Castle, Harris Delaware*. New Castle.

DuPont, Bessie Gardner. 1920. *E. I. Du Pont de Nemours and Company*. . . . Boston: Houghton Mifflin Co.

Eckman, Jeannette. 1951. Life among the Early Dutch at New Castle. *Delaware History* 4:246–302.

"Every Evening", comp. 1894. *History of Wilmington*. New York: Press of Moss Engraving Co.

Federal Writers Project. 1936. *New Castle on the Delaware*. New Castle. Repr. 1983 (NY: AMS Press).

Ferris, Benjamin. 1846. *A History of the Original Settlements on the Delaware. . . and a History of Wilmington*. Wilmington: Wilson and Heald.

Grier, A. O. Herman. 1945. *This was Wilmington*. Wilmington: News Journal Co.

Hoffecker, Carol E. 1974. *Wilmington, Delaware: Portrait of an Industrial City, 1830–1910*. Charlottesville, VA: Eleutherian Mills Historical Library.

Isaacs, I. J., ed. 1887. *The Industrial Advance: A Historical, Statistical, and Descriptive Review of Wilmington*. Wilmington: Commerce Pub. Co.

Janvier, Anne. 1930. *Stories of Old New Castle*. New Castle.

Jones, Theophilus K. 1909. *Recollections of Wilmington from 1845 to 1860*. Wilmington: Historical Society of Delaware.

Kelly, Paul William. 1951. *New Castle, Delaware: A Bibliography*. Newark: Newark Print Co.

Lake, Joseph R. 1976. *Hockessin: A Pictorial History*. Hockessin: Hockessin-Yorklyn-Corner Ketch Bicentennial Committee.

Library of Congress. 1951. *Old New Castle and Modern Delaware, the Tercentenary of the Founding of New Castle by the Dutch*. Washington: US Government Printing Office.

Lincoln, Anna T. 1937. *Wilmington, Delaware: Three Centuries under Four Flags, 1609–1937*. Rutland, VT: Tuttle Pub. Co.

Montgomery, Elizabeth. 1851. *Reminiscences of Wilmington*. Philadelphia: T. K. Collins, Jr.

Nelson, Daniel M. 1968. *A Checklist of Writings on the Economic History of the Greater Philadelphia-Wilmington Region*. Wilmington: Eleutherian Mills Historical Library.

Rodney, Richard. 1919. Historic Notes relating to New Castle. *Philadelphia Geographical Society Bulletin* 17:138–42.

Scott, Henry. 1930. *The Growth of Wilmington during the Last Three Decades*.

Tilly, Charles. 1965. *Migration to an American City*. Newark: University of Delaware Press.

Wolf, George A. 1899. *Ideal New Castle*.

Wolf, George A., comp. 1898. *Industrial Wilmington*. Wilmington: G. A. Wolf.

Wooten, Mrs. Bayard Morgan, and Anthony Higgins. 1939. *New Castle, Delaware, 1651–1939*. Boston: Houghton, Mifflin Co.

1809–1813. *American Watchman*. Wilmington: James Wilson.

1894. *History and Commerce of Wilmington*. NY: A. F. Parsons Pub. Co.

1895. *Cold Facts about Wilmington*. . . . Wilmington: Hawkins and Co.

Wilmington

Ft. Christiana here as early as 1638; settlement of Swedes and Finns. Dutch settlers here c. 1655; English settlers 1664. "Old Swedes Church" est. by 1698. Wilmington laid out 1730s as port for grain trade. Industrial center from late 18th cent. Friends meeting house 1738; Presbyterian church 1740. Incorporated as a borough 1809; as a city 1832. Chesapeake-Delaware Canal 1829; RR from 1830s. Public schools by state law 1829; high schools 1870s. Whaling 1835–45. Good harbor, overshadowed New Castle after 1852. Rapid pop. growth 1830–1900. 14% of pop. foreign born in 1900; Germans (largest body from 1850s), Italians from 1880s, Irish, Jews. AfAm pop. 12 1/2% in 1890. Suburbanization in first half of 20th cent. Products and industries: RR equipment, textiles, paper making, Bethlehem steel, sand, gravel, lime, shipbuilding, machinery, leather, explosives, other chemicals. Pop. 1730: 610, 1775: 1,229, 1850: 13,979, 1880: 42,478, 1910: 87,411, 1930: 106,597, 1960: 95,827.

DE 1A: M, superintendent of transfer companies, PA RR, 70. B. Rose Hill, moved to present residence when 6 yrs. old. — F. b. near Chymont, DE, c. 8 mi. N. (now suburb), moved into city when 15, PGF prob. b. England, PGM b. near Chymont; M. b. east side of Wilmington, MGF, MGF's F. b. S. Jersey, MGM b. near Oxford, PA. — Ed.: local school, 1 yr. h.s. — Working-class type; rather better ed. than FW was looking for, but native American type among urban proletariat is hard to find here. (Mother, 94, still alive but too deaf to talk). — Fairly quick and bright; cooperative, interested, glad to perform; perhaps concealing some coarser speech tendencies. — [vʌː] written for a sound which might just as well be written [ɔˑ˞ə] at times.

DE 1B: M, till 1901 in secret service of PA RR, then reporter and city editor of newspaper, since 1914 asst. sec. of Chamber of Commerce, 63. B. Wilmington. — F. b. Wilmington, PGF b. Zanesville, OH, PGF's F. b. MD, descended from Welshman who came over with Lord Baltimore in 1634, PGM b. Wilmington, PGM's F. b. Phila., PGM's PGF signer of Declaration of Independence; M., MGF, MGM b. Wilmington. — Ed.: public h.s. (finished at 15). — Middle-class; middle-aged; extremely cooperative; quick and intelligent. Feels strongly that DE is a Northern state. Slightly opinionated on a few matters of usage. — Tempo rapid; articulation generally clear; vowels not too short.

DE 1C!: F, housewife, 62. B. same house (1876). — F. b. Brandywine Hundred, just east of city, PGF, PGF's F., PGF's PGF b. Wilmington, of oldest Swedish stock, PGF's M. b. Wilmington, PGM, PGM's F., PGM's PGP b. Brandywine Hundred; M. b. Wilmington, MGF, MGF's F., MGF's M. b. Chester Co., PA, MGM b. Wilmington, sister of PGF. — Ed.: local private h.s. — Episcopalian (her family were Quakers). — Extremely obliging, cultivated, living in house 100 yrs. old, academic associates. Rather free and frank and cooperative in revealing her own speech, but with a few very definite convictions which were imposed on her by schoolteachers. — Tempo very rapid; vowels tend to be short. Mind generally quick, intense concentration, some lapses of memory. — Cultivated.

Red Lion, New Castle Hundred

Hundred settled by Swedes and Dutch in 1650s; area predominantly Dutch into 18th cent. Oldest town in Delaware Valley. Some tracts stayed in families till late 19th cent. Good harbor. Steel, rayon, fiber, aircraft. Red Lion a crossroads hamlet c. 13 mi. from New Castle. Country trading center settled at time of Revolution.

DE 2A: M, small storekeeper, 73. B. here. — F. b. here, PGF b. near Bridgeton or Clayton, NJ, came here as young man, PGM b. NJ (prob. Scottish); M., MGF b. Wilmington (prob. Scottish), MGM b. village of Red Lion (2 mi. from inf.'s home). — Ed.: local schooling till 12, 2 yrs. grammar school in Phila. — Methodist; Odd Fellow, Red Man. — Rather intelligent; reads a bit but treated investigation in plain, matter-of-fact way; tried to be thoroughly honest.

DE 2A*: Harris Corner, 5 mi. N. of Red Lion. — M, retired farmer. — Traveled, well-to-do; not interested enough to continue.

Hockessin, Marshallton P.O., Mill Creek Hundred

Hundred first settled c. 1666; earliest settlers Welsh, Dutch, Swedish; later English, Scots. In NW part of Co., Swedish Church, became Episcopal 1685; Presbyterian 1721; Friends 1730. Shipyard, late 18th cent. Waterpower; many small factories: iron in 18th cent., textiles in late 19th. Hockessin in N. part of Hundred. Orig. part of large Manor given by Wm. Penn to his daughter in 1701. Quaker settlement; rural market. Turnpikes early 19th cent.; RR from 1872. Mushroom farming; paper, mining of kaolin.

DE 2B: M, farmer, 37. B. same house. — F., PGF, PGF's F. b. here (English descent), PGM b. 4 mi. S. of here at Stanton, MGM's F. b. near Middletown (French Huguenot descent); M. b. near Hockessin, 4 mi. NW, MGF, MGF's F. b. near Hockessin (Holland Dutch descent), MGF's M. b. near here (English descent), MGM, MGM's F. b. near Hockessin (Scotch-Irish descent). — Ed.: local schools till 14, then h.s. in Wilmington. — Presbyterian. — Very cooperative; well-to-do farmer's son, living at home, managing farm for aged F. (in FL at time). — Tempo moderately rapid, with tendency to spurt.

DE 2C: Red Lion, New Castle Hundred. — M, farmer, c. 60. B. here. — F. b. here, PGF's F. b. PA (German), just over line; M. b. here. — Incomplete.

3 & 4. Kent County

1st land grants 1671; chiefly English. Also Swedes, Dutch, a few Huguenots among early settlers. Originally a farming area. Some Quakers (abolitionists); 700 AfAms here by 1775. Anglican services by 1705; Presbyterians by 1714. No fixed Co. seat till Dover laid out 1717. Public schools by 1829. 1861–65 neutralists here; DE rejected the 13th, 14th, 15th amendments. Farming and manufacturing. Pop. 1680: c. 99, 1782: 9,782, 1790: 18,920, 1820: 20,793, 1850: 22,816, 1880: 32,874, 1910: 32,751, 1930: 31,841, 1960: 65,651.

Fisher, George Purnell. 1896. *Recollections of Dover in 1824.* Wilmington: Historical Society of Delaware.

Hancock, Harold Bell. 1976. *A History of Kent County Delaware.* Dover: Dover Litho. Printing Co.

Hynson, George, comp. 1899. *Historical Etchings of Milford and Vicinity.* Milford: Hynson and Mears.

Willow Grove, Wyoming P.O., Murderkill Hundred

Murderkill an orig. division of Co. Settled first along streams in 1679. Productive farmland. Shipbuilding till 1880s. Willow Grove 9 1/2 mi. SW of Dover. Scots, English, some Dutch settled first. Methodists early. Cooperage in 19th cent.; small industries, trading center. Wyoming village created by RR and express offices. Largely Baptists; English, Huguenots, some Scots. Large cannery; center of one of richest orchard and dairy regions.

DE 3A: M, farmer, 75. B. 3 mi. E. of Hartly in neighborhood, a few yrs. in New Castle in teens. — F., PGF b. near Hartly (part Irish); M. b. near Kenton, MGF b. near Hartly. — Ed.: sporadic till 21. — Inactive Methodist. — Uneducated, unsophisticated, superstitious.

Bethesda Church, Hartly P.O., West Dover Hundred

W. Dover Hundred created 1877. Largely English stock; part of area disputed with MD to 1763. On watershed between Delaware Bay and Chesepeake Bay. Methodists at least by 1779. Bethesda Church site of Methodist church built 1864; rural, English stock. Hartly patented 1734. RR came through 1882. Trading center; little activity except cannery running during summer.

DE 3B: M, farmer, 38. B. 1/2 mi. N.; once worked in Gastonia, NC. — F., PGF b. 3 mi. E., PGF's F. of Irish descent, PGM b. Co., partly Holland Dutch descent; M. b. Pearsons Corner in Co., MGP b. Co. — Ed.: here till 14. — Methodist. — A very quick, bright man of uneducated background. — Rapid tempo.

Dover

Laid out by Penn. Ordered 1683; site selected 1690; laid out 1717. State capital 1777; incorporated as a town 1817; inc. as city 1920. One of smallest state capitals in US; 2nd oldest state house (1787) in active use in America. Primarily English, some Scots among early settlers. Presbyterian services by 1714; Methodists by 1778. Designed as courthouse town from beginning. Farm marketing center. Products and industries: canning, silk hosiery, mattresses, baskets, automobile bodies, cheese, plumbing supplies, rubber products, foods. Pop. 25% AfAm in 1937. Pop. 1850: 5,207, 1880: 2,811, 1910: 3,720, 1930: 4,800, 1960: 7,250.

DE 3C!: M, farmer and lobbyist at State House, 66. B. Washington, DC. — F., PGF b. Dover, PGM b. Milford, DE; M., MGF, MGF's F., MGF's PGF, MGF's PGF's F. b. Annapolis, MD (his grandfather from Devonshire, England), MGF's PGF's M. b. Salem Co., NJ, MGF's PGM b. Moore Hall, MGM, MGM's F., MGM's M. b. Camden, DE. — Ed: Dover schools; then Wilmington Conference Academy, Dover; Shortledge Academy, Media, PA (15–17); Swarthmore 2 yrs.; Jefferson Medical College, Phila., 3 yrs. (did not graduate); read law 2 yrs. in Dover. — Episcopalian. — Rather sensitive about personal inventions; complacent. — Mother interested in properties of speech. — Cultivated.

Milford Neck, Milford P.O.(Sussex Co.) and Hundred

Milford Hundred formed 1830 from Mispillion Hundred. Landing by Swedes 1638, no settlement. Much of area sold to PA Land Co., which continued in business till c. 1780. 1st land patents 1680–86. 1st settlers chiefly English, some Dutch. Friends settled 1707, but no meeting house till 1790. Methodists by 1777; Baptists by 1781. RR in 1850s. Products and industries: shipping and shipbuilding early, water transportation, farming (mainly fruit) and canning, fertilizer, dental products, paper plates, wooden spoons, dresses, wool yarn, wood veneer products, building materials.

DE 4: M, farmer, 82. B. 1/2 mi. W. — F. b. here; M. b. near Dover. — Little ed. — Methodist. — Very old-fashioned, obliging; memory slightly imperfect.

5 & 6. Sussex County

Formed 1683. Earliest settlement by Dutch in 1631; New Sweden settlement beginning 1638. Dutch and English land grants 1665; also some French. Some Ulster Scot settlers from Long Island. Presbyterians from 1705; Anglicans from 1721; Friends 1721; Methodists later. Border disputes with MD not settled until 1775. Co. seat at Lewes till 1791; then Georgetown. Strong Loyalist sentiment. Public education from 1829; RR at least from 1859. Much pro-Southern feeling (even some Confederate soldiers), but little secessionism. Silk raising 1830–80. Other products and industries: truck farming (largely rural; flattest land in state), soybeans, fruit, broilers, nylon (Dupont plant here). Pop. 1782: 12,660, 1790: 20,488, 1820: 24,057, 1850: 25,396, 1880: 36,018, 1910: 46,413, 1930: 45,501, 1960: 73,195.

Carter, Dick. 1976. *The History of Sussex County*. Selbyville.
Hancock, Harold Bell. 1976. *The History of Sussex County, Delaware*. Dover.

Turner, C. H. B., comp. 1909. *Some Records of Sussex County*. Philadelphia: Allen, Lane and Scott.
1932. *Old Georgetown*. Georgetown: Demonstration School.

Georgetown

Georgetown Hundred formed in 1833. Central in Co.; Co. seat arbitrarily set, for geographical reasons. Elevated sandy plain; watershed between Atlantic and Ches. Bay. 1st land warrants c. 1715; earliest settlers largely English. Diversified farming, fruits and vegetables. Georgetown authorized as Co. seat 1791. Early settlers almost entirely English; a few Germans and Irish. Episcopal church from 1794; Methodists from 1802. Incorporated 1860; growth since 1878. Products and industries: tanning (in past), RR shops, wood products, canning and evaporating fruit, shipping, cooperage, brick making. Pop. 1880: 895, 1910: 1609, 1930: 1763, 1960: 1765.

DE 5A: M, farmer, 77. B. here. — F. b. here, PGF b. Ireland, PGM b. DE; M., MGF, MGF's F., MGM b. here. — Ed.: here till 18. — Methodist. — Lonely, liked to talk. Resembles Midwesterner of similar rural community. Very hearty. — Most tremendously resonant [ɚ·] in FW's experience; [ʉ] in *new, Tuesday* (cf. usage of PA, NJ, and Chincoteague Island, VA); some neutralization of *card/cord* types (cf. Preston, MD). Moderate tempo; vowels moderately prolonged: [ɚ·] prolonged in isolation or postvocalic.

Sunnyside School, Bridgeville P.O., Nanticoke Hundred

NW part of Co.; orig. disputed with MD. Nanticoke Hundred largely rural. Many of earliest settlers (first arrived c. 1705) from VA and MD in 18th cent.; families largely of English descent. Methodists dominant. Ironworks in late 18th cent., abandoned. Shipbuilding, but declined in 19th cent. Slaveholding to 1861. Good farming land: corn, small fruits; iron ore (low grade). Bridgeville began in 1730 with bridge over a branch of the Nanticoke River. Present name 1810. Small industries: canning center, cantaloupe, strawberries, pork packing, shirt factory.

DE 5B: M, farmer, 38. B. 5 mi. N. at Owens Station. — F. b. Co., PGM b. DE; M. b. nearby, MGF b. Co. near Georgetown. — Ed.: here, Bridgeville HS till 15. — Methodist. — Rather unsophisticated, limited experience, unaware of purpose of interview. — Loud reverberant voice.

Newfound, Frankford P.O., Gumboro Hundred

Gumboro smallest hundred in DE, created in 1873. Settlers from mid-18th cent., first settlers largely of English descent. Gumboro village isolated. To 1840, dense forest near swamp; settlement around sawmill. Methodists dominant. First building in Frankford Long's store in 1808; cannery and service shops. Orig. part of Dagworthy's conquest. Box and barrel factory 1870s and 80s.

DE 6A: M, farmer, 70. B. 2 mi. E., near Selbyville. — F. b. head of Sound, near Ocean View, PGF, PGF's F. b. Sinnapuxent Neck, across the line in MD, PGF's PGF b. England, PGF's M. b. MD, nearby, PGM b. St. Martin's Sound, DE (in Co.); M. b. Frankford, MGF b. Baltimore Hundred, DE., MGM b. Selbyville. — Ed.: school only 3 days. — Methodist. — Completely untraveled, unsophisticated, very humble origin. — Articulation somewhat faulty; a little slow at grasping questions.

Sandy Landing, Dagsboro P.O., Baltimore Hundred

Balt. Hundred land orig. claimed by Worcester Co., MD; disputed until 1775. Surveyed for Duke of York in 1683. Settlers began to arrive at least by 1739; by 1785 settlers mainly English, also some Scots, Welsh, Dutch (or Swedes). Presbyterian services by 1767; Baptist by 1778; Methodist by 1784. Largely agricultural and rural; much swampy land (drainage projects). Dagsboro settled 1775; grew up around gristmill. Acquired present name c. 1785. Small industry: distributing center for feed and coal. Nearby holly market, large basket making plant.

DE 6B: M, farmer, 53. B. 2 mi. E. by SE. — F., PGF, PGF's F. b. here, PGM b. near Ocean View; M., MGF b. here (French Huguenot descent), MGM b. Frankford, of ealiest VA stock of local settlers. — Ed.: here till 14, 2 wks. Conference Academy in Dover, c. 14. — Methodist. — Well-to-do from horse trading and money lending, but limited intellectual experience. Cheerful, congenial, slightly slow at comprehending. — Tempo slow, drawling; articulation not very clear.

Bibliographies

Acrelius, Israel. 1874. *A History of New Sweden.* Trans. by William M. Reynolds. Philadelphia: Historical Societies of Pennsylvania and Delaware.

Bevan, Wilson Lloyd. 1929. *History of Delaware, Past and Present....* 4 vols. NY: Lewis Historical Pub. Co.

Conrad, Henry Clay. 1908. *History of the State of Delaware.* 3 vols. Wilmington: Conrad.

Federal Writers Project. 1938. *Delaware: A Guide to the First State.* NY: Viking Press.

Ferris, Benjamin. 1846. *A History of the Original Settlements on the Delaware....* Wilmington: Wilson and Heald.

Frech, Mary L. 1973. *Chronology and Documentary Handbook of the State of Delaware.* Dobbs Ferry, NY: Oceana.

Garber, John Palmer. 1934. *The Valley of the Delaware and Its Place in American History.* Philadelphia: John C. Winston Co.

McCarter, J. M., and B. F. Jackson, eds. 1882. *Historical and Biographical Encyclopedia of Delaware.* Wilmington.

Munroe, John A. 1954. *Federalist Delaware....* New Brunswick, NJ: Rutgers University Press.

Munroe, John A. 1978. *Colonial Delaware: A History.* Millwood, NY: KTO Press.

Munroe, John A. 1979. *History of Delaware.* Newark: University of Delaware Press.

Powell, Walter A. 1928. *A History of Delaware....* Boston: Christopher Pub. House.

Reed, Henry Clay. 1947. *Delaware, a History of the First State...* 3 vols. NY: Lewis Historical Pub. Co.

Ryden, George Herbert. 1938. *Delaware — the First State in the Union.* Wilmington: Delaware Tercentenary Commission.

Scharf, John Thomas. 1888. *History of Delaware.* 2 vols. Philadelphia: L. J. Richards.

Tyler, David Budlong. 1955. *The Bay and the River, Delaware: A Pictorial History.* Cambridge, MD: Cornell Maritime Press.

Vincent, Francis. 1870. *A History of the State of Delaware....* Philadelphia: J. Campbell.

1911–16. *Delaware Archives.* Wilmington: Public Archives Commission.

1946–. *Delaware History.* Wilmington: Historical Society of Delaware.

General Histories

Delan, Paul. 1951. *The Organization of State Administration in Delaware.* Baltimore: Johns Hopkins.

Ferguson, W. 1940. *A Short History of Bridgeville.* For the benefit of St Mary's Parish house fund.

Hitchens, E. Dallas. 1976. *The Milford, Delaware, Area before 1776.* Milford: Shawnee Printing.

Hoffecker, Carol E. 1977. *Delaware: A Bicentennial History.* NY: Norton

Keen, Gregory B. 1884. New Sweden, Or the Swedes on the Delaware. In *A Narrative and Critical History of America,* ed. by Justin Winsor, vol. 4, 443–502.

Kinsman, F. J., and George Gray. 1900. *Landing of the DeVries Colony at Lewes, Delaware.* Wilmington: Historical Society of Delaware.

Palen, Paul. 1956. *The Government and Administration of Delaware.* NY: Crowell.

Powell, Lyman Pierson. 1893. *History of Education in Delaware.* Washington: Govt. Print Office.

Reed, Henry Clay, and Marion B. Reed. 1966. *A Bibliography of Delaware through 1960.* Newark: University of Delaware Press.

Spriuchorn, Carl K. S. 1883. History of the Colony of New Sweden. Trans. by G. B. Keen. *Pennsylvania Magazine of History and Biography* 7:395–419, 8:17–44, 129–59, 241–54.

Wade, William J. 1975. *Sixteen Miles from Anywhere: A History of Georgetown, Delaware.* Georgetown: Countian Press.

Waterston, Elizabeth. 1926. *Churches in Delaware during the Revolution.* Wilmington: Historical Society of Delaware.

Special Studies

Brandt, Francis Burke. 1929. *The Majestic Delaware....* Philadelphia: Brandt and Gummere.

Bumstead, W. F. 1934. *The Diocese of Delaware.* Wilmington: Protestant Episcopal Church.

Clay, Jehu Curtis. 1835. *Annals of the Swedes on the Delaware.* Philadelphia: J. C. Pechin.

Cooper, Alexander B. 1905. *Fort Casimir.* Wilmington: Historical Society of Delaware.

Fisher, Sydney George. 1919. *The Quaker Colonies.* New Haven, CT: Yale University Press.

Gannett, Henry. 1904. *A Gazetteer of Delaware.* Washington: US Geological Survey.

Hancock, Harold Bell. 1977. *The Loyalists of Revolutionary Delaware.* Newark: University of Delaware Press.

Houston, John W. 1879. *Address on the History of the Boundaries of the State of Delaware.* Wilmington: Historical Society of Delaware.

Johnson, Amandus. 1911. *Swedish Settlements on the Delaware.* 2 vols. Philadelphia. Repr. 1969 (Baltimore: Genealogical Pub. Co.).

Johnson, Amandus. 1914. *The Swedes on the Delaware. . . .* Philadelphia: Lenape Press.

Louhi, Evert Alexander. 1925. *The Delaware Finns.* NY: Humanity Press.

Lunt, Dudley Cammett. 1947. *The Bounds of Delaware.* Wilmington: Star Pub. Co.

Munroe, John A. 1965. *Delaware: A Students' Guide to Localized History.* NY: Teachers College Press.

Neuenschwander, John A. 1974. *The Middle Colonies and the Coming of the American Revolution.* Port Washington, NY: Kennikat Press.

Vallandigham, Edward Noble. 1972. *Delaware and the Eastern Shore.* Port Washington, NY: Kennikat Press.

Ward, Christopher. 1930. *The Dutch and Swedes on the Delaware, 1609–64.* Philadelphia: University of Pennsylvania Press.

Ward, Christopher. 1941. *The Delaware Continentals. . . .* Wilmington: Historical Society of Delaware.

Weslager, C. A. 1947. *Delaware's Forgotten River: The Story of the Cristina.* Wilmington: Hambleton Co.

Weslager, C. A. 1961. *Dutch Explorers, Traders and Settlers in the Delaware Valley, 1609–1664.* Philadelphia: University of Pennsylvania Press.

Weslager, C. A. 1967. *The English on the Delaware: 1610–1682.* New Brunswick, NJ: Rutgers University Press.

Wildes, Harry Emerson. 1940. *The Delaware.* NY: Farrar and Rinehart.

Wuorinen, John H. 1938. *The Finns on the Delaware, 1638–1655.* NY: Columbia University Press.

Maryland

1. Cecil County

Spaniards first entered Bay 1575, 1585. Cecil Co. formed 1674. Settlement 1627–28; treaty with Susquehanna Indians 1652. First permanent settlement Carpenter's Point in 1653. A part of "Bohemia Manor", a Jesuit station c. 1660. Labadist (Dutch followers of ex-Jesuit, Jean de Labadie) settlement from 1683; Quakers in late 17th cent. Also Ulster Scots early. Acadians in 1755, went on to Canada and LA. Presbyterian services by 1708. Many from Co. migrated to SC. 1st colonial ironworks here 1715. 1st steamboats 1813; canal by 1829. Co. half in piedmont plateau and half in coastal plain. Products and industries include iron ore, paper making, chrome ore, granite. Pop. 1701: 2,004, 1782: 7,749, 1790: 13,625, 1820: 16,048, 1850: 18,939, 1880: 27,108, 1910: 23,759, 1930: 25,827, 1960: 48,408.

Clark, Charles Branch. 1950. *The Eastern Shore of Maryland and Virginia*. 3 vols. NY: Lewis Historical Pub. Co.

Gifford, G. E., Jr. 1924. *Cecil County, Maryland, 1608–1850, As Seen by Some Visitors*. Rising Sun: Calvert School.

Johnston, George. 1881. *History of Cecil County*. . . . Elkton: The Author.

Miller, Alice Etta. 1949. *Cecil County, a Study in Local History*. Elkton: C. and L. Print. and Specialty Co.

Thurston, W. C., ed. 1938. *The Eastern Shore (of Maryland) in Song and Story*. Federalsburg: J. W. Stowell Printing Co.

1897. *Portrait and Biographical Record of Harford and Cecil Counties*. NY: Chapman Pub. Co.

Battle Swamp, Port Deposit P.O., 7th Dist.

Susquehanna village; Episcopal chapel here 1733 on old Phila. Rd. Basically rural community. Port Deposit incorporated as a town 1813. Port for Susq. R. traffic. Iron mines in 18th cent. Quarries since 1808, only surviving industry.

MD 1A: F, widow at home, 85. B. here. — F. b. here, PGF b. Scotland, PGM, PGM's F. and M. b. here; M., MGF, MGM b. here. — Ed.: here till 16. — Presbyterian. — Occasionally forgetful, but fairly accurate. — Articulation moderately clear.

Rising Sun, 6th Dist.

One of Quaker settlements c. 1727; Presbyterian church by 1741. Banking and trading center for grain-growing farmers. At one time chrome shipped from local mines. Pop. 1930: 565.

MD 1B: M, farmer, 58. B. same house. — F., PGF, PGF's F. b. here (English descent), PGF's M. b. here, PGM b. Co.; M. b. Co., MGF, MGM b. Buck's Co., PA. — Ed.: here, then to Friends Normal Inst. (formerly here), 4 years. — Presbyterian, parents were Friends. — Quick, highly intelligent,

conversational. Solid middle-class type. — Tempo rapid. Vowels short.

2. Kent County

Co. dates from 1642; 2nd oldest in state. 1st E. shore settlement. Smallest no. of farms in MD; largest in average acreage. Quakers 1668; some Scandinavians later from Del. Valley. Declined after Rev., Chestertown overshadowed by Balt. Agriculture: small grains, soybeans, dairying, vegetables; commercial fishing. Pop. 1701: 1,930, 1712: 2,886, 1790: 12,836, 1820: 11,453, 1850: 11,386, 1880: 17,605, 1910: 16,957, 1930: 14,242, 1960: 15,481.

Hanson, George A. 1876. *Old Kent*. Baltimore. Repr. 1967 (Baltimore: Regional Pub. Co.).

Horne, Patricia F. 1973. *The Organization and Development of Kent County, Maryland, 1650–1800*. University of North Carolina dissertation.

Usilton, Fred. G. 1916. *History of Kent County, 1630–1916*.

Skinners Neck, Rock Hall P.O., 5th Dist.

Rock Hall a landing since 1707: former ferry to Annapolis. Terminus of first American turnpike. Fishing: shrimp, fish, crabs, oysters.

MD 2A: M, farmer, 82. B. here, sailed 3 yrs. on the Bay with lumber. — F. b. here, PGF, PGM b. Ireland; M. b. here, MGF, MGM b. MD of English descent. — Ed.: 3 mos. a yr. till 18. — Methodist. — Very quick, intelligent man. Very limited education. — Tempo fairly rapid. Vowels longish; moderately clear articulation. Very open [ɛ˖ɹ] or [ɛˬ˖ɹ].

MD 2B: Blacks Station, Millington P.O., 2nd Dist.–M, farmer, 48. B. 7–8 miles S. of Fair Lea, moved near Fair Lea when 8, then near Tolchester, then at 19 near Chesterton, then at 28 to this neighborhood. — F. b. near Red Lion, DE, came as infant to Quaker Neck in Co., PGF, PGF's F. b. New Castle Co., DE, PGF's M. b. Henderson Pt., Cecil Co., MD (Scotch-Irish descent), PGM b. S. Charles St., Balt.; M. b. Chesterton or nearby, MGF, MGM b. Co. — Ed.: Fair Lea till 12. — Methodist. — Average person. — Moderate tempo, slurred articulation.

3. Queen Annes County

Co. formed in 1706 from Talbot Co. Claiborne setttlement in area c. 1630. Earliest settlements pretty well complete by 1700; early settlers mostly English, with a few Swedes and Dutch (possibly a few Germans). Washington College 1782, joint state and private support. AfAm majority here 1800–1850. Tobacco till 19th cent., but rapid decline after Rev. General farming, stock raising, seafood, fruit, fishing, food processing. Some iron and marl deposits. Pop. 1710: 3,067, 1782: 7,762, 1790: 15,463, 1820: 14,952, 1850: 14,484, 1880: 19,257, 1910: 16,839, 1930: 14,571, 1960: 16,569.

Claiborne, John Herbert. 1917. *William Claiborne of Virginia*. NY: G. P. Putnam's Sons.

Emory, Frederic. 1950. *Queen Anne's County.* . . . Baltimore: Maryland Historical Society.

Gibbons, Boyd. 1977. *Wye Island*. Baltimore: Johns Hopkins University Press.

Isaac, Erich. 1957. Kent Island. *Maryland Historical Magazine* 52:93–119, 210–24.

Dominion, Kent Island, Chester P.O., 4th Dist.

Dominion/Kent Is. oldest settlement in MD; Claiborne settlement here by 1631. Kent I. straddled trading route to Susquehanna; trade and settlement spread here when Great Massacre (1622) checked spread inland from Jamestown. 1st Anglican parish in MD here in 1630s. Reduced by Balt. in 1647. Some trade, tobacco farming early; general farming, livestock imported from VA. Occupied by British 1813; long subject to Indian raids. Prosperous when trade route was north-south; when trade route shifted, Kent I. became a backwater. Many old families; ecological battles today. Pop. Kent I. 1880: 2,137, 1930: 2,196, 1960: 3,114.

MD 3A: M, oysterman, 73. B. here. — F. b. Dorchester Co., came here as half-grown boy, PGF, PGM b. Dorchester Co.; M. b. Dominion, MGF b. Kent I., MGM b. Dominion. — Ed.: a little here till 12. — Methodist since 3 years before interview, change in life. — Quaint, jolly, most willing to talk; slightly forgetful; now very religious (wife superstitious). — Rather rapid tempo, lax articulation.

Prices Station, Church Hill P.O.

Price's Mills here by 1810; RR station. Church Hill a flourishing village. One of few pre-Rev. towns in Co.; location of one of oldest parish churches on E. shore (est. by 1700). Center for rural trade.

MD 3B: M, farmer, 43. B. 12 miles north. — F., PGF b. 12 miles N., PGM b. Co.; M. b. Co., near Kent Co., MGF b. DE, MGM b. France, to NY as a child, then here. — Ed.: till 18. — Methodist. — Obliging, polite, average. Quick, nervous. — Very rapid tempo; somewhat lax articulation; tendency to short vowels.

4. Caroline County

Co. est. 1773. 1st surveys c. 1663; settlement delayed by boundary dispute with DE. Early settlers largely English, many religious refugees (some Quakers). 1/3 of land in cultivation by 1783. Never dominated by plantation system or slavery; Methodists and Quakers dominant by early 19th cent. Some Acadians in 1750s. Only E. shore co. untouched by Ches. Bay. Diversified agriculture by 1840 (no tobacco). General farming: peaches, truck farming, vegetables, grain, poultry. Industry mainly related to farming: fertilizer, flour, fruit and vegetable processing. Pop. 1782: 6,230, 1790: 9,506, 1820: 10,108, 1850: 9,962, 1880: 13,766, 1910: 19,216, 1930: 17,387, 1960: 19,462.

Clark, Raymond B., Jr. 1969. *Caroline County Marriage Licenses. . . and a Short History*. St. Michaels.

Cochrane, Laura C., et al., eds. 1920. *History of Caroline County.* . . . Federalsburg: J. W. Stowell Print. Co.

Hanson, George A. 1876. *Old Kent*. Baltimore. Repr. 1967 (Baltimore: Regional Pub. Co.).

Horsey, Eleanor F. 1974. *Origins of Caroline County*. Denton.

Noble, E. M. 1920. *History of Caroline County*. Federalsburg, Md.: J.W. Stowell.

Williston, Denton P.O., 3rd Dist.

Williston orig. Potter's Landing, an important shipping center in steamboat days; less important when RR supplanted steamboat. Was chief port of Co. for over 100 yrs. Rev. supply depot. Denton orig. called Eden-town (after Robert Eden). Quakers and Roman Catholics in 18th cent. Became Co. seat in 1791. Trading center; canneries, baskets and crates, overalls, pearl buttons.

MD 4A: F, widow, 85. B. 1/4 mile away, in DE, near Smithville, came here at 27 after marriage. — F. b. Talbot Co., Hole-in-the-Wall (S. of Fayton), came to DE as a boy, PGF b. Talbot Co.; M. b. Co., step-PGF lived near Whiteleysburg, MD, in DE. — Ed.: in DE till 16. — Methodist. — Remarkably intelligent; plain, vigorous, outspoken, self-assured; matter-of-fact. Probably deafness increased appreciation of human contact and attention; concentrated on each question as it came along. — Very vigorous articulation; unconscious of old fashioned speech: [aʌʋ˄ aʌɨ] even before voiced consonants and finally.

Burrsville, Denton P.O., 3rd Dist.

Burrsville formed from 2 adjacent villages; named by 1833. Dominated by Methodists.

MD 4B: M, farmer and sawmill worker, 80. B. 2 mi. away. — F. b. 4 mi. W., PGF b. near Whites Church, DE, c. 5 mi. away, PGF's F. b. Ridgly in Co., PGF's M. of Irish descent, PGM b. near Maple Grove, DE, c. 3 mi. away; M. b. Balt., MGF b. Burrsville, MGM b. Elkton, MD. — Ed.: here till 20. — Methodist. — Unable to walk, enjoyed chance for conversation; slightly deaf, quick mind and good memory.

Preston, 4th Dist.

Preston grew up around Bethesda Chapel, an early Methodist church est. by 1800. Named in 1856. Quakers and German Lutherans among settlers in 19th cent. RR in 1890; growth accelerated. Highway by 1916.

MD 4C: M, farmer, 53. B. here. — F., PGF b. Federalstown, MD, PGF's F. b. Sheffield, Yorkshire, came here 1747. PGF's M. b. DE, PGM b. Preston, PGM's F. and M. b. Co.; M., MGF, MGM b. Dorchester Co., MD. — Ed.: here till 17. — Quaker. — Excellent inf., combining naïve rural approachability, intellectual curiosity, enthusiasm and enjoyment of interview. Occasionally slow in reacting, but always with good will. — Strong [ɚ]; neutralization of *card/cord* and the like; initial [ð] becomes [t] or [d], depending on context. Like most American Quakers, uses *thee* for subject and object.

5. Talbot County

Est. 1661. Kent I. trading post in area c. 1630; first settlers on mainland prior to 1658. Terraced plains, unsuccessful attempt to find oil and gas. Orig. tobacco country; then general farming and produce for NY, Phila., and Balt. markets.

Oxford a major port early, now declined. Anglicans by 1650; Quakers by 1657; Roman Church by 1697. Many aristocratic families in 18th cent.; rise of rural elite with diversified sources of wealth. Truck farming; industrialization after 1860, industry with agricultural base (food processing). Shipbuilding. Pop. 1701: 4,862, 1782: 6,744, 1790: 13,084, 1820: 14,389, 1850: 13,811, 1880: 19,065, 1910: 19,620, 1930: 18,583, 1960: 21,578.

Clark, Raymond B., Jr. 1965–67. *Talbot County Marriage Licenses, with a History of Talbot County Churches.* . . . 2 vols. Washington.

Harrison, Samuel A. 1878. *Wenlock Christison and the Early Friends in Talbot County.* Baltimore: Maryland Historical Society.

Higgins, Martin Meginney. 1926. *History of the Reincarnation of Easton.* Easton: Easton Star-Democrat.

Sinclair, Raymond B. 1954. *The Tilghman's Island Story.* . . . Tilghman.

Tilghman, Oswald, comp. 1915. *History of Talbot County.* . . . 2 vols. Baltimore. Repr. 1967 (Baltimore: Regional Pub. Co.).

Tillman, Stephen Frederick. 1946. *Tilghman-Tillman Family.* Ann Arbor: Edwards Brothers.

1967. *Talbot Past and Present.* Easton: Historical Society of Talbot County.

1968. *Guardian of Our Maryland Heritage.* Easton: Talbot County Free Library.

Tilghman Island, Tilghman P.O.
Tilghman I. patented 1659. Formed from Accomack Co., VA, in 17th cent. Low, sandy ground. Fisherman and hunters: oysters, crabs, fish; sport fishing and hunting. Nearly denuded of timber; land divided into small farms. Town of Tilghman a shipping point for seafood; canning of herring roe and tomatoes.

MD 5A: M, waterman, 69. B. here. — F., PGF (prob.), PGM b. Witman, 2 mi. N.; M. b. Island or just across creek at Broad Creek, mainland of Co. — Ed.: very little. — Methodist. — Genial and willing, but tired easily. — Moderate tempo, fairly lax articulation. — Wife, also native, has tendency to open [ɔʊ ɛɪ].

Dover Road, Easton P.O., 1st Dist.
Easton a cathedral town; diocesan city for E. shore. Trading center and port. Quaker community, late 17th cent. Many plantations bought up by New Yorkers, Pittsburghers, etc. Canneries, lumber mill, garment factory. Pop. 1850: 1,413, 1880: 3,005, 1910: 3,083, 1960: 6,337.

MD 5B: M, farmer, 48. B. 8 mi. S. of Easton. — F., M. b. Co. — Ed.: Landing Neck till 18. — Methodist. — Self-made, respectable farmer, prosperous. Genial, quick. — Moderate tempo; somewhat lax articulation.

6. Dorchester County
Co. formed c. 1668. Settlement somewhat delayed because of isolation and Indians. First settlers had arrived by 1659; mostly English stock. Many early settlers from S. MD, Somerset, VA; some Acadians. Anglicans dominant early; Old Trinity Church est. 1692. First Roman Catholic chapel 1769;

Methodists by Revolution. Divided loyalties 1861–65. RR here by 1866. Much swamp and marsh. 2nd only to Louisiana in fur trapping. Cutlery, food producing and processing. Pop. 1701: 2,617, 1712: 3,275, 1782: 8,927, 1790: 15,875, 1820: 17,759, 1850: 18,877, 1880: 23,110, 1910: 28,669, 1930: 26,813, 1960: 29,666.

Jones, Elias. 1925. *Revised History of Dorchester County.* Baltimore. New ed. 1966 (Cambridge, MD: Tidewater Publishers).

Ruelle, Walter E. 1969. *Footnotes to Dorchester History.* Cambridge, MD: Tidewater Publishers.

Wingate, 10th Dist.
Truck farming, oystering, canning.

MD 6A: F, widow, 77. B. Bloodsworth Island (now uninhabited), came to mainland at 30. — F. b. Bloodsworth I., PGF, PGM prob. b. Co.; M., MGF, MGM b. Wingate. — Ed.: Bloodsworth I. till 12 or 13. — Methodist. — Somewhat suspicious; mentally quick. — Rapid tempo; short vowels; fairly clear articulation.

MD 6A*: Fishing Creek (laid out 1707). — M, waterman, 80. B. here. — F., M. b. here. — Illiterate. — Unsophisticated but cordial. Recollections not too clear. — Rather slow tempo; lax articulation.

MD 6B: Salem. — M, farmer and landowner, 58. B. 3 mi. S. — F. b. Vienna in Co., PGF, PGF's F., PGM b. Co.; M. b. Linkwoods in Co., MGF b. Secretary in Co., MGM b. 2 mi. S. — Ed.: Vienna (h.s.) till 20. — Methodist. — Obliging, substantial, self-made. — Moderate tempo and articulation.

7. Wicomico County
Formed 1867 from Somerset and Worcester. 1st settlements in 1660s. City of Salisbury laid out 1732. Early settlers in Co. primarily English and Scots. 1st settlement in America of English Presbyterians in 1683. Episcopal parishes by 1692; Methodists by 1778; Baptist Assn. by 1781. Old industries: iron, grist mills, sugar refining, tanneries. Many water mills in Co. in 19th cent. Has led state in value of farm products: poultry, truck farming, food processing, lumbering, fishing. Most urbanized and populous co. on E. shore. Pop. 1870: 15,802, 1880: 18,016, 1910: 26,815, 1930: 31,229, 1960: 49,050.

Truitt, Charles Jones. 1932. *Historic Salisbury.* . . . Garden City, NY: Country Life Press.

Mt. Pleasant, Willards P.O.
Willards began as RR station. Till 1930 cut pine for mine props. Strawberry marketing, shirt factory.

MD 7A: M, farmer, 73. B. here. — F. b. here, PGF b. Co., PGM b. here; M. b. on island in river near here, on edge of Co., MGF b. Co., MGM b. near here. — Ed.: 2–3 weeks. — Methodist. — Valetudinarian, conscious of advancing age. — Speech archaic, natural: [ɪ] in *room, broom, humor*; [aʊntsə] for *answer*; [ə] usual, except after [-ð-] as in *father, mother*.

Upper Ferry, Salisbury P.O. and Dist.

Upper Ferry a small, rural town on Wicomico. Buildings from early 18th cent. (Salisbury described below.)

MD 7B: M, farmer, 44. B. here. — F., PGF, PGF's F. b. here (Scotch descent), PGM prob. b. here; M., MGF b. Salisbury. — Ed.: here till 7th grade, then 1 yr. Salisbury HS. — Methodist. — Quick, bright, practical; little interest in project. Doesn't consider himself Southern but is identified in Phila. as such. — Fairly rapid tempo; fairly short vowels.

Salisbury

Area first settled 1681; earliest settlers English (some were Penn's colonists, worked way south). Town laid out 1732. Many families assoc. with Wiltshire, England. RR 1860; also fire in 1860, most old buildings lost. Co. seat when Wicomico est. 1867. State Teachers College here. Largest town on E. shore; 2nd largest port in MD. Important shipping point: water, rail, truck, air (airport for S. Delmarva). Supplies farmers all over Delmarva. Products and industries: shipping (esp. fruits and vegetables), lumber, crates, baskets, barrels, meat packing, canneries, garment factories, iron furnace, shipyard. Pop. 1910: 6,690, 1930: 10,997, 1960: 16,302.

MD 7C!: M, interior decorator, 55. B. here; 4 yrs. in Phila. (1903–7). — F. b. 4 mi. W., but owned property in town, PGF, PGF's F. b. 4 mi. W., PGF's PGF's F. of English descent, PGF's M. b. 8 mi. W., PGF's MGF of French Huguenot descent, immigrant from Edinburgh to Northumberland Co., VA, PGM, PGM's F. b. Spring Hill in Co. (latter of English descent), PGM's M. b. Delmar, MD; M., MGF b. Salisbury, MGF's F. b. near Salisbury, MGF's PGF and PGM, MGF's M. b. here, MGM, MGM's F. b. near here, MGM's M. b. 4 mi. E. of Princess Anne, MGM's MGF b. near Princess Anne. — Ed.: local schools till 20, then 4 yrs. at Phila. School of Design. — Episcopalian. — Cultivated local type; rather precise and opinionated but fairly naïve about general usage; honest in reporting. — Cultivated.

8. Worcester County

Co. est. 1742 from E. part of Somerset Co. Land grants under 1651 Act; first settlement 1658; early grants (1660s) to English, Huguenots. Also settlers from Accomack Co., some Acadians. Last E. shore co. to be settled in considerable numbers. Co. name used as early as 1672; initially projected to contain all of territory. Quakers, Presbyterians, Episcopalians, Baptists in 18th cent.; Methodists late 18th cent. (now strongest in Co.); Roman Catholics in late 19th cent. Tobacco important, along with other crops, in 18th cent. Most of Co. within 40 ft. of sea level; barrier island, inlets, marshes. Recreation/resort area. Chiefly agricultural: 2nd in state in value of farm products, 2nd in poultry, truck farming, food processing (esp. tomatoes and poultry). Pop. 1782: 8,561, 1790: 11,640, 1820: 17,421, 1850: 18,859, 1880: 19,539, 1910: 21,841, 1930: 21,624, 1960: 23,733.

Badger, Curtis J. 1974. *Worcester: A Pictorial Review.* Accomac, VA: Eastern Shore News.

Truitt, R. Van J., and M. Callette. 1977. *Worcester County: Maryland's Arcadia.* Snow Hill: Worcester County Historical Society.

MD 8A: West, The Forest, Eden P.O. (Somerset Co.), Atkinsons Dist. — M, farmer, woodsman, huckleberry picker, 70. B. here. — F. b. here, PGF b. perhaps in England; M. b. here, MGF, MGF's F., MGF's M. b. Delaware (latter of Indian descent), MGM b. here, MGM's F. b. Ireland. — Ed.: illiterate, but has committed most of New Testament to memory. — Reared Methodist, then Christian Baptist, then Holiness. — Somewhat suspicious, though enjoyed having someone to talk to; not too interested; slow reactions. No travel, very poor; quarrelsome on religious matters; in 1936 or 1937 won the huckleberry picking championship of the world. — Moderate tempo, articulation, vowel length.

Mile Post Farm, Snow Hill P.O., 2nd Dist.

Snow Hill est. as town in 1683 by General Assembly; Co. seat 1742. Settled 1686; trade and export center; early townsmen Scottish merchants. Anglican parish est. 1692; Episcopal church built 1756. Old houses, seafood, colonial museum. Cypress swamps. Agricultural community; canneries, basket factory, shirt factory. Pop. declining.

MD 8B: M, farmer, 50. B. 10 mi. from Snow Hill. — F. b. W. part of Co., PGF b. Co., PGM b. Somerset Co. (Cornish descent); M., MGF b. Co., MGM b. Accomack Co., VA, near Jinkins Bridge. — Ed.: till 16. — Methodist. — Prosperous, average background. Quick, intelligent, cooperative.

9. Somerset County

Co. est 1666; problem of dividing line with VA resolved 1668. 1st settlement 1661, many Quakers. Early settlers from Accomack and Northampton Cos. AfAms (some free) by 1667. Presbyterians by 1670; 1st Anglican minister 1681. Most settlers were small farmers, some indentured servants; mostly English. Some Acadians in 1755. Ultra-Protestant orientation. Many Tories; many old houses. Tidewater land; income from the waters. Local AfAm community, often called "Liberia" from 1820; made up of freedmen who did not choose recolonization in Liberia; faded away after 1920 (but still large AfAm pop.). Marshes, rivers, bays. Primarily agriculture and fishing. Products and industries: seafood, wildlife preserve, tomatoes, strawberries, potatoes, lumber, broilers. Pop. (AfAm pop. in parens.) 1701: 5,404, 1712: 6,456 (581), 1782: 7,787, 1790: 15,610 (7,338), 1820: 19,579 (9,195), 1850: 22,456 (9,071), 1880: 21,668 (8,694), 1910: 26,455 (9,476), 1930: 23,382 (8,111), 1960: 19,623 (7,300).

Torrence, Clayton. 1935. *Old Somerset on the Eastern Shore of Maryland.* Richmond. Repr. 1966 (Baltimore: Regional Pub. Co.).

Van Ness, Esther Opie. 1958. *William Oppie of Somerset County, New Jersey.*

Wilson, Woodrow T. 1974. *Thirty-Four Families of Old Somerset County.* Baltimore: Johns Hopkins University Press.

Wilson, Woodrow W. 1980. *Quindogue, Maryland.* Baltimore: Johns Hopkins University Press.

Princess Anne

Easiest spot to reach from all of Co.; became Co. seat 1742. Retains 18th cent. plan. Presb. "meeting house" from 1765; Episcopal church from 1767. Maryland State College (now part of U. of MD). Pop. 1880: 751, 1910: 1,006, 1960: 1,351.

MD 9N: F, domestic servant, 70. B. here. — Parents, ancestors as far back as known, b. here. — Ed.: a little private ed. — Trusted old school AfAm family retainer. Quick, nervous, pleasantly irritable when weary. High native intelligence. — Intonation hints at African influence; both /e/ and /o/ difficult to transcribe; postvocalic /r/ variable, though usually absent or weak. Has contrast of *cot/caught, card/cord*.

Deal Island

Settled 1676. Orig. "Devil's Island"; renamed after inhabitants converted to Methodism. Fishing center, almost all watermen. Half marsh; oysters, crabs, muskrat trapping, guides for anglers and hunters (ducks). Pop. 1930: 1,257, 1960: 810.

MD 9A: F, widow, dressmaker, 68. B. here. — F., PGF b. here, PGF's F. b. Tangier I., VA (preached to British occupation troops in 1812 and told them they'd never take Balt.), PGM b. here; M., MGF b. here, MGM b. Dames Quarter, mainland. — Ed.: here till 17. — Methodist. — Old-fashioned, in touch with things. — Tempo fairly rapid; vowels longish; articulation fairly clear; [æ'·ʊ] before /f s t/, etc. Problem: old local drawl or result of contacts with Balt.

MD 9B: Wellington, Princess Anne P.O., Dublin Dist. — M, farmer, 42. B. here. — F., PGF, PGM b. here; M. b. Cokesbury, 3 mi. S., MGF, MGM b. here. — Ed.: here till 14. — Methodist. — Average type; quick; cooperative but not overly enthusiastic. — Slowish tempo; lax articulation.

10. Harford County

Co. est. 1773. Earliest recorded settlements in 1650s. 4/5 of Co. in piedmont plateau; 1/5 in coastal plain. Shoreline occupied by 1700, inland later. Orig. settlers from England, VA, PA. Joppa prosperous port 1709–68; eventually silted up, lost out to Balt.. Church of England by 1671; Presbyterians and Friends in 1730s; others later. 1st gravel road 1815; 1st RR 1836; Susq.-Tidewater Canal 1839. Many 18th cent. buildings. Basically agricultural: dairying, stock raising, gen. farming, vegetables (canning), race horse breeding. Diversified industry. Pop. 1782: 8,377, 1790: 14,976, 1820: 15,924, 1850: 19,356, 1880: 28,042, 1910: 27,965, 1930: 31,603, 1960: 76,722.

Holland, Charles D. 1933. *Some Landmarks of Colonial History in Harford County.* Baltimore: Fosnot and Williams Co.

Mason, Samuel, Jr. 1940. *Historical Sketches of Harford County, Maryland.* Lancaster, PA: Intelligencer.

Preston, Walter W. 1901. *History of Harford County. . . .* Baltimore. Repr. 1972 (Baltimore: Regional Pub. Co.).

Wright, C. Milton. 1967. *Our Harford Heritage.*

Hickory, Forest Hill P.O., 3rd Dist.

Forest Hill a trading and banking center. Canning, fruit packing, nurseries. Pop. 1930: 400.

MD 10A: M, farmer, 82. B. here. — F. b. Sykesville, Howard Co., MD, came here as child, PGF b. England, came to America, settled in Sykesville, PGM b. Co.; M. b. 3 mi. E., MGF b. Co. (English descent), MGM b. 3 mi. E., MGM's F. b. Co. (English descent). — Ed.: 6–18 on and off. — Wealthy landowner, somewhat old-fashioned (keeps oxen); limited contacts: only 3 overnight visits in lifetime to Bel Air (local trading center). Memory failing; euphoric sense of humor at his own mistakes. — Lax articulation.

MD 10B: Benson, 3rd Dist. — M, farmer (asst. superintendent Fresh Air Farms), 41. B. Pylesville, 3 mi. away. — F. b. Bel Air, PGF b. Phila., came here when married, PGF's F. b. Sellarsville, PA, PGF's M. b. PA, PGM b. Phila.; M. b. 5 mi. SE, MGF, MGM b. Co. — Ed.: Bel Air till 17. — Baptist. — Languid looking but mentally sharp; honest and cooperative; thoroughly aware of purpose of interview. — Tempo moderate; articulation lax.

11 & 12. Baltimore County

1st co. in N. MD; one of 4 original cos. in MD; formed c. 1659. 3 cos. eventually taken from it. Balt. 6th largest city; 12th largest urban metropolitan center. Present Co. has no incorporated municipalities; some of largest unincorp. areas in US. Co. and city separated in 1851; Co. tends to be suburbanized. Towson Co. seat. Some iron ore in colonial times. Raided by Confederates in July, 1865. Wealthy colonial families; fox hunting still persists. Diversified industry, including heavy industry (largest steel mill in US), excellent transportation, important port. Pop. 1704: 1,927, 1782: 17,878, 1790: 38,937, 1820: 96,201, 1850: 210,646, 1880: 83,336, 1910: 122,349, 1930: 124,349, 1960: 492,428.

Beirne, Francis F. 1951. *The Amiable Baltimoreans.* NY. Repr. 1968 (Hatboro, PA: Tradition Press).

Beirne, Francis F. 1957. *Baltimore: A Picture History. . . .* NY: Hastings House.

Beirne, Francis F. 1967. *St. Paul's Parish, Baltimore.* Baltimore: Horn-Shafer.

Bowen, E. Bennett, et al. 1956. *Here is Baltimore County.* Towson: Board of Education of Baltimore County.

Chapelle, Howard Irving. 1930. *The Baltimore Clipper.* Salem, MA: Marine Research Society.

Cunz, Dieter. 1940. *History of the Germania Club of Baltimore City, Maryland.* Baltimore: Germania Club.

Hall, Clayton Coleman, ed. 1912. *Baltimore: Its History and Its People.* 3 vols. NY: Lewis Historical Pub. Co.

Hirschfeld, Charles. 1941. *Baltimore, 1870–1900: Studies in Social History.* Baltimore: Johns Hopkins University Press.

Howard, George W. 1873–76. *The Monumental City. . . .* 2 vols. Baltimore: J. D. Ehlers, Printers.

Janvier, Meredith. 1933. *Baltimore in the Eighties and Nineties.* Baltimore: H. G. Roebuck.

Livingood, J. W. 1947. *The Philadelphia-Baltimore Trade Rivalry.* Harrisburg, PA: Pennsylvania Historical and Museum Commission.

Mencken, H. L. *Happy Days, Heathen Days, Newspaper Days.* NY: Knopf.

Offutt, Thieman Scott, et al. 1916. *Baltimore County.* Towson: Jeffersonian Pub. Co.

Owens, Hamilton. 1941. *Baltimore on the Chesapeake.* Garden City, NY: Doubleday, Doran.

Reid, Ira de A. 1935. *The Negro Community of Baltimore*. Baltimore: National Urban League.

Scharf, John Thomas. 1874. *The Chronicles of Baltimore*. Baltimore: Turnbull Bros.

Scharf, John Thomas. 1881. *History of Baltimore City and County*. . . . 2 vols. Philadelphia. Repr. 1971 (Baltimore: Regional Pub. Co.).

Sioussat, Annie Leakin. 1931. *Old Baltimore*. NY: Macmillan Co.

Spencer, Edward, ed. 1881. *Memorial Volume: 1730–1880*. Baltimore: Mayor and City Council.

Thomas, Thaddeus P. 1890. *The City Government of Baltimore*. Baltimore: Johns Hopkins University Press.

Walker, Paul K. 1973. *The Baltimore Community and the American Revolution: A Study in Urban Development*. University of North Carolina dissertation.

1897. *Genealogy and Biography of Leading Families of the City of Baltimore and Baltimore County*. NY: Chapman.

1957. *Baltimore County in the State and Nation*. Towson: Board of Education of Baltimore County.

1978. *The Green Spring Valley: Its History and Heritage*. Baltimore: Maryland Historical Society.

Bluemount, Monkton P.O., 7th Dist.

To N. of Balt., on York Rd. No schools for AfAms before 1867, though over 90% of Balt. AfAms were free.

MD 11: M, retired farmer (also milk business, laid RR ties, worked in local quarry), 77. B. 2 mi. E. — F., PGF b. near Monkton, PGF's F. b. Ireland (Protestant), PGM b. Black Horse, just over line in Harford Co.; M. b. White Hall in Co., MGF b. England, MGM b. near Black Horse. — Ed.: 3 yrs., near here. — Methodist. — Very unsophisticated. Quick, nervous, excitable. — Hard of hearing; lax articulation.

Boring (on Carroll County line), 4th Dist.

Terminus of a turnpike. Western MD RR here from 1880. Named for an early city commissioner.

MD 12A: F, widow, 87. B. 2 1/2 mi. S. of Westminster, Carroll Co. (c. 5 mi. from here). — F. b. Carroll Co., PGF b. MD (English descent), PGM b. MD; M. b. Carroll Co., MGF, MGM b. MD (German descent). — Ed.: till 12. — Methodist. — Has done sewing for better families; better speech than one might expect of poor woman of 87; conceals some of her rusticity.

White House, Upperco P.O.

Late urbanization.

MD 12B: M, farmer, 52. B. same house. — F. b. here, PGF b. 3 mi. away, PGF's F. b. near Towson, PGF's PGF b. near N. Balt., PGF's PGF's F. b. England, PGF's M. b. near Hampstead, just over Carroll Co. line, PGM b. 3 mi. away, PGM's F. b. 3 mi. W. (German descent); M., MGF, MGM b. here, MGM's M. b. near Butler in Co. — Ed.: here till 10. — Baptist. — Frank; genuine open responses after initial timidity allayed.

13. Baltimore City

Laid out 1730; promising harbor (prob. originally to be just another tobacco port). Settlements from 1660s; iron deposits promoted settlement. Slow growth at first (only 200 by 1752). Acadians arrived 1755. Became Co. seat 1768. Early settlers included Quakers, English, French, Germans, Scots. Developed as port in Revolution (privateering center); also during War of 1812. At least 10% of pop. German by 1796 (German spoken, German newspapers); even more strongly German in 19th cent. 3rd largest city in US in 1840, 7th in 1960. Increasing AfAm pop. Separated from Co. in 1851 by new constitution. State Normal School here 1866; Johns Hopkins U. opened 1876. Large numbers of immigrants in early 19th cent. from Russia, SE Europe; many Jews. Diverse shipping. Important port; industrial development as result of access to imported ores, oil, etc. Shipbuilding from 1730. Turnpikes from 1790s; various canals; B&O RR begun 1828. In 19th cent. cotton mfg., clothing, sugar, trade with South. Other products and industries: iron and steel (expanded since WWII), shoes, leather, shipping, copper ore, fertilizer. Pop. (AfAm pop. in parens) 1790: 13,563 (1,578), 1820: 62,738 (14,683), 1850: 169,054 (28,388), 1880: 332,312 (53,716), 1910: 558,485 (84,749), 1930: 804,874 (142,106), 1960: 939,024 (325,589).

See 11 & 12 (Baltimore County) for bibliography.

MD 13A: F, domestic, 70. B. S. Balt., brought up in St. Paul's School (Episcopal orphanage) till 18. — F., M. b. Balt., PGF prob. b. England. — Ed.: till 18. — Conscientious, inclined to be prim.

MD 13B: M, glass cutter, 45. B. NE Balt., has carried papers, worked in printing and auto shops, been chauffeur and shipping clerk; in France during WWI. — F., PGF b. Balt.; M. b. St. Marys Co., moved to Balt. as a child, MGF, MGM b. St. Marys Co. (English descent, MGF prob. Cornish). — Cooperative, recuperating from hospitalization. — Responses to the point. Articulation clear; tempo moderate.

MD 13C: M, salesman, men's clothing co. (formerly woolen buyer), 55. B. on a farm just outside city. — F. b. Balt., PGF b. Balt. Co., PGM b. France, came here at age 21; M., MGF b. Balt., MGF's F. b. Amsterdam, Netherlands, MGM b. Balt., MGM's F. of German descent. — Ed.: parochial school, 3 yrs. Loyola College. — Roman Catholic, formerly Knight of Columbus. — Genial, exuberant; loves talk and good company. — Tempo, stress, articulation moderate.

MD 13D!: F, widow, 70. B. Balt. (after age 6, spent every summer 5 mi. out in country). — F., PGF, PGF's F. b. outside Balt., areas later annexed, PGF's PGF b. Scotland, PGF's PGM b. MD, prob. Balt., PGF's M. b. Camden, NJ, PGM b. Balt. Co.; M. b. Balt., MGF, MGF's F. b. Balt. Co., MGM, MGM's F. b. Balt. — Ed.: French governess and tutor. — Episcopalian. — Cultivated, cooperative; realizes memory failing. — Cultivated.

MD 13E!: F, single, 76. B. near Towson, Balt. Co. When 16, left country estate, and since has lived mostly in Balt.; in 1904–9 traveled in W. Africa, Italy, England, India, China, Palestine. — F., PGF b. here, PGF's F. b. Balt. Co., PGF's PGF b. England, PGF's M. b. Balt. Co., PGM, PGM's F. b. near Annapolis, PGM's M. b. Oak Hill, near Balt.; M., MGF b. Balt., MGF's F. b. Balt. Co., MGF's PGF b. Birmingham,

MGF's PGM b. here, MGF's M. b. Germantown, MGM b. here. — Ed.: governess, brother's tutor, desultory teaching by mother; abroad mostly in France and Italy at ages 12–14. — Episcopalian. — Confirmed spinster of prominent family; not wealthy at present; active in women's work. Cooperative, honest, dependable. — Phonetic pattern, though genuine, not often heard locally, where usually [ɚ·], [ɔ] as in *lord*, [ɛˑʊ] for [ou], etc. Tempo moderate; vowels and diphthongs sometimes prolonged. — Cultivated.

MD 13F!: F, housewife, c. 50. B. Balt., summers at Garrison, 13 mi. NW. — F. b. Balt., PGF, PGF's F. b. Balt. Co., PGF's PGF b. N. Ireland, PGF's M. b. PA, PGF's MGF and MGM b. PA (N. Irish), PGM b. Balt., PGM's F. b. N. Ireland, PGM's M. b. Balt.; M., MGF b. Balt., MGF's F. b. Bremen, Germany, MGM, MGM's F., MGM's PGF b. Balt., MGM's MGF b. N. Ireland (Ulster Scot), MGM's PGM's F. b. Balt. Co., MGM's M. b. Balt., MGM's MGF b. N. Ireland, MGM's MGM b. Accomack Co., VA. — Ed.: governess till 14, Madame Le Febvre's [finishing] School. — St. Paul Episcopal Church. — Husband of ancient and honorable Balt. family; their son a prof. at Johns Hopkins. — Cultivated, middle-aged; poised, assured in speech and manner; fully cooperative in answering questions. — Casual drawling tempo; slight, pleasant nasalization. — Cultivated.

MD 13G: F, housewife and worker in nearby food produce shop. B. same neighborhood, never lived elsewhere. — M., F. b. Balt., grandparents all of native stock, perhaps b. Balt. — Ed.: limited. — Lower middle-class; independent, democratic; glad to talk. No knowledge of country life; never out of Balt., even to shore in summer. Stays in neighborhood. Goes to bed at 6:30 PM, locks doors and windows against neighborhood perils, rises at 5:00 AM. — Speech clear but not vigorous; [ɚ] not strong; [ɪ] in unstressed vowels.

14. Carroll County

Formed 1836 from Baltimore and Frederick Cos. First land grant 1727. Many Germans among early settlers; later English, Irish, Scotch. Some (but not much) tobacco. Turnpike 1805. Western MD College (1866). No large towns, mainly commuting to industrial employment in Balt. Medium-sized farms: grazing, dairying. Iron ores, marble; copper and gold in past. Industry diversified. Pop. 1840: 17,241, 1850: 20,616, 1880: 30,992, 1910: 33,934, 1930: 35,978, 1960: 52,785.

Elderdice, Dorothy. 1937. *The Carroll County Caravan. . . .* Westminster: Times Print. Co.
Klein, Frederic Shriver. 1957. *Union Mills: The Shriver Homestead.* Baltimore: Maryland Historical Society.
Lynch, Branford Gist. 1939. *A Hundred Years of Carroll County.* Westminster: Democratic Advocate Co.
Scharf, John Thomas. 1882. *History of Western Maryland.* 2 vols. Philadelphia: L. H. Everts.
Warner, Mary E., et al. 1976. *Carroll County, Maryland: A History, 1837–1976.* Hadden Crafts: Carroll County Bicentennial Committee.

Silver Run, Westminster P.O., Myers Dist. (Dist. 3)

Dist. predominantly German in origins; English became common only after 1830s. German Reformed and Lutheran.

Silver Run a crossroads; St. Marys Lutheran Church here from 1763. Diversified business in 1880s. Westminster a "prosperous, conservative community". Mainly Scotch, Irish, English, and Dutch. Formed in 1764; renamed just before Rev. Courthouse 1836. 40 stores and 3 banks in 1861.

MD 14: M, farmer, 52. B. here. — F, PGF, PGF's F. b. here, PGF's PGF, PGF's PGF's F. b. Frederick Twp., Montgomery Co., PA, came when PGF's PGF was 2 to Littlestown, Adams Co., PA (5 mi. from here), PGF's PGF's PGF b. Europe, PGF's PGF's PGM b. Rheinpfalz; M. b. 3 mi. W. — Ed.: here till 15. — Reformed-Evangelical. — A plain matter-of-fact man who saw no sense to the questions but answered them quickly and well because he had promised to.

Union Mills

Mill, tannery built 1760 by Shriver family; house continuously occupied by same family. Village developed c. Rev. around mill; flour and grist mill center of 18th cent. economy. Tannery and cannery, abandoned or moved after Civil War. Diversified business.

MD 14*: M, retired farmer, 79. B. in backwoods NE of here. — Parents b. here. — Very little ed. — Lutheran. — Bilingual: Dutch/English. Aged, testy, with aggressive wife; sensitive about "Dutchiness"; translating responses was arduous. — Very harsh, vigorous articulation, with great muscular energy.

15. Howard County

Formed 1851 from Anne Arundel Co. 1st settlers in area (1649) descendants of Anne Arundel Co. Puritans and Quakers. Large estates in present co. in 1687. Many English settlers; many 18th cent. buildings. Church of England here from 1728; Methodists by 1794. Home of Charles Carroll, last signer of Declaration to die. Recently suburbanization between Balt. and Washington. Piedmont; gently to strongly rolling. Primarily agricultural: corn, small grains, dairying, livestock, turkeys, vegetables and fruit on small scale. Some iron ore; small industries. Pop. 1860: 13,338, 1880: 16,140, 1910: 16,106, 1930: 16,169, 1960: 36,152.

Stein, C. F. 1972. *Origin and History of Howard County, Maryland.* Baltimore: Johns Hopkins University Press.
Warfield, Joshua Dorsey. 1905. *The Founders of Anne Arundel and Howard Counties.* Baltimore. Repr. 1967 (Baltimore: Regional Pub. Co.).

MD 15A: Florence, Woodbine P.O., 4th Dist. — M, farm worker, 71. B. 2 mi. N. — F. b. over line in Frederick Co., came here when young man as carpenter, PGF, PGM b. Buckeyestown, Frederick Co.; M. b. over line in Frederick Co., MGF, MGM b. Frederick Co. (MGM of Irish parents). — Ed.: several yrs., off and on. — Methodist. — Genial, fairly bright despite lack of education and social graces. — Articulation not exceptionally clear.

MD 15B: Florence, Woodbine P.O., 4th Dist. — M, farmer, 42. B. here. — F, PGF b. here, PGF's F. b. Albanton, near Ellicott City, PGF's M. b. Frederick Co.; M. b. Poplar springs in Co., MGF, MGF's F. b. Co., MGM, MGM's F. b. Carroll Co. — Very quick, nervous; hearty, enjoyed questioning. — Rapid tempo; vigorous speech.

16 & 17. Frederick County

Formed 1748; originally much larger. Named for last Lord Baltimore. Settlements along Monocacy River as early as 1710; much settlement c. 1730 and later. Many PA Germans; later English and Scotch-Irish, some Swiss; still later Irish and Germans direct from Europe. Presbyterians by 1746. Most populous co. in state in 1790. Ironworks in 18th cent. Turnpike in 1805; B&O RR 1835. Ridge and valley terrain; fertile soil. Wheat, hay, milk, livestock. Iron, copper, zinc, limestone, small amounts of lead. Pop. 1782: 20,495, 1790: 30,791, 1820: 40,459, 1850: 40,987, 1880: 50,482, 1910: 52,673, 1930: 54,440, 1960: 71,930.

Delaplaine, Edward Schley. 1949. *The Origin of Frederick County.* Washington: Judd and Detweiler.

Gordon, Paul, and Rita Gordon. 1971. *The Jews beneath the Clustered Spires.* Hagerstown: Hagerstown Bookbinding and Print. Co.

Gordon, Paul P., and Rita S. Gordon. 1975. *A Textbook History of Frederick County.* Frederick: Board of Education of Frederick County.

Grove, William J. 1928. *History of Carrollton Manor. . . .* Frederick: Marken and Beilfeld.

Helman, James A. 1906. *History of Emmitsburg, Maryland.* Frederick: Citizens Press.

Johnson, William Crawford. 1938. *Old Fredericktown.* Frederick: Maryland School for the Deaf.

Schultz, Edward T. 1896. *First Settlements of Germans in Maryland.* Frederick: D. H. Smith.

Smith, Elizabeth Oakes Prince. 1932. *History of All Saints' Parish.* Frederick: Marken and Bielfeld, Inc.

Williams, Thomas John Chew. 1910. *History of Frederick County. . . .* 2 vols. Frederick. Repr. 1967 (Baltimore: Regional Pub. Co.).

Middletown

Settled in 18th cent., first by English, then Germans, who eventually dominated. Incorporated 1834. Middletown Valley, between Blue Ridge and Catoctin Mtns. Serves prosperous agricultural region.

MD 16: F, farm wife, c. 60. B. Highlands (6 or 7 mi. N.). — Parents b. here (German descent). — Complacent; no curiosity. — Rather old-fashioned and somewhat German speech.

Frederick

Surveyed 1725; town laid out 1745; Co. seat 1748. Settled by Palatine Germans from PA. Evangelical Lutheran and Reformed churches before 1750; others later. Economic ties to Phila. till 1750. At the time of the Rev., German was spoken more generally on the streets of Frederick than was English. B&O RR depot from 1831. Hood College here. Light industry: brushes, hosiery, clothing, cooking; market center. Pop. 1850: 6,028, 1880: 8,659, 1910: 10,411, 1930: 14,434, 1960: 21,744.

MD 17A: M, merchant, 77. B. here. — F., PGF, PGM, M. all b. Frederick (F., PGF of English descent), MGF b. New Market Dist., Frederick Co., MGF's F. b. Chester Co., PA, PGF's PGF b. Baden, Germany (1718), MGF's PGM b. Lancaster Co., PA, MGM b. New Market Dist., Frederick Co.

(PGM, MGF, MGM all of German descent). — Ed.: till 14. — Evangelical and Reformed. — A plain sensible businessman; cooperative but probably not revealing everything.

Yellow Springs, Frederick P.O., Tuscarora Dist.

Tusc. region rich and fertile. Yellow Springs held in high esteem by Indians as "medicine water". Surveyed 1733. Prospected for gold at one time (sulphur?).

MD 17B: M, farmer, 39. B. here. — F., PGF b. here, PGF's F. a Hessian soldier or the son of one; M., MGF, MGM b. here (MGM of French Huguenot descent). — Ed.: till 17. — Lutheran. — Limited intellectual interests, though cooperative.

18. Montgomery County

Formed 1776 from Frederick Co. "Washington's deluxe suburb"; in Washington orbit since 1930s, heavily suburbanized now. 1st reached 1625; 1st settlements 1645; 1st patents 1688. Part ceded to DC in 1791. Settlements near Georgetown from 1680. Orig. tobacco land; edge of plantation culture. Germans took over poor land and farmed it successfully; Friends introduced better farming (grain) in 1840 after many early settlers had emigrated. Canal chartered 1785; RR at least by 1865. Midland belt; general agriculture. Hills, plateaus, rolling country. Heavy maple forests, now cut. Large pop. increase since 1940: proliferation of govt. and flight from District. Highest median income in the state in 1960. Many small towns still; farming still important in N. of Co. (dairying and livestock); some light industry. Pop. 1790: 18,003, 1820: 16,400, 1850: 15,860, 1880: 24,759, 1910: 32,089, 1930: 49,206, 1960: 340,928.

Boyd, Thomas Hulings Stockton. 1879. *The History of Montgomery County. . . .* Clarksburg. Repr. 1968 (Baltimore: Regional Pub. Co.).

Farquhar, Roger Brooke. 1952. *Historic Montgomery County. . . .* Silver Spring.

Farquhar, W. H., et al. 1884–1929. *Annals of Sandy Spring. . . .* 4 vols. Baltimore: Cushings and Bailey.

Hiebert, Ray Eldon, and Richard K. MacMaster. 1976. *A Grateful Remembrance: The Story of Montgomery County, Maryland.* Rockville: Montgomery County Government.

1932. *Greater Montgomery County, Maryland.* Washington: Press of Judd and Detweiler.

Layhill, Silver Spring P.O.

Patented 1716; 1st settlers largely English. Silver Spring has some labs and light industry.

MD 18A: M, dairyman, 65. B. 1 mi. away. — F. b. 2 mi. away, PGF, PGM b. here; M. b. here, MGF, MGF's F. b. Rockville, Montgomery Co., MGM of Protestant Irish descent. — Methodist. — Lifetime of farm labor; shrewd illiterate. — Very rapid clear-cut speech; short vowels.

Sandy Spring, Rockville P.O., 8th Dist.

Settled by Quakers in 1650; meeting house still stands (also some early houses). Poor soil, but improved by intelligent farming. Episcopal parish by 1712; village of Rockford in area by 1726. Rockville Co. seat since 1777.

MD 18B: M, farmer, 49. B. here. — F. b. Germantown, Montgomery Co., moved toward Rockville 1880, PGF b. Frederick Co., PGF's F. b. Georgetown (now Washington DC), of Scots descent, PGM b. Co.; M., MGF b. Co. (latter of French Huguenot descent), MGM, MGM's F. b. Germantown. — Ed.: till 18. — Baptist. — Average middle-class farmer, representing old Quaker stock of W. part of Co. who have become leaders since abolition of slavery and movement of newcomers into area near DC.

19. Prince Georges County

Co. est. 1695; once included all MD to NW. Settled largely by English and people of English descent. Grants from 1641; earliest settlements near Mattaponi Creek. Part ceded to DC in 1791. Iron foundry developed 1731. Tobacco chief crop; also corn, small grains, nursery business. Recent growth rate second only to Montgomery; part of metropolitan Washington: govt. installations, bedroom towns. Andrews Air Force Base. Pop. 1701: 2,358, 1782: 10,011, 1790: 21,344, 1820: 20,216, 1850: 21,549, 1880: 26,451, 1910: 36,147, 1930: 60,095, 1960: 357,395.

> Bowie, Effie Augusta Gwynn. 1947. *Across the Years in Prince George's County*. Richmond: Garrett and Massie.
> Greene, Daniel M. 1941. *A Brief History of Prince George's County*. Avondale: Prince George's Chamber of Commerce.
> Hienton, Louise Joyner. 1972. *Prince George's Heritage*. Baltimore: Maryland Historical Society.

Ritchie, Bennings P.O., Kent Dist.

Rapid growth throughout district 1950–60; Wash. commuters.

MD 19A: M, farmer, 78. B. 3 mi. away near Forestville. — F. b. Co., PGF of Irish descent (Episcopal); M. b. Co. (died when inf. 3 days old), MGM b. Co. Inf. raised by uncle and aunt (his M.'s sister), both b. Co. — Ed.: from 8 to 11. — Episcopal. — Typical old timer, quick and bright. — Fairly rapid tempo; articulation not too clear.

Aquasco, 8th Dist.

Southernmost dist.; slowest growing.

MD 19B: M, farmer, 38. B. 2 mi. E. — F., PGF b. Magruders Ferry in Co., PGM b. Charles Co.; M., MGF, MGM b. Aquasco. — Ed.: Woodville till 22. — Methodist. — Somewhat naive; unaware of purpose of interview. — Articulation very lax.

20. Anne Arundel County

Co. est. 1650. 1st settled 1648 by VA Puritans. Earliest settlers chiefly English, some Quakers. Annapolis (earlier Anne Arundel Town) became state capital in 1695. "Golden age" 1750–75: leading port, social capital, cultural center. Tobacco economy had militated against urbanization. Tobacco, livestock; industrialization in N. of Co. Pop. 1701: 4,121, 1782: 9,370, 1790: 22,598, 1820: 27,165, 1850: 32,393, 1880: 28,526, 1910: 39,553, 1930: 55,167, 1960: 206,634.

> Brown, Vaughan W. 1965. *Shipping in the Port of Annapolis, 1748–1775*. Annapolis: United States Naval Institute.
> Hall, Thomas John. 1944. *History of St. James Parish.*
> Jackson, Elmer Martin, Jr. 1936. *Annapolis*. Annapolis: The Capital-Gazette Press.
> Newman, Harry Wright. 1933. *Anne Arundel Gentry*. Baltimore: Lord Baltimore Press.
> Norris, Walter B. 1925. *Annapolis, Its Colonial and Naval Story*. NY: Thos. Y. Crowell Co.
> Papenfuse, E. L. 1975. *In Pursuit of Profit*. Baltimore: Johns Hopkins University Press.
> Randall, Daniel R. 1886. The Puritan Colony at Annapolis, Maryland. *Johns Hopkins University Studies in History and Political Science* 4.6:211–58.
> Riley, Elihu S. 1887. *"The Ancient City"*. Annapolis: Record Print. Office.
> Riley, Elihu S. 1905. *A History of Anne Arundel County*. Annapolis: C. G. Feldmeyer.
> Stevens, William Oliver. 1937. *Annapolis: Anne Arundel's Town*. NY: Dodd, Mead.
> Taylor, Owen M., ed. 1872. *The History of Annapolis. . . .* Baltimore: Turnbull Bros.

MD 20A: Shady Side, 7th Dist. — M, oysterman and boat builder, 68. B. here. — F. b. Fredericktown, Kent Co., came here when boy; M. b. here, MGF b. Colonial Beach, VA, MGM b. here. — Ed.: to 4th grade. — Indifferent Protestant. — Highly intelligent but eccentric; although children did well in school, refused to send them away for higher ed., believing in working with one's hands; lives in isolated house on water front. Unashamed of speech; gladly cooperative. — Postvocalic /r/ usually lacking, never strong; contrast of *horse* and *hoarse*. A few mi. S., *paws* and *pores* are homonyms.

MD 20B: Tracys Landing, Nutwell P.O., 8th Dist. — M, farmer, 46. B. here. — F., PGF, PGF's F. b. here, PGM b. Co.; M., MGF, MGM b. Churchton. — Quite bright; eager to answer. — Nasal, rapid tempo.

Annapolis

Orig. Providence, when settled by Puritans from VA in 1648; became Anne Arundel town c. 1670; renamed Annapolis (after Queen Anne, rather than Anne Arundel) and became state capital in 1695. Only capital deliberately laid out in colonial times as a seat of govt. Stamp Act protest: burning of the *Peggy Stewart* in 1774. Elegant and sophisticated 18th cent. culture. Plantations: tobacco, slaves, isolation. Many old buildings; preservation movement. St. John's College 1784; US Naval Academy 1845. Business center for S. MD (the western shore); packs seafood, builds small craft. Pop. 1820: 2,260, 1850: 3,011, 1880: 6,642, 1910: 8,609, 1930: 12,531, 1960: 23,385.

MD 20C!: M, clerk, US Naval Engineering Experiment Station, 33. B. Annapolis. — F. b. Annapolis, PGF, PGF's F., PGF's M., PGM, PGM's F. b. South River in Co.; M., MGF, MGF's F. b. Annapolis, MGF's PGF b. in French Switzerland, MGF's PGM b. across Severn River, MGF's M. b. South River, MGF's MGF b. Prince Georges Co., MGM, MGM's F. b. Annapolis. — Ed.: local h.s., 1 1/2 yrs. St. John's College. — Episcopalian. — Of cultivated local family; rather modern, few intellectual interests; takes family background casually; associates largely with young people who come from everywhere geographically. — Distinctly Southern voice quality and intonation, contrasting with cultured infs. of Balt. and Washington. Moderate tempo; slightly lax articulation.

21. Calvert County

Est. 1654; settled earlier by VA dissenters; 1st permanent settlement 1650, largely English. Smallest MD co. Puritan majority early, many Quakers, some Huguenots (c. 1658). Natural forests; good tobacco soil (loam). Presbyterian services by 1668. Dominated by planter oligarchy till Civil War. Products and industries: tobacco, boat building, oyster packing, fishing, oystering, forestry. Pop. 1701: 2,817, 1782: 4,002, 1790: 8,652, 1820: 8,073, 1850: 9,646, 1880: 10,538, 1910: 10,325, 1930: 9,528, 1960: 15,826.

Stein, Charles Francis. 1960. *A History of Calvert County.* Baltimore: Calvert County Historical Society.

Dares Beach Road, Prince Frederick P.O., 2nd Dist.

Prince Frederick first settled by Puritans; main crossroads of Co. in 1680. Became Co. seat 1772. Attacked by British 1814 (courthouse destroyed); disastrous fire 1882.

MD 21A: M, farmer, 85. B. 3 mi. S. — F. b. here, PGF b. Prince Georges Co., PGM, M., MGF, MGM b. here. — Ed.: till 10. — Methodist. — Friendly, cooperative, old-fashioned. — Pretty rapid tempo; rather clear-cut articulation.

MD 21B: Barstow, 2nd Dist. — M, farmer, 48. B. 1 1/4 mi. from Brownsville (c. 4 mi. S. of here); worked in Balt. at age 22–26 as streetcar conductor. — F., PGF, PGM b. Brownsville; M., MGF, MGM b. near Dares Wharf in Co. All old names in Co. — Ed.: Brownsville. — Southern Methodist. — Congenial, cooperative, with no notable education or family background. Truthful but slightly self-conscious, esp. if his school-teacher wife came near. — Tempo rather rapid; lax utterance; nasal.

22. St. Marys County

Co. est 1637; oldest in state. 1st settlement c. 1634 (St. Marys City); spread along Potomac and Patuxent Rivers. Jesuits among early group; also English and Dutch settlers. In 1636 first Roman Catholic church in British N. America here; 1st house 1642. Migration 1790–1810 to KY bluegrass. Steamboat run from 1820s; RR 1881 (never successful). St. Marys College 1839. Much Confed. sentiment (but also Union excitement, including AfAms). Site of military prison and concentration camp in Civil War. Amish and Mennonite colonies in 20th cent. Tobacco oldest crop; some diversification, including dairying. Also seafood: oysters, crab, fish. Pop. 1701: 3,513, 1782: 8,459, 1790: 15,544, 1820: 12,974, 1850: 13,698, 1880: 16,934, 1910: 17,030, 1930: 15,182, 1960: 38,915.

Carr, Lois Greer. 1977. *Inventories and the Analysis of Wealth and Consumption Patterns in St. Marys County, Maryland, 1658–1777.* Baltimore: Johns Hopkins University Press.
Forman, Henry Chandlee. 1938. *Jamestown and St. Mary's.* Baltimore: Johns Hopkins University Press.
Hammett, Regina Combs. 1977. *History of St. Mary's County, Maryland.* Leonardtown: St. Mary's County Bicentennial Commission.

Knight, George Morgan. 1938. *Intimate Glimpses of Old Saint Mary's.* Baltimore: Meyer and Thalheimer.
Pogue, Robert E. T. 1968. *Yesterday in Old St. Mary's County.* NY: Carlton Press.
1953–. *Chronicles of St. Mary's.* Leonardtown: St. Marys County Historical Society.

Beachville

Rural; named for a beech tree.

MD 22N: M, farmer, 92. B. here. — F., M. b. here. — Illiterate. — Roman Catholic. — Rather intelligent; memory just beginning to fail.

Three Notch Road, Ridge P.O., 1st (Long Town) Dist.

Road follows high part of land. Ridge at S. end of dividing ridge of Co.; a crossroads. Largely AfAm parochial school here.

MD 22M: M, farm worker, 83. B. 5 mi. away at Ridge. — F., PGF b. Co.; M. b. near Old Ridge. — No education. — Roman Catholic. — Some defects in memory. Well disposed toward anyone introduced by a priest. — Articulation feeble.

Mattaponi Farm, Pearson P.O., 6th (Patuxent) Dist.

Estate built at Mattaponi Farm in 1642. Orig. site of Indian village granted to Jesuits as mission; grant revoked 1641. Old fortifications; buildings from 1640s.

MD 22A: M, farmer, 76. B. Forest Farm, near Leonardtown (to SE). — F. b. here of local Roman Catholic parentage; M., MGM b. here of local Roman Catholic stock. — Illiterate. — Roman Catholic. — Hard-working poor white, like ancestors; somewhat bitter toward landlord. Genial, hearty, good natured; possibly of Irish descent. Neglected by younger wife. — Archaic use of post-vocalic retroflexion, esp. in emphatic positions. Upgliding diphthong, with increasing rounding in *law*, etc. Linking /r/. Neutralization of *war/wore*, etc.

MD 22B: River Spring, Avenue P.O., 7th Dist. — M, farmer, 54. B. here. — F. b. near Morganza in Co.; M., MGM b. Hilltop in Co. — Ed.: till 16. — Roman Catholic. — Slow, limited intellectual interests, but successful as a farmer. — Articulation very lax, reflecting or portending a stroke.

Leonardtown

Laid out 1708; became Co. seat 1710. Tobacco port; oak and gumwood for piles and RR ties. British landing and looting in 1814. Newspaper since 1839.

MD 22C!: F, housewife, 65. B. 2 mi. N. — F., PGF b. Patuxent Dist. of Co., PGM b. Co.; M. b. Patuxent Dist., MGF, MGM b. Co. — Ed.: governess at home; 3 yrs. at St. Joseph's, Emmitsburg. — Roman Catholic. — Poised and cultivated. — Clear-cut, precise articulation; rapid tempo. — Cultivated.

23 & 24. Charles County

Formed 1658 from St. Marys. First settled c. 1640; earliest settlers largely Anglicans. Port Tobacco a port of entry by 1669; 1st courthouse 1674. Presbyterians by 1657; Methodists by mid-18th cent. Landing of British army here 1814;

secessionist sympathies during the Civil War. RR by 1872. Water transport declined in late 19th cent. as rivers silted up. AfAm majority until 1920. Urbanization in N. part. Tobacco still chief money crop; also forest products, fishing, oystering. Pop. 1701: 2,632, 1782: 9,804, 1790: 20,613, 1820: 16,500, 1850: 16,162, 1880: 18,548, 1910: 16,386, 1930: 16,166, 1960: 32,572.

Klapthor, Margaret Brown. 1958. *The History of Charles County*. La Plata: Charles County Tercentenary.
Newman, Harry Wright. 1940. *Charles County Gentry*. Washington: The Author.
1976. *Charles County, Maryland: A Bicentennial History*. South Hackensack, NJ: Custombook, Inc.

Nanjemoy
Nanjemoy Hundred formed 1657. Parish ("Durham") est. 1692; disrupted by Rev., revived 1790s. Baptist church here by 1837. Fishing.

MD 23A: M, farmer, 79. B. 3 mi. S. — F., M. b. Co. — Ed.: here till 16. — Baptist. — Very excitable, genial, talkative; untraveled and ignorant of outside world. — Very rapid tempo; tendency to short vowels with muscular articulation.

MD 23B: M, farmer and waterman, 70. B. here; has sold seafood in Washington. — F. b. here, but raised across river in Dumfries (Prince William Co.), VA, PGF, PGM, M., MGF, MGM b. here. — Illiterate. — Baptist. — Peculiar, set in his ways; discontinued interview when Episcopal rector discussed project openly in his presence.

Pomfret, 6th Dist.
Roman Catholic chapel here 1763; 1st convent in US (Carmelite) 1790.

MD 23C: M, farmer, 39. B. Gallant Green (18 mi. away), came here at age 19. — F. b. Gallant Green; M. b. Balt., MGF, MGM b. Co. — Ed.: Gallant Green till 14; Notre Dame, Bryantown, 2 yrs.; Leonard Hall, Leonardtown, 1 yr. — Roman Catholic. — Quick, bright. — Uses higher vowel in *law*, etc., than wife does; perhaps the result of schooling.

Gallant Green, Waldorf P.O.
Gallant Green a village in W. part of Co. Waldorf grew with Potomac River Bridge. Roman Catholic from 1700s. Developed after 1820 as trading and shipping center for tobacco; RR station and P.O. by 1880. Baptists in 20th cent. From 1930s, a shopping center for Washington workers.

MD 24: M, farmer, 87. B. here (2 mi. from Prince Georges Co.). — F., PGF b. here, PGF's F. fought with Washington in Rev., PGM b. here; M., MGF b. here, MGM b. near Bryantown, in Co. — Ed.: 2–3 yrs. — Presbyterian. — Slow of thought and association (effect of age); somewhat deaf; docile. — Fairly short vowels; steady tempo; weak articulation.

25 & 26. Washington County
Formed 1776 from Frederick Co. 1st settlement 1735; many Germans from PA. Also diverse other groups among early settlers: Swiss, English, Scotch-Irish, Dutch, French

(from Alsace-Lorraine). Steamboat from 1786; turnpike authorized 1797. Many RRs beginning in 1841; C&O Canal complete 1850. Federalist stronghold. Iron ore, some copper and antimony early. Foot of Alleghenies. Excellent farming: wheat, fruits, dairy products, livestock. Diversified industry, including cement, aircraft, pipe organs. Hagerstown 2nd to Balt. in urban pop. Pop. 1782: 11,488, 1790: 15,822, 1820: 23,075, 1850: 30,848, 1880: 38,561, 1910: 49,617, 1930: 65,882, 1960: 91,219.

Mish, Mary Vernon. 1937. *Jonathan Hager, Founder*. Hagerstown: Hagerstown Bookbinding and Print. Co.
Williams, Thomas J. C. 1906. *A History of Washington County*. 2 vols. Chambersburg, PA. Repr. 1968 (Baltimore: Regional Pub. Co.).

Keedysville, 19th Dist.
S. part of Co. First settled by Germans. Church of the United Brethren est. here in 18th cent. Grazing.

MD 25: M, farmer and dairyman, 78. B. here. — F., PGF b. Keedysville, PGF's F. of English descent, PGM b. Highland, Frederick Co.; M., MGF b. Keedysville. — Ed.: till 16. — United Brethren. — Not highly intelligent; seemed to think questions silly. — Very lax articulation, immobile lips.

Sidelong Hill, Hancock P.O., 5th Dist.
Extreme W. of Co.; semi-mountainous. Ft. here on Potomac in 1755; abandoned after Ft. Frederick built in 1756. Area settled late 18th cent. Stopover point on Cumberland Rd.; C&O Canal here 1839. Limestone and slate; fruit growing.

MD 26A: F, spinster housekeeper for brother, 70. B. here. — F. b. just over line in Fulton Co., PA, came as infant to Allegany Co., MD, 1 mi. from here; when young moved across creek to Washington Co., PGF b. nearby in Allegany Co., MD, PGF's F. of Welsh descent, PGM b. Hancock; M. b. across ridge in this Co., MGF partly of German descent. — Ed.: here till 16. — Methodist. — Timid, isolated person; talked cheerfully to FW after receiving brother's permission (brother was hard of hearing).

Hagerstown
Laid out 1762; RR junction, gridiron pattern, public square. Lutherans from 1770; Episcopalians (from VA) by 1787; Methodists by 1793; Roman Catholics 1794. Shoes and hats in 18th cent. Industries: tanning, iron and steel, machinery, pipe organs, textiles, wood products, paper, cigars. Pop. 1850: 3,879, 1880: 6,627, 1910: 16,507, 1930: 30,861, 1960: 36,660.

MD 26B: M, retired businessman, 80. B. here. — F., M. b. here. — Ed.: local schools. — Episcopalian. — Very intelligent, quick-to-the-point, alert businessman. However, didn't see any point to the study, prob. suspicious and tired (wife has been in hospital); didn't complete interview.

27. Garrett County
Formed 1872 from Allegany Co. Area abandoned by Shawnee c. 1750; 1st settled early 1750s. Ft. Cumberland here 1750. Earliest settlers English, German, Ulster Scots; early

19th cent. Irish, Germans. Amish colony since 18th cent. National Road; pop. loss to westward migration 1800–1810. Coal mining early 19th cent. By 1850, Cumberland 2nd largest town in MD, but growth stopped. Diversified industries; many small ones failed 1929. Coalfields declined in 1920s; glass industry also declined in 19th cent. General economic decline since 1929, exc. WWII. More state-owned land than any other co.; forests and state parks. Most elevated region in state; coal, iron, manganese, cement, limestone. Also dairying, livestock. Only MD natural gas field. Pop. 1880: 12,175, 1910: 20,105, 1930: 19,908, 1960: 20,420.

Stegmaier, Harry I., et al. 1976. *Allegany County: A History.* Parsons, WV: McClain Print. Co.

Dry Run, Swanton P.O., 4th Dist.

Swanton formerly a shipping point for yellow and white pine, esp. ship spars. Named for Swan's Mill.

MD 27A: M, farmer, 76. B. 3 mi. away. — F., PGF b. 10 mi. E. of here, PGF's F. b. Germany (Hessian deserter), PGM, PGM's F. b. near Allegany Co.; M. b. Pea Ridge in Co., MGF b. near Frostburg (English and German ancestry), MGM b. Germany. — Ed.: 3 or 4 winters. — Methodist. — Willing and patient, though memory failing with fatigue; independent mountaineer, isolated, self-sufficient (son very suspicious). — Articulation fairly lax; tempo moderate.

Sander Flats, Deer Park P.O., 10th Dist.

Deer Park developed out of agricultural and lumbering operations. Noted fashionable summer resort in 19th cent.

MD 27B: M, farmer, 39. B. here. — F. b. 5 mi. SE, PGF b. Co., PGF's F. b. Germany, PGM b. Co.; M. b. near Deer Park, MGF, MGM b. Co. — Ed.: here till 16. — Methodist. — Good-natured person when at ease. Became rather self-conscious at times, esp. in presence of wife, because of apparent wish to avoid making a bad showing. Often became evasive; very cautious when pressed. After wife left the room, interview proceeded more rapidly. — One apparent speech defect (prob. not influence of German, since not enough recent contacts): very clear [ḷ] finally, most noticeable after back vowels; results in fronting of the vowel as in [hoḷ] for *whole.* FW suspects this is not typical; with some effort, inf. avoids the extreme type and has upgliding diphthong with less fronting, prob. normal here. Otherwise little distinctiveness of speech.

Bibliographies

Baer, Elizabeth. 1949. *Seventeenth Century Maryland: A Bibliography.* Baltimore: John Work Garrett Library.

Duncan, Richard R., and Dorothy M. Brown. 1970. *Master's Theses and Doctoral Dissertations on Maryland History.* Baltimore: Maryland Historical Society.

Manakee, Harold Randall. 1968. *Maryland: A Students' Guide to Localized History.* NY: Teachers College Press.

Mathews, Edward Bennett. 1897. *Bibliography and Cartography of Maryland.* Baltimore: Johns Hopkins University Press.

Steiner, Bernard C. 1904. *Descriptions of Maryland.* Baltimore: Johns Hopkins University Press.

General Histories

Allen, Ethan. 1866. *Who were the Early Settlers of Maryland?* New Haven, CT.

Andrews, Matthew Page. 1929. *History of Maryland.* Garden City, NY: Doubleday.

Andrews, Matthew Page. 1933. *The Founding of Maryland.* NY: D. Appleton-Century.

Bibbins, Ruthella B. M. 1934. *The Beginnings of Maryland in England and America.* Baltimore: Norman Remington Co.

Bode, Carl. 1978. *Maryland: A Bicentennial History.* NY: American Association for State and Local History.

Browne, William H. 1884. *Maryland.* Boston and NY: Houghton, Mifflin and Co.

Clark, Charles B., ed. 1950. *The Eastern Shore of Maryland and Virginia.* NY: Lewis Historical Pub. Co.

Dozer, Donald Marquand. 1976. *Portrait of the Free State: A History of Maryland.* Cambridge, MD: Tidewater Pub.

Earle, Swepson. 1916. *Maryland's Colonial Eastern Shore.* Baltimore: Munder-Thomsen Press.

Federal Writers Project. 1940. *Maryland, a Guide to the Old Line State.* NY: Oxford University Press.

Fiske, John. 1899. *Old Virginia and Her Neighbors.* 2 vols. NY: Houghton, Mifflin and Co.

Griffith, Thomas Waters. 1821. *Sketches of the Early History of Maryland.* Baltimore: F. G. Schaeffer.

Ives, Joseph Moss. 1969. *The Ark and the Dove.* NY: Cooper Square Publishers.

Land, Aubrey C. 1981. *Colonial Maryland, a History.* Millwood, NY: KTO Press.

McSherry, James. 1849. *History of Maryland.* Baltimore: J. Murphy.

Mereness, Newton Dennison. 1968. *Maryland as a Proprietary Province.* Cos Cob, CT: J. E. Edwards.

Neill, Edward Duffield. 1871. The English Colonization of America during the Seventeenth Century. London: Straham and Co.

Newman, Harry Wright. 1984. *The Flowering of the Maryland Palatinate.* Baltimore: Genealogical Pub. Co.

Radoff, Morris Leon. 1971. *The Old Line State, a History of Maryland.* Annapolis: State Hall of Records Commission.

Scharf, John Thomas. 1879. *History of Maryland.* 3 vols. Baltimore: Johns Hopkins University Press.

Walsh, Richard, ed. 1974. *Maryland, a History 1632–1974.* Baltimore: Maryland Historical Society.

1906–. *Maryland Historical Magazine.* Baltimore: Maryland Historical Society.

Special Studies

Appleby, Joyce Oldham. 1978. *Economic Thought and Ideology in Seventeenth-Century England.* Princeton: Princeton University Press.

Bayloff, William H. 1959. *The Maryland-Pennsylvania and the Maryland-Delaware Boundaries.* 2nd ed. Annapolis: Board of Natural Resources.

Beitzell, Edwin Warfield. 1973. *Life on the Potomac River.* Abell: Beitzell.

Brackett, Jeffrey Richardson. 1889. *The Negro in Maryland.* Baltimore: Johns Hopkins University Press.

Burgess, Robert H. 1963. *This was Chesapeake Bay.* Cambridge, MD: Cornell Maritime Press.

Cain, James M. 1930. *Our Government*. NY: Knopf.

Clark, William B. 1928. *The Geography of Maryland*. Baltimore: Maryland Geological Survey.

Clemens, Paul G. E. 1980. *The Atlantic Economy and Colonial Maryland's Eastern Shore*. Ithaca, NY: Cornell University Press.

Cohen, Edward H. 1975. *Ebenezer Cooke: The Sot-Weed Canon*. Athens, GA: University of Georgia Press.

Cunz, Dieter. 1948. *The Maryland Germans*. Princeton, NJ: Princeton University Press.

De Gast, Robert. 1970. *Oystermen of the Chesapeake*. Baltimore: International Marine Publishing Co.

Earle, Carville. 1975. *The Evolution of a Tidewater Settlement System: All Hallow's Parish, Maryland, 1650–1783*. Chicago: University of Chicago Dept. of Geography.

Earle, Swepson. 1923. *The Chesapeake Bay Country*. Baltimore: Thomsen-Ellis Co.

Eller, Ernest McNeill, ed. 1981. *Chesapeake Bay in the American Revolution*. Centreville: Tidewater Publishers.

Fisher, Richard Swainson. 1852. *Gazetteer of the State of Maryland*. NY: J. H. Colton.

Footner, Hulbert. 1942. *Maryland Main and the Eastern Shore*. NY. Repr. 1967 (Hatboro, PA: Tradition Press).

Gould, C. P. 1913. *The Land System in Maryland, 1720–1765*. Baltimore: Johns Hopkins University Press.

Harvey, Katherine A. 1969. *The Best-Dressed Miners: Life and Labor in the Maryland Coal Region, 1835–1910*. Ithaca, NY: Cornell University Press.

Hoffman, Ronald. 1973. *A Spirit of Dissension*. Baltimore: Johns Hopkins University Press.

Hruschka, P. D. 1975. *The Acquisition and Maintenance of Postiton as Economic Elite: A Study of Four Maryland Families, 1630–1960*. University of Wisconsin dissertation.

Karinen, Arthur E. 1958. *Numerical and Distributional Aspects of Maryland Population, 1631–1840*. University of Maryland dissertation.

Kent, Frank R. 1911. *The Story of Maryland Politics*. Baltimore: Thomas and Evans Print. Co.

Land, Aubrey C. 1955. *The Dulanys of Maryland*. Baltimore. Repr. 1968 (Baltimore: Johns Hopkins Press).

Land, Aubrey C. 1965. Economic Base and Social Structure: The Northern Chesapeake in the Eighteenth Century. *Journal of Economic History* 25:639–54

Martenet, Simon J. 1873. *New Topographical Atlas of the State of Maryland*. Baltimore: Johns Hopkins University Press.

Mathews, Edward Bennett. 1907. *Counties of Maryland*. Baltimore: Johns Hopkins University Press. Reprinted 1967 (Cleveland: Bell and Howell).

McCormack, Eugene I. 1904. *White Servitude in Maryland*. Baltimore: Johns Hopkins University Press.

McGrath, Francis Sims. 1950. *Pillars of Maryland*. Richmond: Dietz Press.

Menard, Russell R. 1973. From Servant to Freeholder: Status Mobility and Property Accumulation in Seventeenth-Century Maryland. *William and Mary Quarterly* 30:37–64.

Middleton, Arthur Pierce. 1984. *Tobacco Coast*. Baltimore: Johns Hopkins University Press.

Mikkelson, Michael A. 1897. *The Bishop Hill Colony*. Baltimore: Johns Hopkins University Press.

Nead, Daniel Wunderlich. 1914. *The Pennsylvania-German in the Settlement of Maryland*. Lancaster, PA: Press of the New Era Print. Co.

Olson, Sherry H. 1980. *Baltimore, the Building of an American City*. Baltimore: Johns Hopkins University Press.

Petrie, George. 1892. *Church and State in Early Baltimore*. Baltimore: Johns Hopkins University Press.

Price, Jacob M. 1973. *France and the Chesapeake: A History of the French Tobacco Monopoly, 1674–1791. . . .* Ann Arbor: University of Michigan Press.

Price, Jacob M. 1980. *Capital and Credit in British Overseas Trade: The View from the Chesapeake, 1700–1776*. Cambridge, MA: Harvard University Press.

Renzulli, L. Marx. 1973. *Maryland: The Federalist Years*. Rutherford, NJ: Fairleigh Dickinson University Press.

Reps, John William. 1972. *Tidewater Towns: City Planning in Colonial Virginia and Maryland*. Williamsburg, VA: Colonial Williamsburg Foundation.

Scarpaci, Jean. 1977. *The Ethnic Experience in Maryland*. Towson: Towson State University.

Scharf, John Thomas. 1882. *History of Western Maryland*. Philadelphia.

Scharf, John Thomas. 1888. *Maryland's Resources*. Annapolis: Maryland Land Office.

Scharf, John Thomas. 1892. *Natural and Industrial Resources and Advantages of Maryland*. Annapolis: Maryland Land Office.

Schoch, Mildred Lilian Cook, comp. 1970. *Ringgold in the United States*. Lutherville.

Schultz, Edward Thomas. 1896. *First Settlements of Germans in Maryland*. Frederick: D. H. Smith.

Skirven, P. P. 1923. *The First Parishes of the Province of Maryland*. Baltimore: Johns Hopkins University Press.

Slaughter, Philip. 1877. *A History of St. Mark's Parish*. Baltimore: Innes and Co.

Slaughter, Philip. 1879. *A History of Bristol Parish*. Richmond: J. W. Randolph and English.

Slaughter, Philip. 1890. *History of St. George's Parish*. Richmond: J. W. Randolph and English.

Sparks, Francis Edgar. 1898. *Causes of the Maryland Revolution of 1689*. Baltimore: Johns Hopkins University Press.

Steiner, Bernard C. 1903. *Beginnings of Maryland*. Baltimore: Johns Hopkins University Press.

Tracy, William P. 1889. *Old Catholic Maryland and Its Jesuit Missionaries*. Swedesboro, NJ.

Warner, William W. 1976. *Beautiful Swimmers: Watermen, Crabs, and the Chesapeake Bay*. Boston: Little, Brown.

Wilstach, Paul. 1931. *Tidewater Maryland*. Indianapolis. Repr. 1945 (NY: Tudor Pub. Co.).

Winsor, Justin. 1887. Maryland and Virginia. In *A Narrative and Critical History of America*, ed. by Justin Winsor, vol. 5, 259–70.

1883–1972. *Archives of Maryland*. 72 vols. Baltimore: Maryland Historical Society.

1968. *The Counties of Maryland and Baltimore City: Their Origin, Growth and Development, 1634–1967*. Baltimore: State Planning Dept.

1973. *Historical Atlas: A Review of Events and Forces That Have Influenced the Development of the State*. Annapolis: Maryland Dept. of Economic and Community Development.

District of Columbia

1. Washington, DC

Founded solely as capital; central to US of 1790. Land grants in present District from 1663. 1st settlements prob. c. 1745; settlement in area began on VA side. 1st proposed as capital site 1783; several settlements before Wash. Georgetown important market, port early; most of DC orig. part of Montgomery Co. Real estate speculation early. 1790 L'Enfant plan generally followed. Congress niggardly about appropriations. Free AfAms set up own school system. Became scientific center; Smithsonian 1840. In 1846, Alexandria Co. re-ceded to VA. Land communications poor: turnpikes 1820s; 1st through rail connections 1855. Primarily a southern village to 1860; S. influence survived heavily till New Deal and WWII. Pop. 33% AfAm by 1890; 60% AfAm by 1965 (90% of public school enrollment). Congressional Library 1897. Union Station 1907; Lincoln Memorial 1922; Arlington Memorial Bridge 1932. Has grown with Fed. govt.; govt. and sightseeing the major industries. Emergence as a social and cultural center: museums, galleries, etc. Pop. 1800: 14,093, 1820: 33,039, 1850: 51,687, 1880: 177,624, 1910: 331,069, 1930: 486,869, 1960: 763,956.

DC 1A: M, retired paperhanger, 89. B. Cherokee Nation, Indian Territory, brought to Washington as infant; had spent yrs. 9–12 in Frederick Co., MD. — F. b. Georgetown (colonial village, incorp. into Washington in late 19th cent.), PGF, PGM b. St. Marys Co., MD, paternal ancestors came to MD with Lord Baltimore in 17th cent.; M. b. Georgetown, MGF b. Cape May, NJ, MGM b. Philadelphia (her F. with Washington at Valley Forge). — Ed.: 9 mos. formal schooling, largely self-educated. — Methodist (father was Roman Catholic); Society of Oldest Inhabitants of the District, works for Prohibition and Ku Klux Klan. — Somewhat pompous. — Speech typical of older residents, not cultivated. Deliberate tempo; vowels tend to be short, esp. [æ]. Weak postvocalic /r/; vowel of *girl* weakly constricted and lightly rounded. Initial /p, t, k/ unaspirated.

Georgetown

Laid out 1751; incorporated 1789. Site of Indian village as early as 1622. Land first patented 1703; first grants 1734. Scotch community in early 18th cent. Rival of Baltimore. Site for Georgetown U. (Roman Catholic) selected 1776. Southern village till incorp. in DC in 1871. Southern-born pop. outnumbered northern-born 15 to 1 in 1861, but Northerners dominated commercial life. Was tobacco port. City canal opened 1815, unsuccessful; declined as port, channel silted up. Influx of AfAms, Irish after 1865. Slum, then following private urban renewal became fashionable; fashionable residences, etc., built up mainly from 1930s on. Has recently tended to become more white, unlike rest of District. Pop. 1810: 3,235, 1820: 4,940, 1850: 8,366, 1880: 12,578 (after, with DC).

DC 1B!: F, funeral director, 50. B. here. — F. b. Georgetown, PGF b. what is now Arlington Co., VA (then part of DC), PGF's F. b. Fairfax Co., VA (perhaps the part ceded to DC, then retroceded), PGM b. Clay Spring, Washington Co., MD; M. b. DC, MGF prob. b. DC, MGM b. Georgetown. — Ed.: Friends School, Washington, 4 yrs. — United Presbyterian. — Very quick, cooperative. — Cultivated businesswoman; rather unctuous form of speech, not atypical of community or profession. — Cultivated.

Bibliographies

Bethel, Elizabeth. Material in the National Archives relating to the Early History of the District of Columbia. *Columbia Historical Society Records* 42:169–87.

Bryan, Wilhelmus Bogart. 1900. *Bibliography of the District of Columbia. . . to 1898*. Washington: Government Printing Office.

General Histories

Brown, George Rothwell. 1930. *Washington, a Not Too Serious History*. Baltimore: Norman Pub. Co.

Bryan, Wilhelmus B. 1930. *Some Myths in the History of Washington*. Washington: Columbia Historical Society.

Bryan, Wilhelmus Bogart. 1914–16. *A History of the National Capital. . ..* 2 vols. NY: Macmillan Co.

Caemmerer, Hans Paul. 1948. *Historic Washington. . ..* Washington: Columbia Historical Society.

Federal Writers Project. 1937. *Washington, City and Capital*. Washington: United States Government Print. Office.

Furer, Howard B. 1975. *Washington, a Chronological and Documentary History. . ..* Dobbs Ferry, NY: Oceana Publications.

Green, Constance McLaughlin. 1976. *Washington*. Princeton, NJ: Princeton University Press.

Lewis, David L. 1976. *District of Columbia: A Bicentennial History*. NY: Norton.

Mackall, Sally Somervell. 1899. *Early Days of Washington*. Washington: Neale Co.

Nicholay, Helen. 1924. *Our Capital on the Potomac*. NY: Century Co.

Proctor, John Clagett. 1930. *Washington, Past and Present*. 4 vols. NY: Lewis Historical Pub. Co.

Reps, John William. 1967. *Monumental Washington*. Princeton, NJ: Princeton University Press.

Tindall, William. 1914. *Standard History of the City of Washington. . ..* Knoxville, TN: H. W. Crew.

Truett, Randall Bond, ed. 1968. *Washington, DC: A Guide to the Nation's Capital*. Rev. ed. NY: Hastings House.

Special Studies

Daley, John M. 1957. *Georgetown University: Origin and Early Years*. Washington: Georgetown University Press.

Durkin, Joseph T. 1963. *Georgetown University: The Middle Years (1840–1900)*. Washington: Georgetown University Press.

Ecker, Grace Dunlop. 1933. *A Portrait of Old George Town*. Richmond: Garrett and Massie.

Green, Constance McLaughlin. 1967. *The Secret City: A History of Race Relations in the Nation's Capital*. Princeton, NJ: Princeton University Press.

Kayser, Elmer Louis. 1970. *Bricks without Straw: The Evolution of George Washington University*. NY: Appleton-Century-Crofts.

Leech, Margaret. 1941. *Reveille in Washington, 1860–1865*. NY: Harper and Bros.

Mitchell, Mary Atkinson. 1968. *Divided Town*. Barre, MA: Barre Publishers.

Smith, Sam. 1974. *Captive Capital: Colonial Life in Modern Washington*. Bloomington: Indiana University Press.

Virginia

1. Arlington County

Ceded to US as part of Washington DC in 1791; retroceded as Alexandria Co. Renamed Arlington Co. in 1920. Tobacco country in 18th cent.; grist mills. Canals 1785; turnpikes 1796. Few slaves 1840–60; AfAm majority c. 1870, but not after 1880. 1870–1900 beginning of suburbanization; govt. installations, etc. Pop. 1800: 5,949, 1820: 9,703, 1850: 10,008, 1880: 17,546, 1910: 10,231, 1930: 26,615, 1960: 163,401.

Alexandria, Virginia. 1960. *City of Alexandria, Virginia: Home Town of George Washington and Robert E. Lee.* Alexandria.

Benham, Mary Louisa Slacum. 1977. *Recollections of Old Alexandria.* Ed. by Elizabeth Jane Stark.

Brockett, F. L. 1883. *A Concise History of the City of Alexandria, Virginia, from 1669 to 1883. . . .* Alexandria: Gazette Book and Job Office.

Chittenden, Cecil. 1946. *Arlington, a New Frontier.* NY: Hobson Book Press.

Cusselman, Ames Burn. 1909. *The Virginia Portion of the District of Columbia.* Washington: Columbia Historical Society.

Davis, Deering, et al. 1946. *Alexandria Houses.* NY: Architectural Book Publishing Co., Inc.

Federal Writers Project. 1939. *Alexandria.* Alexandria: Williams Print. Co.

Harrison, Mrs. Burton. 1892. *Belhaven Tales.* NY: Century Co.

Harvey, Karen G., and Ross Stansfield. 1977. *Alexandria: A Pictorial History.* Norfolk: Donning Co.

McKim, Randolph Harrison. 1877. *Washington's Church: An Historical Record of Old Christ Church.* Germantown, PA: W. H. Bonsall.

Montague, Ludwell Lee. 1976. *Historic Arlington.* Arlington: Arlington County Bicentennial Commission

Moore, Gay (Montague). 1949. *Seaport in Virginia: George Washington's Alexandria.* Richmond: Garrett and Massie.

Powell, Mary G. 1928. *The History of Old Alexandria, Virginia, from July 13, 1749, to May 24, 1861.* Richmond: William Byrd Press.

Rose, Cornelia Bruere. 1976. *Arlington County, Virginia: A History.* Arlington: Arlington Historical Society.

Smoot, Betty Carter (McGuire). 1934. *Days in an Old Town.* Alexandria. Repr. 1972 (Washington: A. H. Smoot).

Voses, Nettie Allan. 1975. *Old Alexandria: Where America's Past is Present.* McLean: EPM Publications.

1907. *A Brief History of Alexandria County.* Falls Church: Alexandria County Board of Supervisors.

Alexandria

Town organized 1749; market town, shipbuilding, important port, sugar refinery. 1st settlers c. 1695. Scots most numerous among early settlers; some Ulster Irish, some Germans, a few French, a few from northern colonies. Turnpike 1785. Included in DC 1791–1846. Presbyterians and Methodists from 1774; Roman Catholics from 1795. Theater here by 1791. Tobacco important early; gave way to wheat by 1770. Chartered as city 1856. Many runaway slaves 1861–65. From 1917 on tied to expansion of Washington; still many old homes and public buildings. Diversified industry; in 1939, 2nd largest freight classification yard in US. Pop. 1850: 8,734, 1880: 13,659, 1910: 15,329, 1930: 29,169, 1960: 91,023.

VA 1!: F, single, "middle-aged". B. here. — F., PGF b. here, PGF's F. b. NJ, came here when young (1796), PGF's M. b. here, PGM b. King George Co.; M. b. here, MGF b. Fauquier Co., came here when young, MGM b. here, MGM's F. from Scotland, MGM's M. b. here. — Ed.: Arlington Inst. here; 1 yr. boarding school in Baltimore. — Episcopal Church; women's club. — Of good old family. Charming; aristocratic interest in her social duties. Very Virginian; not objective in evaluating speech differences. — None of the widespread Georgetown type of speech (the Potomac is still the ancient boundary between MD homonymy of *for* and *four* but contrast with *far* and VA homonymy of *far* and *for* but contrast with *four*). Tendency to drawl long vowels. — Cultivated.

2. Fairfax County

Formed 1742 from Prince William. Many immigrants from NY and PA in 1840s. 1st turnpike charter 1796 (1st in VA). AfAm pop. declined with decline in tobacco economy in early 19th cent.; large estates broken up; wheat, cattle, sheep, grist mills, textile mills. Fishing important early but declined when Potomac overfished. RRs in 1850s. Sharecropping after 1865; dairying in late 19th cent. Suburbanization began 1865–1900. No high school till 1906; accessibility of DC schools delayed development. Farming still important, but not dominant. Pop. 1755: 2,233, 1782: 8,763, 1790: 12,320, 1820: 11,404, 1850: 10,682, 1880: 15,025, 1910: 20,536, 1930: 25,264, 1960: 275,002.

Brown, Stuart, E., Jr. 1965. *Virginia Baron: The Story of Thomas, Sixth Lord Fairfax.* Berryville: Chesapeake Book Co.

Geddes, Jean. 1967. *Fairfax County: Historical Highlights from 1607.* Middleburg: Denlinger's.

Hall, M. D., et al. 1907. *Industrial and Historical Sketch of Fairfax County. . . .* Falls Church: Fairfax County Board of Supervisors.

Kilmer, Kenton, and Ronald Emery. 1975. *The Fairfax Family in Fairfax County.* Fairfax: Fairfax County Office of Comprehensive Planning.

Morrison, Charles. 1970. *The Fairfax Line: A Profile in History and Geography.* Parsons, WV: McClain.

Muir, Dorothy Troth. 1943. *Potomac Interlude.* Washington: Mount Vernon Print Shop.

Netherton, Nan, et al. 1978. *Fairfax County, Virginia: A History*. Fairfax: Fairfax County Board of Supervisors.

Netherton, Russ DeWitt. 1976. *The Calvin Run Mill*. Fairfax: Fairfax County Office of Comprehensive Planning.

Schneider, Lottie M. (Dyer). 1962. *Memories of Herndon, Virginia*. Marion.

Sprouse, Edith Moore. 1975. *Colchester: Colonial Port on the Potomac*. Fairfax: Fairfax County Office of Comprehensive Planning.

———. 1974. *Fairfax County in Virginia. . . 1742–1973*. Fairfax: Office of Comprehensive Planning.

Herndon, Dranesville District

Herndon a new village in 1850s: market center for NW Fairfax. Northerners settled after 1865, many from NJ. RR from Wash. 1856–57; commuters; relatively cosmopolitan. Also center of dairying. Public cannery WWII. Dranesville once part of George Washington's estate. Reverted to wilderness around time of Civil War; reconstructed as part of park system.

VA 2A: M, farmer, cattleman, c. 84. B. Germantown, Fairfax Co. (named for family name *German*: no German settlers, 6 houses), in Co. all his life except 4 yrs. (ages 11–15) during Civil War; took up cobblestones in Washington 1872; worked for Co. supervisor and highway dept. — F. b. Co. (1826), PGF b. Dumfries (1793), PGF's F. b. Dumfries in Stafford Co. (English stock), PGM b. Dumfries (1801), PGM's F. and M. b. England, to VA via Baltimore; M. b. Co. (1832), MGF b. Ireland (Roman Catholic), settled at first in Loudoun Co., MGM b. Goose Creek, Loudoun Co., MGM's F. b. Scotland. — Ed.: 45 days at 5 cents a day; VA seceded on first day he went to school. — Methodist. Social contacts limited to fishing. — Intelligent, successful (only practical ed.); old-fashioned, at ease, quiet, self-assured in speech. — Weak occasional retroflexion seems to point to an old tidewater type (cf. Northumberland Co., Mathews Co., Eastern Shore) that came up the Potomac.

Colchester, Woodbridge P.O., Mt. Vernon District

On Potomac path. Patented 1666; Scots and English among earliest settlers c. 1749. Warehouse for tobacco 1790. 1791 ferry upstream; turnpike 1811. Flour mill 1819. Flourished around time of American Rev.; decline after 1800, now historic site.

VA 2B: M, fisherman, gardener, laborer, 77. B. on the ox road below Burke Station, on road to Courthouse. — F., M. b. near Burke Station; PGF, PGM prob. b. there also. — Ed.: 3 mos. — Simple, kindly old man, little touched by proximity to Alexandria and Washington. — Noteworthy use of lower mid-central vowel with slightly retroflex off-glide in *year* "ear" and *byeard* "beard".

VA 2B*: F, wife of VA 2B. B. here of local parents. — Less old-fashioned.

3. Loudoun County

Formed 1757 from Fairfax Co. Piedmont; ridge between Potomac and Occoquan. 1st settlement (c. 1725–35) in S. part of Co. from E. VA; NW part a German settlement; center Quakers. At Rev., one of most densely populated VA counties. Tobacco and flour important in 18th cent. Quakers and Lutherans among early settlers; 1760–90 Methodists and Baptists became dominant. Farm labor shortage, esp. 1865–1905; interest in improved machinery and farm methods. Turnpikes from 1802; unsuccessful canal and RR projects. Little secession sympathy in 1861; troops on both sides 1861–65. 1869 Loudoun Valley Academy (teacher training). Suburbanization since 1914. Farming: general, dairying, grain, fruits; also timber, iron ore, marble, copper and silver. Pop. 1783: 9,651, 1790: 18,962, 1820: 22,702, 1850: 22,079, 1880: 23,634, 1910: 21,167, 1930: 19,852, 1960: 24,549.

Head, James W. 1909. *History and Comprehensive Description of Loudon County, Virginia*. Washington: Park View Press.

Poland, Charles Preston. 1976. *From Frontier to Suburbia*. Marceline, MO: Walsworth Pub. Co.

Weatherly, Yetive Rockefeller. 1976. *Lovettsville, the German Settlement*. Lovettsville: Lovettsville Bicentennial Committee.

1957. *A Short History of Loudon County, Virginia*. Leesburg: Loudon County Bicentennial Committee.

Point of Rocks Road, Lovettsville P.O. and District

Industrious and progressive German neighborhood; non-slaveholding, opposed secession. Most influential farm lobby org. in Co. here c. 1911.

VA 3A: M, farmer, 73. B. 3 mi. away (Taylortown Dist.). — F., PGF, PGM, M., MGF, MGM b. here, all of German descent. — Ed.: none. — Lutheran. — Highly extroverted, aggressive man, covering German background by clowning (FW had never heard a louder voice). — Moderate tempo.

Goose Creek Meeting neighborhood, Lincoln P.O., Mt. Gilead District

600 ft. above sea level. Quaker settlement in Goose Creek area from 1735. Lincoln begun 1730 by PA Friends; actively anti-slavery in 1847.

VA 3B: F, housewife, 50. B. Silcott Springs, 4 or 5 mi. away. — F., PGF, PGF's F., PGF's M. b. here, orig. settled in Burlington, NJ, in 1680, from Northhants, England, with Society of Friends, PGM b. Purcellville; M. b. Philmont, MGF b. Frederick Co., MGM, MGM's F. b. here, all Society of Friends. — Ed.: Silcott Springs and Purcellville; George School (Friends), Bucks Co., PA, 3 yrs. — Dignified, kind, pleasant, refined; somewhat isolated because lacking Southern sympathies. — Understood purpose of interview; somewhat on guard (conscious of correctness).

VA 3C: Irish Neck, Lovettsville P.O. and Dist. — M, farmer, 75. B. near Hillsville in Co. — Parents b. near Hillsville of old German stock. — Little ed. — Not very alert but well-meaning; unsure of purpose of interview. — Moderate tempo. — Domineering wife forced inf. to discontinue.

4. Prince William County

Formed 1730 from Stafford Co. 1st settler 1651; 1st settlements on rivers. Profitable tobacco plantation country; declined with exhaustion of soil and silting up of Quantico Creek below Dumfries (town and tobacco market c. 1749).

First settlers predominantly English; some Scots, some from MD. Baptists 1760s; Presbyterians 1770s; Methodists later. Civil War battleground. Fine racehorses. Pop. 1755: 2,798, 1782: 4,320, 1790: 11,615, 1820: 9,419, 1850: 8,129, 1880: 9,180, 1910: 12,026, 1930: 13,951, 1960: 50,164.

> Clark, Annye Beatrix. 1933. *History of Prince William County*. Manassas: Prince William County School Board.
> Ewell, Alice Maude. 1931. *A Virginia Scene: Or, Life in Old Prince William*. Lynchburg: J. P. Bell Co.
> Federal Writers Program. 1941. *Prince William, the Story of its People and Its Places*. Richmond: Whittet and Shepperson.
> Harrison, Fairfax. 1924. *Landmarks of Old Prince William*. Repr. 1964 (Berryville)
> Ratcliff, R. Jackson. 1978. *This was Prince William*. Leesburg: Potomac Press.

Hickory Grove (edge of Bull Run Mtns.), Haymarket P.O., Gainesville Dist.

Hickory Grove a crossroads store; site of a plantation (Hundred Oaks) built 1830. Gainesville a "scattered village" in 1930s; battlefield several times 1861–64. Haymarket a small village, burned in 1862. Incorporated 1882; reincorporated 1908.

VA 4N: F, house servant, midwife, 89. B. near Wolsey (5 mi. away). — F., M., MGM (etc.) b. neighboring plantations. — No information on ed. — Baptist. — B. a slave, turned loose after Civil War. Well preserved. Limited intellectual experience, timid. — Prob. retains much old-fashioned speech. Tempo rather rapid, fluctuating intensity. Initial /w v f/ fluctuating in quality, often with coarticulated bilabial spirants.

5. Fauquier County

Formed 1759 from Prince William. 1st explored 1670; proposed Huguenot settlement 1686; actual settlement by 1692. Permanent settlement on a large scale after 1722. Two streams of migration: from PA and from Chesapeake Bay. Mainly PA Germans and Ulster Scots. Baptists by the time of the Rev.; also Presbyterians early. Grain area. Pop. 1782: 6,915, 1790: 17,892, 1820: 23,103, 1850: 20,868, 1880: 22,993, 1910: 22,526, 1930: 21,071, 1960: 24,066.

> Chappelear, B. Curtis. 1954. *Maps and Notes Pertaining to the Upper Section of Fauquier County*. Warrenton: Warrenton Antiquarian Society.
> Day, Annie G. 1908. *Warrenton and Fauquier County, Virginia*. Warrenton: Frank Printing House.
> Evans, Marie Louise. 1955. *An Old Timer in Warrenton and Fauquier County*. Ed. by Charles F. Knox, Jr. Warrenton: Virginia Pub.
> Fauquier County Bicentennial Committee. 1959. *Fauquier County, Virginia, 1759–1959*. Warrenton: Fauquier County Bicentennial Committee and the Board of Supervisors.
> Groome, Harry Connelly. 1927. *Fauquier during the Proprietorship*. Richmond: Old Dominion Press.
> McCarty, Clara S. 1974. *The Foothills of the Blue Ridge in Fauquier County, Virginia*. Warrenton: Faquier Democrat.

> Presley, Alexander Lycurgus. 1926. *Boyhood Memories of Fauquier*. Richmond: Old Dominion Press.

Carters Run Valley, Dudie P.O., Marshall Dist.

Carters Run Valley surveyed and settled c. 1724. Limit of navigation of the upper Rappahannock. On "tobacco road" to Dumfries.

VA 5A: M, farmer, 64. B. 2 mi. SW — F. b. lower end of Co., PGF descended from French Huguenot who had royal land grant in lower Co.; M. of Rappahannock Co. family, MGM b. Rappahannock (all of old VA stock). — Ed.: very little. — Baptist. — Religious enthusiast; very talkative but cooperative. — Folk grammatical forms habitual. Rather clear-cut speech; genuinely old-fashioned.

Warrenton, Center Dist.

Warrenton an outpost of E. VA culture. Incorporated 1810. Courthouse here since creation of Co. Early settlers primarily English and Scots. Orig. a trading post for Dumfries; on important early roads: highway hub in 1839. On branch of Orange and Alexandria RR. Warren Academy here from 1777. Many professional people, esp. lawyers. Pop. 1880: 1,464, 1910: 1,427, 1930: 1,450, 1960: 3,522.

VA 5B: F, housewife, 55. B. 4 mi. from here. — F., PGF, PGF's F., PGF's PGF, PGF's PGF's F. b. Caroline Co., PGF's PGF's PGF b. Fredericksburg, great-(×6)-GF b. Yorkshire, PGF's PGF's PGM b. Gloucester Co., PGF's PGM b. Northumberland House, Northumberland Co.; M., MGF, MGF's M., MGM, MGM's F. b. here, MGM's PGF b. Lancaster Co., MGM's PGF's F. b. England, MGM's M. b. Fitzhugh Hall in Co., MGM's MGF b. Caroline or King and Queen Co., MGM's MGM b. Brandon on James. — Ed.: Fauquier Female Seminary, 2 sessions. — Episcopalian.

6. Madison County

Formed 1793 from Culpeper Co. 1st settled in early 18th cent. German settlers from 1720; first Lutheran settlement in VA here 1740. Also English settlers from E. VA. Baptists by 1765; Episcopalians by Rev. (never flourished). 1st public schools 1870. Corn, wheat, fruit, livestock; small industries: chicken coops, chairs. Pop. 1800: 8,322, 1820: 8,490, 1850: 9,331, 1880: 10,562, 1910: 10,055, 1930: 8,952, 1960: 8,187.

> Davis, Margaret Grier. 1977. *Madison County, Virginia: A Revised History*. Madison, VA: Board of Supervisors of Madison County.
> Yowell, Claude Lindsay. 1926. *A History of Madison County, Virginia*. Strasburg: Shenandoah Pub. House.

Nethers, 7th Dist.
P.O. 1875; rural.

VA 6A: M, farmer, carpenter, mechanic, 81. B. here. — F., PGF b. here, PGM b. here or Culpeper Co. (PGP of English descent); M., MGF, MGM b. here, of local German stock. — Ed.: 6 mos. — Methodist (not member). — Practical.

Madison, Robinson Dist.

Baptist church here 1823; Methodists by 1838. Episcopal church never flourished. 1884 first 2-room school in Co. here.

VA 6B: F, housewife, 55. B. here near Madison. — F., PGF b. here, descended from Spotswood's 18th cent. German colony at Germania, PGM b. here; M. b. Page Co. (over the mtns.), came here as child, MGF, MGM b. Page Co. — Ed.: Culpeper till 14. — Lutheran. — Prosperous middle-class type. — Use of face and throat muscles seems German.

7. Louisa County

Formed 1742 from Hanover Co. 1st grants c. 1720; English settlers from E. VA, Scots after 1745. 1765–68 Patrick Henry as legislator. Some Huguenot settlers. RR from 1836. Vandalized by Feds 1863. Baptists always strong (1st ch. 1770); Quakers 1746–1833. Also Presbyterians, Methodists; Episcopalians present, but faded. Midland VA, in Piedmont between N. and S. Anna Rivers. Tobacco in past, now corn and wheat. Minerals: copper, sulphur, iron, mica, gold, iron pyrite. Pop. 1755: 2,107, 1790: 8,467, 1820: 13,746, 1850: 16,691, 1880: 18,942, 1910: 16,578, 1930: 14,309, 1960: 12,959.

Harris, Malcolm H. 1936. *History of Louisa County.* Richmond: Dietz Press.
Williams, Kathleen Booth. 1959. *Marriages of Louisa County, 1766–1815.* Alexandria.

Bell's Crossroads P.O. and Dist.

An old mtn. road; important c. 1860, now little used.

VA 7A: M, farmer, sawmill operator, 71. B. 2 mi. away on old Patrick Henry place. — F., PGF, PGM, M., MGF, MGM b. here. — Ed.: 5–6 days (illiterate). — Methodist. — Remarkable memory and ability at mental calculation. — Lower low-front vowel in *part, hard, garden* noteworthy (cf. E. New Eng.; also occurs in one Nelson Co. inf.).

Moreland (farm), Louisa P.O., Mineral Dist.

RR station in Mineral Dist. area in 1850s. Iron furnace here 1848. Sulphur and iron pyrites exploited 1865–1900. Mainly Methodists.

VA 7B: F, housewife, 54. B. 1/2 mi. from here. — F., PGF b. here (PGF's M. remotely of Scotch descent), PGM b. here (Irish descent), PGM's M. of German descent; M., MGF, MGM, MGM's F. b. here (last of Scotch descent). — Fairly good family. — Temperamental, high-strung; quick reactions. — Responds spontaneously to questions without stopping to think, but worries when FW probes further. Rapid tempo.

8. Spotsylvania County

Formed in 1721 from Essex. Includes pass over Blue Ridge discovered in 1716. Palatine colonies here 1710–17. Settlement to Blue Ridge 1727; 1st settlement in Shenandoah 1728. In 1729, first general post office in America here. Pop. 1755: 2,133, 1782: 5,410, 1790: 11,252, 1820: 14,254, 1850: 14,911, 1880: 14,828, 1910: 9,935, 1930: 10,056, 1960: 13,819.

Alvey, Edward, Jr. 1976. *History of the Presbyterian Church of Fredericksburg, Virginia, 1808–1976.* Fredericksburg: Session of the Presbyterian Church.
Armstrong, Thomas Field. 1975. *Urban Vision in Virginia.* University of Virginia dissertation.
Carmichael, Virginia. 1957. *This is Fredericksburg.* Richmond: Dietz Press.
Darter, Oscar H. 1957. *Colonial Fredericksburg and Neighborhood in Perspective.* NY: Twayne Publishers.
Embrey, Alvin T. 1937. *History of Fredericksburg, Virginia. . . .* Richmond: Old Dominion Press.
Goolrick, John T. 1922. *Historic Fredericksburg. . . .* Richmond: Whittet and Shepperson..
Hintz, Suzanne Steiner, and Laura Daughtry Smart. 1980. *The Fredericksburg Connection.* Fredericksburg: Historical Fredericksburg Foundation.
Mansfield, James Roger. 1977. *A History of Early Spotsylvania.* Berryville: Virginia Book Co.
Quenzel, Carrol Hunter. 1951. *The History and Background of St. George's Episcopal Church, Fredericksburg, Virginia.* Richmond.
Quinn, Sylvanus Jackson. 1908. *The History of the City of Fredericksburg, Virginia.* Richmond: Hermitage Press.
Vann, Elizabeth Chapman (Denny), and Margaret C. Denny Dixon. 1961. *Virginia's First German Colony.* Richmond.
Wayland, John Walter. 1956. *Germanna, Outpost of Adventure, 1714–1956.* Harrisonburg: Memorial Foundation of the Germanna Colonies in Virginia.

VA 8A: Alsop, Livingston Dist. — M, farmer (son of overseer), 83. B. here — F., M., PGF b. here (M. 1st cousin of F.). — Ed.: 3 mos. (when already a stout boy). — Methodist. — Poor (F. refused to fight in 1861), quiet, restrained, friendly, enjoys good conversation. Although the informant is hard of hearing and his memory is failing, this is a good record. — *Say* with vowel of *set; cot* and *caught* distinguished, as also *cart.* [ei] and [oi] have up-glide followed by in-glide (compare Princess Anne County, MD); high allophone of *cut* vowel.

VA 8B: Post Oak, Berkeley Dist. — M, farmer, 71. B. here. — F., PGF, M., MGF, MGM b. here. — Little ed. — Baptist. — Average background. Crippled yet active, has lived as bachelor for 24 yrs. Rather quick and bright, cooperative, though not interested in abstraction. — Tempo moderate. Vowels and diphthongs short or very short; /ai/ and /au/ distinctly short finally and before voiced sounds, occasionally centering of 1st element (as before voiceless consonant); vowel of *hot* very short.

Fredericksburg

Town authorized 1727; laid out 1728; incorporated 1781. First explored 1670; 1st patent and settlement 1671. German settlement here by 1714. 1st church 1726 (St. George's; German, not Anglican). Lutheran groups in 1717, 1719–20. Baptists by 1768; Disciples by 1832; Presbyterian church by 1833. Inspection site for tobacco by 1730. Steamers to Baltimore till late 19th cent. Wheat trade by 1812; in 19th cent., center for trade from N. Rappahannock Valley. Market center, small industries; old residential community. Pop. 1850: 4,061, 1880: 5,010, 1910: 5,874, 1930: 6,819, 1960: 13,639.

VA 8C!: F, single homemaker, 62. B. here. — F., PGF b. here, PGF's F. b. Essex or Mathews Co., PGF's PGF b. Kelso, Scotland, PGM b. Falmouth, Stafford Co. (just across Rappahannock), PGM's F. of Scottish descent (desc. from 1st settler of

Alexandria), many distinguished lines, PGM's M. of French Huguenot descent; M., MGF b. here, MGF's F. b. Hertfordshire, England (came with British Army, resigned, took up American cause in Rev.), MGF's M. of Gloucester Co., VA, family, MGM b. Middlesex Co., VA. — Ed.: local h.s. — Presbyterian; active in local historical and literary circles. — Provincial cultivated woman, living in an historic house. — Strong distinction between long and short vowels. Broad *a* ultimately, perhaps from M.'s GF, Englishman of Revolutionary period (could be reinforced by her tidewater ancestry, esp. Gloucester); although laughed at by boys at school, she has persisted in using it, but slips occasionally. — Cultivated.

9. Stafford County

Formed 1664 from Westmoreland Co. Jesuit missionaries in the area early. Settled in 1647 by MD dissidents; 1st settlers mostly English, a few Roman Catholics (colony by 1670s). Germans arrived 1719–48. Also Huguenots and Ulster Scots by 1720s. Wealthy in colonial times, family settlements. Falmouth an important colonial tobacco port by 1727. Indentured servants replaced by slaves. Also iron works near Falmouth early. Area occupied during Civil War. Pop. 1699: 1,860, 1755: 2,015, 1785: 2,911, 1790: 9,588, 1820: 9,517, 1850: 8,044, 1880: 7,211, 1910: 8,070, 1930: 8,080, 1960: 16,876.

Goolrick, John Taquette. 1976. *The Story of Stafford. . . .* Fredericksburg: Fredericksburg Press.

Rectory, Aquia Dist.

Roman Catholic colony in 1670s; scene of anti-Catholic tumult in 1688.

VA 9A: M, farmer, sawmiller, 73. B. here. — F., PGF b. here (widespread local family), PGM b. here (family connected with widely publicized suit over inheritance of Lower Manhattan real estate); M. b. Co., MGF b. Ireland, settled here, MGM b. Co. — Ed.: "few days at a time for a few years". — Northern Methodist. — Jolly, good natured, reminding one of a contented rotund English villager; not too sophisticated but always genial and willing to entertain a gentleman.

Aquia Church, Stafford C.H. P.O., Aquia District

Present church from 1757 (1st bldg. 1751). In 1647, first site of settlement by dissident MD Catholics.

VA 9B!: F, housewife, 71. B. Tomahawk (Civil War refugee); a few months after birth brought to old home c. 6 miles from here, on Potomac River; to Aquia when married. — F. b. Falmouth, PGF b. Stafford, PGF's F. b. Aquia Creek (of Williamsburg origin), PGM b. Stafford; M. b. Faquier Co., came here young. — Ed.: here, private tutor. — Episcopalian. — Old-fashioned, provincial, rural, very local, cultivated; keen mind. At ease, natural, understood purpose of project. — Quaint, crackling, rustic gentility of voice; /e·/ and /o·/ tend to be high. — Cultivated.

10. Caroline County

Formed 1727 from several cos. 1st patents in 1650s and 1660s; chiefly English, some Huguenots. Roadbuilding in 1730s. Quakers and other Dissenters arrived in late 1730s. Port Royal tobacco port for Co. Little industry (some gristmills); shortage of skilled labor. Plantation country. Baptists dominant early; also many Anglicans. Steamers through 1920s; RR from 1836. Slovaks (Roman Catholic) c. 1908. Lumber, excelsior among industries. Pop. 1755: 3,682, 1783: 4,677, 1790: 17,489, 1820: 17,982, 1850: 18,456, 1880: 17,243, 1910: 16,596, 1930: 15,263, 1960: 12,725.

Bell, Annie Walker Burns. 1934. *Third Census of the US. . . for the County of Caroline.* Washington.

Campbell, Thomas Elliott. 1954. *Colonial Caroline. . . .* Richmond: Dietz Press.

Collins, Herbert Ridgeway. 1954. *History and Genealogy of the Collins Family of Caroline County, Virginia.* Richmond: Dietz Press.

Wingfield, Marshall. 1924. *A History of Caroline County. . . .* Richmond: Press of Trevvet Christian.

Naulakla, Whites Dist.

Terrell grant 18th cent.; settlement began 1714.

VA 10A: M, farmer, sawmiller, 77. B. Upper Zion (4 mi. W.); did sawmilling in Caroline and on edge of Essex and King and Queen. — F. unknown; M. b. Upper Zion, MGF, MGM b. nearby. — Illiterate. — Baptist. — Primitive, destitute. Rather quick and bright, but slightly hard of hearing and aging. Never quite understood purpose of interview; became somewhat weary. — /au/ with centered beginning before voiceless, but [æ'ʊ] or [æʊ] before voiced and final (sometimes short).

Mulberry Place, De Jarnette P.O., Bowling Green Dist.

Mulberry Place est. 1790, still in same family in 1920s. Bowling Green Village is Co. seat.

VA 10B: F, single homemaker, farmer, 60. B. here. — F. b. here, PGF, PGF's F. b. Co. (Welsh descent), PGM, PGM's F. b. Hanover Co.; M., MGF, MGM b. Hanover Co. — Ed.: till 16 with governess. — Women's Club, UDC. — Youngest of 4 maiden sisters and bachelor brother, all living in fine old family home. Active local social life. — Some affectations of speech, but older sisters (who listened to interview) held her down to natural old childhood speech; despite affectations, easily lapses into rusticity. Mixture of old-fashioned and modern usage; when on guard, some interest in "improving" speech.

11. Hanover County

Formed 1720 from New Kent. Earliest settlement 1676; early shipping port for tobacco. Methodism important by 1780. Home of Patrick Henry. Little foreign settlement between 1st settlement and 1861. Mostly English stock. Randolph-Macon College at Ashland. Vegetables, melons, tobacco, cotton (later), many grist mills. Small industry related to timber: excelsior, paper. Pop. 1755: 3,790, 1782: 8,891, 1790: 14,754, 1820: 15,267, 1850: 15,153, 1880: 18,588, 1910: 17,200, 1930: 17,009, 1960: 27,550.

Lancaster, Robert B. 1976. *A Sketch of the Early History of Hanover County, Virginia. . . .* Richmond: Whitter and Shepperson.

Page, Rosewell. 1926. *Hanover County.* Richmond.

Cold Harbor P.O. and Dist.
    Battlefields here 1862, 1864.

VA 11A: F, housewife, 83. B. 1 1/2 miles from courthouse; has frequently visited relatives in Richmond. — F., PGF b. Cold Harbor, PGF's F. b. Ireland, PGM b. Cold Harbor, Irish descent; M., MGF b. Cold Harbor, MGF's F., M. b. Old Church, Hanover Co., MGM, MGM's F., M. b. Old Church. — Illiterate. — Presbyterian (parents Baptist). — Humble background; very feminine, winsome-looking; very conservative and old-fashioned in speech. Remarkably good health, able to walk miles without tiring. From visits to Richmond (daughter with bureau of taxation) has learned to dress stylishly, look modern, even to talk about things young people do; but when on familiar topic reverts to old-time speech [characteristic Southern decorum?]. — Slight tendency to prolong vowels and diphthongs. Apparent homophony of such pairs as *cart* and *caught.*

VA 11B: Western View, Hanover P.O. — F, housewife, 52. B. here; a few months in Norfolk in 1917. — F. b. here, PGF b. Scotland, came as boy to Elizabeth City and later to Hanover Co., PGM, PGM's F. b. here; M., MGF, MGF's F., MGM, MGM's F. b. here. — Ed.: here till 15, then finished h.s. at Ashland, age 18 (1902). — Episcopalian. — Family ostracized for F.'s Unionist sympathies, though he was landowner of some importance. Honest responses. — Reports some neighbors have centralized beginning of /au/ in all positions, opposed to her typical VA alternation. Perhaps divided usage from beginning of community, with consistent centralization losing out.

12. Westmoreland County

Formed 1653 from Northumberland Co. 1st grant 1669. Patent of 1673, bought out by crown 1684. Iron c. 1700, abandoned 1729 (glass making too?). Birthplace of Washington, Lee. Pop. 1699: 2,541, 1755: 2,532, 1782: 4,946, 1790: 7,722, 1820: 6,901, 1850: 8,080, 1880: 8,846, 1910: 9,313, 1930: 8,497, 1960: 11,042.

Bell, Annie Walker Burns. 1934. *Third Census of the USA, Weston County.* Washington.
Crozier, William Armstrong. 1913. *Westmoreland County.* Hasbouck Heights, NJ. Repr. 1962 (Baltimore: Genealogical Pub. Co.).
Eaton, David W. 1942. *Historical Atlas of Westmoreland County, Virginia.* Richmond: Dietz Press.
Nottingham, Stratton, comp. 1928. *The Marriage License Bonds of Westmoreland County, 1786 to 1850.* Onancock.
Wright, Thomas R. B. 1912. *Westmoreland County, Virginia.* ... Richmond: Whittet and Shepperson.

George Walker's Place, Oldhams P.O.
    Old parish area; glebe house (c. 1655) still remains.

VA 12N: F, housewife, 80+. B. nearby plantation; after Civil War, moved around in county. — F., PGF, M., MGF, MGM slaves on Newtons' plantation. — Illiterate. — Baptist. — Unsophisticated but with native intelligence. Cooperative; very much respectable old servant type. Deeply religious. Not in good health but able to work. — Former field hand, little

contact with housework; speech may reflect either early African or West Indian patterns. Central rather than high-central vowel in weak-stressed syllables, always before [z] and before [d] when back vowel in preceding stressed syllable.

Smith Mount Farm, Horners Mill P.O., Washington Dist.
    Smith Mt. an old plantation, founded c. 1715.

VA 12A: M, farmer, 73. B. 1 or 2 miles from here. — F. b. Caroline Co., came here when married, PGF, PGM b. Caroline County; M. b. King and Queen Co., came here when married, MGF, MGM b. King and Queen Co. — Ed.: "slight". — "Christian". — Of good family (F. a physician) but grew up isolated, without education. — Extremely rapid speech. Quick tempo. Short vowels. Precise articulation. [Among some people in Co., *cot* and *caught*, etc. are homonymous.]

Blenheim Farm, Oak Grove P.O., Washington Dist.
    Blenheim one of Washington plantations, built 1780.

VA 12B!: M, farmer, 51. B. 1/4 mile from here. — F., PGF, PGF's F., PGM, PGM's F., PGM's PGF b. here (latter halfbrother to George Washington), PGM's M. b. Richmond Co., near Warsaw; M., MGF b. King George Co., MGM b. MD of Welsh desc. — Ed.: privately at home. — Episcopalian. — Intelligent, cooperative; Washington connection admitted but not boasted. Rather rustic; lived as a bachelor until his marriage a few years before interview. — Cultivated.

13. Lancaster County

Organized 1652. 1st patent 1642. Indians delayed settlement. Most of earliest settlers were small planters; majority of labor white indentured servants. Heavy settlement 1657–69. Pop. spread from marine fringe toward interior; tendency toward larger estates. Mainly English, some French. After 1669 pop. began to tail off as a result of the tobacco depression (caused by overproduction and poor quality). 1680–1720 decline in no. of middling planters, rise in no. of large; increase in no. of slaves. Oligarchy developed. Pop. 1699: 2,093, 1755: 1,610, 1783: 4,108, 1790: 5,638, 1820: 5,517, 1850: 4,708, 1880: 6,160, 1910: 9,752, 1930: 8,896, 1960: 9,174.

Lee, Ida Johnson. 1959. *Abstracts of Lancaster County, Virginia, Wills 1653–1800.* Richmond: Dietz Press.
Nottingham, Stratton, comp. 1927. *The Marriage License Bonds of Lancaster County, from 1701 to 1848.* Onancock.
Nottingham, Stratton, comp. 1930. *Revolutionary Soldiers and Sailors from Lancaster County, Virginia.* Onancock.
Wheeler, Robert Anthony. 1972. *Lancaster County, Virginia, 1650–1750.* Brown University dissertation.

VA 13A: Corotoman, Weems P.O. — F, housewife, 74. B. Irvington (nearby). — F. b. Richmond Co.; M. b. Irvington, MGF, MGM b. eastern shore of VA. — Ed.: none. — Baptist. — Whimsical, if improverished; very quick. — Rapid tempo, short vowels. Low-back up-gliding rounded diphthong for both *cot* and *caught* types; occasional weak constriction (as in *father*). Double-tap for intervocalic /t/, unusual (no AfAm influence here).

VA 13B: Mollusk, White Chapel Dist. — F, housewife, 57. B. White Plains, 14 miles from here, in Co.; 3 yrs. in Baltimore, c. 1907. — F, PGF, PGM, M., MGF, MGM b. Co. (all of old stock). — Ed.: here till 14 or 15. — Methodist, though raised in Episcopal Church. — Quick, willing, intelligent, of good average family background or better. Never quite sure of purpose of interview. — /w-/ for /hw-/, /j-/ for /hj-/ seems quite local.

14. Northumberland County

Est. 1648. Northern Neck settlement began in late 1620s; part of Culpeper grant in 1660s. Predominantly English, largely secondary settlement; however, mixed pop. origins and mixed 17th cent. politics (many Royalists). Many early settlers from MD. Huguenots, Scotch, Irish; a few Germans, Hollanders, Scandinavians. Most rapidly growing part of colony 1652–74. Tobacco warehouse by 1779. Planter society from beginning; tobacco lands exhausted by end of Rev. Also wheat, flour. Decline from Rev., esp. after 1860. Many Baptists from early 19th cent. Raided and pillaged 1814 by British. Bombarded 1862; raided several times during Civil War. No RRs, low traffic density on highways. Pop. 1699: 2,019, 1755: 2,414, 1782: 7,734, 1790: 9,163, 1820: 8,016, 1850: 7,346, 1880: 7,929, 1910: 10,777, 1930: 11,081, 1960: 10,185.

Brown, Stuart E., Jr. 1965. *Virginia Baron: The Story of Thomas, Sixth Lord Fairfax.* Berryville: Chesapeake Book Co.

Haynie, Miriam (Williams). 1959. *The Stronghold, a Story of Historic Northern Neck of Virginia and Its People.* Richmond: Dietz Press.

1966–. *Bulletin of the Northumberland County Historical Society.* Heathsville: Northumberland County Historical Society.

VA 14A: Callao (crossroads community), Hyacinth P.O., Callao Dist. — F, housewife, 88. B. 3 mi. away, Richmond Co.; has been to Washington and Baltimore to visit children. — F, PGF, PGM, M., MGF, MGM b. here. — Ed.: till 15. — Methodist. — Good mind, sound, though hard of hearing. — Honest, cooperative. — Distinguishes *cot* and *caught* types.

VA 14B: Remo, Wicomico Dist. — F, housewife, 57. B. 2 1/2 miles from here. — F. b. Simpson's Wharf, in Co., PGF b. Co.; M. b. Remo. — Ed.: here till 17 (probably not great). — Baptist. — Quick, bright, but poor, hard working; intelligent, understood purpose of interview; tried to use speech of childhood and of her parents, who had even fewer advantages. — Apparent homonymy of *beer/bare* and the like (cf. southern MD and SC coast). Constriction sometimes suggests spelling pronunciation with its strength, but prob. natural constriction here. *Burg* for *bug* prob. overcorrection or dialect mixture. Some linking /r/; confusion of /v/ and /w/ (as /v/ [with overrounding]). Rather quick, energetic speech (rapid-fire speech apparently a coastal characteristic, not found inland, though some here also speak slowly).

Wicomico Church P.O., Wicomico Dist.

Old village; pre-Revolutionary parish. 1856 Methodist church; 1908 h.s.

VA 14C: F, housewife, 46. B. 1 mi. away; never traveled in VA; took boat twice a yr. to Baltimore to do shopping. — F., PGF, PGF's F., PGF's M., PGM, PGM's F., PGM's M., M., MGF, MGF's F., MGF's M., MGM, MGM's M. b. here; MGM's F. b. Caroline Co. — Ed.: local private school till 17. — Episcopal family, but not a member. — Moderate tempo. Homonymy of *air/ear* and the like. Some consciousness of spelling and correctness (and insecurity) from educated grandmother.

15. Essex County

Formed from Rappahannock Co. First attempt at settlement 1612. Earliest settlers from St. Marys, MD. C. 1646 settlements withdrawn after Indian Wars; treaty abrogated 1649 and permanent settlement followed. Mainly English, but including some French surnames (Huguenots?). Possibly glassmaking in colonial days. Pop. 1699: 2,592, 1755: 2,600, 1785: 5,306, 1790: 9,122, 1820: 9,909, 1850: 10,206, 1880: 11,032, 1910: 9,105, 1930: 6,976, 1960: 6,690.

Dorman, John Frederick. 1959. *Essex County, Virginia Records, 1717–1722.* Washington.

Showell, Virginia. 1924. *Essex Sketches.* Baltimore: Thomas Press.

Warner, Pauline Pearce, and Thomas Hoskins Warner. 1926. *History of Essex County, Virginia.* Dunnsville: Sentinel Press.

Warner, Thomas Hoskins. 1965. *History of Old Rappahannock County, 1656–1692. . . .* Tappahannock: P. P. Warner.

VA 15N: Dunnsville. — F, housewife, former field hand, 88. B. here. — Family b. here. — Illiterate. — Fervently religious (prob. Baptist). Little contact with whites. — Speech prob. shows influence of early type of English spoken by slaves; difficult to say whether it shows African or West Indian influence. Sudden changes in stress, loudness, and pitch, to express emphasis. Before voiced consonants /au/ has lower beginning and shorter first element than usual.

VA 15N*: Dunnsville (mill in 17th cent.). — M, 94. B. here. — Parents b. here. — Illiterate.

Brays P.O.

Bray's Church built here 1693.

VA 15A: M, farmer, 73. B. 1 1/3 mi. away. — F., PGF, PGM, M., MGF, MGM b. here. — Illiterate. — Baptist. — Intelligent. — Moderate tempo. Short vowels and diphthongs.

Wares Wharf, Dunnsville P.O., Rappahannock Dist.

Wares Wharf a landmark from the 17th cent. Mill formerly on river branch here (Kings Swamp).

VA 15B: F, housewife, 45. B. Tappahannock, to Wares Wharf when 21, taught 1 yr. in WV. — F. b. Dunnsville, PGF, PGF's F. b. King and Queen Co., PGM, PGM's F. b. Wares Wharf, PGM's M. b. Co.; M. b. King William Co., MGF b. Galveston, TX, MGF's F., MGM, MGM's F. b. King William Co. — Episcopal School, Winchester, 2 yrs. — Disciples of Christ, formerly Episcopalian. — Good family (husband with fewer advantages); fully cooperative. — Liked her nurse as a child;

thinks she absorbed more of Negro voice quality and laxness of articulation than did others of the family. Moderate tempo; often slow.

16. King and Queen County

Formed in 1691 from New Kent Co. Tidewater co., NE shore of York and Mattaponi Rivers. Baptists here from 1769; now dominant. Methodists by 1790, but never numerous. No Episcopal colonial church survives. Indian lands here till at least 18th cent. General farming, tobacco, timber. Pop. 1699: 3,306, 1755: 3,047, 1782: 3,376, 1790: 9,377, 1820: 11,798, 1850: 10,319, 1880: 10,502, 1910: 9,576, 1930: 7,618, 1960: 5,889.

Bagby, Alfred. 1908. *King and Queen County, Virginia.* NY: Neale Pub. Co.

Fleet, Benjamin Robert. 1962. *Green Mount: A Virginia Plantation Family during the Civil War.* Lexington, KY: University Press of Kentucky.

Harris, Malcolm Hart, comp. 1977. *Old New Kent County: Some Account of the Planters, Plantations and Places in New Kent County.* 2 vols. West Point, VA: M.H. Harris.

Hundley, William Thomas, ed. 1928. *History of Mattaponi Baptist Church, King and Queen County, Virginia.* Richmond: Appeals Press.

Lipscomb, Mary. 1931. *Recollections of Early West Point.* West Point, VA.

1888. *West Point, Virginia, and King William County.* Richmond: E. Waddey.

King and Queen Courthouse P.O., Stephensville

Small courthouse village; courthouse site same since 1691. 1st lands patented 1653. Original community wiped out by Yankee cavalry in 1864: only 1 house left standing. Stephensville Academy well known. Many old houses.

VA 16A: M, farmer, sawmiller, storekeeper, 70. B. here. — F., PGF, PGM, M., MGF, MGM b. here (MGM's F. a seaman). — Ed.: Stephensville till 17; private school afterwards, short terms. — Moderate status, old-fashioned.

(Across the river from) West Point (King Wm. Co.), West Point P.O., Buena Vista Dist.

West Point at confluence of Mattaponi and York Rivers. Colonial grant in 1652 to John West. Townsite and wharf by 1691; est. as port 1705. RR to point 1856; West Point Land and Developing Company est. same year. Town charter 1870. Town declined in late 19th cent.; damaging fires in 1888 and 1903. Pop. 1910: 1,397, 1930: 1,844, 1960: 1,678.

VA 16B: M, bridge tender, former mechanic, 44. B. West Point. — F., PGF b. Co., PGF's F. b. Ireland, PGM b. Co.; M., MGF b. Co., MGM, MGM's F. b. King and Queen or Essex Co. — Ed.: Gloucester Academy, Randolph-Macon Academy, Randolph-Macon College (Ashland) 2 yrs. — Baptist. — Quick, nervous manner. — Rapid speech, clear articulation.

17. King William County

Formed 1701 from King and Queen Co. Pop. 1755: 2,536, 1782: 4,320, 1790: 8,128, 1820: 9,697, 1850: 8,779, 1880: 8,751, 1910: 8,547, 1930: 7,929, 1960: 7,563.

Clarke, Peyton Neale. 1897. *Old King William Homes and Families.* Louisville: J. P. Morton.

Ryland, Elizabeth Hawes, comp. 1955. *King William County, Virginia....* Richmond: Dietz Press.

1888. *West Point, Virginia, and King William County.* Richmond: E. Waddey.

Central Garage (inf. lives in rural area 4 mi. N.), Venter P.O., Aquinton Dist.

Central Garage a crossroads village. Land patent for "Aquinton Quarter" in 1687. Aquinton Church now Methodist. Swamp here.

VA 17A: M, farmer, former carpenter, 64+. B. Manquin (4 or 5 mi. from here), came here as infant; when 18–23 in Hanover Co., near Gethsemane Church. — F. b. here, PGF a Yankee who came before 1860, PGM b. near Lanesville in Co.; M. b. here, MGF, MGM b. Co. — Ed.: none. — Baptist. — Old-fashioned; has lived in woods a long time, isolated. — Though illiterate, says /kælm/. Fairly rapid speech, rather clear articulation. Centralized beginning of /au/ before voiceless consonants; in other positions, first element depends on length, etc., varying from center to front. Confusion of status of *card*, *cord*, *cod* words: at one time, 3-way contrast; now *card* normally = *cord*, but every conceivable intermediate type exists.

Beulahville, Mangohick Dist.

Church here by 1732, now used by AfAm Baptists. Plantation by 1766.

VA 17B: M, farmer, carpenter, 46. B. here. — F. b. near Cold Harbor, Hanover Co.; M., MGM, MGM's F. b. here. — Ed.: here till 16. — Baptist, Jr. Order Mechanics. — Obliging, honest; limited sophistication but good inf. — Slight drawl; /au/ has centralized beginning before voiceless consonants; before voiced and in final position the first element is further front but almost never fully front; it varies with length, etc.

18. Middlesex County

Christ Church parish est. in area 1663. Pop. 1699: 1,541, 1755: 1,527, 1783: 3,449, 1790: 4,140, 1820: 4,057, 1850: 4,394, 1880: 6,252, 1910: 8,852, 1930: 7,273, 1960: 6,319.

Chamberlayne, C. G., ed. 1927. *The Vestry Book of Christ Church Parish, Middlesex County, Virginia....* Richmond: Old Dominion Press.

Saluda

Co. seat from 1852. Courthouse burned 1860s, but records saved. Little change to 1939.

VA 18: M, farmer, 81. B. county, between Saluda and Urbanna. — F. (came here as young man), PGF, PGM, M. (came here when young), MGF, MGM b. Gloucester Co. — Ed.: 10 yrs. — Indigent, blind, but bright and intelligent. — Very quick speech, very rapid tempo; precise articulation, not influenced by spelling. Very short vowels and diphthongs.

19. Gloucester County

Formed 1651 from York Co. Middle peninsula; fertile soil. 1st permanent settlements 1647; Gloucester Pt. est. as pŏrt 1667. Became most populous co. in 1790. Family roots are deep. Gloucester Church 1679; new bldg. 1766. Baptists by 1775; Methodists by 1782. Raided during Civil War. Pop. 1699: 3,770, 1701: 5,720, 1755: 4,421, 1783: 5,915, 1790: 13,498, 1820: 9,678, 1850: 10,527, 1880: 11,876, 1910: 12,477, 1930: 11,019, 1960: 11,919.

Association for the Preservation of Virginia Antiquities. 1959. *Epitaphs of Gloucester and Mathews Counties.* . . . Richmond: Virginia State Library.

Caywood, Louis R. 1955. *Excavations at Green Spring Plantation.* Yorktown: Colonial National Historical Park.

Chamberlayne, G. C., ed. 1933. *The Vestry Book of Petsworth Parish, Gloucester County, Virginia, 1677–1793.* Richmond: Division of Purchase and Printing.

Gray, Mary Wiatt. 1936. *Gloucester County.* Richmond: Cottrell and Cooke.

Mason, G. C., ed. 1946–48. *Records of Colonial Gloucester County.* 2 vols. Newport News: G. C. Mason.

Montague, Ludwell Lee. 1965. *Gloucester County in the Civil War.* Gloucester: DeHardit Press.

Noël Hume, Ivor. 1962. *Excavations at Rosewell in Gloucester County, Virginia, 1957–1959.* Washington: Smithsonian Institution.

Robins, Salley Nelson. 1893. *Gloucester.* Richmond: West, Johnston.

Sinclair, Caroline B. 1974. *Stories of Old Gloucester.* Verona, VA.

Guinea neighborhood, Severn P.O., Abingdon Dist.
Colonial church, built in Abingdon c. 1732, still standing.

VA 19A: M, fisherman, clammer, farmer, 67. B. here. — F., M. b. here; thinks all GP also b. here. — Ed.: 3rd grade. — Baptist and Holiness. — Good citizen; churchgoer (atypical in community). Quick, bright, unguarded. — Tempo rapid to very rapid; vowels short. Note *I'm been thinking* and response *I am* to question "Have you?" Centered beginning of /o/; back beginning of /ai/; *air/ear* homonymy (cf. low-country SC); [v] for both /v/ and /w/; /au/ with centralized beginning in all positions; /e/ in *head*, *bed*, etc.

VA 19B: Friends Church, Achilles P.O., Abingdon Dist. — F, spinster, 61. B. here. — F., PGF, PGM, M., MGF, MGM b. here [M. died 4 yrs. before interview, age 102]. — Ed.: here 6–15. — Recently joined Quakers. — Tense, quick and obliging, unsophisticated; lacked family advantages. — Undulating, ingratiating drawl. /w/ for /v/, open diphthongs, back beginning of /ai/ — all shared by various coastal communities, including NYC.

SE of Gloucester Courthouse, Zanoni P.O., Ware Dist.
Ware Church (1680–90) still standing.

VA 19C!: F, single homemaker, 55. B. Goshen on Ware River (1 mi. from present residence, 3 mi. from courthouse). — F., PGF b. here, PGF's F. b. Co., PGM, PGM's F. b. Middlesex Co., PGM's M. b. Mt. Airy, Richmond; M. b. Petersburg, returned to Gloucester in teens, MGF, MGF's F., MGF's M. b. Co., MGM b. Tappahannock, MGM's F. b. Fredericksburg. — Ed.: here, private school. — Episcopalian, Women's Club,

Garden Club. — Quick, alert, distinctly cultivated; mentality even more quick and direct than in N. Neck communities. — Broad *a* in all or almost all positions where it is found in England; traditional upper-class usage for some generations (other infs., less cultivated, have /æ/ in these words). — Cultivated.

20. Mathews County
Only VA co. where fishing is the major source of income. Pop. 1800: 5,806, 1820: 6,920, 1850: 6,714, 1880: 7,501, 1910: 8,922, 1930: 7,884, 1960: 7,121.

VA 20A: Winter Harbor, Onemo P.O., Chesapeake Dist. — M, farmer, 79. B. here. — F., PGF, PGF's F., M., MGF b. here (believes all lines have been in community a long time). — Genial, enjoyed interview; genuinely old-fashioned. — Complex distribution of allophones of /au/: low-central before /n/, upper low-central before voiced and finally, upper low-central, with rounding, before voiceless.

VA 20B: East River (Ware Point), Port Haywood P.O., Chesapeake Dist. — F, single homemaker, 63 (b. 1873). B. 3 mi. S., always lived in Co. — F. b. Gloucester Pt., PGF b. here, PGM b. Gloucester Pt.; M. b. here (Horn Harbor); MGF b. Co. (English descent). — Ed.: Woodstock Academy (teacher from Clark Co.). — Episcopalian. — Uneasy about local usage, thanks to purism of teacher. Difficult interview.

VA 20C: Mathews Courthouse, Westville Dist. — F, housewife, 45–50. B. here. — Parents b. here. — Perhaps from E. part of Co., where mixing with Eastern Shore people occurs. Difficult interview; self-conscious. — Dubious authenticity. [æ] beginning of /au/ where others have centralized beginning; strong postvocalic /r/ may be genuine. Tempo rather slow.

21. Charles City County
1622 plans for "East Indian School" involved this area. Pop. 1624–25: 236, 1634: 511, 1699: 3,899, 1755: 1,595, 1787: 3,201, 1790: 5,588, 1820: 5,255, 1850: 5,200, 1880: 5,512, 1910: 5,253, 1930: 4,881, 1960: 5,492.

VA 21N: "In de woods", Holdcroft P.O., Chickahominy Dist. — F, housewife, 75. B. 2 mi. away at "Old Neck". — F., PGF, PGM b. Co. (all free renters); M. b. York Co. near Yorktown, MGF b. York Co. (slave), MGM b. York Co. (free). — Illiterate. — Baptist. — Parents suffered discrimination after 1865. Native intelligence, poised, cooperative; understood questions and purpose and tried to give old-style AfAm usage. — Phonetic pattern confused; final voiced plosives and fricatives not distinguished from voiceless counterparts; inf. can distinguish, but not natural. Initial /p   t   k/ usually unaspirated with slight voice; occasionally strongly aspirated with special effort. Initial /b   d   g/ usually very long, very fully voiced. Medially usually no difference between /t   d/; occasionally different in length. Occasional low-pitched glottal rumble. Postvocalic clear [l], initial palatal [n], and [n ⁱ]. /ai/ with slightly centralized beginning (not characteristic of whites), and high second element, before voiced sounds. /au/ with centralized beginning in all positions; different from usage of rural whites.

VA 21A: Gillams, Providence Forge P.O. (New Kent Co.), Tyler Dist. — F, housewife, 80. B. 5 mi. away; always lived here. — F., PGF, PGM, M., MGF, MGF's parents, MGM, MGM's parents b. Co., native stock. — Illiterate. — F. was Baptist. — Shrewd, intelligent, hardworking, without many worldly goods. — Good representative of local uneducated speech. [æ] beginning of /au/ finally and before voiced sounds indicates its antiquity (contrast other E. VA communities). Tendency toward short vowels.

VA 21B: Ruthville, Tyler Dist. — M, retired merchant, 56. B. 6 mi. E. at Clay Yard. — F. b. Co., PGF b. Ireland, came here as young man, PGM, M., MGF, MGM b. Co. — Ed.: here till 16. — Baptist, Mason. — Middle class type. — Enunciation and articulation not too precise; inf. tubercular. Fairly short vowels. Centralized beginning of /au/ before voiceless, less often before voiced. Variation according to speed, length, etc.

22. James City County

Jamestown not the most viable site for a colony; unhealthy. By 1660, all ships reported to James City; afterwards, to the collector of a particular river. Diffused intellectual life in E. VA; more receptive than creative. Pop. 1624–25: 475, 1699: 2,760, 1755: 1,648, 1782: 2,325, 1790: 4,160, 1820: 4,563, 1850: 4,020, 1880: 5,422, 1910: 6,338, 1930: 3,879, 1960: 11,539.

Bridenbaugh, Carl. 1980. *Jamestown.* NY: Oxford University Press.
Dowdey, Clifford. 1957. *The Great Plantation: A Profile of Berkeley Hundred and Plantation Virginia from Jamestown to Appomattox.* NY: Rinehart.

VA 22: Edge of Charles City Co., Diascund P.O., Powhatant Dist. — F, housewife, 86. B. Norge, 3 mi. from village on edge of York Co., lived at Ridge. — Parents, grandparents b. just over line in York Co. — Illiterate. — Baptist (rarely attends). — Extremely unsophisticated; unaware even of names of gospels as given names. Extraordinarily good health; quick mind; immediate spontaneous reactions, but no critical faculties developed. — Rapid tempo. Neutralization of *card/cord* contrast. Palatal stops in *car, garden* with fronting.

23. York County (now City of Poquoson)

Yorktown a tobacco port; had already declined by 1776. Pop. 1699: 1,909, 1755: 2,129, 1782: 2,762, 1790: 5,233, 1820: 4,384, 1850: 4,460, 1880: 7,349, 1910: 7,757, 1930: 7,615, 1960: 21,583.

Bradshaw, Ura Ann, ed. 1957. *York County.* Hampton.
Hopkins, G. E. 1942. *York County Source Book.* Winchester: Privately issued.

Messick, Poquoson Dist.
Richest part of Co. Mostly English, some Holland Dutch among settlers.

VA 23A: F, widow, 107 (by repute). B. 3/4 mi. away; first married at 16, just after battle at Williamsburg. — F., PGF, PGM b. Messicks Point; M., MGF, MGM b. Mathews Co. — Uneducated. — No church or other organizations. — Desperately poor environment in childhood, though they could catch their food (fishing). — Open diphthong; some fronting of centralized beginning of /au/; /ai/ with back beginning; /u/ up-gliding high-central diphthong.

VA 23B: Grafton. — F, widow, 73. B. here. — F. b. here, PGF b. Maine, died when inf.'s father was 6, PGM, PGM's F. b. here (old native stock); M. b. here, MGF, MGM b. Poquoson (all of old native stock). — Ed.: little (11–15). — Christian Church. — Very intelligent, sociable, gracious; reminded FW of better class of New Eng. infs., though social status not very high; but no attempt to conceal speech (as in New Eng.). — Very rapid speech; vowels short to very short; clear utterance. *Cot* type distinguished from *cart, caught* types, which fall together.

24. Warwick County (now City of Newport News)

Formed in 1634; never subdivided. Smallest of 8 shires of 1634. 1st settlements as early as 1611. Irish settlement in Newport News in 17th cent. Newport News a British base in Revolution; became a federal base in 1861. Pop. in 1784 mostly English, a few Germans and French. Co. agricultural till after 1865, though devastation and depression caused many to join westward migration. All pre-1865 development lost as a result of scorched earth policy c. 1865. Area somewhat revived with coming of C&O RR in 1881. Coal port, shipbuilding, major naval installation. In 1958 Warwick merged with the city of Newport News. Pop. (Co.) 1634: 811, 1699: 1,362, 1755: 746, 1782: 1,345, 1790: 1,690, 1820: 1,608, 1850: 1,546, 1880: 2,258, 1910: 6,041, 1930: 8,829; in 1960 Newport News pop. 113,662.

Vollertsen, Arthur. 1977. *Warwick County, Virginia, 1782–1888: Who Was Who.* Fort Eustis: Fort Eustis Historical and Archeological Association.

Denbigh Plantation, Oyster Point P.O., Denbigh Dist.
Co. seat. One of oldest plantations in area, dates from 1622. One of great VA estates. Prob. a church here by 1635; Anglican church certainly by 1774.

VA 24: F, single homemaker, 64. B. here; taught 2 yrs. in 1-room school at Morrison in Co. — F. b. Harpersville, PGF b. Co. (perhaps Scotch descent), PGM, PGM's F. b. Co; M. b. Co., MGF b. Eastern Shore, MGM, MGM's F. b. Co., MGM's PGF, PGM b. Elizabeth City, MGM's M. b. Co. — Ed.: private school in Norfolk. — Episcopalian. — F. owned 3000 acres. Represents only old family of consequence left in neighborhood which is now Mennonite. Bitter about fortunes. Very positive attitudes. — Good speech, some folk forms (e.g., *this-a-way*).

25, 26, 27. Accomack County

Accomack Co. formed 1663; orig. est. as Northampton Co. in 1642. Oldest county records of unbroken continuity (from 1632). 1st explored 1608; 1st settlement c. 1614. Earliest settlers yeomanry; almost 100% English (no Irish). A few Dutch and Germans, some New Eng. Puritans, some Quakers. 1st courthouse 1632. Occasional migration to MD (land boom). By 1666, most densely populated part of VA. Presbyterians by 1684, but Anglicans dominant till Revolution; Methodists and Baptists dominant since. Large estates; 1st AfAms in VA here; many freed AfAms even in 17th cent.

Tobacco early (by 1620), grain later; salt making, shipping, small industries. Harassed by British fleet during Rev., yet some Loyalist sentiment. Occupied by Feds in 1861. E. Shore RR not completed till 1885. In late 19th cent., sweet potatoes, berries, truck farming, poultry, seafood; decline in cattle and hogs. Old families still rooted. Increasing diversification of agriculture in 20th cent.; fishing. Pop. 1624–25: 81, 1634: 396, 1699: 2,668, 1755: 2,641, 1787: 3,561, 1790: 13,959, 1820: 15,966, 1850: 17,890, 1880: 24,408, 1910: 36,650, 1930: 35,854, 1960: 30,635.

Ames, Susie M. 1940. *Studies of the Virginia Eastern Shore in the Seventeenth Century.* Richmond: Dietz Press.

Barnes, Brooks Miles, and W. Robert Keeney, comps. 1976. *A Bibliography of the Eastern Shore of Virginia.* Accomac: Eastern Shore Public Library

Breen, T. H., and Stephen Innes. 1980. *"Myne Owne Ground": Race and Freedom on Virginia's Eastern Shore, 1640–1676.* NY: Oxford University Press.

Crowson, E. T. 1981. *Life as Revealed through Early American Court Records.* Easley, SC: Southern Historical Press.

Forman, Henry Chandlee. 1975. *The Virginia Eastern Shore and Its British Origins: History, Gardens and Antiquities.* Easton, MD: Eastern Shore Publishers' Associates.

Hall, Samuel Warren. 1939. *Tangier Island.* Philadelphia: University of Pennsylvania Press.

Mariner, Kirk. 1968. *Nothing Ever Happened in Arcadia.* Richmond: Cooper-Trent Printers.

Mears, James Egbert. 1937. *Hacks Neck and Its People, Past and Present.* Chicago: J. E. Mears.

Mears, John Neely. 1937. *Tangier Island.* Onancock: J.N. Mears.

Nock, L. Floyd, III. 1976. *Drummondtown, "a One Horse Town": Accomac Court House, Virginia.* Verona: McClure Print. Co.

Nottingham, Stratton, comp. 1929. *Certificates and Rights, Accomack County, 1663–1709.* Onancock.

Nottingham, Stratton, comp. 1930. *Land Causes, Accomack County, Virginia, 1727–1826.* Onancock.

Nottingham, Stratton, comp. 1931. *Accomack Tithables (Tax Lists) 1663–1665.* Onancock.

Nottingham, Stratton, comp. 1931. *Wills and Administrations, Accomack County, 1663–1800.* Onancock.

Nottingham, Stratton, comp. 1965. *The Marriage License Bonds of Accomack County, from 1774 to 1806.* Baltimore: Genealogical Pub. Co.

Pennebaker, Katherine B. 1975. *Homes and Harbors on the Eastern Shore.* Accomac: Eastern Shore News.

Turner, Nora. 1964. *The Eastern Shore of Virginia, 1603–1964.* Onancock: Eastern Shore News.

Whichard, Rogers D. 1959. *The History of Lower Tidewater Virginia.* NY: Lewis Historical Publishing Co.

Whitelaw, Ralph T. 1951. *Virginia's Eastern Shore.* Richmond: Virginia Historical Society.

Wilcher, Talmage S. 1964. *King of Assateague.* NY: Vantage Press.

Wilson, Robert. 1928. *Half Forgotten By-Ways of the Old South.* Columbia, SC: State Co.

Wise, Henry A. 1962. *Over on the Eastern Shore.* Onancock: Eastern Shore News.

Wise, Jennings Cropper. 1911. *Ye Kingdome of Accawmacke.* Richmond: Bell Book and Stationery Co.

Tangier Island, Tangier P.O., Lee Dist.

Tangier I. patented 1675–76 for stock raising. English settlers c. 1666. Now few animals, little gardening. One of smallest inhabited islands: less than 2 sq. mi., 90% marsh. Loyalist in Rev. No participation in Civil War; few slaves, ever. Methodists; fundamentalists. Shoals: largest crabbing center in the world, crabbing and oysters provide bulk of income. Recently tourism a source of income. Declining pop., est. 900 in 1976.

VA 25: M, crabber, 76. B. here. — F., PGF b. here, PGM b. Mathews Co.; M., MGF b. mainland of Co. — Little education. — Methodist. — Sensitive community; interview successful by following recognized protocol. — Strong postvocalic /r/.

VA 25*: F, widow, 85. B. here. — F. b. mainland of Co., came here as young man; M. b. upper end of Island, MGF, MGM b. Island. — Ed.: Sabbath School. — Methodist. — Pleasant, but timid reactions slowed down by age. — Speech rather rapid.

Craddockville, Pungoteague Dist.

Pungoteague the site of an Indian village. Plantation country; boundary of settlement. Fort in Dutch war. St. George's prob. earliest church in Co. British landing in 1814. Unanimously secessionist. Craddockville a small village.

VA 26A: M, painter, 82. B. Co. — F., M. b. here; grandparents of old native stock. — Little education. — Kindly, untraveled; good mental processes despite history of stroke. — Long low-central and low-back vowels fall together; occasional weak postvocalic /r/. Rapid tempo, genuine.

Lee Mont, Justisville P.O., Metompkin Dist.

Plantation country in 17th cent.; Lee Mont a small village.

VA 26B: F, housewife, 78. B. here. — F., PGF, PGF's F., PGF's PGF, PGM, PGM's F., PGM's PGF, PGM's PGM, M., MGF, MGF's F., MGM b. here. — Ed.: 6 mos. — Methodist. — Middle-class background, typical of community. Highly intelligent, industrious, old-fashioned, isolated. — Clear articulation. Initial /p t k/ weakly aspirated; sometimes written [p̥ t̥ k̥].

Accomac P.O., Lee Dist.

Accomac orig. Drummondtown; renamed 1893. 1st patent 1664; courthouse here from 1693. Chartered 1786. Incorporated 1944. HQ of army of occupation 1861–65; some property damage (to Methodist and Presbyterian churches). Small village, Co. seat. Downtown fire 1921.

VA 26C: F, housewife, 47. B. Drummondtown. — F., PGF b. Lee Mont; M. b. Locustville (5 mi. S.), MGF b. Locustville, ancestors came from England with 17th cent. royal grant, ancestors in another line founded Drummondtown (now called Accomac) in 1788, MGM b. Machapungo Creek, MGM's F. and M. b. Co., MGM's ancestors ultimately of New Eng. ancestry. — Ed.: local h.s. — Presbyterian, Women's Club, UDC. — Attractive, energetic, public-spirited woman.

Tried to be natural, but some self-consciousness. — Tempo rapid; clear, vigorous articulation. Extremely variable post-vocalic retroflexion.

Chincoteague, Chincoteague Island (The Islands)

Patented for stock raising by 1670s. Wild ponies by 1680s. Plantation in late 17th cent. Voted overwhelmingly against secession in 1861. Largest marketer of shellfish and broilers; also horse and cattle grazing. Most populous E. Shore VA island. Pop. 1880: 1,662, 1910: 1,419, 1930: 3,182, 1960: 2,131.

VA 27: F, housewife, 88. B. lower part of island. — F. b. Phila. but came here as infant, PGF prob. b. here (English descent), PGM b. lower Co.; M., MGF, MGF's F. b. Assoteague Island (adjacent). — Ed.: none. — Baptist. — Quaint, wizened, remarkable mentality and memory. Dependable once confidence gained (partial record, 2 yrs. earlier, discontinued; filed for comparison). — Normal postvocalic /r/, not exaggerated. *Cot/caught* distinction. After /t d n/ has /u/, often high central.

28. Northampton County

Founded as Accomack; name change 1643; division and formation of Northampton c. 1663. 1st purchase and settlement 1614: fishing and salt works. Some Dutch settlers c. 1650. Basically small farmer country in 1679. Strong Royalists. Bluffs; no marshes. AfAm majority till at least 1960. Base for crab dredging. Pop. 1699: 2,050, 1755: 1,511, 1790: 6,889, 1820: 7,705, 1850: 7,498, 1880: 9,152, 1910: 16,672, 1930: 18,565, 1960: 16,966.

Dalbys, Cape Charles P.O., Capeville Dist.

Dalby plantation site of Co. courthouse after partition (c. 1663). Cape Charles City formed c. 1680; PA RR terminus here 1884.

VA 28A: M, farmer, clammer, oysterman, carpenter, wheelwright, 84. B. Co. between Eastville and Johnsontown; came here when 3 or 4 yrs. old. — F. b. above Eastville, PGF b. Co., PGM b. here; M. b. Eastville, MGM b. here. — Quiet, clear-thinking. — Tempo rather rapid; occasional retroflexion; /ai au/ may have slight lengthening in all positions.

Chatham Plantation, Bridgetown, Eastville P.O.

Chatham first patent 1640. Bridgetown oldest continuous town on E. Shore. Eastville a small, prosperous, rural co. seat; courthouse from 1680. Pop. Chatham 1930: 1,143, 1960: 1,822.

VA 28B: F, single homemaker, 60. B. near Sea View, Capeville Dist., came here at 4. — F., PGF, PGF's F., PGF's PGF b. Sea View, PGF's PGM b. Co., PGF's M., MGF, MGM b. Co. (here since 17th cent.); M. b. below Capeville, MGM's F., M. b. Co. — Ed.: here till 18. — Presbyterian. — Residence quite different from birthplace. Not very alert; somewhat guarded. — Rather slow tempo. No positional variant of /au/, as usual in VA.

29. Henrico County

Early settlements (1609–11) failed; settlement practically wiped out in 1622 massacre. Huguenot settlers in 1690s.

Huguenots at Manakin Town formed an early Anglican parish. 1st settlement above falls in 1720s. Pop. 1624–25: 22, 1634: 419, 1699: 2,222, 1755: 1,427, 1787: 8,300, 1790: 12,000, 1820: 23,667, 1850: 43,572, 1880: 82,703, 1910: 23,437, 1930: 30,310, 1960: 117,339.

Berman, Myron. 1979. *Richmond's Jewry, 1769–1976.* Charlottesville: University Press of Virginia.

Bill, Alfred Hoyt. 1946. *The Beleaguered City, Richmond, 1861–1865.* NY: A. A. Knopf.

Bondurant, Agnes M. 1942. *Poe's Richmond.* Richmond: Garrett and Massie, Inc.

Brock, R. A., ed. 1874. *The Vestry Book of Henrico Parish, 1730–'73. . . .* Richmond.

Burton, L. W. 1904. *Annals of Henrico Parish.* Richmond: Williams Print. Co.

Cabell, James Branch. 1955. *As I Remember It.* NY: McBride.

Chesson, Michael B. 1981. *Richmond after the War, 1865–1890.* Richmond: Virginia State Library.

Christian, William Asbury. 1912. *Richmond, Her Past and Present.* Richmond: L. H. Jenkins.

Cutchins, John A. 1973. *Memories of Old Richmond.* White Marsh: McClure Press.

Dabney, Virginia. 1976. *Richmond, the Story of a City.* Garden City, NJ: Doubleday.

Eckenrode, Hamilton James, ed. 1938. *Richmond, Capital of Virginia.* Richmond: Whittet and Shepperson.

Ernst, William Joel. 1978. *Urban Leaders and Social Change: The Urbanization Process in Richmond, Virginia, 1840–1880.* University of Virginia dissertation.

Ezekiel, Herbert T. 1917. *The History of the Jews of Richmond from 1769 to 1917.* Richmond.

Jones, John Beauchamp. 1866. *A Rebel War Clerk's Diary at the Confederate States Capital.* 2 vols. Philadelphia: J.B. Lippincott.

Little, John P. 1851. *History of Richmond.* Richmond. Repr. 1933 (Richmond: Dietz Print. Co.).

Lutz, Francis Earle. 1937. *A Richmond Album.* Richmond: Garrett and Massie.

Moore, Ernest Walke, comp. 1924. *History of St. John's P. E. Church, Richmond, Virginia.* 2nd ed. Richmond: Christian and Co.

Mordecai, Samuel. 1860. *Virginia, Especially Richmond. . . .* 2nd ed. Richmond: West and Johnston.

Pember, Phoebe Yates. 1959. *A Southern Woman's Story.* Jackson, TN: McCowat-Mercer.

Sanford, James K., ed. 1875. *Richmond: Her Triumphs, Tragedies and Growth.* Richmond: Metropolitan Richmond Chamber of Commerce.

Sheldon, Marianne Patricia Banff. 1978. *Richmond, Virginia: The Town and Henrico County to 1820.* University of Michigan dissertation.

Smith, Leslie Winston. 1974. *Richmond during Presidential Reconstruction, 1865–1867.* Ann Arbor: Xerox University Microfilms.

Stanard, Mary Newton. 1923. *Richmond, Its People and Its Story.* Philadelphia: J. B. Lippincott.

Thomas, Emory M. 1971. *The Confederate State of Richmond.* Austin: University of Texas Press.

Warner, Pauline Pearce. 1959. *The County of Henrico: A History.* Richmond.

Watson, Walter A. 1925. *Notes on Southside Virginia*. Richmond: Virginia State Library.

Weddell, Elizabeth Wright. 1931. *St. Paul's Church, Richmond, Virginia*. Richmond: William Byrd Press.

Deep Run Church, Richmond P.O., Tuckahoe Dist.
  Patent at least by 1695. Manakin Town orig. a Huguenot
settlement; dissipated.

VA 29: M, farmer, trucker, 75. B. 200 yards from here. — F.,
PGF, PGF's F., PGF's PGF, PGM, PGM's F. b. just over line
in Goochland Co.; M., MGF, MGF's F. b. Co. — Ed.: here 3
sessions. — Baptist. — Conservative, old-fashioned farmer;
rather good background; ordinary circumstances. — Regular
distinction of /ai au/ before voiced and voiceless, but not as
marked as in northern and western parts of state. Retracted
low-central or low-back vowel in *hot* (contrast tidewater); up-
gliding rounded diphthong in *all, law*, etc. (characteristic of
Piedmont).

30. City of Richmond
  Smith visited area 1607. 1st settlements 1610–11. 1670
land of Wm. Byrd I: Falls Plantation. Town laid out 1737.
Co. seat 1754; capital 1779; incorporated 1782. Iron works
from 1619. St. John's, Anglican church, proposed 1739;
became a cultural focus of city and state. Only VA town that
properly recovered from Revolution. Baptist congregation by
1780; Methodist cong. by 1800; Roman Catholic church by
1834. 1st steamboat 1815. VA State Library 1827; VA Historical Soc. 1830s. Coal output increased till 1832; also iron,
flour, textiles, tobacco. One of most important coffee ports by
1860; also sugar refining by 1860. Northern and foreign (esp.
Scots) businessmen; Whig stronghold. Many Germans 1836–
60. Little in common with cotton South; segregation developed during reconstruction. 1st school 1759; U. of Richmond
1832; Medical College of VA (1st in South) 1838; VA Union
1865; Union Theological Seminary moved to Richmond 1898.
After 1875, C&O RR to Newport News, port activity declined.
Largest Southern manufacturing center by 1880: tobacco,
flour, iron and steel. Shipbuilding, locomotives into 20th cent.
Suburbanization in 1950s. Diversified industry: financial center, fertilizer, tobacco, publishing, flour. Pop. 1820: 12,067,
1850: 27,570, 1880: 63,600, 1910: 127,628, 1930: 182,929,
1960: 219,958.

See 29 (Henrico County) for bibliography.

VA 30A: M, carpenter, 79. B. here; in Baltimore age 14–17,
from age 22 worked off and on at Dayton Coal Mine on
Henrico-Goochland Co. line. — F. b. New Kent, came here
age 17, PGF b. New Kent; M. b. Hanover Co., near Beaver
Dam, came here as young woman, MGF b. Hanover. — Ed.:
here to 5th grade. — Methodist. — Sturdy, genial; highly
intelligent, quick and alert. — Speech typical of older white
laboring class of Richmond (so far as they survive). Contrasts
cord and *card*.

VA 30B!: F, housewife, 50. B. S. Richmond. — Parents both
b. S. Richmond. — (Husband a florist.) — Slow reactions, self-
conscious, non-commital. — Drawl. — Cultivated.

VA 30C!: F, housewife, 85. B. Richmond, 1916–20 in Nor-
folk, 1920–22 in California. — F. b. Dorchester Co., MD, to
Richmond age 15, PGF, PGM b. Dorchester Co., MD; M. b.
Clarkston, King and Queen Co., to Richmond age 20, MGF,
MGM b. Clarkston. — Ed.: private school, 1 yr. college,
Farmville. — Baptist. — Well-to-do family. Traditional Virginian, loved and respected but temperamentally democratic
and unself-conscious (not so exclusive as Charlestonians).
Honest about speech. — Slight drawl; vowels otherwise short.
Tempo generally slow; utterance lax and slurred with pervasive trace of delicacy. Vowel of *hot* low-central, slight fronting; no contrast of *barn, born*; *cart, caught* in ordinary speech
but sometimes distinguished when conscious of spelling; /e o/
below cardinal point, slight up-glide with trace of centering;
pharyngealization of /au/ in *down*. — Cultivated.

VA 30D!: Single woman of means (inherited), 83. B. Richmond. — F. b. Goochland Co., came here age 16, PGF, PGF's
F., PGF's PGF b. Ditchley, PGM b. Goochland; M. b. Richmond, MGF, MGF's F., MGF's M. b. Cumberland Co., MGM
b. Richmond, MGM's F. b. Nottoway Co., VA, MGM's M. b.
Hanover Co., VA. — Ed.: Misses Grattans School; Southern
Female Institute. — Presbyterian, Colonial Dames, Woman's
Club. — Lady of old Richmond; bedridden with broken hip,
still alert mentally. Loves to talk about past. Precise manner,
opinionated, but gracious and ladylike. Loyal to Confederacy
but (like family) sympathetic toward North. Her love of conversation and personal naiveté allowed FW to elicit most of
her natural speech forms, despite her schoolteaching experience in past. In lengthened, precise style, her /e o/ have up-
glide followed by slight in-glide. — Cultivated.

VA 30E!: F, housewife, 50. B. Richmond (downtown, present
site of Medical College). — F. b. Richmond, PGF b. Cumberland Co., PGM b. Goochland; M. b. Charlotte Co., came here
as child, MGF b. Charlotte Co., MGF's F. b. Henry Co.,
MGF's M. b. Charlotte Co., MGM, MGM's F., MGM's M. b.
Campbell Co. — Ed.: local private school. — Episcopalian;
Garden Club, Women's Club, Colonial Dames. — Honest, distinctly modern type; full of democratic spirit of present-day
Richmond, where most of old class distinctions have disappeared or grown up along new lines. — Cultivated.

31. Chesterfield County
  Co. formed 1749. 1st settlement "Bermuda Hundred" c.
1613; by 1616 largest town in VA. Iron furnace at Falling
Creek by 1619. Huguenots, some Germans c. 1700. British
depredations 1781. Episcopalians by 1723; Presbyterians by
1745; Baptists by 1770; Methodists by 1775. Chiefly agriculture; coal fields, recent industry, some diamonds (largest gem-
stone found in US found here in 19th cent.). Pop. 1755: 2,039,
1783: 10,846, 1790: 14,214, 1820: 18,003, 1850: 17,489, 1880:
25,085, 1910: 21,299, 1930: 26,049, 1960: 71,197.

Bell, Annie Walker Burns. 1934. *Third Census of the US
  (Year 1810) for the County of Chesterfield*. . . . Washington.

Clarke, Ethel Courtney, comp. 1937. *Chesterfield County,
  Virginia, Records*. . . . Richmond.

Gold, Thomas D. 1914. *History of Clarke County*. . . . Berryville: C. R. Hughes.

Historical Records Survey. 1938. *Inventory of the County Archives of Virginia: Chesterfield County*. Charlottesville.

Kerby, Maude L. 1976. *Midlothian: An American Village, 1776–1976*. Richmond: Williams Job Print.

Lutz, Francis Earle. 1954. *Chesterfield, an Old Virginia County*. Richmond: William Byrd Press.

Weaver, Betti, ed. 1954. *Chesterfield County, Virginia: A History*. Richmond:

Beach P.O., Matoaca Dist.

Puritan colonies in Southside area 1618–40. A small farmer area in 17th cent. Truck farming began c. 1850.

VA 31A: M, farmer, 70. B. here. — F., M. and their parents b. neighborhood. — Ed.: here 3 yrs. — Baptist. — Very old-fashioned in speech. Very short [ăʊ̯] in all positions except [æ̃ʊ̃] before /n/ and [aʌʊ̯] or [æ'ʊ̯] after /n/. Vowel somewhat lengthened in *pod, oxen, cottage, frog* [ɑˑ aʌ]; contrast [ɔ·]. — Incomplete (see VA 31C).

VA 31A*: F, widow, 93. B. here, living with daughter (31C) and son-in-law (31A). — Ed.: day student before 1861 at boarding school situated in neighborhood. — Mind still good, but suffers from deafness. — Guarded speech somewhat more conventional than that of son-in-law or daughter. *Card/cord* fall together in her speech but distinguished in children's.

Midlothian P.O. and Dist.

Huguenots into area 1700. Coal discovered early 18th cent.; mines opened 1709; shut down in 1920s. Widely scattered settlement from the early mining days of colony. Residential community in 1950s.

VA 31B: M, rural letter carrier, 55. B. 6 mi. S. — F., M. and their parents all b. Co. — Ed.: here till 17. — Baptist, Mason. — Quick, intelligent, rather modern. — Precise rapid-fire tempo and articulation. Uses short [ǒʊ] in all positions except beside /n/; no trace of Richmond influence in his diphthong. Boundary of 2 types seems to have existed for some time.

VA 31C: Beach, Matoaca Dist. — F, housewife, 70. — F., PGF, PGM b. Co., PGM's M. b. Dinwiddie Co.; M., MGF, MGF's F., MGF's M., MGM, MGM's F., MGM's M. b. Co. — Baptist. — Wife of VA 31A. When husband tired, wife completed interview (see p. 62). Childless couple, living alone save for wife's M. (VA 31A*); have always lived in neighborhood. — Speech less old-fashioned than husband's except occasionally when off-guard.

32. City of Petersburg

Ft. Henry here by 1645. Est. as a village by Wm. Byrd in 1733; incorporated 1784. Producing flour and tobacco by 1775. Seized by British in battle in 1781. By 1860, one of 10 top US tobacco markets. Important in trading area of Southside VA and part of NE NC. Important RR center (RR by 1832). Much farmland abandoned after 1870. Development of manufacturing and distribution of fertilizer 1870–80. Textiles from 1830s (8 cotton mills by 1834); also small-scale ironworks. AfAm majority throughout most of history until 1910. Pop. 1820: 6,690, 1850: 14,010, 1880: 21,656, 1910: 24,127, 1930: 28,564, 1960: 36,750.

Claiborne, John. 1904. *Seventy-Five Years in Old Virginia*. NY and Washington: Neal Publishing Co.

Davis, Arthur Kyle. 1923. *Three Centuries of an Old Virginia Town*. Richmond: W. C. Hill Print. Co.

Federal Writers Program. 1942. *Dinwiddie County, "The Countrey of the Apamatica"*. Richmond: Whittet and Shepperson.

Harrison, Marion Clifford. 1942. *Home to the Cockade City! The Partial Biography of a Southern Town*. Richmond: House of Dietz.

Henderson, William D. 1977. *The Unredeemed City: Reconstruction in Petersburg, Virginia*. Washington: University Press of America.

Henderson, William D. 1980. *Gilded Age City: Politics, Life, and Labor in Petersburg, Virginia, 1874–1889*. Lanham, MD: University Press of America.

Historical Records Survey. 1939. *Inventory of the County Archives of Virginia: Dinwiddie County*. Richmond.

Hughes, Thomas P., comp. 1975. *Dinwiddie County, Virginia, Data, 1752–1865*. Memphis, TN: Hughes.

Jones, Richard Lyon. 1976. *Dinwiddie County, Carrefour of the Commonwealth*. Dinwiddie: Board of Supervisors of Dinwiddie County

Scott, James G. 1960. *Petersburg's Story: A History*. Petersburg.

VA 32!: F, housewife, 70. B. Petersburg. — F., PGF, PGF's F., PGF's PGF b. Dinwiddie Co., PGF's PGF's F. b. England, PGF's PGF's M. b. just outside present limits of Petersburg, PGF's PGM b. Dinwiddie (her parents b. Prince George Co., of Isle of Wight descent), PGM, PGM's F. b. Amelia Co., PGM's M. b. Nottoway Co.; M., MGF b. Dinwiddie Co., MGF's F. b. Gloucester Co., MGF's PGF, PGM b. Prince George Co., MGM b. Petersburg, MGM's F. b. Co., across line from Sussex Co., MGM's M. b. Surry Co. — Ed.: tutor, private school. — Episcopalian; UDC, DAR, Colonial Dames. — Charmingly cultivated; simultaneously young and modern in spirit and delightfully old-fashioned. Typical Petersburg aristocrat. Very quick, intelligent, obliging, interested; thoroughly natural. — Quick, rapid tempo; precise; centered beginning of /au/ always except beside /n/. — Cultivated.

33. Dinwiddie County

1st settlers 1634; by 1639, land patented at the falls of Appomattox. Huguenot settlers in the 18th cent. Quakers by 1757; Methodists by 1765; Baptists by 1773. Devastation 1864–65. Settlers from Austria-Hungary in 1870. Tobacco principal cash crop; also corn and wheat. Little industry outside Petersburg in 1930s. Pop. 1755: 1,959, 1782: 6,586, 1790: 13,934, 1820: 20,482, 1850: 25,118, 1880: 32,870, 1910: 15,442, 1930: 18,492, 1960: 22,183.

See 32 (City of Petersburg) for bibliography.

VA 33A: Dewitt P.O., Rowanty Dist. — F, housewife, 73. B. 5 mi. N. — F., M. and their parents all b. Co. — Ed.: 15 mos. — Methodist. — Limited advantages; tense family situation (difficult interview). Quick, nervous intelligence; excellent folk inf. — Extremely rapid speech, great energy and breath force, clear-cut consonants, short vowels and diphthongs (reminds FW of speech of similar class in NH).

VA 33B: Aspen Hill Plantation, Dinwiddie P.O., Rowanty Dist. — F, housewife, 47. B. here. — F. b. Dinwiddie Courthouse, PGF, PGM b. Co.; M. b. Co., near McKenny, MGF b. Brunswick Co., MGF's F. b. Brunswick Co., lived in MO and came back, MGF's PGM b. England, MGF's M. b. Brunswick, MGM, MGM's F., M. b. Dinwiddie Co. — Ed.: here till 16. — Methodist. — Intelligent, natural. Her M., still alive, somewhat lady of old school; inf. less cultivated than mother. — Quick, rapid-fire speech of Southside.

34. Prince George County

Est. 1702. Some agricultural settlement c. 1610–13. Riddled in massacre of 1622. Plantations patented from 1617 (Londoners). 1657, oldest Prot. church in America est. here. Almost entirely English or English-Welsh in 17th cent.; Scots after 1707. Church of England dominant till 1776; then Baptists. Slow expansion in 17th cent.; AfAm majority by 1755. As with other tidewater counties, agricultural prosperity peaked by the time of the Revolution; thereafter soil exhausted by tobacco. RRs in 1838, 1858, but no effective port development. Little industry by 1861; occupied by Feds during siege of Petersburg. Decline in agriculture after 1860. Czechs and Slovaks from 1882. Industrial lag after WWI; revival c. 1920. Hopewell developed as industrial center by Du Pont. Pop. 1755: 1,788, 1782: 3,779, 1790: 8,173, 1820: 8,030, 1850: 7,596, 1880: 10,054, 1910: 7,848, 1930: 10,311, 1960: 20,270.

Historical Records Survey. 1941. *Inventory of the Colonial Records of Virginia: Prince George County.* Richmond.
Lutz, Earle. 1957. *The Prince George-Hopewell Story.* Richmond: (Hopewell) Area Historical Committee.
Weisiger, Benjamin B., comp. 1975. *Prince George County, Virginia: Records, 1733–1792.* Richmond: Weisiger.
Writers' Program. 1939. *A Guide to Prince George and Hopewell.* Hopewell: Hopewell News.

Prince George Courthouse, Bland District
Co. seat since 1810.

VA 34A: F, housewife, 66. B. Blackwater Dist., 3 mi. away. — F., his parents and GP, M. and her parents b. here, all of old stock. — Ed.: here till 16. — Methodist. — Limited advantages; insecure; nervously quick, occasionally forgetful. — Rapid tempo; short vowels.

VA 34A*: F, 84. — VA 34A's aunt (M.'s sister). — Somewhat better position in community, but same type of speech.

VA 34B: Newville (crossroads village), Disputanta P.O., Brandon Dist. — F, housewife, 45. B. 2 1/2 mi. from here. — F., PGF, PGM, PGM's F. b. over line in Surry Co.; M., MGF b. here. — Ed.: Newville till 17. — Methodist. — Middle class; frank and honest responses. — Rather quick, precise, rapid-fire speech. Somewhat fronted [əʻʊ] in all positions except beside /n/.

35. Isle of Wight County

Original shire, est. 1634. Puritan settlement from London c. 1619; Puritan stronghold under Commonwealth. Severe losses in Indian massacre in 1622. Few land patents by 1634. Some Quakers arrived 1656; offshoots to E. NC 1663. Area raided by Dutch in 1667. C. 1700 indentured whites replaced by AfAm slaves. Anti-slavery but secessionist; attacked but never occupied in Civil War. Smithfield Academy here from 1829. Chiefly agricultural (to 1940): peanuts, potatoes, cotton. Pop. 1699: 2,766, 1755: 1,776, 1782: 6,708, 1790: 9,028, 1820: 10,118, 1850: 9,353, 1880: 10,572, 1910: 14,929, 1930: 13,409, 1960: 17,164.

Boddie, John Bennett. 1938. *Seventeenth Century Isle of Wight County.* Chicago: Chicago Law Print. Co.
Historical Records Survey. 1940. *Inventory of the County Archives of Virginia: Isle of Wight County.* Richmond.
Morrison, E. M. 1907. *Isle of Wight County: 1608–1907.* Norfolk: Jamestown Tercentenary Exposition.

Mills Swamp, Smithfield P.O., Hardy Dist.
Baptist church at Mills Swamp from 1714. Courthouse at Smithfield from 1750. Small, diversified industry. St. Luke's church here oldest American church with original walls: built 1632; restored 1889.

VA 35A: M, farmer, 75. B. 2 mi. E. — F., PGF, PGF's F. b. here, PGM b. just over line in Surry Co., PGM's F. and M. b. Little Surry, Surry Co.; M. b. Surry Co. (between here and Surry Courthouse), MGF, MGM, MGM's F. and M. b. Surry. — Uneducated. — Pentecostal (Baptist as boy). — PGF's F. was very wealthy, but family has gone down since; inf. always poor, lives in woods. Peaceable community: adventurous ones left for NC 200 yrs. ago; those remaining prefer quiet, well-ordered existence. Inf. quick and bright.

VA 35B: Whitleys Store, Windsor P.O. and Dist. — F, housewife, 44. B. 8 mi. from here at Orbit (5 mi. NE of courthouse). — F., PGF, PGM, PGM's F. b. Co.; M. b. Nansemond Co., near Box Elder, MGF, MGM b. Nansemond Co. (MGM's parents came over from England). — Ed.: Isle of Wight HS till 17 (10th grade). — Christian Church. — Very quick, alert, intelligent; thoroughly enjoyed interview. — Quick, crisp speech; /o/ occasionally very slightly fronted. Inf. reports that many in community have trouble distinguishing /v-/ and /w-/; her only problem is *varmints*, where she has /w-/. Cf. VA 21N and Turner's Gullah records for the following: [-ɾɾ-] for /-t-/, [-ɾɾ-] for /-d-/, [ɾ] for /r/ in *three*. *Card* and *cord* are homonyms.

36. Southampton County

Formed 1748 from Isle of Wight Co. No legal settlement by 1700; earliest settlers English stock from Isle of Wight. Quakers early; Baptists flourished from 1791. Shipping in 18th cent.; decline after Rev. Some anti-slavery sentiment in 1790s. Several minor slave uprisings; major revolt in 1799. Many AfAms went to Liberia after Turner revolt. Little tobacco in early 19th cent., yet Co. primarily agricultural. Sweet potatoes, peanuts important crops by 1870; by 1880 over 1/2 farms cultivated by owners. Timber important after 1856. Unsuccessful RR in 1830s. Some Hungarian immigrants by WWI. In 20th cent. no. of farms decreased, size increased. Some diversification of industry. AfAm majority since 1790. Pop. 1755: 2,009, 1784: 10,239, 1790: 12,864, 1820: 14,170, 1850: 13,521, 1880: 18,012, 1910: 26,302, 1930: 26,870, 1960: 27,195.

Historical Records Survey. 1940. *Inventory of the County Archives of Virginia: Southampton County*. Richmond.

Knorr, Catherine Lindsay. 1955. *Marriage Bonds and Ministers' Returns of Southampton County, 1750–1810*. 2nd ed. Pine Bluff, AR.

Parramore, Thomas C. 1978. *Southampton County, Virginia*. Charlottesville: Southampton County Historical Society.

Tragle, Henry Irving. 1971. *The Southampton Slave Revolt of 1831*. Amherst: University of Massachusetts Press.

Drewryville, Boykins P.O., Capron Dist.

Dist. created in 20th cent. Drewryville had a pop. of less than 1,000 in 1957.

VA 36A: M, farmer, 75. B. 6 mi. W. of here; spent 5 yrs. in Greensville Co. 20 yrs. ago. — F., M. and their parents b. here. — Ed.: very little. — Methodist. — Very patient; somewhat hard of hearing and forgetful (a combination which irritated FW) but endured. — Speech very vigorous, in contrast to that of Northampton Co., NC, just across the line. Shibboleth: North Carolinians say [hwɑ˞ᵊt], Virginians [hwʌᵊt]. Community has strong sense of being Virginian rather than North Carolinian.

Courtland P.O., Jerusalem Dist.

Courtland est. as town and Co. seat 1791; incorporated 1888. A tavern first business in area 1749. RR in 1830s; 1st steamboat 1859. Site of Nat Turner trial. Scattered village with courthouse.

VA 36B: F, housewife (widow), 55. B. here. — F. b. Co., between Courtland and Franklin, PGF b. nearby in NC, came here at 18, PGF's F. b. England, came to NC as a child (Christian name suggests German stock), PGF's M. b. Blackwater R. in Co., PGM b. Co. between Courtland and Franklin, PGM's F. and M. b. Co.; M., MGF, MGM, MGM's F. and M. b. Co. — Ed.: here till 17. — Methodist. — Highly intelligent woman; immediately aware of purpose of each question. Very cooperative.

37. *Nansemond County (now City of Suffolk)*

Formed 1639 from Isle of Wight Co. 1st exploration 1607 by Smith; attempt at settlement as early as 1609 (unsuccessful). Massacre by Indians 1622; punitive raids vs. Indians thereafter. Settled 1632 by Puritans from Isle of Wight; waterfront settlements c. 1635 from London and W. England. Anglicans, Quakers, Independents among early settlers. Courthouse burned in British raid, 1779. Brick making in early 20th cent. Gum and cypress (outlet of Dismal Swamp). Agriculture: cotton, corn, peanuts; also seafood, paper products. Pop. 1699: 2,571, 1755: 2,253, 1787: 5,409, 1790: 9,010, 1820: 10,494, 1850: 12,283, 1880: 15,903, 1910: 26,886, 1930: 22,530, 1960: 31,366.

Burton, Ann H., ed. 1970. *History of Suffolk and Nansemond County, Virginia*. Suffolk: Phelps Ideas.

Cross, Evelyn Huff. 1973. *Nansemond Chronicles, 1606–1800, Virginia Colony*. Richmond: E.H. Cross.

Davis, Margaret. 1934. "Great Dismal" Pictures. *South Atlantic Quarterly* 33:171–184.

Dunn, Joseph B. 1907. *The History of Nansemond County*. Suffolk.

Granbery, Julian Hastings. 1964. *John Granbery, Virginia*. NY: A. G. Walter.

Holland P.O., Holy Neck Dist.

Site of chapel in 1794 which later became Methodist. Nat Turner rebellion in 1831. Small village in agr. country. HQ of Ruritan National, a service club for rural communities.

VA 37: M, farmer, 76. B. here. — F. b. Holland, PGM b. Isle of Wight Co., near Carrsville; M., MGM b. here. — Ed.: very little. — Christian Church. — Rather intelligent, but distinctly limited in awareness of things outside own environment. Rather hard of hearing; could not understand why FW asked him to repeat certain words for their sound (thinks higher education spoils people). — /o/ not particularly front, but many others in Co. use front variety (women more than men); front variety more likely in drawled speech (cf. Gates Co., NC). Forms such as [rʉᵘm] and [hwɑ˞ᵊt] are proto-NC.

38. *Norfolk County (now City of Norfolk)*

Norfolk Co. est. 1634; separated from Princess Anne 1691. Elizabeth City est. 1619 in area. 1st settlers in area chiefly English. 1st ferries 1636, important till very recently. Area assoc. with NC (Dismal Swamp); always first port of VA sighted from S. Important tobacco center 1800–1810; declining importance 1850–60. Pop. 1790: 14,524, 1820: 22,936, 1850: 33,036, 1880: 50,657, 1910: 52,744, 1930: 30,082, 1960: 51,612.

Burton, Harrison W. 1877. *The History of Norfolk, Virginia*. Norfolk: Norfolk Virginian Job Print.

Chambers, Lenoir, and Joseph E. Shand. 1967. *Salt Water and Printers Ink . . . Norfolk and Its Newspapers, 1865–1965*. Chapel Hill: University of North Carolina Press.

Emmerson, John Cloyd, Jr., comp. 1948. *Some Fugitive Items of Portsmouth and Norfolk County History*. Portsmouth.

Fleet, Beverley, ed. 1948. *Lower Norfolk County, 1651–1654*. Richmond.

Forrest, William S. 1853. *Historical and Descriptive Sketches of Norfolk and Vicinity*. . . . Philadelphia: Lindsay and Blakiston.

James, Edward Wilson, ed. 1895–1906. *The Lower Norfolk County, Virginia Antiquary*. 5 vols. Baltimore: Friedenwald Co.

Lamb, Robert W., ed. 1887–88. *Our Twin Cities of the Nineteenth Century: (Norfolk and Portsmouth)*. . . . Norfolk: Barcroft

Moore, Gay Montague. 1949. *Seaport in Virginia: George Washington's Alexandria*. Richmond: Garrett, Massie.

Nowitzky, George I. 1888. *Norfolk, the Marine Metropolis of Virginia, and the Sound and River Cities of North Carolina*. Norfolk: G. I. Nowitzky.

Porter, John W. H. 1892. *A Record of Events in Norfolk County, from April 19th, 1861, to May 10th, 1862. . . [those] Who Served in the Confederate States Army or Navy*. Portsmouth: W. A. Fiske.

Read, Helen Calvert Maxwell. 1970. *Memoirs*. Ed. by Charles R. Cross, Jr. Chesapeake: Norfolk Historical Society.

Schlegel, Marvin Wilson. 1951. *Conscripted City: Norfolk in World War II*. Norfolk: Norfolk War History Commission.

Stewart, William H. 1902. *History of Norfolk County, Virginia, and Representative Citizens*. 2 vols. Chicago: University of Chicago Press.

Stewart, William H. 1902. *History of Norfolk County, Virginia, and Representative Citizens*. Chicago: Biographical Pub. Co.

Walter, Alice Granbery, ed. 1967. *Vestry Book of Elizabeth River Parish, 1749–1761*. NY.

Wertenbaker, Thomas J. 1931. *Norfolk: Historic Southern Port*. Durham, NC: Duke University Press.

1934. *St. Paul's Church, 1832, Originally the Borough Church, 1739, Elizabeth River Parish, Norfolk, Virginia*. Norfolk: Altar Guild of St. Paul's Church.

1936. *Through the Years in Norfolk. . . .* Norfolk: Norfolk Advertising Board.

VA 38: Deep Creek. — M, clerk in Navy Yard, 43. B. here. — F. b. Portsmouth, VA, PGF b. Pitt Co., NC, came here at 18, PGM b. Gloucester Co., VA; M., MGF b. Deep Creek, MGF's F. b. here (descended from 1st settler, 1682), MGF's M. b. here, old stock, MGM b. DC (MGM's F.'s family from Princess Anne Co., MGM's M.'s family of old DC stock). — Ed.: h.s. Deep Creek, extension courses William and Mary. — Ancestors Baptists and Methodists; Virginia Historical Soc., Norfolk Soc. of Arts. — Intelligent and honest, but a bit slow in reactions. — Tempo rapid; vowels short; falling together of vowels of *barn*, *pasture* with those of *born*, *law*, yielding slightly rising rounded diphthong with lower low-back beginning; this varies greatly in length and tongue position, perhaps because of spelling-consciousness and attempt to distinguish sounds not really distinguished. A shorter, low-central unrounded vowel in *not*. Striking open diphthongs: *dough* and *door* never alike. [v] most natural realization of both /v/ and /w/. Everybody agrees that inf. uses natural speech of older generation, uncontaminated by outside contacts.

39. City of Norfolk

Town authorized 1680; site purchased 1682; survey complete 1688. Chartered 1736. Many early settlers from Princess Anne Co.; mostly English, some Holland Dutch. Active seaport; many sailors. Large artisan class from the beginning. 1st products timber and naval stores (no local tobacco); port for NE NC. Shipping pt. for W. Indian trade, many Scots merchants. Burned by British fleet and Amer. looters in 1776, suffered severely. 1st church St. Paul's, built 1640. Norfolk Academy est. 1728. Industry in early 19th cent. Dismal Swamp Canal opened 1814; 1st RR authorized 1834. Surrender of Norfolk 1861. Water system est. 1872; sewers 1887. By 1880, chief VA port (esp. cotton). Naval base in WWI. Peanuts, truck farming, shipping, resort trade. Largest city in VA. Pop. 1820: 8,478, 1850: 14,326, 1880: 21,966, 1910: 67,452, 1930: 129,710, 1960: 305,872.

See 38 (Norfolk County) for bibliography.

VA 39!: F, artist, 47. B. Norfolk, spent 1 mo. or more each summer in Wytheville (SW VA). — F. b. Norfolk, PGF, PGF's F. b. Nansemond Co. (plantation people) near Suffolk, PGF's PGF b. Isle of Wight Co., PGF's PGM b. Williamsburg, came here as very small child, PGM b. Petersburg, PGM's F. of Scotch descent; M. b. Hampton, came here as very small child, MGF b. Portsmouth, MGF's F. and M. b. Hampton, MGM b. Gloucester Co., lived in Hampton, MGM's F., M. b. Gloucester Co. — Ed.: Leache-Wood Seminary (defunct). — Episcopalian; art assoc. — Trustworthy, cultivated informant. — Somewhat self-conscious cultivated atmosphere. Homonymy of *card*/*cord* and similar pairs. — Cultivated.

40. Princess Anne County (now City of Virginia Beach)

Formed 1691 from Lower Norfolk. 1st settlers English. 1st parish church 1639. Tory depredations 1777. Naval installations. Recently developed as a resort area and bedroom suburb of Norfolk. Seafood. Pop. 1699: 1,971, 1755: 1,720, 1783: 6,655, 1790: 7,793, 1820: 8,768, 1850: 7,669, 1880: 9,394, 1910: 11,526, 1930: 16,282, 1960: 76,124.

Kellam, Sadie Scott. 1931. *Old Houses in Princess Anne, Virginia*. Portsmouth: Printcraft Press.

Mason, George Carrington, ed. 1949. *The Colonial Vestry Book of Lynnhaven Parish. . . .* Newport News.

VA 40A: Back Bay, Pleasant Ridge Dist. — F, housewife, 81. B. 1 1/2 mi. from here. — F. b. Co.; M. b. near Charity Church, in Co., MGF, MGM b. Co. — Ed.: 3 years "a little". — Methodist. — Rugged Christian folk speaker, rural. Very clear mind, good responses, though many things outside her experience. Difficult interview, because of suspicious son and grandson. — [hwaʌt] rather than typical VA [hwʌᵊt]; [ɚ] with lateral spreading, rather than usual American lateral contraction; [ß] usual for both /w/ and /v/; [æ̆ʊ] used before /-n/; [æʊ] in other positions not a natural sound but an unnatural intrusion.

Back Bay, Pungo Dist.

Early English settlement in Dist. 1st farming in Co. Oysters.

VA 40B: M, student, 18. B. here. — F, PGF, PGF's F., PGF's PGF b. here (Scotch descent), PGF's M. b. Co., west of the river, PGM, PGM's F. b. Co., PGM's M. b. northern part of Co.; M., MGF, MGF's F. b. here, MGF's M. b. Co., MGM b. Co., MGM's F. b. Pasquotank Co., NC, MGM's M. b. Co. — Ed.: freshman, Norfolk branch, William and Mary (now old Dominion U.). — Baptist. — Speech completely different from that of Norfolk; some similarities to that of Knott's Island (NC 1). [FW was referred to inf.'s parents, but both had tooth defects; son's dialect so genuine FW used him.] Very cooperative; genuine local speech. [ɚ] somewhat labialized: begins almost unretroflex [perhaps [ɜɚ] or [ɔɚ] would be more accurate]; somewhat opener than usual one; lacks lateral constriction of most American dialects; has lateral spreading characteristic of most English dialects. /w/ and /v/ distinguished only in conscious speech. Deliberate tempo.

41. Goochland County

Formed 1727 from Henrico Co. Tuckahoe House (Randolph) possibly oldest residence of note and size in VA. Coal discovered 1701; mined beginning 1740. Huguenots in 18th cent. Pop. 1755: 1,504, 1782: 4,466, 1790: 9,053, 1820: 10,007, 1850: 10,352, 1880: 10,292, 1910: 9,237, 1930: 7,953, 1960: 9,206.

Wight, Richard Cunningham. 1935. *The Story of Goochland*. Richmond: Richmond Press.
1962. *Facets of Goochland County's History*. Richmond: Dietz Press.

VA 41A: Hadensville (named for prominent family) P.O., Byrd Dist. — M, farmer, 80. B. 5 miles E. — F. b. near Columbia, Fluvanna Co., came here when 1 yr. old, PGF b. here, PGF's F. of French Huguenot descent, PGM b. here, probably Huguenot descent; M. b. here, MGF b. near Scottsville, Albemarle Co., MGM b. Fluvanna Co. — Very little education. — Christian Church. — Rather intelligent uneducated old man, though deafness hampered interview. Natural. — Has [əʊ] in *cow, houses*: only place north of James where it has turned up in Piedmont.

Tabscott, Kents Store P.O., Byrd Dist.
Gold-bearing quartz discovered early in Tabscott.

VA 41B: M, farmer, 54. B. 1 mi. away, when 22 spent 1 yr. in Louisa Co. — F., PGF, PGM, M., MGF b. here. — Ed.: here till 18 (limited). — Baptist. — Good middle-class person (though some of family once aristocratic). Limited experience, but obliging. — Not very rapid speech. Characteristic Piedmont treatment of /au/ allophones.

42. Buckingham County

Formed 1761 from Albemarle Co. 1st explored c. 1700. Plantations early; small farms later. Baptists from 1772. Iron works, misc. minerals; gold and iron by 1860. Copper, dark tobacco, cattle and sheep. Pop. 1782: 3,919, 1790: 9,779, 1820: 17,569, 1850: 13,837, 1880: 15,540, 1910: 15,204, 1930: 13,315, 1960: 10,877.

Bell, Annie Walker Burns, comp. 1934. *Third Census of the US (Year 1810) for the County of Buckingham. . . .*Washington.
Goldstone, Robert L. 1953. *Historical Geography of Scottsville*. University of Virginia Master's thesis.
Hess, Karl. 1973. *Four Decades of Change: Scottsville, Virginia, 1820–1860*. University of Virginia Master's thesis.
Maloney, Eugene A. 1976. *A History of Buckingham County*. Dillwyn: Buckingham County Bicentennial Commission.
Moore, Virginia. 1969. *Scottsville on the James*. Charlottesville: Jarman Press.
Pennington, Margaret A., and Lorna S. Scott. 1977. *"The Courthouse Burned"*. Waynesboro: Charles F. McClung.

Wingina P.O. (Nelson Co.), James River Dist.
RR station and store at Wingina.

VA 42A: M, farmer, 75. B. 8 mi. south. — F., PGF b. here (Irish descent), PGM b. here; M. b. just across line in Appomattox Co., MGM b. Appomattox Co. — Illiterate. — Baptist. — Pleasant, good natured, good character. Quick and intelligent. Family poor before 1861, didn't feel it was their fight; inf. recognized that only freeing of slaves made it possible for his family to own land and improve their lot (atypical reaction of his class). — Completely natural speech; has heard no other kind than his own; moderate tempo, not very careful enunciation.

VA 42A*: Slate River Dist. — F, 80. — Uneducated. — Poor background.

Mt. Tabor, Scottsville P.O. (Albemarle Co.), Slate River Dist.
Scottsville settled by Edward Scott 1732. In Albemarle Co., but trade magnet for Buckingham. Courthouse for Albemarle Co. here 1744–62. Chief upland port in 1750s; tobacco, prosperous fishing. Tobacco warehouse at ferry on James by 1792. Incorporated 1818. Raided and pillaged by Sheridan 1865. Turnpike and canal traffic rivaled Charlottesville in first part of 19th cent., until introduction of RR. US rubber plant here 1944.

VA 42B: F, housewife, 61. B. near Diana Mills, 8 mi. from here. — F., PGF b. near Buckingham Courthouse, PGM b. Buckingham; M. b. near Buckingham Institute, MGF, MGM b. co. — Ed.: private teacher. — Baptist. — Woman of aristocratic old family with few present advantages; lives quietly at home.

43. Cumberland County

Formed 1749 from Goochland Co. Early settlers chiefly English, some Quakers. Also some Scots. Little settlement to 1727. Agricultural (tobacco county); declining pop. Decline in Episcopalians since Rev.; Presbyterians by 1743; Methodists by 1750; Baptists by 1777. Gold in early 19th cent. Some Germans and other out-of-state immigrants in 20th cent. Pop. 1755: 2,098, 1782: 6,552, 1790: 8,153, 1820: 11,023, 1850: 9,751, 1880: 10,540, 1910: 9,195, 1930: 7,535, 1960: 6,360.

Hopkins, Garland Evans. 1942. *Colonel Carrington of Cumberland*. Winchester: Privately issued.
Hopkins, Garland Evans. 1942. *The Story of Cumberland County*. Winchester: Privately issued.
Vaughan, M. K. 1969. *Crucible and Cornerstone — A History of Cumberland County*. Atlanta: Southern Regional Education Board.
1935. *Today and Yesterday in the Heart of Virginia*. Farmville: Farmville Herald.

VA 43N: Cumberland Courthouse, Madison Dist. — M, farmer, 86. B. on plantation near here. — F., M. and their parents (all slaves) b. on neighboring plantations. — Uneducated. — Baptist. — Intelligent, independent farmer (fairly successful; many contacts with whites, so that speech less old-fashioned than some). — Tempo rather rapid, variable; lax articulation. [ɐʊ] in all positions except [aʊ] before /n/; not as central or as front as that in speech of local whites. /e o/ monophthongal, higher than that among whites; tends to use pure vowels. Generally distinguishes /w f v θ ð/, but sounds often labialized. Good deal of variety in articulation of various phonemes, perhaps because of dialect mixture in family.

Ca Ira, Guinea Mills P.O., Madison Dist.
Plantation country. Grace Church here oldest in Co.

VA 43A: M, farmer, 68. B. here; kept bar 1 yr. at Cumberland Courthouse. — F., PGF, PGM b. here, PGM's F. b. Amelia Co.; M., MGF, MGM b. Co. — Ed.: c. 12 mos. altogether. — Methodist. — Poor; a bit slow but sound in reactions; given to digressions on state of world. — [aʊ] before /n/. Rather clear-cut, well-articulated speech.

VA 43B: Guinea Mills, Madison Dist. — M, farmer, 64. B. here. — F. b. here, PGF b. Scotland, came here when young, PGM b. here; M. b. 2 mi. away, MGF b. here, MGF's F. came from Scotland, MGM b. here. — Ed.: till 18. — Presbyterian. — Family almost only prominent one that remained and made a success of farming after 1865. Quick, intelligent. — Speech quick, brisk; vowels and diphthongs tend to be short; [əʊ˰] in all positions except next to /n/.

44. Appomattox County

Formed 1845 from 4 other cos. English predominant; also some Germans, French, Irish, Scots, and Welsh. Baptists from 1772. Pop. 1850: 9,193, 1880: 10,080, 1910: 8,904, 1930: 8,402, 1960: 9,148.

> Featherston, Nathaniel Ragland. 1948. *The History of Appomattox, Virginia.* . . . Appomattox: American Legion Post 104.
> Stanley, Vera Smith. 1965. *A History of Appomattox County, 1845–1965: Appomattox County, Past, Present, Future.* Appomattox: Times-Virginian.

VA 44A: Wesley Chapel, Appomattox Depot P.O., Southside Dist. — F, housewife, 74. B. near Pamplico in Co., here last 52 yrs. — F. b. Campbell Co., just over line, PGF b. Campbell Co., PGF's F. Welsh, PGM b. Buckingham Co.; M., MGF b. near Pamplico, MGF's F. "Dutch", MGM b. Co., MGM's F. English, MGM's M. b. Powhatan Co. — Genuine old-fashioned inf.; talkative and congenial, but not aware of purpose of questions. Honest, intelligent answers. — Fairly slow; words tend to be lengthened; initial dark [ɫ].

VA 44B: Evergreen, Southside Dist. — M, merchant, postmaster, 65. B. 2 mi. from here. — F., M., MGF, MGM b. here. — Ed.: here till 16. — Baptist, Woodmen of the World. — Friendly, quick, bright, local middle-aged type. — Rather quick tempo and short vowels. Occasionally uses a faint trace of postvocalic retroflexion, chiefly after /a/; FW unsure whether natural survival or spelling pronunciation; doesn't seem characteristic of other speakers.

45. Prince Edward County

Formed 1753 from Amelia Co. 1st settlers English (from coast) and Ulster Scots (from PA). Some Huguenots (from Manakin), Welsh, and Lowland Scots. Many Dissenters. Presbyterians from 1740; Baptists c. 1768. 1787–1878 plans and attempts to open the Appomattox for navigation: expensive, usefulness lost when Southside RR completed 1854. Coal discovered 1833; mined (small scale) 1837–87; also marl, copper. Agricultural experimentation, esp. with strains of fruits and grapes. Self-sufficient farming by 1861. Devastation in last throes of Confederacy, 1865. Spring Creek colony from England revived Episcopal church in 1874. Public school enrollment 2/3 AfAm c. 1890. German immigrants (Lutherans and Roman Catholics) c. 1900. Tobacco principal money crop. Mechanization of agriculture as farm pop. declines. Other industries: dairying, forest products, shoes, pulpwood. Pop. 1755: 826, 1783: 3,020, 1790: 8,100, 1820: 12,577, 1850:

11,857, 1880: 14,668, 1910: 14,266, 1930: 14,520, 1960: 14,121.

> Bradshaw, Herbert Clarence. 1955. *History of Prince Edward County, Virginia.* . . . Richmond: Dietz Press.
> Burrell, Charles Edward. 1922. *A History of Prince Edward County, Virginia.* . . . Richmond: Williams Print. Co.
> Douglas, James W. 1828. *A Manual for the Members of the Briery Presbyterian Church.* . . . Richmond. Repr. 1971 (Memphis, TN: owned by Mrs. George W. Harian).
> DuBois, W. E. B. 1898. The Negroes of Farmville, Virginia: A Social Study. *US Labor Department Bulletin* 3.14:1–38.
> Eggleston, Joseph Dupuy. 1928. *Prince Edward County, Virginia.* Farmville: Farmville Herald.

VA 45A: Throck, Darlington Heights P.O., Hampden Dist. — F, housewife, 67. B. here. — F., M., and their parents b. here, old stock Presbyterians. — Ed.: here till 12. — Presbyterian. — Quick, nervous little woman of least affluent class; satisfied with lot, doesn't believe in modern ways of living and speaking. Believes in sticking to old names for things whether she's called old-fashioned or not. Discerning and discriminating quick mind, though of limited experience. Kindly. — Extremely quick, rapid speech; short vowels and often very short diphthongs. Has two phonemes in traditional /aʊ/ range (FW never encountered this before): [ðʊ˰] in [hðʊ˰s hðʊzɪ˰z], and [æ˰ʉ] in [bæ˰ʉ˰nd]. She uses [ðʊ] regularly in *houses*, but this is the only word where FW found it before voiced. Cf. [θæ˰ʉzənd]: proof of phonemic contrast in her speech.

Rice P.O., Lockett Dist.

Meeting house for Dissenters at Rice by 1775. Sailor Creek Church here 1781. Short-lived Union Baptist church. Rice's Depot a P.O. after RR built. Fighting here in Appomattox campaign. 1st public school diplomas in Co. 1908.

VA 45B: M, farmer, county supervisor, 54. B. here. — F., PGF b. here, PGM b. Cumberland Co.; M., MGF b. here, MGM b. Amelia Co. — Ed. till 17. — Presbyterian. — Middle-aged man; more or less old-fashioned speech. Moderate intelligence, rather self-conscious about revealing himself.

46. Campbell County

Formed 1781 from Bedford Co. 3 groups of settlers: Presbyterians from PA 1742 (also some Baptists); Quakers at least from 1757 (though many left 1835–37 because of the slavery issue); Anglicans, at least by 1750 (New London est. 1757). Eventually settlers from MD and PA; English, Scots, Irish, Welsh, some Germans and Huguenots. New London Academy from 1798; RRs in 1850s. Tobacco country; also fruit, ironworks. Pop. 1782: 2,366, 1790: 7,685, 1820: 16,569, 1850: 23,245, 1880: 36,250, 1910: 23,043, 1930: 22,885, 1960: 32,958.

> Armstrong, Thomas Field. 1975. *Urban Vision in Virginia.* Ann Arbor: University Microfilms.
> Cabell, Margaret Couch (Anthony). 1858. *Sketches and Recollections of Lynchburg: By the Oldest Inhabitant.* Richmond: C. H. Wynne.

Christian, William Asbury. 1900. *Lynchburg and Its People.* Lynchburg: J. P. Bell Co.

Cornelius, Roberta D. 1951. *This History of Randolph-Macon Woman's College from the Founding in 1891 through the Year of 1949–1950.* Chapel Hill: University of N.C. Press.

Early, Ruth Hairston. 1927. *Campbell Chronicles and Family Sketches.* . . . Lynchburg: J. P. Bell Co.

Halsey, D. P. 1935. *Historic and Heroic Lynchburg.* . . . Lynchburg.

Scruggs, Philip Lightfoot. 1973. *Lynchburg, Virginia.* Lynchburg: J. P. Bell.

Yancey, Rosa Faulkner. 1935. *Lynchburg and Its Neighbors.* Richmond: J. W. Fergusson.

Alta Vista, Otter River Dist.

Alta Vista a thriving town in SW part of Co. Many Quakers early, though sect not influential as a group. James River bateaux: important for trade. Water power. 1st rayon-weaving plant in VA. Also cedar works (cedar chests), cotton mills, wood products, warehouses. Pop. 1930: 2,367, 1960: 3,299.

VA 46N: M, farmer, c. 70. B. here. — Local family. — No information on education. — Baptist. — Not too helpful.

Lynch Station, Otter River Dist.

Scots and English settlers early. Station est. with completion of Lynchburg and Danville. Incorporated as a town 1884; charter inactive 1900.

VA 46A: F, housewife, 72. B. foot of Johnson's Mtn. — F. b. here, PGF b. here, of Irish descent, PGM b. Bedford; M. b. here, MGF, MGM b. Bedford. — Ed.: here a few sessions. — Baptist. — Motherly woman of fairly good folk stock, unsophisticated. — Little drawl; articulation fairly clear.

Lynchburg

Est. 1786 around the John Lynch ferry; incorporated 1805. Many Quakers in early days. Center of SW Piedmont; tobacco market from outset. Turnpike from 1817; canal by 1840; 1st RR by 1852 (many Irish came in with RR work). Cotton mill in 1834. Boom in 1850s. Iron industry: small-scale, unsuccessful. VA Theological Seminary and College est. 1888; Lynchburg College 1903. Reliance on tobacco till 1890s; no successful diversification till then. Machinery, shoes, textiles, clothing.

VA 46B!: F, housewife, music teacher (voice), c. 55. B. Lynchburg. — F. b. Co., near Marysville, came to Lynchburg when 27, PGF, PGF's F. b. Co., PGF's M. b. KY and came back, PGM, PGM's F. and M. b. Co.; M., MGF b. Lynchburg, MGM, MGM's F. b. Co., MGM's M., MGM's MGF and MGM b. Charlotte Co., MGM's MGM's M. of illustrious family. — Ed.: Lynchburg public schools, Randolph-Macon College for Women. — Methodist, Women's Club, musical organizations, social welfare organizations. — Fairly intelligent. Singing makes her enunciation somewhat clearer, but she tried to relax and be natural; cooperative. — Loss of /-t/ in *aunt, saint,* etc. may indicate influence of Negro servants. — Cultivated.

47. Lunenburg County

Co. formed 1745–46 from Brunswick Co. Area 1st explored c. 1650. 1st settlers from Lower Piedmont (esp. Prince George Co.); mainly English, Scots, some Huguenots (from Manakin); also some Ulster Scots from PA. All in all, few settlers in 18th cent.; land sales through speculators. Presbyterians by 1746; Baptists by 1766 (flourished); Methodists around time of Rev. In 1738, VA legislature promoted SW settlement; area became a way station for SW settlement. Road to Richmond laid out 1811. Pop. 1755: 2,112, 1782: 4,156, 1790: 8,959, 1820: 10,662, 1850: 11,692, 1880: 11,535, 1910: 12,780, 1930: 14,058, 1960: 12,523.

Bell, Landon C. 1927. *The Old Free State: A Contribution to the History of Lunenburg County and Southside Virginia.* 2 vols. Richmond: William Byrd Press.

Bell, Landon C., ed. 1931. *Sunlight on the Southside: Lists of Tithes, Lunenburg County, 1748–1783.* Philadelphia: George S. Ferguson Co.

Bell, Landon Covington. 1972. *Lunenburg County, Virginia Wills, 1746–1825.* Berryville: Virginia Book Co.

Elliott, Katherine B., comp. 1967. *Early Wills, 1746–1765.* South Hill.

Keysville P.O., Pleasant Grove Dist.

Dist. in NW part of Co. Keysville a tobacco market (actually in Charlotte Co., but near line).

VA 47: M, farmer, 80. B. just over line in Charlotte Co., came when 3 to place about 1 mi. from here. — F., PGF b. here, PGM b. near Lunenburg Courthouse; M. b. 5 mi. from here in Charlotte Co., MGF, MGM b. Charlotte Co. — Ed.: mighty little. — Baptist. — Very bright; quick, rapid, precise articulation.

48. Pittsylvania County

Formed 1767 from Halifax Co. Largest VA Co. 1st explored 1670; settlement slow. Grants to Byrd by 1735; inducements to settle in 1738 brought PA Quakers, Germans, and Ulster Scots (many moved on to Carolinas, where less Indian trouble). Scotch Presbyterians by 1755. Church of England disappeared after 1778; revived 1846. Also Baptists, Methodists. River traffic prosperous till 1860s (some till past WWI). Tobacco mfg.; concentrated in Danville after 1850. Pop. 1782: 7,139, 1790: 11,579, 1820: 21,323, 1850: 28,796, 1880: 52,589, 1910: 50,709, 1930: 61,424, 1960: 58,296.

Cahill, Mary, and Gary Grant. 1977. *Victorian Danville.* Danville: Womack Press.

Clement, Maud (Carter). 1958. *The Turn of the Wheel: Sketches of Life in Southern Virginia, 1756–1956.* Danville: J. T. Townes Ptg. Co.

Clement, Maud Carter. 1929. *The History of Pittsylvania County, Virginia.* Lynchburg: J. P. Bell Co.

Hagan, Jane Gray. 1950. *The Story of Danville.* NY: Stratford House.

Hairston, Lora Beatrice Wade. 1955. *A Brief History of Danville, Virginia, 1728–1954.* Richmond: Dietz Press.

VA 48A: Pullens Old Store, Climax; Chatham P.O., Pigg River Dist. — F, farmhand, take-in-worker, 66. B. Climax (formerly Red Eye), worked on various farms in Co. — F. b. here; M. b. between here and Chatham, MGF, MGM b. here. — Ed.: none (brother taught her to read and write). — Primitive Baptist. — Quick, active; very clear mind but entirely ignorant of outside world. Of good but impoverished family; worked in fields as a child. Most unselfconscious inf. FW had ever encountered, and most mentally alert of any uneducated inf., grasping exactly what he meant and not having to fumble for responses. — Speech genuinely old-fashioned. Note: [ʋˌɝ] in *corn*, [ɡˤˑ] in *barn*, [ɡᶿ] in *rock*.

Danville

Formed 1793; chartered 1833. Built on Dan River; began as planned community. English, Scots, some Germans among settlers. Turnpike from 1830; RR at least by 1856. Presbyterians by 1826; Episc. by 1840; Baptists, Methodists, Disciples shortly thereafter. Confed. supply base 1861–65. Tobacco, cotton; 1st textile mills 1881.

VA 48A*: (West of Danville). — M, farmer, Confederate veteran, 89. B. here. — F. b. here, PGF b. Halifax Co., PGF's F. of "Dutch" descent, PGM b. NC; M., MGF, MGM b. here. — Ed.: here till 13–14. — Has attended all the old Confederate reunions. — Old-fashioned.

VA 48B: Concord Church, Chatham P.O. and Dist. — F, housewife, 62. B. here. — F., PGF b. here, PGF's F. b. Halifax Co. (of Scotch-Irish descent), PGM b. NC; M. b. between here and Chatham, MGF b. here (Scotch-Irish descent), MGM b. here. — Ed.: here till 13–14. — Baptist. — Satisfied middle-aged type. — Rather front articulation.

49. Halifax County

Formed 1752 from Lunenburg Co. Grants from 1746; earliest settlers chiefly English, some Scots. Many went on to W. and SW. Episcopal church oldest; Baptists by 1773. In 1840, largest slaveholdings in VA (14,216). Much illiteracy even into 1920s. Intensive agriculture; water power, copper and gold, mineral springs. Pop. 1755: 770, 1782: 8,625, 1790: 14,722, 1820: 19,060, 1850: 25,962, 1880: 33,588, 1910: 40,044, 1930: 41,283, 1960: 33,637.

Carrington, Wirt Johnson. 1924. *A History of Halifax County*. Richmond. Repr. 1969 (Baltimore: Regional Pub. Co.).

Edmunds, Pocahontas Wight. 1978. *History of Halifax*.

Knorr, Catherine L. 1957. *Marriage Bonds and Ministers' Returns of Halifax County, 1753–1800*. Pine Bluff, AR.

Mathis, Harry, ed. 1964. *Along the Border*. Oxford, NC: Coble Press

Morrison, Alfred J. 1907. *Halifax County: A Handbook....* Richmond: Everett Waddey Co.

Scottsburg, Roanoke Dist.

Market village; tobacco warehouses. Methodist church. Normal College 1890–1910, became h.s.

VA 49A: M, farmer, 62. B. here. — F. b. here, PGF b. Portugal, came to Norfolk as young sailor and settled here, PGM b. here, of old VA stock; M., MGF, MGM b. here. — Ed.: here, very little. — Baptist (never goes to church). — Hard-working small farmer, barely avoiding poverty. Very

quick and intelligent, though without knowledge of outside world. Liked FW, cooperated, though not fully understanding importance of work. Very old-fashioned; never leaves home, even to go to town. — In conversation, consistently has [aˑˑ] for [æə] in all positions.

Younger Store Community, Halifax P.O., Meadville Dist.

W. part of Co. Youngers an old family. Meadesville Presbyterian Church here since 1880.

VA 49B: F, housewife, 48. B. 4 mi. away, near Meadville, came here when married. — F., PGF b. here, PGM b. near News Ferry, nearby; M., MGF, MGM b. here. — Ed.: Meadville, private school corresponding to h.s. — Methodist. — Quick, reserved, religious; well-bred but rather plain. Like middle-class Northern women in her belief in education. Of upper group in her community, but not aristocratic. Cooperative. — Speech prob. more careful than that of most people (better educated); thoroughly natural and honest.

50. Mecklenburg County

Formed 1765 from Lunenburg Co. Many Scotch-Irish, English among early settlers. Presbyterians, Methodists, Baptists in 18th cent.; Episcopalians meager by 1820s. Tobacco roads to Roanoke River. Roanoke Canal 1812–34; fell into disrepair after RRs came in. Horse breeding. One of richest VA cos. to 1861; then decline. Mineral springs, tobacco and tobacco factories, copper and gold. Pop. 1782: 11,324, 1790: 14,733, 1820: 19,786, 1850: 20,630, 1880: 24,610, 1910: 28,956, 1930: 32,622, 1960: 31,428.

Alexander, Charles. 1907. *Mecklenburg County, Virginia: Its History, Resources and Advantages*. Boydton.

Bracey, Susan L. 1977. *Life by the Roaring Roanoke*. Boydton: Mecklenburg County Bicentennial Commission.

Elliott, Katherine B., comp. 1962. *Early Settlers, Mecklenburg County, Virginia*. South Hill: DAR.

VA 50A: Reeks Mills, Chase City P.O., Buckhorn Dist. — M, farmer, 76. B. South Hill (2 1/2 mi. north of here), came here age 2. — F. b. between here and South Hill, PGF, PGM b. NC; M., MGF b. here, MGF's F. of Welsh descent, MGM, MGM's F., MGM's PGF b. here (ancestors had large grant from king). — Ed.: here till 14. — Baptist. — Quick-speaking, nervously conversational. Moderate intelligence; not sure of purpose of interview; somewhat inclined to conceal archaisms. — Tempo rapid; vowels and diphthongs short. Treatment of [æʊ] like Brunswick, Lunenburg, and E. Prince Edward Cos.; sharply different from that of the middle-aged inf. who represents the regional type of Halifax Co., VA, and the one in Warren Co., NC.

VA 50B: Finchley neighborhood, Boydton P.O. and Dist. — F, 58. B. here. — F., PGF, PGM, M., MGF, MGM, MGM's F., MGM's M. b. here. — Ed.: till 20 (h.s. in Boydton). — Baptist. — Cooperative. — Treats [æʊ] as in Halifax Co., VA, unlike the old-fashioned inf. in this co., who has the Brunswick Co. type.

51. Brunswick County

Formed 1720 from Prince George Co. 1st recorded explorations c. 1640. 1st land grant 1715; earliest settlers from E. VA, later Ulster Scots from PA. Settlement slow. Not really suitable for plantation culture: no good port for marketing tobacco. Methodists, Presbyterians, and Baptists by 1775. Several pre-Rev. homes survive. Small raids in Civil War. Still predominantly rural; some tobacco, but diversification; reforestation (pulp wood, wooden pallets). Pop. 1755: 2,275, 1782: 6,449, 1790: 12,827, 1820: 16,687, 1850: 13,894, 1880: 16,707, 1910: 19,244, 1930: 20,486, 1960: 17,779.

Bell, Annie Walker Burns, comp. 1934. *Third Census of the US (Year 1810) for the County of Brunswick.* . . . Washington.

Bell, Edith Rathbun, and William Lightfoot Heartwell, Jr. 1957. *Brunswick Story.* Lawrenceville: Brunswick Times-Gazette.

Knorr, Catherine Lindsay. 1953. *Marriage Bonds. . . of Brunswick County, 1750–1810.* Pine Bluff, AR.

Neale, Gay. 1975. *Brunswick County, Virginia, 1720–1975.* Lawrenceville: Brunswick County Bicentennial Committee.

Ebony P.O. and Dist.

Store, school, and horserace track here c. 1820. P.O. unmanned after 1865: no one would take oath.

VA 51A: M, farmer, 82. B. Rock Shore, 20 mi. NE in Co., to Ebony age 18; 1923–30 in Roanoke Rapids, NC, across line. — F., M. and their parents b. Co. (MGM's family of Irish descent). — Ed.: none. — Methodist. — Quick, bright though illiterate; very naive. — Although only 1/2 mi. from NC, strong in assertion of being [fɛˈdʒɪnəmən]. High, monophthongal /o/, open [ɐʊ æʊ]. Possibly NC influence?

Gholsonville, Meherrin Dist.

Gholsonville named for prominent local family; spreads along the highway.

VA 51B: F, housewife, 62. B. near Valentines, in Co. — F. b. Gholsonville, PGF, PGM b. Lawrenceville; M., MGF b. Co. (MGF an overseer), MGM b. Co. (some Irish ancestry). — Ed.: country school here till 20. — Methodist. — Middle class. — Very lax articulation. — Completed interview when 51C lapsed.

VA 51C: F, widow, 55. — Biog. and family history not obtained; interview interrupted when elderly tenant took FW for rival suitor. — Good local background but unsophisticated. — Slight drawl, lax articulation. Has Petersburg [əʊ] in general, but not always a short sound (cf. similar diphthong in speech of old-fashioned inf. in W. part of Halifax Co., NC).

52. Frederick County

Formed 1738 from Orange Co. Shen. Valley settled primarily from PA. Quaker (Hopewell Friends meeting by 1734) and German settlements by 1731; many Ulster Scots by 1738. Also some English. Roads est. by 1740s; fortifications in 1756. Earliest church Presbyterian in 1736; Lutherans by 1760. Winchester (est. 1738) changed hands 9 times during Civil War period. Products and industries: apples, flour, dairy products, lumber, limestone. Pop. 1755: 2,513, 1782: 5,553, 1790: 19,681, 1820: 24,706, 1850: 15,975, 1880: 17,553, 1910: 12,787, 1930: 13,167, 1960: 21,941.

Bell, Annie Walker Burns, comp. 1934. *Third Census of the US (Year 1810) for the County of Frederick.* Washington.

Cartmell, Thomas Kemp. 1909. *Shenandoah Valley Pioneers and Their Descendants.* Winchester: Eddy Press.

Cartwell, T. K. 1909. *Frederick County.* Winchester: Eddy Press.

Norris, J. E., ed. 1890. *History of the Lower Shenandoah Valley Counties.* . . . Chicago: A. Warner.

Pickeral, John Julian, and Gordon Fogg. 1930. *An Economic and Social Survey of Frederick County.* Charlottesville: University of Virginia.

1936. *Hopewell Friends History, 1734–1934, Frederick County, Virginia.* Strasburg: Shenandoah Pub. House.

Chestnut Grove, Gainesboro P.O. and Dist.

Gainesboro a hamlet; Methodist church. Quaker meeting house here 1777.

VA 52A: M, farmer, 71. B. here. — F., PGF, PGF's F. b. here (German descent); M., MGF, MGM, MGM's F. b. here, MGM's M. b. near Capon, Hampshire Co. (now WV). — Ed.: till 18. — Southern Methodist. — Old-fashioned mountaineer, perhaps better ed. than average of his generation.

Brucetown, Stonewall Dist.

Brucetown a hamlet with an old Methodist church. Tavern here c. 1745. Village once noted for flour mills; also woolen mill at one time.

VA 52B: F, housewife, 50. B. here. — F. b. Warren Co., PGF of English descent, PGM b. Warren Co.; M., MGF b. Clark Co. — Ed.: till 16 here; 2 yrs. Valley Female College, Winchester; 1 yr. Presbyterian College, Winchester. — Methodist. — Obliging but inwardly resisting. Refined person in straitened circumstances. — Speech well-bred; desire to "improve" speech.

Opequon, Shawnee Dist.

Grants to Friends in 1730, 1732, 1735; 1st actual Quaker settlement 1731 in E. part of Co. Also some Ulster Scots. Hopewell monthly meeting by 1734; Presbyterian church by 1736 (one of oldest churches in valley). Union sympathizers.

VA 52C!: F, housewife, 55. B. Opequon, lived about 1 1/2 mi. from Winchester during most of childhood, after marriage spent many winters in Richmond and Norfolk, and 3 yrs. in SC. — F. b. Round Hill in Co., PGF b. Co., PGF's F. b. Westmoreland Co., England, and came via NJ, PGM b. Co. (Scotch-Irish descent); M. b. Greenwood in Co., MGF b. Co., MGF's F. b. England and came to Charles City Co., MGM b. Opequon, MGM's F. b. Ireland (Ulster), MGM's M. b. Ireland (Scotch-Irish). — Ed.: Old Fairfax Hall, Winchester. — Episcopalian. — Feels need to keep playing part of a lady; well and naturally done. — Cultivated.

53. Shenandoah County

Formed 1772 from Frederick. 1st settlement 1734: English from MD. Indian raids 1758. "German regiment" raised in 1776 by Peter Muhlenburg. Much fighting 1861–65. Germans largest group; language survived through 1962. Early settlers Mennonites, Lutherans, Reformed; others later. Iron works to 1900. Agriculture, stock raising. Pop. 1783:

8,255, 1790: 10,510, 1820: 18,926, 1850: 13,768, 1880: 18,204,
1910: 20,942, 1930: 20,655, 1960: 21,825.

> Sherman, Mandel, and Thomas R. Henry. 1933. *Hollow Folk*. NY: Thomas Y. Crowell.
>
> Wayland, John W. 1927. *A History of Shenandoah County, Virginia*. Strasburg: Shenandoah Pub. House.
>
> Wayland, John W. A Chronology of the Shenandoah Valley. *Rockingham Recorder* 1:157–77, 237–57, 293–316.

Stony Creek, Basye P.O., Ashby Dist.

Stony Creek orig. contained a fort against Indians. Primarily German village; United Brethren church here by 1828.

VA 53A: M, farmer, 82. B. near Shenandoah Alum Springs, 2 mi. from here. — F. b. here, PGF of German descent; M. b. here, MGF of Irish descent. — Illiterate. — Lutheran. — Rather willing and intelligent but somewhat feeble with age. — Articulation not very distinct; [aᵛ·ʊᵥ aᶜ·ʊᵥ] indicate old-fashioned uneducated speech (prob. Scotch and German in origin), as compared to cultivated [æ·ʊ], which prob. was introduced by Quakers and other English settlers of the Valley.

Mt. Jackson, Ashby Dist.

An old Indian road ran through Mt. Jackson. Laid out during War of 1812; est. as town 1826. Earliest settlers English and Irish in 1734; Germans later. Crossroads trading center; original terminus of Valley RR.

VA 53B: M, farmer, 56. B. here. — F., PGF b. Rockingham Co., PGM b. Timberlake, Rockingham Co. (possibly of German descent); M. b. 2 mi. W., MGF, MGF's F. b. here, MGM b. Timberlake, Rockingham Co. — Ed.: 2 yrs., Mt. Jackson HS, till 20. — Lutheran; director of farm bureau and bank. — Middle-class successful farmer; typical Valley German, without veneer of cultivation but intelligent. — Slow, mumbling, somewhat self-conscious manner; slurred utterance; /ju/ normal after /t d n/ except when *new* is followed by initial /j/, as in *New York* and *New Year*, where /nu/ occurs.

54. *Warren County*

Formed 1836 from Frederick and Shenandoah Cos. Settled by English from E. VA; also many Germans. Pop. 1840: 5,627, 1850: 6,607, 1880: 7,399, 1910: 8,589, 1930: 8,340, 1960: 14,655.

> Wayland, John Walter, ed. 1930. *Virginia Valley Records*. Strasburg: Shenandoah Publishing House.

VA 54A: Browntown, South River Dist. M, farmer, 62. B. here. — F. b. here, PGF b. Rappahannock Co., just over mtns. (of Dutch [ultimately Long Island Holland Dutch] and Indian descent), PGM b. here, MD Irish descent; M., MGF b. here, MGM b. here (1st cousin of PGM), MD Irish. — Ed.: till 17–18, short terms. — Church of God, PGM's family Dunkards (United Brethren). — Friendly, isolated mountaineer; hearty, vigorous; knew FW a gentleman, glad to have company, invited FW to spend night. Quick to answer all questions, but prob. didn't grasp purpose; ignorant of outside world. — Tempo rather rapid; vowels rather short.

Rockland, Success P.O., Cedarville Dist.

Quaker-led settlement one of earliest in Cedarville area.

VA 54B: M, farmer, stock dealer, 44. B. Front Royal. — F. b. Cedarville, PGF b. Montgomery Co., MD (Scotch-Irish), PGM b. Cedarville, PGM's F. of Scotch-Irish descent; M., MGF b. Middletown, Frederick Co. (German descent), MGM b. Middletown. — Ed.: Richland, Cedarville, Front Royal and prep school at Front Royal. — Methodist. — Good, successful farmer; satisfied. Helpful, intelligent, but without intellectual curiosity. — Speech modern, not emphatic; clear.

55. *Rockingham County*

Formed 1778 from Augusta Co. Possibly German and Swiss settlers as early as 1726. Settlers predominantly German; some Ulster Scots, some Quakers (many Quakers moved on, some to IN). Presbyterians, Lutheran, Reformed by 1750; Baptists by 1756. Least settled of Valley by 1776. Tobacco tried briefly; gave way to wheat. Germans largest group, language still alive in 1960s. Burned and pillaged by Sheridan in 1864; many records lost. After Civil War, flour milling, wood products, coal, clay products, lead, marble; iron foundries. Pop. 1783: 6,832, 1790: 7,449, 1820: 14,784, 1850: 20,294, 1880: 29,567, 1910: 34,903, 1930: 29,709, 1960: 40,485.

> Harrison, John Houston. 1935. *Settlers by the Long Grey Trail*. . . . Dayton, VA: Joseph K. Ruebush Co.
>
> Hess, Nancy B. 1976. *The Heartland's? "Rockingham County"*. Harrisonburg: Park View Press.
>
> May, Clarence Edward. 1976. *Life under Four Flags in North River Basin of Virginia*. Verona: McClure.
>
> Wayland, John W. 1912. *A History of Rockingham County*. Dayton, VA: Ruebush-Elkins Co.
>
> Wayland, John W., ed.-in-chief. 1943. *Men of Mark and Representative Citizens of Harrisonburg and Rockingham County, Virginia*. Staunton: McClue Co.
>
> Wayland, John Walter. 1949. *Historic Harrisonburg*. Staunton: The Author.
>
> 1945–. *The Rockingham Recorder*. Dayton, VA: Rockingham Historical Society.

Rawley Springs Rd., Harrisonburg P.O., Denton Dist.

Harrisonburg est. as town and co. seat 1780. 1st settler arrived c. 1737 from Long Island. Heavy German settlement; also some Ulster Scots early. Methodist and Presbyterian groups by 1789. Diversified industry by 1820. City charter by 1849. Trading center; RR from 1870. Madison College. Center of Valley; fruits, poultry, dairy products, livestock, air conditioning equipment, pottery. Pop. 1880: 2,831, 1910: 4,879, 1930: 7,232, 1960: 11,916.

VA 55A: M, farmer, 72. B. here. — F., PGF b. here, PGF's F. from Germany, settled Shenandoah Co., VA, PGM b. here; M. b. here, MGF, MGM b. Page Co. (all of German descent). — Ed.: till 20. — Presbyterian. — Moderately intelligent; cooperative, sociable, glad to sit up late to answer questions. — Tempo rather rapid; articulation not too precise. *Horse* and *hoarse* types close together but distinct. Some people in community have strong [ɚ·], like those in MD, DE, and PA.

Dayton, Ashby Dist.

Fort located at Dayton from 1748. Episcopal chapel as early as 1778; Presbyterians later. Town chartered 1833. Shenandoah Seminary (1876) later became a jr. college and conservatory. Publishing after 1878 (Shenandoah Press). Carriages and harness co., 1898–1926. Small industries.

VA 55A*: F, housewife, 82. B. here. — F., M. and their parents b. here. — Ed.: limited. — Mennonite. — Typical German Hausfrau. Spoke "Dutch" before English, but only English in last 15 yrs. Likes to be busy all the time. — Very nasal before nasal consonants, esp. in German. In speaking English, voiced /b d g/ and aspirated [pʰ tʰ kʰ] clearly differentiated. In [daɪtʃ], initial and final voiceless sounds only, generally indicated as [b̥ d̥ g̊] before vowels, although before voiceless sounds and finally often as [p t k]; no distinction. (In other words, FW uses [b̥ d̥ g̊] for unvoiced, not necessarily voiceless sounds; here they are fully unvoiced.) In a few words, however (not all have the spelling in German, by any means), aspirated [pʰ tʰ kʰ] occur; FW doesn't know whether from English influence or from some German dialect which distinguishes the sounds.

VA 55B: Harrisonburg. — F, housewife, 62. B. here. — F. b. KY, returned as infant, PGF b. Frederick Co. (Welsh descent), PGM b. Frederick Co.; M., MGF b. here, MGF's F. Huguenot and Scotch-Irish descent, MGM b. here. — Ed.: here, public schools. — Presbyterian. — Superior local type.

56. Highland County

Formed 1847 from Pendleton and Bath Cos. 1st exploration c. 1727; stockade here 1755, though comparatively little Indian trouble. Rapid pop. increase after 1783. Settlers largely Scotch-Irish and German, English less common. First churches Presbyterian and German Reformed (1780s), Methodists by 1832; others later (but no Baptists). Road-building early 19th cent. Unionist in sympathies, but economic ties to E. VA. Near geographic center of old VA; center of Appalachian uplift, between Shenandoah and Allegheny Mtns. Hilly. Many springs, limestone and clay, hardwoods, buckwheat, maple sugar, apples. Pop. 1850: 4,227, 1880: 5,164, 1910: 5,317, 1930: 4,525, 1960: 3,221.

Morton, Oren F. 1922. *A Handbook of Highland County....* Monterey: The Highland Recorder.

Morton, Oren Frederick. 1911. *A History of Highland County.* Monterey: The Author.

Crabbottom, Blue Grass Dist.

Gap in Back Creek Range. 1st settler 1761; German settlement in 18th cent. Crabbottom a local trading center. Good grazing, prosperity. Fertile limestone soil. Pop. 1939: 100.

VA 56A: M, farmer, 71. B. here. — F. b. here, PGF of German descent; M. b. here. — Ed.: here, little. — M. was Methodist. — Genial, quick, hearty, restless, rather intelligent.

Pisgah, High Town P.O., Bluegrass Dist.

Pisgah a rural settlement. High Town on watershed between James and Potomac.

VA 56B: F, housewife, 54. B. Monterey. — F., PGF b. here, PGF's F. b. Co. (Scotch descent, via PA), PGF's M., PGM b. Co. (both Scotch-Irish); M. b. here, MGF, MGF's F. b. Co. (Irish descent — prob. Scotch-Irish — from Tyrone), MGF's M., MGM b. Pochahontas Co. (now WV). — Ed.: Monterey till 18. — Presbyterian. — Middle-aged, fairly intelligent, rather progressive and modern.

57. Augusta County

Formed 1738 from Orange. Earliest settlers c. 1726–32; some from Ireland via PA. Rapid settlement; primarily Ulster Scots at first, but German spoken into 1960s. Indian troubles in 1750s. Presbyterians from 1738 (center of frontier Presbyterianism); Anglicans from 1746; Methodists, German Baptists, Lutherans later 18th cent. Turnpike from at least 1847; RR from 1854. Several major academies by 1860. Occupied by Feds and devastated in 1864. Pop. 1755: 2,313, 1782: 2,493, 1790: 10,886, 1820: 16,742, 1850: 24,610, 1880: 35,710, 1910: 32,445, 1930: 38,163, 1960: 37,363.

Cleek, George Washington. 1957. *Early Western Augusta Pioneers.* Staunton.

Hotchkiss, Jedediah. 1885. *Historical Atlas of Augusta County, Virginia.* Chicago. Repr. 1980 (Chicago: Waterman, Watkins).

Kemper, Charles Edward. Historical Notes from the Records of Augusta County, Virginia. *Lancaster Historical Society* 25:89–92.

Peyton, John Lewis. 1882. *History of Augusta County.* Staunton: S. M. Yost.

Ruffin, Beverley. 1970. *Augusta Parish, Virginia, 1738–1780.* Verona: McClure Press.

Waddell, Joseph Addison. 1886. *Annals of Augusta County. . . .* Richmond. Repr. 1958 (Bridgewater: C. J. Carrier Co.).

Wilson, Howard McKnight. 1954. *The Tinkling Spring, Headwater of Freedom.* Fishersville: Tinkling Spring and Hermitage Presbyterian Churches.

1964–. *Augusta Historical Bulletin.* Staunton: Augusta County Historical Society.

VA 57A: Sherando, Lyndhurst P.O., South River Dist. — F, housewife, 79. B. here. — F. b. here, PGF b. Switzerland, came to PA, PGM b. Germany, came to PA; M. b. New Hope in Co., MGF b. Co., MGF's F. of Scotch-Irish descent, MGF's M. of English descent, MGM b. here ("Dutch" descent). — Ed.: taught herself to read; 4 1/2 days in school; read Bible through 12 times in successive yrs. — Methodist. — Timid, obliging, old-fashioned.

Stuarts Draft, South River Dist.

Stuarts Draft founded pre-Rev. Monadnock formation. P. O. and village 8 mi. from Staunton in 1882. Old order Amish; German still used. Also Scots settlers; Presbyterian church 1890. Mtn. resort in 1950s.

VA 57B: F, housewife, 64. B. here. — F., PGF b. here, PGF's F. b. Ireland (Scotch-Irish), PGM, PGM's F. b. Nelson Co.; M., MGF, MGF's F. b. here (prob. Scotch-Irish descent), MGM, MGM's F. b. Rockbridge Co. (of Scotch-Irish descent). — Ed.: here till 20. — Presbyterian. — Reserved, pious. — Speech timid, weak but determined.

58. Greene County

Est. 1838. Pop. 1840: 4,232, 1850: 4,400, 1880: 5,830, 1910: 6,937, 1930: 5,980, 1960: 4,715.

VA 58: Shiflett Hollow, Mission Home P.O., Monroe Dist. — M, farmer, 73. B. on Greene-Rockingham Co. line (4 mi. from Albemarle). — F. b. Bakins Hollow in Co. (5–6 mi. away), PGF b. Co.; M. b. Co., MGF's F. a Rev. soldier (possible French ancestry). — Illiterate. — Doesn't attend church; United Brethren, Dunkard, and Christian in neighborhood. — Good repute, self-supporting; friendly to Episcopal mtn. mission, but never felt like belonging to a church. Grew up on crest of Blue Ridge and saw only 2 people outside his family until he was grown. Never understood purpose of interview, but decided FW was harmless. — Enunciation not particularly clear; tends to substitute /f/ for /θ/ and /d/ for /ð/ in all positions; /w-/ for /v-/ in *very*. Some Valley characteristics in speech; cf. Nelson Co.

VA 58*: See Albemarle County below.

59. Albemarle County

Formed 1744 from Goochland Co. Settled from tidewater via lower Piedmont. Many early settlers from Ulster Scots PA migration. 1st grants 1727–37, including Henry and Jefferson families. Stronghold of independence and liberalism; cultural center. Many old mansions remain. Tobacco culture lasted briefly; replaced by grain near end of colonial period. Towns slow to develop; agrarian orientation. Some iron c. 1800. Slight AfAm majority 1810–80. 1st purely vocational school in the US here 1878. 19th cent. center for scientific agriculture. Presbyterians early; Baptists most numerous denomination in 20th cent. Soapstone, slate, small amounts of nonferrous metals. Home of Albemarle pippin, famous apple; also peaches, grapes. Some light industry; textiles. Pop. 1755: 2,091, 1782: 5,317, 1790: 12,585, 1820: 19,747, 1850: 25,800, 1880: 32,618, 1910: 29,871, 1930: 29,981, 1960: 30,969.

Alexander, James. 1942. *Early Charlottesville: Recollections. . . 1828–1874.* Charlottesville: Michie Co.

Bruce, Philip Alexander. 1920–22. *History of the University of Virginia, 1819–1919.* 5 vols. NY: Macmillan.

Coddington, Anne Bartlett. 1936. *Genealogical Index to The History of Albemarle County, Virginia by Rev. Edgar Woods.* Philadelphia: Magee.

Federal Writers Program. 1941. *Jefferson's Albemarle. . . .* Charlottesville: Jarman.

Mead, Edward Campbell. 1899. *Historic Homes of the South-West Mountains, Virginia.* Philadelphia: J. B. Lippincott.

Moore, John H. 1976. *Albemarle: Jefferson's County, 1727–1976.* Charlottesville: University Press of Virginia.

Murphy, Mary Catherine, comp. 1924. *Historical Guide to Albemarle County, 1783–1852.* Charlottesville: Albemarle D. A. R. and Colonial Dames.

Norford, William Lindsay. 1956. *Marriages of Albemarle County and Charlottesville, 1781–1929.* Charlottesville.

Rawlings, Mary. 1925. *The Albemarle of Other Days.* Charlottesville: Michie Co.

Rawlings, Mary. 1935. *Ante-Bellum Albemarle.* Charlottesville: Peoples National Bank.

Seamon, W. H. 1888. *Albemarle County.* Charlottesville: Jefferson Book and Job Printing House.

St. Claire, Emily Entwisle. 1932. *Beautiful and Historic Albemarle.* Richmond: Appeals Press.

Watts, Charles Wilder. 1948. *Colonial Albemarle.* University of Virginia Master's thesis.

Woods, Edgar. 1901. *Albemarle County in Virginia.* Charlottesville: Michie Co.

1941–. *The Magazine of Albemarle County History.* Charlottesville: Albemarle County Historical Society.

VA 58*: Doylesville, White Hall Dist. — F, housewife, 80. B. Burns Cove in Albemarle Co., always lived in mtns. nearby. — F. b. Free Union in Albemarle Co.; M. b. Burns Cove in Albemarle Co. — Illiterate. — Very primitive; reactions so slow that FW gave up. FW thinks she is representative of many whites. — No essential difference in speech from nearby AfAm inf. (VA 59N). Articulation very lax.

Batesville, Samuel Miller Dist.

W. part of Co. 1st local land grant 1737. Miller Manual Labor School here (since 1878).

VA 59N: M, farmer, 80. B. here; away a few months at a time. — F., PGF, PGM b. here; M. b. here, MGF b. Goochland Co., MGM b. here. — Ed.: none. — Baptist, loyal and devoted, deacon 40 yrs. — Extremely valuable inf.; understood purpose, glad to cooperate. — Deeply resonant voice; otherwise general phonetic pattern not different from that of white people in community. Chief difficulty: communicating abstract notions. Pronunciation varies; can pronounce [ð]; remembers older AfAms always substituted [d], occasionally substitutes [d̪] or [d] in unstressed words, and FW believes he once heard it in a stressed syllable. Varies between [ɪ˞] and [ə˞] in some words, notably *the* before consonants, possibly indicating imperfect acquisition of English by foreign-speaking people. Distinction between [ʌ] and [ɝ˞ə] often difficult to hear. Vowels tend to be not very long, but may be prolonged. Tempo fairly rapid; nasalization noticeable at times. Articulation of final consonants weak; much slurring. Distinction between *cod* and *card* largely matter of length, but *cod* more central; [ɛ˞] very high, might be written [e˞] at times, but always distinguished from [e e˞] allophones of /e/ phoneme.

Cismont, Rivanna Dist.

Village took name from Cismont Manor in 1890s. Old rural church here.

VA 59A: F, housewife, 46. B. here. — F., PGF, PGM, PGM's F. b. Stony Pt.; M., MGF b. Stony Pt., MGM b. Cowlesville (nearby), MGM's F. b. nearby. — Ed.: here till 16. — Baptist. — Average sort of person, at present in poor circumstances, doing sewing for the "quality" (F. had been respectable superintendent on one of larger places). — Has become self-conscious about speech since many of her clients come from other places. Moderate tempo. Slightly fronted /o/ indicates PA-MD Valley influence.

Dunlora, Charlottesville P.O. and Dist.

Charlottesville est. 1762; Co. seat from beginning. Town chartered 1801; city chartered 1888. 1st settlers 1735. U. of VA est. 1825. 1st church in town consecrated 1826.

University city; little industry. Dunlora contained a colony of free AfAms c. 1865.

VA 59B!: F, housewife, 54. B. here. — F., PGF b. near Scottsville, PGF's F. b. Co., PGF's PGF b. New Kent Co., PGM b. Co., PGM's F. of English descent, PGM's M. b. here (Scotch-Irish stock, first Valley settlers to Albemarle); M. b. here, MGF, MGF's F. b. Louisa Co., MGF's M. b. Louisa Co. (Scotch-Irish descent), MGM b. Scotland (her parents sojourning there), MGM's F. b. Scotland, MGM's M. b. Fredericksburg, VA. — Ed.: here, Piedmont Female Institute; 1 yr. art school in Washington. — Episcopalian; Garden Club, Literary Club. — Aristocratic background; quick and intelligent. Somewhat affected manner of style and speech. Occasionally hesitant before pronouncing a certain sound just as she thought it should be. — Only noticeable distortion of speech from affectation is [æɜ:] or [aɜ:] for [æ] and [æɪ]. Very proud of pronunciations such as [čjaʼɑˤrə] and [jˡˌɜˤəɪ], which have been carefully preserved. Moderately slow tempo; tendency to prolong vowels. Enunciation very precise at times, lax at others. — Cultivated.

60. Bath County

Formed 1790 from several cos. Distinctly Scotch-Irish flavor. 1st settler 1744; many early settlers from PA, MD. Surveys 1745–46, 1750. Most early settlers Presbyterians; 1st church 1752. Indian troubles 1753–63; many settlers moved on to NC. Villages didn't develop till later. Divided loyalties in Civil War. 2 cultures: 1) older farming and stockraising, 2) resort-tourist (with service labor from outside Co.). Lead mines. Many mineral springs, have remained fashionable resorts. Pop. 1800: 5,508, 1820: 5,231, 1850: 3,426, 1880: 4,482, 1910: 6,538, 1930: 8,137, 1960: 5,335.

Brock, Robert A. 1884. *Hardesty's Historical and Geographical Encyclopedia. . . Special Virginia Edition.* NY: H.H. Hardesty and Co.

Morton, Oren F. 1917. *Annals of Bath County.* Staunton: McClure Co.

Burnsville, Williamsville Dist.

Ebbing spring here; intermittent. Early settlement: Scotch, Welsh, English.

VA 60: M, farmer, 80. B. here. — F. unknown; M., MGF b. here (MGF's F. of Scotch-Irish descent), MGF's M. b. here, MGM, MGM's F. b. Rockingham. — Ed.: 10 mos. — Methodist. — Humble, good-natured, unassuming jack-of-all-trades. — Slight whimper.

VA 60*: Dry Run, Burnsville P.O., Williamsville Dist. — F, widow, 72. B. here. — F., PGF b. here (of Scotch-Irish descent), PGM b. Rockingham Co. of Scotch-Irish descent; M. b. Augusta Co., came here as a child, MGF b. PA, German descent, MGM b. Augusta Co., of German descent [although MGF, MGM spoke "Dutch", M. learned to speak English from a AfAm girl who worked for them]. — Ed.: here, 1 term. — Methodist. — Timid. — Old-fashioned, rough speech.

61. Rockbridge County

Formed 1777 from Botetourt and Augusta Cos. 1st important grant 1739; many early settlers from NJ. Predominantly

Scotch-Irish (2/3 of first settlers); also many Germans (some German still spoken). Indian raids 1742–65. Remained more rural and agriculturally oriented than rest of Valley. Presbyterians from 1740s; Co. still largely Presbyterian. Highways in 1820s. Flax and linen into 19th cent. Much Union sympathy; opposed secession. Center of iron making, but still primarily agrarian: tend to big farms and cattle. Last grist mill closed 1969. Tourism recently: Shenandoah Natl. Park, Shenandoah Natl. Forest, Natural Bridge Natl. Forest. Pop. 1782: 1,226, 1790: 6,528, 1820: 11,945, 1850: 16,045, 1880: 20,003, 1910: 21,171, 1930: 20,902, 1960: 24,039.

Allan, Elizabeth Preston. 1903. *The Life and Letters of Margaret Jankin Preston.* NY and Boston: Houghton, Mifflin and Co.

Boley, Henry. 1936. *Lexington in Old Virginia.* Richmond: Garrett and Massie.

Couper, William. 1939. *One Hundred Years of VMI.* 4 vols. Richmond: Garrett and Massie.

Crenshaw, Ollinger. 1969. *General Lee's College.* NY: Random House.

Diehl, George West. 1971. *Old Oxford and Her Families.* Verona: McClure.

Lee, Susan Pendleton. 1893. *Memoirs of William Nelson Pendleton.* Philadelphia: J.P. Lippincott.

Letcher, John Seymour. 1974. *Only Yesterday in Lexington, Virginia.* Verona: McClure.

Lyle, Royster, Jr., and Pamela Hemenway Simpson. 1977. *The Architecture of Historic Lexington.* Charlottesville: Historic Lexington Foundation.

McClung, James W. 1939. *Historical Significance of Rockbridge County, Virginia.* Staunton: McClure Co.

McCulloch, Ruth Anderson. 1972. *Mrs. McCulloch's Stories of Ole Lexington.* Verona: McClure Press.

Morton, Oren F. 1920. *A History of Rockbridge County, Virginia.* Staunton: McClure Co.

Tompkins, Edmund Pendleton. 1952. *Rockbridge County, Virginia: An Informal History.* Ed. by Marshall Fishwick. Richmond: Whittet and Shepperson.

Turner, Charles W. 1977. *Stories of Ole Lexington.* Verona: McClure Press.

1939–. *Rockbridge Historical Society Proceedings.* Lexington: The Society.

Whistle Creek, House Mtn., Kerrs Creek Dist.

1st settlement in dist. c. 1740; one early mill still operating in 1950. Presbyterian church as early as 1750. Damaging Indian raids 1759, 1763. One-time carding factory.

VA 61A: M, truck driver for cleaning and pressing company, 53. B. neighborhood, in Lexington last 35 yrs. — F., M. and their parents b. House Mtn., to west of Lexington. — Little ed. — Methodist; Moose. — Good inf. and very cooperative, but slow reactions; exhausted FW (see 61A*). — Tempo moderately slow; vowels not particularly long. Not much slurring, but weak final articulation. Difficult at times to distinguish between [aᵊ] and [ɒᵊ], or [ɨ] and [ə˞]; [d] for [ð] from inf. never in contact with AfAms suggests German or Irish influence.

Lexington

Est. 1777 as Co. seat. Incorporated 1841. Strongly Presbyterian. Known as "Athens of VA": intellectual society with regard for books. Serious fire 1796: lottery for rebuilding. Washington College became Washington and Lee University in 1812; state arsenal became VMI 1839. In some sense a college town.

VA 61B!: M, hardware merchant, 54. B. Timber Ridge Church area; in town since 1900. — F., PGF b. Co. (Scotch-Irish ancestor at old Timber Ridge Church, 1756), PGM b. Co., old Anglo-Irish (Ulster) stock, family came 1770; M., MGF, MGM b. Co. — Ed.: till 16 or 17. — Presbyterian, Kiwanis, Mason. — Refined, cultivated, local person of better old Scotch-Irish families (related to Mrs. R. B. McCormick of Chicago). — Quiet, rapid speech. — Cultivated.

VA 61C: Kerrs Creek. — M, farmer, 76. B. WV but brought here at age 2, here ever since. — F. b. nearby in Augusta Co., PGF, PGM b. Augusta Co. (both German); M., MGF b. Lexington (Scotch-Irish), MGM b. Lexington, MGM's F. b. Lexington (German), MGM's M. b. Ireland (Roman Cath.). — Ed.: here till 16. — Presbyterian. — Friendly, but suffering from old age. — Tempo moderate.

62. Nelson County

Est. 1807. Pop. 1810: 9,684, 1820: 10,137, 1850: 12,758, 1880: 16,536, 1910: 16,821, 1930: 16,345, 1960: 12,752.

Claiborne, J. G. 1925. *Nelson County.* Lynchburg: Brown-Morrison Co.

Jones, Maupin. 1929. *University of Virginia.* Richmond: County School Board.

Dutch Creek, Rockfish P.O., Elma Dist.

Staunton-Charlottesville Rd. in Rockfish (C&O tunnels underneath).

VA 62A: F, housewife, 77. B. here. — F. b. here, PGF, PGM b. here or from down the James (PGM Irish descent); M., MGF b. here (Scotch descent), MGM of English descent. — Ed.: Elma (pay school) one session. — Methodist. — Rather slow tempo with drawl, causing prolongation of all vowels; FW had not encountered phenomenon east of here; reminded him of PA or NC. Fronted /a/ as in Louisa Co.; /au/ like Greene and Augusta Cos.

VA 62A*: Saunders, Lovingston Dist. — M, farmer, 82. B. here. — F., M. b. here. — Illiterate. — Some travel. Fairly good family, comfortable circumstances. FW stopped because inf. slow and unwell. — [kɐˤʊ̴], [hɐˤʊ̴zɪz], but also [hæʌuˢzɪ̴z]. *Redworm.*

VA 62B: Nellysford, Rockfish Dist. — M, farmer, 55. B. Avon (3 mi. below Afton), came here at age 25. — F. b. Wintergreen, 2 mi. above here, PGF, PGM b. Co.; M. b. Bryants in Co., MGF, MGM b. Co. — Ed.: Avon till 16. — Baptist. — Typical better-class, middle-aged farmer, fairly well-to-do (wife somewhat better family). Rather casual manner, as if nothing mattered. — Lax articulation; nasalization.

63. Craig County

Est. 1851. Harried by Feds in 1864. Pop. 1860: 3,553, 1880: 3,794, 1910: 4,711, 1930: 3,562, 1960: 3,356.

Craigs Creek, Newcastle P.O., Barbours Creek Dist.

Craigs Creek/Newcastle settled by 1750s; one of earliest settlements in area. Named for Presbyterian missionary of 1760s. School here 1846.

VA 63A: M, farmer, 80. B. 1 mi. away. — F. b. Barbours Creek, PGF b. Co., PGM b. Rich Patch on Blue Spring Run (Alleghany Co.); M. b. 1 mi. from here, MGF b. Monroe Co. (now WV), MGM b. Sweet Springs, Monroe Co. (just over line), MGM's F. from Tuckahoe, VA, stock. — No ed. — M. was Dunkard. — Intelligent. — Quick speech.

VA 63B: Paint Bank P.O., 9th Dist. — F, housewife, 73. B. 3 mi. W., near Paint Bank. — F. b. Rich Patch, Alleghany Co., PGF, PGM b. Alleghany Co.; M. b. here (all lines apparently German). — Ed.: Paint Bank till 18. — Christian. — Mtn. woman of the PA-WV type. — Speech very plain, matter-of-fact, homely, coarse, vigorous. Inability to voice /t/ in many words suggests German or other foreign influence.

64. Bedford County

Formed 1754 from Lunenburg and Albemarle Cos. Settlers from E. VA, Shenandoah Valley; primarily English, Ulster Scots. Church of England here by 1762; also Presbyterians. Baptists by 1770; others later. Schools all private till late 19th cent. Canal and RR both by c. 1850. Some plantations; cotton and flax, tobacco money crop. Grazing, timber cut off; minerals, water power. Diversified manufacturing: aluminum, pulp, paper, asbestos. Pop. 1755: 500, 1783: 7,150, 1790: 10,531, 1820: 19,305, 1850: 24,080, 1880: 31,205, 1910: 29,549, 1930: 29,091, 1960: 31,028.

Ackerly, Mary Denham. 1930. *"Our Kin".* Lynchburg: J. P. Bell Co.

Parker, Lula Eastman. 1954. *The History of Bedford County.* Bedford: Bedford Democrat.

1907. *Historical Sketch of Bedford County.* Lynchburg: J. P. Bell Co.

Battery Creek, Big Island P.O., Charlemont Dist.

Pulpwood, paper important industries.

VA 64A: F, housewife, 83. B. here. — F., PGM, M., MGF, MGM, MGM's F. b. here. — One yr. free school when they started (she was 21). — Baptist. — Remarkably young for age; moves gracefully, thinks and acts without effort. Hard-working, never defeated (even when taking care of very ill husband). Calm, serene, made interview easy for FW, though no perceptible intellectual interest. — Natural folk speaker.

VA 64B: Red Lands Farm, Peaks Road, Bedford P.O., Central Dist. — F, housewife, 59. B. Flint Hill in S. part of Co.; lived near Moneta, S. part of Co., in early childhood. — F., M., and their parents b. Co. — Ed.: Moneta. — Baptist (church-worker). — Comfortable middle-class person (type that has risen to dominance since Civil War). — Tendency to constant drawl, with caressing intonation.

65. Roanoke County

Formed 1838 from Botetourt Co. 1st settlement 1740s; earliest settlers Scots, English, Germans from Shen. Valley and E. VA. Also a few French. Forts on Indian frontier in 1750s. Presbyterians predominant in 18th cent.; Baptists c. 1780, Methodists slightly later. Tobacco early, farming became diversified, smaller farms (apples). Hollins College 1842 (1st women's college in VA); Roanoke College 1853. Strongly secessionist vote 1860. Medicinal springs, iron and copper ore; land boom 1880s. Pop. 1840: 5,499, 1850: 8,447, 1880: 13,105, 1910: 19,623, 1930: 35,289, 1960: 61,693.

> Federal Writers Program. 1942. *Roanoke, Story of County and City*. Roanoke: Stone Print. Co.
> Hoffer, Frank William. 1928. *Public and Private Welfare, Roanoke, Virginia*. Roanoke: Stone Printing and Manufacturing Co.
> Jack, George S. 1912. *History of Roanoke County*. Roanoke: Stone.
> McCauley, William, ed. 1902. *History of Roanoke County. . . *. Chicago: Biographical Pub. Co.
> 1922. *Roanoke, Virginia*. Roanoke: Roanoke Booster Club.

VA 65A: Cave Spring. — F, housewife, 70. B. here. — F, PGF b. Bedford Co. (Irish descent), PGM b. Patrick Co.; M., MGF b. Montgomery Co., MGM of German descent. — Ed.: only 1 mo. at a time, by 4 teachers, prob. 18 mos. altogether. — Very bright and willing, though age has slowed her memory. — Moderate tempo. [ɔ] weaker than with most speakers; others have almost none at all. Use of [ɪ˗n dɨ kʌbəd], [ɪ˗n də faˀəɾ] suggests German or Irish influence, since there are no AfAms here.

Upper Back Creek, Salem P.O. and Dist.

Upper Back Creek on colonial road to NC. Salem Co. seat, authorized 1806. Roanoke College 1847. German pop., many Lutherans.

VA 65B: M, farmer, 56. B. here. — F, PGF, M., MGF b. here (PGF German, MGF Irish). — Ed.: moderate. — Mountaineer, not primitive type. Common sense; slow reactions, easy going; not voluble. — Slow tempo; vowels tend to be prolonged. Somewhat nasal. Final articulation rather weak.

Roanoke

Incorporated 1874 as Big Lick; renamed Roanoke in 1882; city charter 1884. 2 streams of settlers: E. VA and Shen. Valley. RR and hwy. junction. Stage stop in 1838; on RR 1852. Heavy growth of pop. in 1890s; rapid and diversified industrialization. Hydro-electric power, factories, RR shops, steel products, textiles, lumber and other wood products. Pop. 1850: 8,477, 1880: 15,533, 1910: 34,874, 1930: 69,206, 1960: 97,110.

VA 65C!: F, housewife, 35. B. Elmwood (old country estate, now houses Roanoke Public Library); has summer home on Bent Mtn. — F. b. Louisa Courthouse, came here age 20, PGF, PGM b. Louisa Courthouse; M. b. Roanoke Co., MGF b. Bedford Co., MGF's F. b. Halifax Co., MGF's M. b. Bedford, MGM, MGM's F. b. Roanoke Co., MGM's PGF b. Rockingham Co. (of German descent), MGM's M. b. Roanoke Co. (of German descent). — Ed.: Roanoke HS, Baldwin School at Bryn Mawr, Barnard College. — Episcopalian; interested in out-patient dept., clinic; Garden Club. — Went away to college and came back to live; much interested in things intellectual. — Rather clear-cut intonation. Family made a point of using broad *a*, but she is not consistent: [aˑ] and [aˀ:] tend to overlap in her speech, since any vowel may be prolonged. — Cultivated.

66. Franklin County

Formed 1786 from Henry and Bedford Cos. 1st grants 1749; earliest settlers Ulster Scots, Germans, Irish (some French). Many German Brethren churches. 1st road surveys 1786. Turnpike 1840; RR 1880–1930. Birthplace of Booker T. Washington. Tobacco the money crop till late 19th cent. Several small factories. Known for illicit whiskey at one time. Iron ore (receded); fruit, furniture, talc mining, mica, leather. Pop. 1790: 6,842, 1820: 12,017, 1850: 17,430, 1880: 25,084, 1910: 26,480, 1930: 24,337, 1960: 25,925.

> Sloan, Raymond. 1977. *Uncle Esom's Grist Mill*.
> Smith, Essie Wade. 1977. *History of Franklin County, Virginia*. Ferrum: Franklin County Bicentennial Commission.
> Wingfield, Marshall. 1964. *Franklin County: A History*. Berryville: Chesapeake Book Co.
> Wingfield, Marshall. 1964. *Pioneer Families of Franklin County*. Berryville: Chesapeake Book Co.

VA 66A: Shooting Creek, Endicott P.O., Long Branch Dist. — F, housewife, 70. B. Patrick Co., 4 mi. from here, here since marriage. — F. b. Patrick Co., 5 mi. from here, PGF b. Greene Co., moved here as little boy, PGF's F., PGF's M. b. Greene Co., PGM, PGM's F., PGM's M. b. Patrick Co. (latter of Irish stock); M., MGF, MGF's F., MGM, MGM's F., MGM's M. b. Patrick Co. — Very little ed. — Primitive Baptist. — Respectable family, among dangerous moonshiners. Timid but sure; talked freely without getting tired. — Speech not especially old-fashioned, but notable for unfamiliarity with such general terms as *hotel*, *theater*, *baker's bread*, which had to be suggested.

VA 66B: Sydnorsville, Rocky Mount P.O., Snow Creek Dist. — M, farmer, 52. B. here; 1 yr. in Ohio when 2 1/2, a time in Roanoke later. — F., PGF b. Co., PGF's F. b. Mecklenburg Co., PGM, PGM's F. b. Co. (Scotch-Irish descent); M., MGF, MGF's F., MGF's M., MGM, MGM's F., MGM's M. b. Co. — Ed.: slight, here, till 15 or 16. — Methodist. — Middle-aged, but rather old-fashioned (sister a teacher). — Speech slow, deliberate, perhaps slightly contaminated.

67. Pulaski County

Co. est. 1839. German settlement from PA in 1745; also some Ulster Scots, English. New Dublin Church (Presbyterian) est. 1768; one of oldest W. of Alleghenies. Limestone, iron, zinc, lead. Pop. 1840: 3,739, 1850: 5,118, 1880: 8,755, 1910: 17,246, 1930: 20,566, 1960: 27,258.

> Smith, Conway Howard. 1975. *Colonial Days in the Land That Became Pulaski County*. Pulaski: Pulaski County Library Board.

Whitmore, E. Pierce. 1974. *Pulaski County*. Radford: Commonwealth Publishers, Inc.

VA 67A: Max Creek, Hiwassee P.O. — M, farmer, 83. B. 2 1/2 mi. from here; when 15, went to WV, lived with uncle and went to school 2 sessions. — F. b. here, PGF b. Carroll Co. (English descent), PGM, PGM's F. b. Wythe Co. (English descent); M., MGF b. here, MGF's F. b. England, MGM, MGM's F. b. here (English descent), MGM's M. b. near Newbern in Co. (English descent). — Primitive Baptist. — Hardworking man, old-fashioned in ways and speech. — Moderate tempo.

Draper, Newbern Dist.

1st colonial settlement W. of Allegheny divide here 1748. Many Germans among earliest settlers. Indian troubles 1755. Old Harmony Church: Presbyterian and Baptist, to 1849.

VA 67B: F, middle-aged. B. 29 mi. from here in Wythe Co. (Barren Springs), age 8–11 in Russellville, TN. — F., PGF b. Wythe Co., PGF's F. and M., PGM b. Carroll Co.; M., MGF b. Pulaski Co. (Irish descent), MGM, MGM's F. b. Wythe Co. (Irish descent). — Ed.: 2–3 yrs. in TN, then in Pulaski Co. till 16. — Christian.

68. Floyd County

Co. est. 1831. In 1951, only S. Blue Ridge Co. predominantly agricultural; no factories. Pop. 1840: 4,453, 1850: 6,458, 1880: 13,255, 1910: 14,092, 1930: 11,698, 1960: 10,462.

VA 68A: Eastview neighborhood, Floyd P.O. and Dist. — F, housewife, 79. B. 2 mi. from here. — F. b. Franklin Co., just over mtns., PGF b. Ireland, as infant to Franklin Co., PGM b. Franklin Co.; M., MGF b. here, MGM, MGM's F., MGM's M. b. NC. — Reads print very little; can't write. — Ironside Baptist. — "Most intelligent woman FW had interviewed in VA" (May 1935). Quick, mentally alert, full of hearty, vigorous, swift intellectual associations typical of rural northern New Eng. In addition, has full power of sympathetic cooperation in intellectual endeavors, typical of PA southern type, lacking New Eng. constant fear of self-expression. Every answer true response of woman who came from poor family and struggled in adversity.

VA 68B: Allum Ridge, Sowers P.O. — M, farmer, 52. B. 300 yds. from here. — F., PGF, PGF's F. b. here, PGF's PGF a Scot, came to Montgomery Co. from N. Ireland, PGM b. here; M. b. Co., MGF b. here, MGF's F. from N. Ireland (brother to PGF's F.), MGM b. here, MGM's M. "Dutch". — Ed.: Oak Hill and Allum Ridge till 18. — Parents were Brethren (German Baptist, Reformed Dunkard). — Quick, bright, believes in giving children good education. — Has retained old type of speech for the most part.

69. Henry County

Formed 1776 from Pittsylvania. Hilly, rolling. 1st settlers upstream from the east (Dan and Smith River Valleys). Few settlers in 1740s, great influx 1750–75. Western boundary not est. till 1854. Baptists strong. Iron furnaces at one time; destroyed by Feds. Tobacco chief money crop and industry; tobacco mfg. ceased 1900–1910. Lumbering, furniture, modular homes, brickmaking, textiles. Pop. 1782: 2,891, 1790:

8,479, 1820: 5,624, 1850: 8,872, 1880: 16,009, 1910: 18,459, 1930: 20,088, 1960: 40,335.

Coe, Malcolm Donald. 1969. *Our Proud Heritage*. Bassett: Bassett Print. Corp.

Hill, Judith Parks America. 1925. *A History of Henry County*. Martinsville.

Pedigo, Virginia G., and Lewis G. Pedigo. 1933. *History of Patrick and Henry Counties, Virginia*. Roanoke: Stone Print. Co.

Thompson, Mrs. J. Frank, ed. 1933. *Copy of the History of Bever Creek Church, 1786, Henry County, Virginia*. Columbia, MO.

Spencer, Horsepasture Dist.

Once important tobacco center. Small village: 1 church, 1 store, RR station 1925.

VA 69A: M, farmer, sawmiller, 76. B. here. — F. b. here (owned 200 slaves and had a tobacco factory), PGF perhaps from Pittsylvania Co.; M., MGF b. here. — No ed.; neighbor woman tried to teach him some, privately. — Christian Church. — Eccentric; hearty but very earthy; showing effects of age. — Some mumbling.

Ridgeway

Trading center of Co. c. 1850; 1st P.O. Large estates by 1861. Incorporated 1890. Methodist Church here 1893. Tobacco market in mid 19th cent., now bedroom community for Danville workers.

VA 69B: M, merchant, 52. B. Irishburg, 10 mi. E. of Martinsville. — F. b. Shady Grove, Franklin Co., PGF b. Franklin Co., descendant of prominent Manhattan resident, PGM, PGM's F. b. Matrimony, NC, 3 mi. from line; M., MGF, MGF's F., MGF's M. b. here, MGM b. SC, came here when married. — Intelligent, cooperative; typical successful middle-aged inf. — Speech average to good.

70. Bland County

Formed 1861 from Giles, Wythe, and Tazewell. Mountainous. Settled in 1740s; raided by Indians 1749. Early settlers Ulster Scots, English, many Germans. Raided by Feds 1863. Methodists, Lutherans, Presbyterians, Christians. Trading center. Salt springs, manganese, lumber; good grazing; small industries. Pop. 1870: 4,000, 1880: 5,004, 1910: 5,154, 1930: 6,031, 1960: 5,982.

1961. *History of Bland County*. Bland: Bland County Centennial Corp.

Bland, Seddon Dist.

Dist. named after VA statesman. Co. seat orig. Seddon; became Bland 1861. Courthouse not built till 1874.

VA 70A: F, housewife, 61. B. here. — F., PGF, PGF's F., PGF's M. b. here, PGM, PGM's F. b. here (German descent); M. b. Pulaski Co. (came here as infant), MGF, MGF's F., MGM, MGM's F. b. Pulaski Co. (German descent). — Ed.: till 19, never graded. — Methodist. — Independent, brawny, German-looking mountaineer. Keener than most of her neighbors, but not well informed about outside world. —

Deliberate tempo; characteristic long vowels, even for /a ai au/.

VA 70B: F, housewife, 48. B. 1 1/2 mi. from here. — F. b. Pulaski Co., PGF of Scotch descent, PGM of German descent; M., MGF b. Mechanicsburg, MGF's F. of Scotch-Irish descent, MGM b. near Mechanicsburg, MGM's F. of German descent. — Ed.: Mechanicsburg till 18. — Christian Church. — Hardworking, self-reliant, respectable. — Rugged speech.

71. Grayson County

Formed 1792 from Wythe Co. Earliest settlers English from E. VA (some from NC), Ulster Scots from the Shen. Valley, and Germans from PA. 1st factory c. 1884. RRs, timber later. Loss of pop. during and after WWI. 1st paved road in 1920s. Copper, iron, lead; some recent industry. Pop. 1800: 3,912, 1820: 5,598, 1850: 6,677, 1880: 13,068, 1910: 19,856, 1930: 20,017, 1960: 17,390.

Fields, Betty Lou. 1976. *Grayson County: A History in Words and Pictures*. Independence: Grayson County Historical Society.
Nuckolls, Benjamin Floyd. 1914. *Pioneer Settlers of Grayson County*. Bristol, TN: King Print. Co.

Chestnut Hill, Independence P.O., Elk Creek Dist.

Independence Co. seat from 1851. Built around courthouse. English, German, Ulster Scots; some settlers from W. NC. Baptists and Methodists. 1st store and hotel 1853. Some industry after 1940.

VA 71A: M, farmer, 75. B. 6 mi. from here on Saddle Creek. — F. b. near here; M. b. Saddle Creek, MGF b. Iredell Co., NC, came here as grown man, MGM b. Iredell Co. — Very little ed. — Baptist. — Unaware. — Old-fashioned speech.

VA 71B: Independence, Elk Creek Dist. — F, housewife, 51. B. 1/2 mi. from here. — F. b. here, PGF b. Bridal Creek (5 mi. W.), PGF's F. b. on New River in Co., near NC, PGF's PGF a surveyor from E. VA, PGF's PGM of Scotch-Irish descent, PGF's M. b. Bridal Creek, on New River (NC descent), PGM b. just over river in Alleghany Co., NC, PGM's F. lived in Alleghany Co., PGM's M. b. Grayson Co. (sister of PGF's M.); M., MGF, MGF's F. b. near Galax, MGF's M., MGM b. Elk Creek, MGM's F. of Baltimore descent. — Ed.: here till 14, then Bridal Creek HS 2 yrs. — Methodist — Open, frank personality. — Fairly modern speech.

72. Buchanan County

Formed 1858 from Tazewell and Russell Cos. Still much wilderness in 1860. Early settlers Methodist and Baptist; settlers included English, Scots, Irish, Germans. Guerilla fighting 1862–65. Limited schooling at the time of WWI; few roads "outside" till 1920s. Lumbering, coal, grazing; now a recreational area. Pop. 1860: 2,793, 1880: 5,694, 1910: 12,334, 1930: 16,740, 1960: 36,724.

Baker, Nancy Virginia. 1976. *Bountiful and Beautiful: A Bicentennial History of Buchanan County, Virginia, 1776–1976*. Grundy: Buchanan County Vocational School.
Compton, Hannibal Albert. 1958. *Looking Back on One Hundred Years: A Brief Story of Buchanan County and Its People*. Grundy: Buchanan County Chamber of Commerce.
Richardson, Alexander Stuart. 1958. *History of Buchanan County*. Grundy: reproduced from typewritten copy.

VA 72A: Stone Coal Branch, Stacy P.O., Grundy Dist. — M, farmer, 82. B. on Dismal River, 15 mi. from here, on top of Keen Mtn. — F. b. Thompson's Cove, Tazewell Co., came here as youth, PGF b. Thompson's Cove, PGM b. Tazewell Co.; M. b. on Clinch R., Tazewell Co., brought to Buchanan Co. as a girl, MGF b. Clinch R., Tazewell Co., MGM, MGM's F. b. Tazewell Co. — Ed.: till 14. — Methodist. — Untraveled. Old-fashioned in manner and speech.

VA 72B: Loggy Bottom Branch, Whitewood P.O., Garden Dist. — M, farmer, commissioner of revenue, 45. B. here. — F. b. Tazewell Co., brought here age 2, PGF b. Tazewell Co., PGF's F. prob. b. Montgomery Co., PGF's PGF of English descent, PGF's M. of Scotch descent, PGM b. Tazewell Co., PGM's F. of English descent, from MD (orig. Catholic); M. b. Ward's Cover, Tazewell Co., brought here age 2, MGF, MGF's F., MGF's PGF b. Tazewell Co., MGF's PGF's F. b. Ireland, MGF's M. b. Tazewell Co., MGF's MGF prob. Scottish, MGM, MGM's F. b. Smyth Co. (Dutch), MGM's PGF b. Smyth Co. (Scottish). — Ed.: here till 20; 2 or more summers Big Stone Gap Normal School. — Baptist father. — Crippled; well-respected, has written mountain novel. Natural, cooperative. — Very drawling, overlong vowels; very central [ʌ] (= [ɜ]) and [ʊ] (= [ʉ]).

73. Russell County

Formed 1786 from Washington Co. English, Scots, a few Germans and Dutch. Indian harassment early. Temporary home of D. Boone in 1770s; fort here 1771; military frontier till 1790. Way station on route to KY and TN. French settlement c. 1800, eventually failed. Few Presbyterians; many Baptists, some Methodists. Farming, coal. Pop. 1790: 3,338, 1820: 5,536, 1850: 11,919, 1880: 13,906, 1910: 23,474, 1930: 25,957, 1960: 26,290.

Addington, John L. 1906. *Honored Family*. Nickelsville: Saratoga Print. Co.
Albert, Anne Roberts, and Ethel Evans Albert. 1973. *Russell County, Virginia, Personal Property and Land Tax List*. Petersburg, VA.
Hagy, James William. 1966. *Castle's Woods: Frontier Virginia Settlement, 1769–1799*. East Tennessee State University thesis.
Pratt, Dot C. 1968. *Russell County, Virginia's Bluegrass Empire*. Bristol, TN: King Print. Co.

Dorton's School, Castlewood P.O., Copper Creek Dist.

Castlewood first and most important settlement in area, 1769. Some problems with land titles in late 18th cent. Settlers Scots, Irish, English.

VA 73: M, farmer, 63. B. N. side of Copper Ridge, 6 mi. from here; 1902–4 to Tom's Creek, Wise Co. — F. b. here, PGF b. Sugar Run, close to where it flows into New River, PGM b. Sugar Run; M. b. Co., MGF b. Castlewood, MGF's F. of

Scottish stock, MGF's M. German stock, MGM b. Co., MGM's F. French descent, MGM's M. prob. German descent. — Ed.: none. — Missionary Baptist. — Independent, cooperative. — Fairly old-fashioned speech.

74. Washington County

Formed 1776 by division of Fincastle Co. Explored 1748–49; first lands surveyed and assigned 1749. 1st settlers Scots (largely from Ulster) from Shen. Valley, PA, and Ireland; also some Germans. Presbyterians dominant, also Baptists and Presbyterians in 1770s. Frontier battles with Indians during Revolution. Salt deposits, gypsum; good soil for cereals, grasses, roots, tobacco. Pop. 1782: 1,445, 1790: 5,625, 1820: 12,444, 1850: 14,612, 1880: 25,203, 1910: 32,830, 1930: 33,850, 1960: 38,076.

> Coale, Charles B. 1878. *The Life and Adventures of Wilburn Waters....* Richmond: G. W. Gray, Printers.
> Neal, John Allen. 1977. *Bicentennial History of Washington County, Virginia, 1776–1976.* Dallas, TX: Taylor Pub. Co.
> Preston, Thomas Lewis. 1900. *Historical Sketches and Reminiscences of an Octogenarian.* Richmond: The Author.
> Summers, Lewis Preston. 1903. *History of Southwest Virginia, 1746–1786: Washington County, 1777–1870.* Richmond. Repr. 1971 (Baltimore: Regional Pub. Co.).

Meadowview, Glade Spring Dist.

Dist. is "bluegrass section". RR junction; shipping pt. for Saltville. Glade Spring incorporated 1865. Meadowview a thriving village.

VA 74A: M, farmer, 77. B. 2 mi. E. of Damascus in Widener Valley, age 6 to Emory, age 9 to Meadowview, age 24 to Poor Valley, only last 6 yrs. in Meadowview again. — F., PGF b. Widener Valley, near Damascus, PGF's F. of English background, PGM b. Damascus (of "Dutch" and English descent); M., MGF b. Damascus, of English descent, MGM b. Damascus, MGM's F. of Irish and Indian descent. — Ed.: a little. — Church of Christ; parents Methodist. — Old-fashioned type; quick and intelligent. Deliberate, reliable; not suggestible, would stick to a point if he knew anything about it. Didn't report on speech of other old people, but simply spoke in his own accustomed manner, so that in some cases responses may seem less old-fashioned than in many previous records. — Tempo deliberate. Vowels generally fairly short, but with a tendency towards prolonging. Voice weak; inf. had TB, FW feared contagion.

Abingdon

Est. 1778. Fort here attacked 1776; burned by Federal raiders in 1864. Early commercial center of district: grew rapidly, several women's colleges here. Iron, marble. Many old homes still; summer experimental theater. Pop. 1880: 1,064, 1910: 1,757, 1930: 2,877, 1960: 4,758.

VA 74B!: F, housewife, 56. B. Panacella (family estate), 1 mi. from Abingdon. — F. b. Buckingham Courthouse, came here age 4, PGF b. Louisa Co., came here as young man (Methodist minister), PGF's F. b. Cub Creek, Louisa Co., PGF's M. b. Augusta Co., PGM b. Hashville, PGM's M. of Irish descent;

M. b. here, MGF b. England, brought as child to E. VA, later here, MGM b. Saltville (Smyth Co.), MGM's F. of Scotch-Irish descent. — Ed.: here, Stonewall Jackson Institute; graduate of Martha Washington College. — Methodist. — Modern, obliging person. — Modern educated speech. Traces of a distinct family/courthouse/urban tradition approaching that of E. VA. — Cultivated.

75. Lee County

Formed 1792 from Russell Co. Early settlers English, Scots, Dutch; some Germans and Holland Dutch. Town burned 1863. Jonesville Institute (Methodist) 1902–11, eventually became a public h.s. Mountains, coal fields, some tobacco. Pop. 1800: 3,538, 1820: 4,256, 1850: 10,267, 1880: 15,116, 1910: 23,840, 1930: 30,419, 1960: 25,824.

> Burns, Annie Walker. 1933 *Southwest Virginia Historical Records: Lee County.* Jonesville.
> Catron, Ada Grace. 1968–72. *Lee County, Virginia: Court Records.* Pennington Gap.
> Laningham, Anne Wynn, and Hattie Byrd Muncy Bales, comps. 1977. *Early Settlers of Lee County, Virginia and Adjacent Counties.* Greensboro.

Thompson's Settlement, Bishop's Store Precinct, Jonesville P.O., White Shoals Dist.

1st land grant here 1793. Baptist church by 1800.

VA 75A: M, farmer, 74. B. Cedar Fork, Claiborne Co., TN (just over line); when age 2 to Sugar Run, N. of Jonesville, when age 4 to Jonesville, when age 5 to Wallen's Creek (4 mi. E. of Stickleyville), when 14 to Scott Co. for a few yrs., settled here when 22 (1883). — F. b. Crab Orchard in Co., PGF b. Co., PGM b. Crab Orchard (both PGP of Dutch descent); M. b. Cedar Fork, Claiborne Co., TN, MGF b. Claiborne Co. (Irish descent), MGM b. Cedar Fork. — Ed.: very little. — Methodist. — Very unsophisticated. — Old-fashioned speech.

VA 75B: Morgan's Store, Jonesville P.O., White Shoals Dist. — M, farmer, 52. B. Rose Hill. — F. b. near Cumberland Gap in Co., PGF b. TN (of English descent), PGM b. Co., near Cumberland Gap (of Irish descent); M. b. here, MGF, MGF's F. b. Co. (E. VA extraction), MGF's M. b. Co., MGF's MGF of English descent, MGM, MGM's F. b. Sugar Run, N. of Jonesville. — Ed.: ages 5–21. — Southern Methodist. — Obliging; fairly cultivated. — Speech weak because of TB.

Bibliographies

Cappon, Lester J., and Dumas Malone. 1930. *Bibliography of Virginia History since 1865.* Charlottesville: Institute for Research in the Social Sciences.

Howe, Henry. 1845. *Historical Collections of Virginia.* Charleston, SC: Babcock and Co.

1971. *Virginia Local History: A Bibliography.* Richmond: Virginia State Library.

General Histories

Andrews, Matthew Page. 1937. *Virginia, the Old Dominion.* Garden City, NY: Doubleday.

Beeman, Richard R. 1972. *The Old Dominion and the New Nation.* . . . Lexington: University Press of Kentucky.

Beverley, Robert. 1722. *The History and Present State of Virginia.* . . . London. Repr. 1971 (Indianapolis: Bobbs-Merrill).

Billings, Warren M. 1975. *The Old Dominion in the Seventeenth Century: A Documentary History of Virginia, 1606–1689.* Chapel Hill, NC: Institute of Early American History.

Bruce, Philip A. 1924. *History of Virginia.* 6 vols. NY and Chicago: American Historical Society.

Cooke, John Esten. 1888. *Virginia: A History of the People.* Boston: Houghton, Mifflin.

Federal Writers Program. 1946. *Virginia: A Guide to the Old Dominion.* NY: Oxford University Press.

Fishwick, Marshall W. 1959. *Virginia: A New Look at the Old Dominion.* NY: Harper.

Rubin, Louis Decimus. 1977. *Virginia: A Bicentennial History.* NY: Norton.

Special Studies

Abernethy, Thomas Perkins. 1940. *Three Virginia Frontiers.* Baton Rouge: Louisiana State University Press.

Alvord, Clarence Walworth, and Lee Bidgood. 1912. *The First Explorations of the Trans-Allegheny Region by the Virginians, 1650–1674.* Cleveland: Arthur H. Clark.

Bailey, Kenneth P. 1939. *The Ohio Company of Virginia.* . . . Glendale, CA: Arthur H. Clark Co.

Bailyn, Bernard. 1958. Politics and Social Structure in Virginia. In J. M. Smith, ed., *Seventeenth Century America* (Chapel Hill: University of North Carolina Press), 90–115.

Ballagh, J. C. 1902. *History of Slavery in Virginia.* Baltimore: John Hopkins University Press.

Ballagh, J. C. 1905. *White Servitude in the Colony of Virginia.* Baltimore: John Hopkins University Press.

Bean, Robert Bennett. 1938. *The Peopling of Virginia.* Boston: Chapman and Grimes.

Blanton, Wyndham Bolling. 1930. *Medicine in Virginia in the Seventeenth Century.* Richmond: William Byrd Press.

Brown, Robert E., and B. Katherine Brown. 1964. *Virginia, 1705–1786: Democracy or Aristocracy?* East Lansing: Michigan State University Press.

Bruce, Kathleen. 1930. *Virginia Iron Manufacture in the Slave Era.* NY: Century Co.

Bruce, Philip Alexander. 1895. *Economic History of Virginia in the Seventeenth Century.* 2 vols. NY: P. Smith.

Bruce, Philip Alexander. 1910. *Institutional History of Virginia in the Seventeenth Century.* 2 vols. NY and London: G. P. Putnam's.

Bruce, Philip Alexander. 1920–22. *History of the University of Virginia.* 5 vols. NY: Macmillan.

Bruce, Thomas. 1891. *Southwest Virginia and the Shenandoah Valley.* Richmond: J. L. Hill Publishing Co.

Brydon, George M. 1947. *Virginia's Mother Church.* 2 vols. Richmond: Virginia Historical Society.

Buck, J. L. Blair. 1952. *The Development of Public Schools in Virginia, 1607–1952.* Richmond: State Board of Education bulletin, vol. 35, no. 1.

Cabell, James Branch. 1947. *Let Me Lie.* NY: Farrar, Straus.

Cappon, Lester J. 1938. The Evolution of County Government in Virginia. In *Inventory of the County Archives of Virginia, Chesterfield County* (Charlottesville: Historical Records Survey), 5–33.

Chalkley, Lyman, ed. 1966. *Chronicles of the Scotch-Irish Settlement in Virginia.* 3 vols. Baltimore: Johns Hopkins University Press.

Chandler, Julian A. C. 1896. *Representation in Virginia.* Baltimore: Johns Hopkins University Press.

Christian, Bolivar. 1860. *The Scotch-Irish Settlers in the Valley of Virginia.* Richmond: Macfarlane and Fergusson.

Couper, William. 1952. *History of the Shenandoah Valley.* 3 vols. NY: Columbia University Press.

Craven, Wesley Frank. 1932. *Dissolution of the Virginia Company.* NY: Oxford University Press.

Craven, Wesley Frank. 1957. *The Virginia Company of London.* . . . Williamsburg: Virginia 350th Anniversary Celebration.

Craven, Wesley Frank. 1971. *White, Red, and Black: The Seventeenth-Century Virginian.* Charlottesville: University Press of Virginia.

Dabney, Virginia. 1971. *Virginia: The New Dominion.* Garden City, NJ: Doubleday.

Davis, Julia. 1945. *The Shenandoah.* NY and Toronto: Farrar and Rinehart Inc.

Davis, Richard Beale. 1972. *Intellectual Life in Jefferson's Virginia, 1790–1830.* Knoxville: University of Tennessee Press.

Dowdey, Clifford. 1969. *The Virginia Dynasties: The Emergence of "King" Carter and the Golden Age.* Boston: Little, Brown.

Durand of Dauphine. 1934. *A Huguenot Exile in Virginia.* [1687] NY: Press of the Pioneers.

Eckenrode, Hamilton James. 1910. *Separation of Church and State in Virginia.* Richmond: D. Bottom, Superintendent of Public Printing.

Eisenberg, W. J. 1967. *The Lutheran Church in Virginia, 1717–1962.* Roanoke.

Eisenberg, William Edward. 1954. *This Heritage.* Winchester: Trustees of Grace Evangelical Lutheran Church.

Flippin, Percy Scott. 1919. *The Royal Government in Virginia, 1624–1775.* NY: Columbia University Press.

Gannett, Henry. 1904. *A Gazetteer of Virginia.* . . . Washington. Repr. 1975 (Baltimore: Genealogical Pub. Co.).

Glassie, Henry H. 1975. *Folk Housing in Middle Virginia.* Knoxville: University of Tennessee Press.

Gottmann, Jean. 1969. *Virginia in Our Century.* Charlottesville: University Press of Virginia.

Hale, John Symonds. 1978. *A Historical Atlas of Colonial Virginia.* Verona: McClure Press.

Hart, Freeman H. 1942. *The Valley of Virginia in the American Revolution.* Chapel Hill: University of North Carolina Press.

Hartwell, Henry, James Blair, and Edward Chilton. 1940 [1697]. *The Present State of Virginia and the College.* Ed. by Hunter D. Farish. Williamsburg: Colonial Williamsburg.

Heatwole, Cornelius J. 1916. *A History of Education in Virginia.* NY: Macmillan.

Heuvener, Ulysses S. A. 1929. *German New River Settlement.* Repr. 1976 (Baltimore: Genealogical Pub. Co.).

Howard, A.E. Dick, et al. 1970. *Virginia's Urban Corridor.* Charlottesville: University Press of Virginia.

Jackson, Luther Porter. 1942. *Free Negro Labor and Property Holding in Virginia, 1830–1860.* NY: Appleton-Century Co.

Johnston, David E. 1906. *A History of Middle New River Settlements and Contiguous Territory.* . . . Huntington, WV: Standard Print.

Kercheval, Samuel. 1833. *A History of the Valley of Virginia.* Winchester: S. H. Davis.

Kingsbury, Susan M. 1906. A Comparison of the Virginia Company with the Other English Trading Companies of the Sixteenth and Seventeenth Centuries. *Annual Report of the American Historical Association* 1:161–176.

Kingsbury, Susan Myra, ed. 1906–35. *The Records of the Virginia Company of London.* . . . Washington: Government Printing Office.

Klein, Herbert S. 1967. *Slavery in the Americas: A Comparative Study of Virginia and Cuba.* Chicago: University of Chicago Press.

Koontz, L. K. 1941. *The Virginia Frontier, 1754–1763.* Baltimore: Johns Hopkins University Press.

Lingley, Charles Ramsdell. 1910. *Transition in Virginia from Colony to Commonwealth.* NY: Columbia University Press.

Mapp, Alf J. 1974. *The Virginia Experiment: The Old Dominion's Role in the Making of America (1607–1781).* 2nd ed. LaSalle, IL: Open Court.

McGregor, James Clyde. 1922. *The Disruption of Virginia.* NY: Macmillan.

Merton, Richard Lee. 1960. *Colonial Virginia.* Chapel Hill: University of North Carolina Press.

Mitchell, Robert D. 1977. *Commercialism and Frontier: Perspectives on the Early Shenandoah Valley.* Charlottesville: University Press of Virginia.

Moger, Allen W. 1968. *Virginia: Bourbonism to Byrd, 1870–1925.* Charlottesville: University Press of Virginia.

Morgan, Edmond Sears. 1975. *American Slavery, American Freedom: The Ordeal of Colonial Virginia.* NY: Norton.

Mullin, Gerald W. 1972. *Flight and Rebellion: Slave Resistance in Eighteenth-Century Virginia.* NY: Oxford University Press.

Noël Hume, Ivor. 1966. *1775: Another Part of the Field.* NY: Knopf.

Nugent, Nell Marion. 1963. *Cavaliers and Pioneers: Abstracts of Virginia Land Patents and Grants, 1623–1666.* 2nd ed. Baltimore: Genealogical Pub. Co.

Page, Thomas Nelson. 1910. *The Old Dominion: Her Making and Her Manners.* NY: Scribner's.

Pendleton, William Cecil. 1920. *History of Tazewell County and Southwest Virginia.* . . . Richmond: W. C. Hill Print. Co.

Pond, George E. 1883. *The Shenandoah Valley in 1864.* NY: Scribner's.

Porter, Albert Ogden. 1947. *County Government in Virginia, 1607–1914.* NY: Columbia University Press.

Rice, Philip Morrison. 1948. *Internal Improvements in Virginia, 1775–1860.* University of North Carolina dissertation.

Robert, Joseph C. 1941. *The Road from Monticello: A Study of the Virginia Slavery Debate of 1832.* Durham, NC: Trinity College Historical Society.

Russell, John Henderson. 1913. *The Free Negro in Virginia.* . . . Baltimore. Repr. 1969 (NY: Dover Publications).

Rutman, Darrett B. 1964. *The Old Dominion: Essays for Thomas P. Abernathy.* Charlottesville: University Press of Virginia.

Schuricht, Herrmann. 1898–1900. *History of the German Element in Virginia.* Baltimore. Repr. 1977 (Baltimore: Genealogical Pub. Co.).

Shanks, Henry Thomas. 1934. *The Secession Movement in Virginia.* . . . Richmond: Garrett and Massie.

Simonini, Rinaldo C. 1958. *Virginia in History and Tradition.* Farmville: Institute of Southern Culture.

Smith, Elmer Lewis, John G. Stewart, and M. Ellsworth Egger. 1964. *The Pennsylvania Germans of the Shenandoah Valley.* Pennsylvania German Folklore Society.

Stanard, Mary M. 1917. *Colonial Virginia, Its People and Customs.* Philadelphia: J. B. Lippincott Co.

Stoner, Robert P. 1967. *A Seed-Bed of the Republic: A Study of the Pioneers in the Upper (Southern) Valley of Virginia.* Roanoke: Roanoke Historical Society.

Swem, Earl G., comp. 1965. *Virginia Historical Index.* 2 vols. Gloucester, MA: P. Smith.

Sydnor, Charles S. 1952. *Gentlemen Freeholders: Political Practices in Washington's Virginia.* Chapel Hill, NC: Institute of Early American History and Culture.

Taylor, Alrutheus Ambush. 1926. *The Negro in the Reconstruction of Virginia.* Washington: Association for the Study of Negro Life.

Topping, Mary. 1971. *Approved Place Names in Virginia.* Charlottesville: University Press of Virginia.

Turner, Charles Wilson. 1956. *Chessie's Road.* Richmond: Garrett and Massie.

Wayland, John W. 1926. *Twenty-Five Chapters on the Shenandoah Valley.* Strasburg.

Wayland, John W. 1967. *The Valley Turnpike.* Winchester: Winchester-Frederick County Historical Society.

Wayland, John Walter. 1907. *The German Element of the Shenandoah Valley of Virginia.* Charlottesville. Repr. (Bridgewater: Carrier).

Weeks, J. Devereux. 1967. *Dates of Origin of Virginia Counties and Municipalities.* Charlottesville: University of Virginia Institute of Government.

Wertenbaker, Thomas Jefferson. 1910. *Patrician and Plebian in Virginia.* Charlottesville: Michie Co.

Wertenbaker, Thomas Jefferson. 1922. *The Planters of Colonial Virginia.* Princeton, NJ: Princeton University Press.

Wertenbaker, Thomas Jefferson. 1958. *The Shaping of Colonial Virginia.* NY: Russell and Russell.

Whichard, Rogers Dey. 1959. *The History of Lower Tidewater Virginia.* 2 vols. NY: Lewis Historical Pub. Co.

William and Mary College. 1870. *The History of the College of William and Mary from Its Foundation, 1693–1870.* Baltimore: Murphy.

Wilstach, Paul. 1945. *Tidewater Virginia.* NY: Tudor Pub. Co.

Wright, Louis B. 1940. *The First Gentlemen of Virginia.* San Marino, CA. Repr. 1964 (Charlottesville: University Press of Virginia).

Wust, Klaus German. 1969. *The Virginia Germans.* Charlottesville: University Press of Virginia.

1969. *Virginia Outdoor Recreation Atlas.* Alexandria: Alexandria Drafting Co.

North Carolina

1 & 2. Currituck County

Earliest settlement in E. NC, c. 1650. Albemarle section plagued with poor transportation: difficult by land and water because of swamps, sandbars. Colonists of various origins: VA and New Eng., some from the British Isles and Bermuda. Later Huguenots, Swiss, Palatinate Germans. Approx. 4,000 settlers in Albemarle section by 1675; religious diversity, Quakers esp. strong. 1st grant in Currituck Co. area made by Gov. Berkeley (VA) in 1663. Currituck inlet important access route early; silted up 1731; finally closed 1821. One of the greatest US wildfowl areas. Drained marshes provide rich land; potatoes, sweet potatoes, fishing. Pop. 1790: 5,219, 1820: 8,098, 1850: 7,236, 1880: 6,476, 1910: 7,693, 1930: 6,710, 1960: 6,601.

Albertson, Catherine. 1914. *Ancient Albemarle*. Raleigh: North Carolina DAR.

Dunbar, Gary S. 1958. *Historical Geography of the North Carolina Outer Banks*. Baton Rouge: Louisiana State University Press.

Edmunds, Pocahontas Wight. 1941. *Land of Sand: Legends of the North Carolina Coast*. Richmond: Garrett and Massie.

Pennington, Edgar Legare. 1937. *The Church of England and the Rev. Clement Hall in Colonial North Carolina*. Hartford, CT: Church Missions Pub. Co.

Powell, William S. 1958. *Ye Countie of Albemarle in Carolina. . . .* Raleigh: State Dept. of Archives and History.

Ray, Worth Stickley. 1947. *Old Albemarle and Its Absentee Landlords*. Austin.

Vaughan, Frank E. 1895. *The Albemarle District of North Carolina*. Elizabeth City.

Vaughan, Frank E., comp. 1884. *The Albemarle Section of North Carolina. . . .* NY: J. C. Rankin.

1973–. *The Journal of the Currituck County Historical Society*. Currituck: The Society.

Fruitville, Knotts Island P.O.

Knotts Island largest island in Currituck Sound. Numerous wildfowl. Fruitville halfway down sound. Pop. Fruitville 1920: 649.

NC 1: F, 66 or older. B. here. — F. b. Knotts Island, PGF, PGM b. here probably; M. b. here, MGF b. near Cape Henry, VA, MGM b. Knotts Island. — Ed.: none. — Methodist. — Untraveled, untutored; conversational, friendly; becoming senile. Likes company, but didn't altogether enjoy questions. — Were it not for her failing teeth, FW would have described her labial sound as [v] everywhere, as he did chiefly in the last part of the record. This record is significant for the history of the [æʊ] sound in VA. On Knotts I. only [ɐʊ˄] or [ɐˢʊ] exists, even before /n/. In Princess Anne Co., VA, [æʊ] appears before /n/, and only before /n/. There is an undulating drawl on the island, often producing peculiar diphthongs. [æ] is very low-central, sometimes written [aʌ·]. Tempo very slow.

Point Harbor, Poplar Branch Twp.

Pt. Harbor at S. tip of W. peninsula. Confluence of 4 sounds. Dangerous coast at Poplar Branch; watermelon shipping. Pop. Pt. Harbor 1930: 60.

NC 2A: M, farmer, hunter, 65. B. here. — F., PGF b. here (of English descent), PGM b. here; M., MGF, MGF's F., MGM all b. here. — Ed.: till 15. — Christian. — Quiet, unassuming, rather quick and intelligent, though quite local. — Fronted [ɜʊ] diphthong (cf. Pasquotank Co., NC, where this is regular. Also cf. the record from Blounts Creek and Vanceboro, NC). The use of postvocalic [r] before p. 69 and postvocalic [ɚ] after p. 69 shows drift in transcription habits. Use of /w/ for /v/ regular. Moderate tempo. Vowels tend to be prolonged.

NC 2A*: Grandy Record, Poplar Branch Twp. — F.

NC 2A**: Jarvisburg, Poplar Branch Twp. — M. — Brother of NC 2A*.

Moyock

Twp. in NW of Co. Amish colony nearby 1907–35. Pop. 1930: 500.

NC 2B: M, farmer, 41. B. here. — F., PGF, PGF's F. b. here (of French Huguenot descent), PGF's step-M., PGM, PGM's F., PGM's M. b. here; M., MGF, MGF's F., MGF's M. b. here, MGM, MGM's F. b. Shawboro, MGM's M. b. here. — Ed.: here till 16. — Baptist. — Middle-class; in bad health. Rather indifferent. — Tempo slow; bad articulation; very nasal. [ɜʊ] before voiceless consonants; varies between [ɜʊ] and [æʊ] before voiced, the latter when longer. (His daughter, who speaks quickly, uses a sound more like the first type in all positions.)

3. Camden County

Formed 1777 from Pasquotank Co. Marshy; Dismal Swamp area. Approx. 60% of farming by tenants in 1925. Diversified agriculture: Irish potatoes, corn, truck crops. Pop. 1790: 4,033, 1820: 6,347, 1850: 6,049, 1880: 6,274, 1910: 5,640, 1930: 5,461, 1960: 5,598.

Pugh, James Forbes. 1957. *Three Hundred Years along the Pasquotank: A Biographical History of Camden County*. Old Trap.

Pugh, Jesse Forbes. 1953. *Journeys through Camden County*. Camden: The Author.

Old Trap, Shiloh Twp.

Twp. has oldest organized Baptist church in NC (1727). Old Trap a truck marketing village with prosperous farms. Indian settlement in 16th cent. Nearby docks; handy to routes to windmills on the river. Much Northern sympathy in 1861. Pop. 1930: 318.

NC 3A: M, farmer, 79. B. South Mills (1 1/2 mi. E.). When 12 yrs. old, moved to Belcross. Has been at Old Trap for 23 yrs. — F. b. Perquimans Co. and came to Courthouse Twp., Camden Co., when 20; M., MGF, MGF's F., MGF's M., MGM, MGM's F., MGM's M. all b. South Mills. — Ed.: none. — Methodist. — Illiterate; well-to-do (owns 8 or 9 farms). Senile, rather slow to grasp some things (his wife assisted in drawing him out). — Natural old-fashioned speech; speaks rapidly with good articulation (perhaps typical of the N. part of Co.; in the S. part most people have a slow drawl).

Belcross, Courthouse Twp.

Twp. est. 1777; smallest co. seat in NC. Potato country. Several homes 1700–1750 vintage. Belcross a rural neighborhood named for Bell family. RR crossing from 1881.

NC 3B: F, homemaker, 37. B. here. — F. b. here, PGF, PGF's F., PGF's PGF b. Pasquotank Co. (ancestors direct from Wales), PGM, PGM's F. b. Co.; M., MGF, MGF's F. all b. Co., MGM b. Shipyard in Co., MGM's F. b. England, MGM's M., MGM's MGF both b. Co. — Ed.: Belcross till 18. — Baptist. — Lives in lovely old home with her father. Good memory; intelligent and cooperative; very friendly, rustic, local. — Speech prob. better than most, yet full of unselfconscious *this-a-way*s and *that-a-way*s. Moderate tempo; considerable nasalization; the [ɐɯ] diphthong has very weak rounding.

4. Gates County

Formed 1779 from 3 other cos. 1st settlers c. 1660 from VA; mainly small farmers. Many small slaveholders. 3 academies. No record of a church until Baptist church in 1806; Methodist and Christian churches shortly thereafter. Numerous swamps; drain into Dismal Swamp. Self-sufficient farm economy; cotton and peanuts, occas. Irish potatoes. Pop. 1786: 4,917, 1790: 5,392, 1820: 6,837, 1850: 8,426, 1880: 8,897, 1910: 10,455, 1930: 10,551, 1960: 9,254.

Harrell, I. S. 1916. Gates County to 1860. In *Historical Papers of the Trinity College Historical Society* vol. 12.

Fort Island, Eure P.O., Hall Twp.

Twp. in W. part of Co.; Eure in NW part of Twp.

NC 4A: M, farmer and fisherman, 83. B. here. — F. b. here, PGF, PGM, PGM's F. all b. Co.; M., MGF, MGM all b. here, MGM's F. b. Co. — Ed.: 19 days (Sunday school). — Baptist. — Old-fashioned, genial; sings ballads. — Has very slight retroflexion, difficult to hear (elsewhere in Gates Co. retroflexion has almost disappeared).

NC 4A*: F, wife of NC 4A. B. here. — F., PGF, PGM all b. here; M. b. Co., MGM, MGM's F. b. here, MGM's M. b. Edgecombe Co.

NC 4B: Trotville, Hunters Mill Twp. (E. central part of Co.). — F, 38. B. here. — F., PGF, PGF's F., PGF's M., PGM, PGM's F. b. here; M., MGF, MGF's F., MGF's M., MGM, MGM's F. all b. here. — Ed.: till 18. — Baptist. — Not very intelligent yet conscientious farm woman Sunday school teacher. Rather self-conscious. — Usually uses [v] in natural speech, but [β] also for both /v/ and /w/. [æ] sound often very

central and distinctly short, not long as it is so frequently in VA. Presumably the [aⱡ·] in [flaⱡ·və] is a member of the [æ] phoneme; not a member of the [aᐣ·ᵊᶜ] or [aᶜ·ᵋᐣ] diphthong. Her [ɐʊ·] diphthong is usually well marked (cf. [kɐʊ·t] = *coat*, [ko·ᵊ·t] = *court*, often [ko·t] = *court*). Her mother uses [a:] where she uses [aᐣ:] or [ɑᶜ:]. Plosives not always very aspirated.

5. Pasquotank County and Perquimans County

Pasquotank County

Formed 1670 as a precinct of Albemarle. 1st known permanent settlement here 1656–59. Settlers from Bermuda 1666. C. 1675 possibly first church (Quaker) in NC; 1st school in NC here 1705. Baptists by 1727. Elizabeth City est. 1793; chartered 1830. Economic ties with Boston in 18th cent.; Dismal Swamp Canal 1790–1825, ties to VA. First rail connections 1881. Generally prosperous since 1880. Not tourist area. Much forest and much low and fertile land; good farming (truck crops). Pulpwood, timber, textiles, shipbuilding. Coast Guard base. Pop. 1786: 4,793, 1790: 5,497, 1820: 8,008, 1850: 8,930, 1880: 10,369, 1910: 16,693, 1930: 19,143, 1960: 25,630.

Flora, Jerome B. 1950. *A Historical Sketch of Ancient Pasquotank County, North Carolina*. Elizabeth City.
Virginia Electric and Power Company. 1967. *Elizabeth City and Pasquotank County, NC: An Economic Data Summary*. Richmond: The Company.
1954–. *Pasquotank Historical Society Yearbook*. Elizabeth City.

Okisko, Elizabeth City, Mount Hermon Twp.

Twp. in the center of Co. Eliz. City only town on Pasquotank R.; excellent inland harbor, Coast Guard HQ and air base. Settlement here 1666 from Bermuda. Town inc. 1793; Co. seat 1799. Burned 1862 before Fed. occupation. Slow growth; till 1920s more closely tied to VA Southside than to rest of NC. Pop. Eliz. City 1930: 10,037.

NC 5A: F, housewife, 74. B. 3 mi. E. — F, M. and their parents b. here. — Ed.: only a little. — Methodist. — Delightful; most revealing, incapable of deception. — Tempo fairly slow.

Perquimans County

Formed 1670 as precinct in Albemarle. 1st settler a Quaker in 1661; some settlers from PA c. 1695. Many Quakers early; still fairly numerous into 20th cent. Berkeley Parish 1715: few Church of England, many Dissenters. Bethel Baptist Church est. 1808. Timber, fishing, sheep, grapes. Pop. 1790: 5,440, 1820: 6,857, 1850: 7,332, 1880: 9,466, 1910: 11,054, 1930: 10,668, 1960: 9,178.

White, Julia Scott. 1908. The Quakers of Perquimans. *North Carolina Booklet* 7:278–289.
Winslow, Ellen Goode (Rawlings). 1931. *History of Perquimans County*. . . . Raleigh: Edwards and Broughton.

Winfall, Parkville Twp.

Winfall a small village in S. part of Twp. At highway bend; sawmill. Quaker settlement at nearby Belvidere in early 18th cent. Pop. 1930: 426.

NC 5B: F, housewife, 44. B. 2 mi. E. — F. b. here, PGF b. England and came as a boy, PGM b. Pasquotank Co.; M., MGF, MGM, MGM's F. b. here. — Ed.: h.s. in Hertford, Littleton Seminary for 3 yrs. — Methodist. — Not very intelligent; loves to talk. — Note how [a] in [naˑt] is often long in this part of NC as compared to the uniformly short [aˏ] in VA nearby. There are some who do not use as much retroflexion and have [ɚ] for [ɜə]. Tempo slow.

6. Chowan County

Orig. formed 1668 as Shaftesbury Precinct of Albemarle. Smallest co. in NC. Earliest settlers from VA by 1650; relative harmony and lack of violence. Little foreign stock, most immigration from VA. Primarily farming by 1880; small farms. Cotton, corn, sweet potatoes, peas, some hay, fruit; cattle, hogs, poultry. By 1915, working of crops improved: machinery for harvesting peanuts, soybeans; oxen gone, horses worked more efficiently. Some industry: bricks, lumber, other building materials. Mainly Baptists and Methodists. Pop. 1786: 3,782, 1790: 5,011, 1820: 6,464, 1850: 10,174, 1880: 7,900, 1910: 11,303, 1930: 11,282, 1960: 11,729.

Boyce, William Scott. 1917. *Economic and Social History of Chowan County, North Carolina, 1880–1915.* NY: Columbia University Press.

Parramore, Thomas C. 1967. *Cradle of the Colony: The History of Chowan County and Edenton.* Edenton: Chamber of Commerce.

Wall, Bennett H. 1950. The Founding of the Pettigrew Plantations. *North Carolina Historical Review* 27:395–418.

Watson, Alfred A. 1901. *The Religious and Historic Commemoration of the Two Hundred Years of St. Paul's Parish, Edenton, North Carolina.* Goldsboro: Nash Brothers.

Edenton

One of the 3 oldest communities in the state. Settlers from Jamestown by 1658. Governor's residence and virtual capital by 1710. Queen Anne's Town to 1722; then inc. as Edenton. Early shipyards, fishing. Cotton-spinning mills. Diversified farming, including corn, soybeans, cotton, tobacco, truck. Largest peanut market in state (2nd in world). Still several pre-Rev. structures. Sport fishing, boating. Pop. 1790: 1,575, 1850: 1,607, 1880: 1,382, 1910: 2,789, 1930: 3,563, 1960: 4,458.

NC 6!: F, 57. B. here. — F. b. Hertford Co. and came to Edenton as a young lawyer, PGF, PGF's F., PGM, PGM's F., PGM's PGF, PGM's PGF's F. all b. Gates Co., PGM's PGF's PGF b. VA, PGM's M. b. Gates Co.; M., MGF, MGF's F., MGF's PGF, MGF's M. b. Edenton, MGM b. Chowan Co. — Ed.: Edenton; then Salem Academy at Winston-Salem, NC, 3 yrs. — Episcopalian. — Part of "gentry" of this small, isolated town. Rather slow; at times seemed to conceal the true nature of her speech; very self-conscious. — Somewhat precise and affected articulation. Phonetic pattern stable except

for the word *father*, which varies from short to long. Unconscious of her [ɚ] diphthong in *bird*, etc. It is interesting that she has no retroflexion, whereas most of the country people in the co. have a little retroflexion and some of the older ones a good deal (cf. Perquimans Co.); Edenton, and Chowan and Gates Co. between Edenton and VA, seems to have been a center from which the type without retroflexion spread in this part of NC; Elizabeth City is another modern center for the type without retroflexion, but Edenton is probably a very old such center. Her speech differs from the country people of adjoining cos. in that she uses a short [aˑ] sound, whereas they frequently lengthen the vowel in *not*. — Cultivated.

7. Bertie County

Formed 1722 from Chowan Co. 1st permanent settlements from VA Southside. Peanuts, tobacco, cotton; fishing and mfg. minor. Pop. 1790: 12,606, 1820: 10,805, 1850: 12,851, 1880: 16,399, 1910: 23,039, 1930: 25,844, 1960: 24,350.

Bell, Mary Best, ed. 1963–65. *Colonial Bertie County, North Carolina.* 4 vols. Windsor.

NC 7A: Trapp, Colerain Twp. — F, 74. B. Suffolk, VA, but came back to Bertie Co. when 2–3 yrs. old (her parents had moved to VA before her birth, but were natives of Bertie Co.). — F., PGF, PGM, M., MGF, MGM all b. Co. — Ed.: very little (2 mos.). — Baptist. — Simple; had sense of inferiority and felt incapable of answering questions. — Slow and drawling speech compared to VA, but diphthongs before voiceless consonants are not usually prolonged.

NC 7A*: M (husband of NC 7A). — Ancestors all the same locality.

Askewville, Windsor Twp.

Twp. in S. central part of Co. Laid out 18th cent.; Co. seat c. 1750. Port of entry before 1861. Cotton, tobacco, peanuts, truck; sawmills, barrel mills, warehouses; fishing, game (deer, squirrel, quail, goose, duck). Askewville in N. part of Twp.

NC 7B: F, housewife, 43. B. Colerain Twp. (4 mi. S.) — F., PGF, PGF's F., PGM, PGM's F. b. Colerain; M. MGF, MGF's F. all b. Colerain, MGM, MGM's F. both b. Hertford Co. — Ed.: Colerain till 18 (grammar school). — Baptist. — Slow, yet considered bright in the community (she says her mother was an educated person); answered questions laboriously and honestly; unaware of the outside world. — As in Perquimans and Currituck Cos., she voices /t/ before /n/, in contrast to Dare and Carteret Cos., where strong glottal stops are used. Slow tempo; peculiar throaty resonance quality (such as in the speech of the sister of the middle-aged informant for Southampton Co., VA).

8. Martin County

Co. formed 1774 from Halifax and Tyrrell Cos. Mostly English, some Scots and Welsh. Over 50% of farms rented. Farm pop. about 50% AfAm in 1925. Tobacco, peanuts, cotton, timber; favorable for stock raising. Pop. 1790: 6,080, 1820: 6,320, 1850: 8,307, 1880: 13,140, 1910: 17,797, 1930: 23,400, 1960: 27,139.

Hughes, Shelby Jean Nelson, ed. 1980. *Martin County Heritage*. Williamston: Martin County Historical Society.

Wheeler, John Hill. 1885. *Reminiscences and Memoirs of North Carolina*. Columbus, OH: Columbus Printing Works.

Old Cotten Plantation, Oak City, Hobgood P.O., Goose Nest Twp.

Oak City estab. in 1860s; inc. 1891 as Conoho; became Oak City 1901. Cotten Plantation named for man who rehabilitated it. Pop. Oak City 1910: 251, 1930: 481, 1960: 574.

NC 8N: M, farmer, 80. B. here, lived in the little hotel at Hamilton until slaves were freed. — F. (his old master) b. Hamilton in Co., PGF, PGM both b. Edgecombe Co.; M., MGM both b. at Cokery, 6 miles SW of here, in Edgecombe Co. — Ed.: very little (3 or 4 mos.). Taught a little at home by old mistress. — Missionary Baptist. — He calls himself a [jæᵊlə nɨɡə], a type of person who used to be important back in slavery times but now is disliked by both races. When 7 yrs. old, he was sold by his own father to pay his debts. Quick, intelligent; full of energy and enthusiasm; polite in the traditional way. — Tempo rapid; vowels fairly long.

Holly Springs, Williamston P.O., Griffin P.O., Williamston Twp.

Williamston Co. seat from 1774; port of entry before Rev. Tobacco market, peanut processing, fertilizer, lumber, commercial fishing. Holly Springs community contains a Methodist church.

NC 8A: F, farm laborer and domestic, 70. B. in the Islands (4 mi. N. of here on the river). — M. b. here (raised by another woman at Hardison Mill, 10 mi. S. of here). — Illiterate. — Baptist (not a member). — Quick, bright woman who has worked hard all her life and knows nothing of the outside world (hasn't been to town once in ten years). — Rather rapid tempo; fairly good enunciation. Some tendency to shortness of vowels and diphthongs. Note the high second element of the [æᵁ˄] and [aᴧɨ] diphthongs.

NC 8B: F, housewife, 41. B. Williamston, Williamston Twp. Until 8 yrs. lived with MGM 3 mi. S. of Williamston, then to present neighborhood, where raised by another woman, not her mother, who died at daughter's birth. — F., PGF b. Pantego, Beaufort Co.; M. b. 3 mi. S. of Williamston. — Ed.: here till 13 or 14. — Methodist. — Quick, intelligent; limited background and community. — Note high second element of [æᵁ˄] and [aɨ] diphthongs and weak retroflexion. Tempo and lengths normal.

NC 8B*: Williamston (5 mi. E.). — F, housewife, middle-aged. B. here. — Parents b. here; all ancestors from this section as far as she can remember. — Intelligent. — Speech indistinct, with several pronounced speech defects. She also had peculiar spelling pronunciations due to schooling. Tempo deliberate; vowels rather short.

9. Tyrrell County

Formed 1729 from 3 cos. Settlers after 1690, largely from upper Albemarle section and from Southside VA; English, some Welsh, Germans. Devastated in Tuscarora War, 1711.

Bridges, ferries, and roads by 1724. 1st church (St. Paul's) by 1716. 1755, discovery of Lake Phelps, freshwater, in swamp (later used by rice planters). Elizabethtown est. 1793 as co. seat; name changed to Columbia 1810. 1st local public schools c. 1878. Predominantly rural and agricultural. 1st through road 1926. Decline in N. of small farms in 20th cent. Most sparsely settled co. in NC. Potatoes, corn, lumbering, pulpwood, commercial fishing, stock raising. Pop. 1786: 3,859, 1790: 4,744, 1820: 4,319, 1850: 5,133, 1880: 4,545, 1910: 5,219, 1930: 5,164, 1960: 4,520.

Davis, David E. 1963. *History of Tyrrell County*. Norfolk, VA: J. Christopher Printing.

Columbia, Alligator Twp.

Columbia in NW corner of Co. Est. as Co. seat, with name of Elizabethtown, 1793; became Columbia 1810. Earlier a landing and trading post. Damaged in Union raid in 1863. Small village in 1880s. 1st h.s. 1915; 1st hwy. connection 1927.

NC 9A: M, farmer, 71. B. 1 mile W. — F., PGF, PGM, M, MGF, MGM's F. all b. here (M.'s family came from Barnstable Co., MA, in 1707, said to be Scotch-Irish). — Ed.: very little. — Baptist. — Delightfully quick and intelligent; uneducated; very honest, trustworthy, cooperative. Represents a genuine lower-class tradition; not afraid to use such words as *bull*, etc. Unaware of outside world. — Fairly rapid tempo. Uses [a] in *not* (cf. inf. from Pitt Co.).

NC 9B: F, widow, 60. B. Alligator (7 1/2 mi. E.), lived there until 16 or 17, then moved to Columbia. — F. b. Edgecombe Co. and came here as a young man; M. b. Alligator, MGF b. Hyde Co., MGM b. Alligator. — Ed.: in Alligator. — Methodist. — Slow. — Her [ʉᶜᵁ] sound is very front sometimes, as in *two* (written [yʾʉᶜ]); it should not be confused with the other peculiar sound [iyʾ˕ᵁ], [i̥yʾ·] or [ɪy·] as in *tube, Tuesday*. Her back [aʾ˩˩] is like the coastal type. Slow tempo; long vowels and diphthongs.

10. Dare County

Formed 1870 from Currituck, Tyrrell, and Hyde Cos. Extreme E. co. of state. Outer Banks constantly shifting: many inlets closed and opened. Earliest settler 1663; cattle raising on Roanoke Island by 1669. Roanoke Inlet closed by 1730. Some British raids during Rev. No church buildings till end of 19th cent. Tourism before 1850. Bridges, hwys. 1927 and after. Families concerned with education: less illiteracy than any other NC co. Important US Coast Guard installations. Resort/vacation pop. grown since 1930. Fishing (tendency to overfishing): shad, porpoise, terrapin, oysters, shrimp, crab. Some agriculture (most farms owned), timber. Pop. 1870: 2,778, 1880: 3,243, 1910: 4,841, 1930: 5,202, 1960: 5,935.

Albertson, Catherine. 1914. *Legend of the Dunes of Dare*. Raleigh: Commercial Printing Co.

Albertson, Catherine. 1934. *Roanoke Island in History and Legend*. Elizabeth City: The Independent Press.

Brown, Arch Burfoot. 1937. *Historic Sands of Eastern Carolina*. Washington.

Bullance, Mildford. 1972. *The Hands of Time*. NY: Vantage Press.

Powell, William S. 1965. *Paradise Preserved*. Chapel Hill: University of North Carolina Press.

Stick, David. 1952. *Fabulous Dare: Graveyard of the Atlantic*. Chapel Hill: University of North Carolina Press.

Stick, David. 1970. *Dare County: A History*. Raleigh: State Dept. of Archives and History.

Wachter, Nell Wise. 1975. *Some Whisper of Our Name*. Manteo: Times Print Co.

1927. *Dare County and Its Matchless History*. Manteo: Dare County Historians.

Kitty Hawk, Atlantic Twp.

Some Germans at Kitty Hawk. Duneland; terrapin fishing. Lifesaving stations. Area of Wright bros. experiments. Now resort area.

NC 10A: M, fisherman, 76. B. here. — Parents and grandparents b. here. — Very intelligent; reliable information; poor health. — Deliberate tempo; use of [ɚ] postvocalically and of open diphthongs noteworthy.

Rodanthe, Kenekeet Twp.

Inhabitants of Rodanthe (Hatteras I.) mainly boatmen ever since colonial times; mainly English. Easternmost point on NC coast. Artificial harbor developed 1936; Coast Guard station. Game refuge; once heavily forested, now cut over. Isolated till recent bridges and hwy.

NC 10B: F, washerwoman, 70. B. Salvo, 3 mi. S.; when 11 lived a year at Stumpy Point, and when 13 lived a year at East Lake. — F. b. near Atlantic (Carteret Co.) and came here as a young man; M. b. Rodanthe, MGF b. Currituck Co., MGM b. Rodanthe. — Methodist. — Sweet-souled religious woman; unaware of the outside world. — The [ɔ:] or [ɔ.·ə] sound as on Tangier Island, VA; not [ɔ˞ɔ]. She uses glottal stops profusely wherever a Cockney would. Is this an early American lower-class type of speech, or is it a later introduction? (Family name is common all along the Carolina coast.) Or, is the glottal stop the result of a person using /d/ for /t/ in medial position, trying to have two separate phonemes, after coming in contact with educated speech? (Cf. [ncʰᵈ dæ·ʊ˞n] with the use of glottals elsewhere.)

Manteo, Nags Head Twp.

Manteo seat of Raleigh's abortive colonies. Cattle raising here as early as 1669. Occupied by Federal forces in 1862. Town permanently settled c. 1865; co. seat when Dare Co. founded in 1870. Inc. 1899. Fishing, hunting; greater variety of fish than in any other US co. Lost Colony pageant from 1930s. Marine science center of E. Carolina U. here. Until recently, accessible only by boat.

NC 10C: F, housewife, 41. B. here. — F. PGF, PGF's F. all b. here (Scotch-Irish descent), PGF's PGM b. here (family from Salem, MA, 1741), PGF's M., PGM, PGM's F., PGM's PGF all b. here, PGM's M. b. Camden Co. or thereabouts; M., MGF, MGF's F. all b. here, MGF's M., MGF's MGF b. Nags Head, MGM, MGM's F., MGM's M. all b. here. — Ed.: here (h.s.). — Baptist. — Attractive; spontaneous; genuine. — Tempo fairly slow. Something of the voice quality and intonation remind FW of the small, quavering voice of the inf. from Chincoteague Island, VA. Wanchese, at the southern tip of the island, has the more extreme, Cockney-like phonetic pattern similar to Tangier Island, VA, and Carteret Co., NC. The [ɔ:] or [ɔ.:] sound is not diphthongal. [ɔɚ] and [oɚ] have fallen together as [ɔ˞ɚ], as in MD.

11. Hyde County

Formed under another name c. 1705; name changed to Hyde c. 1712. Courthouse built 1738. Co. includes mainland and banks. Low, flat; pasturage on islands. Well settled by 1710. Real estate promotions c. 1875 failed. Some Dutch since WWII; Mennonite community est. recently. Now mostly Baptist. 2nd most sparsely settled co. in NC. Logging, grist mills in past; corn, fruit, beans, flax, hunting, fishing. Pop. 1786: 3,421, 1790: 4,120, 1820: 4,967, 1850: 7,636, 1880: 7,765, 1910: 8,840, 1930: 8,550, 1960: 5,765.

Shelby, Marjorie T., et al. 1976. *Hyde County History: A Hyde County Bicentennial Project*. Charlotte: Herb Eaton, Inc.

Simmons, Carolina V. 1907. The Settlement and Early History of Hyde County. In *Reports of the Public Schools of Washington, North Carolina* (Goldsboro: Nash Bros.), 106–14.

1957. Hyde County. *The State*. Aug. 24, 1957.

Near Englehard, Middletown P.O., Lake Landing Twp.

Twp. in ESE part of Co.; one of first parts of Co. to be settled. Agricultural: rice (till early 1900s), cotton, truck, soybeans. Englehard first settled in late 17th cent.; village in 18th cent. Some Quakers in colonial days. Village with 4 churches and a school. Many canals; thousands of truckloads of fish. Pop. 1930: 340.

NC 11A: M, farmer, 82. B. locally. — F, PGF, PGM all b. here; M. b. here, step-M. b. Co. — Ed.: 1 1/2 mos. every summer (18 mos. all together) — Methodist. — Well-preserved physically and mentally; quick, reactive mind; trustworthy responses. — Fairly rapid tempo; vowels and diphthongs prolonged. [æ·ʊ] and [æ̇ʊ˞] both occur, depending on length or tempo. Informant has an [æ] or [æ˞] for standard [eɪ]. Informant has [æ], [æ˞], or [ɐˢ] for /æ/. [ɡˢʊ] is notably front-open, even almost [ɐʊ] for [oʊ] at times. Note [ə] for [ɚ] after [ð] finally. Linking [ˀɚ] when a vowel begins the following word.

Tiny Oak, Swan Quarter P.O. and Twp.

Swan Quarter only inc. place in Co.; Co. seat from 1836. Swann Plantation dates from 1700s. Trading center. Large oyster beds; large wildlife refuge; tobacco, truck, fishing. Tiny Oak a vast farming section. Presbyterians and Baptists. Flower-raising area (peonies).

NC 11B: F, housewife, 39. B. here. — F., PGF, PGF's F., PGF's M. PGF's MGF, PGM all b. here; M. b. Juniper Bay in Co.; MGF, MGM both b. here. — Ed.: here till 17. — Primitive Baptist. — Quick, highly intelligent, with a discriminating mind; cooperative. Very unselfconscious and objective on some points, but in other questions trying to put best foot forward. Five-year-old son caught her up on a few questions and made her admit she used another form. — Tempo fairly rapid; vowels and diphthongs prolonged. [ɚ] in all positions except finally after [ð]. When a word beginning with a vowel follows, a linking [ᵊɚ] is used in this position. The older Hyde Co. inf. agrees in this practice; not encountered elsewhere. Only [æ æᵊ]; there is no distinctive [æɹ] in Hyde Co., in marked contrast to other parts of E. Carolina. An open [ʌ] or [ʌ·] sound is noteworthy.

12. Beaufort County

One of 7 oldest cos.; Beaufort Precinct est. 1705. 1st settlers hunters and traders, then squatters; area known as "County of Bath" c. 1690. Bath oldest town in NC: settled by 1681, inc. 1705. Eventually settlers from Albemarle, also from Cape Fear, Charleston. Chiefly English, both Quakers and Anglicans from earliest times; also Baptists, Presbyterians, Methodists from 1784. Shipbuilding, center of piracy in early 18th cent. Cotton country after 1793 (still today). Public schools from 1840; steamships from 1847. Fisheries, farming, tobacco, mfg. Pop. 1790: 5,462, 1820: 9,850, 1850: 13,816, 1880: 17,474, 1910: 30,877, 1930: 35,026, 1960: 36,014.

Cooper, Francis Hodges. 1916. *Some Colonial History of Beaufort County, North Carolina*. Chapel Hill: University of North Carolina Press.

Reed, C. Wingate. 1962. *Beaufort County: Two Centuries of Its History*. Raleigh.

Beaver Dam, Washington P.O., Long Acre Twp.

Old Zion Chapel located in Beaver Dam; consecrated 1824.

NC 12A: M, farmer, 77. B. locally. — F. b. here, PGF b. Co. (said to be descended from Roanoke Island setters), PGM b. Great Contentnea (inland); M., MGM, MGM's F. all b. here. — Ed.: none. — Disciples. — Strong and healthy; convivial, friendly, and obliging; jolly manner; loves to talk. Simple, untutored mind; knows no other way to talk than his own. Quick and alert in all the simple, spontaneous reactions, but rather slow, having some difficulties with more complex questions. — Tempo fairly slow; tendency to prolong. The [aˑɨ] or [a·ᵊ‘] diphthong varies tremendously due to length/tempo, or to influence of cultivated speech. [æʊ] is frequently [a·ʊ] as often in old-fashioned speech. Informant's grandchildren use a higher [ɔɔ̞] sound and a back [ɑɚ], whereas he uses [ɔ·] and [a̞ᵊ].

NC 12A*: Blounts Creek. — F, 84. B. here. — F., PGF, PGM all b. here; MGF (Irish) probably came from away, MGM b. here. — Ed.: none. — Primitive Baptist. — Simple; reactions somewhat slow; unwilling to make a complete record. — Nervously quick, rapid speech. Beautiful [ɜʊ], [ɵʊ] diphthong similiar to RP /ou/ sound.

Washington P.O. and Twp.

Co. seat, in W. of Co. Town authorized 1771; est. 1775; named 1776. Primarily English and Dutch. Commercial center, naval stores, prospered in Rev. Important port of 1860: handled over half of waterborne commerce of the state. 1st road 1722; 1st RR 1885. Occupied by Feds 1862–65. Pop. 1850: 2,015, 1880: 2,462, 1910: 6,211, 1930: 7,035, 1960: 9,939.

NC 12B: F, housewife, 46. B. locally. — F., PGF both b. here, PGM b. Martin Co.; M., MGF, MGM all b. here. — Ed.: here

at Old Ford (h.s.); summer school at Greenville. — Christian. — Insecure, slow, but cooperative. — Retroflexion marked by dot is extremely weak and can just barely be heard, but seems to be consistently present.

13. Pamlico County

Formed 1872 from Craven and Beaufort Cos. 2nd in state in production of Irish potatoes and in fishing. Pop. 1880: 6,323, 1910: 9,966, 1930: 9,299, 1960: 9,850.

NC 13A: Folly Road (near Florence), Whortonsville P.O. — M, farmer and oysterman, 75. B. locally, on the sound at Springs Creek and Bay River. — F. b. here, PGF b. PA, came by sea (of Irish descent), PGM b. on Bay River, PGM's F. b. Ireland, PGM's M. b. here; M. b. here, MGF b. near Bath (Beaufort Co.), MGM b. here, MGM's F. b. Pamlico Co. (of Scottish descent). — Ed.: 4 sessions, 2 mos. each. — Free Will Baptist. — Quick, nervous, not too clearheaded. — Tempo rapid; not much lengthening. Speech very different from other Pamlico Co. type. Inf. uses [aɨ] as do simple, aged people of Goose Creek Island (Pamlico Co.); roughly similar to cultivated speech of New Bern. Other parts of Pamlico Co. use [a·ɛ’].

Merritt P.O.

At center of Co. Free Will Baptist Church located here.

NC 13B: F, 40. B. locally. — F., PGM both b. here; M. b. Maribel (Pamlico Co.), MGM b. here. — Ed.: here till 18. — Christian. — Intelligent, cooperative. — Long, slow drawl with caressing, undulating intonation similar to that of Knotts Island (Currituck Co.).

Bayboro P.O.

Co. seat. Near head of navigation of Bay River. Commercial fishing, oyster culture, Irish potatoes.

NC 13B*: F, 50. — F., M. both b. here. — Slow, uncooperative; not very natural in her speech.

14. Craven County

Formed 1705 as Archdale, name changed to Craven 1712. 1st grant S. of the Chowan made here 1656; 1st settler arrived 1664 from VA. Huguenot settlers in 1707; later Swiss and many Germans. New Bern founded 1710 (became capital 1763); Welsh Quakers, Puritans from New Eng., NJ. Indian problems during the Tuscarora uprising in 1711. Anglicanism est. early, but no church till 1751; also Methodists, Presbyterians. New Bern very prosperous in early 19th cent.: opposite important inlet. Tobacco, forest products, some commercial fishing. Pop. 1790: 10,469, 1820: 13,394, 1850: 14,709, 1880: 19,729, 1910: 25,594, 1930: 30,665, 1960: 58,773.

Brinson, S. M. 1911. Early Craven County. *North Carolina Booklet* 10:176–95.

Carraway, Gertrude S. 1938. *Historic New Bern*. . . . New Bern: Merchants Association and Chamber of Commerce.

Carraway, Gertrude Sprague. 1940. *Crown of Life: History of Christ Church, New Bern, North Carolina 1715–1940*. New Bern: O.G. Dunn.

Cooper, Francis Hodges. 1920. Some Colonial History of Craven County, North Carolina. *James Sprunt Studies in History and Political Science* 17.1:27–74.

Dill, Alonzo Thomas. 1955. *Governor Tryon and His Palace*. Chapel Hill: University of North Carolina Press.

Graffenried, Christoph. 1973. *Christoph von Graffenried's Account of the Founding of New Bern*. Ed. and trans. by Vincent A. Todd. Spartanburg, SC: Reprint Co.

Todd, Vincent Hollis. 1913. *Baron Christoph von Graffenried's New Bern Adventures*. University of Illinois dissertation.

Vass, Lachlan Cumming. 1886. *History of the Presbyterian Church in New Bern, North Carolina*. Richmond, VA: Whittet and Shepperson.

1900. De Graffenreid and the Swiss and Palatine Settlement of New Bern, North Carolina. *Historical Papers of the Historical Society of Trinity College* 4:64–71.

1941. *New Bern, Cradle of North Carolina*. Raleigh: Garden Club of North Carolina.

Cahoque, Havelock P.O.

During prohibition, Havelock a distributing center for "Craven County Corn" made in local woods and swamps.

NC 14N: M, farmer, 77. B. Harlowe (Carteret Co., just over co. line). Former slave; went as infant to Craven Co. — F., PGM both b. 3 mi. S. of Harlowe; M., MGF, MGM b. Harlowe. — Ed.: very little. — Methodist. — Quick, bright, active; old, somewhat forgetful. Speech not frightfully old-fashioned; parents prob. belonged to educated whites. Inf.'s wife reads; his children have contacts in New Bern. — Tempo rather rapid. Occasional hesitations; otherwise clear utterance. Pronunciation of [nuʃ] is interesting; cf. Wilmington and Charleston. An old English dialect characteristic, or substitution of [nu] for [ɲu]? FW uses [F] for a voiceless labiodental frictionless continuant. /v/ and /w/ are both [v].

NC 14A: Ernul P.O. — M, farmer, 70. B. locally. — F., PGF b. here, PGF's F. b. Ireland (came to VA and then here), PGF's M. b. here, PGM perhaps b. Carteret Co. (of "foreign descent"); M., MGF b. near New Bern, MGF's F. b. Scotland, MGF's M., MGF's MGF both b. Pamlico Co., MGM, possibly MGM's F. b. here. — Ed.: till 20 (very little). — Christian. — Poor, industrious; very clear mind; no pretense or dissimulation; enjoys talking to people. Grasps a point instantaneously, but makes an intellectually evaluated response that is, however, thoroughly natural and fitting. Cooperative, understands purpose of interview. Very observant: frequently states present-day form but also remembers old form. Inf. feels he and his wife use the older words; feels other people do not. — Moderate tempo; slightly slurred utterance. Retroflex vowel in unstressed syllables usually absent. One day, however, he began to use weak ones for several pages.

Vanceboro

Craven County Farm Life School here; educational center of section. Pop. 1930: 742.

NC 14B: F, 75. B. locally (Neuse River Landing). — F. b. Neuse River Landing, PGF, PGM b. England; M., MGF, MGM all b. Kitts Swamp. — Ed.: country school till 12;

Vanceboro later; Greensboro Female College (Guilford Co.) for a short time at age 19. — Methodist. — Highly intelligent; cooperative. Schoolteacher background in family, makes her appear similar to many New Eng. village types. Acts to some extent as expert on local dialect, which she may not always use herself. — Tempo ordinary; vowels tend to be short. Utterance clear. Noteworthy are the open diphthongs, often closing with the [j]. The [oʊ] diphthong generally does not begin at so central a point as in Blounts Creek.

New Bern

One of oldest NC communities. Est. 1710; almost wiped out in 1711 in Tuscarora Wars. Inc. and became Co. seat 1723. Many German settlers: Reformed and "First Day Baptists". Became official capital in 1767. Public schools since 1764. Important trading and cultural (drama, music) center. Active during Rev.: many French "adventurers". Cosmopolitan; largest town in NC in 1815. No damage in Civil War. Decline after RR. Agriculture, fishing, lumber, woodworking. Pop. 1850: 4,681, 1880: 6,443, 1910: 9,961, 1930: 11,981, 1960: 15,717.

NC 14C!: F, single homemaker, 67. — F., PGF, PGF's F. all b. here, PGM b. Co. (descended from an early colonial church warden and high sheriff); M. b. here, MGF, MGF's F. (a doctor), MGM all b. Co. (MGF's PGF's F. lived in Halifax, NC, and was prominent in NC govt.; MGF's paternal line came to RI in 1632, then to Albemarle Sound via VA in 1653). — Ed.: at home and New Bern Academy. — Episcopalian. — Has lived sheltered life centering on family; rather nervous and eccentric; kind and cooperative. Member of one of old families of New Bern. Did not understand purpose of interview for c. first 20 pages. — Doesn't think about her pronunciation, prob. unaware that there is any other way to say *palm* [pæəm], *turn* [tʰɵˑ·i̥ʃn], etc. Rather opinionated in saying, however, that she had never heard anything but *afternoon* used (she was forced to add later, "by those of [her] class"). Unconscious also of her use of [v] for both /w/ and /v/. Rather back [uʃ] very different from [ʮˁʉˀˁ] sound of the surrounding area. Her [aɪ] sound, similar to that of the aged inf. for Pamlico Co., is different from other places around here. — Cultivated.

15. Pitt County

Formed 1760 from Beaufort Co. 1st settler arrived 1714. Some early settlers from MA; pop. English and Scots. Some iron production during Rev. Shipping in 19th cent. Some Civil War skirmishing. Timber cutting. Highest income from major farm products (esp. tobacco) in state. 3/4 of farm pop. tenants; over 50% AfAm. Few industries. Pop. 1790: 8,275, 1820: 10,001, 1850: 13,397, 1880: 21,794, 1910: 36,340, 1930: 54,466, 1960: 69,942.

Duncan, John G. 1966. *Pitt County Potpourri*. Greenville: East Carolina College.

Jenkins, James S. 1965. *Greenville and Pitt County near the Turn of the Century*. Greenville: The Author.

King, Henry T. 1911. *Sketches of Pitt County*. Raleigh: Edward and Broughton Printing Co.

Pitt County Club. 1920. *Pitt County: Economic and Social*. Chapel Hill: University of North Carolina Press.

Williams, Thomas A., ed. 1974. *A Greenville Album: The Bicentennial Book.* Greenville: ERA Press.
1957. Pitt County. *The State* Oct. 5, 1957.

Shelmerdine, Greenville P.O., Chicod Twp.

Shelmerdine a sawmill town; company town for Beaufort Lumber Co. Decline in 20th cent. pop. Greenville 2nd largest bright-leaf market in the world. Founded 1786. E. Carolina U. here.

NC 15A: M, farmer, 74. B. locally. — M., MGF, MGM, MGM's F., MGM's M. all b. here (M's family had large early land grant here). — Ed.: none (completely illiterate). — Free Will Baptist. — Extremely old-fashioned, isolated; genial, cooperative; becoming somewhat forgetful. Humble circumstances, family once better off. Unaware of outside world, though goes to Greenville occasionally now. Daughter and son-in-law cooperated in drawing him out. — Tempo and nasalization moderate. Somewhat slurred utterance.

Winterville P.O. and Twp.

Small town, trading center in NE of Twp. Baptist Academy became Winterville HS in early 20th cent. 1st NC Institute for Teachers here, 1901. Some small mfg.

NC 15B: F, widowed homemaker, 53. B. near Hadock's Crossroads (10 mi. SE of Winterville). — F., PGF, PGM, M., MGF, MGF's F., MGM, MGM's F. all b. Co. — Ed.: at home till 13, then at Free Will Baptist Seminary in Ayden (Pitt Co.) for 2 yrs. — Free Will Baptist. — Sweet, maternal, hospitable; cooperative, natural. — Tempo moderate. Appears to distinguish [æ], [æɨ], and [ɛɨ]. Modern tendency to substitute [æ] for some of the [æɨ] words. Perhaps as a result, many of the [æɨ] words have fallen together with the [ɛɨ] words. This last phenomenon may be due to her consciously trying to use an old-fashioned pronunciation for FW and overstepping the mark, or it may be related to the type of speech of the older Wilson Co. person. (Note: many examples of /e/ in *aunt, can't, haunt* in SAS — RIM). Inf. distinguishes *past* and *paste*, [pæɨ.st], [pɛɨ.st] as well as *asked* [æᵊst]. The older Wilson Co. inf. does not distinguish the first two.

Bethel P.O. and Twp.

Bethel in N. end of Twp. Pop. 1880: 127, 1910: 469, 1930: 1,522, 1960: 1,578.

NC 15C: M, farmer, 84. B. here. — F., M. b. here. — Illiterate. — Social contacts limited. — Intelligent, but extremely deaf; interview discontinued for this reason. — Very good articulation. No retroflexion (except for this northernmost section, Pitt Co. has retroflexion). Uses [oᵛᵊ᷈] where the rest of Pitt Co. uses [ɵ·ʊ᷈], as in *go, slow.* /u/ is not the very front type of the rest of Pitt Co.

16. Greene County

Formed 1799 (was Glasgow, formed 1791). Mostly English by 1800; a few Jews, some Scots and Irish. Little industry; always agriculture. RR's late and unsuccessful. Farm pop. 80% tenants. Tobacco and cotton; recently soybeans. Pop. 1800: 4,218, 1820: 4,533, 1850: 6,619, 1880: 10,037, 1910: 13,083, 1930: 18,656, 1960: 16,741.

Creech, James M. 1979. *History of Greene County, North Carolina.* Baltimore: Gateway Press.

Arba, Snow Hill P.O., Hookerton Twp.

Snow Hill Co. seat. Laid out 1811; inc. 1828. Center of transportation and communication. Arba a small uninc. community; religious; rich farmland. Pop. Arba 1950: c. 200.

NC 16A: F, widowed homemaker, 74. B. locally. — F., PGF, b. here, PGM b. here (of "Croatan" ancestry, but [pæ.ɨ.s fə hwa-ɛ't]); M. b. near Rose Sharon Meeting House (Lenoir Co.), MGF, MGM b. Lenoir Co.. — Ed.: c. 6 mos. — Methodist. — Old-fashioned; quick, alert mind; limited interests. Children did not attend school. Unaware of other types of speech; no effort to "improve" her speech. — Tempo rather slow; tendency to lengthen vowels and diphthongs. Apparent distinction between [ɛ'ɨ.] and [æ·ɨ.], based chiefly on length of first element. Cf. [dʒæ.ɨ.ndʒəz] and [lɛ.ɨ.n]. Although FW did not mark length in the first word, [æ] always implies greater length and more front articulation than [ɛ], cf. [hæ.ɨ.nt] and [kɛɪnt]. FW can't swear, though, to the constancy of a distinction.

NC 16A*: Snow Hill P.O. and Twp. — F, widow, 70+. B. here (in log house). — F., M. b. here. — Becoming slow with age. — Has had slight lisp or indistinctness of pronunciation all her life.

NC 16B: Snow Hill P.O., near Hookerton Twp. — M, farmer, 44. B. locally. — F., PGF b. here, PGM b. Lenoir Co.; M., MGF b. near Snow Hill, MGM b. Greene Co. — Ed.: off and on till 20 (1-2 mos. per yr.). — Christian. — Obliging, earnest, but reactions very slow; religious; possibly self-conscious. — Tempo rather slow; tendency to prolong.

17. Wayne County

Formed 1780 from Dobbs. 1st settlement c. 1730. Slightly over 50% of farm pop. were tenants in 1925. Tobacco, cotton, strawberries, Irish potatoes; leads state in mfg. brick and tile. Pop. 1790: 6,133, 1820: 9,040, 1850: 13,486, 1880: 24,951, 1910: 35,698, 1930: 53,013, 1960: 82,059.

Byrd, Sam. 1942. *Small Town South.* Boston: Houghton, Mifflin.
Daniels, Frank A. 1914. *History of Wayne County.* Goldsboro.

NC 17A: Emmaus Church, Dudley P.O., Indian Springs Twp. (SE part of Co.). — M, farmer, 66. B. locally. — F., PGF b. just across Neuse River (in Co.); M., MGF b. here. — Ed.: little or none. — Free Will Baptist. — Old-fashioned, not very intelligent, becoming senile. — Tempo slow; tendency to lengthen sounds.

Mt. Olive P.O., Brogden Twp.

Mt. Olive at S. end of Twp. Bright-leaf, cotton, berries, melons, vegetables; state's largest bean market. Pop. 1910: 1,071, 1930: 2,685, 1960: 4,673.

NC 17B: M, farmer, 48. B. here. — F. b. here, PGF, PGF's F., PGF's M. PGM all b. Wayne Co.; M. b. here, MGF b. Pitt Co., MGM b. Pitt or Greene Co. — Ed.: till 15. — Presbyterian. —

Quite curious at first, but lost interest during last part of the interview. Average intelligence; more social than industrious. — Tempo moderately slow. Articulation lax. Articulation very indistinct during last interview; claimed to be suffering from hay fever.

18. Duplin County

Formed 1749 from New Hanover. Scotch-Irish settlers direct from Ireland in 1736 (Ulster Presbyterians); later Swiss. Baptists by 1755. Grove Academy from 1786. RRs from 1840; naval stores by 1860. Truck farming, fruits and vegetables (esp. strawberries), poultry; tobacco chief crop. Pop. 1786: 5,248, 1790: 5,662, 1820: 9,744, 1850: 13,514, 1880: 18,773, 1910: 25,442, 1930: 35,103, 1960: 40,270.

> McGowen, Faison Wells, ed. 1971. *Flashes of Duplin's History and Government*. Kenansville: McGowen, Pearl Canady.
> Williams, V. Faison. 1923. Henry McCullough and His Irish Settlement. *North Carolina Booklet* 22:32–39.

NC 18A: Chinquapin P.O., Cypress Creek Twp. — M, farmer, 71. B. here. — F. b. near here, PGF, PGM both b. here; M., MGM b. near here. — Illiterate. — Social contacts limited. — Jolly, obedient, suspicious. Perception not very quick; slightly hard of hearing. — Tempo moderate; tendency to prolong vowels. Says [dⁱʉplɪn], not [duˈplɪn] as in the W. part of the county.

Friendship, Warsaw P.O., Faison Twp.

Twp. in NW part of Co. Faison village founded 1785; one of largest cucumber markets. Friendship uninc.; location of Academy from 1841. Warsaw a truck market center.

NC 18B: F, single, 61. B. here. — F., PGF, PGF's F., PGM b. here (of Scotch-Irish descent on both sides); M., MGF, MGM, MGM's F. b. here. — Ed.: till 20. — Presbyterian. — Of good family; rather conservative. — Moderate tempo; tendency to prolong vowels. [e⌃] and [i], [o⌃] and [uˈ] fall together as [e⌃] and [o⌃], respectively, before nasals.

19. Jones County

Formed 1779 from Craven Co. Huguenots from VA arrived 1707. Farming; well over 50% of farming pop. tenants. Pop. 1790: 4,822, 1820: 5,216, 1850: 5,038, 1880: 7,491, 1910: 8,721, 1930: 10,428, 1960: 11,005.

> Johnson, Talmadge Casey. 1954. *The Story of Kinston and Lenoir County*. Raleigh: Edwards and Broughton Co.
> Powell, William S. 1963. *Annals of Progress, the Story of Lenoir County and Kinston, North Carolina*. Raleigh: State Dept. of Archives and History.

Pleasant Hill, Kinston P.O., Tuckahoe Twp.

Twp. in W. of Co.; Pleasant Hill on E. side of Twp. Kinston in Lenoir Co., where it is Co. seat. Tobacco center. Town authorized 1762; Anglican parish antedates Kinston. Old buggy factory, textile mills, lumber mill, tobacco works, one-time shoe factory.

NC 19A: M, farmer, 69. B. locally. — F. b. Co. (towards Trenton), PGM b. Co.; M., MGF, MGF's F. b. here, MGM b.

Lenoir Co. — Ed.: here till 21 (little). — Christian. — Pleasant, obliging, conversational; good common sense. — Tempo rather slow. His [e⌃ɹ] or [eɪ⌃] diphthong is markedly different from the [ɛɪ] type in Greene, Wilson, and Wayne Cos. No overlapping of [æɪ⌃] and [eɪ], except in *can't*, which is often abnormal. His [ɚ] is strong, frequently transcribed [ɝ], and frequently glides up into the fricative area [ɝɪ]. Is this an English dialect characteristic, or does it bear some relation to the Scotch-Irish settlement of Duplin Co.? FW had not heard anything like it except occasionally in W. PA.

Trenton P.O., Beaver Creek Twp.

Trenton Co. seat. Grist mill here from before 1861; also lumber mills. Swamps and savannas; game and fish thrive. Pop. 1930: 500.

NC 19B: M, farmer, 51. B. here. — F., PGM b. here; M. b. Co., MGF b. Harlowe (Craven Co.), MGM b. near Beaufort (Carteret Co.). — Ed.: here through 7th grade, then to Trenton, then one term military school in Kinston (Lenoir Co.). — Methodist; Mason; Chairman, county commissioners. — Patient, genial, slow to understand questions. — Tempo slow; tendency to lengthen sounds. He has an [iə] diphthong and an [ɛə] diphthong (latter varies somewhat). His [æ] is high, not low-retracted as in most of E. Carolina. Little retroflexion; FW attributes this to cultural spreading from New Bern. [ɒ·ə] in *barn* resembles speech N. and W. of here, as opposed to the older inf. in another part of Jones Co. who uses [a·ɚ] as in Onslow Co.

20. Carteret County

Formed 1722 from Craven Co. Nearly half of area in water. Slow settlement; Tuscarora Indians. Beaufort laid out 1713. 1st settlers Huguenots (from VA) and English. Anticipated boom from Atlantic and NC RR (1858), but war and blockade cut short development. Forest products, biological stations; little mfg.: packing boxes, one knitting mill. Tobacco chief crop, also corn, potatoes, cotton; little livestock. Leads state in commercial fishing. Pop. 1790: 3,732, 1820: 5,609, 1850: 6,939, 1880: 9,784, 1910: 13,776, 1930: 16,900, 1960: 30,940.

> Cobb, Collier. 1915–16. Greek, Roman and Arabian Survivals on the North Carolina Coast. *North Carolina Booklet* 15:218–26.
> Lefferts, Aleeze, et al. 1928. *Carteret County: Economic and Social*. Chapel Hill: University of North Carolina Press.
> Salter, Ben B. 1972. *Portsmouth Island: Short Stories and History*. Atlantic.

Roe, Cedar Island Twp.

Cedar Island most thickly settled section in colonial days. Banks islands heavily subject to erosion; dangerous waters. Portsmouth in 1815 largest seaport in NC; now fishing primarily, home gardens. Pine, cedar, and myrtle cover sand dunes.

NC 20A: M, fisherman, 69. B. here; has been away fishing along NC coast for a few mos. at a time. — F., PGF, PGM b. here (both sides of old stock); M., MGF, MGM all b. North River (E. of Beaufort). — Ed.: about 12 mos. — Social contacts limited. — Average intelligence; quick, nervous, energetic; not loquacious. May have tendency to conceal older things from FW, and not admit things he feels are incorrect. — Tempo extremely rapid; vowels usually short. Speed tends to close up diphthongs which in other individuals are extremely open. Glottalization a regular feature of the speech of Co. Inf. says people do not use /w/ for /v/; FW heard him use it only in [wɛɾɪ] for [vɛɾɪ]. However, island people notice that the people from Atlantic use /w/ all the time. The school superintendent on Cedar Island, originally from Atlantic (B.A. from UNC), said [sælwɪdʒ], [kənwiinjənt] in FW's presence. Some of the people from Atlantic to Harkers Island have a very Cockney speech; e.g. *Boyd* [oʌɪ], *bowed* [æʌʊ], *abode* [ʒʊ] or [ʌʌʊ]. They have [ɤ] in all positions.

Harkers Island (at ferry landing)
Speech old-fashioned due to long isolation. Fishing principal activity. Pop. 1930: 1,200.

NC 20B: M, fisherman, storekeeper, 72. B. here. — F., PGF, PGM, PGF's F. all born here; M. b. here, MGF b. Sea Level (Carteret Co.), MGM b. here. — Ed.: here, 6 or 7 mos. — Methodist. — Intelligent; becoming somewhat senile. Has never traveled or had much schooling, but reads a lot, and tends to put best foot forward. — Rapid tempo; vowels and diphthongs tend to be short. Type of speech probably less extreme than that of descendants of refugees from "Diamond City" shipwreck near here in 1900. Intonation quick, monotonous, lacking polite rise and fall of the usual Southern or New England speaker. Intonation more like that of unaffected Cockney, or of Mid-Atlantic states (e.g., N. MD). The word *hob* [haʔb] turns up for *goal*, as on Chinocoteague Island, VA.

Straits P.O. and Twp.
Isolated farm community opposite Harkers Island.

NC 20C: F, widowed homemaker, 42. B. here. — F. b. Gloucester (2 miles from here), PGF b. here, PGM b. Shalotte (Brunswick Co.); M. b. Gloucester, MGF, MGF's F. both b. Betty (near North River), MGM, MGM's F. both b. Straits, MGM's M. b. here. — Ed.: here till 18. — Methodist. — Extremely gracious; most obliging; conscientious. — Tempo slow. Voice and intonation vaguely reminiscent of Cockney, though inf.'s speech not as extreme as many in area. According to inf. at Atlantic, /w/ and /v/ are neutralized as [w]; in Beaufort, /hw/ merges with /w/.

21. Onslow County
Formed 1734 from New Hanover Co. 1st settlement 1705–6; most early settlers English or German. Settlement primarily along coast. Few Tories. Plantation country; few but powerful planters. Anglicans c. 1731; Baptists 1735–40; Methodists from 1785. Fed. raids 1862–64. RR from 1890. Many dispossessed when Marine base built here. Tobacco leading crop. Pop. 1790: 5,387, 1820: 7,016, 1850: 8,283, 1880: 9,829, 1910: 14,125, 1930: 15,289, 1960: 82,706.

Brown, Joseph Parsons. 1960. *The Commonwealth of Onslow: A History*. New Bern: O. G. Dunn.
1955. Onslow County. *The State*, Mar. 26, 1955.

Grants Creek, Maysville P.O. (Jones Co.), White Oak Twp.
Twp. settled 1720s from E. NC, VA, MD, CT, MA. Timber, sawmills after 1865. Inland waterway. Early Baptist church located in Grants Creek. Farming and lumber milling at Maysville. Savannas and ponds; rice grown here in colonial days.

NC 21A: F, housewife, 71. B. here. — F. b. here, PGF b. Co., PGF's F. b. England, PGF's M. b. Co. (half Indian), PGM b. near Sneads Ferry, PGM's F. b. Co.; M., MGF both b. here, MGM b. just across river, in Jones Co. — Ed.: very little. — Missionary Baptist. — Lovable, very loquacious, utterly unsuspicious. Not very aware of outside world or of purpose of interview, but very obliging and cooperative. FW became acquainted with her informally, offering her a ride to church. — Tempo moderate; tendency to prolong.

Harris Creek, Jacksonville P.O. and Twp.
Free Will Baptist church located at Harris Creek. Jacksonville in W. center of Co.; Co. seat from 1842. Fine oyster beds; tobacco chief money crop.

NC 21B: M, farmer and merchant, 45. B. locally (near Jacksonville). — F., PGF, PGF's F., PGF's M. all b. near Jacksonville, PGM b. Co.; M., MGF b. near Jacksonville, MGF's F., MGM b. Co. — Ed.: till 21; Clemson College (SC) for 4 mos. in 1918 for mechanical training course (military). — Primitive Baptist. — Good middle-aged type; substantial local citizen; quick, intelligent, natural, cooperative. — Fairly rapid tempo. He uses [ɛɤ] for [æɤ] altogether. Words which in most varieties of English have [ɪɤ] have [jɤ] or [ⁱɤ] (two ways of writing much the same phenomenon).

22. Pender County
Formed from New Hanover in 1875. Welsh tract set aside 1725, Welsh settlers 1730. Immigrants from VA c. 1775; also Scottish, Irish. Presbyterians oldest religious group. Strong anti-carpetbag movement here. Experimental agricultural colony est. here at St. Helena in 1906. Timber cutting in past. Diversified crops: cotton, corn, tobacco, strawberries, lettuce. Pop. 1880: 12,468, 1910: 15,471, 1930: 15,686, 1960: 18,508.

Bloodworth, Mattie. 1947. *History of Pender County, North Carolina*. Richmond, VA: Dietz Print. Co.
Waddell, Alfred Moore. 1909. *A History of New Hanover County and the Lower Cape Fear Region: 1723–1800....* Wilmington.

Canetuck, Currie P.O.
Baptist church here. Richest soil in Co.; some swamps.

NC 22A: M, farmer, logger, hunter (guide), 68. B. here. — F. b. here, PGF, PGM from SC; M. b. here. (Wife b. here; PGF, PGM from Stump Sound, Onslow Co.; M., MGF b. Pender Co.). — Baptist; social contacts involving hunting. — Honest, poor family. Unaware of outside world. Inf. accustomed to being guide to a few hunters from Winston-Salem each year. — Tempo slow; vowels long.

Riverside, Burgaw P.O. and Twp.
Burgaw Co. seat; site given by RR, charter 1879. Notable variety of wild flowers and shrubs. St. Helena, agricultural

colony, developed here. NC coastal experiment station. Game refuge with public hunting grounds. Greatest diversification of crops in state (strawberries chief product).

NC 22B: F, housewife, 49. B. locally. — F., PGF b. Topsail Twp. (coast of Pender Co.), PGM b. Wilmington (perhaps New England name); M. b. Holly Twp. (12 miles north), MGF b. Co. (parents from Scotland), MGM b. Holly Twp. — Ed.: here till 18. — Baptist. — Inf. tried to "speak well" for FW; a good record nonetheless. Inf. living in good circumstances. — Tempo moderate; tendency to prolong.

23. New Hanover County

Formed 1729 from Craven Co. One of smallest NC cos. Abortive colonies in area very early: 1526, 1662, 1664–67. By 1720, SC had expanded to bay, with Cape Fear as unofficial boundary. Brunswick settlement here by 1725, with settlers from SC and upper NC. Welsh tract 1730; Highland and Ulster Scots in Wilmington area by 1733. Naval stores port here early. St. James Parish est. 1729 in approx. the area of Co. Many Presbyterians, Baptists by 1760. British occupation of area in 1781. By 1788–89 trade above pre-Rev. level, mostly to Wilmington; dredging of river began. Steam navigation by 1817; RRs by 1840. Strongest NC center of secessionism. Beginning of free public schools 1872. Rice (pre-Civil War), cotton, naval stores, truck farming; but 2nd lowest value of farm crops in NC. Resort areas at beach. Suburban developments; heavy industries WWII and after. Pop. 1786: 5,042, 1790: 6,831, 1820: 10,866, 1850: 17,668, 1880: 21,376, 1910: 32,037, 1930: 43,010, 1960: 71,742.

Connor, Robert W. D. 1907. The Settlement of the Cape Fear. *South Atlantic Quarterly* 6:272–87.

De Rosset, William Lord, ed. 1938. *Pictorial and Historical New Hanover County and Wilmington, North Carolina, 1723–1938*. Wilmington: W.L. DeRosset.

Evans, William McKee. 1967. *Ballots and Fence Rails: Reconstruction on the Lower Cape Fear*. Chapel Hill: University of North Carolina Press.

Hewlett, Crockette W. 1971. *Between the Creeks: A History of Masonboro Sound. . . .* Wilmington: Wilmington Print. Co.

Howell, Andrew J. 1930. *The Book of Wilmington*. Wilmington.

Lee, Lawrence. 1965. *The Lower Cape Fear in Colonial Days*. Chapel Hill: University of North Carolina Press.

Lee, Lawrence. 1971. *New Hanover County: A Brief History*. Raleigh: State Dept. of Archives and History.

Reilly, J. S. 1884. *Wilmington: Past, Present and Future. . . .* Wilmington.

Schaw, Janet. 1921. *Journal of a Lady of Quality. . . .* Ed. by Evangeline Walker Andrews, in collab. with Charles McLean Andrews. New Haven: Yale University Press.

Sprunt, James. 1896. *Tales and Traditions of the Lower Cape Fear. . . .* Wilmington. Repr. 1973 (Spartanburg, SC: Reprint Co.).

Sprunt, James. 1914. *Chronicles of the Cape Fear River. . . .* Raleigh: Edwards and Broughton Print. Co.

Waddell, Alfred Moore. 1908. *Some Memories of My Life*. Raleigh: Edwards and Broughton.

Waddell, Alfred Moore. 1909. *A History of New Hanover County and the Lower Cape Fear Region: 1723–1800. . . .* Wilmington.

Whiskey Creek, Wilmington P.O., Masonboro Twp.

Masonboro location of summer residences of planters.

NC 23A: M, farmer and fisherman, 75. B. Wilmington, but returned here when infant. — F. b. Myrtle Grove, PGF, PGM both b. Co., step-PGM perhaps b. Wilmington (of Irish immigrant stock); M. b. Co., MGF b. Federal Point in Co. — Baptist. — Genial, quick old man whose mind is pretty good, despite heart and blood pressure trouble. — Tempo rather rapid; tendency to short vowels. Pretty clear enunciation. "Retroflexion" weak, variable in presence or absence. [u˂] is farther back than the Wilmington [ʉ], but inf. distinguishes [ᶦʉ] from [u˂] whereas most Wilmington people seem to use [ʉ] for both, just as Bostonians use [u·] for both. [o˯ʊ] often begins more open than indicated; open [ʌ˯]; very open [ɔ˯].

NC 23B: Myrtle Grove Sound, Wilmington P.O., Masonboro Twp. — F, housewife, 46. B. here. — F. b. Duplin Co. (near Wallace) and came here when young, PGF b. Duplin Co. (Scotch-Irish descent), PGM b. Duplin Co.; M. b. Greenville Sound in Co., MGF b. Brunswick Co., MGF's F., MGF's M. both b. near Greensboro, MGM b. Masonboro Sound in Co., MGM's F. b. Onslow Co. (Scotch-Irish descent), MGM's M. b. on Little Sound in Co. — Ed.: till 16. — Presbyterian. — Perhaps somewhat too careful of certain particulars in her speech, though FW believes they are thoroughly natural to her adulthood. — Moderate tempo; some prolonging. Retroflexion variably present, variably intense. Open [ɛ˯]. [ɒ˰·] for [ɔ̈ː].

NC 23B*: F, housewife, 45. — Parents b. here. — Ed.: moderate. — Not very quick or bright, but conscientious. Her husband stopped the interview at p. 30. — Lips immobile; sounds difficult to catch.

Wilmington

1st settlement in area 1730, called Newtown. Surveyed 1733; renamed Wilmington 1739. Became Co. seat 1740. Chartered as a borough 1763; as town 1776; as city 1866. Good harbor, easily accessible from interior. Ironworks (1838) oldest business in city. RRs from 1850; most important RR center in state by 1865. Chief blockade-running port for Confederacy. Free public schools from 1872. Race riot 1898. Largest city in NC till 1910. Turpentine, oil terminals, chemical plants, shipbuilding, shipping, lumber, fertilizer, cotton, shirt factory, naval stores (largest naval stores market in US in 1850s). Pop. 1850: 7,264, 1880: 17,350, 1910: 25,748, 1930: 32,270, 1960: 44,013.

NC 23C!: F, 48. B. here. — F., PGF, PGF's F., PGF's PGF all b. Wilmington, PGF's PGF's F. and M. b. Charleston, SC, PGF's PGM, PGF's M. b. Wilmington, PGF's MGF b. Highlands of Scotland, PGF's MGM b. Cape Fear country, PGM b. Wilmington, PGM's F. b. Brunswick, PGM's PGF b. near Georgetown, SC (All Saints Parish, Scots father), PGM's M., PGM's MGF b. Brunswick Co., PGM's MGF's F. (French Huguenot) and M. both b. near Georgetown, SC, PGM's MGM b. Brunswick Co., PGM's MGM's F. b. near

Georgetown, SC, PGM's MGM's M. b. near Charleston, SC (French Huguenot); M. b. Wilmington, MGF, MGF's F. both b. Brunswick Co., MGF's PGF b. Bladen Co., MGF's PGM, MGF's PGM's F. b. Brunswick Co., MGF's PGM's M. b. New Hanover Co., MGF's M. b. Bladen Co., MGM b. Morristown, NJ, and came here when young, MGM's F. and M. b. Morris Co., NJ — Ed.: here till 17; training as a nurse. — Episcopalian. — Cooperative. — Tempo rather rapid; no particular prolongation. Low [ɛ̬]; [ɐɪ] and [ɐʊ̭] before voiceless cons. [ɛə] appears in natural conversation for both [ɪə] and [ɛə], but [ɪə] is frequently substituted in careful speech. — Cultivated.

NC 23D!: F, 55+. — Parents b. Wilmington. — Episcopalian. — Good background; simple. Her sister is a florist and she felt too busy just before Easter to continue. A good record on the whole. — Moderate tempo. No retroflexion. [ʉ] is substituted for [ɪʌʉ] after /n t d/, although there is an artificial tendency to use [ɪʌu] after /t d/. High [o] and [e] sounds with a tendency to [ə] off-glides often. [ɐʊ̭] and [ɐɪ] before voiceless sounds. [ɛə] is natural for both [ɪə] and [ɛ̬ə], but there is a tendency to use spelling pronunciations and distinguish them. — Cultivated.

24. Brunswick County

Formed 1764 from New Hanover. None of old Brunswick town records preserved; many destroyed by Union soldiers. Many Cape Fear Scots; coast settled by fishermen. Low pop. density; less than 6% of land cultivated. Rural; heavy rainfall; little wealth. High illiteracy. Much timber swamp, absentee landlords. Base for Confederate blockade-running; Fed. invasion 1863. Rice planting, naval stores, lumbering, fishing (2nd in state in fishing revenue). Pop. 1790: 3,071, 1820: 5,480, 1850: 7,272, 1880: 9,389, 1910: 14,432, 1930: 15,813, 1960: 20,278.

> Trussell, Brandon. 1926. *County Government in Brunswick County, North Carolina.* Chapel Hill: University of North Carolina Press.
> Waddell, Alfred Moore. 1890. *A Colonial Officer and His Times, 1754–1773.* Raleigh: Edwards and Broughton.
> 1965. *Bicentennial, Brunswick County, NC: Souvenir Booklet.* Southport: Brunswick Co. Historical Society.

Calabash, Shallotte P.O. and Twp.
Shallotte in SW corner of Twp. Named for Little Charlotta plantation. Fishing area.

NC 24N: M, farmer, 89. B. Columbus Co. on a plantation. At end of war (age 17) came to Little River just over line in SC. After some years, came back here to this part of Brunswick Co. (did not live in Brunswick Co. until grown). — F. b. Columbus Co. (father was sold away so inf. did not know him); M., MGF, MGM all b. in Columbus Co. on same plantation. — Baptist. — Quick; highly intelligent. Cooperative, but tendency not to remember the most old-fashioned forms. — Rapid tempo; some tendency to prolong.

NC 24A: Freeland, Waccamaw Twp. (NW corner of Co.). — F, housewife, 70. B. here. — F. b. on Roanoke River in VA and came here as a small boy (died when inf. was 9 yrs. old), PGF, PGM both b. on Roanoke River in VA; M. b. here,

MGF b. Co., MGM b. Columbus Co., near here. — Ed.: a little. — Missionary Baptist. — Intelligent; obliging. Perhaps not as old-fashioned as FW could have found. — Tempo rather slow; some tendency to prolong.

Royal Oak, Supply P.O., Lockwoods Folly Twp.
Settlement by Lockwood from Barbados c. 1692 destroyed by Indians. Supply a base for deer and quail hunting.

NC 24B: M, farmer and sawmill worker, 45. B. here. — F. b. 10 mi. S. near coast, PGF, PGM b. Co. (PGM's name an old one here); M. b. Supply, MGF, MGM b. Co. — Ed.: here till 18. — Baptist. — Progressive middle-aged type. Slightly hesitant about being fully cooperative at all times. — Tempo fairly rapid; some tendency to prolong.

25. Sampson County

Formed 1784 from Duplin Co. Largest co. in state. Scotch-Irish settlers in 1736, then Swiss. Later some Highlanders, some English from VA, Quakers here. Gun factory during Rev. War. Private school from 1875. One of the most productive NC cos.; cotton chief crop, blueberries. Pop. 1786: 4,268, 1790: 6,065, 1820: 8,908, 1850: 14,585, 1880: 22,894, 1910: 29,982, 1930: 40,082, 1960: 48,013.

> Bass, Cora. 1957. *Sampson County Yearbook, 1956–57.* Clinton: Bass Pub. Co.

Turkey
Pepper market. Pop. 1930: 213.

NC 25N: F, farmer, 60. B. here. — F., PGF, PGM b. here; M. b. Co., MGM lived in Co. — Ed.: till 20 in local school. — Holiness Church (Pentecostal); formerly Baptist. — Shrewd, quick-witted; abundant energy; well-educated for her generation and quite intelligent, but ideas about many things rather vague and judgment is not always to be trusted. Altogether an excellent inf. — Speech is energetic and clear, lacking the extreme mumbling, intoned character of many of her relatives; however, many sounds, particularly final consonants, are very weakly articulated. Nasality often; vowels tend to be lengthened. A number of sound substitutions which inf. employs in common with her companions seem to reflect the phonetic pattern of some group of African languages, namely: [ɲ] for [ɲ̊ʲ], [t] for [θ], [d] for [ð], [f] or [ɸ] for [θ], [s] for [θ], [s] for [ʃ], [tʃ] for [ʃ], [β] for [v], [a˞·β] or [a˞·v] or [a˞·v] for [a̭ʊ]. We may presume that the African language had a [ɲ]; also that there were no [θ], [ð], [ʃ], [ʒ], [ʊ], or [aʊ] sounds. Confusion of /l r n/ in certain words is also noticeable. /l/ is darker than in the speech of whites. The [a˞ʊ] diphthong is never front as in the speech of whites. Uses [ɛ̃˞r] or [ɛ̃˞ə] where white people say [æ̭ə] or [æ̭ər]. Inf. definitely preserves the old "Negro" way of speaking except when consciously correcting herself.

Clinton (14 mi. W.), Mints P.O., McDaniels Twp.
Clinton oldest town in Co. Co. seat from 1818; inc. 1852. Slow growth early, but much expansion since 1910. Tobacco market; livestock, poultry, eggs, fruit, vegetables. Lumber, light (mostly service) industry, meat and poultry packing. Pop. 1880: 620, 1910: 1,101, 1930: 2,712, 1960: 7,461.

NC 25A: M, farmer, sawmill worker, 73. B. here. — F. b. just across river in Cumberland Co., PGF b. near London, England, PGM b. just across river in Cumberland Co.; M., MGF, MGM b. here (MGF's people came from Tar River near present Rocky Mount). — Baptist. — Talkative, somewhat unconnected, but thoroughly capable of answering questions. — Loud, harsh, coarse voice. Tendency to prolong vowels. Note that [æ] is very short and rather open in all positions (never [æɨ]).

NC 25B: Turkey. — M, farmer (Co. Road Commissioner, 20 yrs. Justice of the Peace, State Legislature 1929), 68. B. here. — F., PGF, PGF's F. b. here, PGF's PGF b. Isle of Wight Co., VA (Scotch-Irish), PGF's M. of German descent, PGM, PGM's F. and M. all b. here (English descent); M., MGF, MGF's F., MGF's M., MGF's MGF b. here (latter of "Irish" descent), MGM, MGM's F., MGM's M., MGM's MGF all b. here (English descent). — Ed.: here till 16. — Methodist. — Both parents were college grads. Interested in worthy, intellectual things as his family would have liked him to be. Gr-gr-grandfather a Revolutionary general, buried here on the old place. — Tempo more rapid than most, but rather deliberate at times; vowels usually fairly short. Articulation fairly precise.

26. Cumberland County

Formed 1754 from Bladen County. NC Highlanders. Tourist in 1828 complained that many of the people in a 24-mi. radius spoke only Gaelic. Some slaves acquired Gaelic. 1st Highlanders settled in 1731; some Swiss settlers 1736. More than 5,000 Scots in area by 1740. Center of naval stores production before Civil War. Plank roads by 1850. Fort Bragg est. 1918 (field artillery, paratroops). Agriculture, forestry, plywood and veneer, cottonseed oil. Pop. 1790: 8,671, 1820: 14,446, 1850: 20,610, 1880: 23,836, 1910: 35,284, 1930: 45,219, 1960: 148,418.

> Meyer, Duane Gilbert. 1961. *The Highland Scots of North Carolina, 1732–1776.* Chapel Hill: University of North Carolina Press.
> Myrover, J. H. 1905. *Short History of Cumberland County and the Cape Fear Section.* Fayetteville: Bank of Fayetteville.
> Oates, John Alexander. 1950. *The Story of Fayetteville and the Upper Cape Fear.* Fayetteville.

NC 26A: Chasons Store, Cedar Creek P.O. and Twp. — F, housewife, widow, 70. B. here. — F. b. Cedar Creek, PGF, PGM b. Co.; M. b. here, MGF, MGM b. Co. — Ed.: a little each winter. — Baptist. — Calm, patient and attentive; occasionally slow in understanding. — Lips move only a little, owing to tobacco or pellagra. Vowels and diphthongs decidedly prolonged. The sequence [æɚ] or [ær] does not exist in her speech. It is replaced by [ɛʌɚ] or [ɛʌr] as in *more* [mɛʌɚ], *married* [mɛʌɾɨd]. Also *Cape Fear* [fɛʌɚ], but *afraid* [əfjɚ·d] and *beard* [bjɚ·d]. Tendency for the second element of the [æʊ] diphthong to be slightly raised. [ɑʌ·] as in *long* appears to belong to the /ɑ/ phoneme as in *not*, not to the /ɔʌɔ/ phoneme.

Hope Mills, Rockfish Twp.

Twp. in SW of Co.; Hope Mills a settlement with several churches in center of Twp.

NC 26B: F, housewife, 57. B. 12 mi. N. of Fayetteville in Eastover Twp. near Wade, came here when 16. — F. b. Wade, PGF b. over line in Harnet or Johnson Co., PGM b. over line in Sampson Co.; M. b. near Godwin Sta. in Co., MGF, MGM b. Co. (latter of Scottish descent). — Quick, intelligent, cooperative; occ. somewhat reticent. — Tendency to prolong vowels as in E. Carolina.

Fayetteville, Cross Creek Twp.

Est. 1760 as Cross Creek; chartered as Campbellton 1762; combined with Cross Creek 1778; had received name Fayetteville by 1784. Briefly state capital in late 18th cent. Head of navigation and commercial center. Presbyterian stronghold from beginning; Methodists, Roman Catholics, Baptists, Episcopalians shortly thereafter. Gaelic still spoken around Fayetteville in the 1870s. Textiles by 1824; paper mill at one time. 1st steamboat 1818; RR by 1832. US arsenal 1836–61, Confed. 1861–65. Ft. Bragg nearby, largest military base in US. Pop. 1790: 1,536, 1850: 4,645, 1880: 3,485, 1910: 7,045, 1930: 13,049, 1960: 47,106.

NC 26C!: F, housewife, widow, 37. B. here. — F. b. Fayetteville, PGF b. Bennettsville, SC, came here when young, PGF's F. b. Bennettsville, PGF's PGF from England, PGM, PGM's M. b. Fayetteville; M., MGF, MGF's F. b. Fayetteville, MGF's PGF from Lowlands of Scotland, MGF's MGF and MGM from Highlands of Scotland, MGM b. Fayetteville. — Ed.: here through h.s. — Episcopalian. — Intelligent, cooperative, enjoyed the questions. Family once prominent, but not in last generation. Inf. had to make an effort at first to avoid spelling-pronunciation in *frost*, etc., but got along pretty well. — Pronunciations [hwʌt], [ʌv] resemble VA rather than most NC speech. Also inf.'s [ɐ] is like VA. Around Fayetteville one hears much speech like that of inf. 26A; whether this inf.'s speech represents a class or city dialect in Fayetteville or the regional type W. and N. of Fayetteville is uncertain. In her personal leanings, she is bitterly anti-VA (cf. the cultivated Raleigh inf. for [ɒʊ]). — Cultivated.

27. Bladen County

Formed 1734 from New Hanover Co. 1st grants c. 1732 to Scots; settlement along Cape Fear and South River. 1st courthouse 1738. Whig stronghold during Rev.; battle at Elizabethtown. Presbyterians and Methodists by late 18th cent., Baptists later. Mainly rural; plantation country. Naval stores, tobacco, lumber, cotton, corn, peanuts. Pop. 1790: 5,084, 1820: 7,276, 1850: 9,767, 1880: 16,158, 1910: 18,006, 1930: 22,389, 1960: 28,881.

> Crawford, Clifton E. 1957. *Bladen County.* Elizabethtown: The Author.

Bladenboro

Twp. in SW corner of Co. 1st settled 1779 by English. Grew up as RR station late 19th cent. Cotton mills in 1911.

NC 27A: M, farmer, 70. B. locally. — F. b. here (said his descent was French and "Buckskin"); M. b. locally, MGF, MGM b. Co. — Missionary Baptist. — Quick; humble background. — Tempo moderate; prolongation. [a·ʊ] diphthong; short [ɒ] appears slightly rounded at times; [æ̰] in all positions; the [æ̰ɨ] sound does not exist (this is like New Hanover and Carteret Cos.). FW recorded /r/ postvocalically because it seemed to be made with tongue-tip up. In connected speech, inf. uses a great many more glottal stops for unexploded /t/ in word juncture, even before vowels.

Elizabethtown

Ferry site on Cape Fear River. Settled 1734; named and est. as Co. seat by 1774. Tory center; battle 1781. Formerly lumbering; peanut factory 1931.

NC 27B: F, housewife, 47. B. locally. — F. b. 8 mi. up river on other side, PGF b. Co.; M., MGF b. near White Oak, up across river. — Ed.: Duplin Co. till 19 (Bethel Twp.). — Baptist. — Quick, intelligent, cooperative. — Tempo rather rapid; no great prolongation. [æ⌄] in all positions. No [æ·ɨ] sound (cf. New Hanover and Carteret Cos.).

28. Columbus County

Formed 1808 from Brunswick and Bladen Cos. Visited first c. 1734. Tobacco chief crop. Cotton from 1815, strawberries from 1896; also sweet potatoes, beans, pecans, peanuts. Timber crops. Hunting and sport fishing. Pop. 1810: 3,022, 1820: 3,912, 1850: 5,909, 1880: 14,439, 1910: 28,020, 1930: 37,720, 1960: 48,973.

Rogers, James A. 1946. *Columbus County, North Carolina.* Whiteville: The Author.

Crusoes Island, Old Dock P.O., Lees Twp.

Crusoes Island settled 1792, possibly by refugees from Haiti. Elevated knoll in swamp country. Deer and bears; bearhunting. Old Dock formerly shipping pt. on Waccamaw for naval stores.

NC 28A: M, farmer and fisherman, 76. B. here. — M., MGM b. here. — Ed.: very little. — Baptist. — Quick, bright, intelligent; calm and even disposition; very cooperative. — Tempo deliberate. No particularly great prolongation (unlike many other islanders). Inf. has good, clear articulation except that the lips move little and there is retracted vowel articulation. Inf.'s voice has the rather deep, coarse, harsh quality and resonance with retracted and muffled articulation which one associates with PA and Midwestern speech more than with the South Atlantic. [u˂·] is replaced by [oʌ·] before /m n/; *soon* = [soʌ·n]; *room* and *Rome* both = [roʌ·m]. FW also heard this pronunciation elsewhere.

The Jam (the Corner), Macedonia Church, Boardman P.O., Tatums Twp.

Twp. in NW corner of Co. Boardman now an almost deserted settlement; was busy lumber mill town till mills closed in 1926. Pop. 1930: 158.

NC 28B: M, farmer, 67. B. here. — F. b. 5 mi. E. near Evergreen, PGF b. Co., PGM b. 2 1/2 mi. SE, PGM's F. b. Co.; M. b. 14 mi. away near Cherry Grove, MGF, MGM b. Co. — Ed.: very little. — Baptist. — Very cooperative, fairly intelligent, but quite unaware of the outside world. Loves to talk. — Tempo moderate. Articulation very clear-cut. [ɝ·] rounded usually.

Whiteville, Welch Creek Twp.

Laid out 1810; chartered 1873. Co. seat; first courthouse 1809. Tobacco warehouses, grapes. Pop. 1880: 343, 1910: 1,368, 1960: 4,683.

NC 28C: F, single homemaker, 40. B. here. — F. b. here, PGF b. Co., PGM, step-PGM b. here; M. b. Boardman Co., MGF b. here, MGM b. Boardman Co. — Ed.: here till 16. — Baptist. — Good, local middle-class type; quick, obliging, somewhat timid. Some stubborn spelling pronunciations. — Tempo rather slow; some prolongation.

29. Robeson County

Formed 1786 from Bladen Co. Indian tribe makes up approx. 1/3 pop. of county. 1st European settlers Scots 1726–35. Intermarriage has created a rural proletariat of AfAms and Anglo-Indians. Co. terrorized by Lowrie outlaw gang 1864–74. Flora MacDonald College est. 1896. Swamp drainage 1914–18. Rich agricultural county; tobacco dominant. 2nd in NC in number of tenant farmers; tenants make up over 65% of farm pop. Cotton and corn, in addition to tobacco. Pop. 1790: 5,326, 1820: 8,204, 1850: 12,826, 1880: 23,880, 1910: 51,945, 1930: 66,512, 1960: 89,102.

Farris, James J. 1925. The Lowrie Gang. *Trinity College Historical Society Historical Papers* 15:55–93.

Lawrence, Robert C. 1939. *The State of Robeson.* . . . NY: J. J. Little and Ives.

Locklear, Janie Maynor, and Drenna J. Oxendine. 1975. *Bibliography, Lumbee Indians.* Pembroke: Lumbee Indian Education Project.

Lucas, John Paul, Jr., and Bailey T. Groone. 1940. *The King of Scuffletown.* Richmond: Garrett and Massie.

Magdol, Edward. 1973. Against the Gentry: An Inquiry into a Southern Lower-Class Community and Culture, 1865–1870. *Journal of Social History* 6:259–83.

Norment, Mary C. 1875. *The Lowrie History.* . . . Wilmington: Daily Journal Print.

Sider, G. M. 1974. *The Political History of the Lambee Indians of Robeson County, North Carolina.* New School for Social Research thesis.

Pembroke

Once named Scuffletown. Center of Croatan/Lumbee Indians (origins obscure). State college; at one time had 3 school systems.

NC 29A: M, farmer (public works till married), 78. B. locally. — F. b. here (Lowland Scottish), PGM b. here; M. b. here, MGF b. Scotland (Gaelic), MGM b. Harpers Ferry, just across the creek, MGM's F. Indian, MGM's M. Indian and white. — Ed.: 2 mos. — Baptist; deputy sheriff once. — Kind accommodating; intelligent, responses trustworthy. Rugged: walks 10–15 mi. a day and never feels it. — The use of [ß], [ᵝ] for /w/, not found elsewhere in NC to FW's knowledge, is prob. of Indian origin. Perhaps Gaelic influences the speech of the region, too (in his father's day, preaching was in Gaelic and English). The use of [ɪs] for [ɪz], etc. may be due to a foreign language, unless it is a survival from English dialects.

NC 29A*: F, c. 60. B. here. — Parents and grandparents were Indians here. — Poor, uneducated. Because of inf.'s slow responses, NC 29A was substituted for this locality. — Inf. preserves traces of the foreign speech.

Barker Ten Mile, Lumberton P.O., Howellsville Twp.

Twp. in E. part of Co. In 18th cent., Lumberton a trading point for timber and naval stores; timber rafts and cargo floated down Lumber R. When timber gone, farming and cattle. 1st dry co. in NC, 1886. Textile mills, fertilizer factories, shipping point for truck.

NC 29B: F, housewife, 43. B. here. — F., PGF b. 5 mi. E. (perhaps of Irish descent); M., MGF b. Robeson Co. (perhaps of Irish descent), MGM b. here. — Ed.: till 18. — Methodist. — Timid; worried about her performance. — Rather slow tempo; tendency to prolong.

30. Northampton County

Formed 1741 from Bertie. Over 65% of farm pop. tenants; over 60% AfAm. Cotton and peanuts. Pop. 1786: 7,043, 1790: 9,981, 1820: 13,242, 1850: 13,335, 1880: 20,032, 1910: 22,323, 1930: 29,161, 1960: 26,811.

Johnson, J. Roy, and Tom Parramore. 1962. *The Roanoke-Chowan Story*. Rich Square: Parker Bros.
Stephenson, Grace, and Gilbert Stephenson. 1958. *We Came Home to Warren Place*. Raleigh: A. Williams.
Wilborn, Elizabeth W., et al. 1974. *The Roanoke Valley: A Report for the Historic Halifax State Historic Site*. Raleigh: Division of Archives and History.

NC 30A: Faisons Old Tavern, Conway P.O., Wiccacanee Twp. — M, farmer, 89. B. here. — F. b. here, PGF, PGM b. Gates Co. and came here; M., MGF, MGM b. here. — Baptist. — Well, alert, able to work every day at age 89. Never quite aware of purpose of interview, or convinced that it was worthwhile. Trustworthy responses. — Tempo rather rapid; articulation good. Retroflexion almost absent (occ. a trace). Inf.'s speech very different from that of neighboring Southampton Co., VA, in [ɑv], [hwɑt], and the [aɨ] and [aʊ] diphthongs.

NC 30B: Lasker, Roanoke Twp. — F, 65. B. locally. — F. b. Lasker, PGF, PGM b. Co.; M. b. Rich Square, MGF b. near Ahoskie, Hertford Co., MGF's F. b. Hertford Co., MGM b. Rich Square. — Ed.: Lasker till 16. — Methodist (M. a Quaker). — Motherly, cooperative; middle-aged type; accurate, natural. — Tempo moderate; some prolonging. This part of the county alone has slight retroflexion which does not exist elsewhere in Co.

31. Halifax County

Formed 1757 from Edgecombe Co. 1st settlements c. 1723. Earliest settlers English from VA, some from PA and NJ; also Highlanders from VA. Baptist settlement 1742. Colonial products: rice, corn, cotton, indigo, tobacco, lumber, meat and hides. Overland markets to VA Piedmont. Navigation on Roanoke R.; declined with coming of RRs. Before 1861, more influence in state than any other co. To 1918, numerous governors, congressmen, gov't officials from this co. Rich farmland, cotton, tobacco, peanuts, corn, textiles, forest products, paper. Pop. 1786: 10,327, 1790: 13,965, 1820: 17,237,

1850: 16,589, 1880: 30,300, 1910: 37,646, 1930: 53,248, 1960: 58,956.

Allen, Sidney B., and R. Stanford Trents, Jr. 1920. *Halifax County: Economic and Social*. Durham: Seeman Printery.
Allen, W. C. 1918. *History of Halifax County*. Boston: Cornhill Co.
Gowen, Harry W. 1907. *Story of the Right Worshipful Joseph Montfort*. Halifax: The Author.

Hollister, Essex P.O., Brinkleyville Twp.

Twp. in SW corner of Co. Hollister a small community with some importance as a lumber center.

NC 31A: M, farmer, 68. B. here. — F. b. Northampton Co., near Jackson, came here just after War, PGF, PGF's F. both b. near Petersburg, VA, PGM b. near Jackson in Northampton Co.; M. b. here, MGF b. near Weldon in Co., MGM b. Warren Co. near Warrenton. — Baptist. — Becoming senile. — Deliberate tempo; vowels and diphthongs tend to be short. [æʊ] is treated more or less as in Brunswick Co., VA (similar to Nash Co., NC?). E. part of Halifax Co. has quite a different type.

Darlington, Halifax P.O., Faucett Twp.

Halifax founded 1757 to promote trade and navigation on Roanoke River; successful trade with Edenton and with Southside VA. On main coastal highway. Didn't grow after Rev. Co. seat from 1758. Scene of first constitutional convention in 1776; seat of general assembly 1776–82. Agricultural section, with industries related to agriculture: peanut processing, cottonseed oil mills, fertilizer.

NC 31B: F, 59. B. Scotland Neck Twp. in Co., came to Darlington upon her marriage. — F. b. Scotland Neck, PGF b. prob. in Germany or perhaps from PA (a "Dutchman"), and as a boy came with his father, PGM, PGM's F. b. Scotland Neck; M. b. near Weldon, MGF b. Hamilton, Martin Co., MGM b. Halifax Co. — Ed.: till 15. — Parents Primitive Baptist. — Unselfconscious, cooperative, middle-class type. — Tempo fairly rapid; tendency to prolong vowels. Her speech more likely that of her birthplace (between Scotland Neck and Tarboro) than of community where she now resides. It resembles NC infs. from Northampton Co. (except that she has no retroflexion) and Edgecombe Co. It is completely different from that of the old-fashioned inf. in the W. part of Halifax Co. (NC 31A), who does not use [æʊ] but uses a diphthong rather similar to that of Brunswick Co., VA. The 2 records from Halifax Co., NC, should be regarded as representing 2 completely different speech areas.

32. Edgecombe County

Formed 1741 from Bertie Co. Individual settlers arrived beginning c. 1720; chiefly English, some Irish, French. Enfield co. seat; lost when co. divided. Slavery grew, till AfAm majority in 1860. Early products: naval stores, cattle, hogs, horses (for sport), tobacco. Episc. parish 1741; Baptists 1745; Presbyterians 1754; Methodists 1760. Tarboro head of navigation, furthest inland port. RRs 1880s led to industrialization. Farm pop. 83% tenants. Cotton, stock raising in 19th, 20th cent.; various industries in late 19th cent.:

furniture, textiles. Pop. 1786: 8,480, 1790: 10,255, 1820: 13,276, 1850: 17,189, 1880: 26,181, 1910: 32,010, 1930: 47,894, 1960: 54,226.

Barringer, Bugs, Dot Barringer, and Lela Chesson. 1977. *Rocky Mount: A Pictorial History*. Norfolk, VA: Donning Co.

Bobbitt, William E. 1950. *A Brief History of Rocky Mount, North Carolina*. Rocky Mount: Chamber of Commerce.

Lichtenstein, Gaston. 1908. *Early History of Tarboro, North Carolina*. Richmond, VA: W. E. Jones.

Lichtenstein, Gaston. 1910. *When Tarboro was Incorporated*. Richmond, VA: Capitol Print. Co.

Piehl, Charles. 1979. *White Society in the Black Belt, 1870–1920: A Study of Four North Carolina Counties*. Washington University [St. Louis] dissertation.

Turner, J. Kelly, and J. L. Bridgers. 1920. *History of Edgecombe County*. Raleigh: Edwards and Broughton Print. Co.

Turner, James Kelly. 1916. Slavery in Edgecombe County. *Historical Papers of the Trinity College Historical Society* 12:5–36.

Watson, Joseph W. 1969. *Kinfolks of Edgecombe County, North Carolina. . . .* Rocky Mount.

Rocky Mount P.O. and Twp.

Twp. on W. side of Co. Settled by 1734 at falls of Tar River. RR 1839; town developed with RR: textiles, shoes, tobacco market, Atlantic Coast Line Shops. 1st public school 1901. NC Wesleyan College 1960. Diversified economy: 5th largest bright-leaf market in world, clothing, textiles, cottonseed oil and meal, fertilizer, cordage, and lumber. Pop. 1880: 552, 1910: 8,051, 1930: 21,412, 1960: 32,147.

NC 32A: M, farmer, woodsman, 73. B. here. — F. b. here, PGF b. in mts., settled here as a boy, PGF b. Edgecombe; M., MGF, MGM b. here. — Illiterate. — Social contacts limited. — Jolly, good-natured storyteller; rather slow, but very obliging and patient. 4 mo. interval in interview between 32.4 and 32.5.

Coolmore Farm, Tarboro P.O. and Twp.

Tarboro founded 1760; became Co. seat 1762. Relatively small; some industry: farming (cotton, tobacco, peanuts), tobacco market, cotton mfg., cottonseed products, veneers, cornmeal, feed.

NC 32B!: F, widow, 59. B. 6 mi. SE of Tarboro. — F., PGF, PGF's F. all b. Edgecombe Co. (of VA origin), PGM, PGM's F. b. Edgecombe Co.; M., MGF, MGF's F., MGM b. Edgecombe Co., MGM's M. b. Martin Co. — Ed.: public and private schools here; one session private school in Tarboro; one yr. college at Greensboro. — Baptist. — Although selected as middle-aged type, inf. is in most respects more like cultivated type, although not residing in an urban community. Poised, self-possessed; seemed to thoroughly enjoy interview. Tried to be completely natural in her speech. Interesting that there is no retroflexion in this co., whereas it turns up in most nearby cos. — Cultivated.

33. Wilson County

Formed 1855 from 4 other cos. Tobacco chief crop; city of Wilson a major NC tobacco market. Mainly tenant farming. Pop. 1860: 9,720, 1880: 16,064, 1910: 28,269, 1930: 44,914, 1960: 57,716.

NC 33A: Black Creek P.O. and Twp. — F, 68. B. on Contentnea Creek (4 mi. NW). — F. b. here; M., MGM b. over line in Wayne Co. — Ed.: very little. — Ironside Baptist. — Simple, hardworking; thoroughly natural and cooperative; of humble background but self-assured. — Tempo rather slow; vowels and diphthongs tend to be prolonged. Her speech illustrates with marked clarity the existence of two phonemes in words which ordinarily have [æ]. She uses [æ] or [æᵊ] (a sound slightly low and slightly centralized) in words such as *slam* [slæᵊm], *mercy* [mæᵊsɪ]. There is no [ɪ]-like off-glide even before [k], [g], and [ʃ], as in [sæk̓], [bæᵊˢd̞], [mæ·ʃ]. Another phoneme, realized as [æ·ɪ̯], is used in words such as *last* [læ·ɪ̯st], *calm* [k̓æ·ɪ̯m]. Cf. *platter* [plæțɚ] and *daughter* [dæ·ɪ̯ țɚ]. The same distinction is further carried out between such pairs as *sham* [ʃæᵊm] and *shame* [ʃæ·ɪ̯ m]. [æ·ɪ̯] is not distinctive, however, with respect to [ɛɪ]. Although at first there appeared to be a distinction in certain words based on historical differences or spelling, these differences do not appear to be regular or consistent. [æ·ɪ̯] seems to be a long open allophone of /ɛɪ/ which occurs before [θ f v s m n]. The shorter allophone, [ɛ‘ɪ̯], occurs finally and elsewhere and, when the word is spoken quickly, even before [θ f v s m n]. The amazing thing about this inf. is that she always uses the same phoneme ([æᵊ] or [æ·ɪ̯]) in the same word. There is a clear-cut distinction between these two. Has not tried to tamper with her speech. Inf. NC 15B (in Pitt Co.), on the other hand, often hesitates between the two sounds. See extra pages for further examples.

Evansdale, Wilson P.O., Stantonsburg Twp.

Stantonsburg in SE of Co. Wilson formed 1855. Settled c. 1790, mainly by Irish and English from VA. Largest bright-leaf tobacco market in world; 8 large tobacco warehouses. Cotton and fertilizer factories; redrying plants; bale covering, bus bodies, wagons. Pop. 1930: 12,613.

NC 33B: F, housewife, 40. B. Saratoga (4 mi. E.); when 8 moved to Wilson suburbs. — F. b. Wilson, PGF b. here, PGF's F. b. Ireland; M., MGM b. Wilson. — Ed.: Saratoga, and Maplewood School in Wilson. — Methodist. — Middle class; good tenant farmer. Natural; rather intelligent. — Tempo moderate. Articulation rather good. [æ˞] and [æ˞ɪ̯] (distinctive) are unusually high in beginning.

34. Johnston County

Formed 1746 from Craven Co. Earliest settlers Scots, also some English; names continue from early settlements. First Academy 1809. Last important battle of Civil War here. Tobacco warehouse by 1898; cotton, corn, tobacco, sweet potatoes chief crops. Pop. predominantly rural and agricultural; high illiteracy, birthrate, homicide. 81% of farms cultivated by whites. Lumbering, wood products, cottonseed products. 65% of land cut over, woodlands or scrub timber. Also iron ore; grist and flour mills.

Sanders, William Marsha, Jr. 1922. *Johnston County: Economic and Social.* Smithfield: The Smithfield Observer. 1956. Johnston County. *The State*, Sept. 8, 1956.

Sanders Chapel, Smithfield P.O. and Twp.

Twp. in center of Co.; Sanders Chapel in SE of Twp. (actually across line in Boon Hill Twp).

NC 34A: F, farm laborer, 70. B. Ingrams Twp. (15 mi. SW of here near Benson); came here when 40. — M. b. near Benson (Johnston Co.), MGF b. Harnett Co. — Illiterate. — Primitive Baptist. — Very talkative. Some difficulty understanding more intricate problems, but generally does very well. Humble circumstances; has worked hard at menial tasks all her life and has feeling of obedient inferiority. — Fairly rapid tempo; vowels and diphthongs tend to be long. — Record has second p. 56.

Smithfield

St. Patrick's Parish in area 1746. Town est. 1770; inc. 1775. Head of navigation on Neuse. Tobacco market, art pottery. Pop. 1850: 329, 1880: 485, 1910: 1,347, 1930: 2,543, 1960: 6,117.

NC 34B: F, housewife, 61. B. locally. — F. b. here, PGF b. TN and family later came back here; M., MGF b. here, MGM b. near Princeton in Co. — Ed.: till 15. — Methodist. — Obliging, competent, cooperative. Not always alert. Middle-aged type. — Tempo rather slow; vowels and diphthongs prolonged. The prolongation is a single impulse of breath but does not exhibit the extreme tapering off in breath-impulse and pitch which the VA type shows. Presence and amount of retroflexion extremely variable. Inf. seems to have an /eɹ/ phoneme, an /æ/ phoneme, and an /æɹ/ phoneme, but the 3 overlap in certain words. Both inf. and her husband say *quarter till eleven*; FW hasn't encountered it elsewhere in eastern NC.

35. Harnett County

Formed 1855 from Cumberland Co. 1st settlers English, Welsh, Scots; Quakers and Presbyterians among early settlers. Baptists by 1778, Methodists later. Loyalist activity in Rev. A few large slaveholdings; mostly small farmers. Not much cotton till after 1865; tobacco after 1880. Iron industry briefly c. 1876: rich ore, but vein ran out. Cotton mills in Erwin by 1903; other scattered industries. Pop. 1860: 8,039, 1880: 10,862, 1910: 22,174, 1930: 37,911, 1960: 48,236.

Fowler, Malcolm. 1955. *They Passed This Way: A Personal Narrative of Harnett County History.* Harnett Co. Centennial Inc.

NC 35A: Manchester, Anderson Creek Twp. — F, housewife, 80. B. here. — F. b. Barbecue (in Co., on Cumberland line), PGF, PGM b. Barbecue Church (parents on both sides b. Highlands of Scotland); M., MGF b. Moore Co., MGF's F. and M. Highland Scots, MGM, MGM's F. and M. all b. Cumberland Co., of Highland Scots ancestry. All 4 GPs spoke both Gaelic and English; their parents knew no English before coming. — Ed.: Manchester till 15. — Presbyterian. — Remarkably well-preserved; rugged in mind and personality. Good family, better educated than many of her neighbors.

Aware of FW's purposes and glad to cooperate. — Tempo deliberate; vowels tend to be fairly short, except for emphasis or relaxation. Articulation more precise than by most people. /a/ seems to vary from front to back, as though she had heard both varieties during her life.

Erwin, Grove Twp.

Twp. on E. side of Co. Erwin a cotton mill town from c. 1903.

NC 35B: F, housewife, 44. B. here. — F. b. Grove Twp., PGF b. Harnett Co., PGM b. Almance Co. and came here when married; M. b. Grove Twp., MGF b. here, MGM b. Co. — Ed.: here (not much). — Free Will Baptist. — Quick, reactive, but sometimes rather flighty (perhaps because ill at ease, esp. during last part when sister was listening). — Tempo quick; vowels and diphthongs tend to be long.

36. Scotland County

Formed 1899 from Richmond. Largest proportion of pop. Scotch Presbyterians. C. 80% of farm pop. tenants. Cotton chief crop; also tobacco, melons, cantaloupe. Textile mills from 1828; lumber. Pop. 1900: 12,553, 1910: 15,313, 1930: 20,174, 1960: 25,183.

Nashville, Wagram P.O., Spring Hill Twp.

Spring Hill Church an old Baptist center. Wagram an important shipping point for peaches. Pop. Nashville 1930: 1,137, 1960: 1,423.

NC 36N: M, farmer, 77. B. locally. — F. b. near Wagram; M., MGF b. just across river in Hoke Co. (M. was bought at age 16 by F.'s master). — Ed.: 2 mos. during each of 3 years. — Baptist Missionary. — Above the average; not particularly old-fashioned. Slightly hard of hearing. — Tempo moderate; some tendency to prolong. Unusually high [eˑ iˑ oˑ uˑ].

NC 36A: Gibsons Store, Laurel Hill P.O. and Twp. — M, farmer, 76. B. here. — F. b. near Aberdeen (Moore Co.), PGF b. Isle of Skye, Scotland (Europe) and came here after marriage, PGM b. Scotland (Europe); M., MGF both b. 5 mi. N. of here, MGM b. near Spring Hill Church (now Wagram) 8 mi. NE of here. Families on both sides Highland Scots. — Ed.: 3 mos. — Presbyterian. — Patient, obliging, but somewhat senile. — Tempo deliberate; no particular prolongation. Articulation good. /r/ after a vowel represents a retroflex sound, the tongue tip rising toward or to the post-alveolar ridge.

NC 36B: St. John Church, Gibson P.O., Williamsons Twp. — M, farmer, 43. B. locally. — F., PGF, M., MGF, MGF's F., MGM all b. here. — Ed.: till 16. — Methodist. — Inf. seemed prematurely old; hard of hearing. Did not seem to understand some of the questions, perhaps since purpose of interview misunderstood. — Tempo fairly rapid; some tendency to prolong. Lip action weak; mouth not opened much. Note postvocalic [r] for [ɚ].

37. Warren County

Formed 1779 from Bute. Brief settlement 1728. Other settlers followed from VA and E. NC. Various social classes, mostly English, some Scots; also slaves (slave majority by

1790). Baptists and Methodists in 1780s. Plantation country; tobacco from 18th cent. 1810–20 most powerful co. politically in USA. Agricultural; once 3 resort springs. Pop. 1786: 8,295, 1790: 9,397, 1820: 11,158, 1850: 13,912, 1880: 22,619, 1910: 20,266, 1930: 23,364, 1960: 19,652.

> Montgomery, Lizzie Wilson. 1924. *Sketches of Old Warrenton, North Carolina.* Raleigh: Edwards and Broughton Print. Co.
>
> Vance, Zebulon Baird. 1875. *Sketches of North Carolina.* Norfolk: The Norfolk Landmark.
>
> Wellman, Manly Wade. 1959. *The County of Warren, North Carolina, 1586–1917.* Chapel Hill: University of North Carolina Press.

Wise, Smith Creek Twp.
Twp. in N. part of Co.; settled pre-Rev.

NC 37A: F, housewife, 65. B. locally (4 mi. from the VA line). — F., PGF, PGM, M., MGF all b. Co., MGM b. locally, MGM's F. b. Co. (genealogy not trusted by FW). — Illiterate. — Methodist. — Hardworking, upright; direct, sensible mind; trustworthy inf. — Rather good enunciation and articulation. Inf.'s speech is thoroughly VA in character (of W. Mecklenburg and Halifax Cos. in VA, and in marked contrast to the speech of E. Mecklenburg and of Halifax Co., NC). A clear illustration of the fact that most VA and NC dialects are regional, embracing all classes in the community. It is noteworthy that she uses *minister's face,* a term that turns up chiefly on the lower James and York.

Marmaduke, Fishing Creek Twp. (record made in Warrenton, Shocco Twp., where inf. had lived for the previous 12 yrs.)
Warrenton laid out as Co. seat 1780. Area settled c. 1730s. Methodist, Episcopal, Presbyterian churches in early 19th cent. Center of culture 1800–1860. Once, many private schools and academies. Textile mfg. Pop. 1850: 1,242, 1880: 816, 1910: 807, 1930: 1,072, 1960: 1,124.

NC 37B: M, farmer, 52. B. near Marmaduke. — F. b. 3 mi. SE of Warrenton, PGF, PGM b. Co.; M. b. 12 mi. S. of Warrenton, MGF, MGM b. Co., step-M., step-M.'s F. and M. all b. Halifax Co. — Ed.: here till 20, then Buie's Creek Academy in Harnett Co. for 18 mos. — Baptist. — Inf.'s mother died when he was 4 yrs. old. Good, solid, middle-class farmer; fairly good background; somewhat slow. — Fairly rapid tempo; tendency not to prolong sounds. Inf.'s speech is not quite as thoroughly VA as that of inf. NC 37A.

38. Franklin County
Formed 1779 from Bute. Over 50% of farm pop. tenants. Pop. 1786: 5,475, 1790: 7,557, 1820: 9,741, 1850: 11,713, 1880: 20,829, 1910: 24,692, 1930: 24,456, 1960: 28,755.

Moulton, Louisburg P.O., Sandy Creek Twp.
Louisburg 1st settled 1758. Louisburg College, Methodist and coed., founded c. 1802. Lumber, milling.

NC 38N: M, farmer, 81. B. locally. — F. b. locally (different plantation), PGF, PGM both b. Epsom (NW of here); M., MGF both b. locally on diff. plantations, MGM b. on same plantation as M. and inf. — Illiterate. — Baptist. —

Intelligent, quick; cooperative. Since freedom he has accumulated property and has other AfAms working for him. Polite, humble, well-respected locally. — Tempo moderate; tendency to prolong.

Bunn, Dunn Twp.
Dunn a marketing center for farming region. Founded by descendants of early English and Scotch settlers. Bunn smallest inc. place in Co. in 1920.

NC 38A: M, tenant farmer, 70+. B. here. — Parents b. here. — Illiterate. — Isolated, proud (refused money for the interview, though clearly in need of it), stubborn (stopped in middle of page 88 and refused to continue). — Fairly rapid tempo. Vigorous speech, enunciation not very clear. Slight postvocalic retroflexion is sometimes present, sometimes absent.

NC 38B: F, housewife (formerly seamstress), 58. B. here. — F. b. here, PGF b. Wilson Co. and came here when young, PGM b. just over line in Wake Co.; M., MGF both b. here, MGM b. near Franklinton. — Ed.: here till 16. — Baptist. — Intelligent; cooperative. Wife of local merchant. — Tempo fairly slow; vowels tend to be rather long. Her retroflexion is almost always present, esp. for /ar/, in contrast to the area only a few miles east where practically no retroflexion exists in the speech of the old-fashioned type. Nash Co. preserves greater retroflexion. Presumably the speech in the northern part of the county is more like that of Warren and Granville counties.

39. Granville County
Formed 1746 from Edgecombe County. First white settlers c. 1715–20, from Bath neighborhood. Many settlers from VA in late 1730s. Early settlers predominantly English; some Scotch-Irish, French, Germans; Anglicans, Presbyterians and Baptists all by 1750. One of leading slaveholding cos.: 43% of pop. slaves in 1800. Corn, wheat, tobacco early crops; some soil exhaustion by Rev. Some naval stores; peaches and apples, cider and brandy. Small amount of mineral wealth: iron, copper, gold; rich farm lands. Pop. 1786: 6,247, 1790: 10,982, 1820: 18,222, 1850: 21,249, 1880: 31,286, 1910: 25,102, 1930: 28,723, 1960: 33,110.

> Caldwell, James R. 1968. *A History of Granville County, North Carolina: The Preliminary Phase, 1746–1800.* University of North Carolina dissertation.
>
> Gwynn, Zae Hargett. 1974. *Kinfolks of Granville County, North Carolina, 1765–1826.* Rocky Mount: J. W. Watson.
>
> Hummell, Elizabeth Hicks, comp. 1965. *Hicks History of Granville County, North Carolina.* Oxford, NC.
>
> Lyle, Virginia Reavis. *Granville County, North Carolina Potpourri.* Nashville: Vee El Ancestral Studies.
>
> Ray, Worth Stickley. 1945. *Colonial Granville County and Its People.* Austin, TX. Repr. 1965 (Baltimore: Genealogical Pub. Co.).
>
> Tilley, Nannie May. 1934. The Settlement of Granville County. *North Carolina Historical Review* 11:1–19.

Old Watch Curran Home, Oxford P.O. and Twp.
Oxford co. seat in E. central Co. Named 1764 for plantation. Academy and military school in 19th cent.; tobacco market, mfg.

NC 39A: M, farmer, 77. B. 7 mi. S. of VA line and about same from Person Co. line. Moved part way here when 12 yrs. old; last 20 yrs. here. — F. b. NE corner of Co.; M. b. 5 mi. N. near Mt. Creek Church, MGF b. VA, MGM b. Co. — Illiterate. — Baptist. — Successful tobacco farmer; genial; not very bright; not ever altogether aware of purpose of interview. — Tempo deliberate; vowels and diphthongs tend to be short. None of the drawl of E. Carolina. Speech seems indistinguishable from neighboring VA type.

NC 39B!: Abrams Plains, Stovall (center for tobacco, vegs.) P.O., Sassafras Fork Twp. — F, housewife, 45. B. here. — F. b. here, PGF b. Franklin Co., NC, PGM, PGM's F., PGM's M., PGM's MGM, PGM's MGM's F. b. here, PGM's MGM's PGF b. VA of a 1653 ancestor from Bristol, England; M. b. Miss. and returned here as infant, living over the line in Mecklenburg Co., VA, before married, MGF b. Goshen in Co., MGM b. Mecklenburg Co., VA. — Ed.: Statesville Female College (now Mitchell College) 3 yrs. Previous education by governesses from Richmond and northernmost NC. — Presbyterian. — Charming, delightful; natural speech. — The only thing FW noticed which was not throughly VA about inf.'s speech was a tendency on one or two occasions to lengthen very, very slightly the [ɐɪ] sound before voiceless consonants. This does not appear in the old-fashioned speaker for this co., and it may be due to inf. having been at college with people from other parts of Carolina — an unconscious influence. — Cultivated.

40 & 41 Wake County

Formed 1770 from 3 cos. Early settlers primarily English, some Scots; many from VA. Presbyterians, Methodists, Baptists, Episcopalians all by 1820; Roman Catholic cong. slightly later. Wake Forest College (Baptist) here from 1834; NC State at Raleigh. Electrical power dist. center from 1913; farming; trading rather than mfg. Pop. 1790: 10,192, 1820: 20,102, 1850: 24,888, 1880: 47,939, 1910: 63,229, 1930: 94,757, 1960: 169,082.

Amis, Moses Neal. 1913. *Historical Raleigh. . . with Sketches of Wake County. . . .* Rev. and enl. ed. Raleigh: Commercial Printing Co.

Battle, Kemp P. 1877. *Sketches of the Early History of the City of Raleigh.* Raleigh: Raleigh News Steam Job Print.

Battle, Kemp P. 1902. *Raleigh and the Old Town of Bloomsbury.* Raleigh: Capital Print. Co.

Chamberlain, Hope Summerell. 1922. *History of Wake County, North Carolina. . . .* Raleigh: Edwards and Broughton Print. Co.

Devereaux, Margaret. 1906. *Plantation Sketches.* Cambridge, MA: privately printed at the Riverside Press.

Federal Writers Project. 1942. *Raleigh, Capital of North Carolina.* New Bern: Owen G. Dunn.

Haywood, Marshall De Lancey. 1900. *Joel Lane, Pioneer and Patriot.* Raleigh: Alford, Bynum, and Christophers.

Powell, William S. 1968. *Raleigh-Durham-Chapel Hill: A Student's Guide to Localized History.* NY: Teacher's College Press.

Stolpen, Steve. 1977. *Raleigh: A Pictorial History.* Norfolk, VA: Donning Co.

Swain, David L. 1867. *Early Times in Raleigh.* Comp. by R. S. Tucker. Raleigh: Walters, Hughes.

Waugh, Elizabeth Culbertson, et al. 1967. *North Carolina's Capital, Raleigh.* Chapel Hill: University of North Carolina Press.

1887. *The City of Raleigh.* Raleigh: Edwards and Broughton.

1976. *Raleigh: A Guide to North Carolina's Capital.* Raleigh: Fine Arts Society.

Cary P.O., House Creek Twp.

Cary a farming community 8 mi. N. of Raleigh founded c. 1852. Mill here became Confed. powder factory. RR station some yrs.; town after Civil War. Industrialization post WWII: research triangle of NC State, UNC, Duke.

NC 40A: F, 68. B. here. — F., PGF, PGF's F. b. here (partly Scotch-Irish descent), PGF's M. b. here, PGM, PGM's F. b. Eagle Rock; M., MGF, MGM, MGM's F., MGM's M. b. here. — Ed.: a few yrs. (mos. at a time). — Christian. — Very loquacious, likes attention. Many conversational forms may be gathered, but it is difficult to keep her attention on a specific question. Uncertain and changeable about both her speech and what she thinks. Locally well known as ballad singer; speech undoubtedly influenced by singing and other garnishings of culture. Record resumed p. 88 after 3 mo. interval.

Leesville, Morrisville P.O., Leesville Twp.

Twp. in NW part of Co. RR station c. 1853.

NC 40B: M, farmer, 58. B. here. — F. b. here, PGF either b. here or came from VA (of Scotch-Irish descent), PGM b. here; M. b. near Flat Rock (near Franklintown in Franklin Co.) and came as infant to a point 2 mi. from here in Durham Co. (until 1911 part of Wake Co.), MGF, MGF's F. both b. Franklin Co., MGM b. Wake Co. — Ed.: here till 21 (never more than 3 mos./yr.). — Methodist. — Intelligent; slightly forgetful. — Tempo moderate; no particular prolongation. Occasional slight retroflexion. Is this the E. Carolina type, or a survival of the primitive VA or PA migration?

Raleigh City and Twp.

One of first settlers arrived 1741, est. tavern and church. Wake courthouse est. 1771; Co. coextensive with St. Margaret's parish. 1778 land purchased for state capital; town laid out 1792. Destructive fires in 1818, 1821, 1831. Confed. supply depot. By 1900 cotton and knitting mills, tobacco warehouse, electric power center. Wake Forest Coll., NC State, St. Mary's. Many federal agencies. Cotton goods, cottonseed oil, furniture, building supplies, automobile bodies, publishing; cotton and tobacco market. Pop. 1850: 4,515, 1880: 9,265, 1910: 19,218, 1930: 93,931.

NC 41!: F, widow (for 3 yrs.), works in lawyer's office, 54. B. Raleigh. — F. (trained at Belleview Hospital in NY), PGF both doctors, both b. Raleigh, PGF's F. (State Treasurer of NC), PGF's PGF (a colonel) both b. Edgecombe Co., PGF's PGF's F. b. Barbados, PGF's M. b. Brunswick Co., PGM b. Raleigh, PGM's M. b. Franklin Co.; M. b. Edenton, came to Raleigh age 7, MGF (Princeton grad.) b. Edenton, MGM b. Windsor. — Ed.: Peace Institute (left in Junior yr.); business course at St. Mary's school. — Episcopalian; Colonial Dame. — Reactions not very quick; average intelligence. Very dramatic in a way, with something of the awed, hushed silence in her voice, similar to the speech of the cultivated Albemarle Co., VA, inf. — Tempo slow; some prolongation. — Cultivated.

42. Chatham County

Formed 1770 from Orange Co. 1st settlers 1745–50; 1750–55 settlers well-scattered, esp. in river valleys. Most early settlers came from N. or SE, near "Catawba trading path" from VA and PA (migration from 1735 on). English, Scots, Ulster Scots, some Germans. Plank roads 1850s. Iron ore, coal, exhausted or abandoned. Western RR chartered 1852; to Deep River coalfields 1860; several other RRs followed. Quakers from 1750; Baptists from 1755; Methodists c. 1776. 6 Presbyterian congs. by 1770. Recent diversification of agriculture: larger farms, forage crops, livestock, rabbits, poultry. Other products: plywood, chemicals, clay, brick, tile.

> Hadley, Wade H., Davis G. Horton, and Nell C. Strand. 1921. *Chatham County, 1721–1921.* Durham: Moore Pub. Co.
> Hadley, Wade Hampton, et al. 1976. *Chatham County, 1771–1971.* 2nd ed. Durham: Moore Publishing Co.
> London, Henry Armand. 1894. *An Address on the Revolutionary History of Chatham County.* . . . Sanford: Cole Print. Co.
> London, Henry Armand. 1923. *Historical Background of Chatham County.* Chapel Hill: University of North Carolina Press.

Siler City, Staley P.O., Matthews Twp.

Siler City first settled c. 1754. Inc. 1887. Siler plantation originally a crossroads settlement and station on stage route. Siler's gristmill 1880; RR service c. 1884. Many Methodists c. 1886. Greatest rabbit shipping station on continent. Poultry, flour mills, cotton mills, washboard factory, furniture, foods, wood products, plywood, fabrics, clothing, paper products, shoes. Pop. 1910: 895, 1930: 1,730, 1960: 4,455.

NC 42A: M, farmer, 84. B. locally. — F., PGF b. here, PGF's F. b. Germany or of German descent, PGM b. here (of German descent); M. b. 3 or 4 mi. N. of Staley, in Randolph Co., MGF, MGM b. edge of Randolph Co. — Ed.: very little. — Social contacts limited. — Quick, intelligent, cooperative; occ. "[fə'gɪ'tʃl]". Appears to be in good circumstances. — Strikingly, he uses a more or less monophthongal [e·], not only in *can't, haunt, aunt, chance*, but also in *dance*. [æ·ɨ] does not exist in his speech. In other places FW found [e·ɨ] in all the above words, or [ɛɨ], except *dance*, and so regards the monophthongal type as unusual. Perhaps it represents the PA learning of an E. Carolina type of speech and failing to distinguish [æ·ɨ] and [ɛ·ɨ].

Harpers Crossroads, Bear Creek Twp. (record made near Pittsboro, Hickory Mtn. Twp., where inf. had lived since 20 yrs. old).

Harpers Crossroads a rural community, one-time trading center. Pittsboro Co. seat. Quakers in area in 1750s; settled 1771 by planters from Cape Fear region. Market town; mfg. silk garment labels; hosiery, poultry (processed).

NC 42B: F, housewife (taught school locally for a while when young), 44. B. Harpers Crossroads. — F., PGF, PGM b. Harpers Crossroads (PGF of "Irish" descent); M. b. Siler City, MGF b. on Fall Creek in Co., MGM b. Siler City. — Ed.: Harpers Crossroads till 18. — Methodist. — Quick, intelligent; did not like to elaborate on answers to questions. — Tempo moderate; no particular prolongation. Clear utterance. Community where inf. now lives prob. linguistically closer to Orange and Wake Cos. than where she was born. Her husband tends to use an [ɐʊ] sound, suggestive of VA influence. Whether this is simply an adult-acquired characteristic or affectation (as inf. believes) is doubtful. (Cf. aged Harnet Co. and the cultivated Fayetteville and Raleigh records.)

NC 42B*: Pittsboro, Center Twp. — F, middle-aged. — Rather self-conscious and slow. — Prolongation is of the E. Carolina type.

43. Orange County

Formed 1752 from several cos. 1st settlers in 1740s. By 1751 large migration from PA; Orange the most heavily pop. co. in NC: English, Scotch-Irish, Germans, Highlanders, Irish, Welsh, Quakers. German spoken for some time. Never more than 31% slaves. Decline in agriculture 1860–1930. 3 Church of England congs. before Rev. Presbyterians by 1755; Methodists by 1768; Baptists by 1789; Christians by 1797. UNC Chapel Hill here from 1789. Farms smaller by 1950; tobacco chief crop. Cotton mill from 1837. Hardwood, excelsior, hosiery, furniture, clothing, woolens. Pop. 1790: 12,216, 1820: 23,492, 1850: 17,055, 1880: 23,698, 1910: 15,064, 1930: 21,171, 1960: 42,970.

> Lefler, Hugh, ed. 1953. *Orange County, 1752–1952.* Chapel Hill.
> Nash, Francis. 1903. *Hillsboro, Colonial and Revolutionary.* Raleigh: Edwards and Broughton.
> Nash, Francis. 1903. *Hillsboro, Colonial and Revolutionary.* Raleigh: Edwards and Broughton.
> Prince, William Meade. 1950. *The Southern Part of Heaven.* NY: Rinehart.
> Sanders, Charles R. 1974. *The Cameron Plantation in Central North Carolina.* Durham: Sanders.

NC 43A: Hurdle Mills (Person County), Cedar Grove Twp. — F, housekeeper on a plantation, 80. B. locally. — F. b. here, PGF b. in "the Old Country", PGM b. here; M. b. Rockingham Co., came here young. — Illiterate. — Presbyterian. — Faithful domestic; natural; quick, although somewhat limited. — Tempo moderately rapid; vowels fairly short.

Orange Grove, Hillsborough P.O., Bingham Twp.

Hillsborough laid out 1754; inc. 1759 as Childsborough; received present name 1766; "borough" status 1770. Almost all white pop. descended from Scotch-Irish, Welsh, English, Germans. Center for Regulator disturbances 1768–70. Provincial congress held here 1775; general assembly 1778–84. Cedar chests, oil, flour, timber products, cotton, rayon; granite and sandstone quarries. Pop. 1880: 781, 1910: 857, 1930: 1,232, 1960: 1,349.

NC 43B: M, farmer, 41. B. here. — F. b. 1/2 mi. over the line in Chatham Co., brought to this neighborhood when 1 yr. old,

PGF b. Chatham Co., PGM b. Orange Co.; M., MGF b. locally. — Ed.: till 21 (equiv. of 8th grade). — Baptist. — Quick, obliging, but rather matter-of-fact and not too inspired. — Tempo moderate; no particular prolongation. Occasional weak retroflexion: of E. Carolina origin or of the W. Carolina type? Survival of primitive Virginian?

44. Caswell County

Formed 1777 from Orange Co. 1st settlers English, Dutch (from NY), Ulster Scots, German; possibly some French. Regulator troubles. 1st post-Independence Co. 2nd most populous co. in 1786. Prosperous farming by 1860; one of 16 cos. with slave majority. W. Piedmont. Limestone, slate, misc. minerals, water power; extinct volcano. Some industry since 1939. Recent reforestation and restocking. Tobacco still chief crop. Pop. 1786: 9,839, 1790: 10,096, 1820: 13,253, 1850: 15,289, 1880: 17,825, 1910: 14,858, 1930: 18,214, 1960: 19,912.

> Powell, William S. 1977. *When the Past Refused to Die: A History of Caswell County, North Carolina, 1777–1977.* Durham: Moore Pub. Co.

Old Fitch Store, Yanceyville P.O., Anderson Twp.

Twp. created 1868. Courthouse at Yanceyville 1791; inc. 1810. Never grew; lack of transportation facilities.

NC 44: M, farmer, 49. B. here. — F., PGF, PGM b. here; M., MGF b. locally, MGM b. Alamance Co. — Ed.: till 20 (local academy 2 sessions). — Primitive Baptist. — Genial; somewhat slow. — Tendency to short vowels.

NC 44*: F, 75. — Illiterate. — Somewhat senile. — No retroflexion; uses [oˑ] for [ou], but does not have the fully central [ɐ̯u] of VA.

45. Rockingham County

Formed 1785 from Guilford Co. Moravians here as early as 1752; used German officially till 1856. 1st settlers 1760 from PA and Jerseys. Dissenters; few Episcopalians till end of 19th cent. Plantation country in Dan Valley; textiles, tobacco chief crop. Pop. 1790: 6,187, 1820: 11,474, 1850: 14,495, 1880: 21,744, 1910: 36,442, 1930: 51,083, 1960: 69,629.

> Gardner, Bettie Sue. 1964. *History of Rockingham County, North Carolina.* Reidsville.
> James Hunter Chapter. 1977. *Early Families of the North Carolina Counties of Rockingham and Stokes.* Madison: DAR.

Reidsville

1st settlers c. 1815; town by 1829. Greensboro-Danville RR 1863. Tobacco factory by 1854; one of 3 NC tobacco mfg. centers. Warehouses by 1872. Diversified industries: cotton, silk, rayon, shoe polishes, concrete forms, food products, feedstuffs. Pop. 1880: 1,316, 1910: 4,828, 1930: 6,851, 1960: 14,267.

NC 45A: F, 80. B. locally. Lived most of life on a farm just on the line in Caswell Co. — F. b. locally, PGF of "Irish" descent; M. b. Caswell Co., MGF b. Rockingham Co., MGM perhaps French Huguenot. — Illiterate. — Missionary Baptist. — One of four unmarried sisters, all field hands, poor all their lives. Quick, alert; limited knowledge of outside world. Friendly, cooperative, unsuspicious. Reserved, dignified manner. — Tempo moderately rapid; vowels tend to be short or very short. Articulation inclined to be precise, emphatic, clear-cut. Varies from [aʌu] to [ɐu] dependent on length in all positions (cf. elsewhere in northern NC). [eˀə̯] for [eɨ] occ.

NC 45B: Wentworth. — M, 75. — Uneducated.

46. Guilford County

Formed 1770 from Rowan and Orange Cos. 2 settlement streams: from Lancaster, PA, and from Charleston. Scotch-Irish (central), Germans (east), English Quakers (west); also some Welsh. Whig, Regulator territory. Many slaveholders in E. Guilford; c. 1800, manumission society, underground RR. Many Quakers eventually went NW. Co. "always a great public highway"; coach lines, RR junction. Oldest church Lutheran (1744–45); Presbyterians and Friends by 1751; Methodists by 1773. Quakers very influential in Co.; concern with schools. New Garden Boarding School (1837) became Guilford College 1888. Greensboro Female College (Methodist) 1846; High Point College. Many local schools, gradually merged into public schools. Furs in early days. Textile mills from 1832. High Point center of NC furniture industry since 1867. Wood products, nurseries, fruit growing (esp. peaches), minerals (iron, gold, copper). Pop. 1790: 7,191, 1820: 14,511, 1850: 19,754, 1880: 23,585, 1910: 80,497, 1930: 133,010, 1960: 246,520.

> Albright, James W., comp. 1904. *Greensboro, 1808–1904...* . Greensboro: J. J. Stone.
> Arnett, Ethel Stephens. 1955. *Greensboro, North Carolina, the County Seat of Guilford.* Chapel Hill: University of North Carolina Press.
> Gilbert, Dorothy Lloyd. 1937. *Guilford, A Quaker College.* Greensboro: Printed for Guilford College by J. J. Stone and Co.
> Klain, Zora. 1925. *Quaker Contributions to Education in North Carolina.* Philadelphia: Westbrook Publishing Co.
> Rankin, Samuel Meek. 1934. *History of Buffalo Presbyterian Church.* Greensboro: J. J. Stone.
> Stockard, Sallie W. 1902. *The History of Guilford County, North Carolina.* Knoxville, TN: Gaut-Ogden Co.
> Whitsett, William Thornton. 1925. *History of Brick Church and the Clapp Family.* Greensboro: Harrison Printing Co.

Guilford College, Friendship Twp.

Guilford College settled 1750 by Friends as New Garden. New Garden Boarding School (est. 1837) became Guilford College 1888; oldest and most influential Quaker college in the South.

NC 46A: M, farmer (carpenter as young man), 83. B. 12 mi. E. and brought here as infant. — M., foster father, foster mother all b. Guilford Co. (FW reports many Quakers adopted illegitimate children). — Ed.: 6 mos. — Friends (Quaker). — Genial; eccentric; patient and enduring. — Moderate tempo; no particular lengthening.

NC 46B: M, farmer, 44. B. here. — F., PGF, PGF's F. b. Guilford Co. (of Nantucket, MA, Quaker ancestry); M. b. Deep River (8 mi. W.). — Ed.: till 23 at Guilford College School (1 1/2 yrs. at "College"). — Methodist. — Slow; shy, cautious, and fearful. — Deliberate tempo; vowels tend to be fairly short. Lip action too weak and general articulation too indistinct for good phonetic recording.

Greensboro, Gilmer Twp.

Part of original grant from Earl of Granville in 1749 for settlement of Scotch-Irish Presbyterians. Germans to E., Quakers to W. 1st courthouse 1774, 5 mi. NW of present Greensboro. Co. seat here 1808; town org. 1824; 2nd charter 1837; city charter 1870. Several colleges, some for women. Methodist church by 1830; Baptist by 1859; Episcopalian by 1871. RR by 1856; highway hub; tri-city (Greensboro, Winston-Salem, High Point) airport here 1927. Diversified mfg. by 1830: textiles, lumber, wood products, terracotta, brick, tile, iron and steel products, machinery, carpets, furniture, chemicals, tobacco prods. Wholesale distribution center. Pop. 1880: 2,105, 1910: 15,895, 1930: 53,469, 1960: 119,574.

NC 46C!: F, executive sec. of Girl Scouts, 48. B. here. — F. b. near Greensboro, PGF b. Greensboro, PGF's F. of German descent, PGM, PGM's F. b. near Greensboro, PGM's M. b. Co.; M. b. near Alamance Co., MGF, MGF's F. b. E. Guilford Co., MGF's PGF b. PA (parents from Paisley in Scotland), MGF's PGM rescued from Indians, MGM b. Co. — Ed.: Womans College (Greensboro) 1 yr., Queens College, Charlotte (Mecklenburg Co.), 1 yr., then back here 2 yrs. — Presbyterian (now Methodist). — Father typical merchant. Inf. perhaps somewhat affected. — Tempo moderate; vowels not prolonged. — Cultivated.

47. Randolph County

Formed 1779 from Guilford and Rowan Cos. Settled 18th cent., mainly from PA by Scotch-Irish, Germans, Quakers. Oldest Baptist Assoc. in NC here. Asheboro Co. seat from 1793. Textiles since 1836; 5 cotton mills by 1860. Gold mines, timber, wood products. Agriculture chief work; little tenant farming, over 80% of farmers own their land. Corn, wheat, cotton, flax, tobacco, poultry. Pop. 1790: 7,276, 1820: 11,331, 1850: 15,832, 1880: 20,836, 1910: 29,491, 1930: 36,259, 1960: 61,497.

> Auman, Dorothy, and Walter Auman. 1976. *Seagrove Area.* Asheboro: Village Printing Co.
> Blair, J. A. 1890. *Reminiscences of Randolph County.* Greensboro: Reece and Elam.
> Burgess, Fred. 1924. *Randolph County: Economic and Social.* New Bern: Owen G. Dunn, Printer.
> Jones, Margaret. 1845–1893. *Diary of Margaret Jones. . . Randolph County, North Carolina.*
> 1956. Randolph County. *The State*, July 14, 1956.

Sophia, New Market Twp.

Sophia settled before 1779, mainly by PA Germans. Was in hardwood forests, mostly cut; also smaller oak, cut into cross ties. Pop. 1930: 153.

NC 47: F, housewife, 76. B. here. — F. b. here, PGF "Dutch" (he or PGF's F. b. Europe), PGM b. here (Quaker stock); M.

b. here, MGF from Stanley Co., brother to PGF, MGM b. Stanley Co. (of English stock). — Ed.: very little (ABCs at Marlboro School). — Methodist (F. attended Friends Meeting, although not a member). — Simple, obliging. Unaware of outside speech.

48. Davidson County

Formed 1822 from Rowan Co. Most farmers own land. Furniture, granite, cotton and knitting mills. Pop. 1830: 13,389, 1850: 15,320, 1880: 20,333, 1910: 29,404, 1930: 47,865, 1960: 79,493.

> Leonard, Jacob Calvin. 1927. *Centennial History of Davidson County, North Carolina.* Raleigh: Edwards and Broughton Co.
> Matthews, Mary Green. 1952. *Wheels of Faith and Courage: A History of Thomasville, North Carolina.* Thomasville.
> Sink, Margaret Jewell, and Mary Green Matthews. 1972. *Pathfinders Past and Present: A History of Davidson County, North Carolina.* High Point: Hall Printing Co.

Thomasville

Named after man who supported and helped build NC RR in Co. Settled by Rev.: English, Germans, Quakers. Town planned 1851; inc. 1857. Glen Anna female seminary here 1854. Baptists in area early; built orphanage here. Building materials, furniture; cotton, rayon, and silk mills from 1820s. Pop. 1880: 450, 1910: 3,877, 1930: 10,090, 1960: 18,190.

NC 48: M, farmer, 52. B. here. — F. b. locally, PGF b. here (of Scotch-Irish descent); M. b. locally, MGF, MGM b. Co. — Ed.: here till 18. — Methodist. — Quick, intelligent; interested in talking to FW. Somewhat unaware of the outside world. — Tempo moderate; vowels not particularly prolonged.

49 & 50. Rowan County

Formed 1753 from Anson Co. Indians to 1670. Orig. part of Granville's trust. Settled by 2 streams (poss. as early as 1737): one from SC and one from PA. Scots, Ulster Scots, Germans (1st indisputable record of Germans 1755). Lutheran and Reformed church by 1757 (Reformed more numerous). German spoken till late 19th cent. Presbyterian cong. by 1753; Methodists and Anglicans org. by 1780. Catawba College. Small farming economy; gen. diversified agriculture, though cotton chief crop. Gold mining till Civil War; given up after Calif. discoveries; also some copper and silver mining. Diversified industry, cotton mills, building and crushed stone, plastics, chemicals, furniture, woodworking. Pop. 1790: 15,828, 1820: 26,009, 1850: 13,870, 1880: 19,965, 1910: 37,521, 1930: 56,685, 1960: 82,817.

> Alexander, Samuel Davis. 1855. *An Historical Address. . . Thyatira Presbyterian Church.* Salisbury: Bruner.
> Alexander, Samuel Davis. 1857. *An Historical Address. . . Back Creek Church.* Salisbury. Bound in *History of Back Creek Church.* Mooresville, NC: Enterprise S.J. Prt.
> Brawley, James S. 1953. *The Rowan Story, 1753–1953.* Salisbury: Rowan Print. Co.
> Brawley, James S. 1959. *Old Rowan Views and Sketches.* Salisbury.

Chamberlain, Hope Summerell. 1938. *This Was Home.* Chapel Hill: University of North Carolina Press.

Gehrke, William Herman. 1934. *The Beginnings of the Pennsylvania-German Element in Rowan and Cabarrus Counties, North Carolina.* University of North Carolina Master's thesis.

Hunter, Cyrus Lee. 1877. *Sketches of Western North Carolina.* Raleigh: Raleigh News Steam Job Print.

Lingle, Walter Lee. 1948. *Thyatira Presbyterian Church. . . 1753-1948.* Statesville: Brady Pub. Co.

Ramsey, Robert W. 1964. *Carolina Cradle. . . .* Chapel Hill: University of North Carolina Press.

Rumple, Jethro. 1881. *A History of Rowan County.* Salisbury: J. J. Bruner.

Corinth Church, Gold Hill P.O., Morgan Twp.

Corinth Church a Baptist church 14 mi. E. of Salisbury. Gold Hill a mining camp c. 1842; then shrank to a country village. Copper and gold mining.

NC 49: F, housewife, 79. B. locally. — F., PGF b. Morgan Twp., PGF's F. b. Germany; M., MGF b. Morgan Twp. (German descent), MGM of German descent. — Ed.: a little. — Lutheran. — Sweet, domestic; rather slow, also becoming somewhat childish. — Tempo rather slow; no particular prolongation. A certain even monotony in intonation suggests possible German influence; always hitting the same pitch levels. The articulation is very choppy, and has a certain "clenched" quality which is very un-English, esp. in certain final groups such as /-nts/ pronounced very short with great stress. The entire consonant articulation of alveolars, etc., is very forward in the mouth. These sounds tend to be shorter, more vigorous, and with a "clearer" vowel-resonance than usual. [ə] is used for [ɪ] in all positions. /e/ and /o/ tend to be monophthongs. [v] for /w/ and /v/ frequently (this seems to be German since it is separated geographically from the coastal Carolina type).

Milford Hills, Salisbury P.O., Franklin Twp.

Milford Hills W. of Salisbury, on RR. Scotch-Irish settlement.

NC 50A: M, farmer, 45. B. locally. — F., PGF b. China Grove, PGF's F. of PA German stock, PGM b. locally (German descent); M. b. Franklin, MGF b. Co. (English descent), MGM b. Davie Co. (Irish descent), MGM's M. b. in an English-speaking seaport in Ireland and kidnapped by a sailor and brought to America and sold. — Ed.: till 18. — Baptist. — Quick, highly intelligent, cooperative. — Tempo rather rapid; no particular prolongation.

Salisbury

One of oldest towns of the Piedmont: founded 1753 (as Co. seat); inc. 1755. Important for residence and trade by the Rev.; administrative center. Frontier post in French and Indian War. Lutherans by 1768. Between Scotch-Irish and German settlements; German still spoken in 1880s. 2 colleges. On "Western Great Road"; some trade with SC. Textiles, granite. Pop. 1880: 2,723, 1910: 7,153, 1930: 16,951, 1960: 21,297.

NC 50B!: F, stenographer, 38. B. here. — F. b. here, PGF b. Petersburg, VA, PGM b. Wilmington, NC; M. b. here, MGF b. Scotland, MGM, MGM's F. both b. here, step-M. b. here, step-M.'s F. b. near Organ Church in Co., step-M.'s M. b. Co. — Ed.: h.s. in Salisbury, St. Marys (Raleigh) 1 yr., NC College for Women (Greensboro) 2 yrs. — Episcopalian. — Secluded life until lately; cooperative; surprising rusticity in some instances as compared with Greensboro and Charlotte. — Rather slow tempo; no particular prolongation. A weak [ə] survives postvocalically at times. The tongue is rather heavy, and the mouth large, producing a certain heaviness and immobility, but not a definite speech defect. — Cultivated.

51. Montgomery County

Formed 1779 from Anson County. Settled from E. NC; also Highlanders, Scotch-Irish, some Germans. Co. seat est. at Troy 1842. Rural; small farmers, family farms; some to Georgia 1792. "New Scotch" from Cape Fear c. 1771. Methodists c. 1790; Baptists about same time. Unsuccessful attempts to make the Pee Dee navigable. Naval stores to late 19th cent. Gold mining into 20th cent.; hydroelectric power in 20th cent. Peaches, cotton, poultry. Textiles, lumber, chairs, packaging, service industries. Pop. 1790: 4,725, 1820: 8,693, 1850: 6,872, 1880: 9,374, 1910: 14,697, 1930: 16,218, 1960: 18,408.

Lassiter, Mable S. 1976. *"Patterns of Timeless Moments": A History of Montgomery County.* Montgomery County Board of Commissioners.

Black Ankle, Steeds P.O., Little River Twp.

Twp. in N. center of Co. Black Ankle a gold mining area.

NC 51A: F, housewife, 76. — F. b. over line in Randolph Co., PGF b. Edgecombe Co. and sailed the seas for a time, PGF's M. Irish descent, PGM b. over line in Randolph Co. ("Dutch" descent); M., MGF b. here, MGF's F. b. VA, MGF's M. b. here, MGF's MGF b. nearby in Randolph Co. (English descent), MGM b. W. of here in Randolph Co., MGM's F. b. Rowan Co. ("Dutch" descent), MGM's M., MGM's MGF b. Randolph Co. (Dutch descent). — Ed.: very little. — Holiness. — Quick, bright; somewhat melancholic (a good deal of mental illness in the family); neighborhood desolate and remote. — Moderate tempo; tendency to prolong.

Rubyatt, Candor P.O., Rocky Springs Twp.

Candor a marketing center for peach growers. 1st commercially successful orchard 1928; 200 orchards by 1938. Pottery clay, formerly gold mine. Pop. 1930: 462.

NC 51B: M, farmer, 49. B. locally. — F., PGF b. here, PGF's F. b. Scotland, PGM b. here (Scottish parentage); M., MGF b. Richmond Co. (MGF's parents b. Scotland), MGM b. on Moore-Montgomery Co. line. — Ed.: till 18, Ether Academy 1/2 session. — Presbyterian. — Good-natured, obliging, quick. — Moderate tempo; no great prolongation. Articulation somewhat muffled with inadequate lip motion (possibly Scottish?).

52. Anson County

Formed 1750 from Bladen Co. Catawba country; Catawbas always friendly to whites. First settlers up Pee Dee

c. 1740; others from MD and PA; by 1750 Germans, Ulster Scots, Welsh. Center of Regulator activities 1766. Some Huguenots from SC 1774. Co. seat est. at New Town (later became Wadesboro) 1783. Presbyterians, Quakers early (Quakers left). Relatively small numbers of Presbyterians today; Baptists most numerous. Abortive attempt to develop Pee Dee navigation 1802. Growing prosperity 1820–50. Devastated 1865. RR 1910. Number of farms decreased, average size doubled since 1950; cotton acreage down; soybeans, grazing, poultry. Gold mining, brownstone, sand and gravel, hydroelectric power, textiles, clothing, plywood. Pop. 1790: 5,133, 1820: 12,534, 1850: 13,489, 1880: 17,994, 1910: 25,465, 1930: 29,349, 1960: 24,962.

Boykin, J. G. 1913–14. Anson County. *North Carolina Booklet* 13.4:214–21.

Hadley, Maria L. 1976. *History of Anson County, North Carolina*. Wadesboro: Anson County Historical Society.

East Rocky Ford, Wadesboro P.O. and Twp.

Twp. in center of Co. Courthouse here from 1785 (name originally New Town). Academy 1802. Edge of sand hills; longleaf pine belt.

NC 52N: F, housewife, widow, 90. B. 13 mi. W. on plantation. At age 21, began moving closer to town. — F. b. Richmond, VA, and sold here as a young man; M. b. Richmond Co., NC; MGF lived Richmond Co. — Ed.: none. — Baptist. — Very quick, intelligent; cooperative; extensive contact with white people keeps inf. from having a very old-fashioned type of speech. — Rapid tempo; some tendency to prolong.

Forestville Church, Pee Dee P.O., Lilesville Twp.

Twp. now in agricultural region; prosperous before Rev. Regulator center. Lilesville Baptist Church here from 1771; one of oldest in NC. Lumbering. Forestville Church settled c. 1760, primarily by English. Methodists since 1783.

NC 52A: F, farm laborer, 77. B. locally. — F. b. locally, PGM, PGM's F. b. Co.; M., MGF b. here, MGF's F. of French descent, MGF's M. of Indian descent from Cabarrus Co., MGM b. Jones Creek, S. of Lilesville, MGM's F.'s brother and mother were buried on Sullivan Island, SC, on way to America. — Ed.: learned to read a little at home. — Methodist. — Intelligent; old-fashioned; unmarried; humble background. — Tempo moderate; tendency to prolongation.

Jones Creek, Morven P.O., Gulledge Twp.

Gun and powder factory at Jones Creek in Civil War, not discovered by Feds. Morven (as Old Morven, c. 1800) location of a tavern. Scotch graveyard (Highlanders). New town grew up around RR station 2 mi. E. Burned during Fed. occupation.

NC 52B: M, farmer, 48. B. here. — F., PGF b. Lilesville Twp., PGF's F. b. VA, of a MD family (Irish descent), PGM b. Scotland Co.; M., MGF, MGF's F. all b. Lilesville, MGF's PGF b. VA, MGM b. Morgan Twp., MGF's F. b. Co. — Ed.: here till 15. — Presbyterian. — Well-to-do gentleman of succesful family; only local contacts. — Tempo moderate; prolongation not noticeable. The high [ε˞] and the [a·ʊ˞], etc. seem to point to contacts with SC (boats came up the Pee Dee River from Georgetown) as well as to VA [hwʌt], [ʌv]. Co. seems different from any of the surrounding cos. Extreme NW corner of Co. is like Stanly Co. (PA German).

53. Union County

Formed 1842 from Anson and Mecklenburg Cos. 1st settlements c. 1742; earliest settlers English, Ulster Scots, Scots, Germans. 1st church Presbyterian, c. 1760; later Baptists and Methodists became more numerous. Wingate Jr. College (Baptist). 4 stages of farming: 1) self-sufficient farming, 2) commercial raising of livestock and small grain, 3) cotton (slavery, tenancy), 4) diversification and soil conservation. Timber, gold and silver mining, slate, clay, textiles, metalworking, woodworking. Forestry emphasized after WWII. Pop. 1850: 10,051, 1880: 18,056, 1910: 33,277, 1930: 40,979, 1960: 44,670.

McNeely, R. N. 1912. Union County and the Old Waxhaw Settlement. In *North Carolina Booklet* vol. 12.

Stack, Amos Morehead, and R. F. Beasley. 1902. *Sketches of Monroe and Union County*. Charlotte: Charlotte News and Time.

Walden, H. Nelson. 1964. *History of Union County*. Monroe.

Williams, Robert F. 1902. *Negroes with Guns*. Ed. by Marc Schliefer. NY: Marzani and Munsell.

Winchester, George T. 1937. *A Story of Union County and the History of Pleasant Grove Camp Ground*. Mineral Springs.

1956. Union County. *The State*, Dec. 1, 1956.

NC 53A: New Salem School, Marshville P.O., New Salem Twp. — M, farmer, 82. B. locally. — F. b. just over line in Anson Co., PGF lived in Anson Co. (either he or PGF's F. b. in SC), PGM b. Co.; M., MGF, MGM all b. near Olive Branch, E. of Marshville. — Quick, bright; occ. slightly forgetful; obliging, loves conversation. — Tempo, vowel length, enunciation all moderate.

Wingate, Monroe P.O., Marshville Twp.

Wingate Jr. College est. 1897. Monroe est. 1844 as Co. seat. Named for Pres. Monroe. Settled mid-18th cent., mainly by Ulster Scots from PA and SC. Artesian springs; cotton, lumber, knitting, cottonseed oil, roller mills, marble works, creamery. Pop. 1880: 1,564, 1910: 4,082, 1930: 6,100, 1960: 10,882.

NC 53B: F, housewife, 42. B. here. — F. b. here, PGF b. Union Co. (Scotch-Irish descent), PGM, PGM's F. b. Co. (of VA family); M. b. here, MGF, MGM b. Co. (MGM said to be "Dutch", although name is Welsh). — Ed.: here till 18. — Baptist. — Very quick, intelligent, obliging; glad to cooperate. — Tempo moderate; no great prolongation.

54. Cabarrus County

Formed 1792 from Mecklenburg Co. 1st settlers Germans (east) and Ulster Scots (west). Regulator stronghold. Presbyterians, Lutherans, Reformed. 1st US gold mine here 1799. Lost pop. to west c. 1816, 1832. Textiles, cotton chief crop. Pop. 1800: 5,094, 1820: 7,248, 1850: 9,747, 1880: 14,964, 1910: 28,240, 1930: 44,331, 1960: 68,137.

Corbin St. School Sixth Grade. 1933. *A Short History of Cabarrus County and Concord*. Concord: Snyder Printing Co.

Hammer, Carl, Jr. 1943. *Rhinelanders on the Yadkin*. Salisbury: Rowan Print. Co.

Harris, William S. 1873. *Historical Sketch of Poplar Tent Church*. Charlotte.

Lore, Adelaide, and Eugenia Lore. 1971. *Open the Gate and Roam Cabarrus with Us*. Salisbury: Rowan Business Forms.

Lore, Adelaide, Eugenia Lore, and Robert Hull Morrison. 1950. *The Morrison Family of the Rocky River Settlement of Cabarrus County*. Charlotte: Morrison family.

Rouse, Jordon K. 1966. *North Carolina Picadillo*. Kannapolis.

Rouse, Jordon K. 1970. *Historical Shadows of Cabarrus County, North Carolina*. Charlotte: Crabtree Press.

Concord

Founded 1796. German settlement; Regulator center. Attempt c. 1896–1904 to organize an all-AfAm cotton mill here failed. 20 factories: cotton goods, cottonseed oil, lumber, flour, mattresses. Pop. 1880: 1,264, 1910: 8,715, 1930: 11,820, 1960: 17,799.

NC 54A: M, farmer, 79. B. here. – F. b. here, PGF b. Germany, came here and settled as a young man; M., MGF b. here (of German descent). – Ed.: till 18. – Lutheran. – Whittler and builder. Ingenious in those pursuits, but rather slow in speech and thought.

NC 54B: Cold Springs Church, Concord P.O., Baptist Church Twp. – F, housewife, 41. B. Faggarts Twp. (10 mi. N.). – F. b. near Gold Hill (Rowan Co.), came here as a boy, PGF b. Rowan Co. (German descent); M. b. Faggarts Twp., MGF, MGM b. Co. (German descent). – Ed.: Pinnacle School till 19. – German Reformed. – Energetic; hardworking at manual labor. Quick; somewhat self-conscious at times; essentially honest and truthful. – Rather forward articulation with "clear" quality, suggests German substratum. [oˑu] and [ɛˑɹ] diphthongs tend at times to be very open and prolonged.

55 & 56. Mecklenburg County

Formed 1762 from Anson Co. 1st settler c. 1740; early settlers from VA and PA: English, Ulster Scots, Germans, Huguenots. Also some migration from SC and English from E. NC. Colonial trade with Charleston and Philadelphia. Presbyterians first organized denomination; org. c. 1755. General farming, cotton by 1800. Gold rush 1825. NC RR 1856. 1st public school 1882; school consolidation and bussing in 1920s. Davidson College est. 1837; UNC Charlotte here. Lower percentage of open country dwellers than any surrounding co.; rapidly growing city pop. Agriculture tends to specialize for local market: cotton, corn, wheat; milk cows. Industry well diversified in 1920; more diversification since; includes textiles, hydroelectric power, brickmaking. Pop. 1790: 11,395, 1820: 16,895, 1850: 13,914, 1880: 34,175, 1910: 67,031, 1930: 127,971, 1960: 272,111.

Alexander, John Brevard. 1897. *Biographical Sketches of the Early Settlers of the Hopewell Section. . . .* Charlotte: Observer Print. and Pub. House.

Alexander, John Brevard. 1902. *The History of Mecklenburg County, from 1740 to 1900*. Charlotte: Observer Printing House.

Alexander, John Brevard. 1908. *Reminiscences of the Past Sixty Years*. Charlotte: Ray Printing Co.

Blythe, LeGette, and Charles Raven Brockmann. 1961. *Hornets' Nest: The Story of Charlotte and Mecklenburg County*. Charlotte: Public Library of Charlotte and Mecklenburg County.

Blythe, LeGette, et al. 1967 *Charlotte and Mecklenburg County, North Carolina Today*. Charlotte: Crabtree Press.

Federal Writers Project. 1939. *Charlotte, a Guide to the Queen City of North Carolina*. Charlotte: News Printing House.

Groome, Bailey T. 1931. *Mecklenburg in the Revolution. . . .* Charlotte: Sons of the American Revolution.

Hoyt, William Henry. 1907. *The Mecklenburg Declaration of Independence*. NY: G.P. Putnam's Sons.

King, Victor C. 1954. *Story of the Origin of the City of Charlotte*. Charlotte.

Marsh, Kenneth F., and Blanche Marsh. 1967. *Charlotte, Carolinas' Queen City*. Columbia, SC: R. L. Bryan Co.

Ovens, David. 1957. *If This be Treason: A Look at His Town and Times*. Charlotte: Heritage House.

Sommerville, Charles William. 1939. *The History of Hopewell Presbyterian Church*. Hopewell: Hopewell Presbyterian Church.

Stenhouse, James A. 1951. *Journeys into History*.

Stenhouse, James A. 1952. *Exploring Old Mecklenburg*. Charlotte.

Thompson, Edgar Tristram. 1926. *Agricultural Mecklenburg and Industrial Charlotte: Economic and Social*. Charlotte: Chamber of Commerce.

Tompkins, Daniel Augustus. 1903. *History of Mecklenburg County and the City of Charlotte. . . .* 2 vols. Charlotte: Observer Printing House.

Mint Hill, Matthews P.O., Clear Creek Twp.

Twp. rural; pop. decline 1890–1920. Mint Hill 12 mi. E. of Charlotte. Bain Academy in 1860s.

NC 55: M, tenant farmer, 86. B. Goose Creek Twp. in Union Co. (c. 10 miles away), when married (65 yrs. ago) moved here. – F. b. Goose Creek (Union Co.), PGF b. Union Co. (German descent); M. b. near Monroe in Union Co., MGF of Scotch-Irish descent, MGM b. Stanley Co. on Rocky River. – Illiterate. – Baptist. – Inf. a tenant farmer all his life, living at various points, all within a radius of about 10 miles. – Remarkably powerful, vigorous, resonant voice. Tempo fairly rapid; fairly short vowels and diphthongs. [æˑʏ˔] frequently for [æʊ]. Long /e/ and /o/ tend to monophthongs. [ɨ] is low central. [ʌv] for *of*.

Hopewell, Huntersville P.O., Long Creek Twp.

Hopewell one of earliest settlements in W. NC. Settlers from PA as early as 1762; 1st church (Presbyterian) 1765. Area intensely Presbyterian. Church maintained school till 1904. Huntersville a small town N. of Charlotte near Davidson College.

NC 56A: F, housewife, 60. B. locally. — F. b. Sugar Creek (near Charlotte), PGF b. Co. (Scotch-Irish descent), PGM, PGM's F. b. Co., PGM's PGF b. No. Ireland, PGM's PGM b. here, PGM's M. b. Sugar Creek; M. b. Hopewell, MGF b. Co., MGF's F. b. in Holland and came to PA, MGM, MGM's F. b. here, MGM's PGF b. 1726 in PA, MGM's PGM b. MD, MGM's M. b. south Mecklenburg Co. (Scotch-Irish descent). — Ed.: here till teenager (attended White Hall, a grammar school taught by northerners in Cabarrus Co., and Asheville Normal School (less than 1 yr.)). — Presbyterian. — Cooperative; middle-aged type. — Tempo moderate; no particular prolongation. Articulation mumbling and indistinct as in Scottish speech. Absence of lip movements. [æ‧·u̯ʌ] for [æu] . Strikingly, inf. uses [ə] for [ɨ] in all positions (like the old-fashioned type in Rowan Co.)

Charlotte

1st permanent settlers c. 1748; early settlers Scotch-Irish and Germans from PA, some English, Huguenots, and Swiss from Charleston. Town chartered 1768. One of 3 colonial rifle factories in 1775; center of rev. sentiment. Queens College est. 1775; second in South. Center of gold rush c. 1800; most productive in country to 1848. Branch mint 1836–1913. Founded by Presbyterians; Baptists by far most numerous today. 1st public school 1882; UNC Charlotte est. 1946. City pop. trebled 1865–75; quadrupled 1900–1930. Confederate ordnance plant; textile center in late 19th cent.; ironworks. Market and distribution center, financial center; clay products, peanut products, center of power company, center of Eastern Air Lines. Pop. 1880: 7,094, 1910: 34,014, 1930: 86,675, 1960: 201,564.

NC 56B!: F, housewife (wife of a physician), 45. B. here. — F. b. Orange Co., came here young, PGF b. Orange Co.; M., MGF both b. here (Welsh descent), MGF's M. of New Bern ancestry, MGM b. here, MGM 's F. b. Co., MGM's MGM b. MD and came here as a child. — Presbyterian College (later Elizabeth College); finished junior year. — Baptist (now attends Episcopal church). — Old Charlotte family. Highly intense, jubilant, with an ever-bubbling sense of humor and incessant conversation. — Tempo rapid; vowels often prolonged (vowels can be excessively prolonged for emphasis in emotion). — Cultivated.

57. *Stokes County*

Formed 1789 from Surry Co. Minerals; rural, almost half of farm pop. tenants. Pop. 1790: 8,528, 1800: 11,026, 1820: 14,033, 1850: 9,206, 1880: 15,353, 1910: 20,151, 1930: 22,314.

Danbury P.O., Peters Creek Twp.

Danbury site of Indian village. Trading post here 1790s; boisterous frontier town, flourishing barrooms. Before 1861 iron foundry, limekilns, mica mines, distilleries, quarries. Became Co. seat c. 1852, renamed Danbury.

NC 57A: M, storekeeper, carpenter, and farmer, 81. B. locally. — F. b. locally, PGF perhaps b. England, PGM b. western Co. (VA descent); M. b. Co., MGF b. here, MGF's F. b. Henry Co., VA, MGM b. Patrick Co., VA. — Ed.: 18 days. — Baptist. — Obliging; intelligent. Probably above average, but very old-fashioned in many ways. — Tempo moderate; no particular prolongation.

Piedmont Springs, Danbury P.O. and Twp.

Piedmont Springs a rural settlement; once fashionable.

NC 57B: M, farmer, 36. B. here. — F, PGF, PGM all b. here; M. b. S. of Patrick Co., VA. — Ed.: Danbury till 17. — Baptist. — Obliging "typical citizen". — Moderate tempo; vowels not particularly prolonged.

58. *Surry County*

Formed 1771 from Rowan Co. Area first visited in 1670s. Moravians settled 1750s; also Scotch-Irish and Germans. Frontier against Cherokees; frontier wars 1759–61; further Indian troubles 1765–76. Quakers first denomination, also Baptists early; Methodists, Presbyterians later. Pre-Rev. iron mining. Subsistence farming earliest. To 1812, corn, wheat, oats, some tobacco, no cotton (few slaves). By c. 1840, textile mills, tobacco mfg., furniture, quarrying. Sheep introduced after 1865, woolen mills. RR, hydroelectric power c. 1888. To 1893, tobacco money crop; fruit, esp. apples. Mountainous, cultural isolation till hwys. of 1920s; long toward bottom of state educationally. Pop. 1786: 1,559, 1790: 7,191, 1820: 12,320, 1850: 18,443, 1880: 15,302, 1910: 29,705, 1930: 39,749, 1960: 48,205.

Cox, Aras B. 1900. *Foot Prints on the Sands of Time.* Sparta: Star Pub. Co.

Hollingsworth, Jesse Gentry. 1935. *History of Surry County.* Greensboro: W. H. Fisher.

Taliaferro, Harden. 1859. *Fisher's River. . . .* NY: Harper and Bros.

Sage Creek, Mt. Airy P.O., Stewarts Creek Twp.

Mt. Airy has a granite quarry; also textile mills, furniture factories. Pop. 1880: 2,893, 1910: 3,844, 1930: 6,045, 1960: 7,055.

NC 58A: M, farmer, 72. B. locally (Red Hill Creek). — F. b. locally, PGF, PGM both b. Co.; M. b. locally, MGF, MGM both b. Co. — Ed.: very little. — Baptist. — Quick, intelligent. Poor, untraveled; old-fashioned. — Tempo rapid; vowels and diphthongs fairly short. Good, clear enunciation.

NC 58B: Ladonia, Mt. Airy P.O., Stewarts Creek Twp. — F, 39. B. locally (Round Peak). When 8 yrs. old, moved to Lamsburg, VA, just over line, for 3 yrs.; then back age 11. When 18 yrs., married and came here. — F. b. Round Peak, PGF, PGM both b. Co.; M. b. Round Peak, MGF b. Carrol Co., VA, MGM b. Co. — Ed.: till 12 (Oak Grove School at Round Peak and at Lamsburg). — Missionary Baptist. — Fairly intelligent. Inclined to be secretive about those things she fears may by ungrammatical. — Tempo fairly rapid; no particular tendency toward prolongation.

59. *Yadkin County*

Formed 1850 from Surry Co. 1st expedition in area 1673. 1st settlers in area 1748: Quakers from Chester Co., PA. English, Germans, Moravians (few Scotch-Irish) among petitioners for land in 1751. Quakers still active; Baptists from 1780s; Methodists from 1800s. Iron, tobacco; resort co. Pop. 1860: 10,714, 1880: 12,420, 1910: 15,428, 1930: 18,010, 1960: 22,804.

Hickerson, Thomas Felix. 1940. *Happy Valley, History and Genealogy*. Chapel Hill: The Author.

Hickerson, Thomas Felix. 1962. *Echoes of Happy Valley.* . . . Chapel Hill.

Rutledge, William E., Jr. 1965. *An Illustrated History of Yadkin County, 1850–1965*. Yadkinsville.

Boonville

Est. 1857 as crossroads settlement. English stock; some Germans. Incorp. as town 1895; trading center. Poss. Methodists in 18th cent.; Baptists here by 1849. Boonville Academy 1881. Small mfg., most gone.

NC 59: F, housewife, 86. B. locally. — Both parents b. here (returned here after living in SC); one grandfather (PGF? MGF?) perhaps b. VA and moved here. — Ed.: a few years. — Missionary Baptist. — Alert; quick, plain and direct in answering; acquaintance with outside world very limited, was unable to see the point of the investigation (near the end of the interview refused to answer any more questions). — Use of a strong [ɚ] sound in all positions is noteworthy, and the use of [ʋɚ] for words spelled with both *-or* and *-ar*. Some speakers in the community distinguish these sounds. (It would be interesting to compare certain sections of Indiana and Iowa which were chiefly settled from this region.)

NC 59*: F, c. 80. Native of Boonville. — Descended from natives. — Friend and neighbor of NC 59, who finished record for NC 59.

60. Forsyth County

Formed 1849 from Stokes County. Co. seat, Winston, built N. of Moravian town of Salem. Salem founded 1766 as Moravian trading center. Moravian tract in Co. early; reinforced c. 1753 from ME and MD. Plank road from Fayetteville c. 1852; RRs from 1873. Salem Female Academy and College. Leading industrial county; highest in density of pop. Diversification of agriculture in recent years: cattle, seed corn, soil conservation. Textiles, tobacco, knitwear (underwear and hosiery), brick and tile, pottery, furniture, granite, sand, gravel. Pop. 1850: 11,168, 1880: 18,070, 1910: 47,311, 1930: 111,681, 1960: 189,428.

Fries, Adelaide L. 1898. *Forsyth County*. Winston: Stewarts' Printing House.

Fries, Adelaide L. 1944. *The Road to Salem*. Chapel Hill: University of North Carolina Press.

Fries, Adelaide L., et al. 1949. *Forsyth, a County on the March*. Chapel Hill: University of North Carolina Press.

Siewers, Charles Nathaniel. 1924. *Forsyth County: Economic and Social*. Chapel Hill: University of North Carolina, Dept. of Rural Social Economics.

Tobaccoville P.O., Old Richmond Twp. (inf. b. near Rural Hall).

Twp. named for old Surry Co. seat. Decayed when church left. Rural Hill on edge of 1752 Moravian grant. Evan. Lutheran church org. 1755. Mainly Germans and Scotch-Irish. RR junction; industrial and trading center. Tobaccoville a small settlement W. of Rural Hall on RR. Local farmer pioneered in seed corn.

NC 60: M, farmer, 41. B. near Rural Hall. — F. b. Rural Hall, PGF b. near Germanton, PGF's F. of German descent, lived near Germanton, PGM b. near Germanton in Stokes Co.; M. b. Forsyth or Stokes Co. (spoke German as a child), MGF b. 10 mi. west of Germanton, in Stokes Co., MGM b. near Pfafftown. — Ed.: Rural Hall HS 1 yr.; Bethanis HS 1 yr. — Christian (parents Lutheran). — Either not particularly intelligent, or very self-conscious. — No particular prolongation. Lip movements and articulation generally not vigorous enough for good phonetic recording. Nothing particularly German seems to turn up in his speech; it is the mixed PA-VA type of this region with weak retroflexion.

61. Iredell County

Formed 1788 from Rowan County. 1st settlers c. 1740s; English and Scotch-Irish first, Germans later. Cattle country; Ft. Dobbs a frontier post. Presbyterians 1st sect; by 1860 Methodist church strongest in Co. ("great revival"); also Baptists and Lutherans early. Public schools from 1839; plank roads 1850s; RR from 1858. Cotton after 1877; distilling center, tobacco early. After 1865 farming shifted to money crops: tobacco and cotton. Also some flax and wheat. Small industries by 1858: smiths, leatherwork, clothing, small textile works, sawmills, gristmills, linseed oil. In 20th cent., textiles, clothing, furniture, flour and food, metals; open shop area. Hydroelectric power. Agricultural diversification: cattle and poultry. Pop. 1790: 5,435, 1820: 13,071, 1850: 14,719, 1880: 22,675, 1910: 34,315, 1930: 46,693, 1960: 62,526.

Carter, William Franklin, Jr., and Carrie Young Carter. 1976. *Footprints in the "Hollows"*. Elkin: Northwestern Regional Library.

Evans, Virginia Fraser, comp. 1976. *Iredell County Landmarks*. Statesville: Iredell Co. American Revolution Bicentennial Commission.

Groome, Bailey T. 1928. *Facts and Figures about Statesville and Iredell County*. Statesville: Chamber of Commerce.

Keever, Homer N. 1976. *Iredell: Piedmont County*. Statesville: Brady Printing Co.

1980. *The Heritage of Iredell County*. Statesville: Genealogical Society of Iredell Co.

New Hope P.O. and Twp.

NW corner of Co. Mountainous. 1st settlers from Ireland and VA. Some slaveowners. 1st Baptist church in Co. here.

NC 61A: M, farmer, 74+. B. locally. — F, PGF, M., MGF, MGM all b. here, MGM of German descent. — Illiterate. — Baptist. — Quick, fairly alert. A tenant all his life in same neighborhood; no awareness of the outside world. Very little awareness of purpose of interview. — Tempo moderately rapid. Fairly short vowels. Diphthongs are often shortened, as [aʌʊ] for [æˑʊ].

Trinity Church, Statesville P.O., New Concord Twp.

Twp. a rural school district NW of Statesville. Scotch-Irish settlement named after Concord Church. Statesville area settled 1750 by Scotch-Irish and Germans. Town founded 1789; damaging fire 1852. Women's college est. 1856; also RR. Medicinal roots and herbs. Local industrial center;

brickmaking machinery, cotton mills, furniture. More wheat than any other co.; largest flour mills in state. Trinity Church a Methodist church in NE corner of Twp.

NC 61B: F, housewife, 40. B. locally. — F., PGF both b. here, PGF's F., PGF's PGM both b. Tyrone Co., Ireland, PGF's M. b. Iredell Co., PGM b. Davie Co.; M. b. here, MGF b. Co., MGM b. Sharpsburg Twp. in Co., MGM's M. b. MD. — Ed.: here first, then at Scotts (h.s.). — Methodist (of Presbyterian descent). — Timid. Tendency to conceal some speech habits. — Tempo moderately rapid; no particular prolongation. Slight difficulty in articulation due to recently extracted teeth. Occ. [ǎ˸ˈʊ˔] replaces [æʊ] before voiceless sounds when quick.

62. Ashe County

Formed 1799 from Wilkes Co. 1st recorded visit by a Moravian Bishop in 1752. Earliest settlers English, Scotch-Irish, German; many from PA; 1st permanent settlement 1771. Slow developing, isolated. Baptists early; Presbyterians 1st settlers, but no permanent church till 1899; Methodists 1815–20; Episcopalians by 1861. Iron mined till 1887; lead mine worked 1861–65; copper mine. 1st high schools private; 2 still survive. Rugged terrain, plateau; many mt. peaks. General farming at first; soil adapted to grain, fruit, dairying, stock raising; local cheesemaking, gave way to Kraft, etc. Tobacco from 1930; beans, strawberries, hay, corn. Water power, furniture among industries. Pop. 1800: 2,783, 1820: 4,335, 1850: 8,777, 1880: 14,437, 1910: 19,074, 1930: 21,019, 1960: 19,768.

Fletcher, Arthur L. 1963. *Ashe County, a History*. Jefferson: Ashe County Research Association.

West Jefferson P.O. and Twp.

Twp. developed 1914 by Norfolk and Western. Part of "Watanga settlements", along with settlements in TN. Good grazing country; rich iron deposits; dairy processing.

NC 62A: M, 76. B. 5 mi. south of Glendale Springs (Ashe Co.), just across line in Wilkes Co. When two years old went to head of Reddies River in Wilkes Co. At age 38 came to Ashe Co. Last 15 years in W. Jefferson. — F., PGF both b. in Co., PGF's F. b. England, PGM b. Co.; M., MGF, MGM all b. Wilkes Co. (in Blue Ridge mtns). — Ed: 6 mos. — Missionary Baptist. — An old-fashioned man with some money and a good, solid, common-sense mind. Hard of hearing, but every one of his answers is a good one. — Deliberate tempo; moderate lengths.

Nathans Creek, West Jefferson P.O., Jefferson Twp.

Nathans Creek an old settlement from c. 1789. Consolidated school 1930. Beef cattle developed.

NC 62B: F, housewife (wife of former postmaster), 52. B. Nathans Creek, has lived last 18 yrs. at West Jefferson. — F. b. near Jefferson, PGF b. on Reddies River (Wilkes Co.), PGF's F. b. Wilkes Co., PGF's PGF b. Rowan Co. (now Davidson Co.), PGF's PGF's F. b. Staten Island or NJ, PGF's PGF's PGF b. Staten Island or in England, PGF's PGF's M. b. NJ, PGF's PGM b. Ashe Co. (Scotch-Irish descent), PGF's M. b. Wilkes Co., PGM, PGM's F., PGM's M. all b. Ashe Co. (PGM's M. of German descent); M. b. Nathans Creek, MGF b. Iredell Co., MGM b. Jefferson. — Ed.: Nathans Creek and

Plummer Seminary at Crumpler (Ashe Co.) 2 summers. — Baptist. — Old French Huguenot family (son of man who fought under Cromwell came to Staten Island in 17th cent.; his son stayed on to be the tax collector there). Inf. complacent, obliging, cooperative; not particularly intelligent. — Tempo deliberate; vowels and diphthongs tend to remain short. Good, clear enunciation on the whole.

63. Wilkes County

Formed 1777 from Surry Co. Moravian grants 1752; other settlers English, Ulster Scots, PA Germans. Pop. grew with influx from PA, VA. Gristmills. Baptists early; Presbyterians late. Academies. Farming and livestock to 1880. RR by 1890; trading developed 1900–1914. Industry in 20th cent.; brick, furniture, gristmills, cotton mfg., mirrors, hosiery, poultry processing, wood products. Pop. 1790: 8,156, 1820: 9,967, 1850: 12,097, 1880: 19,181, 1910: 30,282, 1930: 36,162, 1960: 45,269.

Anderson, J. Jay. 1976. *Wilkes County Sketches*. Wilkesboro: Anderson.

Crouch, John. 1902. *Historical Sketches of Wilkes County*. Wilkesboro: J. Crouch.

Ferguson, Thomas Wiley. 1956. *Home on the Yadkin*. Winston-Salem: Clay Printing Co.

Hayes, Johnson J. 1962. *The Land of Wilkes*. Wilkesboro: Wilkes County Historical Society.

1956. Wilkes County. *The State*, Jan. 26, 1956.

NC 63A: Chestnut Mtn. Ridge, Stony Fork P.O. (Watauga Co.), Elk Twp. — F, widow, 74. B. locally. — F. b. just across mtn. in Ashe Co., came here young (during Civil War), PGF of German descent, PGM b. Ashe Co.; M. b. Long Branch, very near here in Co., MGF b. near top of mtn. just across line in Watauga Co., MGF's F. b. prob. Ashe Co., MGM b. Watauga Co. (just across the mtn.), MGM's M. b. Caldwell Co. — Ed.: very little. — Baptist. — Isolated, old-fashioned woman living on top of mtn. which is inaccessible in bad weather. Good mind; quick, alert common sense; independent, not suggestible, yet accommodating. — Tempo deliberate; vowels fairly short. [baʎən], *born*; [staʎəm], *storm*; [maʎənɪŋ], *morning*. Cf. [kɔ˔ˈən], *corn*; [ɔˈətə], *ought to*; [fɔ˞ɚɾɪ], *forty*.

Wilkesboro, Gilreath P.O., Brushy Mtn. Twp.

Twp. isolated area; old Baptist stronghold. Wilkesboro not laid out till 1801.

NC 63B: F, postmistress, 52. B. very near Wilkesboro; when 10 moved from Wilkesboro to Yadkin Valley (Caldwell Co.) on line of Caldwell Co.; when 22 came to live in Gilreath (where record made). — F., PGF both b. Wilkesboro, PGF's F. and M. b. Davie Co. (PGF's F. of English descent), PGM, PGM's F. both b. near Wilkesboro; M. b. near Wilkesboro, MGF b. Scotland, came here when 4 yrs. old, MGM b. near Wilkesboro. — Ed.: in Wilkesboro. — Baptist. — Very intelligent; cooperative; calm, matter-of-fact. Good family background. — Tempo deliberate; vowels fairly short.

64. Catawba County

Formed 1842 from Lincoln Co. 1st settlers 1747 from VA; 1st land grants 1749. Thickly settled by Rev.; Tories active. Settlers mainly German and Scotch-Irish; German spoken for a long time. Germans on W. side of Catawba. Lutheran and Reformed 1st churches; preaching by 1759. Strong support for free schools; several colleges beginning with Catawba College in 1852. Prevailingly agricultural to 1900; mainly small farmers. One of top wheat cos. in 1884. Cotton chief money crop; tobacco till decline of Hickory as a market. Chickens, eggs, apples, peaches. Various minerals: gold, mica, iron, lime, graphite, lead; pottery, sand, gravel. Pop. 1850: 8,862, 1880: 14,946, 1910: 27,918, 1930: 43,991, 1960: 73,191.

> Preslar, Charles J., Jr., ed. 1954. *A History of Catawba County*. Salisbury: Catawba County Historical Association.

Ban Oak, Vale P.O., Bandy Twp.

Ban Oak in SW part of Co.; named for 2 school districts: Bandy and Oak Hill.

NC 64A: M, farmer and cobbler, 86. B. locally. — F. b. here, PGF of German descent, PGM b. here; M., MGF both b. here, MGF's F. of Irish descent, MGM b. here. — Illiterate. — Baptist. — Intelligent; isolated. — Tempo moderate; no particular prolongation.

Hickory/Love, Newton P.O., Caldwell Twp.

Hickory Tavern on Hickory/Love site by 1790. Town of Hickory charter 1873; city charter 1889. Developed as trading center after 1870; industry developed with RR. Patent medicine, tobacco, whiskey. 1st land granted for Newton 1748. Settled mainly by PA Dutch. Catawba College here from 1852 (later moved to Salisbury).

NC 64B: M, farmer, 39. B. near Hickory (Hickory Twp.); when 15 came to Love. — F. b. near Hickory, PGF b. Co. (German descent), PGM b. near Hickory; M., MGF, MGM all b. near Conover in Co. (MGF of German descent), MGM's F. b. Co. (German descent). — Ed.: at Charity School. — Methodist. — Slow, patient, obliging, slightly reticent. — Tempo moderate; no particular prolongation. Articulation not very good. Tends to be "front" in quality, possibly due to German background.

65. *Caldwell County*

Formed 1841 from Burke and Wilkes Cos. Settled by English, Scots, Scotch-Irish, Germans, Welsh, a few French. Mountainous area. Cotton mills, woolens, cordage, furniture. Pop. 1850: 6,317, 1880: 10,291, 1910: 20,579, 1930: 28,016, 1960: 49,552.

> Alexander, Nancy. 1956. *Here Will I Dwell: The Story of Caldwell County*. Salisbury: Rowan Print. Co.
> Hickerson, Thomas Felix. 1962. *Echoes of Happy Valley: Letters and Diaries. . . .* Chapel Hill.
> Scott, William W. 1930. *Annals of Caldwell County*. Lenoir: News-Topic Print.

Green Valley, Colletsville P.O., Johns River Twp.

Colletsville a summer resort area at the confluence of Mulberry Creek and Johns River.

NC 65A: F, housewife, 66. B. here. — F. b. here, PGF, PGM, both b. Caldwell Co.; M. b. locally, MGF b. here, MGM b.

Watauga Co. — Ed.: till 16 (extremely irregular). — Missionary Baptist. — Old-fashioned, but with some education (and therefore some pretense, albeit easily put aside). Family have been opposed to roads and schools, and like the old way of life. — Tempo moderate; no particular prolongation.

Kings Creek, Kings Creek Twp. (record made in Lenoir)

Lenoir Co. scat; surveyed and named 1841; incorp. 1851. Methodists built first church. Davenport College from 1855; combined 1930s with Greensboro College. Textiles; brickmaking. Furniture mfg.; lumber mills and yards. Mountain resorts. Pop. 1880: 422, 1910: 3,364, 1930: 6,532, 1960: 10,257.

NC 65B: F, housekeeper, 64. B. on Kings Creek, came to Lenoir when 29; married when 41, went to Little Creek for 13 yrs, then back to Lenoir. — F., PGF both b. here, PGF's F. b. VA ("Irish" descent), PGM b. here, PGM's F. of "Irish" descent; M. b. here, MGF b. here (Welsh descent), MGM b. here (Irish descent). — Ed.: very little (at Kings Creek). — Adventist. — Slow; complacent. — Speech probably toned down from living in town.

66. *Cleveland County*

Formed 1841 from Rutherford and Lincoln Cos. 1st settlers 1750: Scotch-Irish and Germans. Chiefly from PA; some from Charleston. Baptists, Presbyterians, some Episc. Divided sentiment in Rev. Many textiles by 1871; early hat industry; cotton declined. Vineyards in 19th cent. Mfg. increased during Reconstruction. Resort area to 1929 (coastal planters first). Mountainous; various minerals, including gold, tin, clay, lithium, mica. Pop. 1850: 10,396, 1880: 16,571, 1910: 29,494, 1930: 51,914, 1960: 66,048.

> Davis, J. R. 1914. Reconstruction in Cleveland County. In *Trinity College Historical Society Annual Publication* vol. 10.
> Weathers, Lee Beam. 1956. *The Living Past of Cleveland County. . . .* Shelby: Star Pub. Co.
> 1976. *Our Heritage: A History of Cleveland County*. Shelby: Shelby Daily Star.

NC 66A: Warlick, Lawndale P.O. — M, farmer, 75. B. locally. — F. b. here, PGF b. locally (English descent), PGM b. here (Irish descent); M. b. here, MGF of Scottish descent, MGM b. here (Welsh descent). — Illiterate. — Baptist. — Quick, bright; has visited sons in VA, but remains unchanged. — Tempo moderate; no particular prolongation. Articulation slightly slurred. Note: [wɨð'ɹaɪks].

Boiling Springs

Named for former local springs. Grew up around a Baptist church; town named 1843; inc. early 20th cent. College here descendant of old Baptist Academy.

NC 66B: F, housewife, 53. B. Belwood. When 7, came to Shelby to live; moved here age 25. — F. b. Belwood, PGF b. Bullocks Creek (York Co. SC), came here when young, PGF's F., PGF's PGF, PGF's PGF's F., PGF's PGF's M., PGF's PGM all b. Fitchburg, MA, PGF's M. b. York Co., SC, PGM, PGM's F., PGM's M. all b. Belwood (PGM's F. of German descent); M. b. Belwood, MGF b. Cleveland Co., MGF's F. b. Kings

Mtn., MGM, MGM's F. both b. Lincoln Co. (German descent). — Ed.: 11th grade in Shelby. — Born Methodist; now Baptist. — Middle-aged type; good family background; cooperative. — Rapid tempo; no particular prolongation.

67. Mitchell County

Formed 1861 from Yancey and other cos. Legally opened to settlement 1778. Communication difficult; 1st road 1834. Divided allegiance 1861–65. Diversified agriculture; self-sufficiency. Mountainous; 2nd in state in mining, esp. feld-spar, also mica, kaolin. Pop. 1870: 4,705, 1880: 9,435, 1910: 17,245, 1930: 13,962, 1960: 13,908.

> Dayton, Jason Basil. 1931. *History of the Toe River Valley to 1865.* University of North Carolina Master's thesis.
> Sheppard, Muriel E. 1935. *Cabins in the Laurel.* Chapel Hill: University of North Carolina Press.

NC 67A: Hughes Settlement, Rock Creek, Buladean P.O., Harrell Twp. — M, farmer, 84. B. locally. — F. b. Co. near Relief down on Tow River (10 mi. below here), PGF, PGM both b. Co.; MGM b. Little Rock Creek in Co. — Ed.: none. — Free Will Baptist. — Intelligent; friendly; unsuspicious. He always lived near the crest of the mtns. — Tempo deliberate; vowels have some prolongation. Retroflexion rather weak, beginning unretroflex (note loss of retroflexion after [ð] in unstressed syllables as in Hyde Co.). Both [eˑeˀ] and [oˑo] diphthongs are very interesting.

NC 67B: Honeycutt, Bakersville, Harrell Twp. — M, farmer, 81. B. here. — F. b. here, PGF, PGM both b. VA or KY, came here just after Revolution (PGF Scots-Irish descent); M. b. here, MGF b. locally, MGF's F. a Revolutionary soldier, MGM b. Burke Co., MGM's F. b. in England. — Ed.: little, here. — Methodist, Odd Fellows. — Comparatively well-to-do; interested, honest.

68. McDowell County

Formed 1842 from Rutherford and Burke Cos. 1st explorer 1730. One Rev. skirmish. Goldmining in early 19th cent. 1st RR 1870. Rural, mountainous, scenic. Corn chief crop. Forestry, textiles, furniture, pharmaceuticals, limestone, mica. Pop. 1850: 6,245, 1880: 9,836, 1910: 13,538, 1930: 20,336, 1960: 26,742.

> American Revolution Bicentennial Commission. 1975. *Pictorial History of McDowell County, NC: 1775–1975.* Marion: Heritage Committee.
> Fossett, Mildred B. 1976. *History of McDowell County.* Marion: McDowell County American Revolution Bicentennial Commission.
> Perry, Martha Elmina. 1910. *Christ and Answered Prayer.* Cincinnati: Benson.

NC 68A: Glenswood, Nealsville P.O., Glenwood Twp. — F, housewife, 67. B. Higgins Twp. (7 or 8 mi. NE). — F. b. Higgins Twp., PGF's F. b. in England, PGM b. Higgins Twp.; M., MGF, MGM all b. Co., MGM's F. of English descent. — Ed.: very little, a month or two at a time. — Methodist. — Highly intelligent; old-fashioned with little knowledge of outside world; hospitable, friendly, cooperative; motherly, unsuspicious; quick-thinking, untiring. A very slight palsy. — Tempo

moderate; some prolongation of vowels and diphthongs at times.

Greenlee, Marion P.O., Old Fort Twp.

Greenlee an outpost; old fort here 1776. Named after early settlers. Heavily damaged by 1916 flood. Marion est. 1842; courthouse built 1844. Robert Morris of PA once owned 200,000 acres in region. Textile mfg.

NC 68B: F, housewife, 42. B. here. Has visited considerably in VA, TN, and E. NC. — F. b. North Cove in Co., PGF b. Co., PGF's F. b. Ireland, PGF's M. b. Co., PGM, PGM's F., PGM's M. all b. Co. (Irish descent); M., MGF, MGF's F. b. here, MGM b. Marion, MGM's F. of German descent, MGM's M. b. one of counties east of here. — Ed.: here till 18 (Nebo High School 1 yr.). — Presbyterian. — Very quick-thinking, intelligent; slightly timid and self-conscious, yet anxious to cooperate; slightly "flurried". In spite of her travels, not the type to change her speech. — Tempo rapid; no particular prolongation. Articulation not very clear.

69. Polk County

Formed 1855 from Rutherford and Henderson Cos. 1st settlers c. 1775; Cherokees driven back 1776. Frontier country in Rev. Scotch-Irish, German stock. Settled via SC up-country. Old Buncombe road opened 1793. Few AfAms, few plantations. Gold to 1840. Grapes c. 1896; scenic, resort country. Pop. 1860: 4,043, 1880: 5,062, 1910: 7,640, 1930: 10,216, 1960: 11,395.

> Carver, Helen A. 1948. *Reminiscences.* Saluda: Excelsior Printers.
> Patton, Saide (Smathers). 1950. *Sketches of Polk County History.* Asheville.

Mill Spring, White Oak Twp.

Mill Spring inc. by 1895; relatively small, isolated. 1st settlers by Rev.; Loyalists. 2 churches and a school c. 1920.

NC 69A: M, farmer, 77. B. locally. — F., PGF both lived here; M. b. here, MGF lived here, MGM b. Co., MGM's F. of "Dutch" descent. — Illiterate. — Baptist. — Very slow; talkative. — Tempo rapid; no particular prolongation. Articulation rather clearcut.

Friendship Church, Saluda P.O. and Twp.

Settlement and church at Friendship Church by 1825; org. as town 1834. Saluda developed along with RR in 1870s. Steep grade, deep gorges; fishing, resort area.

NC 69B: F, housekeeper, 57. B. here. — F. b. Henderson Co., 10 mi. from Hendersonville on road to Asheville, came here when 9 yrs. old, PGF b. near Saluda, PGF's F. b. Co., PGM b. Henderson Co.; MGF b. Saluda, MGF's M. b. Co. — Ed.: very little; nearby. — Baptist. — Unmarried, living with aged father. Pretty genuine speech.

70. Madison County

Formed 1851 from Buncombe and Yancey Cos. 1st exploration 1677; 1st settled 1784. Earliest settlers from PA: German and Scotch-Irish. 1st road 1795; turnpike by 1828; RR complete to Knoxville 1882. Many church-founded schools. Ballad collector worked here. Mid point of NC-TN line, scenic, rugged. Mostly farming through 1820s; lumbering after RR (1882). Tobacco (introduced 1872), corn, cotton mills, limestone, chalk, iron. Tourism after 1882. Pop. 1860: 5,908, 1880: 12,810, 1910: 20,132, 1930: 20,306, 1960: 17,217.

> Dykemann, Wilma. 1955. *The French Broad*. NY: Rinehart and Co.
> Wellman, Manly Wade. 1973. *The Kingdom of Madison: A Southern Mountain Fastness and Its People*. Chapel Hill: University of North Carolina Press.

Marshall, formerly White Rock, Shelton Laurel Twp.

Twp. a rugged region; named for settlers c. 1799. Hiding place for outlaws, esp. Unionists; atrocities by Confederate authorities. Moonshining; ballad country.

NC 70A: F, widow, 71. B. locally. — F. b. here, PGF b. Cane River (Yancey Co.), PGM, PGM's F., PGM's M. b. Yancey Co.; M. b. on Little Laurel in Co., MGF b. Co., MGF's M., MGM, MGM's F., MGM's M. b. here (most families said to be "Irish" and "Dutch"). — Illiterate. — Few social contacts. — Quick, bright mind; plenty of common sense. Has lived hard poverty-stricken life; ruggedly individualistic; belligerently old-fashioned. FW approached her through a local merchant who was her former charge. Inf. still lives as though it were 1865, with all the bitter feelings of that era. — Tempo fairly rapid; no particular tendency to prolongation. Enunciation clear, distinct, and forceful. *Or* in some words is [ɞ͜ə], and is distinguished from *ar* [ɑ·ɚ]. [ɚ] is strongly reverberant, and may be produced in a number of ways. It often glides up into a retroflex sound; the ending may be a consonantal glide or fricative or even a tap when a vowel follows, e.g. [ðɚɾ̮ɔ˞un]. Initial /r/ is usually a consonantal glide, but may become a trill, [rr], esp. when [ðə] precedes, or if /d/ or /t/ precede in the sentence. Medial /t/ is often replaced by [ɾ] or [rr]. Some instances of [rr], such as that in the phrase [kʊkt æᵊpḷz] or [kʊkrr æᵊpḷz], sounds quite un-English. It would seem that Scottish (or Irish or German) speakers who use [rr] for an /r/ sound, upon learning a variety of English where [ɾ] is used for medial /t/ have substituted [rr] and used it where no English speakers ever would have used it. Cf. [gɑ˞tɾ̮ræy] or [gɑ˞rɾ̮ræyk]. It is evident that the [r] - [ɾ] phoneme is separate from the [t] - [rr] phoneme. The existence of two trills in a dialect as a result of a foreign language background is exactly comparable to conditions found among the Gullah Negroes of SC, except that in their dialect [r] and [ɾ] are separate phonemes (their [ɾ] is only used for Standard English medial /d/). [s] and [z] are retroflex almost always.

Walnut, Big Laurel Twp.

Walnut once Jewel Hill. Co. seat to 1858. Had private boarding school. School and clutch of churches c. 1920.

NC 70B: M, student, 16. B. here. — F. b. Walnut, PGF, PGF's F. both b. Co., PGM, PGM's F. both b. here, PGM's M. b. Co.; M., MGF, MGF's F. all b. near Marshall, MGF's M. b. near Rutherfordton, MGM b. near Marshall, MGM's F. b. Co., MGM's PGF of a VA family (of "Dutch" descent), MGM's M. b. Co., MGM's MGF of "Irish descent". — Ed.: senior in high school at time of interview. — FW unable to find a suitable middle-aged informant in this area. FW originally directed to

this inf.'s aunt (who has raised inf. from infancy), but the aunt turned out to be unsuitable for interview. Aunt's speech influenced in childhood by Presbyterian missionaries from the North; she says: [rʊᵊm]; [spʊᵊn]; [grijsɪ̮]. Inf. and aunt's mother both laughed at aunt's idiosyncracies as she attempted to answer questions; inf. volunteered to answer questions himself. Inf. is quick, bright, and had a fully scientific and objective attitude toward his answers, with none of his aunt's desire to "put on". He does not want to go on to school; prefers camping in mountains. — Tempo moderate; no particular tendency to prolong.

71. Buncombe County

Formed 1791 from Burke and Rutherford Cos. 1st settlements c. 1781; earliest settlers from PA via VA and from SC; Scotch-Irish, German, and English. Turnpike from 1824; plank road to Greenville 1851; RR at least by 1881. Tobacco culture till c. 1897. Scenic. Industry increased from 1930s. Chief milk-producing co. in state; also cattle, apples, granite, clay, sand, feldspar. Pop. 1800: 5,812, 1820: 10,542, 1850: 13,425, 1880: 21,909, 1910: 49,798, 1930: 97,937, 1960: 130,074.

> Digges, George A. 1935. *Historical Facts concerning Buncombe County Government*. Asheville: Biltmore Press.
> Dykemann, Wilma. 1955. *The French Broad*. NY: Rinehart and Co.
> Mead, Martha Norburn. 1942. *Asheville, in Land of the Sky*. Richmond, VA: Dietz Press.
> Sondley, F. A. 1922 *Asheville and Buncombe County*. Asheville: The Citizen Co.
> Sondley, F. A. 1930. *History of Buncombe County, North Carolina*. 2 vols. Asheville: Advocate Printing Co.
> Wolfe, Thomas. 1929. *Look Homeward, Angel*. NY: Scribner's.

Dillingham P.O., Asheville Twp.

Dillingham contains entrance gate of Mt. Mitchell division of Pisgah National Forest. Tourist area. Pop. 1930: 275.

NC 71A: M, farmer, 78. B. Pensacola, Yancey Co. (just across mountain). When 7 or 8 years old, moved over to this side of mountain in Buncombe Co. — F. b. near Pensacola; M. b. near Pensacola (died at inf.'s birth), step-M. b. Flat Creek in Co.) — Ed.: very little (month or two). — Methodist. — Quick, intelligent, cooperative; little awareness of how antique his speech is. — Moderate tempo; no particular prolongation. Articulation fairly good.

Lower Hominy, Candler P.O., Lower Hominy Twp.

Forge on Hominy Creek by 1800. Candler a conservation area near Pisgah Natl. Forest. First large rayon factory in South nearby from 1929.

NC 71B: M, farmer, 54. B. Newfound (on the Haywood Co. line, northwest of Asheville.). — F., PGF both b. on Hominy in Co., PGF's F. b. here, PGF's PGF b. PA 1755 (of Welsh descent), died Buncombe Co. 1824. — Ed.: Newfound; then 3 years at the Haywood Institute at Clyde (Haywood Co.) — Presbyterian. — Intelligent, sensible. Rather inclined not to give himself away in speech at times; his wife made him admit some things he had not planned to. Perfect calm; he can't be hurried. — Deliberate tempo; no particular prolongation. Good articulation.

Asheville

Economic and cultural center of the 18 mountain cos. Cherokee hunting ground; no settlers before Rev. Co. seat laid out, orig. Morristown; 1797 renamed in honor of Samuel Ashe (gov. 1795–98). Earliest settlers Scotch-Irish and PA Dutch. Turnpike 1824; 1st RR 1880. Large-scale reforestation c. 1892; Biltmore School of Forestry founded 1895. Nucleus of Pigsah Natl. Forest here. Tourism. Once tobacco market; barley by 1931. Industrialization with coming of RR: textiles, lumber, wood products, rayon, paper. Pop. 1850: 502, 1880: 2,616, 1910: 18,762, 1930: 60,192.

NC 71C!: F, housewife, 49. B. here. — F. b. Gudgers Mill (14 mi. W.), PGF b. Co., PGF's F. b. Madison Co. (Scottish descent), PGM, PGM's F. both b. Co. (English descent); M. b. Leicester in Co., MGF b. Co. (Irish descent), MGM b. Henderson Co. — Ed.: city schools until 16; Converse College, Spartanburg, SC, 4 yrs. — Methodist. — Wife of a lawyer; delightful; thoroughly natural; full cooperation. — Tempo rapid; vowels tend to be short. Good enunciation. [ɚ] sound is not particularly strong. — Cultivated.

72. Transylvania County

Formed 1861 from Henderson and Jackson Cos. 1st deed 1788; Indian frontier to 1838. Ulster Scots, English from E. NC, VA, PA. Presbyterians by 1800; Baptists by 1804; Methodists later. RR from 1894. Communication with SC difficult: first real hwy. 1924. Resort area from before 1861. Ironworks to 1896; gold. Hatmaking, lumbering; family farms, corn. Mill for making cigarette paper here from 1939. Pop. 1870: 3,536, 1880: 5,340, 1910: 7,191, 1930: 9,589, 1960: 16,372.

> Dykemann, Wilma. 1955. *The French Broad*. NY: Rinehart and Co.
> Norris, Kevin, and Martin Reidinger. 1973. *Transylvania County: An Early History*. Brevard: History.
> 1961. *Transylvania County Centennial, 1861–1961*. Brevard: Transylvania Historical Commission.

Wilson Street, Brevard, Pisgah Forest P.O., Dunns Rock Twp.

1st hotel in Co. at Dunns Rock. Brevard inc. 1867. Once center of high hat industry. Still no school building in Brevard c. 1889; now Brevard College. Lumber, tanning, cotton. Pisgah Forest a small lumbering community; one entrance to Pisgah Natl. Forest. Papermill. Pop. 1880: 223, 1910: 919, 1930: 2,329, 1960: 4,847.

NC 72A: M, farmer and moonshiner, 74. B. locally. — F. b. here, PGF of Irish descent; M. b. here, MGF b. Gloucester Twp. in Co. (Scottish descent), MGM b. Co., MGM's F. b. here probably. — Ed.: none to speak of. — Methodist. — Mentally a bit slow, though quick in reaction time. Affectionate to those he approves of, yet capable of shooting others. — Tempo moderate; no prolongation to speak of. Articulation rather bad. He has several speech defects in individual words.

NC 72B: Rock Brook, Brevard P.O., Dunns Rock Twp. — F, housewife, 45. B. locally. — F., PGF both b. here, PGF's F. b.

Ireland, PGM b. here; M. b. just over line in SC, MGF, MGF's F., MGF's M. all b. here (MGF's F. of English descent), MGM b. just over line in Pickens Co., SC, MGM's F., MGM's M. both b. SC. — Ed.: here till 16; Brevard Institute 1 term. — Baptist. — Timid; intelligent; cooperative. — Tempo moderate; vowels tend to be short. [ɚ] is not particularly strong. The most notable influence on inf.'s speech has probably been that of a former schoolteacher from Abbeville, SC.

73. Swain County

Formed 1871 from Jackson and Macon Cos. Cherokee reservation. Corn; copper mining, limestone, clay. Scenic, resorts; Fontana Lake here. Pop. 1880: 3,784, 1910: 10,403, 1930: 11,568, 1960: 8,387.

NC 73A: Proctor, Dorsey P.O., Forneys Creek Twp. — F, 86. B. 9 mi. from here; 3 mi. from Bushnell. Lived back and forth between here and Stecoah in Graham Co. from early childhood until few years after marriage. Here for last 53 years. — F. b. Stecoah, Graham Co., PGM lived Graham Co.; M. b. near Chambers Creek on Kirklands Creek, MGF b. near Bushnell (perhaps part Indian). — Very alert, talkative; mind still very clear. Poor health, yet enjoyed FW's visit. — Tempo fairly deliberate; lengths moderate. Articulation pretty clear.

Wadkins, Bryson City, Charleston Twp.

Bryson City center of Co.; Co. seat. Cherokee country; reservation nearby. Woodworking; HQ for copper and feldspar mining. Shipping point for purebred stock. Extensive reforestation began here 1937. Pop. 1910: 612, 1930: 1,806, 1960: 1,084.

NC 73B: M, farmer and carpenter (and cancer-curer), 77. B. here. Lived Haywood Co. age 2 to 19. — F. b. here, PGF b. near Sylva (Jackson Co.), said to have come from NY or somewhere north, but this may have been PGF's F., PGM lived Jackson Co. (Irish descent); M. b. Wilkes Co., came here when 12, MGF b. Wilkes Co. (Irish descent), MGM b. Wilkes Co. ("Black Dutch"). — Ed.: Haywood Co. (a little). — Baptist. — Easy-going; not particularly intelligent. — Tendency to prolong vowels. Slow utterance. Somewhat nasal.

74. Macon County

Formed 1828 from Haywood Co. 1st settlers English, Scotch-Irish, some Germans. Corn chief crop, soapstone, corundum mining from 1870. Summering place for S. Carolinians; Highlands developed by outlanders from KS, MA, MN, IN, etc., as well as by S. Carolinians. Pop. 1830: 5,333, 1850: 6,389, 1880: 8,064, 1910: 12,191, 1930: 13,672, 1960: 14,935.

> Smith, C. D. 1905. *Brief History of Macon County, North Carolina*. Franklin: Franklin Press.
> Wood, Lawrence E. 1972. *Mountain Memories*. Franklin.

Highlands, Satolah (GA) P.O.

Highlands a summer resort town. Forest; wide variety of plant and animal life; spectacular scenery. Museum and Biological Lab. Pop. 1880: 82, 1910: 267, 1930: 1,514, 1960: 1,418.

NC 74A: M, farmer, 71. B. locally. — F. b. Tuckasegee River in Jackson Co. and came here before Civil War, PGF b. NC, perhaps in Jackson Co. ("Dutch"), PGM b. Jackson Co. ("Irish" descent); M. b. Rutherford Co. and came here when young, MGF b. Catawba Co. ("Irish" descent), MGM b. Rutherford Co. (English descent). — Ed.: none. — Methodist parentage; now Baptist. — Quick, bright; old-fashioned, companionable. Suspicious at first, but convinced it was worthwhile when he discovered FW was from Chapel Hill. — Moderate tempo; no particular prolongation.

Cartoogechaye, Franklin P.O. and Twp.

Cartoogechaye in heavily wooded area. Franklin near old Cherokee settlement; twice destroyed and rebuilt. Paper mills, extract factories, talc and mica mines, lumber companies.

NC 74B: F, housewife, 57. B. locally. — F. b. Franklin, PGF b. Co. (Irish descent), PGM, PGM's F. b. Macon Co. (latter of Irish descent), PGM's step-M. b. Co.; M. b. Burke Co. and came here age 3, MGF, MGM both b. Burke Co. (both "Dutch" descent). — Ed.: here, h.s. at Franklin 1 term. — Methodist. — Quick, intelligent; slightly on guard. — Tempo moderate; no prolongation to speak of.

75. Cherokee County

Formed 1839 from Macon Co. Mountainous; towns in lowland. Surveyed 1836 after Cherokees dispossessed. 1st whites in area traders and explorers (some from Charleston). 1st settlements c. 1830: English, Scotch (possibly some Dutch and French) from W. NC, some from PA, VA, TN. Over 80% forested; isolated. 1st turnpike 1839; RR not till 1918. Reforestation. Center of NC Cherokee nation. Most farms for household use (some apples, hens). Textiles, knit goods, hosiery. Minerals: marble, limestone, quartz, sandstone, iron ore, talc, magnesium, gold. Water power, tourism. Pop. 1840: 3,422, 1850: 3,385, 1880: 8,182, 1910: 14,136, 1930: 16,151, 1960: 16,335.

Barclay, E. E. 1946. *Ducktown Back in Raht's Time.* Chapel Hill: University of North Carolina Press.

Browder, Nathaniel C. 1974. *The Cherokee Indians and Those Who Came After: Notes for a History of Cherokee County, North Carolina, 1835–1860.* Hayesville: Browder.

Freel, Margaret (Walker). 1956. *Our Heritage, the People of Cherokee County, North Carolina, 1540–1955.* Asheville: Miller Print. Co.

Lambert, Robert S. 1958. The Oconaluftee Valley, 1800–1860: A Study of the Sources for Mountain History. *North Carolina Historical Review* 35:415–426.

Roach, Hattie Joplin. 1952. *Hills of Cherokee.* Rusk, TX.

Stringfield, William W. 1903. *North Carolina Cherokee Indians.* Raleigh: E. M. Uzzell and Co.

Head of Beaverdam, Grandview P.O., Beaverdam Twp.

Twp. in NW part of Co.; mountainous and rugged. Early settlers English, Scotch, Welsh. Beaverdam Creek best farming land in area. Head of Beaverdam a small settlement.

NC 75A: M, farmer and cattleman, 83. B. here. — F. b. Buncombe Co., came here c. 20 yrs. old, PGF b. Buncombe Co.

("Dutch" descent), PGM of "Dutch" descent; M. b. Yancey Co. — Illiterate. — Humble origin, but has made money raising cattle (has taken cattle to Richmond, but has always come straight back again, uncontaminated). Quick, alert; quick answers, although sometimes forgetful. — Tempo rapid; vowels and dipthongs are very short. Clear articulation. [aⁱ] diphthong is noteworthy.

Peachtree, Murphy P.O. and Twp.

Twp. in central part of Co.; most populous twp. in Co. Varied surface. Murphy est. 1830, orig. an Indian trading post. Peachtree a thickly settled and prosperous agricultural section; rich bottomland; only moderately hilly. Diversified farming. One of most important Indian sites; peach and plum trees when whites arrived. Baptists by 1837; Methodists at least by 1885.

NC 75B: F, housewife (wife of retired Methodist missionary), 52. B. here. — F. b. Marble in Co., PGF b. Lincoln Co. (partly Dutch descent), PGM b. just over line in Tennessee; M. b. here, MGF b. Morgantown (Burke Co.), MGM b. Lenoir (Caldwell Co.). — Ed.: here till 16. — Methodist. — Quick, intelligent, cooperative. This the quickest record FW made in South (3 1/2 hours instead of the ususal 5 or 6). — Moderate tempo; no particular prolongation.

Bibliographies

Jones, H. G. 1966. *For History's Sake: The Preservation and Publication of North Carolina History, 1663–1903.* Chapel Hill: University of North Carolina Press.

Leflor, Hugh T. 1969. *A Guide to the Study and Reading of North Carolina History.* 3rd ed., rev. and enl. Chapel Hill: University of North Carolina Press.

Powell, William S. 1958. *North Carolina County Histories: A Bibliography.* Chapel Hill: University of North Carolina Library.

Stevenson, George. 1984. *North Carolina Local History: A Select Bibliography.* Rev Ed. Raleigh: North Carolina Dept. of Cultural Resources.

Thornton, Mary L. 1958. *A Bibliography of North Carolina, 1889–1956.* Chapel Hill: University of North Carolina Press.

Weeks, Stephen B. 1895. *Bibliography of North Carolina Historical Literature.* Cambridge, MA: Harvard University Press.

1934–. *North Carolina Historical Review Annual Classified Bibliography.* Raleigh: NC Historical Commission.

General Histories

Ashe, Samuel A'Court. 1908–25. *History of North Carolina.* 2 vols. Greensboro. Repr. 1971 (Spartanburg, SC: Reprint Co.).

Burney, Eugenia. 1975. *Colonial North Carolina.* Nashville: T. Nelson.

Connor, R. D. W. 1919. *History of North Carolina. . . .* NY. Repr. 1973 (Spartanburg, SC: Reprint Co.).

Connor, R. D. W. 1929. *North Carolina: Rebuilding an Ancient Commonwealth.* 2 vols. NY. Repr. 1973 (Spartanburg, SC: Reprint Co.).

Henderson, Archibald, ed. 1941. *North Carolina, the Old North State and the New*. 5 vols. Chicago: University of Chicago Press.

Lambeth, Mary Weeks. 1957. *Memories and Records of Eastern North Carolina*. Nashville.

Lefler, Hugh T., and Albert Ray Newsome. 1954. *North Carolina: The History of a Southern State*. Chapel Hill: University of North Carolina Press.

Lefler, Hugh T., and William S. Powell. 1973. *Colonial North Carolina: A History*. NY: Scribner.

Moore, John Wheeler. 1880. *History of North Carolina*. Raleigh: A. Williams and Co.

Powell, William S. 1977. *North Carolina: A Bicentennial History*. NY: Norton.

Williamson, Hugh. 1812. *History of North Carolina*. 2 vols. Philadelphia. Repr. 1973 ((Spartanburg, SC: Reprint Co.).

1901–1971. *The North Carolina Booklet*. Raleigh: NC Society, Daughters of the American Revolution.

Special Studies

Allen, Mary Moore. 1949. *North Carolina Sketches*. Goldsboro.

Arthur, John Preston. 1914. *Western North Carolina*. Raleigh. Repr. 1973 (Spartanburg, SC: Reprint Co.).

Barrett, John Gilchrist. 1963. *The Civil War in North Carolina*. Chapel Hill: University of North Carolina Press.

Bassett, J. S. 1894. The Regulators of North Carolina. In *American Historical Society Annual Report*, pp. 141–212. Washington, DC.

Bassett, J. S. 1896. *Slavery and Servitude in the Colony of North Carolina*. Baltimore: Johns Hopkins Press.

Bassett, J. S. 1898. Landholding in Colonial North Carolina. *Annual Publication of Historical Papers: Trinity College Historical Society* 2:44–61.

Battle, Kemp Plummer. 1907–12. *History of the University of North Carolina*. 2 vols. Raleigh: The Author.

Bernheim, Gotthardt. 1872. *History of the German Settlements and of the Lutheran church in North and South Carolina....* Philadelphia. Repr. 1972 (Spartanburg, SC: Reprint Co.).

Brown, Cecil Kenneth. 1928. *A State Movement in Railroad Development....* Chapel Hill: University of North Carolina Press.

Brown, Cecil Kenneth. 1931. *The State Highway System of North Carolina, Its Evolution and Present Status*. Chapel Hill: University of North Carolina Press.

Bryson, Herman. 1928. *The Story of the Geologic Making of North Carolina*. New Bern: O.G. Dunn, Printer.

Byrd, William. 1929. *William Byrd's Histories of the Dividing Line....* Raleigh: North Carolina Historical Commission.

Cameron, John D. 1893. *Hand-Book of North Carolina*. Raleigh: Edwards and Boughton.

Cathey, Cornelius O. 1956. *Agricultural Developments in North Carolina, 1783–1860*. Chapel Hill: University of North Carolina Press.

Cheshire, Joseph Blount, ed. 1892. *Sketches of Church History in North Carolina*. Wilmington: W. L. DeRosset, Jr.

Connor, R. D. W. 1920. *Race Elements in the White Population of North Carolina*. Greensboro. Repr. 1971 (Spartanburg, SC: Reprint Co.).

Cook, Harvey Toliver. 1924. *The Hard Labor Section*. Greenville, SC.

Corbitt, David Leroy. 1950. *The Formation of the North Carolina Counties, 1663–1943*. Raleigh: State Dept. of Archives and History.

DeMond, Robert O. 1940. *The Loyalists in North Carolina....* Durham: Duke University Press.

Dykeman, Wilma. 1955. *The French Broad*. NY: Rinehart.

Ervine, Samuel J., Jr. The Provincial Agents of North Carolina. *James Sprent Historical Publications, University of North Carolina* 16.3:63–77.

Federal Writers Project. 1939. *North Carolina, a Guide to the Old North State*. Chapel Hill: University of North Carolina Press.

Foote, William Henry. 1846. *Sketches of North Carolina....* NY: R. Carter.

Franklin, John H. 1943. *The Free Negro in North Carolina, 1790–1860*. Chapel Hill: University of North Carolina Press.

Gobbel, Luther L. 1938. *Church-State Relationships in Education in North Carolina since 1776*. Durham: Duke University Press.

Greene, Jack P. 1965. *The Quest for Power: The Lower Houses of Assembly in the Southern Royal Colonies, 1689–1776*. Chapel Hill. Repr. 1972 (NY: W. W. Norton).

Guess, William C. 1911. County Government in Colonial North Carolina. *James Sprunt Historical Publications, University of North Carolina* 11.1:5–39.

Haywood, Marshall de Lancey. 1903. *Governor William Tryon, and His Administration....* Raleigh: E. M. Uzzell.

Hobbs, Samuel Huntington. 1930. *North Carolina, Economic and Social*. Chapel Hill: University of North Carolina Press.

Johnson, Guion Griffis. 1937. *Ante-Bellum North Carolina....* Chapel Hill: University of North Carolina Press.

Johnston, Frances B., and Thomas T. Waterman. 1941. *The Early Architecture of North Carolina....* Chapel Hill: University of North Carolina Press.

Knight, Edgar Wallace. 1916. *Public School Education in North Carolina*. Boston: Houghton Mifflin Co.

Lemmon, Sarah McCulloh. 1951. Genesis of the Protestant Episcopal Diocese of North Carolina, 1707–1823. *North Carolina Historical Review* 28.4:426–62.

Logan, Frenise A. 1964. *The Negro in North Carolina, 1876–1894*. Chapel Hill: University of North Carolina Press.

Lonsdale, Richard E., and John B. Cole. 1967. *Atlas of North Carolina*. Chapel Hill: University of North Carolina Press.

Mabry, William Alexander. 1940. *The Negro in North Carolina Politics since Reconstruction*. Durham: Duke University Press.

Merrens, Harry H. 1964. *Colonial North Carolina in the Eighteenth Century*. Chapel Hill: University of North Carolina Press.

Moore, George E. 1963. *A Banner in the Hills*. NY: Appleton-Century-Crofts.

Moore, James Floyd. 1967. *Sources of Quaker History in North Carolina*. Greensboro: Guilford College.

Nixon, Joseph R. 1912. The German Settlers in Lincoln County and Western North Carolina. *James Sprunt Historical Publications, University of North Carolina* 11.2:28–61.

Noble, H. C. S. 1930. *A History of the Public Schools of North Carolina*. Chapel Hill: University of North Carolina Press.

O'Connell, Jeremiah Joseph. 1879. *Catholicity in the Carolinas and Georgia. . . AD 1820–AD 1878*. NY. Repr. 1972

(Spartanburg, SC: Reprint Co.).

Oliver, David B. 1910. The Society for the Propagation of the Gospel in the Province of North Carolina. *James Sprunt Historical Publications, University of North Carolina* 9.1:7–23.

Ormund, Jesse M. 1931. *The Country Church in North Carolina.* . . . Durham: Duke University Press.

Piehl, Charles. 1979. *White Society in the Black Belt 1870–1920: A Study of Four North Carolina Counties.* Washington University [St. Louis] dissertation.

Powell, William S. 1963. *The Proprietors of Carolina.* Raleigh: Carolina Charter Tercentenary Commission.

Powell, William S. 1968. *The North Carolina Gazetteer.* Chapel Hill: University of North Carolina Press.

Puryear, Elmer L. 1962. *Democratic Party Dissension in North Carolina, 1928–1936.* Chapel Hill: University of North Carolina Press.

Ramsey, Robert W. 1964. *Carolina Cradle, Settlement of the Northwest Carolina Frontier, 1747–1762.* Chapel Hill: University of North Carolina Press.

Rankin, Hugh F. 1962. *Upheaval in Albemarle: The Story of Culpepper's Rebellion, 1675–1684.* Raleigh: Carolina Charter Tercentenary Commission.

Reichel, Levin Theodore. 1857. *The Moravians in North Carolina: An Authentic History.* Philadelphia. Repr. 1968 (Baltimore: Genealogical Pub. Co.).

Rivers, William J. 1887 The Carolinas. In Justin Winsor, ed., *Narrative and Critical History of America* vol 5:285–356.

Salley, Alexander Samuel. 1929. *The Boundary Line between North Carolina and South Carolina.* Columbia, SC: State Co.

Saunders, William Lawrence. 1884. *North Carolina: Its Settlement and Growth.* Raleigh.

Saunders, William Lawrence. 1886–90. *Colonial Records of North Carolina.* 10 vols. Raleigh: P. M. Hale.

Sharpe, Bill. 1951–65. *A New Geography of North Carolina.* 4 vols. Raleigh: Sharpe Pub. Co.

Sitterson, Joseph Carlyle. 1939. *The Secession Movement in North Carolina.* Chapel Hill: University of North Carolina Press.

Skaggs, Marvin Lucian. 1941. *North Carolina Boundary Disputes Involving Her Southern Line.* Chapel Hill: University of North Carolina Press.

Steiner, Jesse F., and Roy M. Brown. 1927. *The North Carolina Chain Gang.* Chapel Hill. Repr. 1970 (Westport CT: Negro Universities Press).

Taylor, Rosser H. 1920. The Free Negro in North Carolina. *James Sprunt Historical Publications, University of North Carolina* 17.1:13–26.

Taylor, Rosser Howard. 1926. Slaveholding in North Carolina: An Economic View. *James Sprunt Historical Publications, University of North Carolina* 18:103–115.

Thompson, Holland. 1906. *From the Cotton Field to the Cotton Mill: A Study of the Industrial Transition in North Carolina.* NY: Macmillan.

Thornburgh, Laura. 1937. *The Great Smoky Mountains.* NY. Rev. and enl. ed. 1984 (Knoxville: University of Tennessee Press).

Troxler, Carole Watterson. 1974. *The Migration of Carolina and Georgia Loyalists to Nova Scotia and New Brunswick.* Chapel Hill: University of North Carolina Press.

Wager, Paul Woodford. 1928. *County Government and Administration in North Carolina.* Chapel Hill: University of North Carolina Press.

Weeks, Stephen Beauregard. 1892. *The Religious Development in the Province of North Carolina.* Baltimore: Johns Hopkins.

Williams, Charles Bray. 1901. *History of the Baptists in North Carolina.* Raleigh: Edwards and Broughton.

Wilson, Louis R. 1957. *The University of North Carolina, 1900–1930: The Making of a Modern University.* Chapel Hill: University of North Carolina Press.

Wooften, Bayard, and Archibald Henderson. 1939. *Old Homes and Gardens of North Carolina.* Chapel Hill: University of North Carolina Press.

Zeigler, Wilbur Gleason, and Ben S. Grosscup. 1883. *The Heart of the Alleghanies.* . . . Raleigh: A. Williams and Co.

South Carolina

1. Horry County

Formed 1785 as Kingston; renamed 1801. Transportation very poor for a long time. Active desertion 1861–65. Tobacco planting since 1869; shipbuilding in 1870s. Lumbering for a time. Also melons, strawberries, truck, cotton, corn. Resort area: Myrtle Beach. Pop. 1810: 4,349, 1820: 5,025, 1850: 7,646, 1880: 15,574, 1910: 26,995, 1930: 39,376, 1960: 68,297.

Epps, Florence Theodora. 1970. *The Independent Republic of Horry, 1670–1970.* Conway: Horry Printers.

Quattlebaum, Paul. 1945. History of Conway and Horry County. *South Carolina Magazine* 8.3:4-5.

Rogers, James S., III. 1972. *The History of Horry County, South Carolina, 1855–1876.* University of South Carolina Master's thesis.

Steanson, O., M. H. Sutherland, and M. C. Rochester. 1934. *Farming Possibilities in Horry County, South Carolina.* South Carolina Agricultural Experiment Station.

Thomas, Bruce G. 1967. *Coastal and Fluvial Landforms: Horry and Merton Counties, South Carolina.* Baton Rouge: Louisiana State University Press.

Willcox, Clark. 1967. *Musings of a Hermit of Three Score and Ten.* 2nd ed. Charleston: Walker Evans.

1967–. *Independent Republic Quarterly.* Conway: Horry County Historical Society.

SC 1A: Burgess P.O. (P.O. abandoned c. 1935), Socastee Twp. — F, housewife, 81. B. other side of Chinus Swamp, further up the Pee Dee River in Horry Co.; moved as an infant, grew up at Pauley's Swamp 5 mi. E. of Pee Dee River and 10 mi. from Conway. Came here in 1893, aged 37. — F., M. b. other side of Chinus Swamp in Co. — Ed.: very little. — Baptist. — Old-fashioned; honest and cooperative. — Moderate tempo; some tendency to prolong.

Spring Branch (Marion Co.), Fair Bluff P.O. (NC), Floyd Twp.
Twp. in NW corner of Co.; completely rural.

SC 1B: F, housewife, 56. B. Duford, 3 mi. S.. — F. b. Duford, PGF b. here, PGM b. just over line in Marion Co., near town of Nichols; M., MGF, MGM b. just over line in Robeson Co., NC. — Ed.: here; 2 yrs. Winthrop College at Rock Hill. — Methodist. — Cooperative, but not too revealing. — Moderate tempo; no great prolongation.

2. Marion County

Created 1785 as Liberty Co.; renamed 1798. First settlements 1735; English and Welsh; many settlers from PA, VA. Chapel built at early Brittons Neck settlement in 1740. Undulating surface, generally level; drained by rivers and inland swamps. High illiteracy till 1920s; high tenancy. Varied agriculture, cotton and tobacco chief money crops, some indigo; stock raising early. Pop. 1800: 6,914, 1820: 10,201, 1850: 17,407, 1880: 34,107, 1910: 20,596, 1930: 27,121, 1960: 32,014.

Davis, Henry Grady. 1927. *The Development of Education in Marion County, South Carolina.* University of South Carolina Master's thesis.

Godbold, Sarah Ellerbee, and Gustavus Adolphus Williamson. 1923. *Marion County: Economic and Social.* Columbia: University of South Carolina.

Sellers, William W. 1902. *A History of Marion County, South Carolina. . . .* Columbia: R. L. Bryan Co.

Stanley, Victor Bland., Jr. 1938. *Marion Churches and Churchmen, 1735–1935.* Charleston: Southern Printing and Publishing Co.

1946. Marion County, "In the Heart of the Pee Dee". *South Carolina Magazine* 9.10:18–.

Davis neighborhood, Centenary P.O., Le Gette Twp.
Twp. one of poorest in Co.

SC 2A: F, housewife, 70. B. 6 mi. N. — F., PGF, PGF's F., PGF's M., PGM b. 6 mi. N.; M., MGF, MGM, MGM's F. b. nearby. — Ed.: none. — Methodist. — Old-fashioned; good memory. — /æ⋅ɪ/ sound is notable, cf. E. NC; it is a separate phoneme from /æ/ and /e⋅/. Inf. pronounces *there* as [de⋅], exactly like *day*, at times. Moderate tempo; utterance clear. Tendency to prolong.

Pinderboro, Marion P.O. and Twp.
Twp. wealthiest in Co. Courthouse at Marion from 1800. Mills, lumber, veneer and brick, ironworks. River and lake fishing.

SC 2B: F, housewife, 48. B. Centenary, came here when married. — F., PGF, PGF's F. b. Centenary, PGM b. here; M., MGF b. Mullins, MGM b. near Mullins, MGM's GF came from Scotland. — Ed.: Centenary till 18. — Baptist. — Tendency to conceal old-fashioned things. — Better-than-average speech from a person of ordinary background. Tempo slowish; some prolonging.

SC 2C: Floyd Twp., near Davis' store. — F, housewife, domestic, 70. B. here. — F., M. b. here. — Old-fashioned speech; not too alert. — Tempo slowish; some prolonging.

3. Florence County

Formed 1880 from Darlington and Marion Cos. Queensborough Twp. laid out 1731–32. Welsh Baptists from PA, some Huguenots arrived 1736–37. Regulator movement. Plantations. RR by c. 1854. Tobacco outstripped cotton in 1890s; also corn, pecans, truck, timber. Industrial diversification. Pop. 1890: 25,007, 1910: 35,621, 1930: 61,027, 1960: 84,438.

Brunson, Mason, Jr. 1948. Florence County, Agricultural and Medical Center. *South Carolina Magazine* 11.11:5.

King, G. Wayne. 1981. *Rise Up So Early: A History of Florence County, South Carolina.* Spartanburg: Reprint Co.

McNeill, James Purdie, Jr., and John A. Cheze, Jr. 1921. *Florence County, Economic and Social.* Columbia: University of South Carolina Press.

SC 3A: Vausetown, Olanta P.O., James Cross Roads Twp. — M, farmer, 72. B. here. — F. b. here, PGF b. Duplin or Lenoir Co., NC (of German descent), PGM b. Green Co., NC; M., MGF, MGM b. here. — Ed.: here, only 2 mos. — Free Will Baptist. — Friendly, talkative; understood purpose of interview. — [r] or [ɚ] unusually penetrating at times; should perhaps be [ɽ] or [ɚ]. No tendency for [e‿·] or [o‿·] to have centering off-glide. Deliberate tempo; vowels tend to be long. Good nasalization in vicinity of nasal consonants. Utterance not slurred, but very much as in New England, with more prominence in unstr. syllables than one would expect in the South. — (PSWS).

Sardis, Timmonsville P.O., James Cross Roads Twp.

Timmonsville a cotton and tobacco market; pecan groves, pepper, cattle.

SC 3B: M, retired farmer, 80. 10 yrs. in state legislature; ran sawmill awhile; 30 yrs. in tobacco business; ran warehouse in Timmonsville. B. same territory; winter in Florida last 5–10 yrs. — F., PGF, PGM b. 2 mi. away in Williamsburg Co., descended from earliest settlers; M. b. Vosstown, MGF large landowner, MGF's F. Swedish, MGM b. around Elam. — Ed.: ordinary pay schools, about 10 yrs., 4–6 mos. a yr. — Baptist, Mason 40 yrs., former member Knights of Pythias, Woodmen of World, Improved Order of Red Men. — Cooperative, natural; enjoyed talking with FW. Warmed up as interview progressed. — Many folk forms and pronunciations. Strong nasality; strong stresses; voice medium register; moderate drawl; stressed vowels prolonged. /ju/ in *Tuesday, news*; /o/ us. up-gliding except in *coat, road, home*; /ɛ/ and /ɪ/ sometimes neutralized before nasals. Up-glide in *eggs*. [ɪ] in *milk*; [æ] and [æɪ] contrast. /a/ us. low-back [ɒ] in *palm, calm*, etc. Retroflexion varying in *Thursday* type. Unstr. [ə] final, less common medially. Long and short /ai/ with low-center or low-front beginning. Unstr. [ɪ] in *Georgia, borrow*. [gl-] (clear [l]) in *glass*; [hw-] and clear [l] in *wheelbarrow*; final /l/ often vocalized. [-r-] weak; some [-r] of varying intensity; intrusive [r] in *swallow it, ought*.

Pee Dee, Coles Crossroads, Florence P.O., Tans Bay Twp.

Florence largest RR transfer pt. in SC; RR shops important to its growth. Area settled in 1732 by Scotch Presbyterians; Welsh Baptists to NW by 1736. Plantations to mid-19th cent. City chartered 1871. Experimental farming; furniture, bakeries, nurseries.

SC 3C!: F (two sisters), widows, one had assisted husband in horse-trading, the other taught school for a short time, 67 and 62. B. on same place. — F., PGF, PGM b. same neighborhood; M. b. Camden, AL, MGF b. on plantation next to inf.'s, MGM b. Halifax, NC, attended Moravian College. — Ed.: 1) Meminger School (women's h.s.) in Charleston, 2 yrs. at Winthrop College; 2) grade and h.s. Florence, Winthrop College grad. — Presbyterians, UDC, various church societies. —

Enthusiastic, cooperative, hospitable; volunteered many synonyms. Contemptuous toward pseudo-learning as exemplified by the local Baptist minister. — Sisters insisted on joint interview; speech so much alike FW made no attempt to distinguish. Knew folk idiom. Strong stresses; wide range of intonation; mocked extreme nasality of "crackers". Stressed vowels generally very long; unstr. vowels shortened. Both ingliding and up-gliding forms of /e o ɔ/. /-l/ often > vowel. /hw-/. /-r-/ weak; no /-r/ or intrusive /r/. — Cultivated.

SC 3C!*: M. Nephew of inf. 3C; former student of FW at the Citadel. — Cultivated.

4. Clarendon County

Formed 1856. Cotton, tobacco, truck. Pop. 1860: 13,095, 1880: 19,120, 1910: 32,188, 1930: 30,036, 1960: 29,490.

Martin, John Bartlow. 1957. *The Deep South says "Never".* NY: Ballantine.

Orvin, Virginia Kirkland Gullachat. 1961. *History of Clarendon County, 1700 to 1961.* Manning.

Wheeler, Kathleen. 1947. Manning: In the Heart of South Carolina. *South Carolina Magazine* 10.4:16–.

1946. Clarendon County, Where Life is Well Balanced. *South Carolina Magazine* 9.11:10–.

Manning

Old country town with country ways. Farming market; lumbering, canning, dairying. Pop. 1880: 1,440, 1910: 1,854, 1930: 1,884, 1960: 3,917.

SC 4A: M, commercial fisherman, farmer, 55. B. Santee Twp. near Richburg. Hardly ever outside Co. — F., M. and their parents all b. Co.; PGF's F. a preacher sent from England, descendants of French Huguenots. — Ed.: country school, c. 4th grade. — No organizations; little reading. — Independent, hard-working, fair-minded, unpretentious. Enjoyed interview after initial suspicions overcome. — Old-fashioned speech; unaffected by children's education. Monotone of medium-high register. Strong stress; drawl; some nasality. Simplification of final consonant clusters; final cons. often cut short or lost. /-t-/ > [-r-]; /ʃr/ = [sw̥-]; /hw-/ even in *whoa*. Postvocalic /l/ sometimes vocalized; /-r/ very rare; slight trace of intrusive [r] in one notation of *ought to*. /ju-/ in *Tuesday*; [ɪ] in *milk*; /ɛ/ sometimes retracted. /a/ us. low-central; rounded vowel [ɒ] in *borrow, pot, rock*. /ʌ/ > /ɛ/ in *shut*; /ʊ/ high in *bull, bushel*; stressed /ɜ/ > [ɜɪ ɜ]. /ai/ us. with low-central beginning; /au/ begins [æ] to [a]; weak stressed [ɪ] in *cabbage, towel*. — Incomplete; systematic interview only 7.6–62.8, many cv. forms.

SC 4B: F, housewife, 81. B. Summerton, a summer resort for planters in pine belt; lived Wright's Bluff till 21. — F. from plantation family along Santee, PGF from Williamsburg, PGF's F. from England; M. from AL. — Ed.: local schools; fair amount of reading; writes poetry. Little travel. — Methodist, former UDC, Missionary Society, Civic League, Library Assn., Vice-Chair Co. Democratic Committee. — Knows community life; enjoys talking. Cooperative, intelligent, interested. — Much folk grammar. Old-fashioned intonation; ingratiating rise-fall patterns (would be classed as "Negro intonation" by those who assert racial differences in speech).

Final clusters simplified. [ʃʃ] us. (palatalization not always marked). /hw-/; /-t-/ often > [-ɾ-]. Both /sr-/ and /ʃr-/. Retroflexion in stressed syllables most common after /ɔ a ɝ/. Intrusive /r/ in *swallow it*. Clear /l/ between front vowels; /-l/ us. dark. /i u e o/ monoph. or in-gliding. /ju/ after /t- d- n-/. /æ/ somewhat low; /a/ low-central or low-central backish; [ɒ] in *rock, strop*; [a ɒ] in *crop*; [ɒ] in *borrow*; /ɔ/ monoph. or in-gliding, range [ɔ˞] to [ɔ˷]; [ɔ, o] distinguished in *morning/mourning*, etc. /ai au/ sometimes with centralized beginning before voiceless, sometimes backish; /ʌ/ med. high; /ʊ u/ us. fronted. Unstr. vowels generally reduced to [ə ɨ ɩ˞ ɪ˞].

SC 4C: M, chief of police, farms on the side (has been carpenter, steel worker), 55. B. Juneville, S. of Manning toward Santee R. — F.'s family earliest settlers near Manning, immediately from PA, orig. from N. Ireland; some of PGM's people from Williamsburg Co.; M., MGF, MGM from Sumter Co. (next W.). — Ed.: local country schools, never finished h.s. Some reading, interested in local traditions. — National Guard, on Mexican border 1916; WWI 30th Division, in France; 2 yrs. Bayonne, NJ; Baptist. — Knows community; good observer, good memory. Able to distinguish words used in other communities from local usage. Good sense of humor; many anecdotes. Minds own business, but generous, hospitable. — Slow speech; several teeth missing. Initial stops less strongly aspirated than in speech of most SC inf.'s. /tʃ/ us. strongly palatalized. /d̪/ for /ð/; /hw /; /-ɾ-/ when on guard, less when speaking informally. Us. /tju dju nju/. In-gliding normal for /e o/. /ʌ/ occ. very high; /a/ occ. rounded, but less often than in speech of Georgetown/Williamsburg areas. Folk preterites; *ain't*; multiple negatives.

5. Williamsburg County

Formed 1785. 1st settlement 1732; others (largely Ulster Scots) 1734. Also Huguenots from S. of Santee by 1737; possibly some Highlanders and Palatines. Anglicans, Baptists, and Presbyterians all by 1737; Methodists in early 19th cent., prob. no Roman Catholic before 1860. 1st slave 1736; more slaves than whites by Rev. 1st public road 1741. Swampy; indigo and rice country, also cattle. Wealthy co. by 1830. Transportation poor until 1850s; RR 1856. After 1900 more land cleared, swamps drained; tobacco introduced c. 1900, now tobacco market. Diversification of crops after boll weevil, c. 1920; truck, fruit, hogs, cattle, poultry, timber; hunting, fishing. Pop. 1810: 6,871, 1820: 8,716, 1850: 12,447, 1880: 24,110, 1910: 37,626, 1930: 34,914, 1960: 40,932.

Boddie, William Willis. 1923. *History of Williamsburg*. Columbia: State Co.

Burgess, James M. 1888. *Chronicles of St. Marks Parish, Santee Circuit, and Williamsburg Township, South Carolina, 1731–1885*. Columbia: C.A. Calvo, Jr., Printer.

Courdin, P. G. 1946. *Life along the Santee in Williamsburg County, South Carolina*. Kingstree: The County Record.

Hadden, H. S. 1939. Kingstree: Noted for Its Hospitality and Peaceful Atmosphere. *South Carolina Magazine* 3.1:24.

McGill, Samuel D. 1897. *Narrative of Reminiscences of Williamsburg County*. Columbia: Bryan Print. Co.

Boyd Community, Spring Gully Dist., Andrews P.O. (Georgetown County), Anderson Twp.

Swamp country; pole-fishing from causeways. Andrews a one-time lumber boom town. Abandoned RR. Market town; now ships pulpwood.

SC 5A: M, farmer, 79. B. Central neighborhood, 6 mi. NW; moved to present community in 1876 (age 7), lived nowhere else. — F., PGM b. Cedar Swamp area (10–12 mi. NW of inf.'s present home); M. from same community, MGF, MGM supposed to have come from NC, nothing much known. — Ed.: local schools, got through blueback speller (c. 4th grade). — Methodist; Presbyterian parents. — Natural. Good knowledge of local culture; almost no contacts outside area. — Deep voice; throaty. Strong stresses. Tempo fast, though not extreme speed of coastal type. Final consonants weakly articulated; final clusters simplified. Prevocalic /v-/ often velarized. No dark [ɫ]; sometimes /tl̩-/ for /kl-/; /sr-/ in *shrimp*, etc. No postvocalic constriction; little linking [-r·]; no intrusive [r]. /u/ in *new*; /u/ generally fronted. [ɒ] in *borrow, pot, vomit, college, palm*; /ʌ/ not as low as in Georgetown. /ɝ/ as [ɝ ɵɪ] in *thirty*; [ɵɪ] in *Thursday*. Low-back /ai/ beginning before zero or voiced consonants; /ai au/ with centered beginning before voiceless consonants.

Kingstree, Kings Twp.

Kingstree Co. seat; site of oldest inland settlement in SC (1732). Town laid out 1788; not inc. till 1866. Some Irish, Huguenots among early settlers. Factionalism among Presbyterians. Area plagued by malaria and typhus early; drainage and sewerage after 1910. Truck raising, tobacco; furniture, veneer, sand refinery; winter colony of northern sportsmen. Pop. 1880: 384, 1910: 1,372, 1930: 2,392, 1960: 3,847.

SC 5B: M, handyman, mechanic, inventor, registrar of vital statistics last 31 years, has run blacksmith shop, 80. B. Gourdin's Depot, Suttons Twp. — F. came to Co. c. 1860 from sea islands near Charleston; M. b. same co., MGF lived in extreme lower edge of Co. — Ed.: rural schools. — Methodist, Shriner, very active in Masons. — A bit tiresome; hard to keep at interview. Courteous and cooperative despite many interruptions. Likes to talk; tends to pontificate; bragged about appetite, Mason involvement. Tends to give spelling pronunciations after giving natural ones. — Tempo variable: fast when talking about everyday things, slow when pontificating. Strong stresses; some retroflexion, strongest when repeating. [i] us. in-gliding or monophthongal; /e o/ us. in-gliding; /u/ often monophthongal, always strongly front, /ju/ after /t/, etc.; /æ/ low; /a/ low-central in *father*, etc.; low-back [ɑ] or rounded [ɒ] in *pot, rock, oxen, watch*; [ʌ] fairly high, but lower than upcountry vowel. /u/ us. high, slightly fronted; little retroflexion in *thirty worms*, etc. /ai/ us. begins low-central; /ai au/ rare with centralized beginning; /ɔi/ us. begins high; /o/ begins high (sometimes at /ʊ/), us. in-glide. [ɨ] in weak-stressed syllables of *bucket, sausage, lettuce*. Many clear [l]s, esp. several final, after front vowels; /-t-/ > [-ɾ-]; palatal [j] in *garden*; /ð-/ > [d̪] in *the*; /hw-/; /sr-/. Intervocalic /r/ often weak, occ. disappearing.

SC 5C: M, retired fertilizer merchant, 61. B. 12 mi. N., came to Kingstree at 22. — F., M. both local descendants of early settlers. — Ed.: country school. — Presbyterian, Mason. —

Nervous; hypertense (high blood pressure). Crowded schedule; couldn't relax during interview because of limited time, yet tried to take lead from FW. Great fund of detail on local customs and farm life. — Fast speech; over-rounding of back vowels (this (perhaps with "inner rounding") is one of the characteristics of what city-bred Low-Countrymen call "Geetchee" dialect). Practically no /-r/. Intervocalic /t/ > [ɾ]; /θr-/ often /sr-/. Many clear /l/s. /au/ with centralized fronted beginning in most positions; voice-voiceless alternation of /ai/, often begins far back. In-gliding /e o/; /u/ fronted.

SC 5D!: F, Co. director American Red Cross, 71. B. plantation 15 mi. S., came here when married. — F. b. Charleston, brought up Buffalo Circle, Berkeley Co., PFG from Co., PGM b. Co.; M. b. Co., MGF built plantation house. — Ed.: private tutor. — Episcopalian; DAR; Colonial Dames. — Active, energetic. Hospitable. Enjoyed interview; likes to talk about old days and present life of community. Has had contact with all sorts of people, both races. Keen sense of humor. Stylistic virtuosity. — Some nasality, /i u/ mostly up-gliding, as well as /ɛ/ before /-g/. In-gliding of /o/, and us. /e/. /ju/ after /t d n/. /æ/ us. low. /a/ low-center to low-back. /ɒ/ in *pot, crop, John, orange, borrow*. /ɔ/ in-gliding. /ʌ/ rather low. /ʊ/ slightly fronted. /ai/ begins centered before voiceless cons., otherwise low-central (back). /au/ centered beginning before voiceless cons., low-central /a/ (occ. /æ/) elsewhere. /t/ *mountain, towel, -ed*. Occ. unstr. diph. as in *Tuesday* /i/. No /-r/. /-t-/ sometimes > [-ɾ-]. /k- g-/ often palatal. /sr-/; /hw-/ exc. in *wharf*. /-r-/ in *swallow it*, not *law and order*. — Cultivated.

SC 5D!*: F. Younger sister of SC5D!; same general background, less alert and less at ease, but authentic. — Cultivated.

6. Georgetown County

Formed 1798. Wealthiest part of state in 1843; 90% AfAm in 1850 (largest AfAm/white ratio in SC). Land grants as early as 1705; Winneau est. as trading post with Indians by 1716. Petition for parish church as early as 1720. Georgetown Dist. est. 1769; later divided into a number of cos. Early settlers individual families: Scots, French, and English; from lower SC or Charleston. Good water transportation. All rivers subject to tidal action. Rice plantations by 1738; historical center of rice culture (plantation country). Also naval stores, timber, indigo early. Some Acadians in 18th cent. Free schools by 1811 (but poorly supported). Peak of rice culture 1850–60; many planters absentee landlords, living in Charleston. Strongly secessionist. Blockaded Dec. 1861; harassment along rivers. Little economic progress of AfAms during Reconstruction; schools declined. RR 1883. Pop. still over 75% AfAm in 1910. AfAms elected to public office till 1902; "fusion" died after racial trouble then. By 1889, Northern capitalists became interested in Southern estates. Rice culture ended with hurricanes 1893–1911. After WWII, paper mills, suburbanization, cattle; industrial diversification; fishing, tourism. Pop. 1790: 22,122, 1820: 22,938, 1850: 20,647, 1880: 19,613, 1910: 22,270, 1930: 21,733, 1960: 34,798.

Allston, Susan Lowndes. 1935. *Brookgreen, Waccamaw, in the Carolina Low Country*. Charleston: Walker, Evans and Cogswell.

Bolick, Julian S. 1946. *Waccamaw Plantations*. Clinton: Vacob Press.

Bull, Henry De Saussure. 1948. *All Saints' Church, Waccamaw*. Charleston: South Carolina Society of Colonial Dames of America.

Childs, Arney Robinson, ed. 1953. *Rice Planter and Sportsman: The Recollections of J. Motte Alston*. Columbia: University of South Carolina Press.

Collins, Elizabeth. 1865. *Memories of the Southern States, 1859–1864*. Tannton, Eng.: Barnicott

Cook, Harry Toliver. 1926. *Rambles in the Pee Dee Basin. . . *. Columbia: State Co.

Devereaux, Anthony Q. 1973. *The Rice Princes*. Columbia: State Printing Co.

Doar, W. W. 1939. Georgetown County, Rich in Romance. *South Carolina Magazine* 3.1:15.

Easterby, J. H., ed. 1945. *The South Carolina Rice Plantation*. Chicago: University of Chicago Press.

Edwards, Sally, and Jean Erwin. 1965. *Pawley's Island*. Charlotte, NC: Heritage.

Funderburk, A. E., Jr. 1941. Georgetown — Historic, Hospitable. *South Carolina Magazine* 4.3:28–29.

Lachicotte, Alberta Morel. 1955. *Georgetown Rice Plantations*. Columbia: State Commercial Print. Co.

Lachicotte, Henry A. 1950. *Genealogy of the Rossignol-Lachicotte Family, with Historical Notes of Localities*. Douglas, GA: Julian W. Frier.

Lathers, Richard. 1907. *Reminiscences of Richard Lathers*. Ed. by Alvah F. Sunbean. NY: Grafton Press.

Prevost, Charlotte Kaminski, and Effie Leland Wilder. 1972. *Pawley's Island. . . a Living Legend*. Columbia: State Print. Co.

Pringle, Elizabeth W. Allston. 1913. *A Woman Rice Planter*. NY: Macmillan Co.

Pringle, Elizabeth W. (Allston). 1922. *Chronicles of Chicora Wood*. NY: C. Scribner's sons.

Rogers, George C., Jr. 1970. *The History of Georgetown County*. Columbia: University of South Carolina Press.

Smith, H. A. M. 1913. The Baronies of South Carolina: Hobean Barony. *South Carolina History and General Magazine* 14:62–80.

Smith, Henry A. M. 1908. Georgetown: The Original Plan and the Earliest Settlers. *South Carolina History and General Magazine* 9:85–101.

Vaughan, Celina McGregor. 1969. *Pawley's. . . As It Was*. Columbia.

Willcox, Clarke A. 1968. *Musings of a Hermit*. 3rd ed. Murrells Inlet: Hermitage.

Winyah Indigo Society. 1938. *Rules of Winyah Indigo Society of Georgetown, South Carolina: With a Short History of the Society and a List of Living and Deceased Members from 1775 to 1938*. Charleston: Walker, Evans and Cogswell.

SC 6N: M, foreman for building supply company (has worked on boats, in mills, and done a little farming), 78. B. on Pee Dee River, 12 mi. from Georgetown, never lived out of Co. — F., M. slaves, b. on Pee Dee, lived all their lives there; little else known. — Ed.: a very little common school (6–9 mos. at most); chiefly self-educated. — African Methodist Episcopal Church. — Well-respected; authority on building materials, river life. Quiet, dignified; religious. Not subservient. Easily tired; a bit suspicious; became restless and broke off interview. — Medium tempo. Little nasality. Strong stresses.

Unstr. vowels short. Some old folk preterites. /w/ in *wheelbar-row*, etc. No /-r/; occ. [ß] for /v/; [d̪] often for /ð/; [t̪] occ. for [θ]. Fewer dark [ɫ]s, many more clear [l]s than in white speech. /ʌ/ medium to low; in-gliding /e o/; less rounding of /a/ than in white speakers of community, though /a/ generally low-back except before [ə] (reflex of /-r/). /ai au/ us. with centralized beginning before voiceless cons.; /au/ often, /ai/ once or twice with centralized beginning when final or before voiced cons. /ai/ sometimes > /a/; occ. /ł/ for stressed /l/.

Hemingway, Carvers Bay

Hemingway inc. 1913. Trading center. Tobacco; as many as 16 vegetables grown, even in coldest mos. Carvers Bay a community of small farmers. Anti-nullification; culturally akin to Horry.

SC 6A: M, farmer, 60. B. here. — F. b. Georgetown (in city), PGF captain on boat between Baltimore and Georgetown, PGM b. Georgetown (in city); M., MGF, MGM b. here. — Ed.: here, a little. — Missionary Baptist; Knights of Pythias, Coroner's Office. — No sophistication; limited cultural experience. Parents very poor. Practically no education. Self-made man; aware of own importance. Sensitive but cooperative when convinced on importance of project. — Rather rapid tempo (cf. region, plus high blood pressure). Archaic speech; variable. Many words have [ʊr] where modern generation uses [ɔr], [ʊ-] similarly used for [ɔ-], [ʊ] for [aˑɪ] before [ɫ]. [ʊr] or [ʊˑ] varies greatly in first element. Seems further forward when spoken quickly or when somewhat assimilated with [-r].

Plantersville, Prince Frederick Parish

Parish est. 1735; chapel from 1835. Orig. a summer resort of planters; inc. 1852. Indigo; then rice, tobacco, cotton. Refuge of Waccamaw people during Civil War. Most old plantations now owned by Northern sportsmen.

SC 6B: F, housewife, 79. B. locally. Always lived in neighborhood, except 1 yr. in Horry Co. — F., PGF b. here, PGM b. Horry Co.; M. raised locally, MGF, MGM prob. b. Horry. — Ed.: till 5th grade. — Episcopalian. — Quick, nervous if sure; slower if unsure. Strong on local details. Little experience outside community. — Tempo generally fast; slurred utterance; nasality; strong stress. Centered beginning of /ai au/ before voiceless cons.; often low-back beginning finally or before voiced. /hw-/ us.; /sr-/. Simplification of final clusters, final cons. often weakly articulated. Much constriction: both *thirty* and *barn*.

Waccamaw Neck, Pawleys Island, All Saints Parish

Waccamaw Neck a populous and productive rice plantation district. Earliest grants on Pawleys Island 1711; chapel of ease by 1739. Center of Georgetown rice culture; summer vacation spot from early 19th cent.: first for planters, now for others. Lumber company here 1889. Paper mills 1936. Diversification after WWII.

SC 6C!: F, housewife, 65. B. Murrell's Inlet. Lived 3 yrs. Bucksport, Horry Co. — F. b. Charleston, PGF b. Savannah, PGM b. Charleston, PGF's F. came to Charleston from Haiti; M. b. Barnwell Co. — Ed.: governess, Waverly School (on island). Summer school at Winthrop. — Episcopalian; Garden Club, UDC, Eastern Star, Pres. Co. Council of

Farmwomen. — Close observer, natural, few taboos. Talked freely, enjoyed interviews. Strong stresses. Wide intonation range. Great deal of apparent inner rounding (tendency to overround back vowels). Very short, weak unstr. vowels. /ai/ often begins far back finally or before voiced cons.: not characteristic of cultivated plantation speech. /ai au/ with centered beginning before voiceless consonants. /w-/ in /hw-/ words. /sr-/ in *shrub*. * forms pp. 7–17 from SC6C*. Many details pp. 7–76 verified by brother, landscape gardener and shopkeeper, 57, ed. at Clemson College (not as quick as sister). — Cultivated.

SC 6C*: M, retired sailor. Lives near SC6C!; interview discontinued because of deafness.

SC 6D: Georgetown. — M, chronically unemployed, 49. B. Carvers Bay. Lived 3 yrs. E. NC, 6 yrs. Sumter. — No family history. — Ed.: w yrs. common school. — Low social standing. — Unreliable. Difficulty understanding questions. — Not very distinct speech; husky, hoarse, semi-whisper. In-gliding /e o/. /ı ɛ/ neutralized before nasals. /æ/ fairly low. Occ. /ɒ/ alternates with /a/. /ai/ us. begins fairly far back. /ju/ after /t/. /hw-/, /sr-/.

7. City of Georgetown

Laid out 1729–34. Co. seat from 1768. Most settlers English; also some Germans, French, Scots. Port for rice and indigo, West Indies and England. Designated a port of entry, 1731. Large slave imports in 1730s. Some shipbuilding in 18th cent. From c. 1780, Jews (Sephardim) important in economic and social life. Many pre-Rev. buildings. Town at apogee in 1820s, declined later (eventually overshadowed by Wilmington and Charleston). By 1850, urban merchants constitute a middle class, inferior to planters. Rich timberlands, cutover; pulp mill. Supported education for the poor; library plundered by army of occupation, 1860s. Some mfg.: turpentine distillery, shoe factory. Pop. 1850: 1,658, 1880: 2,557, 1910: 5,530, 1930: 5,082, 1960: 12,261.

See 6 (Georgetown County) for bibliography.

SC 7N: M, handyman, retired Episcopal church sexton, 83. B. Windsor, 5 mi. NW of town, came to Georgetown at age 22. — Knows nothing about F. or F.'s family; M. a slave, b. on a rice plantation in Co. — Ed.: no formal education; can read a little. — Known by all Georgetonians as a "character". — Extremely deferential, even somewhat scared during interview (called FW /mɔˤːəsə/). Limited intelligence; subsists by wheedling, flattering whites; often teased *re* love affairs. — Articulation impeded by lack of front teeth. Extremely fast speech (all Georgetonians speak fast); extremely wide intonation range; stressed syllables rising very high (in excitement, extreme rise and length). Folk preterites. No /hw-/; /sw-/ for /ʃr-/; some postvocalic /-r/. Central beginnings of /ai au/; in-gliding /i e o/ except occ. as final; low /æ/; [ɒ] in *pot*, etc.

SC 7A: M, retired shopkeeper, 75. B. Georgetown, lived nowhere else. — F., PGF, PGM b. Georgetown, F.'s ancestor a "count" from England (one of earliest colonial judges); M. b. Charleston, came to Georgetown in 1867–68, her people Huguenots from Normandy, MGF (and ancestry) from Charleston, MGM from Clarendon Co. — Ed.: common school. —

No lodges, churches, etc.; well known in community. — Good specimen of decaying old Southern family. Unsuccessful in business; now lives alone; still ferociously independent. Even severest critics concede absolute honesty. Limited comprehension. — Wheezy voice (possibly TB); not very clear articulation (teeth badly neglected), though enough for spirants. Fast tempo; strong stressses. Almost no postvocalic /r/. Frequent clear [l] intervocalically. Us. /w-/ in *wheel*, etc.; /sr-/. Often [ß] for /v/, sometimes for /w/; occ. [ɸ] for /f/ (Negro influence?). Centered beginning of /ai au/: the former before voiceless consonants, the latter always before voiceless, sometimes before voiced. In-gliding /e o/, occ. /i u/; /u/ us. fronted. — Incomplete: original record made on tablets (instead of field book) in emergency.

SC 7B: M, retired storekeeper, also farmed, 85. B. Waccamaw, Mindaville; lived in Plantersville (1886–92), on Black River 3 yrs. (always in Co.). — F. b. Kingston, NY; M. b. NY City; both came S. as teachers. — Ed.: taught at home, no formal schooling. — Mason, Episcopalian, Winyah Indigo Society, Georgetown Historical Society. Has been alderman and magistrate. — Cooperative; natural; no pretensions of correctness. Knows all community; rich fund of anecdotes. — Very fast speech; wide intonation range; weak-stressed syllables short; clear articulation. Occ. double negative is natural; occ. folk preterites. /w-/ normally in *wheel*, etc; some /-r/ (not much); /-t-/ normally [-ɾ-]. Many clear [l]s before front vowels. Some palatalization of /k g/. In-gliding /e o/; low /ʌ/. Fronted /u/; /u/ often after /t d n/ as in *tube, due, new*. /ɪ/ > /i/ often.

SC 7B*: F, 76. B. Plantersville, always lived in Co.; wife of SC7B.

SC 7C!: M, lawyer, 78. B. Black River; some travel, but essentially local. — F. b. Black River, PGF b. edge of town; M. b. Waccamaw Neck (across bay), MGM b. Brook Green Plantation, Waccamaw; all branches of family in Georgetown since 1745. — Ed.: Indigo Society School; Porter Military Academy (Charleston); The Citadel. Read law in Georgetown. — Masons, Winyah Indigo Society, Episcopal Church. Served in SC legislature. — Keen but subtle sense of humor; enjoys telling stories about his experiences. Knows local history, customs, families in detail. — Fast speech. Slightly rasping voice. /p- t- c- k-/ not always aspirated. /hw-/ when careful, not when off guard. (In Georgetown /hw-w-/ alternate, the latter being probably more common; people from S. end of county tend to have less /hw-/ than those from N. and W.). Low vowel in *hat*; in-gliding /e o/. Positional alternation of /ai au/; centered beginning of /au/ before voiced consonants or finally apparently not typical of upper-class Georgetown speech as it is of country speech or lower-class town speech; but attempts to label this feature by social class are treacherous, since family dialect forms are encouraged (as in all plantation SC). /ɪ/ often replaced by [ɪ]. — Cultivated.

SC 7D!: F, housewife, 50. B. here. — F, PGF, M., MGF all Georgetown Co. families. Descendant of prominent early proprietory grantee. — Ed.: Georgetown public schools, Winthrop College. — Episcopalian. — Not sure of purpose of inquiries; somewhat impatient. Little knowledge of farm and

country life. Limited contacts. Good example of cultivated speech, without conscious archaisms, but sure of standing in comm. Interview pp. 7–41 in presence of brother and husband; pp. 44–82 in presence of husband. Their responses not always starred, nor separately identified. Husband is native of Plantersville, ed. locally; brother went to college and law school. All have keen sense of humor, quick minds. — Husband has over-rounding plus inner-rounding, generally characteristic of plantation-type speech. This not shared by inf., bro. or SC7C!*. All have fast speech. Inf. has some /-r/, generally less over-rounding of back vowels than others. Inf. and bro. both have /hw-/. Clear articulation. In-gliding diphthongs. /nj tj dj/, /sr-/. No folk preterites. — Cultivated.

SC 7D!*: Clerk of court, 62. — Keen sense of humor, quick mind. — Fast speech; no /hw-/. — Note: some * responses may have been given by husband and bro. of SC7D! mentioned above. — Cultivated.

8 & 9. Berkeley County

Formed 1882. 1st settlers English, 1670s; many French after 1680. Several Huguenot settlements; over 100 French families in Santee area c. 1700; in Orange Quarter, French used up to middle of 18th cent. Anglican dominated; plantation dominated. Canal 1792–1800, used till c. 1900. Pineland resorts, early 19th cent. Power development 1930s. Naval stores, cattle, rice, indigo early. Cotton, dairying, poultry, trade, timber. Pop. 1910: 23,487, 1930: 22,236, 1960: 38,196.

Dubose, Samuel, and Frederic A. Porcher. 1887. *A Contribution to the History of the Huguenots of South Carolina.* NY: T. Gaillard Thomas.

Dwight, Henry Ravenel. 1921. *Some Historic Spots in Berkeley.* Charleston: J. J. Furley.

Ingle, V. H. 1948. Berkeley County: An Historical Past, an Industrial Future. *South Carolina Magazine* 11.7:20–.

Irving, John B. 1842. *A Day on Cooper River.* Charleston: A. E. Miller.

Kirk, Francis Marion. 1945. *Colonial Education in Berkeley County.* University of South Carolina Master's thesis.

Nelson, Frank P., ed. 1974. *The Cooper River Environmental Study.* Cayce: South Carolina Water Resources Commission.

Orvin, Maxwell C. 1973. *Historic Berkeley County. . . .* Charleston: Comprint.

Ravenel, Henry William. 1947. *The Private Journal of Henry William Ravenel, 1859–1887.* Columbia: University of South Carolina Press.

Smith, Henry A. M. 1908. French James Town. *South Carolina History and General Magazine* 9:220–27.

Macedonia, Bonneau P.O., St. Stephens Parish

Parish est. 1754. Frontier fort before 1715. Acadians settled 1755; colony unsuccessful, though some prospered. Lumber interests, homes of mill executives. St. Stephens Episcopal Church built 1767–69; modeled on St. Michaels in Charleston. Bonneau orig. location of river ferry; named for Huguenot settlers in 18th cent.

SC 8A: F, housewife, 74. B. locally. Lived a short time in St. Stephens. — F. b. Pitt Co., NC, came to SC after Civil War (as did stepfather, also from Pitt Co.); M. b. locally, MGF, MGF's

F. and M. raised locally, MGM b. Horry Co., came to Co. as child. — Ed.: possibly 6 mos.; mostly self-educated. — Macedonia Christian Church. — Practically no travel or knowledge of geography.

Hell Hole, Huger P.O., St. Thomas Parish

St. Thomas church built 1819, replacing one destroyed by fire in 1708. Reputed massacre of colonials by Tories at Hell Hole. Seat of domestic distilling during prohibition.

SC 8B: M, farmer, some work for co. supervisor, 58. B. 10 mi. away. — F. b. Williamsburg Co., came to Co. as baby, PGF, PGM both from same comm.; M. b. Co. — Ed.: till 3rd grade. — Baptist; school trustee. — Little experience. — Complete vocalization of /-l/ in many cv. forms, where direct forms have [-l].

SC 8C: St. Stephens. — M, farmer, telegrapher, and general handyman, 67. B. locally (Russellville). Worked Atlantic Coast from Savannah to Wilmington, lived 4 mos. in Charleston. — F. raised in Russellville, PGF local plantation overseer, lost all siblings to malaria, PGM b. Co.; M., MGF from Russellville, MGM from Darlington Co., Scotch-Irish. — Ed.: about 3 mos. total; reads a lot. — Christian Church. — Independent outlook, serious. Strong local roots. Little travel outside occupation. — Speech very fast.

Pine Ridge School, Summerville P.O. (Dorchester Co.), 2nd St. James Parish

Parish church of St. James, Santee, built by 1706. Summerville originally pineland refuge of planters during malaria season (cf. name). C. 1900 became winter resort of Northerners. Cutting of pine trees forbidden.

SC 9A: M, farmer, 75. B. here. — F. b. here, PGF b. Williamsburg Co., came here at 18 before railroad was built, PGM from Sumter (F.'s family orig. German, came over with Hessians); M., MGF, MGM from same section. — Ed.: till 14 at rural school, 3 mos. a year. — Baptist; Woodmen of the World. — Voice low to mid range, rasping, monotonous. Moderate speed. Strong stresses.

Cross, Eutaw Twp.

Eutaw a plantation area; many bought by Northerners.

SC 9B: M, storekeeper, retired farmer, 65. B. and raised locally. — F. b. Co., PGF, PGM b. England, died while F. young; M. b. Co., MGF b. Ireland, came here as child. — Ed.: about 2nd grade. — Methodist; no lodge, "always refused" public office. — Afraid of women. Anti-Negro. — Fast speech. Not very loud; tends to be indistinct.

Moncks Corner, St. John's Parish

Moncks Corner a pre-Rev. settlement (Continental defeat 1780). Struggling village at first; grew with Santee-Cooper, now HQ for Santee-Cooper power project. Became Co. seat when Mt. Pleasant annexed to Charleston Co. Hunting, fishing.

SC 9C!: M, lawyer, about 50. — Cultivated.

Pinopolis, 2nd St. John's Parish

Pinopolis summer resort of Charleston families c. 1834. Residential; rejected chance to be Co. seat. "Almost idyllic village" before Santee-Cooper.

SC 9D!: M, 73. — Ed.: Union College, Schenectady, NY. — Cultivated.

10 & 11. Charleston County and City

Co. formed 1785; Charlestown became Charleston in 1783 act of incorporation. Plantations laid out along lower 25 mi. of Ashley shortly after 1670 settlement; most date from first 5–7 yrs., though a few not till after 1700. Upper Ashley swampy. Several Quaker families as early as 1675. Many Huguenots beginning in 17th cent. Huguenot church survives; transfer of church of Pons, France. Church of England est. 1706; Anglicanism identified with the gentry. "Free school" 1712; also schools for indigent children; 1st teaching of English grammar in America. 1st library 1700; Charleston Library Society 1748. Many plantations abandoned before 1861, unprofitable and unhealthy; others because of Civil War. Strong Jewish community dates from 1750; most early Charleston Jews from England and from English possessions in the western hemisphere; largest Jewish community in US c. 1800. Over 1,000 Acadians deported to Charleston 1755-56; also German, Scots, Irish, Polish immigration; c. 1752, Charleston 2nd largest port of debarkation for German immigrants (German "2nd language" in city). Very cosmopolitan; more than any other city, product of melting pot. Religious diversity, despite Anglican establishment: Congregational Church by 1680s; Baptists 1688; 1st Presbyterians (Scottish) 1731; Roman Catholics and Lutherans in 18th cent.; Unitarian Church from 1819. Dominated by old families; first planters, then merchants; exclusiveness of society. 3 banks 1792–1812, one of them oldest active banking office in US. Indian trade; Caribbean trade: rice, indigo, naval stores. Economic expansion in 1730s; prosperous export trade; "capital of wealth and ease" by 1800. Emphasis on export crops in early 19th cent. prevented development of industry (incl. shipbuilding). Steady falling off of trade after 1820; southern trade began to use northern ports; New York's rise hastened Charleston's decline. Charleston paralyzed by Civil War; 5 yrs. before train service resumed to Savannah. Theater in 18th cent.; interest in music; publishing center, newspaper (*Courier*) from 1803; Art Association 1857. Dutch influence on architecture. College of Charleston founded 1770; The Citadel 1842. Medical college from 1824; state institution from c. 1915. Despite earthquake (1886), fires (1740), war, many buildings survive from 18th cent. Charleston a city of neighborhoods at least until WWII: businesses concentrated like those of medieval London. Plantation center. Phosphate beds near Charleston, died out c. 1890–1900. Navy yard, port facilities, and military installations; multiplied WWII and after. Agriculture, including sweet potatoes, corn, vegetables; fisheries; hunting. Summer resort area: coast towns, pinelands. Pop. Co. 1790: 46,647, 1820: 80,212, 1850: 72,805, 1880: 102,800, 1910: 88,584, 1930: 101,650, 1960: 216,382. Pop. city of Charleston (settled 1670) 1790: 16,359, 1820: 24,780, 1850: 42,985, 1880: 49,984, 1910: 58,833, 1930: 62,265, 1960: 65,925.

Charleston speech varies greatly. Some upper-middle-class speakers, educated and cultivated people of old stock (but distinctly plainer than the upper classes), use /ß/ in all positions for /w/ and /v/. Many use a back /aˑɨ/ or /ʋˈɨ/.

Ball, William Watts. 1932. *The State That Forgot: South Carolina's Surrender to Democracy*. Chapel Hill: University of North Carolina Press.

Ball, William Watts. 1954. *The Editor and the Republic: Papers and Addresses. . .* Ed. by Anthony Harrigan. Chapel Hill: Bobbs-Merrill Co.

Boggs, Doyle Willard, Jr. 1977. *John Patrick Grace and the Politics of Reform in South Carolina, 1900–1931*. University of South Carolina dissertation.

Bowes, Frederick P. 1942. *The Culture of Early Charleston*. Chapel Hill: University of North Carolina Press.

Burton, E. Milby. 1970. *The Siege of Charleston*. Columbia: University of South Carolina Press.

Cardozo, J. N. 1866. *Reminiscences of Charleston*. Charleston: J. Walker.

Church, Henry F. 1930. *Charleston, South Carolina, 1680–1930. . . .* Charleston: J. J. Furlong.

Clouse, Converse D. 1981. *Measuring Charleston's Overseas Commerce, 1717–1767: Statistics from the Port's Naval Lists*. Washington: University Press of America.

Cohen, Hennig. 1953. *The South Carolina Gazette: 1732–1775*. Columbia: University of South Carolina Press.

Duffy, John Joseph. 1963. *Charleston Politics in the Progressive Era*. University of South Carolina dissertation.

Easterby, J. H. 1935. *A History of the College of Charleston*. Charleston: College of Charleston.

Fraser, Charles. 1854. *Reminiscences of Charleston*. Charleston: J. Russell.

Fraser, Walter J. 1976. *Patriots, Pistols, and Petticoats*. Charleston: Charleston County Bicentennial Committee.

Gougaware, George J. 1933. *The History of the German Friendly Society of Charleston, South Carolina, 1766–1916*. Richmond: Garrett and Massie.

Guilday, Peter. 1927. *Life and Times of John England, First Bishop of Charleston*. NY: America Press.

Hanckel, William H. 1962. *The Preservation Movement in Charleston, 1920–1962*. University of South Carolina dissertation.

Hode, W. S. 1934. *Literary and Cultural Background of Charleston, 1830–1860*. Duke University dissertation.

Holland, Janice. 1955. *Pirates, Planters, and Patriots*. NY: Scribner.

Hoole, William Stanley. 1936. *A Check-List and Finding-List of Charleston Periodicals, 1732–1864*. Durham, NC: Duke University Press.

Irving, John B. 1842. *A Day on Cooper River*. Charleston: A. E. Miller.

Killens, John Oliver, ed. 1970. *The Trial Record of Denmark Vesey*. Boston: Beacon Press.

Land, John E. 1884. *Charleston: Her Trade, Commerce, and Industries, 1883–4*. Charleston: The Author.

Lawsen, Christian L. 1949. *Metropolitan Charleston*. Columbia: University of South Carolina Press.

Leiding, Harriette Kershaw. 1931. *Charleston, Historic and Romantic*. Philadelphia: J. B. Lippincott.

Lesesne, Thomas Petigru. 1931. *History of Charleston County. . . .* Charleston: A. H. Cawston.

Mazyck, Arthur, comp. 1875. *Guide to Charleston. . . .* Charleston: Walker, Evans, and Cogswell.

McCowen, G. S., Jr. 1972. *The British Occupation of Charleston, 1780–82*. Columbia: University of South Carolina Press.

McCrady, Edward. 1897. *A Sketch of St. Philip's Church, Charleston, South Carolina*. Charleston: Incas and Richardson.

McIver, Petrona Rayall. 1960. *History of Mount Pleasant, South Carolina*. Charleston: Ashly Print. Co.

Middleton, Alicia Hopton. 1929. *Life in Carolina and New England during the Nineteenth Century*. Bristol, RI.

Molloy, Robert. 1947. *Charleston, a Gracious Heritage*. NY: D. Appleton-Century Co.

O'Brien, Joseph L. 1934. *John England, Bishop of Charleston*. NY: Edward O'Toole Co.

O'Brien, Joseph L. 1937. *A Chronicle History of Saint Patrick's Parish, Charleston, South Carolina*. Charleston.

O'Cain, Raymond K. 1972. *A Social Dialect Study of Charleston, South Carolina*. University of Chicago dissertation.

Phillips, U. B. 1907. The Slave Labor Problem in the Charleston District. *Political Science Quarterly* 22:416-39.

Ravenel, Beatrice St. Julien. 1945. *The Architects of Charleston*. Charleston: Carolina Art Association.

Ravenel, Harriott Horry R. 1906. *Charleston, the Place and the People*. NY: Macmillan Co.

Reznikoff, Charles. 1950. *The Jews of Charleston*. Philadelphia: Jewish Publication Society of America.

Rhett, Robert Goodwyn. 1940. *Charleston: An Epic of Carolina*. Richmond: Garrett and Massie.

Rogers, George C., Jr. 1980. *Charleston in the Age of the Pinckneys*. Columbia: University of South Carolina Press.

Sass, Herbert Ravenel. 1953. *Outspoken: 150 Years of the News and Courier*. Columbia: University of South Carolina Press.

Sellers, Leila. 1934. *Charleston Business on the Eve of the American Revolution*. Chapel Hill: University of North Carolina Press.

Simons, Albert, and Samuel Lapham. 1927. *Charleston, South Carolina*. NY: Press of the American Institute of Architects.

Simons, Katherine Drayton. 1930. *Stories of Charleston Harbor*. Columbia: State Co.

Smith, Alice R. Huger, and D. E. Huger Smith. 1917. *The Dwelling Houses of Charleston, South Carolina*. Philadelphia: J. B. Lippincott Co.

Smith, Daniel Elliott Huger. 1950. *A Charlestonian's Recollections, 1846–1913*. Charleston: Carolina Art Assoc.

Smith, H. A. M. 1915. Old Charles Town and Its Vicinity. *South Carolina History and General Magazine* 16:1–24, 49–67.

Smith, H. A. M. The Ashley River: Its Seats and Settlements. *South Carolina History and General Magazine* 20:3–51, 75–122.

Smith, H. A. M. The Upper Ashley. *South Carolina History and General Magazine* 20:151–98.

Smith, Henry A. M. 1908. Charleston: The Original Plan and the Earliest Settlers. *South Carolina History and General Magazine* 9:12–27.

Smythe, Augustine Thomas, et al. 1931. *The Carolina Low-Country*. NY: Macmillan.

Stevens, William Oliver. 1939. *Charleston, Historic City of Gardens*. NY: Dodd, Mead, and Co.

Stoney, Samuel Gaillard, and Bayard Wooten. 1937. *Charleston: Azaleas and Old Bricks*. Boston: Houghton Mifflin Co.

Uhlendorf, Bernhard Alexander. 1938. *The Siege of Charleston*. Ann Arbor: University of Michigan Press.

Walker, Cornelius Irvine. 1919. *Guide to Charleston, South Carolina*. Charleston: Walker, Evans and Cogswell Co.

Walsh, Richard. 1959. *Charleston's Sons of Liberty*. Columbia: University of South Carolina Press.

Wannamaker, W. W. J. 1975. *Long Island South: Stories of Sullivan's Island and the Isle of Palms*. Columbia: University of South Carolina Press.

Waring, Joseph I. 1970. *The First Voyage and Settlement at Charles Town, 1670–1680*. Columbia: South Carolina Tricentennial Commission.

Waring, Laura W. 1941. *You Asked for It*. Charleston: Southern Ptg. and Pub. Co.

Waring, Laura Witte. 1980. *The Way It Was in Charleston*. Ed. by Thomas R. Waring, Jr. Old Greenwich, CT: Denvin-Adair.

Webber, Marie L., ed. 1927. Records of the Quakers in Charles Town. *South Carolina History and General Magazine* 28:22–43, 94–107, 176–197.

Williams, George W. 1951. *St. Michael's, Charleston, 1751–1951*. Columbia: University of South Carolina Press.

1880–. *Year Book*. Charleston: City of Charleston, South Carolina.

SC 10A: Awendaw — F, housewife, 14 yrs. "feeder" in tobacco factory, store clerk, 53. B. Co. (Awendaw), came to Charleston at 24. One three-day trip to Washington. — F., PGF b. Awendaw, PGM prob. b. Awendaw; M. b. Awendaw, MGF, MGM came to Awendaw from NC via Clarendon Co., SC. — Ed.: till 6th grade, Awendaw public schools. — No church; active Food Tobacco Agricultural Workers Union; CIO shop steward. — Little education but strong opinions. Key member of FTA strike committee. Matriarchal. Did not understand point of interview, but cooperated. Highly independent. — Hesitancy, guarded response on vocabulary. Recalls old-fashioned words used by parents and grandparents, but not always willing to give them. Grammar naturally old-fashioned. In-gliding diphthongs for /e o/. Positional alternates for /ai au/. *Pot* vowel us. unrounded; rounding less common than with city infs. /ɪ/ for /i/ also less frequent than for city infs. Occ. retroflexing when emphasizing (noticed in other infs. as well). /hw-/ > /w-/ only in *wharf*. /l/ occ. completely vocalized.

SC 10B!: McClellanville, St. James Santee. — M., former surveyor, farmer, ran oyster factory, 85. B. Mt. Pleasant. — F. b. nearby, PGF b. NC, adopted by uncle, moved to Charleston as boy, PGM b. nearby; M., MGF b. nearby, MGF's F. a Charleston doctor, MGM from Charleston. — Ed.: McClellanville College, Hobart College. — Episcopalian; Masons, Knights of Pythias. Town intendant (mayor) 9 yrs. Pres. SC Farmers Union, Pres. SC Sea Island Cotton Growers Assn., Selective Service Board 6 yrs., school board. — Excellent example of cultivated, rural-oriented speech. Interview curtailed by business activity and by deafness of inf. Mod. to rapid tempo.

Pitch low-med. to high, rising very high with excitement, but generally kept quite even. Stresses strong. Nasality. In-gliding /i e ɔ o u/; /u/ in *new tub*; /æ/ very low, often [a]; [a] in *barn, car*; [ɒ] in *pot, crop, college, orange, closet, watch, wash*. /ʌ/ often low and somewhat fronted. Stressed /ɜ/ > [ɜɪ]. "Long" and "short" [ai au] with centered beginning before voiceless cons. /k g/ sometimes fronted. /sr-/; /w-/ in *wheelbarrow*, etc., esp. in cv. forms. Some clear /l/, even postvocalic. /r/ sometimes velarized before /n/. No postvocalic constriction. Linking /r/ in *swallow it*. — Cultivated.

SC 10C!: Mt. Pleasant, Christ Church Parish. — F, widow, taught school 2 yrs. here, 2 yrs. in nearby (6 mi.) Palmetto Grove, 64. B. McClellanville. Moved here at 5. Lived 3 yrs. Sumter, 3 yrs. Charleston. — F. b. here, PGF b. across Shaw Creek, PGF's F. b. here, PGF's PGF from James I., family drifted down from NE, PGM from Christ Church Parish; M. b. St. James Santee Parish, MGF b. locally, MGM b. McClellanville, granddaughter of original settler who fled GA after Indian massacre. — Ed.: 12 yrs. normal school. — Presbyterian; State Bird Chm., Garden Club, life member Huguenot Soc., former UDC, DAR, Historical Research Soc. of Parish (now defunct). — Interested in fieldwork (had done some collecting of Negro idioms). Like most cultivated speakers of Charleston area, knows dialect is different, but has made no effort to change (except the initial cons. of *garden*, altered after other garden club members teased her). Articulation clear. Tempo moderately fast. Stressed vowels fairly long. Some simplification of final cons. clusters, but less than us. in SC. Sometimes /w-/ in *wheel* words. No postvocalic constriction; some linking /r/ before vowels; no intrusive /r/. No dark /-l/; some clear final /l/. /i e ɔ o u/ monoph. or in-gliding; centered beginning of /ai au/ before voiceless cons. — Cultivated.

SC 11N: M, carpenter, 58. B. here. Lived ages 9–16 in Smithville. — F. b. here: free, part Indian; M. b. Sand Island near Georgetown, came here when young, MGF coachman Sand Island, MGM seamstress Sand Island (both at Flagg Estate). — Ed.: privately 7 yrs, white teacher. — Baptist. — A city Negro of the respectable working classes. Likable, quick and imaginative. Not always attentive. Highly superstitious. — Fairly rapid tempo.

SC 11M!: Jasper Court. — M, mail carrier, has sold papers, Fuller brushes, now notary public, 44. B. Charleston, PGF, PGM b. near Moncks Corner; M. b. Charleston, MGF, MGM probably b. Charleston. — Ed.: h.s., Avery Institute. — Methodist; Boy Scouts District Council, administrative council of Avery Inst., USO volunteer host, YMCA, Masons, Natl. Alliance Postal Employees, Natl. Letter Carriers Assn., NAACP. — Dignified; quiet, subtle sense of humor. Free in discussion. Has worked all over Charleston; knows almost everyone in town, AfAm and white. Progressive thinker, but without malice. — Natural, cultivated speech; melodious, soft-spoken. Wide intonation range; strong stresses. Knows folk grammatical forms, but doesn't use them. Offered several lexical items FW had not previously encountered — *gap, pinto, yard-ax*. In-gliding diphthongs; rounded [ɒ] in *pot*, etc. More retroflexion than us. in Charleston, esp. in unstr. syllables (school influence?). — Cultivated.

SC 11A: M, owner and manager of foundry and machineworks, officer in insurance company, 86. B. here. Lived 2 yrs. Florence, SC. — F. b. Ireland, came here in potato famine, PGM b. Scotland; M. b. Ireland, left same time as F. — Ed.: public schools, some private school (no h.s.), Charleston. — Roman Catholic; Knights of Columbus, Rotarian; past pres. Hibernian Soc.; alderman 8 yrs., member State Dem. exec. comm. — Hardworking, thrifty, accommodating. Knows everyone in Charleston. Interview somewhat difficult because of inf.'s deafness. Occ. tendency towards recitative storytelling style when discussing historical events, but generally quite colloquial. Good example of the "Charleston Irish". — Some cultivated forms through reading (not much) and social contacts, but normally no hesitancy about using folk forms. Clear speech, even when rapid. Tempo normally medium or a little slow. Pleasing voice, melodious intonation. In-gliding diphs. [ʌ] rather low; [ai, aʊ] with positional allophones, as us. in Charleston speech; [u] fronted, [ʋ] often in *got, hod*, etc. /-r/ > [ə] or length; [j] occ. before [u] following [t d n], but oftener not. [hw] > [w] us. [ɜɪ] in *hurt, word*, etc. (us. in Charleston).

SC 11A*: M, tinsmith, 86. B. here. — F. b. here, PGF b. Scotland, PGM b. England; M. b. here, MGF b. Scotland, MGM b. near Williston, SC (English descent). — Ed.: till age 12 here. — Episcopalian. — An old confederate soldier, son of a tinsmith. Too feeble to continue. — Deliberate, but short vowels.

SC 11B: M, service station manager, 57. B. Charleston, visits to NY, New Orleans, Miami. — F. b. Sicily; M. b. Charleston (Irish ancestry). — Ed.: 8th grade. — St. Patricks Church, Knights of Columbus, Sec. of Holy Name Society; President of Retail Gas Dealers Assn. — Excellent informant; drank steadily through both sessions, but maintained perfect control of thoughts and articulation. Completely removed from rural South: no recollection of many terms that are generally regarded as Southern. Middle and low-front vowels generally lower than expected norms; seems to have low-back alternates that are not shown in Wetmore's study for E. SC.

SC 11C: Downtown. — F, housewife, 58. B. Charleston, lived in Akron, OH (1913–18), Jacksonville, FL (1931–33). — F. b. en route Germany-America, PGF, PGM b. Germany; M. b. Germany, came to U.S. with parents at age of 9; neither parent lived anywhere but Charleston. — Ed.: 5th grade, Charleston public schools. — St. Lukes Episcopal Church; Typographical Auxiliary. Somewhat limited in social contacts; sticks close to household. — "Good citizen." Likes children. Cooperative; considerate; generally enjoyed interviews, though a little suspicious of items commonly supposed to test "good English". Occ. anecdotes. Little knowledge of rural terms. — High-pitched voice. Stressed syllables very heavily stressed. Staccato speech. In-gliding diphs. /e o/ etc. Positional allophones of /ai, au/ as us. in Charleston. /hw-/ in *wheelbarrow* and other such words, except *wharf*.

SC 11D: M, wholesale cigar and tobacco dealer, ex-farmer, 83. B. Charleston. — F. b. Galicia, came to Charleston c. 1825; M. b. Russia (no foreign languages spoken in family). — Ed.: grammar school. — Well known in town. Jewish, Beth Elohim Temple (President-Emeritus Congregation), President Hebrew Orphan Society (oldest of its kind in N. America —

1801); ex-Pres. Agricultural Society of SC, VP Charleston Agriculture and Fair Assn., VP Charleston-Isle of Palms Traction Co., Woodmen of the World, Masons. — Interested in interviews. Patient with FW; generous with time. Quotes freely from English classics. Tells riddles and anecdotes (somewhat ponderous). Knows Charleston of last 75 years very well; knew everyone of prominence in political and commercial life. Respected in community. A little guarded on folk forms, undoubtedly result of self-education. — Speech generally has modern orientation. Self-education probably responsible for tendency to post-vocalic retroflexion when on guard (less in cv. forms), and for restoration of [h] in such words as *wheelbarrow* (note absence in cv. forms). /k g/ less palatal than in SC11J. Typical Charleston /e o/; tendency to [ʋ] type in *John, God, rock*, though [ɑ] forms do occur. Regular allophonic alternation of /ai au/ in *house, houses; rice, rise*. Low-Country /ʌ/ in *bulge, bulk*; /ʌ/ variable, much lower (as a rule) than in FW's speech. [ɨ] often replaces [ɪ] in stressed syllables, though less than in other Charleston inf.'s (is [ɨ] more "upper class"?).

SC 11E: M, magistrate, has been in insurance, whiskey business, once commissioner state dispensary system (alcohol), 76. B. Charleston, one yr. in Norfolk, VA, summer visits to MA and Adirondacks. — F., PGF b. Charleston, PGF's GF b. Scotland, PGM, PGM's F., PGM's M. b. Charleston; M., MGF, MGF's F., MGF's M., MGM all b. Charleston; all GP, most GGP never left community (inf. has record of family genealogy). — Ed.: Charleston HS, Prof. Maingault (Gibbes St.), no college ("damn glad"). — St. Mary's Roman Catholic; Elk, Hibernian Society, German Rifle Club, "almost everything". — Knows everybody in the co. Has retained position 24 years; best vote-getter in history of Charleston politics. Paternalistic; soft-spoken; courteous; even-tempered. Fond of good eating. Tends to decide realistically, rather than according to letter of law, if there should be a conflict. Many anecdotes; recollects old times, but also keeps up with new slang expressions. Delightful sense of humor. — Even tempo; variation in intensity of stress; clear speech (probably result of years on bench). Free and frank vocabulary, no inhibitions. /aiðər/ (possibly result of travel, summer visits, and other Northern contacts). /k g/ often palatal (recognizes this as old-fashioned). /ə/ for postvocalic /-r/. /a/ low-back, occ. rounded [ʋ]; /ai, au/ alternation according to phonemic environment. /e o/ monoph. or in-gliding; /i/ pure vowel, occ. in-gliding. /-l/ dark, occ. vocalized. /ʌ/ us. fairly low. [ɨ] for /i/. /ju/ often after /t d n/; /j/ occ. omitted.

SC 11F: Fishburne Tract, Northwest. — F, housewife, yeomanette in WWI, substitute church organist, 48. B. Charleston, 3 mos. in OH and short visits. — F. b. Charleston, PGF, PGM b. Germany; M. b. Charleston, MGF b. Germany, MGM b. Bremen, Germany (came to Charleston with sister c. 1870). — Ed.: public schools: Craft School, Meminger HS, Charleston. — Lutheran, Ladies Aid, Missionary Society, other church organizations; American Legion Auxiliary, Garden Club of Charleston, Eastern Star. — Very guarded. Tenseness, noticed in strained huskiness of voice, tendency to over-enunciate. Conscious of notion of "correctness" — Occ. betrayed herself on verb forms. Hospitable. Only one child; husband away a good part of the time. Interested in family background; would like to write it up, but timid about it.

Diffident about her knowledge. — Vowels typically Charleston, except that /i/ is more often rising than us. in Charleston.

SC 11G!: M, physician (intern), 24. B. Charleston. — F., PGF b. Charleston, PGF's parents b. Ireland (M. County Clare), PGM b. Charleston, PGM's F. from England; M. b. Charleston, MGF b. Germany (Hanover), MGM b. Charleston, MGM's F. and M. b. Germany. — Ed.: parochial grammar school, Bishop England HS, College of Charleston, Medical College of SC. — Roman Catholic; θΔΚ (local fraternity, College of Charleston), θΡΣ (medical fraternity). — Good inf. Alert; quick-witted; keen sense of humor. Modest; unexcitable. Enjoyed interviews; understood purpose. Tells a good story; knows younger generation habits, speech, etc. — Knows what grammar books indicate as correct, but gave normal colloquial responses. Some recollection of GM's speech, but otherwise oriented to the present. Few folk grammatical forms. Us. /w-/ in *wheel*, etc. /k g/ not heavily palatalized (apparently palatalization is receding, even in Charleston). No post-vocalic retroflexion. Less [ɨ] for /ɪ/ than in older generation. /e o/ in-gliding; in-gliding /i u/ less common. /ai au/ with normal positional alternations of Charleston speech. [ɒ] in *not*, etc.; /ʌ/ variable, often very low. — Cultivated.

SC 11H!: S. of Broad. — M, Social Security administrator (previously private insurance business), 52. B. Charleston, in army in TX 1916–19. — F. b. Charleston, PFG b. Charleston (ancestor b. PA, settled in SC after Rev.), PGM b. Charleston (17th cent. Huguenot descent); M., MGF, MGM b. Charleston. Family connections well established; F. compiled family records. — Ed.: Charleston schools, 1 yr. prep school VA, U. of SC. — Episcopalian; Soc. of Cincinnati (Jr. steward), Soc. for the Preservation of Spirituals (Pres.), Rotary Club (Sec.), Chamber of Commerce, etc. "Used to belong to everything" — Satisfactory interview. Quick mind. Interested in work of *Atlas*. Many contacts through Social Security work. Slightly nervous, but gracious. Many anecdotes; keen sense of humor. — Knew what interviews were about, but kept completely natural (assurance of the aristocrat who knows his speech is OK). Tempo rapid, with stressed syllables long and unstr. very short (transcriptions tend to under-transcribe the difference, esp. the pronounced in-glide of [e o]); wide intonation range. Melodious; quasi-"Gullah" intonation, a type often met with among cultivated older generation males of upper-class families (less common among females; FW can't recall an instance). Typical Charleston phonemes; /w-/ for /hw-/ not as common as in other infs. of class. — Cultivated.

SC 11I!: S. of Broad. — F, 51. B. here. — F., PGF, PGF's F. b. here (of early Scottish descent), PGM b. here (desc. from early colony); M., MGF (old stock), MGM b. here, MGM's F. b. here (Huguenot stock), MGM's M. English, desc. of signer of Declaration. — Ed.: private finishing school. — Episcopalian. — Highly intelligent and cultivated woman of the old and best families of Charleston. Has never traveled because she has been at home caring for the older members of her own family. Extremely distinguished siblings: schoolmistress, surgeon, history prof., county engineer. Enjoyed interviews. — Extremely quick, rapid speech. — Cultivated.

SC11I!*: F. Maiden lady of cultivated stock living a block away from SC11I!.

SC 11J!: S. of Broad. — F, artist (woodblocks, watercolors), has written several books, 69. B. Charleston. — F., PFG, PGF's F. b. Charleston, PGF's PGF 1st bishop of SC, PGM, PGM's F. Huguenot (PGM's F. anti-nullification but secessionist), PGM's M. descendant of signer of Declaration; M, MGF Charleston Huguenot, MGM descendant of Winthrops of MA. — Ed.: private schools, Charleston ("not so keen on college", "Southern girls didn't go to college in those days"); hon. D.Litt., Mount Holyoke. — Episcopalian; "Everything in Charleston": SC Hist. Soc., Charleston Art Assn., Chas. Museum, Chas. Hist. Soc. (curator), Chas. Lib. Soc., "many charitable things", in *Who's Who* 20 years, exhibits all over US E. of the Mississippi (Boston, NY, Phila., Wash., Richmond, New Orleans, etc.), Huguenot Soc. — Excellent example of female aristocrat of Charleston. Represents the "Old South" in its best aspects. Well-read, entertaining conversationalist sure of her social position. Manners and speech oriented toward past; dominating influence in her life her father and grandmother (GM's parents born before Rev.). Knows all the "nice people" of Charleston and plantations along coast; has painted scenes in most plantations. Hospitable. Many anecdotes, recollections of what parents and grandparents (esp. GM) said. — *Casual* is an epithet of condemnation. No taboo reactions, "not a prude, but some words I just never had occasion to learn". Knows many old-fashioned words, insists on using certain old-fashioned pronunciations (e.g., [læntʃ], [č'æ·m], [p'æ·m]) regardless of fashion or notions of "correctness". Conservative on grammar, said GM had drilled her thoroughly on what was "correct" in grammar: "GM would turn over in her grave if she heard me say [e.nt]." /k g/ often palatal when initial in stressed syllables (more than in any other inf.). /hw-/ us. retained ("GM taught us there should be an [h], not a very strong one but enough to let people know it's there."). No post-vocalic retroflexion. Many clear [l]s. Us. Charleston allophonic variants of /au ai/. In-gliding /e o/; often in-gliding /i u/; [ɨ] for [ɪ] often in stressed syllables (more than in any other speaker interviewed). — Cultivated.

12. Dorchester County

Formed 1897. Old Dorchester, on upper Ashley, settled from Dorchester, MA in 1696 (1st settlement outside Charleston). By 1719, had c. 115 English families and 1500 slaves. Market and fair here by 1727; free school 1734; fortified 1775. C. 1752, most of colony migrated to GA. Decline after Rev.; absorbed in neighboring plantations (rice, indigo). Now small farming: cotton, tobacco, corn, livestock, lumbering. Pop. 1900: 16,299, 1910: 17,891, 1930: 18,956, 1960: 24,383.

Klauber, E. H. 1940. Dorchester County Abounds in History. *South Carolina Magazine* 3.4:24-25.

Smith, Henry A. M. 1905. The Town of Dorchester, in South Carolina. . . . *South Carolina History and Genealogical Magazine* 6:62–95, 127–130.

1947. Dorchester County, a Fascinating Combination of the Old and New in South Carolina. *South Carolina Magazine* 10.4:8–11.

Indian Fields, Harleyville P.O., Carns Twp.

Since 1838, site of SC's oldest camp meeting. Swamp lands. Harleyville a small trading center with self-sufficient agriculture. Settled in 18th cent. by Germans and Swiss; plantations later. Cement plant here since WWII.

SC 12A: M, farmer, 80. B. 2 mi. away, never lived outside neighborhood. — F. b. NC, came to SC long before Civil War; M. b. community, MGF's family from "Clubhouse" section along Edisto R. (fishermen, hunters, phosphate diggers). — Ed.: 8th grade. — Methodist; trustee and steward to Indian Fields Methodist Church and Camp Ground; Mason. — Isolated, rural, old-fashioned speech. Nasality; drawl; strong stresses. Many folk pronunciations and folk gram. forms. Rather monotonous intonation (little range); voice slightly above medium register. /k g/ often palatal. /sr-/, /hw-/; /-l/ often vocalized; /-r-/ often lost (esp. in cv. forms); [-r] us. > [ə]; occ. slight traces of retroflexion; /-r-/ in *swallow it*. /i/ us. in-gliding; /u/ quite fronted, us. monophthongal; /ju/ in *Tuesday, dues, new*; /e o/ in-gliding. /ɛ/ and /ɪ/ sometimes neutralized before nasals; /a/ low-central to low-back. /æ/ in *calm*; [ɒ] in *pot, crop, rock*, etc.; /ʌ/ high, us. slightly rounded (rounding not always transcribed); /ʊ/ fronted. [ɜɪ] in *thirty, Thursday*; /ɛ/ in *squirrel*. /ai au/ us. with centered beginning before voiceless cons.; finally and before voiced cons., /ai/ with low-central (sometimes back) beginning; /au/ as [æʊ a˔·ʊ ʌˀʊ]; /ai/ instead of /ɔi/; unstr. [ɨ] in *china, borrow*.

Byrd Station, St. George P.O., George Twp.

St. George first settled c. 1697. Quiet trading center; base for hunters and fishermen. Agriculture, lumbering, cattle raising.

SC 12B: F, housewife, 70. B. 3 mi. away. — F. b. here, PGF b. St. George, PGF's F. b. Germany, PGM b. St. George; M. b. here, MGF, MGM b. Harleyville. — Ed.: St. George till 16; 1 yr. Meminger HS, Charleston. — Methodist. — Intelligent, interested, natural. Comes of thrifty, respectable ancient German peasant stock in SC. — Speech very dialectal. FW feels some things may be due to her German ancestry, namely the weakly rounded [ʌ] which is hardly high enough to be of Lincoln-Yorkshire origin; also the extraordinary sound used in *sir* (also for *sow*). Slow tempo.

13. Edisto Island (Charleston County)

Edisto I. settled in 1680s by Scots and Irish; Spanish raid in 1686. Few full-time white residents; whites descended from old plantation families remain. Until 1930s, semi-isolated, road not passable at high tide. Large AfAm pop. (Gullah). Rice, indigo, cotton grown on early plantations. Occupied by Feds 1862. Now diversified truck crops, fishing; resorts. Pop. (AfAm pop.): 1910: 3,234, 1930: 1,948 (1,693), 1960: 1,589 (1,306).

Gadsden, Sam. 1974. *An Oral History of Edisto Island*. Goshen, IN: Pinchpenny.

Graydon, Nell S. 1955. *Edisto Island*. Columbia: University of South Carolina Press.

Graydon, Nell S. 1955. *Tales of Edisto*. Columbia: R. L. Bryan Co.

Kenner, H. C. 1975. *Historical Records of Trinity Episcopal Church, Edisto Island, South Carolina*. Rockingham, NC: Dorsett Print. Co.

Mikill, Isaac Jenkins. 1923. *Rumbling of the Chariot Wheels*. Columbia: University of South Carolina Press.

Puckett, Clara Childs. 1978. *Edisto: A Sea Island Principality*. Cleveland: Seaforth Publications.

Seabrook, E. M. 1853. *The History of the Protestant Episcopal Church of Edisto Island*. Charleston: Walker and James.

Webber, Mabel L. 1922–27. Grimball of Edisto Island. South Carolina History Magazine 23:17, 39–45, 94–101, 28:256–58.

SC 13: The Borough, Edisto Island P.O. — M, farmer, 52. B. same locality. — F., PGF, PGM b. Wadmalaw Island (nearest to NE across Edisto I.); M., MGF, MGM b. Edisto. — Ed.: Clemson College 2 yrs. (agriculture). — Episcopalian. — Quick mind; good sense of humor. Cooperative. Knows island intimately. Seemed to enjoy interviews. — Fast tempo; clear articulation; strong stress, pitch range low to medium. Not bookish, but generally uses standard grammatical forms. (FW thinks that perhaps old Edisto is one of the few places where one could really contrast "Standard English" and "AfAm English".)

14. Colleton County

Formed 1798; before the Rev. covered Edisto to Savannah. Settled primarily by Dissenters c. 1682. Cattle ranches after 1694. Rural: timber, cotton, corn, livestock, hunting, fishing, tourists. Pop. 1790: 20,338, 1800: 24,903, 1820: 26,359, 1850: 39,505, 1880: 36,386, 1910: 35,390, 1930: 25,831, 1960: 27,816.

Glover, Beulah. 1963. *Narratives of Colleton County*.

Smoak, W. W. 1940. Walterboro. *South Carolina Magazine* 3.4: 22–23.

1941. Walterboro. *South Carolina Magazine* 4.3:24–.

1947. Colleton County: Center of Expanding Interests. *South Carolina Magazine* 10:10–11.

SC 14A: Hendersonville, Heyward Twp. — M, farmer (clerk when young), 84. B. Hendersonville, lived ages 1–5 in St. Marys, GA (near FL), 5–22 in Walterboro (10 mi. N.), then 3 yrs. in Albany in SW GA, 8 yrs. on Combahee R., SC; in Hendersonville since he was 34. — F. b. Paris, France, died when son was 5 (F. had come to America when 21); M. b. in Co., MGF b. in Co. (Eng. descent), MGM b. in Co. (German descent). — Ed.: Walterboro till 14. — Baptized as Roman Catholic, later Methodist. — Remarkable man: vigorous, active, quick-thinking, quick of speech. Conscious of his planter origin and duty as a gentleman, but aware that children and grandchildren of his "backwoods" neighbors are educated and often smarter than those of his class; yet he mourns that they are lacking in the character which really separates the two classes. — FW distinguishes between planters such as inf. and "backwoods" people, who are often of German descent. Inf.'s speech is quick, short-voweled, precise, with [aʌ ʌ˕ ɜ]; "backwoods" people are slower, laxer, and use [æ· ʌ˕ ɚ·]. FW did not get a local "backwoods" subject; closest would be SC 12B, Dorchester Co.

Walterboro, Verdier Twp.

Walterboro settled early 18th cent.; library society and bldg. by 1820. Now a tourist town and trade center. Popular winter resort (esp. for Northerners); excellent hunting and fishing country. Pop. 1880: 691, 1910: 1,677, 1930: 2,592, 1960: 5,417.

SC 14B: M, clerk at draft board, managed wholesale grocery 17 yrs., ran a moving picture show, 51. B. here. — F., PGF, PGM old local stock, earliest family settlers from bef. 1700; M., MGF, MGM b. Co., MGF's family from Exeter, England after Rev. — Ed.: local schools, U. of SC "just in and out". — Episcopalian; American Legion, Country Club, City Council 4 yrs., mayor pro tem 2. — Level-headed, good judgment. No pretensions of knowledge. Knows local history. Generous with time. — Uses standard forms naturally. Occ. cites differences between usage now and when he was a boy. Good ex. of natural speech of old families without overlay of much formal education. — Tempo mod. rapid. Strong stresses, shortening of unstr. syllables. Wide intonation range. "Throaty quality" (inner rounding) us. associated with plantation-derived White and Negro speech. /p- t- k- tʃ-/ often without marked aspiration. /k g/ often palatalized by following front vowel. Some simplification of final clusters, not as much as us. for SC. [kl- gl-] > [tl- dl-].

15. Bamberg County

Formed 1897 from Barnwell Co. Mixed settlement; small landholdings. Mainly Irish, Germans, English; also some Dutch. Schools c. 1870; Methodists est. congregation at about same time. Mainly Evangelical Protestants. Cotton mill. Watermelons, other truck; livestock, timber. Pop. 1910: 18,544, 1930: 19,410, 1960: 16,274.

> Brabham, Otis, 1952. *Bamberg and Vicinity: The Tale of a Town*. Bamberg.
> Copeland, D. Graham. 1940. *Many Years After — A Bit of History and Some Recollections of Bamberg*. Copeland.
> 1947. Bamberg County, Determined on Progress. *South Carolina Magazine* 10.5:20–.

SC 15A: Colston, Buford's Bridge Twp. — M, farmer (interested in "home doctoring", supervised local roads, sometime juror), 83. B. nearby, a few trips to Charleston and N. Augusta. — F. b. nearby, PGF b. Buford's Bridge section, PGF's F. a scout with Gen. Marion, PGM b. VA, came to Charleston, PGM's F. 1st Methodist minister in Charleston ("back parents" drifted down from VA [Scotch-Irish migration]); M., MGM b., raised in lower part of Co., MGF farmer, died young. — Ed.: about 3rd grade; considerable reading (F. a teacher). — Baptist; local official duties. — Authority on local customs, excellent memory; knows everyone in community. — Drawl.

Bamberg

Military school here. Watermelons (shipped to Europe), livestock. Voorhees College (est 1897), electric utility distribution point nearby. Pop. 1910: 1,977, 1930: 2,450, 1960: 3,081.

SC 15B: M, seed merchant, small store proprietor, 68. B. Bamberg, lived in town all life except for 3 mos. in Hartford, CT. — F. b. Bamberg, PGF b. Germany, PGM b. locally; M. from near Darlington, inf. never knew MGF, MGM ("different part of country"). — Ed.: local schools till 15 (mostly private); studied optics in CT 3 mos. — Methodist; former Knight of Pythias. — Slight nasality; fast speech.

SC 15C: M, retired dry goods merchant, 85. B. Fishpond Twp., 10 mi. SE. — F. b. Fishpond Twp., PGF b. near St. George, owned large plantation in Fishpond Twp., robbed and murdered when F. a baby, PGM b. old Beaufort Dist. (Varnville); M. from Fishpond Twp., MGF from GA, MGM raised in Fishpond section. — Ed.: 3 mos. a yr. for 13 yrs., country school. — Baptist, Sunday School Supt., 40 yrs. on Board of Deacons; Mayor and Councilman several times, 20 yrs. Chm. Board of Health, scientific, literary, and musical Clubs, Mason, Lions, Good Temperance. — Slow, somewhat hesitating.

16. Allendale County

Formed 1919. 1st settlers 1748–60. Cowpens and small farms at first; also plantation country. Baptist Church as early as 1759. C. 1800 "Christian" church as well. Mennonites recent. Watermelons, truck, livestock, timber, hunting. Pop. 1920: 16,098, 1930: 13,294, 1960: 11,362.

> Lawton, Alexania Easterling, and Minnie Reeves Wilson, eds. 1970. *Allendale on the Savannah*. Bamberg: Bamberg Herald Printers.
> Sanders, Sara L. 1978. *The Speech of Fairfax, South Carolina, in Its Subregional Context: Selected Phonological Features*. University of South Carolina Master's thesis.
> Searson, Louis Arthur. 1949. *The Town of Allendale*. Columbia.

Millettville

Millettville settled c. 1770, largely by Scots. Refugee homes for planters.

SC 16N: M, farmer, occ. preacher, 68. B. Millettville, 6 mi. below Hattieville, moved to Hattieville c. 20 yrs. ago. — F., M. b. old Barnwell Co. (now comprising Bamberg, Aiken, Allendale, Barnwell). — Ed.: practically no schooling or travel, hardly over 100 mi. from home. — Baptist, Christian Union Insurance Society. — One of the "character Negroes" of community. Difficulty at beginning of interview, since inf. tended to give responses he thought FW wanted; difficult to get straight answers at first. When this difficulty was bridged, FW found inf. intelligent and cooperative; information given without much ado. Old-fashioned. — Extreme range of tempo and pitch. Under excitement, stressed vowels at extremely high pitch and overlong. Average tempo rapid; stresses strong; unstr. vowels very short. /-t-/ > [-ɾ-]; [-nt-] > [-r̃-]; /-k/ in *closet*; /sr-/ in *throw*; /sw-/ in *shrink*. /hw-/; /-l/ often vocalized; /-r-/ often weak; no /-r/; slight intrusive /r/ in *ought to*. /i/ monoph. or in-gliding; /e/ almost always in-gliding; /u/ fronted, may be in-gliding or up-gliding. /tʃu/ in *Tuesday*; /dʒu-/ in *due*; /nu/ in *New York*. /o/ in-gliding; no /-o/ in unstr. syllables. /a/ low-central to low-back; [ɒ] in *pot, John, tomorrow, borrow, wash*. /ʌ/ generally high, but replaced by /ɛ/ in *shut*. /ɛ/ in *squirrel*. Stressed /ɜ/ > [ɝ] except final and before /-l/, when [ɜ]. No unstr. [ɚ]; /ai/ us. with low-central beginning; /au/ with beginning varying from [æ] to [a]; [ɔɪ] in *oil, joint*, etc. [ɨ] in unstr. syllables of *borrow, mountain, china, towel, bucket*.

Allendale

Co. seat. Planting area in 18th cent. Town moved to RR in 1872. Episcopal congregation 1847. Watermelon fields. Pop. 1910: 1,453, 1930: 2,066, 1960: 3,114.

SC 16: M, farmer, general business/farm products, 69. No place of birth given. — F. b. Bamberg Co.; M. b. here. — Ed.: little if any h.s. — Baptist, Farm Bureau, National Grange. — Good knowledge of agricultural life, and aware of innovation in terminology. Business-like. Concerned about linguistic propriety, but not pretentious or nervous. — Heavy nasality.

17. Hampton County

Formed 1878 from Beaufort Co. Hunting, timber. Varied agriculture: tobacco, peanuts, strawberries, potatoes, cotton. Pop. 1880: 18,741, 1910: 25,126, 1930: 17,243, 1960: 17,425.

> Writers' Program. 1940. *A Guide to Hampton County, South Carolina.* Hampton County.
> 1946. Hampton County: Forest and Field. *South Carolina Magazine* 9.1:24–.
> 1970. *Both Sides of the Swamp.* Columbia: Hampton County Tricentennial Commission.

Hampton, Peeples Twp.
Hampton sawmill country; truck farms, livestock.

SC 17A: F, housewife, former farm worker, 76. B. nearby. Never lived out of Co. — F. b. locally. PGF, PGM b. Crocketville, near Hampton; M., MGF b. Crocketville, MGM b. Pondtown. No family history recorded. — Ed.: local schools, till about 7th grade. — Primitive Baptist Church. — Limited experience. Very poor. Religious; humble. Generous; enjoyed interview but did not understand purpose. Better at concrete objects than abstract. — Old-fashioned speech. Little attempt to guard herself. Some nasality. Final clusters simplified. Folk plural in *fistes, postes.* /-r/ used more consistently than elsewhere in area. /-t-/ > /-ɾ-/. /hw-/. /-r/ in *walnut.* In-gliding /i/; in-gliding /e/ occ. with slight rise, basically high. /u/ fronted, us. monoph. /ju/ after /t- d- n-/. /o/ in-gliding. /æi/ in *dance, chance.* /a/ low-central to low-back. Unrounded in *borrow, oranges.* /ʌ/ high, often rounded. /ʊ/ us. high and fronted. /ɝ/ in stressed syllables. /ai/ us. with low-central beginning; some /ai/ for /ɔi/, /ɔi/ us. high. /au/ begins low-central to upper low-front. /ɨ/ in *-ed.*

SC 17B: M, school janitor, 68. B. near Nixville Crossroads (13–14 mi. W.). Lived in Estille. — F., PGF, PGM, M., MGF, MGM all from Old Beaufort Dist. Not much known about family. — Ed.: Hopewell school, into 5th reader. — Baptist. — Enjoyed interviews. No suspicions, no inhibitions. Although many locals find him difficult to understand, FW had no problem. Interview interrupted repeatedly and finally cut off by meddling school superintendent. — Speaks with close mouth. Speech generally old-fashioned. Nasality. /i/ monoph. or in-gliding. /ju/ after /n/. /o/ high, in-gliding. /a/ low-central to low-back. /ʊ/ rare: *crop, sausage, rock.* /ʌ/ high. /ʊ/ fronted. In-gliding /e/. Both in-gliding and up-gliding /u/. Almost no retroflexion. Sandhi /r/. No intrusive /r/. /ai/ low-central beginning; /au/ beginning varied [æ] to [a]; /ai/ beginning from [oˑ] to [ɔˑ]. Simplification of final clusters. /-t-/ sometimes [-ɾ-]. /hw-/; /-l/ us. dark.

SC 17C: F, hotel manager, 88. B. here. — F. b. nearby; PGF, PGM, b. same comm.; M. b. here, MGF, MGM b. Co. — Ed.: father a teacher, also Mr. Peeple's private school. — Methodist; UDC, WCTU. — Interested in talking about old times, but a difficult informant. Mind tends to wander. Rather deaf. — Slow speech, no drawl. Little nasality. Folk verb forms. /hw-/; no /-r/ except in sandhi; /sr-/; some vocalization of /-l/. Clear intervoc. /l/. /i e o ɔ/ in-gliding or monoph. Some /ɪ ɛ/ neut. before nasals. /u/ fronted, up-gliding or monoph. /ju/ in *new.* /-ə/ in *tomato, borrow,* etc. /a/ us. low central. Rounded /ʋ/ in *pot, oxen, crop, wash, John.* /ai/ us. low-central beginning before voiced or final cons., /ai/ occ. centered before voiceless cons.; /au/ occ. centered beginning. [oɪ]. /ʌ/ extremely variable. /ɨ/ in weak unstr. syllables of *bucket, lettuce, towel, funnel,* etc. [ɝ] in *furniture,* etc.

SC 17D: M, retired sawmill operator and railroad magnate, 78. B. Charleston. Came to Co. at 3, here at 6. — F. b. Williamston, Anderson Co., moved to Charleston 1866. PGF lived Williamston, PGM b. Pickens Co.; M. b. Spartanburg Co., MGF b. Clarendon Co., MGM b. Spartanburg Co. — Ed.: local schools, U. of SC — Baptist; formerly Knights of Pythias and Elks. — Well-respected and liked in comm. Enjoyed interviews. Not caste-conscious. Quick mind. Knows all types of local people. Familiar with folk idiom. Knows what he has heard. — Initial stops less strongly aspirated than us. in SC. Some /-t-/ > /-ɾ-/; /k- g-/ freq. palatal. /sr-/, /hw-/ assimilations and simplifications of final clusters. No /-r/, sandhi /r/ rare; intrusive [r] only in *swallow it.* [ʋ] ~ [a] in many words. /ai au/ occ. with centralized beginning, with /ai/ us. beginning low-central, /au/ varied beginning. /a/ low-central to low-back. /i e u o ɔ/ us. in-gliding. /u/ fronted. /ju/ after /t d n/. /ʌ/ high.

18 & 19. Beaufort County

Co. formed 1785. Sea islands isolated. 1st explored by Spanish. Abortive Fr. settlement 1562. Spanish garrisoned to 1663. Scots colony 1684–86; English, Scots settlers 1698. Attractive harbors. 1715, ravaged in Yamassee War. 1717, 1st lot in Beaufort (city); mixed settlement, including Barbadians. 18th cent crops: naval stores, rice, indigo, sea island cotton. In 1833, probably the richest district in the US excepting the great commercial cities. C. 1860, large plantations: slaveholdings twice state average. Small, close-knit group of planter families. 1862–65 recruiting ground for AfAm troops. Now winter resort area (e.g. Hilton Head). Fishing, canning, lumbering; agriculture: truck, corn, hogs. Pop. 1790: 18,753, 1820: 32,199, 1850: 38,805, 1880: 30,176, 1910: 30,355, 1930: 21,815, 1960: 44,187.

> Bailey, Robert Smith. 1929. *A History of Education in Beaufort County up to the Civil War.* University of South Carolina master's thesis.
> Barnwell, Stephen Bull. 1969. *The Story of an American Family.* Marquette.
> Beaufort Historic Foundation. 1970. *A Guide to Historic Beaufort.* Columbia: State Print. Co.
> Cowley, Charles. 1882. *The Romance of History in "the Black County," and the Romance of War in the Career of Gen. Robert Smalls. . . .* Lowell, MA.
> Federal Writers Project. 1938. *Beaufort and the Sea Islands.* Savannah, GA: Review Print. Co.
> French, Austa. 1862. *Slavery in South Carolina and Ex-Slaves on the Port Royal Mission.* NY: W. M. French.
> Graydon, Nell S. 1963. *Tales of Beaufort.* Beaufort: Beaufort Book Shop.

Harrill, Sophie C. 1921. Beaufort, South Carolina. *House Beautiful* 49:294–300.

Hilton, Mary Kendall. 1970. *Old Homes and Churches of Beaufort County, South Carolina*. Columbia: State Print. Co.

Holland, R. S., ed. 1912. *Letters and Diary of Laura M. Towne*. Cambridge, MA: Harvard University Press.

Inglesby, Edith. 1968. *A Corner of Carolina*. Columbia: State Print. Co.

Johnson, Guion Griffis. 1930. *A Social History of the Sea Islands*. Chapel Hill: University of North Carolina Press.

Jones, Katherine M. 1960. *Port Royal under Six Flags*. Indianapolis: Bobbs-Merrill.

Jordan, Jord. 1937. Beaufort, Unexploited by Industry. *South Carolina Magazine* 1.1:13.

Kiser, Clyde V. 1936. *Sea Island to City. Studies in History and Public Law*. Vol. 4, no. 368. NY: Columbia University Press.

McTeer, J. E. 1972. *Adventure in the Woods and Waters of the Low Country*. Beaufort: Beaufort Book Co.

McTeer, James E. 1971. *Beaufort, Now and Then*. Beaufort: Beaufort Book Co.

McTeer, James Edwin. 1970. *High Sheriff of the Low Country*. Columbia: University of South Carolina Press.

Pearson, Elizabeth Ware. 1906. *Letters from Port Royal. . . .* Boston: W. B. Clarke.

Perry, Grace Fox. 1962. *Moving Finger of Jasper*. Ridgeland: Jasper County Confederate Centennial Commission.

Rose, Willie Lee. 1964. *Rehearsal for Reconstruction: The Port Royal Experiment*. Indianapolis: Bobbs-Merrill Co.

Smith, Henry A. M. 1908. Beaufort — The Original Plan and the Earliest Settlers. *South Carolina History and General Magazine* 9:141–60.

Smith, Henry A. M. 1909. Purrysburgh. *South Carolina History and General Magazine* 10:187–229.

Todd, John R. 1935. *Prince William's Parish and Plantations*. Richmond: Garrett and Massie.

Willet, N. L. 1923. *Beaufort County, South Carolina, Its Shrines and Early History*. Beaufort: Press of Beaufort Gazette.

Willet, Nathaniel Lewis. 1923. *Beaufort County, South Carolina, Its Shrines and Early History*. Beaufort, SC: Press of Beaufort Gazette.

Woofter, Thomas Jackson. 1930. *Black Yeomanry: Life on St. Helena Island*. NY: H. Holt.

Beaufort

Town proposed 1710 (3rd town in SC); chartered 1711. New parish of St. Helena 1712. Encouragement to settlers 1716 after Yamassee war. Granting of lots from 1717; slow growth. Prosperous center for sea island planters. Library society from 1802; mostly destroyed in fire in 1868; rebuilt 1902. Occupied by Federal fleet 1861; property confiscated, some distribution among ex-slaves. Girls school est. 1868; RR to Augusta 1870s. Port Royal deepest natural harbor S. of Charleston. Onetime US naval base; US Marine base 1915. Products and industries (at various times): naval stores, indigo, rice, cotton, phosphate, truck farming, fishing, seafood processing; most recently tourists, canning factories, hunting preserves, resort developments. Pop. 1850: 879, 1880: 2,549, 1910: 2,486, 1930: 2,776, 1960: 6,298.

SC 18N: M, storekeeper; fireman on dredges, worked 6 mos. on English ship, draying, many diff. jobs, 75. B. Lady's Island (across bay). Worked 1 yr. in Savannah. — F. from NJ; M., MGF, MGM b. Lady's Island. — Ed.: till fifth grade. — Baptist; Mason. — Knows all Beaufort, liked and respected by both races. Interview very satisfactory. Some reticence on racial names, but generally cooperative. No other taboos. Not very quick with synonyms. Firmly rejected items not in his vocabulary. Somewhat weak on geography. Interview conducted in store, with many free forms observed (Negro and White). Dignified, soft-spoken, unpretentious. — /-t-/ > [-ɾ-], /-r-/ > [-ɾ-] (often, not always): Gullah infl.? /θ ð/ often [t̪ d̪]. /k g/ quite fronted (under-transcribed?). Clear [l], dark rare. /-r/ > [ə] or length); "linking" [r] only occ.; intrusive /r/ spasmodic (*swallow it*). /i/ fairly high, tense, us. undiph.; /e/ quite high, tense; /æ/ low ([a] or [aᶜⁱ] in many old forms; /u/ fronted; /o/ high, tense, somewhat fronted. /a/ low-back, often [ɒ]. /ʌ/ fronted, often high (but low allophones occur freely). Unstr. /i/ often diph. /ɜ/ high, slightly round.

SC 18A: M, cabinet maker and furniture repairman, 68. B. here. 6 mos. in Charleston, 1 yr. in Navy, 1 yr. merchant marine. Never lived elsewhere. — F., PGF b. here; PGM b. here; M. b. here; MGF, MGM b. Co. — Ed.: 2 yrs. private school in Anderson, SC, 8th grade here (of 9 provided). Little reading. — Baptist (wife and most of F.'s family Episcopalian), church member "or s'posed to be"; former member Sons of Conf. Vets, Spanish-American Vets, Beaufort Historical Society, several labor unions — Frugal, hard-working (at own pace). Family very prominent before Civil War. No animosity toward Negroes, but suspicious of Yankees (strong anti-Yankee sentiment in Beaufort). Although generally very courteous, quite temperamental with varying reactions to interview. Many anecdotes of life at sea, phosphate mines, etc. Knows nothing of inland US. — Touchy on some grammatical points, but proud of old-fashioned pronunciation. Essentially no post-vocalic constriction. /w-/ in *whip*, etc. /v/ us. bilabial [β] (inf. suggests this is due to frequent contacts with Negroes in mines, etc.). /ð/ often [d̪], /θ/ sometimes [t̪]. Would often distinguish betw. "right" form and normal form. In-gliding diphthongs.

SC 18B: M, Clerk of Court for Co.; was pilot on river, store clerk, construction worker, 62. B. here. Lived 2 yrs. in Savannah off and on, short pds. in Charleston, 6 mos. in Havana, Cuba. — F., PGF b. Charleston; PGF's F. b. England; PGF's M. b. Charleston; PGM daughter of an Irish earl who came to Baltimore 1688; M. b. Charleston; MGF b. Charleston, lineage to 1680s there, Beaufort since early 1700s; MGM from Santee-McClellanville area. Full genealogy, back to Norman period. — Ed.: h.s. here. — Episcopalian; Huguenot Soc.; SC Historical Soc., Beaufort Hist. Soc., invited to Cincinnati and St. Cecilia (Charleston). — Quick mind. Large fund of anecdotes. Knows everybody, interested in everything local. Large family; well brought up. Generous with time. More progressive than most of comm., esp. regarding race relations. A bit guarded on grammatical items, which were easily checked against his cv. forms. Definite ideas on whether something occurred locally or not. Mixed speech — seems to prefer informal speech with his many and varied cronies, but is linguistically versatile. Knows Gullah grammar "by ear". — Pitch medium, voice distinct except when tired. Normally strong stresses, increasing to extremely emphatic when on controversial subjects. /k g/ fronted, very seldom fully palatal. Generally pure vowels or in-gliding diphs. /e/ not adequately transcribed by either [e˄ɪ] or [e˄ə]. Probably [e˄ᵃ] better. Very rarely [oᵁ], us. [o· oə] types. Post-vocalic retroflection rare. [u] very fronted (us. in Beaufort). /æ/ varies from [æ] to old-fashioned [a]. /a/ us. low-back, occ. [a] in old-fashioned speech. [ɑ] sometimes alternated with [ɒ].

Port Royal Road, Beaufort Twp.

Port Royal deepest natural harbor S. of Charleston. Scots settlement 1682–83; competed with Charleston for Indian trade until wiped out by Spaniards in 1686 (Charleston did not intervene).

SC 18C!: F, housekeeper, helped take census, has taught school, done miscellaneous writing, 61. B. Beaufort, never any length of time away; "off and on" in Savannah over 8 yr. period, 4 yrs. Birmingham, AL (frequently returning), taught 2 mos. Briarfield, AL. — F, PGF, PGF's F. b. Beaufort, PGF's PGF from France, PGM of old Beaufort family; M. German, from Blackville, near Barnwell (SC 28), d. when inf. 6, little known about family, some of M.'s family in Walterboro (SC 14). — Ed.: Beaufort H.S., grad. Winthrop College, some adult ed. courses, Furman U. (Greenville). — Episcopalian, UDC, Huguenot Society of SC; "don't like meetings". — Seemed to enjoy interview: laughed at certain questions. Lives alone with gt. nephew; independent-minded (expressed great admiration for Mrs. Roosevelt, whose name is anathema among most "respectable people" in SC); reads a great deal. Fond of children; hospitable; very good sense of humor. Quite natural; doesn't care that she's considered a bit eccentric in town. Knows everybody; many anecdotes. — Offers forms, synonyms freely. Knows what's grammatically "correct", but admits use of colloq. forms. Unstr. syllables more distinct than with other infs. Frequent arguments about "correctness", but never so as to interfere with interview. Tempo variable, medium to fast. Has /hw-/, suspects didn't have it as a child, but acquired it (possibly Winthrop College, possibly for own convenience teaching school). /k g/ fronted, not as strongly palatal as in SC 18A. /-t-/ > [-ɾ-], esp. in cv. forms. Linking /r/; retroflexion very seldom, always in stressed syllables. [ɨ] often for /ɪ/ (stressed); /u/ fronted; /ju/ after /t d n/; /e o/ in-gliding; infrequent [ɒ] for [ɑ], [a] for [æ]. [ɵ] "short o" at times in unstr. syllables (prob. occurs oftener than FW recorded it). — Cultivated.

SC 18D!: Beaufort. — F, housekeeper, 85. B. Beaufort; 2 yrs. in Florida; visited Florida, Cape Cod. — F, PGF b. Beaufort, family first in Purrysburg situation (1731), came to Beaufort 1740; M. b. Beaufort, MGF b. MA (old family), MGM old family desc. from a royal surveyor-general. — Ed.: private school in Columbia. — Episcopalian, Women's Aux. and Altar Guild; former member Huguenot Soc. of SC, UDC (vehement), eligible for Colonial Dames, never joined because of expense. — Cultivated.

Hilton Head

Island once plantation, then hunting preserve. Bridge to mainland since WWII; development as expensive resort. Gullah spoken by local AfAms. Pop. 1880: 2,573, 1930: 1,474.

SC 19N: M, farmer, takes clams to Savannah every Saturday on boat, 53. B. Hilton Head. — Parents b. Hilton Head. — Willing inf., but untrustworthy about keeping appointments and giving accurate replies. — Extremely rapid tempo; extremely gesticulatory. The [æ] and [a] phonemes are represented by a single [a] phoneme in his speech.

SC 19A: Beaufort. — F, farm manager and housekeeper, 51. B. Okatie, 25–30 mi. SW. — F., PGF b. Charleston (genealogy recorded, ancestor ordained 1705, 1st rector of St. Thomas and St. Denis), PGM b. Charleston; MGF from GA to Okatie as a young man, MGM from about 10 mi. out of Beaufort (old family, most moved to Orangeburg before 1850). — Ed.: h.s. in Beaufort; Old Confederate Home College, Charleston, 3 yrs. — Episcopalian (Auxiliary), UDC. — Hard-working; sympathetic; likes children. Knows country life; talked freely about old times. Cooperative, generally alert. — Old-fashioned terms; almost always could pin a word or pronunciation down to a definite person she'd heard say it. Few folk forms in gram. items. Tempo moderate to fast; stresses strong; intonation naturally variable — wide range. Palatalization of /k g/ not as extreme as in other informants. /-t-/ often [-ɾ-]. No postvocalic retroflexion. /i u/ monophthongal; /u/ quite fronted; /e o/ in-gliding. [ɝ] in *bird*, etc. (us. some rounding). /ai au/ with positional variants, according to environment.

SC 19B: Beaufort. — M, county auditor, 70. B. Pritchardville, 30 mi. W. Has lived in Bamberg (1914–17), vacationed in Canada, visited daughter frequently in Minneapolis. — F. and M. b. Colleton Co. — Ed.: part of 10th grade, Beaufort HS. — A humorist who performs frequently for local clubs, has a great store of Gullah dialect stories. Intelligent; very good representative of middle class. — Rapid tempo and restrained volume (made transcription difficult at times).

SC 19C: Beaufort. — F, "housekeeper" (housewife, widow), former teacher, 68. B. Blountville, Hampton Co. Came to Beaufort when age 6, home plantation Belleview, Cunningham's Bluff, just beyond Whale Branch, in Mainland. Taught 7–8 yrs. in Bluffton, 7 wks. around Phila., 2 wks. in FL, 1 yr. in Aiken (SC). — F. b. Cunningham's Bluff, PGF b. Bristol, England, PGF's F. b. Scotland, PGF's M. b. Ireland, PGM, PGM's F. b. Cunningham's Bluff, PGM's M. b. Beaufort, PGM's GGM supposedly founded Eastern Star after being caught eavesdropping on Masonic meeting, her 2nd husband's F. from England (cousin of Dr. Samuel Johnson [Dictionary]) and 1st librarian of Philadelphia; M. b. Charleston, MGF, MGF's F., MGF's M. b. St. Helena Island, MGM, MGM's F., MGM's M. b. Beaufort Co. — Ed.: in Charleston. — Episcopalian; Literary Club; "Old Family" of county, knows everybody. — A little timid, doesn't offer much material for getting cv. forms (interference of niece, who thought she was helping with her answers). Cooperative; when not subject to family interruptions, direct questioning proceeded very rapidly. Quick mind. Less vehement about Northerners, New Deal, etc. than us. Beaufort citizen. — A little spelling-bound, influenced somethat by notions of correctness. Definite whether a word is or isn't part of her environment. /p t k/ aspirated initially; /dʒ-/ often retroflex; /tl- dl-/; clear [-l-]; /w-/ for *wheel*; /-r/ > /ə/ or length; occ. sandhi /r/; no intrusive /r/. Normally undiph. vowels; /e/ high and tense, occ. glide to [ɪ˅] or [ə˕]; /u/ quite forward; /ɔ o/ high; /æ/ low to moderate (high occ. before /k g ʒ/); off-glide to /ɛ ə/, occ. to /ɨ/. /ɨ/ often in stressed syllables. /a/ low-back. /au/: [ɐu] voiceless, [a·ʊ] voiced. /ai/: [ɐɪ] voiceless, [a·ɨ] voiced or final. /ɔi/, first element us. long, occ. disyllabic. /ɝ/ unretroflex.

Bluffton P.O.

Summer resort before 1860. Popular with writers and artists. Herbs, paper mill.

SC 19D!: M, rice planter, real estate broker, some work with govt. agencies, 67. B. Savannah; 2 yrs. in Atlanta after college, some travel with govt. agencies. — F. b. on Savannah R. plantation, PGF bought it in 1841, PGM Charleston family (kin to SC 11J); M., MGF, MGM b. Beaufort. — Ed.: Savannah; prep school in Sewanee, Tenn. — Episcopalian; American Legion. — Sure of himself and position of family in community; strong local roots. Slightly nervous. Quick mind; seemed to enjoy interviews. — Good example of locally rooted cultivated speech. Not a great deal of folk vocabulary. Fast; strong stresses. Unstr. vowels us. very short. Pitch range low to medium. — Cultivated.

SC 19E!: Beaufort. — F, housekeeper, widow, former teacher, 73. B. Beaufort (close friend of SC 19C). — Family long prominent in Beaufort history; collateral ancestor outstanding minister in Baptist church. — Episcopalian; literary club, interest in local history, active social life, including frequent visits to Charleston and Savannah. — Quiet, courteous; interested in old times. Health not very good; only 1 brief interview arranged, efforts to arrange others conflicted with inf.'s illness and social commitments. Offered spontaneously several forms peculiar to locality. Interested in etymologies. Somewhat dictionary-bound, notions of correctness. Speech represented cultivated of older generation. No observed archaisms in pronunciation. — Cultivated.

20. Marlboro County

Co. est. 1785. Earliest settlers Welsh Baptists (from PA) at Welsh Neck, 1736. Some Germans c. 1751; also Ulster Scots early. Quaker meetings by 1760. Early crops wheat, corn; then indigo. St. David's Parish est. 1768; dist. courts 1769. 1805–14 entire Quaker comm. left, coincident with rise of slavery and plantation culture. Baptists, Presbyterians early; Methodists later. Cotton, corn, peaches, tobacco, some timber. Pop. 1790: 10,706, 1820: 6,425, 1850: 10,789, 1880: 20,598, 1910: 31,189, 1930: 31,634, 1960: 28,529.

Gregg, Alexander. 1867. *History of the Old Cheraus.* NY. Repr. 1905 (Columbia: University of South Carolina Press).

Hudson, Joshua Hilary. 1903. *Sketches and Reminiscences.* Columbia: University of South Carolina Press.

McColl, Duncan Donald. 1916. *Sketches of Old Marlboro.* Columbia: State Co.

Thomas, J. A. W. 1897. *A History of Marlboro County. . . .* Atlanta: Foote and Davies.

1946. Marlboro County: A Story of Consistent Development for More Than Two Hundred Years. *South Carolina Magazine* 9.5:8.

Lower Brownsville, Brownsville Twp.

Old community, from 1730s.

SC 20A: M, farmer (one year as carpenter), 80. B. here. — F. b. this end of co., PGF b. VA, PGM from Brownsville; M., MGF b. here, MGM b. across the line in "old Marion Co.". — Ed.: neighborhood school, 2–3 mos. in a winter. — Methodist; did belong to Farmers' Alliance. — Serious-minded, solitary. Has lived almost as a recluse for years. Knowledge of local life good; cooperative. — Mid-range voice, near monotone; drawl; overlong stressed vowels; tempo moderate to slow. Nasality. Simplification of final clusters. Slurred utterance. /r/ often velarized (esp. prevocalic). Intervoc. /k/ sometimes spirantized; /hw-/; some vocalization of postvocalic /l/; a few dark positional /-l/'s; some postvocalic constriction (not consistent); sandhi /r/; intrusive /r/ in *swallow it.* Rising diphthongs us.; /ju/ us. after /t d n/; /-ɪʃ/ in *borrow*; /æ/ mod. high; rounded vowel in *barn, strop, rock, borrow*; /ɔ/ almost > /o/ in *storm, moth*; /ʌ/ very high; /ɝ/ type (with and without const.) in *thirty, cur, girl*; /ai/ often with low-back beginning.

Wesley, Clio P.O., Red Bluff Twp.

Wesley/Clio area basically settled by Scottish Highlanders in the 18th cent. (possibly spillover from NC); displaced English and other groups.

SC 20B: M, farmer, surveyor, "newsbutched on RR", has run mill, sawmill, gin; has invented several gadgets (no patents); made brick, 76. B. across the road, 2 yrs. in Clinton, NC. — F, PGF b. 1/2 mi. above, PGF's F. came from Scotland to Wilmington, hence Scotland Co., NC, PGM b. Scotland Co., NC; M., MGF b. neighborhood, MGM b. Hamlet, NC. — Ed.: local schools. — Presbyterian; Farm Bureau, Mason. — Big, good-natured "Highlander type"; used to move PGF's anvil around unaided. Enjoyed interviews; good mind. Tended to get a little sleepy toward end of session. — Overlong stressed vowels. Drawl. Low pitch. Natural use of local idiom (/a/ in *wheelbarrow*). No nasality. Some slurring of utterance; simplification of final consonant clusters, weak articulation of final consonants. Constriction medium to strong; /hw-/; no dark /l/; postvocalic /-l/ sometimes vocalized; no intrusive /r/. /i u ɔ o e/ us. up-gliding diph. (/e i u/ sometimes monophth.). [ʋ] in *vomit, college, borrow, swallow.* /ʌ/ very high; /u/ fronted; /ju/ in *new, tube.* "Long" and "short" /ai/ with "long" form practically monophth. /au/ varies in beginning from [a] to [æ].

Blenheim

Pre-Rev. settlement here, battle. Swamp areas. Present town founded c. 1830; summer village for planters. Trading center; several churches, Presbyterian church from beginning.

SC 20C: M. farmer, 72. B. Brownsville. — F, PGF, PGF's F, PGF's PGF b. Co., of Welsh descent; PGM from established local family, of Scottish descent; M. of English descent — Ed.: local schools, 2 yrs. Clemson College (in first class to enroll). — Methodist; Farmers Federation, no politics. — Quick-minded, good sense of humor, keen observer. Intimate knowledge of local culture, knows and is known by everyone in three cos., talked freely and was very interested in interviews. Sure of self and position in comm.; no hesitation about using folk forms. Some familiarity with speech of other areas; knows what is local and what isn't. — Moderately rapid tempo, slight nasality, strong stress. Slurring, simplification of final consonant clusters. Some postvocalic constriction, velarization of prevocalic /r/; /hw-/; some vocalization of postvocalic /-l/; some postvocalic dark /-l/; /ʃr-/ > /ṣr-/. /ɜ/ as [ɜ-] (both with and without constriction). Both up-gliding and in-gliding /æ/ diphthongs, contrasting phonemically; rounded vowel in *pot* (not in other words of type, though); very high /ʌ/; /ju/; /ai/ generally long; [æo] often. — Pp. 45–104 conducted in presence of (and with some assistance from) SC20C*.

SC 20C*: F. Two older sisters of SC20C. — Same general speech type, but slightly more cultivated; a little more education, and a little less contact with folk mores. Taboo reaction on p. 65. — Responses only marked as AUX when different from brother's.

Bennetsville, Bennett Twp.

Bennetsville part of Welsh Neck settlement in 1730s; also Scots among early settlers. Baptist church 1820; Methodists 1834; Presbyterians 1852. Courthouse site 1820. Partly burned in 1865. One of wealthiest agricultural counties: cotton, corn, yarn, tire fabric, oil mill, veg. cannery, fertilizer, lumber. Pop. 1880: 343, 1910: 2,646, 1930: 3,667, 1960: 6,963.

SC 20D!: M, farmer, fertilizer merchant, 53. B. Blenheim, Red Hill Twp., 1 yr. Charlotte, 2–3 yrs. Columbia, returned to Co. age 20. — F., PGF, PGF's F. b. Bennetsville, PGM b. upper part of Co.; M., MGF b. near Blenheim (MGF Mexican and Conf. War vet), MGM b. Bennetsville. — Ed.: 1 yr. U. of SC. — Baptist Church; Rotary Club, Farm Bureau, Mason-1st degree for 34 yrs. — Well-to-do, somewhat eccentric. Widely read, interested in a tremendous variety of subjects. Aware of cultural differences within SC, and between US and rest of world. Enjoys talking; somewhat restless, tended to get tangential (very good for cv. forms, not too good for progress of interview). Interested in interviews. Good observer. Family well rooted in community. — Completely natural, has made no effort to modify his speech according to patterns elsewhere. Quick speech, "look here" an interjectory mannerism. Strong stresses; unstr. vowels very short. Utterance moderately clear. Knows what's local and what isn't. Final cons. somewhat weakly articulated; simplification of final clusters. /hw-/; /ʃr-/. No postvocalic constriction, linking /r/ or intrusive /r/. Few ingliding diphthongs and monophthongs; generally up-gliding. Final /ə/ in *wheeelbarrow*, etc. Rising off-glide of /æ/; /a/ generally low-back, but [ɒ] in *rock, crop, borrow*. Up-gliding /ɔ/. /ʌ/ very high; /ju/ commoner than /ɪu/. — Cultivated.

21. Chesterfield County

Formed 1798. City of Cheraw laid out 1766; head of navigation on Pee Dee. 1770 St. David's Church est. at Cheraw Hill; 1776 Cheraw courthouse. St. David's (philanthropic) Society est. 1777. Cheraw now a mfg. center. Sand Hills Development Project in Co.: reforestation, game preserve. Cotton, corn, tobacco, some timber. Pop. 1800: 5,216, 1820: 6,645, 1850: 10,770, 1880: 16,345, 1910: 26,301, 1930: 34,334, 1960: 33,717.

Gregg, Alexander. 1867. *History of the Old Cheraus.* NY. Repr. 1905 (Columbia: University of South Carolina Press).

Teal, Isom, et al. 1922. *Chesterfield County: Economic and Social.* Columbia: University of South Carolina Press.

1946. Chesterfield County on US Highway 1. *South Carolina Magazine* 9.1:30.

Black Creek and Green Hill School (Darlington County), Hartsville P.O., Alligator Twp.

SE part of Co. Relatively isolated; small farming, sawmills.

SC 21A: F, farmer, 70. B. here. — F. of Scotch descent; M. b. 5 mi. N., MGF b. Chesterfield Co., MGF's F. of Scotch descent, MGM b. 4 1/2 mi. NE of here (perhaps of Scotch descent). — Ed.: Sunday school. — Baptist. — Very intelligent; no knowledge of outside world. Owns small property. Leads good life, although she was thrown out of church for sins of youth. Honest, cooperative. — Tempo slowish; some prolonging.

Chesterfield P.O., Court House Twp.

Chesterfield settled by Welsh Baptists from DE and Scotch-Irish and English from other states. Good cotton crop: matures too late for boll weevil. Pop. 1910: 618, 1930: 1,090, 1960: 1,532.

SC 21B: F, housewife, 56. B. here. — F., M. and their parents b. here. — Ed.: here till 18. — Baptist. — Quiet, obliging, cooperative; impressed by education, but honest. — One of few people who speak as well as she does. Tempo moderate. Fairly clear utterance. Vowels somewhat prolonged. /o/ difficult to transcribe, narrow diphthong with beginning neither very open nor very central; various transcriptions: [oʌʊ oʌʊ oˢʊ oˁʊ oˢʊ oʊ ʊʊ].

22. Kershaw County

Formed 1791 from Lancaster Co. Earliest settlers Ulster Scots, 1733–50. Irish Quakers 1750. Cotton introduced 1790s; AfAm pop. more than quadrupled in 30 yrs.; AfAm majority to 1930. Textiles; some timber; tourist area. Peaches, pecans, sweet potatoes. Pop. 1800: 7,344, 1820: 12,432, 1850: 14,473, 1880: 21,538, 1910: 27,094, 1930: 32,070, 1960: 33,585.

Ames, Joseph S. 1910. Cantey Family. *South Carolina History and General Magazine* 11:213–258.

Boykin, Edward M. 1876. *A History of the Boykin Family.* Camden: Colin Macrae

Chesnut, Mary Boykin Miller. 1949. *A Diary from Dixie.* Ed. by Ben Ames Williams. Boston: Houghton, Mifflin.

Ernst, Joseph A., and H. Roy Murrens. 1973. "Camden's Turrets Pierce the Skies!": The Urban Process in the Southern Colonies during the Eighteenth Century. *William and Mary Quarterly* 30.4:549–74.

Hull, Edward Boltwood. 1918. *Guide-Book to Camden. . . .* Camden: E. B. Hull.

Inabinet, Glen L., and Joan A. Inabinet. 1976. *Kershaw County Legacy.* Camden: Kershaw County Bicentennial Commission.

Kirkland, Thomas J. 1905–26. *Historic Camden*. 2 vols. Columbia: State Co.

Lewis, Kenneth E. 1976. *Camden: A Frontier Town in Eighteenth Century South Carolina*. Columbia: Universty of South Carolina Institute of Archaeology and Anthropology.

McCormick, Jo Anne. 1975. *The Camden Back Country Judicial Precinct, 1764–90*. University of South Carolina Master's thesis.

Montgomery, Rachel. 1971. *Camden Heritage: Yesterday and Today*. Camden.

Schultz, Judith Jane. 1972. *The Rise and Decline of Camden as South Carolina's Major Inland Trading Center, 1751–1829. . . .* University of South Carolina Master's thesis.

Wittkowsky, George H., and J. L. Mosely, Jr. 1923. *Kershaw County, Economic and Social*. Columbia: University of South Carolina Press.

Camden, De Kalb Twp.

1st landowner 1733; earliest settlers English (1733–34) along Wateree. 1750–51, Irish Quakers at Friends Neck. Next came Presbyterians (congregation by 1788). Early settlers largely from British Isles, a few Germans and Huguenots. Town renamed Camden 1768; inc. 1791; inc. as a city 1890. 14 Revolutionary battles in neighborhood; large estates after Rev. Several fires; devastated 1865 by Fed. troops. Winter resort since at least 1880. Cotton festival in Sept. Flour milling by 1760. Pottery and porcelain mfg. in 18th cent. Textiles, cottonseed oil, iron and brass foundry, veneer; gold mining at one time. Pop. 1850: 1,133, 1880: 1,780, 1910: 3,569, 1930: 5,183, 1960: 6,842.

SC 22N: F, domestic at home, has worked out for others, 65. — F., M. b. here. — Not a very satisfactory subject; judgment not clear enough, and too slow. — Has certain speech habits which throw light on African or Indian sounds (is she part Indian?). Strong aspiration of [sp- st-] etc. interesting when compared with NC 29A of Robeson Co.

SC 22A: Boykin, De Kalb Twp. — M, liquor dealer, has farmed, 62. B. Boykin. — F., PGF, PGF's F. b. Boykin, PGF's M. b. Hopkins, Richland Co., PGM b. Hopkins; M., MGF, MGF's F., MGF's M., MGM b. Camden, MGM's F., MGM's M. came direct from Scotland. Family history written up; inf. has ms. copy. — Ed.: local schools, Camden HS. — Episcopalian; many friends, native and foreign. — Very cooperative. Knows community; family has been associated with county 150 yrs. A little slow at times, but mind alert. — Over-stressing of stressed syllables; relaxation and shortening of unstr. syllables (in conversation as well as in direct responses). Intonation highly variable. Very fast speech; monotonous sing-song. /hw-/; /sr-/. In-gliding /e o/ us.; in-gliding /ɔ/. "Short" and "long" forms of /ai/; /au/ us. as [æo] except [aᶜˑo] before /-l/. No retroflexion.

SC 22B: F, housewife, 65. B. 7 mi. below Camden; when age 7 stayed in city and went to school. — F., M. and their parents b. here. — Ed.: till 17. — Presbyterian. — A rather cultivated woman; old-fashioned rural type. Refused to continue record, pleading illness, but prob. felt self-conscious about her speech because of her sister's remarks (FW feels record as made is

accurate and honest). — Very delicate speech with a slight drawl, but vowels tend to be short.

SC 22C!: M, cotton planter, manager steeplechase race course, taught school 12 yrs. (here, Mullins, Summerville, Charleston), 74. B. Camden, 11 yrs. Charleston (1889–93, 1898–1905), 2 yrs. Warrenton, VA (1895–96), short visits elsewhere (1 winter Summerville, 1 winter Mullins). — F., PGF, PGF's F. b. Camden, PGF's M. lived Camden, PGM b. Clarendon Co. ("old sand hills community where all those politicians used to come from"), PGM's F., PGM's M. sandhillers; M. b. Camden, MGF, MGF's F. b. Charleston, MGF's M. b. lower Santee (near McClellanville), MGM b. Camden, MGM's F., MGM's M. both lived here (one born in Scotland), MGM's M.'s F. from Camden (surgeon in Continental Army); genealogy published in SC Hist. Soc. Mag.; had pre-Rev. mill at Camden, made flour for interior traffic. — Ed.: local schools (Camden, country), the Citadel (class of 1893). — Episcopalian, no clubs or public office. — Likable, courteous, hospitable; enjoyed interviews. Steeped in local history and traditions; knows everybody in Co. and all about them. No inhibitions. — Few notions of "correctness". Knows folk vocab. and folk pronun. of community. Low-country intonation (wide range); strong stresses. No marked nasality. Low-pitched voice. Some tendency to simplify final clusters. Intervocalic /k/ occ. spirantized; /dl-/ in *glass*; /sr-/ in *shrimp, shrink*; /hw-/; clear /-l-/ between front vowels; very little postvoc. retroflexion (only in *word*); no restored sandhi /r/; no intrusive /r/. Both in-gliding and up-gliding /i/; in-gliding /e/; /u/ fronted; /ju/ after /t- d- n-/; in-gliding /o/, /-ə/ in *borrow, tomato*; /a/ us. low-back [-ɑ] in *borrow, tomorrow, oranges*; /ʌ/ us. fairly high, /ʊ/ high and fronted. [ɝ] in *thirty, worms*; [ɜ·] elsewhere; [ɝ] us. rounded; /ai/ with low-central to low-front beginning; short second element before voiced cons.; /ɔi/ with initial element varying from [ɵ·] to [v]. Initial element of /au/ [æ a a]; [ɨ] in unstr. sylls. of *bucket, lettuce*, etc. — Cultivated.

23. Darlington County

Formed 1785. 1st settlers Welsh via Delaware, c. 1735. Also Ulster Scots from VA and through Charleston, and Huguenots and a few German-Swiss early. Jewish settlement c. 1845; very prosperous. Misc. industries; tobacco, cotton, corn, timber. Pop. 1800: 7,631, 1820: 10,949, 1850: 16,830, 1880: 34,485, 1910: 36,027, 1930: 41,427, 1960: 52,928.

Ervin, Eliza Cowan, and Horace Fraser Rudisill. 1964. *Darlingtoniana: A History. . . .* Columbia: R.L. Bryan.

Warr, Osta Lee, et al. 1927. *Darlington County: Economic and Social*. Columbia: University of South Carolina Press.

1874. *History, Description and Resources of Darlington County. . . .* Charleston: News and Courier Job Press.

1946. Darlington County. *South Carolina Magazine* 9.5:28.

Dovesville, Doves Depot P.O., Leavenworth Twp.

Leavenworth land orig. granted 1786. Dovesville a crossroads village, part of orig. Welsh Neck settlement in 1736. Stable Baptist community.

SC 23A: M, storekeeper, retired farmer, 81. B. Dovesville, always lived within 2 mi. — F., PGF b. "Gandy section" about

5 mi. from Dovesville (small comm.), PGF's F. in Gandy section (not native), PGM from Ireland; M. b. Palmetto section, E. of Darlington, MGF from Ireland. — Ed.: about 15 mos. in all, local schools. — Baptist, ex-member Woodmen of World, has been school trustee; "lived a mighty quiet life, don't fly off the handle". — Excellent informant. Darlingtonians classified him as "a man of native intelligence, but somewhat argumentative" (FW found little evidence of latter, avoided religious and moral shibboleths). Drawl. A little slow, mind not as quick as it once was. "Ain't got faith in a doctor." "Haven't even got a dollar of insurance — never tried to accumulate any money." Monotone. Mind quickened during interview, willing informant. Religious, somewhat Puritanical (refused to be interviewed on Sunday; would not let anyone else run his store, for fear that they might sell beer). — Strong stresses, slow drawl, monotone. Simplification of final clusters. /dļ-/ in glass; /hw-/; no /-r-/; intrusive /r/ in swallow it. /i/ is monoph., occ. in-glide or up-glide. /e/ in-glide or up-glide; /u/ fronted; /ju/ in Tuesday, due, new; /o ɔ/ in-glide. /ɪ ɛ/ neutralized before nasals. /a/ low-central to low-back; [ɒ] once in barn; [ɒ] in college, John; [ʌ] often high; [ʊ] fronted; stressed [ɜ] > [ɜɪ] except before /-r- -l/, where [ɜ]; most [ɚ] > [ə]; [aʊ] us. with [æ] beginning, occ. [a] or [ɑ]; long and short forms of [aɪ], both with [aˤ] or [aˀ] beginning; unstr. [ɪ] in lettuce, sausage, unless.

Lynches River, New Market, Pond Hollow, Hartsville P.O. and Twp.

Hartsville one of most prosperous cities in state. Associated with Coker family (cf. Coker College), distinguished agriculturists and economists. Cottonseed breeding, textile mill specialties, fiber mill.

SC 23B: M, farmer, worked for airline as foreman of repair crew, 72. B. Bethune, Kershaw Co. (14 mi. NW), lived in Lynches River area 33 yrs., 18 years as migratory turpentine worker (GA and FL), 22 yrs. in present community. — F., PGF, PGM, from Chesterfield Co., also of Scotch-Irish descent. — Ed.: country school, Bethune. — Methodist. — Practical, hardworking, observant. Keen mind, grasped purpose of interviews and seemed to enjoy them. Not many long anecdotes, easy to focus on topics of conversation. Knows folk vocabulary, comparatively few taboos. Wife (from NC) has apparently tried to improve his speech, with little result; teases him about "talking fancy". — Nasality, strong stresses. Moderate drawl. Low, slightly rasping voice, little intonation range. /hw-/; /-l/ often > vowel; /-r-/ often weak; /-r/ often with strength varying; no intrusive /r/. /i/ monoph. or up-gliding; /e/ occ. up-gliding, more often monoph. or in-gliding; /u/ fronted, us. up-gliding. /ju/ in dues, new, Tuesday; /o/ very occ. up-gliding, more commonly in-gliding; /ł/ in milk; /-ə/ in unstr. sylls. in borrow, remark; /a/ low-central to low-back; [ɒ] in vomit, crop; [ɑ] in shorn; /ɜ/ as retroflex up-gliding diphthong in Thursday and furnishing; unstr. [ə ɘ ɚ]; /ai/ us. with low-front beginning. Tendency for long first member in all positions, /au/ us. as [æʊ]. [ɪ] in unstr. syllables in towel, mountain, careless.

Palmetto, Darlington P.O., Palmetto Twp.

Palmetto a rural area with rich farming; settled 1798, inc. 1835. Welsh Neck affiliates; some Huguenots. Veneer plant, cotton mill, chair factory; tobacco and cotton markets. Stock car race; tennis tournament from 1935.

SC 23C: M, farmer, served on county tax-equalization board, worked briefly for IRS as field deputy, 64. B. same farm. — F.'s family from Williamsburg settlement, came up Black River; M.'s family of German descent, among earliest settlers of Welsh Neck (Society Hill) section, and Marlboro Co. — Ed.: about fifth grade, well-read. — Presbyterian. Not much of a joiner, but interested in history and community affairs; has collected information on family tree. — Talkative, cooperative, hospitable, even-tempered. An excellent farmer, abreast of modern technology. — Extremely slow speech. Strong stresses; stressed vowels overlong, with rise-and-fall intonation. Pleasant voice, with wide range of intonation. /ʃr/ > /sr/; no /-r/, sandhi /r/; intrusive /r/ not observed. /i e ɔ o u/ monophthongal or in-gliding. /ju/ alternates with /u/ in Tuesday. /ə/ in borrow, tomato. /a/ most commonly low-central to low-back (most commonly low-central). Unrounded vowel in rock, pot, strop, borrow, wash. /ʌ/ us. high; /ʊ u/ fronted. [ɜɪ] in thirty, etc. Unstr. /ɚ/ > /ə/. "Long" and "short" forms of /ai/, both us. with low-front beginnings. [æo] common before voiced and voiceless cons., occ. [ao aw]. [ɪ] in unstr. syllables of sausage, bucket, haunted, cabbage, etc.

Auburn, Hartsville Twp.

Auburn a crossroads; woodland and farming area.

SC 23D: M, farmer, 71. B. Marlboro Co., "across the river from Cheraw". Came to Darlington Co. in 1901. — Family plantation people on Upper Pee Dee. — Ed.: info. not obtained. — Episcopalian; Darlington Hist. Soc. — Agreeable personality; interested in antiques (collected old implements, white and Indian). Little folk grammar. — Nasality, strong stresses. Very little /-r/; intervocalic /r/ occ. shortened; /hw-/; some simplification of final clusters. /i u/ monoph. or slightly up-gliding. /u/ fronted; /e o/ us. in-gliding or monoph.; /æ/ moderately low; /a/ us. low-central retracted; /ɔ/ high, in-gliding; /ʌ/ high; /æʊ/; unstr. [ɪˤ] in bucket, towel.

SC 23E!: Palmetto, Darlington P.O., Palmetto Twp. — M, farmer, 75. B. same house. Some travel, but never lived elsewhere. — House in family for 5 generations. — Ed.: info. not obtained. — Respected in community. Leader in developing new farming methods. Somewhat deaf; mind not too alert; cooperative. Unpretentious. — Not a great deal of contact with the folk vocab. Medium to slow speech; strong stresses. Definitely cultivated. No folk grammar. In-gliding or monoph. /i e ɔ o u/; /ju/ after /n-/. No /-r/; /hw-/. Low pitch. — Cultivated.

24. Sumter County

Formed 1785; Sumter District early, became "county" 1868. Earliest settlers from Charleston, New England, VA, England (practically all from other colonies). On Catawba Path between Fredericksburg on Wateree and Williamsburg. Devastation during Rev. Post-1815, settled by New Englanders, Sephardic Jews (from Portugal, Spain), Scotch, Irish. Silk culture attempted 1820s. Almost 1/2 of Co. now in forests. Air base, WWII and after. Lumber, tobacco, corn, cotton, livestock, poultry, squabs. Pop. 1790: 6,940, 1820:

25,369, 1850: 33,220, 1880: 37,037, 1910: 38,472, 1930: 45,902, 1960: 74,941.

Gregorie, Anne King. 1954. *History of Sumter County, South Carolina*. Sumter: Library Board of Sumter Co.

Nicholas, Cassie. 1975. *Historical Sketches of Sumter County*. Columbia: University of South Carolina Press.

Pauleen, Josie Platt. 1939. *The Past Flows By on the Road to Poinsett Park*. Sumter: Knight Brothus.

Ramsey, Ralph, Jr., and A. H. Green. 1922. *Sumter County, Economic and Social*. Columbia: University of South Carolina Press.

Sumter, Thomas Sebastian. 1922. *Stateburg and Its People*. Sumter.

1946. Sumter, the Gamecock County. *South Carolina Magazine* 9.4:12.

Sumter

Settled c. 1785; laid out as Sumterville 1800; inc. 1845. Grew with RRs beginning in 1840s. Large, long-established Jewish community. Morris College (AfAm). Center of lumber industry. US Air Force base here since WWII. Wood products, textiles, canning, brickyard, hogs, sweet potatoes, tree nursery; center for hunting and fishing. Pop. 1850: 1,356, 1880: 2,011, 1910: 8,169, 1930: 11,780, 1960: 23,062.

SC 24N: M, retired railway brakeman, ex-farmer (now too feeble for anything but fishing), 82. B. outside Sumter, worked 23 yrs. Atlantic Coast Line RR. — F., M. were slaves on plantation where he was born (just outside Sumter); knows nothing about family. — Ed.: practically none, local country schools. — Methodist. — Taciturn; hard to work with. Was prompted a good deal by 2 other Negroes who were barbecuing hogs while he was looking on. Generally local whites bait him to give anecdotes, etc. and laugh at him. Good memory of the past. — Genuinely old-fashioned forms. Slow tempo; some nasality. Folk grammar. Simplification of final clusters; /k- g-/ sometimes fully palatalized (as in *girl*); /hw-/; /-l/ > /-r/ > /ə/ in *walnut*; /r-/ > /-r/ > /ə/ in *apron*; /ʃr-/ > /sw-/. No postvoc. /-r/; no intrusive /r/. /i/ monoph. or in-gliding; /e/ monoph. or in-gliding; /u/ monoph. or up-gliding. /ju/ in *Tuesday*. /u/ fronted; /u o/ > /ə/ in unstr. sylls. /o/ monoph. or in-gliding; /ɪɹ/ in *borrow*; stressed /ɪ/ in *milk, sister*. /æ/ ingliding; apparently long/short forms automatically adjusted; /a/ low-central; slightly retracted [ɒ] in *strop, crop, rock, John, oxen, tomorrow, wash*. /ʌ/ slightly fronted or slightly raised. /ɜ/ us. [ɜɪ] before voiceless, [ɜˑ·] before voiced. Unstr. /ə/ > /ə/. /ai au/ us. with low-central advanced or low-front retracted beg., occ. with low-central retracted or low-back advanced (variation free rather than allophonic). [-ɪɹ] in *Georgia*.

SC 24N*: Negro friend of SC24N, visiting while preparing barbecue pit.

SC 24A: M, farmer, occ. barber, 67. B. same farm; travel to FL and CA. — As far back as he knows, all ancestors farmed in this same part of county. — Ed.: 5th grade, country school. — Baptist. — Difficult inf., a little hard of hearing and extremely suspicious. Mumbling and slurring frequently made transcription and communication difficult. — Frequently /d/ for /ð/; /t f/ for /θ/. Up-gliding back vowels.

SC 24B: M, farmer, miller (grist, saw-, syrup, wheat), cotton ginner, 84. B. Shiloh and Lynchburgh Twps., always lived there. — F. b. Lynchburg (or Shiloh) Twp.; PGGF from Ireland; M. b. Shiloh, MGF, MGM b. lower part of Co., maybe Williamsburg. — Ed.: "not much". A little at Shiloh, Lynchburg, Pleasant Grove. — Was Methodist, now Presbyterian; former Woodman of the World. — Enjoyed interviews, though physical condition varied (excellent condition pp. 7–41, poor 44–62, excellent remainder). No pretense at being what he isn't. Little reading, mainly church papers; quit Methodists over reunion with N. Methodists. — Slow speech, strong nasality, limited intonation range. Stressed vowels long, strong stress. /-t-/ occ. > [-ɾ-]; /sr-/; intervoc. /r/ often weak. /i/ us. monophth. or in-gliding; /e o ɔ/ most often in-gliding (a few up-gliding forms); /u/ fronted: /ju/ in *Tuesday, dues*, both /nju nu/. /ə/ in *tomorrow*, /-ə -ɪ/ in *borrow*; /ɪ/ in *milk, children*; /ɜ/ often retroflex; /a/ low-central to low-back; [ɒ] in *pot, rock, crop, oxen, vomit, wash*; /ʌ/ high, /bʌldʒ/ but /bulk/; /ɜ/ > /ɜɪ/, occ. with slight retroflexion, except finally, where [ɜ ɝ]; /ɜ/ in *squirrel*. /ai/ with low-front to low-central beginning (free alternation); "short" and "long" /ai/, us. with high beginning; /au/ with free-alternating beginning [æ˕] to [a˕]; unstr. [ɪ] in *bucket, rinses, sausage, Georgia, towel*; unstr. /ə/ > /ə/. Folk preterites.

Loring Mill, Stateburg P.O. and Twp.

Loring Mill a rural settlement; ex-plantation. Village of Stateburg laid out 1783. Once plantation center; proposed as state capital. Had academy in 1830s; now only a few houses and an 1850 church (some houses from 18th cent.)

SC 24C: M, retired miller, petty storekeeper (calls it a commissary), caretaker of estate relics, a little scratch farming, 65. B. neighborhood. Never lived out of Co.; hardly ever traveled out of Co. — F., M. b. in Co. (F. ran mill before him). — Ed.: attended country school till "10 or 11 or maybe 14". Took a little music, tries to play violin. — No Church affiliation. Contacts include whitest Negroes of community, a few professional people in Sumter. — "Po' buckra". Suspicious, limited intelligence, though reasonably patient. Normally uses folk-grammar forms. — Nasality, strong stresses. Rather high-pitched voice, whining, monotonous intonation. /-t-/ > /-ɾ-/; /k- g-/ often palatalized; simplification of final clusters; /sr-/; /hw-/ us., but /w-/ in one recording of *while*; clear /-l-/ between front vowels; /-l/ sometimes vocalized; /-r-/ often weak or lost. /-l/ > /-ə/ in *walnut* [wɔənət]. No /-r/. /i/ up-gliding or in-gliding, /u/ up-gliding or monophthongal, and fronted; /ɛ/ often somewhat retracted; /ju/ in *new*; /æ/ us. somewhat lowered; rounded vowel in *barn*; /a/ us. low-central; /-ə/ in *tomato*, but [ɪɹ] in *borrow*; /ʌ/ variable: [ʌ] to [ɤˑ], with extremes often occurring in successive uses of the same form; [ɪ] in *sifter, mill*; [ɜɪ] between stops and spirants or [n] and stop or spirant, [ɜ] final or before /-l -m/; /ai/ us. with low-central beginning; beginning of /au/ varies from /æ/ to [a]; unstr. [ɪ] in *bucket, towel, minute, lettuce, haunted*.

SC 24D!: Sumter. — M, lawyer, real estate dealer, 86. B. Stateburg (12 mi. W.). In Columbia, law school and practice, 1880–85; Florence, AL, 18 mos., c. 1890. — F. b. Co. Armagh, Ireland, came to SC at 20, practiced medicine in Camden, then came to Stateburg, set up as physician and married a planter's daughter; M., MGF of plantation comm. at Stateburg. — Ed.:

prep school, Atlanta, GA; law school, U. of SC; well-read in tradition of "Southern gentleman". — Well known in community. Episcopalian (vestry of Sumter and Stateburg Churches; has been on diocesan commissions); knows all prominent people in state. — "Autocrat of the breakfast table" (according to his daughter). Positive in his opinions; dogmatic. Hard to keep on subject; launches into long digressions with or without provocation. Not sure of purpose of interviews; caste-conscious; garrulous. Typical Southern Bourbon: hospitable; likes his liquor; violently anti-Roosevelt (but not anti-Russian). Keeps notebook of anecdotes, many of them salacious. — No affectations in speech; no effort to guard his grammar. Rapid speech; loud, forceful; strong stresses. /-t-/ sometimes [-ɾ-]; /k- g-/ sometimes palatal; /hw-/; [-ɬ-] in *skillet*. In-gliding /e o ɔ/; us. in-gliding /i/; /u/ in *news*; /u/ us. up-gliding, fronted; /a/ low-central to low-back; /ɒ/ *pot, oxen, crop, John*; /ʌ/ high; /ʊ/ slightly fronted. /au/ begins [æ] to [a]; /ai/ begins [aˑ] to [a]. — Cultivated.

25. Richland County

Part of "Dutch Fork", with Lexington and Newberry. 1st settlements c. 1744 all Germans, some English by 1749. First Swiss Reformed, then Lutherans; Lutheran churches from 18th cent. Settlers known for industry and hospitality. Many Loyalists. Richland Co. formed 1785. Fort and trading post here 1718–22, 1748–62. Many Germans; some settlers from coast, most from VA and NC. Stock raising, indigo pre-Rev.; AfAm majority by 1800, with spread of cotton, etc. Baptists, German Reformed, Lutherans, Anglicans early. Cotton, corn, dairy products, poultry, livestock. Pop. 1790: 3,390, 1820: 12,321, 1850: 20,243, 1880: 28,573, 1910: 55,143, 1930: 87,667, 1960: 200,102.

English, Elizabeth D., and E. M. Clark. 1923. *Richland County, Economic and Social.* Columbia: University of South Carolina Press.

Graydon, Nell S. 1964. *Tales of Columbia.* Columbia: R. L. Bryan Co.

Green, Edwin L. 1916. *History of the University of South Carolina.* Columbia: University of South Carolina Press.

Green, Edwin Luther. 1932. *A History of Richland County.* Columbia: R. L. Bryan Co.

Hennig, Helen Kohn, ed. 1936. *Columbia: Capital City of South Carolina, 1786–1931.* Columbia: R. L. Bryan. Repr. with mid-century supplement by Charles E. Lee, 1966 (Columbia: University of South Carolina Press).

Hollis, Daniel W. 1956. *The University of South Carolina.* Columbia: University of South Carolina Press.

Latimer, S. C. 1970. *The Story of* The State, *1891–1969, and the Gonzales Brothers.* Columbia: State Printing Co.

LeConte, Emma. 1957. *When the World Ended.* Diary, ed. by Earl Schenck Miers. NY: Oxford University Press.

McIlwaine, Richard. 1908. *Memories of Three Score Years and Ten.* NY: Neale Publishing Co.

Montgomery, John. 1979. *Illustrated History of the City of Columbia.* Columbia: Windsor Publications.

Salley, A. S., Jr., ed. 1919. *Minutes of the Vestry of St. Helena's Parish, South Carolina, 1726–1812.* Columbia: Historical Commission of South Carolina.

Scott, Edwin J. 1884. *Random Recollections of a Long Life, 1806 to 1876.* Columbia: C. A. Calvo, Jr., Printer.

Selby, Julian A. 1905. *Memorabilia and Anecdotal Reminiscences of Columbia, South Carolina. . . .* Columbia: R. L. Bryan Co.

Simons, Jane Kealhofer, and Margaret Babcock Meriwether. 1943. *A Guide to Columbia. . . .* Rev. ed. Columbia: Chamber of Commerce.

Williams, James Franklin. 1929. *Old and New Columbia.* Columbia: Epworth Orphanage Press.

1946. Richland County and Columbia. *South Carolina Magazine* 9.1:21.

SC 25A: Lykesland. — F, housewife, 78. B. 11 mi. out of Columbia on Old Camden Rd. — F., PGF, PGM b. Cooks Mount, SC (Irish Prot. descent); M., MGF, MGM b. here (Scotch descent). — Ed.: limited, local; chiefly in Sunday school. — Baptist. — Sat puffing away at her pipe, enjoying the questionnaire from beginning to end. Composed, companionable; a sparkle of Irish wit. — Not at all guarded about her speech; speech is quaintly antique and vulgar. Slow speech; long vowels. Nasal in vicinity of nasal consonants. She uses [ɜɪ] and no postvocalic /r/, but many speakers in her community use [ɜ˞] or [ɚ] and postvocalic [rˑ] or [r˞].

White Rock, Fork Twp.

White Rock at edge of "Dutch Fork"; farming. Fishing, water sports, summer resort.

SC 25B: M, farmer, storekeeper, sawmiller (own steam thresher 15 yrs.), 77. B. 1 1/2 mi. NE. — F. b. Anderson Co, moved to comm. at 7, PGF b. here, moved to Anderson Co. but returned, PGF's F. b. locally, son of N. Ireland immigrant, PGM b. 2 mi. down the road, PGM's F., PGM's M. could read and speak German; M, MGF b. locally, MGF's parents or grandparents came from Holland, MGM a sister of PGM. — Ed.: old field school c. 2 yrs.; 3 mos. in senior prep. at Newberry College. — Lutheran; Knights of Pythias. — Big man; still physically vigorous. Keeps good care of fences, farm machinery, farm animals. Adheres to local philosophy of making money by not wasting money. Enjoys talking. Plenty of curiosity. Fair amount of reading. Knows all the old families of the Fork, and is kin to most of them. Appreciated interviews as means of preserving lore about old times. Sure of his position. A good many anecdotes, though generally told with a fairly heavy hand. Independent. A great many interests; respect for learning and scholarship. — No inclination to use anything but local forms, though recognizes differences between local speech and that of other areas. A number of German-derived forms. Many folk grammatical forms. Some drawl and nasality. Tempo slightly on slow side. Voice of basically low pitch, but fairly wide intonation range. Varying constriction of postvocalic /r/. Simplification of final clusters; /sr-/; /hw-/. Both in-gliding and up-gliding diphthongs. Slurred utterance.

Columbia P.O. and Twp.

Settlement in 18th cent; many Germans, Irish among early settlers. Chosen as state capital 1786; head of navigation on Congaree; wide streets to prevent spread of epidemics. Inc. 1805. University chartered, as SC College, 1801; named U. of SC (as at present) 1905. USC oldest educational institution entirely supported by state funds; no endowment till after WWII. By 1802, a market for upcountry produce. Trinity

Church built 1840. Early industries: textiles, cotton market, cattle market. Several other colleges org. in 19th and early 20th cent. Public schools organized 1880. Santee Canal 1820 (Irish-Catholic laborers settled to work on canal); RR to Charleston 1842. Active cultural life by 1865. Ft. Jackson, WWI, important permanent base. Pop. doubled 1910–30; growth, with suburban spread, since WWII; many federal agencies have regional HQ here. Pop. 1880: 10,036, 1930: 51,581, 1960: 97,433.

SC 25C!: F, advertising artist, 30. B. Columbia; 1 yr. in Chicago. — F., PGF, PGM b. Abbeville, SC; M. b. Flat Rock, NC, Charleston (Mt. Pleasant) family, moved to Columbia when 13 or 14, some of M.'s relatives in NJ. — Ed.: Columbia, USC; 6 wks. art in NY (father is Dean of Arts and Sciences at USC). — Episcopalian; AΔπ sorority ("I cannot abide organizations"). — Alive; quick mind. Interested in interviews. Completely natural; assurance of social position. Excellent observer. Keen sense of humor. — Good example of younger generation cultivated city speech. Did not know much of rural vocab.; refused to accept suggestions that were not absolutely familiar to her. Accurate definitions of familiar items. Rapid, clipped speech. Musical, smooth, pleasant voice; pitch fairly low. Wide intonation range; strong stresses. Vowels largely of low-country type. Clear utterance. — Cultivated.

26. Calhoun County

Formed 1908 from Orangeburg Co. Lutheran (German) settlement in 1730s. Subsistence farming till 1787. Indigo culture profitable till 1840s. Pecans, cotton, asparagus, cattle, hogs. Pop. 1910: 16,634, 1930: 16,707, 1960: 12,256.

1946. Calhoun County: Home of Gentlemen Farmers and Gentlemen Jockeys. *South Carolina Magazine* 9.12:8–.

SC 26A: Creston, Lyons Twp. — M, farmer, 72. B. 1 mi. away; rarely away, 60 days in McClellanville, a few days travel on business. — F., PGF, PGF's F. local-born; M., MGF, MGM b. locally; family lines intermarried. — Ed.: in local schools. — Methodist, formerly Lutheran; Woodmen of the World, used to be Knight of Pythias, sixteen years as Co. commissioner. — Well-rooted in community and interested in local affairs; likes to attend livestock sales, political rallies, camp meetings. Talkative, acquainted with most people in Co., well-known for being easy-going and not overly interested in working. Uses local folk-type idiom naturally, wouldn't think of talking any other way, even if he could; easily recognizes "foreign" words. No observable taboo reactions. — Strong stresses, pitch slightly below middle register for male speakers. Tempo very variable (very rapid when on a subject about which he is enthusiastic). Some final consonants weakly articulated, a number of unreleased final stops. Postvocalic /l/ sometimes lost; no observed constriction of postvocalic /r/. Voiceless stops in initial position unaspirated or very weakly aspirated (aspiration seems to be much weaker in low country than in upcountry). Short unstr. vowels; /e ɔ o/ in-gliding. Centered beginning of /ai au/ before voiceless stops.

St. Matthews P.O. and Twp.

Settled by Palatine Germans and Swiss 1730–40. Dominated by cotton warehouses; once center for sea island cotton. Long and short staple cotton (including a weevil resistant type), pecans, cattle, hogs, truck, pulp mills, hunting and fishing. Pop. 1910: 1,377, 1930: 1,750, 1960: 2,433.

SC 26B!: M, farmer, 55. B. here, some travel and military service WWI. — [Data on family history not obtained formally.] F. and M. both from "old Orangeburg Co." (from which Calhoun had recently cut off). Family identified with St. Matthews area since early 18th cent. (one of old German-Swiss families), when Amelia Twp. established. — Ed.: local schools; Wofford College, Spartanburg, SC. — Methodist; Masons. — Prosperous farmer; good manager. Very intelligent; well-read; full of curiosity. Enjoyed afternoon of interviewing, regretted that business made it impossible to complete sessions. Good observer. — Slow speech; very long stressed vowels. Uses folk and standard grammatical forms, apparently shifting according to feeling for context. Natural. Very little nasality. Strong stresses. Wide intonation range. Simplification of final clusters. /sr-/ in *shrunk*; /hw-/; dark [ɫ] rare, if ever; /-l/ occ. vocalized; no intrusive /r/. In-gliding /i e ɔ o u/; /ju/ in *new*, etc.; /u/ fronted; [ɨ] occ. for /ɪ/; /a/ us. low-central. Rounded [ɒ] in *pot*, etc.; /ʌ/ us. very high. No constriction in *father, thirty, barn.* "Short" and "long" forms of /ai/, us. beginning [a]; /au/ beginning varies from [æ̠] to [a̠]. — Cultivated.

27. Orangeburg County

Formed 1785. 1st settlement Lyons Creek as early as 1704. Swiss, German, and Dutch settlers at Edisto by 1735; Scots by 1745; Acadians by 1755; also some Barbadians, Huguenots, Quakers. Some Lutheran ministers became Anglicans. Orangeburg on site of an 18th cent. German village. Small farmers (Swiss) in S. part, and cattle ranges, larger farms with slaves in W. part. 2 AfAm colleges in co. seat of Orangeburg. One of leading agricultural cos. in the South. Pop. 1790: 18,513, 1820: 15,653, 1850: 23,582, 1880: 41,395, 1910: 55,893, 1930: 63,864, 1960: 68,559.

Green, James McKibben, Jr., and William Fletcher Fairey, Jr. 1923. *Orangeburg County: Economic and Social.* Columbia: University of South Carolina Press.

Ristow, Walter William. 1937. *Geographic Studies in Orangeburg County, South Carolina.* Clark University dissertation.

Salley, Alexander Samuel, Jr. 1898. *The History of Orangeburg County, South Carolina, from Its First Settlement to the Close of the Revolutionary War.* Orangeburg: R. L. Berry.

1947. Orangeburg County: Agricultural, Industrial, and Historical. *South Carolina Magazine* 10.2:14–16.

1969–. *The Orangeburg Historical and Genealogical Record.* Orangeburg: Orangeburg Historical and Genealogical Society.

SC 27A: Cordova. — M, farmer, carpenter, 71. B. Co. — F. b. Pine Hill section, PGF, PGM b. Co.; M. b. Pine Hill section, MGF, MGM b. Lexington Co. — Ed.: Middle Willow, 9th grade. — Wesley Grove Methodist. — Authentic rural inf., unpretentious and cooperative. — Nasality noticeable. /d/ for /ð/ often in rapid conversation.

SC 27B: Livingston, North P.O. (crossroads), Hebron Twp. — M, farmer, 75. B. 1/2 mi. NW; some travel within state. — F.

(country doctor), PGF b. in community, PGF's F. one of earliest settlers, PGM from "Forks section" of Orangeburg Co.; M. b. 4–5 mi. away, MGF owned property in NW part of Co., MGM b. Springfield section, W. part of Co. "I'm livin' on land that was taken up by [my ancestors] from George II of England." — Ed.: local one-teacher schools, Beaver Creek, Hebron Church. — Methodist; has been Knight of Pythias, Woodman of the World. — Natural, cooperative, good sense of humor; laughed at himself several times for using euphemisms. Hard-working, religious, knows locality intimately. Quick mind; enjoys talking. Sure of position: a prosperous farmer. Knows local folklore. Strong family pride. — Fast speech, generally in lower range and somewhat monotonous. A little hoarse. Strong stresses; very short unstr. vowels. No postvocalic constriction. In-gliding diphthongs; /ai au/ occ. with centered beginning.

28. Barnwell County

Formed 1785. Many Germans settled area from 1740. US Atomic Energy Installation (along Savannah R.) from late 1940s. Asparagus, melons, cucumbers, cotton, lumber, naval stores. Pop. 1800: 7,376, 1820: 14,750, 1850: 26,608, 1880: 39,857, 1910: 34,209, 1930: 21,221, 1960: 17,659.

Lesesne, Henry. 1947. A Model Mill Community 102 Years Later. *South Carolina Magazine* 10.9:6–.

Workman, William D. 1963. *The Bishop from Barnwell.* Columbia: R. L. Bryan Co.

1946. Barnwell County: Prosperous and Debt-Free — Farms, Frolics, Fabricates. *South Carolina Magazine* 9.8:8–.

SC 28A: Patterson Mill, Martin P.O., Bennett Springs Twp. — F, housewife, 78. B. 15–20 mi. S. (now Allendale Co.); moved to neighborhood as a girl, never lived anywhere else (one mo. 3 mi. away). — F. "Irish"; M. b. in comm., died at Milletville, MGF b. in locality, never left. — Ed.: country schools, "no grades". — Baptist. — Forceful, intelligent character. Was the real head of the household even when her father was living. He was a great story-teller and prevaricator, known all over the co. as "lying Bill"; according to the folk *mythos*, she had to go out to the lot to help him call the hogs: they wouldn't believe him. Hardworking; good manager. Not much cultural contact, but knows details of operating farm. Knows everybody in comm. and all their kindred. Talks freely. Little experience outside her immediate comm. — Many cv. forms. No pretensions; knows children and grandchildren try to "correct" her speech, but generally sticks to folk gram. forms. Fast, high-pitched speech. Slight nasality. Very short unstr. vowels. Stressed vowels relatively long. Slurred utterance. Many unreleased final stops. In-gliding /e o ɔ/.

SC 28B: Meyers Mill, Bennett Springs Twp. — M, storekeeper, has been governor's constable, game warden, magistrate, magistrate's constable, first tax collector of Co., 34. B. in Millettville section of Co. (now Allendale Co.); never lived outside of area. — F. b. Estill (now Hampton Co.), PGF b. Irvington, Estill neighborhood, PGF's F. and PGM from Scotland; M., MGF b. MGM's F. and M. b. Millettville. — Ed.: local schools, Millettville and Meyers Mill; Dunbarton HS. — Methodist, no lodges. — Knows everyone in community, including leaders, and most state political figures as

well. Rooted in folkways of comm., knows what is genuinely local. Quick-minded but not at all bookish. Recognizes a "foreign" word when he hears it. — Some nasality, strong stresses. Quick speech — staccato quality. Generally clear articulation. Final cons. weakly articulated; final clusters simplified. /hw-/; postvoc. /l/ often dark, sometimes lost. No postvocalic constriction, sandhi /r/ or intrusive /r/. In-gliding /i e ɔ o u/, occ. up-gliding /ɔ/; /u/ fronted, /ju/ after /t- d- n-/. Some neutralization of /ɪ/ and /ɛ/ before nasals. /æ/ us. medium or low, some up-glide. /a/ low-central to low-back; /a/ in *orange, watch, tomorrow, laundry.* /ʊ/ in *bulge*, somewhat high. /ʌ/ very high; /ɜ/ as [ɜɪ] in *worm, girl, thirty.* "Long" and "short" alternates of /ai/.

SC 28C: Hattieville, Meyers Mill P.O., Bennett Springs Twp. — M, farmer, former surveyor, 44. B. outside Ellenton, SC. — F., PGF, PGF's F b. 4 mi. E. of Ellenton; PGM b. locally; M. from Ellenton; MGM's M. from Black Island. — Ed.: Bailey Military Academy, Greenwood, SC. — Christian Church ("Campbellite"); Masons. Was councilman at Ellenton for a time. — "Laziest man in Co.", according to wife, but a capable plantation manager. Acknowledged leader of community, well liked by AfAms and whites. Well thought of in Co. seat, often sits on co.-wide improvement committees. Generous and hospitable; wide range of anecdotes, keen sense of humor (especially if joke is on himself). Knows everyone in "river section" of Barnwell, Aiken, and Allendale Cos., and is kin to most of them. Good observer, excellent memory, enjoyed interviews. Unaffected, sure of position in comm., so why pretend? Quick-minded, aware that local speech is different from elsewhere, but makes no effort to change. — Fast speech, slightly slurred utterance. Stressed vowels long, unstr. vowels very short. Final consonants often weakly articulated. /hw-/; no postvoc. constriction of /r/; rare sandhi /r/; no intrusive /r/; postvoc. /l/ generally "dark", sometimes vocalized. /ɔ/ occ. up-gliding, but normally in-gliding, as with /i e o u/; [ɪu] rather than /ju/ in *new*, etc. /ʌ/ very high; /ɪ ɛ/ neutralized before nasals. [ɑ] unrounded in *pot*, etc. /ai/ has "long" and "short" forms: former us. monophth. with short centering off-glide. /ɜ/ = [ɜɪ ɜ·], the latter before voiced cons.

Barnwell

Center of mid-country plantation culture. Burnt by Sherman 1864–65. At one time, many distinguished figures in state political life from Co. Pop. 1880: 648, 1910: 1,324, 1930: 1,834, 1960: 4,568.

SC 28D: F, secretary (to powerful state political figure), 19. B. Barnwell Co., near Elko. Never lived outside Co. — F., PGF, PGM b. Williston; M. b. near Elko, MGF, MGM always lived in same comm. — Baptist. Has many acquaintances among Co. political figures. — Intelligent, quick mind. Good knowledge of local culture, especially allowing for age and occupation. Knows difference between her speech and that of older generation. Natural speech, unaffected, pleasant to listen to. — Slight nasality, wide intonation range. Slurring; fast speech but slight drawl flavor from prolongation of stressed vowels. Weak articulation of final consonants; final cons. clusters simplified. Intervocalic /r/ sometimes weak. No sandhi /r/ or intrusive /r/. /hw-/; many postvocalic dark /l/s; very little postvocalic constriction. Generally in-gliding diphthongs (occ. up-gliding /ɔ/). Generally unrounded vowels in words of *watch, pot, tomorrow* type. High /ʌ/; /æ/ often in-gliding. [ɜɪ] in *thirty*, etc., sometimes with slight constriction. [æo] often /au/.

29. Aiken County

Formed 1871 from several other cos. Settlement from 1735; earliest settlers English, Scots, German. Trading post at Silver Bluff, 18th cent. Beech Island once a summer refuge for rice planters. RR to Charleston 1833. Graniteville mill begun 1845; 1st company-owned mill village; compulsory school system (perhaps first in US). Part of US Atomic Energy Commission installation here. Kaolin deposits. Resort area. Agriculture: cotton, corn, fruit, truck, dairying; cotton-mill villages. Pop. 1880: 28,112, 1910: 41,849, 1930: 47,403, 1960: 81,038.

DuBose, Louise Jones. 1947. Versatile and Progressive Aiken County: A Chronological Account. *South Carolina Magazine* 10.9:8–.

Henderson, F. F. 1951. *A Short History of Aiken and Aiken County.* Columbia: University of South Carolina Press.

Mitchell, Broadus. 1928. *William Gregg. . . .* Chapel Hill: University of North Carolina Press.

Toole, Gasper Laren. 1959. *Ninety Years in Aiken County.* Charleston.

1946. Aiken County and Aiken. *South Carolina Magazine* 9.1:26.

Oakwood, Montmorenci P.O., Windsor Twp.

Montmorenci a center for asparagus since 1900. Rural comm.; local school.

SC 29A: M, farmer, 78. B. Tabernacle Church (Tabernacle Twp.), SE part of Co.; moved to Davis Bridge, 10 mi. SE (Windsor Twp.); 5 yrs. in Kitchenville section, E. part of Co., 1908–12, overseer on farm; 3 mos. in Utah for health; 1914 on in Windsor Twp. — F. b. 8 mi. below Oakwood, PGF came from NC, PGM b. Windsor section; M., MGF, MGM b. Edgefield Dist. (now Saluda Co.), family in section since early 18th cent. — Ed.: Edisto School (3 mi. from home place), 8–9 yrs.; 2–3 yrs. Smythe's Academy. — Baptist. — Famous fiddler at one time. Nervous; taboo reactions. Well known in county. Tries to adapt to modern agricultural methods, not too successfully. Enjoyed interviews. Knows local culture. Hospitable. Plain, simple, hard working. Good observer; good sense of humor, many anecdotes. Respected. Reputation for being a great tease. — Strong nasality. Some slight efforts to conceal folk-grammar, but completely unsuccessful (and gave up before very far along in interview). Speech fairly slow; strong stresses. Weak articulation of final consonants, simplification of final clusters. Constriction of postvocalic /r/; prevocalic /r/ often velarized, sometimes with lateral release. Initial /p/ often lenis, unaspirated. In-gliding /e ʊ ɔ/ us.

Graniteville, Gregg Twp.

Graniteville known for Gregg cotton mill (supported by Charleston capital); long-term success as factory example. Established compulsory education in village; long-term family employment. Pop. 1930: 2,560.

SC 29B: M, shipping clerk, cotton mill (75 yrs. with mill), 87. B. Graniteville, never lived out of Co. — F, PGF, PGM b.

Edgefield Co., moved to Graniteville 1847; M. 1st cousin of F., MGF, MGM also moved to Graniteville from Edgefield in 1847. — Ed.: local schools, age 6–10. — Methodist; Mason, Oddfellows for awhile. — Life centered around mill. Intelligent, alert, able. Some tendency to digress. Good observer. Physically vigorous; religious; has given college ed. to most of children. — Speech somewhat modified from folk type (which is still very strong) in the direction of the cultivated type, esp. in intonation. Loud, resonant, deep voice. Some nasality; strong stresses; tempo moderate. Simplification of final consonant clusters. Stressed vowels generally long.

SC 29C: Warrenville, Gregg Twp. — M, farmer; former overseer in cotton mills, once sold razors, 82. — B. Talatha, Aiken Co. Has lived in other localities in Co.; 4 yrs. in LaGrange, GA. — PGF, PGM "must've been raised here"; MGF from Scotland; MGM of Indian descent (lived to be 114). — Baptist "by faith and by birth". Former member of Jr. Order, Odd Fellows, Red Men. — Ed.: local schools, 3 mos. night school (textile course). Much reading. — Intelligent, honest, straightforward, solid citizen. Prosperous, is known by everyone in Co., well thought of as man with plenty of hard common sense. Respects education, encourages family members to read widely. Has worked on farms and mills and "hates to hear people throwing off on farmers and mill people". Still very active, farm well-kept. Intimate knowledge of local rural culture, knows what is local and what isn't. Natural speech, no attempts to put on. No taboo reactions. Slight deafness did not seem to interfere with speech. Enjoyed interviews, especially as they allowed him to recall old days. Generally uses folk verb forms. — Some nasality. Speech a little above middle range. Drawl, slightly monotonous (although not painfully so). Long stressed vowels. Some postvocalic constriction. Prevocalic /r/ often velarized. /hw-/. More in-gliding than up-gliding diphthongs.

Aiken

Area settled before Rev., mainly by Germans and Swiss. Tory stronghold. Town laid out 1834. Textile mills in 1840s; diversified agriculture; cotton mills, kaolin, granite, lumber. Winter resort for Northerners by 1880s; social center. Aiken Prep. School from 1916.

SC 29D: M, farmer, 77. B. Monetta (NE corner of Co.), farmed all over Co., gradually moving toward Aiken. — Old Aiken (Edgefield Co.) family, Huguenot descent. — Ed.: local schools. — Baptist; knows everybody, many times a juror (his attendance at court prevented a full interview). — Folk type: several folk forms (pronun. and grammar) recorded that don't occur in any other interview in area. Forms obtained almost exclusively in conversation. Very fast speech; strong nasality; generally long stressed vowels. Strongly velarized prevocalic /r/. /ju/; normally /i e ɔ o u/ in-gliding or monoph.

Ellenton

Once cotton-raising center. Riots in 1870s. Taken over c. 1950 by Atomic Energy Commission.

SC 29E: M, inactive farmer, elderly. B. here. — Easily teased (scared out of completing interview by rumor that FW was with FBI); reputation for shiftlessness. Not a very satisfactory inf. — Notions of correctness; scorn for "leegendary" talk. Always trying to offer a "correct" name for an implement, etc., rather than the vernacular. Some folk verb forms, even though on guard. Very little nasality; tempo moderate to fast. /hw-/; no /-r/. /a/ low-central to low-back; /e o/ in-gliding; /au/ with low-front beginning.

30. Edgefield County

Formed 1785. Mixed settlement, both from PA and from coast. Methodists by 1790. Hamburg important at one time as terminus of RR; declined after other RRs built and Augusta Canal opened. Riots 1876. Sparsely settled agricultural region: cotton, asparagus, peaches, timber; cotton mills, textiles.

> Chapman, John A. 1897. *History of Edgefield County. . . to 1897.* Newberry: E. H. Aull.
>
> Cook, Harvey Toliver. 1924. *The Hard Labor Section.* Greenville.
>
> Dubose, Louise Jones. 1948. Edgefield County. *South Carolina Magazine* 11.6:14.
>
> Lett, Stanton N. 1930. *The Development of Education in Edgefield County, South Carolina, 1748–1930.* University of South Carolina Master's thesis.
>
> McClendon, Carlee T. 1977. *Edgefield, South Carolina, in the War of 1812.* Edgefield: Hive Press.
>
> Mims, Julian L. 1964. *Radical Reconstruction in Edgefield County, 1868–1877.* University of South Carolina Master's thesis.
>
> 1946. Edgefield County: Home of Statesmen and Land of Opportunity. *South Carolina Magazine* 9.10:6.

SC 30A: Philipps Church, Johnston P.O. — M, farmer, 63. B. neighborhood. — F. b. Orangeburg Co., came here as boy, PGF b. Orangeburg Co., PGF's F. b. Ireland, PGM b. Aiken Co., of "Dutch" descent; M., MGF b. in Co., of Scottish descent, MGM b. Co., of partial "Dutch" descent. — Ed.: 3–4 yrs. school. — Baptist. — Very quick and bright. Speaks absolutely naturally. Takes no interest in modern way of talking.

Edgefield P.O., Pickens or Wise Twp.

Edgefield had German and French settlers in 18th cent. Home of 12 governors and many other distinguished citizens. Largely agricultural; cotton mill, market.

SC 30B: M, retired contractor, collector for telephone company, former carpenter, 79. B. Antioch, Colliers Twp., Edgefield Co. Has lived for short periods in Lanham Springs (in Co.), Augusta, and VA. — F. b. Montreal, grew up in VT, came to SC as schoolteacher; M. b. Co.; family always lived in SC (MGF had 300 slaves, 2,000–3,000 acres). — Ed.: common schooling to 9 yrs. (only one teacher outside parents). — Council Commander of Woodmen of the World, formerly Knights of Pythias, unsuccessful candidate for mayor. — Cooperative, generous with time, appeared to enjoy interviews. No signs of guardedness, talked freely of old and new. Knows local legends, politics and personalities. Somewhat deaf; questions of synonyms hard to handle. Smoked cigar throughout interview, muffling some responses. — Moderate tempo, slight drawl. /-r/ > /ɜ/, length or zero. /hw-/. /e o/ mixed: occ. in-gliding. "Long" and "short" /ai au/, but only

slight low-country centralized beginnings. /ʌ/ high. No post-vocalic constriction.

SC 30C!: F, housewife, writer of local histories, 73. B. Edgefield, lived in same spot since 4–5 yrs. old; lived 3 yrs. in Charleston while attending school. — F. b. outside Edgefield; PGF b. 12 mi. N. of Edgefield; PGF's F. b. VA, came to Edgefield area before Rev. (land grant from George III); PGF's M. b. "Meeting St." section, 12 mi. N. of Edgefield, family came from VA; PGM b. NH, came S. to teach school; M. b. Sumter, SC, moved to Marion as child; MGF b. Sumter; MGF's F. b. in Waxhaw section before Rev., family came with Scotch-Irish migration; MGM from Sumter, distinguished family of CT ancestry. Several family histories published. — Ed.: had governess; 3 mos. Laurens Female College; 3 yrs. Charleston Female Seminary. — Baptist; UDC, DAR, Civic League (chaired committee that built library), WCTU, Edgefield Hist. Soc., Caroliniana Soc. (Charleston). — Intelligent, knows history well. Interested in interviews, though tended to tire easily (health not good lately); speech slightly more "low-country" than informant SC30B. — Strong nasality. /w-/ in *wharf*. More in-gliding diphthongs /e o/ than in SC30B.

SC 30C!*: Lifelong friend of SC30C!. — Similar background and interests; arranged interviews. — Cultivated.

31. Lexington County

Lutheran settlement c. 1735; also Reformed. Lutheran seminary here 1831. "Dutch Fork" area. Residential and mfg. suburbs of Columbia. Sandhills; cotton, asparagus, peaches. Pop. 1810: 6,641, 1820: 8,083, 1850: 12,930, 1880: 18,564, 1910: 32,040, 1930: 36,494, 1960: 60,726.

> Cromer, Voight Rhodes. 1927. *The Church and a Country Neighborhood.* University of South Carolina Master's thesis.
>
> Eleazer, James M. 1952. *A Dutch Fork Farm Boy.* Columbia: University of South Carolina Press.
>
> Rowell, Percival E. 1891. *Lexington County and Its Towns.*
>
> Scott, Edwin J. 1884. *Random Recollections of a Long Life.* Columbia: C. A. Calvo.
>
> Stockman, J. E., and D. S. Shull. 1923. *Lexington County, Economic and Social.* Columbia: University of South Carolina Press.
>
> 1947. Lexington County Presents a Great Variety of Activities. *South Carolina Magazine* 10.12:20–.

Camp Styx, West Columbia P.O., Congaree Twp.

Settlement very near West Columbia from 1722. Mill center; millworker residence. Expanding metropolitan area.

SC 31A: M, superintendant of fish hatchery, farmer, RR construction worker, some sawmill work, 64. B. same comm., never lived elsewhere. — F. b. in comm., family from Pelion area (c. 12 mi. W.); M., MGF from comm. — Ed.: c. 4th grade, Sand Mt. Country School, 4–5 mos. a year. — Congaree Baptist. — Busy, but hospitable and glad to sit down and talk with fieldworker (eagerness to help probably due partially, at least, to informant's superior, the State Chief Game Warden, who arranged interview). Deeply rooted in local culture, talks freely, using local idiom (knows no other, though recognizes that a lot of people speak differently than he does). No observed profanity; few German words; many Midland vocabulary items. Seemed to enjoy interviews. No pretensions of being better than he is. — Strong stresses. Clear utterances; not much intonation range. Tempo moderate; very little drawl. Simplification of final clusters. Some postvocalic constriction. Prevocalic /r-/ sometimes velarized. /hw-/. A few up-gliding diphthongs.

St. Thomas Church, Chapin P.O., Saluda Twp.

Chapin sawmill comm. on the edge of Dutch Fork. Now caters to trade of metropolitan Columbia.

SC 31B: M, farmer, some cabinetry work, ran sawmill, planing mill, gin, 86. B. in comm., never lived elsewhere. — F., PGF, PGF's F., PGF's M. all b. locally, of German origin; PGM, PGM's F., PGM's M. b. here, of German ancestry; M., MGF, MGF's F. b. here (all within 4 mi.), also German; MGM, MGM's F., MGM's M. all born locally (family history recorded). — Ed.: in local schools, till 14–16. — Lutheran; once belonged to Farmers Union, 2 sessions on grand jury. — Oldest inhabitant of the Dutch Fork. Religious, a little consciously moral (rejected notion of *playing hookey*). Independent, still manages to keep farm self-sufficient. Strong local roots, knows local weather-lore, proverbs, etc. Strong respect for learning. Keenly aware of breakdown of old traditions and folkways; anxious to preserve as much info. as possible about old times. Likes to keep local words and idioms. Not garrulous, but has many anecdotes at his disposal. GM spoke German. — Voice somewhat rough, utterances slurred. Tempo moderate to slow. Stressed vowels fairly long. Simplification of final clusters. Velarization of prevocalic /r/; postvocalic /l/ us. dark. /hw-/. Variable constriction of postvocalic /r/: zero to fairly strong. Intervocalic /r/ often lost. Up-gliding diphthongs us.

32. Fairfield County

Formed 1785; 1st settled from VA and NC. Some Germans among early settlers. Secondary school for AfAms in 1870s. Cotton, corn, beef, granite quarries, timber, textile milling. Pop. 1790: 7,623, 1820: 17,174, 1850: 21,404, 1880: 27,765, 1910: 29,442, 1930: 23,287, 1960: 20,713.

Bolick, Julian Stevenson. 1963. *A Fairfield Sketchbook.* Clinton: Jacobs Bros.

Chappell, Buford Souter. 1971. *The Winns of Fairfield County.* Columbia: R. L. Bryan Co.

Ederington, William. 1961. *History of Fairfield County, South Carolina.* Comp. by B. H. Bosson. Tuscaloosa, AL: Wills Pub. Co.

McMaster, Fitz Hugh. 1946. *History of Fairfield County, South Carolina. . . .* Columbia: State Commercial Print. Co.

Nicholson, S. W., H. M. Faucette, and R. W. Baxter. 1924. *Fairfield County, Economic and Social.* Columbia: University of South Carolina Press.

Obear, Katherine Theus. 1913. *Four Months at Glencairn.* NY: Broadway Publishing Co.

Obear, Katherine Theus. 1940. *Through the Years in Old Winnsboro.* Columbia: R. L. Bryan Co.

1949. *Our Heritage.* Fairfield County, South Carolina.

Winnsboro

Settled c. 1755 from PA and VA; later from low country. Laid out as town 1784. Mt. Zion Academy c. 1777; faded away. Regulator territory. Prosperous in plantation era (county still has heavy AfAm pop.). Pillaged 1865 by Sherman. 1st SC school district after Reconstruction to vote a school tax. Large cotton mill (tire fabric); blue granite. Pop. 1880: 1,500, 1910: 1,754, 1930: 2,344, 1960: 3,479.

SC 32A: M, farmer, grocer, 80. B. 12 mi. SW, Horeb neighborhood. — F. b. Greenville, PGF b. VA, came down to SC, PGM b. Greenville Co., prominent family; M. b. Fairfield Co., MGF b. Ireland, MGM b. Fairfield Co., near river, of prominent family in Co. since mid 18th cent. — Ed.: country schools, Charleston HS, 1 yr. SC college; bus. school, Poughkeepsie, NY. — Presbyterian ("officer in the church, unfortunately for the church"); Mason, mayor 12 yrs., council 2 yrs. (proud of record), has been magistrate in Co. — Enjoyed interviews; very cooperative. — No open taboo reactions, but tendency to avoid forbidden words. Nasality. Strong stresses, with relaxation of most vowels. Str. vowels long; no real drawl. Tendency to simplify cons. clusters (less than us.). /ʃr/ > /sr/; /hw-/; clear /l/ between front vowels; no /-r/. Intrusive /r/ in *swallow it*; restored postvocalic /r/ not observed. Intervocalic /r/ sometimes weak. /r/ < /-t-/ occ. /iy/ normal upglide, occ. in-glide or monoph. /ɪ/ occ. for /ɪ/; /ɪ/ alternates with /ɛ/ freely before nasals. /uw/ fronted; up-glide /juw/ after /t d n/; /ou/ sometimes monoph. Some /ɔw/ but /ɔə/ oftener; unrounded vowel in *pot, college, rock, crop, vomit.* /ʌ/ high. /ɜɪ/ before cons. except /l/ (1st element normally rounded). No retroflexion in stressed or unstr. syllables. /ai/ with intial element from [aʌ] to [aˈ]; short centering element before voiced cons. /oy/ with high beginning; occ. disyllabic /æw/ type in *proud, out,* etc. /ɪ/ in *bucket, careless, haunted*; /ɪʃ/ final in *Tuesday,* etc. — Interviews conducted jointly with bro. and wife; speech-types same exc. she speaks a little faster and has more nasality. Both from same comm.; same type of family background.

SC 32B: M, retired farmer, amateur historian and ornithologist, 86. B. Winnsboro. — Old local family, in comm. since before Rev. Some ancestors from Newberry Co. — Ed.: local schools (Mt. Zion Academy, now local h.s.). — Baptist; well known in comm. — Slightly senile, physically feeble, rather deaf. Enjoyed interviews; talked at length. Interview would have been more successful had wife and daughter not tried to "protect" him (solicitations more taxing on strength than conversations with FW). Many anecdotes about flora and fauna and about Civil War. Positive character. — Voice somewhat hoarse, but articulation normally clear. Strong stresses; little intonation variety. /k- g-/ occ. palatalized; /hw-/; /-l/ occ. partially vocalized; almost no trace of /-r/; no intrusive /r/. /i e u o/ us. up-gliding; /ɔ/ occ. up-gliding, oftener ingliding; diph. [æɛ] common, apparently phonemic as in FW's own dialect. /a/ low back; /ʌ/ very high; /u ʊ/ fronted; /ɜ/ > [ɜ·] or [ɜɪ], both often fully rounded. Unstr. /ɚ/ > /ə/; "short" and "long" forms of /ai/, former occ. slightly centralized. [æo] normal. Weak-stressed [ɪ] in *bucket, sausage, Mrs.*

SC 32C: M, farmer, surveyor (with U.S. Maritime service during WWII), 55. B. Winnsboro. — Descendant of earliest settlers of Co. Both parents b. here, old local families. — Ed.:

local schools, 1 yr. Clemson College. — Episcopalian. — Good mind. Intimate knowledge of county. Talks freely; no affectations; interested in FW's work. Understood purpose of interviews; helped in locating other informants. Even tempered. Many anecdotes. [FW stayed at inf.'s home, a motel/tourist home. Family interested in work, so partial interview obtained by way of demonstration. No evidence of any unnatural reactions: since family is sure of its social status, and as sure that Southern speech is as good as any other, no reason to cover up.] — Uses standard colloquial forms. Moderate to rapid tempo. Strong stresses. Articulation clear. Tendency to simplify final clusters; /hw-/; clear [-l-] between front vowels; /-l/ tends to vocalize before cons.; no /-r/ or intrusive /r/. /i e u o/ up-gliding; /ɔ/ in-gliding; /u/ fronted; /ju/ in *Tuesday*; /-ə/ in *borrow, tomorrow*, etc. Up-gliding /æi/ common, phonemically distinct. /a/ low-back, less often low-central. /ɜ/ us. [ɝ]; /ai au/ us. with low-front beginning. [ɨ] in weak stressed syll. of *mountain, careless, bucket*. /ʌ/ high; /ʊ/ us. fronted.

SC 32D: M, druggist, 78. B. here; 5 yrs. in Columbia, 2–3 yrs. in Wash., 2 yrs. in Phila., 1 NH. — F. b. Winnsboro, PGF b. VT (family in NE since 1636), PGM b. Co. Kent, England; M. b. Chester, MGF b. Pineville, NC-SC line, MGM b. Chester Co. M.'s people in SC since mid 18th cent. ("4 generations of the family have lived in the same house."). No records except family Bible; inf.'s aunt has written a book on history of comm. — Ed.: Mt. Zion Academy (local); 1 yr. Yale (1900–1901) as special student. — Episcopalian; Rotary Club, Masons ("don't attend, though"). — Generous with time. — Somewhat more precise in articulation than us. older generation SC inf.'s. Tendency to label folk-pronun. and folk-vocab. as "characteristic of common people". Seemed to be sure of certain folk forms, but not too extensive an acquaintance with rural life (was surprised at FW's reports of certain forms as Fairfield Co.). Rapid speech; strong stresses, with lengthening of str. vowels. Less simplification of consonant clusters than us. expected. /-t-/ sometimes /-r-/; some palatalization of /k- g-/ (not extreme form); /hw-/; /sr-/; /-l/ tends to be vocalized. No /-r/ or intrusive /r/. /i/ sometimes up-gliding, sometimes in-gliding; /e/ us. up-gliding; /u/ fronted, up-gliding; /ju/ in *new, due, Tuesday*; /o/ up-gliding. Some tendency to neutralize /ɪ/ and /ɛ/ before nasals. /æ/ and /æi/ contrast. /a/ us. low-back, unrounded in *pot, crop, rock, oxen, borrow, wash*. /ʌ/ very high; /ʊ/ raised, slightly fronted. /ɜ/ > [ɝ] finally and before [l r], [ɝ] before other cons. (us. rounded). /-ə/ in *father, borrow*. /ai/ with "long" and "short" forms typical of upcountry speech above folk level, us. with low-front [a] beginning. [æʊ] diph. us. Weak stressed [ɨ] in *sausage, bucket*, etc.

33. Chester County

Formed 1785. Settled largely by Scots and Ulster Scots. RR 1851. Diversified mfg.; electric power; cotton, livestock, oats, corn, dairy products, hay. Pop. 1790: 6,866, 1820: 14,189, 1850: 18,038, 1880: 24,153, 1910: 29,425, 1930: 31,803, 1960: 30,888.

Davidson, Chalmers Gaston. 1956. *Gaston of Chester*. Davidson, NC.

Gaston, David A., and Arthur Cornwell. 1925. *Chester County, Economic and Social*. Columbia: University of South Carolina Press.

Nunnery, Jimmie E. 1975. *Chester County, 1885–1905, Tillman Era*. University of South Carolina Master's thesis.

1946. Chester County. *South Carolina Magazine* 9.7:12.

SC 33A: Armenia, Chester P.O. and Twp. — M, farmer, 75. B. here. — F., M. b. here. — Illiterate. — Methodist. — A poor man who worked and acquired land and money (unusual in this section). Hearty and friendly. — [aː], [a], and [aˑə] groups confused at times, apparently indicating mixed speech antecedents in the comm.

Chester

Settled from PA c. 1755. Cotton, cattle raising; hydroelectric development on Catawba c. 1904. Pop. 1880: 1,899, 1910: 4,754, 1930: 5,528, 1960: 6,906.

SC 33B: M, retired mail carrier, 75. B. Fairfield Co., Blackstock Twp. Left Blackstock at 18, lived in Chester ever since (except 2 yrs. construction work with C & NW RR); never below Ft. Jackson (near Columbia). — F. b. Ireland, landed Charleston c. 1850, came to Blackstock and set up as shoemaker; M. b. Fairfield Co. — Ed.: Woodward (below Blackstock), 7–8 yrs. — Presbyterian; Knights of Pythias, ex-Woodman of the World. — A little perturbed at length of interview (though FW made it one of the most rapid he'd ever conducted). Knows countryside thoroughly. — Bass voice, slightly rasping, resonant. Tempo slightly on the slow side; stresses strong. Simplification of final cons. clusters. Intervocalic /-k-/ often with spirantal off-glide; /k-, g-/ sometimes palatalized; /sr-/; /hw-/. Postvocalic /-l/ tends to vocalize; postvocalic /-r/ rare. /i e ɔ o u/ up-gliding; [ɛ] often retracted before [ə r l]; [ɛ] up-glides in *egg*; /ju/ in *news, dues, Tuesday*; /u/ strongly fronted; [ɨ] in *milk*. [æ]/[œi] contrast; /a/ us. low-back; rounded vowel [ɒ] in *barn, crop, pot, rock, palm, calm, wash*; [ʌ] high; /ʊ/ slightly raised and fronted (occ. retroflexion). Stressed /ɜ/ > us. [ɝ] with first member rounded [not always marked: FW]; [ɜ] before [-r -l] and zero; [-ə] in *father*; "long" and "short" forms of /ai, au/ us. beg. [aʌ] or [æˑ]; [ɔi] sometimes disyllabic before /-l/; unstr. [ɨ] in *towel, sausage, bucket, haunted*, etc.

34. Lancaster County

Formed 1785. Earliest settlement 1750; mainly Ulster Scots, many from Lancaster, PA (also from VA, NC). Presbyterians from 1755; eventually many Baptists and Methodists, also some Lutherans. Franklin Academy est. 1825. Town records lost when courthouse burnt by Sherman's men c. 1865. Some mica and gold mining at one time. Textiles chief industry; timber mfg.; cotton, corn, wheat, oats, hay, tobacco. Pop. 1790: 6,302, 1820: 8,716, 1850: 10,988, 1880: 16,903, 1910: 26,650, 1930: 27,980, 1960: 39,352.

Beaty, Ernest Albert, and Carl W. McMurray. 1923. *Lancaster County, Economic and Social*. Columbia: University of South Carolina Press.

Floyd, Viola C. 1940. Lancaster County: Historical, Romantic, Industrial. *South Carolina Magazine* 4.1:22–.

Floyd, Viola C. 1956. *Lancaster County Tours*. Lancaster: Lancaster County Historical Commission.

Malone, George W. 1900. *An Attractive New Book Describing the Principal Towns of Lancaster County, South
Carolina*. Lancaster: Enterprise Pub. Co.

Springs, Elliott White. 1958. *Clothes Make the Man, or,
How to Put the Broad into Broadcloth*. NY: Empyrean.

Lancaster, Gills Creek Twp.

Lancaster settled c. 1755 from PA; "Waxhaw" settlement,
Ulster Scots. Springs, cotton mills, hydroelectric power
nearby; both old and recent industry. Pop. 1850: 376, 1880:
681, 1910: 2,098, 1930: 3,545, 1960: 7,999.

SC 34A: M, farmer, store clerk, 75. B. Elgin, moved to town
when grown. — F. raised in Co., PGF from NC, PGM b. in
Co.; M., MGF, MGM raised in Co. — Ed.: 4th grade
("blueback speller"). — Methodist; Masons. — Not ideal
informant: 1) somewhat suspicious, 2) rather deaf (strain on
FW), 3) tendency to be overcareful in speech (probably result
of deafness), a little hesitant about using folk words. Cooperative; generous with time. Curiosity about interviews. Religious; hastened to complete interview on Sat. PM because he
wouldn't talk on Sunday. — Strong stresses, strong nasality;
medium- to high-pitched voice; monotonous. Occ. /-t-/ > [-ɾ-
]; /k- g-/ sometimes palatalized; /sr-/; /hw-/; /-l/ sometimes
vocalized; [ɛ] sometimes retroflex before [-r -l]; /-r/ varies,
zero to strong. Intrusive /r/ in *swallow it*. Up-gliding /i u e
o ɔ/; /ju/ in *new, dues, Tuesday*; /u/ fronted; /-ə/ in *borrow*. /ɪ/
and /ɛ/ neutralizing before nasals; /æ æi/ contrast. /a/ us. low-
back; /a/ in *crop, pot, borrow*, alternates with /ɔ/ in *water*; /ʌ/
very high. *Thursday*, etc. sometimes with [ɝ], sometimes [ɜɪ]
squirrel; [æʊ]. "Long" and "short" [ai] with low-front beginning, occ. "long" form before voiceless cons. Unstr. [ɪ] in
bucket, towel, etc.

SC 34B: M, gasoline and oil business, farmed, blacksmith
shop 6–7 yrs., deputy sheriff 2 yrs., sergeant of arms SC House
of Representatives 35 yrs., supt. penitentiary, 73. B. in sight of
town (in Co. all life except one period 200 yards over the line
in Kershaw Co.). — F. b. Co. Antrim, Ireland, 1845 (people
from Scotland), came to Lancaster 1870; M. b. Lancaster Co.,
MGF b. Kershaw Co., 1809 (people all moved W. when he was
a boy), MGM b. Lancaster Co., all Lane Co. people, prob.
came in with Scotch-Irish in 18th cent. — Ed.: common
schools, Lancaster Co. — Presbyterian; Mason, Jr. Order. —
Big; hearty. Knows all politicians of state, big and little. Fund
of anecdotes. — Strong stresses; voice in low-mid range,
resonant. Simplification of final clusters. /-t-/ sometimes [-ɾ-];
[-k-] with spirant off-glide; /hw-/. Some vocalization of /-l/;
clear [-l̩-] between front vowels. Intervocalic /r/ sometimes
weak; /-r/ sporadic in occurrence; no intrusive /r/. /tʃ/ in *Tuesday*. /i e ɔ o u/ up-gliding; /ju/ after /d- n-/; /u/ fronted; /-
ə/ in *borrow*, etc. /ɛ/ in *milk*. Tendency to neutralize [ɪ] and [ɛ]
before nasals. [æˌə] and [æɛ] contrast phonemically; /a/ low-
back; [ɒ] in *pot, John, rock, vomit*; /ʌ/ high; /ʊ/ in *bulge, bulk*.
Only partial constriction in *Thursday* and *father* groups of
words — not consistent either for groups of words or for
repetitions of same word. /ai/ with "short" and "long" forms,
both with low-front beginnings; /au/ with [æ] and [a] beginnings. Weak stressed [ɪ] in *towel, sausage*.

SC 34C: F, retired housewife, 80. B. VA; Columbia, SC, ages
3–14, Winnsboro, SC 14–16; Lancaster Co. ever since, has

lived last 60 yrs. within a block of present home. — F. Presbyterian minister; MGF county ordinary (judge of probate)
Lancaster Co. Inf. "old-family type of Southerner." — Ed.:
National Kollock School for Ladies, Hillsboro, NC, ages 15–
18. — Not too satisfactory an informant. Lacked intimate contact with local culture, or at least tended to talk more about
family connections. Mind slightly wandering. A bit garrulous.
— Doesn't try to conceal natural speech. Strong stresses;
moderate nasality; clear. No *ain't* or double negatives; *it
don't*. Final cons. us. articulated. /hw-/; /-ɪŋ/ natural. Almost
no /-r/ [contrast two other informants — see FW's earlier comments on lack of /-r/ in Upcountry cultivated inf.'s]. Some centralized beginning of /au/, /ai/ us. monoph. (or so tending)
before zero or voiced cons. Us. up-gliding diph., with very occ.
in-gliding /o/.

35. York County

Formed 1785. Catawbas limited to a small reservation by
1763. Successful iron mfg. in 18th, early 19th centuries. Co.
about 1/3 AfAm in 1950. Timber, mfg. (esp. textiles); cotton,
grain, peaches, truck, poultry, dairy products. Pop. 1790:
6,604, 1820: 14,936, 1850: 19,433, 1880: 30,713, 1910: 44,718,
1930: 53,419, 1960: 78,760.

Brown, Douglas Summers. 1953. *A City Without Cobwebs:
A History of Rock Hill, South Carolina*. Columbia: University of South Carolina Press.

Ford, Lacy K., Jr. 1976. *One Southern Profile: Moderniza-
tion and the Development of White Terror in York County,
1856–1876*. University of South Carolina Master's
thesis.

Hartness, George Bowman. 1966. *By Ship, Wagon and Foot
to York County, South Carolina*. Columbia.

Lewis, H. 1955. *Blackways of Kent*. Chapel Hill: University
of North Carolina Press.

Moore, Maurice Augustus. 1871. *Reminiscences of York
District, South Carolina*.

Morland, J. Kenneth. 1958. *The Millways of Kent*. Chapel
Hill: University of North Carolina Press.

1946. York County: Center of Diverse Enterprises. *South
Carolina Magazine* 9.4:6–.

Highland Park Mill, Rock Hill, Catawba Twp.

Rock Hill inc. 1868, with over 300 inhabitants; chartered
as a city 1892. 1st regional settlers in Rock Hill area from PA;
some plantations. Charlotte-Augusta RR 1851. Transfer pt.
for Confederate troops and supplies, 1861–65. 1st cotton mill
1880; 5 by 1900; also an auto company 1916–24, canning,
tobacco. Winthrop College transferred here from Columbia
1895; 2 AfAm colleges est. in 1890s. Hydroelectric power
from 1904; abortive attempt at auto industry in 1920s; cottonseed oil, coathangers, printing and finishing. Pop. 1880:
809, 1910: 7,216, 1930: 11,322, 1960: 29,404.

SC 35A: F, housewife, worked in cotton mill before marriage,
59. B. Lando, Chester Co. Moved to Rock Hill, never lived
anywhere else; never lived in country. — F. b. Chester Co.;
PGF supposed to be descendant of Tory leader, killed in Civil
War; M. from Chester Co. — Ed.: about third grade; had to
go to work in mill at age 9. — Baptist; husband active in textile labor union. — Kind-hearted, generous, limited
intelligence; somewhat suspicious of fieldworker. Talked

freely about family, mill village life, working conditions, etc. Not good at offering synonyms or for direct grammatical questioning, but plenty of folk forms in normal speech. — Strong nasality; monotonous, high-pitched voice; strong stresses; drawl. /-r/ medium to strong when occurring; /hw-/; intrusive /r/ in *wash, swallow it*. /æ/ contrasts with /æ:/; /ɪ ɛ/ neutralized before nasals; /ɔ/ rising diphthong; /e o i u/ us. rising diphthongs; /a/ in *water*; "long" and "short" forms of /ai/, with tendency to long forms everywhere.

SC 35A*: F, millworker. Daughter of SC35A. — Ed.: 6th grade. — Union member.

SC 35B: M., textile worker, 37. B. here, never lived elsewhere. — F. b. Randolph, NC, came to Rock Hill at age 5, worked 45 years at Highland Park Mill; M. b. York Co.; MGF, MGM came from Ireland. — Ed.: to 7th or 8th grade. — Baptist; textile union. — Very cooperative, keen sense of humor. Folk pronun. of many words. — Strong nasality. Drawl, with over-lengthening of stressed syllables, but speech not noticeably slow. Wide intonational rise and fall. Final cons. clusters often simplified. Intervocalic /r/ often weak; /-r/ us. lost within word, moderate to strong at end of word (but sometimes lost, representing inconsistency in areas where /-r/ pronounced in SC). /k- g-/ noticeably fronted before front vowels; /-t-/ occ. > [-ɾ-]; /sr-/; /hw-/; clear /-l-/ in *skillet, gully*; /-l/ sometimes vocalized; intrusive /r/ in *swallow it*. /i/ us. up-gliding; /e/ up-gliding with second element fairly far front; /u/ up-gliding and fronted; /ju/ after /t- d- n-/; /o/ up-gliding (not in unstr. syllables); /æ æ:/ contrast; /a/ low-back; /ɔ/ up-gliding except where /-r/ follows; /ɔ/ in *swallow*. /ʌ/ high; /ɝ/ stressed with slight retroflexion or none; /ai/ us. with low-front beginning, monophthongal before voiced cons. or finally; /ɔi/ often disyllabic before /-l/: [ɔwəl]; /ai/ in *joints*; /æw/ us. in all positions (occ. [a > o]); [ɨ] unstr. in *bucket, careless, haunted*. — Pp. 1–7, 63–104 (exc. cv. forms) from SC35D.

Cotton Belt, Beersheba, York P.O.

York settled c. 1757 around a stagecoach tavern. Little industry or tourism; for some time winter quarters for a circus. Pop. 1930: 2,826.

SC 35C: M, farmer, sometime carpenter, 76. B. York Co. — F., PGF, PGM b. Cotton Belt; M., MGF, MGM b. Bullock Creek, York Co. — Ed.: community school, 7 1/2 yrs. — Beersheba Presbyterian Church. — Postvocalic /-r/ us. lost, occ. preserved; occ. loss of intervocalic /r/.

SC 35D: Highland Park Mill, Rock Hill, Catawba Twp. — M, storekeeper and embalmer. Older bro. of SC35B. — Slightly more traveled than bro. but with a sharper feel for rural speech.

SC 35E: Sharon, Broad River, Sharon Twp. — M, physician, 84. B. Rodman, Chester Co. — Died before FW could complete interview. — Intelligent, natural speech, good knowledge of folk vocabulary. Folk preterites, double negatives. — /ɔ/ rising diphthong; up-gliding /e o/; /a/ us. low-back and

unrounded. /ai/ alternants; /au/ beginning low-central to low-front. Fairly strong retroflexion. /hw-/.

36. Spartanburg County

Formed 1785. Settled from Ireland (via Charleston); also Ulster Scots; settlements by 1755. Baptists from VA arrived 1768. Ironworks at Glendale by 1773; also cattle and tobacco by the time of the Rev. Active guerilla fighting in Rev. Water power, minerals, orchards; several "springs", health resorts. Iron mfg. till 1870s, then textiles (1st textile mill 1820). Occupied by Feds., April 1865. RRs by 1870s (eventually largest RR mileage in SC); unsuccessful attempt to promote immigration from Europe in 1870s. Continued industrialization; mfg. (esp. textiles); peaches, cotton, corn. Pop. 1790: 8,800, 1820: 16,989, 1850: 26,400, 1880: 40,409, 1910: 83,465, 1930: 116,323, 1960: 146,830.

Coates, Kenneth D., ed. 1945. *A City Looks at Itself.* Spartanburg: Chamber of Commerce.

DeLorne, Charles DuBose. 1963. *Development of the Textile Industry in Spartanburg County from 1816 to 1900.* University of South Carolina Master's thesis.

Federal Writers Project. 1940. *A History of Spartanburg County.* Spartanburg: Band and White.

Gwathmey, E. M. 1940. Spartanburg: An Educational Center of the Piedmont. *South Carolina Magazine* 3.2:30.

Howe, George. 1861. *The Scotch-Irish, and Their First Settlements on the Tyger River.* . . . Columbia: Southern Guardian Steam-Power Press.

Landrum, John B. O'Neill. 1897. *Colonial and Revolutionary History of Upper South Carolina.* Greenville: Shannon and Co.

Landrum, John Belton O'Neall. 1900. *History of Spartanburg County.* Atlanta: Franklin Print. and Pub. Co.

Moss, Bobby Gilmer. 1972. *The Old Iron District: A Study of the Development of Cherokee County — 1750–1897.* Clinton: Jacobs Press.

Ruern, Philip. 1950. *Spartanburg County: A Pictorial History.* Virginia Beach, VA: Dannig Co.

Rushton, Jessie Eleanor. 1928. *The Development of Education in Spartanburg County prior to 1876.* University of South Carolina Master's thesis.

Wallace, David Duncan. 1952. *History of Wofford College.* Nashville: Vanderbilt University Press.

1946. Lance and Loom in Spartanburg. *South Carolina Magazine* 9.1:18–.

Holly Springs, Inman P.O., Beech Springs Twp.

Holly Springs an early settlement; large Baptist church by 1804.

SC 36A: M, farmer (has been moonshiner), 73. B. here. — F. b. on SC side in mts., PGF's people came from England ("old set of 'em"), stayed at Firforest near Spartanburg, then moved to mts.; M., MGF, MGM lived in comm. (some people down near Newberry); M. had 7 bros. in Civil War, only 2 survived. — Ed.: one-room schools. — Baptist; formerly school trustee, AAA committeeman, Woodman of the World. — Has kept farm largely self-sustaining, buys only a few luxury foods. Knows comm. thoroughly. Didn't understand purpose of interviews; became somewhat impatient, expected pay (a govt.

surveyor had paid someone in comm. for answering a few questions: comparison to FW's disadvantage). Fairly good memory of oldtime conditions. Little experience outside comm. — Knows occupation vocabulary of moonshining. Speech drawling, high pitched; monotonous, querulous intonation. Strong stresses; rather strong retroflexion. Nasality strong. Little palatalization of /k- g-/; /-n/ us. in participles. /a/ us. low-back, occ. rounded; /ɔ/ rising; /a/ in *there*. Mtn.-type speech. "Long" /ai/ normal in all positions.

SC 36A*: F. Wife of SC36A. B. Welford, about 10 mi. S.

Spartanburg

Town laid out 1785; inc. as Spartanburg 1831; city charter 1880. Earliest settlements 1761; Scotch-Irish from PA and VA. Other settlers from Scotland and Ireland via Charleston. Baptists, Methodists, Presbyterians first; Episcopalians by 1850s. Several academies and colleges est. in 19th cent. Iron mfg. before Rev. Cattle and grain early, then cotton. RR by 1859; trading center for mountaineers. 1880–1900 cotton mills, diversification of farming. Heavy concentration of textile mills. Camps here for both World Wars. Pop. 1850: 1,176, 1880: 3,253, 1910: 17,517, 1930: 28,723, 1960: 44,352.

SC 36B: F, housewife, 76. B. 12 mi. SW near Glenn Springs, moved to Spartanburg 1923. — F. b. same house as inf. in 1812, PGF b. 1757 nearer Glenn Springs, built house and moved there when married (served in Rev.), PGF's F. came in from England, PGM b. somewhere in neighborhood; M. b. upper edge of Spartanburg Co., near Holly Springs, MGF b. in mtns. (had farm near Hogback Mtn.), MGM also b. upper part of Co. (M.'s cousin famous for treatment of pellagra, practiced in Greece). — Ed.: country schools, Pauline, SC, and elsewhere around home. — Baptist, still keeps membership in country church. — Inf. not very talkative; taciturnity seems to run in the family ("when mother would go to visit father's people, they'd sit on the porch for hours without saying a word"). Patient and cooperative. — Slow speech; stresses strongly marked. Not a great variety in intonation. Not much memory of old-fashioned words. Retroflexion moderate to strong. /-l/ occ. vocalized; /k/ rarely palatal. Occ. /ɨ/ for /ɪ/; /ɔ/ rising diphthong; /e o/ normally rising diph., occ. monoph; /ʌ/ very high; /u/ fronted; /ʊ/ high. "Short" and "long" allophones of /ai/ diph., with "long" form tending to appear in all positions: /au/ with varied beginning [æ] to [a], no positional alternation; /ɔi/ occ. disyllabic.

SC 36B*: M, retired farmer, 87. B. lower part of Co. — F. b. lower part of Co. — Senile. Tried to help, but too feeble; memory badly faded. Pitiful.

Reidville

Village laid out for academy in 1851. High school by 1857; Reidville Female College 1859. Center of Farmers Alliance in 1888.

SC 36C: M, farmer, has run stores (came to Reidville intending to run a store, "naturally a country merchant"), taught school 4 yrs., 73. B. about 4 mi. from present home (Ferguson's Creek between Reidville and Woodruff); lived 2 yrs. in Laurens Co. — F. b. 3 mi. below here, PGF, PGF's F. b. Reidville, PGF's PGF F. Chester, family came from PA, there

from N. Ireland, ultimately from France (Huguenots, took up land on royal grant in 18th cent.), PGM b. 5 mi. below here, PGM's PGF killed by Tories and Indians during Rev., people came from N. Ireland same time as PGF's; M. b. Pickens, AL, MGF b. SC, orphan, joined Army, War of 1812, in smallpox and yellow fever epidemics in Battle of New Orleans, then sailor, river boat captain, retired to farm (tortured by Sherman, had 6 sons in Conf. Army), MGM descendant of John Knox of Scotland. — Ed.: Reidville Academy; business college, Rome, GA, finished 1893; some work in math and physics at Presbyterian College (Clinton). — Presbyterian, on Home Mission Board 15 yrs., sec. 3 yrs. (Enoree Presbytery), has been elder and lay preacher, supt. of Sunday School; has been school trustee. Well-known in Co. No politics: refused to be mayor; was alderman once and acting mayor. — Great conversationalist. Inf. and wife very hospitable, made FW perfectly at home, teased and joked with him as man to man. Genuine interest in old-time things. Hearty, genial, no pretense at being "better" than anybody. Sent all children to college and aided in educating 6 others (17 in all); devoted to children and grandchildren. — Wide learning but not interfering with natural use of folk speech. Speech rapid. Intonation varied. Stresses strong. /-l/ sometimes vocalized. Postvocalic retroflexion strong to none. /e o/ us. rising diph.; /ɔ/ rising diph.; /a/ us. low-back, occ. rounded; /u/ fronted, us. diph. — *Auxiliary inf., wife, 64, b. about 6 mi. away.

SC 36D!: Spartanburg. — M, lawyer, 80. B. here; has traveled, but always lived in Spartanburg. — F. moved to Spartanburg, PGF b. Ireland, came to Fairfield Co. 1819; other lines descended from Ulster Scots migration from PA via VA. — Ed.: Wofford College (Spartanburg); Law School, Nashville, TN (University of Nashville). — Oldest law firm in US (founded 1825); knows comm. history and customs in detail. — Very much interested in Atlas work; sorry couldn't give time enough for a full interview. Many cv. forms obtained while inquiring of inf. about possible folk informants in the comm. After interviews with folk informants completed, FW made a partial interview to get samples of diff. between folk and cultivated speech in comm. In Spartanburg, as in Greenville, lack of postvocalic retroflexion is one of the characteristics of cultivated speech as opposed to the folk dialect, of urban speech as opposed to rural, and of the younger generation as opposed to the older. Inf., a keen observer of pronun. and vocab. differences, said that all his life the lack of postvocalic retroflexion was the mark of education and culture. The low-country domination of upcountry cultural centers (Greenville, for instance, was a summer resort for planters before 1860) has perhaps served to accentuate the social significance of lack of postvoc. retroflexion. Inf. has quick mind; familiar with many details of old-fashioned life. Enjoyed interview. — Speech quick, staccato, strongly stressed. Recalls words he picked up out of his native culture-area; able to distinguish between what is native and what isn't. "Long" and "short" /ai/ positionally differentiated. — Cultivated.

37. Union County

Formed 1785. 1st settler from VA c. 1750; also Ulster Scots from Lancaster, PA, early. Also some Quakers, most left by 1800 (opposed slavery). Presbyterians; Baptists from 1770s, dominant. Gold mine by 1860. Broad River imp. as avenue of transportation, esp. taking cotton to Columbia.

Mfg., esp. textiles; cotton, corn, sweet potatoes. Pop. 1790: 7,693, 1820: 14,126, 1850: 19,852, 1910: 29,911, 1930: 30,920, 1960: 30,015.

Foster, Mrs. William Rice, ed. 1977. *A History of Union County, South Carolina*. Greenville: Union County Historical Foundation.

Free, Lousarah Belle. 1929. *Education in Union County prior to 1860*. University of South Carolina Master's thesis.

Hope, Robert M., et al. 1923. Union County, Economic and Social. *South Carolina University Bulletin* 128.

Sims, Caldwell. 1979. *Voices of the Past*. Ed. by James Tichten and Allan D. Charles. Union: Union County Historical Commission.

Sparks, Claude Ezell. 1967. *A History of Padgett's Creek Baptist Church*. Union: Counts Print. Co.

Whaley, Mrs. E. D. 1976. *Union County Cemeteries*. Greenville: A Press.

Buffalo

Settled c. 1791, around Union church. Little mill town; "suburb" of Union (Union became Co. seat 1800).

SC 37: M, retired mill worker (retired as overseer, cloth dept.), 66. B. Union, little travel (visited NY). — F., M. and their parents all from Co. — Excellent inf., rather quiet (little free conversation). — Us. vocalizes final /-l/ or has vocalic-colored /l/. /d t/ frequently replace /ð θ/ in weak stressed cv. forms.

38. *Newberry County*

Est. 1785 as a district. Dutch Fork. Opened to settlement 1742. Settled first from SW movement from PA, then from Germany and Ireland and from Saxe-Gotha (now Columbia). First settlement at Duncan's Creek by 1752. Later English, Ulster Scots, some German from Shenandoah. Some Quakers (eventually moved on to Ohio), Presbyterians; Baptists from c. 1760. Unsuccessful navigation projects. Tobacco 1st money crop; then cotton. Nearly 2/3 AfAm by 1860. Several RRs began 1860. Academies 1795, 1806; still no free school by 1861. Timber, granite, textile mfg.; dairying, poultry, truck, grain, cotton. Pop. 1790: 9,342, 1820: 16,104, 1850: 20,143, 1880: 26,497, 1910: 34,586, 1930: 34,681, 1960: 29,416.

Bedenbough, J. Holland. 1930. *A History of Newberry College*. University of South Carolina Master's thesis.

Carwile, John B. 1890. *Reminiscences of Newberry*. . . . Charleston: Walker, Evans and Cogswell, Printers.

O'Neall, John Belton, and John A. Chapman. 1892. *The Annals of Newberry*. . . . Newberry: Aull and Houseal.

Pope, Thomas A. 1973. *History of Newberry County*. Columbia: University of South Carolina Press.

Summer, George Leland. 1950. *Newberry County, South Carolina, Historical and Genealogical*. Newberry.

1946. Newberry County: Hub of the Highways between the Mountains and the Sea. *South Carolina Magazine* 9.7:20–.

Newberry

Est. as co. seat 1789; inc. 1832. Settled c. 1740 from PA and VA. British base here 1780. Presbyterian, Baptist churches by 1835; St. Luke's Episcopal est. 1858. Many pre-1860 homes. Oldest Lutheran seminary in the South here; Newberry College one of oldest S. Lutheran colleges. RR from 1851. Textile mills, cottonseed oil mills. Pop. 1880: 2,342, 1910: 5,028, 1930: 7,298, 1960: 8,208.

SC 38N: M, fireman, has farmed, done brick work, horse handling, 73. B. here. — b. in countryside, family originally from Long Line Place, about 8 mi. N. of Newberry. MGF from Charleston (a free Negro who bought GM from slavery; their children born free). — Ed.: common school; started 2 terms in Columbia "intermediate dept." — A.M.E. Church, steward 26 yrs., has been Knight of Pythias and Odd Fellow. Travelled throughout SE in horse-handler days. — Amiable, quiet, dignified. Known in comm. as hard worker. Knows horses well. Cooperated generously, though somewhat puzzled about interviews (took a great deal of teasing from white fireman). Efficient, intelligent, clear-minded, careful in attention to details in work. Focused attention on old times: recollections of what life was like as boy, and of what the "old people" told him of life before that. Recalled many old-fashioned words and pronunciations, some of which he still uses. — Soft-spoken, slow speech, slight drawl. Little nasality, marked stresses. Final /-l/ (postvocalic or post-cons.) sometimes vocalized. No postvocalic constriction. Linking /r/ and intrusive /r/ very rare, if ever occurring. Sometimes "New England short [ə]" in *road, home*; /ʌ/ high; /u/ fronted; /ɔ/ us. up-gliding diphthong; /a/ us. low-back. Up-gliding /æi/ and centralizing [æə] varieties of /æ/, probably in phonemic contrast. /ʌ/ very high; /ai/ with us. upcountry allophonic distribution ("short" before voiceless cons., "long" elsewhere; sometimes "long" in all positions). /au/ begins [æ a ɑ] regardless of phonetic environment. Sometimes /ai/ replaces /ɔi/.

SC 38A: M, watchman, farmer, expert at castrating farm animals and spaying sows, worked in livery stable, 94. B. along Enoree River (now part of Co.), lived 2 yrs. Goldville, Laurens Co. — F. b. E. part of Newberry Co., "Maybinton Country"; PGF, PGM b. Scotland, came to US in teens, settled in Newberry Co.; M. b. Ireland (Dublin); MGF, MGM came to Newberry when M. was 6 weeks old. — Ed.: none, illiterate. — No church membership, no organizations; belonged to KKK in Reconstruction, and Hampton's Red Shirts. Never been in politics ("Couldn't a held no office even if I had been elected."). Claims politicians ask him for advice. — Hospitable, invited fieldworker to many meals. Still supervises own farm, rising daily at 6 AM. Has worked 39 years as night watchman, including Sundays, hardly missing a day; refuses to retire, despite urging of children. Independent attitude, deplores passing of self-sustaining farm. Mind tended to wander at times, difficult to hold attention to subject if not interesting. Has a few stock anecdotes that he's told over and over, tends to get off on these. Violently anti-Roosevelt, anti-Northern, anti-Negro; will hold forth at length on how Negroes must be kept in their place. Speech has many old-fashioned forms, sometimes alternating with standard ones. Haranguing style in anecdotes; very profane. Knows superstitions and weather-signs. Brags about what he's been able to do without knowing how to read and write. Probably oldest man in town, one of two survivors of Red Shirts. Knows or pretends to know everyone of importance in Co. and state. A genuine "character"; tends to embroider, but very entertaining. — Strong stresses, some nasality. No teeth, but articulation still good, except for occ. muffling of /θ ð/. Postvocalic /-l/ often vocalized. No intrusive /r/; linking /r/ rare. Constriction does not normally occur in *bid, far, father* words, even if vowel immediately follows. /ai/ often for /ɔi/; /u/ fronted; /ɔ e o/ us. up-gliding, occ. monoph.; /au/ us. with low-front beginning: [æ̆ a̬], occ. [a]. /ai/ us. [aʌ̍] before voiceless cons.; [aʌ·ə] goes to [aʌ̍] before voiced cons. (but occ. before voiceless). /æ/ contrasts with [æə] and [æi]; /ʌ/ very high; /i/ high, up-gliding diphthong.

SC 38B: M, creamery business, farming merchandise, 66. B. Mendenhall Twp., never lived outside Co. — F., PGF b. Mendenhall Twp., PGM b. Newberry Co.; M., MGF, MGM b. Newberry Co. Nothing known earlier. — Ed.: about 7th grade ("didn't have no grades when I was going to school"). — Baptist; Masons. — Very intelligent, knows people and their behavior. Generous with time; guessed purpose of interviews. Generally quick. Alert to present, never the prey of his own anecdotes; good sense of humor. Relish for living. — A little sensitive about some shibboleths, but in general uses folk idioms freely. Could supply contextual forms easily. Admits doesn't always use "right" forms. Little drawl, long vowels fairly long. Some nasality. Many folk preterites. Voiceless stops strong esp. initially; intervocalic /-t-/ us. [-ɾ-]. No postvocalic constriction. Postvocalic /-l/ often vocalized; intervocalic /r/ often weak, sometimes lost. No evidence for linking /r/ or intrusive /r/. /e, o/ us. rising diph., occ. monoph.; /ɨ/ stressed in several words; /æ æə æi/ contrast; /a/ low-back; /u/ fronted.

SC 38C!: M, dean at Newberry College, has been professor, college president, 75. B. Dutch Fork section, lived only in Co. except when away at school. — Ancestors were pioneers in Dutch Fork section (lower Newberry Co., parts of Lexington and Richland Cos.), came in c. 1750 (some direct from Germany, others from German settlements on upper Edisto R.). Ancestors on both sides in Dutch Fork for generations. — Ed.: A.B. Newberry College, M.A. Cornell, Ph.D. Columbia. — Lutheran; knows all Newberry Co., all state political and educational leaders, widely read. — Very courteous, gentlemanly. Invaluable in directing FW to other infs. Enjoyed interviews, would have liked to go through whole set of work sheets, but too many responsibilities at college (Newberry College, one of better small denominational colleges found in South). Representative of better type of enlightened Southern conservative — that is, suspicious of New Deal and labor gains, segregationist on racial matters, but adamant in insistence on impartial justice and of adequate opportunities. Great storyteller; knows Dutch Fork life intimately (attention focused on Dutch Fork usage of his boyhood, rather than on present town usage). Very intelligent; shrewd observations on SC politics and politicians. Hospitable; public-minded; has served on state board of education and as unofficial educational adviser to several governors. — Speech natural and unaffected; no attempts to doctor it. Pleasant soft drawl. Wide variations in pitch, stress, and tempo, according to mood. Some nasality. Long vowels overlengthened under stress; weak stressed vowels us. short. Tendency to vocalize

syllabic or postvocalic /-l/; postvocalic /-r/ rather strong retroflexion, not found in any other Newberry Co. informant (possibly a characteristic of the Dutch Fork). /ɨ/ high; /u/ fronted; /e, o/ generally up-gliding; /ɔ/ up-gliding; /a/ low-back, occ. rounded slightly; /ʌ/ very high and fronted; /ɨ/ for /ɪ/ occ. /au/ low-front raised to upper mid-back or lower high-back; /ai/ has us. upcountry "slow" and "fast" alternation, according to environment. — Cultivated.

SC 38D!: F, librarian, taught voice one year, 59. B. Newberry, also lived in Baltimore 1904–6 (Peabody Conservatory), Winchester, VA 1906–7. — F., PGF b. Cromer Twp., c. 10 mi. out, PGF's F. probably b. same place ("about as far back as they've been in this country"), PGM from Dutch Fork, "all her perople came down from there"; M. b. Charleston, MGF's PGF's F. came from England, MGM b. Charleston. — Ed.: Newberry College; summers at U. of VA, U. of SC; 1 summer Appalachian State. — Lutheran; "Don't belong to anything but church and Red Cross", Am. Library Assn., State Library Assn. — Intelligent, efficient, cooperative. Not very talkative, relatively few cv. forms. Understood purpose of interviews. Not too much familiarity with horses and farming. — Quick, nervous type of speech. Educated speech, practically no concessions to folk dialect, but completely natural. [In the South, FW's impressions (borne out by Newberry and Savannah interviews) are that multidialectism is normal among upper-class males, abnormal among upper-class females. "Genteel tradition"?] Doesn't recall very many old-fashioned words. Only Newberry informant that has /ʃr-/ cluster. /-l/ sometimes vocalized; no postvocalic retroflexion; intervocalic /r/ stronger than in most Newberry informants; occ. linking /r/ and intrusive /r/. Very little nasality. /ɨ/ high; /u/ fronted (sometimes had even high-front beginning. Stressed vowels us. long; stresses strong; /ɔ/ rising diphthong. Positional variants of /ai/; /a/ low-back, normally unrounded. — Cultivated.

SC 38E!: M, lawyer, former member legislature, former Chief Justice, State Supreme Court. B. Newberry. — Newberry family, German descent. — In *Who's Who*. — Only fragmentary notes from conversations; illness and business made formal interview impossible. Very helpful in arranging contacts for FW. — Soft, melodious, drawling voice, educated without affectation. Characteristic of upper-class speech of comm. — Cultivated.

39. *Laurens County*

Formed 1785. Presbyterians 1st denomination, from 18th cent.; Baptists also by 1800. 1844 Harmony Church, Baptists and Presbyterians jointly. Episcopal 1846. Baptists and Methodists now predominant. Mfg., chiefly textiles; cotton, grain, vegetables, peanuts, dairying. Pop. 1790: 9,337, 1820: 17,582, 1850: 23,407, 1880: 29,444, 1910: 41,550, 1930: 42,094, 1960: 47,609.

Bolick, Julian Stevenson. 1973. *A Laurens County Sketchbook*. Clinton: Jacobs Press.

Leland, John A. 1879. *A Voice from South Carolina*. Charleston: Walker, Evans, and Cogswell.

McDavid, R. I., and Rosser H. Taylor, eds. 1938. *Memories of Richard Cannon Watts*. Columbia: University of South Carolina Press.

Tolbert, Marguerite. 1972. *South Carolina's Distinguished Women of Laurens County.* Columbia: R. L. Bryan.
1947. Laurens County Reveals a History of Substantial Development. *South Carolina Magazine* 10.6:6–.

Mountville, Hunter Twp.
Mountville an early village; 1st settled c. 1787.

SC 39A: M, storekeeper, "all sorts of a man": cotton gin, sawmills, farm, barbershop, meat market, deep well contracting; 15 yrs. substitute rural letter carrier, 62. B. Cross Hill Twp., 2 mi. W.; here practically all life except 6 mos. in Spartanburg with So. Rwy. Co. — F., PGF b. Cross Hill, PGF's PGF settled lower part of Co. (family prominent in Co. several generations), PGM b. in Co.; M., MGF, MGM b. Co., all lineages in Co. several generations. — Ed.: 4th or 5th grade, local schools. — Baptist; ran for state legislature, 1920, has been precinct committeeman, state constable, magistrate, former member Woodmen of the World. — Very cooperative. Gregarious. Slightly deaf. Knows everybody in comm., almost everybody in Co. (kin to most of old-timers). Fair-minded storekeeper. Soft-spoken; even-tempered, but strong sense of right and wrong. Good, quick mind; good memory. — /-r/ lacking; /-l/ often vocalized; /-t-/ > [-ɾ-]; /tj- dj- nj-/; /hw-/. /ɪ ɛ/ neutralized before nasals; [i̯ˑ] occ.; /e o/ freq. monophthongal; /ʌ/ high; /u/ fronted.

SC 39B!: M, farmer, landowner (wealthy), 84. B. nearer Beaver Dam Church, 4 1/2 mi. NW; settled 3 mi. below here when started out for himself, settled permanently at Mountville c. 1895. Much travel, esp. for medical attention. — F., PGF b. "Old Mountville", above Beaverdam Church, PGF's F., PGF's M. came from VA, PGM b. about 6 mi. below Mountville, PGM's F. settled about Charleston, then came to Laurens Co., PGM's PGF from Ireland; M. b. near Newberry Co. line, MGF left orphan and raised by brother, left Co. before Civil War and settled in TN, MGM b. on edge of Newberry Co. (Inf. not terribly interested in genealogy.) — Ed.: local schools; Adger College, Walhalla, SC, grad. U. of SC; widely read, considerable travel. — Baptist; literary societies in college; no secret societies or public offices ("all the electioneering I've ever done in my life was to keep from being elected"). — "I could've been big rich." (Actually, wealthiest man in comm. — very successful farmer.) Studied law at U. of SC, but never practiced. Used to write poetry. "Never been a frolic-man or a lady'sm'n." Voracious reader, extremely wide range; allusive memory, always citing incidents from his reading. Intimate and detailed knowledge of local flora and fauna. Lost very large personal library when his home destroyed by fire a few years ago. Now lives in little shanty. Modest wants: was known as "Diogenes" in college and believes firmly that a man can decrease his worries by decreasing his desires. Makes no parade of his learning, though can talk on technical subjects if occasion requires it. Ironist and anecdotist, many tales, which he enjoys telling. A "states-rights" man, but not belligerent about any of the common Southern prejudices. Enjoyed interviews, though not sure what some of the questions were about. Skittish where women concerned: probably result of growing up surrounded by a great many older sisters. Likes to be independent. — His patterns of folk speech largely unaffected by his wide reading and considerable travel. Very large vocabulary, ranging from folk obscenities to highly technical language. Had noticed differences in folk-vocab. in SC, TN, and Charleston; freely offered comparisons. Generally uses folk-grammar, including double negative. Drawl; slow speech. Some nasality. Long vowels quite long; stresses strong. No postvocalic constriction. /ʌ/ high; /ɔ/ upgliding diph., us. fairly high; /a/ variable, occ. low-central before /-r/ reflexes, us. low-back before cons. (often rounded); /o/ up-gliding diph.; /e/ us. slightly up-gliding diph., occ. monoph; /au/ with varied beginning [æ a ɑ], no positional alternation; /ai/ with us. upcountry alternation of "long" and "short" forms, but occ. with "long" form before voiceless cons.; /ɪ/ occ. for /i/ in stressed syllables. — Cultivated.

40. Abbeville County
Formed 1785. Huguenots arrived 1730s; Ulster Scots arrived 1756 from PA, via VA; Germans in 1763–64. Mostly small farmers. River navigation Abbeville to Charleston in 19th cent. Cotton, oats, corn, some mfg. Pop. 1790: 9,191, 1820: 23,167, 1850: 32,318, 1880: 40,815, 1910: 34,804, 1930: 23,323, 1960: 21,417.

Cook, Harvey Toliver. 1924. *The Hard Labor Section.* Greenville.
Julien, Carl Thomas. 1950. *Ninety Six: Landmarks of South Carolina's Last Frontier Region.* Columbia: University of South Carolina Press.

Abbeville
Settled in 1730s by Huguenots: "New Bordeaux". Vineyards successful till "drys" declared the business illegal. Also tried silk. Also Ulster Scot and German migration from PA. Pop. 1850: 1,252, 1880: 1,543, 1910: 4,459, 1930: 4,414, 1960: 5,436.

SC 40A: M, farmer, occ. cattleman, occ. guarded convicts, 63. B. "Old Abbeville Co." (now McCormick Co.), 12 mi. SE of courthouse; a few brief stays in Texas in 20s (longest 10 mos.), 3 three-mo. visits to FL, 1 to MS; 3 mos. Anderson Co. (SC 41). — F. b. 10 mi. S, PGF, PGM b. same neighborhood, ancestors bought land from someone who'd been given it by George III, owned it till 1933, family "Scotch-Irish"; M. b. about 9 mi. S., MGF, MGM b. same neighborhood, "Dutch". — Ed.: 150–200 days in all in country schools. — Knows about everyone in Abbeville. Habitué of courthouse steps, whittling and gossiping. "No church, no lodge, no politics." — Somewhat suspicious of project; afraid it would get him in trouble. Requested FW to have final sessions at his house, after his acquaintances had teased him about it. Somewhat evasive, as if unsure of himself. Tends to be garrulous and get off subject of interview. — Very good cv. forms. Difficult to get taboo words (sister present part of the time). Somewhat ashamed of folk speech (aux. inf., sister, "corrected" him and told him what he said normally). Tempo wavering. Was afraid that he'd be listed as using "incorrect terms" which "other people" used (uses them himself, when off guard). No postvocalic retroflexion. Stressed vowels fairly long. /r/ often lost in initial clusters. Final stops sometimes lost. Final /-l/ weak, often completely vocalized. Some nasality. /ɔ/ rounded and diphthongized; /e/ often monoph.

SC 40A*: F. Sister of SC40A. — Somewhat better educated but less unsure.

SC 40B: Lebanon, Abbeville P.O. and Twp. — F, housekeeper, former teacher, 78. B. Cedar Spring Twp. (near present home, but twp. lines changed). Some travel (VA, NC, SC, GA, FL). — F., PGF b. present McCormick Co. (Old Abbeville Co.), PGF's PGF led Huguenots from France, 1716–18; M. b. Rocky River (Abbeville Co.). MGF, MGM Ulster Scots descent, came from PA via VA. — Ed.: Lebanon School (country school), 3 yrs. Due West College; father had a good library, read a good deal. — Presbyterian; church auxiliaries; formerly Huguenot Society (Charleston). — Dignified; sense of family position, despite present poverty. Somewhat sensitive about current economic status. No pretensions of knowledge more than actually possessed. Somewhat reticent. Strong taboo sense. Some ideas of "correctness" (probably due to past occupation), not always accurate. Knowledge of comm. history and customs good; not prone to gossip about private lives. — Pure speech has strong admixture of folkways (about type II+). Stress strong. Pitch somewhat monotonous (except interjectional sentences). Moderate nasality (not always indicated). /-r-/ quite weak; no postvocalic constriction; /-l/ dark, weak, often vocalized. Initial /p- t- k-/ strongly aspirated; /k g/ fronted (not often marked). Front vowels somewhat retracted, back vowels generally advanced. /i e o u/ up-gliding diphs. /u/ generally high-central; /-ju/ after /t- d- n-/, not after /r- l- s-/; automatic fronting of /u/ after /r- s- ʃ- j-/. /ai/ with us. upcountry positional allophones, but tendency toward "long" diphthong in all positions. No phonemic contrast of [æ] and [æ⁴]; /ɔi/ generally disyllabic; /au/ with wide variation in position of 1st member (free variation); /ɔ/ diphthongal, [-ɔr]/[-or] contrast.

41. Anderson County

Formed from Pendleton District 1826 (Pendleton District, including present Anderson, Pickens, and Oconee Cos., formed 1785). Settlement slow in Pendleton Dist. till after 1783. Several treaties with Indians in 18th cent.; last Indian lands purchased 1817. Pendleton (town) near Clemson, an old cultural center. Silkworm culture attempted, not commercially feasible. Town declined after 1865. In 1826, Anderson Co. had some Dutch, Germans, Scots, Ulster Scots, Irish, English. Orig. small farmers, few slaveholders. Presbyterians first, Baptists from 1789, Quakers. Some strong anti-slavery sentiments here. Tobacco first, then cotton; first cotton mill 1836. Attempt at pioneering auto design. Many cotton mills; cotton, grain, fruit, vegetables. Pop. (Pendleton Dist. 1790: 9,568, 1820: 27,022) Anderson 1830: 17,169, 1850: 21,476, 1880: 33,612, 1910: 69,568, 1930: 80,949, 1960: 98,478.

Dickson, Frank A. 1975. *Journeys into the Past: The Anderson Region's Heritage*. Anderson: Dickson.

Fuller, Elizabeth Belser, ed. 1969. *Anderson County Sketches*. Anderson: Droke House.

Johnston, Olin D., et al. 1923. *Anderson County, Economic and Social*. Columbia: University of South Carolina.

McFall, Pearl Smith. 1953. *So Lives the Dream*. NY: Comet Press Books.

Meeks, Z. W. 1947. Anderson: Where Agriculture and Industry Meet. *South Carolina Magazine* 10.12:15–.

Simpson, R. W. 1913. *History of Old Pendleton District. . . .* Anderson: Oulla Printing and Binding Co.

Stevenson, Mary, comp. 1973. *The Diary of Clarissa Adger Bowen*. Pendleton: S.C. Research and Publication Committee.

Vandiver, Louise Ayer. 1928. *Traditions and History of Anderson County*. Atlanta: Ruralist Press.

Wright, Louis B. 1974. *Barefoot in Arcadia: Memoirs of a More Innocent Era*. Columbia: University of South Carolina Press.

1943. Anderson County Does Outstanding Things. *South Carolina Magazine* 6.1:18–19.

Eureka Church, Anderson P.O. and Twp.

Anderson part of old Cherokee lands, deeded to state in 1777; some prior settlement. Predominantly Scotch-Irish from PA and VA among early settlers. Inc. 1882. Center for horse-breeding and racing. Hydroelectric power plant on Seneca River 1897. Products and industries: textile mills, fruit and vegetables, brooms, mattresses, brick and tile, cottonseed products, fertilizer, meal, flour, metal shingles, eyeglasses, monuments and lumber. Pop. 1880: 1,850, 1910: 9,654, 1930: 14,383, 1960: 41,316.

SC 41A: F, housewife, 79. B. near Keys Lake, 2 mi. W. of Anderson. — F. b. here, PGF b. S. Ireland, PGM prob. b. here, Scotch-Irish stock (had strong brogue); MGF b. Belton, SC (c. 10 mi. E. of Anderson), MGM b. here (prob. all Scotch or Ulster Scots). — Ed.: till 12–13 off and on. — Baptist. — Plain, sensible, serious-minded. Felt she was contributing valuable information and took pains to be thoroughly honest. Intelligent in all she told, but incapable of realizing when she had been tricked into using old-fashioned forms. Belongs to the plantation class, but obviously of common, very respectable stock, with none of the gifts or glamour of the low country. — Tempo deliberate. Vowels and diphthongs rather short us., but sometimes lengthened. Use of [ə] in all positions, and [aə ɔə] etc., even when a vowel follows, is like Midwestern practice. [ə] is slightly higher and further front than in Midwest, strongly cacuminal, not truly retroflex.

SC 41B: Anderson. — M, dairy man, 58. B. Garvin Twp., 12 mi. N. of city; lived in Lee Co. 10 mos. 1918–19, to Anderson 1921. — Family migrated from England to Ireland, to Philadelphia in 1732, thence to Charleston, to Abbeville, to Oconee Co. Family prominent in upcountry: Revolutionary general, governor, etc. Family history published. — Ed.: country school, Garvin Twp. — Methodist; Woodmen of the World, Lions, Farmers Alliance, Grange. — Inf. cooperative; explanations adequate. Somewhat restive (ill). — Speech moderate to slow tempo. Retroflexion moderate to weak. Stressed vowels fairly long, unstr. fairly short. /e o/ only slightly diphthongal (up-gliding), occ. monophthongal. /ʌ/ rather high, occ. slightly fronted and rounded; /u/ high central beginning; /a/ low-central retracted, rather than extreme low-back as in Greenville. /ɔ/ normally diphthongal (up-gliding). /ai/ with normal upcountry positional allophones; /au/ with free variation of beginning. Phonemic contrast of /æ/ and /æi/; insufficient evidence on whether [æ:] also phonemic.

42. Greenville County

Formed 1786 from newly ceded Cherokee lands. Area opened to trade in 1760s; to legitimate white settlement in 1777 (though some settlers arrived earlier). Earliest settlers from PA. Some old families originally in Spartanburg Co. 1st Presbyterian church 1786; Episcopal and Baptist congregations by 1821. 1st crops: tobacco, corn, wheat; slaves and cotton in early 19th cent. Also summer resorts for planters. 1st textile production 1820; intensified by 1873, esp. 1895–1912. 46 plants in Co. by 1971. Military bases here 1898, 1917, 1941. Also some cotton, corn, dairying; N. part still summer resort. Pop. 1790: 6,503, 1820: 14,530, 1850: 20,156, 1880: 37,496, 1910: 68,377, 1930: 117,009, 1960: 209,776.

Barhare, Ralph C. 1926. *Community Welfare Work in the Mill Villages of Greenville, South Carolina*. University of South Carolina Master's thesis.

Barnes, Frank. 1956. *The Greenville Story*. Greenville.

Crittenden, S. S. 1933. *The Greenville Century Book*. Greenville: Greenville Press.

De Forest, J. W. 1868. The Low-Down People. *Putnam's*, June 1868:704–16.

De Forest, John Williams. 1945. *A Union Officer in the Reconstruction*. New Haven: Yale University Press.

Ebaugh, Laura Smith. 1966. *Bridging the Gap: A Guide to Early Greenville, South Carolina*. Greenville: Greater Greenville Chamber of Commerce.

Glenn, L. M. 1939. Greenville County, First in Population. *South Carolina Magazine* 2.1:23–.

Gullick, Guy A. 1921. Greenville County, Economic and Social. *South Carolina University Bulletin* 102.

Jacobs, William Plume. 1935. *The Pioneer*. Clinton: Jacobs and Co. Press.

Marsh, Kenneth Frederick, and Blanche Marsh. 1965. *The New South: Greenville, South Carolina*. Columbia: H. L. Bryan Co.

McGlothlin, William Joseph. 1926. *Baptist Beginnings in Education: A History of Furman University*. Nashville: Sunday School Board of the Southern Baptist Convention.

McKoy, Henry Bacon. 1962. *A History of the First Presbyterian Church in Greenville, South Carolina*. Greenville: Keys Print. Co.

Moseley, A. M. 1966. *The Buncombe Street Methodist Story*. Greenville: Moseley.

Oliphant, Mary C. Simms. 1933. The Genesis of an Up-Country Town. *South Carolina Historical Association Proceedings* 50–62.

Prince, Angela Fowler. 1976. *Greenville: A Portrait of Its People*. Greenville: Keys Print Co.

Richardson, James McDowell. 1930. *History of Greenville County, South Carolina, Narrative and Biographical*. Atlanta: A. H. Cawston.

Tippett, James Sterling. 1936. *Schools for a Growing Democracy*. Boston: Ginn and Co.

Whitmire, B. T. 1976. *The Presence of the Past: Epitaphs of Eighteenth and Nineteenth Century Pioneers in Greenville County, South Carolina, and Their Descendants*. Baltimore: John Hopkins University Press.

Wood, Robert C. 1976. *Parish in the Heart of the City: Christ Church, Greenville, South Carolina*. Greenville: Keys Printing.

1946. Greenville, County and City. *South Carolina Magazine* 9.3:6–.

1962–. *The Proceedings and Papers of the Greenville County Historical Society*. Greenville: The Society.

Greenville

Part of old Cherokee lands; settled first from PA and VA by Scotch-Irish and Germans. 1st settler an Irishman c. 1765; became Tory. Early became summer resort for coastal planters. Village called Pleasantburg 1797; name changed to Greenville and chartered as a town 1831; chartered as city 1868. Episcopalians and Baptists by 1821; Methodists by 1834; Presbyterians by 1848. 1st cotton mill by 1820. Christ Church Parish est. 1825; building 1852. Furman at Greenville from 1851; merged with other local college in 1933. 1st library 1921. Unionist stronghold: many deserters and draft dodgers. Many textile mills after 1880; diversification of industry, including brick and tile, foods and candy, patent medicines, fertilizer, flour, feed, grist, bakery products, paints, meat products. Engineering (mill design, etc.), military bases, shipping center (trucks), center of textile industry. Textile Exhibition and Textile Hall from c. 1920s. Pop. 1850: 1,305, 1880: 6,160, 1910: 15,741, 1930: 29,154, 1960: 66,188.

SC 42N: F, house servant, 54. B. Greenville. — F, PGF, PGM b. Greenville; M. b. Augusta, GA, brought to Greenville age 3, MGF, MGM b. Augusta. — Ed.: 5th grade. — Baptist (enthusiastic), church societies; Lady Knights, knows most of Greenville. — Inf. had worked for FW's family for over 40 yrs. Excellent disposition; never angry; fond of children (reciprocal). Gregarious, very religious, conscious of superior status in AfAm comm.. Most cooperative, almost to excess; could pretend knowledge where there was none. Very good at mimicking. — Like most AfAm house servants, can talk a rather cultivated type of English when on guard, but relaxes among close friends. Not very clear about agricultural terms; very good on cooking. Great variation in pitch and stress; stressed long vowels and diphthongs tend to be over long; unstr. vowels very short. Moderate nasality. Final clusters us. simplified; very little postvocalic constriction. /f/ for /θ/; occ. dental [t̪ d̪ n̪].

SC 42M: F, retired house servant, 100. B. Greenville. Some travel with people for whom she has worked, but essentially has stayed in Greenville. — Born a slave. — Ed.: none. — Methodist. Matriarch of Greenville Negro comm.: knows all AfAms, all whites of older generation. Has worked for many of Greenville's best families from c. 15 yrs. old to 95. — Hearing poor, but eyesight and memory good. Remembers everybody she worked for and all the children she helped raise. Very religious; concerned about wild ways of younger generation. Respected by both races. Enjoys talking about old times. Impossible to conduct regular interview on account of inf.'s poor hearing; all forms cited are forms from her reminiscences. — Some old-fashioned words, generally patterned along speech of upper class whites in pron. Double neg.; folk preterites. Postvocalic /-r/ > /ə/ or length or zero.

SC 42A: Parsons Mill Road, Greenville P.O., Butler Twp. — M, tenant farmer (worked in store 2 yrs., 1 yr. in cotton mill), 69. B. Dunklin Twp., S. part of Co., near Laurens Co. line, moved to Oaklawn Twp. age 11, almost 50 yrs. in Woodville section, moved to Butler Twp. 1937. — F., PGF b. Laurens Co., PGF's F. b. Scotland, came first to AL, thence to Laurens Co., PGM "distantly related to Cherokee Indians"; M., MGF b. Dunklin Twp., MGF's F. b. VA, moved to Greenville Co. — Ed.: 4 terms, 3 mos. ea., country schools. — Baptist;

Woodmen of the World 1908–31, Farmers' Union, strongly rooted in Co. — Knows local families and traditions and places in the comm. Cooperative. Somewhat deferential to FW, perhaps because at one time was tenant of FW's grandfather. Strongly moral and religious, with appreciation for those with views different from his; prefers to know where politicians stand, even though he disagrees with them. — Familiar with farm and local terms; speaks folk idiom naturally although he has some confused notions of "correctness". Strong nasality. Stressed vowels fairly long. Final cons. generally clear. Retroflexion fairly light. Front vowels [i ɪ e] quite close, but generally distinctive. [ʌ] fairly high; [u] somewhat fronted; [a] low-back advanced; [ɔ] clearly diphthongal; [ɔi] disyllabic.

SC 42B!: F, housewife, 67. B. "Happy Home" family estate about 20 mi. N.; in Greenville exc. college and 13 yrs. in Mt. Vernon, OH (1905–18). — F. b. Greenville (possibly Marietta, 15 mi. N.?), PGF b. Greenville, PGF's F. prob. b. VA, PGF's M. Huguenot stock, PGF's MGF 1st grave in Springwood Cemetery, PGM's F. b. Greenville, PGM's PGF a Greenville physician; M. b. Lyman comm., Spartanburg Co., MGF, MGM upper Greenville Co. Family prominent in Greenville. — Ed.: private teacher; Greenville Women's College; Miss Ely's School (finishing), Riverside Drive, NY. — Episcopalian; Woman's Auxiliary, Garden Club, McKissick Book Club, Hopewell Auxiliary; active in charitable organizations, well known in comm. — Independent in thinking; forthright in expression. Cooperative. Intellectually alert. Enjoyed interviews though didn't altogether understand purpose. Few guesses; either knew or didn't know. — Grammar upper-class. Nasality. Strong stresses. Wide range intonation. Phonemic pattern normal for educated speech of area. Little postvocalic constriction. — Cultivated.

SC 42C!: M, industrial lobbyist, 58. B. Oaklawn Twp., about 14 mi. S.; to Greenville age 23. Banking and real estate in Greenville. Good deal of travel, mostly in state and adjacent states. — F., PGF b. Oaklawn Twp. (there since c. 1780, when first of family to settle was killed by Tories), family Ulster Scots, from PA via VA, to Laurens Co., thence Greenville, PGM b. Greenville Co., Welsh descent, all paternal lineages in Co. by 1785; M. b. Greenville Co., MGF Welsh descent, MGM b. Greenville Co., MGM's F. from Charleston, of Holland Dutch descent, MGM's M. from old Charleston family (descended from governor of 1780s). — Ed.: country schools, Clemson College, Davidson College (B.S. 1906). — Episcopalian; Masonic orders (inactive); member city council 4 yrs., state assemblyman 6 yrs. Knows practically every S. Carolinian of prominence. — Strikingly handsome; very intelligent, but lazy. Gregarious when permitted. Hottempered but affectionate; strongly devoted to family. Connoisseur of good food. Many anecdotes. — Speech generally slow, heavily emphasized. Strong nasality (not marked). Postvocalic constriction stronger in direct responses than in conversation or ancedote. Never uses folk grammar except deliberately, for purpose of illustrating anecdotes (common SC trait). — Cultivated.

SC 42D!: M, college teacher, 25. B. Greenville (was teaching in Charleston). — Son of inf. SC42C!. F.'s lineage on SC42C; M. b. Lexington, VA, moved to Greenville age 18 mos. after

PGM died, MGF b. Oswego, NY, MGF's F. b. Prince William Co., VA, army surgeon, son of 18th cent. tobacco merchant, MGM b. Setauket, Long I., NY, MGM's F., MGM's M. of old NY families, lineages ranging back from 1790 to 1630s. — Ed.: Greenville schools; Furman, B.A. 1931; Duke, M.A. 1933, Ph.D. 1935. — Baptist with Episcopal leanings (confirmed following spring); SC Poetry Society, MLA, SAMLA, Linguistic Society; Yachting since in Charleston. — Somewhat guarded in responses, due to harassment by president of college where employed, but grew more relaxed during interview. Enjoyed experience. Reluctant in profession of English; fond of history. — Somewhat hesitant in speech. Drawl; nasality. Vowels of us. upcountry quality. Postvocalic constriction only in *bird* and the like. — Cultivated.

SC 42E!: M, textile executive, 52. B. Conestee, Greenville Co., 8 mi. S.; moved to Greenville age 4. Except for schooling and military service, never out of Co. — F. b. Fairview, Greenville Co., PGF b. Mississippi, moved back to Greenville, PGF's F., PGF's M., PGM b. Fairview; M., MGF, MGM b. Midville, Burke Co., GA. — Ed.: Greenville schools; B.S. Furman, M.S. LSU. — First Baptist Church; Greenville Analysts Society (securities), Piedmont Traffic Club (commercial). — Inf. is a childhood friend of FW; grew up about a block away, they have kept up friendship since 1916. Inf. has remained in comm. except for business travel and military service, little dialectal attrition. — Completely natural; on few occasions (as with *coop*) when he gave an artificial response he spontaneously corrected himself. Wide intonation range. Very heavy primary stresses; stressed vowels prolonged ("Southern drawl"). Excellent example of assured cultivated upcountry speech. — Cultivated.

43. Pickens County

Formed 1826 from Pendleton Dist. Ft. Prince George here 1753; Indians expelled after Rev. Many German immigrants in 19th cent.; also some English, Irish. RR in 1870s; also abortive efforts to build RRs across Blue Ridge. Textile mills 1880s; lumber mills 1920s. State parks, forest; quarries; cotton, corn, poultry. Pop. 1830: 14,473, 1850: 16,904, 1880: 14,389, 1910: 25,422, 1930: 33,709, 1960: 46,030.

Clayton, Frederick Van. 1930. *The Settlement of Pendleton District, 1777–1800.* University of South Carolina Master's thesis.

Klosky, Beth Ann. 1971. *The Pendleton Legacy.* Columbia: Sandlapper Press.

McFall, Pearl Smith. 1959. *It Happened in Pickens County.* Pickens.

McFall, Pearl. 1947. A Brief Sketch of Pickens County, South Carolina. *South Carolina Magazine* 10.1:26.

Reece, Bert Hendricks. 1970. *History of Pumpkintown — Oolenoy.* Pickens: Miracle Hill Print Shop.

Robertson, Ben. 1942. *Red Hills and Cotton: An Up-Country Memory.* NY: A. A. Knopf.

Young, Willie Pauline, comp. 1953. *"Citizenship Papers" of Old Pickens District.* Liberty: E. Clement Young.

Pumpkintown, Pickens P.O.

Pumpkintown mountaineer country; moonshining once. Table Rock State Park here: a summer resort in 1840s; now reservoir and state park.

SC 43A: M, farmer, 100. B. here; except for military service (Confederacy) and marketing trips to Augusta, GA, hardly left the co. in his lifetime. — Family one of earliest in comm. — Inf. rather dull and mind tended to wander, so direct questioning impossible; daughter and grandson got him to telling anecdotes, from which many work sheet items could be transcribed. Thus, every response is conversational. — Phonemic patterns much like those of 43B, a younger neighbor, exc. that 43A much more old-fashioned, as in greater use of /a/ in *there, search, grandfather*, etc.

SC 43B: M, farmer, storekeeper, grist miller, 66. B. here. — F. PGF, PGM, M., MGF, MGM all b. comm. To inf.'s knowledge, none ever came in after comm. settled. — Ed.: 8th grade, Dacusville. — Baptist; Woodmen of the World; knows everybody in comm., goes to Greenville twice a week to sell produce. — Inf. knows commuty and people thoroughly. Interview spasmodic, interrupted by inf.'s business negotiations, which, however, allowed many opportunities to get forms from aux. infs. Inf. apparently quite interested in FW's work: frequently reminisces about interviews, asks FW's father about FW's health, etc. — Tempo moderate to slow, tendency to monotone, nasality (not us. indicated) normal. Stressed vowels long; voiceless stops moderate, esp. in prevocalic position. Back vowels all fronted somewhat. Retroflexion us. moderate to strong, but occ. altogether lacking, as in many examples of *first*. /ɔ/ us. diph., except occ. pre-/-r/ in cv. forms; /e ɪ/ both fairly high, approaching /i/. /j/ before /u/ following /t- d- n-/. /e o/ occ. non-diph., when diph., always rising type. /u/ us. quite back; /ʌ/ high, occ. slight rounding; /æ/ fairly high — phonemic /æ æɛ/ distinction as normal in upcountry South.

SC 43B*: Customers of SC43B. Middle-aged or older; natives of comm.

Dacusville
Old part of Co., near Saluda River. Rural.

SC 43C!: M, country doctor, 69. B. here, lived nowhere else exc. for school. — F. b. 2 mi. from Dacusville, PGF b. Gowansville, N. Greenville Co., PGM b. just across Saluda R., Greenville Co.; M. b. between Dacusville and Saluda R., MGF b. 2 mi. from Dacusville, MGM b. E. Pickens Co.; MGF's, MGM's people original settlers, came from PA via VA. — Ed.: Tusculum College, TN; SC Medical College, Charleston (1 yr.); short term, U. of South, Sewanee, TN. — Woodmen of the World, Mason, Pickens Co. Medical Society; knows about everybody in E. part of Pickens Co. — Big, jovial, hearty. Cooperative, generally very natural. Prob. not too well up on medical scholarship; attitude generally common-sense. Heavy eater; very hospitable to FW. Interested in project, referred FW to possible inf.'s, some of whom were used and all of whom were useful. Record defective; some problems with FW's technique in eliciting morph. items. Lexicon fairly good; items generally well identified and defined. — Speech not a great deal different from that of Greenville, except undiphthongal /e/ and /o/ more common. Generally follows folk type of speech. Final stops us. clear, though non-released. Tempo slow, not much nasality. /u/ and /ʊ/ somewhat centralized, other back vowels less (/ɔ/ perhaps undertranscribed); /a/ well back, before /-r/ as well as before other cons. Aspiration

moderate. /ai/ follows us. Piedmont allophonic pattern; /au/ doesn't vary according to environment. — Cultivated.

44. Oconee County

Formed 1868 from Pickens Co. "Walhalla" settled by German shopkeepers and clerks, many from Charleston, c. 1850. Blue Ridge RR to Knoxville surveyed in 1850s; abandoned after Civil War. Clemson U. (originally a local agricultural school). Summer resort area; timber, cotton and cotton mills, corn, wheat. Pop. 1870: 10,536, 1880: 16,256, 1910: 27,337, 1960: 40,204.

Clayton, Frederick Van. 1930. *The Settlement of Pendleton District, 1777–1800*. University of South Carolina Master's thesis.

Doyle, Mary Cherry. 1935. *Historic Oconee in South Carolina*. Seneca.

Hollenam, Frances. 1946. *The Development of Education in Oconee County*. University of South Carolina Master's thesis.

Jaynes, R. T. 1948. *Brief History of Oconee County*. Seneca.

Klosky, Beth Ann. 1971. *The Pendleton Legacy*. Columbia: Sandlapper Press.

Schlaefer, M. V. 1946. Oconee: Land of Adventure and Romance. *South Carolina Magazine* 9.6:10–.

Seaborn, Margaret Mills. 1973. *Benjamin Hawkins's Journeys through Oconee County, South Carolina, in 1796–1797*. Columbia: R. L. Bryan Co.

Watkins, Jack, Ruth Gaines Davis, and Charles S. Collins, eds. 1968. *Oconee County, South Carolina Centennial, 1868–1968*.

Flat Shoals School, Tamassee, Walhalla P.O., Keowee Twp.
Tamassee a mtn. comm. DAR industrial school. Many Union sympathizers, lukewarm Confederates, and deserters.

SC 44A: M, farmer and carpenter (has made shoes, wagons, done blacksmithing, been road foreman for school district), 70. B. a mile from here; has worked short times in Union, Laurens, and Abbeville Cos. — F. b. Anderson Co., moved here age 8 wks. (1832), PGF raised in Abbeville, lived there till 1830, moved to Anderson, then Oconee, PGM b. NC, raised in Oconee; M. b. Pickens Co. (old Pickensville, S. of Easley), MGF, MGM desc. of SW migration of Ulster Scots. — Ed.: about 2 yrs. altogether; reads a good deal: Bible, newspapers. — Presbyterian; Masons, Woodmen of the World, Farmers' Alliance, Farmers' Union, Grange. — Modest, "good neighbor"; spends a lot of time helping out less fortunate members of the comm. Hospitable, cooperative. Quite conversant with affairs of Co. and comm. and to some extent with world matters. Few inhibitions about taboo matters; recognized existence of taboos, warned FW against complications if he came up against them too abruptly, but showed no hesitation about discussing them himself. Travels very little now; few books, mostly old schoolbooks. Excellent memory. — /p- t- k-/ strongly aspirated; /k g/ fronted (not always indicated); /-r-/ sometimes weak; /-r/ moderate to strong retroflexion; /-l/ dark, sometimes weak. Soft-spoken, low-pitched; moderately variable in pitch. /i e o u/ generally up-gliding, but /e/ frequently monophth. Front vowels generally retracted, /o ʊ/ somewhat fronted (not always marked). /ai/ allophones as us. in Piedmont, some tendency for long [aˑɪ] in all positions. /æ/

and /æi/ phonemic contrast; /ɔi/ us. disyllabic; /au/ with 1st member varying freely from [æ↗] to [a]; /ju/ after /t- d- n-/, not /r- l- s-/; /a/ lower back; /ɔ/ diph.

Richland, Center and Seneca Twps.
    Cotton mills, rich farming at Richland.

SC 44B: M, farmer, "dabbled in politics", 85. B. Tugalow or Sentut (SW of here), always in section. — F. b. 6 mi. S. of inf.'s house, PGF b. Abbeville 1763, settled in Pendleton (Oconee) Dist. after Rev., PGF's F. from PA via E. NC to Abbeville, PGF's M. of Huguenot descent, PGM b. Philadelphia, migrated to Salisbury, then to Waxhaw, then to Abbeville; M., MGF, MGM b. Greenville. — Ed.: 2 yrs. schooling, 3–4 mos. at a time; 1/2 freshman year at Newberry College (at Walhalla), 1874. — No church (boasts of heterodoxy — "Unitarian, like Emerson, Beecher, and Lincoln"); family has strong connections in Greenville, inf. in SC House of Representatives 1896–1900, 1902–6, State Senate, 1914–18. — Inf. consciously a self-made man, self-assured in the tradition of the self-sufficient upcountry farmer. Fancied himself a bit of a writer (interested in family history), somewhat superstitiously deferential to dictionary. A little impatient with slowness of FW, and with inquiries about apparent inconsequentials. Inf., at 82, still did most of responsible farm work, including the milking. In general, very satisfactory. — Retroflexion slight; nasality fairly strong. Quite deliberate, almost pontifical in speech, as befitting a partiarch. /k g/ a bit forward. /a/ quite far back; /e/ frequently monoph., /o/ less freq. — Aux. inf., son, middle 50s, somewhat overshadowed by F., but as cooperative, and more conversant with purpose of Atlas; still lived on home place, seldom traveled, speech not greatly different from F.

Bibliographies

Carroll, B. R., comp. 1836. *Historical Collections of South Carolina.* 2 vols. NY: Harper and Bros.

Cote, Richard N. 1981. *Local and Family History in South Carolina: A Bibliography.* Easley: Southern Historical Press.

Dunlap, Mary M., ed. 1977. *A Catalog of the South Caroliniana Collection of J. Rion McKissick.* Spartanburg: Reprint Co.

Easterby, James Harold. 1950. *Guide to the Study and Reading of South Carolina History.* Columbia. Repr. 1975 (Spartanburg: Reprint Co.).

Jones, Lewis P. 1970. *Books and Articles on South Carolina History.* Columbia: South Carolina Tricentennial Commission.

Moore, John Hammond. 1967. *Research Materials in South Carolina.* Columbia: University of South Carolina Press.

Petty, Julian Jay. 1952. *A Bibliography of the Geography of the State of South Carolina.* Columbia: University of South Carolina Research Committee.

Turnbull, Robert James. 1956–60. *Bibliography of South Carolina, 1563–1950.* 6 vols. Charlottesville: University of Virginia Press.

Whitney, Edson L. 1894. Bibliography of the Colonial History of South Carolina. *Annual Report of the American Historical Association,* 563–86.

General Histories

Ball, William Watts. 1932. *The State That Forgot: South Carolina's Surrender to Democracy.* Indianapolis: Bobbs-Merrill Co.

Bargar, B. D. 1970. *Royal South Carolina, 1719–1763.* Columbia: South Carolina Tricentennial Commission.

Burney, Eugenia. 1970. *Colonial South Carolina.* Camden, NJ: T. Nelson.

Drayton, John. 1802. *A View of South Carolina....* Charleston. Repr. 1972 (Spartanburg: Reprint Co.).

Ermkins, Francis B., and Robert R. Woody. 1939. *Reconstruction in South Carolina.* Chapel Hill: University of North Carolina Press.

Federal Writers Program. 1941. *South Carolina: A Guide to the Palmetto State.* NY: Oxford University Press.

Jones, Lewis P. 1971. *South Carolina: A Synoptic History for Laymen.* Columbia: Sandlapper Press.

Lander, E. M. 1960. *A History of South Carolina, 1865–1960.* Chapel Hill: University of North Carolina Press.

Lander, Ernest McPherson, and Robert K. Ackerman. 1973. *Perspectives in South Carolina History, the First Three Hundred Years.* Columbia: University of South Carolina Press.

Quattlebaum, Paul. 1956. *The Land Called Chicora: The Carolinas under Spanish Rule....* Gainesville, FL: University of Florida Press.

Ramsey, David. 1879. *History of South Carolina, 1670–1808.* Charleston: David Longworth. Repr. 1958 (Newberry, S.C.: W. J. Duffie).

Simms, William Gilmore. 1840. *The History of South Carolina.* Charleston: S. Babcock and Co.

Sirmans, Marion Eugene. 1966. *Colonial South Carolina: A Political History, 1663–1763.* Chapel Hill, NC: Institute of Early American History and Culture.

Smith, William Roy. 1903. *South Carolina as a Royal Province, 1719–1776.* NY: Macmillan.

Snowden, Yates, ed. 1920. *History of South Carolina.* 5 vols. Chicago: Lewis Pub. Co.

Wallace, David Duncan. 1934. *The History of South Carolina.* 4 vols. NY: American Historical Society.

Wallace, David Duncan. 1951. *South Carolina: A Short History, 1520–1948.* Chapel Hill: University of North Carolina Press.

Weston, Plowden Charles Jennett. 1856. *Documents Connected with the History of South Carolina.* London.

Wright, Louis B. 1976. *South Carolina, a Bicentennial History.* Nashville: American Association for State and Local History.

Special Studies

Abbott, Martin. 1967. *The Freedmen's Bureau in South Carolina....* Chapel Hill: University of North Carolina Press.

Andrews, Columbus, and Marion A. Wright. 1933. *Administrative County Government in South Carolina.* Chapel Hill: University of North Carolina Press.

Bacot, Daniel Huger. 1923. The South Carolina Up Country at the End of the Eighteenth Century. *American Historical Review* July 1923:682–98.

Ball, William Watts. 1954. *The Editor and the Republic.* Chapel Hill: University of North Carolina Press.

Betts, Albert D. 1952. *History of South Carolina Methodism.* Columbia: Advocate Press.

Boucher, E. J. 1948. *Vestrymen and Church Wardens in South Carolina, 1706–1778.* University of South Carolina Master's thesis.

Brewster, Lawrence Fay. 1947. *Summer Migration and Resorts of South Carolina Low-Country Planters.* Durham, NC: Duke University Press

Brown, Richard Maxwell. 1963. *The South Carolina Regulators.* Cambridge, MA: Harvard University Press.

Burton, E. Milby. 1942. *South Carolina Silversmiths, 1690–1860.* Charleston: Charleston Museum.

Carlton, David L. 1982. *Mill and Town in South Carolina, 1880–1920.* Baton Rouge: Louisiana State University Press.

Cauthen, Charles E. 1950. *South Carolina Goes to War, 1860–65.* Chapel Hill: University of North Carolina Press.

Channing, Steven A. 1970. *Crisis of Fear: Secession in South Carolina.* NY: Simon and Schuster.

Childs, St. Julien Ravenel. 1940. *Malaria and Colonization in the Carolina Low Country, 1526–1696.* Baltimore: Johns Hopkins University Press.

Childs, St. Julien Ravenel. 1941. Cavaliers and Burghers in the Carolina Low-Country. In Eric F. Goldman, ed. *Historiography and Urbanization: Essays in American History in Honor of W. Stull Holt* (Baltimore: Johns Hopkins University Press), 1–20.

Clark, Thomas Dionysius. 1973. *South Carolina: The Grand Tour, 1780–1865.* Columbia: University of South Carolina Press.

Clowse, Converse D. 1971. *Economic Beginnings in Colonial South Carolina. . . .* Columbia: South Carolina Tricentennial Commission.

Coleman, James K. 1935. *State Administration in South Carolina.* NY: Columbia University thesis.

Cook, Harvey Toliver. 1926. *Rambles in the Pee Dee Basin, South Carolina.* Columbia: State Co.

Cooper, William J., Jr. 1968. *The Conservative Regime: South Carolina 1877–1890.* Baltimore: Johns Hopkins.

Courdin, P. 1946 *Life along the Santee in Williamsburg County, South Carolina.* Kingstree: The County Record.

Dalcho, Frederick. 1820. *An Historical Account of the Protestant Episcopal Church in South-Carolina.* Charleston. Repr. 1972 (NY: Arno Press).

De Vorsey, Louis, Jr. 1982. *The Georgia-South Carolina Boundary: A Problem in Historical Geography.* Athens, GA: University of Georgia Press.

Derrick, Samuel Malanchthon. 1930. *Centennial History of South Carolina Railroad.* Columbia: State Co.

Doar, David. 1936. *Rice and Rice Planting in the South Carolina Low Country.* Charleston: Charleston Museum.

Donnan, Elizabeth. 1928. The Slave Trade into South Carolina before the Revolution. *American Historical Review* 33:804–28.

DuBose, Samuel and Frederick A. Porcher. 1887. *A Contribution to the History of the Huguenots of South Carolina.* NY: T. Gaillard Thomas.

Elzas, Barnett A. 1911. *The Jewish Cemeteries of South Carolina.* Charleston.

Elzas, Barnett Abraham. 1905. *The Jews of South Carolina. . . .* Philadelphia. Repr. 1972 (Spartanburg: Reprint Co.).

Freehling, William W. 1966. *Prelude to Civil War: The Nullification Controversy in South Carolina, 1816–1836.* NY: Harper and Row.

Garber, Paul L. 1943. *James Henley Thornwell: Presbyterian Defender of the Old South.* Richmond.

Glen, James. 1761. *A Description of South Carolina.* London: R. and J. Dodsley.

Gordon, Asa H. 1929. *Sketches of Negro Life and History in South Carolina.* W. B. Conkey.

Griffin, Charles M. 1934. *The Story of South Carolina Baptists, 1683–1933.* Greenwood: Connie Maxwell Orphanage.

Hallman, Samuel Thomas, ed. 1924. *History of the Evangelical Lutheran Synod of South Carolina, 1824–1924.* Columbia: Farrell Printing Co.

Harllee, William Curry, et al. 1934–37. *Kinfolks.* 4 vols. New Orleans: William Curry Harllee.

Harlow, Vincent Todd. 1926. *A History of Barbados, 1625–1685.* Oxford. Repr. 1969 (NY: Negro Universities Press).

Henry, Howell Meadoes. 1914. *The Police Control of the Slave in South Carolina.* Emory, VA.

Heyward, Duncan Clinch. 1937. *Seed from Madagascar.* Chapel Hill: University of North Carolina Press.

Higgins, W. Robert. 1967. *The South Carolina Negro Duty Law.* University of South Carolina Master's thesis.

Higgins, W. Robert. 1971. Geographical Origins of Negro Slaves in Colonial South Carolina. *South Atlantic Quarterly* 70:34–47.

Hirsch, Arthur Henry. 1928. *The Huguenots of Colonial South Carolina.* Durham, NC: Duke University Press.

Hollis, D. 1956. *University of South Carolina.* 2 vols. Columbia: University of South Carolina Press.

Howe, George. 1870. *History of the Presbyterian Church in South Carolina from 1800 to 1865.* Columbia: University of South Carolina Press.

Jacobs, William Plume. *Problems of the Cotton Manufacturer in South Carolina.* Clinton: Jacobs and Co. Press.

Jevvey, Theodore. 1911. White Indentured Servants of South Carolina. *South Carolina History and General Magazine* 12:162–71.

Jones, Frank Dudley, and William Hayne Mills, eds. 1926. *History of the Presbyterian Church in South Carolina since 1850.* Columbia: R. L. Bryan.

Kelsey, R. W. 1922. Swiss Settlers in South Carolina. *South Carolina History and General Magazine* 23:85–91.

Klingberg, Frank Joseph. 1941. *An Appraisal of the Negro in Colonial South Carolina.* Washington: Associated Publishers.

Kohn, August. 1907. *The Cotton Mills of South Carolina.* Columbia. Repr. 1975 (Spartanburg: Reprint Co.).

Lamson, Peggy. 1973. *The Glorious Failure: Black Congressman Robert Brown Elliott and the Reconstruction in South Carolina.* NY: Norton.

Lander, Ernest McPherson. 1969. *The Textile Industry in Antebellum South Carolina.* Baton Rouge: Louisiana State University Press.

Landrum, J. B. O. 1897. *Colonial and Revolutionary History of Upper South Carolina.* Greenville. Repr. 1959 (Spartanburg: Reprint Co.).

Littlefield, Daniel C. 1981. *Rice and Slaves: Ethnicity and the Slave Trade in Colonial South Carolina.* Baton Rouge: Louisiana State University Press.

Logan, John Henry. 1859. *A History of the Upper Country of South Carolina, from the Earliest Periods to the Close of the*

War of Independence. Charleston. Repr. 1980 (Easley: Southern Historical Press).

Meriwether, Colyer. 1889. *History of Higher Education in South Carolina*. . . . Washington. Repr. 1972 (Spartanburg: Reprint Co.).

Meriwether, Robert Lee. 1940. *The Expansion of South Carolina, 1729–1765*. Kingsport, TN: Southern Publishers.

Milliry, Chapman. 1943. *Exile without End*. Columbia: University of South Carolina Press.

Mills, Robert. 1825. *Atlas of the State of South Carolina*. Baltimore: F. Lucas.

Mills, Robert. 1826. *Statistics of South Carolina*. . . . Charleston: Hurlbut and Lloyd.

Moffatt, Josiah. 1934. The Scotch-Irish of the Up-Country. *South Atlantic Quarterly* 33:137–51.

Murray, Chalmers Swinton. 1949. *This is Our Land: The Story of the Agricultural Society of South Carolina*. Charleston: Carolina Art Assn.

Newby, Idus A. 1973. *Black Carolinians: A History of Blacks in South Carolina from 1895 to 1968*. Columbia: South Carolina Tricentennial Commission.

Pike, James Shepherd. 1874. *The Prostrate State: South Carolina under Negro Government*. NY: D. Appleton.

Potwin, Marjorie Adella. 1927. *Cotton Mill People of the Piedmont*. NY: Columbia University Press. London: P. S. King and Son.

Pringle, Elizabeth W. Allston. 1922. *A Woman Rice Planter*. NY. Repr. 1961 (Cambridge, MA: Harvard University Press).

Quint, Howard H. 1958. *Profile in Black and White: A Frank Portrait of South Carolina*. Washington: Public Affairs Press.

Revill, Janie. *South Carolina Counties, Districts, Parishes and Townships*. Columbia: University of South Carolina Press.

Rivers, William James. 1876. *Early History of South Carolina*. Charleston: Walker, Evans, and Cogwell.

Robertson, Ben. 1938. *Travelers' Rest*. Clemson: Cottonfield Publishers.

Robertson, Ben. 1942. *Red Hills and Cotton: An Upcountry Memory*. NY: Knopf.

Rogus, James A. 1978. *Theodosia and Other Pee Dee Sketches*. Columbia: R. L. Bryan.

Salley, Marion. 1970. *The Writings of Marion Salley: The Orangeburg Papers*. Vol. 1. Orangeburg: Orangeburg County Historical and Genealogical Society.

Sass, Herbert Ravenel. 1956. *The Story of the South Carolina Lowcountry*. 3 vols. West Columbia: J. F. Hyer.

Savage, Henry, and Lamar Dodd. 1968. *River of the Carolinas: The Santee*. Chapel Hill: University of North Carolina Press.

Schaper, William H. 1900. Sectionalism and Representation in South Carolina. *Annual Report of the American Historical Association* 1:237–463.

Schultz, Harold Seessel. 1950. *Nationalism and Sectionalism in South Carolina, 1852–1860*. Durham, NC: Duke University Press.

Shipp, Albert Micajah. 1882. *The History of Methodism in South Carolina*. Nashville. Repr. 1972 (Spartanburg: Reprint Co.).

Simkins, Francis Butler. 1944. *Pitchfork Ben Tillman: South Carolinian*. Baton Rouge. Repr. 1967 (Baton Rouge: Louisiana State University Press).

Sirmans, Marion Eugene. 1962. Legal Status of the Slave in South Carolina, 1670–1740. *Journal of Southern History* 28:462–66.

Smith, Alfred Glaze. 1958. *Economic Readjustment of an Old Cotton State: South Carolina, 1820–1860*. Columbia: University of South Carolina Press.

Smith, H. A. M. 1910. The Baronies of South Carolina. *South Carolina History and General Magazine* 11:75–91, 193–202.

Smith, H. A. M. 1931. Some Forgotten Towns in Lower South Carolina. *South Carolina History and General Magazine* 14:134–46.

Smith, Henry A. M. 1910. Rudner, Edmundsburg, Jacksonborough. *South Carolina History and General Magazine* 1139–49.

Smythe, Augustine T., et al. 1931. *The Carolina Low-Country*. NY: Macmillan.

Smythe, Augustine Thomas. 1931. *The Carolina Low-Country*. NY: Macmillan.

Stark, John D. 1968. *Damned Upcountryman: William Watts Ball: A Study in American Conservatism*. Durham, NC: Duke University Press.

Stokes, Thomas L. 1951. *The Savannah*. NY: Rinehart and Co.

Stoney, Samuel Gaillard. 1977. *Plantations of the Carolina Low Country*. 7th ed. Charleston: Carolina Art Assoc.

Sulley, Alexander S., Jr., ed. 1959. *Narratives of Early Carolina, 1650–1708*. NY: Barnes and Noble.

Taylor, Alrutheus Ambush. 1924. *The Negro in South Carolina during the Reconstruction*. Washington: Association for the Study of Negro Life and History.

Taylor, Rosser Howard. 1942. *Ante-Bellum South Carolina: A Social and Cultural History*. Chapel Hill: University of North Carolina Press.

Thomas, Albert S. 1957. *A Historical Account of the Protestant Episcopal Church in South Carolina, 1820–1957*. Columbia: University of South Carolina Press.

Thompson, Henry T. 1927. *The Establishment of the Public School System in South Carolina*. Columbia: University of South Carolina Press.

Tindall, George Brown. 1952. *South Carolina Negroes, 1877–1900*. Columbia: University of South Carolina Press.

Ver Steeg, Clarence Lester. 1975. *Origins of a Southern Mosaic*. Athens, GA: University of Georgia Press.

Voigt, Gilbert P. 1935. *The Germans and the German-Swiss in South Carolina, 1732–1765: Their Contribution to the Province*. Columbia: South Carolina Historical Association.

Walker, Cornelius Irvine. 1915. *The Romance of Lower Carolina. . . Incidents of the Colonial and Revolutionary Eras*. Charleston: Art Pub. Co.

Waterhouse, Richard. 1973. *South Carolina's Colonial Elite: A Study in the Social Structure and Political Culture of a Southern Colony, 1670–1760*. Johns Hopkins University dissertation.

Wikramanayake, Marina. 1973. *A World in Shadow: The Free Black in Antebellum South Carolina*. Columbia: South Carolina Tricentennial Commission.

Williams, George C. 1928. *Social Problems of South Carolina*. Columbia: University of South Carolina Press.

Williams, George Croft. 1946. *A Social Interpretation of South Carolina*. Columbia: University of South Carolina Press.

Williams, Jack Kenny. 1959. *Vogues in Villainy: Crime and Retribution in Ante-Bellum South Carolina*. Columbia: University of South Carolina Press.

Williamson, Joel. 1965. *After Slavery: The Negro in South Carolina during Reconstruction, 1861–1877.* Chapel Hill: University of North Carolina Press.

Wood, Peter H. 1974. *Black Majority: Negroes in Colonial South Carolina from 1670 through the Stono Rebellion.* NY: A. A. Knopf.

1857–97. *Collections of the South Carolina Historical Society.* Charleston: South Carolina Historical Society.

1945. *South Carolina: Economic and Social Conditions in 1944.* Columbia: University of South Carolina Press.

Georgia

1. Chatham County

Co. formed 1777. Orig. Savannah Co. (1741); became St. Philips and Christ Church parishes in 1758. Savannah Co. ran from Savannah to Altamaha; Chatham to Ogeechee. Various ethnic groups among early settlers; attempt at New Eng. village society failed, small settlements absorbed into plantations. Rice, indigo, some cotton. Battles in Rev. Rice culture sagged during War of 1812; agriculture disintegrated after 1865. Fertile swamplands: fruits and vegetables for Northern markets. Pop. 1790: 10,769, 1820: 7,214, 1850: 23,901, 1880: 45,023, 1910: 79,690, 1930: 105,431, 1960: 188,299.

Barrow, Elfrida de Renne. 1923. *Anchored Yesterdays. . . Savannah's Voyage across a Georgia Century. . . .* Savannah: Review Pub. and Print. Co.

Blassingame, John W. 1973. Before the Ghetto: The Making of the Black Community in Savannah, Georgia, 1865–1880. *Journal of Southern History* 6:463–85.

Bowden, Haygood S. 1929. *History of Savannah Methodism. . . .* Macon: Burke.

Cooper, Sherwin H. 1962. The Rural Settlement of the Savannah Country. *Papers of the Michigan Academy of Science, Arts, and Letters* 47:413–25.

Fant, H. B. 1938. Plantation Development in Chatham County. *Georgia Historical Quarterly* 22:305–330.

Federal Writers Project. 1937. *Savannah.* Savannah: Review Print. Co.

Gamble, Thomas. 1901. *A History of the City Government of Savannah, Georgia, from 1790–1901.* Savannah: Savannah City Council.

Georgia Writers Project. 1940. Drake's Plantation. *Georgia Historical Quarterly* 24:207–35.

Granger, Mary, ed. 1947. *Savannah River Plantations.* Savannah: Georgia Historical Society.

Habersham, Josephine Clay. 1987. *Ebb Tide: As Seen through the Diary of Josephine Clay Habersham, 1863.* Repr. Macon: Mercer University Press.

Harden, William. 1913. *A History of Savannah and South Georgia.* Chicago. Repr. 1969 (Atlanta: Cherokee Pub. Co.).

Harden, William. 1934. *Recollections of a Long and Satisfactory Life.* Savannah: Press of Review Print. Co.

Hart, Oliver J. 1925. *History of Christ Church Parish. . . .* Macon: Lyon, Harris and Brook.

Hartridge, Walter Charlton. 1947. *Savannah.* Columbia, SC: Bostick and Thornley.

Holland, James W. 1937. *Key to Our Province, 1736–1776: A Study of a Marsh Island of Georgia.* Savannah: National Park Service.

Jones, Charles C., Jr., and O. F. Vedder. 1890. *History of Savannah, Georgia. . . .* Syracuse, NY: D. Mason.

Lawrence, Alexander A. 1951. *Storm over Savannah: The Story of Count d'Estaing and the Siege of the Town in 1779.* Athens: University of Georgia Press.

Lee, F. D., and J. L. Agnew. 1869. *Historical Record of the City of Savannah.* Savannah: J. H. Estill.

Lowe, Miles, et al. 1969. *Savannah Revisited: A Pictorial History.* Athens: University of Georgia Press.

Perdue, Robert Eugene. 1973. *The Negro in Savannah. . . .* NY: Exposition Press.

Waring, Joseph F. 1974. *Cerveau's Savannah.* Savannah: Georgia Historical Society.

Wilson, Adelaide. 1889. *Historic and Picturesque Savannah.* Boston: Boston Photogravure Co.

1968. *Historic Savannah.* Savannah: Historic Savannah Foundation.

Savannah

Laid out 1733; town plan laid out before arrival of colonists. Jewish settlers from 1740; other early settlers from SC, Ireland, Scotland, MA, other parts of GA; also Huguenots (via Charleston) early. Good harbor; merchants and commerce important from 1744; rice, indigo, then cotton, tobacco. Dependency of Charleston until 1760; thereafter an autonomous trading center; trade somewhat handicapped by sandbars in river. British occupation 1778–82. Seaport: naval stores, lumber after 1865. Many Northerners in leadership by 1860. Large AfAm influx from country after 1864. Public schools organized 1865. Much old architecture preserved. Industrial development accelerated by WWI; paper mill (1930s), misc. factories. Pop. 1820: 7,523, 1850: 15,312, 1880: 30,709, 1910: 65,064, 1930: 85,024, 1960: 149,245.

GA 1N: F, cleaning woman, 40. B. here. — F., PGF, PGM, M., MGF, MGM all b. here (family has lived on the outskirts of Savannah and sea islands). — Ed.: 9th grade, "low level". — Baptist. — Very sincere, kind, religious. Good, cooperative informant. — FW made some of us. beginner's mistakes: not going after potentially familiar synonyms, not allowing inf. to talk about familiar subjects, forcing, or attempting to force, paradigms. Note [β] and [v] where most dialects have [v] and [w].

GA 1A: M, warehouseman, 72. B. here. — F. b. McIntosh Co. (local physician, confed. vet., wrote *Memoirs of a Southerner*, a collection of reminiscences chiefly justifying the "peculiar institution" of the "Old South"), F.'s family from Charleston; M. b. Liberty Co., M.'s family from Liberty Co. (plantation people). — Ed.: 2 yrs. h.s. — Hussars (local Co. militia). — Very profane, brusque, loud-speaking (bark worse than bite). Sure of himself; no pretensions of elegance. Associates mainly with Negroes. Hard-working; loyal to friends and benefactors. Dedicated to memory of father (who attempted to educate all his children, but whose money ran out before inf. could finish h.s.). Had little time, but seemed to enjoy interview. — Strong stresses. Little nasality. /ai au/ show alternation conditioned by voicing of following cons.; ingliding /e o/; /u/ fronted to /ju/ before /t d n/ (apparently a recent innovation); as us. in Savannah speech, /æ/ quite low, often [aʌ]; [ʋ] in many words of the *pot, cot* type; [ɔ] often low. Folk preterites, double negatives, *ain't*.

GA 1A*: M, accountant for Bd. of Ed., 79. — Older bro. of GA 1A. — More education and cultural advantages than 1A. — Worked 12 yrs. in bro.'s business, unsuccessful in attempts to break him of swearing. More interest in project than his bro., but not as good for folk speech. — Softer spoken than bro. Doesn't use folk preterites, *ain't*, or double negative. /æ/ not quite as low as younger bro.'s.

GA 1A**: Black Ankle Dist. — F, housewife. B. here. — Not intelligent enough to catch on quickly. — Quick, nervous tempo (reminiscent of rural NH). Very strong syllabic [ɝ:] either strong- or weak-stressed; very strong postvocalic [ɚ].

GA 1B: F, retired nurse, 77. B. here. — F. b. Rotterdam, Netherlands, came to Savannah as young man, first cellarman in Savannah Brewery; M. b. Bainbridge, GA, raised in Macon orphanage; MGM died in Brunswick in epidemic. — Ed.: parochial schools (till 8th grade), 2 yrs. "Bible College" in Toccoa. — Christian Missionary Alliance (b. Roman Catholic); has worked in dime store, been operator for phone company. — Inf. obsessively though not obtrusively pious. Circumstances of interview poor: in nursing home, with many distractions. FW also felt he did not perform well. — Suprasegmentals gave first impression of upper-class coastal speech, impression soon diffused by large number of folk-grammatical forms. As with other Savannah interviews, coastal pron. overlaid with some features assoc. with inland (occ. /-r/), but genuine local type.

GA 1C: F, housewife, 90. B. here. At about age 70 went to country for husband's health (managed farm there successfully several years). Some travel, esp. business trips with husband. — F. b. Liverpool, England, came to Savannah as a boy; M. b. here (old Savannah family). — Ed.: private governess ("sheltered" as a child), a few yrs. public school. — Episcopal (St. Paul's-High Church parish); full social life: plays cards, many friends, active interest in family. — A little timid and hesitant about interview at first, but enjoyed it. Talked freely about what she knew. Adaptable; sociable. Delightful sense of humor. Fair-minded; no strong "southern prejudices". Determined her children would be able to take care of themselves (inf. "never so much as tied my shoelaces till my nurse died") and succeeded. Banters with grandchildren. Slightly deaf but mind clear. — Nasality fairly strong. Voice shows no enfeeblement of age. Us. coastal allophones of /ai au/ for comm.; /a/ in *calm, palm*, etc.; in-gliding /e o i/; /ɛ/ low; /k-g-/ not palatalized as one would find in Charlestonians her age or even 40 yrs. younger; no postvocalic constriction. Multiple negatives, *ain't*, folk preterites.

GA 1D: M, real estate salesman, formerly accountant (clerk for seaboard RR), 76. B. Granville, Beaufort Co., SC. Moved to Savannah age 3. Some travel (southern resorts). Lived Saluda, NC, ages 26–27. — F. of Huguenot descent; M. related to prominent SC Baptist families. — Ed.: h.s., here. — Alchoholic; lives alone; married daughter keeps house; known as "character". Limited intelligence. Affects "plantation manners", thinks in terms of the past. Long anecdotes. Interview not too satisfactory, impossible to question directly

(some success in letting inf. ramble). — Speech somewhat old-fashioned city type.

GA 1E: F, store manager, 36. B. here. Has made a few trips North on business. — F. b. Austria; M., MGF, MGM all b. NY City (parents moved south on marriage, lived Savannah and vicinity ever since). — Ed.: h.s., one summer Columbia U. — Jewish (Reformed). Knows most Savannians of her generation. (In Savannah, as in Charleston, Jewish comm. dates from 18th cent., long established in business and mercantile world, well integrated into comm.). — Clever, quick mind; intelligent. Enjoyed interviews. Generous. Alert to opportunities. — Notices dialect differences. Has some notion of "correctness", but eschews affected forms (strong common sense!). Good representative of younger middle-class speech. — Rapid tempo. Nasality strong (Savannah voices have much more nasality than Charleston). Centralized beginnings of /au ai/ less in evidence than with older informants; /e o/ generally in-gliding or monophthongal; /æ/ very low (FW thinks often under-transcribed — that [aʌ] ought to replace [æʌ] in most places); varies between /hw-/ and /w-/ in some words. In guarded speech, tends to add retroflexion (influence of business associates?).

GA 1F!: F, single homemaker, 78. B. here. Spent only week or so on rice plantation out of city; often spent summers on farm plantation in N. GA. — F., PGF both b. here; PGF's F. and M. from Wales; PGM b. here; PGM's F. b. England (British Consul in Savannah); PGM's M. b. NY; M. b. here; MGF b. Charleston, SC; MGF's F. and M. lived Charleston; MGM b. here; MGM's F. lived CT; MGM's M. from VA. — Ed.: governess. — Episcopalian. — Knows own mind; exact and objective in reporting what she would naturally say, although easily horrified at things the "common people" say. Prominent family, yet poor all her life since the War; belongs thoroughly to the old tradition. Broader cultural background than her New England counterparts. — Precise utterance, unstressed syllables given due prominence. Interesting tendency to distinguish sharply in length between long and short vowels found in same environment. — Cultivated.

GA 1G!: M, retired cotton broker, had had auto agency, 76. B. here. — F., PGF both b. here; (sea captains, merchant and naval, in both lines and in wife's family. MGF responsible for change from "larboard" to "port"). — Ed.: possibly U. of GA. Some travel, considerable reading. — Episcopalian. — Knows Savannah and country around it. — Natural, old-fashioned speech. Some notions of "proper" words, but colloq. usage; unaffected. — Cultivated. — Interview terminated due to illness.

GA 1I!: F, homemaker, 60. B. here. Travel in East, one trip to Europe. — F., PGF both b. here; PGF's F. came from MA or RI — Seekonk; PGF's M. from SC, was living in Savannah when married; PGM's family from Walterboro, SC; M. b. here; MGF from N. GA, died when M. was a baby. Family history in Harden, *History of Savannah and Southern Georgia*. — Ed.: h.s. here; private tutoring; summer school Harvard, U. of VA; Armstrong Jr. College (Savannah). Father didn't believe in education for women. — Episcopal (formerly Methodist); local Alliance Française; art association; Savannah Forum. — Representative of upper-middle class.

Cooperative. Somewhat inclined to offer "book words", but knows whether used in comm. Not much knowledge of farm implements or animals. No taboos. Unaffected pronunciation. Both inf. and brother (GA 1H!*) generous with information at their disposal and frank in recognizing limitations. — Tempo moderate to slow. Pitch varying: strong contrast between high-pitched stressed and low-pitched weak-stressed syllables. /i/: initial element definitely retracted, probably [ɪy] rather than [iy]. /e/ only slightly diphthongal, rarely with fronted second element (us. in-gliding or up-gliding to high-central). /u/ high-central, [ju] only, as a rule, after /m p b f k/. /o/ slightly diphthongal, often in-gliding. Suspect 3-way contrast of /æ æ: æy/, but evidence inconclusive. /a/ low-back. /ɔ/ us. in-gliding, rarely up-gliding diphthong. /a/ us. before /-rV/. [ʌ] generally raised and centered. /ai au/ often have positional variants, as in eastern VA. Unstressed /-i/ often diphthongal (not always transcribed). /kl- gl-/ often [tl̩ dl̩]. /k- g-/ fronted, often palatalized. Both [wɪθ wɪð] before vowels. [ʃr] on guard, [sr] natural initially. /hw-/ us., except in wharf. Clear /b/ intervocalically before [ɪ]. Little prevocalic constriction; occ. linking /r/; no intrusive /r/. (First field record after interlude; some transcriptions, esp. low-back, questionable.) — Cultivated.

GA 1H!*: M, real estate manager, slightly older than GA 1H! (her brother). — Family same as GA 1H!. — Ed.: law degree, U. of GA (never practiced). — Many business contacts. — Hard-headed businessman, anti-New Deal. Keen interest in guns and horses. Quite cooperative: arranged introductions to local antiquarians, took FW on tour of farm properties, etc. As sister, generous with information, yet recognized limitations of same. — Cultivated.

2. Bryan County

Formed 1793. Drained by Ogeechee River. 2 RRs. Hunting and fishing; rice, cotton, grains. Pop. 1800: 2,836, 1820: 3,021, 1850: 3,424, 1880: 4,929, 1910: 7,702, 1930: 5,952, 1960: 6,226.

Wilson, Caroline Price. 1929. *Abstracts of Court Records of Bryan County, Georgia.* Savannah: Lachlan McIntosh Chapter, DAR.

GA 2N: Lanier (post village). — M, farmer, turpentine worker, 67. B. here. — F. from Bulloch Co.; M. raised locally. — Ed.: 3 wks. — Baptist. — Quicker mind than brother (GA 2N*); more active. Kindly, respectful. Not sure of purpose of interview. — Old-fashioned speech. Strong stresses; little nasality. /a/ sometimes rounded [ɒ]; some /-r/, not always consistent; /hw-/; flap [ɾ] for /-t-/. Folk grammar, multiple negation us.

GA 2N*: M, farmer, 72. B. here. Spent time in Evans Co., picking cotton. — Family same as GA 2N (his bro.). — Ed.: local school for 6 mos. once. — Apparently a little higher on social scale than younger brother. Talks more deliberately and is somewhat more suspicious than bro. Crippled. — Occ. [ai] for [ɔi].

GA 2A: Ellabell (shipping pt.). — M, retired farmer, sawmill and grist mill operator, 78. B. about a mile away. 9 yrs. in Screven Co. (ages 19–28), then returned to Bryan Co. — F. b.

and raised in Co., PGF from (present day) Pierce Co. c. 1820 (cattle driver). — Ed.: common school, locally; 1 mo. h.s. — Methodist (Sunday school superintendent 43 yrs.); Masons; 12 yrs. justice of the peace. — "All around handyman." Crippled (foot amputated); glad to have a chance to talk. Some taboo reactions; pious; quotes scripture freely. Mind tends to wander. Uses folk terms for concrete objects; for mental states, tended to use words picked up from reading. — /a/ occ. rounded, [ɒ]; /ai/ sometimes has centered beginning; [ʌ] lower than in upcountry; /e o/ us. up-gliding. /hw-/; /-r/. Slow speech; tends to overstress when on guard. Folk grammar.

GA 2B: Lanier. — M, farmer, naval stores operator, timberman, general storekeeper, 43. B. here. Managed one of F.'s turpentine stills in Blitchton (c. 7 mi. E.) a few years. — F., M. both from Liberty Co., moved to Bryan Co. c. 1895 when turpentine industry opened up. — Ed.: local schools; Brewton-Parker Junior College, Mt. Vernon (Montgomery Co., GA). — Knows everybody in comm.; member Co. Bd. of Ed.; father, bro. have both been Co. commissioners. — Genial, hospitable. Keen sense of humor, delights in teasing people. Interested in Atlas project, knows local usage. Very intelligent; able, hard-working. No pretensions of "elegance"; sure of position. No attempt to guard responses. — Little nasality. Tempo variable (can talk fast or slow according to mood, us. slow when explaining). Slight stutter, no effect on fluency; hardly noticeable. /e o/ generally up-gliding, occ. slight in-glide. /o/ rather far forward, often [ɵ]. Sometimes, but not uniformly, /ju/ after /t d n/. /hw-/; strong /-r/ (seems to be characteristic of ridge section just W. of Savannah River; not found 60 mi. W.). *Ain't*, folk preterites, multiple negatives.

3. Liberty County

Formed 1777 from St. John, St. Andrew, and St. James parishes. First serious settlement in 1752 in Midway Dist.; Congregationalists from SC. Settlers from Devon, Dorset, Somerset via Dorchester, MA, and "old Dorchester", SC (arrived in SC in 1690s). By 1770s, Midway Dist. possessed nearly 1/3 of wealth of GA. Grew with cotton; center of cotton culture 1805. Prosperous, wealthy to 1860s: rice, sugar, cotton. Suffered war privations, pillaged by Sherman's men; never recovered. Bypassed by RRs, roads not improved. Methodist church dominant. Fish, shellfish, diversified farming, timber. Pop. 1790: 5,355, 1820: 6,695, 1850: 7,926, 1880: 10,649, 1910: 12,924, 1930: 8,135, 1960: 14,487.

Mallard, Robert Q. 1892. *Plantation Life before Emancipation.* Richmond: Whittet and Shepperson.

McIlvaine, Paul. 1971. *The Dead Town of Sunbury, Georgia.* Hendersonville, NC.

Myers, Robert M., ed. 1972. *The Children of Pride.* New Haven: Yale University Press.

Pond, Cornelia Jones. 1974. *Life on a Liberty County Plantation....* Darien: The Darien News.

Stacy, James. 1903. *History of the Midway Congregational Church, Liberty County, Georgia.* Newnan. Repr. 1979 (Spartanburg, SC: Reprint Co.).

Tankersley, Allan P. 1948. Midway District: A Study of Puritanism in Colonial Georgia. *Georgia Historical Quarterly* 32:149–57.

Wilson, Caroline Price. 1969. *Annals of Georgia*. Vol. 1, Liberty County. Repr. (Vidalia: Georgia Genealogical Reprints).

Yarbrough, Bird, and Paul Yarbrough. 1963. *Taylors Creek: Story of the Community and Her People through 200 Years.* . . . Pearson: Atkinson County Citizen.

Flemington

Post village. Pop. 1900: 110.

GA 3A: M, farmer, miller, 80. B. here. Spent winters until 12 yrs. old on plantations in lower part of country. After 1865 never lived there. — F. b. here; PGF b. Sunbury (coastal Liberty Co.); PGF's F. of stock of original settlers; PGM b. here (old stock); M. b. here; MGF b. Eatonton (Putnam Co.). — Ed.: private school at 8 yrs., when 10 to public school till 12 or 13. — Presbyterian (the original Congregational Church became Presbyterian in the 1880s); Mason; tax receiver; magistrate. — A splendidly preserved, intellectually able and rugged figure. Hard of hearing, but has the dignity of the old aristocracy. Was reared with about 70 Negroes, no white companions. His speech is considered notably old-fashioned or Geechee. — Striking characteristics are the clear length distinction between long and short vowels, the rounded [ɒ], the /æ/ phoneme as [aˑ] or [aˑ] distinct from [aˑ:] or [ɑˑ:], and many forms (esp. expletives) suggestive of New England. Rather clear utterance; weak-stressed syllables given their due. [aˑt] for [æt], rather than [ɒt], in weak-stressed syllables suggests African or English dialect.

Hinesville

Lumber belt. Skirmish Dec. 16, 1864. Pop. 1900: 249.

GA 3B: F, housewife, 83. B. and lived Bayview (10 mi. NE) till 21, Taylor's Creek ages 21–25, on Canoochee R. (farm) ages 26–41, then to Hinesville. — F., PGF, PGM all b. SC, family settled in Liberty Co. before 1861; M. b. Liberty Co., MGF moved here from VA. — Ed.: 3 mos. school, about 5th grade. — Methodist; UDC. — Still active housewife despite age. Little knowledge of world, linguistic usage outside her comm. Fairly good knowledge of local life, esp. farm life and cookery. Cooperated as best she could; strong taboo reactions. — Speech shows some evidence of mixed origin of ancestors and comm. Slight deafness. — Strong stresses. Nasality. Tempo moderate. Slurred utterance. Tendency to drawl: over-lengthening of stressed vowels and diphthongs. Simplification of final clusters.

4. McIntosh County

Formed 1793 from Liberty Co. Some attempts at colonization in 1680s and 90s. First English settlement Ft. King George in 1721; abandoned 1727. Scots brought to form a military outpost; some had forfeited their estates by participating in 1715 revolt. 1st coastal highway: Darien to Savannah. Over half of GA legislature Scots, but in 1782 legislature tried to prevent further Scottish migration. Original Scots settlers opposed introduction of slavery. Sawmills 1750–1900; rice mill 1820. Flood 1823; hurricanes 1824, 1898. Sea islands; resort co. Old rice plantations, diversified farming, naval stores. Pop. 1736: 250, 1800: 2,660, 1820: 5,129, 1850: 6,027, 1880: 6,241, 1910: 6,442, 1930: 5,763, 1960: 6,364.

Gordon, G. Arthur. 1936. The Arrival of the Scotch Highlanders at Darien. *Georgia Historical Quarterly* 20:199–209.

King, Spencer Bidwell. 1981. *Darien: The Death and Rebirth of a Southern Town*. Macon: Mercer University Press.

Leigh, Frances (Butler). 1883. *Ten Years on a Georgia Plantation since the War*. London. Repr. 1969 (NY: Negro Universities Press).

Lewis, Bessie May. 1936. Darien: A Symbol of Defiance and Achievement. *Georgia Historical Quarterly* 20:185–198.

Lewis, Bessie. 1975. *They Called Their Town Darien*. . . . Darien: The Darien News.

MacDonald, Alexander R. 1936. The Settlement of the Scotch Highlanders at Darien. *Georgia Historical Quarterly* 20:252–62.

Crescent District

Crescent a village, head of Sapelo Sound. Sapelo Island bought 1788 by French partners. Live oak timber.

GA 4N: M, farmer, fishing guide, 53. B. Sapelo Island. Lived there till 16, then just across on mainland. — F. b. Sapelo Island, PGF b. Africa, came here as a child; M. b. AL, but died when inf. young. — Ed.: illiterate. — Baptist. — Very intelligent and trustworthy. — Speech in most particulars that of the old Negro. Quick speech. Vowels tend to be short. Syllables tend to be rather evenly stressed. /a/ represents both [æ] and [a].

Darien

Settled by Highlanders in 1736. Inc. 1816; Co. seat. Petition against intro. of slavery, 1739. Military importance lost after 1763. Sawmill center; rafting; trading center of Altamaha valley by 1804. Plantation country; timber port after War of 1812, timber again toward end of 19th cent. Regional shipping center by 1836: shipping of rice and cotton. Burned in Civil War. Town rebuilt in 1870s, prosperous in 1880s and 90s. Pop. 1900: 1739, 1930: 937.

GA 4A: M, watchmaker, retired telegrapher (47 yrs. for Western Union in Darien), 77+. B. here. — F. b. McIntosh Co. (prob. Darien); PGM from North (MA) before 1861; M., MGF, MGM all b. Liberty Co. — Ed.: Gainesville, FL, 2 yrs. — Presbyterian; Knights of Pythias. — quick mind; knows Co. and people intimately (not much actual rural experience, but Co. so rural that it is impossible to escape knowledge of rural life). Hard-working, busy, but enjoyed interviews. Moderate amount of reading. Likes people and is well liked. Good upper-middle group older generation coastal type. — Voice medium-low; clear articulation. Wide intonation range (of type associated with "Irish", whether Charleston, SC, or NY City). Strong stresses. Fast speech. All vowels shorter than average, but stressed relatively long, unstressed relatively very short. In-gliding /i e ɔ o u/; /u/ somewhat fronted, /ju/ after /t d n/; [ɒ] in *pot, tomorrow*; back vowels generally over-rounded ("inner rounding"). Occ. /w/ > [β]; many clear /-l/s ([ɫ]); some unreleased final stops; /hw-/; /ʃr-/, /sr-/; very little /-r/ constriction; no sandhi /r/ or intrusive /r/.

The Ridge, Ridgeville

1st station N. of Darien on RR. Residential area; spared during Civil War. Small trading center; some small industries.

GA 4B: M, fisherman, farmer, 72. B. Manchester (c. 2 mi. N.). Never out of Co., except fishing. — F. prob. b. summer home, Putnam Co., lived all life in McIntosh Co.; PGF a Yankee merchant from Waterbury, CT; PGM b. Co., desc. of 18th cent. Highlander settlers; PGM's M. b. NC (Cape Fear Valley), came to GA to marry; M. of Savannah Huguenot family, b. at family summer home, Marietta; MGM of St. Augustine Spanish family, connection with Savannah and Camden Co. families (a CT cousin wrote up the family history). — Ed.: local schools. — Episcopalian. — Strong frame, large hands. Steeped in folk speechways; knows local culture intimately, esp. fishing, shrimping, oyster-gathering. Hard worker; was building a boat when FW called, couldn't spare time for full interview, but glad to give one evening. Enjoyed interview. No influence of other dialects and little influence of books; natural speech of a person assured of place in comm. and not bothering about superficial standards. Dresses and lives simply. — Deep, resonant voice. Very fast speech. Utterance generally clear. Long stressed vowels, short weak-stressed. Low /æ/; /i e ɔ o u/ generally monoph. or in-gliding; [ɪu] in *new*; [ɜɪ] in *thirty, Thursday, colonel*; /ai au/ us. with centered beginning before voiceless cons; /ʌ/ low. Simplification of final cons. clusters; /w-/ in *whip*, etc.; /sr-/; postvocalic constriction unusual.

Valona

Hamlet on Sapelo Sound, 10 mi. NE of Darien.

GA 4C!: F, housewife, 58. B. Manchester (c. 2 mi. N.). Spent 1 yr. in Savannah, 2 yrs. in Burke Co. — Inf. sister of GA 4B: see above for family history. — Ed.: governess; 1 yr. boarding school in Darien. — Episcopalian; "not a joiner". — Very good inf.; fine example of natural, cultivated speech. Rooted in comm. (e.g., husband from Burke Co. and she rejected every "Burke Co." item not found in McIntosh Co.). No taboos. Well-read. Quick mind; good eye for local detail. Keenly interested in interviews. — Very fast speech. Wide intonation range. Unusually pleasant, clear, cultivated voice. Strong stresses. All vowels relatively shorter than in FW's speech. /ai au/ have centered beginnings before voiceless consonants; /i e ɔ o u/ in-gliding or monoph.; us. /ju/ after /t d n/; /ʌ/ often for /ʊ/; /æ/ relatively low; round vowel ([ɒ]) in *pot* type of word; alternates with /a/ in *father*; /ʌ/ generally low; [ɜɪ] in *third*, etc. Some final consonants weakly articulated; final clusters simplified; /-t-/ > /-r-/; /ʃr-/ > /sr-/; /hw-/ (except *wharf*); many clear /l/s ([l̩]), intervoc. and postvoc.; no postvoc. constriction; occ. sandhi /r/, no intrusive /r/. — Cultivated.

5. Glynn County

Co. formed 1777. Strictly plantation in 18th cent. (slaves 2/3 of pop.). Rivers and inlets; marshy territory, much reclaimed and now fertile land. Sea islands, fishing and shellfish, timber. Once rice and sea island cotton (commercial rice planting till 1912); now more diversified agriculture; tourist and resort trade. Pop. 1790: 413, 1820: 3,418, 1850: 4,933, 1880: 6,497, 1910: 15,720, 1930: 19,400, 1960: 41,954.

Cate, Margaret Davis. 1930. *Our Todays and Yesterdays: A Story of Brunswick and the Coastal Islands*. Brunswick: Glover Bros.

Engel, Beth and Geneva Stebbins. 1974. *Pages from the Past, St. Simon's Island, 1880–1886*. Jesup: Sentinel Press.

Hazzard, William W. 1825. *St. Simons Island, Georgia, Brunswick and Vicinity. . . .* Repr. 1974 (Belmont, MA: Oak Hill Press).

House, Albert Virgil, ed. 1954. *Planter Management and Capitalism in Ante-Bellum Georgia: The Journal of Hugh Fraser Grant, Rice Grower*. NY: Columbia University Press.

Hull, Barbara. 1980. *St. Simons, Enchanted Island. . . .* Atlanta: Cherokee Pub. Co.

Huxford, Folks, comp. 1977. *Pioneers of Wiregrass Georgia. . . .* 7 vols. Homerville: Huxford Genealogical Society.

Jones, Charles C. 1878. *The Dead Towns of Georgia*. Savannah: Morning News Steam Printing House.

Lovell, Caroline Couper. 1932. *The Golden Isles of Georgia*. Boston. Repr. 1970 (Atlanta: Cherokee Pub. Co.).

Price, Eugenia. 1978. *St. Simons Memoir. . . .* Philadelphia: Lippincott.

Reese, Trevor R. 1969. *Frederica: Colonial Fort and Town*. St. Simons Island: Fort Frederica Association.

Smith, Joseph W. 1907. *Visit to Brunswick, Georgia, and Travels South*. Boston: A. C. Getchell and Son.

Vanstory, Burnette Lightle. 1956. *Georgia's Land of the Golden Isles*. Athens: University of Georgia Press.

Wylly, Charles Spalding. 1897. *Annals and Statistics of Glynn County. . . .* Brunswick: Press of H. A. Wrench and Sons.

The Beach, St. Simons Island

First settled by Spanish, missions; Spaniards planted orange and olive groves. First English settlement (Ft. Frederica) 1736; Moravians in 1730s; many Scots among early settlers. Frederica garrisoned till 1763, military importance lost thereafter. Intensive plantation agriculture to 1860s. Sawmills in 1880s; tourism from 1880s, resort colony.

GA 5A: M, sailor, contractor, 57. B. Frederica (near old fort and village). In naval service both World Wars; yachting cruises. — F., PGF both b. Frederica; PGF's F. b. England (Sunderland); PGF's M. b. England; PGM b. St. Simons; PGM's F. and M. both b. England; M., MGF, MGM all b. Ware Co. (c. 55 mi. W.); their parents GA people of English descent. — Ed.: h.s., St. Simons; business school, Richmond Business College, Savannah. — Episcopalian; Mason, Sec. Chamber of Commerce and Board of Trade, St. Simons Shooting Club, once KKK. — Very quick, cooperative. Intimate knowledge of locale, also of inland waterways from Charleston to Jacksonville. Fond of sea; brings in sea anecdotes at slightest pretext. Vast fund of stories. Very keen sense of humor. Enjoyed interviews. Excellent inf. — Medium-low pitch. Tempo fast. Slurred articulation very often. Strong stresses. Wide intonation range. Long stressed vowels, very short weak stressed vowels; over-rounding of /ɔ o u/; in-gliding /i e ɔ o u/; /ɪu/ rather than /ju/ after /t d n/; /æ/ low; low-central unrounded /a/ in *car, father*; low-back, rounded [ɒ] in *garden, palm, barn, pot*, etc.; [ɜɪ] even in *cur*; /ai au/ with centered beginnings before voiceless consonants.

Final consonants weakly articulated; final clusters simplified; /sr-/; /w-/ occ. (in *whip*, etc.); no constricted /-r/, sandhi /r/ or intrusive /r/.

GA 5B: St. Simons. — M, hotel keeper, fisherman, 60. B. here (only away during tour in the Coast Guard). — F. b. Germany, came to GA c. 1860, moved to St. Simons; M. of old St. Simons family. — Ed.: local h.s. — Episcopal. — Big, hearty, gregarious. Enjoys talking. Good on details of local culture and knows limitations of knowledge. Good mind. Enjoys pleasures of the senses. — Strong stresses. Very fast speech. Wide intonation range, but basic pitch rather low (no nasality). Strong-stressed vowels long, weak-stressed vowels very short. In-gliding /i e ɔ o u/; /ɪu/ rather than /ju/ in *dues, music, new*; [ɒ] in *barn, father, pot, tomorrow*; /ʌ/ low; [ɜɪ] before all consonants except /-l/; /ai au/ with centered beginning before voiceless consonants. Simplification of final clusters, weak articulation of final consonants; /-t-/ often [-ɾ-]; /l/ never dark; /r-/ sometimes velarized before back rounded vowels; no constricted /-r/; sandhi /r/; intrusive /r/ in *swallow it*.

Brunswick

City laid out 1771; inc. 1813. Designed as a rival to Savannah; declining before Civil War. Shipping center; wood products; transportation center: RR and shipping. Recent resort area. Pop. 1880: 2,891, 1910: 10,182, 1930: 14,022, 1960: 21,703.

GA 5C: M, shipyard custodian, gasoline and tire dealer, 66. B. here. Traveled a good deal, 9 yrs. in FL. Has farmed, timbered. — F. b. Americus, GA; M. raised at Angvilla. — Well rooted in native dialect (though less of folk vocab. than other Glynn Co. inf.'s). Knows many points where his speech differs from that of other areas. Knows intimately both St. Simons rural life and town of Brunswick. Contacts now with business, professional, and industrial people of the town. Busy; well thought of. — Fast, nervous speech. Basic pitch medium to low, ranging up and down, range increasing the more anecdotal he gets. Strong stresses, with weak-stressed vowels cut short. Some final cons. very weakly articulated; simplification of final clusters. Some nasality.

GA 5D!: M, Clerk of Court (49 yrs.), previously worked for a mercantile firm, 80. B. here. — F. b. here; PGF b. Jekyll Island (family came to Jekyll Island c. 1791); M., MGM both b. Savannah; MGM's PGF came to GA from Santo Domingo after slave insurrection. — Ed.: Glynn Academy (Brunswick), Moore's Business U. (Atlanta). — Knows everybody in Co. — One of the local landmarks. Full of anecdotes, providing FW wonderful opportunity to get cv. forms of older generation (hard to hold on track, however). Very busy, real or fancied, but "few minutes" promised FW turned into entire afternoon. Interested in work of FW, but attempted "advising" to concentrate on high spots of local history. No attempt to guard grammar or pronunciation. — Very fast speech. Wide intonation range, widening as he warmed up to his anecdotes. Articulation somewhat slurred. Weak-stressed vowels short, strong-stressed relatively long. Vowel pattern of older generation coastal type: over-rounded back vowels, in-gliding diphthongs, centered beginning of /ai au/ before voiceless

consonants. Final consonants weakly articulated; final clusters often simplified. — Cultivated.

GA 5E!: M, real estate broker, 61. B. here (6th generation). 2 yrs. S. FL. ages 38–40. Has been newspaperman, exporter (crossties and lumber), 12–14 yrs. transportation dept. Atlanta-Birmingham Atlantic RR (now Atlantic Coast Line), grocery store work as a boy. — F. b. here, PGF b. Midway (Liberty Co.), PGF's F. b. Dorchester, SC (family from Dorchester, MA), PGF's M. b. Scotland, married at Midway, PGM from around Midway; M., MGF both b. here, MGF's F. came here 1751 from Haddam, CT, MGF's M., MGM, MGM's F. and M. all of Brunswick. — Ed.: 8th grade, local school; much reading. — Methodist (inactive); Elks, Rotary Club (Sec. 20 yrs.), "used to belong to all dancing societies and clubs". — Quick mind. Knows town life intimately, not much knowledge of country. Enjoyed telling anecdotes, though pressure of work kept him from expanding as freely as he might have liked. Pretty sure of local usage; observant of many features of Negro and poor white speech. Interested in Atlas project. Very intelligent. Very active in local economic and cultural enterprises. Apparently takes business in moderation: doesn't neglect, but doesn't let it prevent full participation in life of comm. Likable and very well-rounded personality. Natural, unaffected. Good example of coastal cultivated speech. — Deep voice, musical fast speech (slightly nervous). Generally very clear articulation. Wide intonation range. /ai au/ have centered beginnings before voiceless consonants; /i e ɔ o u/ in-gliding. Grammar mostly standard. — Cultivated.

6. Camden County

Co. est. 1777. Early settlements on Cumberland Island, c. 1736. Area opened to English settlement in 1748; early settlers from VA, NC, Scotland, GA coast. Tory stronghold to 1778; area ravaged in Rev. Strictly plantation in 18th cent. (slaves 2/3 of pop.). Sugar, cotton, and rice (rice till 1919). Harassment by Union raiders 1862–65; some pop. lost. By 1900 half of land owned by AfAms; self-sufficient small farming. Mostly Baptists, also some Methodists, Evangelicals. Timber and turpentine, paper mill; diversified agriculture; fishing. Sea island co.: resorts now. Pop. 1790: 305, 1820: 3,402, 1850: 6,319, 1880: 6,183, 1910: 7,690, 1930: 6,338, 1960: 9,975.

Huxford, Folks, comp. 1977. *Pioneers of Wiregrass Georgia.* . . . 7 vols. Homerville: Huxford Genealogical Society.

Mayo, Lawrence Shaw. 1914. *The St. Mary's River.* . . . Boston: T. R. Marvin and Son.

Reddick, Marguerite. 1976. *Camden's Challenge: A History of Camden County, Georgia.* Camden County Historical Commission.

Thompson, Shirley Joiner. 1982. *The People of Camden County, Georgia.* . . . Jacksonville, FL.

Vocelle, James T. 1909. *Reminiscences of Old St. Marys.* St. Marys: St. Marys Pub. Co.

Vocelle, James T. 1914. *History of Camden County, Georgia.* Jacksonville, FL: Kennedy Brown-Hall Co.

Cherry Point, Kingsland P.O.

Cherry Point old plantation section, now rural, marshy. Kingsland orig. flag station on Seaboard RR, laid out 1894.

GA 6A: M, riverman, 79 B. about 1 mi. S. on adjacent island. Hauled freight; worked on steamboat; some carpentry, farming, butchering, fishing, stock raising. — F. b. St. Marys (confederate cavalryman), PGF b. St. Augustine, PGM b. St. Marys; M. b. Floyds Neck (Camden Co.), MGF, MGM both from Floyds Neck (MGF's family originally from England, came to McIntosh Co., thence to Camden. M.'s uncle first white man to explore the Okefenokee Swamp.). — Ed.: mostly self-educated; a few terms private teaching. — Methodist (casual); has been justice of the peace; served on a grand jury. — Energetic. Knows his own culture (small farming, fishing, and river traffic) intimately, and little else. Quick at repartee. Seemed to enjoy interview. Very active; enjoys life. Hospitable (set very full table for Sunday dinner!). Unpretentious; natural speech. Some sex taboos (presence of family may have inhibited him somewhat). — Very fast speech. Strong stresses. Clipped utterance. Not very wide range of intonation (except when worked up, telling anecdote). Pitch basically medium to low. All vowels somewhat shorter than FW accustomed to find; weak-stressed vowels particularly short. Generally tidewater in type. A few initial aspirated stops; final stops often not released (or otherwise weakly articulated); final clusters generally simplified.

St. Marys

Some French from Acadia as early as 1755; few stayed. Area organized as St. Marys Parish 1763; laid out as St. Patrick 1788; name changed to St. Marys 1792. Inc. 1802. Presbyterian Church by 1808, 3rd oldest in GA. Grew as port of entry for smugglers, esp. smugglers of slaves; one area that prospered during Embargo. Good harbor; shipbuilding, timber port. Now fishing and shrimp, canneries, paper mill.

GA 6B!: M, merchant, former postmaster, 78. B. here. spent some time out in country ages 8–15 (c. 4 mi. W. in Griffins Neck), RR clerk in Savannah 1 yr., age 19. — F. b. St. Marys; PGF, PGF's F. both came here in 1805 (PGF's F. had left Savannah with death sentence commuted provided he leave state, went to St. Augustine, granted tract of land by British governor, but title lapsed; family ancestral line from France via Spain to FL and GA); M. b. St. Marys, MGF, MGM of pre-Revolutionary local stock (MGF introduced pecans into GA). — Ed.: mostly self-educated; F. had governesses; a little school in St. Marys, chiefly arithmetic and geography; great deal of reading; interested in Indian relics, birds, etc. Has written a number of papers on local history; amateur taxidermist. — Methodist; formerly with Ornithological Society; has been Co. treas., chm. Co. commissioners, city treas., city councilman. — Knows local usage and uses it naturally (on cultivated level); very well rooted in comm.; knows every older resident of area. Likes talking; generous fund of anecdotes. No taboos. Well-read. Enjoyed interviews; had observed several differences between his own speech patterns and those of outsiders. Still very active in mind and body. Quick mind. Knows which forms are "correct", but doesn't hesitate to use folk forms in conversation. Slight tendency to be guarded in grammar, esp. if wife present (FW suspects she may have tried to improve him). — Fast speech. Intonation varies widely; basically a little below medium. Strong stresses; weak-stressed vowels very short. Over-rounding ("inner-rounding"?) of back rounded vowels. /-t-/ often [-ɾ-]; /gl-/ occ.

/dl-/. Folk preterites of many verbs, sometimes alternating with standard forms. — Cultivated.

7. Charlton County

Formed 1854 from Camden Co. Sparsely settled till c. 1850; settled from "upper GA" and the Carolinas, some from VA. Development by Atlantic Coast line c. 1880. Some pop. decline after 1910, with end of sawmill boom. Wiregrass. Part in Okefenokee Swamp; islands, lakes and prairies; swamp now wildlife preserve. Early settlers Baptists and Methodists. Second-growth forestry from 1930s; timber, livestock, tourism. Pop. 1860: 1,780, 1880: 2,154, 1910: 4,722, 1930: 4,381, 1960: 5,313.

Huxford, Folks, comp. 1977. *Pioneers of Wiregrass Georgia.* . . . 7 vols. Homerville: Huxford Genealogical Society.

Mays, Lois Barefoot. 1975. *Settlers of the Okefenokee.* . . . Folkston: Okefenokee Press.

McQueen, Alex S. 1932. *History of Charlton County.* Atlanta: Stein Print. Co.

1972. *Charlton County, Georgia: Historical Notes 1972.* . . . Jesup: Charlton County Historical Commission.

Folkston

Co. seat. Laid out as station on Atlantic Coast line 1884; inc. 1895. No AfAms in town till 1931. Lumbering; stop on tourist route to FL.

GA 7: M, fisherman, handyman, 87. B. Pierce Co. (34 mi. NNW) and moved here age 5. Has always lived in neighborhood, on both sides of St. Marys River. Has cut crossties, farmed, logged (30 yrs.), done carpentry, worked on ship at landing. — F. prob. local (nothing known of family); M., MGF, MGM all from area, MGM's M. an Indian ("nearly full blood"), lived to age 115. — Ed.: on and off 4 yrs; can read and write. — Free-Will Baptist (formerly Missionary Baptist); Farmers Alliance while it lasted. — Mind wavering very slightly, not good on abstracts. Definitely folk type. Good memory for details of rural life; knows everybody. Famous as a fisherman and fishing guide ("best in GA"). Looked up to in comm. as authority on old times despite lack of formal education. Sure old-fashioned ways best; no use for doctors. Independent. — Drawl. Soft speech. Strong stresses. Haunting rising-falling intonation on stressed syllables. Speech slow; pitch basically mid-range. Up-gliding /e o ɔ/. Good deal of /-r/ constriction; unvoicing of final voiced consonants; weak articulation of final consonants; simplification of final clusters. Occurrence of much of the "Midland" vocabulary within a very short distance of the S. GA coast one of the obvious linguistic-cultural features.

8. Wayne County

Est. 1805. English, some Scots and Germans. On Altamaha R. Wiregrass and piney woods; turpentine and sawmills; now tourist office. Diversified agriculture, grazing. Pop. 1810: 676, 1820: 1,010, 1850: 1,499, 1880: 5,980, 1910: 13,069, 1930: 12,647, 1960: 17,921.

Huxford, Folks, comp. 1977. *Pioneers of Wiregrass Georgia.* . . . 7 vols. Homerville: Huxford Genealogical Society.

Jordan, Margaret Coleman. 1976. *Wayne Miscellany*. Jesup: Jordan.

Screven

Inc. 1907. Small town in W. part of Co., trading center.

GA 8A: F, widowed housewife, 86. B. Co. (c. 6 mi. NE). — F., PGF, PGM, M., MGF, MGM all b. Co. — Ed.: local country school (chief reading: pulp magazines). — Baptist; Eastern Star. — Somewhat hesitant; a bit suspicious of strangers, esp. traveling salesmen (thought FW was one). Taboo-reactions. Simple, gentle, kind; perplexed at changes in the world. Reads westerns and movie magazines; would often interrupt FW to tell about some story she'd read. Talked freely once FW accepted. Folk type; knows comm. and people intimately. — Drawl. Nasality. Up-gliding diphthongs (occ. in-gliding /ɔ/). Final cons. not clearly articulated; simplification of final clusters; a good deal of postvocalic constriction.

Jesup

Inc. 1870. RR junction; pine region, naval stores; now on tourist route to FL. Finnish settlement nearby (1920). Pop. 1900: 805, 1930: 2,303, 1960: 7,304.

GA 8B: F, housewife, school teacher (8th grade), 30 yrs. principal of rural school, 50. B. "Old Wayne Co." (now Brantley). Never out of Wayne-Brantley area except when in school. — Ancestors came in with Gen. Wayne and settled on the bank of the Satilla River. F. b. near St Marys, PGF b. Beaufort, SC, came to Camden Co.; M. b. Wayne Co., MGF, MGM both from VA. — Ed.: 3 yrs. Statesboro Teachers College (U. of S. GA) since began teaching. — Methodist; Eastern Star, PTA, NEA, GA Ed. Assn, Farm Bureau, WCTU, DAR, UDC. — Quick mind. Energetic. Knows rural life very well. Combines school duties with full household chores, including butchering. Big-framed, very fat; hearty, good-natured. Enjoyed interviews; interested in what FW was trying to find out (knew enough of other GA dialects from her contacts with other teachers to appreciate what Atlas meant). Very intelligent. One of most respected citizens in comm.; authority on local folkways, which she is interested in preserving. Would not be classified as a cultivated inf., however. — Fast speech. Not much intonation range; monotonous tone. Strong nasality. Short weak-stressed vowels; stressed vowels fairly long; generally up-gliding diphthongs. Much constriction, occ. intrusive (sometimes lacking); intervocalic /r/ often weak or lost. Postvocalic /l/ sometimes vocalized. Final cons. lingers sometimes. Intrusive /-v/; /hw-/; /sr-/.

9. Tattnall County

Formed 1801 from Montgomery, Liberty Cos. Many settlers from SC. Drained by Altamaha and Ogeechee. Terrain hilly to level; diversified agriculture. Pop. 1810: 2,206, 1820: 2,544, 1850: 3,227, 1880: 6,988, 1910: 18,569, 1930: 15,411, 1960: 15,837.

> Hodges, Lucile. 1965. *A History of Our Locale, Mainly Evans County, Georgia.* Macon: Southern Press.

Glennville

Local trading center. Pop. 1910: 640, 1930: 1,503, 1960: 2,791.

GA 9A: F, housewife, school lunchroom worker in Head Start, c. 70. B. Readville, same co., has lived briefly in Brunswick; otherwise always in small communities or country. — F. b. 7–8 mi. away, farmer, inf. barely remembers PGF; M. raised locally, housewife. — Ed.: 8th grade in country school. — Methodist church and neighborhood organization.

GA 9B: Cobbtown (inc. 1905). — M, farm worker, has been carpenter, bus driver, worked in Ft. Stewart, c. 60. B. here. — F. b. here, PGF (a blacksmith), PGM b. in Toombs Co. "across the river"; M., MGF, MGM all b. locally. — Ed.: 9th grade. — Baptist. — Talkative, cooperative, though FW found it impossible to conduct a full-length interview.

10. Evans County

Formed 1914 from Tattnall Co. 1st church (Baptist) est. in 1845. Savannah and Western RR. Canoochee R. Pine barren country, sawmill country; agriculture and timber, subtropical fruits and vegetables, naval stores. Pop. 1930: 7,102, 1960: 6,952.

> Hodges, Lucile. 1965. *A History of Our Locale, Mainly Evans County, Georgia.* Macon: Southern Press.

GA 10A: Manassas (Tatnall County). — M, farmer, 67. B. here. — F. b. here, illegitimate; M., MGF b. Screven Co., c. 30 mi. away, moved here, MGM b. Bulloch Co., close ancestry with MGF. — Ed.: 2–3 mos. a year till 22 yrs. old. — Primitive Baptist. — Limited intelligence and experience. Unused to visitors or diversions; content to sit down (with wife) and spend entire day with FW. Prob. had little idea of what interview was about, but introduction from Co. Tax Commissioner made situation better. — Slow and deliberate speech. Some nasalization and slurring; weak articulation. Lengthening of vowels often.

Bellville, Manassas, Hagan

Bellville a RR town, shipping point. Destroyed by storm 1897–98. Baptists, Methodists. Hagan a RR town. Bellville pop. 1900: c. 300.

GA 10B: M, farmer, 84. B. 1/2 mi. W., moved here at age 22. — F. b. 2 mi. NE, PGF b. 2 mi. E., PGF's F. b. in VA, met SC woman PGF's M., PGM from Jefferson Co., b. near the Canoochee river; M. b. c. 4 mi. NW, MGF came from Jefferson Co., MGM b. SC, moved to GA age 4. — Ed.: 2–3 local schools. — Methodist (trustee Methodist camp ground); has been justice of the peace, constable; before that, asst. tax collector, Tatnall Co., member Evans Co. Welfare Bd. — Cooperative; enjoyed interview. Limited education. Independent: his fight with the state hwy. dept. over relocation of road through his farm is one of the legends of Evans Co. Deeply rooted in comm. Some awe of learning. Talks freely. Many anecdotes about old times. Very hospitable. Strong sense of property. Hard-working. Natural: no effort to be "proper" in speech. Almost no profanity. — Slightly muffled utterance; low pitch. Fairly fast tempo. Strong stresses. Many folk-grammatical forms. In-gliding /e o/. Initial voiceless stops generally aspirated; good deal of postvocalic constriction; /hw-/.

11. Candler County

Formed 1914. On Canoochee R. Agriculture and timber. Pop. 1920: 9,228, 1930: 8,991, 1960: 8,672.

Metter

Inc. 1903. Local trade center. Pop. 1900: 400, 1930: 1,424, 1960: 2,362.

GA 11N: F, housewife, formerly school cook, domestic, 60. B. here. Always in Co., except travel to visit relatives in Pittsburgh. — F., M. both b. Wilkinson Co. — Ed.: till 9th grade, locally. — Baptist; church organizations. — Very likable; knows most people in Co., is liked and respected. Natural responses when FW allowed them. [Interview fairly good, though on several items student FW wasn't aware of import of question. — Note [a] in *aunt* as RIM's observations elsewhere would have led one to expect. Variations in postvocalic /r/. — RIM]

12. Bulloch County

Formed 1797. Settled from VA and the Carolinas. Drained by Ogeechee and Canoochee Rivers. Fishing, timber, fruits and vegetables. Pop. 1800: 2,836, 1820: 2,578, 1850: 4,300, 1880: 8,053, 1910: 26,464, 1930: 26,509, 1960: 24,263.

GA 12A: Stilson. — M, retired insurance man, 54. B. Stilson. Lived in Charlotte (2 1/2 yrs.), Birmingham (5 yrs.), and Atlanta (2 yrs.). Bedridden in Savannah last 10 yrs. (interview took place in the Coffee Bluff section of Savannah). — F. b. Co., PGF, PGM came to GA from Scotland in early 19th cent.; MGM's ancestors settled along Savannah R. c. 1732. — Ed.: 2 yrs. h.s. (U. of GA preparatory course). — Presbyterian; had pretty wide range of social contacts, White and Negro, before illness. — Appealing personality, patient in adversity. Tolerant, understanding. Somewhat well-read, but unaffected (no "hyper" forms). — Nasality. Generally sticks to folk grammar when discussing everyday subjects. /e o/ sometimes monophthongal, but in-gliding and up-gliding varieties also occur; less /ʌ/ than found on coast; /ɔ/ sometimes up-gliding. Strong /-r/ (prob. under-transcribed), could be attributed to Scottish background; /hw-/ regularly.

GA 12A*: F, sister of GA 12A, somewhat older. See GA 12A for family history.

Statesboro

Laid out as Co. seat 1803; inc. 1866. Settled before Rev. Grew with lumber and turpentine; small industries, hunting. U. of S. GA here. Pop. 1880: 1,036, 1910: 2,529, 1930: 3,996, 1960: 8,356.

GA 12B!: M, newspaper editor and publisher, local historian, 61. B. here. Lived in Statesboro except during his education, military service, sanatorium in NC, and 2 yrs. in NYC (training at National City Bank). 4 mos. in New Orleans after service (WWII). — Both sides of family in Co. for at least 4 generations (great-grandparents were Scotch-Irish either by descent or birth). F. successful farmer, cotton gin salesman, promoted cotton development in S. America. — Ed.: 2 yrs. GA Tech; B.A. Newberry College, SC. Has published book on the co.; another, more detailed, to come out shortly. — Primitive Baptist (progressive branch). Most associates GA newspapermen and other writers. — Cultivated.

13. Effingham County

Co. formed 1777; once part of St. Matthew and St. Philip parishes. First settled by 3 groups of Salzburgers (Lutherans), 1734–36; settled Ebenezer (1734), Red Bluff (1736). Attempt at silk culture; abandoned 1790 (devastation during Rev.). 1st Protestant orphanage in America est. 1737; apparently discontinued 1750. Further migrations 1739, 1741, 1751. Germans good planters: diversified crops, experimented with rice and cotton, mills for wheat and rice. Some indentured servants; opposed slavery initially. Jerusalem Church est. 1744, parent Lutheran Church in GA; brick bldg. 1767–69. Church profaned during British occupation 1779–82, rebuilt later. Brief Moravian settlement, opposed by Salzburgers; many Moravians left GA because they refused to bear arms. Became a trading center; road building; sawmills, naval stores, fish, timber. Pop. 1736: 146, 1740: 199, 1742: 256, 1790: 2,424, 1820: 3,018, 1850: 3,864, 1880: 5,979, 1910: 9,971, 1930: 10,164, 1960: 10,144.

Cox, S. P., ed. 1734. *An Extract of the Journals of Mr. Commissary Von Reck. . . and of the Rev. Mr. Bolzius. . . .* London: M. Downing.

Gnann, Pearl Ray. 1956. *Georgia Salzburger and Allied Families.* Savannah.

Hofer, J. M. 1934. The Georgia Salzburgers. *Georgia Historical Quarterly* 18:99–117.

Jones, George Fenwick, ed. 1966. *Henry Newman's Salzburger Letterbooks.* Athens: University of Georgia Press.

Newton, Hester W. 1934. Industrial and Social Influences of the Salzburgers in Colonial Georgia. *Georgia Historical Quarterly* 18:335–53.

Newton, Hester W. 1934. The Agricultural Activities of the Salzburgers in Colonial Georgia. *Georgia Historical Quarterly* 18:248–63.

Strobel, Philip A. 1953. *The Salzburgers and Their Descendents.* Athens: University of Georgia Press.

Urlsperger, Samuel, ed. 1968–72. *Detailed Reports on the Salzburger Emigrants. . . .* Trans. by Hermann J. Lacher and ed. by George Fenwick Jones. Athens: University of Georgia Press.

Wilson, Caroline Price. 1969. *Annals of Georgia.* Vol. 2, Effingham County. Repr. Vidalia: Georgia Genealogical Reprints.

Rincon

Village, local trading center. Pop. 1900: 91, 1930: 317.

GA 13A: M, farmer, 69. B. here. — F., PGF both b. here; PGF's F. and M. both b. Salzburg, Austria; PGM b. here; PGM's F. and M. both b. Salzburg, Austria; M., MGF both b. here; MGF's F. and M. both b. Salzburg, Austria; MGM b. here; MGM's F. and M. both b. Salzburg, Austria. — Ed.: here, about 18 mos. — Lutheran; Woodmen of the World. — Gentle, genial soul. Father always clung tenaciously to the old German customs. — Slow tempo. Rather clear utterance. Some nasalization in the vicinity of nasal consonants. In many words, [e˄·] for /iˑ/, [o˄·] for /uˑ/ (not likely to be older English, may be due to German background); never a /u/ before nasals, e.g. *room* [rō˄·m], *funeral* [fjo˄·nəl]; considerable variation in the exact placement of many vowels, again prob. due to childhood use of a more German type of pronunciation. [ß] prob. used originally for both /v/ and /w/.

Wilson Mill Pond, Oakie, Egypt P.O.
    Village, shipping point for farm produce. Pop. 1900: 250.

GA 13B!: M, retired dental surgeon, 83. B. neighborhood. Practiced in Savannah 50 yrs., but always in touch with Effingham. Has fished and hunted, participated in rifle matches all over. — F., PGF both b. Co.; PGF's F. b. Mecklenburg Co., NC; PGF's M. from neighborhood; PGM from neighborhood (German); M., MGF, MGF's F. and M. all b. Co.; MGM, MGM's F. and M. all b. Bulloch Co. — Ed.: N. GA Military College (Dahlonega); Baltimore Dental College. — Mason, Knights of Pythias, GA Dental Society, Am. Dental Society, Psi Omega (Dental Fraternity), Forest City Gun Club (oldest in US), National Rifle Champion 1897–98. — Extremely hospitable, despite recent illness. — Slight drawl effect: speech mod. rapid, but stressed vowels generally prolonged. Small amount of nasality. Strong stresses. Wide range of tempo and intonation. Occ. centered beginning of /ai au/ before voiceless consonants; in-gliding /i e ɔ o u/ more common than up-gliding; /u/ us. fronted; unrounded vowel in *pot, rock, tomorrow*, rounded in *crop, oxen, John*. Many unreleased final stops; some postvocalic constriction, not consistent; no sandhi /r/ or intrusive /r/; /-t-/ sometimes [-ɾ-]; /hw-/ even in *wharf*; /sɪ-/; some postvocalic /l/ weakened or lost. — Cultivated.

14. Screven County

Co. est. 1793. "Never any one colony or group of people." Ebenezer Germans, Queensboro Scotch-Irish among first settlers; Ulster Scots by 1768. Jacksonborough Co. seat from 1799; Sylvania from 1847. Small farmers till c. 1800; then plantation culture est. Early settlers chiefly Methodists and Baptists. RR 1838–39. Cotton, general farming, fruit; lumber and naval stores; burstone and clay. Pop. 1800: 3,091, 1820: 3,941, 1850: 6,847, 1880: 12,786, 1910: 20,202, 1930: 20,503, 1960: 14,919.

Hollingsworth, Clyde Dixon. 1947. *Pioneer Days: A History of the Early Years in Screven County.*

Sylvania
    Est. 1847 as seat of Screven Co. (centrally located); inc. 1854. Trading and shipping point, small industry; since WWII, tourist traffic, with new bridge across Savannah R. Pop. 1880: 314, 1910: 1,400, 1930: 1,781, 1960: 3,469.

GA 14A: M, farmer, 76. B. near here. — F. b. here, PGF came here from NC, PGF's F. from Scotland, PGM b. here; M. b. here, MGF, MGM both prob. b. here (MGF sheriff of Co. when Co. seat at Jacksonborough). — Ed.: c. 10 mos. — Baptist; formerly Knights of Pythias; has been sheriff, deputy sheriff, police chief; has active interest in politics. — Slightly suspicious of FW at first. Talked freely about old times, politics, farm life, weather signs. Cooperative. Knows everybody in comm., local anecdotes, etc. — Spoke in low tone, not very clear. Chewed cigar steadily during interview. Rapid tempo. Weak-stressed vowels very short. Voice somewhat high-pitched. /e o/ up-gliding; /ju/ us. after /t d n/; [v] us.,

pot, etc.; /ai/ has upcountry alternation. Final consonants often muffled; /hw-/; no /-r/, except occ. linking.

GA 14B: M, retired blacksmith, 70. B. Girard (Burke Co., just across line). Ages 16–19 lived in Augusta (Richmond Co.), then to upper end of Screven Co. (Hiltonia), to Sylvania age 29, has lived here ever since. — F., PGF, PGM, M., MGF, MGM all b. Burke Co. (PGF's PGF in Rev., hung by British). — Ed.: equiv. of 7th grade. Little travel. — Methodist; Woodmen of the World, Masons, active in politics, but never ran for public office. — Knows folklife. Offered many synonyms. Knows what's said and what isn't. Good memory. Pleased with opportunity to talk about old times. Recognizes changes in fashion of pronunciation (knows his own has changed). Talked about interviews to family and friends. Good mind. "Memory ain't as good as it used to be", but generally had a good, sound feeling for current usage as well as what had been said. Sure of position. Frequently corrected from a "standard" form to what he naturally would say. — Drawl. Strong stress, long vowels in stressed syllables. Some nasality. Clear articulation, never forced clearness. Up-gliding /e o/; /ɔ/ fairly high; /ʌ/ high; /ai au/ of upper Piedmont type; /u/ fronted to /ju/ after /t d n/. No /-r/; some tendency to clip final cons.

Middleground Road, Red Bluff, Halcyon Dale
    Halcyon Dale a bustling little comm. in 1840s; orig. station number 5 on Central of GA. Village; local trading center.

GA 14C: F, former farm manager, 88. B. Middleground Road, has spent last 10 yrs. in Sylvania. A few visits to friends in other parts of GA, once to Asheville, NC, a couple of times to Columbia and Charleston, SC. — F., PGF, PGM, M., MGF, MGM all b. Co. Indian descent on F.'s side (talks freely about it). — Ed.: lessons at home, 6 mos. to schoolhouses. — Baptist; DAR, Eastern Star, UDC, Masons (wife and daughter's degree), Red Cross. — Many stories. Proud to be old-fashioned. Independent: "I am what I am". No use for "bought friends"; easy to get along with. Called FW "hon" and "son" affectionately within 15 min. after interview started. Blind, slightly deaf; mind wandered a little, but generally quick. Talked freely. No taboo reactions — "Call an animal what his name is". Knew recipes by heart, could recite ad infinitum. Strong physically. Refuses to have anyone staying with her (somewhat to the consternation of some of the townspeople who think she's just miserly: she's reputedly wealthy). Fond of the past but doesn't live in it. Disapproves of "modern women": "they were ladies in my day". Took FW into confidence about life, home, family, one romance in her life. Appreciates chance to talk about old times: "You got me to remembering things I hadn't thought about in years". Not quite sure of purpose of interview, except that it preserved past; "like to keep old friends and make new ones". Told neighbors about interviews. Very religious, nephew pres. S. Baptist Convention, "but in one thing I'm more a Methodist than a Baptist — I don't believe in closed communion". Hard to get morphological items by questioning. — Soft, melodious voice; haunting, gentle, ingratiating. Distinct utterance. Tempo varying, moderate to slow. /ɛ/ goes to /ɪ/ before /r/, *airs, ears* are homonyms; /e o/ slightly up-gliding, but occ. slightly in-gliding; /u/ fronted to /ju/ us. after /t d n/, but not always;

/a/ occ. rounded, but not as far back, as a rule, as in upcountry speech; /ʜ/ alternates with /h/ in some words. Final cons. clear; /-t-/ often [-ɾ-]; /-r/ sometimes (other informants never).

15. Burke County

Est. 1777. One of first settlements after coast. Laid out 1758 as St. George's Parish. By 1763, immigration from Ireland (via Savannah), VA, PA. Revolutionary skirmishes. RRs 1851, 1854. 1864–65 raids, 1 battle, harassment. Old Church of Eng. parish eventually disestablished; Baptists, Presbyterians, Methodists most numerous. Agriculture (long led GA in acreage and production of cotton); orchards, timber, naval stores. Savannah and Ogeechee Rivers. Pop. 1790: 9,467, 1820: 11,577, 1850: 16,100, 1880: 27,128, 1910: 27,268, 1930: 29,224, 1960: 20,356.

Baldwin, Nell H., and A. M. Hillhouse. 1956. *An Intelligent Student's Guide to Burke County (Ga.) History.* Waynesboro: N. H. Baldwin and A. M. Hillhouse.

Alexander

Site of Alexander Academy, 1840–50. Iron foundry (local iron) during Civil War. Village; sawmill and gristmill, cotton. Pop. 1880: c. 400.

GA 15A: M, farmer, 83. B. here. — F., PGF b. here, PGF's F. b. SC (English descent), PGM, PGM's F. b. here (Carolina descent); M., MGF both b. here, MGF's F. b. Charleston, MGM b. here, MGM's F. of Carolina descent. — Ed.: 2 mos. only. — Baptist. — Very quick and intelligent. Uneducated and natural.

Waynesboro

Laid out 1783; inc. 1812; city charter 1883. Part of plantation belt; was shipping center for cotton marketing. Pop. 1850: 196, 1880: 1,008, 1910: 2,729, 1930: 3,922, 1960: 5,359.

GA 15B: M, farmer (once overseer), 92. B. Sardis, lower edge of Co. Has always lived in Co., moving N.; has been in Waynesboro since age 34. — F. b. Sardis, PGF and 2 bros. came from SC; M. raised in Jefferson Co. (adjacent co. to W.). — Ed.: about 9 mos.; mostly self-educated. Fair amount of reading. — Baptist; Farm Bureau. — Mind alert, mind and hearing clear; tries to be fairly active. Spends a good deal of time supervising farm for grandson. Seemed to enjoy interviews. Well posted on state and local affairs; known and respected throughout Co. — Strong stresses. Nasality. Voice trails off to indistinctness occ. at ends of long sentences. Some harshness; little intonation range. Both in-gliding and up-gliding diphthongs. Initial stops generally strongly aspirated; some postvocalic constriction; /hw-/.

16. Richmond County

Co. est. 1777; orig. St. Pauls Parish. Founded 1735; garrison, trading post, 1736. Quakers from England, later 18th cent. 1st cotton mill 1834; Savannah R. drainage and waterpower led to manufacturing, abortive silk scheme, beet sugar 1839. Vineyard experiments, flowers in middle 19th cent. Peanuts also a money crop. Center of Tobacco Road country. National Golf Course laid out 1932–33: Masters Tournament. Peaches, kaolin; resort for N. tourists. Pop. 1790: 11,317, 1820: 8,608, 1850: 16,246, 1880: 34,665, 1910: 58,886, 1930: 72,990, 1960: 135,601.

Bell, Earl L. 1960. The Augusta Chronicle*: Indomitable Voice of Dixie, 1785–1960.* Athens: University of Georgia Press.

Cashin, Edward J. 1975. *Augusta and the American Revolution: Events in the Georgia Back Country 1773–1783.* Darien: Ashantilly Press.

Cashin, Edward J. 1980. *The Story of Augusta.* Augusta: Richmond County Board of Education.

Clark, Walter A. 1909. *A Lost Arcadia.* Augusta: Chronicle Job Print.

Cumming, Mary G. Smith. 1906. *Two Centuries of Augusta: A Sketch.* Augusta: Ridgely-Tidwell-Ashe Co.

Davidson, Grace Gillam, comp. 1929. *Records of Richmond County, Georgia: Formerly St. Paul's Parish.* Athens. Repr. 1968 (Vidalia: Georgia Genealogical Reprints).

deTreville, John. 1979. *Reconstruction in Augusta, Georgia, 1865–1868.* Chapel Hill, NC: deTreville.

Federal Writers Project. 1938. *Augusta.* Augusta: Tidwell Print. Supply Co.

Fleming, Berry. 1957. *Autobiography of a Colony: The First Half-Century of Augusta, Georgia.* Athens: University of Georgia Press.

German, Richard Henry Lee. 1971. *The Queen City of the Savannah: Augusta, Georgia, during the Urban Progressive Era 1890–1917.* University of Florida dissertation.

Hamilton, William B. 1972. *Political Control in a Southern City: Augusta, Georgia, in the 1890s.* Harvard University Bachelor's thesis.

Jones, Charles C., Jr., and Salem Dutcher. 1890. *Memorial History of Augusta, Georgia. . . .* Syracuse, NY: D. Mason. Repr. 1966 (Spartanburg, SC: Reprint Co.).

Norwood, Martha F. 1975. *History of the White House Tract. . . .* Atlanta: Georgia Department of Natural Resources.

Rowland, Arthur Ray. 1967. *A Guide to the Study of Augusta and Richmond County, Georgia.* Augusta: Richmond County Historical Society.

Walden, Ada Ramp. 1936. *History of Richmond County.*

Werner, Randolph Dennis. 1977. *Hegemony and Conflict: The Political Economy of a Southern Region, Augusta, Georgia, 1865–1895.* University of Virginia dissertation.

Whitson, Mrs. Lorenzo Dow. 1882. *Sketches of Augusta, Georgia.* Augusta.

1947. *Handbook of the Augusta Area.* Augusta: Augusta Herald.

County Home, Augusta

Augusta laid out 1735 (founded as trading post), garrisoned 1736; inc. as town 1789; city charter 1798. Early settlers from PA, Beaufort (SC), NC, E. VA, NJ; Salzburgers. Largest fur-trading center in S. colonies. Highway to Savannah 1740; St. Pauls Church 1750. Tobacco culture since 1780s. Richmond Academy 1783 (later became Augusta College). Augusta *Chronicle* since 1785. Steamboat company on Savannah R. by 1823. On RR by 1837; canal by 1845 (still provides power for mills); Central of GA RR 1854. Was important shipping port for cotton and tobacco; leading Southern textile center by 1860. Burst of industrial expansion by 1880. Diversified manufacturing; machinery, flour, lumber. Cotton mills, cottonseed processing; brick and tile; candy, cannery, ironworks. National Golf Course here from 1933, Masters Tournament. Known as winter resort for wealthy Northerners. Pop. 1880: 21,891, 1910: 41,040, 1930: 60,342, 1960: 70,626.

GA 16A: F, farm housewife, 61. B. Grovetown (NW part of Co.) near Bath. — F. b. Edgefield Co., SC, came to GA age 21 (RR man, sawmill, farmed); M. b. Co., MGF from TN, settled in Grovetown as young man, MGM b. Grovetown. — Ed.: Hood's Chapel School, 1/2 mi. from Blythe (Richmond Co.). — Baptist; once Daughters of America. — Plain, middle-class, substantial people. Some taboo reactions, some attempt to conceal folk grammar and folk vocab. Cooperative. Conservative in thinking. Not much tendency to tell anecdotes. Reasonably bright, alert to changes in comm. as Augusta has grown. Regrets loss of some of old ways, but feels the exchange has been generally favorable. — Tempo moderate. Strong nasality. Drawl. Pitch above medium level. Monotonous. Some unexpected glottalizations. Slurred utterance. Generally in-gliding /e ɔ o/. Simplification of final clusters; some constriction in a few words. — Older bro., farmer, Baptist, gave some responses, not marked AUX.

Bath, Blythe P.O.

Bath settled early 19th cent., one-time summer resort for Burke Co. planters. Had many fine mansions, largely abandoned with end of plantation culture. Blythe a country place for wealthy; continuity of elite. 1st cotton mill 1839; important in cotton trade, 2nd only to Memphis as inland market. Irish successful in politics for a time, but power declined by 1900.

GA 16B: F, housewife and "gentlewoman", 85. B. Richmond, VA; married on visit here during malaria season. Plantation home "Greenscut", Briar Creek (Burke Co.); summer home in Bath. Most of the time and all of the last 61 yrs. in Bath. — F., PGF both b. Burke Co., PGF's F. and M. both from VA, PGM b. Providence, RI; M. b. Savannah; MGF b. Wales, MGM, MGM's F. and M. all from Salzburger colony, Effingham Co. — Ed.: private school, Bath. — Presbyterian; postmistress for 6 yrs. — Enjoys travel and conversation. Strong opinions and prejudices (makes no bones about them). Knows all local lore, all old plantation families of the Richmond-Burke area, most of older names in Augusta. Keenly alert to personalities involved in GA politics; not esp. concerned with issues. Some tendency to confuse present and past. Few taboos. Assurance of a position that no financial difficulties or changes in social system can destroy. Kind and dignified in relations with those she considers not of her caste. Has plantation caste prejudices toward poor whites. Many anecdotes. Well respected in Augusta: "the authority on rural life in Richmond Co.". Devoted to family. Independent: "go where I like anytime I feel like it, nobody's going to stop me". Enjoyed interviews; cooperative. Didn't completely see the point of FW's questions but glad to give time and information. Currently feuding with minister of local Presbyterian church. Has enjoyed life and seems determined to continue enjoying it. — Fast speech. Voice in high register with wide intonation range and definite rise on stressed syllables. Strong stresses. /ai au/ often with centered beginning before voiceless consonants; in-gliding /e o ɔ/.

GA 16C: Augusta. — F, housewife, 72. B. here. — F, PGF b. here, PGM b. Athens; M., MGF, MGM all b. Augusta, family ultimately from Santo Domingo. — Ed.: parochial grammar and h.s., one yr. Notre Dame. — Catholic.

GA 16D!: Augusta. — F, homemaker, 54. B. here. Summers at Flat Rock, NC (Henderson Co.); good deal of travel. — F. b. here, PGF b. Lawrenceville (between Atlanta and Athens), family came down with Ulster Scots migration immediately from Fairview section of Greenville Co., SC, PGM b. here, PGM's F. and M. both from NJ; M. b. here, MGF, MGM both b. Scotland, came to GA as children, MGM's M. had come to US early, then went back to Scotland and married. — Ed.: local schools; part of h.s. in Wilmington, NC; Mary Baldwin College, Stanton, VA. — Presbyterian; garden clubs, knows everybody of old families. — Excellent informant! Very quick mind. One of most enjoyable interviews in FW's experience. Immediate grasp of what was wanted; perfect rapport. Speaks natural upper-class city speech. Keen observer of environment, both in Augusta and in other places, and knows differences between her own speech and other types. Quick to reject suggestions outside her pattern, or to document exactly where she heard them. Assurance of position in local society. No taboos; very widely read. Keeps up with national and international affairs and shows excellent judgment. Found interviews great fun. Tolerant. Hospitable (makes excellent cocktails). Knows Augusta history and society intimately. Keen sense of humor. Interested in Atlas: asked many questions about FW's work. — Fast speech (energetic in speech as in personality); crisp, clipped. Wide intonation range. Centered beginning of /ai au/ before voiceless consonants; /e ɔ o/ us. in-gliding. Clear utterance. Strong stresses. Not the slightest suggestion of drawl. Simplification of final clusters. — Cultivated.

17. Jefferson County

Co. formed in 1796. 1st settlement in 1750s; St. George's Parish 1758. In heart of Ulster settlement ("Queensborough"); Irish settlement 1768–75. Also early settlers from NC. Earliest settlers Presbyterian; now Baptists and Methodists dominate. Some Germans in Co. First GA cotton mill here 1828. Pillaged by Sherman 1864. Cotton till boll weevil; then diversified. Soil depleted by inefficient agricultural practices, being renewed. Now rural, agricultural. Some summer retreats. Pop. 1800: 5,684, 1820: 6,362, 1850: 9,131, 1880: 15,671, 1910: 21,379, 1930: 20,727, 1960: 17,468.

Cofer, Loris D. 1977. *Queensborough: Or, The Irish Town and Its Citizens*. Louisville, GA: Cofer.

Thomas, Z. V. 1927. *History of Jefferson County*. Macon: Press of the J. W. Burke Co.

Louisville

Chartered 1786; state capital 1795–1805. Once prosperous plantation country, now declining. Academy in 1790s. First Presbyterians; Methodists and Baptists later. Cottonseed products, market town. Pop. 1820: 694, 1880: 575, 1910: 1,039, 1930: 1,650, 1960: 413.

GA 17N: F, assistant in antique shop, formerly farm hand (till age 34), 48. B. here; only out of state twice on short visits (NY and SC). — All grandparents from Jefferson or

Washington Cos.; great-grandparents all slaves. — Ed.: through 9th grade (3 yrs. h.s.). — Baptist. — Good rural inf. Refuses to watch TV, although her children do. — Distinct nasalization of vowels. Drawl; vowels sometimes overlong.

GA 17: M, automobile dealer, 71. B. here. Age 22, ages 25–33 lived in Columbia, SC; was with army in France during WWI (age 23). — F.'s ancestry English; M.'s ancestry French, English, Scottish. Ancestors have been in Jefferson Co. for 4 generations. — Ed.: Louisville Academy; 3 yrs. GA Tech. — Natural speech, interesting mixture of folk and cultivated.

18. Emanuel County

Formed 1812 from Bulloch and Montgomery Cos. "Pine barren" region (pine barrens a barrier between coastal plantations and inland cotton belt); relatively isolated till 1870s. Drained by several rivers. Early settlers from Carolinas (chiefly NC); cattle grazing. Pine barren speculations c. 1783. Early settlers largely Baptists, with seasoning of Methodists. Academy authorized 1824. Anti-secession; Co. largely spared by Sherman. No newspapers till 1870s; RR from 1880. Sawmills, naval stores; cotton, corn, soybeans, tobacco. Pop. 1820: 2,928, 1850: 4,577, 1880: 9,759, 1910: 25,140, 1930: 24,101, 1960: 17,815.

Dorsey, James E. 1978. *Footprints along the Hoopee. . . .* Swainsboro: Emanuel Historic Preservation Society.

Dorsey, James E. 1981. *Collections of the Emanuel Historic Preservation Society.* Swainsboro: The Society.

Dorsey, James E., and John K. Derden. 1976. *A Visual Salute to Emanuel County.* Swainsboro: Swainsboro Forest-Blade.

Fountain, G. A. 1950. *A Sketch of Emanuel County and Swainsboro.* Swainsboro: Swainsboro Chamber of Commerce.

Rogers, William. 1976. *Emanuel Memories.* Swainsboro: Swainsboro Forest-Blade.

Woods, Dorothy Woodell. 1981. *Salt of the Earth.* Swainsboro: Emanuel Historic Preservation Society.

Adrian

Inc. 1899. Grew out of RR expansion in late 19th cent.; local trading and shipping center. Pop. 1900: 833.

GA 18A: M, farmer, 82. B. here. — F. b. Green Cove Springs, Clay Co., FL; M., MGF, MGM all b. Treutlen Co. (old Montgomery Co.). — Ed.: till 3rd grade; says can't read. — Baptist. — Inf. doing interview to please grandson; tried very hard to give the "right" responses. Large landowners; prominent. Partly deaf and nearly blind. [FW inexperienced, interview hurried. Inf. still came out with several striking non-standard forms, notably /faut/. — RIM]

GA 18A*: F, 66. Wife of GA 18A. — Family from Johnson Co. — Ed.: till 9th grade. — Baptist.

Swainsboro

Designated as Co. seat 1822; town lots laid out 1833; first general stores by 1838–39. Inc. 1853; new charter 1899. RR junction, trading center; small industries related to cotton, lumber, naval stores. Livestock and poultry. Pop. 1880: 186, 1890: 395, 1900: c. 1,000, 1930: 2,442.

GA 18B: F, housewife, 70. B. Twin City (in Co.), 12 mi. away. Lived Johnson Co. 1 1/2 yrs., age 50; lived Jefferson Co. 1 1/2 yrs., age 55. — F., PGF, PGM all b. Emanuel Co.; M., MGF, MGM all b. Glascock Co. — Ed.: country school till 9th grade. — Pentecostal Holiness Church. — Friendly, cooperative, alert. [Little forcing from FW. Fair amount of dialogue, number of very natural direct responses, fair amount cv. forms. Inf. seemed at ease; no attempt to cover up when ignorant. — RIM]

19. Montgomery County

Formed 1793 from Washington Co. Settlers from VA and NC via Abbeville Dist., SC. Scots after 1810 (from NC). Sparsely settled till 1865. Pine barren speculations early 19th cent.; logging late 19th cent. Several cos. formed from orig. Montgomery Co. (7 1/2 million acres granted, over 18 times present size of Co.). Oconee River valley; staple crops, timber, naval stores. Pop. 1800: 3,180, 1820: 1,869, 1850: 2,154, 1880: 5,381, 1910: 19,638, 1930: 10,020, 1960: 6,284.

Dorsey, James E., and John K. Derden. 1983. *Montgomery County, Georgia: A Source Book of Genealogy and History.* Spartanburg, SC: Magnolia Press.

GA 19A: Kibbee (local trade center). — M, merchant (ran store 32 yrs.), farmer, stock raiser, 71. B. here; has been at Kite, 40 mi. N., off and on. — No time to get family history — see GA 19A* (inf.'s aunt). — Ed.: local school. — Baptist. — Interview was pieced out of three kinsmen (GA 19A*, GA 19A**), all of same small-town comm. and cultural background, because 19A, the principal inf., was reportedly too busy to complete interview. All of same type, locally rooted in what people at Co. seat consider one of the backward areas of the co., and the co. as a whole is not prosperous or modern even by S. GA standards. Principal inf. (19A) had the quickest mind of the three, offered synonyms most freely. In better health of body and mind. — Although a bit nervous, speech still slow and drawling; more staccato than the others; stresses much stronger. Natural use of folk vocab. and folk grammar. Strong nasality. Voice generally rather high-pitched, monotonous. Slurred and somewhat unclear utterance. Up-gliding diphthongs. Simplification of final consonant clusters; weak articulation of final consonants; much postvocalic constriction.

GA 19A*: F, housewife, 78. Aunt of 19A. B. here. Has always lived in vicinity. — F. b. here, PGF, PGM from Carolina; M. b. here, MGF, MGM from Carolina. — Ed.: 8–10 yrs., local schools (3 mos. each yr.). — Missionary Baptist; Eastern Star. — A good, simple housewife who cooperated as well as she knew how. Of the three (GA 19A, 19A*, 19A**) she was the most difficult to work with: mind slowest, was prompted often by her little grandchild. Inf.'s responses and those of GA 19A** indicate that the folk vocab. is still very strongly established in the Kibbee/Tarrytown area.

GA 19A**: Tarrytown (post hamlet on RR). — M, farmer, justice of the peace (40 yrs.), 75+. 2nd cousin (and bro.-in-law) of GA 19A. B. near Kibbee. Never lived out of Co., had farm between Kibbee and Tarrytown. Moved to Tarrytown age 43+. — F. perhaps from NC, came here as baby; M. b. here, MGM raised Jefferson Co. (70 mi. N.). — Ed.: local schools. — Once a Methodist (lost interest when church burned and roll lost); Mason; farm organizations; magistrate; local registrar of vital statistics. — Most cooperative of the three (GA 19A, 19A*, 19A**); most generous with his time and most interested in the implications of Atlas work. — Very strong /-r/.

GA 19B: Seward School, Uvalda (town in S. part of Co.). — M, retired farmer, 72. B. here. — F. b. Emanuel Co., came to Montgomery Co. at close of Civil War (F. anti-slavery); PGF probably b. Emanuel Co. (migrated with F.). — Ed.: till about 8th grade (common school). — Methodist; school trustee several yrs.; served on grand jury. — Not much knowledge of river culture, though always lived within a mile of it. Recalls boyhood and rural ways very well ("only one sawmill in the whole co. when I was a boy"). A very likable person, well thought of in the comm. Bedridden: has little contact with the outside world save through reading and conversation with occ. visitors. Enjoyed interviews, cooperated to the fullest extent of his ability — somewhat apologetic that illness (a kind of general rheumatism which compels him to be drawn up in bed) worse than us. and did not allow him to speak as freely as on his "better days". Knows local culture closely. Has kept his equanimity remarkably well under circumstances. Religious. Likes people. Devoted to family and friends; inspires loyalty. Well-respected in Co. Generous and hospitable. Had been very hardworking till illness. Good observer. One of "old-timers" of Co. — Voice husky (probably from strain of fighting physical pain). Midland type strong stresses. Slow speech. Nasality. Many folk-grammatical forms. Taboo reactions. Up-gliding diphthongs. Postvocalic constriction; weak articulation of final consonants; simplification of final clusters.

20. Telfair County

Organized 1807. Many settlers of Scottish descent from Carolinas. Ocmulgee and Little Ocmulgee drainage; yellow pine and wiregrass. By 1855, largely self-sufficient farming; also timber and turpentine. Pop. 1810: 744, 1820: 2,104, 1850: 3,026, 1880: 4,828, 1910: 13,288, 1930: 14,997, 1960: 11,715.

Mann, Floris Perkins, comp. 1949. *History of Telfair County from 1812 to 1949.* Macon: J. W. Burke. Repr. 1978 (Spartanburg, SC: Reprint Co.).

Cobbville, Milan or Workmore (school dist.), McRae P.O. (used to be Cobbville)

Cobbville a fertile farming comm. in the center of Co., c. 10 mi. S. of McRae. Water power (sawmill, gristmill); cotton and misc. farming.

GA 20A: M, farmer, 77. Has been carpenter; built bridges for Co.; 8 yrs. mail carrier. B. China Hill (c. 2 mi. S.). 2 yrs. in FL ages 55–56; short while Columbus, GA (3–4 mos.); just a few trips. — F. b. here, PGF b. Robeson Co., NC, migrated to GA as a young man, PGF's F. came to Wilmington, NC, as a young man, rebelled against army discipline, PGM raised locally; M. b. China Hill, comm. near Ocmulgee R., MGF of Irish descent. — Ed.: 8–9 yrs., local school (3–4 mos. per year). — Methodist; Farmers Alliance, Farmers Union. — Good feeling for local usage. Very familiar with local culture (and local

proverbs and superstitions). Not so familiar with things outside area. Knows all comm., but minds his own business: never raised political questions with FW (unlike almost everybody else FW encountered in Telfair Co.). Hardworking, independent: "Don't want to stand in the way of my boys", so allowed 2 sons to go off to work as carpenters while he did most of the farm work himself. Father of 18 children, youngest 4 yrs. old. Devoted to family. Proud of accomplishments of self, family as craftsmen. No pretense of being other than what he is. Hospitable. Mind and hearing good. — Speech normally local. Folk grammar as a rule. Articulation fairly clear (except occ. when quid larger than us.). Slight drawl. Nasality. Tempo slow. Not much range of pitch — basically mid-range. Stressed vowels generally long; weak-stressed vowels us. very short; some inter-stress [ə] lost. Final consonants us. articulated clearly; some stops not released; intervocalic /r/ often lost; simplification of clusters.

McRae

Co. seat; inc. 1874. Settled in mid-19th cent. by Scottish Presbyterians from Carolinas. RR from 1869. South Georgia College (Methodist) here from late 19th to early 20th cent. Market and service center for farming area: diversified farming, turpentine, crossties. Pop. 1910: 1,160, 1930: 1,314, 1960: 2,738.

GA 20B: M, retired farmer, c. 75. Has been tax collector, has held other Co. offices. B. lower end of Co. Other than a little travel, has not been out of Co. — F. b. Toombs Co. (c. 40 mi. ENE), came to Telfair Co. as a boy; M. b. Co.; MGF, MGM both b. Hanover Co., NC, migrated to NW AL but, after surviving massacre by Indians, moved to Telfair Co. — Ed.: local schools. — Baptist; Woodsmen of the World, Talmadgite (enthusiastic), probably KKK. — Not a very good informant. Very suspicious (FW suspects "machine" may have assigned inf. to find out FW's mission in comm. and then to break off interview when innocuousness revealed). Inf. repeatedly interrupted interview to go see some Co. official on "business" (the nature of which FW was unable to discover: no evidence of business in inf.'s life); many cv. forms from interview interruptions. — Folk grammar. Pronounced drawl. Slowest speaker of any interviewed so far. Strong nasality. Up-gliding diphthongs /e o ɔ/; /i u/ us. monoph.; /u/ fronted. Final clusters simplified.

21. Laurens County

Organized 1807. Land surrendered by treaty of 1783. Many settlers from NC; also from VA, SC, Savannah, Burke Co. Corn chief crop to 1810; then cotton. Rejected Central of GA RR 1834. Privation 1861–65. Steamboats on Oconee (1st steamboat 1819); many natural springs, recreational areas. Chiefly Baptists and Methodists. Cotton chief crop; some tobacco, general and truck crops. One of 3 largest cotton cos., but production cut by boll weevil. Diversification since 1917. Pop. 1810: 2,210, 1820: 5,436, 1850: 6,442, 1880: 10,053, 1910: 35,501, 1930: 32,693, 1960: 32,313.

Hart, Bertha Sheppard. 1941. *The Official History of Laurens County, Georgia.* . . . Dublin: John Laurens chapter, DAR.

Lollie

A "post hamlet". Small town, inc. and post office 1892.

GA 21A: F, housewife, 71. B. Co. Worked as cook for a while in 1943 after first husband died in '42; worked at naval ordnance plant in Macon (50 mi. away) for 7 yrs. and 5 mos., off and on (commuted between Lollie and Macon whole time). — F. b. Williston, SC; M., MGF, MGM all b. Co. — Ed.: 1st through 10th grade in school her father built (approx. 4 mi. away from home). — Baptist. — Somewhat simple-minded. — Nasality.

Dublin

Co. seat: laid out 1811; chartered 1812; inc. as city 1860. Lumbering in 18th cent.; wood floated down Oconee. Distribution point for river freight. Misc. industry; lumbering, wood products, cotton, diversified farming. Pop. 1880: 574, 1910: 5,795, 1930: 6,681, 1960: 13,814.

GA 21B: F, seamstress, 74. B. here; came to Baldwin Co. when 28; lived in lower part of Co. on a farm until the last few yrs., when moved to Milledgeville. Interview took place in Milledgeville (Baldwin Co.). — F. b. Co., PGF b. NC, PGM raised Co.; M. b. Co. — Ed.: "about through blue-black speller". — Baptist. — Somewhat timid, but cooperative. A few pretensions and attempts to cover up at outset, but soon became natural (excellent rapport). Moderate intelligence, somewhat limited in experience. — Slow speech. Somewhat slurred utterance. Nasality. Stressed vowels overlong; generally up-gliding diphthongs. Simplification of final consonant clusters; slight postvocalic constriction; /hw-/; some intrusive /r/.

22. Houston & Peach Counties

Houston Co. formed 1821; Peach Co. 1924 (youngest GA co.). Creek territory in 18th cent. Flourished as plantation (cotton) country c. 1821. Many settlers from SC, esp. Orangeburg Dist. Baptists early, Methodists later. Baptist college for young ladies here 1854. Steamboats developed river travel. Peaches by 1870, diversified truck farming. 1st public schools 1880s; consolidation 1924. Cotton, grain, cereals, peas; more peach culture than any other part of US; some small industries. Pop. Houston Co. 1830: 7,369, 1850: 16,450, 1880: 22,414, 1910: 23,609, 1930: 11,280, 1960: 39,154; Peach Co. 1930: 10,268, 1960: 13,846.

Flanders, Ralph P. 1928. Two Plantations and a County of Antebellum Georgia. *Georgia Historical Quarterly* 12:1–24.

Hickson, Bobbe Smith. 1977. *A Land So Dedicated: Houston County, Georgia.* Perry: Houston County Library Board.

1972. *History of Peach County, Georgia.* Atlanta: Cherokee Pub. Co.

Fort Valley, Peach Co. (formerly Houston Co.)

Orig. Fox Valley, misread by U.S. Postal Service. Est. 1836, grew when RR arrived (1851), inc. 1856. Disastrous fire 1867. State land grant college for AfAms chartered 1896. Basically marketing and shipping point for area; wood products, chemicals, school buses. Peach growing. Pop. 1880: 1,277, 1910: 2,697, 1930: 4,650, 1960: 8,310.

GA 22A: M, city marshall, c. 60. B. 4 mi. out of Fort Valley in Houston Co., has traveled over GA as state highway patrolman (9 yrs.); also travel in FL, 2 summers work in PA tomato fields. — F. b. SC, came to Houston as a small boy; M. b. Houston Co. (ultimately of Irish ancestry on both sides). — Ed.: till 9th grade (Fort Valley). — Methodist; volunteer fireman, assoc. with all Co. politicians, and through them knows most of Co. — Suspicious of FW at first, but proved most cooperative. Slow, relaxed, and straightforward.

GA 22B: M, farmer, 75. Moved to Bibb Co. age 5; back to Houston after marriage; retired to Bibb Co., Rutland District, Macon P.O. (used to be Walden). Interview took place in Bibb Co. — F. b. Houston Co., PGF b. Washington Co. (PGF, PGM buried near Fort Valley); M. b. in comm., MGM b. Twiggs Co. — Ed.: co. schools, h.s. in Walden. — Methodist; Farm Bureau chairman, School Bd. Houston Co. 10 yrs., Bibb Co. committeeman, Prohibitionist. — Plain, intelligent, hardworking. Great respect for learning (one of sons at Duke with FW); "never used slang". Good farmer: fences, animals, machinery in excellent condition. Proud of being a farmer. Very religious, not ostentatiously so. Minds own business. Knows local folkways; well rooted in comm. Good example of prosperous middle-class farmer. Strong sense of family and comm. responsibility. His integrity and good sense a byword among businessmen in Macon. Easy-going when not working. Somewhat deaf, but did all in power to put FW at ease. Responses normal; no pretensions. Interested in preserving traditions. Alert to changes in comm. — Voice soft. Strong stresses. Generally uses standard grammatical forms. Generally up-gliding /ɔ e o i u/. Simplification of final consonant clusters; no postvocalic constriction.

23. Bibb County

Formed 1822 from Houston Co. Settlers from VA, NC; English, Scots. Ocmulgee R. (fall line at Macon); productive agriculture, orchards, granite. Pop. 1830: 7,154, 1850: 16,699, 1880: 27,147, 1910: 56,646, 1930: 77,042, 1960: 141,249.

Butler, John Campbell. 1879. *Historical Record of Macon and Central Georgia. . . .* Macon: J. W. Burke and Co.

Federal Writers Project. 1939. *The Macon Guide and Ocmulgee National Monument.* Macon: J. W. Burke.

Hart, Oliver James. 1925. *The History of Christ Church Parish, Macon. . . .* Macon: Lyon, Harris and Brook.

Young, Ida, et al. 1950. *History of Macon, Georgia.* Macon: Lyon, Marshall and Brooks.

Fort Hawkins, Macon

Fort Hawkins est. 1806 for frontier defense; nucleus of Macon. Macon fall line for Ocmulgee R. Land cessions by Indians 1802–5. 1st settlers 1818–19; 1821 village of Newtown, E. side of river; 1823 Macon laid out on W. side. Cotton market, river port, RR center (Central of GA). Confederate supply base; Army camps WWI; Air Force Base WWII. Wesleyan College; Mercer U. Varied industries, including textiles, grain mills, canneries, slaughter houses, tanneries, lumber, furniture, etc. Pop. Macon 1850: 5,720, 1880: 12,749, 1910: 40,665, 1930: 53,829, 1960: 69,764.

GA 23A: M, laborer (considers fishing and hunting his profession: one of the "rivermen"), 55. B. Fort Hawkins ("East

Macon"); 8 mos. on RR, otherwise always in Co. — F. b. c. 10 mi. SE of Macon; M. b. Co., N. of Macon. Both came to Macon in early adulthood. Nothing known of grandparents. Ed.: Ft. Hawkins, 8 yrs. — A "river rat" whose life centers around river. Somewhat lazy and undependable except where hunting and fishing are concerned. Easy-going philosophy. Enjoys talking; plenty of anecdotes; profane, no taboos. — Fast speech. Slurred utterance. Relatively few up-gliding diphthongs, more in-gliding than in other Macon inf.'s (dialect seems to have many features not found in other inf.'s in Macon area); weak-stressed vowels very short. Final stops often unreleased; final clusters often simplified.

GA 23B: F, housewife, 80. B. here. — F. b. here; M. b. Monroe (Walton Co.). — Ed.: till 10th grade. Good deal of reading. — Presbyterian. — Confined to wheelchair, but very alert. Easy interview. Voice cracked a little at beginning of interview, but became stronger as interview progressed. — [Inexperienced FW; few cv. forms, little elicitation of synonyms. Inf. beginning senility. Speech natural, characteristic of middle GA. — RIM]

GA 23C: F, housewife, 58. B. here. — F. b. Madison, OH; M. b. Painesville, OH. — Ed.: local schools; h.s. grad. — Methodist. — Inf. fairly religious, though not a regular church-goer. Opposed to drinking, profanity, ethnic slurs. Prefers family and small groups for company. Likes reading, sewing, working in garden, boating. [Few cv. forms, little free conversation, but generally good 1st interview for FW. Good rapport with inf. (a relative); FW knew what questions involved, though didn't often follow up or exploit opportunities for synonyms or alternates. Inf. clearly at ease, made no effort to cover up or pretend; seemed reasonably characteristic of her culture. — RIM]

GA 23D!: F, housewife, 62. B. Mitchell, c. 130 mi. S. Came to Macon when 1 yr. old; had country place at Clinton (c. 20 mi. NE) — a "Northern town" with many N. Eng. artisans. — F. a journalist from Wilkes Co. (near Augusta); PGF, PGM both of Wilkes Co.; M. of Americus, GA; MGF b. Morgan Co. (60 mi. N.); MGM b. Eatonton (40 mi. NE). — Ed.: Wesleyan Co. — Baptist; Col. Dames; UDC. — Quick mind. Generous and hospitable, as one is accustomed to think of old Southern cultivated families. Well-read. Seemed to enjoy interview, regretted that she was tied up with a wedding in the family and was unable to finish. Sure of definitions as a rule; consistently rejected suggestions from husband (native of KY) that didn't fit in with local speechways. — Speech clear. Tempo a little slow, with suggestion of drawl (the "Hollywood type" of Southern drawl seems very pervasive around Macon, esp. among h.s. girls: perhaps influence of *Gone With the Wind*? Woman from the Macon *Telegraph* served as technical asst. on GA culture. Or does GWTW reflect Macon?) Voice basically in mid register; wide intonation range. Up-gliding diphthongs; long stressed vowels. Simplification of final clusters. — Cultivated.

GA 23E!: F, housewife, 67. B. here; lived in NY 2 winters before marriage, 1 1/2 yrs. after; 5 visits to Europe, several weeks each. — F. b. Macon, PGF, PGM both came to Macon in 1855; M. b. Griffin, GA of old Macon family (ancestors came shortly after Macon chartered in 1823); branches of ancestors from MA, VA, NC. — Ed.: h.s. in Macon; 3 yrs. Sweet Briar College, VA. — Episcopalian, church groups; PTA, YWCA, interracial organizations. — Authentic plantation Southern; quite relaxed and straightforward in responses. — Cultivated.

GA 23F!: F, teacher, 24. B. here. — F., PGF both b. here, both worked for RR, PGM b. Thompson, GA; M., MGF, MGM all b. Fort Valley. — Ed.: local schools, state colleges, U of GA. — Baptist; h.s. and college social groups. — Specialist in teaching educable mentally retarded children. Quiet, reserved, deliberate, patient. Has participated in many activities, but comes across as a loner. — [Inf. has limited experience with farm life and some surprising lacunae in knowledge (e.g., "freestone peach"), but quite at ease. Self-assured; no affectations. Talked freely about family, history (note *the War*), teaching experience, etc. — Intonation and vowel qualities normal for middle Georgians of several generations. Some /-r/. — RIM] — Cultivated.

24. Baldwin County

Laid out and settled 1803 (Indians removed by 1802 treaty). Settlers from a variety of places, including VA, SC, NC; Germans, Scotch-Irish. Oconee R. fall line here: water power. Agriculture, but soil depletion; potter's clay. Pop. 1810: 6,356, 1820: 5,665, 1850: 8,148, 1880: 13,808, 1910: 18,354, 1930: 22,878, 1960: 34,064.

Beeson, Leola Selman. 1943. *History Stories of Milledgeville and Baldwin County*. Macon: J. W. Burke Co.

Bonner, James C. 1978. *Milledgeville, Georgia's Antebellum Capital*. Athens: University of Georgia Press.

Cook, Anna Maria (Green). 1964. *The Journal of a Milledgeville Girl, 1861–1867*. Ed. by James C. Bonner. Athens: University of Georgia Press.

Cook, Anna Maria Green. 1925. *History of Baldwin County, Georgia*. Anderson, SC: Keys-Hearn Print. Co.

Hines, Nellie Womack, ed. 1936. *A Treasure Album of Milledgeville and Baldwin County, Georgia*. Milledgeville: J. W. Burke.

Phillips, Ulrich Bonnell. 1903. Historical Notes of Milledgeville, Georgia. *Gulf States Historical Magazine*, November, 1903.

Milledgeville

Laid out as state capital 1804; lost importance when capital moved to Atlanta 1868. Fall line; approx. geographic center of GA. Grew as river town; declined with rise of RRs. Numerous Baptists. Several state institutions, mental hospital, prison. Light industry. Pop. 1820: 2,069, 1850: 2,216, 1880: 3,800, 1910: 4,385, 1930: 5,534, 1960: 11,117.

GA 24N: M, sawmill worker, handyman, gardener, 68. B. Hancock Co. (next co. NE). — F., PGF, PGM, M., MGF, MGM all b. Hancock Co. — Ed.: none. — Methodist (most friends connected with the church). — [Inexperienced FW. — RIM]

GA 24A: Mt. Pleasant Church, Milledgeville P.O. — M, farmer, 64. B. here. — F. b. here, PGF b. AL; M., MGF b. here. — Ed.: illiterate. — Baptist. — Rather quick, bright mind. Friendly and completely subservient in manner, "realizing his duty toward a gentleman".

Carrs Station (Hancock Co.)

Sawmills and gristmills (steam and water), 1880. Shipping point.

GA 24B: M, farmer, 66. B. same house; never lived out of Co. Some work on RR and for Co. (has been chain gang guard); ran sawmill. — F., PGF, PGM all b. same comm.; M. b. Hancock Co. (next E.). — Ed.: illiterate. — Baptist; well-known in Co. — active in politics, a good deal of influence. — Utterly folk type (notice mixture of forms which would be expected along Fall Line). Has worked hard all his life; from very beginning "brought up about as rough as them prisoners on the chain-gang". Frugal: never spared himself till his health finally gave out. A political power in the co.; presumably a strong Talmadgite, but never tried to thrust his views on FW or to learn what FW's views were. No use for traveling salesmen; suspicious of outsiders yet reacted very favorably to FW; cooperated enthusiastically. The Co. judge, "ordinary", was almost afraid to suggest inf.'s name to FW for fear he'd resent interview and take it out on her, yet inf. seemed most appreciative of the introduction. Genuine hospitality: accepted FW as one of the family, made no attempt at company manners (or company vittles), said he reckoned FW would prefer it that way. Knows rural life of Co. intimately and in detail. Talks freely; naturally uninhibited. Surprisingly well informed on world affairs (conversation and radio). Asks intelligent questions. — Extreme drawl. Nasality. Extremely slow speech: double over-long stressed vowels; weak-stressed vowels very short. Simplification of final clusters; weakening of final consonants; postvocalic and final /l/ often vocalized; /f/ often for /θ/.

GA 24B*: F, unmarried housekeeper for brother (24B), 54. — Family history above. — Ed.: 4th grade.

25. Hancock County

Formed 1793 from Washington and Greene Cos. Creek cession 1786. Early settlers from VA, MD, Carolinas; most colonial settlers English, occ. Scots, French. Presbyterians, Methodists, Baptists in late 18th cent. Male and female academies by 1830; Mt. Zion Academy long famous. Fall line; cotton, plus recent diversification; fruit exported. Representative of old cotton belt; progressive and cultivated (Planters Club). Experimental agriculture; intellectual life. Many poor whites left Co. 1850–60; large planters acquired most of unimproved land. Many immigrant tradesmen, occ. became landowners. Pop. 1800: 14,456, 1820: 12,734, 1850: 11,578, 1880: 16,989, 1910: 19,189, 1930: 13,070, 1960: 9,979.

Bonner, James Calvin. 1944. Profile of a Late Ante-Bellum Community. *American Historical Review* 49:663–80.

Smith, Elizabeth Wiley. 1974. *The History of Hancock County, Georgia.* 2 vols. Washington, GA: Wilkes Pub. Co.

Sparta

Co. seat; inc. 1805. Trading center. Dairy products, lumber, sawmills, planing mills, cotton and diversified farming. Formerly very wealthy. Pop. 1900: 1,150, 1930: 1,613.

GA 25N: F, housewife, 71. B. here. — F., M. b. Co. No information about grandparents or remote ancestors. — Ed.: till about 3rd grade. — Baptist. — [FW failed to exploit traditionally productive items, and suggested frequently without getting responses from inf. except *yeah* (a few pronounced suggested responses are suspect, e.g. *chesterfield*). — Heavy nasality; articulation not clear. Many folk forms, esp. when off guard. — RIM]

26. Jasper County

Created 1807 as Randolph, name changed 1812. Cotton and diversification; hay, fruit exported. Pop. 1810: 7,573, 1820: 14,614, 1850: 11,486, 1880: 11,851, 1910: 16,552, 1930: 8,594, 1960: 6,135.

Monticello

Co. seat. Cotton center; small factories. Pop. 1880: 511, 1910: 1,508, 1930: 1,593, 1960: 1,931.

GA 26: M, retired civil servant, 49. B. near here. Practically all his life in Monticello (1 yr. CA, 3 yrs. Birmingham, 2 yrs. in Navy). — F., M. both b. Co. — Ed.: till 8th grade locally. — Primitive Baptist. — Excellent folk inf., quite cooperative and talkative. Heavy nasality. Frequent incidence of /d/ for /ð/, esp. in weak-stressed syllables.

27. Greene County

Organized 1786. Settled early by Virginians and NC Presbyterians; Virginians dominant early, some Tories during Rev. Frontier troubles, 1787–93. Union Academy 1786. Presbyterians first, also Methodists and Baptists by 1800; Episcopalians and Roman Catholics in 2nd half of 19th cent. Tobacco and indigo first crops. 1st paper mill in GA here, faded after War of 1812. Leading cotton co. of GA 1820–60; much land worn out then; pop. decline with N. movement of AfAms. Hard-hit by boll weevil. Several surviving plantation mansions. Cotton, truck and dairy farming, small industry. Pop. 1790: 5,405, 1820: 13,589, 1850: 13,068, 1880: 17,547, 1910: 18,512, 1930: 12,616, 1960: 11,193.

Raper, Arthur F. 1936. *Preface to Peasantry.* Chapel Hill: University of North Carolina Press.

Raper, Arthur F. 1943. *Tenants of the Almighty.* NY: Macmillan Co.

Raper, Arthur F., and Martha J. Raper. 1977. *Two Years to Remember.* Vienna, GA: Jenn Moore.

Rice, Thaddeus Brockett. 1961. *History of Greene County, Georgia, 1786–1886.* Macon: J. W. Burke Co.

Greensboro

Co. seat. Inc. 1803, but older (burned by Indians 1787). P.O. 1792. Prominent social/cultural center. Large cotton mills. Bermuda grass region; market town for area farming. Pop. 1880: 1,621, 1910: 2,120, 1930: 2,137, 1960: 2,773.

GA 27!: M, businessman, 48. B. same house. Has worked as forester, geologist, census taker, miner, lumberman, and in postal service, all in Greensboro. Has traveled to 42 states and has prospected in Mexico. — Family left Mecklenburg Co., VA, in 1780s; were in Greensboro in 1786 when town was burned by Indians. All of Ulster-Scots descent. — Most interesting inf. FW had interviewed. Rapid-talking and completely natural. Preserves many rural expressions from his work in Co. — Cultivated.

28. Wilkes County

Formed 1777 from ceded lands acquired from Creeks in 1773. Earliest grants chiefly to SC (many orig. from VA) and NC; some to VA and PA. One of earliest settlements after coast. Continental stronghold in Rev. Baptists 1st active denomination, also Methodists, Presbyterians early; some Roman Catholics. Tobacco and indigo chief early crops. Eli Whitney sojourned here as tutor. 1st cotton mill in South here 1810; failed. One of dominant counties in state politics 1813–51. Plundered by Confederates 1865. Some gold mining in area c. 1830. Water power; cotton, fruit, timber. Pop. 1790: 31,500, 1820: 16,912, 1850: 12,107, 1880: 15,985, 1910: 23,441, 1930: 15,944, 1960: 10,961.

Andrews, Eliza Frances. 1908. *The Wartime Journal of a Georgia Girl. . . .* NY. Repr. 1960 (Macon: Ardivan Press).

Bowen, Eliza A. 1950. *The Story of Wilkes County, Georgia.* Ed. by Louise Frederick Hays. Marietta: Continental Book Co.

Davidson, Grace Gillam. 1932. *Early Records of Georgia's Wilkes County.* 2 vols. Macon: J. W. Burke Co.

Davis, Robert Scott, comp. 1979. *The Wilkes County Papers, 1773–1833. . . .* Easley, SC: Southern Historical Press.

Federal Writers Project. 1941. *The Story of Washington-Wilkes.* Athens: University of Georgia Press.

Hotz, Alex M. 1956. The Earliest settlements in Wilkes County. *Georgia Historical Quarterly* 40:260–80.

Willingham, Robert Marion. 1969. *We Have This Heritage.* Washington, GA: Wilkes Pub. Co.

Delhi, Washington

Delhi a plantation area; discouraged industry and hotels. Nearby, Eli Whitney workshop. Washington somewhat isolated, eschews tourism. Inc. 1805. Academy 1784. French settlement from Haiti 1790; also Jews from Germany. Center of plantation culture, many homes from early 19th cent. Had theater before any church built. Major stop on post road. Trading center; once a shipping point for cotton. Some textiles. Pop. 1820: 695, 1880: 2,199, 1910: 3,065, 1930: 3,158, 1960: 4,440.

GA 28: M, insurance agent, former storekeeper, 80. B. 16 mi. NE of Wash. in Co. Has lived in Wash. except 4 yrs. in CA and AZ ages 16–20, 18 mos. in Army during WWI. — Family has been in Co. since before the Rev. Ancestors were from VA. — Ed.: through 9th grade (private neighborhood school). — American Legion; Kiwanis (charter member). — Old and rather feeble man, closely watched by wife (which interfered with the interview). Early part of interview marked by the inf.'s frozen style.

29. Lincoln County

Formed 1796 from Wilkes Co. English, Scots, Irish, Germans; 1st settlers from NC and SC. Heavily timbered in 18th cent. Tobacco early, then cotton. Baptists, Methodists, and Presbyterians by early 19th cent. Savannah R. drainage system. Land depleted by cotton farming, slowly recovering; truck farming (esp. for Augusta market), timber, some mining.

Pop. 1800: 4,766, 1820: 6,458, 1850: 5,998, 1880: 6,412, 1910: 8,714, 1930: 7,847, 1960: 5,906.

Coulter, E. Merton. 1965. *Old Petersburg and the Broad River Valley of Georgia: Their Rise and Decline.* Athens: University of Georgia Press.

Perryman, Clinton J. 1933. *History of Lincoln County, Georgia.* Lincolnton. Repr. 1985 (Tignall: Boyd Pub. Co.).

Goshen Highway, Lincolnton

Goshen Highway rural comm.; cotton shipping. Lincolnton inc. 1817. Developed as tobacco market late 18th cent. Academy by 1821.

GA 29A: M, farmer, 87. B. 3 mi. N. of Goshen, upper part of Co.; moved to Auburn, AL, c. 6 wks. old; returned to Lincoln Co. age 6 or less (to GF's home); moved near river when 12 yrs. old; worked on river ages 23–25; moved to Tatum Place (up Washington Rd.); married at 27, moved back to GF's place. Has been living in upper part of Co. till about 3 yrs. ago. — F. b. upper part of Co.; PGF's family from Scotland; M., MGF both b. upper part of Co.; MGM prob. b. upper part of Co. — Ed.: 3–4 terms country (private) school. — Baptist; Mason, Woodmen of the World (not active), justice of the peace, notary public. — Not a planter, but a farmer. Has been hard-working; tries to make himself useful on farm, even if not able to do anything more than pick up pecans. Intimate knowledge of local rural life. Few taboos: very little tendency to use euphemisms. Hospitable. Enjoyed interviews. Religious. Folk type, but lacked some of extreme folk items. Likes to talk. Mind still clear. Remembers old ways very well, including Reconstruction. Not very quick in responses, but sure of what is local and what isn't. Has educated children, and is proud of their achievements and advantages. — Voice a little high-pitched, tends to quaver a little. Drawl. Slurred utterance. Slight nasality. Strong stresses. Some up-gliding diphthongs. Weak articulation of final consonants; simplification of final clusters.

GA 29B: Lincolnton. — F, single housekeeper, 67. B. 6 mi. SE or E. of town. Moved to Lincolnton age 39. — F. b. here, PGF b. Co., PGF's ancestors from SC, PGM, PGM's F. and M. all b. Co.; M., MGF both b. Co., MGF's F. and M. from VA, came to GA on horseback 1794, MGM b. Co., MGM's F. and M. from VA. — Ed.: country school; John Gibson Institute (Bowman); Southern Female College (LaGrange, GA), quit beginning of jr. yr. — Baptist, but goes to Methodist Church. — Interview conducted in joint session with GA 29B* and GA 29B**; the three are inseparable evening companions, and the collaboration prob. resulted in both a speedier interview and a surer approach to local folk items than would otherwise have been possible. All three: assurance of social status. No pretension. Naturally quick minds; keenly interested in interviews and anything connected with local culture. All fairly sure of what is local and what isn't. No extreme taboo reactions, except amusement at tendency of some people to resort to euphemisms. Many Midland vocab. items. — All 3: no drawl. Utterances generally clear. Wide intonation range. Strong stresses. Some up-gliding diphthongs. Simplification of final clusters.

GA 29B*: M, farmer, shoe salesman, 85. B. 3 mi. NE. Cousin of GA 29B. Spent 3 yrs. in Miami, FL, ages 60–63, 1 1/2 yrs. Augusta (clerk), 3 yrs. Washington, GA, 3+ yrs. Sandersville, GA; "a planter — one that never gets through planting". — F., PGF b. Co. (ancestors from England via VA, PGM b. Co., PGM's F. and M. prob. b. Co.; M., MGF b. Co. — Ed.: Co. schools, "about 5th reader". — See general comments above (29B) on character of interview. — Inf. has more of a tendency to use folk grammatical forms than either GA 29B or GA 29B** (the two women). This tendency seems to be more common among males than among females of all cultural levels in the South, prob. because of the tradition at all levels of the "Southern lady", or maybe because at all levels women are more exposed to reading than men were. — Inf.'s stressed vowels slightly longer than those of 29B and 29B**.

GA 29B**: F, housekeeper, 68. B. 2 mi. W. of Lincolnton. Spent 3 yrs in Elbert Co. as a child; went to Bowman for education. Taught school 2 yrs. "years and years ago". — F., PGF b. Co., PGF's F. came from VA, PGF's M. from Wilkes Co. (next co. W.), PGM b. W. part of Lincoln or Wilkes Co.; M., MGF b. Co., MGF's F. from VA, MGF's M. prob b. Co., MGM b. Co., MGM's F. and M. both from VA (German descent). — Ed.: local school; John Gibson Inst. — Baptist. — See comments above (GA 29B) on character of interview.

30. Elbert County

Formed 1790 from Wilkes Co. Settled 1776 from VA; also early settlers from NC, SC (many Scots, as in GA 31 and 32, Hart and Franklin Cos.). Also some of German stock. Baptists strong early, Methodists by 1815. Indian frontier after Rev. Rapidly became cotton country. No devastation 1861–65. Few schools by 1865. Till 1930 almost all pop. descendants of early GA settlers. Savannah and Broad Rivers. Diversified economy including agriculture, orchards (peach), quarrying (blue granite). Pop. 1820: 10,094, 1850: 12,959, 1880: 12,957, 1910: 24,125, 1930: 18,485, 1960: 17,835.

> Davidson, Grace Gillam, ed. 1930. *Records of Elbert County, Georgia. . . .* Atlanta: Stein Print. Co.
>
> McIntosh, John Howes. 1940. *The Official History of Elbert County, 1790–1935.* Elberton. Repr. 1968 (Atlanta: Cherokee Pub. Co.).
>
> Moffat, Charles H. 1948. Charles Tait: Planter, Politician, and Scientist of the Old South. *Journal of Southern History* 14:206–33.

Elberton

Settled 1780s; Co. seat 1790; inc. 1803. Presbyterian church organized 1865. Growth with RR after Civil War. 1st granite quarry 1882; largest granite finishing and shipping pt. in GA. RR junction; was cotton shipping pt. Also textiles, peaches, misc. industry. Pop. 1880: 927, 1910: 6,483, 1930: 4,650, 1960: 7,107.

GA 30A: M, blacksmith, farmer, 71. B. 4 mi. S. of Elberton; to NE of town age 4; to town age 14. Little travel, never lived outside of Co. — F., PGF, PGM all b. Co.; M., MGF both from up in Blue Ridge Mtns. — Ed.: common school (but has sent all his children through college). — Baptist; knows everybody, AfAm and white. — Occ. uses cultivated forms instead of folk forms, undoubtedly influence of children. Cheerful;

hard-working; devout; generous. Religious: refuses to work on Sundays. Glad to help, but time limited. Sense of humor: many anecdotes, even at own expense. — Drawl. Nasality strong. Folk grammar. Up-gliding /i e ɔ o u/; /ju/ after /t d n/; /u/ fronted; /-ə/ in *borrow*, *tomato*; neutralization of /ɪ ɛ/ before nasals; contrast of /æ/ and /æɪ/; /a/ low-central to low-back; /a/ high; [ɝ] before consonants, [ɝˑ] final; /-ə/ in *father*; /ai/ us. Up-Country "short" and "long" forms, but with low-front beginning; /au/ beginning [æ] or [a]; [ɪ] in *bucket*, etc. Tendency to simplify final consonant clusters; palatal /k-g-/ occ.; /hw-/; /sr-/; clear [l] between front vowels; /-l/ tends to vocalize; no /-r/ constriction; intrusive /r/ in *swallow it*.

GA 30B: M, baker, 77. B. Ginntown (N. end of Co.), moved to Elberton age 26; never lived elsewhere; slight travel. — As far as known, family (on all sides) in Co. since before 1800. F. in Civil War. — Ed.: local schools. — Baptist. — Somewhat suspicious of FW at first, but cooperative. Has excellent local reputation. Keen sense of humor. Slight tendency to give book forms. No attempt to cover up natural grammatical usage. — Speech fast; strong stresses. Voice low-pitched, with little variation in intonation. /i/ monoph. or slightly rising diphthong; /e/ slight up-glide, fronted ending; /u/ fronted, up-glide (often monophthongal); /ju/ after /t d n/; /o/ up-gliding, fronted, only in stressed syllables; [æ æᵊ æɪ], but doubtful if in contrast; /a/ range [aˀ] to [ɑ]; /a/ in *pot*, *crop*, etc.; /ɔ/ up-gliding; /ɔ/ in *water*; /ʌ/ high; [ɝ] before consonants, except /-l/; [ɝ] final and before /-l/; /-ə/ in *father*; /ai/ with us. Up-Country allophones; /au/ beginning [æ] or [a]; /ɔi/ with high beginning; [ɪˤ] in *bucket*, etc. Final consonant clusters tend to simplify; clear [l] between front vowels; /sr-/; /hw-/; intervocalic /r/ often weak.

GA 30C!: M, retired newspaperman (but still writes), 76. B. here. Between ages 25–31 lived in Bennettsville, SC; Maxton, NC; Mountain City, GA. — F. b. Anderson, SC (just across river), PGF of Ulster Scot stock; M. b. Anderson, SC, MGF, MGM both from Germany. — Ed.: local schools, 2 yrs. Davidson College. — Presbyterian. — A good, self-made cultivated inf. Very conscious of stylistic differences; a broad understanding of regional varieties. — Alternates between [ɝ] and [ɜ], [ð] and [d] under weak stress. /r/ lost in *through*. Occ. [oɔˤ] or other suggestion of low country /o/. — Cultivated.

GA 30D: Oglesby Quarry, Elberton P.O. — M, farmer, 77. B. same house. — Ed.: country schools. — Occ. goes to town. Wife wanted him to become a druggist.

GA 30E: F, housewife, now bedridden, 87. B. here. — Apparently of old family. — Ed.: general type of education expected of "young ladies of good family". — Baptist. — Very likable, but extremely feeble. Easily tired. Mind fairly good, but beginning to go.

31. Hart County

Formed 1853 from Franklin and Elbert Cos. Only co. in state named for a woman: Nancy Hart, Revolutionary heroine. 1st settled along Savannah c. 1784; many early settlers from VA and Carolinas. Diversified farming till fairly late; tobacco first cash crop; open range till 1886. Sawmills; overcutting of timber led to erosion. RR from 1856. Some anti-secessionist sentiment. In 1930, one of highest percentages of rural pop. in GA. German strain from 18th cent.; immigration from Germany to 1930; also some English, Irish, Scots (Highlanders). Rolling piedmont country; water power. Cotton and corn, some diversification and stock raising, fruit, manufacturing; some textiles, gold mining. Pop. 1860: 6,137, 1880: 9,094, 1910: 16,216, 1930: 15,174, 1960: 15,229.

> Baker, John William. 1933. *History of Hart County, 1933.* Atlanta: Foote and Davies Co.

Sardis, Hartwell

Sardis a rural comm., around Baptist church. Land for Hartwell purchased 1854; inc. 1856. Textile plants, shipping for cotton and corn.

GA 31: F, housewife, 73. B. Loundesville, SC (just across river, about 30 mi. from Hartwell); came to Hartwell as a baby. In last 50 yrs., only out of Hartwell to attend a church convention in Atlanta. — No formal education. — Baptist. — Extremely amiable. Lives with daughter on a small farm. Life centered on church and church activities. — [Inf. naturally good and cooperative. FW unprepared. — RIM]

32. Franklin County

Laid out 1784. Scotch-Irish and English; small farming area. Indian frontier to 1800; few large slaveholdings. Lavonia Institute once well known. Piedmont; misc. agriculture. Pop. 1790: 1,041, 1820: 9,040, 1850: 11,513, 1880: 11,453, 1910: 17,894, 1930: 15,902, 1960: 13,274.

Carnesville

Co. seat; inc. 1808. Mineral springs. Pop. 1900: 305.

GA 32: F, housewife, 61. B. Co. — F, PGF, PGM; M., MGF, MGM all b. in Co. — Ed.: 10th or 11th grade, Franklin Co. School. — Baptist. — Tempo very fast.

33. Madison County

Org. 1811. English, Scots, Germans (numerous) from PA, VA, NC, SC. Cherokee cessions 1773, 1784. Chiefly Protestant Fundamentalists, Baptists most numerous. Academy 1828. Much Union sympathy 1830 and 1860. Pioneer farming (diversified), became cotton farming in early 19th cent.; cotton declined; recently poultry and soybeans. RRs from 1851. Segregation intensified after 1865. Misc. farming: little cotton, some tobacco; some mining: gold, iron, granite, and quartz. Pop. 1820: 3,735, 1850: 5,703, 1880: 7,978, 1910: 16,851, 1930: 14,921, 1960: 11,246.

> Tabor, Paul. 1974. *The History of Madison County, Georgia.*

Colbert

RR junction, S. part of Co.

GA 33A: F, widow, 75. B. here. — F. b. MS, PGF, PGM b. Jackson Co. (next co. W.); M. b. here, MGF, MGM b. Co. — Ed.: till 7th grade, Madison Co. school. — Primitive Baptist. — Lives with sister (mid-sixties); contacts are relatives and friends in Colbert. Spry, soft-spoken, gentle; made FW welcome. Seemed to enjoy people and sharing past experiences. — [FW, like many student interviewers, didn't exploit opportunities for synonyms. Relatively few cv. grammatical forms.

Paradigmatic eliciting of verb forms resulted in prob. much more "standard" grammar than inf. actually uses. — RIM]

GA 33B: F, seamstress, 62. B. Co. — F. b. MS, PGF, PGM b. Jackson Co., MS; M., MGF, MGM all b. Co. — Ed.: Colbert till 9th grade. — Primitive Baptist; few social contacts. — Warm, hospitable, generous; devoted to family; involved in world around her, rooted in her history. Put FW at ease. Interesting mixture of old and new lexicon. — [Few cv. responses or synonyms. In general, interesting and natural speech. Note devoicing of initial consonants and clusters. — RIM]

34. Clarke County

Formed 1801 from Jackson Co. Part of Indian cession of 1784. Immigration begun by 1790s; Baptists chief denomination. 20 churches in Co. by 1850. Cotton came late, after War of 1812. Agricultural decline in 1850s; Northerners, foreign-born more prosperous than natives. War did not redistribute wealth; greater concentration afterwards, esp. in Athens. AfAm opportunites expanded after 1870. Several RRs. Drained by Oconee R.; fertile soil, orchards. Pop. 1810: 7,628, 1820: 8,767, 1850: 11,119, 1880: 11,702, 1910: 23,273, 1930: 25,612, 1960: 45,363.

> Brooks, Robert Preston. 1956. *The University of Georgia under Sixteen Administrations, 1785–1955.* Athens: University of Georgia Press.
>
> Coleman, Kenneth, ed. 1969. *Athens, 1861–1865: As Seen Through Letters in the University of Georgia Libraries.* Athens: University of Georgia Press.
>
> Coleman, Kenneth. 1967. *Confederate Athens.* Athens: University of Georgia Press.
>
> Coulter, E. Merton. 1965. Slavery and Freedom in Athens, Georgia, 1860–66. *Georgia Historical Quarterly* 49:264–93.
>
> Hill, Walter Barnard. 1944–45. *Rural Survey of Athens and Clarke County, Georgia.* . . . Athens: University of Georgia Press.
>
> Huffman, Frank J. 1974. *Old South, New South: Continuity and Change in a Georgia Community.* Yale University dissertation.
>
> Hull, Augustus Longstreet. 1894. *A Historical Sketch of the University of Georgia.* Atlanta: Foote and Davies Co.
>
> Hull, Augustus Longstreet. 1906. *Annals of Athens, Georgia, 1801–1901.* Athens: Banner Job Office.
>
> Hull, Henry. 1884. *Sketches from the Early History of Athens, Georgia.* . . . Ed. by A. L. Hull. Athens: H. L. Cranford.
>
> Hynds, Ernest C. 1974. *Antebellum Athens and Clarke County, Georgia.* Athens: University of Georgia Press.
>
> McGuire, P. S. 1934. Athens and the Railroads. *Georgia Historical Quarterly* 18:1–26, 118–44.
>
> Stegeman, John F. 1964. *These Men She Gave: Civil War Diary of Athens, Georgia.* Athens: University of Georgia Press.
>
> Strahan, Charles Morton. 1893. *Clarke County.* . . . Athens: C. P. Byrd.
>
> Thurmond, Michael L., and Dorothy Sparer. 1978. *A Story Untold: Black Men and Women in Athens History.* Athens: Clarke County School District.

Woofter, T. J., Jr. 1913. *The Negroes of Athens, Georgia.* Athens: Bulletin of the University of Georgia.

1923. *History of Athens and Clarke County.* Athens: H. J. Rowe.

Athens

Laid out 1801 as site of U. of GA. Became Co. seat 1871; inc. as a city 1872. 1st settlers from CT, E. VA; also from NC, Savannah, Ireland; Presbyterians first, Baptists most numerous. 1st cotton mill in GA here, 1829. Town grew with the university; 3 cotton mills by 1840. Trading center from early days; strong civic identity from beginning. Episcopal church by 1843; Roman Catholics by 1873. Harassment by occupation troops. High prices for cotton in 1865, source of cash. University proceeded with no appreciable interruption after 1865; RR connections increased; cosmopolitan. Commercial expansion attracted outside whites; suburbanization begun by 1870. Northerners and foreigners dominated top blue- and white-collar jobs. No public school system till 1886. Through 1910 Clarke Co. had a slight AfAm majority, but Athens somewhat greater white preponderance. Pop. 1880: 6,099, 1910: 14,913, 1930: 18,192, 1960: 31,355.

GA 34N: M, handyman, RR, some farming, 75. B. boundary of Morgan and Greene Cos., c. 30 mi. S.; lived in locality ever since. — F., M., MGF, MGM all b. Greene Co. — Ed: "blue-black speller". — Baptist, Sunday school teacher 12 yrs. — Cooperative, but too garrulous to keep on subject. Combination of Negro folk speech with attempt to imitate whites. Recognizes that language has changed (but not a very accurate assessment of that change). Not adjusted to rowdiness of younger generation (broke off interview when quarrel erupted next door). Plenty of anecdotes, prone to exaggerate. Seemed to enjoy interview. Many features such as *hooks* for *hoops*, traditionally associated with Uncle Remus. Religious. Loyal. — Tempo fast. Strong stress. Slightly slurred articulation. Pitch moderate to high. Natural use of folk verb forms. Stressed vowels gen. long, weak-stressed generally short; up-gliding /i e ɔ o u/. Tendency to simplify final clusters; frequent vocalization of /-l/; much loss of intervocalic /r/.

Bogart, Bradberrys

Bogart a village 6–7 mi. W. of Athens; P.O. in Oconee Co.

GA 34A: F, housewife, 65. B. 8–9 mi. from here in Oconee Co.; moved to Clarke Co. age 3. — F. b. Madison Co., PGM b. Oglethorpe Co.; M. b. here, MGF b. Jackson Co., MGM, MGM's F. b. Co. (MGM's F. owned 10,000 acres here). — Ed.: till 14 (Athens). — Baptist. — Quick, busy, enterprising. Was embarrassed to be "caught" picking cotton by FW, perhaps because family once so prosperous. Although she reads some and feels educated, her speech is genuine. Unconsciously uses the older type of pronunciation.

GA 34B: Hinton Brown School, Bogart P.O., Bradberrys. — M, farmer, 62. B. same district, c. 2 1/2 mi. away. Lived same district all his life except for 2 yrs. of married life in Upper Greene, Lower Oconee Cos.. Some carpentry; has been employed by AAA and soil conservation. — F. from immediate section cut off Oconee near Watkinsville (now Clarke Co.); PGF, PGM b. same section as F.; M. b. here, MGF prob. from VA, MGM b. upper Oconee Co. — Ed.: Cleveland

School (NW corner of Co.). — Baptist; Mason, Farm Bureau, justice of the peace since age 29. — Active, prosperous farmer. Hardworking; limited amount of education, but interested in acquiring more information. Interested in education; seemed to enjoy interviews. Natural speech of middle group: doesn't use many folk-grammatical forms, but no discrepancies noted between direct and cv. forms. Deep roots in area. Some prejudices. Live curiosity. Alert mind: interview passed rather rapidly. Many Midland items of vocab. Active in comm. affairs — judgement respected by Co. officials. — Tempo moderate but slight drawl-effect from long stressed vowels and short weak-stressed vowels. Some nasality. Up-gliding /e o ɔ/. Very little, if any, postvocalic constriction.

35. Walton County

Est. 1818. On old trail from Cherokee country to Augusta. Surveyed 1819; land distributed by 1820 lottery. Early settlers from Middle GA, SC, NC, VA, TN, MD. C. 4,000 slaves by 1850. Raided by Federal troops during Civil War. Baptists, Christians, Holiness, Methodists; decline in Presbyterians. Orig. tobacco, rice; cotton eventually; textiles from 1895. Small streams, fertile bottom land; cotton, general farming, fruit, forage crops. Pop. 1810: 1,026, 1820: 4,192, 1850: 10,821, 1880: 15,622, 1910: 25,393, 1930: 21,118, 1960: 20,481.

Sams, Anita B. 1967. *Wayfarers in Walton: A History of Walton County, Georgia. . . .* Monroe: General Charitable Foundation of Monroe, Georgia.

Thompson, Monroe

Monroe est. 1821 as Co. seat. Cotton market; some manufacturing. Pop. Thompson 1930: 1,914, 1960: 4,522.

GA 35N: M, retired farmer, 80. B. Co. — F., M. b. Co. — Ed.: till 4th grade. — Baptist.

36. Rockdale County

Organized 1870; second smallest in size of GA cos. Named for underlying granite/gneiss. Cherokees till 1834. Early families English, Ulster Scots, often from SC. Methodists by 1818, Baptists and Presbyterians followed. Cotton largely wiped out by boll weevil. "Bedroom co. for Atlanta" since WWII. Granite quarries, water power, cotton, general farming, fruit. Pop. 1880: 6,838, 1910: 8,916, 1930: 7,247, 1960: 10,572.

Barksdale, Margaret G., et al., eds. 1978. *A History of Rockdale County.* Conyers: Tom Hay Pub. Co.

Gibboney, Dorothy G. 1975. *Dial Mill, 1830: The First 100 Years.* Conyers.

Conyers

Co. seat; inc. 1854; city charter 1881. Slight destruction from Sherman. Once center of cotton trade for Co.; recent mills, service industries, farming. Now suburbanized. Pop. 1880: 1,374, 1910: 1,919, 1930: 1,495, 1960: 2,881.

GA 36N: M, quarry worker, 69. B. c. 2 mi. away. Has never been outside Co. — F., M. from S. GA. — Ed.: till 5th grade. — Baptist. — Slightly hard of hearing, but memory good. Very provincial: has never traveled; little knowledge of geography. Extremely patient and agreeable; willing to explain things in detail. Family owns (or owned) most of land in neighborhood; most of neighbors are relatives. Interview rather long [by FW's standards; actually a medium to short interview. — RIM]

37. Fulton and Dekalb Counties (Metropolitan Atlanta)

Dekalb est. 1822. Agriculture and truck farming, giving way to manufacturing (part of Atlanta area); suburban bedroom comm. Fulton formed 1853 from Dekalb. Settled mainly by Georgians; also some Up-Country Carolinians, settlers from VA, PA; many Ulster Scots. Chattahoochee River. Misc. farming, esp. for Atlanta market; copper and iron pyrites, ceramic clay, mineral springs (bottled water). Suburbanized with growth of Atlanta. Pop. Dekalb 1830: 10,042, 1850: 14,328, 1860: 7,806, 1880: 14,497, 1910: 27,881, 1930: 70,278, 1960: 256,782. Fulton 1860: 14,427, 1880: 49,137, 1910: 177,733, 1930: 318,587, 1960: 556,326.

Allen, Ivan, with Paul Hemphill. 1971. *Mayor: Notes on the Sixties*. NY: Simon and Schuster.

Allen, Ivan. 1928. *Atlanta from the Ashes*. Atlanta: Ruralist Press.

Avery, I. W., et al. 1892. *City of Atlanta*. Louisville: Inter-State Pub. Co.

Boylston, Elise Reid. 1968. *Atlanta: Its Lore, Legends, and Laughter*. Doraville: Foote and Davies.

Burgess, Margaret Elaine. 1962. *Negro Leadership in a Southern City*. Chapel Hill: University of North Carolina Press.

Clarke, Edward Young. 1881. *Atlanta Illustrated.* . . . 3rd ed. Atlanta: J. P. Harrison and Co.

Cooper, Walter G. 1934. *Official History of Fulton County*. Atlanta: Walter W. Brown Pub. Co.

DeVane, Ernest E. 1974. *Roswell: Historic Homes and Landmarks*. Roswell: Roswell Historical Society.

Durett, Dan, and Dana F. White. 1975. *Another Atlanta: The Black Heritage: A Bicentennial Tour*. Atlanta: History Group.

Eason, Deborah, and Elton Eason. 1967. *This is Atlanta: A Comprehensive Illustrated Guide*. . . . Atlanta.

Ecke, Melvin W. 1972. *From Ivy Street to Kennedy Center: Centennial History of the Atlanta Public School System*. Atlanta: Board of Education.

Edens, A. Hollis. 1939–40. The Founding of Atlanta. *Atlanta Historical Bulletin* 4:203–31, 225–89, 5:65–85.

Federal Writers Project. 1942. *Atlanta, a City of the Modern South*. NY: Smith and Durrell.

Garrett, Franklin M. 1974. *Yesterday's Atlanta*. Miami, FL: E. A. Seemann Pub.

Garrett, Franklin Miller. 1954. *Atlanta and Environs*. . . . 3 vols. NY: Lewis Historical Pub. Co.

Green, Ruth. 1972. *Footprints*. Decatur: Agnes Lee Chapter, United Daughters of the Confederacy.

Hopkins, Richard J. 1965. Occupational and Geographical Mobility in Atlanta 1870–1896. *Journal of Southern History* 34:200–13.

Hornady, John R. 1922. *Atlanta, Yesterday, Today and Tomorrow*. Atlanta: American Cities Book Co.

Hunter, Floyd. 1953. *Community Power Structure: A Study of Decision Makers*. Chapel Hill: UNC Press.

Knight, Lucian Lamar. 1930. *History of Fulton County*. . . . Atlanta: A. H. Cawston.

Martin, Thomas H. 1902. *Atlanta and Its Builders*. . . . 2 vols. Atlanta: Century Memorial Pub. Co.

McMahan, Chalmers A. 1950. *The People of Atlanta: A Demographic Study of Georgia's Capital City*. Athens: University of Georgia Press.

Porter, Michael Leroy. 1974. *Black Atlanta: An Interdisciplinary Study of Blacks on the East Side of Atlanta, 1890–1930*. Emory University dissertation.

Preston, Howard L. 1979. *Automobile Age Atlanta: The Making of a Southern Metropolis, 1900–1935*. Athens: University of Georgia Press.

Reed, Wallace P., ed. 1889. *History of Atlanta*. . . . Syracuse, NY: D. Mason.

Starbuck, James C. 1974. *Historic Atlanta to 1930: An Indexed Chronological Bibliography*. Monticello, IL: Council of Planning Librarians.

Taylor, Arthur Reed. 1974. *From the Ashes: Atlanta during Reconstruction 1865–76*. Ann Arbor: University Microfilms.

Williford, William Bailey. 1962. *Peachtree Street, Atlanta*. Athens: University of Georgia Press.

Wilson, John Stainback. 1871. *Atlanta As It Is*. . . . NY: Little, Rennie and Co.

Wotten, Grigsby Hart. 1974. *New City of the South: Atlanta 1843–1873*. Ann Arbor: University Microfilms.

1902. *Pioneer Citizens' History of Atlanta, 1833–1902*. Atlanta: Pioneer Citizens' Society of Atlanta.

1927–. *The Atlanta Historical Bulletin*. Atlanta: Atlanta Historical Society.

1955. *Fulton County Centennial, 1854–1954*. Atlanta: Foote and Davies.

Atlanta

Watershed between Atlantic and Gulf (Chattahoochee R.). Creek settlement in area 1782; fort created in 1813, first settlement in Atlanta area. Still Indian lands in 1820; Dekalb Co. formed 1822. Remaining Creek lands ceded 1825–27; assertion of claim to Cherokee lands 1828–32; final removal of Cherokees by 1835. RRs authorized 1825; charter of RR from Ocmulgee to Flint 1827; Central of GA chartered 1833; RR center by 1850s. Natural exchange point for grain and cotton belts. Inc. as town of Marthasville 1843; name became Atlantic City 1845; city charter 1847. 1st free school est. 1845. Growth slow till 1845, phenomenal after; already larger than most fall line cities by 1860. Methodists est. first church; Episcopalians, Baptists, and Presbyterians followed; small churches, no religious segregation. Many Northern settlers by 1860; predominantly commercial city; no real old-line planter or merchant group. Factories and warehouses, base hospital in Civil War. Devastated by fire during siege and capture in 1864. Federal headquarters for Reconstruction 1866; population and trade quickly above pre-war levels. Made state capital 1868. Growth of managerial and clerical white groups: new upper class based on wealth. Trade and transportation tended to be more important than manufacturing in growth. Newspapers est. 1868, 1872. Race riots 1906. Architectural blossoming 1907–20; known for innovative architecture since. Military base, WWI and WWII. Center of higher education: numerous colleges and seminaries, including GA Tech (1885) and Emory (1914). Diversified industry (home of Coca-Cola from 1886); Industrial metropolis and distributing center. Communications hub and most important city of Southeast; largest city between DC and New Orleans. Cultural center; cosmopolitan and energetic society which dominates state. Pop. 1850: 2,572, 1880: 37,409, 1910: 154,839, 1930: 270,366, 1960: 487,455.

GA 37N: F, domestic, 82. B. here. — F., M. not b. Atlanta, but lived here most of their lives. — Ed.: till 7th grade. — A.M.E. Church.

GA 37M!: Washington Park, Adamsville (now absorbed in Atlanta), Atlanta, Fulton Co. — M, elementary school principal, 55. B. Atlanta (campus Morehouse College). Has been social worker, elementary teacher, h.s. counselor, army ed. advisor, Red Cross worker, United Nations Relief Agency (was in Italy and Africa with Red Cross during WWII). — F. b. here (math teacher at Morehouse), PGF, PGM b. here (freedmen), PGF's F. b. here, first AfAm member of the House from GA; M. b. here (teacher in Atlanta public schools), MGF, MGM freedmen. — Ed.: MAs from Atlanta U., Michigan, Wisconsin. — Excellent example of AfAm middle-class speech. Speech an interesting mixture of folk speech and hypercorrect forms (*nuisance* has 3 syllables). Very sure of himself in matters of grammar, speculative about semantics, unsure about pronunciation. — Cultivated.

Doraville, Dekalb Co.

C. 10 mi. N. of Decatur. 1st settlement from Dorchester, England. Rural area to 1946, now suburbanized. Pop. 1900: 110.

GA 37A: M, farmer, 95. B. same house (prob. oldest in upper part of Dekalb Co.). Travel restricted to a few visits to relatives. — F. b. 1805, Anderson Co., SC (anti-slavery); M. "located in Newton Co.", MGF left GA for IL because it was a free state. — Ed.: local schools. — Associate Reformed Presbyterian, has been elder in church, now elder emeritus; Farmers Alliance. — Independent. Definite folk type. Mind still very clear; except for legs, physically vigorous; good memory; keeps present and past well separated. Loves to talk; excellent rapport with FW. Knows local traditions, glad to cooperate in any historical project; prob. oldest living resident of Atlanta area, often consulted on local folk history. Religious. No pretensions; humble; respect for learning and education. — Jerky speech. Strong stresses. Nasality strong. Overlong stressed vowels. Slow tempo. Pitch moderate to high. Drawl. Much constriction; simplification of final clusters; many final stops weakly articulated. Both *ain't* and *hain't*.

Rock Chapel, Lithonia P.O., Diamond, Dekalb Co.

Lithonia has granite quarrying, chiefly for crushed rock. Pop. Lithonia 1930: 1,457.

GA 37B: M, storekeeper, farmer, 75. B. here (200–300 yds. away); worked 3 yrs. in DC census office. — F. b. Hall Co., PGF, PGM both b. VA; M. b. Troup Co., MGF, MGM both from SC. — Ed.: "up to about h.s., a little Latin and algebra". — Methodist. — Well rooted in comm. Occ. writes articles on "old times" for co. newspaper. Full of information; enjoys people and talking; much interested in interviews. — High-

pitched voice. Drawl. Slow speech. Nasality. Strong stresses. Almost always up-gliding /e ɔ o/; /i u/ up-gliding most of time; /u/ fronted; /ju/ after /t d n/; [ɑ] (unrounded) in *pot, oxen, garden, wash, tomorrow*; /ʌ/ very high; [ɜɪ] in *thirty, Thursday, girl, worm*; "long" and "short" /ai/, "long" often a pure vowel; beginning of /au/ varies from [æ] to [a]. Weak articulation of final consonants; simplification of final clusters; /hw-/; /sr-/; no postvocalic constriction, linking /r/ or intrusive /r/.

Avondale Estates, Decatur, Dekalb Co.

Avondale Estates a residential suburb; subdivision 1924, city 1926. Decatur Co. seat; inc. 1823, older than Atlanta. Settled by upcountrymen from VA and Carolinas. Rejected RR. Now residential suburb. Pop. Decatur 1850: 744, 1880: 639, 1930: 13,276, 1960: 23,026.

GA 37C: F, housewife, 45. B. Chamblee, to metropolitan Atlanta as a baby [now Chamblee is part of metropolitan Atlanta], to Avondale age 4. Wide travel (trailer trips West). — F. b. Harlem, GA; M. b. Thompson, GA (McDuffie Co.). Knows little of grandparents and further back. — Ed.: through 11th grade, Avondale. — Baptist. — Patient and helpful. Not bookish; religious. Natural informal usage (mixed social influences). Became a little more self-conscious as interview progressed. Observant, though not intimately familiar with rural life. Recalls much folk vocabulary. — Speech slow. Less nasality than younger generation. Some hyperforms like quin*iron*. /ai/ often monophthongal. Not always constriction; some excrescent /-t/: *clift, acrosst*; occ. intrusive /r/. Often uses folk-grammatical forms, though naturally would use standard. — [FW daughter of inf. One of the better student interviews. — RIM]

Druid Hills, Atlanta, Dekalb Co.

Druid Hills opened 1908 as a real estate development. Emory Campus here. Wooded, open; fine residential area.

GA 37D!: M, university teacher, 59. B. here. — F. b. here, PGF b. OH, PGM b. VA (Scotch-Irish ancestry); M., MGF, MGM all b. here. — Ed.: Atlanta public schools; BA and MA Emory University. — Wide variety of associations: Am. Federation of Teachers, Am. Assn. of University Professors, Natl. Council of Teachers of English, past president of GA Teachers Assn. Belongs to square dancing club. — Cultivated.

GA 37E!: F, teacher, 53. B. here. When married, lived in Columbia, SC, 5 yrs. and Pensacola, FL 5 yrs. — F. b. MI, lived there till 18, PGF, PGM both b. Sweden; M. b. Prosperity, SC, lived most of life in Atlanta, MGF, MGM b. SC. — Ed.: BA, post-grad. courses in ed. — Lutheran. — Interview conducted during inf.'s free hours at school, yet fairly relaxed. Generally alert, intelligent; a pleasure to work with. Interest in and understanding of Atlas project. English teacher; had memorized "correct" forms, but sometimes uninhibited, natural responses overcame her indoctrination. Belief in "language improvement", "correct" vs. "incorrect" came across in her classroom teaching. Knowledge of farm terms limited. — No postvocalic constriction; occ. intrusive /-r/ as in *widow* [wɪdɚ]. — Cultivated.

GA 37F!: Atlanta, Fulton Co. — F, "lady" (husband was one of the empire builders of Atlanta, now living in a nursing home), 84. B. Ringgold, GA (mother's summer home). Grew up in Decatur, later to Atlanta. Spent 1 yr. in Cuba. — F. lived in Atlanta most of his life; M. from Roswell, GA (NE part of Fulton Co.), doesn't remember grandparents. — Ed.: prep school in Abingdon, VA; Agnes Scott College. — Presbyterian. — Pleasant, though somewhat feeble. Seemed to enjoy interview, but tended to tire. Mind variable: sometimes quick, sometimes slow. Not much acquainted with folk speech or rural features, but gladly offered what she could. Natural responses. All manners of an old-time Southern lady — husband was one of the great names, as witnessed by local park and hotel. — Cultivated voice. Voice soft, wide intonation range. Strong stresses. Rather rapid speech for the comm., but not nearly so fast as some of the coastal inf.'s. Clear utterance. Stressed vowels us. long, weak-stressed rather short; us. up-gliding /i e ɔ o u/; high /ʌ/; "long" and "short" /ai/. Some simplification of final cons. clusters; /hw-/; /sr-/. — Cultivated.

GA 37G!: Atlanta, Dekalb Co. — M, university professor (French), 51. B. Roswell (N. end of Fulton Co.); moved around N. GA with F. (Methodist preacher). — F. b. White Plains (Greene Co.); PGF, PGM both b. Greene Co.; M., MGF, MGM all b. Alpharetta, (N. Fulton Co.). — Ed.: Chickamauga, etc.; Emory U., U. of Chicago. — Methodist; ΔΤΔ fraternity, Mason, Modern Lang. Assn., S. Atlantic Modern Lang. Assn., Am. Assn. of Teachers of French, Am. Assn. of Teachers of Spanish, Am. Assn. of University Professors. — Some tendency to be over-careful when attention focused on a particular item. Conversational speech typical of upcountry. Rural background plus cultural contacts in adult life. A little slow and ponderous in thinking and in speech. Conservative in educational practices but endeavors to keep abreast of economic and political developments without violent prejudice. Liberal Protestant in general socio-religious outlook, but more on talking than acting level (Emory has reputation for being safe and conservative). Interested in purpose of Atlas; cooperated gladly and generally tried to be natural during interview. Had not heard of Gilliéron and the French Atlas. Seemed to enjoy interview. — Drawl. Strong stresses. Overlong stressed vowels; /u/ very far forward; up-gliding stressed vowels. Some postvocalic constriction, not consistent — varies from word to word and from utterance to utterance of same word; some palatal /k- g-/; articulation of final cons. and final clusters distinct, but simplification of clusters occurs in colloquial speech. — Cultivated.

GA 37H!: Atlanta, Fulton Co. — M, writer, 73. B. Savannah, Atlanta ages 2–38, NY for a few yrs., some in France, 19 mos. in Army, 9 yrs. Columbus, 7 yrs. Chattanooga (always culturally oriented to Atlanta). Worked on various newspapers (Pulitzer Prize). — F., PGF, PGM all b. Eatonton, GA (NE of Macon); M. French. — Ed.: private. — Roman Catholic; Inquiry Club (literary). — Excellent interview. Both inf. and wife (GA 37H!*) completely natural (teased each other and FW very delightfully). Both sure of own family usage, and each quick to point out where other's background might have been different. Both: sense of humor. Both: very quick minds; excellent grasp of purpose of interview, without slightest effect on naturalness of speech. Both excellent

examples of natural cultivated speech of older generation (upcountry type). — Inf.'s speech somewhat rasping. Both inf. and wife: fast speech; us. strong stresses; stressed vowels prolonged, weak-stressed vowels relaxed and shortened. Upgliding /i e ɔ o u/. Some simplification of final clusters; initial stops less strongly aspirated than us. in comm.; /hw-/. A few low country vocab. items (as us. around cities: 39.5, 36.4). — Cultivated.

GA 37H!*: Atlanta, Fulton Co. — F, wife of GA 37H!, 72. B. here. 4 yrs. in Boston (art school). — F. b. here, PGF lived here most of life; M. b. here, MGF, MGM b. Northeast, came to GA before Confederate War. — Ed.: local finishing school; art school in Boston. — Character sketch: see comments above for GA 37H! on this joint interview. — Speech: see comments above for GA 37H!. /ʌ/ often much more rounded than GA 37H!'s. Aux. responses noted only when different from primary inf.'s (almost always identical). — Cultivated.

GA 37I!: Atlanta. — F, housewife, 59. B. here; has always lived in Atlanta area; extensive travel in the US and Europe. — F. b. Mobile, AL, PGF b. MS, later came to Atlanta, PGM b. AL (prob. Mobile); M. b. Toledo, OH, MGF b. PA, came as contractor to Atlanta, helped build state capitol, stayed, MGM b. Nova Scotia. — Ed.: public school through 10th grade; private schools thereafter. 1 yr. Georgetown Visitation Convent in Washington, DC. — Active in comm. affairs. — Cultivated.

38. Hall County

Est. 1818. Earliest settlers in the 1790s from the upland Carolinas, VA Piedmont. Settlers included English, Ulster-Scots, Irish, Scots; some German and French. Baptists early. Federal road 1805. Apple-growing est. c. 1860. Piedmont: general farming. Gold mining, building stone, mineral springs, lumber, manufacturing (textiles). Brenau College and Conservatory at Gainesville. Pop. 1820: 5,086, 1850: 8,713, 1880: 15,298, 1910: 25,730, 1930: 30,313, 1960: 49,739.

> Brice, William Malcolm, comp. 1936. *A City Laid Waste: Tornado Devastation at Gainesville, Georgia, April 6, 1936.* Atlanta: Webb and Martin.
> McRay, Sybil Wood. 1973. *This 'n That: History of Hall County, Georgia. . . .* Gainesville: Peoples Printing.

Tadmore, Gainesville

Gainesville inc. 1821; made a city 1872. 1848 attracted settlers because of GA gold rush. Market center (esp. chickens and eggs); varied industries including cotton, hosiery. 1st town (1889) S. of Baltimore to have electric street lights. Several private schools; Brenau College est. 1878. Pop. 1880: 1,919, 1910: 5,925, 1930: 8,624, 1960: 16,523.

GA 38: M, retired city employee, 79. B. Co. — F., M. b. Banks Co. (adjoining Hall Co.); grandparents Banks Co. people, but inf. unsure of origins. — Painfully humble: called FW "boss" throughout interview. Spoke freely of himself and his language. Esp. interesting references to "flat talk" (which inf. calls a brogue), a variety of speech he associates with SE Hall Co., characterized by semi-vocalic glide after velars in *cards, garden,* etc. — Frequent /d/ for /ð/ in free conversation; curious alternation of /r/ and /Ø/.

39. Lumpkin County

Formed 1832 from Cherokee Co. Cherokees displaced 1838, after gold strike (1829). Settlers from W. NC, VA, Savannah R. Valley; many settlers very quickly after gold rush. Recurrent interest in mining; few slaves. Baptists by 1830, Methodists and Presbyterians followed within decade. Blue Ridge Mtns. Mineral springs; general farming, fruit. Pop. 1840: 5,671, 1850: 8,955, 1880: 6,526, 1910: 5,444, 1930: 4,927, 1960: 7,241.

Cain, Andrew W. 1932. *History of Lumpkin County for the First Hundred Years, 1832–1932.* Atlanta: Stein Print. Co.

Coulter, E. Merton. 1956. *Auraria: The Story of a Georgia Gold-Mining Town.* Athens: University of Georgia Press.

Harshaw, Lou. 1976. *The Gold of Dahlonega.* . . . Asheville, NC: Hexagon Co.

Dahlonega

Center of GA gold fields: 1st nugget c. 1818; fields discovered 1828–29. Many families from W. NC. Co. seat when Co. created in 1832. Federal mint 1838–61. Mines worked sporadically. North Georgia College here from 1873. Trading center for farmers.

GA 39: M, hotelkeeper, loan company owner, 66. B. here; at age 15 moved to Atlanta for 2 yrs., then to Camilla, GA (SW corner of state); at age 44 returned to Dahlonega (had spent summers in Dahlonega till then). Owned hardware store and funeral home in Camilla (licensed undertaker). — F. b. Ireland; M. b. Minnesota (German); parents met in SD where both families were involved in Black Hills gold rush. F. came to Dahlonega in 1890 as supt. of mining co. — Ed.: h.s. in Dahlonega, Atlanta, and Camilla (h.s. grad.). — Active in comm. affairs, considerable travel, pres. Chamber of Commerce and Rotary in Camilla. — Vigorous speech, us. natural; few inhibitions.

40. Cherokee County

Formed 1831 from Cherokee lands. Orig. contained all Cherokee lands in GA; Cherokees evicted 1802–38. Gold discovered 1828; 24 counties cut out of original co. Most early settlers English, Irish, Scots, Dutch, German; also settled from NC, SC, TN, S. GA, VA. VA settlement in NW of Co. by 1850, slaveowners. Divided loyalties during Civil War. Canton burned by Sherman's orders, May, 1864. Many Baptists, Methodists. First public schools 1872; eventually academies competed with public schools. Broken, irregular terrain; varied flora and fauna. General farming; minerals, including gold, copper, mica, asbestos, marble. Pop. 1840: 5,895, 1850: 12,800, 1880: 14,325, 1910: 16,661, 1930: 20,003, 1960: 23,001.

Marlin, Lloyd G. 1932. *The History of Cherokee County.* Atlanta: Walter W. Brown Pub. Co.

Tate, Luke E. 1935. *History of Pickens County.* Atlanta: W. W. Brown Pub. Co.

1976. Cherokee Territory Bicentennial Issue. *Northwest Georgia Historical and Genealogical Society Publication* 8.3.

GA 40: Ducktown (village at edge of Forsyth Co.). — F, housewife, 72. B. Forsyth Co. — F., M. both b. Forsyth Co., MGF, MGM b. AL (ancestry ultimately Irish). — Ed.: through 9th grade. — Baptist.

41. Gilmer County

Formed 1832 from Cherokee Co. Indian mission station (Presbyterian) 1819–38. Many settlers from W. NC, also from VA; English, Scots, Irish, some Germans. Road building important (and difficult) 1832–50. RR in 1883. Mountain country; forest land; diverse timber, apple growing. Methodists first denomination (1817), Baptists by 1841. Gold after 1842, mining resumed 1879. School system authorized 1860, but education slow to develop. Nuts, grapes, syrup once profitable; many minerals. Divided co. 1861–65: many in Union army, local guerilla war. Wood products, iron, gold, various stones; general farming, fruit, poultry; textiles (but little cotton ever grown). Pop. 1840: 2,536, 1850: 8,440, 1880: 8,386, 1910: 9,237, 1930: 7,344, 1960: 8,922.

Ward, George Gordon. 1965. *The Annals of Upper Georgia Centered in Gilmer County.* Carrollton: Thomasson Print. Co.

Ellijay

Indian village before Cherokees displaced; est. 1834 as Co. seat. Textile mills 1873. Reputation for health resort (mineral springs) in 1890s. Formerly lumbering. Fishing; some industry; canning: peaches, apples. Pop. 1930: 1,298.

GA 41: M, handyman (farmer, sawmill worker, etc.), 81. B. Tails Creek, Leaches Dist. in Co.; grew up in Tails Creek, c. age 12 moved to Ellijay. Always in Co., except 10 mos. work in adjoining Murray Co. and visits to children up North. — F., PGF, PGM all b. Buncombe Co., NC; M., MGF, MGM all b. here. — Ed.: Tails Creek, Ellijay through 7th grade. — Primitive Baptist. — Quite bright; friendly and open. Fairly worldly for folk type, considerable reading. Many relic forms. In direct questioning, sometimes conscious of proper forms, but relaxed in conversation.

42. Fannin County

Formed 1854 from Union and Gilmer Cos. 1st settlers from W. NC; others from VA, SC, W. TN. Gold rush not profitable here. Few AfAms; 2/3 Unionist in 1860. 1st RR 1886. Mountainous, scenic. Self-sufficient farming till 20th cent.; fruit and vegetables exported. Mineral resources, esp. copper from 1850. Pop. 1860: 5,139, 1880: 7,245, 1910: 12,574, 1930: 12,969, 1960: 13,620.

Thompson, Kathleen M. 1982. *In Touch with the Past.* . . . Blue Ridge: Fannin County High School.

Thompson, Kathleen. 1976. *Touching Home: A Collection of History and Folklore from the Copper Basin, Fannin County Area.* Blue Ridge: West Fannin High School.

Mt. Liberty (old Pierceville), Copper Hill, TN, P.O., Mobile Dist.

Pierceville a "post hamlet" in 1900. Isolated rural settlement. Water power; country produce.

GA 42A: F, widow, 74. B. Old Copper Hill, Polk Co., TN. Moved to Mobile Dist. before 2 yrs. old; 8 mos. Bridgeport,

TX (age 22); 4 trips to FL (about a yr. in all); few days in OK, 6 mos. Indian Territory. — F. b. Burke Co., NC (part Indian), PGF, PGM b. perhaps Burke Co.; M. b. Oconee Co., SC. — Ed.: Mobile, GA, Grassy Creek, TN: "got to middle of blue-black speller". — Missionary Baptist; Eastern Star. — Excellent interview. Good example of folk speech, little touched by city culture. ("If you hear a hoot owl in winter, it's fixing to snow.".) Simple personality; familiar with details of rural life, but not much outside her cove. Religious; devoted to family; hospitable (raised retarded orphan, took in a homeless hired man). Many anecdotes. Enjoyed interviews: appreciated FW coming to spend the time with her. Good factual grasp. Speaks naturally with no affectation. Uses local forms: couldn't use any other. — Nasality, slightly querulous tone. Slow, long stressed vowels. Slow speech. Up-gliding diphthongs /i e ɔ o u/; /ju/ after /t d n/; /ʌ/ very high; /u/ fronted; /ai/ generally long; /ɔi/ occ. [aᵊɪ]. Simplification of final clusters; strong constriction; /sr/; /hw-/; /-l/ us. dark, occ. vocalized.

Dial, Blue Ridge

Blue Ridge Co. seat (1895); inc. 1887. Orig. Cherokee stronghold; hunting and fishing. Methodists by 1877. RR junction. Some Union sympathy in Civil War. Farming, timbering, mining.

GA 42B: M, farmer, 73. B. Noontootla Dist., c. 10 mi. SE of Blue Ridge (in mtns.), moved to Blue Ridge age 69; one summer in OH, age 46. — F., PGF, PGM all b. Mitchell Co., NC, whole family, including PGF's F., moved to Fannin Co. when inf. was a boy; M. b. Co, MGF b. Rutherford Co., NC, MGM b. Co. — Ed.: local schools to 18; no h.s. diploma, but passed all h.s. courses except language and geometry. — Methodist; Mason, justice of the peace 22 yrs., school bd. 15 yrs., fair amount of reading. — Cooperative. Slightly deaf. Enjoyed interviews. Good observer: knows comm.; well-known; strong comm. spirit. Hard-headed common sense. Dialect strongly rooted in folk speech; authentic judge of other local usage. — Very strong stresses. Nasality. Slow speech; half drawl; slurring. Up-gliding diphthongs. Simplification of final clusters; strong constriction; /hw-/.

43. Union County

Formed 1832 from Cherokee Co. Most early settlers from NC; Scots, English, Irish. Early gold mining. Mostly Baptists. Mountainous (highest elevation in GA). General farming, stock raising, minerals (esp. gold and marble), timber. Pop. 1840: 3,152, 1850: 7,234, 1880: 6,431, 1910: 6,918, 1930: 6,340, 1960: 6,510.

Collins, C. R., and Jan Devereaux. 1976. *Sketches of Union County History*. Blairsville: Union County Historical Society.

Lonesome Cove, Blairsville P.O., Owltown Dist.

Blairsville laid out 1838, after Cherokee removal. Gold mining suspended, because of litigation over rights. National Forest land: "solitary and spectacularly beautiful". Union sympathies; fierce individualism. Reforestation since 1920s.

GA 43: M, farmer, 85. B. here. — F. b. here, PGF b. Buncombe Co., NC (Irish), PGM b. Buncombe Co., NC ("Black

Dutch"); M. b. here, MGF b. White Co., GA (Irish), MGM, MGM's F. b. White Co. ("Dutch"). — Ed.: here (very little). — Baptist; has been circuit judge. — Rather a high type of citizen compared to the average; very primitive; speech genuinely rustic.

44. Rabun County

Est. 1819. Settlers from England, Scotland, N. Ireland; a few Germans, Dutch Huguenots; almost no AfAms, few Episcopalians. Many settlers from PA and VA, via Carolinas, also directly from NC and SC. Baptists and Methodists; some Presbyterians. Basically self-sufficient farming, no money crop. Gold fever 1830s; unprofitable. Roads laid out 1830s. Rabun Turnpike 1845; unprofitable, discontinued 1857. Few slaves; a Union co. in 1860. Co. in relative isolation until recently; no public school till 1870s. Mountainous and scenic. Fish and game; general farming (no cotton), apples; timber; hydroelectric plants; various minerals, mines and quarries; resort area developed since WWI. Pop. 1820: 524, 1850: 2,448, 1880: 4,634, 1910: 5,562, 1930: 6,331, 1960: 7,458.

Ritchie, Andrew Jackson. 1948. *Sketches of Rabun County History, 1819–1948*. Clayton.

Germany, Persimmon Dist.

Persimmon Dist. in mountainous country 8 mi. NW of Clayton. Germans and Ulster Scots. Old settlement; Baptist Church 1833.

GA 44A: M, farmer, 91. B. Burton Lake (W. part of Co.); spent ages 6–12 in Clayton till step-mother remarried, thence to Germany. Never traveled S. of Atlanta. — F. b. Burton Lake, PGF b. Ireland, PGM b. VA; M. b. Burton Lake. — Ed.: Rabun Gap, 4–5 mo. session. — Baptist; Farmers Union, 24 yrs. Bd. of Ed. — Very intelligent; mind still wonderfully alert. Excellent folk type. Respect for education ("sent all my girls to college"). One of Co. patriarchs. Still likes to help with farm chores; can't bear thought of being a burden on anyone. Keeps up on Co. affairs; many trips to Clayton during court sessions. Advice respected and sought. Hearing surprisingly good. Enjoyed interviews; hospitable; takes pride in setting good table (bachelor son runs farm and household and does cooking). Many anecdotes. Speech locally rooted; not much concern with other forms. Uses folk lexicon naturally and unashamedly. Recalls (with prompting by son, age 55) many folk vocab. items, but has kept up with some of the changes in word fashion. Nonetheless, still primitive, even by Clayton standards. — Drawl. Nasality. Voice a bit rasping, often quavers off for an instant, but utterance us. very clear. /ɛ/ and /ɪ/ often neutralized before nasals. Weak articulation of final consonants; some vocalization or loss of postvoc. /l/; /-f/ often for /-θ/; much postvocalic constriction of /-r/.

GA 44B: Quartz (picturesque post village), Persimmon Dist. — M, farmer, 80. B. here. 1 yr. in CO, 2 yrs. in WA as a child (c. 1878). — F. b. Mecklenburg Co., NC; nothing known about M. — Ed.: common school. — Presbyterian; has been member Co. Bd. of Ed. — Somewhat feeble; very deaf (interview broken off as painful to both inf. and FW). Still tries to help around farm. Good knowledge of local culture; authentic; strongly rooted in his cove. — Drawl. Mid-range, rasping voice, strongly nasalized. Strong stresses, overlong stressed vowels. Many folk pronunciations, like /a/ in *narrow* and *wheelbarrow*. Up-gliding /i e ɔ o u/; fronted /u/; [æʊ] in *asks, can't, laugh*; [ʋ] in *rock, oxen, wash*; /ʌ/ high; [æʊ] us.; /ai/ us. long. Simplification of final cons. clusters; postvocalic /l/ us. vocalized; medium to strong constriction in *thirty, father, barn* types.

Persimmon Creek, Clayton P.O., Persimmon Dist.

Clayton laid out as Co. seat 1823. Area settled principally by New Englanders who previously had lived in the mtns. of VA and by a few Tories who had escaped to the mtns. during the American Rev. A few Cherokees who escaped deportation of 1838 intermarried with whites. Mining unprofitable. Growth with coming of RR; brick kiln. Wood products; various light industries. Summer resort; tourists since c. 1914; camps.

GA 44C: M, farmer, 72. B. Persimmon Dist. Spent 2 mos. in Detroit, 2 mos. Haywood Co., NC in his middle age. — M. came from Haywood Co., NC, raised by a family c. 3 mi. away. — Ed.: Boiling Springs, Hiawassee, Rabun Gap. Finished "what was called High School Course". — Ex-Baptist, now Church of God (Holiness); Farmers Union, has been constable 5 yrs, justice of the peace 5 yrs. — Very religious; favorite diversion is reading Bible and trying to understand it. Minds own business; good neighbor. Likes to help others. Knows local culture, folklore, birds and animals. Has been huntsman. Well-kept house; well-managed farm. Good observer; has noticed changes in speech since boyhood; caught on to purpose of interview very early and freely offered variants from his recollections. Pretty good judgment as to what is locally rooted and what isn't. Completely natural: no effort to be either quaint or correct. Excellent rapport with FW . Many Midland forms, and some (e.g. *devil's darning needle*) FW had not expected. Good mind. Enjoyed interviews; hospitable; generous with time. — Low-pitched voice. Drawl. Long stressed vowels. Slurred utterance. Short weak-stressed vowels. Natural usage, somewhere between folk and intermediate. Final consonants often weakly articulated.

GA 44D: Clayton. — M, former merchant, mail carrier, now justice of the peace, 70. B. here. Spent 4–5 yrs. in Habersham Co. — F. b. Co., PGF came from NC via SC, PGM b. Co., PGM's F. and M. from NC; M., MGF b. Co., MGF's F. b. PA, MGM "Dutch". — Ed.: 1 yr. Young Harris Institute; 2 yrs. Green Institute, Demorest, GA. — Methodist; Mason. — Cooperative; amused by interviews. Knows local usage. No farm experience. Interesting example of the small town inf. in a predominantly rural area. Definitely mtn. type, but with modifications. — Speech indistinct. Strong nasality. Drawl; slurred utterance. Medium to high pitch. Weak articulation of final consonants; simplification of final clusters.

Flat Creek, Lakemont

Lakemont in S. part of Co. Burton Reservoir on Tallulah R. Prosperous farming dist. before power plants.

GA 44E: M, rock mason, former farmer, electrical worker, 72. B. Co. Fair amount of travel. — F., PGF, PGM all b. Co.; M. b. Co., MGF, MGM both b. Wales. — Ed.: through 9th grade. Moderate reading (newspapers, farming and news magazines). — Baptist (inactive). — Good-humored, sharp-witted. Drinks

a good bit (own view), but often moralistic. Well-informed about politics, enjoys discussing recent events. Esp. knowledgeable on the history of the civil rights movement. More liberal than FW expected. — [Inexperienced FW; questions often framed so as to 1) suggest responses, 2) divert attention to irrelevant details. Paradigmatic approach to grammatical questions. — RIM]

Bibliographies

Adams, Marilyn. 1982. *Georgia Local and Family History.* . . . Clarkston: Georgia Heritage Research.

Bonner, James Calvin. 1965. *Georgia: A Students' Guide to Localized History.* NY: Teachers College Press.

DeRenne, Wymberley J. 1911. *Books Relating to the History of Georgia in the Library of Wymberley Jones DeRenne.* Comp. by Oscar Wegelin. Savannah: The Morning News.

Rowland, Arthur Ray. 1978. *A Bibliography of the Writings on Georgia History, 1900–1970.* Rev. and enlarged ed. Spartanburg, SC: Reprint Co.

Taylor, Paul Schuster. 1971. *Georgia Plan: 1732–1752.* Berkeley, CA: Institute of Business and Economic Research.

Thompson, Clara Mildred. 1915. *Reconstruction in Georgia. . . 1865–1872.* NY. Repr. 1971 (NY: Books for Libraries Press).

Thorton, Ella M. 1928. *Finding List of Books and Pamphlets Relating to Georgia and Georgians.* Georgia State Library.

Wegelin, Oscar, comp. 1931. *Catalogue of the Wymberley Jones DeRenne Library.* 3 vols. Savannah: The Morning News.

Woolley, Edwin C. 1907. *The Reconstruction of Georgia.* NY: Columbia University Press.

Yenawine, Wayne Stewart. 1948. *A Checklist of Source Materials for the Counties of Georgia.* Athens: Georgia Historical Society.

Zelinsky, Wilbur, comp. 1950. *A Selected Bibliography of Published Materials Relevant to the Geography of the State of Georgia.* Athens.

1938–48. *Inventory of County Archives of Georgia.* Atlanta: U. S. Historical Records Survey.

General Histories

Anderson, Mary Savage Jones. 1933. *Georgia: A Pageant of Years.* Richmond: Garrett and Massie. Repr. 1974 (Spartanburg, SC: Reprint Co.).

Avery, Isaac Wheeler. 1881. *The History of the State of Georgia from 1850.* . . . NY: Brown and Derby.

Brooks, Robert Preston. 1913. *History of Georgia.* Boston. Repr. 1972 (Spartanburg, SC: Reprint Co.).

Bryan, Thomas Conn. 1953. *Confederate Georgia.* Athens: University of Georgia Press.

Candler, Allen D., and Clement A. Evans. 1906. *Georgia: Comprising Sketches of Counties, Towns, Events, Institutions, and Persons, arranged in Cyclopedic Form.* Atlanta: State Historical Association.

Candler, Allen D., comp. 1904–16. *Colonial Records of the State of Georgia.* 26 vols. Atlanta: C. P. Byrd, State Printer.

Cate, Margaret D. 1931. *Sketches of Coastal Georgia.* Brunswick: Glover Bros.

Cate, Margaret Davis. 1955. *Early Days of Coastal Georgia.* St. Simons Island: Fort Frederica Association.

Coleman, Kenneth. 1958. *The American Revolution in Georgia, 1763–1789*. Athens: University of Georgia Press.

Coleman, Kenneth. 1960. *Georgia History in Outline*. Athens: University of Georgia Press.

Coleman, Kenneth. 1976. *Colonial Georgia: A History*. NY: Scribner.

Cooper, Walter G. 1938. *The Story of Georgia*. 4 vols. NY: American Historical Society.

Coulter, E. Merton. 1933. *A Short History of Georgia*. Chapel Hill: University of North Carolina Press.

Federal Writers Program. 1940. *Georgia: A Guide to Its Towns and Countryside*. Athens: University of Georgia Press.

Fewell, Laura R. 1871. *Aunt Quimby's Reminiscences of Georgia*. Meridian, MS: Repr. 1972 (Spartanburg, SC: Reprint Co.).

Grice, Warren. 1966. *Georgia through Two Centuries*. Ed. by E. Merton Coulter, 3 vols. NY: Lewis Historical Pub. Co.

Harris, Joel Chandler. 1896. *Stories of Georgia*. NY: American Book Co.

Howell, Clark. 1926. *History of Georgia*. 4 vols. Chicago: S. J. Clarke Pub. Co.

Johnson, Amanda. 1938. *Georgia as Colony and State*. Atlanta. Repr. 1970 (Atlanta: Cherokee Pub. Co.).

Jones, Charles C., Jr. 1883. *The History of Georgia*. 2 vols. Boston: Houghton, Mifflin and Co.

Jones, Charles C., Jr. The English Colonization of Georgia 1733–1757. *Winsor* 5:357–92.

Lane, Mills. 1975. *The People of Georgia. . . .* Savannah: Beehive Press.

Lovell, Caroline Couper. 1970. *Golden Isles of Georgia*. Atlanta: Cherokee Pub. Co.

Martin, Harold H. 1977. *Georgia: A Bicentennial History*. NY: Norton.

McCain, James Ross. 1917. *Georgia as a Proprietary Province*. Boston: R. G. Badger.

McCall, Hugh. 1811. *The History of Georgia*. 2 vols. Savannah: Seymour and Williams.

Mitchell, Frances Letcher. 1900. *Georgia Land and People*. Atlanta. Repr. 1974 (Spartanburg, SC: Reprint Co.).

Northen, William J. 1907–12. *Men of Mark in Georgia. . . .* 7 vols. Atlanta. Repr. 1974 (Spartanburg, SC: Reprint Co.).

Steed, Henry Alexis. 1971. *Georgia, Unfinished State*. Atlanta: Cherokee Pub. Co.

Stevens, William Bacon. 1847–59. *A History of Georgia*. 2 vols. Savannah. Repr. 1972 (Savannah: Beehive Press).

Ware, Ethel Kime. 1947. A Constitutional History of Georgia. *Columbia University Studies in History, Economics, and Public Law* 528:199–206.

White, George. 1849. *Statistics of the State of Georgia. . . .* Savannah: W. T. Williams.

White, George. 1854. *Historical Collections of Georgia. . . .* NY: Pudney and Russell.

Wilson, Caroline Price. 1933. *Annals of Georgia*. Savannah. Repr. 1969 (Vidalia: Georgia Genealogical Reprints).

Woodward, Emily. 1936. *Georgia Today in Photographs and Paragraphs*. Atlanta: Ruralist Press.

Special Studies

Abbot, William Wright. 1959. *The Royal Governors of Georgia, 1754–1775*. Chapel Hill: Institute of Early American History.

Arnall, Ellis Gibbs. 1946. *The Shore Dimly Seen*. Philadelphia: Lippincott.

Arnett, Alex Mathews. 1922. *The Populist Movement in Georgia*. NY: Columbia University Press.

Bartley, Numan V. 1970. *From Thurmond to Wallace: Political Tendencies in Georgia, 1948–1968*. Baltimore: Johns Hopkins University Press.

Bartram, William. 1792. *Travels*. Philadelphia. Repr. 1958 (New Haven: Yale University Press).

Bolton, Herbert E., and Mary Ross. 1925. *Arredondo's Historical Proof of Spain's Title to Georgia. . . .* Berkeley, CA: University of California Press.

Bonner, James C. 1964. *A History of Georgia Agriculture, 1732–1860*. Athens: University of Georgia Press.

Bonner, James C. 1975. *Atlas for Georgia History*. Fort Worth, TX: Miran Pub.

Bonner, James C., and Lucien E. Roberts, eds. 1940. *Studies in Georgia History and Government*. Athens. Repr. 1974 (Spartanburg, SC: Reprint Co.).

Brooks, Robert Preston. 1914. *The Agrarian Revolution in Georgia 1865–1912*. Madison, WI. Repr. 1970 (Westport, CT: Negro Universities Press).

Brooks, Robert Preston. 1952. *The Financial History of Georgia, 1732–1950*. Athens: University of Georgia.

Brown, John. 1855. *Slave Life in Georgia. . . .* London. Repr. 1972, ed. by F. N. Boney (Savannah: Beehive Press).

Bush-Brown, Harold. 1937. *Outline of the Development of Early American Architecture in Georgia*. Atlanta.

Callaway, James E. 1948. *The Early Settlement of Georgia*. Athens: University of Georgia Press.

Carry, John P. 1936. Racial Elements in Colonial Georgia. *Georgia Historical Quarterly* 20:30–40.

Chalker, Fussell M. 1970. *Pioneer Days along the Ocmulgee*. Carrollton.

Conway, Alan. 1966. *The Reconstruction of Georgia*. Minneapolis: University of Minnesota Press.

Coulter, E. Merton, ed. 1937. *Georgia's Disputed Ruins. . . .* Chapel Hill: University of North Carolina Press.

Coulter, E. Merton. 1949. *A List of the Early Settlers of Georgia*. Athens: University of Georgia Press.

Coulter, E. Merton. 1956. *Lost Generation. . . .* Tuscaloosa: Confederate Pub. Co.

Crane, Verner W. 1930. The Origins of Georgia. *Georgia Historical Quarterly* 14:93–110.

Davis, Harold E. 1976. *The Fledging Province: Social and Cultural Life in Colonial Georgia. . . .* Chapel Hill: Institute of Early American History and Culture.

Dehats, D. A. 1973. *Elites and Masses: Political Structure, Communication, and Behavior in Ante-Bellum Georgia*. University of Wisconsin dissertation.

Du Bois, W. E. B. 1901. *The Negro Landholder of Georgia*. Washington: Bulletin of the Department of Labor.

Fant, H. B. 1936. Financing the Colonization of Georgia. *Georgia Historical Quarterly* 20:1–29.

Felton, Rebecca Latimer. 1911. *My Memoirs of Georgia Politics*. Atlanta: Index Print. Co.

Felton, Rebecca Latimer. 1919. *Country Life in Georgia in the Days of My Youth*. Atlanta: Index Print. Co.

Flanders, Ralph B. 1933. *Plantation Slavery in Georgia*. Chapel Hill: University of North Carolina Press.

Fries, Adelaide L. 1905. *The Moravians in Georgia 1735–1740*. Raleigh, NC: Edwards and Broughton.

Gilmer, George R. 1855. *Sketches of Some of the First Settlers of Upper Georgia.* . . . NY. Rev. ed. 1926 (Americus: Americus Book Co.).

Gordon, Asa H. 1937. *The Georgia Negro, A History.* Ann Arbor. Repr. 1972 (Spartanburg, SC: Reprint Co.).

Hahn, Steven. 1983. *The Roots of Saturn Populism: Yeoman Farmers and. . . the Georgia Upcountry.* NY: Oxford University Press.

Harper, Roland M. 1930. *The Natural Resources of Georgia.* Athens: University of Georgia School of Commerce, Bureau of Business Research.

Hughes, Melvin Clyde. 1940. *County Government in Georgia.* Athens. Repr. 1975 (Westport, CT: Greenwood Press).

Huxford, Folks. 1977. *Pioneers of Wiregrass Georgia.* . . . 7 vols. Homerville: Huxford Genealogical Society.

Ivers, Larry E. 1974. *British Drums on the Southern Frontier: The Military Colonization of Georgia, 1733–1749.* Chapel Hill: University of North Carolina Press.

Janes, Thomas P. 1876. *Handbook of the State of Georgia.* Atlanta: Georgia Dept. of Agriculture.

Jones, Charles C. 1878. *The Dead Towns of Georgia.* Savannah: Morning News Steam Printing House.

Jones, Charles Edgeworth. 1889. *Education in Georgia.* Washington: Government Printing Office.

Knight Lucian L. 1913–14. *Georgia's Landmarks, Memorials, and Legends.* 2 vols. Atlanta: Byrd Print. Co.

Knight, Lucian L. 1931. *Georgia's Bi-Centennial Memoirs and Memories.* Atlanta: The Author.

Krakow, Kenneth K. 1975. *Derivations of Place Names in Georgia.* Macon.

La Forge, Laurence. 1925. *Physical Geography of Georgia.* Atlanta: Stein Print. Co.

Lanning, John Tate. 1935. *The Spanish Missions of Georgia.* Chapel Hill: University of North Carolina Press.

Lanning, John Tate. 1936. *The Diplomatic History of Georgia.* Chapel Hill: University of North Carolina Press.

Longstreet, Augustus Baldwin. 1892. *Georgia Scenes.* . . . 2nd ed. NY: Harper and Bros.

Mallard, Robert Q. 1892. *Plantation Life before Emancipation.* Richmond: Wittet and Shepperson.

Mauelshagen, Carl. 1962. *Salzburg Lutheran Expulsion and Its Impact.* NY: Vantage Press.

McQueen, Alexander Stephens. 1926. *History of Okefenokee Swamp.* Clinton, SC: Press of Jacobs and Co.

Montgomery, Horace, ed. 1958. *Georgians in Profile.* . . . Athens: University of Georgia Press.

Montgomery, Horace. 1950. *Cracker Parties.* Baton Rouge: Louisiana State University Press.

Moore, Francis. 1744. *A Voyage to Georgia in the Year 1735.* London: J. Robinson.

Myers, Robert Manson. 1972. *The Children of Pride.* . . . New Haven: Yale University Press.

Orr, Dorothy. 1950. *A History of Education in Georgia.* Chapel Hill: University of North Carolina Press.

Parrish, Lydia. 1942. *Slave Songs of the Georgia Sea Islands.* NY: Creative Age Press.

Perkerson, Medora Field. 1956. *White Columns in Georgia.* NY: Bonanza.

Phillips, Ulrich B. 1902. *Georgia and State Rights.* Washington. Repr. 1968 (Yellow Springs, OH: Antioch Press).

Ragsdale, Bartow Davis. 1932–35. *Story of Georgia Baptists.* 2 vols. Macon: Mercer University Press.

Range, Willard. 1954. *A Century of Georgia Agriculture, 1850–1950.* Athens: University of Georgia Press.

Ready, Milton L. 1970. *An Economic History of Colonial Georgia 1732–1754.* University of Georgia dissertation.

Reese, Trevor R., ed. 1973. *The Clamorous Malcontents: Criticisms and Defenses of the Colony of Georgia 1741–1743.* Savannah: Beehive Press.

Reese, Trevor Richard. 1963. *Colonial Georgia.* . . . Athens: University of Georgia Press.

Reese, Trevor, ed. 1972. *The Most Delightful Country of the Universe: Promotional Literature of the Colony of Georgia 1717–1734.* Savannah: Beehive Press.

Roberts, Richard A. 1923. *The Birth of an American State: Georgia.* London: Transactions of the Royal Historical Society.

Ross, Mary. 1950. With Pardo and Bagano on the Fringes of the Georgia Land. *Georgia Historical Quarterly* 14: 267–285.

Saye, Albert Berry. 1943. *New Viewpoints in Georgia History.* Athens: University of Georgia Press.

Saye, Albert Berry. 1970. *A Constitutional History of Georgia, 1732–1968.* Rev. ed. Athens: University of Georgia Press.

Sherwood, Adiel. 1827. *A Gazetteer of the State of Georgia.* Charleston: W. Riley.

Shryock, Richard H. 1926. *Georgia and the Union in 1850.* Durham, NC. Repr. 1968 (NY: AMS Press).

Smith, George G. 1913. *The History of Georgia Methodism from 1786 to 1866.* Atlanta: A. B. Caldwell.

Stacy, James. 1912. *A History of the Presbyterian Church in Georgia.* Elberton: Press of the Star.

Stokes, Anthony. 1784. *A Narrative of the Official Conduct of Anthony Stokes.* London: The Author.

Strickland, Reba Carolyn. 1939. *Religion and the State in Georgia in the Eighteenth Century.* NY: Columbia University Press.

Urlsperger, Samuel, ed. 1968–72. *Detailed Reports on the Salzburger Emigrants.* . . . Trans. by Hermann J. Lacker and ed. by George Fenwick Jones. Athens: University of Georgia Press.

Warren, Mary Bondurant. 1968–72. *Marriages and Deaths Abstracted from Extant Georgia Newspapers.* 2 vols. Danielsville: Heritage Papers.

Zelinsky, Wilbur. 1951. An Isochronic Map of Georgia Settlement 1750–1850. *Georgia Historical Quarterly 35:191–95.*

Zelinsky, Wilbur. 1953. The Settlement Patterns of Georgia. versity of California, Berkeley, dissertation.

1881. *Georgia State Gazetteer and Business Directory.* Atlanta: A. E. Sholes and Co.

1881. *History of the Baptist Denomination in Georgia.* . . . Atlanta: J. P. Harrison and Co.

1974. *The Counties of the State of Georgia.* Savannah: Georgia Historical Society.

Florida

1. Nassau County

Separate county by 1840. RR before 1860. Fernandina a Spanish military base 1586–1601. Amelia Island a Highlander outpost in 1736; overrun by Spaniards. Pop. 1830: 1,511, 1850: 2,164, 1880: 6,635, 1910: 10,525, 1930: 9,375, 1960: 17,189.

> Pink, Helen Ross. 1949. *Amelia Island: A Resource Unit for Teachers in Secondary Schools*. University of Florida Master's thesis.

Fernandina, Amelia Island

Fernandina still Spanish post in 1686. Devastated in colonial wars, deserted by 1730. British garrison 1748–83; Tory refuge. Resort of pirates and smugglers (esp. of slaves). Fortified by US 1847; Union base in Civil War. E. terminus of Florida RR. Pulp mills 1936–37; shrimp canneries; fertilizer, feed, fish oil. Pop. 1880: 2,562, 1910: 3,842, 1930: 3,023, 1960: 7,276.

FL 1: F, storekeeper, 70. B. on mainland, near mouth of Loftin Creek. Moved to Amelia I. age 13. 5 yrs. Tampa. — F. b. near Yulee, beyond inf.'s birthplace, PGF b. Spain, came to US nearly 200 yrs. ago; M. grew up at King's Ferry on St. Marys, MGF from England, MGM of Dutch descent. — Ed.: a few months under teacher F. had hired. — Baptist; Rebecca (women's group, Odd Fellows), has belonged to Maccabees, KKK. — About average intelligence; slow of thought. Dialect shows mixture of coastal and Midland ("wiregrass") types; any white folk speaker in Nassau Co. would have some of latter, since most of Co. pop. is of that derivation. — Slow speech; drawl. Nasality very strong. Often a querulous rising intonation at end of statement. Some up-gliding /i/; /ɔ/ often high, approaching [o]. Weak intervocalic /r/ (often lost).

2. Duval County

Created 1822 from St. Johns. Area a base for slave smuggling before Florida purchase. Citrus early, unsuccessful; reintroduced 1879–81. Largest mfg. center of state; diversified. Pop. 1830: 1,970, 1850: 4,539, 1880: 19,431, 1910: 75,163, 1930: 155,503, 1960: 455,411.

> Davis, T. Frederick. 1925. *History of Jacksonville, Florida and Vicinity, 1513 to 1924*. Jacksonville: Florida Historical Society.
>
> Gold, Pleasant Daniel. 1928. *History of Duval County, Florida*. St. Augustine: Record Co.
>
> Graff, Mary B. 1953. *Mandarin on the St. John's*. Gainesville: University of Florida Press.
>
> Martin, Richard A. 1972. *The City Makers*. Jacksonville: Convention Press.
>
> Rawls, Carolina, comp. 1950. *The Jacksonville Story. . . .* Jacksonville: Jacksonville's Fifty Years of Progress Association.

> 1882. *Into Tropical Florida: Or, A Round Trip Upon the St. John River*. Jacksonville: DeBary-Baya Merchants' Line.

Mandarin, South Jacksonville P.O.

Mandarin named from fruit introduced here. Founded during English occupation 1763–83; inc. 1841. Plantation area by 1860. Flourished 1865–1900 as a winter resort; winter home of Harriet Beecher Stowe after 1867.

FL 2A: F, housewife, 69. B. Mandarin (2 mi. out in the woods). Lived in Jacksonville 4 yrs. (2 stays of 2 yrs. each) at ages 42–44 and 50–52. — F. b. here, PGM b. GA, came here as a baby, PGM's F. and M. both b. GA; M., MGM both b. here. — Ed.: till 8th grade (country school). — Methodist; Community Club. — Unsophisticated but intelligent. Strong minded; knows she is a "Florida cracker" and rather proud of the fact. Rooted definitely in the culture of the non-slaveholding small farmer and content with it. Probably as good an example of locally rooted "Anglo-Saxon" stock as can be found in FL, with both parents from the same community. Interested in way interviews called to mind old and long-forgotten folk words. Taboo reactions. Somewhat suspicious of outsiders. Very active. Glad to help FW, though perfectly frank about loss of time it entailed. Generous and hospitable. Knows local comm. intimately. Generally keeps pretty busy: "try to mind my own business". Devoted to family. Not much reading or formal exposure to learning. Proud of her fruit trees, esp. of the "old-fashioned FL oranges". Not much interested in town life; no desire to go there. Neat. — Nasality. Some drawl, though varied tempo, strong stresses. Does not have centered beginning of /ai/ and /au/ before voiceless consonants noticed in both Jacksonville and St. Augustine; ingliding /e o/. Some postvocalic constriction; simplification of final clusters.

Jacksonville

Surveyed 1822; 1st charter 1832. Fording place on St. Johns R. British land grants 1765; 1st settlers 1816. Earliest settlers from SC, GA (other coastal communities). Trading center; shipping pt. for cotton. Growth during and after Seminole War of 1836. Devastated by fire, yellow fever in 1850s. Military occupation 1862–69. First free public schools 1864. Methodist 1824, Episcopal 1829; Baptist, Presbyterian, Roman Catholic, Congregational, Lutheran followed. Became RR center for FL 1871–1900. Improvement of river channel after 1880. 1st heavily populated area in state. Little affected by 1920s boom or 1930s depression. Important port; transportation center. Varied industry: cigars, petroleum products; largest naval stores yard, largest wholesale lumber market on Atlantic coast. Pop. 1850: 1,045, 1880: 7,650, 1910: 57,699, 1930: 129,549, 1960: 201,030.

FL 2B: M, real estate appraiser and broker, 58. B. Wauchula (S. part of state), moved to Jacksonville when 3 mos. old. — F., PGF b. Lebanon, TN; M., MGF, MGM all b. Key West. —

Ed.: public schools through h.s., BA U. of FL. — Served on Jacksonville Civil Service Commission 25 yrs. — Very alert, well-read; used descriptive and colorful phrases. Honest in his replies. Inf. shied away from using what he considered "uneducated" words. Helpful. Lives in central part of town and has very little contact with rural inhabitants of Co.

FL 2C!: M, retired lumberman, 85. B. Orange Co., (S., near Orlando). 4 yrs. in W. NC and SW VA 1917–21 (ages 55–58) procuring timber for ship contracts. Few mos. at a time in Cuba. Has been in drug manufacturing business. — F. b. Colleton Co., SC, married and came to Jacksonville long before Civil War, PGF b. VA (schoolteacher), PGM b. SC (both came S. in War of 1812); M. b. Colleton Co., MGF from Boston, MGM b. SC. — Ed.: Vanderbilt U. (Nashville, TN); Gordon Military College (Barnesville, GA); Jacksonville. — Methodist; Mason, Odd Fellow, KKK, Golden Eagle, etc. (mostly inactive). — Very intelligent. Full life. Well-known and respected in Jacksonville. One of the "builders of J-ville". A big man, still physically and mentally vigorous. Excellent observer; well-read, wide variety of interests. Enjoyed interviews. Completely natural. Uses a number of folk forms. Few taboos, many anecdotes (enjoys telling them, esp. those of which he was the butt). Keen business sense. Has kept up with world; views it with equanimity. No tendency to live in the past. Generous with his time: hoped FW would come back and talk some more (wonderful source of cv. forms!). Acquainted with both rural and urban life. Enjoys people. Very fine example of coastal cultivated speech (note resemblance to Charleston area). — Tempo moderate. Pitch basically low side of moderate. Some of the hoarseness of age, but still pleasantly resonant. Strong stresses. Utterance generally clear. Weak-stressed vowels very short. Centered beginning of /ai au/ diphthongs very common; in-gliding /e o ɔ i u/ usual; both [ɨu] and [ju] forms. Simplification of final clusters; /w-/ for hw-/. — Cultivated.

3. St. Johns County

Est. 1821. About 4,000 Tories to E. FL c. 1787. Aircraft, ships. Pop. 1830: 2,538, 1850: 2,525, 1880: 4,535, 1910: 13,208, 1930: 18,676, 1960: 30,034.

Brooks, A. M. 1909. *The Unwritten History of Old St. Augustine.* . . . St. Augustine: Record Co.

Deland, Margaret. 1889. *Florida Days.* Boston: Little, Brown.

Dewhurst, William W. 1881. *The History of Saint Augustine, Florida.* . . . NY. Repr. 1969 (Rutland, VT: Academy Books).

Fairbanks, George R. 1881. *History and Antiquities of St. Augustine, Florida.* . . . Jacksonville: H. Drew.

Federal Writers Project. 1937. *Seeing St. Augustine.* St. Augustine: Record Co.

Folsom, Montgomery. 1905. *Old St. Augustine.* Atlanta: Franklin Print. and Pub. Co.

Longworth, Maria Theresa. 1869. *Saint Augustine, Florida.* NY: G.P. Putnam and Son.

Reynolds, Charles Bingham. 1885. *Old St. Augustine: A Story of Three Centuries.* . . . St. Augustine: E. H. Reynolds.

Wright, J. Leitch, Jr. 1975. *British St. Augustine.* St. Augustine: Historic St. Augustine Preservation Board.

1955–. *El Escribano.* St. Augustine: St. Augustine Historical Society.

St. Augustine

Oldest permanent white settlement in US, 1565; 3 rivers, defensible site, shrimp fishing. Minorcans from 1767; Minorcan customs flourished till late 19th cent. Military HQ of Spanish North Am. Town largely abandoned by time of cession to Great Britain; became Tory center. Capital of E. FL till 1824, when Tallahassee became territorial capital. US military post during Seminole War. Occupied by Federals 1862–65. Development as winter resort begun 1880. Port relatively undeveloped; good harbor, cut off from interior by pine barrens. Pop. 1850: 1,934, 1880: 2,293, 1910: 5,494, 1930: 12,111, 1960: 14,734.

FL 3A: M, former farmer, 65. B. 18 mi. W., came to St. Augustine age 15. In Co. all his life, except for occ. trips. — F. b. Co.; PGF's F. came from Spain; M., MGF, MGM all b. Co. — Ed.: country public school. — Roman Catholic; former Elk; knows all older people in Co. Ran prison camp, has been mason, carpenter, painter, builder, clerk. Has spent much time in the woods. — One of old names in Co. Very much interested in work FW doing. Easygoing. Has enough wealth (married it?) so that he doesn't have to work too hard. Lives simply. Enjoys fishing, eating, sitting around talking with cronies. Likable. Local reputation for being a bit of a liar, but FW could detect no tendency to stray from truth so far as purposes of interviews were concerned. Talked freely and naturally. Uses many folk-grammatical forms and items of folk vocab. Knows local culture intimately. Has met all kinds of people from all kinds of places, consequently (being a good observer) has noticed differences in speech. No evidence that his own speech has been at all distorted by these contacts. Self-assurance. Good sense of humor; no taboos; amused by attempts of some people to use euphemisms. Many anecdotes. A bit of a tease. Interested in traditions, but no tendency to live in the past (unless his comments about the lack of cold-resistance in present-day oranges might be so interpreted). — Very fast speech; weak-stressed vowels very sharp. Low pitch. Not much intonation range. Clipped utterance, yet clear; no problem understanding except for the speed. Centered beginning of /ai au/ before voiceless consonants; in-gliding /e o/, etc. Simplification of final clusters; /hw-/.

FL 3B!: M, farmer, surveryor, 76. B. here. Lived here except time away at school; moved to country from townhouse c. age 46. — Ed.: college in Macon, GA; Rock Hill College, Baltimore, MD (possibly seminarian). — Roman Catholic. — Well known in community as antiquarian and authority on local history. Highly thought of. Somewhat eccentric. Lives isolated, hard-working existence on farm outside of St. Augustine. Little time — could give only part of one Sunday PM to interview — though seemed to enjoy the session. Has great deal of old plunder of misc. quality (some excellent, some poor) all of which he carefully treasures. Frugal. Interested in local traditions. Knows a great deal about farm life. Some tendency to be "correct" in direct questioning; more relaxed in conversational forms. Interesting personality: combination of peasant economy with a "gentleman's" wide reading and broad knowledge of the world. — Fast, fluid speech. Pleasant, clear voice. Phonology local. Pitch basically low, rising and falling over fairly wide range. Strong stresses; stressed vowels fairly high pitched. Has centered beginning of /ai au/ before voiceless cons. — Cultivated.

4. *Volusia County*

Co. formed 1854. Atlantic Ocean to St. Johns River. An "isolated Spanish outpost" early. English attempted to promote settlement by c. 1764; land ceded to English c. 1776. Indigo first cash crop of Turnbull colony here. Some 18th cent. plantation culture settlement from SC and GA. English dominance 1783–1819; Spanish authority never stable after 1785. US purchase 1819. Road to New Smyrna 1831, but most transport by water. Cotton; oranges a cash crop by 1830s. Second Seminole War 1835–42; most plantations ravaged. Most Seminoles migrated W. 1850–60. Subsistence agriculture during Reconstruction; introduction of livestock raising; seafood processing. Co. seat to De Land 1889. De Land College est. 1885; Stetson U. 1889. A resort area since 1865: Daytona Beach, Daytona Speedway here. Coastal areas developed with RRs, winter resorts changed to year round traffic. Industrialization during and after WWII. Pop. 1860: 1,158, 1880: 3,294, 1910: 16,510, 1930: 42,757, 1960: 125,319.

Fitzgerald, Thomas Edward. 1937. *Volusia County, Past and Present*. Daytona Beach: The Observer Press.

Fitzgerald, Thomas Edward. 1939. *Historical Highlights of Volusia County*. Daytona Beach: The Observer Press.

Gold, Pleasant Daniel. 1927. *History of Volusia County, Florida*. Deland: E. O. Painter Print. Co.

Hebel, Ianthe (Bond), ed. 1955. *Centennial History of Volusia County, Florida, 1854–1954*. Daytona Beach: College Pub. Co.

Hebel, Ianthe B. 1941. *Presenting Forty Years of Progress, 1901–1941: Volusia County, Florida*. Daytona Beach: Daytona Beach Observer.

Sobern, Michael G. 1976. *A History of Volusia County, Florida*. Florida State University dissertation.

FL 4: Tomoka Farms (formerly Spruce Creek), Daytona Beach P.O. — M, rancher, livestock inspector, 56. B. here. — F. b. Port Orange, PGF, PGM both b. either here or NC; M. b. Osten (E. of Sanford), MGF, MGM came from GA. — Ed.: Spruce Creek School 4 yrs.; Port Orange School through 8th grade. — Cattlemen's Assoc.; Volusia Co. Fair Assoc.; supervisor of Livestock Assoc.

5. *Alachua County*

Organized 1824. Spanish missions initially, abandoned. Cattle free-ranging after 1750. 1814 1st attempt to settle from GA, failed; first permanent settlements c. 1820 (Micanopy settlement). Settlers from a variety of areas, both low and upcountry; mainly SC, GA, NC. Boundaries shrank with creation of other cos. (last 1925). Harassed in Seminole War, 1835–41. Co. seat to Gainesville 1854; Gainesville in 1880s most important city in central FL, cotton shipping. RR opened 1859. Prosperity and rapid growth 1865–1900; diversified farming (N. limit of citrus). 1894, 1899 citrus crop crippled by freezes; boll weevil destroyed Sea Island cotton crop 1920s. Phosphate mining 1890–1920. Leading livestock Co. to 1920. Army base here WWII. Central highland, studded with lakes and lagoons. Hardwood forest area. Not industrialized, agricultural; U. of FL largest employer. Pop.

1830: 2,204, 1850: 2,524, 1880: 16,462, 1910: 34,305, 1930: 34,365, 1960: 74,074.

Aldreth, C. H. 1981. *History of Gainesville, Florida, 1854–1979*. Gainesville: Alachua County Historical Society.

Ashby, John W. 1898. *Alachua, the Garden County of Florida*. NY: South Pub. Co.

Buchholz, Fritz W. 1929. *History of Alachua County, Florida, Narrative and Biographical*. St. Augustine: Record Co.

Davis, Jesse G. 1966. *History of Gainesville, Florida*. . . . Gainesville.

Davis, Jesse G. 1970. *History of Alachua County, 1824–1969*. Gainesville.

Milanich, Jerald T. 1971. *The Alachua Tradition of North-Central Florida*. Gainesville: University of Florida.

Opdycke, John B., ed. 1974. *Alachua County: A Sesquicentennial Tribute*. Gainesville: Alachua County Historical Commission.

Rawlings, Marjorie Kinnan. 1942. *Cross Creek*. NY. Repr. 1974 (Atlanta: Mockingbird Books).

Webber, "Carl". 1883. *The Eden of the South*. . . . NY: Leve and Alden.

Gainesville

Settlement (Hog Town) in area 1830; became Gainesville 1853. Courthouse here 1854; 4th largest city in FL by 1884. Phosphate 1879; orange culture cut back by freezes of 1894 and 1899. U. of FL founded 1905, result of consolidation of several schools. Naval stores, sawmills, cattle, turpentine. Pop. 1930: 10,465.

FL 5A: M, farmer, 26 yrs. railroad construction, logging for big sawmills, 74. B. Bradford Co.; moved to Alachua Co. when 1 yr. old, lived there ever since, in Hague section. Moved to Gainesville when 67 yrs. old. — F. b. at old Noonansville, c. 14 mi. NW, now abandoned, PGF b. Alachua Co. (family came c. 1800 from Holland (German-Dutch)), PGM b. Alachua Co.; M. from Bradford Co., MGM from Stark (M.'s people Scotch-Irish). — Ed.: "5th reader"; a fair amount of reading. — Nazarene Church (had been Baptist); Mason, Woodmen of the World. — Ambivalence: wanted to cooperate, somewhat flattered by appeal to his experience and authority, but also suspicious; complained that interviews made him "nervous" and kept him from sleeping (interview incomplete). Cracker type: hardworking, limited cultural contacts, good deal of practical experience, suspicious of strangers and of too much "learning". Fundamentalist in religion. Well-rooted in local folkways; knows most of old families of Co. Some tendency to dwell in past. Fisherman by avocation. Shrewd and calculating in business transactions. Difficulties in adjusting to contemporary social context. — Moderate tempo. Strong nasality. Drawl; overlong stressed vowels; slurred articulation. Weak final cons.; simplification of final cons. clusters.

Windsor, Gainesville P.O.

Windsor a decaying old town, once prosperous; at one time many fine residences, most of which have been torn down or deteriorated.

FL 5B: M, retired railway expressman, 75. B. here; ages 1–10 moved around with F. through SC, GA; Windsor ever since.

— F. b. here, PGF from SC (Methodist preacher around Columbia), PGM from Blackstock, SC; M. from Chester Co., SC (came to FL to visit aunt, married here). — Ed.: local schools through 5th reader. — Methodist. — Relaxed. Interested in interviews as providing continuity with past. Doesn't like living in town, though goes there on occasion. Well-known and respected. Respects learning; fair amount of reading. Sense of own position. Pleasant; good mind. Keen sense of geography (result of work with express company). Intermediate type: a lot of folk speechways worn off by contacts, some recalled by suggestion. Aware of speech differences, but never consciously tinkered with own speech. Mild profanity. — Speech soft, pleasant to listen to. Clear utterance. Slight drawl. Tempo basically fast; short weak-stressed vowels. Ingliding diphthongs. Simplification of final consonant clusters; /kl-/ goes to /tl-/ fairly often.

Bibliographies

Hanna, Alfred Jackson. 1946. *Recommended Readings for the Florida Centennial.* . . . Winter Park: Union Catalog of Floridana.

Harris, Michael H. 1972. *Florida History: A Bibliography.* Metuchen, NJ: Scarecrow Press.

Yonge, Julien C. 1938. *Catalogue of the Julien C. Yonge Collection, Pensacola, Florida.* Miami.

General Histories

Abbey, Kathryn Trimmer. 1941. *Florida, Land of Change.* Chapel Hill: University of North Carolina Press.

Bennett, Charles E. 1968. *Settlement of Florida.* Gainesville: University of Florida Press.

Brevard, Caroline Mays. 1924–25. *A History of Florida.* 2 vols. Deland: Florida State Historical Society.

Cutler, Harry Gardiner. 1923. *History of Florida, Past and Present, Historical and Biographical.* 3 vols. NY: Lewis Pub. Co.

Douglas, Marjory Stoneman. 1967. *Florida: The Long Frontier.* NY: Harper and Row.

Dovell, Junius Elmore. 1952. *Florida, Historic, Dramatic, Contemporary.* 4 vols. NY: Lewis Historical Pub. Co.

Fairbanks, George R. 1868. *The Spaniards in Florida.* Jacksonville: C. Drew.

Gold, Robert L. 1969. *Borderland Empires in Transition: The Triple-Nation Transfer of Florida.* Carbondale: Southern Illinois University Press.

Jahoda, Gloria. 1976. *Florida: A Bicentennial History.* NY: Norton.

Patrick, Rembert Wallace. 1945. *Florida under Five Flags.* Gainesville: University of Florida Press.

Quattlebaum, Paul. 1956. *The Land Called Chicora.* . . . Gainesville: University of Florida Press.

Tebeau, Charlton, and Ruby L. Carson. 1965. *Florida from Indian Trail to Space Age.* 3 vols. Delray Beach: Southern Pub. Co.

Verrill, A. Hyatt. 1935. *Romantic and Historic Florida.* NY: Dodd, Mead and Co.

Special Studies

Avant, David A. 1979. *Florida Pioneers and Their Alabama, Georgia, Carolina, Maryland and Virginia Ancestors.* Easley, SC: Southern Historical Press.

Cabell, Branch. 1943. *The St. Johns, a Parade of Diversities.* NY: Farrar and Rinehart.

Cline, Howard Francis. 1974. *Provisional Historical Gazeteer with Locational Notes on Florida Colonial Communities.* NY: Garland Pub., Inc.

Johnson, Clifton. 1918. *Highways and Byways of Florida.* NY: Macmillan Co.

Lowery, Woodbury. 1901. *The Spanish Settlements within the Present Limits of the United States.* NY: G. P. Putnam's Sons.

Martin, Sidney Walter. 1944. *Florida during the Territorial Days.* Athens, GA: University of Georgia Press.

Morris, Allen Covington. 1974. *Florida Place Names.* Coral Gables: University of Miami Press.

Nance, Ellwood Cecil, et al. 1962. *The East Coast of Florida, a History, 1500–1961.* 3 vols. Delray Beach: Southern Pub. Co.

Polk, R. L. 1918. *R. L. Polk and Company's Florida State Gazetteer and Business Directory.* Jacksonville: R. L. Polk and Co.

Pyburn, Nita Katharine. 1951. *Documentary History of Education in Florida.* Tallahassee: Florida State University.

Raisz, Erwin Josephus, et al. 1964. *Atlas of Florida.* Gainesville: University of Florida Press.

Roberts, Kenneth. 1926. *Florida.* NY: Harper and Bros.

Smith, Julia Floyd. 1973. *Slavery and Plantation Growth in Antebellum Florida, 1821–1860.* Gainesville: University of Florida Press.

Vance, Maurice M. 1959. Northerners in Late Nineteenth Century Florida: Carpetbaggers or Settlers? *Florida Historical Quarterly* 38:1–14.

Wood, Roland, and Edward A. Fernald. 1974. *The New Florida Atlas.* . . . Tallahassee: Trend Publications.

1908–. *Florida Historical Quarterly.* St. Augustine: Florida Historical Society.